济普查

OMIC CENSUS

您的配合与支持！

ed Your Cooperation&Support!

二产业、第三产业的所有法人单位、产业活动单位和个体工商户，

时、如实地填报第一次全国经济普查表。

湖南省第一次全国经济普查领导小组办公室

OFFICE OF THE LEADING GROUP OF HUNAN PROVINCE FOR THE FIRST NATIONAL ECONOMIC CENSUS

湖南统计年鉴

2004

HUNAN STATISTICAL YEARBOOK

湖南省统计局 编

Edited by

Statistical Bureau of Hunan Province

中国统计出版社

China Statistics Press

湖湘数典

★湖南省生产总值（亿元）

Gross Domestic Product (100 million yuan)

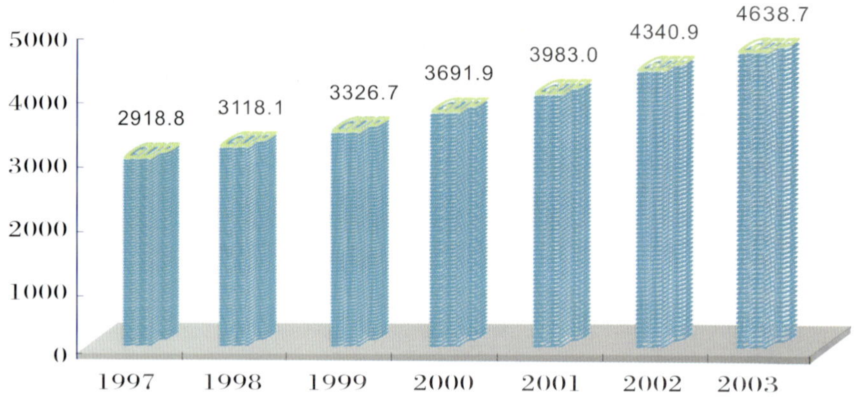

★ 人均生产总值（元）

Per Capita GDP (yuan)

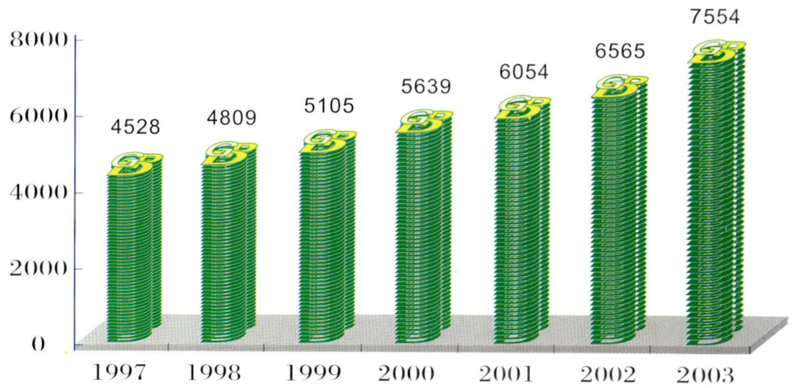

★ 生产总值构成（%）

Composition of GDP (%)

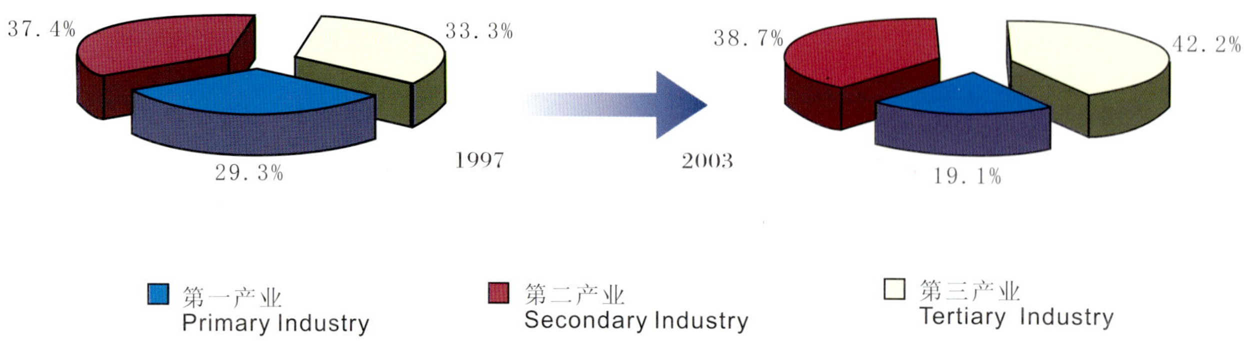

DIGITAL HUNAN

DIGITAL HUNAN

★市镇人口与乡村人口（万人）

Population of Urban and Rural (10 000 persons)

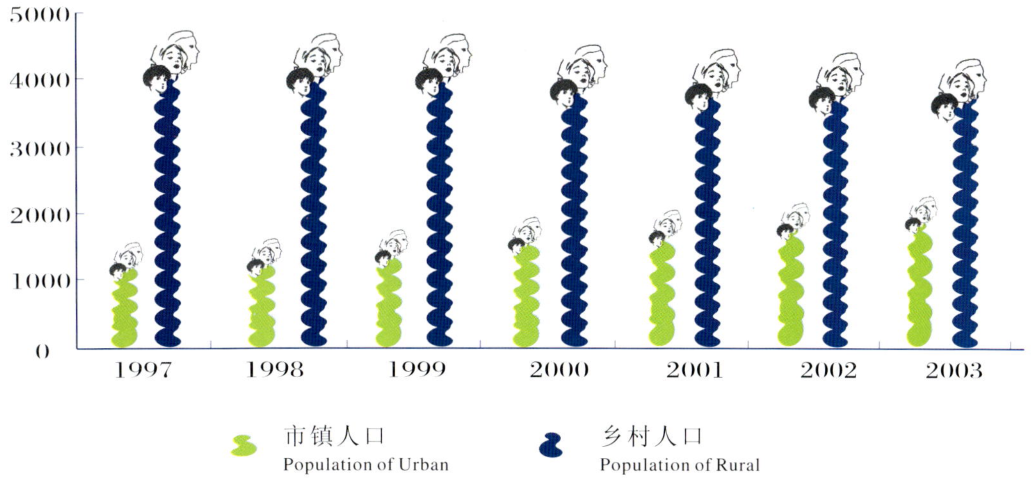

★从业人员与职工人数（万人）

Employees and Staffs （10 000 persons）

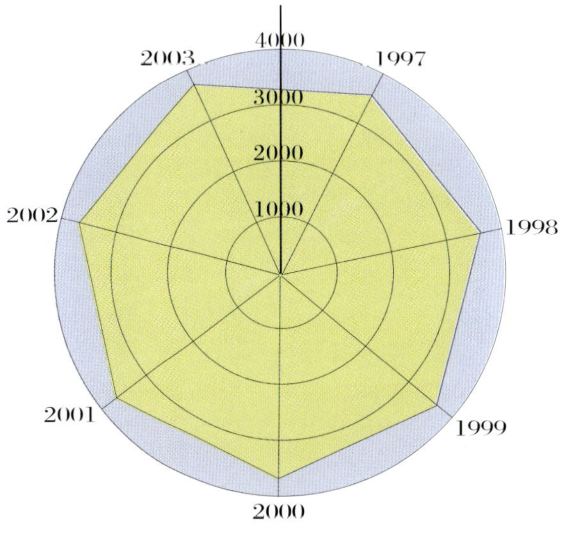

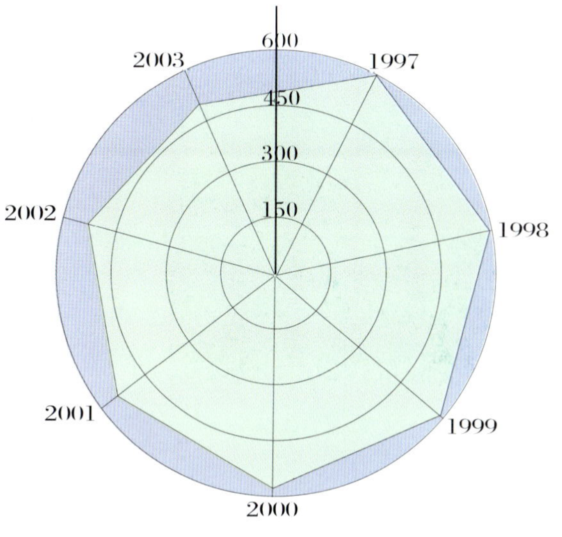

从业人员 Employees　　职工人数 Staffs

★从业人员构成（%）

Composition of Employees （%）

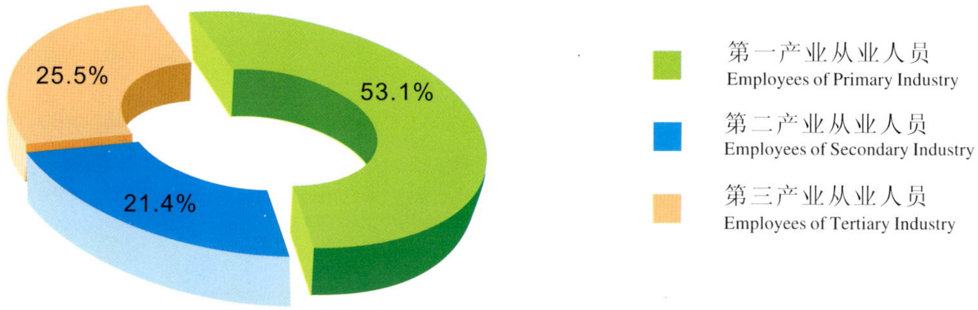

湖湘数典

★财政收入（亿元）

Government Revenue (100 million yuan)

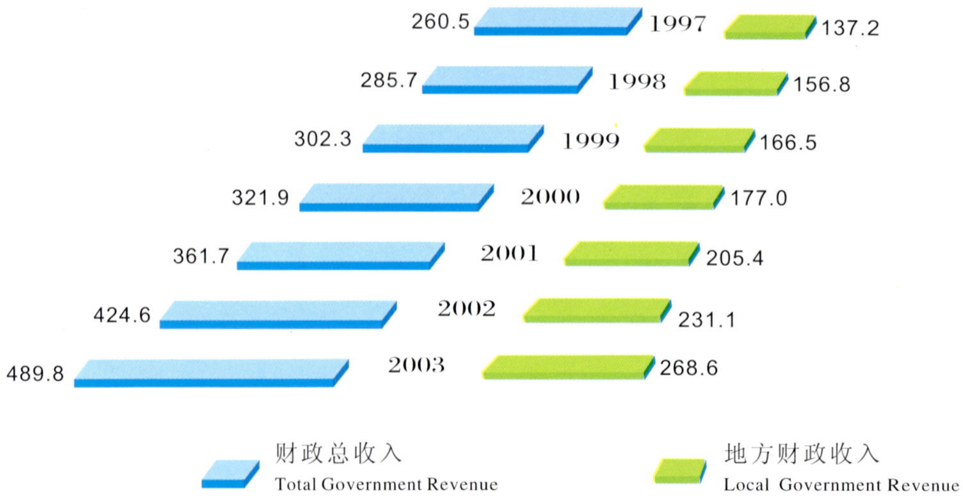

★财政支出（亿元）

Government Expenditures (100 million yuan)

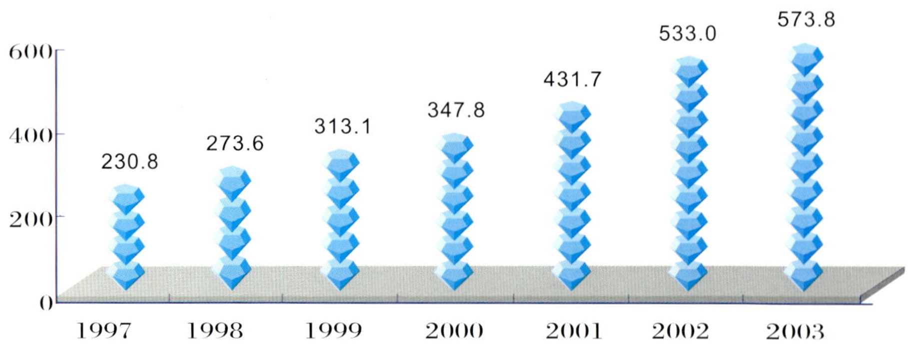

★固定资产投资（亿元）

Investment in Fixed Assets (100 million yuan)

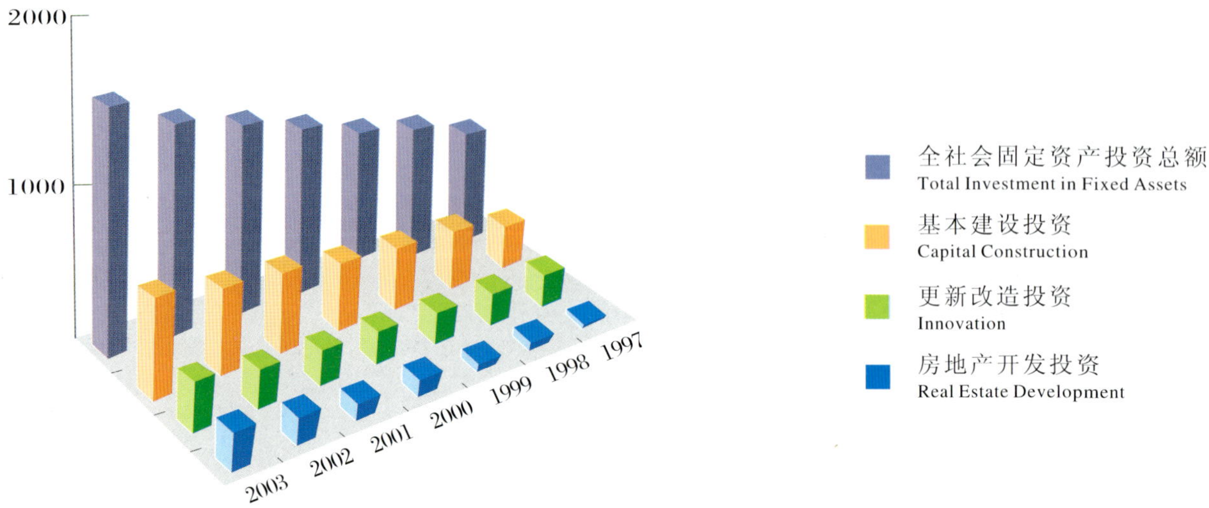

DIGITAL HUNAN

DIGITAL HUNAN

★社会消费品零售总额（亿元）

Total Retail Sales of Consumer Goods (100 million yuan)

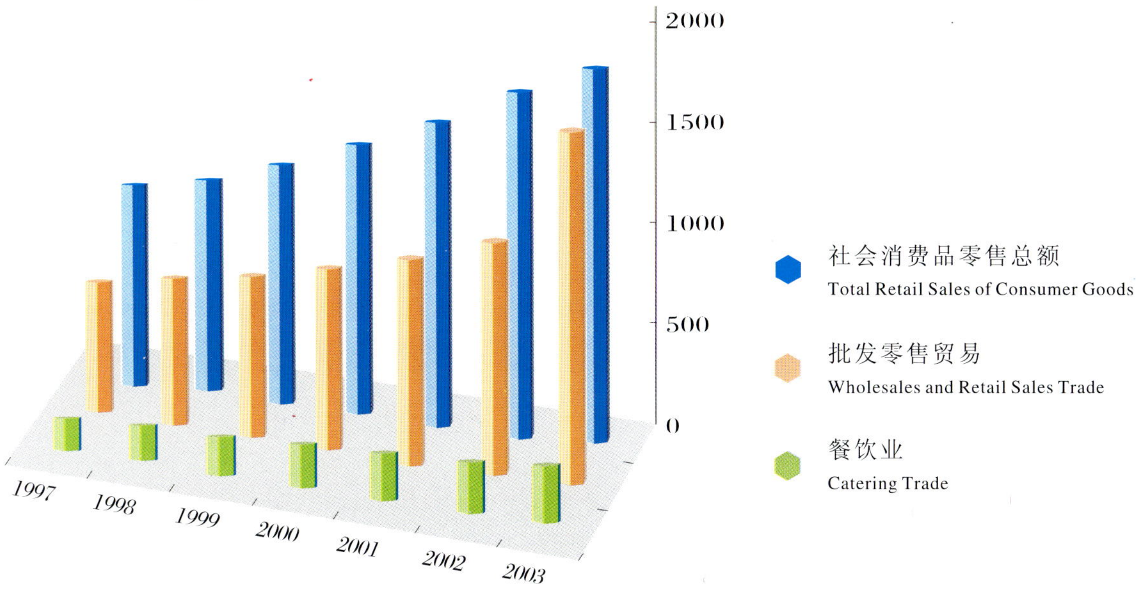

★对外贸易进出口额（亿美元）

Imports and Exports (USD 100 million)

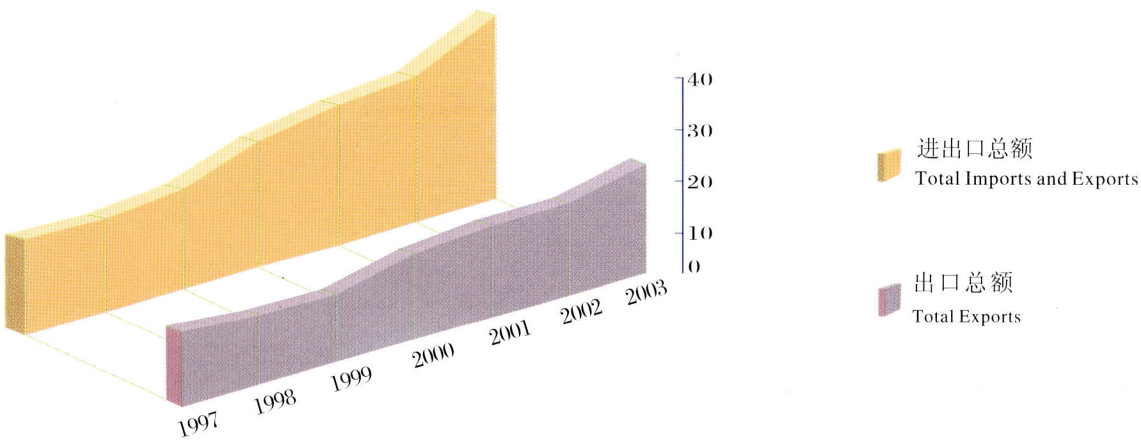

★利用外资（亿美元）

Utilization of Foreign Capital (USD 100 million)

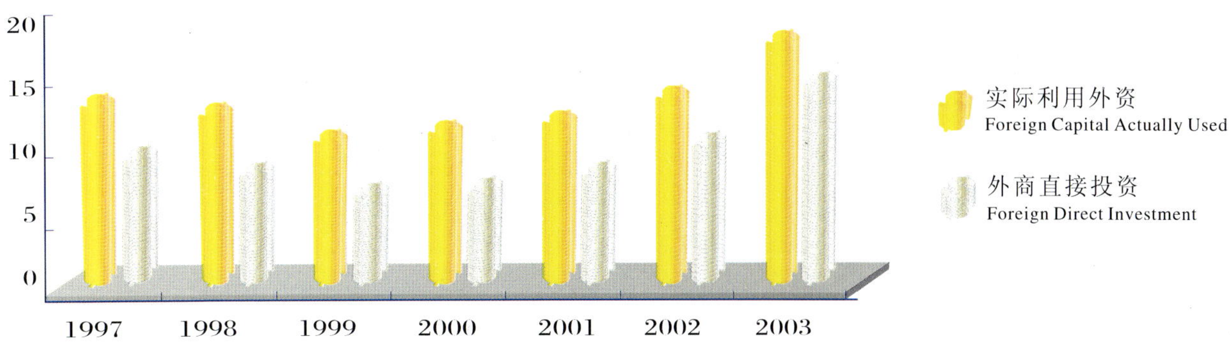

湖湘数典

★居民人均储蓄存款余额（元）

Per Capita Balance of Saving Deposit of Residents (yuan)

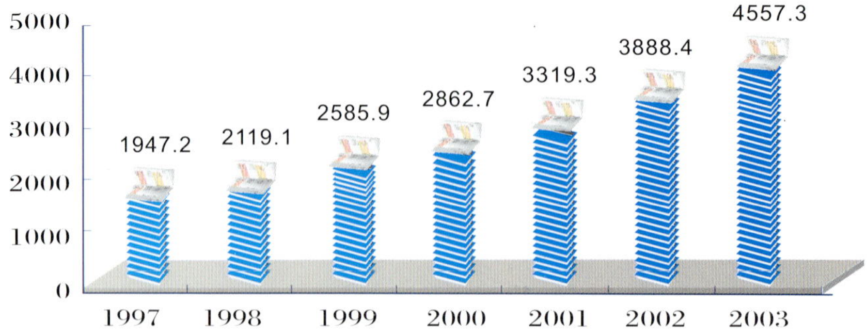

★居民收入（元）

Income of Households (yuan)

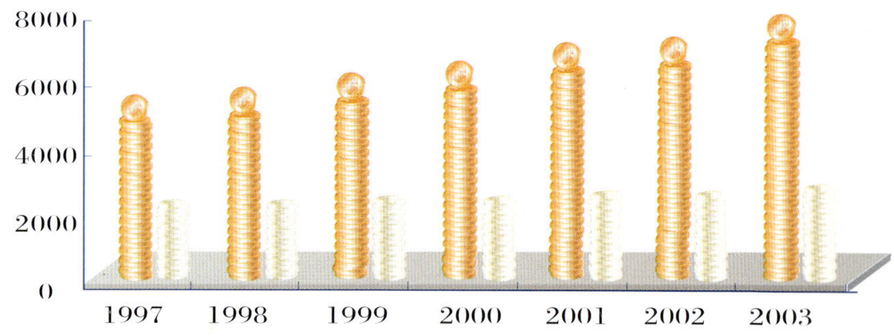

城镇居民家庭人均可支配收入
Per Capita Disposable Income of Urban Households

农村居民家庭人均纯收入
Per Capita Net Income of Rural Households

★居民人均消费支出（元）

Per Capita Annual Living Expenditures for Consumption (yuan)

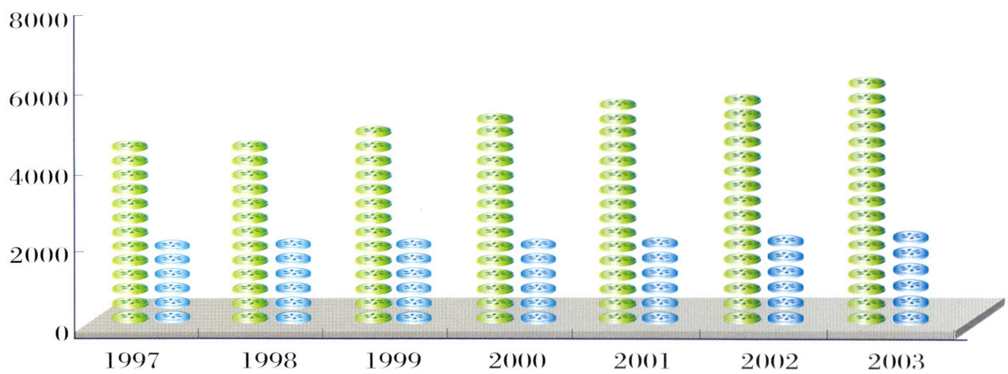

城镇居民
Urban Households

农村居民
Rural Households

DIGITAL HUNAN

★湖南的一天（2003）

Daily Economic Indices of Hunan（2003）

DIGITAL HUNAN

地区生产总值12.71亿元
Gross Domestic Product:1271 million yuan

布93.42万米
Cloth:934.2 thousand meters

原煤6.48万吨
Coal:64.8 thousand tons

地方财政收入7360万元
Local Government Revenue:73.60 million yuan

原油加工量13878吨
Machining Crude Oil:13878 tons

钢16185吨
Steel:16185 tons

机制纸及纸板3405吨
Machine-made Paper and Paperboard:3405 tons

成品钢材15293吨
Steel Products:15293 tons

发电量14349万度
Electricity:143.49 million kw.h

水泥 8.37万吨
Cement :83.7 thousand tons

粮食6.69万吨
Grain:66.9 thousand tons

棉花 446.85吨
Cotton:446.85 tons

苎麻340.55吨
Ramie:340.55 tons

油料 3444吨
O il-bearing Crops:3444 tons

烤烟483.84吨
Flue-cured Tobacco:483.84 tons

茶叶166.03吨
Tea:166.03 tons

柑桔4587.4吨
Oranges:4587.4 tons

猪牛羊肉13312吨
Pork, Beef and Mutton:13312 tons

水产品4290.26吨
Aquatic Products:4290.26 tons

对外贸易进出口总额1023.56万美元
Total Imports and Exports:USD 10235.6 thousand

进口总额435.62万美元
Total Imports:USD 4356.2 thousand

邮电业务总量6417.37万元
Business Volume of Postal and Telecommunications Services: 64173.7 thousand yuan

出口总额587.95万美元
Total Exports:USD 5879.5 thousand

出版报纸311万份
Newspaper Published:3110 thousand copies

城乡居民消费总额5.53亿元
Resident Consumption:553 million yuan

出版图书80.98万册
Books Published:809.8 thousand copies

邮寄函件138.72万份
Post Letters:1387.2 thousand pieces

平均每人消费额9.00元
Per Capita Consumption:9 yuan

出版杂志34.46万册
Magazines Published:344.6 thousand copies

出生人口2152人
Births:2152 persons

（京）新登字041号

图书在版编目（CIP）数据

湖南统计年鉴.2004/湖南省统计局编
北京：中国统计出版社，2004.6
ISBN 7-5037-4337-9
Ⅰ.湖…
Ⅱ湖…
Ⅲ.统计资料—湖南省—2004—年鉴
Ⅳ.C832.64-54
中国版本图书馆CIP数据核字（2004）第032177号

湖南统计年鉴—2004

作　　者/ 湖南统计局
责任编辑/ 蔡启新
E-mail/ yearbook@stats.gov.cn
责任校对/ 李生春
封面设计/ 李生春
出版发行/ 中国统计出版社
通信地址/ 北京市西城区三里河月坛南街75号　中国统计出版社
邮政编码/ 100826
电　　话/（010）63262295
印　　刷/ 湖南彩印厂
经　　销/ 新华书店
开　　本/ 297mm×210mm　1/16
字　　数/ 170万字
印　　张/ 35
印　　数/ 2200
版　　别/ 2004年7月第1版
版　　次/ 2004年7月第1次印刷
书　　号/ ISBN 7-5037-4337-9/F.1802
定　　价/ 220元

《湖南统计年鉴--2004》编辑委员会和编辑工作人员

一、编委会

主任委员

马　勇

副主任委员

吴星明	周菊华	张世平	黎新明	邱运斌
刘志荣	江利国	张松青	张光友	

委　　员　（以姓氏笔划为序）

马爱霞	王立凯	王建春	王晓华	冯文金
叶扬宗	江金生	刘红旗	刘其祝	刘明亮
刘顺国	刘湘林	陈良米	陈建军	李　波
李平安	李机生	李建平	李绍文	李春喜
苏寿泉	肖胜利	张昭红	林定春	林德勇
欧阳美嫔	周海俊	郑红梅	贺友斌	赵子荣
高　勇	高群芳	唐素芳	徐　朋	曾斌求
梁已香	谭蒲辉	廖伟雄	颜宏晖	戴乐平

二、编辑工作人员

总　编　辑	马　勇				
编辑部主任	高　勇				
编辑部副主任	曾斌求	彭积龙	周碧红		
责任编辑	蔡启新				
执行编辑	李生春				
专文特载	高　勇	曾斌求	彭积龙	周曙东	李生春
	彭　刚	唐　颖			
英文翻译	戴乐平	周曙东			
校　　订	高　勇	李生春			

《Hunan Statistical Yearbook -- 2004》 Editorial Board and Staff

编 者 说 明

一、《湖南统计年鉴－2004》是一部全面反映湖南省国民经济和社会发展情况的资料性年刊。收录了全省及各市、州、县2003年经济和社会发展方面的大量统计数据，以及重要历史年份的全省主要统计数据。是一本党政部门、企事业单位、经济研究工作者、教学科研人员及来湘投资者的重要工具书。

二、《湖南统计年鉴－2004》在保持过去历年统计年鉴结构联贯、资料可比的基础上，做了部分补充和调整。首卷为特载《湖南省统计局关于2003年国民经济和社会发展统计公报》。统计资料分19部分，即：1. 综合；2. 国民经济核算；3. 人口就业和职工工资；4. 固定资产投资； 5. 财政、金融、保险； 6. 物价指数； 7. 人民生活； 8. 城市建设，环境保护；9. 农业；10. 工业；11. 建筑业；12. 运输、邮电；13. 国内外贸易、对外经济和旅游；14. 教育和科技；15. 文化、体育、卫生；16. 党群、政法和社会福利；17. 企业调查；18. 各市、州、县主要经济和社会统计指标；19. 各省、市、自治区主要经济和社会统计指标。

三、本《年鉴》资料大部分来自年度统计报表，一部分来自抽样调查。各市、州、县主要经济和社会统计指标是根据当年各地的统计年报资料整理的；全国及各省、市、自治区的年度引用数据是根据国家统计局反馈资料加工的；有些专业性很强的指标是由省直有关业务厅局年报提供的；土地面积、森林资源、河流湖泊状况是按照有关部门近年来普查资料整理的。

四、本《年鉴》中价值指标均按当年价格计算，指数均按可比价格计算。如有变化，表后附有说明。本年鉴数据均为电脑合成，由于单位取舍按四舍五入处理产生的计算误差，均未作机械调整。

五、本《年鉴》是按照《中国统计年鉴》的大体框架和规范要求编辑的。统一使用《中国统计年鉴》指标解释，统一采用国际度量衡标准计量单位，统一使用《中国统计年鉴》规范符号。

“...”表示数据不足本表最小单位数；“#”表示其中的主要项；“空格”表示指标数据不详或无该项统计数据；“※”表示表下有注释。

Preface

Ⅰ.《Hunan Statistical Yearbook-2004》is an annual statistical publication, which provides comprehensive data series in 2003 and some selected data series for historically important years at provincial level and local levels of cities, prefecture and counties. There for, it is an important reference book for party and government departments, enterprises and administrations units, economic and scientific research works, teachers and investment units come to Hunan.

Ⅱ.《Hunan statistical Yearbook-2004》has been adjusted and added partly and it maintains the continuity compared with the yearbooks published before. The first special issue is statistical communique on the National Economy and Social Development of Hunan province Statistical Bureau 2003.

The Statistical figures contains the following 19 parts, 1. General Survey; 2. National Economy Accounting; 3. Population, Employment and Wage; 4. Investment in Fixed Assets; 5. Public Finance, Banking, Insurance; 6. Price Indices; 7. People's Livelihood; 8. Construction of Cities, Environmental Protection; 9. Agriculture; 10. Industry; 11. Construction; 12. Transportation, Post and Telecommunication Services; 13. Domestic Trade, Foreign Trade, Foreign Economy and Tourism; 14. Education and Science; 15. Culture, Sports and Public Health;16.Party and Mass, Politics and Law, Social Welfare; 17. Enterprises Survey; 18. Main Economic and Social Statistics Indicators of Cities, Prefecture and Counties; 19. Main Economic and Social Indicators by Provinces (Municipalities and Autonomous Regions).

Ⅲ. The major data of the book are from annual statistical reports, and some from sampling surveys. Main economic and social statistics indicators of cities, Prefecture and counties are arranged according to their annual statistical reports. Annual data of state, and other provinces, municipalities directly under central government and autonomous regions are quoted from data returned by State Statistical Bureau. Some very specialized indicators are applied by the province directly under administrational annual reports. Area of total land, Forest resources, the condition of rivers and lakes are arranged according to census by the departments concerned in recent years.

Ⅳ. All of the value indicators in this book are calculated by the same year's prices. All of the indices are calculated by the constant price. Explanatory notes are provided behind the list in which if there are changes. Data of the book are composed by computers.

Ⅴ. The book is edited according to the frame and standard of China Statistical Yearbook. The indicator explanatory notes are edited according to China Statistical Yearbook, and the units of measurement are internationally standard measurement units. The notations are standard notations of China Statistical Yearbook.

"…" not large enough to be rounded into the least unit.

"#" of which: major items.

"Space" data not available.

"※"see footnotes below.

目　录

CONTENTS

二、国民经济核算

Chapter 2 National Economic Accounting

三、人口、就业和职工工资

Chapter 3 Population, Employment and Wages of Staff and Workers

四、固定资产投资

Chapter 4 Investment in Fixed Assets

五、财政、金融、保险
Chapter 5 Finance, Banking and Insurance

六、物价指数

Chapter 6 Price Indices

七、人民生活

Chapter 7 People's Livelihood

八、城市建设、环境保护

Chapter 8 Construction of Cities, Environmental Protection

九、农业

Chapter 9 Agriculture

十一、建筑业
Chapter 11 Construction

十二、交通运输、邮电业
Chapter 12 Transportation, Postal and Telecommunication Services

十四、教育和科技

Chapter 14 Education, Science and Technology

十五、文化、体育、卫生
Chapter 15 Culture, Sports and Public Health

十六、党群、政法和社会福利
Chapter 16 Party and Mass, Politics and Law,Social Welfare

十七、企业调查
Chapter 17 Enterprises Survey

十八、各市、州、县主要经济和社会统计指标
Chapter 18 Main Economic and Social Statistics Indicators of Cities,Perfecture and Counties

十九、各省、市、自治区主要经济和社会统计指标

Chapter 19 Main Economic and Social Statistics Indicators by Provinces,Municipalities and Autonomous Regions

湖南省统计局

关于2003年湖南省国民经济和社会发展统计公报

2004年2月10日

2003年，在省委、省政府的正确领导下，全省认真贯彻落实“三个代表”重要思想和党的十六大、十六届三中全会精神，面对突如其来的非典疫情和严重的旱涝灾害，坚持一手抓防治非典不放松，一手抓经济建设不动摇，进一步推进工业化、农业产业化和城镇化进程，加快发展开放型经济、劳务经济和民营经济，国民经济持续快速增长，质量效益同步提高，各项社会事业全面发展，人民生活不断改善。

一、综　合

经济增长加快，内在活力增强。2003年，全省GDP为4633.73亿元，比上年增长9.6%，为1998年以来增速最快的一年，其中第一产业增加值885.87亿元，增长3.6%；第二产业增加值1793.71亿元，增长12.6%；第三产业增加值1954.15亿元，增长9.6%。按常住人口计算，人均GDP为7247元。三次产业结构为19.1∶38.7∶42.2。全省规模工业中非公有制企业增加值增长29.5%，比规模工业快8.8个百分点；非国有经济投资增长24%，占全社会固定资产投资的比重 55%，比上年提高4.1个百分点；全年新增私营企业户数和注册资本金分别增长48.4%和56.4%。全省对外贸易依存度 6.7%，比上年提高0.7个百分点；在（深圳）投资洽谈会上，省级合同引进外资和内资分别为20.9亿美元和119.15亿元。全省农村外出务工人员1199.41万人，增长6%，劳务总收入539亿元，增长8%。

工业化、农业产业化和城镇化取得新进展。工业保持快速增长，全部工业增加值增长12.6%，对经济增长的贡献率为41.4%，推动经济增长4.0个百分点。规模以上工业企业经济效益综合指数121.55%，比上年高11.73个百分点；实现利润100.08亿元，增长43.4%，均创历史最高水平。农业产业化进程稳步推进，全省60家国家和省级龙头企业完成销售收入203亿元，增长12.8%；实现利税12.4亿元，增长6%；共连接基地86.67万公顷，辐射农户400多万户，初步形成以“公司+基地+农户”为纽带的粮食、蔬菜、食用油、畜禽水产乳制品、茶果、竹木林纸六大产业链条；农产品市场体系不断完善，农产品商品率为62%。城市化进程迈出新步伐，城市化水平为33.5%，比上年高1.5个百分点；长株潭三市GDP为1578.36亿元，增长12.8%；占14个市州GDP的比重为33.2%，比上年提高0.4个百分点。

物价总水平适度回升。全省居民消费价格总指数为102.4%，比上年高2.9个百分点，其中食品类价格指数为105.8%，医疗保健价格指数为108.6%；商品零售价格总指数为100.6%；农产品生产者价格指数为106.8%；原材料、燃料、动力购进价格指数为106.7%；工业品出厂价格指数为102.6%；固定资产投资价格指数为102.8%；房地产价格指数为101.4%。

就业再就业工作力度加大。据省劳动和社会保障厅统计，年内新增城镇就业50万人，下岗职工再就业41万人，城镇登记失业人员31.4万人，登记失业率为4.5%。

经济发展环境进一步优化。依法治省积极推进，廉政建设和反腐败斗争的力度加大，从严查处一批大案要案。强化社会治安综合治理，严厉打击各种刑事犯罪和经济犯罪，全省社会治安形势稳定。农村税费改革政策进一步落实，农民负担进一步减轻，人均税费支出81.7元，比上年减少3.2元，下降3.8%。

经济社会发展中存在的主要问题是：经济结构还不合理，制造业整体实力较弱；能源紧缺的矛盾较为突出；农村和农业投资不足，农民收入增长较缓；下岗失业人员和新增劳动力较多，就业压力较大。

二、农　业

农业生产稳定增长。全省粮食总产量2442.73万吨，减少2.3%；油料125.7万吨，增长5.4%；棉花16.31

万吨，增长6.6%；烟叶18.71万吨，增长0.4%；大豆39.72万吨，减少11.5%；蔬菜2291.02万吨，增长5.0%；水果512.38万吨，增长7.0%；出栏肉猪6660.19万头，增长3.3%；出笼家禽52275.76万羽，增长5.8%；出栏牛168.23万头，增长11.2%；出栏羊722.22万只，增长9.8%；禽蛋85.81万吨，增长4.0%；水产品156.59万吨，增长4.7%。

农业结构调整稳步推进。全年粮食作物播种面积4529.79千公顷，减少2.6%，粮食作物占农作物总播种面积的58.6%。稻谷播种面积3409.98千公顷，减少3.7%，其中优质稻播种面积所占比重为39.4%，比上年高1.7个百分点。油料播种面积为867.76千公顷，减少2.9%；药材播种面积为80.77千公顷，棉花播种面积为138.99千公顷，分别增长25.3%和17.3%；麻类播种面积为57.23千公顷，增长0.9%；烟叶播种面积94.06千公顷，蔬菜播种面积为964.26千公顷，分别增长0.5%和7.2%。畜牧业稳定发展，2003年畜牧业增加值增长3.7%，占第一产业增加值的29.4%。农、林、牧、渔比例为55.7∶7.9∶29.4∶7.0。据省乡镇企业局统计，2003年，全省乡镇企业增加值1593.3亿元，增长10.7%。

农村基础设施和生态环境进一步改善。全年开工各类水利工程60.7万处，投入资金43亿元，完成土石方6.51亿立方米，治理水土流失面积527平方公里。全省新增农田有效灌溉面积6.2千公顷；新增节水灌溉面积10.1千公顷。农业机械总动力2664.72万千瓦，增长6.7%。全年化肥施用量（折纯）188.33万吨，增长2.2%；农村用电量53.84亿千瓦小时，增长8.0%。完成造林面积40.96万公顷，年末有林面积986.11万公顷，增长1.5%；森林覆盖率53.67%，比上年高0.54个百分点。

扶贫开发取得新成绩。全年共投入专项扶贫资金11.6亿元，有20万人解决温饱和越过低收入线。

三、工业和建筑业

工业生产快速增长。全年全部工业增加值1455.27亿元，比上年增长12.6%，其中规模以上工业增加值886.52亿元，增长20.7%。在规模以上工业中，轻工业增加值358.14亿元，增长18.4%；重工业增加值528.38亿元，增长21.9%；国有及国有控股企业增加值549.27亿元，增长14.4%；大中型企业增加值504.06亿元，增长14.9%；“十大标志性工程”骨干企业增加值286.71亿元，增长27.4%，拉动全省规模工业增长8.8个百分点。重点行业增长加快，交通运输设备制造业等10大行业拉动全省规模工业增长14.0个百分点。

主要产品产量增长较快。原煤2366.69万吨，增长16.2%；发电量523.73亿千瓦小时，增长19.5%；钢产量590.77万吨，增长8.1%；水泥3054.34万吨，增长11.1%；平板玻璃763.85万重量箱，增长30.9%；机制纸及纸板124.28万吨，增长37.1%；十种有色金属107.18万吨，增长16.4%；汽车4.38万辆，增长76.2%；纱21.99万吨，增长20.1%。

产销衔接良好。规模以上工业企业实现销售产值2639.41亿元，增长23.4%；产品销售率为100.07%，比上年高0.34个百分点。

建筑业快速发展。全年建筑业实现增加值338.44亿元，增长12.5%。具有资质等级的建筑企业1495家，实现利润14.1亿元，增长27.2%；房屋建筑施工面积8970万平方米，增长25.2%；房屋建筑竣工面积3905.6万平方米，增长6.6%。

四、固定资产投资

固定资产投资增速加快。2003年，全社会固定资产投资1556.94亿元，比上年增长14.8%，同比快2.8个百分点。其中国有经济投资701.28亿元，增长5.3%；非国有经济投资855.66亿元，增长24.0%。在非国有经济中，外商、港澳台、联营、股份制经济投资405.28亿元，增长68.4%；集体及个体经济投资450.38亿元，增长0.2%。按管理渠道分，基本建设投资605.2亿元，增长13.1%；更新改造投资301.8亿元，增长32.4%；房地产开发投资230.0亿元，增长52.4%。地方项目投资1444.24亿元，增长21.5%；中央项目投资112.7亿元，下降32.5%。年内新开工项目5653个，全部投产项目4473个。计划总投资亿元以上的基本建设项目392个，完成投资332.9亿元。

重点工程建设进展顺利。50个在建重点工程完成投资327.29亿元，增长12.7%。鲤鱼江电厂扩建、韶山毛泽东诞辰 110 周年建设工程、五城会场馆建设工程、株洲电厂二期和长潭高速公路路面改造工程等项目竣工投产。华菱集团技改工程、县乡公路改造等项目进展顺利。

工业投入力度加大。在国有及其他经济投资中，全部工业完成投资 376.5 亿元，增长 36.9%，其中工业技改投资 239.8 亿元，增长 44%。以煤炭、黑色、有色金属为主的采掘业投资 7.43 亿元，增长 38.7%；以冶金、机械工业为龙头的制造业投资 261.54 亿元，增长 55.3%。支柱产业和优势企业的发展，有力推进了全省工业化进程。

全年主要新增生产能力：发电机组 194.45 万千瓦，11 万伏及以上变电设备能力 308.75 万千伏安；长途光缆 173 公里，程控交换机 50 万线，移动通信基站设备 428 个；新建铁路正式交付运营里程 101.3 公里；新建公路 834.69 公里，其中高速公路 216.12 公里；城市自来水日供水量 41.9 万吨，城市污水日处理量 1 万吨；城市道路扩建长度 540.56 公里。

五、交通、邮电

交通运输业继续发展。2003 年，全社会货物周转量 1368.17 亿吨公里，比上年增长 11.7%，其中铁路运输 783.19 亿吨公里，增长 7.0%；公路运输 460.59 亿吨公里，增长 29.4%；水路运输 122.35 亿吨公里，减少 9.7%；民航运输 1.33 亿吨公里，增长 24.2%。旅客周转量 827.75 亿人公里，增长 0.4%，其中铁路运输 429.95 亿人公里，增长 0.9%；公路运输 382.23 亿人公里，下降 0.7%；水路运输 2.43 亿人公里，下降 24.1%；民航运输 13.14 亿人公里，增长 24.0%。客货运输换算周转量 1838.1 亿吨公里，增长 8.7%。

邮电通信业快速增长。全年完成邮电业务总量 220.14 亿元，增长 21.2%，其中邮政业务总量 21.19 亿元，电信业务总量 198.95 亿元，分别增长 5.3%和 21.7%。局用交换机总容量 1098.81 万门，增加 49.23 万门。固定电话用户数 953.66 万户，增长 20.18%；移动电话用户 791.68 万户，增长 32.3%。电话普及率为 26.3%，其中固定电话普及率为 14.4%，比上年高 2.4 个百分点；移动电话普及率为 11.9%，比上年高 2.9 个百分点；互联网用户数 213.19 万户，增长 68.3%。

六、国内贸易

消费品市场日益活跃。2003 年，全省实现社会消费品零售总额 1816.3 亿元，比上年增长 10.8%，其中城市 997.12 亿元，增长 11.9%。分行业看，批发零售贸易业零售额 1558.4 亿元，增长 10.6%；餐饮业 224.57 亿元，增长 13.3%；其他行业 33.33 亿元，增长 4.7%。以汽车、通讯器材等为代表的新兴消费引领消费市场快速增长。2003 年，限额以上贸易企业的汽车、通迅器材零售额分别增长 46.7%和 56.6%。连锁超市等新型业态显示出巨大活力，全省限额以上连锁商业企业 4 4家，商品销售额 55.23 亿元，增长 51.5%。

七、对外经济贸易和旅游业

对外贸易取得新成绩。2003 年，全省进出口总额为 37.36 亿美元，比上年增长 29.9%，其中出口 21.46 亿美元，增长 19.5%；进口 15.9 亿美元，增长 47.1%。一般贸易进出口额为 32.88 亿美元，增长 33.3%；加工贸易进出口额 3.34 亿美元，增长 24.9%。按企业性质分，国有企业进出口 22.77 亿美元，增长 23.3%；集体企业 2.41 亿美元，增长 36.6%；私营企业 4.49 亿美元，增长 136.9%；外商投资企业 7.69 亿美元，增长 16.0%。出口商品中，农产品出口 1.85 亿美元，增长 20.2%；机电产品 4.31 亿美元，增长 17.7%；服装 1.96 亿美元，增长 30.3%。

招商引资取得新突破。全年协议利用外资 23.76 亿美元，增长 43.3%；实际利用外资 17.9 亿美元，增长 30.0%，其中外商直接投资 14.89 亿美元，增长 44.4%。实际利用内资 335.43 亿元，增长 110.8%。

对外经济合作大幅增长。全年新签对外承包工程、劳务合作、设计咨询的合同金额 3.91 亿美元，增长 25.3%；营业额 3.86 亿美元，增长 30.3%。

旅游业稳步发展。成功举办以“展现绿色潇湘，体验健康之旅”为主题的中国湖南旅游节等系列促销活动，促进和推动了旅游业的发展。全年接待国内外旅游者 5970.39 万人次，增长 3.7%；实现旅游总收入 294.1 亿元，增长 19.7%。

八、金融、证券与保险

金融机构存贷款快速增长,对经济的支持力度加大。年末全省金融机构各项存款余额 4774.8 亿元，新增 747.4亿元，同比多增 141.2 亿元，其中城乡居民储蓄存款余额 3120.8 亿元，新增 457 亿元，同比多增 53.7 亿元；企业存款余额 1185.3 亿元，新增 242.8 亿元。金融机构各项贷款余额 3900.6 亿元，新增 589.2 亿元，同比多增 164.5 亿元。中长期贷款余额 1524.4 亿元，新增 332.2 亿元，同比多增 130.1 亿元，其中基建和技改贷款两项新增 187.3 亿元，同比多增 70 亿元，占全部新增贷款的 33%，比上年高 6 个百分点。个人消费贷款余额 220.8 亿元，新增 90.9 亿元，同比多增 36.2 亿元，其中个人住房贷款余额 136.2 亿元，新增 50.1 亿元，同比多增 15.8 亿元；个人汽车贷款余额 27.7 亿元，新增 14.9 亿元，同比多增 5 亿元。

证券市场融资功能不断增强。年末全省共有境内上市公司 39 家，比上年增加 3 家，其中增发新股一家，境外上市公司 2 家；年末股票市价总值 859 亿元，比上年增加 3.9%；全年通过证券市场募集资金 57.7 亿元，增长 94.2%。

保险事业快速发展。全年保费收入 103.9 亿元，比上年增长 21%，其中财产险保费收入 20.1 亿元，增长 8.1%；人身意外伤害险保费收入 4 亿元，增长 34.5%。各项赔付支出 21.5 亿元，增长 4.9%，其中人身意外伤害险赔款 1.8 亿元，增长 21.7%；财产险赔款 10.7 亿元，增长 12.4%。

九、科学技术和教育

科技成果不断涌现，重大科技专项和科技攻关取得新的突破。全省有县及县以上独立研究与开发机构 308 个，其中社会人文研究机构 3 个，科技信息与文献机构 13 个。拥有国家级重点实验室 3 家，部级重点实验室 7 家，省级重点实验室 29 家，国家（部门）级工程技术研究中心 6 家，省级工程技术研究中心 17 家。全省共取得各类科技成果 836 项，其中“复杂体系成分分析及波谱结构解析的化学计量学研究”获国家自然科学二等奖，“异源四倍体鱼和三倍体鲫（鲤）研究”等 10 个项目获国家科技进步二等奖。全省制造业信息化省级示范企业 84 家；电动汽车的研发和产业化工作有了创造性突破；逐步形成以人类胚胎干细胞为核心、以成体干细胞为辅的研究开发人类干细胞治疗疾病的产业链；血防研究取得重要进展。全年受理专利申请 6080 件，增长 25.1%；专利授权量 3100 件，增长 32.1%。高新技术产业发展步伐加快，全年高新技术产品产值 956 亿元，增长 28.5%。

地质勘探和测绘事业进一步拓展。2003 年，新发现矿产地 13 处，成功预报地质灾害 175 起，全年为经济建设提供数字测绘成果 21186 平方公里/9556MB，绘制各种比例尺地图 13851 幅。

普通高等教育规模继续扩大。全省普通高等学校 73 所，普通高校招生 19.38 万人，增长 23.5%；在校学生 53.72 万人，增长 28.1%；毕业生 9.00 万人，增长 45.0%；全省 10 所普通高校和 5 个科研机构共招收研究生 8597 人，增长 47.4%，其中攻读博士学位 1410 人，攻读硕士学位的 7187 人；毕业研究生 3099 人，其中授予博士学位 384 人；在校研究生 19421 人，增长 37.3%，其中在学博士生 3456 人，增长 25.1%。普通中等专业教育结构日趋合理，教育质量不断提高。全省有普通中等专业学校 81 所，招生 9.22 万人，增长 11.5%，在校学生 22.65 万人，增长 1.3%。中小学教育稳步发展。全省普通中学 4689 所，在校学生 488.77 万人，增长 4.7%；普通初中入学率 96.26%，比上年高 3.03 个百分点；初中在校学生辍学率 1.51%，下降 0.36 个百分点。普通小学 24673 所，减少 2570 所；在校学生 468.69 万人；小学适龄儿童入学率为 98.56%，比上年高 0.92 个百分点；小学在校学生辍学率 0.15 %，下降 0.01 个百分点。

十、文化、卫生和体育

文化事业蓬勃发展。花鼓戏《沥沥太阳雨》获第九届全国精神文明建设“五个一工程”入选作品奖；

木偶剧《石三伢子》获第二届全国木偶皮影比赛金奖；皮影戏《肥猫哥儿》、《会摇尾巴的狼》获第二届全国木偶皮影比赛银奖；舞剧《古汉伊人》获第六届全国舞剧比赛演出大奖；舞剧《边城》获第二届全国舞台美术展览会金奖。成功举办第四届中国金鹰电视艺术节；电视剧《女子乘务组》获中国电视剧飞天奖中篇电视剧三等奖。年末全省艺术表演团体 88 个，文化馆 125 个，群众艺术馆 15 个，博物馆、纪念馆 70 个，公共图书馆 115 个。

广播电视事业日益繁荣。全省拥有广播电台 11 座，中、短波发射台和转播台 25 座，对国内广播节目 53 套，平均每日播音时间 531 小时 55 分，增加 36 小时 50 分；广播综合人口覆盖率 81.79%。全省电视台 15 座，电视发射台和转播台 443 座，电视节目 103 套，增加 2 套，平均每周播出时间 9178 小时 31 分，增加 981 小时 58 分；电视综合人口覆盖率 91.91%；全省有线电视用户 380.68 万户，增加 35.3 万户。

新闻出版事业稳步发展。全年出版图书 3889 种，总印数 33721 万册，增长 3.34%；出版期刊 269 种，总印数 11938 万册，增长 6.52%；出版报纸 106 种，总印数 10.18 亿份，增长 6.9%。湖南少年儿童出版社出版的《无人区科学探险系列》荣获中宣部第九届"五个一工程奖·一本好书奖"二等奖，《波斯经典文库》等 9 种图书获国家图书奖，其中《农村卫生人员预防传染性非典型肺炎必读》获国家图书奖特别奖。

卫生医疗保健事业发展加快。年末全省医疗卫生机构 4272 家，卫生机构床位数 14.36 万张，卫生技术人员 19.24 万人，执业（助理）医师 7.94 万人，注册护士 5.36 万人。全省乡镇卫生院 2532 家，拥有床位数 3.75 万张，增长 1.4%。农村有医疗点的村占总村数的比重为 94.4%，比上年提高 0.9 个百分点。非典防治工作取得阶段性重大胜利，全省没有原发病例，也没有发生二代病例。

体育基础设施建设有较大改观。全省拥有体育场地 29213 个，其中体育场 38 个，体育馆 57 座，成功举办第五届全国城市运动会。全年获得世界冠军 9 个，在重大国际体育比赛中获得金牌 10 枚，银牌 5 枚，铜牌 2 枚；在全国性体育比赛中获得金牌 37 枚，银牌 27 枚，铜牌 28 枚；有 1 人 2 次破 2 项世界纪录。颁布并实施《湖南省全民健身条例》，群众性体育运动进一步普及，经常参加体育活动的人口占总人口的比重为 35.7%，比上年提高 1.8 个百分点。

十一、环境保护

环境治理力度加强，环境质量进一步改善。2003 年，全省环保监测站加强标准化、自动化建设，环保监测站 130 个，环境监测人员 1935 人；完成环境污染限期治理项目 342 个，投资额 9230.5 万元。建成烟尘控制区 194 个，面积 1122.3 平方公里，增长 4.8%；环境噪声达标区 166 个，面积 1096.6 平方公里，增长 0.2%。新上一批清洁燃料、污水处理和垃圾处理等城市环境基础设施项目。全省 14 个地级城市，有 7 个实现地表水按功能区达标，永州、怀化、郴州市实现大气质量按功能分区达标。年末全省建有自然环境保护区 82 个，其中国家级 8 个，省级 35 个；自然环境保护区面积 99.49 万公顷，增长 20.6%。河、湖、空气、重点污染源的监测继续加强。全省工业污染源基本实现达标排放，列入国家考核的 396 家重点企业中，达标 385 家，达标率 97.2%；在国家控制的 12 种污染物中，全省有 11 种控制在国家规定的指标以内。

十二、人口、人民生活和社会保障

据抽样调查，年末全省总人口为 6662.8 万人，比上年末增加 34.3 万人，其中市镇人口 2232.04 万人，乡村人口 4430.76 万人。全省人口出生率为 11.82‰，上升 0.26 个千分点；死亡率为 6.87‰；自然增长率为 4.95‰，提高 0.09 个千分点。年末全省 65 岁及以上老年人口为 556.92 万人，占全省总人口的比重为 8.36%，比上年提高 0.31 个百分点。

人民生活不断改善。2003 年，全省城镇居民人均可支配收入 7674.2 元，增长 10.3%，考虑价格因素，实际增长 8.8%，其中城镇居民人均工薪收入 5553.8 元，增长 10.2%；经营净收入 356.2 元，增长 51.3%；转移性收入 1663.6 元，增长 5.7%。农村居民人均纯收入 2532.9 元，增加 135 元，增长 5.6%，考虑价格因素，实际增长 4.7%，其中工资性收入 988.4 元，增加 74.1 元；家庭经营收入 1427.2 元，增加 50.5 元；转移性和财产性收入 117.3 元，增加 10.4 元。农村居民人均可支配收入 2471.6 元，增加 108.4 元。城乡居民的消费方式、消费渠道和消费结构发生重大变化。2003 年，城镇居民人均消费性支出 6082.6 元，增长 9.1%，考虑价格因素，实际增长 7.6%，其中交通及通信消费支出 680.2 元，教育文化娱乐消费支出 994 元，医疗保健消费支出 391.3 元，分别增长 14.1%、 12.5%和 13.9%；城镇居民恩格尔系数为 35.8%；平均每百户家庭拥有家用汽车 0.27 辆，家用电脑 26.7 台；人均住房建筑面积 23.3 平方米，增加 0.9 平方米。农村居民人均生活消费总支出 2139 元，增长 3.4%；农村居民恩格尔系数为 51.9%；平均每百户家庭拥有彩色电视机 49.6 台，电话机 41.4台，移动电话机 15.4 台；人均住房面积 35 平方米，增加 1 平方米。

社会保障工作得到加强。2003 年，全省参加基本养老保险的人数 634.23 万人，增长 2.9%，其中参加基本养老保险的离退休人员 167.06 万人，增长 5.9%；参加失业保险人数 347.50 万人，增长 6.4%；参加基本医疗保险人数 423.50 万人，增长 6.4%；领取城市最低生活保障费人数 1774 万人次。全年发放企业离退休人员基本养老金 81.4 亿元，国有企业下岗职工基本生活保障资金 12.7 亿元，城市居民最低生活保障资金 9.35 亿元。

注：1、本公报为初步统计数。

2、湖南省 GDP、各产业增加值绝对数按现价计算，增长速度按可比价计算。

STATISTICAL COMMUNIQUE OF HUNAN PROVINCE

ON THE 2003 NATIONAL ECONOMIC AND SOCIAL DEVELOPMENT

PROVINCIAL STATISTICAL BUREAU OF HUNAN

February 10, 2004

In 2003, under the correct leadership of Hunan Provincial committee of CPC and the Government, people al over the province dealt steadily with the serious problems and challenges brought about by the sudden outbreak of SARS epidemic and various natural disasters, implemented the important thought of □Three Represents?and the spirit of the 16th National Congress of CPC and the Third Plenary Session of the 16th CPC Central Committee, insisted on prevention and cure of SARS epidemic and economical construction, pushed on agricultural industrialization, industrialization and urbanization further, and developed the opening economy, the personal service economy and the non -state-owned economy. The national economy maintained a continual and rapid development with further improved quality and vitality. The social affairs developed in an all -round way, and the living standard of people was further improved.

I. General Outlook

The national economy increased by fast speed, and inherent vitality was enhanced. According to preliminary estimation and evaluation, the Gross Domestic Product of the province was 463.37 billion yuan, increased by 9.6 percent over the previous year according to comparable prices, representing the highest grow since 1998. Of this total, the value-added of the primary industry was 88.59 billion yuan, up by 3.6 percent; the value -added of the secondary industry was 179.37 billion yuan, having a increase of 12.6 percent; and that of tertiary industry was 195.42 billion yuan, having increased 9.6 percent. The per-capita GDP at permanent residents (who having been in Hunan for more than half a year) reached 7247 yuan. The structure of the GDP was 19.1:38.7:42.2. The value-added of non-state-owned enterprises of the total industrial enterprises above designated size increased 29.5 percent, or 8.8 percentage points higher over the total industrial enterprises above designated size. The investment of the non-state-owned economy increased 24 percent, accounted for 55 percent of the completed investment in fixed assets, 4.1 percentage points higher over the previous year. The newly added private-owned enterprises and registered capital increased 48.4 percent and 56.4 percent respectively. The ratio of interdependent of foreign trade was 6.7 percent, more than 0.7 percentage points over the previous year. In Shenzhen investment negotiation conference, the foreign capital and internal capital registered with the provincial contracts was 2.1 billion dollar and 11.92 billion yuan respectively. The number o countryside labor worked outside the rural areas was 11.99 million, increased by 6 percent, and the total personal service income was 53.9 billion yuan, up by 8 percent.

A new development was gained in pushing on agricultural industrialization, industrialization and urbanization. Fast growth was registered in industrial production, the gross v alue-added of industrial sectors increased by 12.6 percent, leaded the growth of economy to increase 4.0 percent point; its contribution to the growth of economy reached 41.4 percent. The index of comprehensive economic benefit in the industrial enterprises above designated size was 121.55 percent, or 11.73 percentage points higher over the previous year. The profits of the industrial enterprises above designated size stood at 10.01 billion yuan, increased by 43.4 percent, the two indices were the best records in the history. Agricultural industrialization was pushed steadily. The sixty state and province-level chief enterprises achieved sales revenue 20.3 billion yuan, increased by 12.8%, and gained per-tax profits 1.24 billion yuan, up by 6%. It has connec ted bases 866.7 thousand hectares, and covered farms 4 million or more. Th major six industry chairs of grain, vegetables, eatable oil, animal、fowls、aquatic and dairy products, tea and fruits, and bamboo、 wood、 forest and paper products, linking with □company to base to farm?, have formed initially. The market system of farm crops was further improved, and the commodity ratio of farm crops reached 62 percent. New progress was gained in pushing on urbanization. The urbanization ratio was 33.5 percent, rose by 1.5 percentage points higher over the previous year. The Gross Domestic Product of Changsha and Zhuzhou and Xiangtan was 157.84 billion yuan, up by 12.8 percent. The GDP of three cities accounted for 33.2 percent of the province, or 0.4 percentage points higher over the previous year.

The general prices level increased by small margin. The general level of consumer prices in Hunan of the year was up by 2.4 percent over the previous year. Of this total, the price for food increased by 5.8 percent; the price s for medical, health and personal articles up by 8.6 percent. The general retail price of commodities was up by 0.6 percent. The pr ucers' price index for farm products was 106.8 percent. The purchasing price index for raw materials, fuels and power was 106.7 percent. The ex-factory price index for industrial product was 102.6 percent. The price index for investment in fixed assets was 102.8 percent. The price index for real estate was 101.4 percent.

The work on employment was strengthened. According to the statistics from the B ureau of Labor and Social Security of Hunan Province, the newly-added employed people in urban areas was 0.5 million, and the re-employed people of laid-off workers was 0.41 million by the end of 2003. The total of urban unemployed people through unemployment registration numbered 0.314 million, and the urban unemployment ratio through unemployment registration was 4.5 percent.

The economic environment was further improved. Administering the province according to law was pushed on actively. The construction of incorruptible government and the struggle against corruption were strengthened, and a series of cases with serious problem were investigated earnestly. The comprehensive administration of public security was strengthened, and all kinds of criminal offense and economic crim inals were struck seriously. The situation of public security of the province was steady. The policy of reform for countryside taxs and administrative fees was implemented further, and the burden on the peasants was lightened further. In 2003, the per -capita expenditure of taxs and administrative fees of peasantry was 81.7 yuan, decreased 3.2 yuan over the previous year, down by 3.8 percent.

Main problems that existed in the economic and social development included the unreasonable economic al structure, the general weakling strength of manufacturing sector, the tight relation between the supply and demand of energy, the un-sufficient investment in fixed assets in rural areas and agricultures, the slow growth of farmers' income, the increasing number of laid-off workers of state-owned enterprises and newly-added labor, and the severe situation of employment.

II. Agriculture

Steady progress was gained in agriculture production. The total output of grain amounted to 24. 43 milli tones, decreased by 2.3 percent. The output of oil-bearing seeds was 1.26 million tones, increased by 5.4 perc ent. The output of cotton amounted to 163 .1 thousand tones, up by 6.6 percent. The output of flue-cured tobacco was

187.1 thousand tones, increased by 0.4 percent. The output of vegetables amounted to 22.9 million tones, up by 5.0 percent. The output of fruits was 5.12 million tones, increased by 7.0 percent. The number of slaughtered fattened hogs amounted to 66.6 million heads, up by 3.3 percent. The number of slaughtered fowles was 522.76 million feathers, increased by 5.8 percent. The number of slaughte red beef cattle was 1.68 million heads, up by 11.2 percent. The number of slaughtered sheep and goats was 7.22 million heads, increased by 9.8 percent. The total aquatic products amounted to 1.57 million tones, up by 4.7 percent.

Structural adjustment of agriculture was pushed steadily. In 2003, the sown areas of grain was 4.53 million hectares, decreased by 2.6 percent. The sown areas of grain covered 58.6 percent of that of the whole crop production. The sown areas of rice was 3.41 million hectares, dec reased by 3.7 percent. The sown areas of high quality rice covered 39.4 percent of that of the rice; it was 1.7 percentage points higher over the previous year. The sown areas of oil-bearing crops was 867.76 thousand hectares, decreased by 2.9 percent. The sown areas of medical herbs was 80.77 thousand hectares, and cotton was 138.99 thousand hectares, increased by 25.3 percent and 17.3 percent respectively. The sown areas of ramie was 57.23 thousand hectares, up by 0.9 percent. The sown areas of cured tobacco was 94.06 thousand hectares, and vegetables was 964.26 thousand hectares, increased by 0.5 percent and 7.2 percent respectively. Steady progress was registered in animal husbandry. In 2003, the value -added of animal husbandary increased by 3.7 percent, covered 29.4 percent of that of the primary industry. According to statistics of the Bureau of the township enterprises of Hunan Province, the total value -added of the township enterprises was 159.3 billion yuan, up by 10.7 percent.

The construction of r ural infrastructure facilities and zoology environment was further improved. In 2003, 607 thousand water conservancy projects were started working, 4.3 billion yuan was invested, and 0.65 billion earth-stone cubic metres was finished. The areas of control ling soil erosion reached 527 square kilometers. Over 6,200 hectares of land were converted into farmland with effective irrigation system, another 10100 hectares of land were guaranteed by water -saving irrigation system. The total power of agricultural machinery reached 26.65 million kw, up by 6.7 percent. By the end of 2003, the forestation areas reached 409.6 thousand hectares, the areas with woodland was 9.86 million hectares, up by 1.5 percent. The forest coverage ratio reached 53.6 percent, up by 0.54 percentage points higher over the previous year.

New progress was gained in helping people out of poverty. In 2003, the fund in helping people out of povert y reached 1.16 billion yuan, and 200 thousand of people have solved the problem of adequate fo od and clothing and acrossed the line of low income.

III. Industry and Construction

Fast growth was registered in industrial production. In 2003, the total value-added of the industrial sector was 145.53 billion yuan, up by 12.6 percent over the previous year. The value-added of the industrial enterprises above designated size was 88.65 billion yuan, increased by 20.7 percent. Of which, the value-added of the light industry was 35.81 billion yuan , up by 18.4 percent; the value -added of the heavy industry was 52.84 billion yuan, up by 21.9 percent; the value-added of the state-owned and state-holding enterprises was 54.93 billion yuan, up by 14.4 percent ; the value-added of the large scale enterprises was 50.41 billion yuan up by 14.9 percent. The value-added of ?0 typified industrial enterprises?reached 28.67 billion yuan ,increased by 27.4 percent , leading the industria enterprises above designated size increase 8.8 percentage points. The emphasized sectors increased quickly, the

10 typified sectors including the transport equipment manufacturing industry leading the industria enterprises above designated size increase 14.0 percentage points.

The output of major industrial products increased quickly. The output of coal was 23.67 million tones ,up by 16.2 percent ; the electricity generated for the whole year was 5.24 billion kilowatt-hours, up by 19.5 percent; the output of steel reached 5.91 million tones , up by 8.1 percent ;the output of cement stood at 30.54 million tones ,up by 11.1 percent ; plate glass 7.64 million weight box , up by 30.9 percent ; the output of machine-processed paper and cardboard was 1.24 million tones , up by 37.1 percent ; ten kinds of nonferrous metals 1.07 million tones , up by 16.4 percent ; automobiles 43.8 thousand units , up by 76.2 percent ; yarn 219.9 thousand tones , up by 20.1 percent .

Production and marketing linked tightly. The sales income of industrial enterprises above designated size was 263.94 billion yuan , increased by 23.4 percent . The sales ratio was 100.07 percent , 0.34 percentage points higher over the previous year .

The construction enterprises developed quickly. The value-added of construction enterprises was 33.84 billion yuan, up by 12.5 percent. The number of construction enterprises with certain qualification was 1495 units, and th profit of it was 1.41 billion yuan ,up by 27.2 percent. The floor space of building under construction was 89.7 million square meters, up by 25.2 percent. The floor space of building completed 39.06 million square meters, up by 6.6 percent.

IV. Investment in Fixed Assets

Investment in fixed assets increased quickly. In 2003, the completed investment in fixed assets reached 155.69 billiion yuan, increased by 14.8 percent, or 2.8 percentage points quicker ov er the previous year. Of which, the investment of state-owned units was 70.13 billion yuan,up by 5.3 percent; the investment of non-state-owned units was 85.57 billion yuan, up by 24.0 percent. Among the investment of non-state-owned units, the investment from foreigners, Hong Kong, Macao and Taiwan, joint ownership and share-holding economy was 40.53 billion yuan, up by 68.4 percent; the investment of collective-owned and individual economy was 45.04 billion yuan, up by 0.2 percent. Among the investment of state-owned and other types of units, the investment in capital construction was 60.52 billion yuan, up by 13.1 percent; the investment in technical updating and transformation was 30.18 billion yuan, up by 32.04 percent; the investment in real estate development was 23.00 billion yuan, up by 52.4 percent. The investment in the local projects reached 144.42 billion yuan, up by 21.5 percent, and the investment in the central projects was 11.27 billion yuan, down by 32.5 percent. The newly started projects d uring the year were 5653, and the finished projects reached 4473. The capital projects which investment above 10 0 million yuan 392, and the finished investment 33.29 billion yuan.

The construction of key projects progressed smoothly. The fifty key project s under construction finished investment 32.73 billion yuan, increased by 12.7 percent. The construction projects including the extension of Liyujiang electric factory, the projects in Shao Shan celebrated the 110rd anniversary of Mao Ze Dong'birthday, the stadiums and accommodations for The Fifth Cities'Games, the second period of Zhu Zhou electric factory, and the paving transformation of Chang-Zhu-Tan expressway completed and put into operation. The projects including the technical updating and transformation of Hua Ling Group and the transformation of road in rural areas progressed smoothly.

The investment in industry increased rapidly. Among the investment of state-owned and other types of units, the total investment in industry was 37.65 billion yuan, up by 36.9 percent. Of which, the investment in technical updating and transformation was 23.98 billion yuan, increased by 44 percent. The mining and quarrying investment mainly enganged in coal mining, ferrous metals mining and nonferrous metal was 743 million yuan, up by 38.7 percent; the manufacturing investment mainly eneraged in metallurgy and engineering industry was 26.15 billion yuan, up by 55.3 percent. With the development of the pillared industry and predominant corporation, the progress of industrialization developed by fast speed.

The newly increased annual production capacity in 2003 through capital construction projects included: the capacity of power generating sets 1.95 million kws, the electric substation equipment (equal or larger than 110 thousand v) 3.09 million volt-ampere, the long distance cable was 173 kms, the program controlling exchange 500 thousand lines, the facility of mobile communication base 428 sign paths; new trunk railways put into operation 101.3 kms; newly constructed highways 834.69 kms, including 216.12 kms of express highways ; the capacity of daily city tap water supply 419 thousand tons; the capacity of daily disposal sewer 10 thousand tons; the length of extending city road 540.56 kms.

V. Transportation, Post and Telecommunications

The transportation developed steadily. In 2003, total volume of cargo transported by various means was 136.82 billion ton-kilometers, up by 11.7 percent over the previous year. Of which, the cargo transportation by railways was 78.32 billion ton-kilometers, increased by 7.0 percent; by highways, 46.06 billion ton-kilometers, u by 29.4 percent; by waterways, 12.24 billion ton-kilometers, down by 9.7 percent; and by airways, 0.133 billion ton-kilometers, up 24.2 percent. The volume of passenger transportation was 82.78 billion person-kilometers, an increase of 0.4 percent. Of which, passengers carried by railways were 43.00 billion person-kilometers, up by 0.9 percent; by highways, 38.22 billion person-kilometers, down by 0.7 percent; by waterways 0.243 billion person-kilometers, down by 24.1 percent; by airways, 1.31 billion person-kilometers, up by 24.0 percent. The total conversion of the passenger-kilometers and freight ton-kilometers were 183.81 billion ton-kilometers, up by 8.7 percent.

The posts and telecommunication developed quickly. The business transactions of postal and telecommunication services in 2003 totaled 22.01 billion yuan, up by 21.2 percent over the previous year. Of this total, postal services accounted for 2.12 billion yuan, up by 5.3 percent; telecommunication services accounted fo 19.90 billion yuan, up by 21.7 percent. By the end of 2003, total capacity of office exchanges reached 10.99 million gates, including 492.3 thousand new-installed exchanges; telephone subscribers numbered 9.53 million, up 20.2 percent; mobile telephone users numbered 7.92 million, up 32. 3 percent; internet services users reached 2. 13 million, up 68.3 percent. There were 26.3 telephones per 100 persons in this province. Of which, there were 14.4 telephone subscribers per 100 persons, up 2.4 percentage points higher over the previous year; and 11.9 mobile telephone users per 100 persons, up 2.9 percentage points higher over the previous year.

VI. Domestic Trade

The sales flourished in commodity marketings. In 2003, the total retail sales of consumer goods reached

181.63 billion yuan, up by 10.8 percent over the previous year. Of this total, the retail sales of consumer goods in urban areas reached 99.71 billion yuan, up by 11.9 percent. In terms of different industries, 155.84 billion yuan from wholesale and retail sale trade, an increase of 10.6 percent; 22.46 billion yuan from catering industries, increased by 13.3 percent; 3.33 billion yuan from other industries, up by 4.7 percent. The new consumer goods represented by motor vehicles and telecommunication equipments increased in consumer goods market quickly. In 2003, of the total wholesale and retail sales above designated size, the retail s ales of motor vehicles and telecommunication equipment increased 46.7 percent and 56.6 percent respectively. The new industries, such as store chains and supermarkets developed quickly. In 2003, there were 44 store chains above designated size with 5.52 billion yuan of the retail sales, up by 51.5 percent.

Ⅶ. Foreign Economic Relations and Tourism

New progress was gained in foreign trade. The total volume of export and import in 2003 amounted to 3.74 billion US dollars, up by 29.9 percent over the previous year. Of which, the export value was 2.15 billion US dollars, up by 6.1 percent; the import was 1.59 billion US dollars, up by 47.1 percent. The volume of export and import of general trade was 3.29 billion US dollars, up by 33.3 percent; the volume of export and import of processing trade was 0.334 billion US dollars, up by 24.9 percent. By the types of enterprises, the export and impor of the state-owned corporations was 2.23 billion US dollars, increased by 23.3 percent; the export and import of collective owned enterprises was 241 million US dollars, up by 36.6 percent; the export and import of private enterprises reached 449 million US dollars, up by 136.9 percent; the export and import of foreign investment enterprises was 769 million US dollars, up by 16.0 percent. Of the volume of export , the exp ort of agricultur goods was 185 million US dollars, up by 20.2 percent;

the export of machinery and electronic products was 431 million US dollars, up by 17.7 percent; the export of textile and articles was 196 million US dollars, had an increase of 30.3 percent.

New breakthrough was registered in utilization of foreign capitals. During the year, the contracted foreign capitals reached 2.38 billion US dollars, up by 43.3 percent over the previous year, and that of actually utilized was 1.79 billion US dollars, up by 30.0 percent, of which, the foreign direct investment was 1.49 billion US dollars, increased by 44.4 percent. The internal capitals utilized actually 33.54 billion yuan, increased by 110.8 percent.

Rapid growth was made in foreign economic and technical cooperation. In 2003, the value involved in the ne contracts signed through contracted projects, labor contracts and design and consultancy se rvinces reached 391 million US dollars, up by 25.3 percent; the accomplished business revenue was 386 million US dollars, up 30.3 percent.

Tourism maintained steadily growth. The year 2003 saw 59.7 million domestic tourists and tourists fro overseas , up by 3.7 percent. The total income of tourism reached 29.4 billion yuan, up by 19.7 percent.

VIII. Banking, Security and Insurance

Savings deposits and loans of financial institutions increased by a wide margin, and its support to economic growth was strengthened. By the end of 2003, the savings deposit in Renminbi and foreign exchange in all financial institutions totaled 477.48 billion yuan, creating an increase of 74.74 billion yuan over the beginning of the year, and more than 14.12 billion yuan on comparable basis. Of this total, the savings deposits by urban and rural residents reached 312.08 billion yuan, creating an increase of 74.74 billion yuan, or more than 5.37 billion yuan on comparable basis; the savings deposits by enterprises was 118.53 billion yuan, creating an increase of 24.28 billion yuan. The year-end value of loans stood at 390.06 billion yuan, creating an increase of 58.92 billion yuan during this year, or more than 16.45 billion yuan on comparable basis. The long-term and medium-term loans accounted for 152.44 billion yuan, creating an increase of 33.22 billion yuan during this year, and more than 13.01 billion yuan on comparable basis. The consumption loans totalled 22.08 billion yuan, creating an increase of 9.09 billion yuan, and more than 3.62 billion yuan on comparable basis. Of which, the loans for individual housing were 3.43 billion yuan, creating an increase of 9.09 billion yuan, and more than 3.62 billion yuan on comparable basis; and the loans for automobile purchase were 2.77 billion yuan, creating an increase of 1.49 billion yuan, and more than 0.5 billion yuan on comparable basis.

The financing function of stock exchange continued to strengthen. At the end of the year, the number of internal listed companies in Hunan rose to 39 , an increase of 3 listed companies. Of which, a listed company sended out new stocks, an d two listed companies entered the offshore stock exchange. At the end of the year, the total stock value was 85.9 billion yuan, an increase of 3.9 percent over the previous year. In 2003, funds rose through issuing stocks and share rights were 5.77 billion yuan, increased by 94.2 percent.

The insurance industry gained rapid development. The insurance premium of all the insurance organs of th province reached 10.39 billion yuan, up 21 percent over the previous year. Of this total, the premium of property insurance was 2.01 billion yuan and the premium from health and unforeseen accident insurance was 0.4 billion yuan, up by 8.1 percent and 34.5 percent respectively. The compensation payment reached 2.15 billion yuan, up by 4.9 percent. Of which, the compensation payment from health and unforeseen accident insurance was 0.18 billion yuan, up by 21.7 percent; the compensation payment of property insurance was 1.07 billion yuan, up by 12.4 percent.

IX. Science, Technology and Education

The fruitful re sults of science and technology emerged continually and newly breakthrough was acquired in science and technolog . By the end of 2003, there were 308 independent scientific research institutions at or above county level, among which there were three institutes for social sciences, and 13 institutes for sci-tech intelligence and literature. There were 3 key national laboratories, 7 key labs at the ministerial level, 29 key labs at the province level, six national (ministerial) technical centers, and 17 technical centers at the province level. In 2003, a total of 836 scientific research results were achieved. There were 84 demonstrated enterprises at the province level engaged in the informativation of manufacturing industry, creative breakthrough in the res earch and industrialization of power-driven automobiles. An significant advance was acquired in the prevention and cure of schistosome. Some of 6,080 patent applications were received, of while, 3,100 patents were authorized, up 25.1 percent and 32.1 percent respectively. The development of high-tech industry was speeded up, and the high- tech enterprises realized output value of 9.56 billion yuan, with an increase of 28.5 percent.

New progress was made in geological prospecting and mapping. In 2003, there were 13 newly found places of minerals, and there were 175 geology disasters had been forecasted successfully. There were fruitful results of figure surveying and drawing 21,186 square kilometers per 9556MB provided for economical development. Surveying and mapping departments published 13,851 kinds of maps of various scales .

The scale of common higher education continued to expand. By the end of 2003, there were 73 general universities in Hunan with 537.2 thousand enrolled undergraduate students, up by 28.1 percent, including 193.8 thousand new entrants and 90.0 thousand completed their undergraduate courses, having increased by 23.5 percent and 45.0 percent. There were 10 universities and 5 institutions that offered courses leading to postgraduate degrees, with 8,597 new entrants, having increased by 47.4 percent. Among which, there were 1,410 new entrants to read for doctor degree and 7,187 new entrants to read for master degree. There were 3,099 postgraduates completed their postgraduate courses, of which, 384 postgraduates awarded doctor degree. There were 19,421 enrolled postgraduat students, increased by 37.3 percent, of which, there were 3,456 postgraduate reading for doctor degree, up by 25.1 percent. The structure of common medium education was reasonable day by day, and the quality of education was enhanced. There were 4,689 ordinary schools with 4887.7 thousand enrolled students, up by 4.7 percent. The entrance rate of the ordinary junior middle school was 96.3 percent, having increased 3.03 percentage points over the previous year. The drop-off rate of ordinary junior middle school students was 1.51 percent, having decreased 0.36 percentage points. There were 24,673 ordinary primary schools , having decreased 2 ,570, with 4686.9 thousand students. The enrollment rate of primary-school-age children was 98.56 percent, having increased 0.92 percentage points; and the drop -off rate of primary school students was 0.15 percent, having decreased 0.01 percentage points.

X. Culture, Public Health and Sports

Cultural industry prospered. By the end of 2003, there were 88 art-performing groups, 125 cultural centers, 15 public artistic centers, 70 museums and memorials, and 115 public libraries in Hunan.

Fairly fast development continued in broadcasting, movie and television programs. By the end of 2003, there were 11 radio broadcasting stations, 25 medium and short wave radio transmitting and relaying stations. Th internal broadcasting programs were 53 suits, and the average broadcasting time everyd ay were 531 hours and 55 minutes, increased 36 hours and 50 minutes over the last year. The through out Hunan brought radio programs to 81.79 percent of the total population. There were 15 TV stations and 443 television transmitting and relaying stations. The TV programs were 103 suits, increased 2 suits over the last year; and the average TV broadcasting time per week were 9,178 hours and 31 minutes, increased 981 hours and 58 minutes. The through out Hunan brought TV programs to 91.91 percent of the total population. The users of CATV were 3806.8 thousands, increased 353 thousands over the last year.

The industry of publication and issue developed steadily. All sorts of books issued 3,889 types, the number of copys at one impression was 337.21 millions, up 3.34 percent; magazines, 269 types, 119.38 million copys, up 6.52 percent; newspaper, 106 types, 1,018 million copys, up 6.9 percent.

The development made in medical treatment hygiene and public health work was speeded up. By the end of 2003, there were 4,272 medical treatment hygiene institutions, with a total of 143.6 thousand. There were 192.4 thousand hygiene technical personnel, 79.4 thousand licensed (assistant) doctors, and 53.6 registered nurses throughout province. By the end of 2003, there were 2,532 medical treatment hygiene institutions in villages and towns, with a total of 37.5 thousand beds, increased by 1.4 percent. Rural villages with medical -care stations made up 94.4 percent, up 0.9 percent compared with the previous year. The prev ention and cure of SARS acquired significant success by stages, neither the primary affection reported, nor the second-generation case found.

The construction of sports infrastructure progressed greatl . There were 29,213 places of sports in Hunan. Among which, there were 38 stadiums and 57 gymnasiums. Hunan succeeded in holding the Fifth Nation-wide City Game. In 2003, athletes from Hunan won 9 world champions; 10 gold medals, 5 silver medals and 2 bronze at important international sport games; furthermore, athletes from Hunan won 37 gold medals, 27 silver medals and 28 bronze at national sport games. One athlete and two person-times broke 2 world records. □he whole people body-building regulations of Hunan Province?was issued and brought into practi ce. Sports were further popularized among the masses, 35.7 percent of the population often took part in sports activities, increased 1.8 percentage points over the previous year.

XI. Environment Protection

The environment protection was enhanced, and the environment quality was further improved. In 2003, the environment monitoring stations strengthened the construction of standardization and automatization, there were 130 environmental monitoring stations, and 1,935 people working in environment protection agencies in Hunan. 342 of programs of treating environment pollution were finished with 92.30 million yuan of investment. 194 of smoke/dust control zones were finished, covering an area of 1,122.3 square kilometers, increased by 4.8 percent; and 166 of zones where the noise pollution was controlled within the standard were finished, covering an area of 1,096.6 square kilometers, increased by 0.2 percent. A batch of programs of urb an environment infrastructure including clean fuel, sewage treatment and refuse disposal were began construction. In the 14 Region-level cities o Hunan Province, there were 7 of cities surface water met the standards related according to function zones, and the quality of atmosphere of YongZhou, HuaiHua and ChengZhou met the standards related according to function zones. By the end of 2003, Hunan had 82 natural protection zones (including 8 nation -level ones and 35 province-level ones); the area of the protection zones reached 994.9 thousand hectares, having an increase of 20.6 percent. The all-round monitoring of the rivers, lakes, air and serious pollution area were reinforced continuously. The ou -let of the industual pollution sources met the standards related basically. 385 enterprises reached the state standards among the 396 key enterprises listed into the state survey, accounted for 97.2 percent. Among 12 sorts of the wastes controlled by the state, 11 were restricted within the standards regulated by the state.

XII. Population, People□s Life and Social Security System

According to the sampling survey, at the end of 2003, the total population of Hunan was 66.63 million, and had an increase of 343 thousand. Of which, 22.32 million people lived in cities and towns and 44.31 million people lived in rural areas. A crude birth rate was 11.82 per thousand, up by 0.26 per-thousand-points; the crude death rate was 6.87 per thousand; the natural growth rate was 4.95 per thousand, or 0.09 per -thousand-points higher than that of 2002. The aged population at 65 and over was 5.57 million, accounted for 8.36 percent of the total population or 0.31 percent-points higher than that of 2002.

The living standard of people improved continuall . In 2003, the annual p er capita disposable incomes o urban households was 7,674.2 yuan, increased by 10.3 percent, if excluding the element of the price change, a real increase of 8.8 percent. Of which, the annual per capita net income from wage and stipend was 5 ,553.8 yuan, a n increase of 10.2 percent; the annual per capita net income from household business operation was 356.2 yuan, increased by 51.3 percent; the transfer income was 1,663.6 yuan, increased by 5.7 percent. In 2003, the annual pe capita net income of rural households was 2,532.9 yuan, increased 135 yuan, up by 5.6 percent, if excluding th element of the price change, a real increase of 4.7 percent. Of which, the annual per capita net income from wage and stipend was 988.4 yuan, increased 74.1 yuan; the annual per capita net income from household business operation was 1,427.2 yuan, increased 50.5 yuan; the transfer and property income was 117.3 yuan, increased 10.4 yuan. The annual per capita disposable income of rural households was 2471.6 yuan, increased 108. 4 yuan. The ways, channel and structure o residents consumption have been changed greatly. In 2003, the annual per capit expenditure for consumption of urban households was 6,082.6 yuan, if excluding the element of the price change, real increase of 7.6 percent. Of which, the expenditure of urban households for transportation & telecommunication, education culture & recreation, and medical services were 680.2 yuan, 994 yuan and 391.3 yuan, increased by 14.1 percent, 12.5 percent and 13.9 percent respectively. The Engel coefficient of urban households was 35.8 percent. Averagely, every hundred urban families own 0.27 domestic automobiles and 26.7 computers. Per capita municipal residents?housing area reached 23.3 square meters more 0.9 square meters than last year. The per capita consumption expenditures of rural households were 2,139 yuan, increased by 3.4 percent. The Engel coefficient s (which refers to the proportion of expenditures on food to the total consumption expenditures of households) were 51.9 percent for rural households. Averagely, every hundred rural families numbered 49.6 color TV sets, 41.4 telephones, and 15.4 mobile telephones. The rural resident□s per capital housing areas reached 35 square meter more 1 square meter than last year.

Social security system was further consolidated. By the end of 2003, 6. 34 million staff and workers in urban areas participated in the basic pension programs, increased by 2.9 percent. Of which, including 1.67 million retirees, an increase of 5.9 percent; 3.48 million people participated in unemployment insurance programs, having an increase of 6.4 percent; the basic health programs involved 4. 24 million people, a growth of 4 percent. The retirees from enterprises were paid 8.14 billion yuan as basic pensions, 1.27 billion yuan were paid to lay-off workers from the state-owned enterprises for maintaining basic life during this year. The urban residents received 935 million yuan of the minimum income relief from governments.

Note:

1.All figures in the Communique are preliminary statistics.

2.Figures in value terms on Gross Domestic Product and Value -added of various sectors quoted in the Communique are at current prices, whereas growth rates are calculated at comparable prices.

一、综合

GENERAL SURVEY

资料整理人员： 陈洲艳　梁尔郁　李生春
熊　丽　唐双全　王忠好

1-1 行政区划

Administrative Division

单位：个 (unit)

年份 Year	市州 Cities and A.P	地州数 Number of Prefecture and A.P	地级市 Number of Cities at Prefectural Level	县级市 Number of Cities at County Level	县数 Number of Counties	市辖区数 Districts Under the Jurisdiction of Cities at Prefectural Level	镇数 Number of Towns	乡数 Number of Township
1978		12	3	7	90	13	154	3295
1980		12	5	9	90	22	155	3321
1981		11	5	9	89	22	185	3331
1982		11	5	11	87	22	196	3340
1983		9	6	10	88	22	230	3340
1984		9	6	12	86	27	513	3090
1985		9	6	14	84	27	544	3011
1986		7	6	16	82	27	581	2895
1987		7	6	18	80	26	585	2903
1988		6	8	17	78	30	596	2889
1989		6	8	17	78	30	621	2807
1990		6	8	18	78	29	628	2801
1991		6	8	18	78	29	639	2784
1992		6	8	19	77	26	663	2773
1993		6	8	20	76	26	748	2689
1994		5	9	20	74	28	769	2658
1995		4	10	19	73	30	899	1406
1996		3	11	17	73	32	950	1360
1997		3	11	18	72	32	979	1327
1998		2	12	17	72	33	1001	1350
1999		1	13	16	72	34	1023	1330
2000		1	13	16	72	34	1055	1310
2001		1	13	16	72	34	1087	1275
2002		1	13	16	72	34	1097	1257
2003		1	13	16	72	34	1098	1264
长沙市	Changsha City		1	1	3	5	81	38
株洲市	Zhuzhou City		1	1	4	4	68	69
湘潭市	Xiangtan City		1	2	1	2	35	24
衡阳市	Hengyang City		1	2	5	5	111	74
邵阳市	Shaoyang City		1	1	8	3	94	102
岳阳市	Yueyang City		1	2	4	3	100	75
常德市	Changde City		1	1	6	2	104	106
张家界市	Zhangjiajie City		1		2	2	32	62
益阳市	Yiyang City		1	1	3	2	70	58
郴州市	Chenzhou City		1	1	8	2	86	164
永州市	Yongzhou City		1		9	2	108	80
怀化市	Huaihua City		1	1	10	1	87	237
娄底市	Loudi City		1	2	2	1	56	24
湘西土家族苗族自治州	West Hunan Tujia and Miao A.P	1		1	7		66	151

长沙市 Changsha City

芙蓉区(Furong District)、天心区(Tianxin District)、岳麓区(Yuelu District)、开福区(Kaifu District)、雨花区(Yuhua District)
浏阳市(Liuyang City)、长沙县(Changsha County)、望城县(Wangcheng County)、宁乡县(Ningxiang County)

株洲市 Zhuzhou City

荷塘区(Hetang District)、石峰区(Shifeng District)、芦淞区(LouSong District)、天元区(Tianyuan District)、醴陵市(Liling City)
株洲县(Zhuzhou County)、攸县(Youxiang County)、茶陵县(Chaling County)、炎陵县(Yanling County)

湘潭市 Xiangtan City

雨湖区(Yuhu District)、岳塘区(Yuetang District)、湘乡市(Xiangxiang City)、韶山市(Shaoshan City)、湘潭县(Xiangtan County)

衡阳市 Hengyang City

珠晖区(zhuhui District)、雁峰区（yanfeng District)、石鼓区(shigu District)、蒸湘区（zhengxiang District)
南岳区(Nanyue District)、耒阳市(Leiyang City)、常宁市(Changning City)、衡阳县(Hengyang County)、衡南县(Hengnan County)
衡山县(Hengshan County)、衡东县(Hengdong County)、祁东县(Qidong County)

邵阳市 Shaoyang City

双清区(Shuangqing District)、大祥区(Daxiang District)、北塔区(Beita District)、武冈市(Wugang City)、邵东县(Shaodong County)
新邵县(Xinshao County)、邵阳县(Shaoyang County)、隆回县(Longhui County)、洞口县(Dongkou County)、
新宁县(Xinning County)、绥宁县(Suining County)、城步苗族自治县 (Chengbu Miao Autonomous County)

岳阳市 Yueyang City

岳阳楼区(Yueyanglou District)、云溪区(Yunxi District)、君山区(Junshan District)、汨罗市(Miluo City)、临湘市(Linxiang City)
岳阳县(Yueyang County)、平江县(Pingjiang County)、湘阴县(Xiangyin County)、华容县(Huarong County)

常德市 Changde City

武陵区(Wuling District)、鼎城区(Dingcheng District)、津市市(Jinshi City)、安乡县(Anxiang County)、汉寿县(Huanshou County)
澧县(Li County)、临澧县(Linli County)、桃源县(Taoyuan County)、石门县(Shimen County)

张家界市 Zhangjiajie City

永定区(Yongding District)、武陵源区(Wulingyuan District)、慈利县(Chili County)、桑植县(Shanhzhi County)

益阳市 Yiyang City

资阳区(Ziyang District)、赫山区(Heshan District)、沅江市(Yuanjiang City)、南县(Nan County)、桃江县(Taojiang County)、
安化县(Anhuan County)

郴州市 Chenzhou City

北湖区(Beihu District)、苏仙区(Suxian District)、资兴市(Zixing City)、桂阳县(Guiyang County)、永兴县(Yongxing County)、
宜章县(Yizhang County)、嘉禾县(Jiahe County)、临武县(Linwu County)、汝城县(Rucheng County)、桂东县(Guidong County)、
安仁县(Anren County)

永州市 Yongzhou City

芝山区(Zhishan District)、冷水滩区(Lengshuitan District)、东安县(Dongan County)、道县(Dao County)、
宁远县(Ningyuan County)、江永县(Jiangyong County)、江华瑶族自治县(Jianghua Yao Autonomous County)、
蓝山县(Lanshan County)、新田县(Xintian County)、双牌县(Shuangpai County)、祁阳县(Qiyang County)

怀化市 Huaihua City

鹤城区(Hecheng District)、洪江市(Hongjiang City)、中方县(Zhongfang County)、沅陵县(Yuanling County)、
辰溪县(Shenxi County)、溆浦县(Xupu County)、麻阳苗族自治县(Mayang Miao Autonomous County)、会同县(Huitong County)
新晃侗族自治县(Xinhuang Tong Autonomous County), 芷江侗族自治县(Zhijiang Tong Autonomous County),
靖州苗族侗族自治县(Jinzhou Miao and Tong Autonomous County)、通道侗族自治县(Tongdao Tong Autonomous County)

娄底市 Loudi City

娄星区(Louxing District)、冷水江市(Lengshuijiang City)、涟源市(Lianyuan City)、双峰县(Shuangfeng County)、
新化县(Xinhua County)

湘西土家族苗族自治州 West Hunan Tujia and Miao Autonomous Prefecture

吉首市(Jishou City)、泸溪县(Louxi County)、凤凰县(Fenghuang County)、花垣县(Huayuan County)、保靖县(Baojin County)、
古丈县(Guzhang County)、永顺县(Yongshun County)、龙山县(Longshan County)

1-2 人口和自然资源

Population and Natural Resources

项 目	Item	2003
人口	**Population**	
年底人口数 (万人)	Total Population at the Year-end (10 000 persons)	6662.8
人口密度 (人/平方公里)	Density of Population (person/sq.km)	314.58
土地	**Land**	
土地面积 (万平方公里)	Area of Land (10 000 sq.km)	21.18
耕地面积 (万公顷)	Area of Cultivated Land (10 000 hectares)	383.4
气候	**Climate**	
年平均降水量 (毫米)	Annual Average Precipitation (mm)	1225
年降水总量 (亿立方米)	Annual Total Precipitation (100 million cu.m)	2595
森林	**Forest**	
有林地面积 (万公顷)	Area with woodland (10 000 hectares)	986.11
(万亩)	Area of Forest (10 000 mu)	14791.65
森林覆盖率 (%)	Forest Coverage Rate (%)	53.67
林木蓄积量 (万立方米)	Stock Volume of the Forest (10 000 cu.m)	32318.54
水文、水利	**Water**	
5公里以上河流 (条)	Rivers Over 5 km (unit)	5341
5公里以上河流长度 (万公里)	Total Length of Rivers Over 5 km (10 000 km)	9
河川年径流总量 (亿立方米)	Annual Total Flow of Rivers (100 million cu.m)	2141
淡水总面积 (万公顷)	Total Area of Fresh Water (10 000 hectares)	135.38
(万亩)	Total Area of Fresh Water (10 000 mu)	2030.7
#已放养面积 (万公顷)	# Cultivated Area (10 000 hectares)	42.25
(万亩)	(10 000 mu)	633.72
天然水资源总量 (亿立方米)	Natural Water Volume (100 million cu.m)	1640.4
地表水资源总量 (亿立方米)	Surface Water Volume (100 million cu.m)	1633.8
地下(浅层)水量 (亿立方米)	Shallow Ground Water Volume (100 million cu.m)	396.7
水力资源蕴藏量 (万千瓦)	Hydropower Resources (10 000 kw)	1532.45
#可开发量	#Developable Resources	1083.84
矿产资源保有储量（截至2002年底）	**Mineral Resources Ensured Resources (at the 2002 year-end)**	
煤 (亿吨)	Coal (100 million ton)	29.97
铁矿石 (亿吨)	Iron Ore (100 million ton)	11.06
磷矿石 (亿吨)	Phosphate Ore (100 million ton)	20.32
盐 (亿吨)	Salt (100 million ton)	36.05

注:1.本表淡水面积、可养殖面积、水力资源蕴藏量均为过去清查数，有待进一步普查和勘测。

2.河川年径流总量=省内各水系年径流量+客水+地下水。

3.耕地面积是指年末耕地总资源面积，包括常用耕地和临时性耕地。由国土部门提供（后同）。

a. Figures in this table, except population, cultivated area and mineral resources were obtained from surveys in previous years, and is subject to further verification.

b. The annual total flow of rivers=annual flow of major rivers in our province + branch water + groundwater.

c. The data of cultivated land is actual cultivated land total resources(year end),including common cultivated land and temporary cultivated land. The date came from Hunan Province Territory Resource Burear。The same as in the following table。

1-3 土 地 状 况(2003年)

Land Characteristics (2003)

项 目	Item	总面积 Total Area 万公顷 (10 000 hectares)	万亩 (10 000 mu)	占总面积的% Percentage to Total Area (%)
总面积	**Total Area**	**2118.29**	**31774.35**	**100.0**
按地形分	**By Topographic Feature**			
山地	Mountains	1084.72	16270.80	51.2
盆地	Basins	294.12	4411.73	13.9
平原	Plains	277.86	4167.90	13.1
丘陵	Hills	326.22	4893.28	15.4
水面	Water-face	135.37	2030.64	6.4
按地高分	**By Altitude**			
50米以下	Under 50m	210.65	3159.76	9.9
50-100米	50-100m	235.27	3529.03	11.1
100-300米	100-300m	491.74	7376.09	23.2
300-500米	300-500m	478.36	7175.34	22.6
500-800米	500-800m	390.48	5857.19	18.5
800-1000米	800-1000m	220.58	3308.73	10.4
1000米以上	Above 1000m	91.21	1368.21	4.3
按特征分	**By Land Use**			
耕地	Cultivated Land	383.40	5751.00	18.1
有林地	Woodland	986.11	14791.65	46.6
宜林荒山	Undeveloped Land Usable for Afforestation	14.59	218.85	0.7
疏林	Sparsely Forests	27.86	417.90	1.3
灌木	Shrubbery	131.12	1966.80	6.2
未成林造林地	Afforestation for Undeveloped Forests	49.14	737.10	2.3
淡水总面积	Total Area of Fresh Water	135.38	2030.70	6.4
其他	Others	390.69	5860.35	18.4

注:为使用方便,面积列出万公顷数与万亩数。

Data on area were listed with 10 000 hectares and 10 000 mu for the sake of convenience.

1-4 主要山脉基本情况

Major Mountain Ranges

名称	Name	平均高度(米) Average Height(m)	最高峰(米) Heightest Peak (m)	Heightest Peak
雪峰山	Xuefeng Mountain Range	1500	2021 (城步县二宝顶)	Erbao Peak in Chengbu County
武陵山	Wuling Mountain Range	500--1200	2098.7 (石门县壶瓶山)	Huping Mountain in Shimen County
南岭山脉 (指大庾岭、骑田岭、萌渚岭、都庞岭、越城岭)	Nanling Mountain Range (Dageng Peak,Qitian Peak, Mengzhu Peak, DuPang Peak, Yuecheng Peak)	1000-1500	2009 (道县韭菜岭)	Jiucai Peak in Dao County
幕阜山---罗霄山	Mofu Mountain ---Luoxiao Mountain Range	1000	2052 (炎陵县斗笠顶)	Douli Peak in Yanling County
			2041.1 (桂东县八面山)	Bamian Mountain in Guidong County

1-5 主要河流基本情况

Major Rivers

名称	Item	河长(公里) Length of River (km)	#省内 #In Province	河流条数(条) Number of River (unit)	流域面积(平方公里) Drainage Area (sq.km)	#省内 #In Province	省内年径流量(亿立方米) Annual Flow in Province (100 million cu.m)	水力资源蕴藏量(万千瓦) Hydro-power Resources (10000 kw)	#可开发量 Develop-able Resources
合计	**Total**			**5341**		**211829**	**2560**	**1532.45**	**1083.84**
湘 江	Xiangjiang River	856	670	2157	94660	85383	1059.62	470.7	318.29
资 水	Zijiang River	713	630	771	28142	26738	319.96	201.03	147.71
沅 江	Yuanjiang River	1033	568	1491	89163	51066	609.49	537.51	460.21
澧 水	Lishui River	388	388	326	18496	15505	190.55	152.46	137.11
洞庭湖水系	Water System of Dongting Lake			432		27269	299.71	140.2	13.65
鄱阳湖水系	Water System of Poyang Lake			16		683	10.79	3.12	0.58
珠江水系	Water System of Zhujiang River			148		5185	69.88	27.43	6.29

注: 1.河流条数指河长5公里以上的河流数,河长共9万公里。
2.资水河长以夫夷水作水源计算。
3.据1986年勘定,洞庭湖面积为2691平方公里。

a. Rivers refer to those which are more than 5 km long, and the total length of the rivers are 90 000 km.
b. The length of Zishui River refers to that of Fuyi River.
c. The figure on the area of Dongting Lake was taken from the survey in 1986.

1-6 主要城市平均气温(2003年)

Monthly Average Temperature of Major Cities(2003)

单位:摄氏度 (℃)

城市	City	1月 January	2月 February	3月 March	4月 April	5月 May	6月 June	7月 July
长沙	Changsha	5.6	7.9	10.8	16.9	21.5	26.3	31.3
株洲	Zhuzhou	5.7	8.2	11.2	17.5	21.9	26.5	31.5
湘潭	Xiangtan	5.7	8.0	10.9	17.3	21.6	26.1	31.0
衡阳	Hengyang	6.7	8.9	11.7	18.1	22.5	27.0	32.4
邵阳	Shaoyang	6.3	8.4	10.9	17.4	21.3	25.7	30.4
岳阳	Yueyang	6.2	7.3	10.8	16.8	21.6	26.4	29.8
常德	Changde	6.1	7.3	10.9	16.7	21.3	26.4	29.1
张家界	Zhangjiajie	6.4	8.2	11.1	16.6	20.9	25.5	28.3
益阳	Yiyang	5.6	7.3	10.7	16.7	21.1	26.2	30.2
郴州	Chenzhou	7.4	10.4	12.6	19.2	23.0	26.9	32.3
永州	Yongzhou	6.9	9.5	11.7	18.3	22.1	25.8	31.1
娄底	Loudi	6.4	8.1	11.0	17.4	21.4	26.3	31.4
怀化	Huaihua	5.5	8.2	10.7	16.5	20.7	25.3	29.5
吉首	Jishou	6.0	8.1	10.6	16.4	20.6	24.9	28.0

城市	City	8月 August	9月 September	10月 October	11月 November	12月 December	全年平均 Annual Average	上年平均 Annual Average Preceding Year
长沙	Changsha	29.0	24.4	18.5	13.0	6.7	19.3	17.8
株洲	Zhuzhou	28.9	24.9	18.7	13.4	7.0	19.6	18.1
湘潭	Xiangtan	28.9	24.7	18.7	13.3	6.7	19.3	17.7
衡阳	Hengyang	29.7	25.9	19.8	14.5	7.7	20.3	18.6
邵阳	Shaoyang	28.6	24.5	18.8	13.6	7.2	17.8	17.6
岳阳	Yueyang	28.5	24.6	18.4	12.6	6.7	19.9	17.9
常德	Changde	28.6	24.3	18.5	12.5	6.6	17.4	17.8
张家界	Zhangjiajie	28.7	24.6	18.0	12.6	7.5	17.4	17.7
益阳	Yiyang	28.4	23.9	18.1	12.6	6.3	17.3	17.7
郴州	Chenzhou	28.7	25.0	19.1	14.6	7.8	18.9	18.8
永州	Yongzhou	28.7	25.2	19.0	14.3	7.6	18.4	18.2
娄底	Loudi	29.4	25.2	19.3	13.9	7.3	18.1	18.0
怀化	Huaihua	28.5	24.0	17.9	12.0	6.9	17.1	17.2
吉首	Jishou	28.2	23.7	17.4	12.0	7.5	17.0	17.2

1-7 主要城市降水量 (2003年)

Monthly Precipitation in Major Cities (2003)

单位:毫米 (millimeter)

城市	City	1月 January	2月 February	3月 March	4月 April	5月 May	6月 June	7月 July
长沙	Changsha	70.1	107.8	134.6	190.0	280.3	116.1	5.3
株洲	Zhuzhou	66.5	103.2	128.4	140.7	248.5	255.8	19.3
湘潭	Xiangtan	60.2	110.1	102.8	129.8	275.9	218.8	0.8
衡阳	Hengyang	103.4	126.4	92.2	102.3	240.1	179.6	8.2
邵阳	Shaoyang	71.3	77.1	86.1	135.8	215.5	181.9	15.8
岳阳	Yueyang	56.6	170.6	87.0	286.4	334.9	128.4	104.9
常德	Changde	52.8	118.2	107.1	214.2	263.6	141.0	194.5
张家界	Zhangjiajie	48.4	167.5	64.1	206.1	234.3	269.7	705.4
益阳	Yiyang	95.6	122.1	120.9	237.4	261.6	186.9	113.7
郴州	Chenzhou	78.2	58.0	111.4	121.3	197.3	182.9	2.6
永州	Yongzhou	104.2	101.4	106.0	179.1	292.0	222.7	6.0
娄底	Loudi	68.7	96.5	86.6	126.2	335.6	240.2	19.4
怀化	Huaihua	82.6	78.9	93.6	162.6	260.9	147.2	134.3
吉首	Jishou	53.4	76.1	110.7	151.4	233.6	150.3	218.1

城市	City	8月 August	9月 September	10月 October	11月 November	12月 December	全年 Annual Total	上年全年 Annual Total Preceding year
长沙	Changsha	39.4	39.6	13.9	34.7	33.6	1065.4	1595.3
株洲	Zhuzhou	127.1	50.3	11.3	23.3	32.5	1206.9	1744.3
湘潭	Xiangtan	38.1	36.5	15.3	22.9	35.0	1046.2	1923.3
衡阳	Hengyang	12.1	66.4	15.0	21.7	34.9	1002.3	1836.5
邵阳	Shaoyang	56.9	76.7	10.3	10.1	43.8	981.3	1656.5
岳阳	Yueyang	55.9	19.0	24.0	79.2	25.4	1372.3	2110.2
常德	Changde	54.8	39.6	23.6	35.7	36.8	1472.4	2063.7
张家界	Zhangjiajie	20.8	181.5	52.1	50.1	49.0	2049.0	1982.7
益阳	Yiyang	110.4	59.8	22.7	45.5	28.9	1405.5	2239.0
郴州	Chenzhou	99.3	94.3	37.6	27.6	19.0	1128.8	2176.9
永州	Yongzhou	50.3	27.3	23.4	25.2	24.4	1162.0	2034.8
娄底	Loudi	27.5	40.5	19.7	19.8	41.0	1121.7	1694.2
怀化	Huaihua	15.1	40.5	65.1	36.7	40.7	1158.2	1791.0
吉首	Jishou	53.7	91.1	80.1	44.5	77.7	1340.7	1718.6

1-8 主要城市日照时数 (2003年)

Monthly Sunshine Hours in Major Cities (2003)

单位:小时 (hour)

城市	City	1月 January	2月 February	3月 March	4月 April	5月 May	6月 June	7月 July
长沙	Changsha	76.6	55.5	111.2	100.6	77.4	139.6	283.4
株洲	Zhuzhou	63.2	55.0	101.2	105.7	91.6	148.8	309.2
湘潭	Xiangtan	85.9	64.0	107.4	108.3	104.6	148.8	315.0
衡阳	Hengyang	86.5	63.7	92.5	112.7	94.6	171.0	336.9
邵阳	Shaoyang	90.0	61.4	104.1	118.9	109.2	163.0	325.1
岳阳	Yueyang	113.8	58.9	133.5	118.4	130.0	176.3	270.6
常德	Changde	100.8	59.5	131.4	99.8	88.3	143.0	224.3
张家界	Zhangjiajie	51.1	38.0	101.4	67.8	85.0	112.4	197.4
益阳	Yiyang	97.1	55.1	109.9	107.6	105.3	149.0	277.3
郴州	Chenzhou	73.6	61.5	69.2	116.1	69.7	137.0	310.2
永州	Yongzhou	93.2	62.1	84.2	106.9	81.6	153.0	301.3
娄底	Loudi	89.9	51.0	110.4	110.1	89.6	157.0	302.0
怀化	Huaihua	46.3	34.8	101.7	96.9	80.2	118.2	235.9
吉首	Jishou	26.1	38.8	50.5	73.9	80.6	99.2	190.6

城市	City	8月 August	9月 September	10月 October	11月 November	12月 December	全年 Annual Total	上年全年 Annual Total Preceding year
长沙	Changsha	165.3	140.3	124.4	120.2	75.9	1470.4	1406.4
株洲	Zhuzhou	200.1	174.9	154.8	126.1	91.6	1622.2	1453.2
湘潭	Xiangtan	199.7	176.5	154.7	133.9	87.2	1686.0	1549.8
衡阳	Hengyang	199.0	178.5	137.8	141.4	105.3	1719.9	1472.6
邵阳	Shaoyang	219.3	194.1	156.9	145.3	115.2	1802.5	1421.5
岳阳	Yueyang	192.1	181.0	170.5	133.0	84.2	1762.3	1848.0
常德	Changde	182.4	151.7	146.1	113.3	68.6	1691.6	1676.3
张家界	Zhangjiajie	180.7	157.1	123.1	91.4	65.8	1271.2	1227.2
益阳	Yiyang	159.9	152.6	150.7	111.8	59.5	1535.8	1536.4
郴州	Chenzhou	145.5	142.1	136.8	123.8	120.4	1505.9	1140.8
永州	Yongzhou	176.8	178.5	135.9	136.5	119.8	1629.8	1323.1
娄底	Loudi	194.7	178.6	151.0	128.4	99.8	1662.5	1403.9
怀化	Huaihua	197.5	165.6	122.4	89.3	70.3	1359.1	1419.9
吉首	Jishou	193.5	138.6	104.7	84.3	43.2	1124.0	1206.2

1-9 国民经济和社会发展总量指标

Principal Indicators of National Economy and Social Development

指 标	Item	总量指标 Aggregate Data 2000	2001	2002	2003
人口与就业	**Population and Employment**				
人口 (万人)	**Population (10 000 persons)**				
年底总人口	Population at the Year-end	6562.04	6595.85	6628.50	6662.8
市镇人口	Urban	1952.21	2031.52	2121.12	2232.04
乡村人口	Rural	4609.84	4564.33	4507.38	4430.76
男性人口	Male	3422.77	3409.72	3433.56	3453.33
女性人口	Female	3139.28	3186.13	3194.94	3209.47
就业 (万人)	**Employment (10 000 persons)**				
从业人员数	Employees	3577.58	3607.96	3644.52	3694.78
职工人数	Staff and Workers	580.82	534.22	525.28	500.27
城镇登记失业人员数	Un-employees in Urban	27.57	30.34	30.39	37.13
宏观经济	**Macro-economy**				
国民核算 (亿元)	**National Accounting (100 million yuan)**				
国内生产总值	Gross Domestic Products	3691.88	3983.00	4340.94	4638.73
第一产业	Primary Industry	784.92	825.73	847.25	886.47
第二产业	Secondary Industry	1461.86	1573.00	1737.20	1794.21
第三产业	Tertiary Industry	1445.10	1584.27	1756.49	1958.05
国内支出总额	Total Domestic Expenditure	3691.88	3983.00	4340.94	4638.73
最终消费	Final Consumption	2383.27	2553.14	2762.95	2886.03
居民消费	Households Consumption	1782.77	1871.64	1992.05	2016.88
政府消费	Government Consumption	600.50	681.50	770.90	869.15
资本形成总额	Gross Capital Formation	1274.94	1426.47	1572.89	1738.27
固定资本形成总额	Gross Fixed Capital Formation	1082.00	1233.17	1380.89	1613.12
存货增加	Changes in Inventory	192.94	193.30	192.00	125.15
固定资产投资 (亿元)	**Investment in Fixed Assets (100 million yuan)**				
全社会固定资产投资总额	Total Investment in Fixed Assets	1066.27	1210.63	1355.87	1557
国有单位	State-owned unit	574.12	618.54	665.7	701.33
集体单位	Collective-owned Unit	118.8	145.78	166.92	199.59
个体经济	Individuals	281.89	291.55	282.53	250.8
财政 (亿元)	**Public Finance (100 million yuan)**				
地方财政收入	Local Government Revenue	177.04	205.41	231.15	268.65
地方财政支出	Local Government Expenditure	347.83	431.7	533.02	573.75
物价总指数 (上年=100)	**Price Index (preceding year=100)**				
商品零售价格总指数	General Retail Price Index	99.3	98.8	99.2	100.6
居民消费价格总指数	General Consumer Price Index	101.4	99.1	99.5	102.4
农产品生产者价格指数	Producer Price Indices of Farm Products	-	100.9	99.9	106.76
利用外资 (万美元)	**Utilization of Foreign Capital (USD 10 000)**				
签订利用外资协议额	Amount of Foreign Capital for Utilization Through Signed Contracts or Agreements	109370	133063	165759	237610
实际利用外资额	Amount of Foreign Capital Actually Utilized	110843	118747	137689	179041
产 业	**Industry**				
农业	**Agriculture**				
耕地面积(千公顷)	Cultivated Areas (1 000 hectares)	3921.6	3912.55	3891	3833.74
农林牧渔业从业人员 (万人)	Number of Persons Engaged in Farming, Forestry, Animal Husbandry and Fishery (10 000 persons)	2065.92	2058.67	2019.6	1997.67

1-9 续表 1 continued

指　标	Item	总量指标 Aggregate Data 2000	2001	2002	2003
农林牧渔业总产值(亿元)	Gross Output Value of Farming, Forestry, Animal Husbandry and Fishery (100 million yuan)	1251.89	1313.22	1349.92	1452.96
农业	Planting	633.84	665.7	666.65	671.66
林业	Forestry	51.01	51.88	54.78	81.73
牧业	Animal Husbandry	486.13	510.42	538.64	575.08
渔业	Fishery	80.91	85.23	89.85	96.97
主要农产品产量(万吨)	Output of Major Farm Products (10 000 tons)				
粮食	Grain	2874.97	2700.3	2501.3	2442.73
棉花	Cotton	17.13	19	15.3	16.31
油料	Oil-bearing Crops	139.35	137.39	119.25	125.70
苎麻	Ramie	6.62	9.42	12.81	12.43
黄红麻(熟麻)	Jute and Ambary Hemp	0.23	0.19	0.42	0.38
烤烟	Fluecured Tobacco	15.55	16.28	17.45	17.66
茶叶	Tea	5.73	5.84	6.1	6.06
柑桔	Citrus	125.92	154.15	144.26	167.44
猪牛羊肉	Pork, Beef and Mutton	436.51	452.12	470.23	485.89
水产品	Aquatic Products	133.21	140.96	149.56	156.59
工业	**Industry**				
主要工业产品产量	Output of Major Industrial Products				
布(亿米)	Cloth (100 million m)	3.41	3.05	2.96	3.41
机制纸及纸板(万吨)	Machine-made Paper and Paperboards(10 000 tons)	70.07	77.61	88.54	124.28
糖(万吨)	Sugar (10 000 tons)	4.44	7.19	7.08	3.49
合成洗涤剂(万吨)	Synthetic Detergents (10 000 tons)	8.12	9.27	8.8	22.56
缝纫机(万架)	Sewing Machine (10 000 sets)	1.56	0.94	0.4	0.42
家用电冰箱(万台)	Household Refrigerators (10 000 sets)	44.54	47.79	55.08	44.73
原煤(万吨)	Coal (10 000 tons)	1490.81	1546.11	1845.42	2366.69
发电量(亿千瓦小时)	Electricity (100 million kw.h)	354.42	384.35	425.54	523.73
钢(万吨)	Steel (10 000 tons)	304.13	441.9	546.65	590.77
成品钢材(万吨)	Steel Products (10 000 tons)	299.05	389.01	487.71	558.18
水泥(万吨)	Cement (10 000 tons)	2395.72	2496.02	2746.5	3054.34
独立核算工业企业财务指标	Principal Financial Item of Industrial Enterprises with Independent Accounting Systems				
年底固定资产原价(亿元)	Original Value of Fixed Assets (100 million yuan)	1947.23	2095.68	2268.98	2510.77
年底固定资产净值(亿元)	Net Value of Fixed Assets (100 million yuan)	1268.61	1368.37	1454.92	1558.18
利润和税金总额(亿元)	Profits and Taxes (100 million yuan)	205.87	235.66	268.1	345.67
建筑业	**Construction**				
建筑业企业人数 (万人)	Number of Employed Persons (10 000 persons)	76.3	96.73	92.72	111.95
建筑业总产值 (亿元)	Gross Output Value of Construction (100 million yuan)	354.29	489.79	595.77	818.84
施工房屋面积 (万平方米)	Floor Space of Buildings Under Construction (10 000 m^2)	5087.93	6259.27	7167.52	10051.97
#竣工房屋面积	Floor Space of Buildings Completed	2603.03	3204.6	3665.71	4969.67
交通运输	**Transportation**				
货运量 (万吨)	Freight Traffic (10 000 tons)	51090	50518	52156	59952
铁路	Railways	4676	4965	4942	5214
公路	Highways	42868	41823	42982	51136
水运	Waterways	3406	3572	3760	3600
客运量 (万人)	Passenger Traffic (10 000 persons)	87462	92381	98244	96182
铁路	Railways	5233	5202	5173	4850
公路	Highways	81005	85971	91653	90353
水运	Waterways	1094	1063	1249	793

指　标	Item	总量指标 Aggregate Data			
		2000	2001	2002	2003
邮电通信业	**Postal and Telecommunications Services**				
邮电业务总量　(万元)	Total Business Revenue (10 000 yuan)	1409225	1341636.1	1854712.7	2342342
函件　(万件)	Number of Letters Delivered (10 000 pieces)	21255	39470	49505.24	50634.30
报刊期发数　(万份)	Newspapers and Magazines Distributed (10 000 copies)	1042.72	1022	903.16	834.48
交换机容量　(万门)	Capacity of Office Telephone Exchanges(10 000 lines)	873.2	964.59	1049.23	1085.61
电话机(万部)	Number of Telephone Sets (10 000 units)	700.04	711.94	826.55	902.11
国内商业 (亿元)	**Domestic Trade (100 million yuan)**				
社会消费品零售总额	Total Retail Sales of Consumer Goods	1364.66	1511.07	1678.86	1816.30
对外经济贸易和旅游	**Foreign Trade and Tourism**				
进出口总额　(亿美元)	Total Exports and Imports (USD 100 million)	25.13	27.58	28.76	37.36
进口额	Imports	8.6	10.04	10.81	15.90
出口额	Exports	16.53	17.54	17.95	21.46
国际旅游	International Tourism				
来湘旅游人数(万人次)	Tourism to Hunan　(10 000 person-times)	45.4	50.46	56.62	15.39
旅游外汇收入(亿美元)	Foreign Exchange Earnings from Tourism (USD 100 million)	2.21	2.71	3.11	0.45
金融保险 (亿元)	**Finance and Insurance (100 million yuan)**				
商业银行各项存款	Deposits of Commercial Banks	1905.79	2337.87	2790.71	3362.01
商业银行各项贷款	Loans of Commercial Banks	1479.94	1799.65	2146.71	2538.45
城市信用社各项存款	Deposits of Urban Credit Cooperative	40.14	32.7	4.65	6.01
城市信用社各项贷款	Loans of Urban Credit Cooperative	26.03	15.74	2.7	3.27
农村信用社各项存款	Deposits of Rural Credit Cooperative	560.03	633.26	715.23	825.36
农村信用社各项贷款	Loans of Rural Credit Cooperative	372.04	414.45	459.96	534.04
教育、科技、文化	**Education, Science and Technology, Culture**				
教育	**Education**				
专任教师数(人)	Full-time Teachers (person)				
普通高等学校	Institutions of Higher Education	20317	23878	30557	34816
普通中学	Secondary Schools	223693	236161	248245	259281
小学	Primary Schools	306387	291574	276535	260704
在校学生(万人)	Students Enrollment (10 000 persons)				
普通高等学校	Institutions of Higher Education	25.31	33.13	41.94	53.72
普通中学	Secondary Schools	391.73	425.6	466.91	488.78
小学	Primary Schools	663.93	601.26	529.49	468.69
教育事业费支出(亿元)	Government Expenditures on Education (100 million yuan)	50.88	65.09	82.98	90.06
科技	**Science and Technology**				
各类专业技术人员数(人)	Scientific and Technical Personnel (person)	1093367	1103287	1262050	1212866
科技三项及科学事业费支出(亿元)	Expense on S&T Promotion and Operating Expenses for Sciences (100 million yuan)	5.55	7.42	7.64	7.14
技术市场技术交易成交额(亿元)	Transaction Value in Technical Market (100 million yuan)	10.95	11.31	10.02	18.20
文化	**Culture**				
出版数量	Publications				
图书(万册)	Number of Books (10 000 copies)	24844	23808	32600	29556
杂志(万册)	Number of Magazines (10 000 copies)	10504	10051	11207	12577
报纸(万份)	Number of Newspapers Issue (10 000 copies)	83467	92273	95198	113514
电视节目每周播出时间(小时)	Time for TV Programs Telecasting (hour)	2338	8224	8196	9178

注:对外贸易中的进出口总额,统一按海关统计数据。

Figures on total imports and exports from foreign trade are obtained from the customs statistics.

指 标	Item	总量指标 Aggregate Data			
		2000	2001	2002	2003
家庭、生活、环境	**Family, People's Livelihood and Environment**				
家庭	**Family**				
家庭总户数(万户)	Total Number of Households (10 000 households)	1874.87	1884.47	1899.3	1929.59
城镇居民户均家庭人口(人)	Average Household Size in Urban Areas (person)	3.09	3.06	3.06	3.02
农村居民户均常住人口(人)	Average Household Size in Rural Areas (person)	3.97	3.93	3.93	3.89
婚姻(万对)	**Marriages and Divorces (10 000 couples)**				
结婚数	Number of Marriages	38.31	36.57	36.57	38.38
离婚数	Number of Divorces	6.45	7.34	5.4	6.00
居住(平方米/人)	**Housing (sq.m/person)**				
城市居民人均居住面积	Per Capita Floor Space of Urban Residents	11.75	11.8	12.4	24.43
农村居民人均住房面积	Per Capita Floor Space of Rural Residents	30.92	32.87	34.05	35.09
生活	**People's Livelihood**				
城市居民人均可支配收入(元)	Per Capita Annual Disposable Income of Urban Households(yuan)	6218.7	6780.6	6958.6	7674.20
农村居民人均纯收入(元)	Per Capita Annual Net Income of Rural Households (yuan)	2197.16	2299.46	2397.92	2532.87
城乡储蓄存款余额(亿元)	Outstanding Amount of Saving Deposits in Urban and Rural Areas (100 million yuan)	1874.22	2183.73	2577.44	3036.45
工资福利	**Wages and Welfare**				
工资总额(亿元)	Total Wages (100 million yuan)	377.19	407.58	458.53	494.42
职工平均工资(元)	Average Wage of Staff and Workers (yuan)	6515	7698	8734	9855
离休、退休、退职人数(万人)	Number of Retired & Resigned Staff and Workers (10 000 persons)	153.3	165.26	165.4	195.29
离退休退职人员劳保福利费(亿元)	Pensions, Labour Insurance and Welfare Funds for Retired Staff and Workers (100 million yuan)	103.31	117.2	125.46	156.57
卫生	**Health Care**				
医院与卫生院(个)	Number of Hospitals (unit)	3339	3335	3324	3349
医生(万人)	Number of Doctors (10 000 persons)	8.87	8.95	7.91	7.97
医院床位数(万张)	Number of Hospital Beds (10 000 units)	13.21	13.43	14.3	14.49
市政建设	**City Construction**				
自来水供应量(亿吨)	Volume of Tap Water Supply (100 million tons)	28.24	27.63	26.94	26.27
排水管道长度(公里)	Length of Sewer Pipelines (km)	3754	3854	4089.5	4404.02
城市煤气供气量(万立方)	Volume of Coal Gas Supply in Urban Areas (10 000 cu.m)	60375	48559	41667.6	43529.70
石油液化气用量(万吨)	Volume of Liquefied Petroleum Gas (10 000 tons)	20.2	24.76	29.75	23.11
公共汽车总数(辆)	Total Number of Public Buses (unit)	9083	8616	8099	8995
公交客运总量(万人次)	Total Passenger Traffic of Public Transportation (10 000 person-times)	106227	101835	105522	117635
环境、灾害	**Environment and Disaster**				
治理污染资金使用额(万元)	Actual Investment in Implementation of the Project for Pollution Treatment (10 000 yuan)	54470.2	60090.6	45970.7	34059.6
环境污染事故数(次)	Number of Pollution Accidents (times)	317	238	340	314
环境污染事故罚款金额(万元)	Amount of Reparations and Fines (10 000 yuan)	30.82	29.6	53.8	5034
火灾发生数(次)	Number of Fire Disasters (times)	3440	3979	5040	6221
火灾经济损失(万元)	Loss of Fire Accidents (10 000 yuan)	4799	4397.35	5357	4834.52
交通事故发生数(次)	Number of Traffic Accidents (times)	23938	32504	28056	23224
交通事故经济损失(万元)	Loss of Traffic Accidents (10 000 yuan)	9662	8799.48	9100	10464.79

注：1、2002年起，医生数是指执业医生数。2、城市居民人均居住面积数据由省建设厅提供。

Data of doctors are doctors and assistant doctors since 2002.

The data on per capita living floor space of urban residents are devided by Constructional Bureau of Hunan Province.

1-10 国民经济和社会发展速度指标

Develop Speed of National Economy and Social Development

单位：%　　　　(%)

指　标	Item	指数 Index（2003为下列各年）2003 as percentage of the following years			年均增长速度 Average Annual Growth Rate	
		2000	2001	2002	1996-2000	2001-2003
人口与就业	**Population and Employment**					
人口	**Population and Employment**					
年底总人口	Population at the Year-end	101.54	101.02	100.52	0.53	0.51
市镇人口	Urban	114.33	109.87	105.23	4.71	4.57
乡村人口	Rural	96.12	97.07	98.30	-0.97	-1.31
男性人口	Male	100.89	101.28	100.58	0.60	0.30
女性人口	Female	102.24	100.73	100.45	0.45	0.74
就业	**Employment**					
从业人员数	Employees	103.28	102.41	101.38	0.63	1.08
职工人数	Staff and Workers	86.13	93.64	95.24	-0.56	-4.85
城镇登记失业人员数	Un-employees in Urban	134.68	122.38	122.18	0.12	10.43
宏观经济	**Macro-economy**					
国民核算	**National Accounting**					
国内生产总值	Gross Domestic Products	130.22	119.46	109.60	9.71	9.20
第一产业	Primary Industry	110.55	106.29	103.60	4.06	3.40
第二产业	Secondary Industry	137.49	124.65	112.40	12.17	11.20
第三产业	Tertiary Industry	133.95	121.22	109.70	11.31	10.23
国内支出总额	Total Domestic Expenditure	130.22	119.46	109.60	9.71	9.20
最终消费	Final Consumption	126.44	117.07	107.80	7.70	8.13
居民消费	Households Consumption	119.89	113.42	106.50	6.65	6.23
政府消费	Government Consumption	145.64	126.65	110.90	11.24	13.35
资本形成总额	Gross Capital Formation	137.98	123.97	112.70	9.59	11.33
固定资本形成总额	Gross Fixed Capital Formation	143.39	126.78	113.60	14.70	12.76
存货增加	Changes in Inventory	102.91	101.99	102.30	-8.93	0.96
固定资产投资	**Investment in Fixed Assets**					
全社会固定资产投资总额	Total Investment in Fixed Assets	146.02	128.61	114.83	15.27	13.45
国有单位	State-owned unit	122.16	113.38	105.35	12.62	6.90
集体单位	Collective-owned Unit	168.01	136.91	119.57	24.43	18.88
个体经济	Individuals	88.97	86.02	88.77	18.56	-3.82
财政	**Pubic Finance**					
地方财政收入	Local Government Revenue	151.75	130.79	116.22	10.36	14.91
地方财政支出	Local Government Expenditure	164.95	132.90	107.64	14.87	18.15
物价总指数(上年=100)	**Price Index (preceding year=100)**					
商品零售价格总指数	General Retail Price Index	98.60	99.80	100.60	0.02	-0.47
居民消费价格总指数	General Consumer Price Index	100.97	101.89	102.40	2.49	0.32
农产品生产者价格指数	Producer Price Indices of Farm Products	107.61	106.65	106.76	-	2.48
利用外资	**Utilization of Foreign Capital**					
签订利用外资协议额	Amount of Foreign Capital for Utilization Through Signed Contracts or Agreements	217.25	178.57	143.35	-8.91	29.52
实际利用外资额	Amount of Foreign Capital Actually Utilized	161.53	150.78	130.03	4.94	17.33
产　业	**Industry**					
农业	**Agriculture**					
耕地面积	Cultivated Areas	97.76	97.99	98.53	3.83	-0.75
农林牧渔业从业人员	Number of Persons Engaged in Farming, Forestry, Animal Husbandry and Fishery	96.70	97.04	98.91	-0.47	-1.11

单位：%　　　　1-10 续表 1 continued　　　　(%)

指 标	Item	指数 Index(2003为下列各年) 2003 as percentage of the following years)			年均增长速度 Average Annual Growth Rate	
		2000	2001	2002	1996-2000	2001-2003
农林牧渔业总产值	Gross Output Value of Farming, Forestry,Animal Husbandry and Fishery	110.73	106.50	103.70	5.14	3.46
农业	Farming	106.52	102.91	102.70	3.57	2.13
林业	Forestry	112.17	108.74	104.00	3.36	3.90
牧业	Animal Husbandry	114.16	109.41	104.10	6.36	4.51
渔业	Fishery	119.88	113.63	107.30	11.40	6.23
主要农产品产量	Output of Major Farm Products					
粮食	Grain	84.97	90.46	97.66	0.88	-5.29
棉花	Cotton	95.21	85.84	106.60	-5.18	-1.62
油料	Oil-bearing Crops	90.21	91.49	105.41	4.46	-3.38
苎麻	Ramie	187.81	131.98	97.05	2.57	23.38
黄红麻(熟麻)	Jute and Ambary Hemp	164.61	199.26	90.14	-8.57	18.07
烤烟	Fluecured Tobacco	113.58	108.49	101.22	14.56	4.34
茶叶	Tea	105.71	103.72	99.30	-1.37	1.87
柑桔	Citrus	132.97	108.62	116.07	4.41	9.96
猪牛羊肉	Pork, Beef and Mutton	111.31	107.47	103.33	6.58	3.64
水产品	Aquatic Products	117.55	111.09	104.70	9.20	5.54
工业	**Industry**					
主要工业产品产量	Output of Major Industrial Products					
布	Cloth	100.00	111.80	115.20	-6.96	0.00
机制纸及纸板	Machine-made Paper and Paperboards	177.37	160.13	140.37	-5.71	21.05
糖	Sugar	78.60	48.54	49.29	-6.79	-7.71
合成洗涤剂	Synthetic Detergents	277.83	243.37	256.36	6.06	40.58
缝纫机	Sewing machine	26.92	44.68	105.00	-31.08	-35.43
家用电冰箱	Household Refrigerators	100.43	93.60	81.21	14.86	0.14
原煤	Coal	158.75	153.07	128.25	-23.16	16.66
发电量	Electricity	147.77	136.26	123.07	1.26	13.90
钢	Steel	194.25	133.69	108.07	11.61	24.77
成品钢材	Steel Products	186.65	143.49	114.45	14.11	23.12
水泥	Cement	127.49	122.37	111.21	1.76	8.43
独立核算工业企业财务指标	Principal Financial Item of Industrial Enterprises with Independent Accounting Systems					
年底固定资产原价	Original Value of Fixed Assets	128.94	119.81	110.66	8.71	8.84
年底固定资产净值	Net Value of Fixed Assets	122.83	113.87	107.10	6.93	7.09
利润和税金总额	Profits and Taxes	167.91	146.68	128.93	17.75	18.86
建筑业	**Construction**					
建筑业企业人数	Number of Employed Persons	146.72	115.73	120.74	4.59	13.63
建筑业总产值	Gross Output Value of Construction	231.12	167.18	137.44	13.48	32.21
施工房屋面积	Floor Space of Buildings Under Construction	197.57	160.59	140.24	2.37	25.48
竣工房屋面积	Floor Space of Buildings Completed	190.92	155.08	135.57	2.39	24.06
交通运输	**Transportation**					
货运量	Freight Traffic	117.35	118.67	114.95	0.49	5.48
铁路	Railways	111.51	105.02	105.50	-1.40	3.70
公路	Highways	119.29	122.27	118.97	0.76	6.06
水运	Waterways	105.70	100.78	95.74	-0.72	1.86
客运量	Passenger Traffic	109.97	104.11	97.90	4.09	3.22
铁路	Railways	92.68	93.23	93.76	4.82	-2.50
公路	Highways	111.54	105.10	98.58	4.19	3.71
水运	Waterways	72.49	74.60	63.49	-4.47	-10.17

单位：%　　1-10 续表 2 continued　　(%)

指 标	Item	指数 Index(2003为下列年) 2003 as percentage of the following years)			年均增长速度 Average Annual Growth Rate	
		2000	2001	2002	1996-2000	2001-2003
邮电通信业	**Postal and Telecommunications Services**					
邮电业务总量	Total Business Revenue	166.21	174.59	126.29	34.96	18.46
函件	Number of Letters Delivered	238.22	128.29	102.28	-9.19	33.56
报刊期发数	Number of Newspapers and Magazines Distributed	80.03	81.65	92.40	-6.83	-7.16
交换机容量	Capacity of Office Telephone Exchanges	124.33	112.55	103.47	26.11	7.53
电话机	Number of Telephone Sets	128.87	126.71	109.14	31.38	8.82
国内商业	**Domestic Trade**					
社会消费品零售总额	Total Retail Sales of Consumer Goods	133.10	120.20	108.19	10.26	10.00
对外经济贸易和旅游	**Foreign Trade and Tourism**					
进出口总额	Total Exports and Imports	148.67	135.47	129.91	4.50	14.13
进口额	Imports	184.87	158.36	147.08	8.73	22.73
出口额	Exports	129.84	122.36	119.57	2.64	9.09
国际旅游	International Tourism					
来湘旅游人数	Number of Tourism to Hunan	33.91	30.51	27.19	20.69	-30.27
旅游外汇收入	Foreign Exchange Earnings from Tourism	20.36	16.62	14.47	27.74	-41.17
金融保险	**Finance and Insurance**					
商业银行各项存款	Deposits of Commercial Banks	176.41	143.81	120.47	18.05	20.83
商业银行各项贷款	Loans of Commercial Banks	171.52	141.05	118.25	9.39	19.70
城市信用社各项存款	Deposits of Urban Credit Cooperative	14.97	18.38	129.25	-10.70	-46.90
城市信用社各项贷款	Loans of Urban Credit Cooperative	12.56	20.78	121.11	-9.96	-49.92
农村信用社各项存款	Deposits of Rural Credit Cooperative	147.38	130.34	115.40	11.82	13.80
农村信用社各项贷款	Loans of Rural Credit Cooperative	143.54	128.86	116.11	11.81	12.80
教育、科技、文化	**Education, Science and Technology, Culture**					
教育	**Education**					
专任教师数	Full-time Teachers					
普通高等学校	Institutions of Higher Education	171.36	145.81	113.94	5.83	19.67
普通中学	Secondary Schools	115.91	109.79	104.45	3.35	5.04
小学	Primary Schools	85.09	89.41	94.28	0.56	-5.24
在校学生	Students Enrollment					
普通高等学校	Institutions of Higher Education	212.26	162.16	128.09	14.18	28.51
普通中学	Secondary Schools	124.77	114.84	104.68	9.24	7.66
小学	Primary Schools	70.59	77.95	88.52	-2.06	-10.96
教育事业费支出	Operating Expenses for Education	177.00	138.36	108.53	10.01	20.96
科技	**Science and Technology**					
各类专业技术人员数	Number of Scientific and Technical Personnel	110.93	109.93	96.10	1.14	3.52
科技三项及科学事业费支出	Expense on S&T Promotion and Operating Expenses for Sciences	128.57	96.17	93.40	20.22	8.74
技术市场技术交易成交额	Transaction Value in Technical Market	166.19	160.90	181.61	16.60	18.45
文化	**Culture**					
出版数量	Publications					
图书	Number of Books	118.97	124.14	90.66	-5.90	5.96
杂志	Number of Magazines	119.74	125.13	112.23	6.22	6.19
报纸	Number of Newspapers Issue	136.00	123.02	119.24	5.98	10.79
电视节目每周播出时间	Time for TV Programs Telecasting	392.56	111.60	111.98	12.61	57.75

注:对外贸易中的进出口总额,统一按海关统计数据。

Figures on total imports and exports from foreign trade are obtained from the customs statistics.

单位：% 1-10 续表 3 continued (%)

指 标	Item	指数 Index(2003为下列年) 2003 as percentage of the following years)			年均增长速度 Average Annual Growth Rate	
		2000	2001	2002	1996-2000	2001-2003
家庭、生活、环境	**Family, People's Livelihood and Environment**					
家庭	**Family**					
家庭总户数	Total Number of Households	102.92	102.39	101.59	0.98	0.96
城镇居民平均每户家庭人口	Average Household Size in Urban Areas	97.73	98.69	98.69	-0.63	-0.76
农村居民平均每户常住人口	Average Household Size in Rural Areas	97.98	98.98	98.98	-1.07	-0.68
婚姻	**Marriages and Divorces**					
结婚数	Number of Marriages	100.18	104.95	104.95	-2.63	0.06
离婚数	Number of Divorces	93.02	81.74	111.11	0.38	-2.38
居住	**Housing**					
城市居民人均居住面积	Per Capita Floor Space of Urban Residents	207.91	207.03	197.02	8.68	27.63
农村居民人均住房面积	Per Capita Floor Space of Rural Residents	113.49	106.75	103.05	3.87	4.31
生活	**People's Livelihood**					
城市居民人均可支配收入	Per Capita Annual Disposable Income of Urban Households	123.41	113.18	110.28	3.42	7.26
农村居民人均纯收入	Per Capita Annual Net Income of Rural Households	115.28	110.15	105.63	5.96	4.85
城乡储蓄存款余额	Outstanding Amount of Saving Deposits in Urban and Rural Areas	162.01	139.05	117.81	16.31	17.45
工资福利	**Wages and Welfare**					
工资总额	Total Wages	131.08	121.31	107.83	5.99	9.44
职工平均工资	Average Wage of Staff and Workers	151.27	128.02	112.83	3.79	14.79
离休、退休、退职人员人数	Number of Retired & Resigned Staff and Workers	127.39	118.17	118.07	2.09	8.40
离退休、退职人员劳保福利	Pensions, Labour Insurance and Welfare Funds for Retired Staff and Workers	151.56	133.60	124.80	11.75	14.87
卫生	**Health Care**					
医院与卫生院	Number of Hospitals	100.30	100.42	100.75	-2.95	0.10
医生	Number of Doctors	89.83	89.02	100.73	0.95	-3.51
医院床位数	Number of Hospital Beds	109.71	107.92	101.35	1.18	3.14
市政建设	**City Construction**					
自来水供应量	Volume of Tap Water Supply	93.02	95.08	97.51	-2.33	-2.38
排水管道长度	Length of Sewer Pipelines	117.32	114.27	107.69	5.10	5.47
城市煤气供气量	Volume of Coal Gas Supply in Urban Areas	72.10	89.64	104.47	-2.91	-10.33
石油液化气用量	Volume of Liquefied Petroleum Gas	114.41	93.34	77.68	11.64	4.59
公共汽车总数	Total Number of Public Buses	99.03	104.40	111.06	5.74	-0.32
公交客运总量	Total Passenger Traffic of Public Transportation	110.74	115.51	111.48	2.84	3.46
环境、灾害	**Environment and Disaster**					
治理污染资金使用额	Used Value for Pollution Treatment	62.53	56.68	74.09	7.65	-14.49
环境污染事故数	Number of Pollution Accidents	99.05	131.93	92.35	1.04	-0.32
环境污染事故罚款金额	Amount of Reparations and Fines	16333.5	17006.8	9356.9	-2.51	446.63
火灾发生数	Number of Fire Disasters	180.84	156.35	123.43	24.98	21.83
火灾经济损失	Loss of Fire Accidents	100.74	109.94	90.25	-6.80	0.25
交通事故发生数	Number of Traffic Accidents	97.02	71.45	82.78	18.23	-1.00
交通事故经济损失	Loss of Traffic Accidents	108.31	118.93	115.00	9.27	2.70

1-11 国民经济和社会发展效益指标

Beneficial Indicators of National Economy and Social Development

指 标	Item	2000	2001	2002	2003
人口与就业	**Population and Employment**				
人口出生率(‰)	Birth Rate (‰)	11.45	11.80	11.56	11.82
人口死亡率(‰)	Death Rate(‰)	6.79	6.72	6.70	6.87
人口自然增长率(‰)	Natural Growth Rate(‰)	4.66	5.08	4.86	4.95
就业者负担人口(人)	Dependency Rate(person)	1.83	1.83	1.82	1.80
城镇登记失业率(%)	Unemployment Rate in Urban Areas (%)	3.70	4.00	4.00	4.50
宏观经济	**Macro Economy**				
全社会劳动生产率(元/年人)	Overall Labor Productivity (yuan/person-year)	10285	11086	11971	12641
第一产业	Primary Industry	3785	3933	4120	4437
第二产业	Secondary Industry	17407	19793	23068	23182
第三产业	Tertiary Industry	21373	22685	21500	21812
人均生产总值(元)	Per Capita GDP (yuan)	5639	6054	6565	7554
全社会固定资产投资相当于生产总值(%)	Proportion of Investment in Fixed Assets to GDP (%)	28.88	30.39	31.23	33.57
国有经济项目投产率(%)	Rate of Projects Completed and Put into Use in State-owned Economic (%)	62.3	58.3	59.0	57.8
国有经济固定资产交付使用率(%)	Rate of Fixed Assets Completed and Put into Use in State-owned Economic (%)	69.8	56.5	73.6	66.3
基本建设固定资产交付使用率(%)	Rate of Fixed Assets Completed in Capital Construction and Put into Use (%)	68.4	46.8	75.8	69.0
基本建设项目建成投产率(%)	Rate of Projects Completed in Capital Construction and Put into Use (%)	58.4	50.5	50.8	51.2
地方财政收入相当于生产总值(%)	Proportion of Local Government Revenue to GDP (%)	4.80	5.12	5.32	5.79
地方财政支出相当于生产总值(%)	Proportion of Local Government Expenditures to GDP (%)	9.42	10.84	12.28	12.37
实际利用外资相当于签订合同利用外资额(%)	Proportion of Foreign Capital Actually Used to Total Amount of Foreign Capital for Utilization by Signed Contracts or Agreements (%)	101.35	89.24	83.05	75.35
产 业	**Industry**				
人均耕地面积(公顷)	Per Capita Cultivated Land (hectare)	0.06	0.0593	0.0588	0.0575
农业从业者人均耕地面积(公顷)	Cultivated Land per Agricultural Laborer (hectare)	0.189	0.1899	0.1908	0.1919
农业从业者人均农业总产值(元)	Agricultural Output Value per Agricultural Laborer(yuan)	6048	6367.76	6620.06	7233.569
每公顷耕地农业机械总动力(千瓦)	Total Power of Agricultural Machinery per Hectare Cultivated Land (kw)	5.63	6.02	6.4	6.95
每公顷耕地用电量(千瓦小时)	Electric Power Consumption per Hectare Cultivated Land(kw.h)	1135	1193	1277.2	1404.32
每公顷播种面积化肥施用量(公斤)	Chemical Fertilizer Consumption per Hectare Sown Area (kg)	228	232.29	240.8	243.60
每公顷耕地生产的农业产值(元)	Agricultural Output Value per Hectare Cultivated Land (yuan)	31923	33526	34597	37619
每一农业从业者农产品产量	Output of Farm Products per Agricultural Laborer				
粮食(公斤)	Grain (kg)	1388.86	1309.37	1226.65	1216.11
棉花(公斤)	Cotton (kg)	8.28	9.21	7.50	8.12
油料(公斤)	Oil-bearing Crops (kg)	67.32	66.62	58.48	62.58
肉类(公斤)	Meat (kg)	239.69	250.54	265.58	279.68
水产品(公斤)	Aquatic Products (kg)	64.35	68.35	73.34	77.96
每公顷播种面积农产品产量	Output of Farm Products per Hectare Sown Area				
粮食(公斤)	Grain (kg)	5716	5723	5376	5393
棉花(公斤)	Cotton (kg)	1173	1354	1291	1173
油料(公斤)	Oil-bearing Crops (kg)	1490	1505	1334	1449

1-11 续表1 continued

指 标	Item	2000	2001	2002	2003
独立核算工业企业效益	Economic Efficiency of Industrial Enterprises with Independent Accounting Systems				
固定资产利税率(%)	Rate of Per-tax Profits to Fixed Assets (%)	10.57	11.25	11.82	13.77
全部资金利税率(%)	Rate of Per-tax Profits to Total Assets (%)	8.76	9.54	10.02	11.98
产值利税率(%)	Rate of Per-tax Profits to Output Value (%)	12.65	13.01	12.77	13.24
流动资产周转天数(天)	Number of Days of Turnover Circulating Funds (day)	249	244.82	222	183.45
百元销售收入实现利税(元)	Per-tax profits per 100 Yuan Sales Revenue (yuan)	13.17	13.87	13.54	13.27
工业增加值率(%)	Ratio of Value Added to Gross Industrial Output Value	28.45	28.87	33.66	34.03
工业产品销售率(%)	Proportion of Industrial Products Sold (%)	99.32	99.2	99.6	99.83
全员劳动生产率(元/年人)	Overall Labor Productivity (yuan/person-year)	73284.25	89130	110450	130309
建筑业技术装备率(元/人)	Value of Machinery in Construction per Laborer (yuan/person)	5428	5199.5	8844.52	8820.2
建筑业动力装备率(千瓦/人)	Power of Machinery per Laborer (kw/person)	4.7	4.38	4.96	4.2
建筑业产值利税率(%)	Ratio of Per-tax Profits to Gross Output Value (%)	4.3	5.21	5.35	6.5
建筑业全员劳动生产率(元/人)	Overall Labor Productivity (yuan/person-year)	46436	56128.62	66667.52	74546.3
运输业铁路网密度(公里/万平方公里)	Railway Density in Transportation (km/10 000 sq.km)	138.07	136.65	133.57	130.87
运输业公路网密度(公里/万平方公里)	Highway Density in Transportation (km/10 000 sq.km)	2872.9	3144.15	4004.15	4024.22
全省人均消费品零售额(元)	Per Capita Retail Sales of Consumer Goods (yuan)	2084.39	2296.82	2539.04	2733.07
进出口总额相当于生产总值(%)	Proportion of Total Imports and Exports to GDP (%)	5.63	5.73	5.48	6.67
每一来湘旅游客人次支出(美元)	Expenditure per International Tourist in Hunan (USD)	486.92	536.46	549.4	292.34
教育、科技、文化	**Education, Science and Technology, Culture**				
学龄儿童入学率(%)	Rate of School-age Children Enrollment (%)	98.42	97.9	96.76	98.56
小学升学率(%)	Rate of Graduates of Primary Schools Entering Junior Secondary Schools(%)	97.04	97.89	98.74	99.83
初中升学率(%)	Rate of Graduates of Junior Secondary Schools Entering Senior Secondary Schools(%)	51.15	60.45	62.5	65.71
学校每一专任教师负担学生人数	Number of Students Supported by Each Fulltime Teacher				
#高等学校(人)	Institutions of Higher Education (person)	12.5	13.87	15.70	16.17
普通中学(人)	Secondary Schools (person)	17.5	18.02	18.81	18.85
小学学校(人)	Primary Schools (person)	21.7	20.62	19.15	17.98
教育事业费相当于生产总值(%)	Proportion of Operating Expenses for Education to GDP (%)	1.38	1.63	1.91	1.94
科技三项及科学事业费相当于生产总值(%)	Proportion of Operating Expenses for Sciences and Expenses on S&T Promotion to GDP (%)	0.15	0.19	0.18	0.154
每百万人有艺术表演团体(个)	Number of Troupes per Million Persons (unit)	1.39	1.32	1.32	1.29
每百万人有公共图书馆(个)	Number of Public Libraries per Million Persons (unit)	1.76	1.74	1.74	1.73
家庭、生活、环境	**Family, People's Livelihood and Environment**				
离婚率(‰)	Divorce Rate (?	1.97	2.23	1.64	1.80
离退休职工相当于在岗职工比例(%)	Proportion of the Retired or Resigned to Staff and Workers on the Job (%)	34.74	41.13	42.03	51.47
每万人口中医院卫生院数(个)	Number of Hospitals per 10 000 persons (unit)	0.51	0.51	0.50	0.50
每万人口中医生数(人)	Number of Doctors per 10 000 persons (person)	13.52	13.54	11.96	11.96
每万人口中医院床位数(张)	Number of Hospital Beds per 10 000 persons (unit)	20.13	20.36	21.58	21.75
医院病床使用率(%)	Utilization Rate of Hospital Beds (%)	45.59	57.44	52.56	52.33
城市自来水普及率(%)	Percentage of Households with Access to Tap Water (%)	97.5	97.4	80.70	86.36
城市用气普及率(%)	Percentage of Households with Access to Tap Gas(%)	78.35	57.67	59.69	66.58
人均公共绿地面积(平方米)	Per Capita Public Green Areas (sq.m)	5.1	4.55	4.72	5.07
每起火灾经济损失(万元)	Average Loss of per Fire Disaster (10 000 yuan)	1.4	1.11	1.06	0.78
每起交通事故经济损失(万元)	Average Loss of per Traffic Accident (10 000 yuan)	0.4	0.27	0.32	0.46
每起环境污染事故罚款(万元)	Average Loss of per Pollution Accident (10 000 yuan)	0.097	0.124	0.158	16.03

1-12 国民经济主要比例关系

Main Proportional Relations of National Economy

单位:%　　　　(%)

指　标	Item	2000	2001	2002	2003
生产总值比例	**Ratio of Gross Domestic Products**				
第一产业	Primary Industry	21.3	20.7	19.5	19.1
第二产业	Secondary Industry	39.6	39.5	40.0	38.7
#工业	# Industry	33.3	32.9	33.2	31.3
建筑业	Construction	6.3	6.6	6.8	7.4
第三产业	Tertiary Industry	39.1	39.8	40.5	42.2
#运输邮电业	# Transportation, Post and Telecommunications	7.5	7.4	7.4	7.8
商业	Commerce	9.4	9.6	9.7	10.0
国内支出总额比例	**Ratio of Gross National Expenditure**				
资本形成总额	Gross Capital Formation	34.5	35.8	36.2	37.5
#固定资本形成总额	#Fixed Capital Formation	84.9	86.4	87.8	92.8
存货增加	Changes in Inventories	15.1	13.6	12.2	7.2
最终消费	Final Consumption Expenditure	64.6	64.1	63.6	62.2
#居民消费	#Resident Consumption	74.8	73.3	72.1	69.9
#农民	#Agricultural Resident' Consumption	58.3	56.9	55.5	52.9
非农业居民	Non-agricultural Resident' Consumption	41.7	43.1	44.5	47.1
政府消费	Government Consumption	25.2	26.7	27.9	30.1
全社会固定资产投资的资金来源	**Ratio of Investment in Fixed Assets by Source of Finance**				
国家预算内投资	State Budgetary Appropriation	7.2	7.7	6.7	5.7
国内贷款	Domestic Loans	20.0	17.0	15.6	18.2
债　券	Bunds	0.2	0.1	0.4	0.2
利用外资	Foreign Investment	2.1	2.4	3.2	3.0
自筹投资	Fundraising	58.5	62.6	62.9	60.6
其他投资	Others	12.1	10.2	11.1	12.2
国有经济投资中各行业比例	**Ratio of Investment in Fixed Assets by Sector**				
(国有经济)	(State-owned Economic)				
农　业	Agriculture	0.8	0.7	1.0	2.0
工　业	Industry	23.7	23.4	26.0	27.2
#能源工业	#Energy	15.5	14.3	15.1	11.7
运输、邮电、仓储业	Transportation, Postal and Telecommunications, Storage	42.5	37.3	27.2	30.5
地方财政收入比例	**Ratio of Local Government Revenue**				
工商税收	Industrial and Commercial Tax	54.0	60.6	64.3	64.5
企业所得税	Income Tax of Enterprises	6.8	11.0	6.7	5.0
国有企业亏损补贴	Subsidies to Loss-suffering State-owned Enterprises	-2.8	-2.9	-2.4	-1.5

单位：%　　　　1-12 续表 continued　　　　(%)

指　标		2000	2001	2002	2003
农业总产值中农林牧副渔比例	**Ratio of Agricultural Output Value**				
农业	Agriculture	50.6	50.7	49.4	46.2
#种植业	#Planting	46.3	46.5	45.2	-
林业	Forestry	4.1	4.0	4.1	5.6
牧业	Animal Husbandry	38.8	38.9	39.9	39.6
渔业	Fishery	6.5	6.5	6.7	6.7
规模工业总产值中轻重工业比例	**Ratio of Gross Output Value of Industrial Enterprises above Designated Size**				
轻工业	Light Industry	34.7	35.0	35.6	32.0
以农产品为原料	Using Farm Products as Raw Materials	75.3	76.5	76.5	-
以非农产品为原料	Using Non-Farm Products as Raw Materials	24.7	23.5	23.5	-
重工业	Heavy Industry	65.3	65.0	64.4	68.0
采掘工业	Mining and Quarrying	6.6	6.3	6.9	-
原料工业	Raw Materials Industry	56.0	54.6	51.6	-
加工工业	Manufacturing Industry	37.3	39.1	41.5	-
客运量比例	**Ratio of Total Passenger Traffic**				
铁路	Railways	6.0	5.6	5.3	5.0
公路	Highways	92.6	93.1	93.3	93.9
水运	Waterways	1.3	1.2	1.3	0.8
民用航空	Civil Aviation	0.2	0.2	0.2	0.2
货运量比例	**Ratio of Total Freight Traffic**				
铁路	Railways	9.2	9.4	9.5	8.7
公路	Highways	83.9	83.9	82.4	85.3
水运	Waterways	6.7	6.8	7.2	6.0
货物周转量比例	**Ratio of Total Freight Ton-kilometers**				
铁路	Railways	58.9	59.6	59.8	57.5
公路	Highways	27.7	27.9	29.1	33.5
水运	Waterways	13.4	12.5	11.1	8.9
全社会消费品零售总额比例	**Ratio of Total Retail Sales of Consumer Goods**				
市	City	52.0	52.9	53.8	54.9
县	County	18.7	18.4	18.3	18.3
县以下	Under County Level	29.3	28.7	27.9	26.8
公有经济	Public -Owned Economic	29.1	26.8	24.4	-
#国有经济	#State-owned Economic	17.1	16.3	15.1	-
非公有经济	Non Public-Owned Economic	70.9	73.2	75.6	-

1-13 平均每天主要社会经济活动

Selected Indicators of Average Daily Social and Economic Activities

指　标	Item	2000	2001	2002	2003
全省每天创造的财富	**Daily Production**				
地区生产总值(亿元)	Gross Domestic Product (100 million yuan)	10.11	10.91	11.89	12.71
农业总产值(亿元)	Gross Output Value of Agriculture(100 million yuan)	3.43	3.60	3.70	3.98
地方财政收入(万元)	Local Government Revenue (10 000 yuan)	4850.40	5627.64	6332.76	7360.27
布(万米)	Cloth (10 000 m)	93.42	83.56	81.10	93.42
机制纸及纸板(吨)	Machine-made Paper and Paperboard (ton)	1919.73	2126.30	2425.75	3404.93
原　煤(万吨)	Coal (10 000 tons)	4.08	4.24	5.06	6.48
发电量(万度)	Electricity (10 000 kw.h)	9710.14	10530.10	11658.63	14348.76
原油加工量(吨)	Machining Crude Oil (ton)	14422.47	11943.29	12844.66	13877.53
钢(吨)	Steel (ton)	8331.51	12106.85	14976.71	16185.48
成品钢材(吨)	Steel Products (ton)	8193.15	10657.80	13361.92	15292.60
水　泥(万吨)	Cement (10 000 tons)	6.56	6.84	7.52	8.37
粮　食(万吨)	Grain (10 000 tons)	7.88	7.40	6.85	6.69
棉　花(吨)	Cotton (ton)	469.32	520.55	419.18	446.85
油　料(吨)	Oil-bearing Crops (ton)	3817.81	3764.11	3267.20	3443.84
苎　麻(吨)	Ramie (ton)	181.37	258.08	350.97	340.55
烤　烟(吨)	Flue-cured Tobacco (ton)	426.03	446.03	478.04	483.84
茶　叶(吨)	Tea (ton)	156.99	160.00	167.16	166.03
柑　桔(吨)	Oranges (ton)	3449.86	4223.39	3952.28	4587.40
猪牛羊肉(吨)	Pork, Beef and Mutton (ton)	11959.18	12386.85	12883.01	13312.05
水产品(吨)	Aquatic Products (ton)	3649.59	3861.92	4097.52	4290.26
对外贸易进出口总额(万美元)	Total Imports and Exports (USD 10 000)	688.49	755.62	788.00	1023.56
进口总额(万美元)	#Total Imports (USD 10 000)	235.62	275.07	296.11	435.62
出口总额(万美元)	Total Exports (USD 10 000)	452.88	480.55	491.90	587.95
全省每天消费	**Daily Consumption**				
城乡居民消费总额(亿元)	Resident Consumption (100 million yuan)	4.88	5.13	5.46	5.53
平均每人消费额(元)	Per Capita Consumption (yuan)	7.46	7.79	8.25	9.00
其他经济活动	**Other Daily Economic Activities**				
邮电业务总量(万元)	Business Volume of Postal and Telecommunications Services (10 000 yuan)	3860.89	3675.72	5081.40	6417.37
出版图书(万册)	Books Published (10 000 copies)	68.07	65.23	89.32	80.98
出版杂志(万册)	Magazines Published (10 000 copies)	28.78	27.54	30.70	34.46
出版报纸(万份)	Newspaper Published (10 000 copies)	228.68	252.80	260.82	311.00
邮寄函件(万份)	Post Letters (10 000 pieces)	58.23	108.14	135.63	138.72
全省每天人口变动和婚姻	**Daily Population Changes and Marriages**				
出　生(人)	Births (person)	2054	2121	2094	2152
死　亡(人)	Deaths (person)	1218	1208	1214	1251
结　婚(对)	Marriages (couples)	1050	1002	1002	1052
离　婚(对)	Divorces (couples)	177	201	201	164

1-14 人均主要工农业产品产量

Per Capita Output of Major Agricultural and Industrial Products

指　标	Item	2000	2001	2002	2003
粮食(公斤)	Grain (kg)	439.0	410.4	377.4	366.6
棉花(公斤)	Cotton (kg)	2.6	2.9	2.3	2.5
食用植物油(公斤)	Edible Vegetable Oil (kg)	8.6	8.5	6.9	7.1
甘蔗(公斤)	Sugarcane (kg)	17.7	25.3	27.2	21.4
烤烟(公斤)	Flue-cured Tobacco (kg)	2.4	2.3	2.6	2.7
茶叶(公斤)	Tea (kg)	0.9	0.9	0.9	0.9
水果(公斤)	Fruit (kg)	23.0	75.4	72.3	76.9
#柑桔(公斤)	#Oranges (kg)	19.2	23.4	21.8	25.1
猪牛羊肉(公斤)	Pork, Beef and Mutton (kg)	66.7	68.7	70.9	72.9
#猪肉(公斤)	#Pork (kg)	63.3	65.2	67.0	68.6
禽蛋(公斤)	Poultry Eggs (kg)	11.2	11.7	12.4	12.9
水产品(公斤)	Aquatic Products (kg)	20.3	21.4	22.6	23.5
纱(混合数)(公斤)	Yarn (kg)	2.53	2.53	2.71	3.58
布(混合数)(米)	Cloth (meter)	5.19	4.64	4.47	5.55
针棉织品(折用纱量)(公斤)	Cotton Knitwear (kg)	0.1	0.07	0.1	0.29
机制纸及纸板(公斤)	Machine-made Paper and Paperboard (kg)	10.68	11.79	13.4	20.24
家用电冰箱 (台/百人)	Household Refrigerators (unit / 100 persons)	0.68	0.73	0.83	0.73
合成洗涤剂(公斤)	Synthetic Detergents (kg)	1.24	1.41	1.33	3.67
原盐(公斤)	Salt (kg)	11.11	10.43	10.76	12.86
糖(公斤)	Sugar (kg)	0.68	1.09	1.07	0.57
卷烟(箱 / 百人)	Cigarettes (cases/100 persons)	3.51	3.71	3.74	4.1
原煤(吨)	Coal (ton)	0.23	0.24	0.28	0.39
原油加工量(公斤)	Machining Crude Oil (kg)	80.22	66.25	70.91	82.49
发电量(度)	Electricity (kw.h)	540.11	584.12	643.63	852.89
生铁(公斤)	Pig Iron (kg)	50.7	63.41	75.54	88.06
钢(公斤)	Steel (kg)	46.35	67.16	82.68	96.21
钢材(公斤)	Steel Products (kg)	45.57	59.12	73.77	90.9
水泥(吨)	Cement (ton)	0.37	0.38	0.42	0.5
合成氨(公斤)	Synthetic Ammonia (kg)	25.49	22.68	27.14	26.62
农用化肥(折纯量)(公斤)	Chemical Fertilizers (kg)	21.6	22.21	24.81	27.12
#氮肥(公斤)	#Nitrogen Fertilizers (kg)	17.21	18.14	20.48	22.61
农药(原药折纯量)(公斤)	Chemical Pesticide (kg)	0.7	0.75	0.88	1.11
汽车 (辆/万人)	Motor Vehicles (unit/10 000 persons)	2.68	3.12	4.23	7.13
摩托车 (辆/万人)	Motorcycles (unit/10 000 persons)	21.72	17.68	37.94	42.90

1-15 贫困县市基本情况(2003年)

Basic Statistics on Poverty Counties and Cities (2003)

县 市	Country & City	总人口 (万人) Total Population (10 000 persons)	国内生产总值 (万元) Gross Domestic Products (10 000 yuan)	第一产业增加值 (万元) Added Value of Primary Industry (10 000 yuan)	工业增加值 (万元) Added Value of Industry (10 000 yuan)	财政收入 (万元) Govern-ment Revenue (10 000 yuan)	粮食产量 (万吨) Total Output of Grain (10 000 ton)	农民人均纯收入(元) Per Capita Annual Net Income of Rural Households (yuan)
国家扶贫开发工作重点县	**Key Counties For National Poverty Alleviation Development**							
邵阳县	Shaoyang County	96.36	219935	84125	30650	12894	30.85	1188.32
隆回县	Longhui County	110.54	313433	99092	41181	12393	34.64	1210.37
城步县	Chengbu County	25.72	88613	26683	29873	5313	7.64	1221.09
平江县	Pingjiang County	99.73	399039	124572	98796	16721	42.51	1345.56
桑植县	Shangzhi County	43.17	93683	29607	18426	4555	12.79	1223.29
安化县	Anhua County	95.84	260956	94620	60456	9315	25.60	1392.22
汝城县	Nucheng County	35.80	167485	44285	47929	9296	14.18	1528.24
桂东县	Guidong County	16.95	55546	15702	10972	4000	5.51	1486.56
新田县	Xintian County	36.70	111543	50683	16452	4236	12.17	1451.31
江华县	Jianghua County	45.83	130784	57864	24137	5995	15.84	1341.77
沅陵县	Yuanling County	64.84	348620	61301	197525	11588	20.91	1347.87
通道县	Tongdao County	22.23	57654	24655	10170	3290	7.40	1289.19
新化县	Xinhua County	128.83	317497	110176	48493	13912	35.00	1320.20
泸溪县	Louxi County	28.69	77610	23577	22860	2686	6.93	1245.76
凤凰县	Fenghuang County	37.31	98637	23619	16568	3273	8.82	1354.22
花垣县	Huayuan County	27.08	73357	20696	29207	4927	8.10	1262.24
保靖县	Baojing County	27.41	78078	22249	17936	3449	8.59	1266.87
古丈县	Guzhang County	13.74	33040	11593	4886	1278	3.24	1234.06
永顺县	Yongsun County	49.01	110271	45878	17382	4241	20.66	1337.52
龙山县	Longshan County	53.78	144691	50487	43529	5997	17.12	1464.70
省扶贫开发工作重点县	**Key Counties For Provincial Poverty Alleviation Development**							
茶陵县	Chaling County	57.03	255481	87955	69474	10203	31.88	1866.24
炎陵县	Yanling County	17.70	101326	25994	23076	5288	8.60	1807.94
新邵县	Xinshao County	73.10	247903	68523	47973	7886	25.44	1560.10
新宁县	Xinning County	58.24	167391	57337	21552	8500	28.33	1160.29
石门县	Shimen County	69.20	386150	118871	97384	15308	28.85	2035.22
永定区	Yongding Distract	42.03	183476	49161	32052	7683	14.85	1714.66
武陵源区	Wulingyuan Distract	4.54	74601	4962	1797	7022	1.16	1949.70
慈利县	Cili County	67.69	231868	72401	46554	8735	26.06	1701.38
宜章县	Yizhang County	55.57	306130	64659	83624	20039	22.64	2347.75
安仁县	Anren County	39.49	199258	65802	38198	9996	24.79	1948.87
双牌县	Shuangpai County	17.10	82890	25123	24077	4859	5.56	1665.65
宁远县	Ningyuan County	78.04	208115	80505	28717	8760	22.26	1375.02
辰溪县	Chenxi County	51.81	141674	43148	32339	7050	14.51	1762.00
麻阳县	Mayang County	36.45	98544	40113	15454	4326	10.97	1428.24
新晃县	Xinhuang County	25.61	82417	22380	25334	3571	7.51	1301.87
芷江县	Zhijiang County	35.75	149885	50208	33240	5025	15.00	1776.01
涟源市	Lianyuan City	109.30	335600	89105	92679	15519	35.51	1737.12
吉首市	Jishou City	28.53	210694	25640	64422	8851	4.62	1975.24

1-16 城乡私营企业基本情况(2003年)

Basic Statistics on Private Enterprises in Urban and Rural Areas (2003)

项　目	Item	户　数 (户) Number of Enterprises (unit)	投资者 (人) Employers (person)	雇工人数 (人) Number of Employed Persons (person)	注册资金 (万元) Registered Capital (10 000 yuan)
合计	**Total**	**56535**	**289227**	**802116**	**6953687**
#城镇	Urban	42442	251011	574591	5720318
独资企业	Private-funded Enterprises	9278	9278	114070	432593
合伙企业	Private Partnership Enterprises	4834	19042	66898	188027
有限责任公司	Private Limited Liability Corporations	42372	260388	611790	6130744
股份有限公司	Private Share-holding Corporations Ltd.	51	519	9358	202322

注：本表资料由湖南省工商行政管理局提供。

Data in the table were obtained from the Administrative Bureau for Indestry and Commerce of Hunan Province.

1-17 城乡私营企业生产经营情况(2003年)

Basic Statistics of Production and Operation on Private Enterprises in Urban and Rural Areas (2003)

单位：亿元 (100 million yuan)

项　目	Item	总产值 Total Output Value	#城镇 Urban	销售总额或营业收入 Total Sales	#城镇 Urban	零售额 Retail Sales	#城镇 Urban
合　计	**Total**	**300.12**	**194.27**	**251.63**	**194.97**	**267.46**	**203.42**
农林牧渔业	Farming, Forestry, Animal Husbandry and Fishery	9.02	4.77	5.96	3.00	3.17	1.87
#农林牧渔服务业	#Farming, Forestry, Animal Husbandry and Fishery Service			0.12	0.09	0.12	0.10
采掘业	Mining and Quarrying	22.34	6.07			6.78	4.22
制造业	Manufacturing	209.46	142.41			50.28	28.67
建筑业	Construction	59.30	41.02			17.39	11.44
交通运输、仓储业	Transport, Storage			12.27	9.86	5.66	4.83
#仓储业	#Storage			6.20	5.93	2.96	2.57
批发零售贸易、餐饮业	Wholesale and Retail Trades and Catering Services			168.25	129.35	150.54	123.22
#餐饮业	#Catering Trade			46.93	44.19		
社会服务业	Social Services			47.44	39.37	24.01	20.43
日用品修理业	Commodity Revamp			0.36	0.28	0.23	0.19
旅馆业	Hotels			1.93	1.60	0.73	0.61
娱乐服务业	Recreational Services			2.78	2.50	1.73	1.47
其他行业	Others			17.70	13.39	9.63	8.74

注：本表资料由湖南省工商行政管理局提供。

Data in the table were obtained from the Administrative Bureau for Indestry and Commerce of Hunan Province.

1-18 城乡个体工商业基本情况(2003年)

Basic Statistics on Individuals and Commerce in Urban and Rural Areas (2003)

金额单位：亿元 （100 million yuan）

项 目	Item	户数(户) Number of Enterprise (household)	#城镇 Urban	从业人员(人) Number of Employees (person)	#城镇 Urban	注册资金 Registered Capital	#城镇 Urban
合 计	**Total**	**940403**	**566300**	**1978624**	**1173295**	**195.24**	**131.22**
农林牧渔业	Farming, Forestry, Animal Husbandry and Fishery	3976	1651	12354	5007	1.05	0.4
农林牧渔服务业	Services	177	85	412	156	0.1	0.02
采掘业	Mining and Quarrying	1400	348	6233	1837	1.11	0.3
制造业	Manufacturing	107077	58290	263164	138078	26.5	13.35
建筑业	Construction	1129	652	4706	2191	0.8	0.25
交通运输、仓储业	Transport, Storage	80542	36621	137148	64655	24.15	11.23
仓储业	Storage	7261	3768	11424	5518	2.17	0.85
批发零售贸易、餐饮业	Wholesale and Retail Trades and Catering Services	608430	382793	1269875	777935	116.4	87.4
餐饮业	Catering	127280	82946	349268	189618	26.27	19.28
社会服务业	Social Services	122663	77972	257813	168861	20.85	15.25
日用品修理业	Commodity Revamp	20269	9153	35887	17370	1.76	1
旅馆业	Hotels	7037	3681	16562	8848	2.03	1.09
娱乐服务业	Recreational Services	14751	10130	35269	24453	4.33	3.45
其他行业	Others	15186	7973	27331	14731	4.38	3.04

项 目	Item	总产值 Total Output Value	#城镇 Urban	销售总额或营业收入 Total Sales	#城镇 Urban	零售额 Retail Sales	#城镇 Urban
合 计	**Total**	**288.34**	**132.97**	**829.40**	**466.95**	**623.55**	**336.96**
农林牧渔业	Farming, Forestry, Animal Husbandry and Fishery	13.97	2.40	6.49	1.24	3.86	1.28
农林牧渔服务业	Services			0.39	0.02	0.42	0.03
采掘业	Mining and Quarrying	14.57	3.41			4.47	0.73
制造业	Manufacturing	232.97	111.74			61.28	32.78
建筑业	Construction	26.83	15.42			7.72	5.71
交通运输、仓储业	Transport, Storage			105.69	51.39	35.72	17.83
仓储业	Storage			15.71	7.43	3.58	2.26
批发零售贸易、餐饮业	Wholesale and Retail Trades and Catering Services			615.92	348.03	449.20	235.28
餐饮业	Catering			175.14	102.90		
社会服务业	Social Services			93.01	61.01	55.84	39.74
日用品修理业	Commodity Revamp			11.56	6.43	6.21	3.68
旅馆业	Hotels			6.40	4.06	2.77	1.99
娱乐服务业	Recreational Services			13.30	9.87	8.45	6.35
其他行业	Others			8.29	5.28	5.46	3.61

注：本表资料由湖南省工商行政管理局提供。

Data in the table were obtained from the Administrative Bureau for Indestry and Commerce of Hunan Province.

1-19 三资企业投资基本情况(2003年)

Basic Statistics on Investment of "Three Types of Capital" Enterprises (2003)

类别	Item	项目数(个) Number of Projects (unit)	合同外资(万美元) Contracted Value (USD 10 000)	实际投资(万美元) Used Value (USD 10 000)	年末实有企业数(个) Number of Registered Enterprises (unit)	#本年新增企业 Newly Increase this Year
总 计	**Total**	**558**	**207476**	**148907**	**2337**	**442**
中外合资企业	Joint-venture Enterprises	197	39726	49836	1165	156
中外合作企业	Cooperation Enterprises	43	27018	16451	224	43
外商独资企业	Enterprises with Sole Foreign Investment	316	140609	82456	944	243
按国民经济行业分组	**By Economic Sector**					
农、林、牧、渔业	Farming, Forestry, Animal Husbandry and Fishery	41	11374	7456	78	23
采掘业	Mining and Quarrying	9	2438	2380	23	3
制造业	Manufacturing	285	76579	58342	1204	151
纺织业	Textiles	17	2481	1987	64	7
石油加工及炼焦业	Petroleum Processing and Coking				6	2
化学原料及化学制品	Raw Chemical Materials and Chemical Products	31	6711	5080	115	11
医药制造业	Medical and Pharmaceutical Products	17	6769	3401	43	4
普通机械制造业	Ordinary Machinery	10	529	531	37	8
专用设备制造业	Equipment for Special Purposes	9	752	1637	34	5
交通运输设备制造业	Transport Equipment				56	6
电气机械及器材制造业	Electric Equipment and Machinery				45	3
电子及通信设备制造业	Electronic and Telecommunications Equipment	20	21546	16258	65	9
电力、煤气及水的生产和供应业	Production and Supply of Electric Power, Gas and Water	15	10406	10886	34	5
建筑业	Construction	15	24073	6607	83	14
地质勘查业、水利管理业	Geological Prospecting and Water Conservancy	2	97	60	2	1
交通运输、仓储及邮电通信业	Transportation, Storage, Postal and Telecommunications Services	7	3027	2666	49	7
批发和零售贸易、餐饮业	Wholesales &Retail Trade and Catering Services	17	3648	3019	164	98
房地产业	Real Estate Trade	72	35961	28599	311	44
社会服务业	Social Services	85	34170	24955	336	68
卫生、体育和社会福利业	Health Care, Sports and Social Welfare	3	3049	2586	6	1
教育、文艺及广播电影电视业	Education, Culture and Arts, Radio, Film and Television	3	525	637	7	1
科学研究和综合技术服务	Scientific Research and Polytechnical Services	3	2149	230	20	11
其他	Others	1	-20	484	20	15

类别	Item	项目数（个）Number of Projects (unit)	合同外资（万美元）Contracted Value (USD 10 000)	实际投资（万美元）Used Value (USD 10 000)	年末实有企业数（个）Number of Registered Enterprises (unit)	#本年新增企业 Newly Increase this Year
按国别(地区)分组	**By Country (Territory)**					
亚洲	Asian	443	168807	116241	1901	343
香港	Hong Kong	294	108630	78923	1203	215
澳门	Macao	14	14092	3835	39	9
台湾	Taiwan	81	18984	10714	415	59
日本	Japan	12	2188	2194	59	11
菲律宾	Philippines	4	1474	2655	17	7
泰国	Thailand	4	740	757	19	2
马来西亚	Malaysia	5	4042	598	30	2
新加坡	Singapore	6	1424	4911	45	7
印度尼西亚	Indonesia			1018	4	1
韩国	Republic of Korea	13	16940	10369	35	12
非洲	Africa	3	154	293	10	5
欧洲	Europe	26	8591	11781	107	25
德国	Federal Republic of Germany	2	73	1511	18	2
法国	France	1	8	250	4	1
意大利	Italy	1	2779	18	10	
荷兰	Netherlands	2	177	6310	14	5
英国	United Kingdom	14	4955	3381	32	10
挪威	Norway	1	60	28	4	2
奥地利	Austria	1	14		1	1
拉丁美洲	Latin America	4	3882	3656	46	9
维尔京群岛	Virgin Islands	3	3320	3053	35	6
北美洲	North America	66	21821	11498	235	50
加拿大	Canada	12	4054	2554	40	7
美国	United States	54	17767	8944	195	43
大洋洲	Oceanic	13	4221	5438	37	10
澳大利亚	Australia	11	2874	2491	31	8
新西兰	New Zealand	2	244	230	3	2

二、国民经济核算

NATIONAL ECONOMIC ACCOUNTING

资料整理人员： 肖首雄　刘　杰

2-1 总产出

Gross Output

单位：亿元 (100 million yuan)

年份 Year	总产出 Gross Output	第一产业 Primary Industry	第二产业 Secondary Industry	工业 Industry	建筑业 Construction	第三产业 Tertiary Industry	交通运输仓储邮电业 Transportation,Postal and Telecommunications	批发零售贸易餐饮业 Wholesale, Retail Trade and Catering	其他 Other
1952	39.34	23.79	9.09	8.19	0.90	6.46	1.32	2.79	2.35
1955	49.24	25.83	14.47	12.11	2.36	8.94	2.39	4.50	2.05
1960	113.37	27.78	62.58	48.85	13.73	23.01	6.90	8.45	7.66
1965	107.35	42.70	45.55	38.90	6.65	19.10	5.93	5.35	7.82
1970	162.14	58.22	78.40	68.94	9.46	25.52	7.16	7.71	10.65
1975	234.10	76.06	120.60	105.34	15.26	37.44	9.25	11.23	16.96
1978	289.79	81.91	160.32	142.78	17.54	47.56	11.40	14.45	21.71
1979	347.74	109.18	186.04	164.12	21.92	52.52	12.12	16.05	24.35
1980	376.14	111.14	206.57	177.85	28.72	58.43	12.60	17.81	28.02
1981	408.13	126.36	214.61	187.02	27.59	67.16	12.68	19.77	34.71
1982	449.11	142.71	235.37	205.78	29.59	71.03	13.63	22.68	34.72
1983	498.03	158.16	261.66	221.15	40.51	78.21	15.14	22.84	40.23
1984	562.67	171.26	299.00	255.06	43.94	92.41	18.54	28.72	45.15
1985	698.36	198.44	372.89	314.68	58.21	127.03	26.00	40.52	60.51
1986	810.42	222.68	437.15	368.88	68.27	150.59	28.44	48.42	73.73
1987	980.08	253.39	540.92	456.74	84.18	185.77	32.68	58.96	94.13
1988	1239.59	303.01	690.19	581.85	108.34	246.39	43.09	80.03	123.27
1989	1390.89	337.48	768.85	680.09	88.76	284.56	51.37	85.79	147.40
1990	1571.34	397.42	809.86	712.67	97.19	364.06	56.35	136.70	171.01
1991	1777.40	425.58	928.67	803.71	124.96	423.15	70.50	157.16	195.49
1992	2210.80	471.22	1147.44	970.18	177.26	592.14	90.01	232.92	269.21
1993	2863.77	563.47	1610.45	1364.02	246.43	689.85	142.87	289.82	257.16
1994	3942.50	792.90	2075.56	1757.29	318.27	1074.04	227.34	393.00	453.70
1995	4997.42	1046.97	2569.29	2166.66	402.63	1381.16	283.72	506.55	590.89
1996	6178.52	1226.32	3446.08	2936.18	509.90	1506.12	324.74	590.37	591.01
1997	6932.53	1322.26	3842.26	3279.53	562.73	1768.01	375.85	649.63	742.53
1998	7544.08	1262.46	4273.81	3593.14	680.67	2007.81	419.37	705.80	882.64
1999	8122.44	1200.94	4559.96	3786.19	773.77	2361.54	465.98	773.05	1122.51
2000	9210.52	1251.89	5167.95	4272.00	895.95	2790.68	545.15	859.43	1386.10
2001	9966.39	1313.23	5534.70	4508.70	1026.00	3118.46	582.76	949.15	1586.55
2002	10947.50	1349.92	6095.12	4939.37	1155.75	3502.46	639.98	1061.20	1801.28
2003	11604.82	1425.44	6206.62	4868.00	1338.62	3972.76	714.93	1172.30	2085.53

注：1、由于规模以下工业总产值统计调查方法改变，1992年至1998年的核算数据按国家规定进行了调整，采用时以此年鉴为准。

2、根据国家新的方法制度规定，2003年规模以下工业以抽样调查数据为准。

a、Since the way of researching on industrial total output value was changed, data on national economy in 1992-1998 were adjusted in accordance with the government regulations.Please refer to the yearbook.

b、The data on industrial enterprises under designated size are obtained from the sample surveys in 2003 to the governmnet Regulations.

2-2 总产出构成

Composition of Gross Output

单位：%　　(以总产出为100) (Gross Output=100)　　(%)

年份 Year	总产出 Gross Output	第一产业 Primary Industry	第二产业 Secondary Industry	工业 Industry	建筑业 Construction	第三产业 Tertiary Industry	交通运输仓储邮电业 Transportation,Postal and Telecommunications	批发零售贸易餐饮业 Wholesale, Retail Trade and Catering	其他 Other
1952	100.0	60.5	23.1	20.8	2.3	16.4	3.4	7.1	5.9
1955	100.0	52.5	29.4	24.6	4.8	18.1	4.9	9.1	4.1
1960	100.0	24.5	55.2	43.1	12.1	20.3	6.1	7.5	6.7
1965	100.0	39.8	42.4	36.2	6.2	17.8	5.5	5.0	7.3
1970	100.0	35.9	48.4	42.5	5.9	15.7	4.4	4.8	6.5
1975	100.0	32.5	51.5	45.0	6.5	16.0	4.0	4.8	7.2
1978	100.0	28.3	55.3	49.2	6.1	16.4	3.9	5.0	7.5
1979	100.0	31.4	53.5	47.2	6.3	15.1	3.5	4.6	7.0
1980	100.0	29.5	54.9	47.3	7.6	15.6	3.3	4.7	7.6
1981	100.0	31.0	52.6	45.8	6.8	16.4	3.1	4.8	8.5
1982	100.0	31.8	52.4	45.8	6.6	15.8	3.0	5.0	7.8
1983	100.0	31.8	52.5	44.4	8.1	15.7	3.0	4.6	8.1
1984	100.0	30.4	53.1	45.3	7.8	16.5	3.3	5.1	8.1
1985	100.0	28.4	53.4	45.1	8.3	18.2	3.7	5.8	8.7
1986	100.0	27.5	53.9	45.5	8.4	18.6	3.5	6.0	9.1
1987	100.0	25.9	55.2	46.6	8.6	18.9	3.3	6.0	9.6
1988	100.0	24.4	55.7	47.0	8.7	19.9	3.5	6.5	9.9
1989	100.0	24.3	55.3	48.9	6.4	20.4	3.7	6.2	10.5
1990	100.0	25.3	51.5	45.3	6.2	23.2	3.6	8.7	10.9
1991	100.0	23.9	52.2	45.2	7.0	23.9	4.0	8.8	11.1
1992	100.0	21.3	51.9	43.9	8.0	26.8	4.1	10.5	12.2
1993	100.0	19.7	56.2	47.6	8.6	24.1	5.0	10.1	9.0
1994	100.0	20.1	52.6	44.6	8.0	27.3	5.8	10.0	11.5
1995	100.0	21.0	51.4	43.4	8.0	27.6	5.7	10.1	11.8
1996	100.0	19.8	55.8	47.5	8.3	24.4	5.3	9.6	9.5
1997	100.0	19.1	55.4	47.3	8.1	25.5	5.4	9.4	10.7
1998	100.0	16.7	56.7	47.6	9.1	26.6	5.6	9.4	11.6
1999	100.0	14.8	56.1	46.6	9.5	29.1	5.7	9.5	13.9
2000	100.0	13.6	56.1	46.4	9.7	30.3	5.9	9.3	15.1
2001	100.0	13.2	55.5	45.2	10.3	31.3	5.9	9.5	15.9
2002	100.0	12.3	55.7	45.1	10.6	32.0	5.8	9.7	16.5
2003	100.0	12.3	53.5	41.9	11.6	34.2	6.2	10.1	17.9

2-3 总产出发展速度

Growth Rate of Gross Output

单位：%　　(以上年为100)(precending year=100)　　(%)

年份 Year	总产出 Gross Output	第一产业 Primary Industry	第二产业 Secondary Industry	工业 Industry	建筑业 Construction	第三产业 Tertiary Industry	#交通运输仓储邮电业 Transportation,Postal and Telecommunications	#批发零售贸易餐饮业 Wholesale, Retail Trade and Catering
1952	100.0	121.3	151.9	132.3	236.8	100.0	129.3	107.7
1955	115.1	118.5	111.8	105.8	154.5	110.2	118.8	99.5
1960	105.2	84.7	117.1	112.3	140.5	105.3	96.6	109.8
1965	115.5	104.4	126.1	127.9	114.5	112.2	109.6	105.0
1970	124.3	105.0	142.3	144.6	123.3	100.9	116.6	109.1
1975	117.4	104.6	128.4	131.2	111.3	112.9	109.6	106.3
1978	114.8	110.2	117.0	115.6	130.3	115.8	113.2	113.2
1979	110.4	106.3	112.9	112.1	120.0	108.7	106.6	109.5
1980	105.8	98.1	109.8	108.0	123.6	104.8	102.6	104.8
1981	105.6	106.1	103.2	104.0	98.4	112.9	98.8	109.2
1982	108.7	110.1	109.2	109.6	106.3	104.4	108.3	112.8
1983	108.9	105.0	111.4	107.8	137.6	108.2	110.3	107.6
1984	110.7	105.7	112.2	112.6	104.3	115.1	122.3	121.9
1985	114.5	104.9	116.1	116.4	114.3	125.9	140.3	127.0
1986	110.6	105.4	112.1	113.0	106.3	113.6	111.6	114.1
1987	113.3	103.3	116.2	116.9	111.4	117.8	109.2	110.1
1988	111.0	100.5	114.6	115.3	110.0	112.6	118.7	107.8
1989	104.3	105.1	103.1	106.7	76.6	107.2	109.7	90.8
1990	103.9	101.9	104.7	105.0	100.9	103.8	109.4	91.2
1991	109.5	103.9	111.9	111.2	117.3	110.5	112.9	110.4
1992	112.6	103.8	116.3	115.6	121.5	113.6	121.5	132.4
1993	115.3	105.3	119.1	121.0	105.8	116.5	119.6	109.4
1994	113.4	106.4	116.0	116.3	113.8	113.7	110.8	109.0
1995	112.4	110.2	113.6	113.5	114.6	111.3	108.1	111.6
1996	118.9	108.4	126.4	127.5	117.1	108.9	112.7	108.7
1997	113.4	108.3	114.8	115.6	108.1	113.4	113.5	106.7
1998	111.2	101.5	113.3	113.0	116.1	113.0	115.7	111.0
1999	109.8	103.4	109.5	109.3	111.4	115.2	110.1	112.1
2000	111.0	104.3	111.2	111.1	112.4	114.7	119.0	112.0
2001	110.0	104.0	110.0	109.4	113.0	112.8	110.9	111.8
2002	110.1	102.7	110.7	110.5	112.0	112.2	110.2	112.7
2003	111.4	103.7	114.2	114.7	112.4	110.0	110.0	109.8

2-4 总产出指数

Indices of Gross Output

单位：%　　(1952 =100)　　(%)

年份 Year	总产出 Gross Output	第一产业 Primary Industry	第二产业 Secondary Industry	工业 Industry	建筑业 Construction	第三产业 Tertiary Industry	#交通运输仓储邮电业 Transportation,Postal and Telecommunications	#批发零售贸易餐饮业 Wholesale, Retail Trade and Catering
1952	100.0	100.0	100.0	100.0	100.0	100.0	100.0	100.0
1955	126.2	108.7	175.7	163.0	283.3	132.4	191.6	147.7
1960	260.8	103.1	773.1	619.0	1514.3	320.5	549.6	261.1
1965	213.6	116.7	541.0	477.6	644.7	248.7	452.9	151.3
1970	341.1	151.4	1015.3	926.6	917.7	350.7	543.7	218.8
1975	494.8	186.5	1573.9	1456.6	1480.3	532.0	702.5	319.8
1978	622.9	209.5	2104.0	1981.4	1716.6	675.6	863.9	410.9
1979	687.6	222.7	2375.4	2220.8	2060.1	734.3	921.0	450.0
1980	727.5	218.4	2608.1	2398.2	2546.6	769.6	944.5	471.5
1981	768.2	231.6	2691.6	2493.0	2504.9	868.8	933.6	514.7
1982	835.1	255.1	2939.3	2732.4	2663.9	907.1	1010.9	580.6
1983	909.4	267.9	3274.3	2946.3	3666.3	981.5	1115.1	624.9
1984	1006.7	283.1	3673.8	3347.1	3825.3	1129.7	1363.9	762.0
1985	1152.7	297.0	4265.3	3894.3	4371.0	1422.2	1913.4	967.7
1986	1274.9	313.2	4781.4	4401.3	4647.3	1615.7	2136.1	1103.8
1987	1444.4	323.5	5556.6	5144.4	5177.6	1903.3	2331.9	1214.8
1988	1603.3	325.2	6367.2	5931.2	5695.4	2143.1	2768.0	1309.6
1989	1672.3	341.8	6564.5	6328.6	4362.7	2297.4	3036.5	1189.1
1990	1737.5	348.3	6873.1	6647.7	4401.9	2384.7	3321.9	1084.5
1991	1902.6	361.9	7691.0	7302.2	5163.4	2635.1	3750.4	1197.3
1992	2142.3	375.6	8944.6	8441.3	6273.6	2993.5	4556.8	1585.2
1993	2470.1	395.5	10653.0	10214.0	6637.4	3487.4	5449.9	1734.2
1994	2801.1	420.8	12357.5	11878.9	7553.4	3965.2	6038.5	1890.3
1995	3148.4	463.7	14038.1	13482.6	8656.2	4413.2	6527.6	2109.6
1996	3743.4	502.7	17744.2	17190.3	10136.4	4806.1	7356.6	2293.1
1997	4245.0	544.4	20370.3	19872.0	10957.4	5450.1	8349.7	2446.7
1998	4720.4	552.6	23079.5	22455.4	12721.5	6158.6	9660.6	2715.8
1999	5183.0	571.4	25272.1	24543.8	14171.8	7094.7	10636.3	3044.4
2000	5753.1	596.0	28102.6	27268.2	15929.1	8137.6	12657.2	3409.7
2001	6328.4	619.8	30912.9	29831.4	17999.9	9179.2	14036.8	3812.0
2002	6967.6	636.5	34220.6	32963.7	20159.9	10299.1	15468.6	4296.1
2003	7761.9	660.1	39079.9	37809.4	22659.7	11329.0	17015.5	4717.1

2-5 地区生产总值

Gross Domestic Product

单位：亿元 (100 million yuan)

年份 Year	地区收入总值 Gross National Income	地区生产总值 Gross Domestic Product	第一产业 Primary Industry	第二产业 Secondary Industry	工业 Industry	建筑业 Construction	第三产业 Tertiary Industry	交通运输仓储邮电业 Transportation,Postal and Telecommunications	批发零售贸易餐饮业 Wholesale, Retail Trade and Catering
1978	146.99	146.99	59.83	59.82	51.94	7.88	27.34	5.91	9.71
1979	178.01	178.01	79.40	68.42	59.23	9.19	30.19	6.47	10.85
1980	191.72	191.72	81.14	76.99	65.31	11.68	33.59	6.77	11.73
1981	209.68	209.68	93.29	77.78	67.19	10.59	38.61	6.93	13.42
1982	232.52	232.52	107.99	82.51	71.31	11.20	42.02	7.61	12.81
1983	257.43	257.43	117.79	93.37	78.84	14.53	46.27	8.16	12.56
1984	287.29	287.29	128.28	104.34	90.79	13.55	54.67	9.30	15.40
1985	349.95	349.95	147.72	127.08	110.05	17.03	75.15	13.23	22.94
1986	397.68	397.68	165.28	143.31	124.30	19.01	89.09	15.00	27.60
1987	469.44	469.44	187.09	172.45	149.67	22.78	109.90	20.13	34.56
1988	584.07	584.07	217.03	221.28	190.40	30.88	145.76	24.12	46.61
1989	640.80	640.80	234.31	238.15	212.21	25.94	168.34	26.81	45.48
1990	744.44	744.44	279.09	249.98	220.69	29.29	215.37	32.27	62.94
1991	833.30	833.30	301.02	281.95	242.96	38.99	250.33	41.68	73.91
1992	986.98	986.98	323.91	337.17	284.66	52.51	325.90	51.29	104.96
1993	1259.55	1259.55	383.68	470.25	398.79	71.46	405.62	72.47	123.71
1994	1666.64	1666.64	532.89	590.29	497.99	92.30	543.46	99.63	167.75
1995	2151.43	2151.43	685.30	771.55	654.76	116.79	694.58	132.39	211.37
1996	2584.98	2584.98	793.98	946.25	808.93	137.32	844.75	168.88	245.95
1997	2918.83	2918.83	855.75	1092.80	944.95	147.85	970.28	195.38	270.12
1998	3118.09	3118.09	828.31	1200.86	1024.30	176.56	1088.92	216.49	291.73
1999	3326.75	3326.75	778.25	1297.74	1096.56	201.18	1250.76	240.40	315.04
2000	3691.88	3691.88	784.92	1461.86	1230.71	231.15	1445.10	277.69	348.10
2001	3983.00	3983.00	825.73	1573.00	1309.50	263.50	1584.27	294.90	382.40
2002	4340.94	4340.94	847.25	1737.20	1440.80	296.40	1756.49	322.58	422.55
2003	4638.73	4638.73	886.47	1794.21	1452.86	341.35	1958.05	359.83	465.83

单位：亿元　　　　　　　　　　　　　2-5 续表　continued　　　　　　　　　　　　　(100 million yuan)

年份 Year	金融保险业 Banking and Insurance	房地产业 Real Estate Trade	社会服务业 Social Services	卫生体育和社会福利事业 Health Care, Sports and Social Welfare	教育文化艺术和广播电影电视业 Education, Culture, Arts, Radio, Film and Television	科学研究和综合技术服务业 Scientific Research and Poly-technical Services	国家机关政党机关和社会团体 Government Agencies, Party Agencies, and Social Organizations	其他 Others	人均国内生产总值(元) Per Capita Gross Domestic Product (yuan)
1978	2.55	2.03	0.62	1.05	3.21	0.20	1.86	0.20	286
1979	2.50	2.10	0.68	1.24	3.72	0.28	2.10	0.25	343
1980	2.70	2.32	0.83	1.54	4.46	0.31	2.63	0.30	365
1981	3.60	3.56	0.95	1.72	4.83	0.36	2.89	0.35	394
1982	5.02	3.96	1.06	1.96	5.60	0.39	3.21	0.40	430
1983	5.66	5.18	1.17	2.33	6.40	0.49	3.87	0.45	470
1984	6.53	5.76	1.58	2.58	7.57	0.57	4.88	0.50	519
1985	8.85	7.84	3.34	2.87	9.13	0.68	5.67	0.60	626
1986	12.55	7.93	3.39	3.26	10.80	0.84	6.75	0.97	703
1987	15.94	8.53	3.91	3.84	12.61	0.99	8.14	1.25	818
1988	20.91	9.96	6.55	5.08	17.61	3.99	10.93		999
1989	26.94	11.00	8.73	6.04	21.61	6.07	13.86	1.80	1074
1990	31.01	16.25	10.84	7.98	17.43	7.36	26.51	2.78	1228
1991	38.26	17.73	10.88	9.02	19.14	7.45	29.08	3.18	1357
1992	49.01	20.57	16.52	11.35	23.02	9.41	34.72	5.05	1595
1993	63.47	25.73	18.54	14.08	27.55	10.93	43.96	5.18	2023
1994	73.60	32.30	24.84	20.72	42.37	15.78	59.70	6.77	2656
1995	90.15	40.90	29.39	25.47	55.99	19.86	79.98	9.08	3400
1996	105.14	57.37	33.11	33.84	67.21	8.62	99.78	24.85	4033
1997	119.22	65.75	39.66	40.62	80.27	10.23	119.35	29.68	4528
1998	125.62	75.67	47.05	48.19	97.97	12.07	139.39	34.74	4809
1999	129.76	86.98	66.31	61.50	124.12	14.79	172.20	39.66	5105
2000	140.70	97.14	82.87	77.11	154.16	17.38	203.67	46.28	5639
2001	143.16	108.00	91.98	85.60	170.20	17.90	241.35	48.78	6054
2002	145.63	125.46	102.19	95.87	196.95	19.69	273.36	52.21	6565
2003	157.40	137.71	193.86	113.69	219.99	23.28	228.04	58.42	7554

注：2003年人均生产总值按常住人口计算。 The data of per capita GDP are calculated at dejure population since 2003.

2-6 地区生产总值构成

Composition of GDP

单位：% (GDP=100) (%)

年份 Year	地区生产总值 Gross Domestic Product	第一产业 Primary Industry	第二产业 Secondary Industry	工业 Industry	建筑业 Construction	第三产业 Tertiary Industry	交通运输仓储邮电业 Transportation,Postal and Telecommunications	批发零售贸易餐饮业 Wholesale, Retail Trade and Catering
1978	100.0	40.7	40.7	35.3	5.4	18.6	4.0	6.6
1979	100.0	44.6	38.4	33.3	5.1	17.0	3.6	6.1
1980	100.0	42.3	40.2	34.1	6.1	17.5	3.5	6.1
1981	100.0	44.5	37.1	32.0	5.1	18.4	3.3	6.4
1982	100.0	46.4	35.5	30.7	4.8	18.1	3.3	5.5
1983	100.0	45.8	36.3	30.6	5.7	17.9	3.2	4.9
1984	100.0	44.7	36.3	31.6	4.7	19.0	3.2	5.4
1985	100.0	42.2	36.3	31.4	4.9	21.5	3.8	6.6
1986	100.0	41.6	36.0	31.3	4.7	22.4	3.8	6.9
1987	100.0	39.9	36.7	31.9	4.8	23.4	4.3	7.4
1988	100.0	37.2	37.9	32.6	5.3	24.9	4.1	8.0
1989	100.0	36.6	37.2	33.1	4.1	26.2	4.2	7.1
1990	100.0	37.5	33.6	29.6	4.0	28.9	4.3	8.5
1991	100.0	36.1	33.8	29.2	4.6	30.1	5.0	8.9
1992	100.0	32.8	34.2	28.8	5.4	33.0	5.2	10.6
1993	100.0	30.5	37.3	31.7	5.6	32.2	5.8	9.8
1994	100.0	32.0	35.4	29.9	5.5	32.6	6.0	10.1
1995	100.0	31.9	35.9	30.4	5.5	32.2	6.2	9.8
1996	100.0	30.7	36.6	31.3	5.3	32.7	6.5	9.5
1997	100.0	29.3	37.4	32.4	5.0	33.3	6.7	9.3
1998	100.0	26.6	38.5	32.9	5.6	34.9	6.9	9.4
1999	100.0	23.4	39.0	33.0	6.0	37.6	7.2	9.5
2000	100.0	21.3	39.6	33.3	6.3	39.1	7.5	9.4
2001	100.0	20.7	39.5	32.9	6.6	39.8	7.4	9.6
2002	100.0	19.5	40.0	33.2	6.8	40.5	7.4	9.7
2003	100.0	19.1	38.7	31.3	7.4	42.2	7.8	10.0

单位：%　　　　　　　　　　　　　　　　2-6 续表 continued　　　　　　　　　　　　　　　　(%)

年份 Year	金融保险业 Banking and Insurance	房地产业 Real Estate Trade	社会服务业 Social Services	卫生体育和社会福利事业 Health Care, Sports and Social Welfare	教育文化艺术和广播电影电视业 Education, Culture, Arts, Radio, Film and Television	科学研究和综合技术服务业 Scientific Research and Poly-technical Services	国家机关政党机关和社会团体 Government Agencies, Party Agencies, and Social Organizations	其他 Others
1978	1.7	1.4	0.4	0.7	2.2	0.1	1.3	0.2
1979	1.4	1.2	0.4	0.7	2.1	0.2	1.2	0.1
1980	1.4	1.2	0.4	0.8	2.3	0.2	1.4	0.2
1981	1.7	1.7	0.5	0.8	2.3	0.2	1.4	0.1
1982	2.2	1.7	0.5	0.8	2.4	0.2	1.4	0.1
1983	2.2	2.0	0.5	0.9	2.5	0.2	1.5	0.0
1984	2.3	2.0	0.5	0.9	2.6	0.2	1.7	0.2
1985	2.5	2.2	1.0	0.8	2.6	0.2	1.6	0.2
1986	3.2	2.0	0.9	0.8	2.7	0.2	1.7	0.2
1987	3.4	1.8	0.8	0.8	2.7	0.2	1.7	0.3
1988	3.6	1.7	1.1	0.9	3.0	0.7	1.9	0.0
1989	4.2	1.7	1.4	0.9	3.4	0.9	2.2	0.3
1990	4.2	2.2	1.5	1.1	2.3	1.0	3.6	0.4
1991	4.6	2.1	1.3	1.1	2.3	0.9	3.5	0.4
1992	5.0	2.1	1.7	1.1	2.3	1.0	3.5	0.5
1993	5.0	2.0	1.5	1.1	2.2	0.9	3.5	0.4
1994	4.4	1.9	1.5	1.2	2.5	0.9	3.6	0.5
1995	4.2	1.9	1.4	1.2	2.6	0.9	3.7	0.3
1996	4.1	2.2	1.3	1.3	2.6	0.3	3.9	1.0
1997	4.1	2.3	1.4	1.4	2.8	0.4	4.1	0.8
1998	4.0	2.4	1.5	1.5	3.1	0.4	4.5	1.2
1999	3.9	2.6	2.0	1.8	3.7	0.4	5.2	1.3
2000	3.8	2.6	2.2	2.1	4.2	0.5	5.5	1.3
2001	3.6	2.7	2.3	2.1	4.3	0.4	6.1	1.3
2002	3.4	2.9	2.4	2.2	4.5	0.5	6.3	1.2
2003	3.4	3.0	4.2	2.5	4.7	0.5	4.9	1.2

2-7 地区生产总值发展速度

Growth Rate of GDP

单位：% (以上年为100) (precending year=100) (%)

年份 Year	地区收入总值 Gross National Product	地区生产总值 Gross Domestic Product	第一产业 Primary Industry	第二产业 Secondary Industry	工业 Industry	建筑业 Construction	第三产业 Tertiary Industry	交通运输仓储邮电业 Transportation,Postal and Telecommunications	批发零售贸易餐饮业 Wholesale, Retail Trade and Catering
1978	116.4	116.4	111.7	121.8	121.6	123.3	115.5	110.7	120.4
1979	109.1	109.1	106.8	111.4	111.3	112.1	109.0	109.3	110.1
1980	105.2	105.2	98.9	111.0	109.7	119.9	105.5	104.5	102.5
1981	105.5	105.5	107.0	100.2	101.4	92.7	113.3	102.6	112.6
1982	109.4	109.4	113.0	106.0	106.1	105.0	107.5	109.6	94.0
1983	109.2	109.2	103.7	116.7	114.8	130.2	108.2	107.2	95.8
1984	109.4	109.4	106.6	109.7	113.0	89.8	115.6	113.9	119.3
1985	112.0	112.0	103.7	113.6	114.3	108.7	127.2	140.6	134.8
1986	108.1	108.1	105.2	107.7	108.5	101.6	114.1	112.6	114.6
1987	109.3	109.3	102.9	112.8	113.3	108.6	114.0	127.1	113.8
1988	108.2	108.2	97.7	115.0	115.3	112.6	112.6	120.4	108.9
1989	103.6	103.6	105.7	101.2	103.0	79.3	105.0	97.3	90.6
1990	104.0	104.0	103.2	104.6	104.5	106.1	103.8	113.7	83.7
1991	107.9	107.9	105.6	108.5	107.4	116.7	110.5	118.6	112.0
1992	111.1	111.1	103.5	117.3	116.8	120.4	114.1	112.8	110.0
1993	112.6	112.6	104.3	118.2	120.0	105.5	116.1	125.2	110.8
1994	110.6	110.6	105.4	115.4	115.9	111.7	110.3	110.6	109.0
1995	110.4	110.4	106.5	113.5	113.4	114.6	110.4	116.3	109.1
1996	112.1	112.1	106.2	116.3	116.8	112.3	112.6	117.8	109.0
1997	110.7	110.7	106.1	113.3	114.3	104.4	111.5	115.0	109.5
1998	108.5	108.5	100.9	111.5	111.2	114.1	111.0	113.4	110.3
1999	108.3	108.3	103.3	109.3	109.0	111.7	110.9	108.0	110.5
2000	109.0	109.0	103.9	110.6	110.5	111.5	110.6	114.5	111.4
2001	109.0	109.0	104.0	110.3	109.9	112.3	110.5	110.2	111.3
2002	109.0	109.0	102.6	110.9	111.0	110.4	110.5	109.9	111.5
2003	109.6	109.6	103.6	112.4	112.7	111.2	109.7	110.3	109.6

单位：%　　　　　　　　　　2-7 续表 continued　　　　　　　　　　(%)

年份 Year	金融保险业 Banking and Insurance	房地产业 Real Estate Trade	社会服务业 Social Services	卫生体育和社会福利事业 Health Care, Sports and Social Welfare	教育文化艺术和广播电影电视业 Education, Culture, Arts, Radio, Film and Television	科学研究和综合技术服务业 Scientific Research and Poly-technical Services	国家机关政党机关和社会团体 Government Agencies, Party Agencies, and Social Organiza-tions	其他行业 Others
1978	115.3	104.0	100.0	113.4	115.8	115.1	116.9	100.0
1979	96.5	101.7	101.9	115.9	113.6	137.9	111.2	125.0
1980	97.8	110.4	104.8	113.5	110.0	103.7	115.3	112.0
1981	131.0	146.4	151.3	110.4	106.6	114.5	108.2	116.7
1982	137.3	110.3	110.2	112.1	114.3	105.8	109.1	111.4
1983	110.1	128.5	128.5	116.0	111.8	124.7	117.7	112.8
1984	111.9	110.0	108.8	107.9	114.9	114.0	122.7	106.6
1985	122.1	128.4	125.9	100.9	109.5	109.0	106.1	110.6
1986	135.3	100.9	97.4	109.4	113.0	118.6	113.7	157.7
1987	114.9	105. 0	99.4	107.0	106.2	107.4	109.8	118.3
1988	104.6	109.5	149.8	107.1	112.6	131. 1	108.5	112.4
1989	150.6	86.7	122.5	113.6	117.5	146.3	120.8	101.8
1990	109.0	109.0	104.3	110.2	107.3	108.9	110.4	115.3
1991	115.5	106.1	100.0	107.8	104.9	100.0	106.0	107.6
1992	130.3	110.6	116.7	104.4	106.3	108.7	116.8	107.8
1993	121.3	124.0	107.1	116.8	113.1	108.4	113.3	101.0
1994	105.7	112.0	107.4	117.9	123.2	125.5	109.2	104.6
1995	106.0	114.7	102.4	106.5	104.4	104.4	116.0	116.2
1996	110.6	117.1	107.1	126.3	114.1	117.5	110.3	106.6
1997	110.3	110.2	111.3	112.4	114.9	113.0	111.1	108.1
1998	105.2	113.3	114.0	112.5	115.7	111.7	110.7	111.1
1999	105.1	117.3	121.6	112.8	115.4	112.0	112.0	111.7
2000	106.0	109.2	111.2	111.6	111.4	106.5	109.0	109.6
2001	103.5	109.3	111.5	109.5	108.9	103.9	117.8	105.8
2002	103.2	111.2	111.1	110.4	114.1	110.6	111.7	107.2
2003	105.4	109.0	110.0	112.0	111.7	115.5	111.7	100.2

2-8 地区生产总值指数

Gross Domestic Product Indices

单位：% (1978 =100) (%)

年份 Year	地区收入总值 Gross National Income	地区生产总值 Gross Domestic Product	第一产业 Primary Industry	第二产业 Secondary Industry	工业 Industry	建筑业 Construction	第三产业 Tertiary Industry	交通运输仓储邮电业 Transportation,Postal and Telecommunications	批发零售贸易餐饮业 Wholesale, Retail Trade and Catering
1978	100.0	100.0	100.0	100.0	100.0	100.0	100.0	100.0	100.0
1979	109.1	109.1	106.8	111.4	111.3	112.1	109.0	109.3	110.1
1980	114.8	114.8	105.6	123.6	122.1	134.4	115.0	114.2	112.9
1981	121.0	121.0	113.0	123.9	123.8	124.6	130.4	117.2	127.1
1982	132.4	132.4	127.7	131.3	131.4	130.8	140.2	128.4	119.4
1983	144.6	144.6	132.5	153.3	150.8	170.3	151.7	137.7	114.4
1984	158.2	158.2	141.2	168.1	170.4	153.0	175.4	156.8	136.5
1985	177.2	177.2	146.4	191.0	194.7	166.3	223.0	220.5	184.0
1986	191.7	191.7	154.1	205.8	211.3	168.9	254.5	248.3	210.9
1987	209.5	209.5	158.5	232.2	239.4	183.5	290.0	315.6	240.0
1988	226.7	226.7	154.9	267.0	276.1	206.6	326.6	379.9	261.4
1989	234.9	234.9	163.8	270.2	284.3	163.8	342.9	369.1	236.8
1990	244.3	244.3	169.1	282.7	297.1	173.8	355.9	420.3	198.2
1991	263.6	263.6	178.5	306.7	319.1	202.8	393.3	498.5	222.0
1992	292.9	292.9	184.8	359.8	372.7	244.2	448.7	562.3	244.2
1993	329.8	329.8	192.7	425.3	447.2	257.6	520.9	704.0	270.6
1994	364.8	364.8	203.1	490.8	518.3	287.7	574.6	742.0	295.0
1995	402.7	402.7	216.3	557.1	587.8	329.7	634.3	863.3	321.8
1996	451.4	451.4	229.7	647.9	686.6	370.3	714.2	1017.0	350.8
1997	499.7	499.7	243.7	734.1	784.8	386.6	796.3	1169.6	384.1
1998	542.2	542.2	245.9	818.5	872.7	441.1	883.9	1326.3	423.7
1999	587.2	587.2	254.0	894.6	951.2	492.7	980.2	1432.4	468.2
2000	640.0	640.0	263.9	989.4	1051.1	549.4	1084.1	1640.1	521.6
2001	697.6	697.6	274.5	1091.3	1155.2	617.0	1197.9	1807.4	580.5
2002	760.4	760.4	281.6	1210.3	1282.3	681.2	1323.7	1986.3	647.3
2003	833.4	833.4	291.7	1360.4	1445.2	757.5	1452.1	2190.9	709.4

单位：%　　　　2-8 续表 1 continued　　　　(%)

年份 Year	金融保险业 Banking and Insurance	房地产业 Real Estate Trade	社会服务业 Social Services	卫生体育和社会福利事业 Health Care, Sports and Social Welfare	教育文化艺术和广播电影电视业 Education, Culture, Arts, Radio, Film and Television	科学研究和综合技术服务业 Scientific Research and Poly-technical Services	国家机关政党机关和社会团体 Government Agencies, Party Agencies, and Social Organizations	其他行业 Others
1978	100.0	100.0	100.0	100.0	100.0	100.0	100.0	100.0
1979	96.5	101.7	101.9	115.9	113.6	137.9	111.2	125.0
1980	94.4	112.3	106.8	131.5	125.0	143.0	128.2	140.0
1981	123.6	164.4	161.6	145.2	133.2	163.7	138.7	163.4
1982	169.7	181.3	178.1	162.8	152.3	173.2	151.4	182.0
1983	186.9	233.0	228.8	188.8	170.2	216.0	178.1	205.3
1984	209.1	256.3	248.9	203.8	195.6	246.3	218.6	219.3
1985	255.4	329.1	313.4	205.6	214.2	268.4	231.9	242.5
1986	345.5	332.0	305.0	224.9	242.0	318.4	263.7	382.4
1987	397.0	348.6	303.4	240.7	257.0	341.9	289.5	452.4
1988	415.2	381.7	454.5	257.8	289.4	448.3	314.1	508.5
1989	625.3	331.0	556.8	292.8	340.0	655.8	379.5	517.7
1990	681.6	360.8	580.7	322.7	364.8	714.2	419.0	596.9
1991	787.2	382.8	580.7	347.8	382.7	714.2	444.1	642.3
1992	1025.7	423.4	677.7	363.1	406.8	776.3	518.7	692.4
1993	1244.2	525.0	725.8	424.1	460.1	841.5	587.7	699.3
1994	1315.1	588.0	779.5	500.0	566.8	1056.1	641.8	731.5
1995	1394.0	674.4	798.2	532.5	591.8	1102.6	744.5	850.0
1996	1541.8	789.7	854.9	672.5	675.2	1295.6	821.2	906.1
1997	1700.6	870.2	951.5	755.9	775.8	1464.0	912.4	979.5
1998	1789.0	985.9	1084.7	850.4	897.6	1635.3	1010.0	1088.2
1999	1880.2	1156.5	1319.0	959.3	1035.8	1831.5	1131.2	1215.5
2000	1993.0	1262.9	1466.7	1070.6	1153.9	1950.5	1233.0	1332.2
2001	2062.8	1380.3	1635.4	1172.3	1256.6	2026.6	1452.5	1409.5
2002	2128.8	1534.9	1816.9	1294.2	1433.8	2241.4	1622.4	1511.0
2003	2243.8	1673.0	1998.6	1449.5	1601.6	2588.8	1812.2	1514.0

单位：%　　2-8 续表 2 continued (1952 =100)　　(%)

年份 Year	地区收入总值 Gross National Income	地区生产总值 Gross Domestic Product	第一产业 Primary Industry	第二产业 Secondary Industry	工业 Industry	建筑业 Construction	第三产业 Tertiary Industry	#交通运输仓储邮电业 Transportation,Postal and Telecommunications	#批发零售贸易餐饮业 Wholesale, Retail Trade and Catering
1952	100.0	100.0	100.0	100.0	100.0	100.0	100.0	100.0	100.0
1955	126.1	126.1	110.3	190.0	165.0	331.5	150.4	192.5	140.2
1960	197.5	197.5	90.4	765.8	671.7	1274.9	292.1	506.9	229.1
1965	170.1	170.1	111.7	558.4	570.3	417.8	186.1	274.9	116.7
1970	247.0	247.0	139.5	1005.8	1057.3	569.4	245.9	363.1	179.7
1975	307.6	307.6	162.4	1325.9	1329.2	1142.5	309.9	449.5	232.0
1978	390.3	390.3	184.3	1903.0	1949.8	1427.7	392.8	538.3	308.6
1979	425.7	425.7	196.8	2119.1	2169.4	1600.1	428.2	588.3	339.8
1980	448.0	448.0	194.6	2352.0	2380.0	1918.7	451.9	614.8	348.3
1981	472.4	472.4	208.3	2357.8	2414.0	1779.3	512.1	630.5	392.2
1982	516.7	516.7	235.4	2498.9	2561.8	1868.4	550.6	690.8	368.7
1983	564.4	564.4	244.2	2917.3	2939.9	2432.2	595.9	740.7	353.2
1984	617.4	617.4	260.2	3198.9	3321.7	2184.7	688.9	843.8	421.4
1985	691.8	691.8	269.9	3634.5	3795.5	2375.4	875.9	1186.1	568.0
1986	748.1	748.1	284.0	3916.1	4119.2	2414.5	999.7	1335.2	650.9
1987	817.8	817.8	292.2	4418.7	4668.6	2622.1	1139.2	1697.3	740.7
1988	884.9	884.9	285.5	5081.5	5382.9	2952.5	1282.7	2043.5	806.6
1989	916.8	916.8	301.8	5142.5	5544.4	2341.3	1346.8	1988.3	730.8
1990	953.1	953.1	311.6	5380.0	5793.9	2484.2	1397.9	2260.7	611.7
1991	1028.4	1028.4	329.0	5837.3	6222.6	2899.1	1544.7	2681.2	685.1
1992	1142.6	1142.6	340.5	6847.2	7268.0	3490.5	1762.5	3024.4	753.6
1993	1286.6	1286.6	355.1	8093.4	8721.6	3682.5	2046.3	3786.5	835.0
1994	1423.0	1423.0	374.3	9339.8	10108.3	4113.4	2257.1	4187.9	910.2
1995	1571.0	1571.0	398.6	10600.7	11462.8	4713.9	2491.8	4870.5	993.0
1996	1761.1	1761.1	423.3	12328.6	13388.6	5293.7	2805.8	5737.4	1082.4
1997	1949.5	1949.5	449.1	13968.3	15303.2	5526.6	3128.5	6598.0	1185.2
1998	2115.2	2115.2	453.1	15574.7	17017.2	6305.9	3472.6	7482.1	1307.3
1999	2290.8	2290.8	468.1	17023.1	18548.7	7043.7	3851.1	8080.7	1444.6
2000	2497.0	2497.0	486.3	18827.5	20496.3	7853.7	4259.3	9252.4	1609.3
2001	2721.7	2721.7	505.8	20766.7	22525.4	8819.7	4706.5	10196.1	1791.2
2002	2966.7	2966.7	519.0	23030.3	25003.2	9736.9	5200.7	11205.5	1997.2
2003	3251.5	3251.5	537.7	25886.1	28178.6	10827.4	5705.2	12359.7	2188.9

2-9 地区生产总值构成项目表

Structure of Gross Domestic Product

单位：亿元 (100 million yuan)

指 标	Item	2000	2001	2002	2003
地区生产总值	**Gross Domestic Product**	**3691.88**	**3983.00**	**4340.94**	**4638.73**
劳动者报酬	Compensation of Laborers	2287.45	2491.25	2667.31	2803.7
固定资产折旧	Depreciation of Fixed Assets	578.46	600.74	671.73	717.99
生产税净额	Net Taxes on Production	465.18	493.34	555.43	596.35
营业盈余	Operating Surplus	360.79	397.67	446.47	520.69
第一产业	**Primary Industry**	**784.92**	**825.73**	**847.25**	**886.47**
劳动者报酬	Compensation of Laborers	691.52	727.39	738.04	771.8
固定资产折旧	Depreciation of Fixed Assets	31.40	33.56	35.26	37.43
生产税净额	Net Taxes on Production	15.70	15.87	24.33	26.22
营业盈余	Operating Surplus	46.30	48.91	49.62	51.02
第二产业	**Secondary Industry**	**1461.86**	**1573.00**	**1737.20**	**1794.21**
劳动者报酬	Compensation of Laborers	712.74	775.86	853.71	878.62
固定资产折旧	Depreciation of Fixed Assets	219.10	232.11	257.12	259.78
生产税净额	Net Taxes on Production	330.10	366.89	405.80	418.08
营业盈余	Operating Surplus	199.92	198.14	220.57	237.73
#工业增加值	**# Added Value of Industry**	**1230.71**	**1309.50**	**1440.80**	**1452.86**
劳动者报酬	Compensation of Laborers	578.44	622.01	681.50	679.95
固定资产折旧	Depreciation of Fixed Assets	200.61	210.83	233.41	232.47
生产税净额	Net Taxes on Production	303.98	318.21	351.56	355.95
营业盈余	Operating Surplus	147.68	158.45	174.33	184.49
#建筑业增加值	**# Added Value of Construction**	**231.15**	**263.50**	**296.40**	**341.35**
劳动者报酬	Compensation of Laborers	134.30	153.85	172.21	198.67
固定资产折旧	Depreciation of Fixed Assets	18.49	21.28	23.71	27.31
生产税净额	Net Taxes on Production	26.12	48.68	54.24	62.13
营业盈余	Operating Surplus	52.24	39.69	46.24	53.24
第三产业	**Tertiary Industry**	**1445.10**	**1584.27**	**1756.49**	**1958.05**
劳动者报酬	Compensation of Laborers	883.19	988.00	1075.56	1153.28
固定资产折旧	Depreciation of Fixed Assets	327.96	335.07	379.35	420.78
生产税净额	Net Taxes on Production	119.38	110.58	125.30	152.05
营业盈余	Operating Surplus	114.57	150.62	176.28	231.94
#交通运输仓储邮电业增加值	**# Added Value of Transport,Storage, Postal and Telecommunications**	**277.69**	**294.90**	**322.58**	**359.83**
劳动者报酬	Compensation of Laborers	163.54	160.55	173.88	187.65
固定资产折旧	Depreciation of Fixed Assets	109.73	119.32	133.71	140.55
生产税净额	Net Taxes on Production	20.40	20.74	22.17	23.98
营业盈余	Operating Surplus	-15.98	-5.71	-7.18	7.65
#批发零售贸易餐饮业增加值	**# Added Value of Wholesale, Retail Trade and Catering Services**	**348.10**	**382.40**	**422.55**	**465.83**
劳动者报酬	Compensation of Laborers	211.32	231.80	255.60	281.38
固定资产折旧	Depreciation of Fixed Assets	45.28	49.57	54.50	60.42
生产税净额	Net Taxes on Production	52.28	57.48	63.58	69.12
营业盈余	Operating Surplus	39.22	43.55	48.87	54.91

单位：亿元　　2-9 续表 continued　　(100 million yuan)

指 标	Item	2000	2001	2002	2003
#金融保险业增加值	**# Added Value of Finance and Insurance**	**140.7**	**143.16**	**145.63**	**157.4**
劳动者报酬	Compensation of Laborers	44.93	61.78	49.13	57.36
固定资产折旧	Depreciation of Fixed Assets	33.04	9.58	12.47	20.39
生产税净额	Net Taxes on Production	13.15	15.39	16.97	21.48
营业盈余	Operating Surplus	49.58	56.41	67.06	58.17
#房地产业增加值	**# Added Value of Real Estate Trade**	**97.14**	**108**	**125.46**	**137.71**
劳动者报酬	Compensation of Laborers	5.9	6.88	8.3	9.83
固定资产折旧	Depreciation of Fixed Assets	84.93	93.63	108.14	116.75
生产税净额	Net Taxes on Production	2.9	3.37	4.04	5.22
营业盈余	Operating Surplus	3.41	4.12	4.98	5.91
#社会服务业增加值	**# Added Value of Social Services**	**82.87**	**91.98**	**102.19**	**193.86**
劳动者报酬	Compensation of Laborers	28.42	37.68	34.95	65.52
固定资产折旧	Depreciation of Fixed Assets	7.46	9.2	10.22	19.77
生产税净额	Net Taxes on Production	27.62	10.34	15.2	28.5
营业盈余	Operating Surplus	19.37	34.76	41.82	80.07
#卫生体育福利业增加值	**# Added Value of Health Care,Sports and Social Welfare**	**77.11**	**85.6**	**95.87**	**113.69**
劳动者报酬	Compensation of Laborers	61.72	68.57	76.7	90.95
固定资产折旧	Depreciation of Fixed Assets	0.54	9.84	11.32	13.64
生产税净额	Net Taxes on Production	9.02	0.6	0.58	0.68
营业盈余	Operating Surplus	5.83	6.59	7.27	8.42
#教育文艺广播电影电视业增加值	**# Added Value of Education,Culture and Arts,Radio, Film and Television**	**154.16**	**170.2**	**196.95**	**219.99**
劳动者报酬	Compensation of Laborers	133.96	147.73	171.15	187.87
固定资产折旧	Depreciation of Fixed Assets	16.96	18.72	21.66	24.64
生产税净额	Net Taxes on Production	0.77	1.02	0.99	1.1
营业盈余	Operating Surplus	2.47	2.73	3.15	6.38
#科学研究和综合技术服务业增加值	**# Added Value of Scientific Research and Polytechnical Services**	**17.38**	**17.9**	**19.69**	**23.28**
劳动者报酬	Compensation of Laborers	12.53	12.91	14.18	17.46
固定资产折旧	Depreciation of Fixed Assets	2.38	2.43	2.7	3.19
生产税净额	Net Taxes on Production	0.54	0.55	0.61	0.7
营业盈余	Operating Surplus	1.93	2.01	2.2	1.93
#国家政党机关和社会团体增加值	**# Added Value of Government Agencies, Party Agencies and Social Organizations**	**203.67**	**241.35**	**273.36**	**228.04**
劳动者报酬	Compensation of Laborers	188.67	223.49	253.13	211.85
固定资产折旧	Depreciation of Fixed Assets	14.26	17.62	19.13	15.05
生产税净额	Net Taxes on Production	0.2	0.24	0.28	0.23
营业盈余	Operating Surplus	0.54		0.82	0.91
#其他增加值	**# Added Value of Others**	**46.28**	**48.78**	**52.21**	**58.42**
劳动者报酬	Compensation of Laborers	32.2	36.61	38.54	43.41
固定资产折旧	Depreciation of Fixed Assets	4.9	5.16	5.5	6.38
生产税净额	Net Taxes on Production	0.98	0.85	0.88	1.04
营业盈余	Operating Surplus	8.2	6.16	7.29	7.59

2-10 地区生产总值(支出法)

GDP (by Expenditure Approach)

单位：亿元 (100 million yuan)

年份 Year	地区生产总值 GDP by Expenditure Approach	最终消费 Final Consumption Expenditure	居民消费 Household Consumption	农业居民 Agricultural	非农业居民 Non-agricultural	政府消费 Government Consumption
1978	146.99	100.83	93.93	70.87	23.06	6.90
1980	191.72	136.94	125.42	93.15	32.27	11.52
1985	349.95	263.11	240.71	182.85	57.86	22.40
1986	397.68	290.14	265.54	196.12	69.42	24.60
1987	469.44	328.34	298.85	218.93	79.92	29.49
1988	584.07	399.15	364.37	256.19	108.18	34.78
1989	640.80	439.54	393.49	270.81	122.68	46.05
1990	744.44	564.70	454.90	314.05	140.85	109.80
1991	833.30	621.93	500.84	340.27	160.57	121.09
1992	986.98	725.60	582.91	379.23	203.68	142.69
1993	1259.55	885.05	706.55	442.35	264.20	178.50
1994	1666.64	1113.62	883.46	534.34	349.12	230.16
1995	2151.43	1396.88	1108.78	674.09	434.69	288.10
1996	2584.98	1753.27	1409.44	896.48	512.96	343.83
1997	2918.83	1956.22	1540.67	970.95	569.72	415.55
1998	3118.09	2062.84	1601.83	1009.06	592.77	461.01
1999	3326.75	2212.47	1690.66	1021.56	669.10	521.81
2000	3691.88	2383.27	1782.77	1038.80	743.97	600.50
2001	3983.00	2553.14	1871.64	1065.00	806.64	681.50
2002	4340.94	2762.95	1992.05	1105.18	886.87	770.90
2003	4638.73	2886.03	2016.88	1067.23	949.65	869.15

年份 Year	资本形成总额 Gross Capital Formation	固定资本 Fixed Capital	存货增加 Changes in Inventories	货物和服务净出口 Net Export of Goods&Services	资本形成率(投资率)% Rate of Capital Formation (%)	最终消费率(消费率)% Rate of Final Consumption(%)
1978	42.41	27.68	14.73	3.75	28.9	68.6
1980	40.02	32.76	7.26	14.76	20.9	71.4
1985	92.19	58.14	34.05	-5.35	26.3	75.2
1986	115.02	75.57	39.45	-7.48	28.9	73.0
1987	139.84	91.79	48.05	1.26	29.8	69.9
1988	184.75	114.73	70.02	0.17	31.6	68.3
1989	169.41	83.19	86.22	31.85	26.4	68.6
1990	184.12	122.82	61.30	-4.38	24.7	75.9
1991	224.80	160.49	64.31	-13.43	27.0	74.6
1992	291.04	228.29	62.75	-29.66	29.5	73.5
1993	396.00	330.54	65.46	-21.50	31.4	70.3
1994	553.74	422.61	131.13	-0.72	33.2	66.8
1995	756.23	534.12	222.11	-1.68	35.2	64.9
1996	833.12	678.32	154.80	-1.41	32.2	67.8
1997	947.22	725.73	221.49	15.39	32.5	67.0
1998	1038.75	846.37	192.38	16.50	33.3	66.2
1999	1130.67	956.10	174.57	-16.39	34.0	66.5
2000	1274.94	1082.00	192.94	33.67	34.5	64.6
2001	1426.47	1233.17	193.30	3.39	35.8	64.1
2002	1572.89	1380.89	192.00	5.10	36.2	63.6
2003	1738.27	1613.12	125.15	14.43	37.5	62.2

2-11 最终消费构成项目

Compostion of Final Consumption

单位：亿元 (100 million yuan)

年份 Year	最终消费 Final Consumption Expenditure	居民消费 Household Consumption	农业居民 Agricultural Households	自给性消费 Self-Sufficient	商品性消费 Commodity Consumption	文化生活服务 Cultural,Life and Services
1978	100.83	93.93	70.87	46.07	19.35	1.91
1980	136.94	125.42	93.15	50.67	33.72	1.77
1985	263.11	240.71	182.85	81.13	89.85	2.87
1986	290.14	265.54	196.12	82.54	100.88	3.56
1987	328.34	298.85	218.93	85.01	117.40	6.38
1988	399.15	364.37	256.19	89.98	145.58	8.94
1989	439.54	393.49	270.81	90.88	154.75	11.81
1990	564.70	454.90	314.05	136.03	152.46	12.44
1991	621.93	500.84	340.27	145.00	166.39	14.44
1992	725.60	582.91	379.23	153.78	173.94	35.72
1993	885.05	706.55	442.35	173.97	203.25	46.55
1994	1113.62	883.46	534.34	218.72	239.01	54.05
1995	1396.88	1108.78	674.09	256.35	311.44	70.56
1996	1753.27	1409.44	896.48	346.21	367.75	121.20
1997	1956.22	1540.67	970.95	351.51	410.07	147.95
1998	2062.84	1601.83	1009.06	351.60	438.59	148.12
1999	2212.47	1690.66	1021.56	329.30	463.32	147.38
2000	2383.27	1782.77	1038.80	249.05	504.23	187.87
2001	2553.14	1871.64	1065.00	244.43	519.74	194.96
2002	2762.95	1992.05	1105.18	235.86	550.80	204.26
2003	2886.03	2016.88	1067.23	213.45	528.17	203.57

年份 Year	住房及水电消费 Housing Water and Electricity	非农业居民 Non-Agricultural Households	商品性消费 Commodity Consumption	文化生活服务 Cultural Life and Services	住房及水电消费 Housing Water and Electricity	政府消费 Government Consumption
1978	3.54	23.06	20.96	1.59	0.51	6.90
1980	6.99	32.27	29.40	2.19	0.68	11.52
1985	9.00	57.86	51.75	4.77	1.34	22.40
1986	9.14	69.42	61.92	6.29	1.21	24.60
1987	10.14	79.92	70.46	7.64	1.82	29.49
1988	11.69	108.18	97.08	8.95	2.15	34.78
1989	13.37	122.68	109.30	9.82	3.56	46.05
1990	13.12	140.85	125.82	11.06	3.97	109.80
1991	14.44	160.57	142.58	13.50	4.49	121.09
1992	15.79	203.68	169.99	27.59	6.10	142.69
1993	18.58	264.20	221.65	35.39	7.16	178.50
1994	22.56	349.12	282.11	54.49	12.52	230.16
1995	35.74	434.69	362.77	56.61	15.31	288.10
1996	61.32	512.96	418.38	50.01	44.57	343.83
1997	61.42	569.72	439.82	80.04	49.86	415.55
1998	70.75	592.77	441.57	95.24	55.96	461.01
1999	81.56	669.10	467.17	157.55	44.38	521.81
2000	97.65	743.97	509.76	184.77	49.44	600.50
2001	105.87	806.64	533.43	207.97	65.24	681.50
2002	114.26	886.87	612.13	218.24	56.50	770.90
2003	122.04	949.65	659.87	223.61	66.17	869.15

2-12 最终消费发展速度及指数

Growth Rate and Indices of Final Consumption Expenditure

单位:% (%)

年份 Year	以上年为100 (preceding year=100) 最终消费 Final Consumption Expenditure	居民消费 Household Consumption	农业居民 Agricultural	非农业居民 Non-Agricultural	政府消费 Government Consumption	以1952年为100 (1952=100) 最终消费 Final Consumption Expenditure	居民消费 Household Consumption	农业居民 Agricultural	非农业居民 Non-Agricultural	政府消费 Government Consumption
1978	112.5	112.9	111.0	118.7	107.7	258.5	246.2	211.6	490.9	677.9
1979	112.3	110.8	110.3	112.2	131.4	290.3	272.8	233.4	550.8	890.8
1980	108.9	108.5	109.2	106.5	112.8	316.2	296.0	254.8	586.6	1004.8
1981	111.2	111.3	113.0	106.5	109.9	351.6	329.4	288.0	624.8	1104.3
1982	111.8	111.3	113.4	105.0	116.5	393.0	366.6	326.5	656.0	1286.5
1983	107.5	107.7	108.8	104.2	104.7	422.5	394.8	355.3	683.5	1347.0
1984	108.9	108.8	108.3	110.2	110.6	460.1	429.6	384.8	753.3	1489.8
1985	108.3	108.4	107.6	111.3	106.6	498.3	465.7	414.0	838.4	1588.1
1986	104.5	104.5	101.8	113.3	104.3	520.7	486.6	421.5	949.9	1656.4
1987	102.3	102.1	101.2	104.5	104.5	532.7	496.9	426.5	992.6	1730.9
1988	98.3	98.2	95.6	105.4	99.4	523.7	487.9	407.7	1046.2	1720.5
1989	97.7	96.8	97.0	96.2	107.9	511.6	472.3	395.5	1006.5	1856.5
1990	105.9	105.0	101.7	113.8	114.0	541.8	495.9	402.2	1145.4	2116.4
1991	105.4	105.3	104.1	108.0	106.0	571.1	522.2	418.7	1237.0	2243.4
1992	103.9	103.5	101.4	108.3	105.4	593.3	540.5	424.6	1339.7	2364.5
1993	105.3	104.5	100.7	112.2	108.9	624.8	564.8	427.5	1503.1	2575.0
1994	105.8	105.9	100.6	115.5	105.6	661.0	598.1	430.1	1736.1	2719.2
1995	108.6	108.7	109.2	107.8	108.4	717.9	650.2	469.6	1871.5	2947.6
1996	113.8	114.4	120.7	104.4	111.3	817.0	743.8	566.8	1953.8	3280.7
1997	108.0	106.2	105.7	107.3	115.1	882.4	790.0	599.1	2096.4	3776.1
1998	105.6	104.9	105.7	103.4	108.2	931.8	828.7	633.2	2167.7	4085.7
1999	105.7	104.5	101.3	110.5	110.1	984.9	866.0	641.4	2395.3	4498.4
2000	105.6	103.6	100.7	108.7	112.3	1040.1	897.2	645.9	2603.7	5051.7
2001	108.0	105.7	102.7	109.8	115.0	1123.3	948.3	663.3	2858.9	5809.5
2002	108.6	106.5	103.8	110.2	114.2	1219.9	1009.9	688.5	3150.5	6634.4
2003	107.8	106.5	101.5	112.7	110.9	1315.1	1075.5	698.8	3550.6	7357.5

2-13 居民消费水平

Household Consumption

年份 Year	按当年价计算 At Current Prices			以上年为100 Preceding Year=100			以1952年为100 1952=100		
	居民消费水平(元) Household Consumption Level (yuan)	农业居民 Agricultural Households	非农业居民 Non-Agricultural Households	居民消费水平(%) Household Consumption Level (%)	农业居民 Agricultural Households	非农业居民 Non-Agricultural Households	居民消费水平(%) Household Consumption Level (%)	农业居民 Agricultural Households	非农业居民 Non-Agricultural Households
1978	183	154	427	111.7	110.0	115.4	153.4	134.7	252.9
1979	211	181	454	109.6	110.0	104.5	168.2	148.2	264.3
1980	239	201	523	107.3	108.8	100.1	180.4	161.2	264.6
1981	268	229	552	109.9	112.0	102.4	198.3	180.6	270.9
1982	295	257	567	109.5	111.8	101.7	217.2	201.9	275.5
1983	326	287	603	106.2	107.4	102.4	230.6	216.8	282.1
1984	360	317	650	107.7	108.0	104.3	248.4	234.2	294.3
1985	430	379	751	107.3	107.6	102.9	266.5	252.0	302.8
1986	469	404	866	103.3	101.1	108.9	275.3	254.7	329.8
1987	521	446	969	100.7	100.0	101.6	277.2	254.7	335.0
1988	623	514	1256	96.4	94.2	101.0	267.2	239.9	338.4
1989	660	534	1372	100.0	103.6	91.8	267.2	248.6	310.6
1990	750	611	1533	103.6	100.0	111.9	276.9	248.6	347.6
1991	816	654	1714	104.0	102.9	105.9	288.0	255.8	368.1
1992	942	726	2106	102.7	101.1	104.9	295.8	258.6	386.1
1993	1134	849	2598	103.9	100.8	106.6	307.3	260.7	411.6
1994	1408	1027	3260	105.0	100.8	109.6	322.7	262.8	451.1
1995	1752	1294	3884	107.8	109.0	103.2	347.9	286.5	465.5
1996	2199	1710	4395	113.0	119.9	100.1	393.1	343.5	466.0
1997	2390	1851	4746	105.6	105.7	104.3	415.1	363.1	486.0
1998	2471	1921	4813	104.3	105.6	100.8	432.9	383.4	489.9
1999	2594	1945	5290	104.0	101.3	107.6	450.2	388.4	527.1
2000	2723	1981	5705	103.2	100.8	105.5	464.6	391.5	556.1
2001	2845	2037	5974	105.2	103.0	106.0	488.8	403.2	589.5
2002	3013	2119	6346	106.0	104.0	106.4	518.1	419.3	627.2
2003	3284	2227	7040	106.4	102.4	108.7	551.3	429.4	681.8

2-14 按三次产业分的资本形成总额

Total Capital by Type of Industry

单位：亿元 (100 million yuan)

年份 Year	合计 Total 资本形成总额 Gross Capital Formation	固定资本 Fixed Capital	存货增加 Changes in Inventories	第一产业 Primary Industry 资本形成总额 Gross Capital Formation	固定资本 Fixed Capital	存货增加 Changes in Inventories
1978	42.41	27.68	14.73	4.59	3.43	1.16
1980	40.02	32.76	7.26	3.58	3.31	0.27
1985	92.19	58.14	34.05	2.71	1.45	1.26
1986	115.02	75.57	39.45	6.28	1.51	4.77
1987	139.84	91.79	48.05	6.37	2.48	3.89
1988	184.75	114.73	70.02	5.24	3.56	1.68
1989	169.41	83.19	86.22	13.70	2.41	11.29
1990	184.12	122.82	61.30	7.99	3.45	4.54
1991	224.80	160.49	64.31	12.01	3.91	8.10
1992	291.04	228.29	62.75	15.73	8.45	7.28
1993	396.00	330.54	65.46	32.27	15.73	16.54
1994	553.74	422.61	131.13	83.95	69.37	14.58
1995	756.23	534.12	222.11	150.04	95.46	54.58
1996	833.12	678.32	154.80	78.31	28.64	49.67
1997	947.22	725.73	221.49	126.93	32.15	94.78
1998	1038.75	846.37	192.38	125.17	30.64	94.53
1999	1130.67	956.10	174.57	101.15	29.42	71.73
2000	1274.94	1082.00	192.94	126.50	48.36	78.14
2001	1426.47	1233.17	193.30	132.11	53.94	78.17
2002	1572.89	1380.89	192.00	117.98	42.41	75.57
2003	1738.27	1613.12	125.15	102.58	54.40	48.18

年份 Year	第二产业 Secondary Industry 资本形成总额 Gross Capital Formation	固定资本 Fixed Capital	存货增加 Changes in Inventories	第三产业 Tertiary Industry 资本形成总额 Gross Capital Formation	固定资本 Fixed Capital	存货增加 Changes in Inventories
1978	20.15	17.68	2.47	17.67	6.57	11.10
1980	16.23	15.36	0.87	20.21	14.09	6.12
1985	38.93	32.73	6.20	50.55	23.96	26.59
1986	58.05	47.08	10.97	50.69	26.98	23.71
1987	69.19	59.48	9.71	64.28	29.83	34.45
1988	92.67	75.03	17.64	86.84	36.14	50.70
1989	101.59	56.24	45.35	54.12	24.54	29.58
1990	110.18	78.61	31.57	65.95	40.76	25.19
1991	116.64	99.02	17.62	96.15	57.56	38.59
1992	132.22	119.42	12.80	143.09	100.42	42.67
1993	185.25	127.78	57.47	178.48	187.03	-8.55
1994	191.33	145.74	45.59	278.46	207.50	70.96
1995	219.99	158.33	61.66	386.20	280.33	105.87
1996	257.01	205.55	51.46	497.80	444.13	53.67
1997	317.18	215.69	101.49	503.11	477.89	25.22
1998	305.60	190.62	114.98	607.98	625.11	-17.13
1999	297.00	216.79	80.21	732.52	709.89	22.63
2000	321.76	232.04	89.72	826.68	801.60	25.08
2001	377.01	286.84	90.17	917.35	892.39	24.96
2002	459.77	368.24	91.53	995.14	970.24	24.90
2003	577.67	517.22	60.45	1058.02	1041.50	16.52

2-15 生产总值(支出法)构成

Composition of GDP (by Expenditure Approach)

单位:% (%)

年份 Year	以生产总值为100 GDP=100			以最终消费为100 Final Consumption Expenditure=100		以居民消费为100 Household Consumption=100	
	最终消费 Final Consumption Expenditure	资本形成总额 Gross Capital Formation	货物和服务净出口 Net Export of Good and Services	居民消费 Household Consumption	政府消费 Government Consumption	农业居民 Agricultural Households	非农业居民 Non Agricultural Households
1978	68.6	28.9	2.5	93.2	6.8	75.4	24.6
1979	66.7	23.5	9.8	92.3	7.7	76.0	24.0
1980	71.4	20.9	7.7	91.6	8.4	74.3	25.7
1981	74.3	19.6	6.1	91.7	8.3	75.2	24.8
1982	75.1	21.7	3.2	91.3	8.7	76.5	23.5
1983	75.8	22.0	2.2	91.5	8.5	77.2	22.8
1984	75.9	20.6	3.5	91.4	8.6	76.8	23.2
1985	75.2	26.3	-1.5	91.5	8.5	76.0	24.0
1986	73.0	28.9	-1.9	91.5	8.5	73.9	26.1
1987	69.9	29.8	0.3	91.0	9.0	73.3	26.7
1988	68.3	31.6	0.1	91.3	8.7	70.3	29.7
1989	68.6	26.4	5.0	89.5	10.5	68.8	31.2
1990	75.9	24.7	-0.6	80.6	19.4	69.0	31.0
1991	74.6	27.0	-1.6	80.5	19.5	67.9	32.1
1992	73.5	29.5	-3.0	80.3	19.7	65.1	34.9
1993	70.3	31.4	-1.7	79.8	20.2	62.6	37.4
1994	66.8	33.2	0.0	79.3	20.7	60.5	39.5
1995	64.9	35.2	-0.1	79.4	20.6	60.8	39.2
1996	67.8	32.2	0.0	80.4	19.6	63.6	36.4
1997	67.0	32.5	0.5	78.8	21.2	63.0	37.0
1998	66.2	33.3	0.5	77.7	22.3	63.0	37.0
1999	66.5	34.0	-0.5	76.4	23.6	60.4	39.6
2000	64.6	34.5	0.9	74.8	25.2	58.3	41.7
2001	64.1	35.8	0.1	73.3	26.7	56.9	43.1
2002	63.7	36.2	0.1	72.1	27.9	55.5	44.5
2003	62.2	37.5	0.3	69.9	30.1	52.9	47.1

2-16 资本形成总额发展速度及指数

Growth Rate and Indices of Gross Capital Formation

单位:% (%)

年份 Year	以上年为100 (Preceding year=100) 资本形成总额 Gross Capital Formation	固定资本 Fixed Capital	存货增加 Changes in Inventories	以1952年为100 (1952=100) 资本形成总额 Gross Capital Formation	固定资本 Fixed Capital	存货增加 Changes in Inventories
1952				100.0	100.0	100.0
1955	172.8	84.5	514.0	322.3	170.1	860.5
1960	86.5	106.0	40.0	1351.5	1610.6	762.6
1965	119.4	120.8	114.1	752.8	825.8	631.5
1970	169.6	177.2	149.1	1705.4	1783.3	1751.5
1975	113.5	115.8	99.6	1761.3	2102.2	1014.7
1978	154.2	156.3	148.0	2708.0	2749.5	2992.9
1979	98.0	106.2	75.9	2653.9	2920.0	2270.6
1980	96.1	105.9	58.4	2550.4	3092.3	1327.0
1981	95.8	84.2	176.5	2443.2	2603.7	2342.7
1982	122.7	122.4	123.7	2997.9	3186.9	2898.9
1983	113.5	125.0	75.4	3402.6	3983.6	2186.4
1984	99.6	93.9	130.4	3389.0	3740.6	2850.1
1985	138.0	125.6	185.8	4676.8	4698.2	5295.1
1986	119.7	123.6	110.1	5598.1	5807.0	5828.1
1987	113.7	113.7	113.3	6365.0	6602.6	6602.0
1988	114.1	109.7	127.4	7262.5	7243.0	8409.8
1989	81.2	68.6	113.3	5897.1	4968.7	9525.7
1990	88.1	90.9	86.0	5195.4	4516.6	8192.1
1991	115.4	121.4	103.4	5995.5	5483.2	8470.6
1992	112.3	122.1	89.1	6732.9	6694.9	7547.3
1993	115.8	123.2	91.7	7796.7	8248.2	6920.9
1994	118.7	112.6	144.9	9254.7	9287.5	10028.4
1995	122.0	114.5	147.4	11290.7	10634.2	14781.9
1996	113.7	124.5	85.6	12837.5	13239.6	12653.3
1997	114.2	105.1	148.6	14660.4	13914.8	18802.8
1998	108.7	113.9	94.7	15935.9	15848.9	17806.3
1999	109.6	112.7	99.7	17465.7	17861.7	17752.9
2000	110.1	110.9	107.0	19229.7	19808.6	18995.6
2001	111.3	113.1	100.9	21402.7	22403.5	19166.6
2002	110.0	111.6	99.7	23543.0	25002.3	19109.1
2003	112.7	113.6	102.3	26533.0	28402.6	19548.6

2-17 各市、州全社会总产出及指数(2003年)

Gross Output of Society and Its Indices of Cities and Prefecture (2003)

市州	Cities and Prefecture	总产出(万元) Gross Output (10 000 yuan)	第一产业 Primary Industry	第二产业 Secondary Industry	工业 Industry	建筑业 Construction	第三产业 Tertiary Industry	#交通运输仓储邮电 Transport Postal and Telecommunications	#批发零售贸易餐饮 Wholesale Retail Trade and Catering	总产出指数(以上年为100) Gross Output Indices (preceding year=100)
长沙市	Changsha	25247307	1353366	13981067	9377570	4603497	9912874	1009544	4599268	117.3
株洲市	Zhuzhou	10455965	754406	6688444	5663639	1024805	3013115	771916	878585	112.1
湘潭市	Xiangtan	6302904	607955	3513835	2945516	568319	2181114	569811	666710	113.7
衡阳市	Hengyang	10543799	1658378	5177392	4091948	1085444	3708029	764441	1009932	112.1
邵阳市	Shaoyang	5686930	1308457	2252785	1805398	447387	2125688	338682	669898	107.7
岳阳市	Yueyang	11920346	1649241	7314068	6174012	1140056	2957037	689551	767823	113.0
常德市	Changde	11229884	1780424	6043310	4609860	1433450	3406150	553780	985964	112.2
张家界	Zhangjiajie	1902742	248496	701766	410966	290800	952480	233743	268961	110.2
益阳市	Yiyang	5510549	898442	2485508	1948855	536653	2126599	699154	600144	110.7
郴州市	Chenzhou	7476042	1006823	4312271	3208379	1103892	2156948	602588	490341	114.5
永州市	Yongzhou	5756810	1368743	2582987	1905819	677168	1805080	480964	579631	113.6
怀化市	Huaihua	5409165	867672	2448227	1912058	536169	2093266	573798	502246	112.0
娄底市	Loudi	4856426	602823	2856761	2139740	717021	1396842	465654	345186	110.8
湘　西	West Hunan	2068908	356979	1123779	764913	358866	588150	155395	180458	112.7

2-18 各市、州生产总值及构成(2003年)

Gross Domestic Products and Its Composition of Cities and Prefecture (2003)

市州	Cities and Prefecture	地区生产总值(万元) GDP (10 000 yuan)	第一产业 Primary Industry	第二产业 Secondary Industry	工业 Industry	建筑业 Construction	第三产业 Tertiary Industry	#交通运输仓储邮电 Transport Postal and Telecommunications	#批发零售贸易餐饮 Wholesale Retail Trade and Catering	人均生产总值(元) Per Capita GDP (yuan)
长沙市	Changsha	9294858	832886	3936734	2682806	1253928	4525238	678255	1401333	14810
株洲市	Zhuzhou	3830868	496005	1877981	1577713	300268	1456882	404183	322857	10707
湘潭市	Xiangtan	2676868	369788	1086831	859818	227013	1220249	197874	256776	10056
衡阳市	Hengyang	4454628	1051355	1573436	1304750	268686	1829837	423475	414287	6754
邵阳市	Shaoyang	2850856	852893	824401	626174	198227	1173562	160426	268659	4338
岳阳市	Yueyang	4951877	1046632	2108831	1816632	292199	1796414	454772	400327	9860
常德市	Changde	4865833	1157149	1976756	1600695	376061	1731928	296854	379062	9229
张家界	Zhangjiajie	819087	154551	205923	133223	72700	458613	110027	118743	5708
益阳市	Yiyang	2396731	577990	696894	523809	173085	1121847	321973	259087	5840
郴州市	Chenzhou	3242609	642645	1257165	1047407	209758	1342799	390183	324188	7597
永州市	Yongzhou	2803566	853117	756971	572388	184583	1193478	292427	334454	5607
怀化市	Huaihua	2496138	567534	709601	549889	159712	1219003	358192	256777	5621
娄底市	Loudi	2112509	388584	890554	682618	207936	833371	279502	175803	5634
湘　西	West Hunan	826378	223739	304768	216790	87978	297871	63559	70879	3393

2-19 各市、州生产总值指数(2003年)

Indices of Gross Domestic Products of Cities and Prefecture(2003)

以上年为100 (preceding year=100)

市州	Cities and Prefecture	地区生产总值 Gross Domestic Products	第一产业 Primary Industry	第二产业 Secondary Industry	工业 Industry	建筑业 Construction	第三产业 Tertiary Industry	#交通运输仓储邮电 Transport Postal and Telecommunications	#批发零售贸易餐饮 Wholesale Retail Trade and Catering	人均生产总值 Per Capita GDP
长沙市	Changsha	114.0	104.8	120.2	118.8	123.8	110.8	107.8	111.5	113.6
株洲市	Zhuzhou	111.1	103.5	113.5	112.5	119.3	110.8	109.5	109.7	110.8
湘潭市	Xiangtan	111.2	104.2	114.9	114.3	117.0	110.5	111.8	110.8	111.1
衡阳市	Hengyang	110.1	103.1	116.2	117.3	111.2	109.4	108.0	110.6	109.7
邵阳市	Shaoyang	109.3	103.1	114.2	111.8	122.5	111.0	110.2	109.9	108.7
岳阳市	Yueyang	111.0	104.4	115.1	116.0	109.4	110.5	110.8	109.6	110.5
常德市	Changde	111.3	105.3	115.6	114.6	120.3	110.8	109.3	108.8	111.0
张家界	Zhangjiajie	110.3	103.0	121.7	120.1	124.5	108.8	108.3	107.9	110.0
益阳市	Yiyang	109.4	104.0	113.5	114.1	111.7	109.9	109.0	110.0	109.0
郴州市	Chenzhou	111.3	103.4	117.1	116.5	120.0	110.3	110.0	109.3	111.0
永州市	Yongzhou	110.6	103.7	118.8	117.5	123.2	110.7	109.2	110.2	110.3
怀化市	Huaihua	109.8	103.0	115.9	115.6	117.2	109.7	109.0	108.7	109.5
娄底市	Loudi	109.0	99.5	114.3	110.9	126.6	108.5	110.3	106.8	108.7
湘　西	West Hunan	108.1	102.9	111.0	104.6	131.9	109.6	109.6	106.6	108.0

2-20 各市、州支出法生产总值(2003年)

Gross Domestic Expenditures of Cities and Prefecture(2003)

市州	Cities and Prefecture	支出法生产总值(万元) GDP by Expenditure Approach (10 000 yuan)	最终消费 Final Comsumption Expenditure	资本形成总额 Gross Capital Formation	货物和服务净出口 Net Export of Goods and Services	投资率(%) Capital Formation Rate (%)	消费率(%) Comsumption Rate (%)
长沙市	Changsha	9294858	4253574	4255870	785414	45.8	45.8
株洲市	Zhuzhou	3830868	1963308	1477377	390183	38.6	51.2
湘潭市	Xiangtan	2676868	1555225	1082321	39322	40.4	58.1
衡阳市	Hengyang	4454628	3520584	1367692	-433648	30.7	79.0
邵阳市	Shaoyang	2850856	2262051	601322	-12517	21.1	79.3
岳阳市	Yueyang	4951877	3107116	1788227	56534	36.1	62.7
常德市	Changde	4865833	2835298	1735100	295435	35.7	58.3
张家界	Zhangjiajie	818491	447055	361399	10037	44.2	54.6
益阳市	Yiyang	2396731	1858285	664819	-126373	27.7	77.5
郴州市	Chenzhou	3242609	2046112	1392382	-195885	42.9	63.1
永州市	Yongzhou	2803566	2000838	799308	3420	28.5	71.4
怀化市	Huaihua	2496138	1864195	595947	35996	23.9	74.7
娄底市	Loudi	2112509	1331263	799056	-17810	37.8	63.0
湘　西	West Hunan	826378	698626	314121	-186369	38.0	84.5

2-21 各市、州生产总值项目构成(2003年)

Item Composition of Gross Domestic Products of Cities and Prefecture(2003)

单位：万元 (10 000 yuan)

市州	Cities and Prefecture	地区生产总值 Gross Domestic Products	劳动者报酬 Compensation of Laborers	固定资产折旧 Depreciation of Fixed Assets	生产税净额 Net Taxes on Production	营业盈余 Operating surplus
长沙市	Changsha	9294858	5258842	1131334	1356790	1547892
株洲市	Zhuzhou	3830868	2005988	504080	453781	867019
湘潭市	Xiangtan	2676868	1567577	516333	249753	343205
衡阳市	Hengyang	4454628	2683308	808009	428157	535154
邵阳市	Shaoyang	2850856	1869827	372568	290128	318333
岳阳市	Yueyang	4951877	2935504	759295	665946	591132
常德市	Changde	4865833	2648369	729031	816611	671822
张家界	Zhangjiajie	819087	547401	109671	56853	105162
益阳市	Yiyang	2396731	1558939	423144	218755	195893
郴州市	Chenzhou	3242609	1799823	657806	384575	400405
永州市	Yongzhou	2803566	1914554	386564	263419	239029
怀化市	Huaihua	2496138	1432785	312516	228521	522316
娄底市	Loudi	2112509	1322203	345854	199772	244680
湘　西	West Hunan	826378	551944	93194	81977	99263

2-22 各市、州支出法生产总值结构(2003年)

Structure of gross Domestic Expenditures of Cities and Prefecture (2003)

单位：万元 (10 000 yuan)

市州	Cities and Prefecture	资本形成总额 Gross Capital Formation				最终消费 Final Consumption Expenditure					
		绝对数 Absolute Figure		比重 Proportion (%)		绝对数 Absolute Figure				比重 Proportion (%)	
		固定资本 Fixed Capital	存货增加 Changes in In-ventories	固定资本 Fixed Capital	存货增加 Changes in In-ventories	居民消费 House-hold Consump-tion	农业居民 Agri-cultural	非农居民 Non-agri cultural	政府消费 Govern-ment Consump-tion	居民消费 House-hold Consump-tion	政府消费 Govern-ment Consump-tion
长沙市	Changsha	3688315	567555	86.7	13.3	3147149	1277305	1869844	1106425	74.0	26.0
株洲市	Zhuzhou	1067005	410372	72.2	27.8	1587567	828159	759408	375741	80.9	19.1
湘潭市	Xiangtan	761452	320869	70.4	29.6	1301649	680098	621551	253576	83.7	16.3
衡阳市	Hengyang	1177448	190244	86.1	13.9	2883239	1708375	1174864	637345	81.9	18.1
邵阳市	Shaoyang	479794	121528	79.8	20.2	2019696	1381987	637709	242355	89.3	10.7
岳阳市	Yueyang	1481041	307186	82.8	17.2	2592335	1044378	1547957	514781	83.4	16.6
常德市	Changde	1226070	509030	70.7	29.3	2482443	1091711	1390732	352855	87.6	12.4
张家界	Zhangjiajie	314897	46502	87.1	12.9	381833	236811	145022	65222	85.4	14.6
益阳市	Yiyang	605300	59519	91.0	9.0	1405853	827112	578741	452432	75.7	24.3
郴州市	Chenzhou	1358130	34252	97.5	2.5	1581854	719232	862622	464258	77.3	22.7
永州市	Yongzhou	677815	121493	84.8	15.2	1646457	946933	699524	354381	82.3	17.7
怀化市	Huaihua	478913	117034	80.4	19.6	1508809	886827	621982	355386	80.9	19.1
娄底市	Loudi	769605	29451	96.3	3.7	1160556	663539	497017	170707	87.2	12.8
湘　西	West Hunan	300778	13343	95.8	4.2	463058	281544	181514	235568	66.3	33.7

三、人口、就业与职工工资

POPULATION, EMPLOYMENT AND WAGES OF STAFF AND WORKERS

资料整理人员： 石　梅　　欧阳普

3-1 年末人口数

Population at the Year-end

年份 Year	总户数（万户） Households (10 000 households)	总人口（万人） Total Population (10 000 persons)	男 Male	女 Female	市镇 Urban	乡村 Rural
1978	1167.53	5165.91	2684.80	2481.11	593.86	4572.05
1980	1197.88	5280.95	2740.40	2540.55	671.05	4609.90
1985	1334.54	5622.49	2928.44	2694.05	915.90	4706.59
1990	1661.65	6110.89	3178.31	2932.58	1072.46	5038.43
1991	1697.69	6166.33	3208.42	2957.91	1147.86	5018.47
1992	1725.72	6207.78	3231.73	2976.05	1217.74	4990.04
1993	1745.47	6245.58	3249.20	2996.38	1205.95	5039.63
1994	1765.67	6302.58	3279.07	3023.51	1356.56	4946.02
1995	1796.19	6392.00	3322.27	3069.73	1550.99	4841.01
1996	1799.97	6428.00	3339.25	3088.75	1606.95	4821.05
1997	1798.83	6465.00	3356.43	3108.57	1629.00	4836.00
1998	1809.00	6502.00	3374.33	3127.67	1684.00	4818.00
1999	1814.64	6532.00	3389.32	3142.68	1724.00	4808.00
2000	1874.87	6562.05	3422.77	3139.28	1952.21	4609.84
2001	1884.47	6595.85	3409.72	3186.13	2031.52	4564.33
2002	1899.30	6628.50	3433.56	3194.94	2121.12	4507.38
2003	1929.59	6662.80	3453.33	3209.47	2232.04	4430.76

注：1995年以前的人口数均为年报数；2000年的人口数根据第五次人口普查有关数据推算，其余各年人口数均根据人口变动抽样调查资料推算。

The data on the total population are collected from the year-reports before 1995.

The data 2000 are estimated on the data collected from fifth population surveys.

The data of other years are estimated on the basis of the data collected from the sample surveys on population changes.

3-2 人口出生率、死亡率、自然增长率

Birth Rate,Death Rate and Natural Growth Rate of Population

单位:

年 份 Year	出生率 Birth Rate	死亡率 Death Rate	自然增长率 Natural Growth Rate
1978	17.40	7.01	10.39
1980	17.68	6.88	10.80
1985	18.16	6.47	11.69
1990	23.93	7.23	16.70
1991	20.50	7.30	13.20
1992	16.70	7.30	9.40
1993	14.08	7.13	6.95
1994	13.88	7.03	6.85
1995	13.02	7.15	5.87
1996	12.81	7.20	5.61
1997	12.59	6.99	5.60
1998	12.31	7.10	5.21
1999	11.72	7.12	4.60
2000	11.45	6.79	4.66
2001	11.80	6.72	5.08
2002	11.56	6.70	4.86
2003	11.82	6.87	4.95

3-3 1-4次全国人口普查人口基本情况

Basic Statistics on National Population Census in 1953,1964,1982 and 1990

单位：万人 (10 000 persons)

指 标	Item	第一次 1953 First	第二次 1964 Second	第三次 1982 Third	第四次 1990 Fourth
总户数 (万户)	**Total Households (10 000 households)**	836.11	916.20	1233.88	1573.79
家庭户	Family Households			1227.89	1564.88
集体户	Non-Family Households			5.99	8.91
总人口	**Total Population**	3322.69	3718.23	5401.05	6065.80
男性人口	Male	1752.64	1931.70	2805.23	3149.76
女性人口	Female	1570.05	1786.53	2595.82	2916.04
#育龄妇女(15—49岁)	#Women at Childbearing Age (Age 15-49)	750.73	819.43	1301.08	1607.99
各年龄组人口	**Population by Age**				
0—6岁	Age 0-6	669.02	706.05	701.81	869.47
7—14岁	Age 7-14	519.19	768.91	1131.16	826.93
劳动年龄人口	Population within Working Age	1720.75	1878.68	2936.91	3618.26
男60、女55岁以上人口	Males Age 60 and Females Age 55 and Over	319.57	285.00	503.39	628.16
民族人口	**Population by Nationality**				
汉族	Han Nationality	3254.67	3589.80	5180.92	5583.42
少数民族	Minority Nationalities	68.02	128.43	220.13	482.38
15岁以上婚姻人口	**Marital Status of Population Aged 15 and Over**				
未婚	Unmarried			1009.86	1099.89
有配偶	Married			2271.76	2963.86
丧偶	Widowed			262.16	278.87
离婚	Divorced			24.31	26.77
6岁以上文化程度人口	**Population Aged 6 and Over by Educational Level**				
大学本科	University		} 9.77	} 24.56	20.72
大学专科	Three Years College				48.27
中专	Specialized Secondary School		} 40.99	} 353.64	81.82
高中	Senior Secondary School				404.79
初中	Junior Secondary School		160.27	932.53	1370.42
小学	Primary School		1256.03	2325.78	2552.16
不识字或识字很少	Illiterate and Semi-Illiterate		1255.57	1173.52	822.76
#文盲、半文盲人口	#Illiterate and Semi-Illiterate Aged 15 and Over		1255.57	943.97	742.56
在业人口	**Employed Population**			2827.75	3489.74
不在业人口	**Unemployed Population**			740.34	879.65
市镇县人口	**Population of Cities,Towns and Counties**				
市	Cities	134.97	161.31	507.43	765.62
镇	Towns	157.57	160.79	260.00	328.20
县	Counties	3030.15	3396.13	4633.62	4971.98

注：1. 劳动年龄人口指男16-59岁，女16-54岁人口。
2. 各年龄组人口缺15岁人口和年龄不详人口，加总不等于总人口。
3. 由于四次普查所设指标不同，故此表空栏处均表示该年度普查无此调查项目。
4. 1964年人口普查时，6-12岁不在校儿童没有调查其相当的文化程度，故各项文化程度人口加总不等于6周岁及以上人口数。

a.Working age range refers to 16-59 years for men and 16-54 years for women.

b. The sum of the population of the age group is not equal to the total population, because the population aged 15 is not shown and there is population whose true age is unknown.

c. Since the quota in the four population censuses were set differently, the blank space indicates the absence of this item of the year.

d. Data in 1964 excludes the children in school aged from 6-12, thus the sum of the population at all education levels does not equal to the population aged above six.

3-4 第五次全国人口普查基本情况

Basic Statistics on National Population of Fifth Censuses

指标	Item	数量 Volume
总户数（万户）	**Number of Households (10 000 households)**	**1800.38**
家庭户	Family Households	1766.21
集体户	Non-Family Households	34.17
总人口（万人）	**Total Population (10 000 persons)**	**6327.42**
家庭户人口	Population of Family Households	6106.15
集体户人口	Population of Non-Family Households	221.27
平均家庭户规模（人/户）	**Average Family Size (person/household)**	**3.46**
总人口中：男性人口（万人）	**In Total: Male (10 000 persons)**	**3299.37**
女性人口（万人）	Female (10 000 persons)	3028.05
性别比	Sex Ratio	108.96
总人口中：汉族人口（万人）	**In Total: Han Nationality (10 000 persons)**	**5686.35**
少数民族人口（万人）	Minority Nationalities (10 000 persons)	641.07
少数民族人口比重（%）	Percentage of Minonrity Nationalities Population (%)	10.13
总人口中：市镇人口（万人）	**In Total: Urban Population (10 000 persons)**	**1915.92**
乡村人口（万人）	Rural Population (10 000 persons)	4524.15
总人口中：0—5岁人口（万人）	**In Total: Age 0-5 (10 000 persons)**	**387.71**
6—14岁人口（万人）	Age 6-14 (10 000 persons)	1012.25
15—64岁人口（万人）	Age 15-64 (10 000 persons)	4454.8
65岁以上人口（万人）	Aged 65 and Over (10 000 persons)	472.66
6周岁及以上人口（万人）	**Population Aged 6 and Over by Educational Level (10 000 persons)**	**5939.70**
未上过学（万人）	Unschool (10 000 persons)	298.22
扫盲班（万人）	Literacy Courses (10 000 persons)	67.69
小学（万人）	Primary School (10 000 persons)	2421.99
初中（万人）	Junior Secondary School (10 000 persons)	2259.38
高中和中专（万人）	Senior and Specialized Secondary School (10 000 persons)	707.25
大专及以上（万人）	College and Over (10 000 persons)	185.17
每十万人口中：小学文化（人）	**Per 100000 Population: Primary School (person)**	**38278**
初中文化（人）	Junior Secondary School (person)	35708
高中和中专（人）	Senior and Specialized Secondary School (person)	11177
大专及以上（人）	College and Over (persons)	2926
文盲、半文盲人口（万人）	**Population of Illiterate and Semi Literate (10 000 persons)**	**294.96**
文盲率（%）	**Illiterate Rate (%)**	**5.99**
普查年度出生率（‰）	**Birth Rate in Census Year（‰）**	**11.45**
普查年度死亡率（‰）	**Death Rate in Census Year（‰）**	**6.79**
普查年度自然增长率（‰）	**Natural Growth Rate in Census Year（‰）**	**4.66**

注：1. 表中的各项数据均按普查登记的口径计算，不包括本省外出的人口，包括外省来本省的人口。

2. 普查年度是指1999年11月1日0时至2000年10月31日24时。

3. 城乡人口是按国家统计局1999年发布的《关于统计上划分城乡的规定（试行）》计算。

a. The data in table are calculated according to the approach of censuses. The data excluded the population of going to other provinces and included the population from other provinces.

b. The censuses year is 1999-11-1 zero o'clock to 2000-10-31 24 o'clock.

c. The urban population and rural population are calculated according to the <regulations concerning plot out urban and rural in the statistical(test run) > promulgated in 1999.

3-5 年末从业人员人数

Number of Employed Persons at the Year-end

单位：万人 (10 000 persons)

		从业人员人数 Number of Employed Persons	职工人数 Number of Staff and Workers	国有经济 State-owned Economic Units	城镇集体经济 Urban Collective-owned Economic Units	其他经济类型 Economic Units of Other Types	城镇个体私营企业从业人员 Employees in Urban Private Enterprises and Self-Employed Individuals	农村从业人员 Employees in Rural	其他从业人员 Other Employees
1978		2280.05	363.78	282.06	81.72		0.35	1915.92	
1980		2399.95	409.16	316.80	92.36		1.81	1988.98	
1981		2449.46	426.88	332.46	94.42		3.43	2019.15	
1982		2541.05	441.48	344.41	97.07		5.21	2094.36	
1983		2594.37	447.81	348.97	98.84		9.72	2136.84	
1984		2672.86	460.71	340.94	119.75	0.02	13.18	2198.97	
1985		2728.71	475.15	352.73	122.34	0.08	16.19	2237.37	
1986		2808.87	492.79	367.31	125.25	0.23	18.44	2297.64	
1987		2904.10	515.22	386.34	128.60	0.28	24.72	2364.16	
1988		2998.64	530.20	401.75	128.14	0.31	30.75	2437.69	
1989		3091.37	536.64	411.34	124.81	0.49	30.43	2524.30	
1990		3158.42	551.03	422.28	128.07	0.68	31.94	2575.45	
1991		3222.43	567.07	435.66	130.35	1.06	32.52	2622.84	
1992		3278.83	579.74	447.88	130.43	1.43	39.93	2659.16	
1993		3345.61	588.87	454.26	126.70	7.91	60.42	2675.75	20.57
1994		3400.29	589.48	459.14	121.57	8.77	106.51	2685.54	18.76
1995		3467.31	597.50	466.00	119.13	12.37	133.86	2717.38	18.57
1996		3514.16	596.84	471.55	114.47	10.82	166.21	2732.35	18.76
1997		3560.29	597.48	471.52	110.48	15.48	200.36	2744.33	18.12
1998		3603.17	594.16	461.65	101.21	31.30	222.46	2772.59	13.96
1999		3601.39	590.75	461.83	96.01	32.91	210.29	2784.00	16.35
2000		3577.58	580.82	456.28	90.33	34.21	148.54	2832.04	16.18
2001		3607.96	534.22	407.55	70.95	55.72	199.76	2856.70	17.28
2002		3644.52	525.28	398.42	66.19	60.67	231.87	2870.32	17.05
2003		3694.78	500.27	379.72	56.55	64.00	335.94	2836.36	22.21
长沙市	Changsha	356.35	76.08	49.07	8.14	18.87	46.48	230.50	3.28
株洲市	Zhuzhou	208.10	35.85	23.69	4.74	7.42	17.15	152.83	2.26
湘潭市	Xiangtan	171.89	31.99	23.89	4.96	3.14	15.98	123.39	0.53
衡阳市	Hengyang	379.81	56.39	39.93	8.22	8.23	22.24	298.16	3.03
邵阳市	Shaoyang	411.13	42.45	34.07	5.18	3.20	15.57	351.69	1.42
岳阳市	Yueyang	257.75	38.70	31.16	3.91	3.63	14.34	202.13	2.58
常德市	Changde	306.91	27.32	20.99	2.24	4.08	21.29	257.46	0.84
张家界市	Zhangjiajie	84.79	8.79	6.85	0.92	1.02	3.31	72.62	0.07
益阳市	Yiyang	248.39	37.85	29.86	4.96	3.03	7.97	201.80	0.77
郴州市	Chenzhou	262.68	29.70	24.49	2.54	2.67	19.05	212.53	1.40
永州市	Yongzhou	303.39	29.75	24.82	2.58	2.34	6.98	265.72	0.94
怀化市	Huaihua	265.11	28.94	21.52	3.64	3.78	9.29	225.75	1.13
娄底市	Loudi	216.22	29.52	24.61	3.22	1.69	8.98	175.35	2.37
湘西州	West Hunan	157.83	15.09	12.92	1.28	0.89	16.10	125.97	0.67
其他	Others	12.77	11.86	11.86					0.91

注：全省从业人员人数及分三次产业从业人数根据劳动力抽样调查资料推算。

The data of total employees and employees by type of industry are estimated on the data collected from the sample surveys on labor.

3-6 按三次产业分的年末从业人员

Employees by Type of Industry at the Year-end

		年末从业人员(万人)				构成(以合计为100)			
		Employees at the Year-end (10000 persons)	第一产业 Primary Industry	第二产业 Secondary Industry	第三产业 Tertiary Industry	Composition in Percentage (total=100)	第一产业 Primary Industry	第二产业 Secondary Industry	第三产业 Tertiary Industry
1978		2280.05	1788.17	305.37	186.51	100.0	78.4	13.4	8.2
1980		2399.95	1846.46	339.06	214.43	100.0	77.0	14.1	8.9
1981		2449.46	1887.54	339.52	222.40	100.0	77.0	13.9	9.1
1982		2541.05	1955.49	350.79	234.77	100.0	77.0	13.8	9.2
1983		2594.37	1966.48	361.77	266.12	100.0	75.8	13.9	10.3
1984		2672.86	1971.93	414.00	286.93	100.0	73.8	15.5	10.7
1985		2728.71	1946.85	458.68	323.18	100.0	71.4	16.8	11.8
1986		2808.87	1969.64	494.51	344.72	100.0	70.1	17.6	12.3
1987		2904.10	2011.35	531.70	361.05	100.0	69.3	18.3	12.4
1988		2998.64	2050.72	550.38	397.54	100.0	68.4	18.4	13.2
1989		3091.37	2104.60	550.26	436.51	100.0	68.1	17.8	14.1
1990		3158.42	2176.70	553.83	427.89	100.0	68.9	17.5	13.6
1991		3222.43	2219.82	570.35	432.26	100.0	68.9	17.7	13.4
1992		3278.83	2213.42	613.57	451.84	100.0	67.5	18.7	13.8
1993		3345.61	2140.76	679.22	525.63	100.0	64.0	20.3	15.7
1994		3400.29	2076.14	731.01	593.14	100.0	61.1	21.5	17.4
1995		3467.31	2071.61	756.54	639.16	100.0	59.8	21.8	18.4
1996		3514.16	1994.90	810.38	708.88	100.0	56.8	23.0	20.2
1997		3560.29	1998.59	802.25	759.45	100.0	56.1	22.5	21.4
1998		3603.17	2002.51	822.49	778.17	100.0	55.6	22.8	21.6
1999		3601.39	2026.09	839.09	736.21	100.0	56.3	23.3	20.4
2000		3577.58	2120.98	840.52	616.08	100.0	59.3	23.5	17.2
2001		3607.96	2078.36	748.90	780.70	100.0	57.6	20.8	21.6
2002		3644.52	2034.04	757.26	853.22	100.0	55.8	20.8	23.4
2003		3694.78	1961.93	790.68	942.17	100.0	53.1	21.4	25.5
长沙市	Changsha	356.35	139.12	84.68	132.55	100.0	39.0	23.8	37.2
株洲市	Zhuzhou	208.10	91.70	55.40	61.00	100.0	44.1	26.6	29.3
湘潭市	Xiangtan	171.89	79.54	50.21	42.14	100.0	46.3	29.2	24.5
衡阳市	Hengyang	379.81	208.57	72.27	98.97	100.0	54.9	19.0	26.1
邵阳市	Shaoyang	411.13	262.08	43.26	105.78	100.0	63.8	10.5	25.7
岳阳市	Yueyang	257.75	140.91	38.10	78.74	100.0	54.7	14.8	30.5
常德市	Changde	306.91	180.04	38.05	88.82	100.0	58.7	12.4	28.9
涨家界市	Zhangjiajie	84.79	55.65	6.36	22.78	100.0	65.6	7.5	26.9
益阳市	Yiyang	248.39	140.10	40.24	68.05	100.0	56.4	16.2	27.4
郴州市	Chenzhou	262.68	133.89	50.7	78.09	100.0	51.0	19.3	29.7
永州市	Yongzhou	303.39	183.46	39.61	80.32	100.0	60.5	13.1	26.5
怀化市	Huaihua	265.11	181.47	29.32	54.32	100.0	68.5	11.1	20.4
娄底市	Loudi	216.22	124.28	35.29	56.65	100.0	57.5	16.3	26.2
湘西州	West Hunan	157.83	101.15	14.77	41.91	100.0	64.1	9.4	26.6

注：全省从业人员人数及分三次产业从业人数根据劳动力抽样调查资料推算。

The data of total employees and employees by type of industry are estimated on the data collected from the sample surveys on labor.

3-7 年末城镇从业人员

Number of Employed Persons in Urban Areas at the Year-end

		城镇从业人员合计 (万人)								
		Number of Employed Persons in Urban Areas (10 000 persons)	国有经济 State-owned Economic	城镇集体经济 Urban Collective-owned Economic	其他经济 Economic Units of Other Types	内资经济 Domestic Funded Economic	港澳台投资经济 Economioc With Funded From H.K, Macao and Taiwan	外商投资经济 Economic With Funded Foreign	城镇私营经济 Urban Private Economic	城镇个体经济 Urban Individuals Economic
1995		749.93	482.68	120.83	12.56	6.62	2.73	3.21	17.6	116.26
1996		781.81	487.94	116.61	11.05	5.12	2.59	3.34	22.8	143.41
1997		815.96	486.58	113.19	15.83	9.23	2.96	3.64	26.94	173.42
1998		830.58	472.37	103.56	32.19	25.21	3.2	3.78	36.89	185.57
1999		817.39	474.23	98.95	33.92	27.54	3.19	3.19	34.52	175.77
2000		745.54	467.98	92.99	36.04	29.81	3.07	3.16	33.54	114.99
2001		751.26	419.71	73.62	58.17	52.35	3.15	2.67	44.43	155.33
2002		774.20	410.13	68.73	63.47	56.88	3.51	3.08	65.63	166.24
2003		858.42	395.39	59.65	67.45	60.04	3.50	3.90	87.56	248.38
长沙市	Changsha	125.85	51.62	8.46	19.29	16.17	1.47	1.65	24.22	22.26
株洲市	Zhuzhou	55.28	24.98	5.17	7.98	6.81	0.28	0.89	5.84	11.31
湘潭市	Xiangtan	48.50	24.17	5.06	3.29	3.11	0.14	0.03	5.56	10.42
衡阳市	Hengyang	81.65	41.58	9.00	8.83	8.07	0.43	0.33	7.73	14.51
邵阳市	Shaoyang	59.44	35.05	5.47	3.35	3.21	0.02	0.13	2.53	13.04
岳阳市	Yueyang	55.62	33.33	4.09	3.86	3.39	0.15	0.32	3.01	11.33
常德市	Changde	49.44	21.60	2.30	4.26	3.80	0.17	0.29	5.43	15.86
张家界市	Zhangjiajie	12.17	6.91	0.92	1.03	0.88	0.13	0.02	1.30	2.01
益阳市	Yiyang	46.59	30.28	5.05	3.29	3.07	0.19	0.03	2.25	5.72
郴州市	Chenzhou	50.15	25.43	2.69	2.98	2.44	0.42	0.12	3.50	15.55
永州市	Yongzhou	37.66	25.50	2.76	2.42	2.37	0.05	0.00	1.60	5.38
怀化市	Huaihua	39.37	22.32	3.78	3.98	3.91	0.01	0.05	1.97	7.32
娄底市	Loudi	40.86	26.51	3.46	1.91	1.87	0.02	0.02	2.86	6.12
湘西州	West Hinan	31.86	13.34	1.44	0.98	0.93	0.02	0.03	2.52	13.58
其 他	Others	12.77	12.77							

3-8 按类型分的年末从业人员

Employees by Type at the Year-end

单位：万人 (10 000 persons)

类 别	Item	2002 合计 Total	2002 #城镇 Urban	2003 合计 Total	2003 #城镇 Urban
从业人员总计	**Total Number of Employed Persons**	**3644.52**	**774.2**	**3694.78**	**858.42**
按就业身份分	**By Status**				
在岗职工	Staff and Workers on the Job	393.54	393.54	379.43	379.43
离开本单位保留劳动关系职工	Staff and Workers Left Self Unit and Remind Labor Relations	131.74	131.74	120.84	120.84
私营业主	Private Enterprises Owner	16.83	13.91	28.92	25.10
个体户主	Self-Employed Individuals	85.77	49.07	94.04	56.63
私营企业和个体从业人员	Number of Employees in Private Enterprises and Self-Employed Individuals	259.9	146.89	327.87	213.99
乡镇企业从业人员	Number of Employees in Township Enterprises	192.62		191.18	
农村劳动力	Laborer in Rural	2525.07		2490.07	
其他从业人员	Others	39.05	39.05	62.43	62.43
#再就业的离退休人员	#Retired Persons of Reemployment	1.06	1.06	1.01	1.01
按经济类型分	**By Economic Types**				
国有经济	State-owned Economy	410.13	410.13	395.39	395.39
集体经济	Collective-owned Economy	2786.42	68.73	2740.9	59.65
私营经济	Private Enterprises	89.72	65.63	114.14	87.56
个体经济	Self-Employed Individuals	294.78	166.24	376.91	248.38
联营经济	Joint Ownership Enterprises	1.01	1.01	0.7	0.7
股份制经济	Share-holding Corporations Enterprises	49.6	49.6	53.55	53.55
外商投资经济	Enterprises With Foreign Investment	3.08	3.08	3.5	3.5
港、澳、台投资经济	Enterprises With Investment from Hong Kong, Macao and Taiwan	3.51	3.51	3.9	3.9
其他经济类型	Enterprises of Other Types of Ownership	6.27	6.27	5.79	5.79
按国民经济行业分	**By Sector**				
农、林、牧、渔业	Agriculture,Forestry,Farming of Animals and Fishing	2038.41	23.43	1961.93	19.81
采矿业	Mining	78.41	22.88	67.08	19.85
制造业	Manufacturing	493.7	168.91	502.04	162.67
电力、燃气及水的生产和供应业	Production and Distribution of Electricity,Gas and Water	12.37	12.37	12.98	12.98
建筑业	Construction	172.78	41.85	208.58	44.31
交通运输、仓储和邮政业	Traffic,Transport, Storage and Post	5.45	5.45	114.78	45.34
信息传输、计算机服务和软件业	Information Transfer,Computer Services and Software	101.68	42.96	9.21	8.37
批发和零售业	Wholesale and Retail Trade	292.31	186.36	250.22	144.29
住宿和餐饮业	Accommodation and Restaurants	14.99	14.99	115.93	77.81
金融业	Finance	5.42	5.42	15.08	15.08
房地产业	Real Estate Trade	215.37	67.52	5.31	5.31
租赁和商务服务业	Tenancy and Business Services	29.21	24.51	6.93	6.93
科学研究、技术服务和地质勘查	Scientific Research,Technical Service and Geologic Perambulation	75.47	75.47	7.92	7.92
水利、环境和公共设施管理业	Management of Water Conservancy,Environment and Public Establishment	5.18	5.18	8.13	8.13
居民服务和其他服务业	Resident Services and Other Services	84.93	59.89	179.93	82.12
教育	Education			67.37	67.37
卫生、社会保障和社会福利业	Sanitation,Social Security and Social Welfare	18.84	17.01	29.42	24.47
文化、体育和娱乐业	Culture,Sports and Entertainment			41.52	40.34
公共管理和社会组织	Public Management and Social Organization			90.42	65.32
国际组织	International Organizations				

3-9 各行业年末从业人员及构成(2003年)

Number of Employees and Its Composition by Sector at the Year-end (2003)

行业	Sector	从业人员 Employees	职工 Staff and Workers	城镇个体私营企业 Urban Private and Individuals	农村从业人员 Employees in Rural	其他从业人员 Other Employees
总计(绝对数,万人)	**Total (ABS,10 000 persons)**	**3694.78**	**500.27**	**335.94**	**2836.36**	**22.21**
农、林、牧、渔业	Agriculture,Forestry,Farming of Animals and Fishing	1961.93	17.63	1.21	1942.12	0.97
采矿业	Mining	67.08	18.14	1.22	47.23	0.49
制造业	Manufacturing	502.04	128.74	31.28	339.37	2.65
电力、燃气及水的生产和供应业	Production and Distribution of Electricity, Gas and Water	12.98	12.82			0.16
建筑业	Construction	208.58	31.96	6.38	164.27	5.97
交通运输仓储和邮政业	Traffic,Transport, Storage and Post	114.78	31.06	12.63	69.44	1.65
信息传输、计算机服务和软件业	Information Transfer,Computer Services and Software	9.21	5.33	2.55	0.84	0.49
批发和零售业	Wholesale and Retail Trade	250.22	43.43	99.76	105.93	1.10
住宿和餐饮业	Accommodation and Restaurants	115.93	7.12	70.36	38.12	0.33
金融业	Finance	15.08	12.30			2.78
房地产业	Real Estate Trade	5.31	5.16			0.15
租赁和商务服务业	Tenancy and Business Services	6.93	5.65			1.28
科学研究、技术服务和地质勘查业	Scientific Research,Technical Service and Geologic Perambulation	7.92	7.51			0.41
水利、环境和公共设施管理业	Management of Water Conservancy, Environment and Public Establishment	8.13	7.66			0.47
居民服务和其他服务业	Resident Services and Other Services	179.93	4.48	77.52	97.81	0.12
教育	Education	67.37	65.99			1.38
卫生、社保和社会福利	Sanitation,Social Security and Social Welfare	29.42	23.86		4.95	0.61
文化、体育和娱乐业	Culture,Sports and Entertainment	41.52	7.12	33.03	1.18	0.19
公共管理和社会组织	Public Management and Social Organization	90.42	64.31		25.10	1.01
构成(以合计为100)	**Composition in Percentage (total=100)**	**100.0**	**13.5**	**9.1**	**76.8**	**0.6**
农、林、牧、渔业	Agriculture,Forestry,Farming of Animals and Fishing	100.0	0.9	0.1	99.0	
采矿业	Mining	100.0	27.0	1.8	70.4	0.7
制造业	Manufacturing	100.0	25.6	6.2	67.6	0.5
电力、燃气及水的生产和供应业	Production and Distribution of Electricity, Gas and Water	100.0	98.8			1.2
建筑业	Construction	100.0	15.3	3.1	78.8	2.9
交通运输、仓储和邮政业	Traffic,Transport, Storage and Post	100.0	27.1	11.0	60.5	1.4
信息传输、计算机服务和软件业	Information Transfer,Computer Services and Software	100.0	57.9	27.7	9.1	5.3
批发和零售业	Wholesale and Retail Trade	100.0	17.4	39.9	42.3	0.4
住宿和餐饮业	Accommodation and Restaurants	100.0	6.1	60.7	32.9	0.3
金融业	Finance	100.0	81.6			18.4
房地产业	Real Estate Trade	100.0	97.2			2.8
租赁和商务服务业	Tenancy and Business Services	100.0	81.5			18.5
科学研究、技术服务和地质勘查业	Scientific Research,Technical Service and Geologic Perambulation	100.0	94.8			5.2
水利、环境和公共设施管理业	Management of Water Conservancy, Environment and Public Establishment	100.0	94.2			5.8
居民服务和其他服务业	Resident Services and Other Services	100.0	2.5	43.1	54.4	0.1
教育	Education	100.0	98.0			2.0
卫生、社保和社会福利	Sanitation,Social Security and Social Welfare	100.0	81.1		16.8	2.1
文化、体育和娱乐业	Culture,Sports and Entertainment	100.0	17.1	79.6	2.8	0.5
公共管理和社会组织	Public Management and Social Organization	100.0	71.1		27.8	1.1

3-10 年末城乡劳动力资源与分配

Resources and Distribution of Labor Force in Urban and Rural Areas at theYear-end

单位:万人 (10 000 persons)

类别	Item	合计 Total		城镇 Urban		乡村 Rural	
		2002	2003	2002	2003	2002	2003
总计	**Total**	**4997.89**	**5063.73**	**1527.21**	**1607.07**	**3470.68**	**3456.66**
经济活动人口	Economy Active Population	3674.91	3731.91	804.59	895.55	2870.32	2836.36
从业人员	Employees	3644.52	3694.78	774.20	858.42	2870.32	2836.36
失业人员	Unemployment	30.39	37.13	30.39	37.13		
非经济活动人口	Non-Economy Active Population	1322.98	1331.82	722.62	711.52	600.36	620.30

3-11 年末城镇各单位按行业分组的女性从业人员(2003年)

Number of Female Employees by Sector at the Year-end (2003)

单位:万人 (10 000 persons)

行业	Sector	各单位女性从业人员 Number of Female Employees in Units	国有经济 State-owned Economic Units	城镇集体 Urban Collective-owned Economic Units	其他经济 Economic Units of Other Types
总计	**Total**	**142.59**	**111.25**	**11.79**	**19.55**
农、林、牧、渔业	Agriculture,Forestry,Farming of Animals and Fishing	6.78	6.61	0.13	0.04
采矿业	Mining	2.85	2.16	0.16	0.53
制造业	Manufacturing	30.11	14.95	3.87	11.29
电力、燃气及水的生产和供应业	Production and Distribution of Electricity,Gas and Water	3.96	3.45	0.08	0.43
建筑业	Construction	4.38	2.31	1.27	0.80
交通运输仓储和邮政业	Traffic,Transport, Storage and Post	8.11	6.97	0.57	0.57
信息传输、计算机服务和软件业	Information Transfer,Computer Services and Software	1.80	1.17	0.04	0.59
批发和零售业	Wholesale and Retail Trade	8.41	4.60	1.79	2.02
住宿和餐饮业	Accommodation and Restaurants	3.07	1.74	0.22	1.11
金融业	Finance	6.49	3.76	1.62	1.11
房地产业	Real Estate Trade	1.14	0.78	0.06	0.30
租赁和商务服务业	Tenancy and Business Services	1.45	0.98	0.22	0.25
科学研究、技术服务和地质勘查业	Scientific Research,Technical Service and Geologic Perambulation	2.26	2.08	0.03	0.15
水利、环境和公共设施管理业	Management of Water Conservancy, Environment and Public Establishment	2.68	2.45	0.15	0.08
居民服务和其他服务业	Resident Services and Other Services	0.26	0.14	0.08	0.04
教育	Education	27.51	27.33	0.06	0.12
卫生、社保和社会福利	Sanitation,Social Security and Social Welfare	12.95	11.60	1.34	0.01
文化、体育和娱乐业	Culture,Sports and Entertainment	2.71	2.57	0.03	0.11
公共管理和社会组织	Public Management and Social Organization	15.67	15.60	0.07	
国际组织	International Organization				

3-12 各行业年末在岗职工(2003年)

Total Number of Staff and Workers on the Job by Sector at the Year-end (2003)

单位：万人 (10 000 persons)

行业	By Sector	全部在岗职工 Number of Staff and Workers on the Job	国有经济 State-owned Economic	城镇集体 Urban Collective-owned Economic
总计	**Total**	**379.43**	**297.52**	**31.28**
农、林、牧、渔业	**Agriculture, Forestry, Farming of Animals and Fishing**	**17.12**	**16.37**	**0.64**
农业	Agriculture	11.39	11.32	0.07
林业	Forestry	2.00	1.95	0.05
畜牧业	Farming of animals	0.32	0.21	0.05
渔业	Fishing	0.57	0.52	0.04
农、林、牧、渔服务业	Service Activities for Agriculture,Forestry, Farming of Animals and Fishing	2.83	2.37	0.43
采矿业	**Mining**	**11.67**	**9.26**	**0.39**
煤炭开采和洗选业	Mining and Washing of Coal	8.86	6.99	0.15
黑色金属矿采选业	Mining of Ferrous Metal Ores	0.20	0.17	0.03
有色金属矿采选业	Mining of Non-ferrous Metal Ores	2.05	1.72	0.15
非金属矿采选业	Mining and Processing of Nonmetal Ores	0.53	0.35	0.07
其他采矿业	Mining of Other Ores N.E.C	0.03	0.03	
制造业	**Manufacturing**	**77.35**	**39.74**	**8.67**
农副食品加工业	Processing of Food from Agricultural Products	1.85	1.09	0.02
食品制造业	Manufacture of Foods	1.38	0.55	0.02
饮料制造业	Manufacture of Beverage	1.11	0.42	0.02
烟草制品业	Manufacture of Tobacco	1.14	1.09	0.01
纺织业	Manufacture of Textile	5.22	2.49	0.38
纺织服装、鞋、帽制造业	Manufacture of Textile Wearing Apparel,Footware and Caps	0.83	0.14	0.28
皮革毛皮羽毛(绒)及其制品业	Manufacture of Leather,Fur,Feather and Its Products	0.45	0.02	0.16
木材加工及木、竹、藤、棕、草制品业	Processing of Timbers,Manufacture of Wood,Bamboo, Rattan,Palm and Straw Products	0.56	0.06	0.07
家具制造业	Manufacture of Furniture	0.06	0.06	0.02
造纸及纸制品业	Manufacture of Paper and Paper Products	2.53	1.51	0.14
印刷业和记录媒介的复制	Printing,Reproduction of Recording Media	1.30	0.50	0.47
文教体育用品制造业	Manufacture of Articles for Culture,Education and Sport Activity	0.11	0.01	0.03
石油加工、炼焦及核燃料加工	Processing of Petroleum,Coking,Processing of Nucleus Fuel	2.16	1.74	0.01
化学原料及化学制品制造业	Manufacture of Chemical Raw Material and Chemical Products	7.84	2.94	0.78
医药制造业	Manufacture of Medicines	1.96	0.53	0.09
化学纤维制造业	Manufacture of Chemical Fiber	0.80	0.11	
橡胶制品业	Manufacture of Rubber	0.75	0.49	0.18
塑料制品业	Manufacture of Plastic	0.85	0.10	0.38
非金属矿物制品业	Manufacture of Non-metallic Mineral Products	7.94	4.19	1.28
黑色金属冶炼及压延加工业	Manufacture and Processing of Ferrous Metals	6.22	4.19	0.55
有色金属冶炼及压延加工业	Manufacture and Processing of Non-ferrous Metals	5.52	3.68	0.25
金属制品业	Manufacture of Metal Products	1.01	0.37	0.38
通用设备制造业	Manufacture of General Purpose Machinery	5.26	1.85	0.88
专用设备制造业	Manufacture of Special Purpose Machinery	6.31	4.58	0.35
交通运输设备制造业	Manufacture of Transport Equipment	7.15	4.32	0.74
电气机械及器材制造业	Manufacture of Electrical Machinery and Equipment	4.04	1.76	0.73

单位：万人　　　　3-12 续表 1　continued　　　　(10 000 persons)

行业	By Sector	全部在岗职工 Number of Staff and Workers on the Job	国有经济 State-owned Economic	城镇集体 Urban Collective-owned Economic
通信设备、计算机及其他电子设备制造业	Manufacture of Communication Equipment,Computer and Other Electronic Equipment	2.03	0.54	0.23
仪器仪表及文化、办公用机械制造业	Manufacture of Measuring Instrument and Machinery for Cultural Activity and Office Work	0.69	0.40	0.08
工艺品及其他制造业	Manufacture of Artwork,Other Manufacture N.E.C	0.28	0.08	0.14
废弃资源和废旧材料回收加工	Recycling and Disposal of Waste	0.02		0.02
电力、燃气及水的生产和供应	**Production and Distribution of Electricity,Gas and Water**	**11.22**	**9.64**	**0.24**
电力、热力的生产和供应业	Production and Supply of Electric Power and Heat Power	8.50	7.14	0.18
燃气生产和供应业	Production and Distribution of Gas	0.43	0.28	
水的生产和供应业	Production and Distribution of Water	2.29	2.23	0.05
建筑业	**Construction**	**25.28**	**12.26**	**7.17**
房屋和土木工程建筑业	Construction of Building and Civil Engineering	23.87	11.45	6.88
建筑安装业	Architectural Installation	1.14	0.69	0.28
建筑装饰业	Architectural Decoration	0.15	0.01	0.02
其他建筑业	Other Construction	0.12	0.11	
交通运输、仓储和邮政业	**Traffic,Transport,Storage and Post**	**23.87**	**19.93**	**2.34**
铁路运输业	Transport Via Railway	7.88	7.86	0.02
道路运输业	Transport Via Road	7.46	5.81	0.62
城市公共交通业	Urban Public Traffic	2.32	1.97	0.05
水上运输业	Water Transport	1.27	0.66	0.54
航空运输业	Air Transport	0.43	0.32	
装卸搬运和其他运输服务业	Loading,Unloading,Portage and Other Transport Services	1.55	0.47	1.05
仓储业	Storage	0.74	0.66	0.03
邮政业	Post	2.21	2.19	0.02
信息传输计算机服务和软件业	**Information Transfer,Computer Services and Software**	**4.26**	**2.85**	**0.08**
电信和其他信息传输服务业	Telecom and Other Information Transfer Services	3.21	2.34	
计算机服务业	Computer Services	0.45	0.37	0.06
软件业	Software Industry	0.60	0.14	0.02
批发和零售业	**Wholesale and Retail Trade**	**18.43**	**10.80**	**3.86**
批发业	Wholesale	10.97	7.34	1.92
零售业	Retail Trade	7.47	3.46	1.94
住宿和餐饮业	**Accommodation and Restaurants**	**5.13**	**2.91**	**0.34**
住宿业	Accommodation	3.79	2.29	0.26
餐饮业	Restaurants	1.35	0.62	0.08
金融业	**Finance**	**11.33**	**6.92**	**3.26**
银行业	Bank	9.93	6.23	3.22
证券业	Securities	0.16	0.03	
保险业	Insurance	1.13	0.59	
其他金融活动	Other Financial Activities	0.11	0.07	0.04
房地产业	**Real Estate**	**3.09**	**2.00**	**0.16**
房地产开发经营	Real Estate Exploitation Management	1.83	0.95	0.11
物业管理	Management Concerning Dwelling	0.63	0.46	0.04
房地产中介服务	Real Estate Agency Service	0.12	0.11	
租赁和商务服务业	**Tenancy and Business Services**	**4.37**	**3.19**	**0.55**
租赁业	Tenancy	0.13	0.10	0.01
商务服务业	Business Service	4.24	3.09	0.53

单位：万人　　3-12 续表 2　continued　　(10 000 persons)

行 业	By Sector	全部在岗职工 Number of Staff and Workers on the Job	国有经济 State-owned Economic	城镇集体 Urban Collective-owned Economic
科研、技术服务和地质勘查业	**Scientific Research,Technical Service&Geologic Perambulation**	**6.37**	**5.91**	**0.15**
研究与试验发展	Research and Experimental Development	2.01	1.95	
自然科学研究与试验发展	R&D on Physical Science	0.45	0.41	
工程和技术研究与试验发展	R&D on Engineering and Technical Research	0.64	0.63	
农业科学研究与试验发展	R&D on Agricultural Science Research	0.51	0.51	
医学研究与试验发展	R&D on medical research	0.16	0.15	
社会人文科学研究与发展	R&D on Social Science and Humanities	0.26	0.24	
专业技术服务业	Professional Technique Services	2.59	2.46	0.02
气象服务	Weather Services	0.16	0.16	
地震服务	Earthquake Services	0.02	0.02	
测绘服务	Plotting Services	0.17	0.17	
技术检测	Technique Detection	0.28	0.27	0.01
环境监测	Environmental Monitoring	0.11	0.11	
工程技术与规划管理	Engineering Technic and Programming Management	1.81	1.69	0.01
科技交流和推广服务业	Services of S&T Intercommunion and Generalization	0.65	0.54	0.10
地质勘查业	Geologic Perambulation	1.12	0.96	0.02
水利、环境和公共设施管理业	**Management of Water Conservancy,Environment and Public Establishment**	**6.48**	**5.92**	**0.36**
水利管理业	Management of Water Conservancy	2.33	2.21	0.12
环境管理业	Environmental Management	2.19	1.99	0.17
公共设施管理业	Management of Public Establishment	1.96	1.73	0.07
居民服务和其他服务业	**Resident Services and Other Services**	**0.66**	**0.46**	**0.14**
居民服务业	Resident Services	0.30	0.18	0.08
其他服务业	Other Services	0.36	0.28	0.07
教育	**Education**	**64.27**	**63.93**	**0.12**
初等教育	Primary Education	26.97	26.92	0.02
中等教育	Secondary Education	29.65	29.47	0.03
高等教育	Higher Education	5.66	5.60	0.03
卫生、社会保障和社会福利业	**Sanitation,Social Security and Social Welfare**	**22.36**	**19.79**	**2.55**
卫生	Sanitation	21.61	19.05	2.54
社会保障业	Social Security	0.40	0.40	
社会福利业	Social Welfare	0.34	0.34	
文化、体育和娱乐业	**Culture, Sports and Entertainment**	**6.28**	**5.93**	**0.08**
#新闻出版业	Journalism and Publishing Activities	0.66	0.57	
广播、电视、电影和音像业	Broadcasting,Movies,Television and Audiovisual Activities	3.97	3.80	0.02
文化艺术业	Culture and Art	1.30	1.24	0.05
体育	Sports Activities	0.23	0.22	
娱乐业	Entertainment	0.11	0.10	0.01
公共管理和社会组织	**Public Management and Social Organization**	**59.90**	**59.72**	**0.18**
#中国共产党机关	Organ of Communist Party of China	2.19	2.19	0.00
国家机构	Organ of State	55.62	55.49	0.13
人民政协和民主党派	People's Political Consultative Conference and Democratic Party	0.50	0.50	
群众团体社会团体和宗教组织	Mass Community,Social Community and Religion Organizations	0.66	0.61	0.05
国际组织	International Organizations			

3-13 城镇新就业人数及登记失业人员

Number of New Employees and Registered Unemployment in Urban Areas

单位：万人 (10 000 persons)

指标	Item	2000	2001	2002	2003
城镇新就业人数合计	**Total Number of New Employees in Urban Areas**	**29.05**	**27.66**	**39.39**	**67.99**
按来源分：	**By Source**				
从城镇招收	Recruitment from Urban	2.04	1.95	2.38	2.68
从农村招收	Recruitment from Rural	2.06	2.26	2.78	3.67
大中专技校毕业生	Graduates of University,College, Specialized Secondary Schools and Technical Secondary Schools	6.16	4.13	3.81	3.75
其他	Others	18.79	19.32	30.42	57.89
按就业去向分：	**By Outlet of New Employees**				
国有经济	State-owned Unit	13.11	9.92	10.21	10.08
城镇集体经济	Urban Collective-owned Unit	2.40	1.49	1.30	8.85
其他经济类型	Units of Other Types of Ownership	2.12	3.02	4.19	8.52
从事个体劳动	Self-Employed Individuals	11.42	13.23	23.69	40.54
城镇登记失业人员	**Number of Registered Unemployment in Urban Areas**	**27.57**	**30.34**	**30.39**	**37.13**
城镇登记失业率(%)	**Rate of Registered Unemployment (%)**	**3.7**	**4.0**	**4.0**	**4.5**

3-14 职业介绍服务机构及劳动力交流情况

Employment Services and Labor Force Exchanges

项 目	Item	2000	2001	2002	2003
职业介绍服务机构(个)	**Number of Employment Services (unit)**	**788**	**788**	**910**	**815**
#劳动部门办	# Run by Labor Departments	374	508	603	679
其他组织办	Run by Other Organization	231	90	104	30
公民个人办	Run by Private	183	190	203	106
本年登记求职人数 (万人次)	**Registered Persons in This Year (10 000 person-times)**	**81.18**	**87.03**	**88.21**	**90.34**
#下岗职工	#Laid-off Workers	18.04	20.70	23.30	29.58
失业人员	Former Unemployed	26.56	26.09	30.39	45.03
获得职业资格人员	Persons with Certificates	11.14	18.87	24.27	28.01
本年介绍成功人数 (万人次)	**Number of Persons Actually Employed (10 000 person-times)**	**39.79**	**27.15**	**29.39**	**35.08**
#女性	#Female	21.10	17.48	16.51	17.74
#下岗职工	#Laid-off Workers	9.48	10.53	12.45	12.14
失业人员	Former Unemployed	13.43	12.58	12.97	18.35
获得职业资格人员	Persons with Certificates	5.61	10.52	14.74	18.21

3-15 职工工资总额及年平均工资

Total Wages and Average Annual Wage of Staff and Workers

年份 Year 市州 Cities and Prefecture		全部职工工资总额 (亿元) Totel Wages of Staff and Workers (100 million yuan)	国有经济 State-owned Economic	城镇集体经济 Urban Collective-owned Economic	其他经济 Economic Units of Other Types	全部职工年平均工资 (元) Average Annual Wages of Staff and Workers (yuan)	国有经济 State-owned Economic	城镇集体经济 Urban Collective-owned Economic	其他经济 Economic Units of Other Types
1978		20.33	16.29	4.04		563	589	474	
1980		28.73	23.09	5.64		718	746	625	
1985		49.30	38.36	10.93	0.01	1059	1111	912	1270
1986		58.80	45.97	12.81	0.02	1220	1281	1043	1078
1987		70.14	55.16	14.94	0.04	1400	1470	1190	1483
1988		87.38	69.78	17.54	0.06	1688	1777	1407	1966
1989		96.78	78.66	18.02	0.10	1836	1945	1475	2125
1990		108.97	88.92	19.91	0.14	2014	2141	1593	2089
1991		119.67	97.57	21.91	0.19	2152	2278	1727	2361
1992		143.69	118.37	24.96	0.36	2526	2686	1966	2852
1993		181.84	148.64	29.51	3.69	3142	3324	2379	4970
1994		238.22	198.56	34.76	4.90	4104	4388	2910	5762
1995		282.05	233.48	41.12	7.45	4797	5082	3525	6259
1996		299.57	251.74	41.59	6.24	5100	5412	3724	5897
1997		314.91	265.53	40.70	8.68	5326	5683	3736	5733
1998		323.76	269.17	35.94	18.65	5473	5849	3585	5994
1999		349.06	293.70	34.55	20.81	5939	6385	3627	6403
2000		377.19	318.62	34.21	24.36	6515	6999	3800	7217
2001		407.58	335.75	29.00	42.83	7698	8295	4146	7825
2002		458.53	374.41	30.05	54.07	8734	9403	4522	8958
2003		494.42	400.01	29.04	65.37	9855	10484	5108	10327
长沙市	Changsha	108.16	78.36	4.88	24.91	14181	15967	5883	13185
株洲市	Zhuzhou	39.01	28.55	2.92	7.55	10591	11673	5949	10095
湘潭市	Xiangtan	29.57	24.24	2.52	2.82	9215	10065	5205	8884
衡阳市	Hengyang	45.88	35.27	3.85	6.76	8189	8836	4712	8510
邵阳市	Shaoyang	30.42	26.41	1.99	2.02	7206	7798	3805	6480
岳阳市	Yueyang	36.15	29.69	2.21	4.26	9282	9460	5623	11688
常德市	Changde	31.22	26.02	1.62	3.58	11257	12155	6806	9067
张家界市	Zhangjiajie	9.71	8.16	0.55	1.00	10996	11773	6056	10086
益阳市	Yiyang	24.65	20.99	1.66	2.00	6527	6986	3360	7191
郴州市	Chenzhou	30.22	26.22	1.36	2.65	10163	10683	5386	9902
永州市	Yongzhou	25.23	21.70	1.22	2.31	8481	8720	4804	9949
怀化市	Loudi	25.10	19.86	1.82	3.42	8598	9143	4957	9005
娄底市	Huaihua	26.25	23.23	1.69	1.33	8986	9560	5200	7997
湘西州	West Hinan	13.95	12.42	0.77	0.77	9194	9548	5897	8817
其他	Others	18.91	18.91			15834	15834		

3-16 职工实际工资总额指数

Total Wage Indices of Staff and Workers

年份 Year	以1978年为100 (1978 =100)			以上年为100 (preceding year=100)			
	全部职工 Total Number of Staff and Workers	#国有经济 State-owned Units	#城镇集体经济 Urban Collective-owned Units	全部职工 Total Number of Staff and Workers	国有经济 State-owned Units	城镇集体经济 Urban Collective-owned Units	其他经济类型 Units of Other Types of Ownership
1978	100.0	100.0	100.0	106.1	121.5	72.3	
1980	121.4	121.8	120.0	108.6	109.9	101.5	
1990	213.5	217.4	196.3	111.9	112.3	99.4	139.2
1995	268.0	276.9	196.6	100.3	99.6	100.1	128.7
1996	265.6	278.6	185.4	99.1	100.6	94.3	78.1
1997	269.6	283.7	175.4	102.3	102.6	95.2	135.3
1998	275.3	285.6	153.8	102.3	100.9	87.9	213.8
1999	298.0	312.9	148.4	107.8	109.1	96.1	111.6
2000	317.9	335.1	145.1	106.7	107.1	97.7	115.6
2001	347.3	357.0	124.3	109.3	106.5	85.7	177.8
2002	392.7	400.1	129.5	113.1	112.1	104.1	126.9
2003	413.5	417.5	122.2	105.3	104.3	94.4	118.1

3-17 职工年平均工资指数

Average Annual Wage Indices of Staff and Workers

年份 Year	货币工资指数 Indices of Average Money Wage				实际工资指数 Indices of Average Real Wage			
	全部职工 Total Number of Staff and Workers	国有经济 State-owned Units	城镇集体经济 Urban Collective-owned Units	其他经济类型 Units of Other Types of Ownership	全部职工 Total Number of Staff and Workers	国有经济 State-owned Units	城镇集体经济 Urban Collective-owned Units	其他经济类型 Units of Other Types of Ownership
1978=100								
1990	357.7	363.5	336.1		141.4	143.7	132.9	
1995	852.0	862.7	743.4		164.6	166.7	143.7	
1996	905.9	918.8	785.7		163.3	165.5	141.5	
1997	946.0	964.9	788.2		164.7	168.0	137.2	
1998	972.1	993.0	756.3		168.0	171.7	130.7	
1999	1054.9	1084.0	765.2		183.1	188.1	132.8	
2000	1157.2	1188.3	801.7		198.3	203.6	137.3	
2001	1367.3	1408.3	874.7		236.8	243.9	151.5	
2002	1551.3	1596.4	953.8		270.1	277.9	166.1	
2003	1750.4	1780.0	1077.6		297.6	302.6	183.2	
以上年为100	**preceding year=100**							
1990	109.7	110.1	108.0	98.3	109.0	109.4	107.3	97.7
1995	116.9	115.8	121.1	108.6	99.0	98.1	102.5	92.0
1996	106.3	106.5	105.6	94.2	99.2	99.3	98.5	87.9
1997	104.4	105.0	100.3	97.2	101.6	102.1	97.6	94.6
1998	102.8	102.9	96.0	104.6	102.2	102.4	95.5	104.0
1999	108.5	109.2	101.2	106.8	109.0	109.6	101.6	107.3
2000	109.7	109.6	104.8	112.7	108.3	108.2	103.4	111.3
2001	118.2	118.5	109.1	108.4	119.5	119.8	110.3	109.6
2002	113.5	113.4	109.0	114.5	114.1	113.9	109.6	115.0
2003	112.8	111.5	113.0	115.3	110.2	108.9	110.3	112.6

3-18 各行业在岗职工工资总额(2003年)

Total Wages of Staff and Workers on the Job by Sector (2003)

单位：万元 (10 000 yuan)

行业	By Sector	全部在岗职工 Number of Staff and Workers on the Job	国有经济 State-owned Economic	城镇集体 Urban Collective-owned Economic
总计	**Total**	**4649940**	**3769310**	**267326**
农、林、牧、渔业	**Agriculture, Forestry, Farming of Animals and Fishing**	**91281**	**86893**	**3321**
农业	Agriculture	50289	49931	318
林业	Forestry	11402	11120	282
畜牧业	Farming of animals	2430	1430	236
渔业	Fishing	3958	3657	240
农、林、牧、渔服务业	Service Activities for Agriculture,Forestry, Farming of Animals and Fishing	23202	20755	2245
采矿业	**Mining**	**107480**	**83235**	**2653**
煤炭开采和洗选业	Mining and Washing of Coal	80712	60987	814
黑色金属矿采选业	Mining of Ferrous Metal Ores	1290	1148	142
有色金属矿采选业	Mining of Non-ferrous Metal Ores	20392	17258	1330
非金属矿采选业	Mining and Processing of Nonmetal Ores	4557	3314	367
其他采矿业	Mining of Other Ores N.E.C	529	529	
制造业	**Manufacturing**	**888620**	**488838**	**68907**
农副食品加工业	Processing of Food from Agricultural Products	18001	10768	124
食品制造业	Manufacture of Foods	13947	4480	114
饮料制造业	Manufacture of Beverage	11727	3796	109
烟草制品业	Manufacture of Tobacco	36622	36237	63
纺织业	Manufacture of Textile	34065	14138	2261
纺织服装、鞋、帽制造业	Manufacture of Textile Wearing Apparel,Footware and Caps	7006	1366	1990
皮革毛皮羽毛(绒)及其制品业	Manufacture of Leather,Fur,Feather and Its Products	3159	134	909
木材加工及木、竹、藤、棕、草制品业	Processing of Timbers,Manufacture of Wood,Bamboo, Rattan,Palm and Straw Products	4051	347	422
家具制造业	Manufacture of Furniture	411	1	61
造纸及纸制品业	Manufacture of Paper and Paper Products	27495	18249	946
印刷业和记录媒介的复制	Printing,Reproduction of Recording Media	13927	6199	3127
文教体育用品制造业	Manufacture of Articles for Culture,Education and Sport Activity	1087	37	253
石油加工、炼焦及核燃料加工	Processing of Petroleum,Coking,Processing of Nucleus Fuel	42840	31837	138
化学原料及化学制品制造业	Manufacture of Chemical Raw Material and Chemical Products	76827	25626	7269
医药制造业	Manufacture of Medicines	19669	4817	657
化学纤维制造业	Manufacture of Chemical Fiber	7962	682	1
橡胶制品业	Manufacture of Rubber	7270	5212	1168
塑料制品业	Manufacture of Plastic	7196	743	2681
非金属矿物制品业	Manufacture of Non-metallic Mineral Products	62050	34959	8271
黑色金属冶炼及压延加工业	Manufacture and Processing of Ferrous Metals	103774	81564	4892
有色金属冶炼及压延加工业	Manufacture and Processing of Non-ferrous Metals	81076	55782	2738
金属制品业	Manufacture of Metal Products	8441	2845	2786
通用设备制造业	Manufacture of General Purpose Machinery	55067	15452	6847
专用设备制造业	Manufacture of Special Purpose Machinery	69598	41841	3144
交通运输设备制造业	Manufacture of Transport Equipment	101213	62567	7010
电气机械及器材制造业	Manufacture of Electrical Machinery and Equipment	41468	19665	7525

单位：万元 3-18 续表 1 continued (10 000 yuan)

行 业	By Sector	全部在岗职工 Number of Staff and Workers on the Job	国有经济 State-owned Economic	城镇集体 Urban Collective-owned Economic
通信设备、计算机及其他电子设备制造业	Manufacture of Communication Equipment,Computer and Other Electronic Equipment	22989	4610	1742
仪器仪表及文化、办公用机械制造业	Manufacture of Measuring Instrument and Machinery for Cultural Activity and Office Work	7749	4410	797
工艺品及其他制造业	Manufacture of Artwork,Other Manufacture N.E.C	1722	445	720
废弃资源和废旧材料回收加工	Recycling and Disposal of Waste	214	30	146
电力、燃气及水的生产和供应	**Production and Distribution of Electricity,Gas and Water**	**168926**	**140301**	**3070**
电力、热力的生产和供应业	Production and Supply of Electric Power and Heat Power	130503	104478	2502
燃气生产和供应业	Production and Distribution of Gas	5513	3599	44
水的生产和供应业	Production and Distribution of Water	32909	32224	524
建筑业	**Construction**	**227150**	**114186**	**56658**
房屋和土木工程建筑业	Construction of Building and Civil Engineering	207464	102236	53144
建筑安装业	Architectural Installation	17035	10732	3344
建筑装饰业	Architectural Decoration	1384	97	170
其他建筑业	Other Construction	1267	1122	
交通运输、仓储和邮政业	**Traffic,Transport,Storage and Post**	**303607**	**270062**	**13774**
铁路运输业	Transport Via Railway	130724	130347	274
道路运输业	Transport Via Road	74820	60380	4022
城市公共交通业	Urban Public Traffic	25150	18807	293
水上运输业	Water Transport	10691	7566	2675
航空运输业	Air Transport	6464	4705	27
管道运输业	Transport Via Pipeline	6	6	
装卸搬运和其他运输服务业	Loading,Unloading,Portage and Other Transport Services	12442	6272	5782
仓储业	Storage	8564	7670	343
邮政业	Post	34746	34309	359
信息传输计算机服务和软件业	**Information Transfer,Computer Services and Software**	**90309**	**59573**	**601**
电信和其他信息传输服务业	Telecom and Other Information Transfer Services	76536	53467	15
计算机服务业	Computer Services	5358	4605	400
软件业	Software Industry	8415	1502	186
批发和零售业	**Wholesale and Retail Trade**	**197131**	**124516**	**28830**
批发业	Wholesale	132609	94690	15310
零售业	Retail Trade	64521	29827	13520
住宿和餐饮业	**Accommodation and Restaurants**	**49330**	**27242**	**2879**
住宿业	Accommodation	37807	22277	2417
餐饮业	Restaurants	11523	4965	462
金融业	**Finance**	**208843**	**133346**	**50169**
银行业	Bank	184219	122101	49770
证券业	Securities	4219	598	
保险业	Insurance	19059	9701	
其他金融活动	Other Financial Activities	1345	945	400
房地产业	**Real Estate**	**39533**	**26257**	**1462**
房地产开发经营	Real Estate Exploitation Management	22585	11425	937
物业管理	Management Concerning Dwelling	8084	6296	425
房地产中介服务	Real Estate Agency Service	1691	1600	29
租赁和商务服务业	**Tenancy and Business Services**	**57956**	**42348**	**4600**
租赁业	Tenancy	1759	1414	84
商务服务业	Business Service	56197	40934	4516

行 业	By Sector	全部在岗职工 Number of Staff and Workers on the Job	国有经济 State-owned Economic	城镇集体 Urban Collective-owned Economic
科研、技术服务和地质勘查业	**Scientific Research,Technical Service&Geologic Perambulation**	**95300**	**89901**	**1097**
研究与试验发展	Research and Experimental Development	30534	29827	51
自然科学研究与试验发展	R&D on Physical Science	5911	5610	
工程和技术研究与试验发展	R&D on Engineering and Technical Research	13177	13007	
农业科学研究与试验发展	R&D on Agricultural Science Research	5749	5749	
医学研究与试验发展	R&D on medical research	2477	2426	51
社会人文科学研究与发展	R&D on Social Science and Humanities	3220	3034	
专业技术服务业	Professional Technique Services	45359	42960	221
气象服务	Weather Services	2405	2405	
地震服务	Earthquake Services	475	475	
测绘服务	Plotting Services	2496	2496	
技术检测	Technique Detection	4194	4154	29
环境监测	Environmental Monitoring	1718	1718	
工程技术与规划管理	Engineering Technic and Programming Management	33508	31201	139
科技交流和推广服务业	Services of S&T Intercommunion and Generalization	7497	6728	656
地质勘查业	Geologic Perambulation	11910	10387	170
水利、环境和公共设施管理业	**Management of Water Conservancy,Environment and Public Establishment**	**63548**	**58248**	**2771**
水利管理业	Management of Water Conservancy	21724	20934	767
环境管理业	Environmental Management	20997	19178	1476
公共设施管理业	Management of Public Establishment	20827	18135	528
居民服务和其他服务业	**Resident Services and Other Services**	**7463**	**5752**	**1283**
居民服务业	Resident Services	3757	2598	781
其他服务业	Other Services	3707	3154	502
教育	**Education**	**855289**	**851333**	**1330**
初等教育	Primary Education	297218	296845	230
中等教育	Secondary Education	400692	398267	447
高等教育	Higher Education	131243	130619	356
卫生、社会保障和社会福利业	**Sanitation,Social Security and Social Welfare**	**336235**	**314573**	**21430**
卫生	Sanitation	326292	304701	21368
社会保障业	Social Security	5454	5433	20
社会福利业	Social Welfare	4489	4439	42
文化、体育和娱乐业	**Culture, Sports and Entertainment**	**94507**	**87125**	**642**
#新闻出版业	Journalism and Publishing Activities	16708	14708	
广播、电视、电影和音像业	Broadcasting,Movies,Television and Audiovisual Activities	59730	54998	186
文化艺术业	Culture and Art	14015	13532	398
体育	Sports Activities	2880	2775	7
娱乐业	Entertainment	1175	1113	51
公共管理和社会组织	**Public Management and Social Organization**	**767433**	**765582**	**1852**
#中国共产党机关	Organ of Communist Party of China	27301	27285	15
国家机构	Organ of State	712382	710983	1400
人民政协和民主党派	People's Political Consultative Conference and Democratic Party	7138	7138	
群众团体社会团体和宗教组织	Mass Community,Social Community and Religion Organizations	8408	7972	436
国际组织	International Organizations			

3-19 各行业在岗职工年平均工资(2003年)

Average Annual Wage of Staff and Workers on the Job by Sector (2003)

单位：元 (yuan)

行业	By Sector	全部在岗职工 Number of Staff and Workers on the Job	国有经济 State-owned Economic	城镇集体 Urban Collective-owned Economic
总计	**Total**	**12221**	**12604**	**8546**
农、林、牧、渔业	**Agriculture, Forestry, Farming of Animals and Fishing**	**5357**	**5333**	**5140**
农业	Agriculture	4450	4446	4763
林业	Forestry	5668	5671	5551
畜牧业	Farming of animals	7529	6626	4570
渔业	Fishing	6919	7066	5592
农、林、牧、渔服务业	Service Activities for Agriculture,Forestry, Farming of Animals and Fishing	8189	8764	5174
采矿业	**Mining**	**9189**	**8970**	**6768**
煤炭开采和洗选业	Mining and Washing of Coal	9097	8707	5490
黑色金属矿采选业	Mining of Ferrous Metal Ores	6269	6553	4641
有色金属矿采选业	Mining of Non-ferrous Metal Ores	9947	10101	9035
非金属矿采选业	Mining and Processing of Nonmetal Ores	8480	9220	5565
其他采矿业	Mining of Other Ores N.E.C	16854	16854	
制造业	**Manufacturing**	**11312**	**11951**	**7889**
农副食品加工业	Processing of Food from Agricultural Products	9343	9563	5710
食品制造业	Manufacture of Foods	11038	7788	5459
饮料制造业	Manufacture of Beverage	10209	8508	4760
烟草制品业	Manufacture of Tobacco	30503	31166	8117
纺织业	Manufacture of Textile	6349	5409	6145
纺织服装、鞋、帽制造业	Manufacture of Textile Wearing Apparel,Footware and Caps	8561	10009	6867
皮革毛皮羽毛(绒)及其制品业	Manufacture of Leather,Fur,Feather and Its Products	6947	7506	5887
木材加工及木、竹、藤、棕、草制品业	Processing of Timbers,Manufacture of Wood,Bamboo, Rattan,Palm and Straw Products	7341	5343	6372
家具制造业	Manufacture of Furniture	6941	1500	3020
造纸及纸制品业	Manufacture of Paper and Paper Products	11147	12511	6508
印刷业和记录媒介的复制	Printing,Reproduction of Recording Media	10685	12102	6666
文教体育用品制造业	Manufacture of Articles for Culture,Education and Sport Activity	9841	5271	7340
石油加工、炼焦及核燃料加工	Processing of Petroleum,Coking,Processing of Nucleus Fuel	18416	16718	9483
化学原料及化学制品制造业	Manufacture of Chemical Raw Material and Chemical Products	9761	8567	9211
医药制造业	Manufacture of Medicines	9904	8995	7663
化学纤维制造业	Manufacture of Chemical Fiber	9869	5794	1500
橡胶制品业	Manufacture of Rubber	9255	9996	6563
塑料制品业	Manufacture of Plastic	8215	7197	6886
非金属矿物制品业	Manufacture of Non-metallic Mineral Products	7534	7909	6455
黑色金属冶炼及压延加工业	Manufacture and Processing of Ferrous Metals	16731	19639	8738
有色金属冶炼及压延加工业	Manufacture and Processing of Non-ferrous Metals	14345	14736	10194
金属制品业	Manufacture of Metal Products	8600	7637	7750
通用设备制造业	Manufacture of General Purpose Machinery	10272	8158	7790
专用设备制造业	Manufacture of Special Purpose Machinery	10882	8952	8613
交通运输设备制造业	Manufacture of Transport Equipment	13886	13978	9381
电气机械及器材制造业	Manufacture of Electrical Machinery and Equipment	10218	11005	10234

行 业	By Sector	全部在岗职工 Number of Staff and Workers on the Job	国有经济 State-owned Economic	城镇集体 Urban Collective-owned Economic
通信设备、计算机及其他电子设备制造业	Manufacture of Communication Equipment,Computer and Other Electronic Equipment	11243	8358	7473
仪器仪表及文化、办公用机械制造业	Manufacture of Measuring Instrument and Machinery for Cultural Activity and Office Work	11248	10687	11024
工艺品及其他制造业	Manufacture of Artwork,Other Manufacture N.E.C	5701	5656	5123
废弃资源和废旧材料回收加工	Recycling and Disposal of Waste	9995	8444	9831
电力、燃气及水的生产和供应	**Production and Distribution of Electricity,Gas and Water**	**15022**	**14547**	**12817**
电力、热力的生产和供应业	Production and Supply of Electric Power and Heat Power	15311	14632	13649
燃气生产和供应业	Production and Distribution of Gas	12628	12762	11000
水的生产和供应业	Production and Distribution of Water	14402	14499	10034
建筑业	**Construction**	**9328**	**9735**	**7990**
房屋和土木工程建筑业	Construction of Building and Civil Engineering	9069	9422	7827
建筑安装业	Architectural Installation	14078	14143	11970
建筑装饰业	Architectural Decoration	9547	9298	7825
其他建筑业	Other Construction	10342	10226	
交通运输、仓储和邮政业	**Traffic,Transport,Storage and Post**	**12565**	**13343**	**5907**
铁路运输业	Transport Via Railway	16231	16244	12009
道路运输业	Transport Via Road	9984	10318	6304
城市公共交通业	Urban Public Traffic	10805	9509	5404
水上运输业	Water Transport	8209	10911	5073
航空运输业	Air Transport	15131	14772	7417
管道运输业	Transport Via Pipeline	5700	5700	
装卸搬运和其他运输服务业	Loading,Unloading,Portage and Other Transport Services	8035	13251	5555
仓储业	Storage	10735	10725	12353
邮政业	Post	15712	15700	20746
信息传输计算机服务和软件业	**Information Transfer,Computer Services and Software**	**21361**	**21112**	**7203**
电信和其他信息传输服务业	Telecom and Other Information Transfer Services	24093	23082	10714
计算机服务业	Computer Services	11928	12541	6902
软件业	Software Industry	13981	10865	7722
批发和零售业	**Wholesale and Retail Trade**	**10337**	**10911**	**7362**
批发业	Wholesale	11593	12212	7800
零售业	Retail Trade	8454	8154	6923
住宿和餐饮业	**Accommodation and Restaurants**	**9638**	**9320**	**8550**
住宿业	Accommodation	10006	9717	9385
餐饮业	Restaurants	8599	7876	5833
金融业	**Finance**	**18159**	**18785**	**15440**
银行业	Bank	18257	19040	15507
证券业	Securities	25806	21364	
保险业	Insurance	16761	16499	
其他金融活动	Other Financial Activities	12272	13544	10040
房地产业	**Real Estate**	**12959**	**13190**	**8990**
房地产开发经营	Real Estate Exploitation Management	12497	12022	8833
物业管理	Management Concerning Dwelling	12991	13875	9725
房地产中介服务	Real Estate Agency Service	14090	14024	10556
租赁和商务服务业	**Tenancy and Business Services**	**13380**	**13350**	**8462**
租赁业	Tenancy	13994	14520	6704
商务服务业	Business Service	13361	13313	8503

行 业	By Sector	全部在岗职工 Number of Staff and Workers on the Job	国有经济 State-owned Economic	城镇集体 Urban Collective-owned Economic
科研、技术服务和地质勘查业	**Scientific Research,Technical Service&Geologic Perambulation**	**14853**	**15046**	**7449**
研究与试验发展	Research and Experimental Development	15067	15097	11545
自然科学研究与试验发展	R&D on Physical Science	12867	12912	
工程和技术研究与试验发展	R&D on Engineering and Technical Research	20657	20734	
农业科学研究与试验发展	R&D on Agricultural Science Research	11097	11097	
医学研究与试验发展	R&D on medical research	15869	15995	11545
社会人文科学研究与发展	R&D on Social Science and Humanities	12621	12435	
专业技术服务业	Professional Technique Services	17553	17420	10208
气象服务	Weather Services	15000	15000	
地震服务	Earthquake Services	27605	27605	
测绘服务	Plotting Services	14715	14715	
技术检测	Technique Detection	15044	15398	3868
环境监测	Environmental Monitoring	15750	15750	
工程技术与规划管理	Engineering Technic and Programming Management	18567	18346	15584
科技交流和推广服务业	Services of S&T Intercommunion and Generalization	11456	12402	6335
地质勘查业	Geologic Perambulation	10345	10481	9567
水利、环境和公共设施管理业	**Management of Water Conservancy,Environment and Public Establishment**	**9890**	**9926**	**7808**
水利管理业	Management of Water Conservancy	9325	9487	6334
环境管理业	Environmental Management	9785	9880	8765
公共设施管理业	Management of Public Establishment	10681	10541	8072
居民服务和其他服务业	**Resident Services and Other Services**	**11274**	**12333**	**8784**
居民服务业	Resident Services	12345	14315	10126
其他服务业	Other Services	10362	11070	7283
教育	**Education**	**13309**	**13314**	**11571**
初等教育	Primary Education	10885	10888	9488
中等教育	Secondary Education	13606	13603	13581
高等教育	Higher Education	23661	23780	12909
卫生、社会保障和社会福利业	**Sanitation,Social Security and Social Welfare**	**15122**	**15992**	**8437**
卫生	Sanitation	15186	16097	8432
社会保障业	Social Security	13387	13376	17000
社会福利业	Social Welfare	13202	13254	8936
文化、体育和娱乐业	**Culture, Sports and Entertainment**	**15082**	**14712**	**8390**
#新闻出版业	Journalism and Publishing Activities	25403	26041	
广播、电视、电影和音像业	Broadcasting,Movies,Television and Audiovisual Activities	15023	14472	9608
文化艺术业	Culture and Art	10835	10966	7735
体育	Sports Activities	12559	12683	9000
娱乐业	Entertainment	10702	10701	10327
公共管理和社会组织	**Public Management and Social Organization**	**12818**	**12825**	**10478**
#中国共产党机关	Organ of Communist Party of China	12415	12417	10267
国家机构	Organ of State	12825	12830	10750
人民政协和民主党派	People's Political Consultative Conference and Democratic Party	14473	14473	
群众团体社会团体和宗教组织	Mass Community,Social Community and Religion Organizations	12912	13150	9698
国际组织	International Organizations			

3-20 离休、退休、退职人员人数及保险福利费(2003年)

Number of Retired and Resigned Persons and Social Insurance and Welfare Funds (2003)

项目	Item	总计 Total	企业 Enterprises	国有企业 State-owned Enterprises	集体企业 Collective-owned Enterprises	其他企业 Other-owned Enterprises	事业 Institutions	机关 Agencies and Organization
离退休年末人数（万人）	**Number of Retired&Resigned Persons (10 000 persons)**	**195.29**	**142.96**	**104.58**	**29.16**	**8.79**	**38.13**	**14.20**
离休人员	Number of Retired Veterans	4.44	2.07	1.81	0.17	0.08	1.32	1.05
退休人员	Number of Retired Persons	188.63	138.99	101.35	28.58	8.64	36.63	13.01
领取定期生活费的退职人员	Resigned Persons Receiving Periodical Living Expenses	2.22	1.90	1.42	0.41	0.07	0.18	0.14
保险福利费合计（万元）	**Social Insurance and Welfare Funds（10 000 yuan)**	**1565749**	**950184**	**743044**	**150074**	**54440**	**461258**	**154307**
离休金	Pensions for Retired Veterans	72851	30925	26829	2731	1268	25223	16703
退休金	Pensions for Retired Persons	1331393	826716	634199	139587	50486	388097	116580
退职生活费	Resignation Allowances for Living Expenses	7548	5575	4236	1063	252	1042	931
医疗卫生费	Expenses for Medical Care	91352	55146	48934	4473	1691	22627	13579
其他	Others	62605	31822	28846	2220	743	24269	6514

3-21 离开本单位仍保留劳动关系的职工情况(2003年)

Basic Indicators of Staff and Workers Left Self Unit and Remind Labor Relations (2003)

单位：万人 (10 000 persons)

市州	Cities and Prefecture	合计 Total	国有经济 State Owned Units	中央 Centre Genus	省属 Province Genus	地属 Prefecture Genus	县属 County Genus	城镇集体经济 Urban Collective Owned Units	其他经济类型 Units of Other Types of Ownership
合计	**Total**	**120.84**	**82.20**	**7.84**	**12.13**	**27.77**	**34.47**	**25.27**	**13.37**
长沙市	Changsha City	16.25	9.40	1.15	2.90	4.20	1.15	3.98	2.87
株洲市	Zhuzhou City	9.54	5.84	1.04	1.30	2.50	1.02	1.91	1.79
湘潭市	Xiangtan City	9.04	6.21	0.61	1.99	2.88	0.73	2.16	0.67
衡阳市	Hengyang City	16.60	10.83	0.52	0.86	5.93	3.52	3.42	2.35
邵阳市	Shaoyang City	13.32	8.93	0.11	0.83	4.36	3.62	3.12	1.27
岳阳市	Yueyang City	8.01	5.88	1.11	0.27	1.53	2.97	1.32	0.81
常德市	Changde City	4.19	2.92	0.39	0.30	0.28	1.96	0.76	0.51
张家界市	Zhangjiajie City	1.32	1.01	0.03	0.01	0.07	0.90	0.26	0.05
益阳市	Yiyang City	11.81	8.30	0.25	0.67	2.06	5.32	2.85	0.67
郴州市	Chenzhou City	6.21	4.41	0.51	0.61	1.14	2.15	1.13	0.67
永州市	Yongzhou City	6.80	5.14	0.24	0.12	1.39	3.38	1.06	0.60
怀化市	Huaihua City	6.42	4.14	0.31	0.19	0.49	3.15	1.64	0.64
娄底市	Loudi City	7.16	5.68	0.25	2.04	0.61	2.79	1.15	0.32
湘西自治州	West Hunan A.P	2.97	2.30	0.12	0.04	0.34	1.81	0.51	0.15
其他单位	Other Units	1.20	1.20	1.20					

四、固定资产投资

INVESTMENT IN FIXED ASSETS

资料整理人员： 吴　超　向延华　彭　蕾　陈立恒

4-1 全社会固定资产投资

Total Investment in Fixed Assets

指 标	Item	2000	2001	2002	2003	2003年比上年±% Increase Rate in 2003 over 2002 (%)
投资总额（亿元）	**Total Investment (100 million yuan)**	**1066.27**	**1210.63**	**1355.87**	**1557.00**	**14.8**
按经济类型分	**Grouped by Ownership**					
国有经济	State-Owned Units	574.12	618.54	665.70	701.33	5.4
集体经济	Collective-Owned Units	118.80	145.78	166.92	199.59	19.6
城镇	Urban	18.77	18.64	15.02	24.76	64.8
农村	Rural	100.02	127.14	151.90	174.83	15.1
个体经济	Individuals	281.89	291.56	282.53	250.80	-11.2
城镇	Urban	79.49	86.43	74.73	70.57	-5.6
农村	Rural	202.40	205.13	207.79	180.23	-13.3
联营经济	Joint Owned Economic Units	1.36	1.42	3.98	7.52	88.9
股份制经济	Share Holding Economic Units	49.80	113.59	177.48	313.35	76.6
外商投资经济	Foreign Funded Economic Units	24.72	17.54	25.98	21.81	-16.1
港澳台投资经济	Economic Units Funded by Entrepreneurs from Hong Kong,Macao and Taiwan	13.69	20.18	26.64	51.63	93.8
其他经济	Others	1.91	2.02	6.64	10.96	65.1
按管理渠道分	**Grouped by Channel of Management**					
基本建设	Capital Construction	403.96	476.70	535.26	605.22	13.1
更新改造	Innovation	175.20	198.31	227.96	301.87	32.4
房地产开发	Real Estate Development	74.83	107.41	150.92	230.03	52.4
其他投资	Others	412.28	428.21	441.72	419.88	-4.9
按资金来源分	**Grouped by Source of Funds**					
国家预算内投资	State Budgetary Appropriation	76.49	93.43	91.15	89.27	-2.1
国内贷款	Domestic Loans	213.41	206.10	211.12	283.50	34.3
债券	Bonds	2.34	1.48	5.91	3.70	-37.5
利用外资	Foreign Investment	22.01	29.22	43.95	47.25	7.5
自筹投资	Fundraising	623.37	757.56	853.04	943.80	10.6
#股票	#Shares	4.29	3.75	7.19	1.53	-78.7
其他资金	Others	128.65	122.48	150.70	189.48	25.7
按构成分	**Grouped by Use of Funds**					
建筑安装工程	Construction and Installation	759.94	829.11	928.28	1007.30	8.5
设备、工器具购置	Purchase of Equipment and Instruments	198.68	232.39	251.88	312.20	23.9
其他费用	Others	107.65	149.14	175.72	237.50	35.2
按隶属关系分	**Grouped by Administrative Relationship**					
中央	Central	248.26	225.54	166.88	114.09	-31.6
地方	Local	818.02	985.09	1188.98	1442.91	21.4
按用途分：住宅	**Grouped by Industry: Residential Buildings**	**297.00**	**300.62**	**308.00**	**298.76**	**-3.0**
房屋建筑面积(万平方米)	**Floor Space of Buildings (10 000 sq.m)**					
施工面积	Floor Space Under Construction	13170.34	12870.57	14608.52	12818.92	-12.3
竣工面积	Floor Space Completed	10892.52	10216.65	10752.78	8570.03	-20.3
#住宅	# Residential Buildings	9117.54	8344.88	8366.02	6099.02	-27.1

4-2 各种分组的全社会固定资产投资及构成(2003年)

Total Investment in Fixed Assets and Its Composition (2003)

类别	Item	全省总计 Total	国有 State-owned	#基本建设 Capital Construction	#更新改造 Innovation
绝对数	**Absolute Figure**				
投资总额(亿元)	**Total Investment (100 million yuan)**	**1557.00**	**701.33**	**480.54**	**164.75**
按资金来源分	**Grouped by Source of Funds**				
#国家预算内投资	#State Budgetary Appropriation	89.27	71.37	61.58	8.49
国内贷款	Domestic Loans	283.50	179.71	133.41	34.45
债 券	Bonds	3.70	3.70	2.80	0.15
利用外资	Foreign Investment	47.25	17.97	16.05	1.26
自筹投资	Fundraising	943.80	359.27	219.24	117.11
#股票	#Shares	1.53	0.14	0.06	0.08
其他资金	Others	189.48	69.31	47.47	3.29
按构成分	**Grouped by Use of Funds**				
#建安工程	#Construction and Installation	1007.30	480.72	367.21	73.44
设备、工具、器具购置	Purchase of Equipment and Instruments	312.20	112.13	31.89	78.14
其他费用	Others	237.50	108.48	81.43	13.16
按用途分：住宅	**Grouped by Industry:Residential Buildings**	298.76	50.30	23.73	0.16
房屋建筑面积(万平方米)	**Floor Space of Buildings (10 000 sq.m)**				
#施工面积	#Floor Space Under Construction	12818.92	2556.09	1933.68	112.56
竣工面积	Floor Space Completed	8570.03	1042.26	800.73	45.34
#住宅	#Residential Buildings	6099.02	451.02	276.38	4.07
构成(%)	**Percentage(%)**	**100.0**	**100.0**	**100.0**	**100.0**
投资总额	**Total Investment**				
按资金来源分	**Grouped by Source of Funds**				
#国家预算内投资	#State Budgetary Appropriation	5.7	10.2	12.8	5.2
国内贷款	Domestic Loans	18.2	25.6	27.8	20.9
债 券	Bonds	0.2	0.5	0.6	0.1
利用外资	Foreign Investment	3.0	2.6	3.3	0.8
自筹投资	Fundraising	60.6	51.2	45.6	71.1
#股票	#Shares	0.1			
其他资金	Others	12.2	9.9	9.9	2.0
按构成分	**Grouped by Use of Funds**				
#建安工程	#Construction and Installation	64.7	68.5	76.4	44.6
设备、工具、器具购置	Purchase of Equipment and Instruments	20.1	16.0	6.6	47.4
其他费用	Others	15.3	15.5	16.9	8.0
按用途分：住宅	Grouped by Industry:Residential Buildings	19.2	7.2	4.9	0.1

注：其他含联营经济、股份制经济、中外合资经营、中外合作经营、外资、与大陆合资经营、与大陆合作经营、港澳台独资等经济。

Other types of ownership refer to the types of ownership of joint-owned economic units, share holding economic units, economic units funded by Chinese and foreign ventures, Chinese-foreign joint ventures, foreign-funded economic units, and the economic units funded by enterpriser from Hong Kong, Macao and Taiwan.

类 别	Item	集体 Collective Owned	#农村 Rural	个体 Individuals	#农村 Rural	其他 Other Types of Ownership
绝对数	**Absolute Figure**					
投资总额(亿元)	**Total Investment (100 million yuan)**	**199.59**	**174.83**	**250.80**	**180.23**	**405.28**
按资金来源分	**Grouped by Source of Funds**					
#国家预算内投资	#State Budgetary Appropriation	16.68	16.68			1.22
国内贷款	Domestic Loans	13.62	9.97	17.27	3.31	72.90
债 券	Bonds					
利用外资	Foreign Investment	5.16	5.16	0.59		23.53
自筹投资	Fundraising	145.50	133.87	211.18	174.83	227.85
#股票	#Shares					1.39
其他资金	Others	18.64	9.15	21.76	2.09	79.78
按构成分	**Grouped by Use of Funds**					
#建安工程	#Construction and Installation	118.07	99.94	178.67	130.79	229.84
设备、工具、器具购置	Purchase of Equipment and Instruments	66.79	64.86	41.91	35.70	91.36
其他费用	Others	14.73	10.03	30.22	13.74	84.07
按用途分：住宅	**Grouped by Industry:Residential Buildings**	10.24	2.13	148.97	117.88	89.24
房屋建筑面积(万㎡)	**Floor Space of Buildings (10 000 sq.m)**					
#施工面积	#Floor Space Under Construction	1416.64	1143.00	6238.21	5345.00	2607.98
竣工面积	Floor Space Completed	1180.47	1092.00	5401.21	5091.00	946.09
#住宅	#Residential Buildings	119.97	54.00	5029.83	4825.00	498.20
构成(%)	**Percentage (%)**					
投资总额	**Total Investment**	**100.0**	**100.0**	**100.0**	**100.0**	**100.0**
按资金来源分	**Grouped by Source of Funds**					
#国家预算内投资	#State Budgetary Appropriation	8.4	9.5			0.3
国内贷款	Domestic Loans	6.8	5.7	6.9	1.8	18.0
债 券	Bonds					
利用外资	Foreign Investment	2.6	3.0	0.2		5.8
自筹投资	Fundraising	72.9	76.6	84.2	97.0	56.2
#股票	#Shares					0.3
其他资金	Others	9.3	5.2	8.7	1.2	19.7
按构成分	**Grouped by Use of Funds**					
#建安工程	#Construction and Installation	59.2	57.2	71.2	72.6	56.7
设备、工具、器具购置	Purchase of Equipment and Instruments	33.5	37.1	16.7	19.8	22.5
其他费用	Others	7.4	5.7	12.0	7.6	20.7
按用途分：住宅	**Grouped by Industry:Residential Buildings**	5.1	1.2	59.4	65.4	22.0

4-3 各行业基本建设投资(2003年)

Capital Construction Investment by Sector (2003)

单位:万元 (10 000 yuan)

行业	Sector	总计 Total	长沙市 Changsha City	株洲市 Zhuzhou City	湘潭市 Xiangtan City
总计	**Total**	**6052244**	**1990527**	**201919**	**210861**
农、林、牧、渔业	Agriculture,Forestry,Farming of Animals and Fishing	135238	13813	6322	4637
采矿业	Mining	12793		156	500
制造业	Manufacturing	483664	165633	17154	24118
电力、燃气及水的生产和供应业	Production and Distribution of Electricity,Gas and Water	872232	40215	13045	18011
建筑业	Construction	77992	71943	758	60
交通运输、仓储和邮政业	Traffic,Transport, Storage and Post	1671763	489142	42466	27134
信息传输、计算机服务和软件业	Information Transfer,Computer Services and Software	55430	20705	220	984
批发和零售业	Wholesale and Retail Trade	258481	136379	12758	9037
住宿和餐饮业	Accommodation and Restaurants	82711	26533	300	14872
金融业	Finance	21759	8688	1238	
房地产业	Real Estate Trade	86247	84217		
租赁和商务服务业	Tenancy and Business Services	173811	34236	2800	20750
科学研究、技术服务和地质勘查	Scientific Research,Technical Service and Geologic Perambulation	41566	30518	770	634
水利、环境和公共设施管理业	Management of Water Conservancy,Environment and Public Establishment	768894	224001	49893	45817
居民服务和其他服务业	Resident Services and Other Services	14611	6842	180	
教育	Education	342183	95554	24857	16051
卫生、社会保障和社会福利业	Sanitation,Social Security and Social Welfare	120860	56738	3202	916
文化、体育和娱乐业	Culture,Sports and Entertainment	219841	162524	7940	3250
公共管理和社会组织	Public Management and Social Organization	609568	320246	17860	24090
国际组织	International Organizations	2600	2600		

行业	Sector	衡阳市 Hengyang City	邵阳市 Shaoyang City	岳阳市 Yueyang City	常德市 Changde City
总计	**Total**	**327884**	**223774**	**410732**	**434907**
农、林、牧、渔业	Agriculture,Forestry,Farming of Animals and Fishing	10100	26765	5784	6292
采矿业	Mining	1200	3537		
制造业	Manufacturing	4279	6675	65878	100009
电力、燃气及水的生产和供应业	Production and Distribution of Electricity,Gas and Water	141840	42126	22696	56120
建筑业	Construction	345	173	133	570
交通运输、仓储和邮政业	Traffic,Transport, Storage and Post	86161	48892	97324	83174
信息传输、计算机服务和软件业	Information Transfer,Computer Services and Software	4931	5853		1617
批发和零售业	Wholesale and Retail Trade	3750	3030	19272	8515
住宿和餐饮业	Accommodation and Restaurants	50	700	9525	762
金融业	Finance	940	3018	1653	868
房地产业	Real Estate Trade				
租赁和商务服务业	Tenancy and Business Services	1297	5032	25710	12757
科学研究、技术服务和地质勘查	Scientific Research,Technical Service and Geologic Perambulation	1839	664	360	50
水利、环境和公共设施管理业	Management of Water Conservancy,Environment and Public Establishment	20495	24188	89848	88786
居民服务和其他服务业	Resident Services and Other Services	2312	500	600	410
教育	Education	11497	27317	24014	34984
卫生、社会保障和社会福利业	Sanitation,Social Security and Social Welfare	7495	5407	7440	12229
文化、体育和娱乐业	Culture,Sports and Entertainment	3284	1477	8135	8065
公共管理和社会组织	Public Management and Social Organization	26069	18420	32360	19699
国际组织	International Organizations				

单位:万元　　4-3 续表　continued　　(10 000 yuan)

行业	Sector	张家界市 Zhangjiajie City	益阳市 Yiyang City	郴州市 Chenzhou City	永州市 Yongzhou City
总计	**Total**	**105639**	**207080**	**540360**	**258881**
农、林、牧、渔业	Agriculture,Forestry,Farming of Animals and Fishing	147	3222	13831	7592
采矿业	Mining			4857	1630
制造业	Manufacturing	1413	17026	53025	19749
电力、燃气及水的生产和供应业	Production and Distribution of Electricity,Gas and Water	9934	32532	165107	48864
建筑业	Construction	504	70	370	190
交通运输、仓储和邮政业	Traffic,Transport, Storage and Post	15077	34682	74326	65915
信息传输、计算机服务和软件业	Information Transfer,Computer Services and Software		6709	2398	8890
批发和零售业	Wholesale and Retail Trade	8172	3921	45344	2220
住宿和餐饮业	Accommodation and Restaurants	8720		15017	3624
金融业	Finance	385	1647	619	1744
房地产业	Real Estate Trade		2030		
租赁和商务服务业	Tenancy and Business Services	2015	5775	22907	21596
科学研究、技术服务和地质勘查	Scientific Research,Technical Service and Geologic Perambulation	83	3336	2171	
水利、环境和公共设施管理业	Management of Water Conservancy,Environment and Public Establishment	41277	47964	36754	33902
居民服务和其他服务业	Resident Services and Other Services	5	500	170	900
教育	Education	8563	17904	35253	16766
卫生、社会保障和社会福利业	Sanitation,Social Security and Social Welfare	4626	4180	3033	3488
文化、体育和娱乐业	Culture,Sports and Entertainment	1811	3128	6419	3399
公共管理和社会组织	Public Management and Social Organization	2907	22454	58759	18412
国际组织	International Organizations				

行业	Sector	怀化市 Huaihua City	娄底市 Loudi City	湘西自治州 West Hunan A.P	不分地区 Not Classified by Region
总计		**177241**	**118762**	**245921**	**597756**
农、林、牧、渔业	Agriculture,Forestry,Farming of Animals and Fishing	6512	6437	23784	
采矿业	Mining	100	813		
制造业	Manufacturing	2105	4745	1855	
电力、燃气及水的生产和供应业	Production and Distribution of Electricity,Gas and Water	55854	12368	77885	135635
建筑业	Construction	2226	400	250	
交通运输、仓储和邮政业	Traffic,Transport, Storage and Post	38567	45732	61050	462121
信息传输、计算机服务和软件业	Information Transfer,Computer Services and Software	1233	1240	650	
批发和零售业	Wholesale and Retail Trade	2007	3171	905	
住宿和餐饮业	Accommodation and Restaurants	1487		1121	
金融业	Finance	331	288	340	
房地产业	Real Estate Trade				
租赁和商务服务业	Tenancy and Business Services	14730	2230	1976	
科学研究、技术服务和地质勘查	Scientific Research,Technical Service and Geologic Perambulation	928		213	
水利、环境和公共设施管理业	Management of Water Conservancy,Environment and Public Establishment	22677	16366	26926	
居民服务和其他服务业	Resident Services and Other Services	43	794	1355	
教育	Education	8521	9165	11737	
卫生、社会保障和社会福利业	Sanitation,Social Security and Social Welfare	6509	1021	4576	
文化、体育和娱乐业	Culture,Sports and Entertainment	2108	3280	5021	
公共管理和社会组织	Public Management and Social Organization	11303	10712	26277	
国际组织	International Organizations				

4-4 各行业基本建设新增固定资产(2003年)

Newly Increased Fixed Assets through Capital Construction by Sector (2003)

单位:万元 (10 000 yuan)

行业	Sector	总计 Total	长沙市 Changsha City	株洲市 Zhuzhou City	湘潭市 Xiangtan City
总计	**Total**	**4177211**	**1150554**	**149625**	**127067**
农、林、牧、渔业	Agriculture,Forestry,Farming of Animals and Fishing	96074	12387	5099	4337
采矿业	Mining	9338		356	500
制造业	Manufacturing	235753	45132	13628	16208
电力、燃气及水的生产和供应业	Production and Distribution of Electricity,Gas and Water	741693	11530	9413	5170
建筑业	Construction	14283	9783	758	540
交通运输、仓储和邮政业	Traffic,Transport, Storage and Post	1407946	405310	26575	8059
信息传输、计算机服务和软件业	Information Transfer,Computer Services and Software	50160	30430	965	818
批发和零售业	Wholesale and Retail Trade	164885	91447	9440	10218
住宿和餐饮业	Accommodation and Restaurants	47457	11770		13300
金融业	Finance	13399		3706	
房地产业	Real Estate Trade	17070	16120		
租赁和商务服务业	Tenancy and Business Services	49500	11620		8100
科学研究、技术服务和地质勘查	Scientific Research,Technical Service and Geologic Perambulation	10726	4040	770	751
水利、环境和公共设施管理业	Management of Water Conservancy,Environment and Public Establishment	514289	178594	24494	23073
居民服务和其他服务业	Resident Services and Other Services	9667	2000	180	
教育	Education	259315	69535	19329	18042
卫生、社会保障和社会福利业	Sanitation,Social Security and Social Welfare	60152	15099	3350	916
文化、体育和娱乐业	Culture,Sports and Entertainment	98085	60028	2916	3000
公共管理和社会组织	Public Management and Social Organization	374819	173129	28646	14035
国际组织	International Organizations	2600	2600		

行业	Sector	衡阳市 Hengyang City	邵阳市 Shaoyang City	岳阳市 Yueyang City	常德市 Changde City
总计	**Total**	**320940**	**137648**	**273732**	**306908**
农、林、牧、渔业	Agriculture,Forestry,Farming of Animals and Fishing	6315	16114	3944	3959
采矿业	Mining		2330		
制造业	Manufacturing	3877	4045	34997	55387
电力、燃气及水的生产和供应业	Production and Distribution of Electricity,Gas and Water	96020	30008	20973	50836
建筑业	Construction	360		228	330
交通运输、仓储和邮政业	Traffic,Transport, Storage and Post	140968	16841	71221	84460
信息传输、计算机服务和软件业	Information Transfer,Computer Services and Software	1837	5157		2272
批发和零售业	Wholesale and Retail Trade	1364	2267	7948	2810
住宿和餐饮业	Accommodation and Restaurants		409	4000	
金融业	Finance	300	2461	1558	1320
房地产业	Real Estate Trade				
租赁和商务服务业	Tenancy and Business Services	1200	3280	2720	5555
科学研究、技术服务和地质勘查	Scientific Research,Technical Service and Geologic Perambulation	1627		360	60
水利、环境和公共设施管理业	Management of Water Conservancy,Environment and Public Establishment	14685	14097	80730	49762
居民服务和其他服务业	Resident Services and Other Services	500		720	328
教育	Education	11091	20175	9667	23881
卫生、社会保障和社会福利业	Sanitation,Social Security and Social Welfare	10208	6514	6420	4147
文化、体育和娱乐业	Culture,Sports and Entertainment	5510	750	3660	6396
公共管理和社会组织	Public Management and Social Organization	25078	13200	24586	15405
国际组织	International Organizations				

单位:万元　　　　4-4续表　continued　　　　(10 000 yuan)

行业	Sector	张家界市 Zhangjiajie City	益阳市 Yiyang City	郴州市 Chenzhou City	永州市 Yongzhou City
总计	**Total**	**67666**	**134110**	**492137**	**105224**
农、林、牧、渔业	Agriculture,Forestry,Farming of Animals and Fishing	102	3222	9641	6241
采矿业	Mining			4274	1630
制造业	Manufacturing	198	14467	27585	14598
电力、燃气及水的生产和供应业	Production and Distribution of Electricity,Gas and Water	2320	29894	278418	25849
建筑业	Construction	4		200	
交通运输、仓储和邮政业	Traffic,Transport, Storage and Post	6276	3408	39500	15609
信息传输、计算机服务和软件业	Information Transfer,Computer Services and Software		5094	1388	
批发和零售业	Wholesale and Retail Trade	4605	1647	25588	1959
住宿和餐饮业	Accommodation and Restaurants	6300		9366	510
金融业	Finance	385		826	1410
房地产业	Real Estate Trade		950		
租赁和商务服务业	Tenancy and Business Services	696	1685	3409	5669
科学研究、技术服务和地质勘查	Scientific Research,Technical Service and Geologic Perambulation		610	1932	
水利、环境和公共设施管理业	Management of Water Conservancy,Environment and Public Establishment	36881	37972	27311	7287
居民服务和其他服务业	Resident Services and Other Services	975	3300	500	560
教育	Education	4059	13902	26213	10358
卫生、社会保障和社会福利业	Sanitation,Social Security and Social Welfare	761	4570	3284	1963
文化、体育和娱乐业	Culture,Sports and Entertainment	1611	1172	6490	1289
公共管理和社会组织	Public Management and Social Organization	2493	12217	26212	10292
国际组织	International Organizations				

行业	Sector	怀化市 Huaihua City	娄底市 Loudi City	湘西自治州 West Hunan A.P	不分地区 Not Classified by Region
总计	**Total**	**223052**	**77491**	**114779**	**496278**
农、林、牧、渔业	Agriculture,Forestry,Farming of Animals and Fishing	5407	5825	13481	
采矿业	Mining		248		
制造业	Manufacturing	1425	2831	1375	
电力、燃气及水的生产和供应业	Production and Distribution of Electricity,Gas and Water	176812	3462	988	
建筑业	Construction	1400	430	250	
交通运输、仓储和邮政业	Traffic,Transport, Storage and Post	9934	31818	51689	496278
信息传输、计算机服务和软件业	Information Transfer,Computer Services and Software	834	1070	295	
批发和零售业	Wholesale and Retail Trade	2136	1970	1486	
住宿和餐饮业	Accommodation and Restaurants	741		1061	
金融业	Finance	285	388	760	
房地产业	Real Estate Trade				
租赁和商务服务业	Tenancy and Business Services	3510	1780	276	
科学研究、技术服务和地质勘查	Scientific Research,Technical Service and Geologic Perambulation	418		158	
水利、环境和公共设施管理业	Management of Water Conservancy,Environment and Public Establishment	1155	8672	9576	
居民服务和其他服务业	Resident Services and Other Services		604		
教育	Education	7608	9863	15592	
卫生、社会保障和社会福利业	Sanitation,Social Security and Social Welfare	878	533	1509	
文化、体育和娱乐业	Culture,Sports and Entertainment	411	2180	2672	
公共管理和社会组织	Public Management and Social Organization	10098	5817	13611	
国际组织	International Organizations				

4-5 基本建设项目个数、项目投产率(2003年)

Number of Capital Construction Projects, Rate of Projects Put into Use (2003)

市州及行业	Cities, Prefecture and Sector	投资额(亿元) Investment (100 millions yuan)	施工项目(个) Projects under Construction (unit)	全部建成投产项目(个) Projects Completed and Put into Uses (unit)	项目建成投产率(%) Rate of Project Completed and Put into Uses (%)	新增固定资产(亿元) Newly Increase Fixed Assets (100 million yuan)	固定资产交付使用率(%) Rate of Fixed Assets Turn Over to Uses (%)
总计	**Total**	**605.22**	**4482**	**2294**	**51.2**	**417.72**	**69.0**
按地市分	**By Region**						
长沙市	Changsha City	199.05	651	293	45.0	115.06	57.8
株洲市	Zhuzhou City	20.19	246	155	63.0	14.96	74.1
湘潭市	Xiangtan City	21.09	145	79	54.5	12.71	60.3
衡阳市	Hengyang City	32.79	225	128	56.9	32.09	97.9
邵阳市	Shaoyang City	22.38	465	251	54.0	13.76	61.5
岳阳市	Yueyang City	41.07	416	236	56.7	27.37	66.6
常德市	Changde City	43.49	420	241	57.4	30.69	70.6
张家界市	Zhangjiajie City	10.56	117	61	52.1	6.77	64.1
益阳市	Yiyang City	20.71	177	98	55.4	13.41	64.8
郴州市	Chenzhou City	54.04	478	252	52.7	49.21	91.1
永州市	Yongzhou City	25.89	385	171	44.4	10.52	40.6
怀化市	Huaihua City	17.72	286	120	42.0	22.31	125.8
娄底市	Loudi City	11.88	191	77	40.3	7.75	65.2
湘西自治州	West Hunan A.P	24.59	273	131	48.0	11.48	46.7
不分地区	Not Classified by Region	59.78	7	1	14.3	49.63	83.0
按行业分	**By Sector**						
农、林、牧、渔业	Agriculture,Forestry,Farming of Animals and Fishing	13.52	175	91	52.0	9.61	71.0
采矿业	Mining	1.28	25	13	52.0	0.93	73.0
制造业	Manufacturing	48.37	355	184	51.8	23.58	48.7
电力、燃气及水的生产和供应业	Production and Distribution of Electricity, Gas and Water	87.22	345	143	41.4	74.17	85.0
建筑业	Construction	7.80	32	13	40.6	1.43	18.3
交通运输、仓储和邮政	Traffic,Transport, Storage and Post	167.18	669	283	42.3	140.79	84.2
信息传输、计算机服务和软件业	Information Transfer,Computer Services and Software	5.54	70	41	58.6	5.02	90.5
批发和零售业	Wholesale and Retail Trade	25.85	251	139	55.4	16.49	63.8
住宿和餐饮业	Accommodation and Restaurants	8.27	70	33	47.1	4.75	57.4
金融业	Finance	2.18	51	33	64.7	1.34	61.6
房地产业	Real Estate Trade	8.62	24	10	41.7	1.71	19.8
租赁和商务服务业	Tenancy and Business Services	17.38	120	37	30.8	4.95	28.5
科学研究、技术服务和地质勘查业	Scientific Research,Technical Service and Geologic Perambulation	4.16	51	22	43.1	1.07	25.8
水利、环境和公共设施管理业	Management of Water Conservancy, Environment and Public Establishment	76.89	497	237	47.7	51.43	66.9
居民服务和其他服务业	Resident Services and Other Services	1.46	25	11	44.0	0.97	66.2
教育	Education	34.22	682	472	69.2	25.93	75.8
卫生、社保和社会福利	Sanitation,Social Security and Social Welfare	12.09	191	92	48.2	6.02	49.8
文化、体育和娱乐业	Culture,Sports and Entertainment	21.98	149	68	45.6	9.81	44.6
公共管理和社会组织	Public Management and Social Organization	60.96	699	372	53.2	37.48	61.5
国际组织	International Organizations	0.26	1			0.26	100.0

4-6 各种分组的更新改造投资(2003年)

Technical Updates and Innovation Investment by Various Characteristics (2003)

单位:万元 (10 000 yuan)

市州	Cities and Prefecture	投资额 Total Investment	按构成分 Grouped by Use of Funds 建安工程 Construction and Installation	设备工器具购置 Purchase of Equipment& Instruments	其他费用 Others	按建设性质分 Grouped by Type of Construcyion 新建 New Construction	扩建 Expansion	改建 Re-construction
全 省	**Total**	**3018682**	**1303722**	**1418536**	**296424**	**668826**	**1256368**	**1008567**
长沙市	Changsha	679852	357876	234906	87070	186974	381805	87725
株洲市	Zhuzhou	297705	111934	146612	39159	52891	144368	94514
湘潭市	Xiangtan	242247	93791	125920	22536	570	51632	187318
衡阳市	Hengyang	217821	74133	116452	27236	12239	96109	106617
邵阳市	Shaoyang	47239	13439	29851	3949	8183	21707	11322
岳阳市	Yueyang	379483	173374	166562	39547	130981	161773	82999
常德市	Changde	168682	70489	85618	12575	14517	95945	51459
张家界市	Zhangjiajie	38526	12818	24366	1342	10811	16989	8759
益阳市	Yiyang	72272	27261	42025	2986	19563	20649	23886
郴州市	Chenzhou	157848	59236	77926	20686	26059	63816	65173
永州市	Yongzhou	81823	33154	44485	4184	6586	33292	31450
怀化市	Huaihua	125865	63308	53756	8801	14647	59576	44632
娄底市	Loudi	423843	182889	220057	20897	167245	51062	205536
湘西	West Hunan	77422	28560	43964	4898	9506	57645	7177
不分地区	Not Classified	8054	1460	6036	558	8054		

市州	Cities and Prefecture	按资金来源分 Grouped by Source of Funds 国家预算内 State Budgetary Appropriation	国内贷款 Domestic Loans	利用外资 Foreign Investment	自筹资金 Fundraising	其他投资 Others	按隶属关系分 Grouped by Administrative Relationship 中央项目 Central Projects	地方项目 Local Projects
全 省	**Total**	**88688**	**538989**	**79985**	**2228966**	**130379**	**587574**	**2431108**
长沙市	Changsha		69520	14870	560598	36940	102509	577343
株洲市	Zhuzhou	28661	102757	100	163351	13532	126177	171528
湘潭市	Xiangtan	15200	40621	5540	196626	2430	32731	209516
衡阳市	Hengyang	8724	38945	14470	148141	16612	22682	195139
邵阳市	Shaoyang	990	12690	1596	23565	9004	7317	39922
岳阳市	Yueyang	650	56362	6630	295910	23983	84434	295049
常德市	Changde	780	5591	2075	156226	5427	72113	96569
张家界市	Zhangjiajie	2260	13101	400	17369	555	26	38500
益阳市	Yiyang	2430	12567	100	47748	4198	4582	67690
郴州市	Chenzhou	1930	14890	21101	116477	10317	14744	143104
永州市	Yongzhou	3455	16829	11112	38913	3101	22696	59127
怀化市	Huaihua	6631	39441		83345	3330	52699	73166
娄底市	Loudi		98187		337474		20029	403814
湘西	West Hunan	16977	17488	1991	37036	950	16781	60641
不分地区	Not Classified				6187		8054	

4-7 更新改造完成投资及新增固定资产（2003年）

Technical Updates and Innovation and Newly Increased Fixed Assets (2003)

市州及行业	Cities, Prefecture and Sector	投资额（亿元） Investment (100 millions yuan)	施工项目（个） Projects under Construction (unit)	全部建成投产项目（个） Projects Completed and Put into Uses (unit)	项目建成投产率(%) Rate of Project Completed and Put into Uses (%)	新增固定资产（亿元） Newly Increase Fixed Assets (100 million yuan)	固定资产交付使用率(%) Rate of Fixed Assets Turn Over to Uses (%)
全省总计	**Total**	**301.87**	**3161**	**1958**	**61.9**	**193.11**	**64.0**
按地市分	**By Region**						
长沙市	Changsha City	67.99	284	98	34.5	32.19	47.4
株洲市	Zhuzhou City	29.77	252	140	55.6	23.18	77.9
湘潭市	Xiangtan City	24.22	241	187	77.6	13.14	54.2
衡阳市	Hengyang City	21.78	486	282	58.0	16.53	75.9
邵阳市	Shaoyang City	4.72	275	253	92.0	2.41	51.0
岳阳市	Yueyang City	37.95	520	393	75.6	22.90	60.3
常德市	Changde City	16.87	244	150	61.5	20.54	121.8
张家界市	Zhangjiajie City	3.85	73	49	67.1	1.80	46.6
益阳市	Yiyang City	7.23	64	28	43.8	4.59	63.5
郴州市	Chenzhou City	15.78	332	168	50.6	11.89	75.3
永州市	Yongzhou City	8.18	57	22	38.6	3.91	47.8
怀化市	Huaihua City	12.59	82	46	56.1	5.83	46.3
娄底市	Loudi City	42.38	138	106	76.8	27.87	65.8
湘西自治州	West Hunan A.P	7.74	86	20	23.3	5.83	75.3
不分地区	Not Classified by Region	0.81	27	16	59.3	0.50	62.4
按行业分	**By Sector**						
农、林、牧、渔业	Agriculture,Forestry,Farming of Animals and Fishing	0.47	8	5	62.5	0.25	52.8
采矿业	Mining	5.91	101	55	54.5	5.29	89.5
制造业	Manufacturing	211.91	1557	795	51.1	134.03	63.2
电力、燃气及水的生产和供应业	Production and Distribution of Electricity, Gas and Water	22.85	304	182	59.9	13.29	58.2
建筑业	Construction	0.32	3	2	66.7	0.24	73.5
交通运输、仓储和邮政	Traffic,Transport, Storage and Post	11.72	140	82	58.6	8.30	70.8
信息传输、计算机服务和软件业	Information Transfer,Computer Services and Software	34.87	896	774	86.4	24.51	70.3
批发和零售业	Wholesale and Retail Trade	3.62	61	17	27.9	1.81	50.0
住宿和餐饮业	Accommodation and Restaurants	2.87	10	7	70.0	0.97	33.8
金融业	Finance	0.13				0.13	100.0
房地产业	Real Estate Trade					0.00	
租赁和商务服务业	Tenancy and Business Services	0.45	11	2	18.2	0.19	42.9
科学研究、技术服务和地质勘查业	Scientific Research,Technical Service and Geologic Perambulation	0.48	5	1	20.0	0.02	3.4
水利、环境和公共设施管理业	Management of Water Conservancy, Environment and Public Establishment	3.05	36	19	52.8	1.69	55.3
居民服务和其他服务业	Resident Services and Other Services	0.03	1	1	100.0	0.03	100.0
教育	Education	0.24	2	2	100.0	0.12	49.9
卫生、社保和社会福利	Sanitation,Social Security and Social Welfare	1.64	8	6	75.0	1.18	72.0
文化、体育和娱乐业	Culture,Sports and Entertainment	0.68	8	4	50.0	0.47	69.1
公共管理和社会组织	Public Management and Social Organization	0.62	10	4	40.0	0.59	95.2
国际组织	International Organizations						

4-8 国有经济固定资产投资及构成

Investment in Fixed Assets and Its Composition of State – owned Units

年份 Year	固定资产投资总额 Total Investment in Fixed Assets	基本建设 Capital Construction	更新改造 Innovation	房地产开发 Real Estae Development	其他 Others	新增固定资产 Newly Increased Fixed Assets	基本建设 Capital Construction	更新改造 Innovation	房地产开发 Real Estae Development	其他 Others
绝对数(亿元)	**Absolute Figure (100 million yuan)**									
1978	14.71	13.51	1.20			10.56	9.65	0.91		
1980	20.32	15.53	4.79			15.24	11.98	3.26		
1985	43.86	25.58	16.20		2.08	30.66	16.91	12.19		1.56
1990	72.01	43.11	25.24	2.14	1.52	47.27	25.68	18.81	1.37	1.41
1991	94.85	56.10	32.45	3.20	3.10	82.36	50.75	27.20	2.19	2.22
1992	149.72	90.89	49.17	7.42	2.24	117.07	75.01	36.25	4.05	1.76
1993	203.17	122.75	61.72	15.12	3.58	125.96	69.83	45.07	7.75	3.31
1994	251.21	162.99	70.63	13.81	3.78	154.80	92.09	51.48	7.66	3.57
1995	316.90	209.70	79.85	21.61	5.74	202.81	117.55	68.57	11.88	4.81
1996	375.27	245.10	104.67	17.50	8.00	269.99	163.23	86.82	13.12	6.82
1997	366.34	238.01	89.42	15.79	23.12	269.20	156.86	93.81	11.16	7.37
1998	457.00	306.81	106.43	17.61	26.15	290.91	192.02	75.06	13.57	10.26
1999	522.95	348.31	127.29	22.17	25.18	348.43	233.99	90.40	17.47	6.57
2000	574.12	376.40	145.29	25.21	27.22	388.40	245.12	117.79	16.38	9.11
2001	618.54	433.90	146.88	25.25	12.51	349.76	203.59	115.39	18.69	12.09
2002	665.70	478.34	141.86	31.38	14.12	489.89	377.67	84.43	17.59	10.20
2003	701.33	480.54	164.75	37.57	18.48	465.20	322.21	115.51	16.45	10.99
构成(%)	**Composition in Percentage (%)**									
1978	100.0	91.8	8.2			100.0	91.4	8.6		
1980	100.0	76.4	23.6			100.0	78.6	21.4		
1985	100.0	58.3	36.9		4.8	100.0	55.1	39.8		5.1
1990	100.0	59.9	35.0	3.0	2.1	100.0	54.3	39.8	2.9	3.0
1991	100.0	59.1	34.2	3.4	3.3	100.0	61.6	33.0	2.7	2.7
1992	100.0	60.7	32.8	5.0	1.5	100.0	64.0	31.0	3.5	1.5
1993	100.0	60.4	30.4	7.4	1.8	100.0	55.4	35.8	6.2	2.6
1994	100.0	64.9	28.1	5.5	1.5	100.0	59.5	33.3	4.9	2.3
1995	100.0	66.2	25.2	6.8	1.8	100.0	58.0	33.8	5.8	2.4
1996	100.0	65.3	27.9	4.7	2.1	100.0	60.4	32.2	4.9	2.5
1997	100.0	65.0	24.4	4.3	6.3	100.0	58.3	34.8	4.1	2.7
1998	100.0	67.1	23.3	3.9	5.7	100.0	66.0	25.8	4.7	3.5
1999	100.0	66.6	24.3	4.2	4.8	100.0	67.2	25.9	5.0	1.9
2000	100.0	65.6	25.3	4.4	4.7	100.0	63.1	30.3	4.2	2.4
2001	100.0	70.1	23.7	4.1	2.0	100.0	58.2	33.0	5.3	3.5
2002	100.0	71.9	21.3	4.7	2.1	100.0	77.1	17.2	3.6	2.1
2003	100.0	68.5	23.5	5.4	2.6	100.0	69.3	24.8	3.5	2.4

注:1997年—2000年，其他投资中含50万元以下项目投资。

The investments beyond 500,000 yuan were included in other types of investment from 1997 to 2000.

4-9 国有经济各种分组的固定资产投资

Investment in Fixed Assets of State - owned Units by Various Characteristics

指 标	Item	2000	2001	2002	2003	2003年比上年±% Increase Rate in 2003 over 2002 (%)
投资总额(亿元)	**Total Investment (100 million yuan)**	**574.12**	**618.54**	**665.70**	**701.33**	**5.4**
按资金来源分	**Grouped by Source of Funds**					
国家预算内投资	State Budgetary Appropriation	57.21	69.34	69.26	71.37	3.0
国内贷款	Domestic Loans	180.12	159.89	153.46	179.71	17.1
债　券	Bonds	2.34	1.37	5.83	3.70	-36.5
利用外资	Foreign Investment	13.67	18.68	24.45	17.97	-26.5
自筹投资	Fundraising	240.50	311.58	350.26	359.27	2.6
股票	Shares	3.65	1.40	1.89	0.14	-92.5
其他投资	Others	80.28	57.68	62.44	69.31	11.0
按隶属关系分	**Grouped by Administrative Relationship**					
中央项目	Central Government Projects	246.75	217.45	163.56	98.74	-39.6
地方项目	Local Projects	327.37	401.10	502.14	602.60	20.0
按构成分	**Grouped by Use of Funds**					
建筑安装工程	Construction and Installation	394.25	409.64	460.52	480.72	4.4
设备、工具、器具购置	Purchase of Equipment and Instruments	119.42	127.63	110.71	112.13	1.3
其他费用	Others	60.45	81.27	94.47	108.48	14.8
按建设性质分	**Grouped by Type of Construction**					
新建	New Construction	177.16	229.62	261.48	344.15	31.6
扩建	Expansion	186.39	198.75	207.49	158.87	-23.4
改建	Reconstruction	132.98	128.41	129.69	138.55	6.8
按国民经济主要行业分	**Grouped by Main Sector**					
农业	Agriculture	4.42	4.50	6.38	13.82	116.6
工业	Industry	136.29	144.25	173.26	190.87	10.2
#能源工业	Energy	75.46	88.36	100.82	81.78	-18.9
运输邮电业	Transportation,Postal and Telecommunications Services	242.17	227.60	178.92	213.82	19.5
新增固定资产(亿元)	**Newly Increased Fixed Assets (100 million yuan)**	**388.40**	**349.76**	**489.89**	**465.20**	**-5.0**
房屋建筑面积(万平方米)	**Floor Space of Buildings (10 000 sq.m)**					
施工面积	Floor Space Under Construction	2429.83	2283.26	2530.98	2556.09	1.0
竣工面积	Floor Space Completed	1262.35	1094.14	1135.21	1042.26	-8.2
#住宅	# Residential Buildings	718.01	606.58	539.46	451.02	-16.4

4-10 国有经济各行业固定资产投资(2003年)

Investment in Fixed Assets of State-owned Units by Sector (2003)

行业	Sector	固定资产投资额 Investment in Fixed Assets	基本建设 Capital Construction	更新改造 Innovation
绝对数(亿元)	**Absolute Figure (100 million yuan)**			
全省总计	**Total**	**701.33**	**480.54**	**164.75**
农、林、牧、渔业	Agriculture,Forestry,Farming of Animals and Fishing	13.82	11.67	0.26
采矿业	Mining	2.92	0.21	2.67
制造业	Manufacturing	104.11	9.57	94.48
电力、燃气及水的生产和供应业	Production and Distribution of Electricity,Gas and Water	83.84	62.89	20.65
建筑业	Construction	3.15	3.07	0.09
交通运输、仓储和邮政业	Traffic,Transport, Storage and Post	180.69	160.39	10.52
信息传输、计算机服务和软件业	Information Transfer,Computer Services and Software	34.31	4.60	29.71
批发和零售业	Wholesale and Retail Trade	11.22	10.71	0.52
住宿和餐饮业	Accommodation and Restaurants	3.10	2.81	0.12
金融业	Finance	2.30	2.17	0.13
房地产业	Real Estate Trade	44.78	7.05	
租赁和商务服务业	Tenancy and Business Services	12.82	11.95	0.19
科学研究、技术服务和地质勘查	Scientific Research,Technical Service and Geologic Perambulation	3.06	2.04	0.19
水利、环境和公共设施管理业	Management of Water Conservancy,Environment and Public Establishment	75.99	70.38	2.61
居民服务和其他服务业	Resident Services and Other Services	0.68	0.68	
教育	Education	32.63	32.18	0.24
卫生、社会保障和社会福利业	Sanitation,Social Security and Social Welfare	13.29	10.87	1.40
文化、体育和娱乐业	Culture,Sports and Entertainment	18.50	18.02	0.35
公共管理和社会组织	Public Management and Social Organization	60.12	59.28	0.62
国际组织	International Organizations			
构成 (%)	**Composition in Percentage (%)**			
全省总计	**Total**	**100.00**	**100.00**	**100.00**
农、林、牧、渔业	Agriculture,Forestry,Farming of Animals and Fishing	1.97	2.43	0.16
采矿业	Mining	0.42	0.04	1.62
制造业	Manufacturing	14.84	1.99	57.35
电力、燃气及水的生产和供应业	Production and Distribution of Electricity,Gas and Water	11.95	13.09	12.53
建筑业	Construction	0.45	0.64	0.05
交通运输、仓储和邮政业	Traffic,Transport, Storage and Post	25.76	33.38	6.39
信息传输、计算机服务和软件业	Information Transfer,Computer Services and Software	4.89	0.96	18.03
批发和零售业	Wholesale and Retail Trade	1.60	2.23	0.32
住宿和餐饮业	Accommodation and Restaurants	0.44	0.58	0.07
金融业	Finance	0.33	0.45	0.08
房地产业	Real Estate Trade	6.39	1.47	
租赁和商务服务业	Tenancy and Business Services	1.83	2.49	0.12
科学研究、技术服务和地质勘查	Scientific Research,Technical Service and Geologic Perambulation	0.44	0.42	0.12
水利、环境和公共设施管理业	Management of Water Conservancy,Environment and Public Establishment	10.84	14.65	1.58
居民服务和其他服务业	Resident Services and Other Services	0.10	0.14	
教育	Education	4.65	6.70	0.15
卫生、社会保障和社会福利业	Sanitation,Social Security and Social Welfare	1.89	2.26	0.85
文化、体育和娱乐业	Culture,Sports and Entertainment	2.64	3.75	0.20
公共管理和社会组织	Public Management and Social Organization	8.57	12.34	0.38
国际组织	International Organizations			

4-11 国有经济各行业新增固定资产(2003年)

Newly Increased Fixed Assets of State-owned Units by Sector (2003)

行业	Sector	新增固定资产 Newly Increased Fixed Assets	#基本建设 Capital Construction	#更新改造 Innovation
绝对数(亿元)	**Absolute Figure (100 million yuan)**			
全省总计	**Total**	**465.20**	**322.21**	**115.55**
农、林、牧、渔业	Agriculture,Forestry,Farming of Animals and Fishing	9.71	8.08	0.09
采矿业	Mining	2.48	0.09	2.36
制造业	Manufacturing	70.49	4.94	65.55
电力、燃气及水的生产和供应业	Production and Distribution of Electricity,Gas and Water	39.64	26.97	12.38
建筑业	Construction	0.69	0.69	
交通运输、仓储和邮政业	Traffic,Transport, Storage and Post	149.58	137.13	7.89
信息传输、计算机服务和软件业	Information Transfer,Computer Services and Software	28.05	4.68	23.37
批发和零售业	Wholesale and Retail Trade	9.60	9.36	0.23
住宿和餐饮业	Accommodation and Restaurants	1.62	1.58	0.05
金融业	Finance	1.47	1.34	0.13
房地产业	Real Estate Trade	18.06	1.45	
租赁和商务服务业	Tenancy and Business Services	3.06	2.81	0.19
科学研究、技术服务和地质勘查	Scientific Research,Technical Service and Geologic Perambulation	0.87	0.85	0.02
水利、环境和公共设施管理业	Management of Water Conservancy,Environment and Public Establishment	51.55	47.89	1.50
居民服务和其他服务业	Resident Services and Other Services	0.75	0.75	
教育	Education	24.91	24.59	0.12
卫生、社会保障和社会福利业	Sanitation,Social Security and Social Welfare	8.50	5.85	0.94
文化、体育和娱乐业	Culture,Sports and Entertainment	7.00	6.72	0.14
公共管理和社会组织	Public Management and Social Organization	37.17	36.44	0.59
国际组织	International Organizations			
构成 (%)	**Composition in Percentage (%)**			
全省总计	**Total**	100.00	100.00	100.00
农、林、牧、渔业	Agriculture,Forestry,Farming of Animals and Fishing	2.09	2.51	0.08
采矿业	Mining	0.53	0.03	2.04
制造业	Manufacturing	15.15	1.53	56.73
电力、燃气及水的生产和供应业	Production and Distribution of Electricity,Gas and Water	8.52	8.37	10.71
建筑业	Construction	0.15	0.21	
交通运输、仓储和邮政业	Traffic,Transport, Storage and Post	32.15	42.56	6.83
信息传输、计算机服务和软件业	Information Transfer,Computer Services and Software	6.03	1.45	20.23
批发和零售业	Wholesale and Retail Trade	2.06	2.90	0.20
住宿和餐饮业	Accommodation and Restaurants	0.35	0.49	0.04
金融业	Finance	0.32	0.42	0.11
房地产业	Real Estate Trade	3.88	0.45	
租赁和商务服务业	Tenancy and Business Services	0.66	0.87	0.16
科学研究、技术服务和地质勘查	Scientific Research,Technical Service and Geologic Perambulation	0.19	0.26	0.02
水利、环境和公共设施管理业	Management of Water Conservancy,Environment and Public Establishment	11.08	14.86	1.30
居民服务和其他服务业	Resident Services and Other Services	0.16	0.23	
教育	Education	5.35	7.63	0.10
卫生、社会保障和社会福利业	Sanitation,Social Security and Social Welfare	1.83	1.82	0.81
文化、体育和娱乐业	Culture,Sports and Entertainment	1.51	2.09	0.12
公共管理和社会组织	Public Management and Social Organization	7.99	11.32	0.52
国际组织	International Organizations			

4-12 国有经济房屋建设指标(2003年)

Indicators of Building Construction of State - owned Units (2003)

指 标	Item	合 计 Total	基本建设 Capital Construction	更新改造 Innovation	房地产开发 Real Estate Development	其他固定资产投资 Others
施工房屋面积(万平方米)	Floor Space of Buildings under Construction (10 000 sq.m)	2556.09	1933.68	112.56	497.80	12.05
住宅	Residential Buildings	1076.31	617.99	6.78	444.71	6.83
竣工房屋面积(万平方米)	Floor Space Completed (10 000 sq.m)	1042.26	800.73	45.34	192.46	3.73
住宅	Residential Buildings	451.02	276.38	4.07	170.11	0.46
竣工房屋价值(万元)	Value of Buildings Completed (10 000 yuan)	891303	681891	71872	135740	1800
住宅	Residential Buildings	267680	152131	2468	112897	184
房屋建筑面积竣工率(%)	Rate of Floor Space of Buildings Completed (%)	40.78	41.41	40.28	38.66	30.95
住宅	Residential Buildings	41.90	44.72	60.03	38.25	6.73
竣工房屋单位面积造价(元/平方米)	Cost of Buildings Completed (yuan/sq.m)	855.16	851.59	1585.18	705.29	482.57
住宅	Residential Buildings	593.50	550.44	606.39	663.67	400.00

4-13 国有经济分地市项目个数、项目投产率及固定资产交付使用率(2003)

Number of Projects, Rate of Projects Put into Use and Rate of Fixed Assets Put into Use of State—owned Units (2003)

市州	Cities and Prefecture	施工项目个数(个) Number of Projects under Construction (unit)	全投项目个数(个) Number of Projects Completed and Put into Use (unit)	项目投产率(%) Rate of Projects Completed and Put into Use (%)	固定资产交付使用率(%) Rate of Fixed Assets Put into Use (%)
全省总计	**Total**	6039	3489	57.8	66.3
长沙市	Changsha	676	298	44.1	60.2
株洲市	Zhuzhou	410	252	61.5	75.3
湘潭市	Xiangtan	313	216	69.0	49.7
衡阳市	Hengyang	455	277	60.9	94.3
邵阳市	Shaoyang	662	464	70.1	60.5
岳阳市	Yueyang	704	503	71.4	66.9
常德市	Changde	488	309	63.3	97.3
张家界市	Zhangjiajie	171	101	59.1	62.9
益阳市	Yiyang	188	100	53.2	63.2
郴州市	Chenzhou	582	320	55.0	63.4
永州市	Yongzhou	398	183	46.0	41.0
怀化市	Huaihua	310	134	43.2	39.4
娄底市	Loudi	323	182	56.3	68.6
湘西自治州	West Hunan	325	133	40.9	52.5
不分地区	Not Classified by Region	34	17	50.0	82.7

注: 施工、全投项目及项目投产率未包括房地产开发统计资料。

The data of projects under construction, projects completed put into use and rate of projects completed put into use excluded information of real estate development.

4-14 国有经济基本建设投资

Investment in Capital Construction of State – owned Units

类别	Item	2000	2001	2002	2003
投资总额(亿元)	**Total Investment (100 million yuan)**	**376.40**	**433.90**	**478.34**	**480.54**
按资金来源分	**Grouped by Source of Funds**				
国家预算内投资	State Budgetary Appropriation	52.44	59.45	56.67	61.58
国内贷款	Domestic Loans	118.63	116.99	123.38	133.41
债券	Bonds	2.06	1.14	5.08	2.80
利用外资	Foreign Investment	12.42	17.76	17.63	16.05
自筹投资	Fundraising	147.32	198.06	233.01	219.24
其他投资	Others	43.53	40.50	42.57	47.47
按隶属关系分	**Grouped by Administrative Relationship**				
中央项目	Central Government Projects	142.03	122.78	97.90	43.60
地方项目	Local Projects	234.37	311.12	380.44	436.93
按构成分	**Grouped by Use of Funds**				
建筑安装工程	Construction and Installation	286.10	333.93	376.04	367.22
设备、工器具购置	Purchase of Equipment and Instruments	46.90	41.22	34.00	31.89
其他费用	Others	43.39	58.76	68.29	81.43
按建设性质分	**Grouped by Type of Construction**				
新建	New Construction	174.39	220.42	247.85	306.68
扩建	Expansion	93.58	128.97	146.16	95.36
改建	Reconstruction	81.21	58.58	61.28	61.75
按大中小类型分	**Grouped by Sized**				
大中型项目	Large and Medium Sized	54.79	17.05	34.24	31.37
小型项目	Small Sized	320.56	414.93	443.89	448.55
按行业主要门类分	**Grouped by Main Sector**				
农业	Agriculture	3.85	4.19	5.77	11.67
工业	Industry	83.49	73.83	82.77	72.66
轻工业	Light Industry	5.02	3.50	5.71	6.29
重工业	Heavy Industry	78.47	70.33	77.05	66.37
#能源工业	Energy Industry	74.90	66.71	73.85	59.14
运输邮电仓储业	Transportation,Postal, Telecommunications and Storage	150.90	158.33	136.82	164.87
新增固定资产（亿元）	**Newly Increased Fixed Assets (100 million yuan)**	**245.12**	**203.59**	**377.66**	**322.21**
建设项目个数（个）	**Number of Projects (unit)**				
施工项目	Number of Projects under Construction	4057	4043	3825	3789
大中型项目	Large and Medium Sized	29	19	17	25
全部建成投产项目	Number of Projects Completed and Put into Use	2380	2051	1992	1969
大中型项目	Large and Medium Sized	8	1		4
房屋建筑面积（万m²）	**Floor Space of Buildings (10 000 sq.m)**				
施工面积	Floor Space Under Construction	1898.50	1804.22	2045.35	1933.68
#住宅	Residential Buildings	861.52	705.90	788.96	617.99
竣工面积	Floor Space Completed	984.46	829.35	906.29	800.73
#住宅	Residential Buildings	510.31	413.44	379.17	276.38

4-15 国有经济基本建设项目计划总投资完成情况

Situation in Completion of Investment in Capital Construction of Projects of State-owned Units and Situation Completed

单位：亿元 (100 million yuan)

指　标	Item	2000	2001	2002	2003
基本建设项目	**Capital Construction Projects**				
计划总投资	Panning Gross Investment	1407.95	1578.83	1685.83	1722.87
累计完成投资	Accumulative Investment Actually Made	845.87	898.15	1146.65	1117.58
本年完成投资	Investment Made in This Year	376.4	433.9	478.34	480.54
本年新开工项目投资	Started Projects This Year	137.19	131.2	166.64	227.78
累计新增固定资产	Accumulative Newly Increased Fixed Assets	370.32	262.27	506.42	503.41
未完工程投资	Investment of Uncompleted Projects	434.43	546.73	563.43	589.21
全部建成尚需投资	Further Investment Required for the Completion of Construction	572.14	703.79	565.34	645.95
未完工程占用率 (%)	Rate of Investment in Projects Uncompleted (%)	115.42	126	117.79	122.61
建设周期（年）	Period to Complete Panning Gross Investment (year)	3.74	3.64	3.52	3.59
基本建设大中型项目	**Large and Medium Capital Construction Projects**				
计划总投资	Panning Gross Investment	344.3	187.14	206.38	205.14
累计完成投资	Accumulative Investment Actually Made	220.73	69.39	101.64	103.42
本年完成投资	Investment Made in This Year	54.79	17.05	34.24	31.37
本年新开工项目投资	Started projects This Year	2.43	2.09	2.4	6.01
累计新增固定资产	Accumulative Newly Increased Fixed Assets	101.86	12.22	37.36	52.16
未完工程投资	Investment of Uncompleted Projects	115.92	56.81	63.89	50.60
全部建成尚需投资	Further Investment Required for the Completion of Construction	123.23	121.23	108.41	104.04
未完工程占用率（%）	Rate of Investment in Projects Uncompleted (%)	211.57	333.2	186.59	161.30
建设周期（年）	Period to Complete Panning Gross Investment (year)	6.28	10.98	6.03	6.54

4-16 国有经济重点行业固定资产投资

Investment in Fixed Assets of State—Owned Units in Key Sector

项目	Item	2000	2001	2002	2003
投资额（亿元）	**Investment (100 million yuan)**				
农 业	Agriculture	4.42	4.50	6.38	13.82
轻工业	Light Industry	13.70	19.52	30.80	27.60
重工业	Heavy Industry	122.59	124.73	142.46	163.27
能源工业	Energy Industry	88.95	88.36	100.82	81.78
运输邮电仓储业	Transportation,Postal and Telecommunications, Storage	244.10	230.48	181.40	214.87
构成（%）	**Percentage (%)**				
农 业	Agriculture	0.8	0.7	1.0	2.0
轻工业	Light Industry	2.4	3.2	4.6	3.9
重工业	Heavy Industry	21.4	20.2	21.4	23.3
能源工业	Energy Industry	15.5	14.3	15.1	11.7
运输邮电仓储业	Transportation,Postal and Telecommunications Storage	42.5	37.3	27.2	30.6
基本建设投资额(亿元)	**Investment in Capital Construction (100 million yuan)**				
农 业	Agriculture	3.85	4.19	5.77	11.67
轻工业	Light Industry	5.02	3.50	5.71	6.29
重工业	Heavy Industry	78.47	70.33	77.05	66.37
能源工业	Energy Industry	74.90	66.71	73.85	59.14
运输邮电仓储业	Transportation,Postal and Telecommunications Storage	150:90	158.33	136.82	164.87
构成（%）	**Percentage (%)**				
农 业	Agriculture	1.0	1.0	1.2	2.4
轻工业	Light Industry	1.3	0.8	1.2	1.3
重工业	Heavy Industry	20.8	16.2	16.1	13.8
能源工业	Energy Industry	19.9	15.4	15.4	12.3
运输邮电仓储业	Transportation,Postal and Telecommunications Storage	40.1	36.5	28.6	34.3

4-17 基本建设新增生产能力(2003年)

Newly Increased Production Capacity in Capital Construction (2003)

生产能力(或效益)名称	Item	合计 Total	国有经济 State-owned Economic	其他经济 Other Types of Ownership
原煤开采(万吨/年)	Loal Mining (10000 tons/year)	6		6
铁矿石原矿开采(万吨/年)	Iron Ore Mining(10000 tons/year)	4.5		4.5
铁矿选矿处理量(万吨/年)	Selection of Iron Ore(10000 tons/year)	1.7		1.7
人造富铁矿(万吨/年)	Man-made Ferrous Ore(10000 tons/year)	64	64	
其中:烧结铁矿(万吨/年)	Scorch Iron Ore(10000 tons/year)	56	56	
炼铁(万吨/年)	Iron-making(10000 tons/year)	2	1	1
连铸(万吨/年)	Casting(10000 tons/year)	1.2		1.2
铅锌采矿(原矿)(万吨/年)	Lead&Zinc Mining(10000 tons/year)	12		12
铅锌选矿:处理原矿(万吨/年)	Selection of Lead&Zinc(10000 tons/year)	15		15
铅含量(吨/年)	Lead Content(ton/year)	2400		2400
锌含量(吨/年)	Zinc Content(ton/year)	1900		1900
铅冶炼(吨/年)	Lead-making(ton/year)	260		260
锡含量(吨/年)	Tin Content(ton/year)	12		12
电解铝(吨/年)	Electronlyted Al(ton/year)	50000		50000
工业锅炉(蒸吨)	Industrial Boiler(ton)	100		100
水力发电(万千瓦)	Hydropower (10000kw)	7.4	3.31	4.09
火力发电(万千瓦)	Thermal (10000kw)	90	30	60
输电线路长度(11万伏及以上)(公里)	Transmission Line (>110000 v) (km)	3709.2	3709.2	
变电设备能力(11万伏及以上)(万千伏安)	Electric Substation Equipment (>110000 v) (10000 kva)	319.8	319.8	
人造板装饰加工板(万立方米/年)	Man-made Decoration Boards(10000 m3/year)	2	2	
塑料树脂及共聚物(吨/年)	Plastics(ton/year)	10		10
医药中间体(吨/年)	Medium Medicine(ton/year)	26		26
电力电缆(公里)	Electric Power Cables(km)	0.4		0.4
化学纤维(吨/年)	Chemical Fiber (ton/year)	120		120
食用植物油(日处理原料:吨)	Edible Vegetable Oil(handle in a day:ton)	5		5
(日精炼油:吨)	(purify in a day:ton)	4.5		4.5
肉加工品(吨/年)	Meat Products(ton/year)	10	10	
罐头(万吨/年)	Canned Food(10000 tons/year)	8		8
其他乳制品(吨/年)	Dairy Products(ton/year)	25550		25550
软饮料(吨/年)	Soft Drinks(ton/year)	7800		7800
其中:瓶装(或罐装)饮用水(吨/年)	Drinking Water by bottle(or tin)	7800		7800
机制纸(万吨/年)	Machine-made Paper (10000 tons/year)	2		2
机制纸板(万吨/年)	Machine-made Paper Boards(10000 tons/year)	1		1
塑料制品(万吨/年)	Plastics Products(10000 tons/year)	2		2
日用陶瓷器(万件/年)	Daily-use Ceramics(10000 pcs/year)	4000		4000
日用玻璃制品(万吨/年)	Household Glass Products(10000 tons/year)	10		10
移动通信基站设备(信道/年)	Basic Station of Mobile Telephone(unit/year)	10		10
程控交换机(万线/年)	Autoexchage of Telephone Capacity(10000 lines/year)	1	1	

4-17 续表 continued

生产能力(或效益)名称	Item	合计 Total	国有经济 State-owned Economic	其他经济 Other Types of Ownership
新建公路(公里)	Length of New Highways (km)	857.67	851.42	6.25
其中:高速公路(公里)	Expressway	203.3	203.3	
一级公路(公里)	First-class Highway	40.89	40.89	
二级公路(公里)	Second-class Highway	185.04	185.04	
改建公路(公里)	Length of Reconstructed Highways (km)	704.78	704.78	
一级公路(公里)	First-class Highway	135.64	135.64	
二级公路(公里)	Second-class Highway	270.57	270.57	
新建独立公路桥梁(延长米)	Newly Build Highway Bridge (extend metre)	2025	2025	
(座)	(set)	5	5	
新(扩)建客、货运站(个)	Newly Build or Expanded Passenger and Freight Station	3	1	2
(平方米)	(sq.m)	22260	460	21800
长途电缆(延长公里)	Long Distance Cables(km)	20	5	15
新建微波电路(公里)	New Microwave Lines(km)	2	2	
商品蛋鸡场(万公斤蛋/年)	Commodity egg Farm(10000 kg/year)	0.5	0.5	
耕地面积(万亩)	Cultivated Land Area (10000 mu)	0.2	0.2	
造林面积(万亩)	Afforested Area (10000 mu)	5.8	5.8	
水库容量(总库容)(亿立方米)	Reservoir Capacity (100 million m3)	1.74	1.74	
有效灌溉面积(万亩)	Effective Irrigated Area (10000 mu)	76.48	76.48	
除涝面积(万亩)	Flooded or Water Logged Area Under Control (10000 mu)	0.2	0.2	
商业石油库(万立方米)	Commercial Oil Depot(10000 m3)	0.09	0.09	
粮食仓库(万公斤)	Grain Storehouse (10000 kg)	4700	4700	
(平方米)	(sq.m)	10720	10720	
高等院校:学生席位(个)	Number of Student seat of Universit and College	31050	31050	
建筑面积(平方米)	(sq.m)	95395	95395	
中等学校:学生席位(个)	Number of Student seat of Regular Secondary School	105448	103228	2220
建筑面积(平方米)	(sq.m)	463181	442224	20957
小学校:学生席位(个)	Number of Student seat of Primary School	52615	51415	1200
建筑面积(平方米)	(sq.m)	128438	121838	6600
其他院校:学生席位(个)	Number of Student seat of Other School	3260	3260	
建筑面积(平方米)	(sq.m)	14386	14386	
文化馆(平方米)	Cultural Centre(sq.m)	600	600	
医院病床(张)	Number of Hospital Bed	3639	3639	
疗养院、所病床(张)	Number of Sanatorium Bed(unit)	480	480	
宾馆、旅馆、招待所客房数(间)	Number of Hotel Guest-Room (unit)	114	54	60
(平方米)	(sq.m)	17790	6790	11000
城市自来水供水能力(万吨/日)	Capacity of City Tap Water Supply (10000 tons/day)	8.5	8.5	
城市自来水管道长度(公里)	Length of City Tap Water Pipe (km)	69.2	69.2	
城市公共交通车辆购置(辆)	Purchase of City Bus (unit)	95	95	
城市道路扩建长度(公里)	Length of City Road Extended (km)	180.12	178.92	1.2
城市道路扩建面积(万平方米)	Area of City Road Extended (10000 sq.m)	395.07	393.46	1.61
城市排水管道铺设长度(公里)	Length of Sewer Pipelines (km)	23.68	23.68	
城市永久性桥梁(座)	Number of City Bridge (unit)	3	3	
城市防洪堤长度(公里)	Length of City Embarkment (km)	52.53	52.53	

4-18 更新改造新增生产能力(2003年)

Newly Increased Production Capacity in Innovation (2003)

生产能力(或效益)名称	Item	合计 Total	国有经济 State-owned Economic	其他经济 Other Types of Ownership
原煤开采(万吨/年)	Loal Mining (10000 tons/year)	41.4	22	19.4
焦炭(万吨/年)	Coke(10000 tons/year)	60	60	
油罐容量(万立方米)	Capacity of Oil Pot(10000 m3/year)	0.01	0	0.01
人造富铁矿(万吨/年)	Man-made Ferrous Ore (10000 tons/year)	197	197	
其中:烧结铁矿(万吨/年)	Scorch Iron Ore(10000 tons/year)	197	197	
炼铁(万吨/年)	Iron-making(10000 tons/year)	270	270	
炼钢(万吨/年)	Steel-making(10000 tons/year)	100	100	
初轧(万吨/年)	Steel Rolling(10000 tons/year)	4		4
铁合金(万吨/年)	Iron Alloy(10000 tons/year)	1		1
粗铜(吨/年)	Copper(ton/year)	1		1
钢丝(万吨/年)	Steel Wire(10000 tons/year)	0.3	0.3	
铜加工(吨/年)	Copper-making(ton/year)	2000	2000	
铜管材(吨/年)	Copper Products(ton/year)	2000	2000	
铅锌采矿(原矿)(万吨/年)	Lead&Zinc Mining(10000 tons/year)	6	6	
铅锌选矿:(1)处理原矿(万吨/年)	Selection of Lead&Zinc(10000 tons/year)	17.6	6	11.6
(2)铅含量(吨/年)	Lead Content(ton/year)	1000		1000
(3)锌含量(吨/年)	Zinc Content(ton/year)	400		400
铅冶炼(吨/年)	Lead-making(ton/year)	560		560
锌冶炼(吨/年)	Zinc-making(ton/year)	20319		20319
其中:电解锌(吨/年)	Electronlyted Zn(ton/year)	20000		20000
锡采矿(原矿)(万吨/年)	Tin Mining(10000 tons/year)	5	5	0
锡选矿:(1)处理原矿(万吨/年)	Selection of Tin(10000 tons/year)	455	5	450
(2)锡含量(吨/年)	Tin Content(ton/year)	2500		2500
电解铝(吨/年)	Electronlyted Al(ton/year)	11000		11000
铝加工(吨/年)	Al-making(ton/year)	37500		37500
铝型材(吨/年)	Al Products(ton/year)	37500		37500
金采矿(原矿)(万吨/年)	Gold Mining(10000 tons/year)	700	500	200
金选矿:(1)处理原矿(吨/年)	Selection of Gold(ton/year)	600	500	100
(2)金含量(公斤/年)	Gold Content(kg/year)	530	480	50
黄金(公斤/年)	Gold(kg/year)	185	160	25
矿山成品金(公斤/年)	End Products of Gold in Mine(kg/year)	185	160	25
银选矿:(1)处理原矿(吨/年)	Selection of Silver(ton/year)	1		1
(2)银含量(公斤/年)	Silver Content(kg/year)	300		300
原料云母(吨/年)	Mica(ton/year)	1500		1500
水力发电(万千瓦)	Hydropower (10000kw)	3.61	0.31	3.3
变电设备能力(11万伏及以上)(万千伏安)	Electric Substation Equipment(>110000 v)(10000 kva)	11	11	0
水　泥(万吨/年)	Cement (10000 tons/year)	134.92	0.52	134.4
釉面砖(万平方米)	Glazed Bricks(10000 sq.m)	1	1	0
墙地砖(万平方米)	Wall Bricks(10000 sq.m)	90		90
耐火材料制品(吨/年)	Fire-resistant Material Products(ton/year)	3000	3000	0
胶合板(万立方米/年)	Deadlocked Boards(10000 m3/year)	6.8		6.8
纤维板(万立方米/年)	Fibre Boards(10000 m3/year)	8.3		8.3
家具(万件/年)	Furnitures(10000 units/year)	6.33	1.13	5.2
硫　酸(吨/年)	Sulfuric Acid (ton/year)	62000		62000
合成氨(吨/年)	Synthetic Ammonia (ton/year)	3500		3500
氮肥(吨/年)	Nitrogen Fertilizer (ton/year)	330500		330500
磷肥(吨/年)	Phosphate Fertilizer (ton/year)	150000		150000
钾肥(吨/年)	Potash Fertilizer (ton/year)	2000		2000
精甲醇(吨/年)	Carbinol(ton/year)	5650	2650	3000
油 漆(吨/年)	Paint(ton/year)	10000	10000	0
塑料树脂及共聚物(吨/年)	Plastics(ton/year)	2500		2500

生产能力(或效益)名称	Item	合计 Total	国有经济 State-owned Economic	其他经济 Other Types of Ownership
松香(吨/年)	Rosin(ton/year)	20000		20000
化学原料药(吨/年)	Chemical Medicine (ton/year)	200		200
化学药制剂：粉针剂(万瓶/年)	Powdery Injection(10000 units/year)	1500		1500
注射液(万支/年)	Injection Liquid(10000 units/year)	5000		5000
片剂(万片/年)	Tablets(10000 units/year)	180000		180000
输液(万瓶/年)	Infusion(10000 units/year)	2000		2000
胶囊剂(万粒/年)	Capsule(10000 units/year)	40000		40000
医药中间体(吨/年)	Medium Medicine(ton/year)	30		30
中成药(吨/年)	Chinese Herbal Medicine(ton/year)	1020.3	1000	20.3
电力电缆(公里)	Electric Power Cables(km)	4600	0	4600
柴油机制造(台/年)	Diesel Engine Manufacture(unit/year)	20000	20000	0
(万千瓦/年)	(10000kw/year)	1200	1200	0
泵(台/年)	Pump(unit/year)	315200	1000	314200
风机(台/年)	Fan(unit/year)	10000	0	10000
建筑机械制造(台/年)	Architecture Machinery Manufacture(unit/year)	1000	0	1000
其它汽车制造(辆/年)	Others Vehicle Manufacture(unit/year)	250	250	0
化学纤维(吨/年)	Chemical Fiber (ton/year)	2000		2000
其中:合成纤维(吨/年)	Synthetic Fiber(ton/year)	2000		2000
棉纺锭(锭)	Cotton Spindles (unit)	40350		40350
棉印染(万米/年)	Printing and Dyeing of Cotton(10000 m/year)	1702		1702
毛纺锭(锭)	Woolen Spindles(unit)	15000		15000
食用植物油(日处理原料:吨)	Edible Vegetable Oil(handle in a day:ton)	25.55		25.55
(日精炼油:吨)	(purify in a day:ton)	23		23
罐头(万吨/年)	Canned Food(10000 tons/year)	91.26		91.26
饼　干(吨/年)	Biscuit(ton/year)	23		23
白　酒(万吨/年)	Wine (10000 tons/year)	0.1		0.1
冷冻饮品(吨/年)	Freezing Drink(ton/year)	1200		1200
方便主食品(吨/年)	Instant Food(ton/year)	2400		2400
机制纸浆(万吨/年)	Machine -made Paper Pulp(10000 tons/year)	2		2
机制纸(万吨/年)	Machine -made Paper (10000 tons/year)	1.25	0.01	1.24
合成洗涤剂(万吨/年)	Synthetic Detergents(10000 tons/year)	1.5		1.5
轻革(万平方米/年)	Leather(10000 sq.m/year)	1.06		1.06
皮　鞋(万双/年)	Leather Shoes(10000 pairs/year)	11.2		11.2
服　装(万件/年)	Clothes(10000 pcs/year)	3.6		3.6
塑料制品(万吨/年)	Plastics Products(10000 tons/year)	0.5		0.5
日用陶瓷器(万件/年)	Daily -use Ceramics (10000 pcs/year)	1000		1000
灯泡(万只/年)	Light Bulb(10000 units/year)	1800	1800	
灯管(万只/年)	Light Pipe(10000 units/year)	720	720	
家用空气调节器(万台/年)	Air Conditioners(10000 units/year)	1.2		1.2
移动通信基站设备(信道/年)	Basic Station of Mobile Telephone(unit/year)	71	71	
程控交换机(万线/年)	Autoexchage of Telephone Capacity(10000 lines/year)	22.62	22.62	
改建公路(公里)	Length of Reconstructed Highways (km)	463.28	463.28	
二级公路(公里)	Second-class Highway(km)	5.08	5.08	
长途电缆(延长公里)	Long Distance Cable(km)	20	20	
新建微波电路(公里)	New Microwave Lines(km)	10	10	
造林面积(万亩)	Afforested Area (10000 mu)	4.85	4.85	
医院病床(张)	Number of Hospital Bed(unit)	200	200	
宾馆、旅馆、招待所客房数(间)	Number of Hotel Guest-Room	50		50
(平方米)	(sq.m)	2150		2150
城市自来水供水能力(万吨/日)	Capacity of City Tap Water Supply (10000 tons/day)	9	9	
城市自来水管道长度(公里)	Length of City Tap Water Pipe (km)	56.5	56.5	
城市公共交通车辆购置(辆)	Purchase of City Bus (unit)	180	100	80
城市道路扩建长度(公里)	Length of City Road Extended (km)	10.51	10.51	
城市道路扩建面积(万平方米)	Area of City Road Extended (10000 sq.m)	154.7	154.7	
城市防洪堤长度(公里)	Length of City Embarkment (km)	1.98	1.98	

4-19 基本建设大中型、更新改造限额以上及重点项目基本情况(2003年)

项 目 名 称	Item
基本建设大中型项目:	**Capital Construction of Large and Medium Projects:**
湖南旺旺医院	Hunan Wangwang Hospital
长沙市红星国际物流中心	Changsha Hongxing International Centre of Interflow of Goods and Materials
长沙丰升置业有限公司国际汽车城	International Vehicle Centre of Changsha Fengsheng Limited Liability Corp.
湖南HEG电子玻璃有限公司	Hunan HEG Electron Glass Limited Liability Corp.
湖南出版基地建设工程	Construction Projrct of Hunan Publishing Base
株洲天元体育产业体育中心	Zhuzhou Tianyuan Sports Centre
湘潭市自来水公司一水厂搬迁	NO.1 Factory Removal Project of Xiangtan Tap Water Corporation
湖南五凌水电开发有限责任公司近尾洲水电站	Jinweizhou Hydropower Station of Hunan Wuling Hydropower Development Limited Liability Corp.
耒阳电厂二期	Second Phrase of Leiyang Electric Power Corp.
湖南巫水流域水利水电开发有限责任公司白云电站	Baiyun Hydropower Station of Hunan Wushui Hydropower and Conservancy Limited Liabity Corporation
邵阳市大圳灌区工程	Irrigation Project of Dazhen Irrigation District in Shaoyang City
湘阴县湘江大桥	Xiang River Bridge in Xiangyin County
湘阴县临资口大桥	Linzikou Bridge in Xiangyin County
常德市穿紫河综合治理一期工程	First Phrase of Chuanzi River Comprehensive Treatment
常德市自来水公司第四水厂建设	No. 4 Factory Construction of Changde Tap Water Corporation
常德桥南汽车中心站	Bus Centre Station in Qiaonan of Changde City
常德创元铝业有限公司	Chuangyuan Aluminum Corp. in Changde
湖南省澧水公司皂市水库水利枢纽工程	Conservancy Project of Zaoshi Reservoir
湖南省石门电厂二期工程	Second phrase of Shimen Electric Power Corp.
慈利县茶林河水电站	Chalin River Hydropower Station in Cili County
江垭水库	Jiangya Reservoir
益阳市资阳区自来水厂	Ziyang District Tap Water Corp. in Yiyang City
益阳市茅草街大桥	Yiyang Maocao Street Bridge
桃江县资江大桥	Taojiang Zi River Bridge
宜章县康达水泥厂	Kangda Cement Factory in Yizhang
郴州鲤鱼江电厂	Liyu River Electric Power Corp.in Chenzhou County
资兴市程江口电站	Chengjiangkou Hydropower Station in Zixing City
潇湘水电站	Xiaoxiang Hydropower Station
怀化市第二人民医院	The No.2 People Hospital in Huaihua County
怀化市芷江机场改建	Zijiang Airfield Repair Project in Huaihua County
☆洪江水电站	Hongjiang Hydropower Station
湖南华达机械总厂整体脱险搬迁二期工程	Second Phrase of Hunan Huada Mechanical Factory Removal for Safety
保靖碗米坡电站	Baojing Wangmipo Hydropower Station
永顺县高家坝防洪水库工程	Control Flood Project of Yongshun Gaojia Dam
湖南常鲇航运建设工程	Construction Projrct of Shipping of Hunan Changzhan
株洲航电枢纽建设工程	Pivotal Construction Projrct of Zhuzhou Hangdian
更新改造限额以上项目	**Above Normal Innovation Projects**
中汽长电汽车电机	Vehicle Generator of Changsha

Basic Statistics on Investment in Capital Construction of Large and Medium Projects,and Technical Updating and Innovation in Above - norm (2003)

开工时间 (年·月) Starting Date (y .m)	投产时间 (年·月) The Date for Put into Use (y .m)	计划总投资 (万元) Total Investment Planned (10 000 yuan)	累计完成投资 (万元) Accumulative Investment Acually Made (10 000 yuan)	本年完成投资 (万元) Investment Made this Year (10 000 yuan)
		46000	8625	8625
200305		28000	16484	16484
200303		320000	21000	21000
200304		136950	10613	10613
200206		28100	22054	22054
200309		49000	4277	4277
199903		11014	11108	1508
199410	200304	75967	75067	7077
200106	0	239885	188568	95382
199001	200312	43000	43000	315
196510		12300	12476	566
200010	200309	16846	19888	4138
200306		18500	2802	2802
200303		28886	1000	1000
199812	200312	17025	17025	125
200310		22000	800	800
200110		110000	90000	70000
		310978	25484	9817
200310		248523	27341	27341
200305		36000	6083	6083
199208	200301	331372	318637	5
		13000	400	400
200011		37630	22246	9256
200304		6188	937	937
200110		72000	33691	17922
200111	200309	253780	250254	98623
200112		20000	9516	5428
199310		61952	54847	980
200307		15000	950	950
200301		16200	7300	7300
199801		199500	173562	37440
198512		11176	13006	145
200008		201478	133245	55630
200205		22685	2030	1350
200112		29964	13776	5409
200208		194694	62522	41200
200306		12307	1676	1676

项目名称	Item
株洲硬质合金厂钨钼异型大制品深加工工程	Tungsten and Molybdenum Product Finishing Project of Zhuzhou Rigid Alloy Factory
株洲硬质合金厂高性能精密可转位刀片及刀具配套生产线	Blade and Cutter Matching Manufacture Line of Zhuzhou Rigid Alloy Factory
中国南方航空动力机械公司WS11航空技改项目	WS11 Air Technical Revolution Project of China South Air Power Machine Company
中国南方航空动力机械公司WZ9航空技改项目	WZ9 Air Technical Revolution Project of China South Air Power Machine Company
株洲电厂二期工程技改	Second Phrase of Zhuzhou Power Station Technical Revolution Project
株洲电力机车厂地铁项目	Local Railway Project of Zhuzhou Electric Vehicle Factory
株洲冶炼厂铅烧结烟气综合治理	Fume Control Project of Zhuzhou Smelting Work
湘潭电机厂城轨项目	City Track Project of Xiangtang Electric Machine Factory
湘潭电机厂城轨项目二期	Second City Track Project of Xiangtang Electric Machine Factory
湖南金迪化纤50000吨/年直纺涤纶短纤维项目	50000 tons Annual Polyester Short Fibre Project of Hunan Jindi Chemical Fibre Factory
湖南韶峰水泥集团二号窑技改工程	Technical Innavation Project of No.2 Kiln of Hunan Shaofeng Cement Group
湖南铁合金厂有毒铬渣处理工程	Harmful Chromium Waste Disposal Project of Hunan Iron Alloy Factory
衡阳有色冶金机械总厂卷取机生产线	Manufacture Line of Hengyang Nonferrous Metals Smelting and Pressing Machine Factory
衡阳华菱钢管Φ100无缝钢管机组技术改造	Φ100 Seamless Steel Tube Technological Transformation of Hengyang Steel Tube Factory
水口山有色金属有限责任公司铅冶炼烟气治理工程	Fume Control Project of Lead Smelting of Shuikoushan Nonferrous Metals Limited Liability Company
岳阳纸业集团子公司综合技术改造	Comprehensive Technological Transformation of Yueyang Paper Limiited Group Corp.
岳阳巴陵公司煤代油工程	Coal Instead of Oil Project of Yueyang Baling Corp.
岳阳纸业年产12万吨系列胶印书刊纸工程	120 Tousand Tons Newsprint Paper Project of Yueyang Paper Limited Group Corporation
岳阳市鸿仪实业有限公司技术改造	Technological Transformation of Yueyang Hongyi Limited Corp.
湖南科伦制药有限公司技改	Technological Transformation of Hunan Kelun Medicine Limited Corp.
岳阳大陆激光科技有限公司激光设备购置与技术引进	Laser Equipment Purchase of Yueyang Dalu Laser Hi-tech Limited Corp.
岳阳高新区景达生物科技开发有限公司	Jingda Biological Hi-tech Develop Limited Corp. in Yueyang
张家界铝业有限公司3万吨电解铝改造二期工程	Transformation Project of 30000 tons Electrolyted Al in Zhangjiajie Al- Products Limited Corp.
怀化市恒裕实业汽车销售改装维修	Hengyu Vehicle Sale and Reform and Maintain Corp.
湖南怀化莱孚铝业电解铝锭生产	Hunan Huaihua Laifu Al-products Corp.
湖南凤滩水电厂扩机工程	Reconstruction Project of Hunan Fengtai Hydropower Factory
涟源钢铁集团有限公司二号焦炉易地改造	No.2 Furnace Repair Project of Lianyuan Steel Limited Group Corp.
湖南华菱涟钢薄板有限公司	Liangyuan Steel Limited Liability Conmpany of Hunan Hualing
涟源钢铁集团有限公司300立方米高炉大修改造工程	Overhaul and Innovation Project of 300 Cubic Meter High Furnace of Liangyuan Steel Limited Group Corporation
涟源钢铁集团有限公司三号转炉工程	No.3 Steel Converter Project of Liangyuan Steel Limited Group Corp.
涟源钢铁集团有限公司原料厂大修改造工程	Overhaul and Innovation Project of Materials Room of Liangyuan Steel Limited Group Corporation
涟源钢铁集团有限公司2×40平方米烧结机易地大修改造工程	Overhaul and Innovation Project Exchange Space of 2×40 Square Meter Sinter Machine of Liangyuan Steel Limited Group Corporation
涟源钢铁集团有限公司铁路运输系统改造	Reform of Railway Transport System of Lianyuan Steel Limited Group Corporation
双峰海螺新型干法水泥	New Technical Innavation of Shuangfeng Hailuo Cement Corp.
湖南金信化工填平补齐工程	Fill Project of Hunan Jinxin Chemistry Factory
重点项目	**Main Projects**
“五城会”体育场馆	Stadiums and Gymnasiums of Fifth City Sports Meetting
长沙市二环线道路工程	Changsha the Second Loop Line Project
株洲市城市快速环道一期工程	First Phrase of Zhuzhou City Quick Loop Line Project
衡大高速公路	Expressway from Hengyang to Dapu
永州市永连公路指挥部	Yongzhou Highway Commanding Department
潭邵高速公路	Expressway from Xiangtang to Shaoyang
衡枣高速公路	Expressway from Hengyang to Zaomupu
常张高速公路	Expressway from Changde to Zhangjiajie
湖南主电网建设	Construction Project of Hunan Main Electrified Wire Netting

continued

开工时间 (年·月) Starting Date (y .m)	投产时间 (年·月) The Date for Put into Use (y .m)	计划总投资 (万元) Total Investment Planned (10 000 yuan)	累计完成投资 (万元) Accumulative Investment Acually Made (10 000 yuan)	本年完成投资 (万元) Investment Made this Year (10 000 yuan)
200010	200312	5000	4500	447
200012	200312	21000	20358	2552
200101		14700	13248	1542
200108		28100	26684	4806
200106		226426	187435	77245
200205		28983	15692	7192
200009	200308	15396	15396	377
200001		5006	5006	1242
200106		5377	5362	4611
200310		18696	738	738
200212		47076	332	10
199912		8380	3720	1510
200011		5669	1170	80
200310		130200	10009	10009
200304		31722	5487	4294
200209		33576	20390	10662
200301		113379	9320	2520
200001	200312	145100	145100	49852
200302		5300	4280	4280
200305		12000	10800	10800
200207	200304	3000	3000	2000
200301		7160	3000	3000
200101		23769	8880	3200
200306		8500	3097	3097
199608		23500	23497	50
200201		83396	45044	30125
200102	200307	39500	39500	7285
200203		554500	235245	167245
200206	200312	100000	100000	73431
200210	200312	13500	13500	11752
200210	200311	11000	11000	10305
200210	200312	20000	20000	19262
200302	200311	11500	11500	11500
200305		80000	25000	25000
199801		12977	11950	2
200105		296100	207213	57113
199412		414318	355522	26858
199902		185357	86956	23784
200306		94591	27096	27096
199805		106000	92135	9321
200007		609957	597957	54203
200012	200312	512563	496278	172367
200301		687368	212696	183092
200101		502673	423286	135635

4-20 城镇集体各行业项目个数、投资额及新增固定资产(2003年)

Number of Projects, Investment and Newly Increased Fixed Assets of Urban Collective – owned Units by Sector (2003)

指标	Item	施工项目个数(个) Number of Projects under Construction (unit)	全投项目个数(个) Number of Projects Completed and Put into Use (unit)	固定资产投资(万元) Investment in Fixed Assets (10 000 yuan)	新增固定资产(万元) Newly Increased Fixed Assets (10 000 yuan)
总计	**Total**	**118**	**61**	**247639**	**132685**
农、林、牧、渔业	Agriculture,Forestry,Farming of Animals and Fishing	4	1	2160	490
采矿业	Mining	5	2	2268	1314
制造业	Manufacturing	42	27	37892	24803
农副食品加工业	Processing of Food from Agricultural Products	1		380	
食品制造业	Manufacture of Foods	4	2	2490	2190
纺织业	Manufacture of Textile	2	2	3357	3550
皮革毛皮羽毛(绒)及其制品业	Manufacture of Leather,Fur,Feather and Its Products	1	1	170	650
木材加工及木、竹、藤、棕、草制品业	Processing of Timbers,Manufacture of Wood,Bamboo, Rattan,Palm and Straw Products	1	1	400	400
印刷业和记录媒介的复制	Printing,Reproduction of Recording Media	3		800	
化学原料及化学制品制造业	Manufacture of Chemical Raw Material and Chemical	4	2	5405	5480
医药制造业	Manufacture of Medicines	2	2	420	420
化学纤维制造业	Manufacture of Chemical Fiber	1	1	900	900
非金属矿物制品业	Manufacture of Non-metallic Mineral Products	5	3	3548	1848
黑色金属冶炼及压延加工业	Manufacture and Processing of Ferrous Metals	1	1	1530	1530
有色金属冶炼及压延加工业	Manufacture and Processing of Non-ferrous Metals	1	1	500	500
金属制品业	Manufacture of Metal Products	3	2	4740	1940
通用设备制造业	Manufacture of General Purpose Machinery	4	3	6230	1370
专用设备制造业	Manufacture of Special Purpose Machinery	1		2227	
交通运输设备制造业	Manufacture of Transport Equipment	2	1	1100	500
电气机械及器材制造业	Manufacture of Electrical Machinery and Equipment	4	4	2545	2545
通信设备、计算机及其他电子设备制造业	Manufacture of Communication Equipment, Computer and Other Electronic Equipment	1		170	
废弃资源和废旧材料回收加工	Recycling and Disposal of Waste	1	1	980	980
电力、燃气及水的生产和供应业	Production and Supply of Electricity,Gas and Water	24	7	23792	5360
建筑业	Construction	3	1	3350	1100
交通运输、仓储和邮政业	Traffic,Transport, Storage and Post	4	1	23790	25684
批发和零售业	Wholesale and Retail Trade	7	4	8376	3770
住宿和餐饮业	Accommodation and Restaurants	3	2	11766	3550
金融业	Finance	1		201	
房地产业	Real Estate Trade	1	1	118892	51620
租赁和商务服务业	Tenancy and Business Services	6	6	1970	2850
科学研究、技术服务和地质勘查	Scientific Research,Technical Service and Geologic Perambulation	1	1	700	1200
水利、环境和公共设施管理业	Management of Water Conservancy,Environment and Public Establishment	9	3	2052	1384
居民服务和其他服务业	Resident Services and Other Services	1		960	460
教育	Education	2	1	170	700
卫生、社会保障和社会福利业	Sanitation,Social Security and Social Welfare	1	1	400	400
文化、体育和娱乐业	Culture,Sports and Entertainment	1		900	
公共管理和社会组织	Public Management and Social Organization	3	3	8000	8000

注:施工、全投项目个数中未含房地产开发项目。

Data on real estate development were not included in the data on construction and fully constructed projects.

4-21 房地产开发情况(2003年)

Real Estate Development (2003)

市州	Cities and Prefecture	开发公司个数(个) Number of Development Enterprises (unit)	国有经济 State-owned Enterprises	集体经济 Collective-owned Enterprises	外商投资经济 Foreign Funded Enterprises	港澳台投资经济 Funded by Entrepreneurs from Hong Kong, Macao and Taiwan	年末从业人员数(人)	房地产开发投资(万元) Investment (10 000 yuan)
全省总计	**Total**	**1157**	**196**	**89**	**31**	**88**	**41700**	**2300324**
长沙市	Changsha	285	51	15	6	28	8895	1108269
株洲市	Zhuzhou	103	14	9	4	2	3220	199636
湘潭市	Xiangtan	61	13	6	1	6	2615	118651
衡阳市	Hengyang	112	19	17	6	7	4275	115094
邵阳市	Shaoyang	45	9	5	1	1	1375	47027
岳阳市	Yueyang	84	18	5		6	1710	118558
常德市	Changde	120	14	6	1	8	3250	146735
张家界市	Zhangjiajie	37	5	2		2	499	41894
益阳市	Yiyang	72	6	9	2	2	2573	64050
郴州市	Chenzhou	85	8	5	6	10	5491	156017
永州市	Yongzhou	29	10		1	3	818	25405
怀化市	Huaihua	37	11	3			3358	73828
娄底市	Loudi	46	7	5	2	12	2269	40099
湘　西	West Hunan	41	11	2	1	1	1352	45061

市州	Cities and Prefecture	经营总收入(万元) Total Revenue (10 000 yuan)	土地转让收入 Land Transferred	商品房屋销售收入 Commercial Houses Sold	房屋出租收入 Houses Leased	其他收入 Others	税金及附加(万元) Taxes and Extra Charges (10 000 yuan)	利润总额(万元) Total Profits (10 000 yuan)
全省总计	**Total**	**1330404**	**105646**	**1159731**	**11273**	**53754**	**71762**	**-1266**
长沙市	Changsha	656538	60651	578781	5717	11389	35932	
株洲市	Zhuzhou	123205	4707	115946	246	2306	6953	
湘潭市	Xiangtan	87105	2839	82240	102	1924	3933	
衡阳市	Hengyang	62890	4824	54079	2143	1844	3172	
邵阳市	Shaoyang	33901	3103	30548	19	231	1669	
岳阳市	Yueyang	75878	15774	35433	610	24061	3244	
常德市	Changde	123143	3735	114778	615	4015	6926	
张家界市	Zhangjiajie	14614	897	13392	69	256	1215	
益阳市	Yiyang	14698	1050	12893	459	296	985	
郴州市	Chenzhou	71545	1000	67183	1126	2236	4699	
永州市	Yongzhou	8676	1618	6378	61	619	240	
怀化市	Huaihua	26769	1195	22058		3516	1467	
娄底市	Loudi	17549	2882	14361	25	281	781	-1266
湘　西	West Hunan	13893	1371	11661	81	780	546	

4-22 房地产开发统计主要指标(2003年)

Major Statistics Indicators of Real Estate Development (2003)

单位:万元 (10 000 yuan)

指标	Item	合计 Total	国有 State-owned	集体 Colective-owned	其他 Other Types of Ownership
计划总投资	**Panning Gross Investment**	**7902119**	**1617336**	**379726**	**5905057**
实际需要的总投资	Gross Investment in Actual Need	8044224	1627024	393359	6023841
累计完成投资	Accumulative Investment Completed	4362650	653018	216575	3493057
累计新增固定资产	Accumulative Newly Increased Fixed Assets	1982903	263499	84106	1635298
本年底未完工程累计投资	Accumulative Investment of Projects Uncompleted	2165035	360899	123866	1680270
本年计划投资	Planning Investment in the year	2987263	479874	172335	2335054
本年完成投资	Investment Made in This Year	2300324	375691	118402	1806231
按构成分:	Group by Form:				
建筑工程	Construction	1502998	235343	84880	1182775
安装工程	Installation	77240	13640	1967	61633
设备、工具器具购置	Purchase of Equipment,Tools,Apparatus	33185	6837	1510	24838
按工程用途分:	Group by use of Projects				
住宅	Residential Buildings	1457959	259556	70435	1127968
办公楼	Business Buildings	73970	13107	9688	51175
商业营业用房	Commercial Buildings	479640	25920	26465	427255
其他	Others	288755	77108	11814	199833
房地产开发企业本年资金来源	Group by Source of Funds	2537745	399121	144991	1993633
国内贷款	Domestic Loans	561418	103628	31243	426547
债券	Bond	119			119
自筹资金	Fund Raising	971465	144137	48513	778815
本年土地开发投资	Investment in Development of Land	300718	60337	10024	230357
本年新增固定资产	Newly Increased Fixed Assets	1392836	164492	51130	1177214
本年施工房屋面积(平方米)	Floor Space of Buildings Under Construction	31188733	4977972	2177154	24033607
#住宅	Residential Buildings	23325553	4447080	1737179	17141294
本年竣工房屋面积(平方米)	Floor Space of Buildings Completed	11423020	1924598	623572	8874850
#住宅	Residential Buildings	8764214	1701070	546767	6516377
本年竣工房屋价值	Value of Buildings Completed	1114571	135740	44350	934481
#住宅	Residential Buildings	771566	112897	35518	623151
土地开发面积(平方米)	Area of Land Development	9807749	2361329	392284	7054136
商品房销售额	Total Sales of Commercial House	1198667	152636	57887	988144
商品房销售建筑面积(平方米)	Floor Space of Selling Commercial House	8484713	1513557	516003	6455153

4-23 商品房屋销售情况(2003年)

Sales of Commercial House (2003)

市州	Cities and Prefecture	实际销售商品房屋面积(平方米) Floor Space of Selling Commercial House (sq.m)	#住宅 Residential Buildings	个人购买商品房住宅(平方米) Commercial Houses Purchased by Individuals(sq.m)	商品房屋销售额(万元) Total Sales of Commercial House (10 000 yuan)	#住宅 Residential Buildings
全省总计	**Total**	**8484713**	**7252769**	**6755653**	**1198667**	**861836**
长沙市	Changsha	3274626	2911844	2758560	668185	520048
株洲市	Zhuzhou	996035	923569	923154	105985	89817
湘潭市	Xiangtan	655191	554831	551690	67258	49554
衡阳市	Hengyang	435727	383362	383362	40854	28171
邵阳市	Shaoyang	255603	196168	173648	24782	15573
岳阳市	Yueyang	459186	365541	290217	42179	27487
常德市	Changde	814877	675482	629421	96105	51209
张家界市	Zhangjiajie	164188	128857	97567	23347	10117
益阳市	Yiyang	187443	154470	147023	9370	6885
郴州市	Chenzhou	547079	395198	387198	66646	30323
永州市	Yongzhou	120223	110563	12146	5541	4898
怀化市	Huaihua	277517	218464	167247	23622	14507
娄底市	Loudi	180098	142080	142080	11485	7131
湘西自治州	West Hunan A.P	116920	92340	92340	13308	6116

4-24 房地产开发建设房屋建筑面积和造价(2003年)

Floor Space of Building and Cost of Real Estate Development (2003)

市州	Cities and Prefecture	施工房屋面积(平方米) Floor Space of Buildings under Construction (sq.m)	竣工房屋面积(平方米) Floor Space of Buildings Completed (sq.m)	房屋建筑面积竣工率(%) Rate of Floor Space of Buildings Completed (%)	竣工房屋价值(万元) Value of Buildings Completed (10 000 yuan)	竣工房屋造价(元/平方米) Cost of Buildings Completed (yuan/sq.m)
全省总计	**Total**	**31188733**	**11423020**	**36.6**	**1114571**	**975.7**
长沙市	Changsha	11408778	4397448	38.5	563451	1281.3
株洲市	Zhuzhou	3448422	1183197	34.3	87306	737.9
湘潭市	Xiangtan	1801347	781099	43.4	63859	817.6
衡阳市	Hengyang	2745278	845747	30.8	55650	658.0
邵阳市	Shaoyang	738591	342914	46.4	23943	698.2
岳阳市	Yueyang	1667974	531051	31.8	49757	937.0
常德市	Changde	2392800	1033987	43.2	84398	816.2
张家界市	Zhangjiajie	578475	169625	29.3	16458	970.3
益阳市	Yiyang	1064579	317023	29.8	19881	627.1
郴州市	Chenzhou	2375815	991597	41.7	89626	903.9
永州市	Yongzhou	415146	149209	35.9	8331	558.3
怀化市	Huaihua	987732	146570	14.8	8848	603.7
娄底市	Loudi	633359	306077	48.3	20613	673.5
湘西自治州	West Hunan A.P	930437	227476	24.4	22450	986.9

4-25 城镇集体单位固定资产投资和房屋建筑面积(2003年)

Investment in Fixed Assets and Floor Space of Buildings of Urban Collective - owned Units (2003)

市州	Cities and Prefecture	本年完成投资(万元) Investment Completed this Year (10 000 yuan)				房屋建筑面积(万平方米) Floor Space of Building Construction (10 000 sq.m)			
		合计 Total	建筑安装工程 Construction and Installation	设备工具器具购置 Purchase of Equipment and Instruments	其他费用 Others	施工面积 Floor Space under Construction	#住宅 Residential Buildings	竣工面积 Floor Space Completed	#住宅 Residential Buildings
全省总计	**Total**	**247639**	**181271**	**19323**	**47045**	**273.64**	**189.76**	**88.47**	**65.97**
长沙市	Changsha	86786	61979	1919	22888	56.10	36.55	15.60	14.14
株洲市	Zhuzhou	26481	17247	3951	5283	41.01	33.55	9.74	6.03
湘潭市	Xiangtan	16973	10176	2074	4723	23.99	10.43	14.36	7.06
衡阳市	Hengyang	19554	14489	2149	2916	47.10	35.22	11.22	8.19
邵阳市	Shaoyang	10214	6244	2610	1360	17.85	14.22	4.81	3.60
岳阳市	Yueyang	20333	18320	1340	673	7.73	1.26	0.48	0.48
常德市	Changde	19823	15147	2008	2668	31.93	26.75	19.66	17.69
张家界市	Zhangjiajie								
益阳市	Yiyang	7276	5500		1776	13.96	7.30	6.49	5.52
郴州市	Chenzhou	23555	17396	3272	2887	16.94	9.99	4.70	2.99
永州市	Yongzhou	7475	7475						
怀化市	Huaihua	2945	2945			11.54	11.30	0.24	
娄底市	Loudi	3199	2075		1124	1.31	0.28	0.90	
湘　西	West Hunan	3025	2278		747	4.19	2.92	0.27	0.27

4-26 国有农林牧渔业基本建设、更新改造投资及新增固定资产

Investment in Capital Construction, Technical Updating and Transformation and Newly Increased Fixed Assets of State-owned Units of Farming, Forestry, Animal Husbandry, Fishery

单位：万元 (10 000 yuan)

行　业	Sector	固定资产投资总额 Investment of Fixed Assets 2002	2003	新增固定资产 Newly Increased Fixed Assets 2002	2003
基本建设	**Investment in Capital Construction**	**57669**	**116710**	**26064**	**80751**
#农业	#Farming	23219	24975	9724	18376
林业	Forestry	22620	60281	12759	41861
畜牧业	Animal Husbandry	3477	5162	1647	3250
渔业	Fishery	3352	550		510
农林牧渔服务业	Services	5001	25742	1934	16754
更新改造	**Technical Updating and Transformation**	**949**	**2619**	**643**	**860**
#农业	#Farming				
林业	Forestry	137	1349	137	360
畜牧业	Animal Husbandry				
渔业	Fishery				
农林牧渔服务业	Services	812	1270	506	500

4-27 国有农林牧渔业投资额施工投产项目和固定资产交付使用率(2003年)

Investment，Projects Put into Operation and Rate of Fixed Assets Turned over to Uses of State—owned Units of Farming，Forestry，Animal Husbandry，Fishery (2003)

行业	Sector	投资额合计(万元) Total Investment (10 000 yuan)	#住宅 Residential Buildings	施工项目个数(个) Number of Projects Under Construction (unit)	全部建成投产项目个数(个) Projects Completed and Put into Production (unit)	项目投产率(%) Rate of Project Put into Production (%)	固定资产交付使用率(%) Rate of Fixed Assets Turn Over to Uses (%)
总计	**Total**	**138183**	**965**	**168**	**90**	**53.6**	**70.2**
农业	Farming	27675		35	21	60.0	70.7
林业	Forestry	75201	678	74	39	52.7	73.4
畜牧业	Animal Husbandry	7085		10	2	20.0	54.7
渔业	Fishery	760		5	3	60.0	153.9
农林牧渔服务业	Services	27462	287	44	25	56.8	62.8

4-28 城镇和工矿区私人建房情况(2003年)

Building Construction by Individuals in Cities and Industrial Mining Areas (2003)

市州	Cities and Prefecture	城镇、工矿区个数(个) Number of Cities and Industrial Mining Areas (unit)	本年竣工房屋建筑面积(万平方米) Floor Space of Buildings Completed This Year (10000 sq.m)		本年竣工房屋价值(万元) Value of Buildings Completed This Year (10000 yuan)		建房户数(户) Number of Households of Building Construction (household)
			合计 Total	#住宅 Residential Buildings	合计 Total	#住宅 Residential Buildings	
全省总计	**Total**	**167**	**1009.20**	**882.13**	**395815**	**347754**	**35868**
长沙市	Changsha	4	77.31	75.72	34285	31432	3245
株洲市	Zhuzhou	6	69.04	67.72	30832	30113	2540
湘潭市	Xiangtan	8	7.86	7.76	3265	3185	417
衡阳市	Hengyang	12	91.55	87.05	34863	31681	3117
邵阳市	Shaoyang	20	118.73	99.40	56692	46676	5454
岳阳市	Yueyang	8	79.83	68.34	30986	28002	2978
常德市	Changde	14	54.04	53.25	20750	20255	2542
张家界市	Zhangjiajie	4	26.73	25.68	10568	10166	645
益阳市	Yiyang	6	63.04	61.48	27310	26095	2804
郴州市	Chenzhou	16	78.12	62.26	36446	30547	2401
永州市	Yongzhou	16	230.54	173.04	67573	52119	5878
怀化市	Huaihua	15	30.65	27.32	12204	10224	1259
娄底市	Loudi	23	38.45	32.28	14973	12987	992
湘西自治州	West Hunan A.P	15	43.31	40.83	15068	14272	1596

注：本表不含镇级。 The Figures in this Table Excluding Information of Towns.

4-29 国有工业施工、投资项目及项目投产率(2003年)

Projects Under Construction,Put into Use and Rate of Projects Put into Use of State – Owned Industrial Enterprises (2003)

指 标	Item	施工项目个数(个) Number of Projects Under Construction(unit)	全投项目个数(个) Projects Completed and Put into Production(unit)	项目投产率(%) Rate of Project Put into Production(%)
总 计	**Total**	**1212**	**608**	**50.2**
采掘业	**Mining**	70	31	44.3
煤炭采选业	Coal Mining and Dressing	38	21	55.3
黑色金属矿采选业	Mining and Dressing of Ferrous Metals	1	0	0.0
有色金属矿采选业	Mining and Dressing of Nonferrous Metals	25	7	28.0
非金属矿采选业	Mining and Dressing of Nonmetal Minerals	6	3	50.0
制造业	**Manufacturing**	**677**	**353**	**52.1**
#食品加工业	Food Processing	20	6	30.0
食品制造业	Food Production	8	4	50.0
饮料制造业	Beverages	4	1	25.0
烟草加工业	Tobacco	86	52	60.5
纺织业	Textiles	13	9	69.2
木材加工及竹、藤、棕、草制品业	Timber Processing, Bamboo, Cane, Palm Fiber and Straw Products	9	3	33.3
造纸及纸制品业	Papermaking and Paper Products	11	4	36.4
印刷业、记录媒介的复制	Printing and Record Medium Reproduction	3	3	100
石油加工及炼焦业	Petroleum Processing and Coking	26	4	15.4
化学原料及化学制品制造业	Raw Chemical Materials and Chemical Products	70	27	38.6
医药制造业	Medical and Pharmaceutical Products	14	3	21.4
化学纤维制造业	Chemical Fiber	1	0	0.0
橡胶制品业	Rubber Products	1	1	100.0
塑料制品业	Plastic Products	0	0	
非金属矿物制品业	Nonmetal Mineral Products	17	10	58.8
黑色金属冶炼及压延加工业	Smelting and Pressing of Ferrous Metals	152	114	75.0
有色金属冶炼及压延加工业	Smelting and Pressing of Nonferrous Metals	120	53	44.2
金属制品业	Metal Products	3	3	100.0
通用设备制造业	Manufacture of General Purpose Machinery	14	9	64.3
专用设备制造业	Equipment for Special Purposes	36	15	41.7
交通运输设备制造业	Transport Equipment	49	27	55.1
电气机械及器材制造业	Electric Equipment and Machinery	13	3	23.1
电子及通信设备制造业	Electronic and Telecommunications Equipment	1	0	0.0
仪器仪表及文化、办公用机械制造业	Instruments, Meters, Cultural and Office Machinery	1	1	100.0
工艺品及其他制造业	Manufacture of Arts and Grafts	2	1	50.0
废弃资源和废旧材料回收加工业	Recycling and Disposal of Waste	1	0	0.0
电力、燃气及水的生产和供应业	**Production and Supply of Electricity,Gas and Water**	**465**	**224**	**48.2**
电力、热力的生产和供应业	Production and Supply of Electric Power,Heat Power	338	185	54.7
燃气生产和供应业	Production and Distribution of Gas	6	1	16.7
水的生产和供应业	Production and Distribution of Water	121	38	31.4

4-30 农村固定资产投资情况

Investment of Fixed Assets in Rural Areas

单位：万元、万平方米 (10 000 yuan, 10 000 sq.m)

		2002年		2003年	
		总计 Total	#非农户 Non Agricultural Household	总计 Total	#非农户 Non Agricultural Household
本年新增固定资产	**Newly Increase Fixed Assets this Year**	**3217165**	**991766**	**2978745**	**1234401**
本年固定资产投资完成额	**Completed Investment this Year**	**3596926**	**1518987**	**3550566**	**1748286**
按投资来源分	**Grouped by Source of Funds**				
#国家资金	State Capital	224247	224247	166848	166848
国内贷款	Domestic Loans	110917	64700	132735	99680
利用外资	Foreign Investment	19902	19902	51643	51643
自筹资金	Fundraising	3066358	1066601	3087067	1338733
按投资构成分	**Grouped by Use of Funds**				
#建筑工程	Construction	2555161	964773	2253581	946093
安装工程	Installation	55854	53793	53696	53313
设备工器具购置	Purchase of Equipment and Instruments	760207	426344	1005565	648585
按投资方向分	**Grouped by Direction of Investment**				
#农业	Agriculture	332945	62595	369793	117506
采矿业	Mining and Quarrying	120252	115488	170929	132628
制造业	Manufacturing	412085	378177	705313	693523
电力、煤气及水的 生产和供应业	Production and Supply of Electricity,Gas and Water	109993	109993	133253	132487
建筑业	Construction	38054	32957	48264	44192
交通运输、仓储和邮政业	Transport,Storage, Post and Telecommunication	235061	110005	269554	114125
信息传输、计算机服务和软件业	Data Transmission, Computer Service and Software	4826	650	5827	771
批发零售业	Wholesale and Retail Trade	52960	41295	58305	46337
住宿和餐饮业	Hotel and Catering Services	25934	7123	26994	8227
金融业	Banking	2503	2503	4556	4556
房地产业	Real Estate	1435737	68802	1316707	40576
租赁和商务服务业	Leasing and Business Services	8582	3254	9692	3564
科学研究技术服务和地质勘查业	Scientific Research,Technical Services and Geological Prospecting	280	280	294	294
水利、环境和公共设施管理业	Water Conservancy,Environment and Public Utility Management	132520	132412	146530	143849
居民服务业和其他服务业	Personal and Other Services	27362	15230	28622	16165
教育	Education	91242	91242	75801	75801
卫生、社会保障和社会福利业	Public Health,Social Seccurities and Social Welfare	9530	9530	9765	9765
文化、体育和娱乐业	Culture,Sports and Entertainment	56320	50102	57709	51261
公共管理与社会组织	Public Administration and Social Organizations	91213	91213	112639	112639
按具体投资项目分	**Grouped by Item of Investment**				
#房屋	Residential House	1952027	450013	1613480	343937
道路	Roadways	176821	173066	183333	183333
桥梁	Bridges	11719	6544	12120	12120
设备	Equipment	760207	426344	1005565	648585
水利	Water Conservancy	296409	223678	143021	120638
本年施工房屋面积	**Floor Space of Buildings Under Construction in Current Year**	**8561**	**1675**	**6488**	**1143**
#住宅	Residential House	6880	347	5108	66
本年竣工房屋面积	**Floor Space of Buildings Completed in Current Year**	**7741**	**1238**	**6183**	**1092**
#住宅	Residential House	6458	268	4879	54
本年竣工房屋投资完成额	**Investment Made of Building Completed in Current Year**	**1794860**	**341926**	**1533361**	**302415**
#住宅	Residential House	1490781	98292	1200032	21255

五、财政、金融、保险

FINANCE，BANKING AND INSURANCE

资料整理人员：　李生春

5-1 地方财政收支总额

Total Local Government Revenue and Expenditures

单位：亿元 (100 million yuan)

年份 Year / 市州 Cities and Prefecture		总收入(亿元) Total Revenue	#企业收入 Revenue form Enterprises	#各项税收 Taxes Revenue	总支出(亿元) Total Expenditure	#基本建设支出 Expenditure for Capital Construction	#支援农村生产支出及农业事业费 Expenditure for Supporting Agricultural Production and Agricultural Operating Expenses	#文教科学卫生事业费 Operating Expenses for Culture, Education Science and Health Care	#行政管理费 Expenditure for Government Administration
	1978	28.98	9.68	17.17	24.46	7.62	3.57	4.33	1.88
	1980	29.86	9.58	19.53	23.71	4.86	3.44	6.68	2.66
	1981	31.40	9.10	21.49	21.39	3.00	3.07	6.81	2.90
	1982	30.33	5.11	24.48	23.26	3.12	2.95	7.91	3.03
	1983	29.27	2.25	26.16	25.31	3.48	3.26	8.79	3.58
	1984	32.85	2.74	29.12	30.04	4.43	3.21	9.86	4.87
	1985	39.19	1.61	36.83	40.09	4.60	4.01	12.53	5.20
	1986	47.65	4.08	42.26	54.29	5.80	4.52	14.22	5.54
	1987	54.38	4.37	48.36	55.93	4.65	3.09	14.88	6.22
	1988	56.54	-0.47	54.25	64.89	5.21	5.88	18.30	6.13
	1989	68.86	-1.48	64.88	74.23	5.44	6.91	20.69	6.43
	1990	70.07	-3.70	67.33	80.08	5.60	8.17	21.92	6.82
	1991	80.52	-0.91	74.14	88.58	6.16	8.81	24.47	7.80
	1992	92.78	-0.78	84.90	99.10	6.23	9.86	28.42	11.03
	1993	127.56	-0.66	116.31	132.03	7.73	12.89	32.96	13.18
	1994	85.89	2.70	65.04	151.49	7.89	13.74	42.54	17.79
	1995	108.16	2.74	78.05	173.94	9.65	14.55	47.87	21.46
	1996	130.36	2.30	88.00	217.74	13.33	17.09	53.70	24.27
	1997	137.16	2.72	105.75	230.82	13.78	17.66	58.75	26.20
	1998	156.77	3.63	102.95	273.64	28.75	22.16	61.94	26.88
	1999	166.50	6.04	105.50	313.12	37.66	21.49	66.40	29.36
	2000	177.04	8.60	111.57	347.83	38.08	22.15	73.55	32.78
	2001	205.41	19.35	124.45	431.70	39.40	25.55	91.62	41.42
	2002	231.15	14.16	148.61	533.02	58.26	40.59	113.12	50.63
	2003	268.65	14.69	173.15	573.75	51.40	36.21	124.62	59.15
长沙	Changsha	59.89	3.57	44.41	78.42	6.32	4.68	13.32	9.34
株洲	Zhuzhou	16.82	2.22	10.75	30.72	1.66	1.74	6.13	3.35
湘潭	Xiangtan	10.07	0.29	6.59	19.41	0.30	1.09	3.85	1.77
衡阳	Hengyang	14.94	0.18	9.83	33.60	0.21	1.87	8.43	4.49
邵阳	Shaoyang	11.96	0.16	6.49	31.41	0.16	2.25	8.97	4.67
岳阳	Yueyang	20.58	0.85	11.61	36.42	2.52	2.98	8.26	3.70
常德	Changde	19.29	0.79	13.30	35.92	0.33	2.69	9.43	5.01
张家界	Zhangjiajie	3.79	0.38	2.52	10.74	0.05	0.77	3.03	1.38
益阳	Yiyang	7.46	0.18	5.71	21.19	0.26	1.42	6.86	3.08
郴州	Chenzhou	21.49	1.24	12.69	35.07	0.52	2.95	9.48	3.94
永州	Yongzhou	10.81	0.15	6.44	27.32	0.23	1.85	8.30	3.93
怀化	Huaihua	9.20	0.27	6.36	25.23	0.03	1.71	7.17	3.54
娄底	Loudi	9.13	0.23	4.97	19.86	0.16	1.18	5.67	3.33
湘西	West Hinan	4.14	0.04	3.28	20.67	0.04	1.97	5.65	3.02

5-2 财政收入及构成

Government Revenue and Its Composition

项目	Item	财政收入(万元) Government Revenue (10 000 yuan) 2002	2003	2003年比上年增长% Increase Rate in 2003 over 2002(%)	收入构成(%) Composition (%) 2002	2003
本年地方财政收入合计	**Total Local Government Revenue**	**2311459**	**2686469**	**16.22**	**100.00**	**100.00**
#增值税	#Value Added Tax	318967	361183	13.24	13.80	13.44
营业税	Operating Tax	484238	602304	24.38	20.95	22.42
企业所得税	Income Tax of Enterprises	154343	134574	-12.81	6.68	5.01
企业所得税退税	Return for Enterprises' Income Tax	-10		-		
个人所得税	Individual Income Tax	139322	121622	-12.70	6.03	4.53
资源税	Resources Tax	7447	9089	22.05	0.32	0.34
固定资产投资方向调节税	Tax on the Adjustment of the Investment in the Fixed Assets	242	3	-98.76	0.01	□
城市维护建设税	Tax on Town Maintenance and Construction	145369	163264	12.31	6.29	6.08
房产税	Tax on Real Estates	54225	65418	20.64	2.35	2.44
印花税	Stamp Tax	15998	18550	15.95	0.69	0.69
城镇土地使用税	Tax on the Use of Urban Land	23767	23111	-2.76	1.03	0.86
土地增值税	Land Value Added Tax	1756	4317	145.84	0.08	0.16
车船使用税	Tax on the Use of Vehicles and Ships	4832	5601	15.91	0.21	0.21
屠宰税	Slaughter Tax	5442	20	-99.63	0.24	□
筵席税	Banquet Tax					
农业税	Agricultural Tax	174252	181682	4.26	7.54	6.76
农业特产税	Tax on Special Agricultural Products	53403	80452	50.65	2.31	2.99
牧业税	Tax on the Animal Husbandry					
耕地占用税	Tax on Occupancy of Cultivated Land	22408	39369	75.69	0.97	1.47
契税	Contract Tax	36284	55541	53.07	1.57	2.07
国有资产经营收益	State-owned Assets Profits	42137	52136	23.73	1.82	1.94
国有企业计划亏损补贴	Planning Subsidies to Loss-suffering State-owned Enterprises	-54789	-39804	-27.35	-2.37	-1.48
行政性收费收入	Income from Administrative Fees	279415	348640	24.77	12.09	12.98
罚没收入	Penalty and Confiscation Income	212688	228507	7.44	9.20	8.51
土地和海域有偿使用收入	Income on the Use of Land and Sea Area	1035	228	-77.97	0.04	0.01
专项收入	Expert Project Income	82387	99509	20.78	3.56	3.70
其他收入	Other Income	108192	131153	21.22	4.68	4.88
上划中央□两税□收入	**Value Added Tax and Consumption Tax of Turn in Central Government**	**1655484**	**1836924**	**10.96**		
#增值税	#Value Added Tax	956899	1083554	13.24		
消费税	Consumption Tax	698585	753370	7.84		
上划中央所得税	**Income Tax of Turn in Central Government**	**279414**	**374105**	**33.89**		
财政总收入	**Total Government Revenue**	**4246357**	**4897498**	**15.33**		

5-3 地方财政支出及构成

Local Government Expenditure and Its Composition

科 目	Item	财政支出(万元) Government Expenditure (10 000 yuan)		2003年比上年增长% Increases Rate in 2003 over 2002(%)	支出构成(%) Composition (%)	
		2002	2003		2002	2003
地方财政支出合计	**Total Local Government Expenditure**	**5330229**	**5737453**	**7.64**	**100.00**	**100.00**
#基本建设支出	#Expenditure for Capital Construction	582565	513964	-11.78	10.93	8.96
企业挖潜改造资金	Expenditure for Innovation Enterprises	89418	101835	13.89	1.68	1.77
地质勘探费	Expenditure for Geological Prospecting	54853	53731	-2.05	1.03	0.94
科技三项费用	Expenditure for Science and Technology Promotion	53007	49090	-7.39	0.99	0.86
支援农村生产支出	Expenditure for Supporting Agricultural Production	74053	-	-	1.39	-
农业综合开发支出	Expenditure for Comprehensive Development of Agriculture	44518	-	-	0.84	-
农林水利气象等部门的事业费	Operating Expenses for Agriculture, Forestry, Water Conservancy and Meteorology	287352	362098	26.01	5.39	6.31
工业交通等部门的事业费	Operating Expenses for Departments of Industry and Transportation	51962	58892	13.34	0.97	1.03
流通部门事业费	Operating Expenses for Department of Commerce	15948	18599	16.62	0.30	0.32
文体广播事业费	Operating Expenses for Departments of Culture,Sport and Broadcasting	130981	155101	18.41	2.46	2.70
教育事业费	Operating Expenses for Education	829801	900570	8.53	15.57	15.70
科学事业费	Operating Expenses for Science	23388	22267	-4.79	0.44	0.39
卫生经费	Operating Expenses for Public Health	147068	168303	14.44	2.76	2.93
税务等部门的事业费	Operating Expenses for Department of Revenue,Statistic,Finance and Audit	294395	332605	12.98	5.52	5.80
抚恤和社会福利救济费	Pensions, Social and Relief Funds for Social Welfare	153532	218603	42.38	2.88	3.81
行政事业单位离退休经费	Expenditure for Retired Persons in Administrative Department	300306	339042	12.90	5.63	5.91
社会保障补助支出	Expenditure on Subsidies to Social Security Programs	488001	478624	-1.92	9.16	8.34
行政管理费	Expenditure for Government Administration	506316	591494	16.82	9.50	10.31
外交外事支出	Expenditure for Foreign Affairs	1466	1651	12.62	0.03	0.03
城市维护费	Expenditure for City Maintenance	177463	234149	31.94	3.33	4.08
政策性补贴支出	Expenditure for Price Subsidies	155412	140698	-9.47	2.92	2.45
支援不发达地区	Expenditure for Supporting Underdeveloped Areas	57968	62699	8.16	1.09	1.09
土地和海域开发建设支出	Expenditure for Developing Land and Sea Area	85	98	15.29	…	…
专项支出	Expenditure for Special Items	79729	89750	12.57	1.50	1.56
其他支出	Other Expenditure	730642	843590	15.46	13.71	14.70

5-4 金融机构信贷收支

Credit Income and Expenditures of Financial Institutions

单位：万元 (10 000 yuan)

项目	Item	2002		2003	
		年末余额 Balance at the Year-end	比年初增减 Increase Over the Year-beginning	年末余额 Balance at the Year-end	比年初增减 Increase Over the Year-beginning
各项存款	**Deposits**	**39231683**	**5947456**	**46690016**	**7462506**
企业存款	Deposits of Enterprises	9302506	904198	11693785	2398514
活期存款	Demand Deposits	7480618	679760	9208251	1739176
定期存款	Fixed Deposits	1821888	224437	2485535	659338
财政存款	Treasury Deposits	575412	47579	536700	-38713
机关团体存款	Deposits of Government	1351851	541458	1511228	159377
储蓄存款	Savings Deposits	25774354	3941918	30364513	4601485
活期储蓄	Demand Saving	8624112	1798747	10656138	2035854
定期储蓄	Fixed Saving	17150242	2143171	19708375	2565631
农业存款	Agricultural Deposits	775658	122470	966729	191048
信托存款	Trusted Deposits	-	-	-	-
委托存款	Commission Deposits	236396	31162	-18418	-253579
其他存款	Other Deposits	1215507	358673	1635209	404375
金融证券	Financial Bonds	81	-14	-398716	-39856
应付及暂收款	Payable & Actually Received Funds	546107	-27382	601589	55144
#应付及预收利息	#Payable Interest	191973	38927	209814	18383
流通中货币	Currency in Circulation	-	-	-	-
各项准备	All Plans	191568	18594	161858	-33155
#贷款呆帐准备金	#Plan Funds for Loans	191530	22050	161202	-30220
所有者权益	Creditors' Equity	-1452777	10959	-1243798	40826
实收资本	Total Capital Hold	428245	-9870	449860	21621
当年结益	Current Retained Profits	-468703	-463850	-168623	-168623
其他	Others	-3571691	-1466882	-4453007	-1776559
资金来源总计	**All Sources**	**34944971**	**4482731**	**42001714**	**5565803**

项目	Item	2002		2003	
		年末余额 Balance at the Year-end	比年初增减 Increase Over the Year-beginning	年末余额 Balance at the Year-end	比年初增减 Increase Over the Year-beginning
各项贷款	**Loans**	**32274589**	**4266901**	**37963140**	**5664531**
短期贷款	Short-term Loans	19499884	2313007	21566601	2181128
工业贷款	Industry Loans	4676080	826522	5279628	597226
商业贷款	Commercial Loans	5538404	-225545	5396255	-142509
#农副产品贷款	Loans of Agricultural and Sideline Products	3407625	-47295	3236738	-170887
建筑业贷款	Construction Loans	458879	260889	600455	133630
农业贷款	Agricultural Loans	2742276	410045	3318586	576195
乡镇企业贷款	Loans to the Township Enterprises	1187735	-26267	1212658	24919
三资企业贷款	Loans to Sino-foreign Joint Venture and Cooperative Enterprises and Foreign-funded Enterprises	107167	-79383	64950	-42217
私营企业及个体贷款	Loans to Private Enterprises and Individuals	108593	3288.91	146475	37882
其他短期贷款	Other Short-term Loans	4680749	1143457	5547595	996003
#个人消费贷款	#Loans to Personal Expenditure	173556	70624	245032	71723
中期流动资金贷款	Medium-term Circulating Funds of Loans	1856576	50293	1855211	30612
中长期贷款	Medium-term and Long-term Loans	9956771	1949684	13238527	3257347
基本建设贷款	Capital Construction	6250983	1155181	8116895	1857666
技术改造贷款	Technical Innovation	329859	20786	344616	14757
其他中长期贷款	Other Medium-term&Long-term Loans	3375929	773717	4777016	1384924
#个人消费贷款	#Loans to Personal Expenditure	1125177	477145	1963310	837704
信托贷款	Trusted Loans	29061	94	22185	-6876
融资租赁	Circulating Funds Tenancy	-	-	-	-
委托贷款	Commission Loans	231100	16781	12819	-218281
票据融资	Financing From Bills	612639	-59768	1192943	434304
#贴现	#Discount	612639	-59768	1192943	434304
各项垫款	All Funds Advanced to Be Paid Back Later	88557	-3190	74854	-13703
有价证券及投资	Securities and Investment	1490515	361379	1259185	31755
应收及预付款项	Account Receivable and Advance Payment	733574	-156752	658151	-75697
#应收利息	#Receivable Interest	490631	83971	370547	-120371
委托投资	Consigned Investment	13117	-9916	13117	-
金银占款	Purchase of Gold and Silver	3354	-14770	1	-3353
外汇占款	Purchase of Foreign Exchanges	4383	-7734	3660	-723
库存现金	Vault Cash	425440	43624	487751	62408
财政借款	Government Debt				
资金运用总计	**All Uses**	**34944971**	**4482731**	**42001714**	**5565803**

5-5 商业银行信贷收支

Credit Income and Expenditures of Commercial Banks

单位：万元 (10 000 yuan)

项目	Item	2002		2003	
		年末余额 Balance at the Year-end	比年初增减 Increase Over the Year-beginning	年末余额 Balance at the Year-end	比年初增减 Increase Over the Year-beginning
各项存款	**Deposits**	**27907107**	**4528450**	**33620139**	**5713034**
企业存款	Deposits of Enterprises	8893757	808490	11132589	2246041
活期存款	Demand Deposits	7200945	607199	8817229	1627801
定期存款	Fixed Deposits	1692811	201290	2315360	618240
机关团体存款	Deposits of Government	1318752	534198	1470826	152073
储蓄存款	Savings Deposits	16429243	2834427	19331245	2910104
活期储蓄	Demand Saving	6260852	1314211	7726637	1474439
定期储蓄	Fixed Saving	10168391	1520216	11604608	1435666
农业存款	Agricultural Deposits	91317	1344	98565	7248
其他存款	Other Deposits	1174038	349991	1586914	397568
代理财政性存款	Agent of Government Deposits	49443	-66	36121	-13322
发行金融债券	Issuance Financial Bonds	76	-13	71	-4
#发行政策性金融债券	#Policy Financial Bonds				
应付及暂收款	Payable & Actually Received Funds	255654	-42950	279827	24099
#应付及预收利息	#Payable Interest	60723	32443	79699	18940
卖出回购证券	Selling Debits of Buy-return	363800	-43200	311100	-10900
向中央银行借款	Debit from Central Banks	10950	-36155	24483	13533
同业往来	Same Trade Current Account	1188726	-162757	987698	-217253
同业存放款	Deposits	1178326	-160457	987198	-207353
同业拆借	Debit	10400	-2300	500	-9900
委托存款及委托投资基金（净额）	Commission Deposits and Commission Investment Funds (Net Value)	-47118	38733	-46107	1886
委托存款级委托投资基金	Commission Deposits and Commission Investment Funds	196249	26071	344383	155363
委托贷款及委托投资	Commission Loans and Commission Investment	243367	-12662	390490	153477
代理金融机构贷款基金	Loan Funds in Agent of Financial Institutions	11077	-222	7529	-3548
#中央银行委托贷款基金	#Commission Loan Funds in Central Banks	11077	-222	7529	-3548
各项准备	All Plans	115297	3406	97063	-21775
其中：贷款呆帐准备金	Plan Funds for Loans	115262	3410	96408	-18842
所有者权益	Creditors' Equity	-910209	232928	-899511	14227
实收资本	Total Capital Hold	82583	29215	90583	7999
当年结益	Current Retained Profits	-262999	-258147	-193254	-193254
其他	Others	-4391192	-1075261	-5284302	-944858
资金来源总计	**All Sources**	**24553611**	**3442894**	**29134111**	**4555119**

单位：万元 5-5 续表 continued (10 000 yuan)

项目	Item	2002 年末余额 Balance at the Year-end	2002 比年初增减 Increase Over the Year-beginning	2003 年末余额 Balance at the Year-end	2003 比年初增减 Increase Over the Year-beginning
各项贷款	**Loans**	**21467059**	**3470562**	**25384462**	**3891767**
短期贷款	Short-term Loans	11834128	1997124	13291394	1571542
工业贷款	Industrial Loans	4641481	828947	5250778	602975
商业贷款	Commercial Loans	2404162	-153840	2421396	16874
#收购贷款	#Buying Loans	298080	-3719	287439	-10641
建筑业贷款	Construction Loans	458737	260747	600172	133489
农业贷款	Agricultural Loans	322190	-10179	362812	40616
乡镇企业贷款	Loans to Township Enterprises	259066	8898	268984	9917
三资企业贷款	Loans to Sino-foreign Joint Venture and Cooperative Enterprises and Foreign-funded Enterprises	107167	-79383	64950	-42217
私营企业及个体贷款	Loans to Private Enterprises and Individuals	98205	8033	133936	35731
其他短期贷款	Other Short-term Loans	3543120	1133902	4188367	774157
个人消费贷款	Loans to Personnal Expenditure	173556	70624	245032	71723
中期流动资金贷款	Medium-term Circulating Funds of Loans	1856576	50293	1855211	30612
中长期贷款	Medium-term & Long-term Loans	7105852	1193062	9294245	2162505
基本建设贷款	Capital Construction	3686543	442142	4549374	854585
技术改造贷款	Technical Innovation	296679	29026	310536	13857
其他中长期贷款	Other Medium-term&Long-term Loans	3122630	721894	4434335	1294063
#个人消费贷款	#Loans to Personnal Expenditure	1113311	476193	1951202	837462
票据融资	Financing From Bills	581947	233273	868758	140811
#贴现	#Discount	581947	233273	868758	140811
各项垫款	All Funds Advanced to Be Paid Back Later	88557	-3190	74854	-13703
有价证券及投资	Securities and Investment	952757	64342	930869	-21888
应收及预付款	Receivable and Advance Payment	567556	-145205	458849	-108745
#应收利息	#Receivable Interest	425070	-76473	324340	-100757
买入返售证券	Buying Securities of Resold	70205	30926	329633	259428
缴存准备金存款	Hand in Deposits of Prepared Funds	986238	-84138	1450880	464642
存放中央银行特种存款	Special Deposits in the Central Banks				
存放中央银行财政性存款	Treasury Deposits in the Central Banks	50048	21564	91365	41316
同业往来	Same Trade Current Account	228621	72961	234014	5593
存放同业	Deposits	6635	-5699	6822	387
拆放同业	Debit	221986	78660	227192	5206
代理金融机构贷款	Loans from Agent of Financial Institutions	9613	5225	4246	-5367
#代理人行专项贷款	#Loans for Special Items from Agent of People's Bank	9613	5225	4246	-5367
库存现金	Vault Cash	217132	14390	246133	29096
外汇占款	Purchase of Foreign Exchanges	4383	-7734	3660	-723
资金运用总计	**All Uses**	**24553611**	**3442894**	**29134111**	**4555119**

5-6 政策性银行信贷收支

Credit Income and Expenditures of Policy-based Banks

单位：万元

项目	Item	2002 年末余额 Balance at the Year-end	2002 比年初增减 Increase Over the Year-beginning	2003 年末余额 Balance at the Year-end	2003 比年初增减 Increase Over the Year-beginning
各项存款	**Deposits**	**248744**	**87561**	341613.88	92870.25
企业存款	Deposits of Enterprises	248303	87486	341613.88	92870.25
#活期存款	# Demand Deposits	248303	87486	341613.88	92870.25
其他存款	Other Deposits	441	75	211	-220
代理财政性存款	Agent of Government Deposits	145022	74617	72674	-72348
应付及暂收款	Payable & Actually Received Funds	21993	6449	10405.46	-11587.09
#应付及预收利息	#Payable Interest	13553	-110	0	-13553
同业往来	Same Trade Current Account	78	49	419.58	341.39
#同业存放款	# Deposits	78	49	419.58	341.39
各项准备	All Plans	17719	17719	0	-17719
#贷款呆帐准备金	#Plan Funds for Loans	17719	17719	0	-17719
所有者权益	Creditors' Equity	58549	17249	83665.32	25116.18
实收资本	Total Capital Hold	38099	16539	38753	654
当年结益	Current Retained Profits	16016	16016	42371.32	42371.32
其他	Others	5409170	561479	6422225.69	1013055.42
资金来源总计	**All Sources**	**5901275**	**765124**	6931003.93	1029729.15
各项贷款	**Loans**	**5836576**	**738614**	6811315	974739
短期贷款	Short-term Loans	3207741	11164	3165095	-42646
商业贷款	Commercial Loans	3133544	-43836	2973298	-160246
#收购贷款	#Buying Loans	3109545	-43576	2973298	-160246
其他短期贷款	Other Short-term Loans	74197	55000	191797	117600
中长期贷款	Medium-term & Long-term Loans	2628835	727450	3646220	1017385
基本建设贷款	Capital Construction	2562006	727737	3565366	1003360
技术改造贷款	Technical Innovation	19780	-4240	25580	5800
其他中长期贷款	Other Medium-term&Long-term Loans	47049	3953	55274	8225
应收及预付款	Receivable and Advance Payment	26808	3277	7716.25	-19091.53
#应收利息	#Receivable Interest	22077	2177	8520	-14557
缴存准备金存款	Hand in Deposits of Prepared Funds	33760	21904	107468.32	73707.89
同业往来	Same Trade Current Account	3625	1572	4061.36	436.79
#存放同业	#Deposits	3625	1572	4061.36	436.79
库存现金	Vault Cash	506	-243	443	-63
资金运用总计	**All Uses**	**5901275**	**765124**	**6931003.93**	**1029729.15**

5-7 城乡信用社信贷收支情况（2003年）

Credit Income and Expenditures of Credit Cooperative (2003)

单位：万元 (10 000 yuan)

项目	Item	城市信用社 Urban Credit Cooperative		农村信用社 Rural Credit Cooperative	
		年末余额 Balance at the Year-end	比年初增减 Increase Over the Year-beginning	年末余额 Balance at the Year-end	比年初增减 Increase Over the Year-beginning
各项存款	**Deposits**	**60075**	**16857**	**8253628**	**1101300**
企业存款	Deposits of Enterprises	33865	9760	159973	48166
活期存款	Demand Deposits	28293	10310	13	13
定期存款	Fixed Deposits	5572	-550	159960	48153
机关团体存款	Deposits of government			35210	8679
储蓄存款	Savings Deposits	25709	6694	7142709	854032
活期存款	Demand Saving	11494	2722	1849826	268237
定期存款	Fixed Saving	14215	3972	5292883	585795
农业存款	Agricultural Deposits			868164	183800
其他存款	Other Deposits	501	403	47573	6624
代理财政性存款	Agent of Government Deposits			8146	3059
发行金融债券	Issuance Financial Bonds				
发行政策性金融债券	Policy-based Financial Bonds				
应付及暂收款	Payable & Actually Received Funds	648	-159	261344	34711
#应付及预收利息	#Payable Interest	148	-57	127176	13053
卖出回购证券	Selling Debits of Buy-return				
向中央银行借款	Debit from Central Banks			458386	45230
同业往来	Same Trade Current Account			356333	-11463
同业存放款	Deposits			276715	140983
同业拆借	Debit			79618	-152446
委托存款及委托投资基金（净额）	Commission Deposits and Commission Investment Funds (Net Value)			3493	3097
委托存款级委托投资基金	Commission Deposits and Commission Investment Funds			31339	9063
委托贷款及委托投资	Commission Loans and Commission Investment			27846	5966
代理金融机构贷款基金	Loan Funds in Agent of Financial Institutions			14986	3080
#中央银行委托贷款基金	#Commission Loan Funds in Central Banks			36	-16
各项准备	All Plans	327	74	63494	5895
其中：贷款呆帐准备金	Plan Funds for Loans	327	74	63494	5895
所有者权益	Creditors' Equity	1081	108	-561718	-6098
实收资本	Total Capital Hold	2129		197519	12968
当年结益	Current Retained Profits	108	108	-21307	-21307
其他	Others	-1028	3570	-377662	-57437
资金来源总计	**All Sources**	**61103**	**20450**	**8480431**	**1121375**

单位：万元　　5-7 续表　continued　　(10 000 yuan)

项目	Item	城市信用社 Urban Credit Cooperative 年末余额 Balance at the Year-end	城市信用社 Urban Credit Cooperative 比年初增减 Increase Over the Year-beginning	农村信用社 Rural Credit Cooperative 年末余额 Balance at the Year-end	农村信用社 Rural Credit Cooperative 比年初增减 Increase Over the Year-beginning
各项贷款	**Loans**	**32678**	**7346**	**5340376**	**740738**
短期贷款	Short-term Loans	30523	7625	5051871	649113
工业贷款	Industrial Loans	1512	-864		
商业贷款	Commercial Loans	1181	483		
收购贷款	Buying Loans				
建筑业贷款	Construction Loans	283	141		
农业贷款	Agricultural Loans			2955774	535579
乡镇企业贷款	Loans to Township Enterprises			943674	15002
三资企业贷款	Loans to Sino-foreign Joint Venture and Cooperative Enterprises and Foreign-funded Enterprises				
私营企业及个体贷款	Loans to Private Enterprises and Individuals	12539	2151		
其他短期贷款	Other Short-term Loans	15008	5714	1152423	98532
个人消费贷款	Loans to Personnal Expenditure				
中期流动资金贷款	Medium-term Circulating Funds of Loans				
中长期贷款	Medium-term & Long-term Loans	2155	-279	264567	75003
基本建设贷款	Capital Construction	2155	-279		
技术改造贷款	Technical Innovation				
其他中长期贷款	Other Medium-term&Long-term Loans			264567	75003
#个人消费贷款	#Loans to Personnal Expenditure			12108	242
票据融资	Financing From Bills			23938	16622
#贴现	#Discount			23938	16622
各项垫款	All Funds Advanced to Be Paid Back Later				
有价证券及投资	Securities and Investment	4070	2000	639706	82936
应收及预付款	Receivable and Advance Payment	422	-59	105235	-1826
#应收利息	#Receivable Interest	121	-2	38123	-4859
买入返售证券	Buying Securities of Resold				
缴存准备金存款	Hand in Deposits of Prepared Funds	15324	10392	1105565	253499
存放中央银行特种存款	Special Deposits in the Central Banks				-112800
存放中央银行财政性存款	Treasury Deposits in the Central Banks			47	-217
同业往来	Same Trade Current Account	8004	789	1034760	127633
存放同业	Deposits	8004	789	1015244	134931
拆放同业	Debit			19516	-7298
代理金融机构贷款	Loans from Agent of Financial Institutions			15454	-2021
#代理人行专项贷款	#Loans for Special Items from Agent of People's Bank			35	-15
库存现金	Vault Cash	605	-18	239288	33433
外汇占款	Purchase of Foreign Exchanges				
资金运用总计	**All Uses**	**61103**	**20450**	**8480431**	**1121375**

5-8 金融机构现金收支情况（2003年）

Cash Income and Expenditures of Financial Institutions(2003)

单位：万元 (10 000 yuan)

项目	Item	本年累计 Add up this Year	比上年增减额 Increase Over the Year-beginning	比上年增减% Increase Rate in 2003 over 2002 (%)
收入合计	**Total Income**	**151033260**	**19387283**	**14.73**
商品销售收入	Income from Commodity Sales	11805746	1579293	15.44
服务业收入	Income from Service Trade	7086273	851404	13.66
税款收入	Income from Taxes	1011794	143332	16.5
城乡个体经营收入	Income from Urban and Rural Individual Business	2895291	558933	23.92
储蓄存款收入	Income from Saving Deposits	114763803	21199965	22.66
其他金融机构收入	Income from Other Financial Institutions	1014010	-35517	-3.38
居民归还贷款收入	Income from Repayment of Loans by Residents	2884480	644799	28.79
汇兑收入	Income from Remittances	1050490	-423770	-28.74
有价证券收入	Income from Securities	204619	16809	8.95
其他收入	Other Income	8316755	-5147965	-38.23
#兑换外币收入	#Income from Exchange of Foreign Currencies	62914	24894	65.48
支出合计	**Total Expenditure**	**148726556**	**19317159**	**14.93**
工资性支出	Expenditure for Wages	9046190	1409058	18.45
#国家工资及奖金支出	#Expenditure for Wages and Bounties of Government	5148997	808516	18.63
国家对个人其他支出	Other Payments to Individuals of Government	1463276	81907	5.93
部队存款支出	Expenditure for Army Deposits	182559	-10980	-5.67
其他单位工资性支出	Expenditure for Wages of Other Units	2251358	529614	30.76
农副产品采购支出	Purchases of Agricultural and Sideline Products	2421755	451746	22.93
工矿及其他产品采购支出	Expenditure for Purchases of Industrial and Mineral Products	1893723	271926	16.77
行政企事业管理费支出	Government and Enterprises Overhead	5955127	914306	18.14
城乡个体经营支出	Expenditure for Individual Business	3688094	661697	21.86
储蓄存款支出	Expenditure for Savings Deposits	110847348	21152520	23.58
其他金融机构支出	Expenditure for Other financial Institutions	802198	-559566	-41.09
居民提取贷款支出	Expenditure for Repayment of Loans by Residents	3079255	587747	23.59
汇兑支出	Expenditure for Remittances	1492074	-127361	-7.86
有价证券支出	Expenditure for Securities	138614	10691	8.36
其他支出	Other Expenditure	9362178	-5455604	-36.82
#兑换外币支出	#Expenditure for Exchange of Foreign Currencies	80617	53872	201.43
附：代发工资	**Supersede Pay Wages**	**2485404**	**543266**	**27.97**

5-9 国家银行现金收支情况(2003年)

Cash Income and Expenditures of State Banks (2003)

单位：万元 (10 000 yuan)

项目	Item	本年累计 Add up this Year	比上年增减额 Increase Over the Year-beginning	比上年增减% Increase Rate in 2003 over 2002 (%)
收入合计	**Total Income**	**116465509**	**13973016**	**13.63**
商品销售收入	Income from Commodity Sales	9292038	1242136	15.43
服务业收入	Income from Service Trade	5885743	790945	15.52
税款收入	Income from Taxes	776565	98569	14.54
城乡个体经营收入	Income from Urban and Rural Individual Business	933137	244345	35.47
储蓄存款收入	Income from Saving Deposits	91586346	17334866	23.35
其他金融机构收入	Income from Other Financial Institutions	898884	27238	3.12
居民归还贷款收入	Income from Repayment of Loans by Residents	408771	92878	29.40
汇兑收入	Income from Remittances	1004889	-422782	-29.61
有价证券收入	Income from Securities	125753	-4698	-3.60
其他收入	Other Income	5553384	-5430480	-49.44
#兑换外币收入	#Income from Exchange of Foreign Currencies	61571	24048	64.09
支出合计	**Total Expenditure**	**113418623**	**13529220**	**13.54**
工资性支出	Expenditure for Wages	7395867	1111449	17.69
#国家工资及奖金支出	#Expenditure for Wages and Bounties of Government	4615979	724970	18.63
国家对个人其他支出	Other Payments to Individuals of Government	1289645	84172	6.98
部队存款支出	Expenditure for Army Deposits	175382	-13034	-6.92
其他单位工资性支出	Expenditure for Wages of Other Units	1314861	315341	31.55
农副产品采购支出	Purchases of Agricultural and Sideline Products	1735275	417386	31.67
工矿及其他产品采购支出	Expenditure for Purchases of Industrial and Mineral Products	1403903	228449	19.43
行政企事业管理费支出	Government and Enterprises Overhead	4656879	518779	12.54
城乡个体经营支出	Expenditure for Individual Business	1306130	408400	45.49
储蓄存款支出	Expenditure for Savings Deposits	88888023	16683300	23.11
其他金融机构支出	Expenditure for Other financial Institutions	590013	31115	5.57
居民提取贷款支出	Expenditure for Repayment of Loans by Residents	315396	71675	29.41
汇兑支出	Expenditure for Remittances	1429516	-118742	-7.67
有价证券支出	Expenditure for Securities	99453	-15540	-13.51
其他支出	Other Expenditure	5598168	-5807052	-50.92
#兑换外币支出	#Expenditure for Exchange of Foreign Currencies	78195	52676	206.42
附：代发工资	**Supersede Pay Wages**	**2278895**	**498117**	**27.97**

5-10 城乡居民年末储蓄存款余额

Outstanding Amount of Saving Deposits in Urban and Rural Households at the Year-end

单位：亿元 (100 million yuan)

市州	Cities and Prefecture	2002			2003		
		合计 Total	定期 Fixed	活期 Demand	合计 Total	定期 Fixed	活期 Demand
合计	**Total**	**2577.44**	**1715.02**	**862.41**	**3036.45**	**1970.84**	**1065.61**
长沙市	Changsha City	544.99	336.98	208.01	658.18	394.86	263.32
株洲市	Zhuzhou City	197.82	130.05	67.77	233.28	148.02	85.26
湘潭市	Xiangtan City	159.54	124.90	34.64	182.74	142.35	40.39
衡阳市	Hengyang City	275.89	195.78	80.11	323.48	226.64	96.83
邵阳市	Shaoyang City	202.35	138.15	64.19	239.56	161.60	77.96
岳阳市	YueYang City	173.77	115.22	58.55	200.76	132.51	68.25
常德市	Changde City	204.23	139.80	64.43	236.51	161.06	75.46
张家界市	Zhangjiajie City	36.27	20.91	15.36	43.03	24.59	18.43
益阳市	Yiyang C ity	130.87	91.78	39.09	150.58	104.37	46.21
郴州市	Chenzhou City	176.47	108.65	67.82	203.29	118.83	84.46
永州市	Yongzhou City	151.43	104.44	46.99	180.63	117.50	63.13
怀化市	Huaihua City	135.06	81.44	53.62	158.39	92.42	65.98
娄底市	Loudi City	133.05	97.28	35.76	158.14	111.38	46.76
湘西自治州	West Hunan A.P	55.71	29.65	26.06	67.88	34.72	33.16

5-11 保险机构与人员

Institutions and Personnel of Insurance System

项　目	Item	2000	2001	2002	2003
保险机构数（个）	Number of Institutions of Insurance System (unit)	395	407	374	383
省级公司	Provincial Branches	7	10	10	10
地市级公司	Prefecture/City Branches	63	72	76	86
县支公司及营业部	County Branches	325	325	288	287
年底实有职工人数（人）	Employees at the Year-end (person)	6522	6532	8008	8041

5-12 财产保险业务主要指标（2003年）

Major Indicators of Property Insurance Business (2003)

指标	Item	承保数量（件）Number of Insuance (case)	保险金额（万元）Insurance Value (10 000 yuan)	保费收入（万元）Premiums (10 000 yuan)	赔款件数（件）Number of Indemnity (case)	赔款支出（万元）Indemnity Expenditure (10 000 yuan)
合 计	**Total**	**4178645**	**74330749**	**211169**	**26789**	**107840**
财产险	**Property Insurance**	**818889**	**33851715**	**42887**	**1775**	**20449**
企业财产险	Enterprises Property Insurance	22479	27544218	24888	1268	17482
家庭财产险	Family Property Insurance	788519	3519102	5905	220	1904
船舶险	Ships Insurance	223	45317	319	13	203
航天保险	Insurance of Spacefligt					
核电站险	Insurance of Nuclear Power Plant					
能源保险	Energy Property Insurance					
飞机及飞机责任险	Airplane Insurance	-	10000	133	2	4
其他财产保险	Other Property Insurance	7668	2733079	1642	1775	20449
机动车辆险	**Motor Vehicle Insurance**	**1401496**	**24360136**	**126059**	**24385**	**74470**
车损险	Insurance of Motor Vehicle Damage	205796	13108861	42522	599	26635
法定三责险	Insurance of Legal Third Party's Liability	21588	-	3322	-	1138
商业三责险	Insurance of Commercial Third Party's Liability	406841	17540	29759	484	24518
附加险	Additional Insurance	705156	10123492	34204	454	10302
其他机动车险	Other Motor Vehicle Insurance	62115	1110242	16251	22852	11877
责任保险	**Liability Insurance**	**33719**	**221435**	**9014**	**484**	**5454**
公众责任保险	Public Liability Insurance	1136	93937	822	167	498
产品责任保险	Products Liability Insurance	24	69581	368	12	173
雇主责任保险	Employer Liability Insurance	7331	59730	4083	287	2769
职业责任保险	Occupation Liability Insurance	12002	-	2558	-	1333
其他责任保险	Other Liability Insurance	13226	-	1184	18	681
建、安工程险	**Projects Responsibility Insurance**	**109**	**1140082**	**3134**	**38**	**1279**
信用保险	**Credit Insurance**	**-**	**200000**	**573**	**-**	**259**
保证保险	**Guarantee Insurance**	**5389**	**419202**	**1802**	**27**	**497**
货运险	**Freight Transport Insurance**	**90211**	**8003973**	**13185**	**141**	**3337**
农业险	**Agriculture Insurance**	**510000**	**66000**	**891**	**-**	**449**
种植业保险	Planting Insurance	510000	66000	875	-	448
养殖业保险	Cultivation Insurance			16	-	1
其他农业保险	Other Agriculture Insurance					
其他险种	**Other Insurance**	**1331580**	**6100206**	**13627**	**795**	**1647**
分期付款购车保险	Insurance of Buy Cars by Stages	7712	84706	1985	10	86
抵押贷款住房综合保险	Insurance of Mortgage Loans for Housing	20929	414194	1183	4	18
短期健康保险	Insurance of Short-term Health	1162	127027	390	209	30
意外保险	Accident Insurance	1303311	5480509	9765	293	1359
其他	Other Insurance	5710	185847	304	279	163

5-13 人身保险业务主要指标（2003年）

Major Indicators of Life Insurance Business (2003)

单位：万元 (10 000 yuan)

指标	Item	保费收入 Premiums	赔款支出 Indemnity Expenditure	退保金 Withdrawal Amount Insured	年金给付 Annuity Payment	满期给付 Mature Payment	死伤医疗给付 Payment for Death,Injury and Medical Treatment
合 计	**Total**	**825874.1**	**32173.3**	**63485.2**	**40409.5**	**17673.6**	**40641.3**
个人业务	**Personal Business**	**699010.7**	**9923.8**	**47671.6**	**36032.3**	**11933.1**	**21651.0**
人寿保险	Life Insurance	656788.4	29.1	46838.3	36032.3	11933.1	15221.8
非分红产品	Non Bonus Products	236677.4	1.8	26520.7	35097.5	10105.6	13529.3
定期寿险	Term Life Insurance	1587.6	1.8	38.1	0.2	2.7	619.9
两全寿险	Endowment Life Insurance	85219.8		13142.4	15000.2	6898.8	4246.9
终身寿险	Whole Life Insurance	119662.0		5628.0	14707.6	1239.9	8019.4
年金	Annuity	30208.0		7712.1	5389.5	1964.2	643.1
分红产品	Bonus Products	416259.6	27.3	20039.1	934.9	1426.5	1655.1
定期寿险	Term Life Insurance	798.0		2.0			35.0
两全寿险	Endowment Life Insurance	402456.0	27.3	19757.5	885.9	1421.5	1217.5
终身寿险	Whole Life Insurance	9629.6		238.5	32.0	5.0	346.6
年金	Annuity	3376.0		41.2	18.0		56.0
意外伤害保险	Accidence Injury Insurance	2949.0	1215.9	0.8			
一年期以内	Within One Year Period	638.2	104.0				
一年期	One Year Period	2310.8	1111.9	0.8			
健康保险	Health Insurance	39273.3	8678.8	832.5			6429.2
一年期及以内	One Year Period and	13735.4	8636.2	2.0			5521.1
	Within One Year Period						908.0
一年期以上	Over One Year Period	25537.9	42.7	830.5			
团体业务	**Group Insurance**	**126863.4**	**22249.5**	**15813.6**	**4377.2**	**5740.5**	**18990.3**
人寿保险	Life Insurance	86028.0	20.3	15727.7	4377.2	5740.5	373.9
非分红产品	Non Bonus Products	24749.6		12460.8	4050.1	5622.8	346.8
定期寿险	Term Life Insurance	353.6		1.0	5.1	1.0	287.5
两全寿险	Endowment Life Insurance	4402.6		48.2	600.4	336.2	8.9
终身寿险	Whole Life Insurance	207.4		1.8		-0.4	14.1
年金	Annuity	19786.0		12409.8	3444.6	5286.0	36.3
分红产品	Bonus Products	60942.0	20.3	3132.3	305.1	100.0	24.9
定期寿险	Term Life Insurance						
两全寿险	Endowment Life Insurance	42301.8	20.3	182.4			
终身寿险	Whole Life Insurance						
年金	Annuity	18640.2		2949.9	305.1	100.0	24.9
意外伤害保险	Accidence Injury Insurance	26737.9	15092.7	0.3			14406.4
一年期以内	Within One Year Period	2901.2	696.0				499.4
一年期	One Year Period	23836.7	14396.7	0.3			13907.0
健康保险	Health Insurance	14097.6	7136.4	85.7			4210.0
一年期及以内	One Year Period and Within One Year Period	12719.5	7110.3	0.2			4008.2
一年期以上	Over One Year Period	1378.1	26.1	85.5			201.8

六、物价指数

PRICE INDICES

资料整理人员： 陈　浩　陈　军　傅磊峰
刘征宇　蔡月娥

6-1 各种物价总指数

Overall Price Indices

年 份 Year	商品零售价格指数 General Retail Price Index	城市居民消费价格指数 Urban Consumer Price Index	农村居民消费价格指数 Rural Consumer Price Index	农产品收购价格指数 General Purchasing Price Index of Farm Products	农村工业品零售价格指数 General Rural Retail Price Index of Industrial Products	农产品成交价格指数 Farm Products Trade Price Index	工农业商品综合比价指数 General Price Parity Index of Industrial and Farm Products
以上年为100	**Preceding year =100**						
1985	111.1	111.9	110.2	111.6	106.1	118.7	95.1
1986	104.8	105.4	105.3	105.7	103.3	104.7	97.7
1987	110.6	111.3	108.8	110.2	109.9	119.3	99.7
1988	125.9	125.7	125.4	123.1	123.6	136.7	100.4
1989	118.1	117.3	119.1	106.8	120.9	110.8	113.2
1990	99.4	100.6	100.2	94.1	99.7	94.1	106.0
1991	104.1	105.1	103.8	94.3	103.1	99.6	109.3
1992	109.5	113.5	107.9	99.1	104.9	107.8	105.9
1993	115.1	117.4	116.4	114.7	114.9	113.9	100.2
1994	124.5	124.8	125.6	144.1	117.2	135.5	81.3
1995	115.5	118.1	119.5	117.2	116.7	125.2	99.6
1996	105.2	107.2	108.2	104.9	105.1	101.1	100.2
1997	100.3	103.0	102.5	95.3	100.4	95.0	105.4
1998	97.9	100.5	100.1	90.4	97.5	91.7	107.9
1999	97.6	99.6	101.4	91.1	97.0	93.7	106.5
2000	99.3	101.3	101.4	96.8	98.8	95.7	102.1
2001	98.8	98.9	99.3	-	-	96.0	-
2002	99.2	99.6	99.4	-	-	99.1	-
2003	100.6	101.4	104.1	-	-	-	-
以1978年为100	**1978 =100**						
1985	137.1	145.2	113.4	190.3	116.2	157.8	61.1
1986	143.7	153.0	119.4	201.1	120.0	165.2	59.7
1987	158.9	170.3	129.9	221.6	131.9	197.1	59.5
1988	200.1	214.1	162.9	272.8	163.0	269.4	59.7
1989	236.3	251.1	194.0	291.4	197.1	298.5	67.6
1990	234.9	252.6	194.4	274.2	196.5	280.9	71.6
1991	244.5	265.5	201.8	258.6	202.6	279.8	78.3
1992	267.7	301.3	217.7	256.3	212.5	301.6	82.9
1993	308.2	353.7	253.4	294.0	244.2	343.5	83.1
1994	383.6	441.4	318.2	423.7	286.2	465.4	67.6
1995	443.1	521.3	380.2	496.6	334.0	582.7	67.3
1996	466.1	558.8	411.4	520.9	351.0	589.1	67.4
1997	467.5	575.6	421.7	496.4	352.4	559.6	71.0
1998	457.7	578.5	422.1	448.7	343.6	513.6	76.6
1999	446.7	576.2	428.0	408.8	333.3	480.9	81.5
2000	443.6	583.7	434.0	395.7	329.3	460.2	83.2
2001	438.3	577.3	431.0	-	-	441.8	-
2002	434.8	575.0	428.4	-	-	437.8	-
2003	437.4	583.0	446.0	-	-	-	-

6-2 零售物价分类指数(2003年)

Overall Retail Indices by Category of Commodities (2003)

类 别	Item	全省 Total Indices		城市 Urban Indices		农村 Rural Indices	
		以上年为100 Preceding year=100	以1978年为100 1978=100	以上年为100 Preceding year=100	以1978年为100 1978=100	以上年为100 Preceding year=100	以1978年为100 1978=100
零售价格总指数	**General Retail Price Indices**	**100.6**	**437.4**	**100.1**	**460.6**	**101.1**	**409.5**
食品类	Food	104.2	635.9	103.7	684.5	104.7	553.6
粮食	Grain	102.2	821.4	101.8	709.4	103.0	579.7
油脂类	Oil or Fat	110.5	497.3	109.9	458.6	111.1	672.3
肉禽蛋	Meal, Poultry and Eggs	106.0	709.7	103.6	701.6	108.6	708.7
水产品	Aquatic Products	97.9	565.3	96.9	552.4	99.1	593.5
鲜菜	Fresh Vegetables	119.6	1890.9	122.2	1757.5	115.9	
干菜	Dried Vegetables	99.1	497.9	96.3	475.1	101.1	531.3
鲜果	Fresh Fruits	110.0	619.0	110.0	594.0	110.0	378.3
干果	Dried Fruits	102.7	469.9	100.0	474.2	108.6	412.5
其他食品类	Other Food	97.1	446.4	98.5	523.6	95.4	361.2
饮食业	Catering Trade	98.8		97.0		100.1	
饮料、烟酒	Beverages,Tobacco and Liquor	99.5	232.4	99.9	239.4	99.2	183.1
服装、鞋帽类	Garments,shoes and Hats	99.4	224.8	97.1	219.0	101.6	241.6
纺织品类	Textiles	99.3	303.6	98.5	301.3	100.0	299.4
家用电器及音像器材	Electronic Household Appliances	94.6	99.1	93.8	104.6	95.5	95.5
文化办公用品	Cultural Office Articles	98.0	157.1	98.1	155.1	97.8	161.6
日用品	Articles for Daily Use	99.4	262.1	99.9	245.4	99.0	279.0
体育娱乐用品	Sports and Recreation Articles	98.9	158.5	98.4	155.6	99.9	165.0
交通、通信用品	Transportation and Communications Articles	93.4		92.2		95.3	
家具	Furniture	98.1		96.7		99.8	
化妆品类	Cosmetics	99.9		99.7		100.2	
金银珠宝类	Jewelry	110.0		111.7		105.2	
药品及医疗保健类	Medicines and Medical Health Care Medicines	94.0	361.3	95.5	337.5	91.4	394.7
书报杂志及电子出版物	Newspapers and Magazines,	99.5	1619.8	100.0	1466.7	98.4	1828.1
燃料类	Fuels	109.2	634.3	109.8	627.5	108.5	555.1
建筑材料及五金电料类	Building Materials,Hardware,Electric Materials	100.9		101.4		100.4	

6-3 农业生产资料价格指数(2003年)

Price Indices of Agricultural Means of Production (2003)

类 别	Item	以上年价格为100 Preceding year=100	以1978年价格为100 1978 year=100
总指数	**General Indices**	**102.6**	**398.0**
小农具	Small Farm Tools	103.1	459.5
饲料	Forage	101.0	
幼禽家畜	Young Livestock and Fowls	110.2	
大牲畜	Large Animals	109.5	
半机械化农具	Semi-mechanized Farm Tools	102.1	518.5
机械化农具	Mechanized Farm Machinery	99.5	238.8
化肥	Chemical Fertilizer	100.5	325.0
农药及农药械	Pesticide and Its Appliances	101.8	242.6
#化学农药	Chemical Pesticide	101.8	248.1
农药械	Its Appliances	101.6	184.4
农用机油	Oil for Farm Machinery	104.2	1176.6
其他	Others	107.0	381.1

6-4 居民消费价格总指数

Overall Consumer Price Indices

年份 Year	居民消费价格总指数 Overall Consumer Price Indices	城市 Urban	农村 Rural	服务项目价格指数 Services Price Indices
以上年为100	**Preceding year =100**			
1985	110.9	111.9	110.2	106.5
1986	105.3	105.4	105.3	106.7
1987	109.8	111.3	108.8	116.4
1988	125.6	125.7	125.4	125.6
1989	118.2	117.3	119.1	131.3
1990	100.4	100.6	100.2	113.9
1991	104.4	105.1	103.8	106.2
1992	110.7	113.5	107.9	119.1
1993	116.8	117.4	116.4	130.0
1994	125.3	124.8	125.6	125.5
1995	119.0	118.1	119.5	124.8
1996	107.7	107.2	108.2	112.4
1997	102.8	103.0	102.5	112.5
1998	100.2	100.5	100.1	113.4
1999	100.5	99.6	101.4	116.5
2000	101.4	101.3	101.4	113.6
2001	99.1	98.9	99.3	102.5
2002	99.5	99.6	99.4	103.0
2003	102.4	101.4	104.1	103.3
以1985年为100	**1985 =100**			
1985	100.0	100.0	100.0	100.0
1986	105.3	105.4	105.3	106.7
1987	115.6	117.3	114.6	124.2
1988	145.2	147.5	143.7	156.0
1989	171.6	173.0	171.1	204.9
1990	172.3	174.0	171.4	233.4
1991	179.9	182.9	178.0	247.8
1992	199.2	207.6	192.0	295.1
1993	232.6	243.7	223.5	383.7
1994	291.5	304.1	280.7	481.5
1995	346.9	359.2	335.7	601.0
1996	373.6	385.1	363.2	675.4
1997	384.1	396.7	372.3	759.8
1998	384.9	398.7	372.7	861.7
1999	386.8	397.1	377.9	1003.9
2000	392.2	402.3	383.2	1140.4
2001	388.7	397.9	380.5	1168.9
2002	386.8	396.3	378.2	1204.0
2003	396.1	401.8	393.7	1243.7

6-5 居民消费价格分类指数(2003年)

Consumer Price Indices by Category (2003)

类别	Item	全省 Total Indices		城市 Urban Indices		农村 Rural Indices	
		以上年为100 Preceding year=100	以1978年为100 1978=100	以上年为100 Preceding year=100	以1978年为100 1978=100	以上年为100 Preceding year=100	以1978年为100 1978=100
居民消费价格总指数	**General Consumer Price Indices**	**102.4**	**449.8**	**101.4**	**582.7**	**104.1**	**445.9**
食品	Food	105.8	604.8	104.4	658.7	107.8	533.1
粮食	Grain	103.4	817.8	103.0	741.9	105.0	552.2
淀粉及薯类	Starches and Tubers	100.7	0.0	97.1	0.0	108.4	0.0
干豆类及豆制品	Bear and Its Products	106.5	0.0	107.2	0.0	105.2	0.0
油脂类	Oil or Fat	113.7	472.2	111.4	448.1	115.4	620.4
肉禽及其制品	Meal,Poultry and Their Products	109.4	774.2	106.1	756.8	113.6	798.7
蛋类	Eggs	100.5	0.0	99.2	0.0	102.0	0.0
水产品类	Aquatic Products	98.5	550.9	97.4	526.8	100.1	591.2
菜类	Vegetables	118.4	1554.5	118.7	702.9	115.3	0.0
调味品	Flavoring	98.7	355.5	99.3	1381.0	98.2	377.9
糖类	Carbohydrate	95.2	361.9	96.1	495.7	94.4	342.1
烟草类	Tobacco	100.5	231.7	100.9	340.4	100.0	191.4
酒	Wine	98.1	197.5	98.4	213.2	97.8	176.7
茶和饮料	Tea and Beverages	98.8	195.0	100.3	215.7	97.2	170.5
干鲜瓜果类	Dried and Fresh Melons and Fruits	111.2	619.3	104.9	554.7	130.0	510.5
糕点类	Cake	99.3	477.0	98.3	561.5	101.1	365.2
奶及奶制品	Milk and Its Products	98.4	325.1	98.2	347.7	102.5	302.8
其他食品	Other Food	97.0	203.3	99.2	431.2	94.2	293.5
饮食业	Catering Trade	99.4	0.0	98.2	0.0	100.4	0.0
衣着	Clothing	98.8	238.4	97.3	225.5	102.3	254.4
家庭设备、用品	Household Facilities and Article	97.2	155.4	96.6	186.9	98.7	185.3
医疗保健	Medicine and Medical Articles	105.9	445.0	103.4	366.9	109.2	520.4
交通和通信	Means of Transportation&Communication	98.0	0.0	97.6	0.0	98.8	0.0
娱乐、教育文化用品	Recreation, Education and Culture Articles	100.4	189.2	99.4	178.4	102.2	200.2
居住	Residence	103.1	0.0	104.8	0.0	101.5	0.0
服务项目	Services	103.3	1199.8	101.4	1442.6	107.3	1756.2

6-6 十四个调查市县价格指数

Price Indices in 14 Cities and Counties Under Investigation

(以上年价格为100) (preceding year=100)

市县	Cities and counties	居民消费价格指数 Consumer Price Index		商品零售指数 General Retail Price Index		农业生产资料价格指数 Agricultural Means of Production Price Index	
		2002	2003	2002	2003	2002	2003
长沙市	Changsha City	99.2	100.9	98.6	99.2		
株洲市	Zhuzhou City	97.3	101.7	97.3	100.1		
湘潭市	Xiangtan City	100.3	101.7	100.8	100.2		
衡阳市	Hengyang City	99.8	101.9	99.9	100.4		
邵阳市	Shaoyang City	98.9	102.6	98.2	100.9		
岳阳市	Yueyang City	101.1	102.4	99.1	101.8		
常德市	Changde City	100.0	100.7	99.3	99.5		
益阳市	Yiyang City	100.1	102.2	100.1	100.2		
郴州市	Chenzhou City	99.6	101.3	99.1	99.7		
怀化市	Huaihua City	100.0	101.9	99.8	99.4		
耒阳市	Leiyang City	99.4	102.1	99.4	101.0	99.5	101.5
慈利县	Cili County	100.4	102.1	99.6	100.9	99.0	105.0
道　县	Daoxian County	99.9	102.1	99.4	99.6	102.0	99.3
新化县	Xinhua County	99.1	104.4	98.8	102.6	94.3	105.1

6-7 农业生产资料价格指数(2003)

Price Indices of Agricultural Means of Production (2003)

(以上年价格为100) (preceding year=100)

类 别	Item	道县 Dao County	耒阳市 Leiyang City	新化县 Xinhua County	慈利县 Cili County
农业生产资料价格指数	**Price Indices of Agricultural Means of Production**	**99.3**	**101.5**	**105.1**	**105.0**
小农具	Small Farm Tools	97.3	107.7	114.5	101.7
饲料	Forage	98.1	101.0	99.0	105.1
幼禽家畜	Young Livestock and Fowls	98.9	130.8	106.2	113.7
大牲畜	Large Animals	116.2	100.0	107.4	110.2
半机械化农具	Semi-mechanized Farm Tools	101.0	110.4	100.0	98.9
机械化农具	Mechanized Farm Machinery	103.5	91.4	100.0	99.9
化肥	Chemical Fertilizer	95.5	95.1	106.3	103.8
农药及农药械	Pesticide and Its Appliances	97.6	101.2	103.5	101.5
农用机油	Oil for Farm Machinery	107.1	109.1	112.1	92.3
其他	Others	101.4	105.2	107.1	124.7

6-8 农产品生产者价格指数

Producer Price Indices of Farm Products

以上年为100 Preceding year=100

项目	Item	2001	2002	2003
生产者价格总指数	**Overall Producer Price Indices**	**100.94**	**99.91**	**106.76**
农业产品	**Farming Products**	**101.88**	**99.91**	**108.76**
谷物（原粮）	Cereals	111.49	101.18	104.45
小麦	Wheat	98.47		
稻谷	Paddy	112.19	101.32	104.44
#早籼稻	Early Season Rice	107.76	103.20	102.64
晚籼稻	Late Season Rice	112.49	99.08	105.72
其它稻谷	Other Rice	122.90	101.03	95.40
玉米	Maize	99.51	92.70	105.33
薯类	Tubers	103.34	93.31	104.55
#红薯	Sweet Potato	104.36	91.11	106.02
马铃薯	Potatoes	100.63	116.10	100.70
豆类	Beans	94.58	92.56	123.75
#大豆	Soja	95.37	92.76	124.00
绿豆	Mung Bean	89.56	99.62	114.68
油料	Oil-bearing Crops	90.04	109.91	119.85
#花生	Peanut	74.76	106.61	124.35
油菜籽	Rapeseed	96.99	109.01	115.21
棉花	Cotton	55.72	102.21	131.04
麻类	Fiber Crops	93.16	93.76	122.30
糖料	Sugar	91.95	89.76	83.57
烟叶	Tobacco	85.38	146.42	84.88
中药材	Medicinal herbs	99.37	95.87	100.96
#金银花	Honeysuckle	99.62	100.00	100.96
白术	Lagehead Atractylodes	98.68	89.06	
蔬菜	Vegetables	97.67	100.55	110.34
叶菜类	Greenstuff	95.89	89.61	119.94
瓜菜类	Melon and Fruit	89.63	113.67	125.00
块根、块茎菜类	Tuber	114.86	110.82	100.50
茄果菜类	Nightshade	98.46	122.81	102.87
菜用豆类	Navy Bean	84.46	105.44	101.79
水生菜类	Aquicolous Vegetable	95.47	112.58	106.44
食用菌 （干鲜混合）	Mushroom (dried and fresh)	102.45	105.30	115.94
水果	Fruits	91.19	111.47	107.73
柑桔类	Citrus	108.41	104.96	107.77
果用瓜	Fruit Melons	78.35	127.16	99.71
其它水果	Other fruits	90.53	109.85	110.10
茶叶（干品）	Tea (dried tea)	96.79	115.66	98.67
林业产品	**Forestry Products**	**96.62**	**97.21**	**101.01**
木材	Timber	99.06	96.68	100.10
竹材	Bamboo	97.43	94.80	98.88

6-8 续表 (以上年为100 Preceding year=100) continued

项目	Item	2001	2002	2003
#毛竹（楠竹）	Phyllostachys	97.43	104.73	98.88
林产品	Forest Products	94.12	95.32	106.56
工业用原料	Industry Raw Materials	95.36	102.87	107.09
#油桐籽	Tung-oil Seeds	98.89	87.20	113.64
油茶籽	Tea-oil Seeds	95.49	101.16	103.90
坚果	Nut	74.49	97.26	107.00
其它林产品	Other Forest Products	99.04	95.69	
竹笋干	Dried Bamboo Shoot	99.04	100.00	
牧业（畜产品）	**Animal Husbandry**	**100.54**	**99.70**	**107.36**
成年役畜、产品畜	Draught Animals and Commodity Animals	100.22	119.19	
#役用牛	Draught Cattle	100.22	120.87	
肉畜（毛重）	Fatstock (gross weight)	100.81	98.38	102.36
#猪	Hogs	100.81	98.33	107.87
肉牛	Beef Cattle	102.16	94.56	101.53
山羊	Goat	100.23	104.28	103.72
家禽（毛重）	Fowl (gross weight)	99.47	116.38	100.61
#鸡	Hen	98.34	111.48	103.71
鸭	Duck	100.63	122.02	97.02
其它饲养动物	Other Feeding Animals	101.80	101.91	102.85
#兔	Rabbit	101.54	113.38	108.13
狗	Dog	100.64	104.73	101.35
蛇	Snake	103.78	89.78	100.50
蛋类	Poultry Eggs	99.64	95.28	104.30
#鸡蛋	Hens' Egg	99.81	95.84	103.15
鸭蛋	Ducks' Egg	99.36	93.81	104.82
奶类	Milk	97.12	84.19	105.90
#牛奶	Cow Milk	97.12	84.19	105.90
渔业产品	Fishery Products	**98.63**	**92.93**	**97.60**
淡水鱼类	Freshwater Fish	98.28	92.62	97.60
#青鱼	Mackerel	99.67	111.14	82.50
草鱼	Grass Carp	100.33	94.73	94.73
鲤鱼	Carp	92.81	101.24	95.52
鲢鱼	Silver Carp	99.45	88.56	104.71
鲫鱼	Crucian	97.75	75.70	104.44
鳙鱼	Bighrad Carp	96.03	86.40	133.12
其它淡水养殖产品	Other Freshwater Aquatic Products Cultured	100.87	93.70	103.30
#甲鱼	Turtle	100.30	80.00	103.71
黄鳝	Yellow Eel	103.80	80.21	106.82
泥鳅	Loach	99.54	82.12	99.38

6-9 主要原材料、燃料、动力购进价格指数

Principal Raw and Processed Materials, Fuel, Power Purchasing Price Indices

(以上年为100) (preceding year=100)

类 别	Item	2000	2001	2002	2003
全部原材料	**General Purchasing Price Indices**	**106.7**	**101.1**	**99.3**	**106.7**
#燃料动力类	Fuels and Motive Power	108.6	101.5	102.8	108.9
黑色金属材料类	Ferrous Metals Materials	102.8	102.3	99.4	108.8
有色金属材料类	Nonferrous Metals Materials and Electric Wire	113.5	97.5	96.7	105.5
化工原料类	Chemical Raw Materials	115.4	98.7	99.0	104.1
木材及纸浆类	Logging and Paper Pulp	102.0	100.6	99.4	100.2
建材及非金属矿类	Building and Nonmetal Materials	99.3	98.6	101.5	99.4
其它工业原料及半成品类	Other Industry Raw Materials & Semi-Finished Products	100.4	102.1	99.4	102.2
农副产品类	Farm Products	104.5	103.2	96.8	110.7
纺织原料类	Textile Raw Materials	101.8	102.3	93.7	101.3

6-10 工业品出厂价格指数

Ex-Factory Price Indices of Industrial Products

(以上年价格为100) (preceding year=100)

行业	Sector	2000	2001	2002	2003
全部工业品	**General Industrial Products**	**102.9**	**99.8**	**99.2**	**102.6**
生产资料	Means of Production	104.1	99.8	99.2	103.7
采掘工业	Mining and Quarrying Industry	99.4	104.4	106.4	106.1
原材料工业	Raw Materials Industry	108.5	99.3	98.4	107.0
加工工业	Manufacturing Industry	98.2	99.6	99.4	100.6
生活资料	Means of Subsistence	99.1	99.9	99.1	99.5
食品类	Food	98.5	100.7	100.8	100.8
衣着类	Clothing	101.4	98.7	99.3	98.3
一般日用品	Articles for Daily use	98.1	100.1	98.6	100.2
耐用消费品	Durable Consumer Goods	97.4	97.8	92.3	93.5
按工业部门分:	**by Sector**				
冶金工业	Manufacturing Industry	102.6	100.9	97.9	111.2
电力工业	Power Industry	101.4	100.1	99.5	100.2
煤炭及炼焦工业	Coal Industry	97.6	102.8	111.7	106.7
石油工业	Petroleum Industry	140.7	96.8	96.6	110.1
化学工业	Chemical Industry	99.1	99.0	98.8	101.3
机械工业	Machine Building Industry	99.0	98.9	99.0	97.7
建材工业	Building Materials Industry	96.2	100.7	98.7	101.3
森林工业	Timber Industry	101.1	92.5	96.7	97.7
食品工业	Food Industry	98.3	101.2	100.5	100.3
纺织工业	Textile Industry	108.3	94.7	95.2	103.8
缝纫工业	Tailoring Industry	93.3	96.8	98.1	97.2
皮革工业	Leather Industry	110.4	109.9	102.9	102.1
造纸工业	Paper Industry	98.8	100.0	97.3	100.1
文教艺术用品工业	Cultural, Educational & Handicrafts Articles Industry	98.9	98.5	98.3	97.9
其他工业	Others	107.7	102.3	106.4	104.0

6-11 主要工业产品分行业出厂价格指数

Major Industrial Products Price Indices by Sector

(以上年为100) (preceding year=100)

行业	Sector	2000	2001	2002	2003
煤炭采选业	Coal Mining and Dressing	97.70	102.64	113.13	106.39
黑色金届矿采选业	Ferrous Metals Mining and Dressing	87.48		96.85	118.67
有色金属矿采选业	Nonferrous Metals Mining and Dressing	104.94	110.65	100.03	107.44
建筑材料及其它非金属矿采选业	Nonmetal Minerals Mining and Dressing	88.99	93.65	98.28	101.14
采盐业	Salt Mining	102.69	97.67		
木材及竹材采运业	Logging and Transport of Wood and Bamboo	101.08	101.62	99.71	
自来水生产与供应业	Production and supply of Tap Water	120.15	102.36	109.57	106.53
食品制造业	Food Production	88.02	102.37	100.10	99.45
饮料制造业	Beverage Production	100.51	101.02	98.88	99.04
烟草加工业	Tobacco Processing	103.40	99.07	101.01	98.68
饲料工业	Feed Industry	97.97	102.56		
纺织业	Textile Industry	107.52	94.73	95.36	103.80
缝纫业	Garments and other Fiber products	94.38	96.84		
皮革、毛皮及其制品业	Leather, Furs and Related Products	118.27	109.88	102.88	102.15
木材加工及竹藤棕草制品业	Timber Processing, Bamboo, Cane, Palm Fiber & Straw Products	100.08	89.01	95.69	97.57
家具制造业	Furniture Manufacturing	102.14	99.09	97.53	97.02
造纸及纸制品业	Papermaking and Paper Products	98.44	100.03	97.22	100.09
文教体育用品制造业	Cultural, Educational and Sports Articles	97.90	98.52	99.86	100.01
电力、蒸气、热水生产和供应业	Production and supply of Electric Power	101.48	99.74	99.53	100.18
石油加工业	Petroleum Processing and coking	137.98	96.76	96.76	111.02
炼焦、煤气及煤制品业	Production and suppiy of gas	98.41	102.29		
化学工业	Raw Chemical Materials and Chemical products	99.35	99.78	99.76	101.26
医药工业	Medical and Pharmaceutical products	96.71	96.33	95.64	101.32
化学纤维工业	Chemical Fiber	108.43	89.97	96.87	103.07
橡胶制品业	Rubber Products	97.19	100.10	99.35	99.70
塑料制品业	Plastic Products	105.41	102.25	94.86	100.97
建筑材料及其它非金属矿制品业	Nonmetal Mineral Products	97.14	100.65	98.74	100.82
黑色金属冶炼及压延加工业	Smelting and Pressing of Ferrous Metals	101.00	101.32	98.54	120.48
有色金属冶炼及压延加工业	Smelting and Pressing of Nonferrous Metals	105.80	97.34	97.27	106.88
金属制品业	Metal Products	96.81	99.20	97.85	100.66
机械工业	Machine Buiding Industry	99.61	99.09	99.13	97.68
交通运输设备制造业	Transportation Equipment Manufacturing	99.00	98.98	100.21	95.61
电气机械及器材制造业	Electric Machinery and Equipment	100.58	99.20	96.62	98.62
电力及通讯设备制造业	Electronic and Telecommunications Equipment	98.71	97.30	96.42	97.02
仪器仪表及其它计量器具制造业	Instruments, Meters and Calculating Equipment	103.53	100.32	97.62	97.34
工艺美术制造业	Arts and Crafts	101.97		98.19	104.07

6-12 主要市州房地产价格指数

Real Estate Price Indices of Major Cities

(以上年为100) (preceding year =100)

市	Cities	销售价格指数 Selling Price Indices		租赁价格指数 Venting Price Indices		土地交易价格指数 Transaction Price Indices of Land	
		2002	2003	2002	2003	2002	2003
全 省	**Total**	**99.7**	**101.3**	**101.7**	**101.5**	**102.2**	**103.6**
长沙市	ChangSha City	101.1	100.5	101.7	101	101.1	100.9
株洲市	ZhuZhou City	101.4	101.6	101.3	100.6	100.9	101.9
湘潭市	XiangTan City	103.6	107.8	100.0	101.1	101.3	113.3
岳阳市	YueYang City	104.3	100.9	103.7	104.4	105.4	102.9
郴州市	ChenZhou City	100.9	100.0	104.9	95.9	100.1	100.7
衡阳市	HengYang City	102.8	106.6	103.5	102.7	108.5	107.9
娄底市	LouDI City	100.3	100.2	99.0	98.9	100.0	105.9
邵阳市	ShaoYang City	100.2	101.8	100.4	103.1	100.9	103.7
怀化市	HuaiHua City	108.8	102.7	99.2	100.6	100.6	100.8
常德市	ChangDe City	100.4	101.6	100.2	99.4	103.1	102.3
益阳市	YiYang City	95.0	101.7	101.8	100.3	104.2	105.7
永州市	YongZhou City	102.7	109.5	104.8	106.3	103.1	108.3

注:张家界市、湘西自治州因各种原因数据空缺。

Data of Zhangjiajie city and West Hunan A.P is missing for some reason.

6-13 固定资产投资和建筑业价格指数

Price Indices of Investment in Fixed Assets and Construction

(以上年为100) (preceding year=100)

项 目	Item	2000	2001	2002	2003
固定资产投资价格总指数	**Price Indices of Investment in Fixed Assets**	**102.3**	**100.3**	**100.4**	**102.8**
建筑安装工程	Construction and Installation	103.3	101.8	100.9	104.4
设备、工具、器具购置	Purchase of Equipment,Tools and Instruments	99.0	99.1	99.0	97.7
其他投资	Others	101.4	101.1	99.1	101.8
建筑业价格总指数	**Price Indices of Construction**				
直接费用指数	Direct Costs	102.8	102.0	100.8	-
人工费	Manpower	105.6	107.4	104.3	103.1
材料费	Materials	101.3	100.8	99.6	107.1
其他费用指数	Others Costs	106.2	100.4	101.6	100.6
主要材料费用价格指数	**Price Indices of Main Material Costs**				
钢 材	Steel Products	103.1	99.3	97.5	111.2
木 材	Timber	95.4	95.2	100.1	102.0
水 泥	Cement	100.6	102.0	100.1	105.4
地方材料	Local Materials	99.5	103.1	101.0	103.2
其他材料	Others	99.7	99.4	102.4	103.2

七、人民生活

PEOPLE'S LIVELIHOOD

资料整理人员：　夏　卫　彭安玲　熊　丽

7-1 人民物质文化生活提高情况

Improvement in People's Material and Cultural Life

指 标	Item	2000	2001	2002	2003
就业	**Employment**				
每一农村劳动力负担人数(人)	Number of Dependents Per Rural Laborer(person)	1.46	1.45	1.44	1.42
每一城镇就业者负担人数(人)	Number of Dependents Per Urban Employee(person)	1.71	1.77	1.97	1.89
城镇失业率(%)	Urban Unemployment Rate (%)	3.7	4.0	4.0	4.5
收入 (元)	**Income**				
农村居民家庭人均可支配收入	Annual Per Capita Disposable Income of Rural Residents	2159	2264.71	2363.17	2471.59
农村居民家庭人均纯收入	Annual Per Capita Net Income of Rural Residents	2197.16	2299.46	2397.92	2532.87
城镇居民家庭人均可支配收入	Annual Per Capita Disposable Income of Urban Residents	6218.7	6780.6	6958.56	7674.2
职工年平均货币工资	Average Money Wage of Staff and Workers	6515	7698	8734	9855
城乡居民年底人均储蓄存款余额	Per Capita Balance of Saving Deposit in Urban and Rural Residents at Year-end	2862.71	3319.26	3888.42	4557.32
全省居民消费水平 (元)	**Consumption Level (yuan)**	**2723**	**2845**	**3013**	**3284**
住房 (平方米)	**Per Capita Living Floor Space (sq.m)**				
农村居民平均每人住房面积	Rural Residents	30.92	32.87	34.05	35.09
城市居民平均每人居住面积	Urban Residents	11.75	11.8	12.4	24.43
交通	**Traffic**				
农村居民每百户拥有摩托车 (辆)	Motor Cycles per 100 Households in Rural (unit)	10.51	12.41	14.19	17.49
城镇居民每百户拥有摩托车 (辆)	Motor Cycles per 100 Households in Urban (unit)	13.2	15.5	13.69	14.75
城市每万人拥有公共车辆 (标台)	Buses per 10 000 persons in Cities (unit)	10.43	10.39	6.65	7.50
城市公用事业	**Public Utilities in Urban Areas**				
自来水普及率 (%)	Rate of Access to Tap Water (%)	97.5	97.4	80.7	86.36
用气普及率 (%)	Rate of Access to Gas and Liquefied Gas (%)	78.35	57.67	59.69	66.58
每人拥有公共绿地 (平方米)	Per Capita Green Areas (sq.m)	5.1	4.55	4.72	5.02
文化	**Culture**				
城镇居民每百户有彩色电视机(台)	Color TV Sets per 100 Households in Urban (unit)	109.4	112.6	120.03	124.82
农村居民每百户有电视机 (台)	TV Sets per 100 Households in Rural (unit)	97.11	100.35	104.41	107.46
城镇居民每百户有录音机 (台)	Tape Recorders per 100 Households in Urban (unit)	37.8	36.7	34.59	37.91
城镇居民每百户有家用电脑 (台)	Computers per 100 Households in Urban (unit)			19.73	26.67
城镇居民每百户有普通电话 (部)	Telephone per 100 Households in Urban (unit)			91.41	92.36
城镇居民每百户有移动电话 (部)	Mobile Telephone per 100 Households in Urban (unit)			79.09	102.66
农村居民每百户有收录机 (台)	Radio&Recorders per 100 Households in Rural (unit)	13.11	12.89	12.62	10.86
平均每人每年发函件数 (件)	Letters per Person per Year (piece)	3.25	6	7.49	7.62
平均每百人每年报刊期发数 (份)	Newspapers per 100 Persons per Year (piece)	15.93	15.53	13.66	12.56
教育	**Education**				
学龄儿童入学率 (%)	Enrollment Ratio of School-age Children (%)	98.42	97.9	96.76	98.56
每万人口有在校大学生数 (人)	University Students Enrollment per 10 000 Persons (person)	38.7	50.22	63.43	80.63
卫生	**Public Health**				
每万人口拥有医院病床数 (张)	Number of Hospital Beds per 10 000 Persons (unit)	20.13	22.17	21.63	21.75
每万人口拥有医生数 (人)	Number of Doctors per 10 000 Persons (person)	13.52	13.57	11.96	11.96

注：1、2002年起，医生数是指执业医生数。2、城市居民人均居住面积数据由省建设厅提供。

Data of doctors are doctors and assistant doctors since 2002.

7-2 城镇居民生活

Urban Households' Life

年 份 Year	平均每人每年（元）Average per Person per Year (yuan)					每一就业者负担人数(人) Persons Supported by Per Employee (person)	人均居住面积(平方米) Per Capita Living Floor Space of Residents (sq.m)
	全部收入 Total Income	可支配收入 Disposable Income	指数(1978年为100) Indices (1978=100)	消费支出 Living Expenditure	#食品支出 Food		
1978	323.88	323.9	100.0	289.56	166.10	1.90	3.90
1980	475.92	475.9	125.2	425.52	244.10	1.76	4.30
1985	760.80	760.8	161.8	685.32	366.48	1.88	6.00
1990	1591.45	1591.5	194.5	1294.00	720.30	1.80	6.91
1995	4705.20	4699.2	278.7	3886.00	1898.10	1.67	7.75
1996	5060.00	5052.1	279.2	4098.00	1986.60	1.64	8.06
1997	5248.90	5209.7	280.1	4317.20	1972.80	1.64	8.66
1998	5474.60	5434.3	290.7	4371.00	1907.60	1.62	9.91
1999	5855.70	5815.4	312.2	4800.00	1942.20	1.66	10.77
2000	6261.20	6218.7	328.9	5218.80	1943.70	1.71	11.75
2001	6832.60	6780.6	362.6	5546.20	1943.60	1.77	11.80
2002	7371.84	6958.6	399.7	5574.72	1985.88	1.97	12.40
2003	8145.07	7674.2	434.7	6082.62	2179.28	1.89	24.43

注：1、1991年及以前的可支配收入均系全部收入。

2、2002年起，可支配收入剔除了出售财物收入和个人交纳的社会保障支出，消费支出中，居住支出剔除了自有房屋折算金。

3、城镇居民人均居住面积由建设厅提供。

Data on disposable income prior to 1991 refer to those on the total income.

Since 2002,Data on disposable income exclude income of selling property and individul expenditure for social security programs.

In expenditure for consumption,Data on expenditure for residence exclude convert value of self-owned house.

The data on per capita living floor space of urban residents came form Constructional Bureau of Hunan Province.

7-3 农村居民生活

Rural Households' Life

年 份 Year	平均每人每年（元）Per Capita Annual (Yuan)					每一劳动力负担人数(人) Number of Dependents Per Laborer (person)	农村人均居住面积(平方米) Per Capita Living Floor Space of Residents (sq.m)
	纯收入 Net Income	纯收入指数(1978年为100) Index of Net Income (1978=100)	总支出 Gross Expenditure	生活消费支出 Living Expenditure	#食品支出 Food		
1978	142.56	100.0	167.10	140.07	97.93	2.33	10.50
1980	219.72	147.6	236.13	192.95	127.70	2.09	11.15
1985	395.26	239.4	519.85	348.45	219.43	1.69	18.20
1990	545.69	229.4	780.77	504.60	288.32	1.65	22.27
1995	1425.16	270.4	2203.36	1367.30	823.91	1.60	25.57
1996	1792.25	292.8	2784.64	1736.71	1025.32	1.56	26.88
1997	2037.06	318.9	2853.42	1815.79	1078.00	1.56	27.37
1998	2064.85	326.6	2829.93	1889.18	1107.23	1.54	28.79
1999	2147.18	344.6	2772.35	1920.15	1122.96	1.52	29.88
2000	2197.16	361.1	2964.85	1942.94	1053.37	1.46	30.92
2001	2299.46	379.5	3030.13	1990.33	1053.15	1.45	32.87
2002	2397.92	398.5	3114.74	2068.74	1086.11	1.44	34.05
2003	2532.87	417.2	3184.26	2139.15	1111.27	1.42	35.09

7-4 城镇居民家庭基本情况

Basic Indicators of Urban Households

项目	Item	2000	2001	2002	2003
调查户数(户)	**Number of Households Surveyed (household)**	**1000**	**1000**	**1000**	**1000**
平均每户家庭人口(人)	**Average Household Size (person)**	**3.09**	**3.06**	**3.06**	**3.02**
平均每户就业人口(人)	**Average Number of Employees Per Household (person)**	**1.81**	**1.73**	**1.55**	**1.59**
平均每户就业面(包括就业者)(%)	**Percentage of Employed Persons Per Household (%)**	**58.6**	**56.5**	**50.7**	**52.6**
平均每人全部年收入(元)	**Per Capita Annual Income(yuan)**	**6261.2**	**6832.6**	**7371.8**	**8145.1**
#可支配收入	#Disposable Income	6218.7	6780.6	6958.6	7674.2
总收入中：工薪收入	Among the Total Income: Wages			5408.2	5984.8
经营净收入	Net Income of Buesness			235.4	356.2
财产性收入	Property Income	158.8	239.5	111.0	100.7
转移性收入	Transfer Income	1008.1	1254.7	1617.4	1703.4
平均每人消费支出(元)	**Per Capita Annual Living Expenditures for Consumption (yuan)**	**5218.8**	**5546.2**	**5574.7**	**6082.6**
#食品	#Food	1943.7	1943.6	1985.9	2179.3
衣着	Clothing	495.2	551.5	577.7	621.3
家庭设备用品及服务	Household Facilities and Daily Articles	544.5	460.1	420.4	420.2
医疗保健	Medicine and Medical Service	270.2	328.6	343.7	391.3
交通和通信	Transportation and Communications	395.6	474.7	596.0	680.2
教育文化娱乐服务	Education,Cultural,Recreation Service	753.8	826.9	883.6	993.9
居住	Residence	576.7	662.4	581.9	586.9
杂项商品和服务	Miscellaneous Commodities and Services	239.1	298.4	185.6	209.5

7-5 城镇居民可支配收入指数

Indices of Disposable Incomes of Urban Households

年 份	以上年为100 preceding year=100		以1978年为100（1978 =100)	
	货币收入	实际收入	货币收入	实际收入
Year	Money Income	Real Income	Money Income	Real Income
1995	121.0	102.5	1452.6	278.7
1998	104.3	103.8	1677.8	290.7
1999	107.0	107.4	1795.2	312.2
2000	106.9	105.5	1919.9	328.9
2001	109.0	110.2	2092.7	362.6
2002	109.8	110.2	2298.6	399.7
2003	110.3	108.8	2534.9	434.7

注:实际收入指数,指扣除价格上涨因素后的指数。

The real income is calculated without the factor of price increase.

7-6 城镇居民调查户基本情况 (2003年)

Basic Indicators of Urban Households From Sample Survey (2003)

项 目	Item	居民家庭总平均 Average	按可支配收入高低分组 By Level of Disposable Income			
			最低收入 Lowest Income	#更低 Lower Income	低收入 Low Income	中等偏下 Lower Middle Income
调查户数(户)	Households Surveyed (household)	12000	1154	573	1195	2410
平均每户家庭人口（人）	Average Household Size (person)	3.02	3.36	3.29	3.39	3.08
#就业人口	#Employees	1.59	1.27	1.12	1.47	1.49
家庭总收入（元）	**Per Capita Annual Income (yuan)**	**8145.07**	**2896.90**	**2376.54**	**4221.64**	**5745.69**
#可支配收入	#Disposable	7674.20	2798.65	2300.03	4049.48	5463.98
总收入中：工薪收入	Among the Total Income: Wages	5984.82	1817.22	1521.36	2938.53	3935.79
经营净收入	Net Income of Buesness	356.17	211.38	124.49	322.03	392.01
财产性收入	Property Income	100.65	54.86	5.06	5.97	62.53
转移性收入	Transfer Income	1703.42	813.43	725.63	955.11	1355.37
家庭人均总支出(元)	**Per Capita Annual Expenditure(yuan)**	**8441.58**	**3015.92**	**2550.86**	**4238.94**	**5936.85**
#消费支出	Living Expenditures for Consumption	6082.62	2592.41	2246.49	3551.61	4556.60
#服务性消费支出	#Services	1730.28	571.97	474.87	966.21	1151.90
#旅游花费	#Cast for Tour	88.05	3.69		6.44	33.28
#食品	#Food	2179.28	1353.60	1163.56	1624.47	1968.24
衣着	Clothing	621.33	168.70	142.62	303.38	430.33
家庭设备用品及服务	Household Facilities and Daily Articles	420.19	116.09	116.07	167.09	264.91
医疗保健	Medicine and Medical Service	391.29	167.49	152.38	210.97	280.15
交通和通信	Transportation and Communications	680.21	159.62	121.32	302.09	474.02
教育文化娱乐服务	Recreation, Education and Cultural Service	993.94	335.45	300.60	529.32	597.09
居住	Residence	586.90	224.26	202.57	332.67	396.19
杂项商品和服务	Miscellaneous Commodities and Services	209.48	67.19	47.37	81.62	145.66

项 目	Item	按可支配收入高低分组 By Level of Disposable Income				
		中等收入 Middle Income	中等偏上 Upper Middle Income	高收入 High Income	最高收入 Highest Income	#更高 Higher Income
调查户数(户)	Households Surveyed (household)	2434	2423	1200	1184	580
家庭人口（人）	Average Household Size (person)	3.00	2.90	2.77	2.60	2.47
#就业人口	#Employees	1.71	1.73	1.64	1.70	1.68
家庭总收入（元）	**Per Capita Annual Income (yuan)**	**7873.56**	**10311.13**	**13006.40**	**18603.83**	**21637.50**
#可支配收入	#Disposable	7370.70	9646.86	12128.57	17580.66	20444.13
总收入中：工薪收入	Among the Total Income: Wages	5999.36	7929.09	9469.36	13886.53	16896.37
经营净收入	Net Income of Buesness	233.86	453.09	489.01	473.45	468.54
财产性收入	Property Income	55.30	107.96	174.34	416.31	689.35
转移性收入	Transfer Income	1585.04	1820.99	2873.69	3827.54	3583.24
家庭人均总支出(元)	**Per Capita Annual Expenditure(yuan)**	**7911.78**	**11332.40**	**13708.60**	**18442.02**	**21856.58**
消费支出	Living Expenditures for Consumption	5808.03	7622.43	10067.41	12005.22	14140.93
#服务性消费支出	#Services	1646.59	2246.69	2934.51	3841.98	4688.44
#旅游花费	#Cast for Tour	50.77	112.77	265.76	320.93	467.25
#食品	#Food	2148.32	2547.23	2989.27	3203.04	3539.93
衣着	Clothing	654.48	767.45	1037.22	1417.12	1785.73
家庭设备用品及服务	Household Facilities and Daily Articles	377.79	568.05	761.70	1056.51	1210.73
医疗保健	Medicine and Medical Service	399.06	532.82	517.62	806.98	973.35
交通和通信	Transportation and Communications	635.08	812.60	1509.13	1501.71	1882.09
教育文化娱乐服务	Recreation, Education and Cultural Service	940.83	1344.29	1837.63	2132.60	2336.83
居住	Residence	484.27	780.43	1069.60	1294.05	1733.59
杂项商品和服务	Miscellaneous Commodities and Services	168.20	269.57	345.22	593.22	678.67

7-7 城镇居民消费支出构成（2003年）

Composition of Consumption Expenditures of urban Households (2003)

单位：%　　　　　　　　　　　　　　　　　　　　　　　　　　　　(%)

项 目	Item	居民家庭总平均 Average	按人均生活费收入分组 By Level of Income 最低收入 Lowest Income	更低 Lower Income	低收入 Low Income	中等偏下 Lower Middle Income
消费支出	**Expenditure for Consumption**	**100.00**	**100.00**	**100.00**	**100.00**	**100.00**
#服务性消费支出	#Services	28.45	22.06	21.14	27.20	25.28
食品	**Foods**	**35.83**	**52.21**	**51.79**	**45.74**	**43.20**
粮油类	Grain, Oil and Fats	5.45	11.92	11.98	8.49	7.33
肉禽蛋水产品类	Meat, Poultry,Eggs and Aquatic Products	10.05	17.07	17.17	15.41	13.68
蔬菜类	Vegetables	3.93	7.16	8.02	5.27	4.62
调味品	Condiments	0.38	0.63	0.68	0.50	0.50
糖烟酒饮料类	Sugar,Tobacco,Liquor and Beverages	3.57	4.87	4.16	3.94	4.28
干鲜瓜果类	Dried and Fresh Melons and Fruits	3.06	3.85	3.45	3.53	3.65
糕点、奶及奶制品	Cake,Milk and Its Products	2.06	1.64	1.45	1.55	2.30
其他食品	Other Foods	1.25	0.80	0.99	0.75	1.07
饮食服务	Catering Trade Services	6.07	4.27	3.88	6.31	5.76
非食品类	**Non-foods**	**64.17**	**47.79**	**48.21**	**54.26**	**56.80**
衣着	**Clothing**	**10.21**	**6.51**	**6.35**	**8.54**	**9.44**
服装	Garments	7.38	4.39	4.22	5.79	6.72
衣着材料	Clothing Material	0.14	0.11	0.05	0.17	0.15
鞋类	Footgear and Shoes	2.26	1.63	1.77	2.27	2.11
其他衣着用品	Other Clothing Articles	0.33	0.27	0.28	0.26	0.37
衣着加工服务费	Clothing Manufacturing Services	0.09	0.11	0.04	0.06	0.08
家庭设备用品及服务	**Household Facilities,Articles and Services**	**6.91**	**4.48**	**5.17**	**4.70**	**5.81**
耐用消费品	Durable Consumer Goods	3.44	1.02	1.37	1.94	2.51
室内装饰品	Interior Decorations	0.22	0.05	0.01	0.06	0.17
床上用品	Bed Articles	0.55	0.34	0.18	0.31	0.46
家庭日用杂品	Daily Use Household Articles	2.18	2.72	3.30	2.05	2.29
家具材料	Furniture Material	0.02			…	…
家庭服务	Household Services	0.50	0.35	0.31	0.35	0.39
医疗保健	**Medicine and Medical Services**	**6.43**	**6.46**	**6.78**	**5.94**	**6.15**
医疗器具	Medical Instrument	0.07	…	…	…	…
保健器具	Health Care Appliances	0.09	…	…		0.05
药品	Medicines	4.30	4.79	4.52	4.12	4.52
滋补保健品	Health Care Medicines	0.45	0.49	0.59	0.22	0.28
医疗费	Medical Treatment	1.47	1.16	1.64	1.59	1.26
其他	Others	0.05	0.03	0.03	0.01	0.03
交通和通信	**Transport,Post and Communication Services**	**11.18**	**6.16**	**5.40**	**8.51**	**10.40**
交通	Transportation	4.29	2.18	2.12	2.98	3.45
通信	Telecommunication	6.89	3.98	3.28	5.53	6.95
教育文化娱乐服务	**Education, Culture and Recreational Services**	**16.34**	**12.94**	**13.38**	**14.90**	**13.10**
文化娱乐用品	Culture and Recreational Articles	4.05	1.65	0.94	1.52	2.69
文化娱乐服务	Culture and Recreational Services	3.32	1.29	1.37	1.37	2.23
教育	Education	8.98	10.00	11.06	12.02	8.19
居住	**Residence**	**9.65**	**8.65**	**9.02**	**9.37**	**8.69**
住房	Residential Building	3.52	1.32	0.41	2.67	2.12
水电燃料及其他	Water,Electricity and Fules	5.85	7.22	8.53	6.34	6.38
居住服务费	Residence Services	0.28	0.11	0.08	0.36	0.19
杂项商品和服务	**Miscellaneous Commodities and Services**	**3.44**	**2.59**	**2.11**	**2.30**	**3.20**
杂项商品	Miscellaneous Commodities	2.25	1.72	1.79	1.53	2.03
服务	Services	1.19	0.88	0.32	0.76	1.17

7-7 续表 continued

项目	Item	中等收入 Middle Income	中等偏上 Upper Middle Income	高收入 High Income	最高收入 Highest Income	更高 Higher Income
消费性支出	**Expenditure for Consumption**	**100.00**	**100.00**	**100.00**	**100.00**	**100.00**
#服务性消费支出	#Services	28.35	29.47	29.15	32.00	33.16
食品	**Foods**	**36.99**	**33.42**	**29.69**	**26.68**	**25.03**
粮油类	Grain, Oil and Fats	5.56	4.46	3.89	2.90	2.27
肉禽蛋水产品类	Meat, Poultry,Eggs and Aquatic Products	10.61	8.58	7.33	5.81	4.80
蔬菜类	Vegetables	4.14	3.51	3.19	2.61	2.15
调味品	Condiments	0.43	0.33	0.29	0.25	0.19
糖烟酒饮料类	Sugar,Tobacco,Liquor and Beverages	3.37	3.39	3.44	2.95	2.55
干鲜瓜果类	Dried and Fresh Melons and Fruits	3.23	2.96	2.45	2.56	2.44
糕点、奶及奶制品	Cake,Milk and Its Products	2.33	2.12	2.13	1.76	1.71
其他食品	Other Foods	1.42	1.34	1.35	1.37	1.42
饮食服务	Catering Trade Services	5.89	6.74	5.62	6.46	7.51
非食品类	**Non-foods**	**63.01**	**66.58**	**70.31**	**73.32**	**74.97**
衣着	**Clothing**	**11.27**	**10.07**	**10.30**	**11.80**	**12.63**
服装	Garments	8.08	7.25	7.58	8.89	9.53
衣着材料	Clothing Material	0.17	0.16	0.12	0.09	0.10
鞋类	Footgear and Shoes	2.59	2.23	2.19	2.35	2.47
其他衣着用品	Other Clothing Articles	0.34	0.34	0.29	0.38	0.42
衣着加工服务费	Clothing Manufacturing Services	0.09	0.09	0.12	0.10	0.11
家庭设备用品及服务	**Household Facilities,Articles and Services**	**6.50**	**7.45**	**7.57**	**8.80**	**8.56**
耐用消费品	Durable Consumer Goods	3.16	3.76	4.54	4.64	4.14
室内装饰品	Interior Decorations	0.20	0.24	0.32	0.28	0.43
床上用品	Bed Articles	0.49	0.69	0.52	0.69	0.67
家庭日用杂品	Daily Use Household Articles	2.33	2.28	1.69	2.09	1.92
家具材料	Furniture Material	0.03	0.03	0.05	…	…
家庭服务	Household Services	0.29	0.44	0.45	1.09	1.39
医疗保健	**Medicine and Medical Services**	**6.87**	**6.99**	**5.14**	**6.72**	**6.88**
医疗器具	Medical Instrument	0.03	0.02	…	0.37	0.66
保健器具	Health Care Appliances	0.07	0.08	0.02	0.27	0.26
药品	Medicines	4.65	4.90	3.35	3.61	3.04
滋补保健品	Health Care Medicines	0.33	0.34	0.45	1.00	1.05
医疗费	Medical Treatment	1.70	1.56	1.30	1.47	1.85
其他	Others	0.09	0.09	0.02	0.02	0.03
交通和通信	**Transport,Post and Communication Services**	**10.93**	**10.66**	**14.99**	**12.51**	**13.31**
交通	Transportation	3.39	3.55	8.19	5.09	5.57
通信	Telecommunication	7.55	7.11	6.80	7.42	7.74
教育文化娱乐服务	**Education, Culture and Recreational Services**	**16.20**	**17.64**	**18.25**	**17.76**	**16.53**
文化娱乐用品	Culture and Recreational Articles	3.16	4.93	5.69	5.56	5.80
文化娱乐服务	Culture and Recreational Services	3.48	3.03	4.58	4.98	4.93
教育	Education	9.56	9.67	7.99	7.22	5.80
居住	**Residence**	**8.34**	**10.24**	**10.62**	**10.78**	**12.26**
住房	Residential Building	1.71	4.40	5.11	5.33	6.78
水电燃料及其他	Water,Electricity and Fules	6.38	5.55	5.16	5.10	5.12
居住服务费	Residence Services	0.25	0.29	0.35	0.35	0.35
杂项商品和服务	**Miscellaneous Commodities and Services**	**2.90**	**3.54**	**3.43**	**4.94**	**4.80**
杂项商品	Miscellaneous Commodities	2.08	2.13	2.49	3.08	2.83
服务	Services	0.82	1.40	0.94	1.86	1.97

7-8 城镇居民平均每人全年购买商品数量(2003年)

Per Capita Annual Purchases of Commodities of Urban Households (2003)

项 目	Item	居民家庭总平均 Average	按家庭人均可支配收入分组 By Level of Income 最低收入 Lowest Income	更低收入 Lower Income	低收入 Low Income	中等偏下 Lower Middle Income	中等收入 Middle Income	中等偏上 Upper Middle Income	高收入 High Income	最高收入 Highest Income
粮食(千克)	**Grain (kg)**	79.89	86.90	81.40	78.72	85.12	76.01	78.87	82.97	66.79
大米	Rice	63.08	69.64	64.94	64.54	69.66	59.71	61.32	61.33	48.80
面粉	Flour	0.85	0.65	0.31	0.51	0.81	1.06	1.05	0.89	0.78
其他粮食	Other Grain	1.34	0.84	0.42	0.89	1.33	1.12	1.63	2.09	1.92
粮食制品	Grain Products	14.62	15.76	15.72	12.78	13.32	14.13	14.87	18.67	15.28
淀粉及薯类(千克)	**Starches and Tubers (kg)**	3.96	5.35	3.82	4.33	4.08	3.29	3.09	4.38	4.08
油脂类(千克)	**Oil and Fats (kg)**	11.29	10.29	9.15	11.02	11.75	11.68	11.98	12.03	9.00
食用植物油	Edible Vegetable Oil	9.20	6.91	7.19	8.00	9.61	9.87	10.19	10.65	8.28
食用动物油	Edible Animal Oil	2.09	3.38	1.96	3.02	2.14	1.81	1.79	1.37	0.72
肉类(千克)	**Meal (kg)**									
猪肉	Pork	28.88	23.60	20.96	29.01	30.13	28.29	29.93	32.54	28.94
牛肉	Beef	1.98	1.42	1.23	2.29	2.22	2.02	1.88	2.16	1.73
羊肉	Mutton	0.34	0.20	0.25	0.26	0.33	0.34	0.41	0.52	0.41
其他肉	Other Meal	0.22	0.21	0.21	0.20	0.18	0.19	0.32	0.30	0.23
肉制品	Meal Products	2.50	1.22	1.29	1.58	2.30	2.72	2.89	3.78	3.57
禽类(千克)	**Poultry (kg)**	9.17	6.29	4.94	8.58	9.71	9.43	9.90	10.73	9.38
鸡	Chicken	5.03	4.07	3.12	5.09	5.46	4.91	5.24	5.18	5.01
鸭	Duck	2.83	1.79	1.36	2.64	3.12	3.11	3.10	3.27	2.35
其他禽类	Other Poultry	0.12	0.06	0.05	0.11	0.06	0.12	0.11	0.24	0.20
禽制品	Poultry Products	1.19	0.37	0.42	0.73	1.07	1.28	1.44	2.03	1.83
蛋类(千克)	**Eggs (kg)**	7.16	6.37	5.60	6.42	7.03	7.28	7.36	7.74	8.49
鲜蛋	Fresh Egge	6.55	5.98	5.25	5.71	6.42	6.70	6.72	7.17	7.66
蛋制品	Eggs Products	0.61	0.39	0.35	0.71	0.61	0.58	0.64	0.57	0.83
水产品类(千克)	**Aquatic Products (kg)**									
鱼	Fish	9.15	8.14	7.21	9.31	9.45	8.90	9.56	9.49	8.98
虾	Shrimp	0.51	0.19	0.19	0.24	0.47	0.50	0.70	0.81	0.84
其他水产品	Others	1.12	0.93	0.67	0.76	1.06	1.05	1.35	1.50	1.35
蔬菜类(千克)	**Vegetables (kg)**									
鲜菜	Fresh Vegetables	111.43	100.03	97.26	98.94	102.78	108.39	119.44	139.34	129.47
干菜	Dried Vegetables	0.56	0.35	0.22	0.46	0.61	0.56	0.60	0.66	0.70
酒类(千克)	**Liquor (kg)**	4.59	2.30	2.10	3.93	6.27	3.82	5.13	5.94	4.21
白酒	Spirit	1.49	0.88	0.80	1.41	2.13	1.14	1.67	1.96	0.91
果酒	Fruit Wine	0.15	0.07	0.03	0.07	0.12	0.14	0.18	0.30	0.24
啤酒	Beer	1.95	0.82	0.96	0.90	2.22	1.96	2.66	2.19	2.71
其他酒	Other Liquor	1.00	0.53	0.31	1.56	1.79	0.58	0.61	1.48	0.35

项 目	Item	居民家庭总平均 Average	按家庭人均可支配收入分组 By Level of Income 最低收入 Lowest Income	更低收入 Lower Income	低收入 Low Income	中等偏下 Lower Middle Income	中等收入 Middle Income	中等偏上 Upper Middle Income	高收入 High Income	最高收入 Highest Income
饮料(千克)	**Drinks (kg)**									
碳酸饮料	Carbonic Acid Drinks	0.77	0.35	0.14	0.52	0.54	1.07	0.96	1.12	0.84
果蔬饮料	Fruit&Vegetable Drinks	0.80	0.32	0.28	0.39	0.66	1.05	0.89	1.15	1.42
瓶装饮用水	Drinkable Water	4.00	0.89	0.13	1.94	2.99	5.41	3.64	6.33	9.35
茶叶	Tea	0.12	0.10	0.09	0.06	0.10	0.12	0.13	0.16	0.16
干鲜瓜果类(千克)	**Dried & Fresh Melons and Fruits (kg)**									
鲜果	Fresh Fruits	40.02	25.72	17.87	33.25	37.17	38.90	46.77	49.30	56.90
鲜瓜	Fresh Melons	23.77	16.88	14.85	19.21	24.86	24.68	26.63	26.95	26.74
干果	Dried Fruits	0.85	0.67	0.34	0.71	0.74	0.81	1.00	1.23	0.94
瓜果制品	Melon & Fruit Products	0.34	0.12	0.10	0.14	0.23	0.31	0.48	0.62	0.78
坚果及果仁	Nuts and Kernels	2.60	1.86	1.41	2.09	2.35	2.73	2.95	2.87	3.77
糕点(千克)	**Cakes (kg)**	2.82	1.67	1.46	1.71	2.47	2.86	3.30	4.28	4.40
奶及奶制品(千克)	**Milk and Milk Products(kg)**									
鲜乳品	Fresh Milk	6.28	1.08	0.90	1.58	4.43	6.76	8.86	11.09	13.97
奶粉	Milk Powder	1.10	0.45	0.37	0.67	1.11	1.28	1.32	1.89	1.01
酸奶	Sour Milk	1.20	0.21	0.19	0.39	1.09	1.36	1.52	2.17	2.17
服装(件)	**Clothing (piece)**									
男士服装	Men's Clothing	2.82	1.34	1.09	2.23	2.45	2.99	3.40	3.68	4.23
女士服装	Women's Clothing	3.53	1.56	1.35	2.40	3.01	3.75	3.99	4.77	6.71
童装	Children's Clothing	0.92	0.53	0.62	0.54	0.93	0.88	1.16	1.35	1.22
鞋类(双)	**Shoes (pair)**	2.70	1.61	1.74	2.25	2.37	2.78	2.98	3.64	4.01
居住	**Residence**									
水(吨)	Water (ton)	41.98	23.96	25.05	30.42	33.78	44.36	47.60	60.31	69.81
电(度)	Electricity (kw□our)	321.58	130.38	127.11	168.96	235.98	339.55	384.19	501.49	683.41
煤炭(千克)	Coal (kg)	188.22	304.42	300.90	254.25	279.40	142.84	113.96	101.75	50.39
液化石油气(千克)	Liquefied Petroleum Gas(kg)	23.96	7.66	7.30	11.42	20.47	27.87	32.41	35.63	36.46
管道煤气(立方)	Coal Gas Through Pipelines (m^3)	15.50	4.35	3.78	9.57	7.62	19.93	22.98	20.48	28.44
手表(只)	**Watches (piece)**	0.02	0.01	0.00	0.01	0.01	0.02	0.03	0.04	0.05

7-9 城镇居民平均每百户拥有耐用消费品数量（2003年）

Number of Durable Consumer Goods Owned Per 100 Urban Households (2003)

项 目	Item	居民家庭总平均 Average	按家庭人均可支配收入分组 By Level of Income 最低收入 Lowest Income	更低收入 Lower Income	低收入 Low Income	中等偏下 Lower Middle Income	中等收入 Middle Income	中等偏上 Upper Middle Income	高收入 High Income	最高收入 Highest Income
成套家具（套）	Composite Furniture (set)	82.98	66.20	59.33	67.58	73.26	93.45	92.35	90.11	94.16
摩托车（辆）	Motorcycle (unit)	14.75	11.19	14.03	13.13	13.59	13.36	14.59	18.74	22.60
自行车（辆）	Bicycles (unit)	67.61	53.21	62.72	72.46	67.78	68.25	69.39	72.94	68.57
助力车（辆）	Semi-power Bicycles (unit)	2.01	1.32			1.32	1.98	3.22	0.90	5.35
家用汽车（辆）	Automobile (unit)	0.27					0.28		1.18	1.12
洗衣机（台）	Washing Machine (unit)	95.25	78.48	78.19	90.00	95.12	97.85	100.26	97.58	103.92
电风扇（台）	Electric Fan (unit)	253.57	233.57	219.11	254.07	252.46	263.02	250.51	250.80	268.38
电冰箱（台）	Refrigerator (unit)	87.06	57.95	60.15	70.40	82.39	95.31	96.49	101.63	101.12
冰柜（台）	Freezer (unit)	6.65	12.42	9.51	5.99	6.42	6.31	4.71	6.97	5.34
彩色电视机（台）	Color TV set (unit)	124.82	100.68	94.36	109.09	113.60	128.56	132.36	143.83	154.08
影碟机（台）	Video Disc Player (unit)	61.20	34.78	26.76	47.66	53.08	66.67	79.69	71.07	67.56
录音机（台）	Tape Recorder (unit)	37.91	25.11	15.88	20.28	28.76	42.04	50.98	43.38	52.85
录放像机（台）	Video Recorder (unit)	12.96	1.55	1.53	2.99	11.92	13.19	16.63	27.64	18.51
家用电脑（台）	Computer (set)	26.67	6.11	3.31	2.49	9.97	30.37	35.68	53.17	62.92
组合音响（套）	Hi-Fi Stereo Component System (unit)	34.52	8.67	10.36	21.54	24.82	39.49	48.97	56.35	40.49
摄像机（架）	Pickup Camera (unit)	1.31				0.76	0.90	0.56	2.89	6.36
照相机（架）	Camera (unit)	38.70	10.36	8.15	17.33	26.44	47.11	45.25	57.19	74.73
钢琴（架）	Piano (unit)	1.47			0.47	0.87	1.82	0.59	1.18	6.93
其他中高档乐器（件）	Other Medium and High Grade Musical Instrument (unit)	6.65	2.26	3.58	0.72	6.06	6.38	6.88	9.04	17.81
微波炉（台）	Oven (unit)	30.81	4.90	2.01	5.78	16.95	34.96	42.44	50.67	68.75
空调器（台）	Air Conditioner (unit)	55.38	4.90	5.32	9.02	30.15	64.89	75.99	99.63	118.78
取暖器（台）	Warming Appliances(unit)	68.59	19.46	21.19	35.20	47.46	83.32	86.62	104.64	109.09
电炊具（台）	Electric Cooking Appliances(unit)	57.90	18.45	17.82	41.45	41.56	60.06	74.07	77.56	101.94
淋浴热水器(台)	Shower (unit)	64.02	24.19	15.17	41.10	51.79	71.41	83.14	81.40	93.39
排油烟机（台）	Smoke Absorber (unit)	35.68	15.23	10.20	18.70	30.25	42.03	45.01	51.91	43.97
消毒碗柜（台）	Disinfect Cupboard (unit)	17.85	2.52	3.31	10.52	12.11	22.97	23.50	25.56	27.36
洗碗机（台）	Dishes Washing Machines (set)	0.44					1.39			1.78
饮水机（台）	Drinkable Water Machines (set)	23.35	4.40	1.79	11.70	14.63	26.36	31.48	34.96	43.91
吸尘器（台）	Dust Catcher (unit)	4.26				0.96	6.16	3.87	9.65	12.81
健身器材（套）	Healthy Equipment (set)	2.64				0.42	3.49	3.38	2.57	10.29
普通电话（部）	Fixed Telephone (set)	92.36	68.24	64.02	87.06	91.33	97.67	97.36	101.16	100.00
移动电话（部）	Mobile Telephone (set)	102.66	28.65	26.39	59.55	85.20	112.49	134.58	141.97	155.39
使用互联网(条)	Internet User (line)	9.8	0	0	1	4	10	11	14	30
传真机（部）	Fax Machines (set)	0.17					0.32	0.56		
人均住房面积（平方米）	Per Capita Living Floor Space (m^2)									
建筑面积	Building Space	26.55	21.10	22.58	19.43	26.13	27.38	28.15	31.04	36.80
使用面积	Using Space	20.15	16.24	17.19	14.87	20.14	20.55	21.10	23.33	28.01

7-10 城镇居民家庭平均每人全年现金收入和支出

Per Capita Annual Cash Revenue and Expenditures of Urban Household

单位：元 (yuan)

项 目	Item	2002	2003
期初手存现金	**Initial Hands Store Cashes**	**438.71**	**473.27**
家庭总收入	**Total Income**	**7371.84**	**8145.07**
#可支配收入	#Disposable Income	6958.56	7674.20
工薪收入	Income of Wages	5408.16	5984.82
工资及补贴收入	Salary and replenishing incomes	5167.20	5769.39
其他劳动收入	Other incomes from work	240.96	215.44
经营净收入	Net Income of Buesness	235.44	356.17
财产性收入	Property Income	111.00	100.65
利息收入	Interest income	15.48	5.71
股息与红利收入	Dividend and dividend income	24.84	34.30
保险收益	Insurance Income	1.80	1.66
其它投资收入	Other Revenue From Investments	4.44	6.78
出租房屋收入	Let Income	58.08	46.96
知识产权收入	Intellectual Property Income		0.25
其他财产性收入	Other Property Incomes	6.24	5.00
转移性收入	Transfer Income	1617.36	1703.42
养老金或离退休金	Pension or Retired Pay	1033.44	1190.94
社会救济收入	The Society Relieves Incomes	16.32	13.75
辞退金	Payment of Dismissing	12.48	26.27
赔偿收入	Compensation Income	0.24	0.26
保险收入	Insurance Income	12.72	11.43
#失业保险金	#Unemployment Insurance	11.40	10.79
赡养收入	Support Incomes	97.32	79.73
捐赠收入	Present Incomes	333.48	286.04
亲友搭伙费	Relatives and Friends Join as Partner to Spend	28.68	28.36
提取住房公积金	Draw the Public Accumalation Fund for Housing Construction	5.28	3.96
记帐补贴	Allowance of Keeping Accounts	43.56	39.89
其他转移性收入	Other Transfer Income	33.84	22.79
出售财物收入	**Incomes of Selling Property Incomes**	**19.68**	**92.85**
出售住房收入	Income of Selling the House	16.68	89.79
出售其他物品收入	Income of Selling Other Articles	3.00	3.05
借贷收入	**Debt-credit income**	**1692.36**	**1926.53**
提取储蓄存款	Draw the Savings Account	1249.56	1597.56
借入款	Debit Fund	215.16	188.77
收回借出款	Regain Found of Lending Out	33.60	16.37
收回储蓄性保险本	Regain the Saving Insurance Cost	3.12	2.29
兑售有价证券	Change and Sell the Securities with Price		0.30
收回投资本金	Regain the Investment Principal	5.88	14.08
住房贷款	Loan for Purchasing House	135.48	89.46
汽车贷款	Loan for Purchasing Car		
教育贷款	Education Loan		0.04
其他贷款	Other Loan	1.56	0.85
其他借贷收入	Other Debt-credit Income	47.88	16.80

项 目	Item	2002	2003
家庭总支出	**Family's Total Expenditure**	**7583.64**	**8441.58**
消费支出	Consumption Expenditure	5574.72	6082.62
#服务性消费支出	Service	1566.72	1730.28
食品	Foods	1985.88	2179.28
衣着	Clothing	577.68	621.33
家庭设备用品及服务	Household Facilities and Service	420.36	420.19
医疗保健	Medicine and Medical Service	343.68	391.29
交通和通信	Transportation and Communications	596.04	680.21
教育文化娱乐服务	Recreation, Education and Cultural Service	883.56	993.94
居住	Residence	581.88	586.90
杂项商品和服务	Miscellaneous Commodities and Services	185.64	209.48
购房与建房支出	The Expenditure of Purchasing and Building House	403.56	486.60
购房	Purchase House	401.40	479.46
建房	Building House	2.16	7.14
转移性支出	Transfer expenditure	1255.44	1463.75
交纳的个人收入税	Personal Income Tax	26.76	31.00
捐赠支出	Present	874.08	952.25
购买彩票	Lottery Tickets	6.24	4.75
赡养支出	Support	303.00	398.48
#在外就学子女费用	#Go to School Children's Expenses Outside	173.16	254.67
各种非储蓄性保险支出	Various Kinds of Saving Insurance Expenditure	14.64	22.72
#车辆保险支出	#Vehicle Insurance		1.92
其他转移性支出	Other Transfer Expenditure	30.48	54.54
财产性支出	Property Expenditure	6.96	8.64
非生产性利息支出	Unproductive Interest	0.48	1.82
其他	Other	6.48	6.81
社会保障支出	Social Security Expenditure	342.96	399.97
个人交纳的养老基金	Pension Fund Which the Individual Paid	151.32	176.97
个人交纳的住房公积金	Public Accumalation Fund for Housing Construction Which the Individual Paid	128.04	141.37
个人交纳的医疗基金	Medical Fund Which the Individual Paid	45.48	62.09
个人交纳的失业基金	Unemployment Fund Which the Individual Paid	10.08	14.13
其他社会保障支出	Other Social Security Expenditure	8.04	5.42
借贷支出	**Debt-credit Expenditure**	**1436.40**	**1616.02**
存入储蓄款	Deposit	1052.28	1199.62
借出款	Lending	13.08	11.93
归还借款	Return the Borrowed Money	97.32	80.59
储蓄性保险支出	Saving Insurance Expenditure	101.16	124.11
购买有价证券	Securities	13.20	34.52
其它投资支出	Other Investment Expenditure	15.48	28.35
归还住房贷款	Return the Housing Loan	57.96	94.31
归还汽车贷款	Return the Loan for Purchasing Car		
归还教育贷款	Return the Education Loan	0.60	
归还其他贷款	Return the Other Loan	2.40	2.70
其他借贷支出	Other Debt-credit Expenditure	82.92	39.89
期末手存现金	**Hands Store Cashes at the End of Term**	**444.02**	**482.17**

7-11 各调查市县城镇居民家庭生活基本情况(2003年)

Basic Indicators of Urban Households' Life of Cities and Prefecture (2003)

市县	Cities and Counties	平均每户家庭人口(人) Average Household Size (person)	平均每户就业人口(人) Average Number of Employees Per Household (person)	平均每一就业者负担人数(人) Average Number of Persons Supported by Each Employee (person)	平均每百户电脑拥有量(台) Number of Computers per 100 Household in Urban (set)	平均每百户固定电话(部) Number of Fixed Telephone Per 100 Household in Urban (set)	平均每百户移动电话(部) Number of Mobile Telephone Per 100 Household in Urban (set)	人均住房使用面积(平方米) Per Capita Using Floor Space in Urban Resident (m^2)
长沙市	Changsha City	3.04	1.63	1.87	42.00	98.50	117.00	18.01
株洲市	Zhuzhou City	3.01	1.74	1.73	30.00	98.00	115.00	17.67
邵阳市	Shaoyang City	2.95	1.47	2.01	23.00	87.00	102.00	18.28
岳阳市	Yueyang City	2.92	1.73	1.69	29.00	97.00	112.00	22.75
常德市	Changde City	2.94	1.28	2.30	20.00	91.00	87.00	20.72
郴州市	Chenzhou City	2.87	1.64	1.75	39.00	93.00	120.00	22.36
怀化市	Huaihua City	3.02	1.83	1.65	19.00	90.00	83.00	21.02
衡阳市	Hengyang City	3.03	1.49	2.03	13.08	96.25	84.17	19.82
湘潭市	Xiangtan City	2.96	1.29	2.29	20.67	92.83	73.08	17.51
益阳市	Yiyang City	3.05	1.60	1.91	31.08	103.25	125.33	22.12
永州市	Yongzhou City	3.37	1.75	1.93	19.31	86.67	108.19	24.22
娄底市	Loudi City	3.10	1.42	2.18	22.00	100.83	103.67	20.43
吉首市	Jishou City	3.46	1.80	1.92	18.00	99.33	71.67	19.80
张家界市	Zhangjiajie City	3.55	1.58	2.25	7.33	86.67	100.17	47.13
资兴市	Zixing City	2.68	1.27	2.11	27.00	83.67	57.67	22.91
冷水江市	Lengshuijiang City	3.21	1.89	1.70	20.00	100.67	78.83	20.79
津 市	Jinshi City	2.91	1.16	2.51	10.00	92.17	53.17	19.21
耒阳市	Leiyang City	3.15	1.46	2.16	14.00	88.00	98.00	32.05
慈利县	Cili County	2.99	1.48	2.02	12.00	90.00	104.00	36.29
道 县	Daoxian County	3.12	1.66	1.88	6.00	88.00	90.00	27.01
新化县	Xinhua County	3.25	1.65	1.97	12.00	88.00	78.00	16.43
南 县	Nanxian County	3.00	1.30	2.31	10.50	85.67	73.67	26.40
临湘市	Linxiang City	3.19	1.77	1.80	12.00	93.00	118.17	35.81
溆浦县	Xupu County	3.28	1.84	1.78	10.00	92.00	75.83	26.21
武冈市	Wugang City	3.19	1.63	1.96	17.67	90.33	75.67	31.12
攸 县	Youxian County	3.18	1.59	2.00	10.00	102.50	92.67	46.00
湘乡市	Xiangxiang City	3.12	1.70	1.84	16.00	98.33	101.17	20.08
凤凰县	Fenghuang County	3.77	1.59	2.37	9.83	95.00	66.50	24.42

7-12 各调查市县城镇居民平均每人全年家庭收入来源(2003年)

Per Capita Annual Income in Urban Households of Cities and Counties (2003)

单位:元

市县	Cities and Counties	家庭总收入 Total Income	可支配收入 Disposable Income	工薪收入 Income of Wages	经营净收入 Net Income of Bucsness	财产性收入 Property Income	转移性收入 Transfer Income
长沙市	Changsha City	10671.45	9942.51	7577.15	212.45	111.77	2041.15
株洲市	Zhuzhou City	9440.17	8785.77	6791.42	105.97	62.56	1825.82
邵阳市	Shaoyang City	6821.82	6495.58	4606.00	61.87	103.97	1723.75
岳阳市	Yueyang City	9581.05	8981.15	6885.42	353.39	103.86	1638.48
常德市	Changde City	7443.59	7085.26	4225.02	540.85	109.07	2210.32
郴州市	Chenzhou City	8216.47	7559.39	5904.09	451.10	85.30	1118.90
怀化市	Huaihua City	7557.66	7214.05	5460.24	684.89	45.47	1023.46
衡阳市	Hengyang City	7457.04	7205.04	4914.24	176.40	43.68	2070.72
湘潭市	Xiangtan City	8042.40	7670.40	4669.80	335.64	73.80	2591.16
益阳市	Yiyang City	7996.20	7424.28	5767.56	47.04	100.92	1508.76
永州市	Yongzhou City	5816.76	5541.60	4730.16	206.16	61.32	543.96
娄底市	Loudi City	7951.20	7251.72	4670.04	92.04	12.48	2477.16
吉首市	Jishou City	6237.36	5986.20	4742.88	253.20	114.12	876.00
张家界市	Zhangjiajie City	6482.28	6356.04	3526.44	459.60	618.48	1751.52
资兴市	Zixing City	8567.52	7960.20	7092.24	310.56	13.44	543.96
冷水江市	Lengshuijiang City	6726.96	6433.44	4779.00	217.08	168.48	1268.88
津 市	Jinshi City	5936.88	5699.76	3204.24	30.60	26.28	2438.64
耒阳市	Leiyang City	7415.14	7258.59	4345.38	1066.21	268.33	1578.36
慈利县	Cili County	7290.94	6955.31	4371.66	861.08	142.54	1580.03
道 县	Daoxian County	5763.38	5515.66	4060.76	404.92	85.42	964.56
新化县	Xinhua County	5807.28	5532.14	3752.14	431.06	45.14	1303.81
南 县	Nanxian County	6330.36	6029.40	3144.12	1327.32	32.64	1525.32
临湘市	Linxiang City	6610.44	6451.32	5455.44	342.84	58.44	594.60
溆浦县	Xupu County	5881.08	5660.04	4552.08		66.00	1041.96
武冈市	Wugang City	6346.68	5875.92	4660.92	223.56	35.64	955.80
湘乡市	Xiangxiang City	7898.76	7503.48	5587.44	165.36	101.52	1649.16
攸 县	Youxian County	7097.28	6696.72	3980.76	349.44	234.96	2131.56
凤凰县	Fenghuang County	5015.52	4879.32	2731.44	385.80	9.00	1753.08

7-13 各调查市县城镇居民平均每人全年消费支出(2003年)

Per Capita Annual Living Expenditure for Consumption in Urban Households of Cities and Counties (2003)

单位:元

市县	Cities and Counties	消费支出 Living Expenditure for Consumption	食品 Foods	衣着 Clothing	家庭设备用品及服务 Household Facilities Articles and Services	医疗保健 Medicine and Medical Services	交通和通信 Transport Post and Communication Services	教育文化娱乐服务 Education and Culture Recreation Services	居住 Residence	杂项商品和服务 Miscellaneous Commodities and Services
长沙市	Changsha City	8557.60	2708.17	807.54	586.64	621.69	1138.78	1617.12	793.75	283.92
株洲市	Zhuzhou City	6759.70	2348.19	656.05	440.02	354.07	788.37	1267.20	673.06	232.73
邵阳市	Shaoyang City	5159.90	1970.12	582.35	315.68	312.71	515.70	842.87	413.74	206.74
岳阳市	Yueyang City	6797.17	2336.47	809.94	438.62	426.98	795.01	1138.93	604.02	247.20
常德市	Changde City	5796.43	2157.59	499.48	465.12	340.10	585.39	738.40	781.27	229.09
郴州市	Chenzhou City	6197.09	2275.29	671.21	547.49	383.36	516.68	912.23	707.14	183.70
怀化市	Huaihua City	4997.38	1869.98	612.03	370.80	314.35	460.82	877.28	343.77	148.35
衡阳市	Hengyang City	5799.12	2066.52	415.92	548.16	302.64	565.32	658.92	1084.80	156.84
湘潭市	Xiangtan City	6426.72	2251.56	471.36	548.76	424.68	632.64	830.04	1073.52	194.28
益阳市	Yiyang City	6007.68	1947.12	657.96	358.08	279.36	647.40	1408.08	565.44	144.24
永州市	Yongzhou City	4119.96	1594.80	532.92	368.52	195.60	450.12	563.28	292.08	122.76
娄底市	Loudi City	5569.20	1789.80	727.08	571.20	439.80	547.92	852.36	466.68	174.36
吉首市	Jishou City	5134.92	1887.72	597.96	339.84	260.40	455.64	1145.04	320.64	127.68
张家界市	Zhangjiajie City	4703.28	1549.44	381.48	293.04	401.64	427.68	771.12	827.88	51.24
资兴市	Zixing City	5306.76	1778.64	404.76	538.44	493.68	447.60	1181.04	347.88	114.84
冷水江市	Lengshuijiang City	4649.16	1882.32	455.40	466.68	279.36	342.96	883.44	240.24	98.64
津市	Jinshi City	4163.16	1850.52	394.08	294.96	241.80	384.60	366.12	491.04	140.28
耒阳市	Leiyang City	4750.79	1653.22	665.70	318.41	343.44	497.75	559.33	509.02	203.92
慈利县	Cili County	4809.01	1726.27	530.07	285.90	238.88	597.13	680.77	630.77	119.23
道县	Daoxian County	3283.11	1499.75	227.61	205.47	216.76	331.54	531.40	211.64	58.94
新化县	Xinhua County	4306.93	1897.94	372.79	262.74	257.57	453.62	529.13	410.66	122.48
南县	Nanxian County	4155.48	1876.80	438.60	370.80	133.32	371.04	431.28	427.80	105.84
临湘市	Linxiang City	4558.92	1784.52	566.52	304.20	178.08	442.56	736.20	326.76	220.20
溆浦县	Xupu County	4089.96	1776.00	496.68	266.88	191.28	335.64	543.24	373.80	106.32
武冈市	Wugang City	4393.80	1726.92	344.04	268.68	380.04	604.20	558.36	369.84	141.84
湘乡市	Xiangxiang City	5450.76	1941.36	494.04	498.72	364.32	465.00	833.88	610.68	242.76
攸县	Youxian County	4649.88	1761.96	467.16	364.92	341.04	605.76	557.04	422.76	129.12
凤凰县	Fenghuang County	3224.40	1262.04	229.56	281.76	149.64	274.68	538.56	406.80	81.36

7-14 农村居民家庭基本情况

Basic Indicators of Rural Households

项 目	Item	2000	2001	2002	2003
调查村数（个）	**Number of Villages Surveyed (unit)**	**370**	**370**	**370**	**370**
已通电话村所占比重（%）	Proportion of Villages Provided with Telephone (%)	95.70	97.57	97.84	98.65
已通公路村所占比重（%）	Proportion of Villages Provided with Highways (%)	98.60	99.19	99.19	99.19
调查户数（户）	**Number of Households Surveyed(household)**	**3700**	**3700**	**3700**	**3700**
调查户人口(常住人口)（人）	Number of Residents Surveyed (person)	14694	14544	14559	14383
平均每户常住人口（人）	Average Number of Permanent Residents per Household (person)	3.97	3.93	3.93	3.89
平均每户整半劳动力（人）	Average Number of Able-bodied and Semi-ablebodied Laborers per Household(person)	2.72	2.71	2.74	2.74
平均每个劳动力负担人口(人)	Number of Dependents per Laborer (person)	1.46	1.45	1.44	1.42
每百个常住人口中乡村企业从业人数(人)	Number of Employed Persons in Township Enterprises per 100 Permanent Residents(person)	1.13	1.66	1.73	1.78
每百个常住人口中在外从事其他劳动人数(人)	Number of Employed Outgoing Persons per 100 Permanent Residents(person)	11.23	11.97	14.39	16.16
平均每人经营耕地面积(亩)	Area of Cultivated Land Under Management per Capita (mu)	1.09	1.09	1.09	1.08
平均每人经营山地面积(亩)	Hilly Area Under Management per Capita (mu)	0.39	0.38	0.36	0.34
平均每人经营水面面积(亩)	Water Area Under Management per Capita (mu)	0.05	0.04	0.04	0.03
平均每户年末拥有生产性固定资产原值(元)	Original Value of Productive Fixed Assets per Household at the Year-end (yuan)	3006.28	3106.38	3192.01	3165.65
平均每百个劳动力中：	**In Per 100 Rural Labor Force :**				
不识字或识字很少（人）	Illiterate and Semi-illiterate (person)	3.38	3.13	3.19	2.87
小学程度（人）	Primary School (person)	34.00	32.85	32.04	31.86
初中程度（人）	Junior Secondary School (person)	48.88	49.71	50.25	50.50
高中程度（人）	Senior Secondary School (person)	11.47	11.85	11.90	12.17
中专程度（人）	Specialized Secondary school (person)	1.75	1.85	2.05	2.13
大专以上（人）	College and Higher Level (person)	0.52	0.61	0.56	0.47
按纯收入分组户数占调查户比重(%)	**Percentage of Households Group by per Capita Annual Net Income (%)**				
100元以下	Under 100 Yuan	0.00	0.03	0.03	0.05
100—200元	100—200 Yuan	0.03	0.00	0.03	0.08
200—300元	200—300 Yuan	0.05	0.00	0.03	0.11
300—400元	300—400 Yuan	0.11	0.22	0.14	0.22
400—500元	400—500 Yuan	0.46	0.22	0.30	0.49
500-600元	500—600 Yuan	0.97	0.68	0.68	0.89
600—800元	600—800 Yuan	4.65	2.65	3.22	2.14
800—1000元	800—1000 Yuan	3.70	4.35	4.24	3.62
1000—1200元	1000—1200 Yuan	5.78	6.57	5.22	4.89
1200—1300元	1200—1300 Yuan	3.81	3.35	3.59	2.70
1300—1500元	1300—1500 Yuan	7.35	7.24	6.86	6.27
1500—1700元	1500—1700 Yuan	8.84	8.54	6.97	6.76
1700-2000元	1700-2000 Yuan	13.19	12.32	11.59	9.81
2000-2500元	2000-2500 Yuan	19.24	18.78	18.00	17.03
2500-3000元	2500-3000 Yuan	11.81	12.54	12.81	14.19
3000—3500元	3000—3500 Yuan	8.32	7.94	8.97	10.43
3500-4000元	3500-4000 Yuan	4.30	5.43	6.22	7.46
4000-4500元	4000-4500 Yuan	2.68	3.00	3.95	4.54
4500-5000元	4500-5000 Yuan	1.59	2.03	2.27	2.27
5000元以上	5000 Yuan and Over	3.11	4.11	4.89	6.05

7-15 农村居民主要农、牧产品出售情况

Sales of Major Farming, Animal Husbandry Products per Rural Household

项 目	Item	2000	2001	2002	2003
粮食（公斤／人）	Grain Crops (kg/person)	111.59	134.58	127.04	145.46
棉花（公斤／人）	Cotton (kg/person)	2.92	3.26	3.98	10.61
油料（公斤／人）	Oil-bearing Crops (kg/person)	9.26	8.93	8.75	5.60
麻类（公斤／人）	Fiber Crops (kg/person)	0.52	0.82	1.62	1.58
糖料（公斤／人）	Sugar Crops (kg/person)	8.76	4.04	5.68	5.61
烟叶（公斤／人）	Tobacco (kg/person)	5.01	4.43	5.56	5.84
蔬菜（公斤／人）	Vegetables (kg/person)	72.03	76.44	85.87	84.51
水果（公斤／人）	Fruits (kg/person)	33.37	32.55	39.42	33.91
茶叶（公斤／人）	Tea (kg/person)	0.24	0.12	0.10	0.08
猪肉（公斤／户）	Pork (kg/household)	199.61	216.11	233.43	199.63
牛肉（公斤／户）	Beef (kg/household)	-	0.69	2.09	0.85
羊肉（公斤／户）	Mutton(kg/household)	0.07	1.15	2.52	1.18
家禽（公斤／户）	Poultry(kg/household)	9.22	8.84	15.13	17.03
禽蛋（公斤／户）	Poultry Eggs (kg/household)	7.31	5.19	4.52	5.65
水产品（公斤／户）	Aquatic Products (kg/household)	25.17	24.80	26.52	24.89

7-16 农村居民平均每人总收入及总支出

Per Capita Annual Revenue and Expenditures of Rural Household

单位：元 (yuan)

项 目	Item	2000	2001	2002	2003
平均每人总收入	**Per Capita Gross Income**	**3195.13**	**3305.65**	**3389.14**	**3515.52**
工资性收入	Salary Income	789.74	840.11	914.31	988.35
在非企业组织中得到	From Non-enterprise Organization	-	87.44	87.72	72.26
在本地企业中得到	From Local Enterprises	-	175.21	175.22	330.55
在常住人口外出从业得到	Permanent Resident	-	452.00	503.52	585.54
其他	Others	-	125.48	129.04	-
家庭经营收入	From Household Business Operation	2130.06	2191.47	2178.84	2254.58
转移性和财产性收入	Transfer Income and Property Income	275.33	274.07	295.99	272.60
平均每人总支出	**Per Capita Gross Expenditure**	**2964.85**	**3030.13**	**3114.74**	**3184.26**
#家庭经营费用支出	Expenditure for Household Business	642.17	665.53	663.16	691.40
购置生产用固定资产支出	Expenditure for Purchase of Productive Fixed Assets	40.54	52.00	47.83	55.21
税费支出	Tax and Fee	-	101.93	84.89	81.68
各种税款	Tax	-	39.38	65.48	68.38
筹资、收费	Funds and Charges	-	62.55	19.41	13.30
生活消费支出	Expenditure for Consumption	1942.94	1990.33	2068.74	2139.15
转移性和财产性支出	Transfer and Property Expenditure	230.87	220.34	250.11	216.57
寄给、带给在外人口	Post & Bring to Outgoing Person	5.47	3.39	5.07	16.73
赠送农村外部亲友	Giving Non-Rural Friends and Relatives	3.74	4.49	5.03	4.66
其他支出	Other Expenditure	-	10.82	9.56	-

7-17 农村居民平均每人纯收入来源构成

Source and Condition of per Capita Net Income of Rural Household

单位:元 (yuan)

项 目	Item	2000	2001	2002	2003
平均每人纯收入	**Per Capita Net Income**	**2197.16**	**2299.46**	**2397.92**	**2532.87**
按纯收入来源分	**Grouped by Source of Income**				
工资性收入	Salary Income	789.74	840.11	914.31	988.35
在非企业组织中得到	From Non-enterprise Organization	-	87.44	87.72	72.26
在本地企业中得到	From Local Enterprises	-	175.21	175.22	330.55
在常住人口外出从业得到	Permanent Resident	-	452.00	503.52	585.54
其他	Others	-	125.48	129.04	-
家庭经营纯收入	Income from Household Business Operation	1329.10	1371.84	1376.71	1427.21
农业收入	Farming	605.37	642.07	635.60	698.09
林业收入	Forestry	16.35	13.33	15.56	22.48
牧业收入	Animal Husbandry	247.67	255.43	248.78	236.55
渔业收入	Fishery	34.82	25.71	28.00	31.85
手工业收入	Handicraft	17.06	18.09	10.37	-
采集捕猎收入	Gathering and Hunting	17.29	18.34	10.60	-
工业收入	Industry	55.97	58.86	59.26	61.10
建筑业收入	Construction	126.02	126.54	144.78	144.10
交通运输及邮电业收入	Transportation and Telecommunication	53.50	59.69	61.37	56.84
批发零售贸易餐饮业收入	Wholesale & Retail Sales and Catering Trade	85.15	93.65	98.38	99.46
社会服务业收入	Social Service Business	47.54	42.06	45.81	49.85
其他家庭经营收入	Others	22.36	18.07	18.20	26.89
转移性收入和财产性收入	Transfer Income and Property Income	78.32	87.51	106.90	117.31
按纯收入性质分	**Grouped by Type of Income**				
生产性纯收入	Productive Income	2071.30	2169.89	2245.21	2373.61
非生产性纯收入	Non-productive Income	125.86	129.54	152.71	159.26
按现金和实物分	**Grouped by Modality of Income**				
现金纯收入	Net Cash Income	1569.13	1643.62	1810.92	2040.07
实物纯收入	Net Income in Kind	630.03	655.84	567.00	492.81

7-18 农民人均纯收入指数

Indices of Net Income of Rural Household Per Capita

年 份 Year	以上年为100 Preceding year=100		以1978年为100 1978 =100	
	按当年价格计算 At Current Year Prices	扣除价格因素 Subtract Price Affection	按当年价格计算 At Current Year Prices	扣除价格因素 Subtract Price Affection
1995	123.4	105.2	999.7	270.4
1998	101.4	102.4	1448.4	326.6
1999	104.0	105.5	1506.3	344.6
2000	102.3	104.8	1540.8	361.1
2001	104.7	105.1	1613.2	379.5
2002	104.3	105.0	1682.0	398.5
2003	105.6	104.7	1776.2	417.2

7-19 农村居民家庭平均每人生活消费支出

Per Capita Living Expenditures of Rural Household

单位：元 (yuan)

项目	Item	2000	2001	2002	2003
生活消费支出	**Living Expenditure**	**1942.94**	**1990.33**	**2068.74**	**2139.15**
按消费类别分：	**By Category of Consumption**				
食品	Food	1053.37	1053.15	1086.11	1111.27
#主食	Staple Food	244.26	253.47	245.08	
副食	Non-staple Food	469.55	449.81	456.23	
其他食品	Other food	122.49	119.82	124.48	
衣着	Clothing	89.78	93.38	97.85	106.16
居住	Residence	251.92	268.72	271.28	271.97
家庭设备用品及服务	Household Facilities,Articles and Services	78.05	80.76	84.79	79.63
医疗保健	Medicines and Medical Services	82.23	95.71	102.81	105.23
交通通信	Transportation and communications	99.38	102.44	118.57	146.85
文教娱乐用品及服务	Cultural,Educational and Recreational Articles and Services	222.50	234.40	248.60	270.54
其他商品及服务	Other Commodities and Services	65.72	61.76	58.73	47.51
按消费性质分：	**By Source of Consumption**				
货币性消费	**Consumption paid in Money**				
食品	Food	590.19	602.69	641.58	672.05
衣着	Clothing	89.61	93.30	97.79	106.09
居住	Residence	240.26	251.79	263.58	265.80
家庭设备用品及服务	Household Facilities,Articles and Services	78.04	80.73	84.97	79.60
医疗保健	Medicines and Medical Services	82.23	95.71	102.81	105.23
交通通信	Transportation and communications	99.38	102.44	118.57	146.85
文教娱乐用品及服务	Cultural,Educational and Recreational Articles and Services	222.50	234.40	248.60	270.54
其他商品及服务	Other Commodities and Services	65.72	61.76	58.73	46.18
实物性消费	**Consumption in kind**				
食品	Food	463.18	450.46	444.53	439.22
衣着	Clothing	0.17	0.08	0.06	0.07
居住	Residence	11.66	16.93	7.70	6.17
家庭设备用品及服务	Household Facilities,Articles and Services	0.01	0.03	-	0.03
医疗保健	Medicines and Medical Services				
交通通信	Transportation and communications				
文教娱乐用品及服务	Cultural,Educational and Recreational Articles and Services				
其他商品及服务	Other Commodities and Services				1.33

7-20 农村居民平均每人现金收入

Per Capita Cash Revenue of Rural Household

单位:元 (yuan)

项 目	Item	2000	2001	2002	2003
平均每人现金收入	**Per Capita Cash Revenue**	-	**2549.76**	**2731.68**	**2866.96**
工资性收入	Salary Income	789.54	839.79	914.23	987.79
在非企业组织中得到	From Non-enterprise Organization	-	87.32	87.67	72.07
在本地企业中得到	From Local Enterprises	-	175.18	175.22	330.55
在常住人口外出从业得到	Permanent Resident	-	451.83	503.49	585.17
其他	Others	-	125.46	147.85	-
家庭经营收入	Income from Household Business Operation	-	1438.14	1522.83	1610.25
出售产品收入	From Sales Production	904.48	952.67	1000.57	1031.32
出售种植业产品收入	From Farming Production	317.14	335.00	369.39	429.67
出售牧业产品收入	From Animal Husbandry Production	492.42	524.87	531.94	544.38
工业加工费的现金收入	From Industry Processing	58.29	57.60	53.35	47.18
建筑业的现金收入	From Construction	129.35	133.52	152.91	147.95
交通运输及邮电业收入	Transportation and Telecommunication	93.19	90.17	97.74	89.98
批发零售贸易餐饮业收入	Wholesale & Retail Sales and Catering Trade	109.81	124.61	133.06	132.67
社会服务业的现金收入	Social Service Business	41.19	41.90	48.77	49.26
其他家庭经营现金收入	Others	-	26.01	25.70	-
转移性和财产性收入	Transfer Income and Property Income	273.42	271.92	294.62	268.93
非收入所得	From non-income	553.12	516.79	509.61	564.23
银行信用社得到的贷款	From Banks	31.83	29.86	36.36	35.01
借入款	From Lending	277.52	249.96	240.26	203.60
收回借出款	From Getting in Debt	126.73	118.99	101.40	116.35
从银行信用社取回存款	From Taking out Savings	96.03	91.97	102.63	100.65
收回投资款	From Payback	0.57	0.22	2.36	0.89

7-21 农村居民平均每人现金支出

Per Capita Cash Expenditures of Rural Household

单位: 元 (yuan)

项 目	Item	2000	2001	2002	2003
平均每人现金支出	**Per Capita Cash Expenditure**	-	**2424.31**	**2543.87**	**2607.77**
生产费用支出	Productive Costs	563.83	584.64	595.63	619.89
家庭经营费用支出	Expenditure for Household Business	523.29	532.64	547.80	564.43
种植业生产支出	Expenditure for Farming	190.58	190.95	199.20	222.24
牧业生产支出	Expenditure for Animal Husbandry	217.80	227.53	234.87	231.78
购置生产用固定资产支出	Purchase Fixed Assets	40.54	52.00	47.83	55.21
税费支出	Tax and Fee	-	98.11	83.32	81.23
各种税款	Tax	-	37.03	64.72	67.93
筹资、收费	Funds and Charges	-	61.08	18.60	13.30
生活消费支出	Expenditure for Consumption	1467.92	1522.83	1616.45	1692.34
财产性转移性支出	Transfer and Property Expenditure		218.74	248.47	214.30
寄给、带给在外人口	Post & bring to Outgoing Person	5.42	3.26	4.96	16.59
赠送农村以外亲友	Giving Non-Rural Friends and Relatives	3.61	4.36	4.38	4.47
非消费性现金支出	Expenditure From non-comsumption	511.96	525.59	614.09	706.75
归还银行信用社贷款	Return Banks' Loans	23.53	26.95	29.18	29.28
借出款	Lending	59.23	48.29	75.48	65.05
归还款	Payback	211.46	216.85	222.76	205.52
存入银行信用社款	Savings	213.57	227.62	281.49	320.36
支出投资款	Investment	4.14	5.87	5.18	2.05

7-22 农村住户平均每户购买商品情况

Per Capita Purchases of Commodities of Rural Household

项 目	Item	2002		2003	
		实物量 Object Volume	金额(元) value (yuan)	实物量 Object Volume	金额(元) Value (yuan)
购买食品	**Purchase of Food**		**1499.06**		**1555.11**
粮食(原粮)(公斤)	Grain (Unprocessed) (kg)	29.40	31.13	100.27	123.98
食用植物油(公斤)	Edible Vegetable Oil (kg)	5.04	32.17	5.65	43.43
动物油(公斤)	Edible Animal Oil (kg)	19.73	119.96	17.69	121.84
蔬菜(公斤)	Vegetables (kg)	39.17	62.03	33.92	58.04
豆制品(公斤)	Bean and Its Products (kg)	10.35	21.23		19.03
猪肉(公斤)	Pork (kg)	45.68	384.91	40.75	376.07
牛肉(公斤)	Beef (kg)	1.03	12.30	0.77	10.96
羊肉(公斤)	Mutton (kg)	0.28	4.02	0.31	4.57
家禽(公斤)	Poultry (kg)	5.43	51.26	6.06	57.58
鲜蛋(公斤)	Eggs (kg)	4.36	27.79	4.91	31.36
鲜活鱼类(公斤)	Fresh Fish (kg)	16.75	91.22	18.33	105.95
食糖(公斤)	Sugar (kg)	5.50	17.43	4.40	15.85
糕点(公斤)	Cake (kg)	3.77	25.44		27.00
糖果(公斤)	Candy (kg)	2.48	16.87		20.18
卷烟(盒)	Cigarette (pack)	91.83	169.98	87.39	173.20
酒(公斤)	Liquor (kg)	14.79	66.82	13.98	66.91
啤酒(公斤)	Beer (kg)	4.63	15.03	5.60	17.32
茶叶(公斤)	Tea (kg)	0.31	3.64	0.29	4.39
水果(公斤)	Fresh Fruits (kg)	35.95	64.07	35.17	66.60
鲜奶(公斤)	Milk (kg)	0.02	0.20	0.15	0.51
奶制品(公斤)	Dairy Products (kg)	0.40	5.37		
购买衣着和床上用品	**Purchase of Clothing and Bed Articles**		**420.63**		**406.44**
棉布服装(件)	Cotton Clothing (piece)	0.43	10.32		
化纤布服装(件)	Chemical Fiber Clothing (piece)	6.15	185.55		
毛料服装(件)	Woolen Fabric Clothing (piece)	0.06	4.55		
皮料服装(件)	Leather Clothing (piece)	0.01	2.47		

项 目	Item	2002 实物量 Object Volume	2002 金额(元) value (yuan)	2003 实物量 Object Volume	2003 金额 (元) Value (yuan)
购买文化体育用品	**Purchase of Culture and Sports Goods**		**228.46**		**216.36**
黑白电视机(台)	B&W TV Sets (unit)		0.91		1.03
彩色电视机(台)	Color TV Sets (unit)	0.04	68.27	0.05	68.60
收录机(台)	Radio & Type Recorder (unit)	0.01	0.72	0.01	0.83
录放象机(台)	Video-recorder (unit)				0.16
购买建筑材料	**Purchase of Building Materials**		**521.63**		**415.14**
水泥(公斤)	Cement (kg)	382.83	86.12	285.45	63.57
玻璃(平方米)	Glass (sq)	0.35	4.32	0.20	2.61
购买燃料	**Purchase of Fuels**		**156.06**		**167.90**
煤炭(公斤)	Coal (kg)	557.80	136.02	658.02	149.32
购买日用品	**Purchase of Articles for Daily Use**		**519.87**		
自行车(辆)	Bicycle (unit)	0.04	8.47	0.04	7.25
缝纫机(架)	Sewing Machine (unit)		0.43		0.10
洗衣机(台)	Washing Machine (unit)	0.01	7.10	0.02	10.61
电风扇(台)	Electric Fan (unit)	0.07	3.89	0.08	4.70
电冰箱(台)	Refrigerator (unit)		7.14		7.29
摩托车(辆)	Motor Cycle (unit)	0.02	85.49	0.02	76.57
购买药品及医疗用品	**Purchase of Drug and Medical Articles**		**255.23**		**246.46**
药品(元)	Medicine (yuan)		251.67		243.26
购买生产资料	**Purchase of means of production**		**1943.44**		**1828.78**
化肥(公斤)	Chemical Fertilizer (kg)	473.81	361.77	496.62	389.27
饼肥(公斤)	Cake Fertilizer (kg)	1.79	1.37	1.56	1.41
农药(公斤)	Pesticide (kg)	11.84	116.68		137.32
农用薄膜(公斤)	Farming Pellicle (kg)	0.82	6.03	0.86	6.71
生产用燃料(公斤)	Fuels for Farm Machinery (kg)	128.17	83.13		94.82
每百户购买商品	**Purchase of Goods per 100 Households**				
汽车(辆)	Motor Vehicles (unit)	0.19	4048.65	0.20	4357.84
小型和手扶拖拉机(台)	Small and Walking Tractors (unit)	0.30	809.11	0.42	1520.27
机动脱粒机(台)	Motorized Threshing Machines (unit)	0.47	199.46	0.86	403.51
胶轮大车(辆)	Carts with Rubber Tires (unit)	0.03	2.43	0.08	36.49
水泵(台)	Pumps (unit)	1.15	279.51	2.51	762.47
役畜(头)	Draught Animals (head)	2.04	1902.27	1.79	1782.09
产品畜(头)	Commodity Animals (head)	8.54	1264.70	2.49	1592.31

7-23 农村居民平均每人全年主要消费品消费量

Per Capita Annual Consumption of Major Consumer Goods of Rural Household

单位：公斤 (kg)

指 标	Item	2000	2001	2002	2003
粮食(原粮)	Grain (Unprocessed)	287.45	278.00	269.09	247.70
小麦	Wheat	2.25	1.91	2.18	1.47
稻谷	Rice	274.86	267.45	258.53	240.69
玉米	Corn	1.85	0.87	0.78	0.81
薯类	Potato	3.84	2.38	2.21	1.05
豆类及豆制品	Legume	2.14	1.74	3.91	1.69
#大豆	Soja	1.93	1.09	0.87	1.20
蔬菜	Vegetables	156.18	161.47	170.22	149.44
油脂类	Oil and Fats	9.68	9.25	9.25	8.35
#植物油	Vegetable Oil	3.85	3.32	3.42	3.80
动物油	Animal Oil	5.84	5.93	5.83	4.55
肉禽及其制品	Meat , Poultry and Related Products	22.74	23.02	23.50	22.58
#猪肉	Pork	18.27	18.54	18.99	17.18
牛肉	Beef	0.33	0.32	0.26	0.23
羊肉	Mutton	0.14	0.11	0.12	0.10
家禽	Poultry	3.70	3.77	3.85	3.89
肉禽制品	Meat and Poultry 's Products	0.13	0.11	0.13	1.18
蛋类及蛋制品	Eggs and Its Products	3.55	3.64	3.39	3.28
奶和奶制品	Milk and Dairy Products	0.07	0.09	0.11	0.16
水产品	Aquatic Products	4.76	4.98	5.95	6.89
#鱼类	Fish	4.47	4.70	5.52	6.52
虾贝类	Shrimps,Prawns and Crabs， Shell-fish	0.06	0.06	0.10	0.09
澡类	Algae	0.06	0.06	0.07	0.08
其他水产品	Others	0.16	0.15	0.26	0.20
糖类	Sugar	1.95	1.91	2.03	
#食糖	Sugar	1.31	1.27	1.40	1.13
糖果	Candy	0.64	0.64	0.63	
酒和饮料	Liquor and Beverage	7.63	6.46	6.88	
#白酒	Liquor	3.85	3.55	3.24	2.14
啤酒	Beer	1.09	1.05	1.18	1.44
果酒	Fruit Wine	0.02	0.01	0.02	0.02
其他饮料	Other Beverages	1.06	1.01	0.99	
糕点	Cake	0.87	0.86	0.96	
干鲜瓜果类	Melons and Fruits	18.76	26.05	20.92	22.48
坚果及果仁制品	Nuts and Kernels' Products	1.15	0.89	0.76	0.74

7-24 农村居民平均每百户年末拥有耐用消费品数量

Year – End Number of Durable Consumer Goods Per 100 Rural Households

品名	Item	2000	2001	2002	2003
自行车(辆)	Bicycle (unit)	80.59	81.49	81.38	80.30
吸尘器(台)	Dust Catcher (unit)	-	-	0.08	-
微波炉(台)	Microwave Oven (unit)	-	0.05	0.08	0.08
热水器(台)	Water Heater (unit)	-	1.43	1.43	2.00
影碟机(台)	Vieo-Disc Machine (unit)	-	12.86	15.14	19.14
电风扇(台)	Electric Fan(unit)	171.11	176.68	180.22	187.00
洗衣机(台)	Washing Machine(unit)	15.94	16.92	17.78	20.73
电冰箱(台)	Refrigerator(unit)	6.84	7.68	8.05	9.03
摩托车(辆)	Motor Cycle(unit)	10.51	12.41	14.19	17.49
大型家具(件)	Large-Scale funiture (unit)	-	536.14	548.43	548.48
中高档乐器(件)	Medium-to-High Grade musical instrument	-	0.46	0.38	0.30
黑白电视机(台)	B&W Television Set(unit)	66.78	65.54	63.41	57.86
彩色电视机(台)	Color Television Set(unit)	30.32	34.81	41.00	49.59
收录机(台)	Type Recorder(unit)	13.11	12.89	12.62	10.86
照相机(架)	Camera(unit)	1.59	1.59	1.51	1.35
录放像机(台)	Video-recorder(unit)	2.43	2.30	2.41	2.08
组合音响(台)	Hi-Fi Stereo Component System (set)	5.70	6.73	7.35	8.03
空调机(台)	Air Conditioner(unit)	0.11	0.19	0.35	0.51
抽油烟机(台)	Smoke Absorber(unit)	0.51	0.54	0.81	0.76
家用计算机(台)	Computer (set)	0.22	0.38	0.32	0.43
寻呼机(台)	Beep-Pager (unit)	7.59	7.81	6.14	3.97
电话机(台)	Telephone (unit)	23.13	27.84	33.59	41.35
移动电话机(台)	Mobile Telephone (unit)	1.54	4.14	7.7	15.38

注：无数据项均为当年度无此调查项目。

The item of missing data didn't surveyed at current year.

7-25 农村居民住房情况

Living Conditions of Rural Households

指 标	Item	2000	2001	2002	2003
平均每人新建房屋面积(平方米)	Per Capita Newly Built Floor Space of Houses (sq.m)	1.20	1.35	1.16	0.96
#砖木结构面积(平方米)	#Brick and Wood Structure	0.50	0.58	0.39	0.31
钢筋混凝土面积(平方米)	Concrete Structure	0.70	0.76	0.75	0.65
楼房面积(平方米)	Areas of Floor Space of Multi-floor Building	0.99	1.13	1.03	0.87
平均每人年末住房面积(平方米)	Per Capita Floor Space of Residential Building at the Year-end (sq.m)	30.92	32.87	34.05	35.09
#砖木结构面积(平方米)	Brick and Wood Structure (sq.m)	19.76	21.22	21.06	21.00
钢筋混凝土面积(平方米)	Reinforced Concrete Structure (sq.m)	9.05	9.55	10.90	11.80
年末房屋价值(元/平方米)	Value Per Room (Yuan)	162.88	164.65	161.31	167.68

7-26 农村居民拥有生产性固定资产

Production Fixed Assets of Per Capita Rural Household

指 标	Item	2000	2001	2002	2003
按原值计算(每户拥有)	**Group by Original Value (per household)**				
合 计(元)	**Total (yuan)**	**3006.28**	**3106.38**	**3192.01**	**3165.65**
#役畜、产品畜	#Draught Animals & Commodity Animals	318.57	335.48	339.96	329.62
大中型铁木农具	Large(Medium) Ironwood Farm Tools	305.80	306.46	313.62	307.62
农林牧渔机械	Agricultural Machinery	281.66	322.36	338.99	382.75
工业机械	Industrial Machinery	167.51	225.33	210.11	-
运输机械	Transportation Machinery	601.13	518.14	525.02	-
生产用房	Buildings for Productive Purpose	1112.87	1139.93	1144.81	1191.35
其他	Others	218.74	258.68	319.50	-
按实物统计(每百户拥有)	**Number of Productive Fixed Assets (per 100 household)**				
#汽车(辆)	#Motor Vehicles (unit)	1.03	0.91	1.00	0.80
大中型拖拉机(台)	Large(Medium) Tractors (unit)	0.26	0.03	0.03	0.46
小型和手扶拖拉机(台)	Mini and Walking Tractors (unit)	3.31	3.21	3.08	2.72
机动脱粒机(台)	Motorized Threshing Machine (unit)	16.24	3.74	4.18	17.10
胶轮大车(辆)	Carts with Rubber Tires (unit)	3.86	4.01	4.07	4.00
农用动力机械（台）	Agricultural Motive Power Machine (unit)	-	14.27	14.67	18.94
水泵(台)	Water Pumps (unit)	15.33	16.53	16.85	16.11
收割机(台)	Reaping Machine (unit)	-	0.11	0.12	0.56
役畜(头)	Draught Animals (head)	15.58	23.40	22.09	22.37
产品畜(头)	Commodity Animals (head)	23.47	26.02	26.46	19.92

八、城市建设、环境保护

CONSTRUCTION OF CITIES AND ENVIRONMENTAL PROTECTION

资料整理人员： 陈洲艳　蔡红宇

8-1 城市公用事业基本情况

Basic Statistics for urban Public Utilities

指标名称	Item	2000	2001	2002	2003
城市个数(个)	**Number of Cities (unit)**				
省辖市	Cities Under the Jurisdiction of Province	13	13	13	13
县级市	Cities at County Level	16	16	16	16
城市规模	**City Size**				
城市人口(万人)	Population of Cities (10 000 persons)	1196.68	1028.12	1051.98	1009.79
#非农业人口	#Non-agricultural Population	691.72	702.02	719.75	753.3
城市面积(平方公里)	Total Areas of Cities (sq.km)	12733.44	8426.25	8955.48	8992.38
#建成区面积	#Developed Areas	799.27	847.47	897.63	959.38
房屋建筑	**Buildings**				
人均居住面积(平方米)	Per Capita Living Space (sq.m)	11.75	11.8	12.4	24.43
供水	**Water Supply**				
综合生产能力(万立方米/日)	Production Capacity of Tap Water (10 000 cu.m/day)	1162.21	1263.39	1239.42	1213.9
#地下水	#Shallow Ground Water	103.78	101.33	96.25	107.37
供水管长度(公里)	Length of Water Supply Pipelines (km)	7650	9664.5	8563.4	9341.8
供水总量(万立方米)	Total Annual Volume of Water Supply (10 000 cu.m)	282357	276325	269403	262691
#生产用量	# For Production	-	157973	143391	134226
公共服务用量	For Republic Services	-	18743	22678	16426
家庭用量	For Family Use	-	85723	81006	82785
人均日生活用水量(升)	Per Capita Daily Consumption of Tap Water for Residential Use (liter)	310.87	339.35	334.62	311.68
用水普及率(%)	Percentage of Population with Access to Tap Water (%)	97.5	97.4	80.7	86.36
供煤气、液化石油气	**Coal Gas and Liquefied Petroleum Gas Supply**				
供气总量	Total Gas Supply				
煤气(万立方米)	Coal Gas (10 000 cu.m)	60375	48559.3	41667.6	43529.7
#家庭用	#Consumption for Residential Use	28521	7746.66	6559.3	7565.7
液化石油气(吨)	Liquefied Petroleum Gas (ton)	202033	247606	297511	231109.4
#家庭用	#Consumption for Residential Use	189827	223912	250337	177248.9
煤气管道长度(公里)	Length of Coal Gas Pipelines (km)	1116	1155.8	1220	1141
石油液化气管道长度(公里)	Length of Liquefied Petroleum Gas Pipelines (km)	216	461.9	506.79	625.59
用气普及率(%)	Percentage of Population with Access to Gas (%)	78.35	57.67	59.69	66.58
公共交通	**Public Traffic**				
运营车辆合计(辆)	Number of Public Transportation Vehicles (unit)	9083	8616	8099	8995
#汽车	#Buses	9083	8616	8099	8995
小公共汽车	Small Buses	5228	4302	3722	3434
折运营标台(标台)	Convert into Standard Unit (unit)	7212	7021	7000	7571
运营线路长度(公里)	Length of Public Transportation Lines (km)	3713	3169	3559	8839
出租汽车总计(辆)	Total of Taxi (unit)	19534	22663	21412	22715
每万人拥有公共交通车辆(标台)	Number of Public Transportation Vehicles (unit) per 10 000 persons (unit)	10.43	10.39	6.65	7.5
公交客运总量(万人次)	Number of Passengers Carried (10 000 person-times)	106227	101835	105522	117634.5

指标名称	Item	2000	2001	2002	2003
市政设施	**Municipal Engineering**				
道路长度(公里)	Length of Paved Roads (km)	4739	4836.97	4978.57	5368.9
道路面积(万平方米)	Area of Paved Roads (10 000 sq.m)	4815.93	6200.13	6900.4	7980.8
人行道面积(万平方米)	Area of Sidewalk (10 000 sq.m)	1426.82	1713.24	1810.5	1892.5
桥梁数(座)	Number of bridges (unit)	637	520	538	541
#立交桥	#Cloverleaf Junction	82	68	72	74
路灯(盏)	Number of Street Lights (unit)	115147	119336	178122	224858
排水管道长度(公里)	Length of Sewer Pipelines (km)	3754.31	3854.31	4089.54	4404.02
污水排放量(万立方米)	Number Volume of Let Sewage (10 000 cu.m)	165902	119082.7	139159	50235.48
污水处理厂(座数)	Number of Sewage Disposal Farm (unit)	21	13	13	13
处理能力(万立方米/日)	Daily Disposal Capacity of Sewage (10 000 cu.m/day)	61.15	54.4	64.4	73.4
设施能力(万立方米/日)	Capacity of Engineering (10 000 cu.m/day)	83.9	129	103.49	149.64
污水年处理量(万立方米)	Annual Volume of Sewage Treated (10 000 cu.m)	45316	26262	26340.47	40284.96
防洪堤长度(公里)	Length of Banks to Prevent or Control Flood (km)	602.77	528.46	541.5	761.27
#百年一遇以上	# Befall 100 Years and Over	107.03	25.73	49.9	21.7
人均拥有道路(平方米)	Per Capita of Road Areas (sq.m)	6.96	6.03	6.56	7.9
排水管密度(公里／平方公里)	Density of Drainage Pipelines (km/sq.km)	4.7	4.55	4.56	4.59
污水处理率(%)	Rate of Sewage Disposal (%)	27.31	22.05	18.93	26.81
园林绿化	**Parks, Gardens and Green Areas**				
绿化覆盖面积(公顷)	Coverage Space of Green Areas (hectare)	49290	35433.72	37760.1	39544.9
#建成区	#Developed Area	22646	23854.02	25671.3	28827
园林绿地面积(公顷)	Area of Parks,Gardens and Green Areas in Cities (hectare)	44672	30185.38	31825.5	34254.8
#建成区	#Developed Area	19450	20592.56	22434.3	25050.8
公共绿地面积(公顷)	Public Green Areas (hectare)	3525	4680.93	4970.26	5116.29
公园个数(个)	Number of Parks (unit)	116	109	122	129
公园面积(公顷)	Area of Parks (hectare)	2646.41	2547.84	3222.86	3513.39
人均公共绿地面积(平方米)	Per Capita Public Green Areas (sq.m)	5.1	4.55	4.72	5.07
建成区绿地率(%)	Rate of Green Areas Developed (%)	24.33	24.3	24.99	26.11
建成区绿化覆盖率(%)	Coverage Rate of Green Areas Developed (%)	28.33	28.15	28.6	30.05
环境卫生	**Environmental Sanitation**				
实际清扫面积(万平方米)	Area Under Cleaning Program (10 000 sq.m)	3236.22	3804.61	4627.7	5402.1
#机械清扫	Machine Cleaning	411.77	310.6	656.3	814.6
生活垃圾清运量(万吨)	Volume of Garbage Disposal (10 000 tons)	358.46	1048.3	459	444
粪便清运量(万吨)	Volume of Excrement and Urine Disposal (10 000 tons)	24.25	41.3	50.3	64.1
垃圾无害化处理场(座数)	Number of Factories to Treat Garbage Harmlessly(unit)	15	35	26	2
#处理能力(吨/日)	Daily Disposal Capacity (ton/day)	4427	10332	7736	2762
垃圾无害处理量(万吨)	Volume of Garbage Harmlessly Treatment (10 000 tons)	180.91	878.92	252.22	100
粪便无害化处理量(万吨)	Volume of Urine Harmlessly Treatment (10 000 tons)	8.31	31.78	48.2	61.2
公共厕所数(座)	Number of Public Lavatories (unit)	3001	2438	2465	2538
#水冲式	# Water Closet	1771	1720	1822	1919
环卫机械总数(台)	Environmental Sanitation Equipment (unit)	1213	1131	1012	867
年末环卫工人数(人)	Environmental Sanitation Workers at Year-end (person)	11356	17187	19885	19300
生活垃圾无害化处理率(%)	Ratio of Garbage Harmlessly Treatment (%)	50.47	83.8	54.9	24.17
粪便处理率(%)	Ratio of Urine Harmlessly Treatment (%)	34.27	76.95	95.83	92.49

8-2 城市规模和建设用地(2003年)

Urban Scale and Construction Land (2003)

单位：平方公里 (sq.km)

城市	Cities	城市人口 Population in Cities (10 000 persons)	#非农人口 Non-Agricultural Population	城市面积 Area of City	建成区面积 Developed Areas	建设用地面积 Area of Construction Use Land			
						居住用地 Living Space	公共设施用地 Public Engineering	道路广场用地 Road and Plaza	绿地 Green Areas
长沙市	Changsha	188.98	156.22	556.33	135.84	37.64	34.29	15.23	12.91
浏阳市	Liuyang	14.75	7.36	35.00	16.00	5.90	3.60	1.34	0.50
株洲市	Zhuzhou	78.17	59.00	462.00	76.90	1.02	3.87	0.55	0.07
醴陵市	Liling	18.00	13.00	47.00	17.10	4.65	2.82	0.90	0.28
湘潭市	Xiangtan	70.19	57.54	278.77	63.40	17.36	6.30	3.76	3.36
湘乡市	Xiangxiang	11.60	7.53	68.00	27.74	8.13	3.78	4.36	4.12
韶山市	Shaoshan	10.45	3.50	70.00	4.69	0.76	0.43	0.52	0.92
衡阳市	Hengyang	92.34	65.69	557.30	89.93	24.10	4.80	10.20	2.83
耒阳市	Leiyang	24.60	12.22	30.00	24.60	7.47	5.18	3.50	2.88
常宁市	Changning	7.31	7.24	25.20	8.26	1.50	1.62	0.90	1.70
邵阳市	Shaoyang	62.65	36.18	424.20	37.00	11.30	5.30	4.10	1.30
武冈市	Wugang	13.61	8.55	40.00	13.20	4.80	0.50	2.08	3.02
岳阳市	Yueyang	66.41	43.09	1241.84	74.54	26.70	8.62	7.19	6.87
汨罗市	Miluo	12.60	6.10	20.00	13.01	4.83	1.56	1.46	0.32
临湘市	Linxiang	9.20	7.40	25.00	10.31	2.10	1.00	1.10	1.11
常德市	Changde	53.76	39.38	2749.00	55.90	17.35	9.67	6.84	2.24
津市市	Jinshi	13.31	12.36	68.30	10.64	5.80	1.86	1.00	1.06
张家界市	Zhangjiajie	17.23	12.69	145.88	19.10	4.77	4.28	1.45	0.60
益阳市	Yiyang	41.00	34.00	70.00	41.00	10.85	7.52	4.12	2.63
沅江市	Yuanjiang	12.01	8.97	18.00	10.56	3.30	2.20	0.72	0.36
郴州市	Chenzhou	30.00	26.00	1313.00	30.12	12.00	5.00	1.56	1.43
资兴市	Zixing	12.92	9.29	146.00	18.50	6.40	1.80	3.70	0.10
永州市	Yongzhou	32.12	26.75	72.17	36.23	11.61	4.93	3.11	4.20
娄底市	Loudi	31.89	25.83	143.69	40.00	15.05	7.09	4.94	3.03
冷水江市	Lengshuijiang	13.26	12.29	31.00	18.50	4.83	1.12	0.85	3.55
涟源市	Lianyuan	10.20	7.10	18.00	10.50	4.10	2.50	2.20	1.53
怀化市	Huaihua	32.44	28.29	52.00	30.60	12.86	2.66	2.18	2.09
洪江市	Hongjiang	13.19	7.38	129.70	7.21	2.75	0.68	0.53	0.53
吉首市	Jishou	15.60	12.35	155.00	18.00	5.60	1.91	1.66	0.63

8-3 城市设施水平(2003年)

Indicators of Municipal Public Utilities Level (2003)

城市	Cities	人口密度(人/平方公里) Population Density (person/sq.km)	人均拥有城市维护建设资金(元) Per Capita Funds for Construction and Maintenance (yuan)	人均日生活用水量(升) Per Capita Water Consumption for Residential Use (liter)	用水普及率(%) Percentage of Population with Access to Tap Water (%)	每万人拥有公共交通车辆(标台) Number of Public Transportation Vehicles Per 10000 persons (unit)	用气普及率(%) Percentage of Population with Access to Gas (%)
长沙市	Changsha	3397	2925	276.79	100.00	9.45	93.60
浏阳市	Liuyang	4214	2735	289.43	52.88	3.05	59.66
株洲市	Zhuzhou	1692	1268	372.60	75.48	8.10	72.21
醴陵市	Liling	3830	308	193.98	95.56	4.28	44.44
湘潭市	Xiangtan	2518	1312	396.16	99.99	6.97	68.61
湘乡市	Xiangxiang	1706	261	103.01	86.21	5.78	95.69
韶山市	Shaoshan	1493	899	138.47	35.41	0.77	24.88
衡阳市	Hengyang	1657	427	297.01	96.20	6.78	41.27
耒阳市	Leiyang	8200	123	109.93	65.04	2.85	15.45
常宁市	Changning	2901	246	157.24	94.39	6.57	49.25
邵阳市	Shaoyang	1477	464	210.81	72.63	4.53	36.55
武冈市	Wugang	3402	278	103.09	99.19	7.35	33.06
岳阳市	Yueyang	535	516	627.86	99.68	7.98	87.68
汨罗市	Miluo	6300	308	169.05	74.60	3.89	82.54
临湘市	Linxiang	3680	263	143.59	90.22	5.33	97.83
常德市	Changde	196	1258	373.30	71.99	6.36	56.79
津市市	Jinshi	1949	315	152.16	96.99	17.66	49.06
张家界市	Zhangjiajie	1181	745	232.75	87.17	16.77	45.85
益阳市	Yiyang	5857	677	227.76	80.98	7.51	59.76
沅江市	Yuanjiang	6672	107	149.65	88.26	7.49	54.12
郴州市	Chenzhou	228	221	375.07	87.53	13.80	75.70
资兴市	Zixing	885	131	313.20	100.00	7.04	27.09
永州市	Yongzhou	4451	1001	730.24	32.47	9.37	71.51
娄底市	Loudi	2219	1396	257.14	86.23	3.92	83.73
冷水江市	Lengshuijiang	4277	356	208.58	83.41	7.01	60.33
涟源市	Lianyuan	5667	615	218.85	82.35	5.00	72.55
怀化市	Huaihua	6238	1166	291.61	98.64	9.74	83.05
洪江市	Hongjiang	1017	1895	168.89	55.34	1.74	40.18
吉首市	Jishou	1006	1196	409.04	91.67	2.12	66.09

城市	Cities	人均拥有道路面积(平方米) Per Capita Area of Paved Roads (sq.m)	排水管道密度(公里/平方公里) Density of Sewer Pipelines (km/sq.km)	污水处理率(%) Ratio of Sewage Treatment (%)	园林绿化 Parks, Gardens and Green Areas			生活垃圾无害化处理率(%) Ratio of Garbage Harmlessly Treatment (%)
					人均公共绿地面积(平方米) Per Capita Public Green Areas (sq.m)	建成区绿地率(%) Ratio of Green Area in Developed Areas (%)	建成区绿化覆盖率(%) Green Area Coverage Rate in Developed Areas (%)	
长沙市	Changsha	10.48	5.01	19.66	6.51	30.82	36.62	100.00
浏阳市	Liuyang	6.90	2.56		5.76	19.38	25.44	
株洲市	Zhuzhou	7.54	5.12	68.21	5.00	29.18	31.56	
醴陵市	Liling	4.06	3.57		4.11	28.89	30.94	
湘潭市	Xiangtan	7.31	5.36		5.83	40.63	44.18	
湘乡市	Xiangxiang	2.76	1.61		4.48	5.16	5.88	
韶山市	Shaoshan	5.32	13.65	71.72	2.97	33.69	35.61	
衡阳市	Hengyang	5.63	3.94		2.59	19.53	22.80	98.00
耒阳市	Leiyang	7.43	8.01		3.61	21.60	24.83	
常宁市	Changning	16.46	8.78		1.23	9.93	30.27	
邵阳市	Shaoyang	5.80	3.38		3.79	17.23	18.75	
武冈市	Wugang	14.46	4.11		5.73	22.35	26.73	
岳阳市	Yueyang	4.61	4.25	27.47	6.27	25.22	36.38	
汨罗市	Miluo	7.86	4.46		6.20	14.76	19.06	
临湘市	Linxiang	5.87	2.72		5.54	4.95	7.27	
常德市	Changde	9.00	5.83	71.10	5.65	33.41	38.35	
津市市	Jinshi	6.07	6.02		5.46	20.86	21.24	
张家界市	Zhangjiajie	10.71	4.59		2.59	16.52	18.12	
益阳市	Yiyang	9.39	5.82		5.27	30.51	32.67	
沅江市	Yuanjiang	5.08	2.18		5.41	22.54	25.47	
郴州市	Chenzhou	7.41	5.51		6.27	41.77	38.18	
资兴市	Zixing	7.64	1.92		6.25	27.51	28.11	
永州市	Yongzhou	10.76	4.14		4.67	17.78	23.68	
娄底市	Loudi	11.38	6.00	83.67	5.99	30.07	33.08	
冷水江市	Lengshuijiang	5.59	2.43		5.00	22.32	24.97	
涟源市	Lianyuan	6.08	3.50		0.99	21.95	24.18	
怀化市	Huaihua	6.07	2.45		4.32	29.25	31.21	
洪江市	Hongjiang	5.88	3.47		4.02	28.02	31.76	
吉首市	Jishou	10.17	3.35		4.20	14.75	16.14	

8-4 城市供水(2003年)

Tap Water Supply in Cities (2003)

城市	Cities	综合生产能力(万立方米/日) Production Capacity of Tap Water (10 000 cu.m/day)	#地下水 Shallow Ground Water	供水管道长度(公里) Length of Water Supply Pipelines (km)	供水总量(万立方米) Total Annual Volume of Water Supply (10 000 cu.m)	#生产用量 For Productive Use	#公共服务用量 For Republic Services	#家庭用量 For Family Use	用水人口(万人) Number of Residents with Access to Tap Water (10 000 persons)
长沙市	Changsha	137.00		1291.64	38845	9476	373	18719	188.98
浏阳市	Liuyang	4.50	1.50	66	929	85	165	659	7.80
株洲市	Zhuzhou	250.70	0.20	673	39085	28727	2148	5876	59.00
醴陵市	Liling	8.50		197.7	1965	705	40	1115	17.20
湘潭市	Xiangtan	103.00	63.90	988	51804	41434	3737	6411	70.18
湘乡市	Xiangxiang	4.00		48	526	108	271	105	10.00
韶山市	Shaoshan	3.00	1.70	78	286	80	48	139	3.70
衡阳市	Hengyang	102.69	13.70	628	21578	8335	779	8851	88.83
耒阳市	Leiyang	5.30	0.25	96.05	733	74	26	616	16.00
常宁市	Changning	3.30	0.10	5.6	722	280	137	259	6.90
邵阳市	Shaoyang	67.04	0.65	456.48	11858	4889	399	3102	45.50
武冈市	Wugang	8.60	1.40	187	713	102	212	296	13.50
岳阳市	Yueyang	197.20	3.15	660.45	41204	22657	4148	11023	66.20
汨罗市	Miluo	11.30	3.80	68	968	325	26	554	9.40
临湘市	Linxiang	5.50		575	574	119	23	412	8.30
常德市	Changde	47.50		453.22	7350	1857	946	4327	38.70
津市市	Jinshi	21.00	1.00	102	4769	3927	89	628	12.91
张家界市	Zhangjiajie	12.80		303.5	1818	193	357	919	15.02
益阳市	Yiyang	40.20	1.50	233.52	4559	1141	346	2414	33.20
沅江市	Yuanjiang	3.00	3.00	43	592	8	29	550	10.60
郴州市	Chenzhou	53.17	8.38	402.1	7622	3686	707	2888	26.26
资兴市	Zixing	9.60	0.70	193	2545	1066	52	1425	12.92
永州市	Yongzhou	31.00	0.34	306.14	7644	2010	184	2596	10.43
娄底市	Loudi	20.00		257	3354	301	391	2190	27.50
冷水江市	Lengshuijiang	7.00		89.5	1183	236	52	790	11.06
涟源市	Lianyuan	5.00		59	793	102	41	630	8.40
怀化市	Huaihua	25.20		550	4685	1141	135	3271	32.00
洪江市	Hongjiang	10.30		93	822	318	220	230	7.30
吉首市	Jishou	16.50	2.10	237.9	3165	844	345	1790	14.30

8-5 城市公共交通(2003年)

Public Traffic in Cities (2003)

城市	Cities	公共汽车 Buses 运营车数 合计(辆) Number of Public Tran-sportation Vehicles (unit)	#小公共汽车 Small Buses	标准运营车数(标台) Number of Vehicles Convert into Standard unit (unit)	运营线路网长度(公里) Length of Public Tran-sportation Lines (km)	客运总量(万人次) Number of Passengers Carried (10 000 person-times)	#小公共汽车 Small Buses	出租汽车数(辆) Number of Taxis (unit)
长沙市	Changsha	1785		1785	1127	37540.69	1350	6257
浏阳市	Liuyang	51	18	45	63	800	300	400
株洲市	Zhuzhou	641	206	633	330	10260	506	1960
醴陵市	Liling	110	110	77	30	300		500
湘潭市	Xiangtan	535	154	489	316	6440	1300	907
湘乡市	Xiangxiang	93	93	67	118	565	565	286
韶山市	Shaoshan	25	25	8	11	180	180	35
衡阳市	Hengyang	621	163	626	164	8144	273	1394
耒阳市	Leiyang	99	99	70	41	990	990	480
常宁市	Changning	68	68	48	20	345	345	330
邵阳市	Shaoyang	294	52	284	67	3600	600	899
武冈市	Wugang	160	158	100	49	460		186
岳阳市	Yueyang	588	583	530	3882	9500		1256
汨罗市	Miluo	90	78	49	43	660	565	60
临湘市	Linxiang	70	70	49	44	500	500	240
常德市	Changde	834	168	342	355	3774	993	1173
津市市	Jinshi	317	285	235	380	668	586	130
张家界市	Zhangjiajie	299	30	289	133	1490	20	753
益阳市	Yiyang	315	10	308	184	3176.8	73	765
沅江市	Yuanjiang	128	128	90	520	520	520	728
郴州市	Chenzhou	546	261	414	116	6720	1322	1000
资兴市	Zixing	108	62	91	52	351	70	80
永州市	Yongzhou	492	360	301	174	6398	4690	120
娄底市	Loudi	130	13	125	97	1700	70	810
冷水江市	Lengshuijiang	128	117	93	119	1320	1098	181
涟源市	Lianyuan	68	57	51	50	980	710	278
怀化市	Huaihua	324		316	290	7802		800
洪江市	Hongjiang	30	22	23	36	490	370	107
吉首市	Jishou	46	44	33	28	1960	1060	600

8-6 城市市政设施(2003年)

Urban Civil Facilities (2003)

城市	Cities	道路长度(公里) Length of Streets (km)	道路面积(万平方米) Area of Streets (10 000 sq.m)	人行道面积(万平方米) Area of Sidewalk (10 000 sq.m)	桥梁数(座) Number of Bridges (unit)	#立交桥 Cloverleaf Junction	路灯盏数(盏) Number of Street Lights (unit)	排水管道长度(公里) Length of Sewer Pipelines (km)	污水年排放量(万立方米) Annual Volume of Sewage Discharged (10 000 cu.m)
长沙市	Changsha	1188.00	1980.10	491.60	73	22	37215	681.00	11
浏阳市	Liuyang	48.00	101.80	29.00	4		1484	41.00	
株洲市	Zhuzhou	504.26	589.40	150.20	48	12	18000	393.49	
醴陵市	Liling	74.00	73.00	13.00	28	3	600	61.00	59
湘潭市	Xiangtan	275.00	513.00	107.00	4		18901	340.00	25
湘乡市	Xiangxiang	25.22	32.00	10.60	3		2438	44.68	44.5
韶山市	Shaoshan	44.80	55.60	12.60	9		475	64.00	29
衡阳市	Hengyang	447.98	520.00	84.40	18	10	12398	354.19	
耒阳市	Leiyang	104.16	182.80	43.30	3		4129	197.04	
常宁市	Changning	80.50	120.30	20.20	8	2	880	72.50	22
邵阳市	Shaoyang	249.76	363.30	139.10	14		4800	125.20	5.5
武冈市	Wugang	51.50	196.80	60.20	16		690	54.20	
岳阳市	Yueyang	235.01	305.90	41.30	8	5	7259	317.00	20
汨罗市	Miluo	49.00	99.00	29.00	12	3	610	58.00	38
临湘市	Linxiang	53.00	54.00	3.00	5	1	1150	28.00	
常德市	Changde	315.18	484.00	142.90	24		11519	326.06	233.54
津市市	Jinshi	93.00	80.80	19.50	8		6700	64.00	
张家界市	Zhangjiajie	170.69	184.50	31.10	29		4805	87.68	12.21
益阳市	Yiyang	203.78	385.00	58.20	4		12259	238.45	
沅江市	Yuanjiang	50.00	61.00	20.00	9		1251	23.00	4
郴州市	Chenzhou	147.31	222.20	56.40	58	4	21641	166.00	4.8
资兴市	Zixing	87.48	98.70	33.00	10		2490	35.44	18.14
永州市	Yongzhou	213.00	345.50	88.80	16	1	6192	150.00	
娄底市	Loudi	185.00	363.00	58.00	15		30600	240.00	120
冷水江市	Lengshuijiang	81.60	74.10	25.60	13	1	2500	45.00	19
涟源市	Lianyuan	75.00	62.00	11.10	25	2	1317	36.80	7.5
怀化市	Huaihua	143.40	196.90	41.00	30	2	6000	75.00	
洪江市	Hongjiang	64.30	77.50	9.60	4	1	1532	25.00	20
吉首市	Jishou	108.97	158.60	62.80	43	5	5023	60.29	4.4

城市	Cities	污水处理厂 Sewage Disposal Factory 座数(座) Number of Units (unit)	#生化处理 Biological and Chemical Disposal	处理能力(万立方米/日) Disposal Capacity (10 000 cu.m/day)	#生化处理 Biological and Chemical Disposal	污水处理设施处理能力(万方/日) Capacity of Engineering (10 000 cu.m/day)	污水年处理量(万方) Annual Volume of Sewage Disposal (10 000 cu.m)	防洪堤长度(公里) Length of Banks to Prevent or Control Flood (km)	#百年及以上一遇 Befall 100 Years and Over
长沙市	Changsha	2	2	32.00			6100	127.00	
浏阳市	Liuyang							3.00	
株洲市	Zhuzhou	2	1	11.20	10.00	60.14	10611.96	33.00	
醴陵市	Liling							6.00	
湘潭市	Xiangtan							19.00	5.00
湘乡市	Xiangxiang							10.30	0.30
韶山市	Shaoshan	1	1	1.50	1.50	38.00	312		
衡阳市	Hengyang							110.84	7.00
耒阳市	Leiyang							1.48	
常宁市	Changning								
邵阳市	Shaoyang							9.60	
武冈市	Wugang							17.00	1.00
岳阳市	Yueyang	6	6	3.70	3.70	8.00	4121	125.00	
汨罗市	Miluo								
临湘市	Linxiang							4.00	4.00
常德市	Changde	1	1	15.00	15.00		3260	240.74	3.37
津市市	Jinshi							17.00	
张家界市	Zhangjiajie							9.43	0.23
益阳市	Yiyang								
沅江市	Yuanjiang								
郴州市	Chenzhou							14.60	0.40
资兴市	Zixing								
永州市	Yongzhou	1	1	10.00	10.00			1.00	
娄底市	Loudi					43.50	15880	3.90	
冷水江市	Lengshuijiang							1.88	
涟源市	Lianyuan							0.40	0.40
怀化市	Huaihua								
洪江市	Hongjiang							6.10	
吉首市	Jishou								

8-7 城市园林绿化(2003年)

Urban Parks, Gardens and Green Areas (2003)

城市	Cities	绿化覆盖面积(公顷) Coverage Space of Green Areas (hectare)	#建成区 Developed Areas	园林绿地面积(公顷) Area of Parks, Gardens and Green Areas (hectare)	#建成区 Developed Areas	公共绿地面积(公顷) Public Green Areas (hectare)	公园个数(个) Number of Parks (unit)	公园面积(公顷) Area of Parks (hectare)
长沙市	Changsha	6096	4974.3	5712	4186.3	1229.45	14	904.00
浏阳市	Liuyang	489	407	410	310	85.00	3	67.10
株洲市	Zhuzhou	2427.3	2427.3	2244.1	2244.1	391.20	4	245.18
醴陵市	Liling	529	529	494	494	74.00	1	55.00
湘潭市	Xiangtan	4379	2801	4166	2576	409.00	15	261.00
湘乡市	Xiangxiang	226.6	163	205.7	143	52.00	2	28.00
韶山市	Shaoshan	178	167	162	158	31.00	8	22.00
衡阳市	Hengyang	2104.6	2050.8	1757.4	1756.4	238.92	10	118.40
耒阳市	Leiyang	640.8	610.8	561.4	531.4	88.69	4	65.30
常宁市	Changning	310	250	98	82	9.00	1	7.00
邵阳市	Shaoyang	693.6	693.6	637.6	637.6	237.60	6	172.60
武冈市	Wugang	352.8	352.8	295	295	78.00	3	54.00
岳阳市	Yueyang	5256	2712	3364	1879.9	416.48	6	129.00
汨罗市	Miluo	248	248	192	192	78.10	1	66.70
临湘市	Linxiang	1856	75	1829	51	51.00	1	24.00
常德市	Changde	2143.9	2143.9	1877.6	1867.6	303.80	5	255.12
津市市	Jinshi	669	226	662	222	72.70	4	58.30
张家界市	Zhangjiajie	893.4	346	722.8	315.6	44.70	4	28.39
益阳市	Yiyang	1344.2	1339.3	1255.7	1250.8	215.89	4	177.29
沅江市	Yuanjiang	348	269	318	238	65.00	2	58.10
郴州市	Chenzhou	1155	1150	1265.1	1258.1	188.00	4	160.00
资兴市	Zixing	526.6	520	513.1	509	80.77	3	58.00
永州市	Yongzhou	883	858	669	644	150.00	6	74.00
娄底市	Loudi	2230	1323	1530	1203	191.14	6	171.54
冷水江市	Lengshuijiang	580	462	506	413	66.25	2	52.60
涟源市	Lianyuan	276.4	253.9	245.5	230.5	10.10	2	5.90
怀化市	Huaihua	1692.2	955	1564.4	895	140.00	5	125.87
洪江市	Hongjiang	230	229	209	202	53.00	1	29.00
吉首市	Jishou	786.5	290.5	788.4	265.5	65.50	2	40.00

8-8 城市燃气使用情况(2003年)

Urban Coal Gas and Liquefied Petroleum (2003)

城市	Cities	煤气 Coal Gas					
		供气总量 (万立方米) Total Gas Supply (10 000 cu.m)	#家庭用量 Consumption for Residential Use	用气户数 (户) Number of Household with Access to Gas (household)	#家庭用户 Consumption for Residential Use	用气人口 (万人) Population with Access to Gas (10000 persons)	管道长度 (公里) Length of Pipelines (km)
长沙市	Changsha	3373	2152	99249	99114	34.69	63
浏阳市	Liuyang						
株洲市	Zhuzhou	2587	1677	77548	77408	27.20	302
醴陵市	Liling						
湘潭市	Xiangtan	34164	1112	42366	42336	13.64	445
湘乡市	Xiangxiang						
韶山市	Shaoshan						
衡阳市	Hengyang						
耒阳市	Leiyang						
常宁市	Changning						
邵阳市	Shaoyang	895.7	895.7	22000	22000	6.90	129
武冈市	Wugang						
岳阳市	Yueyang						
汨罗市	Miluo						
临湘市	Linxiang						
常德市	Changde						
律市市	Jinshi						
张家界市	Zhangjiajie						
益阳市	Yiyang						
沅江市	Yuanjiang						
郴州市	Chenzhou						
资兴市	Zixing						
永州市	Yongzhou						
娄底市	Loudi	1510	1441	42410	42400	16.90	189
冷水江市	Lengshuijiang	1000	288	4050	4000	1.20	13
涟源市	Lianyuan						
怀化市	Huaihua						
洪江市	Hongjiang						
吉首市	Jishou						

城市	Cities	液化石油气 Liquefied Petroleum Gas					
		供气总量 (吨) Total Gas Supply (ton)	#家庭用量 Consumption for Residential Use	用气户数 (户) Number of Household with Access to Gas (household)	#家庭用户 Consumption for Residential Use	用气人口 (万人) Population with Access to Gas (10 000 persons)	管道长度 (公里) Length of Pipelines (km)
长沙市	Changsha	23786	23786	168504	168504	142.20	70
浏阳市	Liuyang	1865	1865	33000	33000	8.80	8
株洲市	Zhuzhou	12458		82725	82725	29.25	6.4
醴陵市	Liling	7000	4900	35000	34000	8.00	
湘潭市	Xiangtan	14008	12708	105900	105900	34.52	16
湘乡市	Xiangxiang	0.4	0.35	37500	37000	11.10	
韶山市	Shaoshan	1590	1480	5430	5280	2.60	
衡阳市	Hengyang	21226	4290	164120	109635	38.11	175.6
耒阳市	Leiyang	1100	1100	9600	9600	3.80	
常宁市	Changning	550	485	9956	8736	3.60	
邵阳市	Shaoyang	5300	5300	50060	50060	16.00	
武冈市	Wugang	2000	2000	11000	11000	4.50	
岳阳市	Yueyang	57846	49700	271000	214600	58.23	88.58
汨罗市	Miluo	4010	3980	16020	15980	10.40	
临湘市	Linxiang	2950	2850	58000	57560	9.00	
常德市	Changde	22070	18850	161350	150345	30.53	223.51
津市市	Jinshi	2019	2019	17856	17856	6.53	30
张家界市	Zhangjiajie	3210	2610	21698	19617	7.90	
益阳市	Yiyang	8760	8400	70062	70000	24.50	5.5
沅江市	Yuanjiang	1200	1200	26000	26000	6.50	
郴州市	Chenzhou	10975	6825	64830	60950	22.71	
资兴市	Zixing	1550	800	18000	10000	3.50	
永州市	Yongzhou	2615	2400.5	42068	40890	22.97	
娄底市	Loudi	2800	2700	28200	25200	9.80	
冷水江市	Lengshuijiang	1000	800	20000	19000	6.80	
涟源市	Lianyuan	980	900	21600	20600	7.40	
怀化市	Huaihua	14000	11200	72000	71000	26.94	2
洪江市	Hongjiang	1741	1600	13200		5.30	
吉首市	Jishou	2500	2500	22000	22000	10.31	

8-9 工业三废及工业污染治理情况

Statistic on Industrial Waste Water,Waste Gas, Solid Waste and Treatment of Industrial Pollution

指 标	Item	2000	2001	2002	2003
汇总企业数 (个)	**Number of Enterprises Counted (unit)**	**2891**	**2818**	**2801**	**3102**
工业废水	**Industrial Waste Water**				
治理设施数 (套)	Number of Facilities for Treatment (unit)	3034	2846	2825	2942
治理设施设备原价 (万元)	Original Value of Facilities (10 000 yuan)	248232	34993	44138.6	52537.6
工业废水排放总量 (万吨)	Total Volume of Industrial Waste Water Discharged (10 000 tons)	112563	107175	111787.65	124132.35
工业废水排放达标率 (%)	Percentage of Industrial Waste Water up to the Standards for Discharge (%)	66.09	74.52	77.62	79.86
工业废水处理排放达标量 (万吨)	Volume of Treated Waste Water up to the Discharge Standards (10 000 tons)	45647	79870.25	-	99127.32
工业废气、粉尘 (亿标立方米)	**Waste Gas and Industrial Dust (100 million cu.m)**				
工业废气排放总量	Total Volume of Industrial Waste Gas Discharge	3569	3959	4190	4603
燃料燃烧过程中废气排放量	Volume of Waste Gas in the Process of Fuel Burning	1718	1848	2048	2497
生产工艺过程中废气排放量	Volume of Waste Gas from the Process of Production	1851	2111	2142	2105
工业粉尘排放量 (万吨)	Volume of Industrial Dust Discharge (10 000 tons)	63.97	62.7	60.83	69.9
工业固体废物	**Industrial Solid Waste**				
工业固体废物产生量 (万吨)	Volume of Solid Wastes Produced (10 000 tons)	2355	2463	2434	2754
工业固体废物处置量 (万吨)	Volume of Solid Wastes Treated (10 000 tons)	137.32	221.47	240.35	247.41
工业固体废物处置率 (%)	Percentage of Solid Wastes Treated (%)	5.83	8.99	9.87	8.98
工业固体废物贮存量 (万吨)	Volume of Solid Wastes Accumulated (10 000 tons)	534.23	697.47	550.24	717.61
工业固体废物贮存率 (%)	Percentage of Solid Wastes Accumulated (%)	22.69	28.32	22.61	26.06
工业固体废物综合利用量 (万吨)	Volume of Solid Wastes Utilized (10 000 tons)	1106	1531	1577	1749
工业固体废物综合利用率 (%)	Percentage of Solid Wastes Utilized (%)	46.96	59.58	63.51	63.04
工业固体废物排放量 (万吨)	Volume of Solid Wastes Discharged (10 000 tons)	138.82	135.81	133.23	89.5
工业三废综合利用产品产值 (万元)	**Output Value of Products Made from Waste Gas, Waste Water and Solid Wastes (10 000 yuan)**	**116153**	**123434**	**134641**	**153129.3**
污染治理资金来源总计 (万元)	**All Sources of Funds (10 000 yuan)**	**54470.2**	**60090.6**	**45970.7**	**34059.6**
基本建设资金	Capital Construction	3156.6	13053	1898.9	940
环保补助资金	Subsidy of Environmental Protection	1541.7	621.8	289.8	1906.8
贷款	Loans	6723.3	2216.3	3709.6	12063.5
其 他	Others	37651.3	44199.5	40072.4	31212.8
污染治理资金使用总计(万元)	**All Uses of Funds (10 000 yuan)**	**54470.2**	**60090.6**	**45970.7**	**34059.6**
治理废水	Treatment of Waste Water	22668.2	21306.9	20022.4	14262.5
治理废气	Treatment of Waste Gas	28223	35583	16903.8	12331.1
治理固体废物	Treatment of Solid Wastes	2978.8	2834.1	7121.5	5569.9
治理噪声	Treatment of Noise Pollution	149.4	168.7	737.1	439
其 他	Treatment of Other Pollution	450.8	163.2	1185.9	1457.1
污染治理概况	**Situation of Pollution Treatment**				
本年施工项目总数 (个)	Projects Under Construction this Year(unit)	995	468	423	398
本年竣工项目数 (个)	Projects Completed this Year (unit)	893	419	354	326
治理废水	Treatment of Waste Water	359	161	163	143
治理废气	Treatment of Waste Gas	438	205	190	116
治理固体废物	Treatment of Solid Wastes	62	24	37	46
治理噪声	Treatment of Noise Pollution	16	16	18	14
污染情况	**Situation of Pollution**				
污染事故 (次)	Pollution Accidents (times)	317	238	340	314
污染赔款总额 (万元)	Amount of Reparations (10 000 yuan)	442.58	473.7	871	15579.2
污染罚款总额 (万元)	Amount of Fines (10 000 yuan)	30.82	29.6	53.8	5034

注:本表统计范围为有污染的县及县以上工业企业。

Data in this table refer to the data of the enterprises at and above county levels.

8-10 13个地级市及长沙、株洲、湘潭三城市基本情况(2003年)

Basic Statistics on 13 Prefecture–Level Cities and Basic Indicators of Changsha,Zhu zhou and Xiangtan (2003)

指标	Item	13个城市合计 Total on 13 Cities 全市 Cities Total	市辖区 Districts	长沙市 Changsha City 全市 Cities Total	市辖区 Districts
人口、劳动力及土地面积	**Population,Labor and Land Area**				
年末总人口(万人)	Total Population at the Year-end (10 000 persons)	6368.34	1157.62	601.76	196.26
#非农业人口	#Non-agricultural Population	1470.16	663.86	205.83	162.44
年平均人口(万人)	Annual Average Population (10 000 persons)	6346.21	1124.56	598.61	192.62
暂住人口(一个月以上)(万人)	Temporary Population (10 000 persons)	118.53	69.16	40.3	35.3
年出生人口(人)	Number of Births (person)	634286	104087	49683	14334
年死亡人口(人)	Number of Deaths (person)	350675	46820	40064	5635
年末总户数(万户)	Total Households at the Year-end (10 000 households)	1858.24	364.65	177.1	57.27
年末单位从业人员数(万人)	Employed Persons at the Year-end (10 000 persons)	377.23	165.66	63.12	47.9
第一产业	Primary Industry	17.9	2.45	0.3	0.12
第二产业	Secondary Industry	131.24	74.04	23.45	18.46
采矿业	Mining	12.07	1.38	0.65	0.06
制造业	Manufacturing	78.55	48.75	13.02	9.12
电力燃气及水的生产和供应业	Production and Distribution of Electricity,Gas and Water	10.58	4.01	0.97	0.68
建筑业	Construction	30.04	19.9	8.81	8.6
第三产业	Tertiary Industry	228.09	89	39.37	29.32
交通运输、仓储及邮政业	Traffic,Transport, Storage and Post	16.75	9.33	3.06	2.16
信息传输计算机服务和软件业	Information Transfer,Computer Services and Software	4.23	2.94	1.29	1.17
批发和零售业	Wholesale and Retail Trade	19.01	9.23	4.18	3.69
住宿、餐饮业	Accommodation and Restaurants	5.47	3.93	2.13	2.03
金融业	Finance	13.57	6.68	2.14	1.72
房地产业	Real Estate Trade	3.23	2.22	1.04	0.88
租赁和商业服务业	Tenancy and Business Services	5.41	3.91	1.41	1.31
科研、技术服务和地质勘查业	Scientific Research,Technical Service and Geologic Perambulation	6.28	4.27	2.67	2.43
水利、环境和公共设施管理业	Management of Water Conservancy, Environment and Public Establishment	6.79	2.72	0.69	0.39
居民服务和其他服务业	Resident Services and Other Services	0.73	0.47	0.2	0.19
教育	Education	63.58	15.8	8.56	4.68
卫生、社会保障和社会福利业	Sanitation,Social Security and Social Welfare	21.65	6.98	3.18	2.16
文化、体育和娱乐业	Culture,Sports and Entertainment	5.06	2.99	1.99	1.87
公共管理和社会组织	Public Management and Social Organization	56.33	17.53	6.83	4.64
私营和个体从业人员(人)	Employees in Private Enterprises and Individuals (person)	2741265	1145093	580620	428275
年末城镇登记失业人员数(人)	Un-employees in Urban at the year-end (person)	309464	127842	52310	31982
行政区域土地面积(平方公里)	Area of Land (sq.km)	196425	17711	11819	556
#建成区面积	#Developed Areas		788		135
城市建设用地面积(平方公里)	Area of Land for Urban Construction (sq.km)		808		158
居住用地面积	Area of Land for Residential Housing		251		46
公共设施用地面积	Area of Land for Public Utilities		123		34
工业用地面积	Area of Land for Industry		171		20
综合经济	**General Survey Economy**				
地区生产总值(万元)	Gross Domestic Product (10 000 yuan)	46796428	18990957	9294858	5523787
第一产业增加值	Primary Industry	9047340	1083701	832886	87064
第二产业增加值	Secondary Industry	17902078	8346827	3936734	2112716
#工业增加值	#Industry	13977922	6329180	2682806	1336513
第三产业增加值	Tertiary Industry	19847010	9390548	4525238	3324007
交通运输仓储及邮政业	Traffic,Transport, Storage and Post	3607210	1595217	444214	337603
信息传输计算机服务和软件业	Information Transfer,Computer Services and Software	1395260	810880	318993	255194

8-10 续表 1 continued

指标	Item	13个城市合计 Total on 13 Cities 全市 Cities Total	13个城市合计 市辖区 Districts	长沙市 Changsha City 全市 Cities Total	长沙市 市辖区 Districts
金融业	Finance	1992313	1121146	551957	399203
房地产业	Real Estate Trade	1655659	505871	242125	63492
科研、技术服务和地质勘查业	Scientific Research,Technical Service and Geologic Perambulation	264226	181025	130197	104158
人均地区生产总值(元)	Per Capita GDP (yuan)	7554	16202	14810	24312
生产总值增长率(%)	Growth Rate of GDP (%)	10.63	11.76	14	14.5
财政、金融、保险	**Fiscal ,Financial and Insurance**				
地方财政收入（万元）	Local Government Revenue (10 000 yuan)	2153740	1115360	598930	464498
财政支出（万元）	Government Expenditure (10 000 yuan)	4052129	1778504	784168	538922
基本建设支出	Expenditure for Capital Construction	127442	97811	63225	49619
企业挖潜改造资金	Expenditure for Innovation Enterprises	46889	34782	18416	16744
科技三项费用	Expenditure for Science and Technology Promotion	37393	25219	18032	15374
城市维护费	Expenditure for City Maintenance	229788	179866	93817	87335
科学支出	Operating Expenses for Science	9138	6340	2688	2431
教育支出	Operating Expenses for Education	732084	182713	90804	41534
医疗卫生支出	Operating Expenses for Public Health	132623	63241	21637	14207
抚恤和社会福利救济	Pensions, Social and Relief Funds for Social Welfare	201636	73080	30344	18383
社会保障补助支出	Expenditure on Subsidies to Social Security Programs	351744	205054	44612	33595
政策性补贴支出	Expenditure for Price Subsidies	17055	8990	5369	4077
年末金融机构存款余额(万元)	Deposits of Financial Institutions (10 000 yuan)	46609026	27304083	15987000	12789600
#城乡居民储蓄年末余额	Saving Deposits in Urban and Rural Residents	30442648	15748325	7048500	5596509
年末金融机构贷款余额(万元)	Loans of Financial Institutions (10 000 yuan)	37051822	24209443	16294200	13035360
保费收入(万元)	Premiums (10 000 yuan)	995617	532345	283028	218215
财产险	Property Insurance	196251	109673	56166	42686
人身险	Life Insurance	793346	418775	226862	175529
赔款、给付(万元)	Indemnity and Payment (10 000 yaun)	208635	104351	45198	34848
财产险	Property Insurance	93017	47835	27660	20745
人身险	Life Insurance	111440	52858	17538	14103
农业	**Agriculture**				
年末耕地总资源（千公顷）	Cultivated Resource at the Year-end (1 000 hectare)	2950		237	
蔬菜产量(吨)	Output of Vegetable (tons)	22324727		3431256	
水果产量(吨)	Output of Fruit (ton)	4757102		177726	
肉类总产量(吨)	Output of Pork ,Beef and Mutton (ton)	5517757		544077	
奶类产量(吨)	Output of Milk (ton)	51601		15124	
水产品产量(吨)	Output of Aquatic Product (ton)	1547931		94235	
工业	**Industry**				
国有及年销售收入500万元以上非国有工业企业数（个）	Industry Enterprises of State-owned and Non State-owned with the Sales Revenue of over 5 Million Yuan (unit)	5573	1955	912	375
内资企业	Domestic Funded Enterprises	5267	1787	820	340
港、澳、台商投资企业	Enterprises with Investment from Hong Kong、Macao and Taiwan	181	94	48	19
外商投资企业	Enterprises with Foreign Investment	125	74	44	16
工业总产值（万元）	Gross Output Value (10 000 yuan)	25412605	15273552	5339304	3094384
内资企业	Domestic Funded Enterprises	22943211	14043519	4255611	2869116
港、澳、台商投资企业	Enterprises with Investment from Hong Kong、Macao and Taiwan	1076892	581763	357538	124771
外商投资企业	Enterprises with Foreign Investment	1392502	648270	726155	100497
从业人员年平均人数(万人)	Annual Average Staff and Workers (10 000 persons)	151.5	71.21	24.67	11.03
流动资产年平均余额(万元)	Annual Average Balance of Circulating Funds(10 000 yuan)	12879017	8970944	3437007	2373517
固定资产净值年平均余额(万元)	Average Balance of Net Value of Fixed Assets(10 000 yuan)	14823093	8884410	2180141	1134263
产品销售收入(万元)	Sales Revenue (10 000 yuan)	25109635	15647597	5194488	3050561
产品销售税金及附加（万元）	Sales Tax and Extra Charges (10 000 yuan)	1046033	923541	395269	368916
本年应交增值税(万元)	Value Added Tax Payable (10 000 yuan)	1213075	820269	250262	161679
利润总额(万元)	Total Profits (10 000 yuan)	1048269	673989	400102	220707

指标	Item	13个城市合计 Total on 13 Cities 全 市 Cities Total	市辖区 Districts	长沙市 Changsha City 全 市 Cities Total	市辖区 Districts
交通运输、邮电通信和电力	**Transportation,Post, Telecommunication, Energy and Electric Power**				
铁路客运量(万人)	Railway Passenger Traffic (10 000 persons)	5024.11		942	
铁路货运量(万吨)	Railway Freight Traffic (10 000 tons)	5846		189	
境内铁路里程(公里)	Lengh of Railways in Operation (km)	2821		251	
民用汽车拥有量(辆)	Civil Motor Vehicles Owned (unit)	1037873		141300	
#私人汽车拥有量(辆)	#Private Vehicles (unit)	733132		82336	
公路客运量(万人)	Highway Passenger Traffic (10 000 persons)	85929.59		9351	
公路货运量(万吨)	Highway Freight Traffic (10 000 tons)	49795		9572	
境内公路里程公里	Lengh of Highways (km)	73166		5443	
#境内高速公路里程	#Lengh of Expressway	1365		223	
内河港口货物吞吐量(万吨)	Volume of Freight Handled in River Ports (10 000 tons)	2360		314	
水运客运量(万人)	Waterway Passengers Traffic (10 000 persons)	773.2		17	
水运货运量(万吨)	Waterway Freight Traffic (10 000 tons)	3195		866	
民用航空货邮运量(吨)	Freight Traffic by Civil Aviation (ton)	37130		34988	
民用航空客运量(人)	Passengers Traffic by Civil Aviation (person)	3719741		2992543	
年末邮政局(所)数(处)	Number of Postal Offices at the Yearend (unit)	8980	1095	782	187
邮政业务收入(万元)	Total Business Revenue of Postal (10 000 yuan)	194728	86600	41040	27703
电信业务收入(万元)	Revenue of Telecommunications Service (10 000 yuan)	1581606	901236	370004	279390
固定电话用户数(万户)	Number of Fixed Telephone (10 000 households)	919.81	316.95	160	86
年末移动电话用户数(万户)	Number of Mobile Telephone (10 000 households)	788.08	387.99	196.79	110.96
国际互联网用户数(万户)	Number of Internet User (10 000 households)	169.53	106.52	65.44	57.96
能源消费量(万吨/标准煤)	Total Energy Consumption (10 000 tons of SCE)	7049	3628	253	86
全年用电量(万千瓦时)	Consumption Volume of Energy (10 000 kw.h)	4048794	2064440	696000	439000
工业用电	Used in Industry	2689216	1395060	354800	201500
城乡居民生活用电	Used in Living	852232	438712	260300	154200
内外贸易、外经、旅游	**National Trade,Foreign Trade and Tourists**				
限额以上批发零售贸易业商品销售总额(万元)	Total Sales of Above-Norm Wholesale and Retail Trade Enterprisese (10 000 yuan)	12136470	8204135	5681637	5192791
社会消费品零售额(万元)	Total Retail Sales of Consumer Goods(10 000 yuan)	17747180	9113511	4519993	3522069
批发零售贸易企业法人数(个)	Enterprisese of Wholesale and Retail Trade (unit)	751	410	229	196
零售业按经营方式分组	Retial Trade By Chain Form:				
连锁商店(个)	Chain Store (unit)	55	50	17	16
非连锁商店(个)	Non-chain Store (unit)	353	200	69	66
按零售业态分组	Retial Trade By Operation Form:				
百货商店(个)	Department Store (unit)	116	64	10	5
超级市场(个)	Supermarket (unit)	91	61	19	14
进口总额 (万美元)	Total Volue of Imports (USD 10 000)	159396		94595	
出口总额 (万美元)	Total Volue of Exports (USD 10 000)	219376		109811	
当年新签项目(合同)数(个)	Number of Newly-signed Items(Contracts) (item)	582	243	122	76
当年合同外资金额(万美元)	Contract Value (USD 10 000)	203614	74462	77674	33487
当年实际使用外资金额(万美元)	Used Value (USD 10 000)	154200	71922	50209	27124
年末已投产企业数(个)	Number of Enterprises Put into Production (unit)	1700	1121	648	524
从业人员数(人)	Number of Employed Persons (person)	183256	108017	58000	34165
海外游客人数(人)	Number of International Tourists (person)	551456		48481	
外国人	#Foreigner	347818		33304	
港、澳、台同胞	From Hong Kong,Macao and Taiwan	203638		15177	
国际旅游外汇收入(万美元)	Revenue of International Tourist (USD 10 000)	12695		2384	
星级饭店数(个)	Number of Tourist Hotels (unit)	404		61	

8-10 续表 3 continued

指标	Item	13个城市合计 Total on 13 Cities 全市 Cities Total	市辖区 Districts	长沙市 Changsha City 全市 Cities Total	市辖区 Districts
固定资产投资	**Investment in Fixed Assets**				
全社会固定资产投资总额(万元)	Total Investment in Fixed Assets (10 000 yuan)	15894033	8215868	4949713	3073642
#城镇固定资产投资	#Investment in Fixed Assets of Urban	12103004	7167743	4339489	2979901
#房地产开发投资	#Investment in Real Estate Development	2402335	2001084	1225551	1103388
#住宅	#Residential Buildings	1380574	1115316	732833	645502
全年新增固定资产(万元)	Newly Increased Fixed Assets (10 000 yuan)	9304134	4635877	2350330	1865769
本年施工住宅面积(万平方米)	Floor Space of Residential Building Under Construction	5873.67	2851.76	1063.8	865.76
本年竣工住宅面积(万平方米)	Floor Space of Residential Building Completed	3956.79	1507.42	417.65	304.27
商品房屋销售面积(万平方米)	Floor Space of Selling Commercial House (10 000 sq.m)	832.23	575.04	325.82	247.97
#销售给个人	#Commercial Houses Purchased by Individuals	773.84	534.45	304.49	228.77
商品房屋空置面积(万平方米)	Floor Space of Empty Commercial House(10 000 sq.m)	206.44	174.5	79.95	70.18
商品房屋销售额(万元)	Total Sales of Commercial House (10 000 yuan)	1170630	965218	666279	591653
#销售给个人	#Commercial Houses Purchased by Individuals	1061355	876161	595179	521207
教育、科技、文化、卫生	**Education,Science and Technology, Culture,Health Care**				
学校数(所)	Number of Schools (unit)				
高等学校	Institutions of Higher Education	75	70	37	33
中等职业学校	Secondary Specialized Schools	608	269	105	54
普通中学	Regular Secondary Schools	4500	752	358	84
小学	Primary Schools	22681	2576	1580	234
专任教师数(人)	Number of Full-time Teachers (person)				
高等学校	Institutions of Higher Education	32366	31730	16055	15419
中等职业学校	Secondary Specialized Schools	26627	14835	3710	2073
普通中学	Regular Secondary Schools	250114	52864	24392	7015
小学	Primary Schools	247249	48209	18265	6605
在校学生数	Number of Students Enrollment				
高等学校(人)	Institutions of Higher Education (person)	519196	504694	268613	255611
中等职业学校(人)	Secondary Specialized Schools (person)	532762	310193	107475	66424
普通中学(万人)	Regular Secondary Schools (10 000 persons)	462.06	86.69	43.28	11.37
小学(万人)	Primary Schools (10 000 persons)	438.89	81	31.36	10.71
成人高等教育在校学生数(人)	Students Enrollment in Adult Education Schools(person)	170831	162565	23867	22311
各类专业技术人员(人)	Various Specialized Technical Personnel (10 000 persons)	1851079	768534	265583	204726
#中级职称以上	#Persons with Above Middle Rank Titles	508764	267726	112131	92045
体育场馆数(个)	Number of Stadiums and Gymnasiums (unit)	4898	1910	0	0
剧场、影剧院数(个)	Number of Theaters and Music Halls (unit)	155	62	12	10
公共图书馆图书总藏量(千册)	Total Collections in Public Libraries (1000 volumes)	14670	7256	3774	3335
医院、卫生院数(个)	Number of Hospitals (unit)	3521	964	282	119
医院、卫生院床位数(张)	Number of Beds in Hospitals (sheet)	138393	66711	21024	16987
医生数(人)	Number of Doctors (person)	92668	42501	11655	8685
人民生活、社会保障	**The People's Living and Social Security**				
在岗职工平均人数(万人)	Average Persons on the Job (10 000 persons)	360.37	160.17	60.04	45.23
在岗职工工资总额(万元)	Total Wages of Workers on the Job（10 000 yuan)	4359807	2328711	1019924	795129
居民人均可支配收入(元)	Per Capita Disposable Income in Urban Residents(yuan)		7674		9932
居民人均消费支出(元)	Per Capita Living Expenditures for Consumption (yuan)		6083		8330
食品	Foods		2179		2629
衣着用品	Clothing		621		778
家庭设备、用品及服务	Household Facilities,Articles and Services		420		558
医疗保健	Medicine and Medical Services		391		607
交通和通讯	Transportation and Telecommunication		680		1115
娱乐、教育、文化服务	Recreation,Education and Cultural Service		994		1574
居住	Residence		587		792
百户居民家庭拥有家用汽车(辆)	Family Automobile Per 100 Households (unit)		0.27		0.75
百户居民家庭拥有家用电脑(台)	Personnel Computer Per 100 Households (unit)		27		38
人均住房使用面积(平方米)	Per Capita Floor Space of Residential Building (sq.m)		20		18
居民消费价格指数(上年为100)	General Consumer Price Index (preceding year =100)		102.4		100.9

指标	Item	13个城市合计 Total on 13 Cities 全市 Cities Total	市辖区 Districts	长沙市 Changsha City 全市 Cities Total	市辖区 Districts
年末离退休、退职人员数(万人)	Retired and Resigned Persons at the Yearend(10 000 persons)	162.15	86.9	28.58	24.12
社会保险参保人数（人）	N umber of Participants in Social Insurance (person)				
基本养老保险参保人数	Participant in Basic Pension Insurance	3965886	1974424	517957	338724
基本医疗保险参保人数	Participants in Basic Medicare Insurance	3737926	1931446	622317	496356
失业保险参保人数	Participants in Unemployment Insurance	3285306	1825235	494535	411280
社会福利院数(个)	Number of Social Welfare Institutions (unit)	1407	229	138	20
社会福利院床位数(张)	Beds in Social Welfare Institutions (sheet)	31670	9921	4807	2224
社区服务设施数(个)	Number of Community Service Installations (unit)	19565	11795	1714	1637
最低生活保障线以下人数(人)	Persons Under the Line of Lowest Living Security(person)	1497047	553096	143336	76063
社会治安	**Public Security**				
交通事故件数(件)	Number of Traffic Accidents (case)	25832	10850	7775	4592
交通事故死亡人数(人)	Number of Deaths on Traffic Accidents (person)	3964	1246	632	244
刑事案件立案数(件)	Number of Criminal Cases (case)	179901	89477	46618	33841
犯罪人数(人)	Number of Criminals (person)	57008	23125	4792	2129
市政公用事业	**Municipal Public Utilities**				
城市维护建设资金支出(万元)	Expenditure for City Maintenance&Construction(10 000 yuan)		1032372		573952
年末城市道路面积(万平方米)	Area of Paved Roads at the Yearend (10 000 sq.m)		6141		1980
排水管道长度(公里)	Length of Sewer Pipelines (km)		3616		769
供水综合生产能力(万立方米)	Production Capacity of Tap Water (10 000 cu.m/day)		1130.69		165
供水总量(万立方米)	Total Annual Volume of Water Supply (10 000 cu.m)		243639		38845
#居民家庭用水量	#Consumption for Residential Use		73548		18719
用水人口(万人)	Pupolation Using Tap Water (10 000 persons)		746.88		188.98
煤气供气总量(万立方米)	Total Coal Gas Supply (10 000 cu.m)		63776		3373
#家庭用量	#Consumption for Residential Use		11583		2152
用煤气人口(人)	Pupolation Using Coal Gas (persons)		1417496		346900
液化石油气供气总量(吨)	Total Liquefied Petroleum Gas Gas Supply (ton)		735024		75668
#家庭用量	#Consumption for Residential Use		306175		74165
用液化气人口(人)	Pupolation Using Liquefied Petroleum Gas (persons)		4674355		1422000
年末公共汽车营运车辆数(辆)	Number of Public Transportation Vehicles (unit)		7292		1785
全年公共汽车客运总量(万人次)	Number of Passengers Carried (10 000 person-times)		106545.9		37541
年末实有出租汽车数(辆)	Number of Taxi at the Yearend (unit)		18830		6257
园林绿地面积(公顷)	Area of Parks,Gardens and Green Areas in Cities (hectare)		27255		5712
#公共绿地面积	# Public Green Areas		4659		1229
建成区绿化覆盖面积(公顷)	Coverage Space of Green Areas in Developed Area(hectare)		23499		4974
环境保护	**Environmental Protection**				
污染源治理本年投资总额(万元)	Actual Investment for Pollution Treatment (10 000 yuan)	141647		36772	
城市环境基础设施建设本年完成投资额(万元)	Actual Investment in Base Facilities Construction of Urban Environment (10 000 yuan)	465661		138391	
三废综合利用产品产值(万元)	Output Value of Products Made From Waste Water, Waste Gas and Solid Wastes (10 000 yuan)	153129		3099	
工业废水排放量(万吨)	Volume of Industrial Waste Water Discharged (10 000 tons)	121884		4006	
工业废水排放达标量(万吨)	Volume of Waste Water up to the Discharge Standards	99008		3510	
工业二氧化硫去除量(吨)	Volume of Sulphur Dioxide Removed (ton)	493872		25309	
工业二氧化硫排放量(吨)	Volume of Sulphur Dioxide Emission (ton)	519567		54465	
工业烟尘去除量(吨)	Volume of Industrial Soot Removed (ton)	3171727		23867	
工业烟尘排放量(吨)	Volume of Industrial Soot Emission (ton)	382862		40407	
工业固体废物综合利用率(%)	Percentage of Industrial Solid Wastes Utilized (%)	63		99	
烟尘控制区总面积(平方公里)	Total Area of Soot Control (sq.km)	916		173	
高污染燃料禁烧区(平方公里)	Area of Inhibit Burn Hi-pollution Fuel (sq.km)	215		0	
噪声达标区总面积(平方公里)	Area of Environmental Noise up to the Standard (sq.km)	615		97	
生活污水处理率(%)	Rate of Sewage Disposal (%)	27		45	
生活垃圾无害化处理率(%)	Rate of Garbage Harmlessly Treatment (%)	55		76	

指标	Item	株洲市 Zhuzhou City 全市 Cities Total	#市辖区 Districts	湘潭市 Xiangtan City 全市 Cities Total	#市辖区 Districts
人口、劳动力及土地面积	**Population,Labor and Land Area**				
年末总人口(万人)	Total Population at the Year-end (10 000 persons)	373.6	80.2	282.03	70.19
#非农业人口	#Non-agricultural Population	99.31	59	80.05	57.54
年平均人口(万人)	Annual Average Population (10 000 persons)	370.47	77	281.6	69.7
暂住人口(一个月以上)(万人)	Temporary Population (10 000 persons)	9.8	8.3	2.51	1.95
年出生人口(人)	Number of Births (person)	32478	6122	22043	5114
年死亡人口(人)	Number of Deaths (person)	18842	2102	16252	2705
年末总户数(万户)	Total Households at the Year-end (10 000 households)	104.8	24.85	84.97	21.5
年末单位从业人员数(万人)	Employed Persons at the Year-end (10 000 persons)	28.59	18.88	23.48	14.24
第一产业	Primary Industry	0.45	0.01	0.09	0.04
第二产业	Secondary Industry	14.28	11.93	12.76	9.15
采矿业	Mining	0.27	0.12	0.52	0.04
制造业	Manufacturing	11.15	9.57	8.96	7.31
电力燃气及水的生产和供应业	Production and Distribution of Electricity,Gas and Water	0.85	0.5	0.42	0.31
建筑业	Construction	2.01	1.74	2.86	1.49
第三产业	Tertiary Industry	13.86	6.94	10.63	5.05
交通运输、仓储及邮政业	Traffic,Transport, Storage and Post	1.31	0.81	0.71	0.35
信息传输计算机服务和软件业	Information Transfer,Computer Services and Software	0.24	0.16	0.12	0.11
批发和零售业	Wholesale and Retail Trade	1.02	0.67	0.9	0.62
住宿、餐饮业	Accommodation and Restaurants	0.48	0.38	0.21	0.15
金融业	Finance	1.07	0.58	0.88	0.55
房地产业	Real Estate Trade	0.3	0.26	0.17	0.13
租赁和商业服务业	Tenancy and Business Services	0.38	0.29	0.17	0.13
科研、技术服务和地质勘查业	Scientific Research,Technical Service and Geologic Perambulation	0.52	0.46	0.39	0.36
水利、环境和公共设施管理业	Management of Water Conservancy, Environment and Public Establishment	0.5	0.29	0.33	0.18
居民服务和其他服务业	Resident Services and Other Services	0.1	0.07	0.04	0.03
教育	Education	3.16	0.89	3.03	1.03
卫生、社会保障和社会福利业	Sanitation,Social Security and Social Welfare	1.23	0.47	1.04	0.45
文化、体育和娱乐业	Culture,Sports and Entertainment	0.32	0.16	0.13	0.08
公共管理和社会组织	Public Management and Social Organization	3.23	1.45	2.51	0.88
私营和个体从业人员(人)	Employees in Private Enterprises and Individuals (person)	401346	119371	113107	88628
年末城镇登记失业人员数(人)	Un-employees in Urban at the year-end (person)	27847	14417	15968	9562
行政区域土地面积(平方公里)	Area of Land (sq.km)	11272	542	5015	279
#建成区面积	#Developed Areas		77		63
城市建设用地面积(平方公里)	Area of Land for Urban Construction (sq.km)		77		61
居住用地面积	Area of Land for Residential Housing		20		17
公共设施用地面积	Area of Land for Public Utilities		12		6
工业用地面积	Area of Land for Industry		21		23
综合经济	**General Survey Economy**				
地区生产总值(万元)	Gross Domestic Product (10 000 yuan)	3830868	1890642	2676868	1498863
第一产业增加值	Primary Industry	506373	45171	369788	29079
第二产业增加值	Secondary Industry	1877981	1044033	1086831	719328
#工业增加值	#Industry	1577713	891109	859818	584492
第三产业增加值	Tertiary Industry	1446514	801438	1220249	750456
交通运输仓储及邮政业	Traffic,Transport, Storage and Post	348976	210296	138010	58422
信息传输计算机服务和软件业	Information Transfer,Computer Services and Software	80336	50513	59864	42283

8-10 续表 6 continued

指标	Item	株洲市 Zhuzhou City 全市 Cities Total	#市辖区 Districts	湘潭市 Xiangtan City 全市 Cities Total	#市辖区 Districts
金融业	Finance	102701	53164	253721	206581
房地产业	Real Estate Trade	89778	36259	80615	35377
科研、技术服务和地质勘查业	Scientific Research,Technical Service and Geologic Perambulation	36003	33122	12346	8700
人均地区生产总值(元)	Per Capita GDP (yuan)	10707	21516	10056	21209
生产总值增长率(%)	Growth Rate of GDP (%)	11.1	11.8	11.2	11.6
财政、金融、保险	**Fiscal ,Financial and Insurance**				
地方财政收入(万元)	Local Government Revenue (10 000 yuan)	168180	107272	100736	63353
财政支出(万元)	Government Expenditure (10 000 yuan)	307238	181881	196970	114318
基本建设支出	Expenditure for Capital Construction	16645	10126	2977	2740
企业挖潜改造资金	Expenditure for Innovation Enterprises	2269	1843	3534	3340
科技三项费用	Expenditure for Science and Technology Promotion	4480	3398	2139	1705
城市维护费	Expenditure for City Maintenance	31925	28744	11938	8443
科学支出	Operating Expenses for Science	728	675	493	405
教育支出	Operating Expenses for Education	42680	13244	26763	7210
医疗卫生支出	Operating Expenses for Public Health	9820	5704	5940	3461
抚恤和社会福利救济	Pensions, Social and Relief Funds for Social Welfare	12300	5584	11371	7494
社会保障补助支出	Expenditure on Subsidies to Social Security Programs	38172	28393	23882	19515
政策性补贴支出	Expenditure for Price Subsidies	838	419	559	532
年末金融机构存款余额(万元)	Deposits of Financial Institutions (10 000 yuan)	3391137	2322722	2738198	1734051
#城乡居民储蓄年末余额	Saving Deposits in Urban and Rural Residents	2332823	1441364	2029140	1148087
年末金融机构贷款余额(万元)	Loans of Financial Institutions (10 000 yuan)	2125393	1589020	1771626	1257594
保费收入(万元)	Premiums (10 000 yuan)	91925	59751	64025	43865
财产险	Property Insurance	16144	11300	13445	10482
人身险	Life Insurance	75781	45468	50581	33383
赔款、给付(万元)	Indemnity and Payment (10 000 yaun)	16484	10715	14478	9411
财产险	Property Insurance	7467	5223	6652	4324
人身险	Life Insurance	8763	5257	7826	5087
农业	**Agriculture**				
年末耕地总资源(千公顷)	Cultivated Resource at the Year-end (1 000 hectare)	153		119	
蔬菜产量(吨)	Output of Vegetable (tons)	1338778		1052458	
水果产量(吨)	Output of Fruit (ton)	203914		61520	
肉类总产量(吨)	Output of Pork ,Beef and Mutton (ton)	288511		323481	
奶类产量(吨)	Output of Milk (ton)	718		2321	
水产品产量(吨)	Output of Aquatic Product (ton)	56345		63380	
工业	**Industry**				
国有及年销售收入500万元以上非国有工业企业数(个)	Industry Enterprises of State-owned and Non State-owned with the Sales Revenue of over 5 Million Yuan (unit)	521	210	400	209
内资企业	Domestic Funded Enterprises	483	190	380	191
港、澳、台商投资企业	Enterprises with Investment from Hong Kong、Macao and Taiwan	26	12	11	9
外商投资企业	Enterprises with Foreign Investment	12	8	9	9
工业总产值(万元)	Gross Output Value (10 000 yuan)	2620980	2091790	2025508	1578233
内资企业	Domestic Funded Enterprises	2347048	1875452	1942685	1499847
港、澳、台商投资企业	Enterprises with Investment from Hong Kong、Macao and Taiwan	141559	104428	43637	39200
外商投资企业	Enterprises with Foreign Investment	132373	111910	39186	39186
从业人员年平均人数(万人)	Annual Average Staff and Workers (10 000 persons)	18.24	10.96	13.32	9.5
流动资产年平均余额(万元)	Annual Average Balance of Circulating Funds(10 000 yuan)	1657829	1464122	1131860	931362
固定资产净值年平均余额(万元)	Average Balance of Net Value of Fixed Assets(10 000 yuan)	1321486	1169017	1397622	1213947
产品销售收入(万元)	Sales Revenue (10 000 yuan)	2659386	2212389	2064764	1674798
产品销售税金及附加(万元)	Sales Tax and Extra Charges (10 000 yuan)	22821	15161	17311	12426
本年应交增值税(万元)	Value Added Tax Payable (10 000 yuan)	119055	100151	111572	98713
利润总额(万元)	Total Profits (10 000 yuan)	116230	101660	47979	46143

指标	Item	株洲市 Zhuzhou City 全市 Cities Total	株洲市 Zhuzhou City #市辖区 Districts	湘潭市 Xiangtan City 全市 Cities Total	湘潭市 Xiangtan City #市辖区 Districts
交通运输、邮电通信和电力	**Transportation,Post, Telecommunication, Energy and Electric Power**				
铁路客运量(万人)	Railway Passenger Traffic (10 000 persons)	517.65		144.03	
铁路货运量(万吨)	Railway Freight Traffic (10 000 tons)	575		614	
境内铁路里程(公里)	Lengh of Railways in Operation (km)	318		147	
民用汽车拥有量(辆)	Civil Motor Vehicles Owned (unit)	48267		33023	
#私人汽车拥有量(辆)	#Private Vehicles (unit)	25911		20940	
公路客运量(万人)	Highway Passenger Traffic (10 000 persons)	5639.85		2711	
公路货运量(万吨)	Highway Freight Traffic (10 000 tons)	3256		2644	
境内公路里程公里	Lengh of Highways (km)	3947		2717	
#境内高速公路里程	#Lengh of Expressway	72		119	
内河港口货物吞吐量(万吨)	Volume of Freight Handled in River Ports (10 000 tons)	255		155	
水运客运量(万人)	Waterway Passengers Traffic (10 000 persons)	12.54		0	
水运货运量(万吨)	Waterway Freight Traffic (10 000 tons)	148		239	
民用航空货邮运量(吨)	Freight Traffic by Civil Aviation (ton)				
民用航空客运量(人)	Passengers Traffic by Civil Aviation (person)				
年末邮政局(所)数(处)	Number of Postal Offices at the Yearend (unit)	208	48	122	37
邮政业务收入(万元)	Total Business Revenue of Postal (10 000 yuan)	12269	5950	12128	5633
电信业务收入(万元)	Revenue of Telecommunications Service (10 000 yuan)	153480	99762	106116	62332
固定电话用户数(万户)	Number of Fixed Telephone (10 000 households)	74.94	35.94	52.26	23.09
年末移动电话用户数(万户)	Number of Mobile Telephone (10 000 households)	588590	318360	432014	262248
国际互联网用户数(万户)	Number of Internet User (10 000 households)	145700	112537	146778	106086
能源消费量(万吨/标准煤)	Total Energy Consumption (10 000 tons of SCE)	496	403	734	636
全年用电量(万千瓦时)	Consumption Volume of Energy (10 000 kw.h)	492959	364482	390016	312482
工业用电	Used in Industry	351245	293675	303912	273521
城乡居民生活用电	Used in Living	57317	28770	38486	24246
内外贸易、外经、旅游	**National Trade,Foreign Trade and Tourists**				
限额以上批发零售贸易业商品销售总额(万元)	Total Sales of Above-Norm Wholesale and Retail Trade Enterprisese (10 000 yuan)	738178	543721	309442	221961
社会消费品零售额(万元)	Total Retail Sales of Consumer Goods(10 000 yuan)	1400470	728493	902986	535920
批发零售贸易企业法人数(个)	Enterprisese of Wholesale and Retail Trade (unit)	53	38	28	16
零售业按经营方式分组	Retial Trade By Chain Form:				
连锁商店(个)	Chain Store (unit)	3	3	3	3
非连锁商店(个)	Non-chain Store (unit)	20	13	8	6
按零售业态分组	Retial Trade By Operation Form:				
百货商店(个)	Department Store (unit)	3	2	1	1
超级市场(个)	Supermarket (unit)	11	7	3	2
进口总额 (万美元)	Total Volue of Imports (USD 10 000)	13176		12960	
出口总额 (万美元)	Total Volue of Exports (USD 10 000)	36543		17732	
当年新签项目(合同)数(个)	Number of Newly-signed Items(Contracts) (item)	43	31	28	9
当年合同外资金额(万美元)	Contract Value (USD 10 000)	14181	8061	20405	3521
当年实际使用外资金额(万美元)	Used Value (USD 10 000)	9007	7096	11116	8629
年末已投产企业数(个)	Number of Enterprises Put into Production (unit)	110	70	131	104
从业人员数(人)	Number of Employed Persons (person)	29764	18069	13000	11200
海外游客人数(人)	Number of International Tourists (person)	9360		527	
外国人	#Foreigner	4585		212	
港、澳、台同胞	From Hong Kong,Macao and Taiwan	4775		315	
国际旅游外汇收入(万美元)	Revenue of International Tourist (USD 10 000)	203		21	
星级饭店数(个)	Number of Tourist Hotels (unit)	22		14	

8-10 续表 8 continued

指标	Item	株洲市 Zhuzhou City 全市 Cities Total	株洲市 Zhuzhou City #市辖区 Districts	湘潭市 Xiangtan City 全市 Cities Total	湘潭市 Xiangtan City #市辖区 Districts
固定资产投资	**Investment in Fixed Assets**				
全社会固定资产投资总额(万元)	Total Investment in Fixed Assets (10 000 yuan)	1048635	652982	898413	562019
#城镇固定资产投资	#Investment in Fixed Assets of Urban	823635	622699	628976	496177
#房地产开发投资	#Investment in Real Estate Development	184631	150013	118657	101075
#住宅	#Residential Buildings	90363	71920	75842	53995
全年新增固定资产(万元)	Newly Increased Fixed Assets (10 000 yuan)	785490	439588	355510	266796
本年施工住宅面积(万平方米)	Floor Space of Residential Building Under Construction	580.62	274.08	180.14	126.88
本年竣工住宅面积(万平方米)	Floor Space of Residential Building Completed	419.52	146.32	173.92	124.76
商品房屋销售面积(万平方米)	Floor Space of Selling Commercial House (10 000 sq.m)	91.61	79.02	65.53	44.71
#销售给个人	#Commercial Houses Purchased by Individuals	91.49	78.9	62.89	43.37
商品房屋空置面积(万平方米)	Floor Space of Empty Commercial House(10 000 sq.m)	11.84	10.7	24.16	21.45
商品房屋销售额(万元)	Total Sales of Commercial House (10 000 yuan)	99285	87713	67258	52456
#销售给个人	#Commercial Houses Purchased by Individuals	99169	87597	64489	50680
教育、科技、文化、卫生	**Education,Science and Technology, Culture,Health Care**				
学校数(所)	Number of Schools (unit)				
高等学校	Institutions of Higher Education	7	7	4	4
中等职业学校	Secondary Specialized Schools	41	17	59	34
普通中学	Regular Secondary Schools	236	52	232	42
小学	Primary Schools	1029	116	734	115
专任教师数(人)	Number of Full-time Teachers (person)				
高等学校	Institutions of Higher Education	2646	2646	3279	3279
中等职业学校	Secondary Specialized Schools	2453	1854	1791	1576
普通中学	Regular Secondary Schools	15088	3120	12073	3896
小学	Primary Schools	11421	2748	9872	3041
在校学生数	Number of Students Enrollment				
高等学校(人)	Institutions of Higher Education (person)	45006	45006	68223	68223
中等职业学校(人)	Secondary Specialized Schools (person)	50962	41314	37902	37000
普通中学(万人)	Regular Secondary Schools (10 000 persons)	29.88	5.73	22.79	7.59
小学(万人)	Primary Schools (10 000 persons)	22.39	5.43	17.63	5.18
成人高等教育在校学生数(人)	Students Enrollment in Adult Education Schools(person)	25214	25214	22011	22011
各类专业技术人员(人)	Various Specialized Technical Personnel (10 000 persons)	182156	98571	71971	50315
#中级职称以上	#Persons with Above Middle Rank Titles	59856	40365	30711	20714
体育场馆数(个)	Number of Stadiums and Gymnasiums (unit)	1826	1370	17	13
剧场、影剧院数(个)	Number of Theaters and Music Halls (unit)	8	5	5	4
公共图书馆图书总藏量(千册)	Total Collections in Public Libraries (1000 volumes)	1033	424	910	570
医院、卫生院数(个)	Number of Hospitals (unit)	204	95	134	54
医院、卫生院床位数(张)	Number of Beds in Hospitals (sheet)	9920	7079	7890	4420
医生数(人)	Number of Doctors (person)	4805	3010	4059	1939
人民生活、社会保障	**The People's Living and Social Security**				
在岗职工平均人数(万人)	Average Persons on the Job (10 000 persons)	26.75	17.32	22.87	14.24
在岗职工工资总额(万元)	Total Wages of Workers on the Job（10 000 yuan)	359855	257960	272925	178008
居民人均可支配收入(元)	Per Capita Disposable Income in Urban Residents(yuan)		8786		7671
居民人均消费支出(元)	Per Capita Living Expenditures for Consumption (yuan)		6760		6427
食品	Foods		2350		2252
衣着用品	Clothing		656		471
家庭设备、用品及服务	Household Facilities,Articles and Services		440		549
医疗保健	Medicine and Medical Services		354		425
交通和通讯	Transportation and Telecommunication		788		633
娱乐、教育、文化服务	Recreation,Education and Cultural Service		1267		830
居住	Residence		673		1074
百户居民家庭拥有家用汽车(辆)	Family Automobile Per 100 Households (unit)				2
百户居民家庭拥有家用电脑(台)	Personnel Computer Per 100 Households (unit)		29		21
人均住房使用面积(平方米)	Per Capita Floor Space of Residential Building (sq.m)		18		18
居民消费价格指数(上年为100)	General Consumer Price Index (preceding year =100)		101.7		102

指标	Item	株洲市 Zhuzhou City 全市 Cities Total	株洲市 Zhuzhou City #市辖区 Districts	湘潭市 Xiangtan City 全市 Cities Total	湘潭市 Xiangtan City #市辖区 Districts
年末离退休、退职人员数(万人)	Retired and Resigned Persons at the Yearend(10 000 persons)	14.96	10.02	12.68	9.57
社会保险参保人数（人）	N umber of Participants in Social Insurance (person)				
基本养老保险参保人数	Participant in Basic Pension Insurance	326994	211959	254414	170105
基本医疗保险参保人数	Participants in Basic Medicare Insurance	341900	267881	244081	182966
失业保险参保人数	Participants in Unemployment Insurance	343647	265805	254359	202065
社会福利院数(个)	Number of Social Welfare Institutions (unit)	68	6	108	14
社会福利院床位数(张)	Beds in Social Welfare Institutions (sheet)	2223	832	2349	808
社区服务设施数(个)	Number of Community Service Installations (unit)	5932	5075	1808	177
最低生活保障线以下人数(人)	Persons Under the Line of Lowest Living Security(person)	92042	45561	79813	57267
社会治安	**Public Security**				
交通事故件数(件)	Number of Traffic Accidents (case)	1197	586	2627	1073
犯罪人数(人)	Number of Criminals (person)	21514	11237	2228	1064
市政公用事业	**Municipal Public Utilities**				
城市维护建设资金支出(万元)	Expenditure for City Maintenance&Construction(10 000 yuan)		92615		90876
年末城市道路面积(万平方米)	Area of Paved Roads at the Yearend (10 000 sq.m)		589		513
排水管道长度(公里)	Length of Sewer Pipelines (km)		393		340
供水综合生产能力(万立方米)	Production Capacity of Tap Water (10 000 cu.m/day)		250.7		103
供水总量(万立方米)	Total Annual Volume of Water Supply (10 000 cu.m)		39085		51804
#居民家庭用水量	#Consumption for Residential Use		5876		6411
用水人口(万人)	Pupolation Using Tap Water (10 000 persons)		78.18		70.18
煤气供气总量(万立方米)	Total Coal Gas Supply (10 000 cu.m)		2587		34164
#家庭用量	#Consumption for Residential Use		1677		1112
用煤气人口(人)	Pupolation Using Coal Gas (persons)		272000		136400
液化石油气供气总量(吨)	Total Liquefied Petroleum Gas Gas Supply (ton)		12409		14008
#家庭用量	#Consumption for Residential Use		12036		12708
用液化气人口(人)	Pupolation Using Liquefied Petroleum Gas (persons)		292500		345200
年末公共汽车营运车辆数(辆)	Number of Public Transportation Vehicles (unit)		641		535
全年公共汽车客运总量(万人次)	Number of Passengers Carried (10 000 person-times)		10260		6440
年末实有出租汽车数(辆)	Number of Taxi at the Yearend (unit)		1960		907
园林绿地面积(公顷)	Area of Parks,Gardens and Green Areas in Cities (hectare)		2635		4166
#公共绿地面积	# Public Green Areas		391		560
建成区绿化覆盖面积(公顷)	Coverage Space of Green Areas in Developed Area(hectare)		2427		2576
环境保护	**Environmental Protection**				
污染源治理本年投资总额(万元)	Actual Investment for Pollution Treatment (10 000 yuan)	12404		13152	
城市环境基础设施建设本年完成投资额(万元)	Actual Investment in Base Facilities Construction of Urban Environment (10 000 yuan)	10714		59969	
三废综合利用产品产值(万元)	Output Value of Products Made From Waste Water, Waste Gas and Solid Wastes (10 000 yuan)	12969		23000	
工业废水排放量(万吨)	Volume of Industrial Waste Water Discharged (10 000 tons)	9435		14960	
工业废水排放达标量(万吨)	Volume of Waste Water up to the Discharge Standards	7708		12659	
工业二氧化硫去除量(吨)	Volume of Sulphur Dioxide Removed (ton)	318567		7852	
工业二氧化硫排放量(吨)	Volume of Sulphur Dioxide Emission (ton)	77373		37285	
工业烟尘去除量(吨)	Volume of Industrial Soot Removed (ton)	588291		539770	
工业烟尘排放量(吨)	Volume of Industrial Soot Emission (ton)	41430		48551	
工业固体废物综合利用率(%)	Percentage of Industrial Solid Wastes Utilized (%)	75		73	
烟尘控制区总面积(平方公里)	Total Area of Soot Control (sq.km)	81		52	
污染燃料禁烧区面积(平方公里)	Area of Inhibit Burn Hi-pollution Fuel (sq.km)	19		0	
噪声达标区总面积(平方公里)	Area of Environmental Noise up to the Standard (sq.km)	49		12	
生活污水处理率(%)	Rate of Sewage Disposal (%)	63		2	
生活垃圾无害化处理率(%)	Rate of Garbage Harmlessly Treatment (%)	77		83	

九、农业

AGRICULTURE

资料整理人员： 梁尔郁　龙立珍　陈　军　张吉世

9-1 农村基层组织与劳动力

Grassroots Units and Labor Force of Rural Areas

指 标	Item	2000	2001	2002	2003
农村基层组织	**Grassroots Units of Rural Areas**				
#乡(镇)个数 (个)	Number of Township (Town Governments) (unit)	2353	2358	2364	2357
#乡个数	Number of Township	1314	1286	1257	1259
#民族乡	Number of National Township	104	103	103	103
镇个数	Number of Town Governments	1039	1072	1097	1098
村(居)民委员会个数 (万个)	Number of Villagers(Residential) Committees (10 000 units)	5.01	5.01	5.11	5.13
#村民委员会 (万个)	Number of Villagers Committees (10 000 units)	4.75	4.74	4.73	4.66
#村民小组 (万个)	Number of Villagers Groups (10 000 units)	47.51	46.35	45.77	44.89
乡村户数、人口、劳动力	**Rural Households、Population、Laborers**				
#乡村户数 (万户)	Number of Rural Households (10 000 households)	1444	1455.39	1459.07	1468.71
#农业户	Agricultural Households	1362.38	1367.51	1364.59	1363.35
非农业户	Non- Agricultural Households	81.62	87.88	94.48	105.36
乡村人口 (万人)	Rural Population (10 000 persons)	5386.21	5413.75	5420.79	5425.86
#农业人口	Agricultural Population	5106.54	5109.08	5089.58	5077.75
乡村从业人员数 (万人)	Number of Rural Laborers (10 000 persons)	2850.93	2877.58	2898.23	2914.38
按性别分:	By sex:				
#男劳力	Male	1545.29	1560.42	1571.86	1579.05
女劳力	Female	1305.64	1317.16	1326.37	1335.33
按国民经济行业分:	By Nationality Economy Sector:				
#农林牧渔业劳动力	Farming ,Forestry,Animal Husbandry and Fishery Laborers	2065.92	2058.67	2019.6	1997.67
工业劳动力	Industry Laborers	191.6	194.96	215.51	224.94
建筑业劳动力	Construction Laborers	126.34	130.74	142.05	148
交通运输、仓储、邮电通信业劳动力	Transportation,Storage,Post and Telecommunications Laborers	51.65	54.57	59.93	61.99
批发零售贸易业餐饮业劳动力	Wholesale,Retail and Catering Trades Laborers	85.11	91.6	106.49	150.1
其他非农行业劳动力	Other Non-Agricultural Trades Laborers	330.31	347.04	354.65	331.68
农村社会基础设施	**Country Society Basic Establishment**				
#自来水受益村数 (万个)	Villages Tap Water Benefited (10 000 units)	1.17	1.24	1.35	1.45
通汽车村数 (万个)	Villages Car Available (10 000 units)	4.41	4.44	4.48	4.52
通电话村数 (万个)	Villages Telephone Available (10 000 units)	4.05	4.26	4.4	4.48

注:乡村劳动力未包括国有农场劳动力。

Rural laborers not included laborers in State-owned farm.

9-2 农业基本情况

Basic Indicators of Agriculture

年 份 Year	农林牧渔业劳动力（万人）Number of Laborers (10 000 persons)	年末实有耕地面积（万公顷）Cultivated Areas (yearend) (10 000 hectares)	当年减少耕地面积（万公顷）Decrease in Cultivated Area by Cause (10 000 hectares)	农作物播种面积（万公顷）Total Sown Areas (10 000 hectares)	#粮食作物 Grain Corps	#经济作物 Economical Crops	造林面积（万公顷）Afforestation Areas (10 000 hectares)
1980	1764.83	342.48		790.95	545.13	58.45	24.52
1985	1908.43	334.17		747.71	516.14	72.94	34.40
1990	2133.07	331.23	1.16	795.18	536.56	98.99	37.59
1995	2114.71	324.97	1.83	784.04	511.56	125.01	10.95
1996	2089.33	323.94	1.86	792.74	513.39	131.00	5.29
1997	2074.12	323.01	1.66	800.90	515.53	136.64	4.29
1998	2074.51	321.87	1.64	793.63	507.48	131.03	2.86
1999	2074.13	321.32	1.30	802.77	513.52	127.81	2.74
2000	2065.92	392.16	1.18	800.21	502.99	129.30	5.15
2001	2058.67	391.26	1.73	793.17	480.28	130.54	7.56
2002	2019.60	389.10	2.80	777.92	465.26	126.82	10.09
2003	1997.67	383.37	6.46	773.12	452.98	-	40.96

注：从2000年起，耕地面积为国土资源厅统计数据(后同)。

The data of cultivated land from Hunan Province Territory Resource Bureau since 2000.The same as in the following table.

9-3 农业生产条件

Condition of Agricultural Production

年份 Year	农业机械总动力（万千瓦）Total Power of Agricultural Machinery (10 000 kw)	有效灌溉面积（千公顷）Effective Irrigated Area (1000 hectares)	化肥施用量（万吨）Consumption of Chemical Fertilizers (10 000 tons)	农村用电量（万度）Electricity Consumed in Rural Areas (10 000 kwh)	每公顷面积产量（公斤）Yield per hectare (kg) 粮食 Grain Crops	棉花 Cotton	油料 Oil-bearing Crops
1980	588.99	2742.73	361.04	96674	3900	540	570
1985	892.02	2771.18	369.64	150648	4875	990	1005
1990	1209.17	2676.22	126.09	233704	5025	1020	990
1995	1532.54	2680.03	167.91	376414	5380	1206	1258
1996	1616.29	2630.42	167.08	389147	5262	1090	1252
1997	1692.84	2672.38	175.39	416758	5581	1448	1352
1998	1825.57	2675.14	179.93	420064	5553	969	1323
1999	2006.97	2665.4	180.87	429687	5632	1121	1391
2000	2209.74	2677.46	182.15	445291	5716	1173	1490
2001	2358.02	2676.35	184.25	467348	5622	1271	1505
2002	2498.09	2675.61	184.32	498337	5376	1291	1334
2003	2664.45	2675.34	188.33	538375.49	5393	1173	1449

注:化肥施用量1989年及以前均为实物量,1990年及以后为折纯量。

Data of consumption of fertilizers refer to the consumption in quantity prior to 1989, and the consumption in purity in and after 1990.

9-4 农林牧渔业总产值、指数及构成

Indices and Composition of Gross Output Value of Agriculture

年 份 Year	农林牧渔业总产值 Gross Output Value	农业 Farming	种植业 Planting	副业 Sideline Occupations	林业 Forestry	牧业 Animal Husbandry	渔业 Fishery
总产值(按当年价格计算，亿元)	**Gross Output Value (by current prices, 100 million yuan)**						
1990	397.42	241.21	219.17	22.04	25.89	117.22	17.10
1995	1046.97	579.92	543.16	36.76	42.58	369.54	54.93
1996	1226.32	649.38	608.71	40.67	45.71	460.82	70.41
1997	1322.26	660.02	618.52	41.50	47.98	538.15	76.10
1998	1262.46	628.98	582.78	46.20	48.20	505.71	79.57
1999	1200.94	624.70	578.46	46.24	48.20	458.62	69.42
2000	1251.89	633.84	579.81	54.03	51.01	486.13	80.91
2001	1313.23	665.70	611.22	-	51.88	510.42	85.23
2002	1349.92	666.65	609.72	-	54.78	538.64	89.85
2003	1452.96	671.66	-	-	81.73	575.08	96.97
指数(按可比价格计算，%)	**Indices (by comparable prices ,%)**						
以上年为100	**Preceding year=100**						
1990	105.1	101.3	100.3	111.0	97.4	103.4	103.0
1995	108.8	104.3	104.2	106.1	102.3	115.4	121.4
1996	108.4	103.2	102.1	111.8	103.2	115.0	120.7
1997	108.3	108.1	108.3	106.9	101.5	109.2	110.4
1998	101.5	98.7	97.1	111.2	102.4	104.1	107.1
1999	103.4	105.0	105.3	102.5	105.5	100.2	107.8
2000	104.3	103.2	103.1	105.0	104.3	103.9	111.5
2001	104.0	103.5	103.8	-	103.2	104.3	105.5
2002	102.7	100.2	99.4	-	104.6	105.1	105.9
2003	103.7	102.7	-	-	104.0	104.1	107.3
以1978年为100	**1978年 ＝100**						
1990	166.2	169.3	136.2	499.9	119.5	239.0	447.8
1995	221.3	203.4	156.5	672.5	153.0	387.5	803.6
1996	239.9	209.9	159.8	751.9	157.9	445.6	969.9
1997	259.8	226.9	173.1	803.8	160.3	486.6	1070.8
1998	263.7	224.0	168.1	893.8	164.1	506.6	1146.8
1999	272.7	235.2	177.0	916.1	173.1	507.6	1236.3
2000	284.4	242.7	182.5	961.9	180.5	527.4	1378.5
2001	295.8	251.2	189.4	-	186.3	550.1	1454.3
2002	303.8	251.7	188.2	-	194.8	578.2	1540.1
2003	315.0	258.5	-	-	202.6	601.9	1652.5
构成(按当年价格计算，%)	**Composition (by current prices, %)**						
1990	100.0	60.7	55.1	5.6	5.5	29.5	4.3
1995	100.0	55.4	51.9	3.5	4.1	35.3	5.2
1996	100.0	53.0	49.7	3.3	3.7	37.6	5.7
1997	100.0	49.9	46.8	3.1	3.6	40.7	5.8
1998	100.0	49.9	46.2	3.7	3.8	40.0	6.3
1999	100.0	52.0	48.2	3.8	4.0	38.2	5.8
2000	100.0	50.6	46.3	4.3	4.1	38.8	6.5
2001	100.0	50.7	46.5	-	4.0	38.9	6.5
2002	100.0	49.4	45.2	-	4.1	39.9	6.7
2003	100.0	46.2	-	-	5.6	39.6	6.7

注：2003年起，农林牧渔业总产值包含农林牧渔服务业。

Output value of agricultural Services included in the data of gross output value since 2003.

9-5 农林牧渔业分项产值（2003年）

Output Value of Farming, Forestry, Animal Husbandry, and Fishery by Branch (2003)

单位：万元 (10 000 yuan)

项目	Item	总产值 Gross Output Value	商品产值 Commodity Output Value
农林牧渔业合计	**Tatol**	**14529641**	**9011845**
农业产值	**Output Value of Farming**	**6716612**	**3316639**
谷物及其他作物	Cereal and Other Crops	3646521	1732072
谷物	Cereal	2392772	877209
#小麦	#Wheat	17482	8531
稻谷	Rice	2123989	790359
玉米	Corn	141407	62389
薯类	Tubers	169000	64389
油料	Oil-bearing Crops	292791	176972
#花生	#Peanuts	89389	53634
油菜籽	Rapeseeds	187757	120727
豆类	Beans	146596	80396
#大豆	#Soja	109969	63782
棉花	Cotton	222056	193600
麻类	Fiber Crops	77180	72974
糖料	Sugar Crops	55986	50639
烟草	Tobacco	152548	136997
其他农作物	Other Crops	137591	78896
蔬菜园艺作物	Vegetables and Gradening Plantations	2351192	1015869
蔬菜(含菜用瓜)	Vegetables	2233094	907219
花卉园艺作物	Flowers and Plants	118098	108650
水果、坚果、饮料和香料作物	Fruits,Nuts and Crops of Beverage&Perfumery	532349	391474
水果、坚果(含果用瓜)	Fruits and Nuts	483447	354112
茶及其他饮料	Tea and Other Beverage	48902	37362
#茶	#Tea	48902	37362
中药材	Medicinal Materials	186551	177223
林业产值	**Output Value of Forestry**	**817311**	**382311**
林木的培育和种植	Forest Planting and Cultivating	151755	
育种育苗	Grow Seedlings and Seed Cultivation	50161	
造林	Cultivate Forest	65532	
抚育和管理	Cultivation and Management	36062	
竹木采运	Bamboo Cutting and Transportation	309818	228953
林产品	Forest Products	355738	153358
牧业产值	**Output Value of Animal Husbandry**	**5750773**	**4301795**
牲畜饲养	Livestock Rasing	343042	243689
牛的饲养	Cattle Raising	240985	164203
羊的饲养	Sleeps and Goats Raising	86522	64891
其他牲畜饲养	Other Livestock Raising	463	116
奶产品	Milk Products	14965	14396
毛绒产品	Wool Products	106	83
猪的饲养	Hogs Rasing	4107474	3172918
家禽饲养	Poultry Rasing	1212366	815927
肉禽	Poultry for Meat	671762	483455
禽蛋	Poultry Egges	540604	332472
羽绒	Feather		
狩猎和捕捉动物	Hunting and Catching of Wild Animals	5180	4973
其他畜牧业	Other Animal Husbandry	82711	64287
渔业产值	**Output Value of Fishing**	**969744**	**735900**
#养殖	#Cultivation	827267	498842
鱼类	Fish	838148	628611
虾蟹类	Shrimps,Prawns and Crabs	45047	31533
贝类	Shell-fish	1912	1720
其他	Others	84638	74036
农林牧渔服务业产值	**Output Value of Services**	**275200**	**275200**

9-6 农村非农行业总产值

Gross Output Value of Non – Agriculture of rural Areas

单位：万元 (10 000 yuan)

指 标	Item	2000	2001	2002	2003
非农行业总产值	**Gross Output Value of Non-Agriculture**	**47976577**	**39999369**	**42501568**	**44683668**
农村工业总产值	**Gross Industrial Output Value of Rural Areas**	**29678442**	**22996299**	**24593002**	**25432112**
#乡办工业总产值	Gross Industrial Output Value of Townships	6599866	5570179	6006231	6398946
村办工业总产值	Gross Industrial Output Value of Villages	4542582	3760431	4344066	4696311
村以下办工业总产值	Gross Industrial Output Value of Villages Lower Levels	18535994	13665689	14242705	14336855
农村建筑业总产值	**Gross Constructional Output Value of Rural Areas**	**6902456**	**6325388**	**6450776**	**6958852**
#建筑安装工程产值	Output Value of Construction Installation Projects	6419770	5892877	5993142	6470460
#兴建房屋产值	Output Value of House Building	4898662	4418284	4484382	4875515
农田水利工程产值	Output Value of Irrigation and Water Conservancy Works	804368	802438	821916	847968
其他建筑安装工程产值	Output Value of Other Construction Installation Projects	716741	672154	686845	746978
其他基本建设产值	Output Value of Other Basic Constructions	482686	432511	457634	488392
#开垦荒地产值	Output Value of Reclaim Wastelands	34649	64882	66931	81018
农村运输业总产值	**Gross Output Value of Transportation of Rural**	**4370090**	**4091113**	**4321603**	**4569172**
#乡办运输企业货运产值	Output Value of Goods Transportation of Township's Transportation Enterprise	119054	117081	131902	174255
村办运输企业货运产值	Output Value of Goods Transportation of Villages' Transportation Enterprise	167748	149204	173582	191291
村以下办运输企业货运产值	Output Value of Goods Transportation of Villages Lower Levels' Transportation Enterprise	4083288	3824829	4016119	4203626
农村批发零售贸易业、餐饮业总产值	**Gross Output Value of Wholesale, Retail and Catering Trades**	**7025588**	**6586569**	**7136186**	**7723531**
#批发零售贸易业产值	Output Value of Wholesale, Retail and Trades	5108046	4739215	5163624	5761126
#农村供销社产值	Rural Supply and Marketing Cooperative	617597	575450	555854	518356
餐饮业产值	Output Value of Catering	1917543	1847354	1972562	1962405
#农村供销社产值	Rural Supply and Marketing Cooperative	86757	79528	84180	100118

9-7 农林牧渔业增加值(2003年)

Added - Value of Farming, Forestry, Animal Husbandry, and Fishery (2003)

单位：万元 (10 000 yuan)

指 标	Item	总产值 Gross Output Value	中间消耗 Material Consump-tion	中间物质消耗 Middle Material Consump-tion	中间非物质部门劳务支出 Middle Non-material Department Service Payout	增加值 Added Value
合计	**Total**	**14529641**	**5513617**	**4979382**	**534234**	**9016024**
农业	Farming	6716612	1780883	1574934	205949	4935730
林业	Forestry	817311	144168	116371	27796	673144
牧业	Animal Husbandry	5750773	3103518	2960976	142542	2647255
渔业	Fishery	969744	361208	327101	34107	608536
服务业	Services	275200	123840		123840	151360

9-8 耕 地 面 积

Cultivated Areas

单位：千公顷 (1 000 hectares)

指　标	Item	2000	2001	2002	2003
年初实有耕地总资源	**Actual Cultivated Land Total Resources at The Year Beginning**	**3926.52**	**3921.60**	**3912.55**	**3891.00**
年内增加耕地总资源	**Increased Cultivated Land Total resources This Year**	**6.85**	**8.22**	**6.44**	**7.30**
新开荒	Reclaim Wastelands	4.37	5.03	4.01	3.24
年内减少耕地总资源	**Decrease in Cultivated Land Total resources This Year**	**11.77**	**17.27**	**27.99**	**64.56**
国家建设占地	Capital Construction of the Government	4.59	5.82	1.49	3.53
其它基建占地	Village Collective Construction	2.30	2.35	1.88	0.50
年末实有耕地总资源	**Actual Cultivated Land Total Resources at The Year End**	**3921.60**	**3912.55**	**3891.00**	**3833.74**
#水田	Paddy Fields	2962.79	2959.90	2951.39	2936.63
常用耕地	Common Cultivated land	3418.09	3417.85	3408.20	3390.70
#水田	Paddy Fields	2661.57	2659.56	2652.20	2644.32
临时性耕地	Temporary Cultivated land	503.51	494.70	482.80	443.04

9-9 农 田 基 本 建 设

Capital Construction On Farmland

单位：千公顷 (1 000 hectares)

指　标	Item	2000	2001	2002	2003
农田有效灌溉面积	Effective Irrigated Areas on Farmland	2677.46	2676.35	2675.61	2675.34
#当年实灌	Actual Irrigated Areas That Year	2491.81	2496.65	2504.15	2506.02
旱涝保收面积	Areas Ensure Stable Yields Despite Drought or Water Logging	2191.02	2205.39	2206.21	2213.86
易涝面积	Area Liable to Flooding or Water Logging	526.05	526.05	526.44	533.25
除涝面积	Flooded or Waterlogged Area Under Control	454.74	456.5	456.85	464.68
机电排灌面积	Mechanical and Electrical Irrigated and Drainage Areas	1163.26	1164.29	1155.95	1181.15
#机电灌溉面积	Mechanical and Electrical Irrigated Areas	1028.43	1029.75	1021.26	1017.74
机灌	Mechanical Irrigation	215.78	216.73	211.03	200.82
电灌	Electrical Irrigation	812.65	813.02	810.23	817.12
固定站	Fixed Stations	800.29	824.43	793.59	792.48
流动机	Mobile Stations	201.72	205.32	202.46	199.75
喷滴灌	Sprinkling and Drip Irrigation	26.42	25.89	25.21	25.51
纯排面积	Simple Irrigated Areas	134.83	134.54	134.69	163.41
水轮泵灌溉面积	Turbine Pump Irrigated Areas	83.16	82.87	81.57	74.51

9-10 农村主要能源及物资消耗

Consumption of Major Energy and Materials of Rural Areas

指 标	Item	2000	2001	2002	2003
农村电气化情况	**Electric Situation of Rural Areas**				
农村用电量(万度)	Electricity Consumed in Rural Areas (10000 kwh)	445290.53	467347.6	498337.4	538375.4
年末乡办水电站(个)	Number of Hydropower Station in Rural Areas at the Yearend (unit)	1086	1049	1076	1085
装机容量(千瓦)	Capacity of Power Generating Sets (kw)	327843	330423	348237	364584
发电量(万度)	Generated Energy (10000 kwh)	109998.37	110693	117195.5	102253.20
村及村以下办水电站(个)	Number of Water Power Stations of Village and Lower Levels (unit)	3423	3129	3039	2827
装机容量(千瓦)	Capacity of Power Generating Sets (kw)	92073	87118	109738	131993
发电量(万度)	Generated Energy (10000 kwh)	30556.95	28699.74	32066.89	38429.85
农用化肥施用量	**Consumption of Agricultural Chemical Fertilizer**				
按实物量计算(吨)	Calculated at Actual Quantity in Natural Form (ton)	6954529	6933887	6862793	6886111
#氮肥(吨)	Nitrogenous Fertilizer (ton)	3906876	3862813	3779405	3724197
#尿素	Carbide	1115457	1140628	1136167	
氨水	Ammonia	7450	7361	8524	
碳氨	Carbon Ammonia	2714051	2678983	2591437	
磷肥(吨)	Phosphate Fertilizer (ton)	1777537	1757300	1732478	1723682
钾肥(吨)	Potash Fertilizer (ton)	600221	611626	608377	631073
复合肥(吨)	Compound Fertilizer (ton)	669895	701148	742533	807159
每亩播种面积施用量(公斤)	Consumption of Per-mu Sown Areas (kg)	57.9	58.3	58.8	59.38
按折纯量计算(吨)	Calculated at Quantity of 100% Content (ton)	1821508	1842457	1843234	1883338
#氮肥(吨)	Nitrogenous Fertilizer (ton)	980845	986014	974618	976301
#尿素	Carbide	507306	517521	513794	
氨水	Ammonia	949	932	1079	
碳氨	Carbon Ammonia	455329	447902	431433	
磷肥(吨)	Phosphate Fertilizer (ton)	242760	239579	235872	234808
钾肥(吨)	Potash Fertilizer (ton)	298514	303984	301891	312669
复合肥(吨)	Compound Fertilizer (ton)	299389	312880	330853	359560
农用薄膜使用量(吨)	**Consumption of Agricultural Films (ton)**	**40446**	**43011**	**47568**	**50609**
#地膜使用量(吨)	Consumption of Ground Films (ton)	25309	27663	31078	33484
地膜覆盖面积(公顷)	Ground Film Covered Areas (hectare)	313340	349343	391683	405769
农药使用量(吨)	**Consumption of Pesticide (ton)**	**85611**	**85591**	**86972**	**95360**
农用柴油使用量(吨)	**Consumption of Agricultural Diesel Oil (ton)**	**224315**	**247428**	**255044**	**276834**

9-11 农业机械年末拥有量

Year – End Possession of Agriculture Machinery

指 标	Item	2000	2001	2002	2003
农业机械总动力合计(千瓦)	**Total Power of Agricultural Machinery (kw)**	**22097435**	**23580223**	**24980879**	**26644540**
柴油发动机(千瓦)	Diesel Engines (kw)	15719714	16928064	18128174	19379715
汽油发动机(千瓦)	Gasoline Engines (kw)	2310250	2266035	2339783	2405175
电动机(千瓦)	Electric motor (kw)	3959172	4258519	4393665	4748961
其他机械(千瓦)	Other Machinery (kw)	108299	127605	119257	110689
机械分类	**Machinery by Tybe**				
大中型拖拉机 (混合台)	Large and Medium Tractors (mixed unit)	15149	18395	26972	37231
(千瓦)	(kw)	381244	450534	686980	1004220
#轮式拖拉机 (混合台)	Wheeled Tractors (mixed unit)	5012	6501	10327	11851
(千瓦)	(kw)	122689	150811	256785	318880
小型及手扶拖拉机 (混合台)	Mini and Walking Tractors (mixed unit)	209271	205585	192762	175603
(千瓦)	(kw)	1916099	1899036	1785179	1672729
#小四轮拖拉机 (台)	Mini Four-wheel Tractors (unit)	17828	23611	22766	24004
(千瓦)	(kw)	206373	264405	244684	278030
耕整机 (台)	Tillage Machinery (unit)	536557	593159	599747	637196
(千瓦)	(kw)		1970833	2025882	2180139
机耕(滚)船 (艘)	Wet-field Tractors (unit)	40778	48341	55680	59375
(千瓦)	(kw)		170261	188331	194781
大中型拖拉机配套农具(部)	Farm Tools for Large and Medium Tractors (unit)	6428	5151	6604	6827
小型拖拉机配套农具 (部)	Necessary Farm Tools for Mini Tractors (unit)	63865	48793	47567	49199
农用排灌动力机械 (台)	Motor Machinery for Drainage&Irrigation (unit)	1158134	1220879	1279642	1366626
(千瓦)	(kw)	5664559	5891642	6173225	6511616
#柴油机 (台)	Diesel Engines (unit)	742261	786497	814927	871023
(千瓦)	(kw)	3508951	3686890	3945954	4152778
电动机 (台)	Electric Motors (unit)	404862	421942	453107	483897
(千瓦)	(kw)	2116140	2163060	2187119	2318812
汽油机 (台)	Gasoline Engines (unit)	11011	12440	11608	3936
(千瓦)	(kw)	39468	41692	40152	40026
#农用水泵 (台)	Pumps (unit)	1208900	1273184	1317562	1412265
喷灌机械 (套)	Machinery for Sprinkling Irrigation (unit)	9672	8192	7253	6572
联合收获机 (台)	Machinery for Combine Harvesters (unit)	3049	4925	7021	9616
(千瓦)	(kw)	43837	85867	127295	210001
饲料粉碎机 (台)	Fodder Grinders (unit)	132399	133717	149171	165705
牧草收割机 (台)	Herbage Harvesters (unit)	82	97	98	52
渔用机动船 (艘)	Motorized Fishing Boats (unit)	12216	13457	13949	14734
(吨)	(ton)	26788	27608	30643	31092
(千瓦)	(kw)	57491	63770	67831	72899
池塘增氧机 (台)	Machinery for Pond Oxygen Increase (unit)		8082	9803	11804
池渠清淤机 (台)	Cleaners for Ponds and Canals (unit)				1607
农产品加工动力机械 (千瓦)	Motorized Machinery for Products Processing (kw)	3525247	3657373	3886869	4073329
#柴油机动力 (千瓦)	Diesel Engines Power (kw)	2006630	2057474	2175717	2236557
农用载重汽车 (辆)	Trucks for Agricultural use (unit)	69479	73028	76585	78954
(千瓦)	(kw)	5504159	5770143	6053954	6218303
#柴油汽车 (辆)	Diesel Trucks (unit)	45730	49925	53321	55272
(千瓦)	(kw)	3666220	3984472	4250185	4394148
机动运输船 (艘)	Motorized Transport Ships (unit)	19743	20750	21343	21755
(吨)	(ton)	275220	273046	299870	301007
(千瓦)	(kw)	223778	235805	258270	268304
农用运输车 (辆)	Transport Trucks for Agriculture Use (unit)	83944	87492	95166	101304
(千瓦)	(kw)	1602332	1727609	1922071	2148729
推土机 (台)	Bulldozers (unit)	3688	4112	4498	4964
(千瓦)	(kw)	216591	242673	277294	309213

9-12 农作物生产情况(2003年)

Basic Indicators of Farm Corp Production (2003)

指标	Item	播种面积 (千公顷) Sown Area (1 000 hectares)	单产 (公斤/公顷) Per Unit Area Yield (kg/hectare)	总产量 (吨) Total Output (ton)
农作物总播种面积	**Total Sown Area**	**7731.24**	**-**	**-**
粮食作物	**Grain Crops**	**4529.79**	**5393**	**24427300**
#谷物	Cereal	3835.88	5802	22256000
#稻谷	Rice	3409.98	6071	20701800
#早稻	Early Season Rice	1173.33	5295	6212500
#杂交稻	Hybrid Rice	581.57	6002	3490800
优质稻	High Quality Rice	519.03	5739	2978700
中稻与一季晚稻	Middle Season Rice and Late Rice of One-season	834.52	7644	6378700
#杂交稻	Hybrid Rice	668.33	6103	4078800
优质稻	High Quality Rice	270.51	6223	1683300
晚稻	Late Season Rice	1402.13	5784	8110600
#杂交稻	Hybrid Rice	1059.29	6626	7018300
优质稻	High Quality Rice	554.8	6404	3552900
小麦	Wheat	86.33	1910	164900
玉米	Corn	289.77	4436	1285500
高粱	Sorghum	12.24	2819	34500
其他谷物	Other Cereal	37.56	1845	69300
#大麦	Barley	8.27	2104	17400
豆类	Soybeans	293.46	1912	561000
#大豆	Beans	198.21	2003	397000
杂豆	Mixed Beans	95.25	1722	164000
#绿豆	Mung Beans	25.96	1703	44200
薯类(按折粮薯类计算)	Tubers(Converted into Grain)	400.45	4021	1610200
#红薯	Sweet Potatoes	290.99	4337	1261900
马铃薯	Potatoes	109.46	3182	348300
油料	**Oil-bearing Crops**	**867.76**	**1449**	**1257028**
#花生果	Peanuts	145.87	2091	305083
油菜籽	Rapeseeds	711.13	1320	938783
芝麻	Sesame	8.81	1206	10627
向日葵	Sunflower	0.24	963	231
其他油料	Other Oil-bearing Crops	1.71	1347	2304
棉花	**Cotton**	**138.99**	**1173**	**163100**
麻类	**Fiber Crops**	**57.23**	**2353**	**134660**
#黄、红麻	Jute and Ambary Hemp	1.29	2935	3786
苎 麻	Ramie	53.97	2304	124327
甘蔗	**Sugarcane**	**28.64**	**49684**	**1422960**
烟叶	**Tobacco**	**94.06**	**1989**	**187091**
#烤烟	Flue-cured Tobacco	87.07	2029	176622
晒(土)烟	Sun-cured Tobacco	6.99	1498	10469
药材	**Medicinal Herbs**	**80.77**	**5499**	**444168**
蔬菜瓜类	**Vegetables and Melons**	**1094.43**	**23693**	**25930033**
#蔬菜(包括菜用瓜)	Vegetables(include Snake Melons)	964.26	23759	22910187
果用瓜	Fruit Melons	130.17	23199	3019846
其他作物:	**Other Crops**	839.57		
#青饲料	Succulence	266.27		
绿肥	Green Manure	490.49		
#草籽留种	Grass-seed Stock			

9-13 主要农产品产量

Output of Major Farm Products

单位：万吨 (10 000 tons)

年份 year	粮食 Grain	#小麦 Wheat	#稻谷 Rice	棉花 Cotton	油料 Oil-bearing	甘蔗 Sugarcane	茶叶 Tea	水果 Fruit
1990	2692.67	28.56	2517.26	12.01	72.22	127.76	7.39	56.61
1995	2752.09	31.02	2515.34	22.35	112.04	141.52	6.14	272.14
1996	2820.62	30.42	2559.03	18.96	118.12	129.17	5.49	271.88
1997	2953.28	32.11	2668.20	25.57	129.26	174.53	5.55	329.43
1998	2818.19	28.33	2516.30	19.25	120.74	188.41	5.85	307.37
1999	2892.35	25.19	2549.10	17.70	130.17	168.47	5.63	384.47
2000	2874.97	23.31	2528.08	17.13	139.35	115.85	5.73	382.50
2001	2700.30	21.40	2328.90	19.00	137.39	166.41	5.84	496.32
2002	2501.30	18.34	2119.15	15.30	119.25	180.38	6.10	479.01
2003	2442.73	16.49	2070.18	16.31	125.70	142.30	6.06	512.39

9-14 林业情况

Basic Indicators of Forestry

面积单位：千公顷 (1 000 hectares)

指 标	Item	2000	2001	2002	2003
当年造林面积总计	**Total Afforestation Areas of the Current Year**	**51.54**	**75.63**	**100.85**	**409.58**
#工程造林	Engineering Afforestation	24.37			
竹林	Bamboo Forest	2.18	3.95	4.29	26.27
按主要林种用途分	**By the Use of Main Forestry**				
用材林	Timber Forest	22.21	20.43	16.58	52.34
#速生丰产林	Quick and High Yield Forest	10.74	9.12	10.08	0.54
经济林	Economic Forest	12.07	10.82	9.01	45.06
防护林	Shelter-forest	17.13	44.11	74.62	307.39
薪炭林	Charcoal Forest	0.01		0.25	0.05
特种用途林	Special Use Forest	0.12	0.27	0.38	4.74
迹地更新面积	Slash Reforestation Areas	31.82	30.63	13.56	13.93
封山育林面积	Close Hillsides to Facilitate Afforestation Areas	121.83	2077.75	1056.52	728.16
#本年新封	New Closed Areas of the Current Year	99.72	905.24	17.83	12.12
零星(四旁)植树(万株)	Oddly (all around) Tree Planting (10 000 roots)	27187	16202	14801	13583
林木种子采集量(吨)	Forestry Seed Collection (ton)	678	560	1140	1242
育苗面积	Grow Seedlings Areas	2.85	8.1	8.68	10.56
#本年新育面积	New Grow Seedlings Areas of the Current Year	1.78	3.02	4.57	6.61
幼林抚育实际面积	Actual Areas of Young Growth Fostering	205.03	247.3	252.35	388.16
幼林抚育作业面积	Operative Areas of Young Growth Fostering	274.27	458.4	326.28	475.77
成林抚育面积	Mature Timber Fostering Areas	346.2	146.89	214.77	203.84
#中幼林抚育面积	Areas of Middle and Young Growth Fostering	301.77	107.77	176.14	165.1
低产林改造面积	Low Yield Timber Remaking Areas	219.51	97.26	211.62	58.93
抚育改造出材量(万方)	Fostering and Remaking Yields (10 000 cu.m)	27	28	55.78	29.39
#中幼林改造出材量	Middle and Young Growth Remaking Yields	26	20	39.53	15.18
年末实有母树林面积	**Actual Mother Woods Areas at the Yearend**	**9.22**	**2.74**	**2.39**	**2.90**
年末实有种子园面积	**Actual Seed Garden Areas at the Yearend**	**3.03**	**2.07**	**1.18**	**0.67**

9-15 林产品产量(2003年)

Output of Major Forestry Products (2003)

名称	Item	数量 Number	名称	Item	数量 Number
生漆(公斤)	Lacquer (kg)	153000	白果(公斤)	Ginkgo (kg)	386000
油桐籽(吨)	Tung-oil Seeds (ton)	37713	杏仁(公斤)	Almond (kg)	111000
油茶籽(吨)	Tea-oil Seeds (ton)	339716	肉桂(公斤)	Cinnamon (kg)	75000
乌桕籽(吨)	Tallow Tree Seeds (ton)	1640	黄柏(公斤)	Golden Cypress (kg)	527000
五倍子(吨)	Gall (ton)	820	杜仲(公斤)	Gutta-percha (kg)	1370500
棕片(吨)	Palm Leaf (ton)	7622	白蜡(公斤)	Inesctwax (kg)	80000
松脂(吨)	Pine Resin (ton)	17399	杂木棍(万根)	Mixed Cardstock (10 000 roots)	64080.7
竹笋干(吨)	Bamboo Shoots (ton)	14410	桎木条(吨)	Wood Lath (ton)	16117
核桃(吨)	Walnuts (ton)	3945	小杂竹(吨)	Small Mixed Bamboo (ton)	95723
板栗(吨)	Chestnuts (ton)	29369	楠竹尾(吨)	Tails of Phyllostachys Pubescens (ton)	50109
紫胶(吨)	Shellacs (ton)	347	村及村以下竹木采伐量	Logging Volume of Timber and Bamboo in Village and Lower Level	
山苍子(吨)	Fructus Litseae (ton)	6975			
香菇(公斤)	Mushroom (kg)	4499000	#木材采伐量(万方)	Woods Cuts (10 000 cu.m)	412.1
花椒(公斤)	Prickly Ashes (kg)	298000	竹材(万根)	Bamboo (10 000 roots)	7064.34
黑木耳(公斤)	Black An Edible Fungus (kg)	1296000	#楠竹(万根)	Phyllostachys Pubescens (10 000 roots)	1455.14
八角(公斤)	Anise(kg)	406000	篙竹(万根)	Pole-bamboo (10 000 roots)	

9-16 茶叶、水果生产情况(2003年)

Output of Tea and Fruit (2003)

单位：吨 (ton)

名称	Item	数量 Number	名称	Item	数量 Number
茶叶产量	**Output of Tea**	**60573**	**水果产量**	**Output of Fruits**	**5123842**
红毛茶、红碎茶原料	Black Tea and It's Raw Material	12486	柑桔	Citrus	1674387
			柚子	Pomeloes	53325
绿毛茶	Green Tea	30097	桃子	Peaches	74305
乌龙毛茶	Oolong Tea	523	李子	Plums	76438
紧压茶原料	Raw Material of Impacted Tea	8455	梨	Pears	70750
			葡萄	Grapes	36944
其他茶	Other tea	9012	红枣	Red Chinese Dates	18925
			柿子	Fresh Persimmons	8428
			枇杷	Loquates	3844
			其他水果	Other Fruits	3106496

9-17 畜牧业主要产品产量

Output of Major Animal Husbandry Products

名 称	Item	2000	2001	2002	2003
当年出栏猪头数 (万头)	Number of Slaughtered Fattened Pigs of the Current Year (10 000 heads)	6299.70	6495.78	6698.38	6921.45
出栏肉猪	Slaughtered Fattened Hogs	6042.18	6257.54	6447.12	6660.19
出口中仔猪	Exported Middle Piglets	257.52	238.24	251.26	261.26
出售和自宰肉用牛 (万头)	Beef Slaughtered by Peasants Themselves & Sold (10 000 heads)	131.63	137.73	151.22	168.23
出售和自宰肉用羊 (万头)	Mutton Slaughtered by Peasants Themselves & Sold (10 000 heads)	519.23	569.15	658.02	722.22
出售和自宰肉用驴 (匹)	Donkey Slaughtered by Peasants Themselves & Sold (head)	483	496	995	1658
出售和自宰肉用骡 (匹)	Mule Slaughtered by Peasants Themselves & Sold (head)	263	234	114	131
马 (匹)	Horses (head)	883	771	891	1181
家禽 (万羽)	Poultry (10 000 piece)	41855.42	44903.53	49400.71	52275.76
兔 (万只)	Rabbits (10 000 heads)	93.92	105.71	189.66	247.25
当年肉类总产量 (吨)	Total Output of Meat (ton)	4961622	5166968	5415545	5617823
猪肉产量	Output of Pork	4146788	4289639	4439334	4568810
#肉猪产量	Output of Hogs	4091543	4238208	4385573	4512507
出口中仔猪产量	Exported Middle Piglets Output	55245	51431	53761	56303
牛肉产量	Beef Output	138606	144323	161587	177953
羊肉产量	Mutton Output	79737	87266	101332	112130
驴肉产量	Meat of Donkey	39	51	107	149
骡肉产量	Meat of Mule	29	26	11	12
马肉产量	Meat of Horse	91	79	81	88
禽肉产量	Meat of Poultry	595096	636851	697069	741647
兔肉产量	Meat of Rabbits	1236	1351	1588	2108
牛奶产量 (吨)	Cow Milk Output (ton)	10552	18462	34673	52508
羊毛产量 (吨)	Wool Output (ton)	21	2	11	13
山羊毛	Goat Wool	18		8	10
绵羊毛	Sheep Wool	3	2	3	3
蜂蜜产量 (吨)	Honey Output (ton)	5308	7663	9598	8741
蜂蜡产量 (公斤)	Beeswax Output (kg)	114870	144243	143539	158815
禽蛋产量 (吨)	Poultry Eggs Output (ton)	734890	768126	825070	858102
兔毛产量 (吨)	Rabbit Wool Output (ton)	7	2	10	6
蚕茧产量 (吨)	Silkworm Cocoons (ton)	453	509	968	1543
#桑蚕茧 (吨)	Mulberry Silkworm Cocoons (ton)	450	509	967	1542

9-18 畜牧业年末存栏情况(2003年)

Year - end Animals in Stock (2003)

项 目	Item	合计 Total	能繁母畜 Breeding Dams	当年生仔畜 Young Animals Be Born in the Current Year
大牲畜总头数(头)	Number of Large Animals (head)	5403906		
#从事劳役的(头)	Draught Animals (head)	3862482		
牛(头)	Cattle and Buffaloes (head)	5363254		
#从事劳役	Draught Animals	3837413		
黄牛	Ox	3302846	1361375	669420
#菜牛	Beef Cattle	278961		
水牛	Buffaloes	2035220	833780	376777
乳牛	Dairy Cattle	25188	19200	3360
马(匹)	Horses (head)	33591	7704	2346
驴(匹)	Donkeys (head)	5162	1328	305
骡(匹)	Mules (head)	1899		152
生猪(万头)	Hogs (10 000 heads)	3924.1	338.41	
羊(万只)	Goats and Sheep (10 000 heads)	588.37	283.25	
山羊	Goats	588.25	283.21	
绵羊	Sheep	0.12	0.04	

9-19 主要牲畜存栏和水产品产量

Number of Livestock and Output of Aquatic Products

年 份 Year	年底大牲畜头数(万头) Large Animals (year-end) (10 000 heads)	#牛 Cattle and Buffaloes (10 000 heads)	年底猪头数(万头) Hogs(year-end) (10 000 heads)	年底羊只数(万只) Sheep and Goats (year-end) (10 000 heads)	猪牛羊肉(万吨) Pork,Beef, and Mutton (10 000 tons)	水产品(万吨) Aquatic Products (10 000 tons)
1990	400.65	399.25	2798.27	66.46	189.47	53.01
1995	432.65	430.46	3391.10	214.76	317.36	86.27
1996	471.78	469.43	3545.55	390.23	366.46	98.25
1997	496.54	493.73	3632.01	461.31	404.02	110.76
1998	504.02	500.93	3692.24	449.75	429.03	116.78
1999	511.39	508.17	3567.53	466.93	420.56	124.45
2000	522.85	519.29	3694.56	501.27	436.51	133.21
2001	526.10	522.43	3770.44	518.33	452.12	140.96
2002	521.83	517.90	3845.68	603.46	470.23	149.56
2003	540.39	536.33	3924.10	588.37	485.89	156.60

9-20 渔业生产情况

Basic Indicators of Fishery Production

名称	Item	2000	2001	2002	2003
水产品总产量 (吨)	**Total Aquatic Products (ton)**	**1332133**	**1409648**	**1495595**	**1565947**
淡水产品捕捞产量 (吨)	**Freshwater Aquatic Products Caught (ton)**	**150442**	**156497**	**170346**	**175582**
#鱼类	Fish	127725	134883	147548	152614
虾蟹类	Shrimps,Prawns and Crabs	9474	9066	10508	9698
贝类	Shellfish	10659	10743	10330	11131
其他	Others	2584	1805	1960	2139
淡水产品养殖产量 (吨)	**Freshwater Aquatic Products Cultured (ton)**	**1181691**	**1253151**	**1325249**	**1390365**
#鱼类	Fish	1145678	1214533	1281060	1348098
虾蟹类	Shrimps,Prawns and Crabs	11396	14264	18236	14662
贝类	Shellfish	12902	14283	13513	14201
其他	Others	11715	10071	12440	13404
淡水产品中:珍珠产量(公斤)	**Freshwater Aquatic Pearl Products (kg)**	**92015**	**186968**	**360005**	**488424**
淡水养殖面积合计 (千公顷)	**Freshwater Cultured Area (1 000 hectares)**	**413.18**	**422.48**	**437.32**	**448.52**
#池塘养殖	**Pond Cultivated**	**214.96**	**221.4**	**236.14**	**241.47**
#渔业专用塘	Fishery Ponds for Special Use	112.02	130.37	140.8	141.55
湖泊养殖	Lake Cultivated	55.85	55.08	55.86	57.05
#粗养	Extensive Cultivated	32.8	36.92	32.2	30.95
河沟养殖	Brook Cultivated	20.74	18.61	20.48	20.85
水库养殖	Reservoir Cultivated	102.23	106.23	106.51	109.72
#粗养	Extensive Cultivated	48.01	52.58	49.31	49.37
其他养殖	Other Cultivated	19.4	21.16	18.33	19.43
附：稻田养殖	**Enclose: Paddy Cultivated**	**189.76**	**202.2**	**214.41**	**191.22**
#鱼种池面积	Areas of (fish) Fry Ponds	14.98	16.88	18.12	19.32
成鱼面积	Growth Fish Areas	116.24	133.34	139.29	135.19

9-21 按全省人口平均的主要农产品产量

Per Capita Output of Major Farm Products

单位：公斤/人 (kg/person)

产品名称	Item	2000	2001	2002	2003
粮食	Grain	439.00	410.40	377.36	366.62
#谷物	Cereal	403.66	373.57	342.23	334.03
#稻谷	Rice	386.00	354.00	319.70	310.71
棉花	Cotton	2.60	2.90	2.31	2.50
食用植物油(包括料折油及茶油)	Edible Vegetable Oil (Include Material Converted to Oil and Tea-seed Oil)	8.60	8.50	6.90	7.10
甘蔗	Sugarcane	17.70	25.29	27.21	21.40
烤烟	Tobacco	2.40	2.30	2.63	2.70
茶叶	Tea	0.90	0.90	0.92	0.90
水果	Fruit	23.00	75.40	72.26	76.90
#柑桔	Citrus	19.20	23.40	21.76	25.10
猪牛羊肉	Pork,Beef and Mutton	66.70	68.70	70.94	72.90
#猪肉	Pork	63.30	65.20	66.97	68.60
禽蛋	Poultry Eggs	11.20	11.70	12.45	12.90
水产品	Aquatic Products	20.30	21.40	22.56	23.50

9-22 自然灾害情况

Statistics on Natural Disaster

名称	Item	2000	2001	2002	2003
受灾面积合计 (千公顷)	**Total Areas Covered (1 000 hectares)**	**3170.11**	**3774.75**	**5203.96**	**6747.7**
旱 灾 (千公顷)	Drought (1 000 hectares)	649.71	1015.67	139.28	1895.08
水 灾 (千公顷)	Flood (1 000 hectares)	292.76	426.80	1711.87	911.49
风雹灾 (公顷)	Windstorm (hectares)		34.78	874.03	212.49
病 虫 (千公顷)	Plant Diseases and Insect Pests (1 000 hectares)	1871.07	2232.89	2256.53	3617.14
霜 冻 (公顷)	Frost (hectares)				
其 他 (公顷)	Others (hectares)	356.57	64.61	222.25	111.5
成灾面积 (千公顷)	**Areas Affected (1 000 hectares)**	**759.23**	**795.07**	**1591.48**	**1910.8**
旱 灾 (千公顷)	Drought (1 000 hectares)	231.44	396.80	63.1	984.51
水 灾 (千公顷)	Flood (1 000 hectares)	128.06	207.02	952.32	530.55
风雹灾 (公顷)	Windstorm (hectare)		13.44	293.07	81.23
霜 冻 (公顷)	Frost (hectare)				
病虫 (千公顷)	Plant Diseases and Insect Pests (1 000 hectares)	222.43	152.16	146.59	296.93
其他 (千公顷)	Others (1 000 hectares)	177.30	25.65	136.49	17.58
因灾减产粮食 (万吨)	**Grains Reduced of Disaster (10 000 tons)**	**112.68**	**148.05**	**357.14**	**280.72**
死亡人数 (人)	**Number of Dead Population (person)**	**176**	**202**	**341**	**172**
死亡大牲畜 (头)	**Dead Large Animals (head)**	**59689**	**82800**	**189981**	**-**
倒塌房屋 (间)	**Collapsed Houses (unit)**	**149806**	**174900**	**341485**	**247000**
损坏房屋 (间)	**Destroyed Houses (unit)**	**436459**	**573700**	**1003464**	**714000**
成灾人口合计 (人)	**Total Population Affected (person)**	**22237689**	**23480000**	**30399754**	**23819000**
因灾缺粮数量 (吨)	**Grains Quantities Shorted of Disaster (ton)**	**1568465**	**192000**	**977545**	**518420**
因灾缺粮人口 (人)	**Population of Grains Shorted of Disaster (person)**	**9374555**	**6800000**	**10936508**	**8373000**
因灾经济损失合计 (万元)	**Total Economic Loss of Disaster (10 000 yuan)**	**1081796**	**940000**	**2262112**	**2321000**
#水灾损失 (万元)	Flood Loss (10 000 yuan)	662662	450000	1881486	-

9-23 洞庭湖区主要社会经济指标

Major Economic Indicators and Social Indicatiors on The DongTing Lake Area

指标	Item	2000	2001	2002	2003
总户数（万户）	Total Number of Households (10 000 households)	445.30	450.25	460.01	472.58
总人口（万人）	Total Number of Population (10 000 persons)	1504.30	1502.40	1508.70	1510.30
#乡村人口	#Number of Rural Population	1213.70	1228.20	1229.80	1236.70
乡村从业人员数（万人）	Employment of Rural Population (10 000 persons)	634.76	645.83	647.41	652.37
#农林牧渔业	#Farming,Forestry,Animal Husbandry,Fishery	457.18	457.71	440.07	436.61
有效灌溉面积（千公顷）	Effective Irrigated Area (1 000 hectares)	863.13	876.82	876.85	873.33
地区生产总值（亿元）	Gross Domestic Products (100 million yuan)	981.39	1080.60	1251.88	1363.57
#第一产业增加值	#Added-Value of First Industry	260.21	276.23	283.02	303.24
第二产业增加值	Added-Value of Second Industry	394.52	418.31	509.90	567.64
第三产业增加值	Added-Value of Third Industry	326.66	386.06	458.96	492.69
农业机械总动力（万千瓦）	Total Power of Major Agriculture Machinery (10 000 kw)	785.00	744.30	861.30	897.80
农作物总播种面积（千公顷）	Total Sown Area of Crops (1 000 hectares)	2380.14	2350.80	2243.46	2254.76
粮食作物播种面积（千公顷）	Sown Area of Grain Crops (1 000 hectares)	1330.21	1215.81	1168.61	1164.80
#稻谷	#Paddy	1165.77	1057.13	1005.94	998.59
玉米	Corn	40.77	36.22	35.18	41.43
油料播种面积（千公顷）	Sown Area of Oils-bearing (1 000 hectares)	375.15	362.35	349.43	332.59
棉花播种面积（千公顷）	Sown Area of Cotton (1 000 hectares)	115.83	118.80	94.56	115.32
粮食总产量（万吨）	Total Output of Grain (10 000 tons)	778.63	707.68	661.25	671.86
#稻谷	Paddy	720.06	652.82	600.84	611.79
玉米	Corn	19.15	17.27	18.78	20.20
油料产量（万吨）	Output of Oils-bearing (10 000 tons)	57.18	55.21	43.60	48.13
棉花产量（万吨）	Output of Cotton (10 000 tons)	13.49	16.52	13.46	16.30
肉类总产量（万吨）	Total Output of Meat (10 000 tons)	127.02	133.33	144.21	151.11
水产品总产量（万吨）	Total Output of Aquatic Products (10 000 tons)	66.70	70.77	75.20	79.48
水果产量（万吨）	Output of Fruits (10 000 tons)	33.95	154.02	133.09	144.19
地方财政收入（亿元）	Local Government Revenue (100 million yuan)	24.42	28.04	33.78	46.02
国有及年销售收入500万元及以上的非国有工业企业总产值(亿元)	Gross Output Value of State-owned Industrial Enterprises and Non State-owned Industrial Enterprises with an Annual Sales Income of Over 5 Million yuan (100 million yuan)	554.55	662.11	736.63	939.52
普通中学在校学生数（人）	Student Enrollment in General Secondary Schools (person)	897821	1004420	1106964	1133328
小学在校学生人数（人）	Student Enrollment in Primary Schools (person)	1417139	1267109	1097182	970028
医院、卫生院床位数（张）	Hospital Beds (unit)	26203	26584	30185	25563
医院、卫生院技术人员数(人)	Medical Technical Personnel in Hospitals (person)	42438	42073	39351	38116

十、工业

INDUSTRY

资料整理人员：　殷智敏　杨　未　罗　骁

10-1 独立核算工业企业各种分组的主要生产指标(2003年)

Major Production Indicators of Industrial Enterprises with Independent Accounting Systems by Various Characteristics (2003)

单位:亿元 (100 million yuan)

指标	Item	企业单位数(个) Number of Enterprises (unit)	#亏损企业 Loss-making Enterprises	工业总产值(现价) Gross Industrial Output Value (current price)	工业增加值(生产法) Value Added of Industry (by producing)
总计	**Total**	**5967**	**1313**	**2611.45**	**888.56**
按登记注册类型:	**Grouped by Registration**				
内资企业	Internal-invested Enterprises	5662	1232	2361.92	814.62
国有企业	State-owned Enterprises	1295	548	762.13	345.48
中央企业	Central Enterprises	85	35	328.76	200.23
地方企业	Local Enterprises	1210	513	433.37	145.25
集体企业	Collective-owned Enterprises	905	153	184.64	59.50
股份合作企业	Enterprises Cooperated by Joint-stock	339	42	77.63	25.08
联营企业	Cooperative Enterprises	42	6	7.43	2.42
有限责任公司	Limited Liability Company	711	190	457.90	127.72
股份有限公司	Company Limited by Shares	303	78	454.58	129.47
私营企业	Individual-owned Enterprises	2034	210	410.60	122.81
其他企业	Enterprises of Other Types of Ownership	33	5	7.01	2.13
港、澳、台投资经济	Enterprises Funded by Entrepreneurs From Hong Kong,Macao and Taiwan	181	50	108.81	36.07
外商投资经济	Enterprises funded by Foreigners	124	31	140.72	37.87
按经济组织类型:	**Grouped by Ownership**				
独资企业	Enterprises Owned by a Sole Investor	3141	791	1149.88	465.47
合作、合伙企业	Enterprises of Partnership	831	89	160.51	51.12
股份有限公司	Company Limited by Shares	475	97	515.37	149.13
有限责任公司	Limited Liability Company	1520	336	785.69	222.85
国有及国有控股企业	**State-owned or Controlling Share Hold Enterprises**	**1642**	**662**	**1391.74**	**523.60**
农村工业	**Rural Industry Light & Heavy Industry**	**652**	**56**	**149.23**	**47.16**
按轻重工业分组	**Grouped by of Enterprises**				
轻工业	Enterprises of Light Industry	2048	489	834.72	325.60
重工业	Enterprises of Heavy Industry	3919	824	1776.74	562.96
按企业规模分:	**Grouped by Size of Enterprises**				
大型企业	Large Enterprises	56	17	892.36	339.31
中型企业	Medium-sized Enterprises	479	122	720.61	232.09
小型企业	Small Enterprises	5432	1174	998.49	317.16

注：本表综合范围为全部国有工业企业及年产品销售收入500万元及以上的非国有工业企业。

All state-owned and the non-state-owned industrial enterprises with an annual sales income of over 5 million yuan.

单位:亿元　　10-1 续表 1　continued　　(100 million yuan)

指标	Item	企业单位数(个) Number of Enterprises (unit)	#亏损企业 Loss-making Enterprises	工业总产值(现价) Gross Industrial Output Value (current price)	工业增加值(生产法) Value Added of Industry (by producing)
按行业划分:	**Grouped by Sector**				
煤炭开采和洗选业	Mining and Washing of Coal	295	49	65.78	25.41
黑色金属矿采选业	Mining of Ferrous Metal Ores	24	6	3.88	1.20
有色金属矿采选业	Mining of Non-ferrous Metal Ores	158	13	35.27	11.79
非金属矿采选业	Mining and Processing of Nonmetal Ores	108	9	25.44	8.54
其他采矿业	Mining of Other Ores N.E.C				
农副食品加工业	Processing of Food from Agricultural Products	363	78	137.18	34.92
食品制造业	Manufacture of Foods	145	17	47.30	14.55
饮料制造业	Manufacture of Beverage	114	27	40.49	15.44
烟草制品业	Manufacture of Tobacco	12	3	182.03	131.78
纺织业	Manufacture of Textile	221	67	77.71	19.57
纺织服装、鞋、帽制造业	Manufacture of Textile Wearing Apparel,Footware and Caps	67	12	15.20	4.42
皮革、毛皮、羽毛及其制品	Manufacture of Leather,Fur,Feather and Its Products	71	5	21.71	6.53
木材加工及木、竹、藤、棕、草制品业	Processing of Timbers,Manufacture of Wood, Bamboo, Rattan,Palm and Straw Products	200	24	31.99	8.99
家具制造业	Manufacture of Furniture	42	1	10.37	3.06
造纸及纸制品业	Manufacture of Paper and Paper Products	220	47	74.04	20.57
印刷业和记录媒介的复制	Printing,Reproduction of Recording Media	111	25	24.03	9.88
文教体育用品制造业	Manufacture of Articles for Culture, Education and Sport Activity	16	2	1.50	0.42
石油加工炼焦及核燃料加工	Processing of Petroleum,Coking,Processing of Nucleus Fuel	15	5	178.18	45.88
化学原料及化学制品制造业	Manufacture of Chemical Raw Material and Chemical Products	720	116	216.70	64.14
医药制造业	Manufacture of Medicines	140	33	56.03	19.51
化学纤维制造业	Manufacture of Chemical Fiber	11	3	20.02	3.34
橡胶制品业	Manufacture of Rubber	47	16	13.46	4.27
塑料制品业	Manufacture of Plastic	122	41	22.54	7.12
非金属矿物制品业	Manufacture of Non-metallic Mineral Products	725	158	147.68	45.50
黑色金属冶炼及压延加工业	Manufacture and Processing of Ferrous Metals	181	33	209.83	69.71
有色金属冶炼及压延加工业	Manufacture and Processing of Non-ferrous Metals	232	32	163.70	43.83
金属制品业	Manufacture of Metal Products	174	33	40.04	11.95
通用设备制造业	Manufacture of General Purpose Machinery	300	77	70.77	21.71
专用设备制造业	Manufacture of Special Purpose Machinery	201	50	131.80	41.42
交通运输设备制造业	Manufacture of Transport Equipment	209	69	193.61	49.87
电气机械及器材制造业	Manufacture of Electrical Machinery and Equipment	200	50	79.31	22.31
通信设备、计算机及其他电子设备制造业	Manufacture of Communication Equipment,Computer and Other Electronic Equipment	76	21	74.14	15.72
仪器仪表及文化、办公用机械制造业	Manufacture of Measuring Instrument and Machinery for Cultural Activity and Office Work	44	8	10.63	3.28
工艺品及其他制造业	Manufacture of Artwork,Other Manufacture N.E.C	32	8	7.22	2.01
废弃资源废旧材料回收加工	Recycling and Disposal of Waste	5	1	3.23	0.97
电力、热力的生产和供应业	Production and Supply of Electric Power and Heat Power	249	107	159.56	89.68
燃气生产和供应业	Production and Distribution of Gas	7	4	2.80	0.68
水的生产和供应业	Production and Distribution of Water	110	63	16.26	8.61

单位:亿元 10-1 续表 2 continued (100 million yuan)

指标	Item	工业中间投人 Industrial Intermediate Input	本年应付工资 Wages Payable in This Year	本年应付福利费 Welfarisms Payable in This Year	全部从业人员年均人数(万人) Average Number of Employees (10 000 persons)
总计	**Total**	**1850.43**	**169.28**	**22.70**	**158.45**
按登记注册类型:	**Grouped by Registration**				
内资企业	Internal-invested Enterprises	1664.33	159.54	21.35	150.08
国有企业	State-owned Enterprises	474.81	66.25	9.03	53.82
中央企业	Central Enterprises	160.85	19.51	2.85	10.15
地方企业	Local Enterprises	313.96	46.74	6.18	43.68
集体企业	Collective-owned Enterprises	130.99	12.88	1.53	16.51
股份合作企业	Enterprises Cooperated by Joint-stock	55.34	4.62	0.60	5.38
联营企业	Cooperative Enterprises	5.33	0.44	0.06	0.70
有限责任公司	Limited Liability Company	349.93	33.57	4.90	29.02
股份有限公司	Company Limited by Shares	342.06	18.04	2.20	13.98
私营企业	Individual-owned Enterprises	300.84	23.29	2.98	30.10
其他企业	Enterprises of Other Types of Ownership	5.04	0.44	0.05	0.56
港、澳、台投资经济	Enterprises Funded by Entrepreneurs From Hong Kong,Macao and Taiwan	77.55	4.76	0.71	4.24
外商投资经济	Enterprises funded by Foreigners	108.55	4.99	0.65	4.13
按经济组织类型:	**Grouped by Ownership**				
独资企业	Enterprises Owned by a Sole Investor	754.34	89.66	11.89	83.00
合作、合伙企业	Enterprises of Partnership	114.85	9.72	1.26	12.40
股份有限公司	Company Limited by Shares	385.45	20.53	2.57	16.97
有限责任公司	Limited Liability Company	595.78	49.37	6.98	46.07
国有及国有控股企业	**State-owned or Controlling Share Hold Enterprises**	**954.12**	**102.92**	**13.83**	**81.28**
农村工业	**Rural Industry**	**106.73**	**8.80**	**1.12**	**10.92**
按轻重工业分组	**Grouped by of Enterprises**				
轻工业	Enterprises of Light Industry	550.47	42.17	5.13	46.76
重工业	Enterprises of Heavy Industry	1299.96	127.11	17.57	111.68
按企业规模分:	**Grouped by Size of Enterprises**				
大型企业	Large Enterprises	610.68	52.63	7.11	30.66
中型企业	Medium-sized Enterprises	524.50	49.12	6.75	43.18
小型企业	Small Enterprises	715.25	67.53	8.84	84.61

指标	Item	工业中间投入 Industrial Inter-mediate Input	本年应付工资 Wages Payable in This Year	本年应付福利费 Welfarisms Payable in This Year	全部从业人员年均人数(万人) Average Number of Employees (10 000 persons)
按行业划分:	**Grouped by Sector**				
煤炭开采和洗选业	Mining and Washing of Coal	44.63	13.03	1.82	13.78
黑色金属矿采选业	Mining of Ferrous Metal Ores	2.88	0.51	0.04	0.43
有色金属矿采选业	Mining of Non-ferrous Metal Ores	25.03	3.22	0.49	3.19
非金属矿采选业	Mining and Processing of Nonmetal Ores	17.77	1.81	0.17	2.37
其他采矿业	Mining of Other Ores N.E.C	0.00	0.00	0.00	0.00
农副食品加工业	Processing of Food from Agricultural Products	103.89	3.71	0.49	4.57
食品制造业	Manufacture of Foods	34.59	2.45	0.39	3.58
饮料制造业	Manufacture of Beverage	27.12	2.31	0.24	2.06
烟草制品业	Manufacture of Tobacco	70.77	4.88	0.66	1.27
纺织业	Manufacture of Textile	59.76	5.73	0.63	9.15
纺织服装、鞋、帽制造业	Manufacture of Textile Wearing Apparel,Footware and Caps	11.22	1.25	0.15	1.58
皮革、毛皮、羽毛及其制品	Manufacture of Leather,Fur,Feather and Its Products	15.63	0.88	0.11	1.32
木材加工及木、竹、藤、棕、草制品业	Processing of Timbers,Manufacture of Wood, Bamboo, Rattan,Palm and Straw Products	23.84	1.55	0.18	2.48
家具制造业	Manufacture of Furniture	7.54	0.59	0.04	0.60
造纸及纸制品业	Manufacture of Paper and Paper Products	56.44	4.32	0.52	4.21
印刷业和记录媒介的复制	Printing,Reproduction of Recording Media	15.46	1.35	0.14	1.23
文教体育用品制造业	Manufacture of Articles for Culture, Education and Sport Activity	1.11	0.09	0.01	0.17
石油加工炼焦及核燃料加工	Processing of Petroleum,Coking,Processing of Nucleus Fuel	138.64	5.08	0.75	2.08
化学原料及化学制品制造业	Manufacture of Chemical Raw Material and Chemical Products	160.99	15.46	1.89	17.87
医药制造业	Manufacture of Medicines	39.48	3.05	0.31	2.56
化学纤维制造业	Manufacture of Chemical Fiber	17.30	0.79	0.11	0.93
橡胶制品业	Manufacture of Rubber	9.62	1.00	0.12	1.15
塑料制品业	Manufacture of Plastic	16.07	1.26	0.18	1.37
非金属矿物制品业	Manufacture of Non-metallic Mineral Products	108.62	13.50	2.07	19.14
黑色金属冶炼及压延加工业	Manufacture and Processing of Ferrous Metals	153.77	13.71	1.74	8.67
有色金属冶炼及压延加工业	Manufacture and Processing of Non-ferrous Metals	126.49	8.95	1.18	6.56
金属制品业	Manufacture of Metal Products	29.18	2.32	0.29	2.39
通用设备制造业	Manufacture of General Purpose Machinery	51.87	6.56	0.96	5.91
专用设备制造业	Manufacture of Special Purpose Machinery	94.53	10.32	1.31	8.56
交通运输设备制造业	Manufacture of Transport Equipment	150.59	12.74	1.79	8.73
电气机械及器材制造业	Manufacture of Electrical Machinery and Equipment	59.83	4.98	0.66	4.76
通信设备、计算机及其他电子设备制造业	Manufacture of Communication Equipment,Computer and Other Electronic Equipment	60.80	2.36	0.37	2.20
仪器仪表及文化、办公用机械制造业	Manufacture of Measuring Instrument and Machinery for Cultural Activity and Office Work	7.85	0.89	0.22	0.93
工艺品及其他制造业	Manufacture of Artwork,Other Manufacture N.E.C	5.42	0.38	0.04	1.01
废弃资源废旧材料回收加工	Recycling and Disposal of Waste	2.31	0.11	0.02	0.05
电力、热力的生产和供应业	Production and Supply of Electric Power and Heat Power	88.62	14.83	2.19	9.14
燃气生产和供应业	Production and Distribution of Gas	2.26	0.24	0.03	0.31
水的生产和供应业	Production and Distribution of Water	8.50	3.05	0.40	2.15

10-2 独立核算工业企业各种分组的资本金与资产(2003年)

Capital Fund and Fixed Assets of Industrial Enterprises with Independent Accounting Systems by Various Characteristics (2003)

单位:亿元 (100 million yuan)

指标	Item	流动资产年均余额 Annual Average Balance of Circulating Funds	实收资本 Total Capital Hold	流动资产合计 Total Circulating Funds	固定资产 Fixed Assets 原价合计 Original Value	固定资产 Fixed Assets 净值余额 Annual Average Balance of Net Value
总计	**Total**	**1327.44**	**841.37**	**1430.33**	**2510.77**	**1558.18**
按登记注册类型:	**Grouped by Registration**					
内资企业	Internal-invested Enterprises	1225.01	718.51	1312.85	2285.18	1415.68
国有企业	State-owned Enterprises	550.62	262.14	588.84	1233.32	739.23
中央企业	Central Enterprises	253.75	91.05	261.64	572.99	333.37
地方企业	Local Enterprises	296.87	171.09	327.19	660.33	405.86
集体企业	Collective-owned Enterprises	55.38	32.82	59.18	71.26	45.98
股份合作企业	Enterprises Cooperated by Joint-stock	19.77	22.25	21.77	69.15	57.20
联营企业	Cooperative Enterprises	2.04	1.28	2.17	3.17	2.07
有限责任公司	Limited Liability Company	240.91	172.61	256.51	442.91	283.31
股份有限公司	Company Limited by Shares	246.32	140.34	260.55	315.13	177.44
私营企业	Individual-owned Enterprises	107.95	85.33	121.65	147.68	108.70
其他企业	Enterprises of Other Types of Ownership	2.03	1.74	2.18	2.56	1.76
港、澳、台投资经济	Enterprises Funded by Entrepreneurs From Hong Kong,Macao and Taiwan	46.76	43.22	56.50	79.21	58.42
外商投资经济	Enterprises funded by Foreigners	55.67	79.64	60.99	146.39	84.07
按经济组织类型:	**Grouped by Ownership**					
独资企业	Enterprises Owned by a Sole Investor	648.60	337.67	695.13	1369.23	830.11
合作、合伙企业	Enterprises of Partnership	38.38	40.87	41.97	101.08	80.52
股份有限公司	Company Limited by Shares	264.71	156.43	281.68	341.85	194.20
有限责任公司	Limited Liability Company	375.75	306.40	411.55	698.60	453.34
国有及国有控股企业	**State-owned or Controlling Share Hold Enterprises**	**915.97**	**513.20**	**969.27**	**1901.90**	**1148.50**
农村工业	**Rural Industry**	**31.36**	**22.20**	**33.91**	**44.99**	**29.39**
按轻重工业分组	**Grouped by of Enterprises**					
轻工业	Enterprises of Light Industry	400.11	258.16	438.16	494.96	310.00
重工业	Enterprises of Heavy Industry	927.33	583.21	992.17	2015.81	1248.18
按企业规模分:	**Grouped by Size of Enterprises**					
大型企业	Large Enterprises	518.88	235.93	539.38	897.28	504.83
中型企业	Medium-sized Enterprises	453.93	296.96	505.98	884.40	541.88
小型企业	Small Enterprises	354.63	308.47	384.98	729.08	511.46

单位:亿元 10-2 续表 1 continued (100 million yuan)

指标	Item	流动资产年均余额 Annual Average Balance of Circulating Funds	实收资本 Total Capital Hold	流动资产合计 Total Circulating Funds	固定资产 Fixed Assets 原价合计 Original Value	净值余额 Annual Average Balance of Net Value
按行业划分:	Grouped by Sector					
煤炭开采和洗选业	Mining and Washing of Coal	32.19	23.95	30.15	56.99	37.04
黑色金属矿采选业	Mining of Ferrous Metal Ores	2.02	1.22	2.14	2.71	1.54
有色金属矿采选业	Mining of Non-ferrous Metal Ores	9.28	10.23	9.61	19.52	12.72
非金属矿采选业	Mining and Processing of Nonmetal Ores	6.79	4.61	6.74	12.02	7.20
其他采矿业	Mining of Other Ores N.E.C					
农副食品加工业	Processing of Food from Agricultural Products	35.59	30.18	38.72	44.35	31.47
食品制造业	Manufacture of Foods	15.59	14.42	17.56	19.78	11.92
饮料制造业	Manufacture of Beverage	32.14	20.75	32.05	31.48	21.97
烟草制品业	Manufacture of Tobacco	109.91	31.51	114.74	84.46	40.14
纺织业	Manufacture of Textile	34.01	18.34	38.38	36.49	24.95
纺织服装、鞋、帽制造业	Manufacture of Textile Wearing Apparel,Footware and Caps	4.93	2.99	5.44	3.91	2.68
皮革、毛皮、羽毛及其制品	Manufacture of Leather,Fur,Feather and Its Products	4.64	3.00	4.98	4.68	3.58
木材加工及木、竹、藤、棕、草制品业	Processing of Timbers,Manufacture of Wood, Bamboo, Rattan,Palm and Straw Products	6.98	10.57	7.08	18.68	14.78
家具制造业	Manufacture of Furniture	2.31	1.32	2.32	2.05	1.69
造纸及纸制品业	Manufacture of Paper and Paper Products	37.65	32.11	48.04	57.69	36.75
印刷业和记录媒介的复制	Printing,Reproduction of Recording Media	10.46	7.25	11.96	17.30	9.89
文教体育用品制造业	Manufacture of Articles for Culture, Education and Sport Activity	0.42	0.32	0.44	0.50	0.42
石油加工炼焦及核燃料加工	Processing of Petroleum,Coking,Processing of Nucleus Fuel	52.45	22.18	51.98	116.06	66.25
化学原料及化学制品制造业	Manufacture of Chemical Raw Material and Chemical Products	107.49	92.82	112.96	215.72	121.63
医药制造业	Manufacture of Medicines	35.64	21.05	39.47	35.26	26.66
化学纤维制造业	Manufacture of Chemical Fiber	8.69	7.63	8.22	27.89	16.65
橡胶制品业	Manufacture of Rubber	8.77	3.63	9.02	6.83	4.29
塑料制品业	Manufacture of Plastic	11.36	12.61	12.62	16.72	11.90
非金属矿物制品业	Manufacture of Non-metallic Mineral Products	61.18	50.12	65.41	126.44	80.16
黑色金属冶炼及压延加工业	Manufacture and Processing of Ferrous Metals	87.49	32.65	99.25	201.30	113.96
有色金属冶炼及压延加工业	Manufacture and Processing of Non-ferrous Metals	67.21	50.27	72.06	95.55	59.69
金属制品业	Manufacture of Metal Products	16.66	11.99	16.69	21.61	16.62
通用设备制造业	Manufacture of General Purpose Machinery	59.69	26.74	67.49	52.19	31.43
专用设备制造业	Manufacture of Special Purpose Machinery	81.68	25.07	90.74	72.68	45.65
交通运输设备制造业	Manufacture of Transport Equipment	130.55	72.42	137.00	113.86	69.99
电气机械及器材制造业	Manufacture of Electrical Machinery and Equipment	50.69	35.40	54.94	56.38	33.40
通信设备、计算机及其他电子设备制造业	Manufacture of Communication Equipment,Computer and Other Electronic Equipment	44.00	36.02	43.89	68.93	49.73
仪器仪表及文化、办公用机械制造业	Manufacture of Measuring Instrument and Machinery for Cultural Activity and Office Work	5.92	4.21	10.50	6.10	3.27
工艺品及其他制造业	Manufacture of Artwork,Other Manufacture N.E.C	1.49	1.50	1.61	2.17	1.59
废弃资源废旧材料回收加工	Recycling and Disposal of Waste	0.16	0.06	0.18	1.16	0.44
电力、热力的生产和供应业	Production and Supply of Electric Power and Heat Power	135.52	101.09	147.62	798.58	506.98
燃气生产和供应业	Production and Distribution of Gas	2.56	4.04	3.61	4.54	2.52
水的生产和供应业	Production and Distribution of Water	13.34	17.08	14.71	58.12	36.64

单位:亿元　　10-2 续表 2　continued　　(100 million yuan)

指标	Item	累计折旧 Add up Deprecia-tion of Fixed Assets	#本年折旧 Deprecia-tion of this Year	流动负债 Total Liquid Liabilities	长期负债 Long-term Liabilities	所有者权益 Creditors Equity
总计	**Total**	**868.99**	**120.93**	**1471.89**	**798.85**	**1314.10**
按登记注册类型:	**Grouped by Registration**					
内资企业	Internal-invested Enterprises	790.60	108.97	1354.10	746.01	1186.81
国有企业	State-owned Enterprises	438.20	59.01	649.98	482.23	473.28
中央企业	Central Enterprises	214.69	28.53	216.45	290.00	185.42
地方企业	Local Enterprises	223.51	30.48	433.52	192.23	287.86
集体企业	Collective-owned Enterprises	24.70	3.56	61.60	19.18	36.43
股份合作企业	Enterprises Cooperated by Joint-stock	16.93	1.98	21.23	19.88	46.48
联营企业	Cooperative Enterprises	1.03	0.11	2.50	0.60	1.69
有限责任公司	Limited Liability Company	152.04	19.83	290.81	123.96	231.99
股份有限公司	Company Limited by Shares	125.39	16.21	217.76	78.10	251.94
私营企业	Individual-owned Enterprises	31.65	8.17	108.05	21.67	142.80
其他企业	Enterprises of Other Types of Ownership	0.68	0.10	2.18	0.39	2.19
港、澳、台投资经济	Enterprises Funded by Entrepreneurs From Hong Kong,Macao and Taiwan	18.36	4.28	51.73	24.40	54.92
外商投资经济	Enterprises funded by Foreigners	60.02	7.68	66.06	28.45	72.38
按经济组织类型:	**Grouped by Ownership**					
独资企业	Enterprises Owned by a Sole Investor	479.19	67.11	756.23	510.27	563.39
合作、合伙企业	Enterprises of Partnership	24.41	3.58	39.52	24.44	73.06
股份有限公司	Company Limited by Shares	132.85	17.91	239.08	80.86	277.45
有限责任公司	Limited Liability Company	232.54	32.33	437.07	183.28	400.21
国有控股企业	**State-owned or Controlling Share Hold Enterprises**	**693.21**	**89.29**	**1043.49**	**642.68**	**831.82**
农村工业	**Rural Industry**	**14.21**	**2.82**	**30.78**	**9.11**	**33.35**
按轻重工业分组	**Grouped by of Enterprises**					
轻工业	Enterprises of Light Industry	169.26	23.50	382.90	108.68	443.31
重工业	Enterprises of Heavy Industry	699.73	97.44	1088.99	690.17	870.79
按企业规模分:	**Grouped by Size of Enterprises**					
大型企业	Large Enterprises	341.33	49.11	529.53	254.25	486.57
中型企业	Medium-sized Enterprises	321.54	42.49	504.36	338.97	430.35
小型企业	Small Enterprises	206.12	29.33	438.00	205.64	397.19

单位:亿元 10-2 续表 3 . continued (100 million yuan)

指标	Item	累计折旧 Add up Depreciation of Fixed Assets	#本年折旧 Depreciation of this Year	流动负债 Total Liquid Liabilities	长期负债 Long-term Liabilities	所有者权益 Creditors Equity
按行业划分:	**Grouped by Sector**					
开采和洗选业	Mining and Washing of Coal	18.50	2.26	30.81	9.28	35.07
黑色金属矿采选业	Mining of Ferrous Metal Ores	1.03	0.10	2.89	0.49	0.96
有色金属矿采选业	Mining of Non-ferrous Metal Ores	6.66	0.89	10.84	2.38	12.41
非金属矿采选业	Mining and Processing of Nonmetal Ores	4.49	0.48	6.67	2.04	6.80
其他采矿业	Mining of Other Ores N.E.C					
农副食品加工业	Processing of Food from Agricultural Products	10.31	1.79	42.71	8.52	33.42
食品制造业	Manufacture of Foods	5.26	0.74	19.49	2.97	20.81
饮料制造业	Manufacture of Beverage	9.39	1.93	28.21	4.98	31.10
烟草制品业	Manufacture of Tobacco	43.81	5.15	55.76	7.41	121.55
纺织业	Manufacture of Textile	11.32	1.77	44.71	9.57	21.90
纺织服装、鞋、帽制造业	Manufacture of Textile Wearing Apparel,Footware and Caps	1.02	0.21	5.63	0.45	3.46
皮革、毛皮、羽毛及其制品	Manufacture of Leather,Fur,Feather and Its Products	0.93	0.25	5.48	0.99	3.16
木材加工及木、竹、藤、棕、草制品业	Processing of Timbers,Manufacture of Wood, Bamboo, Rattan,Palm and Straw Products	4.13	0.74	8.91	2.88	11.27
家具制造业	Manufacture of Furniture	0.36	0.13	2.06	0.17	2.21
造纸及纸制品业	Manufacture of Paper and Paper Products	18.63	1.89	41.54	26.65	54.90
印刷业和记录媒介的复制	Printing,Reproduction of Recording Media	7.62	1.11	10.88	1.38	11.90
文教体育用品制造业	Manufacture of Articles for Culture, Education and Sport Activity	0.09	0.01	0.52	0.06	0.35
石油加工炼焦及核燃料加工	Processing of Petroleum,Coking,Processing of Nucleus Fuel	47.96	5.56	71.25	14.93	34.65
化学原料及化学制品制造业	Manufacture of Chemical Raw Material and Chemical Products	91.92	9.17	126.72	29.28	102.06
医药制造业	Manufacture of Medicines	7.49	1.35	32.93	9.19	42.08
化学纤维制造业	Manufacture of Chemical Fiber	10.46	1.31	11.58	6.95	12.65
橡胶制品业	Manufacture of Rubber	2.01	0.29	5.91	0.71	8.94
塑料制品业	Manufacture of Plastic	4.48	0.82	11.98	5.96	14.40
非金属矿物制品业	Manufacture of Non-metallic Mineral Products	45.42	6.13	78.60	29.18	60.94
黑色金属冶炼及压延加工业	Manufacture and Processing of Ferrous Metals	68.36	14.77	134.45	42.16	95.76
有色金属冶炼及压延加工业	Manufacture and Processing of Non-ferrous Metals	31.17	4.50	71.43	33.54	67.64
金属制品业	Manufacture of Metal Products	4.68	0.93	20.19	4.26	14.93
通用设备制造业	Manufacture of General Purpose Machinery	20.16	2.81	67.51	12.47	33.47
专用设备制造业	Manufacture of Special Purpose Machinery	25.01	3.63	91.25	13.78	54.17
交通运输设备制造业	Manufacture of Transport Equipment	40.62	6.50	154.49	21.26	93.80
电气机械及器材制造业	Manufacture of Electrical Machinery and Equipment	21.57	2.57	55.07	10.94	43.77
通信设备、计算机及其他电子设备制造业	Manufacture of Communication Equipment,Computer and Other Electronic Equipment	18.30	3.74	47.54	16.26	51.79
仪器仪表及文化、办公用机械制造业	Manufacture of Measuring Instrument and Machinery for Cultural Activity and Office Work	2.04	0.14	11.34	1.39	4.32
工艺品及其他制造业	Manufacture of Artwork,Other Manufacture N.E.C	0.41	0.06	1.55	0.40	1.65
废弃资源废旧材料回收加工	Recycling and Disposal of Waste	0.71	0.01	0.44	0.00	0.20
电力、热力的生产和供应业	Production and Supply of Electric Power and Heat Power	264.34	34.63	141.39	450.51	167.88
燃气生产和供应业	Production and Distribution of Gas	1.32	0.09	3.81	0.18	3.76
水的生产和供应业	Production and Distribution of Water	16.99	2.48	15.35	15.30	33.98

10-3 独立核算工业企业各种分组的主要财务指标(2003年)

Major Financial Industrial Enterprises with Independent Accounting Systems by Various Characteristics (2003)

单位:亿元 (100 million yuan)

指标	Item	产品销售收入 Sales Revenue	销售费用 Cost of Sales	销售税金及附加 Sales Tax and Extra Charges
总计	**Total**	**2604.98**	**97.33**	**106.88**
按登记注册类型:	**Grouped by Registration**			
内资企业	Internal-invested Enterprises	2372.02	87.14	105.73
国有企业	State-owned Enterprises	866.26	21.18	82.08
中央企业	Central Enterprises	427.03	8.87	78.37
地方企业	Local Enterprises	439.24	12.31	3.72
集体企业	Collective-owned Enterprises	169.19	7.75	3.08
股份合作企业	Enterprises Cooperated by Joint-stock	74.01	2.58	0.93
联营企业	Cooperative Enterprises	6.66	0.28	0.17
有限责任公司	Limited Liability Company	448.19	15.21	4.80
股份有限公司	Company Limited by Shares	428.77	20.89	7.99
私营企业	Individual-owned Enterprises	372.58	18.84	6.63
其他企业	Enterprises of Other Types of Ownership	6.37	0.40	0.05
港、澳、台投资经济	Enterprises Funded by Entrepreneurs From Hong Kong,Macao and Taiwan	100.21	5.44	0.44
外商投资经济	Enterprises funded by Foreigners	132.75	4.74	0.70
按经济组织类型:	**Grouped by Ownership**			
独资企业	Enterprises Owned by a Sole Investor	1223.70	38.59	88.74
合作、合伙企业	Enterprises of Partnership	146.68	5.81	2.31
股份有限公司	Company Limited by Shares	483.14	24.09	8.48
有限责任公司	Limited Liability Company	751.46	28.82	7.35
国有控股企业	**State-owned or Controlling Share Hold Enterprises**	**1499.44**	**43.03**	**93.13**
农村工业	**Rural Industry**	**135.13**	**7.74**	**2.35**
按轻重工业分组	**Grouped by of Enterprises**			
轻工业	Enterprises of Light Industry	776.60	44.01	84.26
重工业	Enterprises of Heavy Industry	1828.38	53.32	22.62
按企业规模分:	**Grouped by Size of Enterprises**			
大型企业	Large Enterprises	979.57	22.37	84.32
中型企业	Medium-sized Enterprises	739.30	34.33	9.67
小型企业	Small Enterprises	886.11	40.63	12.89

单位:亿元 10-3 续表 1 continued (100 million yuan)

指标	Item	产品销售收入 Sales Revenue	销售费用 Cost of Sales	销售税金及附加 Sales Tax and Extra Charges
按行业划分:	**Grouped by Sector**			
开采和洗选业	Mining and Washing of Coal	61.96	2.20	1.13
黑色金属矿采选业	Mining of Ferrous Metal Ores	3.70	0.16	0.06
有色金属矿采选业	Mining of Non-ferrous Metal Ores	34.89	1.38	0.68
非金属矿采选业	Mining and Processing of Nonmetal Ores	24.04	1.89	0.70
其他采矿业	Mining of Other Ores N.E.C			
农副食品加工业	Processing of Food from Agricultural Products	121.41	5.51	0.59
食品制造业	Manufacture of Foods	43.26	5.40	0.55
饮料制造业	Manufacture of Beverage	37.91	3.76	2.10
烟草制品业	Manufacture of Tobacco	186.83	6.90	77.53
纺织业	Manufacture of Textile	69.24	2.04	0.43
纺织服装、鞋、帽制造业	Manufacture of Textile Wearing Apparel,Footware and Caps	14.61	1.01	0.15
皮革、毛皮、羽毛及其制品	Manufacture of Leather,Fur,Feather and Its Products	19.30	0.58	0.26
木材加工及木、竹、藤、棕、草制品业	Processing of Timbers,Manufacture of Wood, Bamboo, Rattan,Palm and Straw Products	28.11	0.99	0.40
家具制造业	Manufacture of Furniture	9.60	0.84	0.12
造纸及纸制品业	Manufacture of Paper and Paper Products	70.03	2.21	0.62
印刷业和记录媒介的复制	Printing,Reproduction of Recording Media	22.01	0.33	0.09
文教体育用品制造业	Manufacture of Articles for Culture, Education and Sport Activity	1.44	0.04	0.01
石油加工炼焦及核燃料加工	Processing of Petroleum,Coking,Processing of Nucleus Fuel	179.82	1.45	6.73
化学原料及化学制品制造业	Manufacture of Chemical Raw Material and Chemical Products	208.35	8.38	3.62
医药制造业	Manufacture of Medicines	46.05	7.96	0.30
化学纤维制造业	Manufacture of Chemical Fiber	19.23	0.44	0.21
橡胶制品业	Manufacture of Rubber	13.64	0.58	0.08
塑料制品业	Manufacture of Plastic	19.16	0.69	0.19
非金属矿物制品业	Manufacture of Non-metallic Mineral Products	133.36	7.18	1.66
黑色金属冶炼及压延加工业	Manufacture and Processing of Ferrous Metals	225.18	3.53	1.38
有色金属冶炼及压延加工业	Manufacture and Processing of Non-ferrous Metals	162.57	4.26	1.19
金属制品业	Manufacture of Metal Products	37.25	1.77	0.46
通用设备制造业	Manufacture of General Purpose Machinery	62.94	4.63	0.49
专用设备制造业	Manufacture of Special Purpose Machinery	111.80	6.78	0.55
交通运输设备制造业	Manufacture of Transport Equipment	184.80	4.29	1.95
电气机械及器材制造业	Manufacture of Electrical Machinery and Equipment	70.85	4.36	0.44
通信设备、计算机及其他电子设备制造业	Manufacture of Communication Equipment,Computer and Other Electronic Equipment	75.55	2.83	0.12
仪器仪表及文化、办公用机械制造业	Manufacture of Measuring Instrument and Machinery for Cultural Activity and Office Work	8.84	0.95	0.04
工艺品及其他制造业	Manufacture of Artwork,Other Manufacture N.E.C	7.08	0.47	0.22
废弃资源废旧材料回收加工	Recycling and Disposal of Waste	3.30	0.03	0.01
电力、热力的生产和供应业	Production and Supply of Electric Power and Heat Power	269.21	0.77	1.64
燃气生产和供应业	Production and Distribution of Gas	2.85	0.12	0.02
水的生产和供应业	Production and Distribution of Water	14.83	0.64	0.14

单位:亿元 10-3 续表 2 continued (100 million yuan)

指标	Item	管理费用 Overhead Expenses	财务费用 Financial Expenses	利润总额 Total Profits	利税总额 Total Per-tax Profits
总计	**Total**	**187.38**	**46.64**	**111.25**	**345.67**
按登记注册类型:	**Grouped by Registration**				
内资企业	Internal-invested Enterprises	173.36	42.03	91.33	314.09
国有企业	State-owned Enterprises	83.39	16.63	40.25	180.50
中央企业	Central Enterprises	30.95	5.46	34.82	145.50
地方企业	Local Enterprises	52.44	11.17	5.43	34.99
集体企业	Collective-owned Enterprises	7.72	2.34	4.75	13.68
股份合作企业	Enterprises Cooperated by Joint-stock	3.59	0.81	1.77	5.48
联营企业	Cooperative Enterprises	0.24	0.09	0.18	0.68
有限责任公司	Limited Liability Company	35.92	9.68	9.23	33.78
股份有限公司	Company Limited by Shares	27.44	7.80	20.04	44.98
私营企业	Individual-owned Enterprises	14.74	4.63	14.93	34.60
其他企业	Enterprises of Other Types of Ownership	0.32	0.05	0.18	0.39
港、澳、台投资经济	Enterprises Funded by Entrepreneurs From Hong Kong,Macao and Taiwan	6.30	1.53	9.98	15.23
外商投资经济	Enterprises funded by Foreigners	7.72	3.08	9.95	16.35
按经济组织类型:	**Grouped by Ownership**				
独资企业	Enterprises Owned by a Sole Investor	97.77	21.12	52.37	211.05
合作、合伙企业	Enterprises of Partnership	6.34	1.59	4.07	11.84
股份有限公司	Company Limited by Shares	30.04	8.52	24.65	52.33
有限责任公司	Limited Liability Company	53.22	15.40	30.16	70.45
国有控股企业	**State-owned or Controlling Share Hold Enterprises**	**132.49**	**30.61**	**52.68**	**231.80**
农村工业	**Rural Industry**	**5.02**	**1.74**	**5.92**	**12.94**
按轻重工业分组	**Grouped by of Enterprises**				
轻工业	Enterprises of Light Industry	49.64	10.90	42.72	168.33
重工业	Enterprises of Heavy Industry	137.74	35.74	68.54	177.33
按企业规模分:	**Grouped by Size of Enterprises**				
大型企业	Large Enterprises	75.57	13.77	53.67	195.64
中型企业	Medium-sized Enterprises	58.50	16.25	32.39	78.03
小型企业	Small Enterprises	53.31	16.62	25.19	72.00

单位:亿元　　10-3 续表 3　continued　　(100 million yuan)

指标	Item	管理费用 Overhead Expenses	财务费用 Financial Expenses	利润总额 Total Profits	利税总额 Total Per-tax Profits
按行业划分:	**Grouped by Sector**				
开采和洗选业	Mining and Washing of Coal	9.25	0.65	2.02	7.41
黑色金属矿采选业	Mining of Ferrous Metal Ores	0.38	0.06	-0.12	0.14
有色金属矿采选业	Mining of Non-ferrous Metal Ores	2.71	0.47	1.39	3.62
非金属矿采选业	Mining and Processing of Nonmetal Ores	1.43	0.38	0.40	1.97
其他采矿业	Mining of Other Ores N.E.C				
农副食品加工业	Processing of Food from Agricultural Products	4.15	1.47	1.61	3.83
食品制造业	Manufacture of Foods	2.73	0.55	1.59	3.98
饮料制造业	Manufacture of Beverage	3.05	0.79	2.79	6.95
烟草制品业	Manufacture of Tobacco	13.86	1.03	22.17	120.22
纺织业	Manufacture of Textile	3.40	0.71	-0.69	1.35
纺织服装、鞋、帽制造业	Manufacture of Textile Wearing Apparel,Footware and Caps	0.73	0.18	0.43	1.02
皮革、毛皮、羽毛及其制品	Manufacture of Leather,Fur,Feather and Its Products	0.52	0.17	0.67	1.38
木材加工及木、竹、藤、棕、草制品业	Processing of Timbers,Manufacture of Wood, Bamboo, Rattan,Palm and Straw Products	1.05	0.39	0.59	1.83
家具制造业	Manufacture of Furniture	0.32	0.25	0.36	0.71
造纸及纸制品业	Manufacture of Paper and Paper Products	3.97	1.31	3.34	6.93
印刷业和记录媒介的复制	Printing,Reproduction of Recording Media	1.48	0.20	3.50	4.90
文教体育用品制造业	Manufacture of Articles for Culture, Education and Sport Activity	0.04	0.01	0.03	0.07
石油加工炼焦及核燃料加工	Processing of Petroleum,Coking,Processing of Nucleus Fuel	5.74	2.12	0.15	13.23
化学原料及化学制品制造业	Manufacture of Chemical Raw Material and Chemical Products	16.62	3.72	-1.27	10.78
医药制造业	Manufacture of Medicines	4.39	0.92	3.70	6.96
化学纤维制造业	Manufacture of Chemical Fiber	1.02	0.59	-1.02	-0.19
橡胶制品业	Manufacture of Rubber	0.95	0.07	0.80	1.31
塑料制品业	Manufacture of Plastic	1.83	0.39	0.19	1.02
非金属矿物制品业	Manufacture of Non-metallic Mineral Products	9.99	2.17	2.92	11.03
黑色金属冶炼及压延加工业	Manufacture and Processing of Ferrous Metals	16.02	3.54	8.51	23.54
有色金属冶炼及压延加工业	Manufacture and Processing of Non-ferrous Metals	8.44	3.00	6.05	13.86
金属制品业	Manufacture of Metal Products	1.98	0.69	0.79	2.33
通用设备制造业	Manufacture of General Purpose Machinery	7.01	1.20	2.64	5.94
专用设备制造业	Manufacture of Special Purpose Machinery	15.42	1.79	8.38	13.08
交通运输设备制造业	Manufacture of Transport Equipment	18.09	3.12	11.62	20.43
电气机械及器材制造业	Manufacture of Electrical Machinery and Equipment	6.56	1.33	2.26	5.53
通信设备、计算机及其他电子设备制造业	Manufacture of Communication Equipment,Computer and Other Electronic Equipment	5.64	1.65	5.20	7.70
仪器仪表及文化、办公用机械制造业	Manufacture of Measuring Instrument and Machinery for Cultural Activity and Office Work	1.65	0.36	0.65	1.18
工艺品及其他制造业	Manufacture of Artwork,Other Manufacture N.E.C	0.19	0.04	0.12	0.55
废弃资源废旧材料回收加工	Recycling and Disposal of Waste	0.01	0.00	0.08	0.13
电力、热力的生产和供应业	Production and Supply of Electric Power and Heat Power	13.09	10.43	18.89	39.26
燃气生产和供应业	Production and Distribution of Gas	0.22	0.03	0.15	0.30
水的生产和供应业	Production and Distribution of Water	3.45	0.87	0.38	1.37

10-4 各市、州独立核算工业主要经济指标(2003年)

Major Ecomomic Indicators of Industrial Enterprises with Independent Accounting Systems by Region (2003)

单位：亿元 (100 million yuan)

指标	Item	全省总计 Total	长沙市 Changsha City	株洲市 Zhuzhou City	湘潭市 Xiangtan City	衡阳市 Hengyang City
企业单位数 (个)	Number of Enterprises (unit)	5967	1096	521	400	533
#大型企业	#Largest Enterprise	56	7	9	7	6
#中型企业	#Medium-sized Enterprises	479	100	42	24	46
#小型企业	#Small Enterprises	5432	989	470	369	481
#亏损企业	#Loss-making Enterprises	1313	226	113	99	110
工业总产值(现价)	Gross Industrial Output Value	2611.45	564.33	262.10	202.55	211.20
内资企业	Internal-invested Enterprises	2361.92	452.93	234.70	194.27	198.46
国有企业	State-owned Enterprises	762.13	128.28	60.86	95.91	68.92
集体企业	Collective-owned Enterprises	184.64	17.03	13.50	9.34	34.62
股份合作企业	Enterprises Cooperated by Joint-stock	77.63	12.05	8.19	12.52	2.72
联营企业	Cooperative Enterprises	7.43	0.87	0.00	0.05	1.33
有限责任公司	Limited Liability Company	457.90	90.97	67.53	43.84	26.65
股份有限公司	Company Limited by Shares	454.58	119.60	57.05	6.18	19.27
私营企业	Individual-owned Enterprises	410.60	83.68	27.04	26.33	44.47
其他内资企业	Enterprises of Other Types of Ownership	7.01	0.44	0.54	0.10	0.49
港澳台商投资企业	Enterprises Funded by Entrepreneurs From Hong Kong,Macao and Taiwan	108.81	36.98	14.16	4.36	6.66
外商投资企业	Enterprises funded by Foreigners	140.72	74.42	13.24	3.92	6.09
工业总产值指数（%）	Index of Industrial Output Value	122.78	132.86	108.99	116.10	127.22
工业增加值(生产法)	Value Added of Industry	888.56	203.10	77.51	64.37	65.50
内资企业	Internal-invested Enterprises	814.62	174.38	69.50	62.31	61.02
国有企业	State-owned Enterprises	345.48	79.38	19.48	34.69	22.84
集体企业	Collective-owned Enterprises	59.50	5.98	4.60	3.01	11.52
股份合作企业	Enterprises Cooperated by Joint-stock	25.08	3.68	2.22	3.89	0.95
联营企业	Cooperative Enterprises	2.42	0.36	0.00	0.01	0.45
有限责任公司	Limited Liability Company	127.72	25.92	18.90	9.98	7.29
股份有限公司	Company Limited by Shares	129.47	34.76	14.75	2.06	6.29
私营企业	Individual-owned Enterprises	122.81	24.16	9.36	8.64	11.54
其他内资企业	Enterprises of Other Types of Ownership	2.13	0.15	0.19	0.03	0.15
港澳台商投资企业	Enterprises Funded by Entrepreneurs From Hong Kong,Macao and Taiwan	36.07	11.97	4.05	1.38	2.02
外商投资企业	Enterprises funded by Foreigners	37.87	16.75	3.95	0.68	2.46
工业销售产值	Industrial Sales Value	2607.09	557.89	258.85	205.46	208.55
实收资本	Total Capital Hold	841.37	176.73	100.33	57.68	63.83
#外商资本	#Foreign Capital	46.92	22.39	5.39	2.75	1.49
工业中间投入	Industrial Input	1850.43	389.74	196.5	149.34	152.72

单位：亿元　　10-4 续表 1　continued　　(100 million yuan)

指标	Item	邵阳市 Shaoyang City	岳阳市 Yueyang City	常德市 Changde City	张家界市 Zhangjiajie City	益阳市 Yiyang City
企业单位数　（个）	Number of Enterprises (unit)	419	489	388	82	382
#大型企业	#Largest Enterprise		8	4		
#中型企业	#Medium-sized Enterprises	31	26	49	4	29
#小型企业	#Small Enterprises	388	455	335	78	353
#亏损企业	#Loss-making Enterprises	109	83	107	30	90
工业总产值(现价)	Gross Industrial Output Value	84.51	435.91	220.45	15.78	83.11
内资企业	Internal-invested Enterprises	83.39	401.65	195.41	14.00	77.62
国有企业	State-owned Enterprises	24.95	49.79	102.53	4.52	24.23
集体企业	Collective-owned Enterprises	6.87	31.93	13.06	0.45	11.23
股份合作企业	Enterprises Cooperated by Joint-stock	2.28	13.63	4.06	1.68	1.90
联营企业	Cooperative Enterprises	0.06	1.33	0.55	0.00	1.03
有限责任公司	Limited Liability Company	7.86	102.06	27.22	2.55	24.14
股份有限公司	Company Limited by Shares	11.77	150.30	19.41	0.49	4.75
私营企业	Individual-owned Enterprises	29.44	51.14	26.84	4.32	10.33
其他内资企业	Enterprises of Other Types of Ownership	0.16	1.48	1.75	0.00	0.00
港澳台商投资企业	Enterprises Funded by Entrepreneurs From Hong Kong,Macao and Taiwan	0.42	7.30	19.49	1.42	2.53
外商投资企业	Enterprises funded by Foreigners	0.70	26.95	5.56	0.36	2.96
工业总产值指数（%）	Index of Industrial Output Value (%)	119.74	115.99	117.46	144.29	125.05
工业增加值(生产法)	Value Added of Industry	27.23	126.64	101.94	6.68	23.35
内资企业	Internal-invested Enterprises	26.89	114.74	93.06	5.95	21.99
国有企业	State-owned Enterprises	8.94	15.38	67.38	2.45	7.49
集体企业	Collective-owned Enterprises	2.27	9.59	3.71	0.14	2.98
股份合作企业	Enterprises Cooperated by Joint-stock	0.78	4.17	2.09	0.58	0.48
联营企业	Cooperative Enterprises	0.02	0.35	0.17	0.00	0.30
有限责任公司	Limited Liability Company	2.30	27.80	7.67	1.09	6.97
股份有限公司	Company Limited by Shares	3.60	41.05	4.78	0.22	1.21
私营企业	Individual-owned Enterprises	8.94	15.86	6.78	1.47	2.58
其他内资企业	Enterprises of Other Types of Ownership	0.05	0.53	0.48	0.00	0.00
港澳台商投资企业	Enterprises Funded by Entrepreneurs From Hong Kong,Macao and Taiwan	0.15	2.42	7.26	0.56	0.55
外商投资企业	Enterprises funded by Foreigners	0.18	9.49	1.61	0.16	0.80
工业销售产值	Industrial Sales Value	84.84	438.25	220.03	15.62	82.92
实收资本	Total Capital Hold	25.17	122.56	76.35	8.17	27.49
#外商资本	#Foreign Capital	0.17	1.57	11.13	0.64	0.64
工业中间投入	Industrial Input	60.82	323.03	133.68	9.97	63.35

单位：亿元　　10-4 续表 2　continued　　(100 million yuan)

指标	Item	郴州市 Chenzhou City	永州市 Yongzhou City	怀化市 Huaihua City	娄底市 Loudi City	湘西州 West Hunan A.P
企业单位数　(个)	Number of Enterprises　(unit)	591	300	314	220	232
#大型企业	#Largest Enterprise	5	1	1	6	2
#中型企业	#Medium-sized Enterprises	41	25	24	23	15
#小型企业	#Small Enterprises	545	274	289	191	215
#亏损企业	#Loss-making Enterprises	35	76	88	59	88
工业总产值(现价)	Gross Industrial Output Value	167.59	98.77	87.06	139.06	39.03
内资企业	Internal-invested Enterprises	153.67	95.16	82.87	138.91	38.86
国有企业	State-owned Enterprises	44.48	23.19	35.77	82.40	16.31
集体企业	Collective-owned Enterprises	27.58	3.76	4.81	9.72	0.74
股份合作企业	Enterprises Cooperated by Joint-stock	14.18	1.13	1.13	1.51	0.67
联营企业	Cooperative Enterprises	1.11	0.24	0.06	0.28	0.51
有限责任公司	Limited Liability Company	5.84	11.54	20.40	25.66	1.64
股份有限公司	Company Limited by Shares	8.03	38.46	6.74	7.90	4.63
私营企业	Individual-owned Enterprises	52.29	16.84	12.68	11.20	14.01
其他内资企业	Enterprises of Other Types of Ownership	0.17	0.00	1.28	0.25	0.34
港澳台商投资企业	Enterprises Funded by Entrepreneurs From Hong Kong,Macao and Taiwan	13.01	1.89	0.28	0.14	0.17
外商投资企业	Enterprises funded by Foreigners	0.91	1.72	3.91	0.00	0.00
工业总产值指数（%）	Index of Industrial Output Value	142.63	125.27	123.60	117.78	109.81
工业增加值(生产法)	Value Added of Industry	61.07	31.67	38.18	47.42	13.90
内资企业	Internal-invested Enterprises	56.00	30.43	37.07	47.40	13.86
国有企业	State-owned Enterprises	19.88	10.27	19.76	31.31	6.25
集体企业	Collective-owned Enterprises	9.44	1.11	1.81	3.15	0.20
股份合作企业	Enterprises Cooperated by Joint-stock	4.66	0.34	0.42	0.44	0.38
联营企业	Cooperative Enterprises	0.44	0.09	0.02	0.10	0.12
有限责任公司	Limited Liability Company	1.39	3.64	8.36	5.97	0.45
股份有限公司	Company Limited by Shares	2.81	9.79	2.61	3.08	2.45
私营企业	Individual-owned Enterprises	17.34	5.17	3.79	3.25	3.92
其他内资企业	Enterprises of Other Types of Ownership	0.05	0.00	0.31	0.09	0.09
港澳台商投资企业	Enterprises Funded by Entrepreneurs From Hong Kong,Macao and Taiwan	4.83	0.74	0.06	0.02	0.04
外商投资企业	Enterprises funded by Foreigners	0.24	0.50	1.04	0.00	0.00
工业销售产值	Industrial Sales Value	167.46	100.77	86.69	138.55	41.22
实收资本	Total Capital Hold	55.52	28.63	43.99	35.66	19.25
#外商资本	#Foreign Capital	0.28	0.19	0.29	0	0
工业中间投入	Industrial Input	116.97	72.19	53.29	100.96	27.87

单位：亿元　　10-4 续表 3 continued　　(100 million yuan)

指标	Item	全省总计 Total	长沙市 Changsha City	株洲市 Zhuzhou City	湘潭市 Xiangtan City	衡阳市 Hengyang City
全部从业人员年平均人数 (万人)	Annual Average Number of Obtain Employees (10 000 persons)	158.45	27.66	18.27	13.32	16.96
流动资产	Liquid Assets	1430.33	377.28	170.7	122.76	107.53
#存货	#Inventory	430.21	129.17	47.98	34.38	31.91
产成品	Products	135.88	44.33	14.62	9.9	13.67
流动资产年平均余额	Annual Average Balance of Circulating Funds	1327.44	336.62	165.78	113.19	99.32
固定资产	Fixed Assets	1840.95	277.59	169.67	164.75	160.39
固定资产原价合计	Original Value of Fixed Assets	2510.77	381.75	231.95	232.26	193.41
#生产经营用固定资产	#Production and Operating Fixed Assets	2083.61	334.37	182.29	176.19	144.98
累计折旧	Add up Depreciation of Fixed Assets	868.99	130.27	88.88	85.42	64.47
#本年折旧	#Depreciation of the Year	120.93	20.79	13.03	11.94	8.52
固定资产净值年平均余额	Annual Average Balance of Net Value of Fixed Assets	1558.18	241.12	132.15	139.76	111.28
无形资产	Invisible Assets	136	41.36	18.71	8.16	9.02
资产总计	Total Assets	3642.69	758.29	407.96	304.67	283.88
流动负债合计	Total Liquid Liabilities	1471.89	322.05	188.67	135.88	121.69
长期负债	Long-term Liabilities	798.85	92.84	80.75	49.91	81.09
所有者权益	Creditors Equity	1314.1	343.4	138.55	103.66	77.73
产品销售收入	Sales Revenue	2604.98	567.9	265.94	206.48	197.26
产品销售费用	Cost of Sales	97.33	31.83	9.14	6.26	7.86
产品销售税金及附加	Sales Tax and Extra Charges	106.88	40.26	2.28	1.73	1.27
管理费用	Administrative Expense	187.38	42.78	24.02	18.14	15.94
利息支出	Interest	43.13	6.42	4.27	4.07	3.34
营业利润	Operating Profit	104.76	47.82	7.3	5.66	3.48
利润总额	Total Profit	111.25	47.02	11.62	4.8	6.29
利税总额	Total of Profit and Tax	345.67	115.79	25.81	17.69	14.57
应交所得税	Income Tax Payable	26.07	8.04	1.87	1.88	1.79
本年应付工资总额	Total Wages Payable of the Year	169.28	31.18	23.1	14.48	15.39
本年应付福利费	Fringe Benefits Payable of the Year	22.7	4.63	3.3	1.76	1.88
工业增加值率 (%)	Ratio of Added Value to Gross Output Value (%)	34.03	35.99	29.57	31.78	31.01
每百元固定资产原价实现利税 (元)	Per-tax Profits per 100 yuan of Original Volue of Fixed Assets (yuan)	13.77	30.33	11.13	7.62	7.53
每百元销售收入实现利税 (元)	Per-tax Profits per 100 yuan of Sales Revenue (yuan)	13.27	20.39	9.71	8.57	7.39
流动资金周转天数 (天)	Days of Turnover Circulating Funds (day)	183.45	213.39	224.41	197.35	181.26
全部资金利税率 (%)	Ratio of Per-tax Profits to Total Capital (%)	11.98	20.04	8.66	6.99	6.92
产值利税率 (%)	Ratio of Per-tax Profits to Output Value (%)	13.24	20.52	9.85	8.73	6.9
全员劳动生产率(元/人年)	Overall Labor Productivity (yuan/person-year)	130309	198001	126180	120871	100967

单位：亿元　　10-4 续表 4　continued　　(100 million yuan)

指标	Item	邵阳市 Shaoyang City	岳阳市 Yueyang City	常德市 Changde City	张家界市 Zhangjiajie City	益阳市 Yiyang City
全部从业人员年平均人数 (万人)	Annual Average Number of Obtain Employees (10 000 persons)	8.88	13.67	10.49	1.77	6.76
流动资产	Liquid Assets	44.17	158.87	110.78	9.79	49.55
#存货	#Inventory	12.48	46.17	46.06	1.41	12.59
产成品	Products	4.98	13.97	8.77	0.42	5.78
流动资产年平均余额	Annual Average Balance of Circulating Funds	42.05	150.68	106.02	8.58	38.71
固定资产	Fixed Assets	63.99	201.07	171.57	52.29	79.28
固定资产原价合计	Original Value of Fixed Assets	84.08	330.75	221.05	58.3	105.66
#生产经营用固定资产	#Production and Operating Fixed Assets	74.45	306.37	169.56	45.93	94.78
累计折旧	Add up Depreciation of Fixed Assets	26	142.47	68.38	9.05	33.81
#本年折旧	#Depreciation of the Year	2.84	14.28	11.09	2.07	4.67
固定资产净值年平均余额	Annual Average Balance of Net Value of Fixed Assets	56.39	182.77	157.73	48.46	71.83
无形资产	Invisible Assets	3.21	13.84	10.83	1.71	4.3
资产总计	Total Assets	116.19	410.96	307.79	64.67	138.52
流动负债合计	Total Liquid Liabilities	55.18	167.74	105.23	7.2	55.99
长期负债	Long-term Liabilities	26.62	77	69.03	18.64	50.4
所有者权益	Creditors Equity	32.85	138.92	133.54	38.81	30.52
产品销售收入	Sales Revenue	83.18	417.7	214.02	14.23	79.65
产品销售费用	Cost of Sales	4.2	11.5	7.63	0.35	3.18
产品销售税金及附加	Sales Tax and Extra Charges	1.25	8.76	34.92	0.15	0.71
管理费用	Administrative Expense	6.07	18.71	13.79	0.79	4.9
利息支出	Interest	0.93	5.92	2.89	1.14	2.49
营业利润	Operating Profit	0.67	1.31	14.27	-0.54	-0.53
利润总额	Total Profit	0.61	0.46	12.83	-0.48	0.01
利税总额	Total of Profit and Tax	5.4	22.98	62.91	0.54	4.31
应交所得税	Income Tax Payable	0.36	1.2	4.29	0.05	0.5
本年应付工资总额	Total Wages Payable of the Year	6.85	16.78	11.28	1.16	5.6
本年应付福利费	Fringe Benefits Payable of the Year	0.95	2.08	1.27	0.14	0.67
工业增加值率 (%)	Ratio of Added Value to Gross Output Value (%)	32.22	29.05	46.24	42.33	28.1
每百元固定资产原价实现利税 (元)	Per-tax Profits per 100 yuan of Original Volue of Fixed Assets (yuan)	6.42	6.95	28.46	0.93	4.08
每百元销售收入实现利税 (元)	Per-tax Profits per 100 yuan of Sales Revenue (yuan)	6.49	5.5	29.39	3.79	5.41
流动资金周转天数 (天)	Days of Turnover Circulating Funds (day)	181.99	129.87	178.33	217.06	174.96
全部资金利税率 (%)	Ratio of Per-tax Profits to Total Capital (%)	5.49	6.89	23.85	0.95	3.9
产值利税率 (%)	Ratio of Per-tax Profits to Output Value (%)	6.39	5.27	28.54	3.42	5.19
全员劳动生产率(元/人年)	Overall Labor Productivity (yuan/person-year)	74899	205428	125462	56045	109571

单位：亿元　　10-4 续表 5　continued　　(100 million yuan)

指标	Item	郴州市 Chenzhou City	永州市 Yongzhou City	怀化市 Huaihua City	娄底市 Loudi City	湘西州 West Hunan A.P
全部从业人员年平均人数（万人）	Annual Average Number of Obtain Employees (10 000 persons)	12.16	6.44	6.95	11.17	3.95
流动资产	Liquid Assets	67.13	59.06	32.21	73.6	46.91
#存货	#Inventory	16.13	14.33	6.58	20.96	10.06
产成品	Products	5.2	4.21	2.86	4.41	2.73
流动资产年平均余额	Annual Average Balance of Circulating Funds	64.01	56.1	30.41	69.75	46.23
固定资产	Fixed Assets	125.8	65.24	124.38	128.57	56.36
固定资产原价合计	Original Value of Fixed Assets	167.02	80.09	180.74	179.19	64.53
#生产经营用固定资产	#Production and Operating Fixed Assets	151.14	64.34	141.42	158.51	39.27
累计折旧	Add up Depreciation of Fixed Assets	48.33	25.18	61.27	70.75	14.7
#本年折旧	#Depreciation of the Year	7.17	2.85	6.85	12.35	2.49
固定资产净值年平均余额	Annual Average Balance of Net Value of Fixed Assets	111.78	52.1	115.57	90.66	46.57
无形资产	Invisible Assets	3.14	3.42	3.1	2.11	13.09
资产总计	Total Assets	205.91	134.51	167.68	221.62	120.04
流动负债合计	Total Liquid Liabilities	64.02	61.58	36.28	104.22	46.17
长期负债	Long-term Liabilities	64.63	35.68	73.1	52.1	27.07
所有者权益	Creditors Equity	77.26	36.07	53.67	63.15	45.97
产品销售收入	Sales Revenue	178.03	98.79	77.37	159.06	45.37
产品销售费用	Cost of Sales	6.04	2.4	2.16	2.76	2.03
产品销售税金及附加	Sales Tax and Extra Charges	7.89	3.92	1.01	1.21	1.53
管理费用	Administrative Expense	11.66	7.55	5.26	14.35	3.44
利息支出	Interest	2.74	1.82	3.48	2.11	1.53
营业利润	Operating Profit	11.12	7.75	0.65	5.9	-0.12
利润总额	Total Profit	9.52	8.01	4.44	6.4	-0.28
利税总额	Total of Profit and Tax	27.86	17.02	9.87	16.92	3.99
应交所得税	Income Tax Payable	1.19	2.58	0.46	1.58	0.29
本年应付工资总额	Total Wages Payable of the Year	14.21	5.78	6.11	13.59	3.77
本年应付福利费	Welfare Funds Payable of the Year	2.08	0.64	0.73	2.25	0.33
工业增加值率　(%)	Ratio of Added Value to Gross Output Value (%)	36.44	32.06	43.85	34.1	35.61
每百元固定资产原价实现利税 (元)	Per-tax Profits per 100 yuan of Original Volue of Fixed Assets (yuan)	16.68	21.25	5.46	9.44	6.18
每百元销售收入实现利税　(元)	Per-tax Profits per 100 yuan of Sales Revenue (yuan)	15.65	17.23	12.76	10.64	8.79
流动资金周转天数 (天)	Days of Turnover Circulating Funds (day)	129.44	204.43	141.5	157.86	366.82
全部资金利税率　(%)	Ratio of Per-tax Profits to Total Capital (%)	15.85	15.73	6.76	10.55	4.3
产值利税率　(%)	Ratio of Per-tax Profits to Output Value (%)	16.62	17.23	11.34	12.17	10.22
全员劳动生产率(元/人年)	Overall Labor Productivity (yuan/person-year)	100074	147795	88072	74002	77570

10-5 独立核算工业企业各种分组的主要经济效益指标(2003年)

Major Economic Indicators of Industrial Enterprises with Independent Accounting Systems (2003)

指标	Item	工业增加值率(%) Ratio of Value Added to Gross Industrial Output Value (%)	每百元固定资产原价实现的利税(元) Per-tax Profits per 100 Yuan of Original Value of Fixed Assets (yuan)	每百元销售收入实现的利税(元) Per-tax Profits per 100 Yuan of Sales Revenue (yuan)	流动资金周转天数(天) Number of Days of Turnover Circulating Funds (day)
总计	**Total**	**34.03**	**13.77**	**13.27**	**183.45**
按登记注册类型:	**Grouped by Registration**				
内资企业	Internal-invested Enterprises	34.49	13.74	13.24	185.92
国有企业	State-owned Enterprises	45.33	14.64	20.84	228.83
中央企业	Central Enterprises	60.9	25.39	34.07	213.92
地方企业	Local Enterprises	33.52	5.3	7.97	243.31
集体经济	Collective-owned Enterprises	32.22	19.2	8.09	117.84
股份合作企业	Enterprises Cooperated by Joint-stock	32.31	7.92	7.4	96.17
联营企业	Cooperative Enterprises	32.57	21.45	10.21	110.27
有限责任公司	Limited Liability Company	27.89	7.63	7.54	193.51
股份有限公司	Company Limited by Shares	28.48	14.27	10.49	206.81
私营企业	Individual-owned Enterprises	29.91	23.43	9.29	104.31
其他企业	Enterprises of Other Types of Ownership	30.39	15.23	6.12	114.73
港、澳、台投资经济	Enterprises Funded by Entrepreneurs From Hong Kong,Macao and Taiwan	33.15	19.23	15.2	167.98
外商投资经济	Enterprises funded by Foreigners	26.91	11.17	12.32	150.97
按经济组织类型:	**Grouped by Ownership**				
独资企业	Enterprises Owned by a Sole Investor	40.48	15.41	17.25	190.81
合作、合伙企业	Enterprises of Partnership	31.85	11.71	8.07	94.2
股份有限公司	Company Limited by Shares	28.94	15.31	10.83	197.24
有限责任公司	Limited Liability Company	28.36	10.08	9.38	180.01
国有控股企业	**State-owned or Controlling Share Hold Enterprises**	**37.62**	**12.19**	**15.46**	**219.91**
农村工业	**Rural Industry**	**31.6**	**28.76**	**9.58**	**83.55**
按轻重工业分组	**Grouped by of Enterprises**				
轻工业	Enterprises of Light Industry	39.01	34.01	21.68	185.47
重工业	Enterprises of Heavy Industry	31.69	8.8	9.7	182.59
按企业规模分:	**Grouped by Size of Enterprises**				
大型企业	Large Enterprises	38.02	21.8	19.97	190.69
中型企业	Medium-sized Enterprises	32.21	8.82	10.55	221.04
小型企业	Small Enterprises	31.76	9.88	8.13	144.08

10-5 续表 1 continued

指标	Item	工业增加值率(%) Ratio of Value Added to Gross Industrial Output Value (%)	百元固定资产原价实现利税(元) Per-tax Profits per 100 Yuan of Original Value of Fixed Assets (yuan)	每百元销售收入实现的利税(元) Per-tax Profits per 100 Yuan of Sales Revenue (yuan)	流动资金周转天数(天) Number of Days of Turnover Circulating Funds (day)
按行业划分:	**Grouped by Sector**				
开采和洗选业	Mining and Washing of Coal	38.63	13	11.96	187.03
黑色金属矿采选业	Mining of Ferrous Metal Ores	30.93	5.17	3.78	196.54
有色金属矿采选业	Mining of Non-ferrous Metal Ores	33.43	18.55	10.38	95.75
非金属矿采选业	Mining and Processing of Nonmetal Ores	33.57	16.39	8.19	101.68
其他采矿业	Mining of Other Ores N.E.C				
农副食品加工业	Processing of Food from Agricultural Products	25.46	8.64	3.15	105.53
食品制造业	Manufacture of Foods	30.76	20.12	9.2	129.74
饮料制造业	Manufacture of Beverage	38.13	22.08	18.33	305.21
烟草制品业	Manufacture of Tobacco	72.39	142.34	64.35	211.78
纺织业	Manufacture of Textile	25.18	3.7	1.95	176.83
纺织服装、鞋、帽制造业	Manufacture of Textile Wearing Apparel,Footware and Caps	29.08	26.09	6.98	121.48
皮革、毛皮、羽毛及其制品	Manufacture of Leather,Fur,Feather and Its Products	30.08	29.49	7.15	86.55
木材加工及木、竹、藤、棕、草制品业	Processing of Timbers,Manufacture of Wood, Bamboo, Rattan,Palm and Straw Products	28.1	9.8	6.51	89.39
家具制造业	Manufacture of Furniture	29.51	34.63	7.4	86.63
造纸及纸制品业	Manufacture of Paper and Paper Products	27.78	12.01	9.9	193.55
印刷业和记录媒介的复制	Printing,Reproduction of Recording Media	41.12	28.32	22.26	171.09
文教体育用品制造业	Manufacture of Articles for Culture, Education and Sport Activity	28	14	4.86	105
石油加工炼焦及核燃料加工	Processing of Petroleum,Coking,Processing of Nucleus Fuel	25.75	11.4	7.36	105.01
化学原料及化学制品制造业	Manufacture of Chemical Raw Material and Chemical Products	29.6	5	5.17	185.73
医药制造业	Manufacture of Medicines	34.82	19.74	15.11	278.62
化学纤维制造业	Manufacture of Chemical Fiber	16.68	-0.68	-0.99	162.68
橡胶制品业	Manufacture of Rubber	31.72	19.18	9.6	231.47
塑料制品业	Manufacture of Plastic	31.59	6.1	5.32	213.44
非金属矿物制品业	Manufacture of Non-metallic Mineral Products	30.81	8.72	8.27	165.15
黑色金属冶炼及压延加工业	Manufacture and Processing of Ferrous Metals	33.22	11.69	10.45	139.87
有色金属冶炼及压延加工业	Manufacture and Processing of Non-ferrous Metals	26.77	14.51	8.53	148.83
金属制品业	Manufacture of Metal Products	29.85	10.78	6.26	161.01
通用设备制造业	Manufacture of General Purpose Machinery	30.68	11.38	9.44	341.41
专用设备制造业	Manufacture of Special Purpose Machinery	31.43	18	11.7	263.01
交通运输设备制造业	Manufacture of Transport Equipment	25.76	17.94	11.06	254.32
电气机械及器材制造业	Manufacture of Electrical Machinery and Equipment	28.13	9.81	7.81	257.56
通信设备、计算机及其他电子设备制造业	Manufacture of Communication Equipment,Computer and Other Electronic Equipment	21.2	11.17	10.19	209.66
仪器仪表及文化、办公用机械制造业	Manufacture of Measuring Instrument and Machinery for Cultural Activity and Office Work	30.86	19.34	13.35	241.09
工艺品及其他制造业	Manufacture of Artwork,Other Manufacture N.E.C	27.84	25.35	7.77	75.76
废弃资源废旧材料回收加工	Recycling and Disposal of Waste	30.03	11.21	3.94	17.45
电力、热力的生产和供应业	Production and Supply of Electric Power and Heat Power	56.2	4.92	14.58	181.22
燃气生产和供应业	Production and Distribution of Gas	24.29	6.61	10.53	323.37
水的生产和供应业	Production and Distribution of Water	52.95	2.36	9.24	323.83

指标	Item	全部资金利税率(%) Ratio of Per-tax Profits to Total Capital (%)	产值利税率(%) Ratio of Per-tax Profits to Gross Output Value (%)	全员劳动生产率(元/人·年) Overall Labor Productivity (yuan/person·year)
总计	**Total**	**11.98**	**13.24**	**130309.25**
按登记注册类型:	**Grouped by Registration**			
内资企业	Internal-invested Enterprises	11.89	13.3	117213.49
国有企业	State-owned Enterprises	13.99	23.68	90382.76
中央企业	Central Enterprises	24.78	44.26	175349.75
地方企业	Local Enterprises	4.98	8.07	70618.13
集体经济	Collective-owned Enterprises	13.5	7.41	86644.46
股份合作企业	Enterprises Cooperated by Joint-stock	7.12	7.06	113494.42
联营企业	Cooperative Enterprises	16.55	9.15	91428.57
有限责任公司	Limited Liability Company	6.44	7.38	129965.54
股份有限公司	Company Limited by Shares	10.61	9.89	255901.29
私营企业	Individual-owned Enterprises	15.97	8.43	106744.19
其他企业	Enterprises of Other Types of Ownership	10.29	5.56	106785.71
港、澳、台投资经济	Enterprises Funded by Entrepreneurs From Hong Kong,Macao and Taiwan	14.48	14	215023.58
外商投资经济	Enterprises funded by Foreigners	11.7	11.62	519225.18
按经济组织类型:	**Grouped by Ownership**			
独资企业	Enterprises Owned by a Sole Investor	14.27	18.35	95201.20
合作、合伙企业	Enterprises of Partnership	9.96	7.38	101975.81
股份有限公司	Company Limited by Shares	11.4	10.15	239805.54
有限责任公司	Limited Liability Company	8.5	8.97	160883.44
国有控股企业	**State-owned or Controlling Share Hold Enterprises**	**11.23**	**16.66**	**123196.36**
农村工业	**Rural Industry**	**21.3**	**8.67**	**104432.23**
按轻重工业分组	**Grouped by of Enterprises**			
轻工业	Enterprises of Light Industry	23.7	20.17	131054.32
重工业	Enterprises of Heavy Industry	8.15	9.98	130008.95
按企业规模分:	**Grouped by Size of Enterprises**			
大型企业	Large Enterprises	19.11	21.92	224823.87
中型企业	Medium-sized Enterprises	7.84	10.83	137711.90
小型企业	Small Enterprises	8.31	7.21	92282.24

10-5 续表 3 continued

指标	Item	全部资金利税率(%) Ratio of Per-tax Profits to Total Capital (%)	产值利税率(%) Ratio of Per-tax Profits to Gross Output Value (%)	全员劳动生产率(元/人·年) Overall Labor Productivity (yuan/person·year)
按行业划分:	Grouped by Sector			
开采和洗选业	Mining and Washing of Coal	10.7	11.26	27394.78
黑色金属矿采选业	Mining of Ferrous Metal Ores	3.93	3.61	70232.56
有色金属矿采选业	Mining of Non-ferrous Metal Ores	16.45	10.26	82821.32
非金属矿采选业	Mining and Processing of Nonmetal Ores	14.08	7.74	80464.14
其他采矿业	Mining of Other Ores N.E.C			
农副食品加工业	Processing of Food from Agricultural Products	5.71	2.79	226214.44
食品制造业	Manufacture of Foods	14.47	8.41	101927.37
饮料制造业	Manufacture of Beverage	12.84	17.16	149902.91
烟草制品业	Manufacture of Tobacco	80.12	66.04	554881.89
纺织业	Manufacture of Textile	2.29	1.74	72907.10
纺织服装、鞋、帽制造业	Manufacture of Textile Wearing Apparel,Footware and Caps	13.4	6.71	78291.14
皮革、毛皮、羽毛及其制品	Manufacture of Leather,Fur,Feather and Its Products	16.79	6.36	132500.00
木材加工及木、竹、藤、棕、草制品业	Processing of Timbers,Manufacture of Wood, Bamboo, Rattan,Palm and Straw Products	8.41	5.72	101653.23
家具制造业	Manufacture of Furniture	17.75	6.85	133500.00
造纸及纸制品业	Manufacture of Paper and Paper Products	9.31	9.36	146033.25
印刷业和记录媒介的复制	Printing,Reproduction of Recording Media	24.08	20.39	166341.46
文教体育用品制造业	Manufacture of Articles for Culture, Education and Sport Activity	8.33	4.67	70000.00
石油加工炼焦及核燃料加工	Processing of Petroleum,Coking,Processing of Nucleus Fuel	11.15	7.43	396201.92
化学原料及化学制品制造业	Manufacture of Chemical Raw Material and Chemical Products	4.7	4.97	104353.67
医药制造业	Manufacture of Medicines	11.17	12.42	229765.63
化学纤维制造业	Manufacture of Chemical Fiber	-0.75	-0.95	242473.12
橡胶制品业	Manufacture of Rubber	10.03	9.73	105739.13
塑料制品业	Manufacture of Plastic	4.39	4.53	135474.45
非金属矿物制品业	Manufacture of Non-metallic Mineral Products	7.8	7.47	61776.38
黑色金属冶炼及压延加工业	Manufacture and Processing of Ferrous Metals	11.69	11.22	157854.67
有色金属冶炼及压延加工业	Manufacture and Processing of Non-ferrous Metals	10.92	8.47	204085.37
金属制品业	Manufacture of Metal Products	7	5.82	132845.19
通用设备制造业	Manufacture of General Purpose Machinery	6.52	8.39	111472.08
专用设备制造业	Manufacture of Special Purpose Machinery	10.27	9.92	146600.47
交通运输设备制造业	Manufacture of Transport Equipment	10.19	10.55	227720.50
电气机械及器材制造业	Manufacture of Electrical Machinery and Equipment	6.58	6.97	146428.57
通信设备、计算机及其他电子设备制造业	Manufacture of Communication Equipment,Computer and Other Electronic Equipment	8.22	10.39	782681.82
仪器仪表及文化、办公用机械制造业	Manufacture of Measuring Instrument and Machinery for Cultural Activity and Office Work	12.84	11.1	95698.92
工艺品及其他制造业	Manufacture of Artwork,Other Manufacture N.E.C	17.86	7.62	54653.47
废弃资源废旧材料回收加工	Recycling and Disposal of Waste	21.67	4.02	482000.00
电力、热力的生产和供应业	Production and Supply of Electric Power and Heat Power	6.11	24.61	73435.45
燃气生产和供应业	Production and Distribution of Gas	5.91	10.71	51935.48
水的生产和供应业	Production and Distribution of Water	2.74	8.43	23302.33

10-6 工业产品产量

Output of Industrial Products

产品	Item	2000	2001	2002	2003
化学纤维 (万吨)	Chemical Fiber (10 000 tons)	7.79	6.97	9.02	8.3
纱(混合数) (万吨)	Yarn (10 000 tons)	16.63	16.67	17.89	21.99
纯棉纱 (万吨)	Pure Cotton Yarn (10 000 tons)	-	-	-	-
布(混合数) (亿米)	Cloth (100 million m)	3.41	3.05	2.96	3.41
纯棉布 (亿米)	Pure Cotton Cloth (100 million m)	0.7	0.49	0.58	1.24
针棉织品(折用纱量) (万吨)	Cotton Knitwear (10 000 tons)	0.65	0.64	0.66	1.81
毛巾 (万条)	Towel (10 000 cartons)	5394	5304	5582	11029
袜子 (万双)	Socks (10 000 pairs)	-	-	-	-
服装 (万件)	Clothes (10 000 pieces)	1151	2094	4383	5970
毛线 (吨)	Knitting Wool (ton)	1242	1466.94	1206	1557.3
呢绒 (万米)	Woden Piece Goods (10 000 m)	-	-	-	-
麻袋 (万条)	Gunny-bag (10 000 cartons)	339.75	165.97	273	318.62
丝(不包括土丝) (吨)	Silk (tons)	-	-	-	-
丝织品 (万米)	Silk Fabrics (10 000 m)	10	-	-	-
机制纸浆 (万吨)	Machine_made Paper Pulp (10 000 tons)	31.9	34.94	37.05	50.65
机制纸及纸板 (万吨)	Machine_made Paper and Paper boards (10 000 tons)	70.07	77.61	88.54	124.28
缝纫机 (万架)	Sewing Machine (10 000 units)	1.56	0.94	0.4	0.42
自行车 (万辆)	Bike (10 000 units)	-	-	0.16	-
手表 (万只)	Watch (10 000 units)	-	-	-	-
日用搪瓷制品 (吨)	Household enamel Product (ton)	3187.7	3062	2742	2008
日用陶瓷器 (亿件)	Household Ceramics (100 million units)	9.28	9.61	11.5	13.69
日用精铝制品 (吨)	Household Aluminium Product (10 000 tons)	2479.5	979	827	649
日用玻璃制品 (万吨)	Household Glass Product (10 000 tons)	5.4	4.16	6.11	6.72
保温瓶 (万个)	Vacuum Flask (10 000 units)	1300.69	1330	1342	448.73
自来水笔 (万支)	Pen (10 000 units)	-	94	153	164
圆珠笔 (万支)	Ball-point pen (10 000 units)	-	-	-	-
灯泡 (万只)	Lamp bulb (10 000 units)	12961	10511	13185	16843
合成洗涤剂 (万吨)	Synthetic Detergents (10 000 tons)	8.12	9.27	8.8	22.56
肥皂 (万吨)	Soap (10 000 tons)	1.1	0.67	0.53	0.49
牙膏 (万支)	Toothpaste (10 000 units)	2299.61	2179.67	2677.43	2361.51
火柴 (万件)	Match (10 000 units)	46.03	40.21	39.65	45.44
干电池 (亿只)	Dry Cell (100 million units)	0.57	0.31	0.4	1.46
大米 (万吨)	Rice (10 000 tons)	102.4	97.46	75	70.91
原盐 (万吨)	Salt (10 000 tons)	72.93	68.64	71.12	78.94
糖 (万吨)	Sugar (10 000 tons)	4.44	7.19	7.08	3.49
卷烟 (万箱)	Cigarettes (10 000 cases)	230.43	244.22	247.51	251.63
罐头 (万吨)	Canned Food (10 000 tons)	4.21	5.4	9.86	12.22
软饮料 (万吨)	Soft Drinks (10 000 tons)	12.4	16.36	16.41	16.97

注:2000至2003年产品产量统计口径为全部国有及年产品销售收入500万元以上的非国有工业企业。

Data of product output in 2000-2003 refer to those from all state-owned and the non-state-owned industrial enterprises with an annual sales income of over 5 million yuan.

10-6 续表 1 continued

产品	Item	2000	2001	2002	2003
饮料酒 (万吨)	Liquor (10 000 tons)	30.21	30.68	40.59	44.92
白酒(商品量) (万吨)	Spirit (10 000 tons)	3.76	2.67	2.53	2.61
啤酒 (万吨)	Beer (10 000 tons)	26.42	27.98	37.9	42.21
乳制品 (吨)	Dairy Products (tons)	5577	7182	12446	31057
味精 (吨)	Aginomoto (ton)	4452	3764	4224	1668
食用植物油 (万吨)	Edible Vegetable Oil (10 000 tons)	20.14	19.89	21.32	27.93
化学原料药(24大类) (吨)	Chemical Medicine (ton)	1964.76	1525.02	1619.9	3144.10
中成药 (吨)	Traditional Chinese Medicine (10 000 tons)	11744.53	11118.31	18503.84	18925.15
配混合饲料 (万吨)	Fixed-Forage (10 000 tons)	163.62	186.77	209.68	199.57
塑料制品 (万吨)	Plastics Products (10 000 tons)	7.29	8.28	9.22	10.39
皮鞋 (万双)	Leather Shoe (10 000 units)	429.49	421.43	393.51	556.06
胶鞋 (万双)	Rubber Overshoes (10 000 units)	2782.89	2842	3141.54	3180.53
家用电冰箱 (万台)	Household Refrigerators (10 000 units)	44.54	47.79	55.08	44.73
电风扇 (万台)	Electric Fans (10 000 units)	4.64	12.83	11.84	3.72
房间空气调节器 (台)	Air Conditioners (unit)	34696	17214	-	-
收音机 (万台)	Radio (10 000 units)	-	-	-	-
收录放机 (万台)	Radio Cassette Player (10 000 units)	66	1.5	-	-
电视机 (万台)	Television Sets (10 000 units)	-	0.87	-	-
原煤 (万吨)	Coal (10 000 tons)	1490.81	1546.1	1845.42	2366.69
烟煤 (万吨)	Bituminous Coal (10 000 tons)	778.2	691.64	787.14	869.31
无烟煤 (万吨)	No-Bituminous Coal (10 000 tons)	712.05	854.07	1055.31	1493.38
原油加工量 (万吨)	Crude Process (10 000 tons)	526.42	435.93	468.83	506.53
汽油 (万吨)	Gasoline (10 000 tons)	120.19	108.65	116.33	124.27
柴油 (万吨)	Diesel oil (10 000 tons)	215.53	192.33	185.83	178.87
发电量 (亿千瓦小时)	Electricity (100 million kwh)	354.42	384.35	425.54	523.73
水电 (亿千瓦小时)	Hydro-power (100 million kwh)	191.15	195.27	227.93	232.33
火电 (亿千瓦小时)	Thermal Power (100 million kwh)	163.27	189.07	197.61	291.4
生铁 (万吨)	Pig Iron (10 000 tons)	332.72	417.26	499.44	540.77
钢 (万吨)	Steel (10 000 tons)	304.13	441.9	546.65	590.77
成品钢材 (万吨)	Steel Products (10 000 tons)	299.05	389.01	487.71	558.18
铁道用钢材 (万吨)	Railway Steel (10 000 tons)	1.41	1.65	1.65	2.14
普通大型钢材 (万吨)	Ordinary Large Rolled Stell (10 000 tons)	2.26	2.43	0.55	1.34
普通中型钢材 (万吨)	Ordinary Medium Rolled Stell (10 000 tons)	46.67	73.57	71.76	50.34
普通小型钢材 (万吨)	Ordinary Small Rolled Stell (10 000 tons)	72.91	102.76	133.65	196.73
优质型钢材 (万吨)	High Quality Section Steel (10 000 tons)	12.11	12.79	12.06	12.51
线材 (万吨)	Wire Rod (10 000 tons)	97.24	120.99	168.08	186.72
钢带 (万吨)	Steel Band (10 000 ton)	31.76	34.87	54.66	61.63
无缝钢管 (万吨)	Seamless Steel Pipe (10 000 tons)	31.63	37.74	41.36	42.21
焊接钢管 (万吨)	Welding Steel Pipe (10 000 tons)	2.17	1.68	1.81	2.16

10-6 续表 2 continued

产品	Item	2000	2001	2002	2003
机制焦炭 (万吨)	Machine made Coke (10 000 tons)	207	200.23	200.88	246.86
煤气 (亿立方米)	Coal Gas (100 millions cm)	3.2	3.23	3.41	4.36
铁矿石(成品矿) (万吨)	Iron Mineral (10 000 tons)	4.27	4.31	6.85	13.35
水泥 (万吨)	Cement (10 000 tons)	2395.72	2496.02	2746.5	3054.34
平板玻璃 (万重量箱)	Plate Glass (10 000 weight cases)	735.34	857.93	583.61	763.85
硫酸(折100%) (万吨)	Sulfuric Acid (10 000 tons)	128.17	141.27	124.94	139.61
纯碱 (万吨)	Sode Ash (10 000 tons)	13.03	12.47	14.44	15.78
烧碱(折100%) (万吨)	Caustic Soda (10 000 tons)	20.96	21.53	25.63	25.12
合成氨 (万吨)	Synthetic Ammonia (10 000 tons)	167.3	149.23	179.43	163.5
农用化肥(折纯量) (万吨)	Chemical Fertilizer (10 000 tons)	141.74	146.11	164.04	166.53
氮肥	Nitrogen Fertilizers (10 000 tons)	112.9	119.37	135.41	138.81
磷肥	Phosphate Fertilizers (10 000 tons)	27.57	25.7	27.56	26.51
化学农药(原药折纯量) (万吨)	Chemical Pesticide (10 000 tons)	4.58	4.91	5.81	6.83
电石 (万吨)	Calcium Carbide (10 000 ton)	10.44	11.03	13.12	15.99
塑料树脂及共聚物 (万吨)	Plastics (10 000 tons)	23.1	19.77	23.93	26.22
合成橡胶 (万吨)	Synthetic Rubber (10 000 tons)	9.83	11.17	12.47	14.75
轮胎外胎 (万条)	Tires (10 000 units)	6.74	6.18	6.7	4.89
矿山设备 (吨)	Mining Equipment (ton)	9911.6	9149.1	7504.3	8827.73
起重设备 (吨)	Jack-up Eguiprent (ton)	14810.2	27068.64	39400.3	53991.00
冶炼设备 (吨)	Smelt Equipment (ton)	4540	3016	4136	7602
化工设备 (吨)	Equipment for Chemical Industry (ton)	4292.64	4254	4249	8499
发电设备 (万千瓦)	Power Generating Equipment (10 000 kw)	9.92	5.62	10.82	19.07
交流电动机 (万千瓦)	AC Electric Motor (10 000 kw)	137.59	179.84	238.32	367.49
变压器 (万千伏安)	Transformer (10 000 kva)	494.96	822.58	1162.43	1830.1
泵 (万台)	Pump (10 000 units)	14.24	14.8	13.98	14.41
金属切削机床 (台)	Metal-cutting Machine Tools (unit)	907	1367	1586	992
锻压机械 (吨)	Forging and Pressing Equipment (ton)	1577	1628	2009	1838
汽车 (辆)	Motor Vehicles (unit)	17614	20514	27952	43788
摩托车 (辆)	Motorcycles (unit)	142452	116358	250833	263427
轴承 (万套)	Bearing (10 000 sets)	1940.13	1546.97	1591	1145.52
小型拖拉机 (万台)	Small Tractor (10 000 units)	0.45	0.33	0.17	0.59
内燃机 (万千瓦)	Internal Combustion Engines (10 000 kw)	175.94	140.26	175.45	188.03
工矿电机车 (辆)	Industrial and Mineral Electric Locomotive (unit)	-	-	-	-
铁路机车 (万千瓦)	Railway Locomotive (10 000 KW)	68.96	123.76	131.5	134.26
铁路货车 (辆)	Railway Freight wagons (unit)	3486	3957	2373	2853
民用钢质船舶 (综合吨)	Civil Plate ship (ton)	13541	10733	9191	10023
工业锅炉 (蒸吨)	Industrial Boiler (ton)	2976	3616.85	3911.86	4514.95

10-7 各市、州主要工业产品产量(2003年)

Output of Major Industrial Products (2003)

市州	City and Autonomic Prefect	纱(万吨) Yarn (10 000 tons)	布(亿米) Cloth (100 million meters)	针棉织品(折用纱线)(万吨) Cotton Knitwear (10 000 tons)	机制纸及纸板(万吨) Machine-made Paper and Paperboard (10 000 tons)	缝纫机(万架) Sartorius (10 000 units)	日用陶瓷器(亿件) Household Ceramics (100 million pieces)	灯泡(万只) Lighting Service (10 000 units)
长沙市	Changsha City	1.82	0.11	0.59	7.40		0.42	
株洲市	Zhuzhou City	0.56		0.19	1.41		9.20	253
湘潭市	Xiangtan City	1.87	0.85		0.53	0.10	0.22	
衡阳市	Hengyang City	0.45	0.08		3.19		2.15	12366
邵阳市	Shaoyang City	0.68	0.14	0.01	18.28			
岳阳市	Yueyang City	3.79	0.13		37.89		0.05	
常德市	Changde City	6.77	1.05		18.47	0.32		3754
张家界市	Zhangjiajie City							
益阳市	Yiyang City	2.42	0.12		13.17		0.12	470
郴州市	Chenzhou City	0.80	0.14		4.94		0.02	
永州市	Yongzhou City	0.62	0.34		6.19		0.42	
娄底市	Loudi City	0.62			0.28		0.21	
怀化市	Huaihua City	1.33	0.42	1.02	3.66		0.74	
湘西自治州	West Hunan A.P	0.26	0.05	0.01	0.05		0.15	

市州	City and Autonomic Prefect	糖(万吨) Sugar (10 000 tons)	卷烟(万箱) Cigarettes (10 000 cases)	化学原料药(吨) Chemical Medicine (ton)	食用植物油(万吨) Edible Vegetable Oil (10 000 tons)	配混合饲料(万吨) Mixed Fodder (10 000 tons)	钢(万吨) Steel (10 000 tons)	生铁(万吨) Pig Iron (10 000 tons)
长沙市	Changsha City		102.51	473.25	1.90	32.48	0.06	
株洲市	Zhuzhou City			17.00	0.10	33.12	1.96	1.18
湘潭市	Xiangtan City				0.03	3.65	263.32	251.08
衡阳市	Hengyang City			36.00		7.63	32.04	1.75
邵阳市	Shaoyang City		2.03	40.00		9.76		5.10
岳阳市	Yueyang City	0.46		2377.58	17.63	82.80		
常德市	Changde City	1.30	85.52	131.00	5.56	7.13	0.04	
张家界市	Zhangjiajie City				0.40	1.13		
益阳市	Yiyang City	1.73			1.53	3.31		
郴州市	Chenzhou City		28.23			3.74		3.82
永州市	Yongzhou City		23		0.57	2.97		8.51
娄底市	Loudi City					1.12	291.56	269.33
怀化市	Huaihua City		5.80	65.47	0.06	10.24	1.80	
湘西自治州	West Hunan A.P		4.55	3.80	0.15	0.48		

市州	City and Autonomic Prefect	原煤(万吨) Coal (10 000 tons)	发电量(亿千瓦时) Electricity (100 million kw.h)	#水电 Hydro-power	成品钢材(万吨) Steel Products (10 000 tons)	水泥(万吨) Cement (10 000 tons)	平板玻璃(万重量箱) Plate Class (10 000 weight cases)	硫酸(万吨) Sulfuric Acid (10 000 tons)	烧碱(万吨) Caustic Sode (10 000 tons)
长沙市	Changsha City	209.21	1.24	0.95	3.15	451.68			
株洲市	Zhuzhou City	130.38	28.68	2.02	3.90	154.50	483.94	50.48	9.59
湘潭市	Xiangtan City	70.88	42.83	1.17	233.27	237.32		1.95	0.11
衡阳市	Hengyang City	488.12	38.38	10.62	44.23	149.78		29.61	1.84
邵阳市	Shaoyang City	166.40	10.22	7.74	0.92	171.23	69.45	5.32	
岳阳市	Yueyang City		61.05	1.07		72.85		1.74	9.75
常德市	Changde City	99.12	51.03	16.24		436.32	15.07	8.05	
张家界市	Zhangjiajie City	33.34	13.47	13.10		65.59			
益阳市	Yiyang City	22.50	57.90	24.40	1.62	244.68		0.48	
郴州市	Chenzhou City	729.49	59.94	32.35	9.81	348.65	195.35	13.13	2.12
永州市	Yongzhou City	28.82	16.34	16.15	10.55	264.56	0.03	0.82	
娄底市	Loudi City	316.01	34.76	0.82	250.51	230.02		7.57	0.86
怀化市	Huaihua City	62.64	100.82	98.79		171.89		1.73	0.71
湘西自治州	West Hunan A.P	9.78	7.08	6.91	0.22	55.27		18.72	0.14

市州	City and Autonomic Prefect	化学农药(原药)(万吨) Chemical Pesticide (10 000 tons)	化学肥料(折纯量)(万吨) Chemical Fertilizers (10 000 tons)	氮肥 Nitrogen Fertilizers	磷肥 Phosphate Fertilizers	电石(万吨) Calcium Carbide (10 000 tons)	塑料树脂及共聚物(吨) Plastics (ton)	矿山设备(吨) Mining Equipment (ton)	金属切削机床(台) Metal-Cutting Machine Tools (unit)
长沙市	Changsha City	0.63	2.56	1.28	1.28			596	639
株洲市	Zhuzhou City	0.80	18.04	15.20	2.83	4.71	43087		
湘潭市	Xiangtan City	0.30	2.66	2.66		0.01	2	1558	
衡阳市	Hengyang City	0.67	17.50	15.64	1.86			3188	
邵阳市	Shaoyang City		5.60	5.01	0.59				
岳阳市	Yueyang City	3.21	38.19	37.83	0.36		199060		
常德市	Changde City	0.26	14.25	7.63	6.62			2419	
张家界市	Zhangjiajie City		9.65	9.65					
益阳市	Yiyang City	0.64	3.71	3.52	0.19				353
郴州市	Chenzhou City	0.22	14.45	10.94	2.37	2.77	20018	474	
永州市	Yongzhou City		7.99	5.04	2.95				
娄底市	Loudi City	0.08	18.07	16.41	1.66			505	
怀化市	Huaihua City	0.01	12.44	7.99	4.37	8.50		88	
湘西自治州	West Hunan A.P		1.42		1.42				

10-8 国有及国有控股独立核算工业企业主要指标(2003年)

单位:亿元 (100 million yuan)

指标	Item	企业单位数(个) Number of Enterprises (unit)	#亏损企业 Loss-making Enterprises	工业总产值(现价) Gross Industrial Output Value (current price)
总计	**Total**	**1642**	**662**	**1391.74**
在总计中：轻工业	Light Industry	572	221	383.08
重工业	Heavy Industry	1070	441	1008.66
在总计中：大型企业	Large Enterprises	53	16	808.43
中型企业	Medium-sized Enterprises	273	91	389.74
小型企业	Small Enterprises	1316	555	193.57
煤炭开采和洗选业	Mining and Washing of Coal	85	37	33.72
黑色金属矿采选业	Mining of Ferrous Metal Ores	6	4	1.05
有色金属矿采选业	Mining of Non-ferrous Metal Ores	26	9	7.62
非金属矿采选业	Mining and Processing of Nonmetal Ores	16	5	3.84
农副食品加工业	Processing of Food from Agricultural Products	126	39	41.00
食品制造业	Manufacture of Foods	27	5	8.51
饮料制造业	Manufacture of Beverage	39	14	11.60
烟草制品业	Manufacture of Tobacco	10	3	181.54
纺织业	Manufacture of Textile	50	25	18.29
纺织服装、鞋、帽制造业	Manufacture of Textile Wearing Apparel,Footware and Caps	7	3	1.07
皮革、毛皮、羽毛及其制品	Manufacture of Leather,Fur,Feather and Its Products	4	1	0.73
木材加工及木、竹、藤、棕、草制品业	Processing of Timbers,Manufacture of Wood, Bamboo, Rattan,Palm and Straw Products	17	8	4.03
家具制造业	Manufacture of Furniture	2		0.10
造纸及纸制品业	Manufacture of Paper and Paper Products	36	10	31.87
印刷业和记录媒介的复制	Printing,Reproduction of Recording Media	56	16	11.37
文教体育用品制造业	Manufacture of Articles for Culture,Education and Sport Activity	2	1	0.01
石油加工炼焦及核燃料加工	Processing of Petroleum,Coking,Processing of Nucleus Fuel	6	3	175.72
化学原料及化学制品制造业	Manufacture of Chemical Raw Material and Chemical Products	123	44	90.23
医药制造业	Manufacture of Medicines	33	7	27.53
化学纤维制造业	Manufacture of Chemical Fiber	5	2	13.49
橡胶制品业	Manufacture of Rubber	12	7	5.99
塑料制品业	Manufacture of Plastic	15	9	2.69
非金属矿物制品业	Manufacture of Non-metallic Mineral Products	145	50	42.58
黑色金属冶炼及压延加工业	Manufacture and Processing of Ferrous Metals	46	17	165.34
有色金属冶炼及压延加工业	Manufacture and Processing of Non-ferrous Metals	41	11	85.97
金属制品业	Manufacture of Metal Products	31	12	6.11
通用设备制造业	Manufacture of General Purpose Machinery	83	35	20.27
专用设备制造业	Manufacture of Special Purpose Machinery	82	32	76.51
交通运输设备制造业	Manufacture of Transport Equipment	83	39	134.38
电气机械及器材制造业	Manufacture of Electrical Machinery and Equipment	52	22	25.10
通信设备、计算机及其他电子设备制造业	Manufacture of Communication Equipment,Computer and Other Electronic Equipment	32	15	13.79
仪器仪表及文化、办公用机械制造业	Manufacture of Measuring Instrument and Machinery for Cultural Activity and Office Work	15	6	2.07
工艺品及其他制造业	Manufacture of Artwork,Other Manufacture N.E.C	4	3	0.08
废弃资源废旧材料回收加工	Recycling and Disposal of Waste			
电力、热力的生产和供应业	Production and Supply of Electric Power and Heat Power	214	102	130.26
燃气生产和供应业	Production and Distribution of Gas	4	3	1.71
水的生产和供应业	Production and Distribution of Water	107	63	15.54

Major Indicators of State - owned and State Holding Industrial Enterprises with Independent Accounting Systems (2003)

单位:亿元 (100 million yuan)

工业增加值(生产法) Value Added of Industry (by producing)	工业中间投入 Industrial Inter-mediate Input	本年应付工资 Wages Payable in This Year	本年应付福利费 Welfare Funds Payable in This Year	全部从业人员年均人数(万人) Average Number of Employees (10 000 persons)	固定资产净值年均余额 Annual Average Balance of Net Value of Fixed Assets	流动负债 Total Liquid Liabilities	长期负债 Long-term Liabilities	所有者权益 Creditors' Equity
523.60	**954.12**	**102.92**	**13.83**	**81.28**	**1148.50**	**1043.49**	**642.68**	**831.82**
191.61	220.01	19.14	2.35	16.75	184.11	223.87	76.80	269.33
331.99	734.11	83.78	11.48	64.52	964.39	819.62	565.88	562.49
320.46	543.05	50.77	6.87	29.54	456.40	492.17	242.51	447.23
132.32	279.64	32.52	4.41	27.01	398.20	345.11	258.60	239.50
70.82	131.43	19.64	2.55	24.72	293.90	206.20	141.57	145.08
13.11	23.01	9.22	1.28	9.66	26.21	25.89	7.99	22.25
0.28	0.81	0.30	0.02	0.16	1.12	2.20	0.44	0.36
3.03	4.97	1.65	0.22	1.69	6.45	5.66	1.38	5.06
1.39	2.79	0.54	0.08	0.63	4.11	3.96	1.55	2.79
10.75	30.39	0.97	0.08	1.39	13.99	22.81	3.98	10.88
2.72	6.21	0.40	0.04	0.42	3.36	6.08	1.27	2.42
4.62	7.97	1.15	0.07	1.05	10.11	18.18	2.78	16.21
131.54	70.52	4.86	0.66	1.25	40.02	55.61	7.32	121.47
3.53	15.31	1.81	0.22	3.06	8.42	17.52	5.86	2.22
0.24	0.87	0.12	0.02	0.18	0.29	1.41	0.12	-0.14
0.29	0.45	0.02		0.06	0.27	0.78	0.07	-0.22
0.88	3.31	0.32	0.05	0.39	8.37	4.85	0.76	5.68
0.02	0.08	0.01		0.01	0.12	0.06		0.13
8.63	24.75	2.22	0.29	1.87	22.62	25.85	25.03	37.27
5.01	6.96	0.83	0.07	0.70	5.53	6.71	0.74	4.95
	0.01			0.01	0.15	0.21	0.00	0.02
44.68	137.30	5.04	0.74	2.02	66.01	70.43	14.90	34.31
23.53	69.90	7.29	0.93	6.89	87.51	83.11	22.37	59.91
9.54	19.83	1.41	0.16	1.19	15.52	19.35	3.42	24.28
1.54	12.30	0.61	0.08	0.55	11.80	7.24	5.72	9.24
2.20	3.98	0.54	0.05	0.59	2.12	3.48	0.08	3.50
0.79	1.99	0.21	0.03	0.22	1.91	1.77	0.82	0.96
12.00	32.98	4.61	0.57	6.13	38.94	46.67	15.75	28.40
57.63	119.92	11.56	1.51	6.54	105.33	119.38	40.64	88.15
20.05	70.04	6.61	0.94	4.46	38.06	48.25	25.73	38.98
2.19	4.20	0.61	0.08	0.73	7.76	8.73	2.38	4.04
5.94	15.11	2.56	0.36	2.75	15.25	40.57	9.08	2.41
25.33	53.66	7.79	1.05	6.47	36.13	75.52	10.79	29.27
36.04	103.59	9.53	1.27	5.72	55.29	119.73	17.85	60.78
6.43	19.86	2.54	0.41	2.20	17.52	34.37	5.66	17.97
3.36	10.92	0.97	0.12	1.07	8.34	16.30	5.06	21.24
0.66	1.51	0.48	0.06	0.45	2.23	6.85	0.96	0.69
0.03	0.06	0.02	0.00	0.02	0.20	0.09	0.01	0.37
76.81	69.17	12.90	1.95	8.33	450.12	125.97	387.34	140.36
0.64	1.20	0.19	0.03	0.28	2.31	3.65	0.18	3.33
8.17	8.19	3.03	0.40	2.14	35.02	14.28	14.65	32.26

单位:亿元　　10-8 续表　continued　　(100 million yuan)

指标	Item	流动资产年均余额 Annual Average Balance of Circulating Funds	实收资本 Total Capital Hold	流动资产合计 Total Circulating Funds
总计	**Total**	915.97	513.20	969.27
在总计中：轻工业	Light Industry	251.43	135.74	273.51
重工业	Heavy Industry	664.54	377.46	695.76
在总计中：大型企业	Large Enterprises	490.65	213.71	509.55
中型企业	Medium-sized Enterprises	298.89	174.07	325.53
小型企业	Small Enterprises	126.42	125.41	134.19
煤炭开采和洗选业	Mining and Washing of Coal	25.04	16.67	23.78
黑色金属矿采选业	Mining of Ferrous Metal Ores	1.46	0.86	1.45
有色金属矿采选业	Mining of Non-ferrous Metal Ores	4.10	4.67	4.24
非金属矿采选业	Mining and Processing of Nonmetal Ores	3.54	1.68	3.31
农副食品加工业	Processing of Food from Agricultural Products	16.65	14.93	17.37
食品制造业	Manufacture of Foods	4.99	3.31	5.42
饮料制造业	Manufacture of Beverage	20.99	8.25	20.07
烟草制品业	Manufacture of Tobacco	109.73	31.36	114.58
纺织业	Manufacture of Textile	10.51	5.68	13.07
纺织服装、鞋、帽制造业	Manufacture of Textile Wearing Apparel,Footware and Caps	0.85	0.32	1.02
皮革、毛皮、羽毛及其制品	Manufacture of Leather,Fur,Feather and Its Products	0.21	0.08	0.20
木材加工及木、竹、藤、棕、草制品业	Processing of Timbers,Manufacture of Wood, Bamboo, Rattan,Palm and Straw Products	2.71	6.16	2.45
家具制造业	Manufacture of Furniture	0.07	0.02	0.07
造纸及纸制品业	Manufacture of Paper and Paper Products	25.24	20.63	34.06
印刷业和记录媒介的复制	Printing,Reproduction of Recording Media	4.65	4.11	5.22
文教体育用品制造业	Manufacture of Articles for Culture,Education and Sport Activity	0.07	0.04	0.07
石油加工炼焦及核燃料加工	Processing of Petroleum,Coking,Processing of Nucleus Fuel	51.61	21.93	51.14
化学原料及化学制品制造业	Manufacture of Chemical Raw Material and Chemical Products	70.15	64.95	69.82
医药制造业	Manufacture of Medicines	20.59	10.53	23.46
化学纤维制造业	Manufacture of Chemical Fiber	5.95	5.32	5.27
橡胶制品业	Manufacture of Rubber	4.10	1.65	4.34
塑料制品业	Manufacture of Plastic	1.58	1.40	1.29
非金属矿物制品业	Manufacture of Non-metallic Mineral Products	35.84	26.03	38.04
黑色金属冶炼及压延加工业	Manufacture and Processing of Ferrous Metals	75.96	24.93	86.69
有色金属冶炼及压延加工业	Manufacture and Processing of Non-ferrous Metals	42.90	28.79	44.10
金属制品业	Manufacture of Metal Products	6.02	4.14	5.80
通用设备制造业	Manufacture of General Purpose Machinery	26.01	9.36	29.90
专用设备制造业	Manufacture of Special Purpose Machinery	59.49	17.99	65.33
交通运输设备制造业	Manufacture of Transport Equipment	102.49	46.88	106.60
电气机械及器材制造业	Manufacture of Electrical Machinery and Equipment	29.22	13.55	29.94
通信设备、计算机及其他电子设备制造业	Manufacture of Communication Equipment,Computer and Other Electronic Equipment	21.13	13.91	19.10
仪器仪表及文化、办公用机械制造业	Manufacture of Measuring Instrument and Machinery for Cultural Activity and Office Work	3.76	2.55	4.20
工艺品及其他制造业	Manufacture of Artwork,Other Manufacture N.E.C	0.21	0.30	0.21
废弃资源废旧材料回收加工	Recycling and Disposal of Waste	0.00	0.00	0.00
电力、热力的生产和供应业	Production and Supply of Electric Power and Heat Power	113.20	80.05	120.48
燃气生产和供应业	Production and Distribution of Gas	2.22	3.52	3.31
水的生产和供应业	Production and Distribution of Water	12.75	16.67	13.86

单位:亿元 10-8 续表 continued (100 million yuan)

固定资产原价合计 Original Value of Fixed Assets	累计折旧 Add up Depreciation of Fixed Assets	#本年折旧 Depreciation of this Year	产品销售收入 Sales Revenue	#销售税金及附加 Sales Tax and Extra Charges	利润总额 Total Profits	利税总额 Total Profits and Tax
1901.90	693.21	89.29	1499.44	93.13	52.68	231.80
310.38	119.69	13.90	377.51	80.21	25.86	134.61
1591.52	573.52	75.39	1121.93	12.92	26.82	97.18
830.75	324.14	45.59	907.64	84.20	45.34	184.62
649.85	239.82	30.80	422.07	7.27	7.10	36.59
421.30	129.26	12.90	169.73	1.66	0.24	10.59
42.84	15.43	1.40	31.32	0.29	-0.19	2.49
2.17	0.89	0.06	0.83		-0.23	-0.19
11.44	4.94	0.41	7.42	0.06	0.14	0.59
7.56	3.30	0.26	3.67	0.14	-0.20	0.28
19.07	4.42	0.40	35.95	0.10	0.13	0.38
4.23	0.94	0.10	8.74	0.07	0.70	1.18
15.13	5.22	0.81	12.25	1.43	0.05	2.46
84.23	43.70	5.14	186.69	77.53	22.16	120.21
13.62	5.54	0.58	17.34	0.08	-0.69	-0.07
0.58	0.24	0.03	1.15	0.01	0.01	0.07
0.42	0.10		0.72	0.01	-0.01	0.01
10.68	2.68	0.28	3.46	0.02	-0.15	0.02
0.12	0.01		0.11			
36.83	13.79	0.78	33.22	0.26	1.64	3.42
9.91	4.44	0.71	10.72	0.03	1.20	1.83
0.19	0.04					
115.73	47.87	5.52	177.22	6.72	0.07	13.05
162.08	74.86	6.59	92.72	0.48	-7.18	-3.50
21.57	5.32	0.80	24.08	0.17	1.88	3.89
20.31	7.60	0.87	13.11	0.03	-1.22	-0.84
3.26	1.10	0.14	6.36	0.02	0.23	0.43
3.16	1.20	0.09	2.15	0.01	-0.54	-0.45
65.27	25.94	2.64	39.59	0.36	-0.23	2.53
189.41	65.64	14.18	174.02	1.10	7.06	20.37
67.27	25.40	3.10	89.15	0.24	3.03	7.39
9.97	2.41	0.33	5.88	0.14	-0.30	0.12
26.39	10.82	1.49	16.91	0.09	-0.72	0.15
59.80	22.23	2.86	71.57	0.28	3.65	6.42
88.08	31.49	4.57	135.61	1.63	7.96	14.84
30.87	12.94	1.12	25.56	0.13	0.19	1.50
14.20	6.38	0.48	15.32	0.05	-0.27	0.27
4.35	1.65	0.06	1.87	0.01	-0.17	-0.06
0.28	0.09	0.01	0.08		-0.01	-0.01
700.60	226.95	31.06	238.73	1.50	14.38	31.60
4.22	1.21	0.08	1.74	0.02	0.16	0.30
56.03	16.46	2.32	14.18	0.13	0.16	1.11

10-9 独立核算国有及国有控股工业企业

主要经济效益指标(2003年)

Major Economic Benefit Indicators of

State – owned and State Holding Industrial Enterprises (2003)

单位：% (%)

指标	Item	工业增加值率 Ratio of Added to Gross Industrial Output Value	总资产贡献率 Ratio of Total Assets to Industrial Output Value	总资产负债率 Assets-Liability Ratio	成本费用利润率 Ratio of Profits to Cost
总计	**Total**	**37.62**	**10.24**	**67.56**	**3.94**
按登记注册类型：	**Grouped by Registration**				
内资企业	Internal-invested Enterprises	37.64	10.20	67.91	3.82
国有企业	State-owned Enterprises	45.33	11.97	70.88	5.58
中央企业	Central Enterprises	60.90	21.48	73.78	12.03
地方企业	Local Enterprises	33.52	4.83	68.65	1.26
集体经济	Collective-owned Enterprises	34.00	7.36	74.15	3.39
股份合作企业	Enterprises Cooperated by Joint-stock	48.70	-0.12	40.86	-8.65
联营企业	Cooperative Enterprises	28.53	4.81	70.54	0.34
有限责任公司	Limited Liability Company	27.36	5.61	67.74	0.69
股份有限公司	Company Limited by Shares	27.93	9.10	58.72	2.94
私营企业	Individual-owned Enterprises	30.44	8.38	40.85	0.44
港、澳、台投资经济	Enterprises Funded by Entrepreneurs From Hong Kong,Macao and Taiwan	37.91	20.31	49.01	14.01
外商投资经济	Enterprises funded by Foreigners	34.53	8.63	24.35	5.39
按经济组织类型：	**Grouped by Ownership**				
独资企业	Enterprises Owned by a Sole Investor	45.28	11.96	70.88	5.58
合作、合伙企业	Enterprises of Partnership	41.13	1.31	40.95	-3.29
股份有限公司	Company Limited by Shares	27.95	9.08	58.66	2.94
有限责任公司	Limited Liability Company	28.15	6.08	65.98	1.31
按轻重工业分组	**Grouped by of Enterprises**				
轻工业	Enterprises of Light Industry	50.02	24.05	53.01	9.47
重工业	Enterprises of Heavy Industry	32.91	6.14	71.75	2.52
按企业规模分：	**Grouped by Size of Enterprises**				
大型企业	Large Enterprises	39.64	13.50	62.94	6.00
中型企业	Medium-sized Enterprises	33.95	7.74	72.14	1.72
小型企业	Small Enterprises	36.59	3.67	70.86	0.14

单位：%　　　　10-9 续表 1　　　　(%)

指标	Item	工业增加值率 Ratio of Added to Gross Industrial Output Value	总资产贡献率 Ratio of Total Assets to Industrial Output Value	总资产负债率 Assets-Liability Ratio	成本费用利润率 Ratio of Profits to Cost
按行业划分:	**Grouped by Sector**				
开采和洗选业	Mining and Washing of Coal	38.88	4.77	60.61	-0.58
黑色金属矿采选业	Mining of Ferrous Metal Ores	26.67	-1.65	88.00	-20.91
有色金属矿采选业	Mining of Non-ferrous Metal Ores	39.76	5.49	58.25	1.92
非金属矿采选业	Mining and Processing of Nonmetal Ores	36.20	5.43	67.48	-5.25
农副食品加工业	Processing of Food from Agricultural Products	26.22	1.49	71.35	0.36
食品制造业	Manufacture of Foods	31.96	14.06	75.36	8.93
饮料制造业	Manufacture of Beverage	39.83	6.98	56.46	0.46
烟草制品业	Manufacture of Tobacco	72.46	67.22	34.14	25.47
纺织业	Manufacture of Textile	19.30	0.56	91.45	-3.76
纺织服装、鞋、帽制造业	Manufacture of Textile Wearing Apparel,Footware and Caps	22.43	5.11	109.93	0.88
皮革、毛皮、羽毛及其制品	Manufacture of Leather,Fur,Feather and Its Products	39.73	0.80	133.33	-1.35
木材加工及木、竹、藤、棕、草制品业	Processing of Timbers,Manufacture of Wood, Bamboo, Rattan,Palm and Straw Products	21.84	0.72	50.00	-3.95
家具制造业	Manufacture of Furniture	20.00	0.00	36.84	0.00
造纸及纸制品业	Manufacture of Paper and Paper Products	27.08	5.60	58.08	5.20
印刷业和记录媒介的复制	Printing,Reproduction of Recording Media	44.06	14.82	60.26	12.63
文教体育用品制造业	Manufacture of Articles for Culture, Education and Sport Activity	0.00	0.00	87.50	
石油加工炼焦及核燃料加工	Processing of Petroleum,Coking,Processing of Nucleus Fuel	25.43	12.04	72.24	0.04
化学原料及化学制品制造业	Manufacture of Chemical Raw Material and Chemical Products	26.08	-0.50	67.91	-7.15
医药制造业	Manufacture of Medicines	34.65	10.47	48.46	8.48
化学纤维制造业	Manufacture of Chemical Fiber	11.42	-1.91	58.40	-8.98
橡胶制品业	Manufacture of Rubber	36.73	6.40	50.42	3.78
塑料制品业	Manufacture of Plastic	29.37	-10.04	73.70	-19.42
非金属矿物制品业	Manufacture of Non-metallic Mineral Products	28.18	3.14	69.17	-0.58
黑色金属冶炼及压延加工业	Manufacture and Processing of Ferrous Metals	34.86	10.83	64.52	4.34
有色金属冶炼及压延加工业	Manufacture and Processing of Non-ferrous Metals	23.32	8.44	65.60	3.50
金属制品业	Manufacture of Metal Products	35.84	2.56	73.44	-5.06
通用设备制造业	Manufacture of General Purpose Machinery	29.30	1.15	95.40	-4.07
专用设备制造业	Manufacture of Special Purpose Machinery	33.11	8.19	74.68	5.22
交通运输设备制造业	Manufacture of Transport Equipment	26.82	8.44	69.39	6.08
电气机械及器材制造业	Manufacture of Electrical Machinery and Equipment	25.62	3.76	69.05	0.75
通信设备、计算机及其他电子设备制造业	Manufacture of Communication Equipment,Computer and Other Electronic Equipment	24.37	1.36	50.68	-1.73
仪器仪表及文化、办公用机械制造业	Manufacture of Measuring Instrument and Machinery for Cultural Activity and Office Work	31.88	1.36	91.76	-6.91
工艺品及其他制造业	Manufacture of Artwork,Other Manufacture N.E.C	37.50	-1.63	21.74	-9.09
废弃资源废旧材料回收加工	Recycling and Disposal of Waste				
电力、热力的生产和供应业	Production and Supply of Electric Power and Heat Power	58.97	6.17	79.02	7.27
燃气生产和供应业	Production and Distribution of Gas	37.43	5.34	53.49	9.47
水的生产和供应业	Production and Distribution of Water	52.57	3.33	47.48	1.12

10-9 续表 2 continued

指标	Item	产品销售率(%) Proportion of Products Sold (%)	流动资金周转次数(次) Number of Times of Annual of Turnover Circulating Funds (time)	全员劳动生产率(元/人年) Overall Labor Productivity (yuan/ person-year)
总计	**Total**	**100.51**	**1.64**	**123196.36**
按登记注册类型:	**Grouped by Registration**			
内资企业	Internal-invested Enterprises	100.54	1.64	120935.24
国有企业	State-owned Enterprises	100.33	1.57	90382.76
中央企业	Central Enterprises	100.62	1.68	175349.75
地方企业	Local Enterprises	100.12	1.48	70618.13
集体经济	Collective-owned Enterprises	96.50	2.49	70434.78
股份合作企业	Enterprises Cooperated by Joint-stock	99.68	3.16	138666.67
联营企业	Cooperative Enterprises	98.27	2.77	140000.00
有限责任公司	Limited Liability Company	100.54	1.69	133935.88
股份有限公司	Company Limited by Shares	100.87	1.74	314506.85
私营企业	Individual-owned Enterprises	118.89	3.14	118750.00
港、澳、台投资经济	Enterprises Funded by Entrepreneurs From Hong Kong,Macao and Taiwan	96.27	1.87	301785.71
外商投资经济	Enterprises funded by Foreigners	103.38	1.43	324878.05
按经济组织类型:	**Grouped by Ownership**			
独资企业	Enterprises Owned by a Sole Investor	100.32	1.58	90362.36
合作、合伙企业	Enterprises of Partnership	99.33	2.76	145438.60
股份有限公司	Company Limited by Shares	100.86	1.74	313478.26
有限责任公司	Limited Liability Company	100.65	1.70	142030.11
按轻重工业分组	**Grouped by of Enterprises**			
轻工业	Enterprises of Light Industry	101.15	1.50	152734.33
重工业	Enterprises of Heavy Industry	100.26	1.69	115547.12
按企业规模分:	**Grouped by Size of Enterprises**			
大型企业	Large Enterprises	100.85	1.85	176682.46
中型企业	Medium-sized Enterprises	100.14	1.41	121343.95
小型企业	Small Enterprises	99.80	1.34	61351.13

指标	Item	产品销售率(%) Proportion of Products Sold (%)	流动资金周转次数(次) Number of Times of Annual of Turnover Circulating Funds (time)	全员劳动生产率(元/人年) Overall Labor Productivity (yuan/person-year)
按行业划分:	**Grouped by Sector**			
开采和洗选业	Mining and Washing of Coal	100.00	1.25	14461.70
黑色金属矿采选业	Mining of Ferrous Metal Ores	100.00	0.57	53750.00
有色金属矿采选业	Mining of Non-ferrous Metal Ores	102.23	1.81	34319.53
非金属矿采选业	Mining and Processing of Nonmetal Ores	99.22	1.04	45238.10
农副食品加工业	Processing of Food from Agricultural Products	103.61	2.16	206115.11
食品制造业	Manufacture of Foods	100.82	1.75	148333.33
饮料制造业	Manufacture of Beverage	116.81	0.58	84095.24
烟草制品业	Manufacture of Tobacco	100.23	1.70	561040.00
纺织业	Manufacture of Textile	103.50	1.65	63627.45
纺织服装、鞋、帽制造业	Manufacture of Textile Wearing Apparel,Footware and Caps	94.39	1.35	62222.22
皮革、毛皮、羽毛及其制品	Manufacture of Leather,Fur,Feather and Its Products	98.63	3.43	121666.67
木材加工及木、竹、藤、棕、草制品业	Processing of Timbers,Manufacture of Wood, Bamboo, Rattan,Palm and Straw Products	101.49	1.28	96923.08
家具制造业	Manufacture of Furniture	110.00	1.57	90000.00
造纸及纸制品业	Manufacture of Paper and Paper Products	105.08	1.32	152620.32
印刷业和记录媒介的复制	Printing,Reproduction of Recording Media	98.33	2.31	147428.57
文教体育用品制造业	Manufacture of Articles for Culture,Education and Sport Activity	100.00	0.00	10000.00
石油加工炼焦及核燃料加工	Processing of Petroleum,Coking,Processing of Nucleus Fuel	101.56	3.43	398366.34
化学原料及化学制品制造业	Manufacture of Chemical Raw Material and Chemical Products	100.64	1.32	120754.72
医药制造业	Manufacture of Medicines	96.33	1.17	293865.55
化学纤维制造业	Manufacture of Chemical Fiber	99.56	2.20	316000.00
橡胶制品业	Manufacture of Rubber	103.51	1.55	99830.51
塑料制品业	Manufacture of Plastic	100.00	1.36	124090.91
非金属矿物制品业	Manufacture of Non-metallic Mineral Products	100.00	1.10	61745.51
黑色金属冶炼及压延加工业	Manufacture and Processing of Ferrous Metals	100.73	2.29	158776.76
有色金属冶炼及压延加工业	Manufacture and Processing of Non-ferrous Metals	99.34	2.08	159573.99
金属制品业	Manufacture of Metal Products	94.60	0.98	74383.56
通用设备制造业	Manufacture of General Purpose Machinery	97.34	0.65	81163.64
专用设备制造业	Manufacture of Special Purpose Machinery	97.58	1.20	124049.46
交通运输设备制造业	Manufacture of Transport Equipment	100.28	1.32	259318.18
电气机械及器材制造业	Manufacture of Electrical Machinery and Equipment	102.23	0.87	113409.09
通信设备、计算机及其他电子设备制造业	Manufacture of Communication Equipment,Computer and Other Electronic Equipment	103.26	0.73	201214.95
仪器仪表及文化、办公用机械制造业	Manufacture of Measuring Instrument and Machinery for Cultural Activity and Office Work	99.52	0.50	45555.56
工艺品及其他制造业	Manufacture of Artwork,Other Manufacture N.E.C	100.00	0.38	35000.00
废弃资源废旧材料回收加工	Recycling and Disposal of Waste			
电力、热力的生产和供应业	Production and Supply of Electric Power and Heat Power	100.06	2.11	62845.14
燃气生产和供应业	Production and Distribution of Gas	94.74	0.78	26071.43
水的生产和供应业	Production and Distribution of Water	95.11	1.11	20700.93

10-10 大中型工业企业主要指标及在工业中的地位(2003年)

指标	Item	企业单位数(个) Number of Enterprises (unit)	在工业中的地位 Status in Industry (%)	工业总产值(现价)(亿元) Gross Industrial Output Value (current price) (100 million yuan)	在工业中的地位 Status in Industry (%)
总计	**Total**	**535**	**8.97**	**1612.96**	**61.76**
按登记注册类型:	**Grouped by Registration**				
内资企业	Internal-invested Enterprises	489	8.64	1452.5	61.50
国有企业	State-owned Enterprises	203	15.68	627.18	82.29
集体企业	Collective-owned Enterprises	24	2.65	23.56	12.76
股份合作企业	Enterprises Cooperated by Joint-stock	11	3.24	12.03	15.50
有限责任公司	Limited Liability Company	111	15.61	326.04	71.20
股份有限公司	Company Limited by Shares	89	29.37	395.68	87.04
私营企业	Individual-owned Enterprises	48	2.36	64.35	15.67
其他企业	Enterprises of Other Types of Ownership	3	9.09	3.66	52.21
港、澳、台投资企业	Enterprises Funded by Entrepreneurs From Hong Kong,Macao and Taiwan	23	12.71	59.77	54.93
外商投资企业	Enterprises funded by Foreigners	23	18.55	100.69	71.55
按经济组织类型:	**Grouped by Ownership**				
独资企业	Enterprises Owned by a Sole Investor	247	7.86	680.73	59.20
合作、合伙企业	Enterprises of Partnership	19	2.29	22.52	14.03
股份有限公司	Company Limited by Shares	104	21.89	425.8	82.62
有限责任公司	Limited Liability Company	165	10.86	483.91	61.59
按轻重工业分:	**Grouped by Light and Heavy Industry**				
轻工业	Light Industry	169	8.25	459.39	55.04
重工业	Heavy Industry	366	9.34	1153.57	64.93
按行业划分:	**Grouped by Sector**				
煤炭开采和洗选业	Mining and Washing of Coal	18	6.10	29.55	44.92
黑色金属矿采选业	Mining of Ferrous Metal Ores	1	4.17	0.54	13.92
有色金属矿采选业	Mining of Non-ferrous Metal Ores	7	4.43	7.67	21.75
非金属矿采选业	Mining and Processing of Nonmetal Ores	3	2.78	3.67	14.43
农副食品加工业	Processing of Food from Agricultural Products	12	3.31	33.56	24.46
食品制造业	Manufacture of Foods	16	11.03	23.89	50.51
饮料制造业	Manufacture of Beverage	13	11.40	20.64	50.98

Main Indicators of Large and Medium – Sized Enterprises and Status in Industry (2003)

工业增加值（生产法）（亿元） Value Added of Industry (by production) (100 million yuan)	在工业中的地位 Status in Industry (%)	全部从业人员年平均人数（万人） Average Number of Employees (10 000 persons)	在工业中的地位 Status in Industry (%)	固定资产原价合计（亿元） Original Value of Fixed Assets (100 million yuan)	在工业中的地位 Status in Industry (%)	利税总额（亿元） Total Pre-tax Profits (100 million yuan)	在工业中的地位 Status in Industry (%)
571.4	**64.31**	**73.83**	**46.60**	**1781.68**	**70.96**	**273.67**	**79.17**
525.03	64.45	69.81	46.52	1610.62	70.48	249.47	79.43
294.94	85.37	33.74	62.69	920.68	74.65	173.26	95.99
7.62	12.81	1.79	10.84	12.61	17.70	2	14.62
3.89	15.51	0.52	9.67	8.22	11.89	1.47	26.82
88.11	68.99	18.53	63.85	352.26	79.53	25.22	74.66
110.75	85.54	10.27	73.46	278.39	88.34	40.44	89.91
18.66	15.19	4.69	15.58	38	25.73	6.89	19.91
1.06	49.77	0.28	50.00	0.47	18.36	0.18	46.15
20.42	56.61	1.52	35.85	49.25	62.18	11.54	75.77
25.95	68.52	2.51	60.77	121.81	83.21	12.66	77.43
312.18	67.07	37.18	44.80	948.1	69.24	178.21	84.44
6.92	13.54	1.09	8.79	15.18	15.02	1.98	16.72
120.7	80.94	11.17	65.82	294.8	86.24	45.68	87.29
131.6	59.05	24.39	52.94	523.61	74.95	47.8	67.85
215.54	66.20	18.31	39.16	316.44	63.93	150.08	89.16
355.86	63.21	55.52	49.71	1465.25	72.69	123.59	69.69
11.21	44.12	6.77	49.13	37.97	66.63	2.37	31.98
0.13	10.83	0.09	20.93	0.53	19.56	0	0.00
2.76	23.41	1.19	37.30	10.15	52.00	0.59	16.30
1.31	15.34	0.37	15.61	5.18	43.09	0.47	23.86
7.9	22.62	0.88	19.26	13.71	30.91	0.89	23.24
7.8	53.61	1.7	47.49	9.94	50.25	2.6	65.33
8.21	53.17	1.01	49.03	22.57	71.70	4.67	67.19

10-10 续表

指标	Item	企业单位数(个) Number of Enterprises (unit)	在工业中的地位 Status in Industry (%)	工业总产值(现价)(亿元) Gross Industrial Output Value (current price) (100 million yuan)	在工业中的地位 Status in Industry (%)
烟草制品业	Manufacture of Tobacco	9	75.00	181.22	99.56
纺织业	Manufacture of Textile	28	12.67	33.79	43.48
纺织服装、鞋、帽制造业	Manufacture of Textile Wearing Apparel,Footware and Caps	4	5.97	3.02	19.87
皮革、毛皮、羽毛及其制品	Manufacture of Leather,Fur,Feather and Its Products	3	4.23	2.88	13.27
木材加工及木、竹、藤、棕、草制品业	Processing of Timbers,Manufacture of Wood, Bamboo, Rattan,Palm and Straw Products	4	2.00	2.5	7.81
家具制造业	Manufacture of Furniture	1	2.38	1.11	10.70
造纸及纸制品业	Manufacture of Paper and Paper Products	19	8.64	40.85	55.17
印刷业和记录媒介的复制	Printing,Reproduction of Recording Media	5	4.50	15.4	64.09
文教体育用品制造业	Manufacture of Articles for Culture, Education and Sport Activity				
石油加工炼焦及核燃料加工	Processing of Petroleum,Coking,Processing of Nucleus Fuel	5	33.33	175.66	98.59
化学原料及化学制品制造业	Manufacture of Chemical Raw Material and Chemical Products	56	7.78	108.88	50.24
医药制造业	Manufacture of Medicines	16	11.43	24.34	43.44
化学纤维制造业	Manufacture of Chemical Fiber	6	54.55	17.94	89.61
橡胶制品业	Manufacture of Rubber	2	4.26	5.37	39.90
塑料制品业	Manufacture of Plastic	5	4.10	5.19	23.03
非金属矿物制品业	Manufacture of Non-metallic Mineral Products	48	6.62	45.18	30.59
黑色金属冶炼及压延加工业	Manufacture and Processing of Ferrous Metals	20	11.05	169.51	80.78
有色金属冶炼及压延加工业	Manufacture and Processing of Non-ferrous Metals	25	10.78	109.19	66.70
金属制品业	Manufacture of Metal Products	6	3.45	6.77	16.91
通用设备制造业	Manufacture of General Purpose Machinery	23	7.67	31.01	43.82
专用设备制造业	Manufacture of Special Purpose Machinery	29	14.43	106.91	81.12
交通运输设备制造业	Manufacture of Transport Equipment	40	19.14	163.59	84.49
电气机械及器材制造业	Manufacture of Electrical Machinery and Equipment	22	11.00	39.81	50.20
通信设备、计算机及其他电子设备制造业	Manufacture of Communication Equipment,Computer and Other Electronic Equipment	13	17.11	63.11	85.12
仪器仪表及文化、办公用机械制造业	Manufacture of Measuring Instrument and Machinery for Cultural Activity and Office Work	2	4.55	4.47	42.05
工艺品及其他制造业	Manufacture of Artwork,Other Manufacture N.E.C	1	3.13	3.39	46.95
废弃资源废旧材料回收加工	Recycling and Disposal of Waste				
电力、热力的生产和供应业	Production and Supply of Electric Power and Heat Power	64	25.70	121.69	76.27
燃气生产和供应业	Production and Distribution of Gas	1	14.29	1.28	45.71
水的生产和供应业	Production and Distribution of Water	8	7.27	9.39	57.75

continued

工业增加值（生产法）（亿元） Value Added of Industry (by production) (100 million yuan)	在工业中的地位 Status in Industry (%)	全部从业人员年平均人数（万人） Average Number of Employees (10 000 persons)	在工业中的地位 Status in Industry (%)	固定资产原价合计（亿元） Original Value of Fixed Assets (100 million yuan)	在工业中的地位 Status in Industry (%)	利税总额（亿元） Total Pre-tax Profits (100 million yuan)	在工业中的地位 Status in Industry (%)
131.23	99.58	1.24	97.64	84.23	99.73	120.21	99.99
7.71	39.40	4.24	46.34	18.48	50.64	0.67	49.63
0.78	17.65	0.35	22.15	1.04	26.60	0.22	21.57
0.84	12.86	0.21	15.91	1.11	23.72	0.44	31.88
0.46	5.12	0.26	10.48	9.11	48.77	0.08	4.37
0.26	8.50	0.04	6.67	0.24	11.71	0.12	16.90
11.55	56.15	1.99	47.27	41.08	71.21	4.87	70.27
7.28	73.68	0.36	29.27	9.77	56.47	4.35	88.78
44.66	97.34	2.01	96.63	115.69	99.68	13.03	98.49
29.43	45.88	6.85	38.33	168.47	78.10	0.43	3.99
8.9	45.62	1.03	40.23	17.05	48.36	4.14	59.48
2.97	88.92	0.85	91.40	24.78	88.85	-0.32	168.42
2.01	47.07	0.43	37.39	2.52	36.90	0.42	32.06
1.84	25.84	0.22	16.06	5.08	30.38	0.55	53.92
13.54	29.76	4.95	25.86	59.68	47.20	3.79	34.36
58.09	83.33	6.5	74.97	187.33	93.06	21.63	91.89
26.24	59.87	4.58	69.82	75.81	79.34	8.93	64.43
1.85	15.48	0.52	21.76	7.07	32.72	0.6	25.75
9.92	45.69	1.95	32.99	24.5	46.94	3.69	62.12
33.98	82.04	6.01	70.21	56.58	77.85	11.85	90.60
41.58	83.38	5.98	68.50	93.14	81.80	19.48	95.35
10.92	48.95	2.4	50.42	38.84	68.89	2.84	51.36
12.41	78.94	1.35	61.36	61.05	88.57	7.13	92.60
1.34	40.85	0.19	20.43	1.23	20.16	0.8	67.80
0.98	48.76	0.49	48.51	0.58	26.73	0.34	61.82
65.77	73.34	5.95	65.10	540.31	67.66	30.47	77.61
0.4	58.82	0.12	38.71	1.69	37.22	0.33	110.00
5.13	59.58	0.76	35.35	35.13	60.44	1	72.99

10-11 按全省人口平均的主要产品产量

Per Capita Output of Major Industrial Products

产品	Item	2000	2001	2002	2003
化学纤维（公斤/人）	Chemical Fiber (kg / person)	1.19	1.06	1.36	1.35
纱(混合数)（公斤/人）	Yarn (kg / person)	2.53	2.53	2.71	3.58
纯棉纱（公斤/人）	Pure Cotton Yarn (kg / person)				
布(混合数)（米/人）	Cloth (m / person)	5.19	4.64	4.47	5.55
针棉织品(折用纱量)（公斤/人）	Cotton Knitwear (kg / person)	0.1	0.07	0.10	0.29
丝织品(不包括土丝织品)（米/人）	Silk Fabrics (m/ person)	0.002			
机制纸及纸板（公斤/人）	Machine-made Paper and Paperboards (kg/person)	10.68	11.79	13.40	20.24
缝纫机（架/百人）	Sewing Machine (unit / 100 persons)	0.02	0.01	0.01	0.01
自行车（辆/百人）	Bicycle (unit / 100 persons)				
手表（只/百人）	Watch (leather / 100 persons)				
日用陶瓷器（件/人）	Household Ceramics (piece / person)	14.14	14.60	17.40	22.29
日用精铝制品（公斤/百人）	Household Aluminium Products (kg/100 persons)	3.78	1.49	1.25	1.06
合成洗涤剂（公斤/人）	Synthetic Detergents (kg / person)	1.24	1.41	1.33	3.67
原盐（公斤/人）	Salt (kg / person)	11.11	10.43	10.76	12.86
糖（公斤/人）	Sugar (kg / person)	0.68	1.09	1.07	0.57
卷烟（箱/百人）	Cigarette (case /100 persons)	3.51	3.71	3.74	4.10
家用电冰箱（台/百人）	Household Refrigerators (unit / 100 persons)	0.68	0.73	0.83	0.73
电视机（台/百人）	Television (unit / 100 persons)				
原煤（吨/人）	Coal (ton / person)	0.23	0.24	0.28	0.39
原油加工量（公斤/人）	Processing Output of Crude Oil (kg / person)	80.22	66.25	70.91	82.49
发电量（千瓦小时/人）	Electricity (kwh / person)	540.11	584.12	643.63	852.89
生铁（公斤/人）	Pig Iron (kg / person)	50.7	63.41	75.54	88.06
钢（公斤/人）	Steel (kg / person)	46.35	67.16	82.68	96.21
成品钢材（公斤/人）	Steel Products (kg / person)	45.57	59.12	73.77	90.90
水泥（吨/人）	Cement (ton / person)	0.37	0.38	0.42	0.50
平板玻璃（重量箱/人）	Plate Glass (weight case / person)	0.11	0.13	0.09	0.12
硫酸(折100)（公斤/人）	Sulfuric Acid (kg / person)	19.53	21.47	18.90	22.74
纯碱（公斤/人）	Soda Ash (kg / person)	1.99	1.90	2.19	2.56
烧碱(折100)（公斤/人）	Caustic Soda (kg / person)	3.19	3.27	3.88	4.09
合成氨（公斤/人）	Synthetic Ammonia (kg / person)	25.49	22.68	27.14	26.62
农用化肥(折纯量)（公斤/人）	Chemical Fertilizer (kg / person)	21.6	22.21	24.81	27.12
氮肥（公斤/人）	Nitrogen Fertilizer (kg / person)	17.21	18.14	20.48	22.61
磷肥（公斤/人）	Phosphate Fertilizer (kg / person)	4.2	3.91	4.17	4.32
化学农药(原药折纯量)（公斤/人）	Chemical Pesticide (kg / person)	0.7	0.75	0.88	1.11
塑料树脂及共聚物（公斤/人）	Plastics (kg / person)	3.52	3.00	3.62	4.26
合成橡胶（公斤/人）	Synthetic Rubber (kg/person)	1.5	1.70	1.89	2.40
汽车（辆/万人）	Motor Vehicles (unit/10 000 persons)	2.68	3.12	4.23	7.13
摩托车（辆/万人）	Motorcycles (unit/10 000 persons)	21.72	17.68	37.94	42.90

注:人均的主要产品产量统计口径为全部国有及年产品销售收入500万元以上的非国有工业企业,其中2003年按常驻人口计算。

Data of per capita output of major industrial products refer to those from all state-owned and the non-state-owned industrial enterprises with annual sales income of over 5 million yuan. The data are based on the permanent population in 2003.

10-12 工业企业能源购进、消费及库存(2003年)

Energy Purchase,Consumption and Stock of Industry (2003)

指标	Item	年初库存 Stock at the Beginning of the Year	购进量实物量 Total Purchase	消费量合计 Total Consumption	#生产消费 For Production	#原材料 Material Use	年末库存 Stock at the End of the Year
能源合计 (吨标准煤)	**Total Energy (ton of SCE)**	**2096324**	**49551054**	**55791773**	**55103033**	**3408934**	**1997141**
原煤 (吨)	Raw Coal (ton)	1847263	34406166	34720746	34524590	3129847	1932168
洗精煤 (吨)	Cleaned Coal (ton)	221886	3609152	3656779	3656673	337137	280022
其他洗煤 (吨)	Other Washed Coal (ton)	473	10461	8575	8487	759	2358
型煤 (吨)	Briquettes (ton)						
焦炭 (吨)	Coke (ton)	105388	2107305	3943733	3910401	187227	135515
其他焦化产品 (吨)	Other Coking Products (ton)	240	7779	5938	5938		157
焦炉煤气 (万立方米)	Coke Oven Gas (10 000 cu.m)		2287	81669	79438		
高炉煤气 (万立方米)	High Oven Gas (10 000 cu.m)		25738	841792	837996		
其他煤气 (万立方米)	Other Coal Gas (10 000 cu.m)		18056	34641	34511		
天然气 (万立方米)	Natural Gas (10 000 cu.m)						
原油 (吨)	Crude Oil (ton)	194745	5315378	5067164	5067148		83302
汽油 (吨)	Gasoline (ton)	19247	50017	54463	28223	5438	12351
煤油 (吨)	Kerosene (ton)	3820	5605	5754	5382	12	1573
柴油 (吨)	Diesel Oil (ton)	27887	165069	162098	136116	9809	20460
燃料油 (吨)	Fuel Oil (ton)	30959	183807	225327	225278		61380
液化石油气 (吨)	Liquefied Petroleum Gas (ton)	578	280965	261668	261101		529
炼厂干气 (吨)	Refinery Gas (ton)		24298	184234	184234		
其他石油制品 (吨)	Other Petroleum Products (ton)	33505	157523	404873	404873	130631	27152
热力 (百万千焦)	Heat (million kilo-joule)		6702432	37977567	37030351		
电力 (万度)	Electricity (10 thousand kwh)		2644412	3031598	2933856		
其他燃料 (吨标准煤)	Other Fuel (ton of SCE)	41321	571057	575863	572732	3500	27919

注:本表统计范围为全部国有工业企业及年产品销售收入500万元及以上的非国有工业企业。

All state-owned and the non-state-owned industrial enterprises with annual sales income of over 5 million yuan.

10-13 主要能源按工业行业分组消费量(2003年)

指标	Item	原煤(吨) Raw Coal (ton)	洗精煤(吨) Cleaned Coal (ton)	其他洗煤(吨) Other Washed Coal (ton)	型煤(吨) Briquettes (ton)	焦炭(吨) Coke (ton)
煤炭开采和洗选业	Mining and Washing of Coal	2271566	316303			206
黑色金属矿采选业	Mining of Ferrous Metal Ores	6227				24915
有色金属矿采选业	Mining of Non-ferrous Metal Ores	44310				3941
非金属矿采选业	Mining and Processing of Nonmetal Ores	423959				315
其他采矿业	Mining of Other Ores N.E.C					
农副食品加工业	Processing of Food From Agricultural Products	130634	15			
食品制造业	Manufacture of Foods	96650				1284
饮料制造业	Manufacture of Beverage	108353	500			210
烟草制品业	Manufacture of Tobacco	92995		2104		2446
纺织业	Manufacture of Textile	416323		300		
纺织服装、鞋、帽制造业	Manufacture of Textile Wearing Apparel, Footware, and Caps	6548	5			
皮革毛皮羽绒及其制品业	Manufacture of Leather,Fur,Feather and Its Products	14882				9
木材加工及木、竹、藤、棕草制品业	Processing of Timbers,Manufacture of Wood, Bamboo, Rattan, Palm, and Straw Products	204340		458		
家具制造业	Manufacture of Furniture	8320				
造纸及纸制品业	Manufacture of Paper and Paper Products	1451520				1223
印刷业、记录媒介的复制	Printing,Reproduction of Recording Media	14469				133
文教体育用品制造业	Manufacture of Articles for Culture,Education and Sport Activity	970				20
石油加工、炼焦及核燃料加工业	Processing of Petroleum ,Coking,Processing of Nucleus Fuel	1122691	448016			
化学原料及化学制品制造业	Manufacture of Chemical Raw Material and Chemical Products	5553789	61587	1114		128711
医药制造业	Manufacture of Medicines	168296				20710
化学纤维制造业	Manufacture of Chemical Fiber	285244				47692
橡胶制品业	Manufacture of Rubber	64300				
塑料制品业	Manufacture of Plastic	19778		44		333
非金属矿物制品业	Manufacture of Non-metallic Mineral Products	5599382	25808	3959		26680
黑色金属冶炼及压延加工业	Manufacture and Processing of Ferrous Metals	1224467	2533925			3262861
有色金属冶炼及压延加工业	Manufacture and Processing of Non-ferrous Metals	621502	48781	283		306471
金属制品业	Manufacture of Metal Products	74271	61			7152
通用设备制造业	Manufacture of General Purpose Machinery	46092	1430			29294
专用设备制造业	Manufacture of Special Purpose Machinery	42241	230			11899
交通运输设备制造业	Manufacture of Transport Equipment	66298		313		11137
电气机械及器材制造业	Manufacture of Electrical Machinery and Equipment	105952	9643			28722
通信设备、计算机及其他电子设备制造业	Manufacture of Communication Equipment, Computer and Other Electronic Equipment	66408				17
仪器仪表及文化、办公用机械制造业	Manufacture of Measuring Instrument and Machinery for Cultural Activity and Office Work	3650	260			120
工艺品及其他制造业	Manufacture of Artwork,Other Manufacture N.E.C	4950	76			30
废弃资源和废旧材料回收加工业	Recycling and Disposal of Waste	153				
电力、热力的生产和供应业	Production and Supply of Electric & Heat Power	14310822				992
煤气生产和供应业	Production and Distribution of Gas	48116	210139			26210
水的生产和供应业	Production and Distribution of Water	278				

注:本表统计范围为全部国有工业企业及年产品销售收入500万元及以上的非国有工业企业。

Consumption of Energy and Its Main Varieties by Sector (2003)

其他焦化产品 (吨) Other Coking Products (ton)	焦炉煤气 (万立方) Coke Oven Gas (10 000 cu.m)	高炉煤气 (万立方) High Oven Gas (10 000 cu.m)	其他煤气 (万立方) Other Coal Gas (10 000 cu.m)	天然气 (万立方) Natural Gas (10 000 cu.m)	原油 (吨) Crude Oil (ton)	汽油 (吨) Gasoline (ton)	煤油 (吨) Kerosene (ton)	柴油 (吨) Diesel Oil (ton)	燃料油 (吨) Fuel Oil (ton)
	200					1626	162	3941	8
						265		460	
1080						1182	250	2657	2
	40					1004		3765	
						1327		7721	13
825			2		15	1084	10	927	2440
						586		1012	6500
						457		11426	
231					6	929	140	1317	21
						389		543	
		100				75		175	
161	300					295	2	297	
						157	10	155	
1113						799	11	1879	628
						618	15	732	7
						15		6	
					5064969	5624	67	6691	54062
	1163				1855	8080	196	18637	27569
						825	6	1724	
						829	4	762	5163
					32	1346	3	93	
					12	537	37	5723	320
		22075			58	4254	504	21096	74129
1128	73150	819103	81		5	1885	109	6868	42000
904			34324			2862	891	9485	5821
			105			512	417	742	160
496		514			4	2262	457	4017	120
						2236	162	2525	212
					8	5012	2119	8066	4040
						1436	48	1686	72
			129		200	665	60	16275	
						249	9	58	
						201	5	204	
						55			
						3551	41	19637	2040
	6816					189		433	
						1045	19	363	

All state-owned and the non-state-owned industrial enterprises with annual sales income of over 5 million yuan.

10-13 续表 continued

指标	Item	液化石油气（吨）Liquefied Petroleum Gas (ton)	其他石油制品（吨）Other Petroleum Products (ton)	热力（百万千焦）Heat (million kilo-joule)	电力（万度）Electricity (10 000 kwh)	其他燃料（吨标准煤）Other Fuel (ton of SCE)
煤炭开采和洗选业	Mining and Washing of Coal		9		127233	
黑色金属矿采选业	Mining of Ferrous Metal Ores				10143	
有色金属矿采选业	Mining of Non-ferrous Metal Ores				44279	
非金属矿采选业	Mining and Processing of Nonmetal Ores			138608	20580	114
其他采矿业	Mining of Other Ores N.E.C					
农副食品加工业	Processing of Food From Agricultural Products	8		123	21389	11881
食品制造业	Manufacture of Foods	1551			9431	1569
饮料制造业	Manufacture of Beverage	2406			7895	
烟草制品业	Manufacture of Tobacco	189			15909	
纺织业	Manufacture of Textile	72		359708	71428	146
纺织服装、鞋、帽制造业	Manufacture of Textile Wearing Apparel, Footware, and Caps				3202	
皮革毛皮羽绒及其制品业	Manufacture of Leather,Fur,Feather and Its Products			3428	3292	
木材加工及木、竹、藤、棕草制品业	Processing of Timbers,Manufacture of Wood, Bamboo, Rattan, Palm, and Straw Products				18554	1000
家具制造业	Manufacture of Furniture				2566	2
造纸及纸制品业	Manufacture of Paper and Paper Products	3851		5716799	126181	9986
印刷业、记录媒介的复制	Printing,Reproduction of Recording Media	61	1		7077	
文教体育用品制造业	Manufacture of Articles for Culture,Education and Sport Activity				301	
石油加工、炼焦及核燃料加工业	Processing of Petroleum ,Coking,Processing of Nucleus Fuel	227927	239579	9015723	139865	464622
化学原料及化学制品制造业	Manufacture of Chemical Raw Material and Chemical Products	1334	163783	12894190	483253	36431
医药制造业	Manufacture of Medicines	8		21411	27372	5636
化学纤维制造业	Manufacture of Chemical Fiber			701290	46704	
橡胶制品业	Manufacture of Rubber			600694	5226	
塑料制品业	Manufacture of Plastic				12567	419
非金属矿物制品业	Manufacture of Non-metallic Mineral Products	9066	57	125	332187	23420
黑色金属冶炼及压延加工业	Manufacture and Processing of Ferrous Metals	30	975	8059291	511409	
有色金属冶炼及压延加工业	Manufacture and Processing of Non-ferrous Metals	722	1	124297	493492	516
金属制品业	Manufacture of Metal Products		2	5272	16415	
通用设备制造业	Manufacture of General Purpose Machinery	9	6	1527	27987	218
专用设备制造业	Manufacture of Special Purpose Machinery	56	61	19	39597	
交通运输设备制造业	Manufacture of Transport Equipment	101	44	3628	51782	
电气机械及器材制造业	Manufacture of Electrical Machinery and Equipment	3630	350	2433	25397	4717
通信设备、计算机及其他电子设备制造业	Manufacture of Communication Equipment, Computer and Other Electronic Equipment	6165			39241	
仪器仪表及文化、办公用机械制造业	Manufacture of Measuring Instrument and Machinery for Cultural Activity and Office Work				2313	
工艺品及其他制造业	Manufacture of Artwork,Other Manufacture N.E.C				1680	
废弃资源和废旧材料回收加工业	Recycling and Disposal of Waste				54	
电力、热力的生产和供应业	Production and Supply of Electric & Heat Power		5	166510	230522	15186
煤气生产和供应业	Production and Distribution of Gas	4481		162491	1320	
水的生产和供应业	Production and Distribution of Water	1			53755	

十一、建筑业

CONSTRUCTION

资料整理人员： 孙　靖

11-1 建筑企业概况

General Survey of Construction Enterprises

指标	Item	2000	2001	2002	2003
总产值（万元）	**Gross Output Value of Construction (10 000 yuan)**	**3542866**	**4897879**	**5957743**	**8188402**
#国有企业	State owned Enterprises	1581149	1849867	2100886	2877589
集体企业	Collective owned Enterprises	1509253	1473883	1321090	1472517
股份合作企业	Cooperative Enterprises	49773	88884	156314	239979
联营企业	Joint Ownership Enterprises	20538	25156	61306	44643
有限责任公司	Limited Liability Corporations	152616	835981	1460900	2094822
股份有限公司	Share-holding Corporations Ltd.	174020	389794	549066	895130
私营企业	Private Enterprises	41503	211184	279220	534994
其他企业	Others Enterprises	566	1975	3248	12614
港澳台商投资企业	Funded by Entrepreneurs from Hong kong,Macao and Taiwan	13448	21155	25713	16114
外商投资企业	Enterprises with Foreign Investment				
增加值（万元）	**Value Aded of construction (10 000 yuan)**	**967249**	**1307738**	**1533593**	**1726051**
#本年内提取的固定资产折旧	Depreciation of Fixed Assets Of the Year	77163	92710	111715	134607
应付工资	Wages Payable	490810	606021	685060	984922
应付福利费	Welfare Expenses Payable	42946	60940	72144	113210
管理费用中的劳动待业保险费	Labor and Unemployment Insurance in Management Expenses	28358	37760	37952	39157
工程结算税金及附加	Taxes and Extra Charges on Project Settlement Accounts	101064	158977	191707	278347
工程结算利润	Profits of Project Setlement Accounts	250524	341678	418848	157782
管理费用中的税金	Taxes in Management Enpenses	8007	9652	16167	18026
#国有企业	State owned Enterprises	428924	459865	471573	479615
集体企业	Collective owned Enterprises	412859	408047	364023	353203
股份合作企业	Cooperative Enterprises	14906	27628	46005	60270
联营企业	Joint Ownership Enterprises	6498	7410	18378	14081
有限责任公司	Limited Liability Corporations	63649	233063	386455	475383
股份有限公司	Share-holding Corporations Ltd.	44109	107564	154254	215271
私营企业	Private Enterprises	10393	60650	86059	123415
其他企业	Others Enterprises	98	534	934	2117
港澳台商投资企业	Funded by Entrepreneurs from Hong kong,Macao and Taiwan	5813	2977	5912	2696
外商投资企业	Enterprises with Foreign Investment				
实收资本（万元）	**Capital Stock (10 000 yuan)**	**1004829**	**1521243**	**1881801**	**2340739**
#国有企业	State owned Enterprises	337826	481956	507454	657989
集体企业	Collective owned Enterprises	488259	502047	511735	493054
股份合作企业	Cooperative Enterprises	17883	32150	60183	71126
联营企业	Joint Ownership Enterprises	5754	7000	14611	18232
有限责任公司	Limited Liability Corporations	48338	255107	427332	587615
股份有限公司	Share-holding Corporations Ltd.	69068	178893	239848	336657
私营企业	Private Enterprises	30891	59966	106152	159652

注：1995年至2001年，建筑施工企业为资质等级四级及以上的建筑施工企业，从2002年起，建筑施工企业的统计范围为具有新资质等级的施工总承包和专业承包企业。以后各表均同。

Construction enterprises refer to the fourth and higher grade construction enterprises between 1995 and 2001.

The Statistical Coverage of Construction Enterprises Just Included the New Grade Construction Enterprises of Overall Contract and Special Contract Since 2002. The Same as in the following table.

指标	Item	2000	2001	2002	2003
其他企业	Others Enterprises	100	334	1036	3205
港澳台商投资企业	Funded by Entrepreneurs from Hong kong,Macao and Taiwan	6710	3790	13450	13209
外商投资企业	Enterprises with Foreign Investment				
资产合计 (万元)	**Total Assets (10 000 yuan)**	**3552544**	**4478393**	**5383758**	**6760984**
#流动资产	Circulating Funds	2311307	2835012	3321246	4287889
#固定资产	Fixed Assets	1032597	1326687	1659436	1980973
#专项工程	Special Projects	34894	43056		
#无形及递延资产	Intangible and Deferred Assets	43736	138502	223605	238808
#国有企业	State owned Enterprises	1807419	1953296	2261694	2838151
集体企业	Collective owned Enterprises	1301816	1198775	1165091	1109353
服份合作企业	Cooperative Enterprises	43725	68947	120399	135318
联营企业	Joint Ownership Enterprises	11063	12668	29310	31553
有限责任公司	Limited Liability Corporations	138182	689782	1069671	1545919
股份有限公司	Share-holding Corporations Ltd.	182134	352124	459399	688200
私营企业	Private Enterprises	58761	186398	252061	382039
其他企业	Others Enterprises	155	1448	2527	5721
港澳台商投资企业	Funded by Entrepreneurs from HongKong,Macao and Taiwan	9287	14955	23606	24730
外商投资企业	Enterprises with Foreign Investment				
负债合计 (万元)	**Total Liabilities (10 000 yuan)**	**2287791**	**2642947**	**2994334**	**3796776**
#流动负债	Liquid Liabilities	2064425	2426394	2719603	3520555
长期负债	Long-term Liabilities	223366	216553	274731	276221
#国有企业	State owned Enterprises	1355446	1367100	1527310	1990133
集体企业	Collective owned Enterprises	697271	591717	510023	506224
股份合作企业	Cooperative Enterprises	21781	34298	54752	49897
联营企业	Joint Ownership Enterprises	4977	4057	10176	10552
有限责任公司	Limited Liability Corporations	82412	380900	571338	761196
股份有限公司	Share-holding Corporations Ltd.	103449	143555	187534	295098
私营企业	Private Enterprises	19869	109171	122550	170327
其他企业	Others Enterprises	50	1032	980	1951
港澳台商投资企业	Funded by Entrepreneurs from HongKong,Macao and Taiwan	2535	11117	9671	11398
外商投资企业	Enterprises with Foreign Investment				
所有者权益 (万元)	**Creditors' Equity (10 000 yuan)**	**1264753**	**1835445**	**2389424**	**2964208**
#国有企业	State owned Enterprises	451973	586196	734384	484018
集体企业	Collective owned Enterprises	604545	607058	655068	603129
股份合作企业	Cooperative Enterprises	21945	34649	65647	85421
联营企业	Joint Ownership Enterprises	6086	8611	19134	21001
有限责任公司	Limited Liability Corporations	55770	308882	498333	784723
股份有限公司	Share-holding Corporations Ltd.	78685	208568	271865	393102
私营企业	Private Enterprises	38893	77227	129511	211712
其他企业	Others Enterprises	105	416	1547	3770
港澳台商投资企业	Funded by Entrepreneurs from HongKong,Macao and Taiwan	6752	3838	13935	13332
外商投资企业	Enterprises with Foreign Investment				
企业总收入 (万元)	**Total Income of Enterprises (10 000 yuan)**	**3061339**	**4647297**	**5526543**	**7692633**
#工程结算收入	Revenue of Project Settlement accounts	3049291	4517943	5416568	7573605
工程结算成本	Costs of Project Settlement Accounts	2697703	4017288	4806013	6746447
工程结算利润	Profits of Project Setlement Accounts	250524	341678	418848	278347
其他业务收入	Revenue from Other Business	112048	129354	109975	119028
其他业务利润	Profit from Other Business	28626	23325	22859	23136

11-1 续表 2 continued

指标	Item	2000	2001	2002	2003
#国有企业	State owned Enterprises	1476206	1750730	2018137	2706400
集体企业	Collective owned Enterprises	1281118	1354172	1182732	1396371
股份合作企业	Cooperative Enterprises	47570	82441	139196	222831
联营企业	Joint Ownership Enterprises	17549	30623	72142	46656
有限责任公司	Limited Liability Corporations	133184	848990	1325717	1983779
股份有限公司	Share-holding Corporations Ltd.	152984	390089	502730	844934
私营企业	Private Enterprises	38906	167863	263853	468828
其他企业	Others Enterprises	374	1643	3092	11250
港澳台商投资企业	Funded by Entrepreneurs from Hong Kong,Macao and Taiwan	13448	20746	18944	11584
外商投资企业	Enterprises with Foreign Investment				
利税总额合计 (万元)	**Total pre-tax Profits (10 000 yuan)**	**152949**	**255109**	**318920**	**452511**
#利润总额	Total Profits	43878	86481	111046	156138
工程结算税金及附加	Taxes and Extra Charges on Project Settlement Accounts	101064	158977	191707	278347
管理费用中的税金	Taxes in Management Enpenses	8007	9651	16167	18026
产值利税率(%)	Ratio of Pretax Profits to Output Value(%)	4.3	5.2	5.4	5.5
资产利税率(%)	Ratio of tax Profits to Assets	4.7	5.7	5.9	6.7
#国有企业	State owned Enterprises	42940	64225	82785	117796
集体企业	Collective owned Enterprises	82842	86750	79113	85502
股份合作企业	Cooperative Enterprises	3077	5519	9596	16674
联营企业	Joint Ownership Enterprises	1146	1609	5445	3637
有限责任公司	Limited Liability Corporations	7781	51887	83494	130288
股份有限公司	Share-holding Corporations Ltd.	11236	19853	33994	60013
私营企业	Private Enterprises	2585	20794	22403	37674
其他企业	Others Enterprises	14	68	174	483
港澳台商投资企业	Funded by Entrepreneurs from Hong kong,Macao and Taiwan	1344	804	1916	444
外商投资企业	Enterprises with Foreign Investment				
利润总额合计 (万元)	**Total Profits (10 000 yuan)**	**43878**	**86481**	**111046**	**156138**
#国有企业	State owned Enterprises	2640	13035	20068	22776
集体企业	Collective owned Enterprises	29367	32813	27593	29214
股份合作企业	Cooperative Enterprises	1437	2529	4160	7100
联营企业	Joint Ownership Enterprises	444	840	2358	1235
有限责任公司	Limited Liability Corporations	2627	22872	30420	52791
股份有限公司	Share-holding Corporations Ltd.	5540	8805	13861	24778
私营企业	Private Enterprises	1024	5259	11357	18040
其他企业	Others Enterprises		6	48	128
港澳台商投资企业	Funded by Entrepreneurs from Hong kong,Macao and Taiwan	799	322	1181	76
外商投资企业	Enterprises with Foreign Investment				
工程结算利润总计 (万元)	**Profits of Project Setlement Accounts (10 000 yuan)**	**250524**	**341678**	**418848**	**548811**
#国有企业	State owned Enterprises	118218	125675	140794	174553
集体企业	Collective owned Enterprises	98208	95478	83030	84807
股份合作企业	Cooperative Enterprises	4060	5883	9693	13904
联营企业	Joint Ownership Enterprises	1864	1973	5764	5185
有限责任公司	Limited Liability Corporations	11112	70462	111636	158868
股份有限公司	Share-holding Corporations Ltd.	11382	26552	39442	66817
私营企业	Private Enterprises	3186	14067	25748	42632
其他企业	Others Enterprises	42	133	236	501
港澳台商投资企业	Funded by Entrepreneurs from Hong kong,Macao and Taiwan	2453	1455	2505	1544
外商投资企业	Enterprises with Foreign Investment				

11-2 建筑施工企业个数和平均人数

Number of Construction Enterprises and Its Average Annual Staff and Workers

年 份 Year	总 计 Total	国有经济 State-owned	集体经济 Collective-owned	其他经济 Others owned	建筑业活动单位 Active unit
施工企业个数(个) Number of Enterprises (unit)					
1995	1283	216	1023	3	41
1996	1811	278	1347	31	155
1997	1748	296	1425	27	…
1998	1840	317	1407	116	…
1999	1812	317	1335	160	…
2000	1812	313	1241	258	…
2001	1628	305	829	494	…
2002	1442	262	532	648	
2003	1593	257	470	866	
施工企业人数(万人) Staff and Workers (10 000 persons)					
1995	61.33	22.29	38.52	0.16	0.36
1996	78.88	24.32	50.72	0.90	2.94
1997	81.22	25.08	55.37	0.77	…
1998	82.72	24.93	53.20	4.59	…
1999	77.18	22.98	47.19	7.01	…
2000	76.30	22.66	41.98	11.66	…
2001	96.73	25.01	38.86	32.86	
2002	92.72	21.56	28.70	42.46	
2003	111.95	28.67	27.53	55.75	

11-3 建筑施工企业主要效益指标(2003年)

Major Benefit Indicators of Construction Enterprises (2003)

指 标	Item	总 计 Total	国有经济 State-owned	集体经济 Collective-owned	其他经济 Other owned
年末固定资产原值(万元)	Original Value Fixed Assets at the Yearend (10 000 yuan)	2551515	1027189	452968	1071358
年末固定资产净值(万元)	Net Value of Fixed Assets at the Yearend (10 000 yuan)	1727254	653955	329379	743920
流动资产年末合计(万元)	Circulating Funds at the Yearend (10 000 yuan)	4287889	1909631	640214	1738044
利润总额 (万元)	Total Profits (10 000 yuan)	156138	22776	29214	104148
利税总额 (万元)	Total Pre-tax Profits (10 000 yuan)	452511	117796	85502	249213
资金利润率(元/百元)	Ratio of Fund to Profits (yuan/100 yuan)	2.6	0.9	3.0	4.2
产值利润率 (%)	Ratio of Profit to Gross Output Value (%)	1.9	0.8	2.0	2.7
产值利税率 (%)	Ratio of Pre-tax Profit to Output Value (%)	5.5	4.1	5.8	6.5
年底自有机械设备(台)	Machinery and Equipment Owned at the Year-end (set)	386720	84404	111007	191309
年底自有机械设备净值 (万元)	Net Value of Machinery and Equipment Owned at the Year-end (10 000 yuan)	988718	299168	199514	490036
期末技术装备率(元/人)	Value of Machines Per Laborer (yuan/person)	8831.6	10363.7	7248.1	8820.2
期末动力装备率(kw/人)	Power of Machines per Laborer (kw/person)	4.7	6.0	4.2	4.2
按施工产值计算的劳动生产率 (元/人年)	Overall Labor Productivity in Terms of Total Output Value (yuan /person-year)	74546.3	107348.3	55568.1	67889.1
按增加值计算的劳动生产率 (元/人年)	Overall Labor Productivity in Terms of Added-Value (yuan /person-year)	15713.8	17892.0	13328.8	15798.9
人均竣工面积 (平方米/人)	Floor Space of Buildings Completed per Laborer (sq.m/person)	45.2	32.6	56.1	47.0

注:本表不包括建筑业活动单位。Enterprises engaged in construction were excluded.

11-4 国有建筑企业主要经济指标

Major Economic Indicators on State – owned Construction Enterprises

指 标	Item	2000	2001	2002	2003
国有建筑施工企业	**State-owned**				
施工产值 (亿元)	Output Value of Projects (100 million yuan)	158.11	184.99	210.00	287.76
全员劳动生产率 (元/人)	Overall Labor Productivity (yuan/person)	69792	79318	98358	107348
计算劳动生产率的平均人数 (万人)	Average Number of Staff and Workers by Calculating Labor Productivity (10 000 person)	22.66	23.32	21.36	26.81
房屋建筑施工面积 (万平方米)	Floor Space of Buildings Under Construction (10 000 sq.m)	1287.31	1459.86	1492.90	2403.74
房屋建筑竣工面积 (万平方米)	Floor Space of Buildings Completed (10 000 sq.m)	580.12	575.96	557.76	872.54
#住宅	Residential Buildings				427.00
地方国有建筑施工企业	**Local State-owned**				
施工产值 (亿元)	Output Value of Projects (100 million yuan)	92.10	120.96	133.16	190.59
全员劳动生产率(元 / 人)	Overall Labor Productivity (yuan/person)	59094	71891	88998	95793
计算劳动生产率的平均人数 (万人)	Average Number of Staff and Workers by Calculating Labor Productivity (10 000 person)	15.59	16.83	14.96	19.90
房屋建筑施工面积 (万平方米)	Floor Space of Buildings Under Construction (10 000 sq.m)	1036.99	1199.90	1245.10	1869.84
房屋建筑竣工面积 (万平方米)	Floor Space of Buildings Completed (10 000 sq.m)	481.60	518.98	499.16	723.67
#住宅	Residential Buildings				354.21

11-5 建筑业总产值和增加值(2003年)

Gross Output Value and Added - Valueof Construction Enterprises (2003)

单位：万元 (10 000 yuan)

指 标	Item	总 计 Total	国 有 State-owned	集 体 Collective-owned	其他经济 Others owned
建筑业总产值(施工产值)	**Gross Output Value of Construction (Output Value of Projects)**	**8188402**	**2877589**	**1472517**	**3838296**
建筑工程产值	Output Value of Construction Engineering	6904174	2422767	1224922	3256485
安装工程产值	Output Value of Installation Engineering	594925	266217	107652	221056
其他工程产值	Output Value of Other Engineering	689303	188605	139943	360755
增加值	**Value Aded of construction**	**1726051**	**479615**	**353203**	**893233**
本年提取折旧	Depreciation of Fixed Assets Of the Year	134607	50363	19554	64690
应付工资	Wages Payable	984922	254081	221841	509000
应付福利费	Welfare Expenses Payable	113210	34134	22056	57020
管理费用中劳动待业保险费	Labor and Unemployment Insurance in Management Expenses	39157	22128	4234	12795
工程结算税金及附加	Taxes and Extra Charges on Project Settlement Accounts	278347	90007	52876	135464
管理费用中：税金	Taxes in Management Enpenses	18026	5013	3412	9601
工程结算利润	Profits of Project Setlement Accounts	157782	23889	29230	104663

11-6 房屋建筑面积

Floor Space of Building Construction

单位:万平方米 (10 000 sq.m)

年份 Year / 市州 Cities and Prefecture		房屋建筑面积 Floor Space of Building Construction		国有经济 State-owned		集体经济 Collective-owned	
		施工面积 Floor Space Under Construction	竣工面积 Floor Space Completed	施工面积 Floor Space Under Construction	竣工面积 Floor Space Completed	施工面积 Floor Space Under Construction	竣工面积 Floor Space Completed
1990		1159.10	558.70	572.40	233.50	586.70	325.20
1991		1282.70	653.20	577.20	269.50	705.50	383.70
1992		1554.00	711.30	699.40	279.80	854.60	431.50
1993		1869.50	802.20	867.90	334.60	1001.60	467.60
1994		2081.50	868.30	1011.10	378.40	1068.40	489.30
1995		4507.41	2313.70	1094.50	361.20	3223.05	1835.33
1996		4662.00	2393.05	1285.16	467.04	3333.59	1898.28
1997		4719.57	2279.89	1236.68	465.95	3444.90	1783.44
1998		5067.56	2382.33	1397.64	530.70	3373.22	1701.44
1999		5180.91	2681.81	1333.55	561.10	3417.60	1900.54
2000		5087.93	2603.08	1287.31	580.12	3017.81	1634.32
2001		6259.27	3204.60	1459.86	575.96	2734.12	1548.82
2002		7167.52	3665.71	1492.90	557.76	2342.29	1375.27
2003		10051.97	4969.67	2403.74	872.54	2667.99	1487.17
长沙	Changsha	3434.15	1473.58	1112.86	376.03	430.40	245.39
株洲	Zhuzhou	583.83	285.70	134.74	48.38	104.64	60.11
湘潭	Xiangtan	605.54	312.94	80.91	32.85	203.81	112.97
衡阳	Hengyang	1260.22	607.03	314.14	102.52	662.74	345.66
邵阳	Shaoyang	570.33	306.88	155.58	55.74	217.58	127.14
岳阳	Yueyang	658.04	442.88	67.15	17.76	224.69	173.64
常德	Changde	630.08	387.07	14.93	14.70	39.04	22.48
张家界	Zhangjiajie	120.91	75.70			31.92	22.06
益阳	Yiyang	449.08	250.28	51.62	13.79	93.99	46.84
郴州	Chenzhou	519.92	264.58	169.30	91.68	182.00	98.75
永州	Yongzhou	376.13	149.20	110.54	27.56	146.60	63.36
怀化	Huaihua	271.72	123.30	48.01	20.40	85.19	41.88
娄底	Loudi	399.01	212.33	126.17	61.96	159.35	80.57
湘西自治州	West Hunan	173.01	78.20	17.79	9.17	86.04	46.32

11-7 国有、集体建筑企业生产指标(2003年)

Production Indicators of State－owned and Collective－owned Construction Enterprises (2003)

指标	Item	总计 Total	国有经济 State-owned Economic	中央 Central	地方 Local	集体经济 Collective Owned Economic
企业个数 (个)	Number of Enterprises (unit)	1593	257	41	216	470
建筑业总产值(万元)	Gross Output Value of Construction (10 000 yuan)	8188402	2877589	971717	1905872	1472517
#建筑工程	Construction projects	6904174	2422767	818253	1604514	1224922
安装工程	Installation projects	594925	266217	94690	171527	107652
其他	Others	689303	188605	58774	129831	139943
竣工产值 (万元)	Output Value Completed (10 000 yuan)	6299377	2099347	635995	1463352	1211227
房屋建筑施工面积 (万平方米)	Floor Space of Buildings Under Construction (10 000 sq.m)	10051.97	2403.74	533.91	1869.83	2667.99
#本年新开工面积	Floor Space of Buildings Started in Current Year	6011.1	1310.13	260.43	1049.7	1633.38
#投标承包的面积	Floor Space of Bidding Buildings	7780.24	2110.07	526.80	1583.27	2096.6
#本年新开工	Started in Current Year	5019.81	1172.33	258.67	913.66	1353.38
房屋建筑竣工面积 (万平方米)	Floor Space of Buildings Completed (10 000 sq.m)	4969.67	872.54	148.88	723.66	1487.17
自有机械设备年末总台数 (台)	Number of Machinery and Equipment Owend at the Year-end (unit)	386720	84404	19110	65294	111007
自有机械设备年末总功率 (万千瓦)	Power of Machinery and Equipment Owned at the Yearend (10 000 kw)	522.01	173.87	72.02	101.85	114.81
#施工机械功率	Power of Construction Machines	430.8	135.86	58.97	76.89	92.44
自有机械设备净值 (万元)	Net Value of Machinery and Equipment Owned (10 000 yuan)	988718	299168	97389	201779	199514
计算建筑业劳动生产率的平均人数 (万人)	Average of Staff and Workers by Calculating Construction Labor Productivity (10 000 persons)	109.84	26.81	6.91	19.9	26.5

11-8 建筑业企业分行业生产指标(2003年)

指标	Item	房屋和土木工程建筑业 Construction of Building and Civil Engineering	房屋工程建筑业 Building Engineering Construction	土木工程建筑业 Civil Engineering Construction	铁路公路隧道桥梁建筑业 Construction of Railways, Roads, Tunnels and Bridgeworks
企业个数（个）	**Number of Enterprises (unit)**	**1347**	**1123**	**224**	**99**
建筑业总产值(万元)	**Gross Output Value of Construction (10 000 yuan)**	**7691784**	5644029	2047755	**1371693**
#建筑工程	Construction Projects	6752340	5031608	1720732	1256252
安装工程	Installation Projects	286546	168283	118263	5832
其他	Others	652898	444138	208760	109609
竣工产值（万元）	**Output Value Completed (10000 yuan)**	**5867461**	**4250443**	**1617018**	**1149651**
房屋建筑施工面积（万平方米）	**Floor Space of Buildings Under Construction (10 000 sq.m)**	**9992.09**	**9923.84**	**68.26**	**21.29**
#本年新开工面积	Floor Space of Buildings Started in Current Year	5976.31	5941.34	34.97	7.12
#投标承包的面积	Floor Space of Bidding Buildings	7731.06	7688.47	42.6	17.78
#本年新开工	#Started in Current Year	4990.92	4973.21	17.7	4.02
房屋建筑竣工面积（万平方米）	**Floor Space of Buildings Completed (10 000 sq.m)**	**4955.8**	**4919.2**	**36.6**	**7.89**
自有机械设备年末总台数（台）	**Total Number of Machinery and Equipment Owned at the Yearend (unit)**	**357113**	**305366**	**51747**	**190847**
自有机械设备年末总功率（万千瓦）	**Total Power of Machinery and Equipment Owned at the Yearend (10 000 kw)**	**493.73**	**335.56**	**158.17**	**79.65**
#施工机械功率	#Power of Construction Machines	410.77	280.83	129.95	61.97
自有机械设备净值（万元）	**Net Value of Machinery and Equipment Owned (10 000 yuan)**	**937614**	**631623**	**305991**	**190847**
计算建筑业劳动生产率的平均人数（万人）	**Average of Staff and Workers by Calculating Construction Labor Productivity (10 000 persons)**	**104.44**	**87.99**	**16.45**	**10.13**

Production Indicators of Construction Enterprises by Sector (2003)

11-8 续表 continued

				建筑安装业 Architectural Installation	建筑装饰业 Architectural Decoration	其他建筑业 Other Construction			
水利和港口建筑业 Construction of Water Conservancy and Harbor Engineering	工矿工程建筑业 Construction of Industry and Mining Projects	架线和管道工程建筑业 Construction of Wire Laying and Pipework	其他土木工程建筑业 Construction of Other Civil Engineering				工程准备 Engineering Preparation	提供施工设备服务 Service of Supplying Construction Equipment	其他未列明的建筑活动 Other Construction Activities N.E.C
60	**12**	**24**	**29**	**133**	**87**	**26**	**11**	**2**	**13**
385517	**79154**	**152879**	**58512**	**391028**	**77925**	**27665**	**16497**	**761**	**10407**
299833	543737	79440	30834	79617	49337	22880	16344	761	5775
12200	17366	60932	21933	293467	13446	1466			1466
73484	7415	12507	5745	17944	15142	3319	153		3166
238735	**54510**	**126659**	**47463**	**335740**	**71566**	**24610**	**14908**	**761**	**8941**
14.14	**17.75**	**2.99**	**12.08**	**59.66**		**2136**	**2136**		
6.11	11.28	0.4	10.06	34.58		0.2	0.2		
10.27	6.27	2.25	6.03	49.17		0	0		
5.98	2.11	0.35	5.24	28.89		0	0		
12.29	**10.62**	**2.64**	**3.17**	**13.66**		**0.2**	**0.2**		
84557	**8563**	**14096**	**7928**	**39100**	**6608**	**5396**	**2444**	**227**	**2725**
65.72	**3.02**	**4.56**	**5.22**	**22.47**	**3.04**	**2.76**	**1.95**	**0.06**	**0.76**
57.57	2.17	3.85	4.39	15.46	2.52	2.05	1.28	0.06	0.72
84557	**8563**	**14096**	**7928**	**39100**	**6608**	**5396**	**2444**	**227**	**2725**
3.71	**0.76**	**1.17**	**0.67**	**3.85**	**1.1**	**0.46**	**0.27**	**0.02**	**0.18**

十二、交通运输、邮电

TRANSPORTATION，POSTAL AND TELECOMMUNICATION SERVICES

资料整理人员：　　刘华娟

12-1 运输线路基本情况

Basic Statistics on Transportation Routes

单位：公里 (km)

指标	Item	2000	2001	2002	2003
铁路营业里程	**Lengh of Railways in Operation**	**2924.33**	**2894.4**	**2829.06**	**2771.73**
地方铁路	Lengh of Local Railway	379.5	349.5	276.4	-
复线里程	Double-Track	1836.16	1281.6	1281.6	1272.60
自动闭塞里程	Automatic Switching	1750.52	2253.4	2509.96	1569.48
电气化线路里程	Lengh of Electrified Railway	671.99	1211	1467.6	1424.30
内燃机牵引线路里程	Lengh of Diesel Engine	3086	1057.9	1083.3	1120.60
无缝线路里程	Lengh of Seamless Track	869.49	951.1	1007.38	1373.02
公路线路里程	**Lengh of Highways**	**60848**	**66593**	**84808**	**85233**
有路面里程	Paved Highways	59923	64821	82649	83081
#高级次高级路面	High and Secondary Grade	18349	20587	21789	23183
无路面里程	Non-Paved Highway	925	1772	2159	2152
等级公路	Expressway and Class Ⅰ to Ⅳ Highway	33380	36800	38433	39689
高速	Expressway	449	585	1012	1218
一级	First Class	239	335	412	468
二级	Second Class	3761	4705	4958	5173
等外路	Highway Below Class Ⅳ	27468	29793	46375	45544
内河航道	**Lengh of Navigable Inland Waterway**	**10041**	**10041**	**10041**	**11968**
管道线路里程	**Lengh Of Petroleum And Gas Pipeline**	**163.5**	**164**	**167.6**	**167.6**

12-2 铁路机车拥有量

Number of Railway Locomotives

指标	Item	2000	2001	2002	2003
中央铁路	**Central Railway**				
蒸汽机车（台）	Steam Locomotives (unit)		16		-
内燃机车（台）	Diesel Locomotives (unit)	529	376	374	356
客　车　（辆）	Passenger Coaches (unit)	1335	1443	2073	2080
电力机车(辆)	Electric Locomotives (unit)	120	296	337	503
地方铁路(窄轨)	**Local Railway Locomotives (narrow gauge)**				
蒸汽机车(台)	Steam Locomotives (unit)	15	15		-
内燃机车(台)	Diesel Locomotives (unit)	12	12	7	-
客　车(辆)	Passenger Coaches (unit)	27	27	18	-
货　车(辆)	Freight Cars (unit)	339	303	193	-

12-3 各市州公路长度(2003年)

Length of Highways by Region (2003)

单位：公里 (km)

市州	Cities	里程总计 Total Length of Highways	等级公路 高速公路 Express-way	一级公路 First Class	二级公路 Second Class	三级公路 Third Class	四级公路 Fourth Class	等外路 Highway Below Class Ⅳ
全省合计	**Total**	**85233**	**1218**	**468**	**5173**	**5515**	**27315**	**45544**
长沙市	Changsha	5443	224	32	467	451	2185	2086
株洲市	Zhuzhou	3921	68	51	266	93	1794	1649
湘潭市	Xiangtan	2705	122	10	244		804	1525
衡阳市	Hengyan	7976	228	37	562	282	1815	5052
邵阳市	Shaoyang	7973	82	7	537	739	2587	4020
岳阳市	Yueyang	7840	134	85	543	509	3097	3473
常德市	Changde	7430	55	136	444	474	1736	4585
张家界市	Zhangjiajie	4069		4	164	143	918	2840
益阳市	Yiyang	3934	56	30	328	163	1962	1395
郴州市	Chenzhou	6425	102	8	470	761	1915	3170
永州市	Yongzhou	6788	107	23	334	619	2733	2974
怀化市	Huaihua	9530			344	594	1913	6678
娄底市	Loudi	4635	41	47	299	292	2079	1878
湘西州	West Hunan	6564			172	396	1777	4219

注：资料来源于省交通厅。 Figures in this table form Transpotation Bureau of Hunan Province

12-4 民用车辆拥有量(2003年)

Number of Civil Motor Vehicles (2003)

指标	Item	全省总计 Total	营业性 Business	非营业性 Non-Business	特种车 Special Motor Vehicles	总计中：In Total #个体 Individual	#新注册 New Registr-ation
合计	**Total**	**2417267**	**407844**	**1994715**	**14708**	**1942995**	**358724**
民用汽车 (辆)	Civil Motor Vehicles (unit)	650784	226963	411471	12350	360076	90878
载客汽车 (辆)	Passenger Vehicles (unit)	367876	114911	242980	9985	191374	64960
#大型	#Large	28126	16671	11375	80	4550	3768
中型	Medium	23702	17166	6303	233	9306	6483
轿车	Cars	161870	29830	127821	4219	89375	33997
载客量 (客位)	Passenger Vehicles Seats (seat)						
载货汽车 (辆)	Trucks Vehicles (unit)	274007	111028	162395	584	167494	25148
#重型	#Heavy	37832	14337	23474	21	20483	1561
中型	Medium	110098	52021	58002	75	70698	11219
#普通载货	#Ordinary Trucks	167583	54300	112938	345	97531	7784
载重量 (吨位)	General Trucks (ton)						
摩托车 (辆)	Motors (unit)	1526751	28234	1496599	1918	1410152	258148
农用运输车 (辆)	Agricultural Motor Vehicles(unit)	112703	73466	39237		79560	4600
拖拉机 (辆)	Tractors (unit)	121264	77518	43746		90879	4032
挂车 (辆)	Truck Trailer (unit)	2431	918	1509	4	1054	369
其他类型车 (辆)	Other Motors Vehicles (unit)	3334	745	2153	436	1274	697

12-5 各市州民用车辆拥有量(2003年)

Number of Civil Motor Vehicles by Region (2003)

市州	Cities	总 计（辆）Total (unit)	汽车 Civil Motor Vehicles 载客 Passenger Vehicles	载货 Trucks Vehicles	摩托车 Motors	农用车 Agri-cultural Motor Vehicles	拖拉机 Tractors	其他类型车 Other Motor Vehicles	机动车驾驶员（人）Number of Motor Drivers (person)	#汽车驾驶员 Automobile Drivers
全省合计	**Total**	**2417267**	**367876**	**274007**	**1526751**	**112703**	**121264**	**3334**	**3070910**	**1680213**
长沙市	Changsha	354645	102764	39236	192116	10748	7271	621	500414	352393
株洲市	Zhuzhou	251608	24502	23374	185131	11597	5024	964	298359	145003
湘潭市	Xiangtan	198322	16649	16060	151467	8365	5304	116	238511	103021
衡阳市	Hengyan	232844	26714	30197	158066	11790	4916	75	305993	165444
邵阳市	Shaoyang	162405	22745	15818	109280	9026	5031	110	182395	113658
岳阳市	Yueyang	156562	21132	19413	97436	8166	9692	76	240277	124648
常德市	Changde	213361	26193	19853	146785	7675	11574	154	305801	135121
张家界市	Zhangjiajie	51226	8693	5479	28232	4402	4137	134	58188	32555
益阳市	Yiyang	125910	16371	9448	78906	4531	16344	54	190714	85202
郴州市	Chenzhou	163295	22992	37098	77548	8376	16549	145	173939	107160
永州市	Yongzhou	180448	15928	12033	124817	12902	14219	78	166015	79483
怀化市	Huaihua	131004	16148	16140	83915	4984	9280	37	167951	92422
娄底市	Loudi	114724	18692	19637	64495	4890	6189	328	159937	96600
湘西州	West Hunan	55297	10079	9275	24674	5251	5734	168	67229	34327

12-6 水路运输工具拥有量(2003年)

Number of Civil Transport Vessels (2003)

指标	Item	总 计 Total	#个体 Individual	总计中：In Total 内河运输 Reiver Shipping	#个体 Individual	远洋运输 Ocean Shipping
机动船　（艘）	**Motor Vessels　（unit）**	**8676**	**7299**	**8673**	**7299**	**3**
净载重量　（吨位）	Net Haulage Capacity　(ton)	532624	311129	420484	311129	112140
载客量　（客位）	Passenger Capacity　(seat)	73866	62521	73866	62521	
功率　（千瓦）	Power　(kw)	308942	212696	284360	212696	24582
客船　（艘）	Passenger Ship　(unit)	2482	2277	2482	2277	
载客量　（客位）	Passenger Capacity　(seat)	73466	62521	73466	62521	
功率　（千瓦）	Power　(kw)	60402	47740	60402	47740	
客货船　（艘）	Passenger And Cargo Vessel　(unit)	2		2		
净载重量　（吨位）	Net Haulage Capacity　(ton)	10		10		
载客量　（客位）	Passenger Capacity　(seat)	400		400		
功率　（千瓦）	Power　(kw)	235		235		
货船　（艘）	Cargoboat　(unit)	6075	5000	6072	5000	
净载重量　（吨位）	Net Haulage Capacity　(ton)	532614	311129	420474	311129	112140
功率　（千瓦）	Power　(kw)	232170	162982	207588	162982	24582
货船中：油船（艘）	Oil Tanker　(unit)	66	23	66	23	
净载重量（吨位）	Net Haulage Capacity　(ton)	18647	7077	18647	7077	
功率　（千瓦）	Power　(kw)	9143	3110	9143	3110	
拖船　（艘）	Drawing　(unit)	117	22	117	22	
功率　（千瓦）	Power　(kw)	16135	1974	16135	1974	
驳船　（艘）	**Barges　(unit)**	**353**	**16**	**353**	**16**	
净载重量　（吨位）	Net Haulage Capacity　(ton)	77982	3720	77982	3720	

12-7 营业性公路客货运输量(2003年)

Passenger and Freight Traffic of Highway Transportation for Buseness(2003)

指标	Item	2002		2003	
		合计 Total	#个体 Individual	合计 Total	#个体 Individual
客运量 (万人)	Passenger Traffic (10 000 persons)	91653	58436	90353	50623
汽车	Motor Vehicles	86376	53159	85388	45658
其他机动车	Other Motor Vehicles	5277	5277	4965	4965
旅客周转量 (亿人公里)	Passenger Kilometers (100 million persons-km)	384.91	146.93	384.67	131.23
汽车	Motor Vehicles	382.52	144.54	381.71	128.26
其他机动车	Other Motor Vehicles	2.39	2.39	2.96	2.96
货运量 (万吨)	Freight Traffic (10 000 tons)	42982	24648	34911	27463
汽车	Motor Vehicles	34875	16541	26373	18925
其他机动车	Other Motor Vehicles	1817	1817	2114	6424
轮胎式拖拉机	Tyre Tractors	6290	6290	6424	6424
货物周转量 (亿吨公里)	Total Freight Ton-kilometers (100 million ton-km)	355.96	206.4	328.71	259.80
汽车	Motor Vehicles	341.48	191.92	313.05	244.13
其他机动车	Other Motor Vehicles	5.51	5.51	6.52	6.52
轮胎式拖拉机	Tyre Tractors	8.98	8.98	9.14	9.14

12-8 水路客货运输量(2003年)

Passenger and Freight Traffic of Waterway Transportation (2003)

指标	Item	合计 Total	内河运输 Reiver Shipping	#个体 Individual	远洋运输 Ocean Shipping
客运量 (万人)	Passenger Traffic (10 000 persons)	793	793	581	
机动船	Motor Vessels	793	793	581	
驳船	Bages				
旅客周转量 (万人公里)	Passenger Kilometersc (10 000 persons-km)	24341	24341	12664	
机动船	Motor Vessels	24341	24341	12664	
驳船	Bages				
货运量 (万吨)	Freight Traffic (10 000 tons)	3600	3505	2511	95
机动船	Motor Vessels	3423	3328	2511	95
驳船	Bages	177	177		
货物周转量 (万吨公里)	Total Freight Ton-kilometers (10 000 ton-km)	1217435	513017	307997	704418
机动船	Motor Vessels	1127034	422616	307997	704418
驳船	Bages	90401	90401		

12-9 旅客运量和旅客周转量

Passenger Traffic and Turnover Volume of Passenger Traffic

年份 Year	合计 Total	铁路 Railway	中央 Central	地方 Local	公路 Highway	水运 Waterway	民用航空 Civil Aviation
客运量(万人)	**Total Passenger Traffic (10 000 persons)**						
1980	32776	3434	3271	163	27590	1750	2
1981	33546	3723	3520	203	27871	1950	2
1982	37286	3898	3677	221	31380	2006	2
1983	40380	4117	3895	222	33955	2306	2
1984	43333	4368	4154	214	36497	2466	2
1985	48666	4686	4461	225	41520	2458	2
1986	50903	4368	4159	209	44464	2066	5
1987	53600	4586	4397	189	47071	1935	8
1988	56236	4937	4739	198	49182	2109	8
1989	54084	4357	4205	152	47865	1855	7
1990	54161	3474	3389	85	49112	1568	7
1991	54710	3514	3437	77	49566	1621	9
1992	52641	3638	3564	74	47366	1615	22
1993	55896	4022	3949	73	50252	1562	60
1994	64757	4176	4105	71	59028	1481	72
1995	71566	4135	4083	52	65971	1375	85
1996	76377	3892	3846	46	71087	1298	100
1997	79250	4488	4444	44	73233	1357	172
1998	79540	4497	4469	28	73681	1260	102
1999	87806	5022	5000	22	81675	1002	107
2000	87462	5233	5216	17	81005	1094	130
2001	92381	5202	5188	14	85971	1063	145
2002	98244	5173	5161	13	91653	1249	169
2003	96182	4850	4850	-	90353	793	186
周转量(亿人公里)	**Total Passenger-kilometers (100 million passenger-km)**						
1980	133.68	65.47	65.12	0.35	62.90	5.25	0.06
1981	149.19	73.21	72.80	0.41	70.20	5.71	0.07
1982	159.66	78.05	77.61	0.44	75.62	5.92	0.07
1983	179.81	90.95	90.51	0.44	82.10	6.69	0.07
1984	204.68	104.85	104.42	0.43	93.08	6.68	0.07
1985	254.53	132.78	132.32	0.46	114.95	6.72	0.08
1986	275.38	140.09	139.65	0.44	128.68	6.38	0.23
1987	310.57	161.86	161.45	0.41	142.66	5.74	0.31
1988	354.23	191.21	190.79	0.42	156.57	6.11	0.34
1989	350.34	181.09	180.78	0.31	163.48	5.38	0.39
1990	339.86	162.32	162.17	0.15	172.73	4.25	0.56
1991	378.20	189.29	189.16	0.13	184.27	3.94	0.70
1992	435.19	228.39	228.24	0.15	200.09	4.87	1.84
1993	490.26	270.82	270.68	0.14	209.34	4.58	5.52
1994	539.02	291.44	291.29	0.15	237.00	3.90	6.68
1995	555.13	301.60	301.49	0.11	242.46	3.66	7.41
1996	538.29	262.99	262.89	0.10	263.48	3.45	8.37
1997	592.16	305.06	304.97	0.09	274.68	3.69	8.73
1998	610.53	319.67	319.61	0.06	279.69	3.49	7.68
1999	676.04	353.87	353.83	0.04	310.69	3.76	7.72
2000	724.06	394.00	393.96	0.04	318.37	3.55	8.14
2001	761.62	410.65	410.62	0.03	337.90	3.23	9.84
2002	827.55	428.84	428.81	0.03	384.91	3.20	10.60
2003	831.24	431.00	431.00	-	384.67	2.43	13.14

12-10 货物运量和货物周转量

Freight Traffic and Turnover Volume of Freight Traffic

年份 Year	合计 Total	铁路 Railway	中央 Central	地方 Local	公路 Highway	水运 Waterway	民用航空 Civil Aviation
货运量(万吨)	**Total Freight Traffic (10 000 tons)**						
1980	23650	3778	3594	184	16576	3261	
1981	24633	3573	3408	165	18067	2955	
1982	26951	3783	3616	167	20054	3076	
1983	29100	3876	3710	166	22095	3089	
1984	31800	3977	3826	151	24655	3128	
1985	32902	4218	402	126	35699	2945	
1986	34902	4346	4213	133	27140	3372	
1987	35747	4485	4354	131	27525	3693	
1988	39020	4522	4401	121	30922	3531	
1989	37842	4731	4567	164	29453	3671	
1990	37708	4771	4597	174	29679	3217	
1991	41219	4777	4614	163	33224	3177	
1992	42548	4906	4787	119	33788	3821	
1993	46074	4982	4886	96	37582	3441	1
1994	48448	4929	4841	88	39912	3536	1
1995	49885	5017	4904	113	41272	3531	1
1996	50454	4893	4830	63	42191	3301	1
1997	48980	4535	4495	40	41340	3034	2
1998	49147	4408	4360	48	41610	2990	1
1999	51183	4456	4424	32	43296	3178	1
2000	51228	4676	4628	48	42868	3406	2
2001	53035	4965	4913	52	44340	3572	2
2002	52156	4942	4905	37	42982	3760	2
2003	59952	5214	5214	-	51136	3600	2
周转量(亿吨公里)	**Total Freight Ton-kilometers (100 million ton-km)**						
1980	331.43	272.42	271.02	1.40	33.95	24.98	
1981	340.22	274.11	272.87	1.24	39.57	26.54	
1982	359.71	286.44	285.24	1.20	43.83	29.35	
1983	388.55	302.28	301.10	1.18	50.56	35.61	
1984	435.78	335.83	334.83	1.00	59.70	40.15	
1985	512.03	392.52	391.73	0.79	75.55	43.86	
1986	582.44	438.71	437.83	0.88	91.91	51.72	
1987	637.60	481.87	480.96	0.91	103.91	51.66	
1988	690.60	504.58	503.74	0.84	134.16	51.76	
1989	730.40	544.44	543.57	0.87	129.58	56.29	
1990	774.81	590.33	589.44	0.89	137.02	47.37	
1991	830.64	621.98	621.18	0.80	164.42	44.15	
1992	901.85	656.29	655.50	0.79	191.53	53.95	
1993	951.86	683.10	682.49	0.61	209.85	58.66	0.07
1994	1003.47	720.46	719.87	0.59	221.78	60.98	0.07
1995	1043.67	751.84	751.24	0.60	235.52	56.06	0.09
1996	1029.32	728.91	728.46	0.45	240.13	60.10	0.11
1997	998.72	690.80	690.47	0.33	244.86	62.78	0.12
1998	978.89	652.98	652.66	0.32	256.56	68.92	0.09
1999	967.68	624.14	623.89	0.25	272.71	70.08	0.11
2000	1074.50	632.12	631.94	0.18	297.79	143.76	0.11
2001	1132.18	674.39	674.25	0.14	316.03	141.22	0.14
2002	1223.09	730.86	730.76	0.10	355.96	135.48	0.16
2003	1361.12	782.60	782.60	-	455.45	121.74	1.33

12-11 各市、州邮电业务量(2003年)

Volume of Postal and Telecommunications Services by Region (2003)

市州	Cities and Prefecture	邮电业务总量（万元）Revenue From Postal and Telecommu-nication (10 000 yuan)	函件（万件）Letters (10 000 pieces)	报刊期发数（万份）Parcels (10 000 copies)	移动电话用户（万户）Mobile Telephone Subscribers (10 000 subscribers)	本地电话用户（万户）Local Telephone Subscribers (10 000 subscribers)
合计	**Total**	**2342341.65**	**50634.30**	**834.48**	**791.68**	**944.13**
长沙市	Changsha	570044.78	18000.10	84.09	185.13	161.31
株洲市	Zhuzhou	178406.63	1696.10	50.24	59.09	77.38
湘潭市	Xiangtan	127532.02	3722.30	40.80	41.46	52.45
衡阳市	Hengyang	199791.46	2770.70	80.69	75.25	90.05
邵阳市	Shaoyang	147224.91	2588.20	84.34	47.70	71.75
岳阳市	Yueyang	198927.44	2504.30	44.59	67.60	82.28
常德市	Changde	189621.38	1018.00	120.59	68.62	99.40
张家界市	Zhangjiajie	49379.30	2016.20	12.20	16.56	19.71
益阳市	Yiyang	127186.92	2221.70	36.34	44.49	60.55
郴州市	Chenzhou	148428.41	3371.50	56.65	55.19	58.75
永州市	Yongzhou	113352.15	2394.10	71.90	39.40	48.65
怀化市	Huaihua	127936.51	3416.20	78.20	38.34	56.20
娄底市	Loudi	101350.71	3261.10	43.98	33.61	43.07
湘西自治州	West Hunan A.P	63159.04	1653.80	29.85	19.24	22.58

12-12 邮电通信水平

Development of Postal and Telecommunications Services

指　标	Item	2003
平均每一邮电局所服务面积 （平方公里）	Average Area Served by Every Post Office (sq.km)	70.20
平均每一邮电局所服务人口 （万人）	Average People Served by Every Post Office (10 000 persons)	2.04
平均每人每年发函件数 (件)	Annual Average Number of Letters Mailes Per Capita (piece)	8.25
平均每百人每年订购报刊数 (份)	Annual Average Number of Newspaper and Magazine Subscribers Per 100 Persons (copy)	13.59
设有邮电局、所的乡镇比重 (%)	Percentage of Townships with Post and Telecommunication Office	100.00
平均每百人拥有电话机数（含移动）(部)	Number of Telephones Sets Owend Per 100 Persons (unit) (Including Mobile Telephones)	28.27
移动电话普及率 (部/百人)	Number of Mobile Telephones Owend per 100 Persons (unit)	12.89
进入长途电话自动网的县(市)比重 (%)	Percentage of Townships with Connected Autoexchange Net of Long Distance Call (%)	100.00
已通电话的乡(镇)比重 (%)	Percentage of Townships with Telephone Communication (%)	100.00

12-13 邮政业务基本情况

Basic Statistics of Postal Business

指标	Item	2002	2003
邮政局、所 （处）	**Number of Post Offices (unit)**	**3028**	**3017**
#设在农村的局、所(处)	#Rural Post Offices (unit)	2216	2206
邮政局（处）	Post Bureaus (unit)	108	108
邮政支局（处）	Branch of Post Bureaus (unit)	893	896
自办邮政所（处）	Post Places (unit)	1003	991
代办邮政所（处）	Agency of Post Places (unit)	1016	1020
其他邮政局、所（处）	Other Post Places (unit)	8	2
邮路总长度 （公里）	**Length of Postal Routes (km)**	**100249**	**96018**
农村投递路线总长度（公里）	**Length of Rural Delivery Routes (km)**	**218508**	**219859**
邮政业务总量 （万元）	**Revenue of Postal Business (10 000 yuan)**	**201785.05**	**211687.60**
包裹业务合计 （万件）	**Total of Parcels (10 000 pieces)**	**397.16**	**371.30**
国内内地包裹（万件）	Parcels for Internal Business (10 000 pieces)	394.23	368.80
港、澳、台包裹（万件）	Parcels for HK,Macao and Taiwan Business (10 000 pieces)	1.69	0.70
国际包裹（万件）	Parcels for International Business (10 000 pieces)	1.25	1.80
报刊业务	**Business of Newspaper and Magazine**		
报纸累计份数（万份）	Total of Newspapers (10 000 copies)	72871.12	67100.40
杂志累计份数（万份）	Total of Magazines (10 000 copies)	8044.01	6368.30
报纸期发份数（万份）	Number of Newspapers in one period (10 000 copies)	462.01	500.40
杂志期发份数（万份）	Number of Magazines in one period (10 000 copies)	441.15	334.10
报刊流转额（万元）	Revenue of Newspaper and Magazine in Circulation (10 000 yuan)	63426.19	64179.80
邮政储蓄业务	**Postal Deposits Business**		
邮政储蓄网点数 （个）	Number of Places (unit)	1932	1945
邮政储蓄年末余额 （万元）	Balance at the year-end (10 000 yuan)	3068901.81	3866964
物流运输业务量（万吨公里）	**Total of Interflow Transpotation Business (10 000 ton-km)**	**12074.48**	**3668.70**
邮政其他业务量 （万元）	**Revenue of Other Postal Business (10 000 yuan)**	**17538.04**	**21698.50**
#代办电信业务量（万元）	#Revenue of Telecommunication Agency (10 000 yuan)	3661.88	5925.80

12-14 电信业务基本情况

Basic Statistics of Telecommunication

指标	Item	2002	2003
销售营业网点数（处）	**Number of Selling Places (unit)**	**6967**	**5341**
自办营业网点数（处）	Main Selling Places (unit)	1186	1449
租用营业网点数（处）	Rend Selling Places (unit)	621	539
电信业务代办网点数（处）	Agency of Telecommunication Places (unit)	5160	5465
分组交换节点机端口数（个）	**Number of Packet Switch boards (unit)**	**5502**	**5472**
长途电信设备	**Equipment of Long Distance Telecommunication**		
长途自动电话交换机容量（路端）	Autoexchange of Long Distance Telephone Capacity (line)	325330	370750
数字微波线路长度（公里）	Length of Digital Microwave lines (km)	8879.5	10620
长途光缆线路长度（公里）	Length of Long Distance Optical Cables (km)	18594.81	21172.61
长途业务电路（路）	Long Distance lines (line)	659106	569385
长途电话业务电路（路）	Long Distance telephone lines (line)	223665	168796
数据通信网长途电路（路）	Long Distance lines of Data Communication Network (line)	255315	177621
本地电话设备	**Equipment of Local Telephone**		
局用交换机容量（万门）	Local Switch Boards Capacity (10 000 lines)	1049.23	1085.61
电话机总数（万部）	Total of Telephone (10 000 sets)	826.55	902.11
移动通信主要设备	**Main Equipment of Mobile Communication**		
移动电话网络容量（门）	Network of Mobile Telephone Capacity (line)	8358820	10508000
#GSM（门）	#GSM (line)	7535190	9256000
移动电话基站（个）	Basic Station of Mobile Telephone (unit)	6971	8373
#GSM（个）	#GSM (unit)	6173	7100
移动电话信道（个）	Mobile Telephone Channel (unit)	264693	360831
移动电话交换机容量（门）	Switch Boards Capacity of Mobile Telephone (line)	8398630	10508000
无线寻呼设备	**Equipment of Wireless Paging**		
无线寻呼系统容量（个）	Wireless Paging System Capacity (unit)	7040000	6280000
无线寻呼终端（部）	Wireless Paging Terminal (unit)	147732	
无线寻呼基站（个）	Basic Station of Wireless Paging (unit)	654	495
电信业务总量 （万元）	**Revenue of Telecommunication Business (10 000 yuan)**	**1652927.69**	**2130654.05**
公众电报 （份）	Express Mail of Public (copies)	325541	47871
用户电报 （份）	Express Mail of Fixed User (copies)	2416	944
长途电话 （万次）	Long Distance Telephone (10 000 times)	79874.03	99396.81
IP电话 （万次）	IP Telephone (10 000 times)	39435	47866
无线寻呼年末用户（万户）	Wireless Paging User at the year-end (10 000 households)	367.04	8.93
移动电话年末用户（万户）	Mobile Telephone User at the year-end (10 000 households)	598.21	840.44
#数字移动电话年末用户	#Digital Mobile Telephone User at the year-end	598.21	791.68
本地电话用户 （万户）	Local Telephone User (10 000 households)	808.67	943.65
住宅电话用户 （万户）	Fixed Telephone User (10 000 households)	661.43	728.55
公用电话用户 （万户）	Public Telephone User (10 000 households)	61.02	71.61
国际互联网用户 （万户）	Internet User (10 000 households)	242.64	211.04

十三、国内、外贸易
对外经济和旅游

DOMESTIC TRADE，FOREIGN TRADE，
FOREIGN ECONOMY AND TOURISM

资料整理人员： 王忠好　唐双全　曾晓林　郭文峰

13-1 国内贸易基本情况

Basic Statistics on Domestic Trade

项 目	Item	2000	2001	2002	2003
社会消费品零售总额（亿元）	**Total Retail Sales of Consumer Goods (100 million yuan)**	**1364.66**	**1511.07**	**1678.86**	**1816.30**
按地区分	**By Location**				
市	City	710.06	800.06	903.06	997.12
县	Country	255.10	278.01	307.01	332.48
县以下	Under Country Lever	399.50	433.00	468.79	486.70
按行业分	**By Sector**				
批发零售贸易业	Wholesales and Retail Sales Trade	885.05	985.14	1100.05	1558.40
餐饮业	Catering Trade	139.55	161.08	187.53	224.57
制造业	Manufacturing	69.76	77.93	81.23	-
其他行业	Others	270.30	286.92	310.05	33.33
农民对非农业居民零售	Retail Sales of Peasantry to Non-peasantry	243.15	257.58	278.34	-
消费品市场个数(个)	**Number of Consumable Markets (unit)**	**3682**	**3691**	**3444**	**3550**
城市	Urban Areas	1095	1122	1135	1406
乡村	Rural Areas	2587	2569	2309	2144
消费品市场成交额(亿元)	**Transaction Value of Consumable Markets (100 million yuan)**	**880.93**	**855.74**	**911.77**	**958.11**
按城乡分：	**By Urban or Rural Areas:**				
城市	Urban Areas	484.07	466.73	600.86	606.76
乡村	Rural Areas	396.86	389.01	310.91	351.35
按商品类别分：	**By Types of Goods:**				
粮食类	Grain	38.69	42.19	40.33	57.68
油脂油料类	Oils	25.07	23.47	25.37	37.37
棉烟麻类	Cotton, Tobacco and Hemp	6.63	5.80	24.31	16.70
肉食禽蛋类	Meat,Poultry and Eggs	192.53	184.04	179.72	440.61
水产品类	Aquatic Products	68.28	68.38	61.85	85.48
蔬菜类	Vegetables	97.86	99.78	91.40	119.18
干鲜果类	Dried and Fresh Fruits	103.05	99.03	101.10	122.53
大牲畜类	Large Domeestic Animals	10.31	8.74	12.79	34.50
家畜类	Domeestic Animals	18.71	19.16	19.20	195.68
工业品类	Industrial Products	277.02	269.66	283.06	258.14
其他类	Others	42.80	35.51	72.66	49.62
成交额为社会消费品零售总额(%)	**Proportion of Transaction Value to Total Retail Sales of Consumer Goods (%)**	**64.60**	**56.60**	**54.30**	**52.80**

注：2003年，社会消费品零售总额统计口径进行了调整，分行业的部分数据不可比。

The statistical requirement of total retail sales of consumer goods has been regulated in 2003,the data by sector are not comparable.

13-2 限额以上批发零售贸易、餐饮业基本情况(2003年)

Basic Statistics on Gross Value of Purchases, Sales and Inventory of Wholesale and Retail Trade (2003)

指标	Item	法人单位(个) Number of Corporation (Unit)	产业活动单位(个) Number of Active Units (unit)	从业人数(人) Persons Engaged (person)
总 计	**Total**	**932**	**3047**	**180774**
批发业	**Wholesale Trades**	**414**	**1309**	**59459**
内资企业	Domestic Funded Enterprises	414	1308	59380
国有企业	State-owned Enterprises	227	734	32706
集体企业	Collective-owned Enterprises	32	68	5406
股份合作企业	Cooperative Enterprises	6	7	738
联营企业	Joint Ownership Enterprises			
国有与集体联营企业	Joint State-collective Enterprises			
有限责任公司	Limited Liability Corporations	68	195	8927
国有独资企业	State-funded Corporations	4	87	475
其他有限责任公司	Other Limited Liability Corporations	64	108	8452
股份有限公司	Share-holding Corporations Ltd.	65	279	10445
私营企业	Private Enterprises	16	25	1158
私营有限责任公司	Private Limited Liability Corporations	12	16	760
零售业	**Retail Sale Trades**	**358**	**1411**	**76561**
内资企业	Domestic Funded Enterprises	351	1402	74245
国有企业	State-owned Enterprises	155	734	22071
集体企业	Collective-owned Enterprises	23	89	6495
股份合作企业	Cooperative Enterprises	3	3	121
联营企业	Joint Ownership Enterprises	1	2	100
有限责任公司	Limited Liability Corporations	47	170	9613
其他有限责任公司	Other Limited Liability Corporations	46	166	9567
股份有限公司	Share-holding Corporations Ltd.	35	234	16779
私营企业	Private Enterprises	85	168	18694
私营有限责任公司	Private Limited Liability Corporations	46	112	11870
外商投资企业	Enterprises with Foreign Investment	4	6	2114
中外合资经营企业	Joint-venture Enterprises	4	5	1850
餐饮业	**Catering Trades**	**160**	**327**	**44754**
内资企业	Domestic Funded Enterprises	149	274	35765
国有企业	State-owned Enterprises	26	88	11617
集体企业	Collective-owned Enterprises	3	13	1222
联营企业	Joint Ownership Enterprises		1	181
国有联营企业	Collective Joint Ownership Enterprises		1	181
有限责任公司	Limited Liability Corporations	30	44	7624
其他有限责任公司	Other Limited Liability Corporations	30	44	7624
股份有限公司	Share-holding Corporations Ltd.	8	19	3240
私营企业	Private Enterprises	72	95	9962
私营有限责任公司	Private Limited Liability Corporations	21	26	3780
港、澳、台商投资企业	Enterprises with Investment from Hongkong,Macro and Taiwan	6	19	4852
合资经营企业(港或澳、台资)	Joint-venture Enterprises (with Funds from HongKong,Macao and Taiwan)	4	14	4089
合作经营企业(港或澳、台资)	Cooperative Enterprises (with Funds from HongKong,Macao and Taiwan)		1	353
外商投资企业	Enterprises with Foreign Investment	5	34	4137
中外合资经营企业	Joint-venture Enterprises	1	3	708
中外合作经营企业	Cooperative Enterprises	1	13	1080
外资企业	Enterprises with Sole Foreign Investment	1	16	2178

13-3 限额以上批发零售贸易业商品购进、销售、库存总额(2003年)

Total Value of Purchases Sales and Inventory of above Designated Size in Wholesale and Retail Sales Trade (2003)

单位：亿元 (100 million yuan)

指标	Item	商品购进总额 Total Purchases	商品销售总额 Total Sales	批发 Wholesale Trade	零售 Retail Trade	年末库存总额 Inventory Year-end
总 计	**Total**	**975.80**	**1038.24**	**784.42**	**253.81**	**98.14**
国有及国有控股	State-owned Enterprises (including enterprises with controlling share hold by the state)	778.50	816.15	658.12	158.03	61.29
按登记注册类型分组	**By Status of Registration**					
内资企业	Domestic Funded Enterprises	960.15	1022.18	781.08	241.10	96.78
国有企业	State-owned Enterprises	392.63	418.21	352.63	65.58	39.59
集体企业	Collective-owned Enterprises	32.52	38.52	27.00	11.52	8.44
股份合作企业	Cooperative Enterprises	4.03	4.84	1.98	2.86	0.35
联营企业	Joint Ownership Enterprises	0.19	0.19		0.19	…
集体联营企业	Collective Joint Ownership Enterprises					
国有与集体联营	Joint State-collective Enterprises	0.05	0.05		0.05	…
有限责任公司	Limited Liability Corporations	170.63	174.28	138.14	36.14	24.91
国有独资企业	State-funded Corporations	2.45	3.17	3.01	0.15	0.09
其他有限责任公司	Other Limited Liability Corporations	168.18	171.11	135.12	35.99	24.83
股份有限公司	Share-holding Corporations Ltd.	311.62	331.78	239.68	92.11	16.30
私营企业	Private Enterprises	48.01	53.89	21.65	32.23	7.09
私营有限责任公司	Private Limited Liability Corporations	29.84	35.51	13.41	22.10	3.54
外商投资企业	Enterprises with Foreign Investment	15.19	15.60	3.10	12.51	1.35
中外合资经营企业	Joint-venture Enterprises	13.10	13.48	3.10	10.38	0.90
按国民经济行业分组	**By Sector**					
批发业	**Wholesale Trade**	**807.09**	**855.50**	**758.90**	**96.60**	**73.36**
农畜产品批发业	Farming Products and Animal Products	20.51	30.37	29.97	0.40	8.82
食品、饮料及烟草制品	Foods、Beverages and Tobaccos	211.45	237.46	233.17	4.29	20.23
纺织、服装及日用品	Textiles,Garments and Daily Consumer Goods	40.04	28.92	26.81	2.10	1.77
文化、体育用品及器材	Goods and Appliancea of Cultural and Sports	24.12	24.01	21.43	2.58	2.20
医药及医疗器材	Medicines and Medical Appliances	65.49	62.96	52.54	10.42	17.52
矿产品、建材及化工产品	Mineral Products,Building and Chemical Materials	315.07	335.38	282.03	53.35	13.85
机械、五金交电及电子产品	Machinery,Hardware,Transport,Electric Products	122.04	117.98	96.17	21.81	8.62
其他批发业	Others	8.36	18.42	16.77	1.65	0.33
零售业	**Retail Trade**	**168.71**	**182.74**	**25.52**	**157.21**	**24.78**
综合零售业	General Retail Trade	86.76	95.02	5.79	89.23	9.19
百货零售业	Retail of Consumer Goods	44.86	50.20	4.32	45.87	3.42
超级市场零售业	Retail of Super Markets	40.75	43.57	0.56	43.02	5.55
食品、饮料及烟草制品	Foods、Beverages and Tobaccos	7.22	8.07	3.08	4.99	2.05
纺织、服装及日用品	Textiles,Garments and Daily Consumer Goods	8.83	8.05	1.29	6.76	1.51
文化、体育用品及器材	Goods and Appliancea of Cultural and Sports	16.96	16.60	2.28	14.33	4.75
医药及医疗器材专门零售业	Medicines and Medical Appliances	16.72	18.18	1.72	16.46	2.96
#药品零售业	#Medicines	16.72	18.18	1.72	16.46	2.96
汽车、摩托车、燃料及零配件	Motor Vehicles,Motorcycles and Parts,Fuels	22.52	25.45	7.57	17.88	1.67
#汽车零售业	#Motor Vehicles	8.18	9.54	1.51	8.03	1.07
机动车燃料零售业	Retail of Motor Vehicles Fules	13.91	15.48	6.00	9.48	0.57
家用电器及电子产品	Electronic Household Appliances and Products	4.91	6.44	1.45	4.99	1.64
五金、家具及室内装修材料	Hardware,Furniture and Fittering Material	4.71	4.84	2.35	2.49	1.02
无店铺及其他零售业	Others	0.07	0.08		0.08	…

13-4 限额以上批发零售贸易企业商品销售数量

Total Value of Wholesale above Designated Size in Wholesale and Retail Trade

指标	Item	合计 Total		批发 Wholesale Trade		零售 Retail Trade	
		2002	2003	2002	2003	2002	2003
粮食(吨)	Grain (ton)	301333	648892	241773	525321	59560	123571
食用植物油(吨)	Edible Vegetable Oil (ton)	18725	41333	10904	28253	7821	13080
食糖(吨)	Sugar (ton)	17778	18034	15476	15887	2302	2147
棉花(吨)	Cotton (ton)	115152	166618	115127	166595	25	23
电视机(台)	Television (unit)	357526	354464	120605	107239	236921	247225
组合音响(台)	Hi-Fi Stereo Component	19166	28579	248	652	18918	27927
摄像机(台)	Pickup Camera (unit)	1320	2429		167	1320	2262
录像机(台)	Video Recorder (unit)	2365				2365	
影碟机(台)	Video Disc Player (unit)	75450	98321	3836	6931	71614	91390
家用电冰箱(台)	Household Refrigerator (unit)	237358	213390	111837	87228	125521	126162
家用洗衣机(台)	Household Washing Machine (unit)	270698	251696	128300	112142	142398	139554
房间空调器(台)	Room Air Conditioner (unit)	374060	544947	230458	351902	143602	193045
微波炉(台)	Micro-oven (unit)	166522	155152	39838	87490	126684	67662
微型计算机(台)	Personal Computer (unit)	76887	38872	54949	30415	21938	8457
普通电话机(台)	Telephone (unit)	87667	108812		378	87667	108434
移动电话机(台)	Hand Telephone (unit)	266530	517919	231904	389060	34626	128859
寻呼机(台)	Beep-Pager (unit)	1396				1396	
煤炭(吨)	Coal (ton)	241506	171172	241506	151872		19300
木材(立方米)	Wood (cu.m)	20026	19426	20026	19426		
汽油(吨)	Gasoline (ton)	2089545	2737817	1685954	2116876	403591	620941
柴油(吨)	Diesel (ton)	4145536	5060238	3747449	4292500	398087	767738
化学肥料(吨)	Chemical Fertilizers (ton)	844389	531601	844389	531601		
农用薄膜(吨)	Farming Pellicle (ton)	248	160	248	160		
化学农药(吨)	Chemical Pesticide (ton)	9872	9439	9872	9439		
钢材(吨)	Steel (ton)	607295	622572	580914	602588	26381	19984
铜(吨)	Copper (ton)	9361	5137	9361	5137		
铝(吨)	Aluminum (ton)	6102	25080	6102	25080		
水泥(吨)	Cement (ton)	122525	64118	120376	62546	2149	1572
汽车(辆)	Motor Vehicles (unit)	43971	119923	14319	65951	29652	53972
#轿车(辆)	Car (unit)	13254	73808	4909	32449	8345	41359
摩托车(辆)	Motor (unit)	94521	125417	91256	121866	3265	3551
拖拉机(辆)	Tractors (unit)	1558	1697	1558	1697		

13-5 限额以上餐饮企业销售情况

Sales Statistics of above Designated Size in Catering Enterprises

单位：万元 (10 000 yuan)

指标	Item	营业总收入 Total Operating Revenue		商品零售额 Retail Trade	
		2002	2003	2002	2003
总计	**Total**	**213639.8**	**283006.5**	**184305.2**	**250798.1**
按登记注册类型分组	**By Status of Registration**				
内资企业	Domestic Funded Enterprises	159243.7	217901.7	133140.5	187135.0
国有企业	State-owned Enterprises	58106.7	63137.6	46413.4	48646.0
集体企业	Collective-owned Enterprises	4495.2	5033.0	4409.2	4950.0
股份合作企业	Cooperative Enterprises	5647.0	11278.6	5647.0	11127.8
联营企业	Joint Ownership Enterprises	3686.1	802.4	3275.5	802.4
国有联营企业	State Joint Ownership Enterprises	1221.0	802.4	1221.0	802.4
集体联营企业	Collective Joint Ownership	1740.0		1740.0	
其他联营企业	Other Joint Ownership Enterprises	725.1		314.5	
有限责任公司	Limited Liability Corporations	32625.7	45564.2	24463.0	36547.1
其他有限责任公司	Other Limited Liability Corporations	32625.7	45564.2	24463.0	36547.1
股份有限公司	Share-holding Corporations Ltd.	22920.0	27089.0	19811.3	24600.7
私营企业	Private Enterprises	31763.0	61258.5	29121.1	58310.8
私营独资企业	Private Exclusively Funded Enterprises	8807.6	16982.9	8188.2	16547.3
私营合伙企业	Private Partnership Enterprises	4432.8	10556.3	4432.8	10556.3
私营有限责任公司	Private Limited Liability Corporations	15542.4	26172.5	13857.5	24045.6
私营股份有限公司	Private Share Holding Limited Companies	2980.2	7546.8	2642.6	7161.6
其他企业	Other Enterprises		3738.4		2150.2
港、澳、台商投资企业	Enterprises with Investment from Hongkong,Macro and Taiwan	24911.1	25143.8	22446.0	23702.1
合资经营企业（港或澳、台资）	Joint-venture Enterprises (with Funds from HongKong,Macao and Taiwan)	16146.5	20746.9	14707.7	19305.2
合作经营企业（港或澳、台资）	Cooperative Enterprises (with Funds from HongKong,Macao and Taiwan)	5391.4	1086.5	4365.1	1086.5
独资经营企业	Ventures Exclusively Funded	411.8	690.6	411.8	690.6
投资股份有限公司	Share Holding Limited Companies	2961.4	2619.8	2961.4	2619.8
外商投资企业	Enterprises with Foreign Investment	29485.0	39961.0	28718.7	39961.0
中外合资经营企业	Joint-venture Enterprises	1386.1	6046.9	1254.5	6046.9
中外合作经营企业	Cooperative Enterprises	13578.7	14571.9	12944.0	14571.9
外资企业	Enterprises with Sole Foreign Investment	13814.8	18136.8	13814.8	18136.8
外商投资股份有限公司	Share Holding Limited Companies	705.4	1205.4	705.4	1205.4
按国民经济行业分组	**By Sector**				
正餐	Dinner	171993.5	240564.9	143717.1	210626.0
快餐	Snack	26688.5	29413.3	26268.5	28759.1
饮料及冷饮	Beverage and Cold Drinks		3208.9		3208.9
其他餐饮	Others	14957.8	9819.4	14319.6	8204.1

13-6 限额以上批发零售贸易企业财务状况(2003年)

单位：万元

项 目	Item	合 计 Total	内资企业 Domestic Funded Enterprises	国有企业 State-owned Enterprises	集体企业 Collective Owned Enterprises	股份合作企业 Cooperative Enterprises
流动资产合计	Total Circulating Funds	3312176.2	3284605.8	1677266.7	434368.7	10638.0
#存货	#Inventories	835826.9	826445.5	380962.6	100393.3	3511.5
长期投资	Long-term Investment	328472.4	327477.1	213082.8	11741.3	383.9
固定资产合计	Total Fixed Assets	1325675.3	1269404.8	543594.4	66210.6	4623.6
固定资产原价	Original Value of Fixed Assets	1564900.9	1494579.9	663313.6	81249.9	5655.2
累计折旧	Total Depreciation	403413.9	389145.0	209603.6	26512.7	1146.7
#本年折旧	#Depreciation This Year	67630.7	62734.6	32926.0	2201.4	192.6
资产总计	**Total Assets**	**5531288.0**	**5418536.7**	**2534791.2**	**548819.9**	**16557.8**
负债合计	**Total Liabilities**	**4326173.9**	**4254062.7**	**2095546.3**	**568577.7**	**10856.9**
所有者权益合计	**Total Creditors Equity**	**1205114.1**	**1164474.0**	**439244.9**	**-19757.8**	**5700.9**
实收资本	Capitals Hold	798131.3	747329.7	256064.8	43838.8	3422.0
国家资本	State Capital	389500.1	379569.3	208770.6	5830.9	83.5
外商资本	Foreign Capital	33723.2				
商品销售收入净额	Net Sales Revenue	9100437.2	8980884.7	3792301.8	316715.3	44654.8
商品销售成本	Cost of Sales	8239513.4	8138431.0	3345607.1	300598.9	41148.2
经营费用	Management Cost	345068.8	333709.2	145340.6	11123.9	1989.3
商品销售税金及附加费	Sales Tax and Extra Changes	16787.5	16527.7	6823.3	449.0	73.0
商品销售利润	Total Profits	499067.5	492216.8	294530.8	4543.5	1444.3
代购代销收入	Income from Buy on Sb and Sell Goods on a Commission Basis	7022.6	7022.6	2755.4	796.8	
主营业务利润	Major Business Profits	506090.1	499239.4	297286.2	5340.3	1444.3
其他业务利润	Other Business Profits	40808.6	36456.2	9463.9	1930.8	31.0
管理费用	Overhead Expenses	337105.1	326397.5	197205.4	14832.1	849.0
税金	Taxes	9255.2	8700.4	5194.2	288.3	34.5
财产保险费	Premiums of Property Insurance	3782.3	3591.3	2396.4	194.4	3.4
劳动、待业保险费	Premiums of Labor Insurance	28610.5	28430.5	18824.9	1671.4	10.8
财务费用	Financial Expenses	63189.3	63160.6	28621.2	13251.2	19.7
利息支出	Expenses for Interest	55913.7	54964.1	32360.3	5680.8	18.3
营业利润	Operating Profits	146604.3	146137.5	80923.5	-20812.2	606.6
补贴收入	Subsidies	25020.6	25007.8	22633.4	977.4	3.8
利润总额	Total Profits	95072.3	93960.8	46087.7	-23333.6	590.5
本年应付工资总额	Total Wages Payable this Year	142465.7	139476.7	70294.0	8118.1	737.0
本年应付福利费总额	Welfare Expenses Payable this Year	35203.9	35097.5	15546.7	1362.8	99.6
本年应缴增值税额	Value-added Tax Payable	138402.4	135674.8	71914.2	2527.3	575.0
本年进项增值税额	Value-added Tax from Buying	1222894.3	1205129.3	466113.3	28965.2	6590.5
本年销项增值税额	Value-added Tax from Selling	1315120.5	1294956.0	496870.5	31476.8	7172.4

Financial Affairs of above Designated Size in Wholesale and Retail Trade Enterprises (2003)

(10 000 yuan)

					批发业				
				外商投资		农畜产品	食品饮料烟草	纺织服装日用品	文体用品器材批发
联营企业 Joint Ownership Enterprises	有限公司 Limitied Liability Corporation	股份公司 Share-holding Corporation Ltd.	私营企业 Private Enterprises	Foreign Investment	Wholesale Trade	Farming Products and Animal Products	Foods, Beverages, and Tobaccos	Textiles, Garments, and Daily Consumer Goods	Cultural and Sports Goods
331764.1	438432.7	549854.1	171650.3	21829.6	2666323.1	591921.9	830965.6	176497.2	51917.0
94283.9	125067.8	161619.2	53973.0	6321.4	613395.5	100966.4	229038.9	23944.7	13897.6
20942.3	24263.4	73477.1	4528.6	845.8	283666.7	7868.7	97404.2	31777.6	5533.9
48732.4	83472.5	523440.8	47368.6	44117.5	775728.4	60470.8	259327.0	17862.7	26057.9
56133.5	95826.8	597850.9	49911.5	56003.4	926151.0	79265.3	317412.5	23329.3	39403.4
12057.7	21117.8	124554.8	6131.7	12103.3	265732.1	25243.7	90971.8	6827.8	13604.7
3040.5	5482.0	19421.6	2449.0	2879.5	40381.3	1191.9	15889.1	758.1	2904.7
421070.8	**572974.4**	**1509926.6**	**230355.1**	**92579.2**	**4164708.5**	**694301.7**	**1225990.6**	**237133.9**	**88629.9**
323803.2	**441816.5**	**947864.4**	**184201.0**	**51304.8**	**3373634.1**	**822919.0**	**785808.0**	**239353.8**	**43482.2**
97267.6	**131157.9**	**562062.2**	**46154.1**	**41274.4**	**791074.4**	**-128617.3**	**440182.6**	**-2219.9**	**45147.7**
78567.2	100944.8	290084.0	52811.0	46201.6	571363.7	39688.2	136175.2	17168.4	10886.1
28529.7	30809.2	134075.1		8430.8	329399.6	12651.6	125917.7	12745.5	8966.8
				33723.2					
1195331.9	1444766.4	2926614.5	449560.0	119227.2	7493710.1	267739.2	2218523.7	224418.1	177551.6
1130598.6	1350676.8	2690129.8	404570.6	99702.6	6856206.0	259573.5	1893734.8	211306.2	156887.5
45553.8	64427.5	81712.7	28117.1	10628.1	232567.7	13607.1	77910.7	7937.2	6425.5
939.7	1847.3	5427.9	1873.9	21.4	10221.3	297.0	4908.9	30.2	284.9
18239.8	27814.8	149344.1	14998.4	8875.1	394715.1	-5738.4	241969.3	5144.5	13953.7
625.9	625.9	2632.3	203.0		5614.9	859.0	1637.6	5.6	
18865.7	28440.7	151976.4	15201.4	8875.1	400330.0	-4879.4	243606.9	5150.1	13953.7
3123.1	11675.0	9062.2	3607.2	4279.8	12234.8	377.4	2812.3	388.9	716.7
19682.2	32390.3	67160.7	13478.4	9287.4	233804.8	28528.9	123036.6	5111.4	9565.3
628.0	835.2	2010.8	332.0	554.4	5411.2	213.0	3086.3	203.0	255.8
67.3	128.1	795.6	73.4	189.5	2767.0	275.6	1645.0	99.6	52.4
1591.5	2260.1	5475.2	159.2	178.4	21605.0	1926.0	13978.5	151.1	1250.3
1810.9	2375.3	16329.3	2565.7	1178.9	45980.9	16866.6	14297.9	3909.0	45.4
995.0	1433.8	14379.6	1093.2	949.6	40372.3	9327.1	17555.3	4156.8	59.3
495.7	5350.1	77548.6	2764.5	2688.6	132779.1	-49897.5	109084.7	-3481.4	5059.7
458.0	489.8	798.4	105.0	0.0	23204.1	4995.0	16744.5	239.9	27.0
-3443.3	-678.8	68871.5	2684.1	3322.4	85332.4	-61932.8	89970.9	-3184.4	4160.0
9808.7	17739.5	29345.1	12785.9	2854.8	85652.2	5525.7	39967.8	2109.9	5093.5
2168.8	11901.5	4540.6	1606.2	93.3	18666.4	734.5	9383.2	945.2	917.8
7358.9	13764.2	41231.4	5389.4	2703.5	102098.2	4743.6	48301.0	150.8	2798.1
168055.3	211328.2	425749.6	65617.3	17673.2	1010527.8	24059.6	291395.2	22241.4	23896.8
188090.7	234817.2	451611.7	71987.0	20050.8	1069895.9	25319.9	320924.6	6252.3	25806.0

项 目	Item	医药医疗器材批发 Medicines and medical Appliances	矿产品建材及化工产品 Mineral Products, Building and Chemical Materials	机械五金交电及电子批发 Hardware, Transport and Electric	零售业 Retail Trade	综合零售 General Retail Trade
流动资产合计	Total Circulating Funds	206696.7	365524.3	414711.4	645853.1	396849.5
#存货	#Inventories	64427.9	90618.1	86974.5	222431.4	140041.0
长期投资	Long-term Investment	6630.1	33977.9	85486.7	44805.7	35428.7
固定资产合计	Total Fixed Assets	58589.3	279075.2	57137.7	549946.9	395033.5
固定资产原价	Original Value of Fixed Assets	47735.0	324695.9	69643.9	638749.9	463115.7
累计折旧	Total Depreciation	15857.1	88485.5	17010.9	137681.8	93088.0
本年折旧	Depreciation This Year	1260.9	8584.0	7907.7	27249.4	21031.7
资产总计	**Total Assets**	**287108.8**	**991971.2**	**570689.3**	**1366579.5**	**921021.9**
负债合计	**Total Liabilities**	**228744.3**	**669095.8**	**559148.4**	**952539.8**	**634756.2**
所有者权益合计	**Total Creditors Equity**	**58364.5**	**322875.4**	**11540.9**	**414039.7**	**286265.7**
实收资本	Capitals Hold	56467.5	234766.2	44558.8	226767.6	139818.7
国家资本	State Capital	16468.5	121816.1	10012.2	60100.5	27008.4
外商资本	Foreign Capital	0.0	0.0	0.0	33723.2	33723.2
商品销售收入净额	Net Sales Revenue	565269.6	2885069.4	1093375.4	1606727.1	894169.2
商品销售成本	Cost of Sales	533806.9	2706753.2	1038880.9	1383307.4	759951.0
经营费用	Management Cost	17052.7	63438.1	41832.1	112501.1	63881.4
商品销售税金及附加费	Sales Tax and Extra Changes	322.6	3493.5	836.1	6566.2	4725.4
商品销售利润	Total Profits	14087.4	111384.6	11826.3	104352.4	65611.4
代购代销收入	Income from Buy on Sb and Sell Goods on a Commission Basis	0.0	2930.4	177.3	1407.7	501.8
主营业务利润	Major Business Profits	14087.4	114315.0	12003.6	105760.1	66113.2
其他业务利润	Other Business Profits	818.0	2345.7	3859.4	28573.8	21948.0
管理费用	Overhead Expenses	14700.3	37488.1	12637.1	103300.3	62400.1
税金	Taxes	177.5	854.3	502.9	3844.0	2630.1
财产保险费	Premiums of Property Insurance	90.4	476.6	119.2	1015.3	727.8
劳动、待业保险费	Premiums of Labor Insurance	679.9	2827.6	688.6	7005.5	4439.2
财务费用	Financial Expenses	2311.8	6789.2	1668.7	17208.4	13361.9
利息支出	Expenses for Interest	1991.7	4921.0	2019.1	15541.4	12859.1
营业利润	Operating Profits	-2106.7	72383.4	1557.2	13825.2	12299.2
补贴收入	Subsidies	113.2	374.6	144.1	1816.5	764.9
利润总额	Total Profits	-1502.6	62562.5	-5677.8	9739.9	11838.2
本年应付工资总额	Total Wages Payable this Year	6001.9	19535.1	6241.3	56813.5	31758.9
本年应付福利费总额	Welfare Expenses Payable this Year	1631.7	3931.7	1012.4	16537.5	4195.2
本年应缴增值税额	Value-added Tax Payable	1729.0	37845.7	6379.1	36304.2	17987.9
本年进项增值税额	Value-added Tax from Buying	62672.1	406600.9	175393.2	212366.5	110558.4
本年销项增值税额	Value-added Tax from Selling	81566.4	428309.1	177195.6	245224.6	126085.5

continued (10 000 yuan)

食品饮料烟草 Foods, Beverages, and Tobaccos	纺织服装日用品 Textiles, Garments, and Daily Consumer Goods	文体用品器材 Cultural and Sports Goods	医药医疗器材 Medicines and medical Appliances	汽车摩托及燃料 Motor Vehicles, Motorcycles and Fuels	家用电器及电子产品 Electronic Household Appliance, Electronic Products	五金家具室内装修 Hardware Furniture and Fittering Material	按零售业态 百货商店 Consumer Goods Shoping	超级市场 Super Markets	专业专卖 Specialized Trade
22866.7	33023.8	58937.7	37094.2	48803.7	29419.8	18614.5	207687.5	158636.8	115274.9
6905.8	9242.3	24479.7	17709.5	13561.2	6998.1	3454.1	52817.9	65710.5	45222.7
200.3	23.0	1954.9	2441.9	2388.6	1165.5	1053.3	33142.1	2052.0	6016.7
21420.1	16494.9	43701.4	16029.4	27966.3	25777.7	3384.8	245611.4	70821.8	65292.5
22240.6	16627.2	57166.7	18434.8	31782.6	25409.2	3674.6	287380.1	76614.7	78188.2
3922.0	3848.2	19968.5	5231.2	5405.3	5474.9	584.0	66430.2	11798.7	22095.4
442.6	788.0	2578.3	740.8	959.6	550.7	147.0	11912.4	4590.6	3964.2
45677.2	**55765.3**	**111702.2**	**58539.4**	**88648.5**	**60953.9**	**23739.6**	**549326.2**	**252146.2**	**200600.3**
38782.9	**46808.7**	**53888.9**	**46109.8**	**66017.1**	**43377.9**	**22625.7**	**408881.5**	**193257.9**	**138643.3**
6894.3	**8956.6**	**57813.3**	**12429.6**	**22631.4**	**17576.0**	**1113.9**	**140444.7**	**58888.3**	**61957.0**
8009.4	12983.5	17129.5	13499.6	13619.5	18994.2	1713.2	87951.0	46490.3	35108.2
3758.6	1504.1	14981.2	5315.2	3662.0	2116.9	1304.1	28915.0	5269.0	14588.1
							33723.2		
63404.9	70994.1	134937.0	100704.0	239977.4	65321.6	36393.8	542033.6	439495.0	354209.4
58504.4	61319.1	101592.1	87797.8	222561.4	56786.4	34061.4	458162.5	383228.8	310447.4
4075.4	8456.8	12513.4	8708.3	8128.5	4949.2	1710.0	31966.7	43557.0	22103.8
93.5	88.1	595.7	294.9	370.3	358.0	40.3	2517.2	1970.0	1093.3
731.6	1130.1	20235.8	3903.0	8917.2	3228.0	582.1	49387.2	10739.2	20564.9
	31.7	26.6		847.6			69.8	371.6	954.3
731.6	1161.8	20262.4	3903.0	9764.8	3228.0	582.1	49457.0	11110.8	21519.2
973.7	2998.1	1199.0	456.8	214.7	537.7	237.2	10256.5	13961.3	1437.4
4492.8	2500.3	17735.6	5304.0	6179.1	2943.5	1683.1	41819.9	19905.0	21361.4
72.5	134.7	663.8	127.6	110.5	58.6	45.8	2078.3	545.9	697.0
8.0	14.4	119.7	60.8	77.8	3.8	2.4	543.8	111.7	134.4
275.0	277.6	1002.8	463.2	466.5	25.5	55.7	3735.2	698.8	1422.6
521.7	717.7	266.3	532.1	486.8	924.6	396.9	7961.1	2496.0	1329.6
309.1	532.8	426.8	444.2	486.3	428.8	54.3	8214.2	1460.0	982.1
-3309.2	941.9	3459.5	-1476.3	3313.6	-102.4	-1260.7	9932.5	2671.1	265.6
705.3	6.0	53.2	3.4	4.5	0.0	266.4	73.5	24.9	464.3
-4661.9	374.0	3576.8	-1779.2	1699.2	-379.0	-900.7	10103.3	1728.4	-2892.4
1944.8	2380.5	9235.9	5758.6	2872.9	1701.0	1101.7	17557.4	18662.4	13182.8
362.5	245.0	1308.0	1043.5	333.1	8878.8	169.7	2417.8	2187.2	2098.1
1061.3	1509.8	4812.2	1512.3	7657.7	1405.4	336.8	9181.3	9540.9	8574.2
4341.3	7955.5	12670.9	15850.0	38610.1	18008.0	4284.6	65854.7	64843.9	52549.7
4948.0	8342.7	17562.4	18406.0	44515.7	20560.2	4695.6	75245.2	74137.7	59234.5

13-7 限额以上餐饮企业财务状况(2003年)

单位：万元

项 目	Item	合 计 Total	内资企业 Domestic Funded Enterprise	国有企业 State-owned Enterprises	集体企业 Collective-Owned Enterprises	股份合作企业 Coopera-tive Enterprises
流动资产合计	Total Circulating Funds	66552.6	57969.2	9044.9	343.3	1423.6
存货	Inventories	8945.1	6638.0	1478.7	53.0	282.6
长期投资	Long-term Investment	1630.6	1330.6	317.9		
固定资产合计	Total Fixed Assets	164644.4	123598.2	35490.5	304.6	1638.3
固定资产原价	Original Value of Fixed Assets	191266.0	141575.1	37719.3	371.6	1876.1
累计折旧	Total Depreciation	36787.2	26641.7	7664.2	113.3	372.6
本年折旧	Depreciation This Year	7636.3	6313.1	639.7	25.8	91.8
资产总计	**Total Assets**	**262113.2**	**205154.3**	**48826.6**	**791.5**	**3441.6**
负债合计	**Total Liabilities**	**169953.4**	**125328.5**	**34559.9**	**549.0**	**1797.3**
所有者权益合计	**Total Creditors Equity**	**92159.8**	**79825.8**	**14266.7**	**242.5**	**1644.3**
实收资本	Capitals Hold	77617.5	64206.2	16496.5	203.0	928.0
国家资本	State Capital	24093.7	22614.7	11808.3		
港澳台资本	HongKong,Macao and Taiwan	2907.8	480.9			
外商资本	Foreign Capital	4792.6	220.5			
营业收入	Operating Revenue	161161.9	121952.9	18653.2	972.0	5497.7
营业成本	Operating Cost	83000.4	66819.2	9579.1	598.0	3461.2
营业费用	Expenses for Operating	47613.6	34445.6	5693.2	343.1	1527.9
营业税金及附加费	Tax and Extra Changes	8451.5	6496.6	718.0	56.9	256.2
经营利润	Management Profits	22096.4	14191.5	2662.9	-26.0	252.4
管理费用	Overhead Expenses	21486.8	16733.4	3562.6	1.9	421.8
税金	Taxes	978.9	974.0	70.1		190.0
财务保险费	Premiums of Property Insurance	174.3	144.0	18.1		8.0
劳动、待业保险费	Premiums of Labor Insurance	584.0	358.4	109.5		7.7
财务费用	Financial Expenses	4488.9	2854.9	1143.1	12.0	71.5
利息支出	Expenses for Interest	4444.9	2819.3	1116.2	12.0	18.0
营业利润	Operating Profits	-3879.3	-5396.8	-2042.8	-39.9	-240.9
利润总额	Total Profits	-4627.3	-5573.6	-2997.2	-40.7	-183.5
本年应付工资总额	Total Wages Payable this Year	17016.4	13782.7	1740.1	135.1	372.1
本年应付福利费总额	Welfare Expenses Payable this Year	3149.2	1977.0	491.4	9.4	27.4

Financial Affairs of above Designated Size in Catering Enterprises (2003)

(10 000 yuan)

有限公司 Limited Liability Corporation	股份公司 Share holding Corporation Ltd.	私营企业 Private Enterprises	港澳台 Enterprises With Investment from HongKong Macao and Taiwan	外商投资 Foreign Investment	正餐 Dinner	快餐 Snack	饮料冷饮	其他餐饮 Others
32098.5	4027.2	11013.5	3603.7	4979.7	56998.4	5999.2	575.2	2979.8
2362.8	556.8	1898.4	416.6	1890.5	7060.8	1486.5	29.1	368.7
26.0	80.6	903.3	300.0		1015.6			615.0
55637.0	10244.1	20273.7	33003.8	8042.4	123337.9	10154.4	1227.1	29925.0
64660.4	14595.7	22325.0	40121.5	9569.4	141131.9	12277.7	1001.5	36854.9
9835.6	5137.7	3500.3	7626.6	2518.9	25849.8	3116.6	390.9	7429.9
3635.5	476.3	1435.0	911.7	411.5	5992.8	631.9	25.2	986.4
99457.7	**16856.3**	**35748.1**	**36976.0**	**19982.9**	**199238.0**	**24452.0**	**3603.4**	**34819.8**
55476.4	**13482.6**	**19443.3**	**32538.5**	**12086.4**	**128975.4**	**14183.6**	**2973.4**	**23821.0**
43981.3	**3373.7**	**16304.8**	**4437.5**	**7896.5**	**70262.6**	**10268.4**	**630.0**	**10998.8**
32737.5	2268.3	11561.1	8639.2	4772.1	60920.4	6501.6	600.0	9595.5
10720.0	36.0	40.0	1479.0		16201.1	456.1	120.0	7316.5
480.0			2426.9		1591.8		480.0	836.0
220.0				4572.1	568.5	4224.1		
35201.9	11720.9	49688.7	5981.1	33227.9	114478.3	36920.1	3208.9	6554.6
17226.0	5955.4	29844.5	1915.8	14265.4	61815.9	16837.5	1843.6	2503.4
11171.6	2851.8	12822.9	1625.7	11542.3	32485.7	12155.3	921.4	2051.2
1947.9	591.7	2912.5	315.9	1639.0	6251.9	1752.9	151.3	295.4
4856.4	2322.0	4108.8	2123.7	5781.2	13924.8	6174.4	292.6	1704.6
7609.7	1301.1	3817.9	2793.0	1960.4	16392.3	2283.4	270.0	2541.1
220.8	111.8	368.5	4.1	0.8	902.1	60.7	3.3	12.8
36.0	28.9	51.8	15.4	14.9	147.1	17.0	4.5	5.7
184.5	24.3	28.2	8.2	217.4	217.0	289.6	67.8	9.6
603.9	282.3	742.1	1417.3	216.7	3343.3	266.1	35.4	844.1
751.8	279.0	642.3	1411.2	214.4	3308.8	258.7	35.3	842.1
-3357.2	738.6	-451.2	-2086.6	3604.1	-5810.8	3624.9	-12.8	-1680.6
-3342.5	935.0	55.3	-2043.2	2989.5	-5976.2	2965.1	17.7	-1633.9
4538.2	1240.3	5730.0	856.3	2377.4	13049.9	2775.1	199.6	991.8
421.2	154.9	869.3	910.6	261.6	2782.4	270.6	28.0	68.2

13-8 限额以上贸易、餐饮企业增加值

Added Value of above Designated Size in Trade and Catering Enterprises

单位：万元 (10 000 yuan)

指 标	Item	2000	2001	2002	2003
批发零售贸易业	**Wholesales and Retail Trade**				
增加值合计	Total Value-added	301524	385100	473500	598600
本年提取固定资产折旧	Depreciation this Year	42315	47740	58966	67631
本年应付工资总额	Total Wages Payable this Year	116876	135113	126481	142466
本年应付福利费总额	Welfare Expenses Payable this Year	16175	18970	20579	35204
劳动就业保险费	Premiums of Labor Insurance	21813	21399	23596	28610
商品销售税金及附加	Sales Tax and Extra Changes	11327	13213	14646	16788
利润总额	Total Profits	22576	64060	114242	95072
管理费用中税金	Taxes in Overhead Expenses	7610	7689	8317	9255
餐饮业	**Catering Trade**				
增加值合计	Total Value-added	12392	19100	27400	34400
本年提取固定资产折旧	Depreciation this Year	2347	3682	4822	7636
本年应付工资总额	Total Wages Payable this Year	9371	10047	14202	17016
本年应付福利费总额	Welfare Expenses Payable this Year	784	1135	2001	3149
劳动就业保险费	Premiums of Labor Insurance	579	352	471	584
商品销售税金及附加	Sales Tax and Extra Changes	2968	4643	7265	8451
利润总额	Total Profits	-3011	-1993	-479	-4627
管理费用中税金额	Taxes in Overhead Expenses	132	468	572	979

13-9 各市州限额以上批发零售贸易业商品购销存总额（2003年）

Total Purchases,Sales and Inventory of Enterprise above Designated Size in Wholesale and Retail Trade by Region (2003)

单位：万元 (10 000 yuan)

市州	Item	购进总额 Total Goods Purchase	销售总额 Total Sales	批发业 Wholesale	零售业 Retail Trade	年末库存总额 Inventory at the Year-end
全省合计	**Total**	**9757962**	**10382361**	**7844216**	**2538145**	**981387**
长沙市	Changsha City	5556463	5681638	4344734	1336904	489822
株洲市	Zhuzhou City	679232	738178	577387	160792	39135
湘潭市	Xiangtan City	293834	308598	218567	90031	14293
衡阳市	Hengyang City	529524	565619	386194	179425	70044
邵阳市	Shaoyang City	294065	327662	252695	74967	27943
岳阳市	Yueyang City	454289	560595	416875	143720	31239
常德市	Changde City	491264	574872	451770	123102	141422
张家界市	Zhangjiajie City	97121	106623	82302	24320	10257
益阳市	Yiyang City	210615	252721	169867	82855	18382
郴州市	Chenzhou City	403570	468446	337767	130679	65236
永州市	Yongzhou City	232019	248472	193989	54483	17169
怀化市	Huaihua City	206128	210923	182006	28917	33955
娄底市	Loudi City	195692	211723	124472	87251	12461
湘西州	West Hunan A.P	114147	126291	105591	20700	10030

13-10 各市州限额以上批发零售贸易、餐饮业法人企业数（2003年）

Number of Corporation Units above Designated Size in Wholesale and Retail Trade,Catering Services by Region (2003)

单位：家 (unit)

市州	Item	合计 Total	批发业 Wholesale Trade	零售业 Retail Trade	餐饮业 Catering Services
全省合计	**Total**	**932**	**414**	**358**	**160**
长沙市	Changsha City	320	143	86	91
株洲市	Zhuzhou City	65	25	28	12
湘潭市	Xiangtan City	28	15	10	3
衡阳市	Hengyang City	84	32	39	13
邵阳市	Shaoyang City	50	30	19	1
岳阳市	Yueyang City	43	21	22	0
常德市	Changde City	81	33	35	13
张家界市	Zhangjiajie City	17	6	4	7
益阳市	Yiyang City	28	14	13	1
郴州市	Chenzhou City	62	27	31	4
永州市	Yongzhou City	51	20	25	6
怀化市	Huaihua City	41	25	13	3
娄底市	Loudi City	38	10	22	6
湘西州	West Hunan A.P	24	13	11	

13-11 各市州限额以上批发零售贸易、餐饮业从业人员（2003年）

Number of Persons Employed in Enterprises Units above Designated Size in Wholesale and Retail Trade,Catering Services by Region (2003)

单位：人 (person)

市州	Item	合计 Total	批发业 Wholesale Trade	零售业 Retail Trade	餐饮业 Catering Services
全省合计	**Total**	**180774**	**59459**	**76561**	**44754**
长沙市	Changsha City	65992	23016	21806	21170
株洲市	Zhuzhou City	12068	2526	4922	4620
湘潭市	Xiangtan City	8952	2061	5378	1513
衡阳市	Hengyang City	21583	4326	11790	5467
邵阳市	Shaoyang City	6029	3694	2188	147
岳阳市	Yueyang City	12880	3219	8215	1446
常德市	Changde City	12609	5273	4658	2678
张家界市	Zhangjiajie City	2170	776	386	1008
益阳市	Yiyang City	5621	2454	2834	333
郴州市	Chenzhou City	9903	3603	4105	2195
永州市	Yongzhou City	7285	3911	1937	1437
怀化市	Huaihua City	5601	2020	2253	1328
娄底市	Loudi City	7601	1010	5179	1412
湘西州	West Hunan A.P	2480	1570	910	

13-12 限额以上连锁店(公司)商品销售情况(2003年)

Statistics On Sales Of Chain Stores (Companies) Above Designated Size (2003)

项目	Item	连锁总店数(个) Number Of General Chain Stores (Unit)	连锁门店数(个) Branch Chain Stores (unit)	从业人数(人) Persons Engaged (person)	销售总额或营业总收入(万元) Total Sales (Business Revenue) (10 000 yuan)
总计	**Total**	**44**	**583**	**38366**	**53.49**
零售业	**Retail Trade**	**39**	**534**	**35331**	**51.42**
#国有及国有控股	#State-owned and State-holding	6	150	5436	12.49
按零售业态分组	**By Operation Form:**				
百货商店	Department Store	2	28	784	0.53
超级市场	Supermarket	24	254	30851	42.71
专业店	Specialized Store	10	215	3239	7.33
专卖店	Monopoly Store	1	21	230	0.45
其他	Others	2	16	227	0.4
餐饮业	**Catering**	**5**	**49**	**3035**	**2.07**
#正餐	#Dinner	3	13	791	0.4

13-13 各市州星级宾馆数(2003年)

The Number of Tourist Hotels by Region (2003)

单位：家 (unit)

市州	Item	星级宾馆合计 Total Number of Tourist Hotels	五星级 Five Star	四星级 Four Star	三星级 Three Star	二星级 Two Star
全省合计	**Total**	**359**	**7**	**15**	**115**	**202**
长沙市	Changsha City	60	5	6	35	14
株洲市	Zhuzhou City	18	1	1	7	9
湘潭市	Xiangtan City	14	1		3	9
衡阳市	Hengyang City	31		1	5	23
邵阳市	Shaoyang City	13			3	9
岳阳市	Yueyang City	29		1	20	8
常德市	Changde City	24		2	6	16
张家界市	Zhangjiajie City	54		2	16	30
益阳市	Yiyang City	11		1	2	8
郴州市	Chenzhou City	20		1	5	9
永州市	Yongzhou City	22				20
怀化市	Huaihua City	25			8	15
娄底市	Loudi City	13			3	9
湘西州	West Hunan A.P	25			2	23

13-14 对外经济贸易和旅游概况

A Surrey on Foreign Trade and Tourists

指 标	Item	2000	2001	2002	2003
进出口总额 (亿美元)	**Total Imports And Exports (USD 100 million)**	**25.13**	**27.58**	**28.76**	**37.36**
出口总额	Total Exports	16.53	17.54	17.95	21.46
进口总额	Total Imports	8.6	10.04	10.81	15.9
进出口差额	Balance	7.93	7.5	7.14	5.56
对外签订利用外资协议项目 (个)	**Number of Projects for Utilization of Foreign Capital in the Signed Agreements & Contracts (unit)**	**336**	**356**	**428**	**574**
对外借款	Foreign Loans	16	18	14	16
外商直接投资	Foreign Direct Investments	320	338	414	558
外商其他投资	Other Foreign Investments				
对外签订利用外资协议金额 (亿美元)	**Total Amount of Foreign Capital to Be Utilized in the Signed Agreements & Contracts (USD 100 million)**	**10.94**	**13.3**	**16.58**	**23.76**
对外借款	Foreign Loans	3.37	3.47	3.46	3.01
外商直接投资	Foreign Direct Investments	6.67	9.53	13.12	20.75
外商其他投资	Other Foreign Investments	0.9	0.3		
实际利用外资 (亿美元)	**Total Amount of Foreign Capital Actually Used (USD 100 million)**	**11.08**	**11.87**	**13.77**	**17.9**
对外借款	Foreign Loans	3.37	3.47	3.46	3.01
外商直接投资	Foreign Direct Investments	6.82	8.1	10.31	14.89
外商其他投资	Other Foreign Investments	0.89	0.3		
外商投资企业基本情况	**Registered Foreign-funded Enterprises**				
年底登记户数 (户)	Number of Registered Enterprises (unit)	2316	2080	2152	2337
投资总额 (亿美元)	Total Investment (USD 100 million)	73.06	65.67	86.81	102.14
注册资本 (亿美元)	Registered Capital (USD 100 million)	43.38	37.7	48.53	58.67
#外方	#Capital from Foreign Partners	26.51	23.13	33.33	42.3
对外经济合作合同金额 (亿美元)	**Contracted Value of Economic Cooperation With Foreign Countries & Territories (USD 100 million)**	**1.87**	**2.7**	**3.12**	**3.91**
对外承包工程	Contracted Projects	1.49	2.27	2.58	3.12
对外劳务合作	Labor Services	0.34	0.36	0.39	0.26
设计咨询	Design Consultation	0.04	0.07	0.15	0.53
国际旅游人数 (万人次)	**Total Number of International Tourists (10 000 person-times)**	**45.4**	**50.46**	**56.62**	**15.39**
外国人	Foreigners	15.79	18.85	22.38	10.54
港澳台同胞	Compatriots from HongKong,Macao and Taiwan	29.61	31.61	34.24	4.86
旅游外汇收入总额 (亿美元)	**Foreign Exchange Earnings from International Tourism (USD 100 million)**	**2.21**	**2.71**	**3.11**	**0.45**
星级宾馆(个)	Total Number of Tourist Hotels (unit)	212	270	321	359

注：外贸进出口资料统一按长沙海关统计数据，以下同。

Figures on total imports and exports form foreign trade are obtained from the Changsha Customs statitics.The same as in the following table.

13-15 进出口商品总值

Total Value of Imports and Exports

单位：万美元 (USD 10 000)

项 目	Item	2000	2001	2002	2003
进出口总值	**Imports & Exports**	**251259**	**275841**	**287621**	**373617**
#出口	Exports	165309	175400	179542	214626
进口	Imports	85951	100441	108079	158990
进出口差额	**Balance**	**79358**	**74959**	**71463**	**55636**

13-16 进出口商品主要产销国别(地区)总值

Value of Imports and Exports by Main Producer and Sales Countries(Regions)

单位：万美元 (USD 10 000)

国 家 (地区)	Country (Region)	2002		2003		比上年(+、-)% Increase Rate over 2002	
		进 口 Imports	出 口 Exports	进 口 Imports	出 口 Exporst	进 口 Imports	出 口 Exports
合 计	**Total**	**108079**	**179542**	**158990**	**214626**	**47.1**	**19.5**
香 港	Hong Kong	2713	29134	1266	38010	-53.4	30.5
日 本	Japan	17687	16448	36033	21616	103.7	31.4
菲律宾	Philippines	314	1325	795	1508	153.3	13.8
新加坡	Singapore	577	3972	600	3763	-5.3	3.9
韩 国	Republic of Korea	29483	10852	27838	10600	-5.6	-2.3
台湾省	Taiwan ,China	2051	5749	3325	6664	62.1	15.9
英 国	United Kingdom	1725	4442	2468	4900	43.1	10.3
德 国	Germany	7448	6256	24027	7557	222.6	20.8
法 国	France	1258	1882	1776	1916	41.2	1.8
意大利	Italy	3430	3389	6086	3266	77.4	-3.6
荷 兰	Netherlands	971	5937	1027	8027	5.7	35.2
俄罗斯	Russia	408	2496	867	4357	112.6	74.5
加拿大	Canada	1843	4998	2449	5554	32.9	11.1
美 国	United States	7410	28940	10192	29614	37.5	2.3
澳大利亚	Australia	5397	1891	5862	1971	8.6	4.2
沙特阿拉伯	Saudi Arabia	384	1416	842	2145	119.2	51.5
阿联酋	United Arab Emirates		2385		2741		14.9
比利时	Belgium	298	1073	929	1795	212.1	67.3
西班牙	Spain	201	2185	533	2792	165.1	27.8
马来西亚	Malaysia	1463	2596	2428	2834	66	9.2

13-17 进出口商品机电电子产品情况

Import and Export Value of Machinery and Electrical Products

单位：万美元 (USD 10 000)

指标	Item	2002		2003		比上年(+、-)% Increase Rate in 2003 Over 2002	
		进口 Imports	出口 Exports	进口 Imports	出口 Exports	进口 Imports	出口 Exports
机电产品	**Mechanical & Electrical Products**	**60066**	**36609**	**101336**	**43078**	**68.7**	**17.7**
金属制品	Metal and Related Products	852	9701	1948	11923	128.7	22.9
机电仪器产品及设备	Machinery and Electrical Instruments and Equipment	59214	26908	99388	31155	67.8	15.8
机械及设备	Machinery and Equipment	26832	6474	43508	7738	62.2	19.5
电器及电子产品	Electrical Products	12400	12080	20508	13390	65.4	10.8
运输工具	facilities of Transportation	7805	5808	20394	7290	161.3	25.5
仪器仪表	Instruments and Meters	4552	487	4983	591	9.5	21.5
其他	Others	7626	2060	9995	2146	31.1	4.2

13-18 进出口商品贸易方式

Value of Imports and Exports by Trade Ways

单位：万美元 (USD 10 000)

贸易方式	Trade Ways	2002		2003	
		进口 Imports	出口 Exports	进口 Imports	出口 Exports
一般贸易	Original Trade	84681	161953	135062	193740
国家间、国际组织无偿援助和赠送的物资	Assistant Goods from International Organization	15	82	10	
华侨、港、澳同胞、外籍华人捐赠物资	Assistant Goods from Overseas Chinese, Compatriots from Hongkong, Macao and Taiwan	16		2	
补偿贸易	Compensation Trade				
来料加工装配贸易	Processing and Assembly Trade Provided with Raw Material	2546	4230	2482	3857
进料加工贸易	Processing Trade of Imported Material	6771	13218	10131	16951
寄售、代销贸易	Consign and Commission Trade				
边境小额贸易	Frontier Small Value Trade				
加工贸易进口的设备	Processing and Assembling Import Equipment Provided with Material	3		13	
对外承包工程出口货物	Constructed Projects in Foreign Countries		1		
租赁贸易	International Lease		57	8	
外商投资企业作为投资进口的设备、物品	Imported Equipment and Materials as Investment of Foreign Investment Enterprises	12933		8114	
出料加工贸易	Processing Trade of Exported Material				
易货贸易	Barter				
免税外汇商品	Tax Free Foreign Exchange Commodities				
保税仓库进出境货物	Import & export Commodities in Protective Tariff Zone	895		2562	78
其它贸易	Others Trade	219			

13-19 主要出口商品总值

Major Exports Commodities in Value

单位：万美元 (USD 10 000)

商品名称	Name of Commodities	2000	2001	2002	2003
活猪(种猪除外)	Live Hogs (excluded seed hogs)	4709	4305	4482	4481
鲜、冻猪肉	Fresh Frozen Pork	999	881	1232	1767
水海产品	Aquatic Products	23	33	15	22
谷物及谷物粉	Cereals and Cereals Flour	1862	397	80	411
大米	Rice	1846	375	55	370
鲜、干水果	Vegetables , Fruit & Nuts , Fresh or Dried	165	122	141	142
茶叶	Tea	1310	1602	1526	1903
烤烟	Flue-cured Tobacco	400	277	244	287
黏土及其耐火矿物	Clay and Other Refractory Minerals	1099	1484	1336	1342
天然石墨	Nutural Graphite	1091	1474	1290	1296
仲钨酸铵	Tungstates	597	476	238	461
氧化锌及过氧化锌	Zinc Oxide and Zinc Peroxide	1146	623	336	267
医药品	Medical and Pharmaceutical Products	1730	2124	1577	1653
烟花、爆竹	Fireworks and Firecrackers	8186	8518	9883	12027
松香及树脂酸	Resin and Resin Acids	354	426	362	250
家用或装饰用木制品	Woodwork for Family and Decorating	555	765	841	1033
纺织纱线、织物及制品	Textile Yarn,Textile and Related Products	13344	15859	17256	19932
亚麻及苎麻纱线	Flax and Ramine Yarn	1278	1158	797	865
棉纺机织物	Cotton Textile Machine Woven	3604	4681	5472	6045
其他棉纺机织物	Other Cotton Textile Machine Woven	3541	4614	5391	5859
亚麻及苎麻机织物	Flax and Ramine Machine Woven	2612	2978	2571	2223
棉浴巾	Cotton Bath Towels	708	1242	1912	2939
家用陶瓷器皿	Porcelain and Pottery Ware for Household Use	7184	7920	9056	10146
钢材	Rolled Steel	3121	3769	6924	12070
未锻造的锌及锌合金	Unwrought Zinc and Zinc Alloys	15099	12855	9609	8358
未锻造的锡及锡合金	Unwrought Tin and Tin Alloys	527	223	118	11
未锻造的锑	Unwrought Antimony	781		349	707
未锻造的锰	Unwrought Manganese	5524	8444	7791	12120
手用或机用工具	Hand Tools and Tools for Machines	2452	1964	2047	2701
轴承	Bearings	891	827	769	606
印刷电路	Electrocircuit of Presswork	1234	1192	1349	1365
通断及保护电器装置及零件	Eletrical Apparatus for Switching or Protecting Electrical Circuits	440	660	822	770
汽车零件	Parts of Motor Vehicles	965	1175	1157	1186
摩托车	Motorcycles	1543	2525	3257	4401
船舶	Ships	201	69	251	2
旅行用品及箱包	Travel Goods	1333	1211	1375	1375
服装及衣着附件	Articles of Apparel & Clothing Accessories	13027	15165	15002	19555
织物制服装	Garments with Textile	9536	9786	11585	13681
非针织钩编织物服装	Garmens with Non-Kniting or Crocheting	5403	5342	6127	6929
针织或钩编的服装	Garments with Kniting or Crocheting	4133	4444	5458	6752
皮革服装	Leather Garments	2322	3964	1766	3538
鞋类	Footware	4436	4171	4552	4738
鞋	Shoes	4266	4115	4489	4668
以橡胶或塑料制的鞋	Shoes with Rubber or Plastic Materials	2311	2459	2689	2836
橡胶或塑料底纺织材料为面的鞋	Shoes with Tread of Rubber or Plastic Materials and Surface of Textile Materials	1441	1108	1311	1178
塑料制品	Plastic Articles	770	848	1015	1284

13-20 主要进口商品总值

Major Imports Commodities in Value

单位：万美元 (USD 10 000)

商品名称	Name of Commodities	2000	2001	2002	2003
食用植物油	Edible Vegetable Oil	129	91	366	1143
豆油及其分离品	Bean Oil and Related Separate Articles	42			214
饲料用鱼粉	Flours and Meals of Fish for Animal Food	1600	1046	964	971
原木	Logs	240	482	162	17
纸浆	Paper Pulp	451	2459	1363	2330
二醋酸纤维丝束	Two of Cellulose Diacetate	992	1181	97	
铁矿砂	Iron Ore	5079	8903	10839	11233
铬矿砂	Chromium Ores	823	343	185	166
成品油	Petroleum Products Refined	34	32	16	38
乙二醇	Ethylenc Glycol	463	1022	877	2350
对苯二甲醇	Telephthalic Acid	1106	1817	2438	994
初级形状的塑料	Primary Plastic	569	450	432	904
农药	Pesticides	112			10
纸及纸板(未切成形的)	Paper and Paperboard	717	874	1295	614
无机物涂布纸	Papers with Mineral Coat	687	789	1237	598
棉机织物	Cotton Textile Machine Woven	970	602	667	809
针织或钩编织物	Kniting or Crocheting	363	341	305	272
钢材	Rolled Steels	3805	4016	3979	6073
钢铁板材	Steel-Board	3608	3874	3841	5688
钢铁制标准紧固件	Nails ,Bolts ,etc	520	261	205	774
未锻造的铜及铜材	Unwrought Copper and Rolled Copper	588	499	710	356
铜材	Rolled Copper	513	456	477	356
活塞式内燃机的零件	Accessories of Gas Engine with Piston	421	335	137	82
液泵及液体提升机	Liquid Pump and Machine with Liquid Exaltation	249	468	548	1591
机械提升搬运装卸设备及零件	Portage ,Load and Unload Equipments and Accessories with Machine Exaltation	366	277	227	709
建筑及采矿用机械	Machinery for Counstruction and Mining	456	970	1367	3657
制造纸及纸制品用机械	Paper and Pulp Mill Machinery	110	172	1748	1005
印刷、装订机械	Printing and Binding Machinery	601	1050	745	696
金属加工机床	Machine Tools for Processing Metals	833	1258	1242	2655
烟草加工机械	Machine Tools for Processing Tobacco	294	1059	235	208
模型及金属铸造用型箱	Models and Patterns	165	521	124	427
阀门	Valves	203	96	186	564
自动数据处理设备及其部件	Automatic Data Processing Equipments and Accessories	2952	930	2873	1162
数字式自动数据处理设备	Digital Automatic Data Processing Equipment	1495	336	2514	615
输入或输出部件	Accessories of I/O Equipments	921	508	31	30
有线电话或电报交换机	Lineate Telephones or Telegram Exchanges	356			
有线电话电报设备的零附件	Accessories of Lineate Telephones and Telegrams	454	480	200	3
电视显像管	Kinescope	104	2		
彩色显像管	Color Kinescope	104	2		
集成电路及微电子组件	Integrated Circuit and Microelectronics Device	1052	1105	1016	1111
汽车零件	Parts of Motor Vehicles	6374	6809	4943	9328
医疗仪器及器械	Medical Instruments and Appliances	1014	2041	1550	1177
计量检测分析自动仪器及器具	Measuring and Checking	1718	1583	2538	3408
印刷品	Pressworks	477	186	220	37
塑料制品	Articles of Plastics	297	272	317	317

13-21 进出口商品分地区情况(2003年)

Import and Expert Value by Region (2003)

市州	Cities and Prefecture	进出口总值 万美元 Total Exports and Imports (USD 10 000)	出口 Exports	进口 Imports	比上年增减 (%) Increase Rate in 2003 Over 2002 (%)
总计	**Total**	**373617**	**214626**	**158990**	**29.9**
长沙	Changsha City	204406	109811	94595	22.9
株洲	Zhuzhou City	49719	36543	13176	30.8
湘潭	Xiangtan City	30692	17732	12960	42.4
衡阳	Hengyang City	10788	8068	2720	18.9
邵阳	Shaoyang City	4022	2780	1242	122.5
岳阳	Yueyang City	15950	4410	11540	85.7
常德	Changde City	8888	6562	2326	17.6
张家界	Zhangjiajie City	310	234	76	1531.6
益阳	Yiyang City	8783	4451	4332	22.8
郴州	Chenzhou City	9716	7026	2690	57.5
娄底	Loudi City	10373	4471	5902	32.1
永州	Yongzhou City	8745	1376	7369	98.8
怀化	Huaihua City	2337	2294	43	13.9
湘西自治州	West Hunan A.P	8886	8867	19	26.6

13-22 利用外资概况

Utilization of Foreign Capital

项目	Item	2000	2001	2002	2003
利用外资签订合同项目(个)	**Number of Projects for Utilization of Foreign Capital in the Signed Agreements & Contracts (case)**	**336**	**356**	**428**	**574**
对外借款	Foreign Loans	16	18	14	16
外商直接投资	Foreign Direct Investments	320	338	414	558
外商其他投资	Other Foreign Investments				
协议利用外资合同金额(万美元)	**Total Amount of Foreign Capital to be Utilized in the Signed Agreement & Contracts (USD 10 000)**	**109370**	**133063**	**165759**	**237610**
对外借款	Foreign Loans	33700	34700	34600	30134
外商直接投资额	Foreign Direct Investments	66709	95327	131159	207476
外商其他投资额	Other Foreign Investments	8961	3036		
实际利用外资金额(万美元)	**Total Amount of Foreign Capital Actually Used (USD 10 000)**	**110843**	**118747**	**137689**	**179041**
对外借款	Foreign Loans	33700	34700	34600	30134
外商直接投资额	Foreign Direct Investments	68182	81011	103089	148907
外商其他投资额	Other Foreign Investments	8961	3036		

13-23 外商直接投资签订合同情况(分国别、地区)(2003年)

Basic Statisics on Signed Contracts of Direct Foreign Investment(by Country or Region) (2003)

国别(地区)	Countries (Region)	项目(合同)个数 Number of Projects (case)	合同外资金额 Contract Value (USD 10 000)	实际外资金额 Used Value (USD 10 000)
总 计	**Total**	**558**	**207476**	**148907**
香港(地区)	Hongkong	294	108630	78923
澳门(地区)	Macro	14	14092	3835
台湾(地区)	Taiwan	81	18984	10714
菲律宾	Philippines	4	1474	2655
泰 国	Thailand	4	740	757
马来西亚	Malaysia	5	4042	598
新加坡	Singapore	6	1424	4911
日 本	Japan	12	2188	2194
德 国	Germany	2	73	1511
意大利	Italy	1	2779	18
英 国	United Kingdom	14	4955	3381
加拿大	Canada	12	4054	2554
美 国	United States	54	17767	8944
澳大利亚	Australia	11	2874	2491
维尔京群岛	Virgin Islands	3	3320	3053

13-24 外商直接投资分地区情况(2003年)

Foreign Direct Investment by Region (2003)

市州	Cities and Prefecture	项目个数(个) Number of Projects (case)	合同外资额(万美元) Agreement Amount (USD 10 000)	实际利用(万美元) Actually Used Amount (USD 10 000)	比上年增减(%) Increase Rate in 2003 Over 2002(%)
总 计	**Total**	**558**	**207476**	**148907**	**44.4**
长沙市	Changsha City	122	77672	50011	52.6
株洲市	Zhuzhou City	42	14181	9007	26.4
湘潭市	Xiangtan City	29	20405	11116	84.8
衡阳市	Hengyang City	102	21387	14588	32.6
邵阳市	Shaoyang City	33	3726	4198	19.6
岳阳市	Yueyang City	26	12593	11062	21.2
常德市	Changde City	34	14540	10452	72.7
张家界市	Zhangjiajie City	15	4157	1544	136.4
益阳市	Yiyang City	21	2374	3616	11.8
郴州市	Chenzhou City	53	16409	20065	30.3
永州市	Yongzhou City	35	7490	5075	151.5
怀化市	Huaihua City	9	2407	1820	0.1
娄底市	Loudi City	31	8798	5057	51.3
湘西自治州	West Hunan A.P	6	1337	1296	28.3

13-25 对外承包工程、劳务合作和设计咨询

Contracted Projects, Labor Service Cooperation, Designs Consultation with Foreign Countries

项 目	Item	2000	2001	2002	2003
对外承包工程、劳务合作和设计咨询合同 (个)	Number of Contracts (case)	1096	1101	889	1148
对外承包工程、劳务合作和设计咨询合同金额 (万美元)	Contracted Value (USD 10 000)	18707	27000	31200	39109
实际完成营业额 (万美元)	Value of Businness Fulfilled (USD 10 000)	13845	26500	29616	38593
年末在外人数 (人)	Number of Abroad Person at Year-end (person)	4318	6200	7167	9018
全年派出人次 (人次)	Number of Delegation Person-times All-year (person-time)	2280	3163	4166	5027

13-26 旅 游 业 基 本 情 况

Basic Statistics of Tourism

项 目	Item	2000	2001	2002	2003
接待旅游总人数 (万人)	**Number of Tourists (10 000 persons)**	**4695.4**	**5035.52**	**5756.97**	**5970.11**
#接待海外游客	International Tourists	45.4	50.46	56.62	15.39
#接待国内游客	Domestic Tourists	4650	4985.06	5700.35	5954.72
旅游业总收入(人民币亿元)	**Income of Tourism (100 million yuan)**	**148.8**	**210.4**	**245.97**	**294.07**
#旅游创汇(亿美元)	Earnings from International Tourism (USD 100 million)	2.21	2.71	3.11	0.45
#国内旅游收入 (人民币亿元)	Earnings from Domestic Tourism (RMB 100 million yuan)	130.46	188.09	220.23	290.32

13-27 国际旅游人数和人天数

Number of International Tourists and Days of Tourism

项 目	Item	2000	2001	2002	2003
接待国际旅游人数合计 (人次)	**Total of International Tourist Arrivals (person-time)**	**454008**	**504554**	**566229**	**153931**
#外国人	Foreigners	157899	188485	223812	105368
港澳台同胞	Compatriots From Hongkong,Macao and Taiwan	296109	316069	342417	48563
#台胞	Compatriots from Taiwan	172731	180004	186884	34762
国际旅游人天数合计 (人天)	**Total of International Tourist Arrivals (person-day)**	**1443640**	**1728126**	**1847446**	**269506**
#外国人	Foreigners	596216	640849	738580	188752
港澳台同胞	Compatriots From Hongkong,Macao and Taiwan	847424	1087277	1108866	80754
#台胞	Compatriots from Taiwan	465221	666015	620406	48670

注：从2000年起，华侨并入外国人统计。 Overseas chinese are bring into foreigners since 2000.

13-28 接待外国人按国别分组

Number of Foreign Tourists by Country

单位：人次 (person-time)

国 别	Country	2000	2001	2002	2003
外国人合计	**Total**	**157899**	**188485**	**223812**	**105368**
#日 本	Japan	25006	32549	30121	9196
菲律宾	Philippines	1707	936	1453	270
新加坡	Singapore	11813	8927	6239	1463
泰 国	Thailand	5431	3083	1718	417
印度尼西亚	Indonesia	1181	2474	1296	510
美 国	United States	18942	31264	57700	12161
加拿大	Canada	9611	10793	13876	2486
德 国	Germany	5519	4087	4690	1857
英 国	United Kingdom	5318	2707	2609	1498
法 国	France	1529	2256	3986	1369
意大利	Italy	1132	1408	1237	636
俄罗斯	Russia	1030	1025	373	751
澳大利亚	Australia	5103	2474	1839	1188
新西兰	New Zealand	575	321	395	211
其 他	Others	64002	84181	96280	71355

13-29 各市州接待游客人数

Number of Tourists by Cities and Prefeture

市州	Cities and Rrefeture	2002		2003	
		接待国内游客 (万人次) Domestic Tourists (10 000 person-times)	接待境外游客 (人次) Foreign Tourists (person-times)	接待国内游客 (万人次) Domestic Tourists (10 000 person-times)	接待境外游客 (人次) Foreign Tourists (person-times)
合 计	**Total**	**5700.35**	**566229**	**5954.72**	**153931**
长沙市	Changsha City	1823.76	341359	1541.89	48481
株洲市	Zhuzhou City	269.81	12325	359.58	11726
湘潭市	Xiangtan City	315.22	3890	401.07	527
衡阳市	Hengyang City	902.02	9486	509.66	3792
邵阳市	Shaoyang City	231.56	259	339.22	254
岳阳市	Yueyang City	308.7	23985	404.49	12667
常德市	Changde City	447.88	14436	427.35	962
益阳市	Yiyang City	168.67	124	203.9	3123
郴州市	Chenzhou City	321.06	8919	345.04	9823
张家界市	Zhangjiajie City	286.73	146966	184.03	59332
永州市	Yongzhou City	98.98	416	229.56	720
怀化市	Huaihua City	138.56	34	355.75	128
娄底市	Loudi City	198.43	1075	334	394
湘西自治州	West Hunan A.P	188.99	2955	319.19	2002

十四、教育、科技

EDUCATION，SCIENCE AND TECHNOLOGY

资料整理人员：　蔡冬娥　陈洲艳　朱继无

14-1 各级学校单位数及教职工数

Number of Schools and School Staff

年 份 Year	普通高等学校 Regular Institution of Higher Education	普通中等专业学校 Secondary Schools	职业中学 Vocational Secondary Schools	技工学校 Technical Schools	普通中学 Regular Secondary Schools	普通小学 Primary Schools	特殊教育学校 Special Education Schools	幼儿园 Kinder-gartens
单位数(所)	**Number of Schools (unit)**							
2000	52	144	539	167	4505	34521	57	5473
2001	61	125	434	167	4695	29340	59	1333
2002	60	113	398	133	4712	27243	54	1506
2003	73	81	464	136	4689	24673	55	2331
教职工数(人)	**Number of Teachers and Staff (person)**							
2000	46642	21078	22375	10050	259989	324199	1203	39790
2001	53119	17137	21542	10003	276672	309106	1201	28017
2002	56590	15817	20993	8666	288804	292796	1236	18496
2003	66084	11471	23143	8185	301306	275811	1219	24208
专任教师数(人)	**Number of Full-time Teachers(person)**							
2000	20317	10775	15795	6117	223693	306387	918	33928
2001	23878	9036	14395	6069	236161	291574	905	20307
2002	30557	8598	14266	5514	248245	276535	922	9590
2003	33229	6377	15814	5306	259281	260704	923	12662

注：本表高等学校含3所部属院校，不含军事院校、分院校和大专班。

Regular institutions of higher education includes three institutions managed by the national ministry,excluding military institutions, branches and Specialized Subject class.

14-2 各级学校在校学生、招生及毕业生数

Student Enrollment, New Student Enrollment and Graduates

单位：人 (person)

年 份 Year	普通高等学校 Regular Institution of Higher Education	普通中等专业学校 Secondary Schools	职业中学 Vocational Secondary Schools	技工学校 Technical Schools	普通中学 Regular Secondary Schools	高中 Senior Secondary Schools	初中 Junior Secondary Schools	普通小学 Primary Schools	特殊教育学校 Special Education	幼儿园 Kinder-gartens
在校学生数	**Student Enrollment**									
2000	253084	258342	213898	51237	3917326	625719	3291607	6639289	12179	628744
2001	331301	240910	198813	60193	4255858	752579	3503279	6012579	14635	600570
2002	419437	223697	220167	78117	4669124	914730	3754394	5294879	14294	569064
2003	537220	226487	299145	87931	4887766	1065740	3822026	4686892	13634	657070
招生数	**New Student Enrollment**									
2000	101020	63625	93447	26683	1518734	260515	1258219	717496	2090	583324
2001	117299	71374	100209	32509	1648254	323625	1324629	723570	2194	530097
2002	156946	82740	112935	41090	1764249	382673	1381576	708909	2244	494160
2003	193830	92245	160504	47807	1714186	422322	1291864	714944	2154	566568
毕业生数	**Graduates**									
2000	42428	73076	68800	20479	1000980	145587	855393	1302004	1138	-
2001	49703	80906	59447	19011	1034231	168166	866065	1357129	1273	-
2002	62098	80118	55289	20618	1169802	187847	981955	1403093	1574	-
2003	90035	60664	69488	22831	1325552	233929	1091623	1294814	2192	-

14-3 研　究　生

Number of Postgraduates

单位：人　　(person)

年 份	招生数 New Student Enrollment	毕业生数 Graduates	在学人数 Student Enrollment
1980	77		347
1985	1104	296	2016
1986	950	377	2583
1987	874	666	2771
1988	769	1067	2538
1989	600	862	2311
1990	705	812	2165
1991	687	783	2035
1992	734	543	2168
1993	911	668	2357
1994	1209	630	2864
1995	1209	710	3307
1996	1400	876	3775
1997	1383	1087	4027
1998	1723	1131	4552
1999	2380	1394	5585
2000	3475	1311	7729
2001	4575	1639	10589
2002	5832	1942	14147
2003	8597	3099	19421

14-4 普通高等学校分科在校学生、招生及毕业生数

Student Enrollment, New Student Enrollment and Graduates of General Institutions of Higher Education by Field of Study

单位：人　　(person)

项目	Item	在校学生数 Student Enrollment		招收学生数 New Student Enrollment		毕业生数 Graduates	
		2002	2003	2002	2003	2002	2003
合　计	**Total**	**419437**	**537220**	**156946**	**193830**	**62098**	**90035**
哲　学	Philosophy	221	210	65	49	43	57
经济学	Economics	23965	31668	10354	12575	3304	4638
法　学	Law	23838	26528	7265	8050	4507	5840
教育学	Education	21329	26890	7816	10105	4273	6028
文　学	Literature	70188	90462	26456	33812	10633	16006
历史学	History	1605	1407	376	330	399	473
理　学	Science	35471	42404	12775	14623	5033	7251
工　学	Engineering	146864	184418	55931	65339	20841	30464
农　学	Agriculture	7829	8835	2573	2779	1565	1952
医　学	Medicine	33773	46081	11557	15313	4468	6303
管理学	Administration	54354	78317	21778	30855	7032	11023

14-5 普通高等学校、中等专业学校教职工

Staff and Workers in General Institutions of Higher Education and Specialized Secondary Schools

单位：人 (person)

类 别	Item	高等学校 General Institutions of Higher Education			中等专业学校 Specialized Secondary Schools		
		2001	2002	2003	2001	2002	2003
教职工	**Staff and Teachers**	**53119**	**56590**	**66084**	**17137**	**15817**	**11471**
#校部教职工	#Staff and Workers	45982	48592	57484	16120	14852	10662
#专任教师	#Full-time Teachers	23878	26715	33229	9036	8598	6377
教辅人员	Auxiliary Teaching Staff	6144	6681	7459	1500	1406	889
行政人员	Administrative Personnel	8584	8441	10093	3036	2693	1864
工勤人员	Logistics Personnel	7376	6755	6703	2548	2155	1532

14-6 普通高等学校分科专任教师(2003年)

Full – Time Teachers in General Institutions of Higher Education by Field of Study (2003)

单位：人 (person)

类 别	Item	合 计 Total	正高级 Professors	副高级 Asso. Professors	中 级 Lecturers	初 级 Assistants	无职称 Instructors
合 计	**Total**	**33229**	**3019**	**10089**	**11356**	**6138**	**2627**
哲 学	Philosophy	1186	106	416	426	158	80
经济学	Economics	2198	156	688	823	399	132
法 学	Law	1282	92	330	510	257	93
教育学	Education	2894	129	904	1010	618	233
文 学	Literature	6813	418	1724	2329	1659	683
历史学	History	423	68	162	120	33	40
理 学	Science	4408	495	1494	1373	695	351
工 学	Engineering	9565	947	2943	3261	1631	783
农 学	Agriculture	869	133	341	294	73	28
医 学	Medicine	2245	358	699	689	363	136
管理学	Adminstration	1346	117	388	521	252	68

14-7 普通中等专业学校专任教师和学生数(2003)

Students and Full-Time Teachers in General Specialized Secondary Schools (2003)

单位：人 (person)

类 别	Item	招生数 New Student Enrollment	毕业生数 Graduates	在校学生数 Student Enrollment	专任教师 Full-time Teachers
总 计	**Total**	**92245**	**60664**	**226487**	**3961**
农林类	Denomination of Agriculture and Forestry	1411	1152	3834	125
资源与环境类	Denomination of Natural Resources and Environment	138	807	929	10
能源类	Denomination of Energy Sources	488	587	1393	78
土木水利工程类	Denomination of Civil and Water Conservancy Engineering	1611	2161	4383	209
加工制造类	Denomination of Processing and Manufacture	16025	7762	32773	336
交通运输类	Denomination of Transportation	694	692	2143	71
信息技术类	Denomination of Information Technique	22316	18588	59897	807
医药卫生类	Denomination of Sanitation and Medicines	13700	9515	35678	596
商贸与旅游类	Denomination of Trade and Tourists	9904	4448	24506	246
财经类	Denomination of Economics and Finance	7614	3863	18216	421
文化艺术与体育类	Denomination of Culture,Arts and Sports	5360	3999	12719	516
社会公共事业类	Denomination of Social Public Facilities	5405	2539	13114	102
师范类	Denomination of Normal Schools	4972	2265	11114	392
其他	Other Denomination	2607	2286	5788	52

14-8 普通中学、小学按城乡和主办部门分组的情况（2003年）

Basic Statistics on General Secondary Schools, Primary Schools by Urban and Rural Area and by Department (2003)

单位：人 (person)

类 别	Item	合 计 Total	按城乡分 By Urban and Rural Areas 城市 Urban Areas	县镇 Counties and Towns	农村 Rural Areas	按主办部门分 By Departments 教育部门和集体办 Schools Run by Educational Departments	其他部门和民办 Schools Run by Other Departments
普通中学	**Regular Secondary Schools**						
学校数(所)	Number of Schools(unit)	4689	607	1366	2716	4183	506
教职工数	Number of Staff and Teachers	301306	52913	116370	132023	277604	23702
#专任教师数	#Full-time Teachers	259281	42081	97869	119331	241239	18042
招生数	New Student Enrollment	1714186	275595	675436	763155	1576961	137225
毕业生数	Number of Graduates	1325552	201220	484157	640175	1249004	76548
在校学生数	Student Enrollment	4887766	772354	1865046	2250366	4532156	355610
普通中学中：高中	**Senior Secondary Schools**						
学校数(所)	Number of Schools(unit)	327	63	186	78	284	43
专任教师数	Full-time Teachers	56185					
招生数	New Student Enrollment	422322	125865	228435	68022	371683	50639
毕业生数	Number of Graduates	233929	69725	126834	37370	211235	22694
在校学生数	Student Enrollment	1065740	321099	573563	171078	952239	113501
普通中学中：初中	**Junior Secondary Schools**						
学校数(所)	Number of Schools(unit)	3347	200	914	2233	3176	171
专任教师数	Full-time Teachers	203096					
招生数	New Student Enrollment	1291864	149730	447001	695133	1205278	86586
毕业生数	Number of Graduates	1091623	131495	357323	602805	1037769	53854
在校学生数	Student Enrollment	3822026	451255	1291483	2079288	3579917	242109
小 学	**Primary Schools**						
学校数(所)	Number of Schools(unit)	24673	922	2222	21529	24218	455
教职工数	Number of Staff and Teachers	275811	35713	58346	181752	262375	13436
#专任教师数	#Full-time Teachers	260704	32097	54231	174376	249509	11195
招生数	New Student Enrollment	714944	94396	134852	485696	679324	35620
毕业生数	Number of Graduates	1294814	123841	279586	891387	1251095	43719
在校学生数	Student Enrollment	4686892	603812	973164	3109916	4468314	218578

14-9 各级学校在校女学生和女教师

Number of Females Students and Teachers by Level of School

类别	Item	2000	2001	2002	2003
女学生(万人)	**Number of Female Students (10 000 persons)**	**531.25**	**519.19**	**526.82**	**502.7**
普通高等学校	Regular Institutions of Higher Education	9.58	13.04	34.4	23.85
普通中等专业学校	Regular Specialized Secondary Schools	15.06	13.77	12.64	12.62
普通中学	Regular Secondary Schools	179.12	198.06	218.87	230.28
职业中学	Vocational Secondary Schools	9.68	9.69	11.12	15.24
普通小学	Primary Schools	317.81	284.63	249.79	220.71
女学生占全部学生(%)	**Percentage of Female Students to Total Students(%)**	**47.09**	**47.03**	**48.66**	**47.26**
普通高等学校	Regular Institutions of Higher Education	37.85	39.35	44.19	44.4
普通中等专业学校	Regular Specialized Secondary Schools	58.29	57.16	56.51	55.72
普通中学	Regular Secondary Schools	45.73	46.54	46.88	47.11
职业中学	Vocational Secondary Schools	45.26	48.74	50.52	50.95
普通小学	Primary Schools	47.87	47.34	47.18	47.1
女教师(万人)	**Number of Female Teachers (10 000 persons)**	**24.79**	**28.66**	**28.99**	**29.05**
普通高等学校	Regular Institutions of Higher Education	0.69	2.16	2.58	2.74
普通中等专业学校	Regular Specialized Secondary Schools	0.43	0.71	0.66	0.47
普通中学	Regular Secondary Schools	8.13	9.9	10.54	11.19
职业中学	Vocational Secondary Schools	0.59	0.82	0.81	0.93
普通小学	Primary Schools	14.95	15.07	14.4	13.72
女教师占全部教师(%)	**Percentage of Female Teachers to Total Teachers(%)**	**42.97**	**42.31**	**42.95**	**42.83**
普通高等学校	Regular Institutions of Higher Education	33.96	40.64	40.6	41.45
普通中等专业学校	Regular Specialized Secondary Schools	39.9	41.19	41.7	40.87
普通中学	Regular Secondary Schools	36.34	35.77	36.49	37.14
职业中学	Vocational Secondary Schools	37.35	38.1	38.35	39.24
普通小学	Primary Schools	48.79	48.76	49.2	49.75

14-10 平均每万人口中在校学生

Student Enrollment Per l0,000 Population

项目	Item	2000	2001	2002	2003
各类普通学校在校学生占全省人口(%)	**Students as Percentage of Total Population (%)**	**17.24**	**16.74**	**16.34**	**15.97**
平均每万人口中在校学生(人)	**Student Enrollment Per l0 000 Population (person)**				
普通高等学校	Regular Institutions of Higher Education	38.7	50.2	63.27	80.63
中等学校	Regular Secondary Schools	665.5	711.9	771.36	812.48
普通小学	Primary Schools	1014.4	911.6	798.81	703.44

注: 1.本表未包括技工学校在校学生。

2.各类普通学校在校学生数包括普通高校、普通中专、职业中学、普通中小学的在校学生数。

a. Secondary schools excludes schools for skilled workers.

b. The number of student enrollment refers to that of students enrolled in regular institutions of higher education, specialized secondary schools, vocational schools, regular secondary schools and primary schools.

14-11 民办(私立)学校情况

Statistics on Private Schools

单位：人 (person)

项目	Item	2000	2001	2002	2003
普通中学	**Regular Secondary Schools**				
学校数(所)	Number of Schools(unit)	166	251	275	298
教职工数	Staff and Teachers	4845	9301	11306	14283
专任教师数	Full-time Teachers	3367	6567	8167	10356
毕业生数	Graduates	9035	18274	29513	43723
招生数	New Student Enrollment	43333	66519	78661	96558
在校学生数	Student Enrollment	90112	146984	182284	238731
普通小学	**Primary Schools**				
学校数(所)	Number of Schools(unit)	213	261	245	231
教职工数	Staff and Teachers	2451	4074	4235	4600
专任教师数	Full-time Teachers	1713	2914	3046	3246
毕业生数	Graduates	6183	7820	11061	12685
招生数	New Student Enrollment	5572	8919	9464	10534
在校学生数	Student Enrollment	45911	59962	60551	64309

14-12 特殊教育学校基本情况

Basic Statistics on Schools for Special Education

单位：人 (person)

项目	Item	2000	2001	2002	2003
各类特殊学校数(所)	Number of Schools for Special Education(unit)	57	59	54	55
教职工数	Staff and Teachers	1203	1201	1236	1219
专任教师数	Full-time Teachers	918	905	922	923
毕业生数	Graduates	1138	1273	1574	2192
招生数	New Student Enrollment	2090	2194	2244	2154
在校学生数	Student Enrollment	12179	14635	14294	13634

14-13 各类学校代课教师及临时工人数

Provisional Teachers and Temporary Workers by Type of School

单位：人 (person)

项 目	Item	2000	2001	2002	2003
普通中学	**Regular Secondary Schools**				
代课教师	Provisional Teachers	2593	2803	4626	4400
临时工	Temporary Workers	1564	1248	-	-
兼任教师	Part-time Teachers	440	674	1267	1065
职业中学	**Vocational Secondary Schools**				
代课教师	Provisional Teachers	194	247	510	3
临时工	Temporary Workers	227	196	-	-
兼任教师	Part-time Teachers	1283	941	1190	4
技工学校	**Various Technical Schools**				
兼职教师	Part-time Teachers	1233	1301	1103	1063
普通小学	**Primary Schools**				
代课教师	Provisional Teachers	15718	9118	8697	4278
临时工	Temporary Workers	2415	1374	-	-
兼任教师	Part-time Teachers	71	118	1157	631

14-14 平均每一教职工负担学生

Student/ Staff and Worker Ratio

单位：人 (person)

项目	Item	2000	2001	2002	2003
平均每一教职工负担的学生	**Student - Teacher Ratio**				
普通高等学校	Regular Institutions of Higher Education	5.5	6.2	7.4	8.1
普通中等专业学校	Regular Specialized Secondary Schools	12	14.1	14.1	19.7
普通中学	Regular Secondary Schools	15.1	15.4	16.2	16.2
普通小学	Primary Schools	20.5	19.5	18.1	17
平均每一专任教师负担的学生	**Student - Full-time Teacher Ratio**				
普通高等学校	Regular Institutions of Higher Education	12.5	13.9	15.7	16.17
普通中等专业学校	Regular Specialized Secondary Schools	23.97	26.7	26	35.52
普通中学	Regular Secondary Schools	17.5	18	18.8	18.85
普通小学	Primary Schools	21.7	20.6	19.15	17.98

14-15 初中和小学毕业生升学率及学龄儿童入学率

Percentage of Graduates of Junior Middle Schools and Primary Schools Entering Higher Level Schools,Percentage of School - Age Children Enrolled

项目	Item	2000	2001	2002	2003
初 中	**Junior Middle Schools**				
毕业生数（万人）	Number of Graduates (10 000 persons)	85.77	86.61	98.36	109.25
高级中等学校招生数（万人）	New Student Enrollment of Senior Secondary Schools (10 000 persons)	43.87	52.36	61.48	71.79
升学率 (%)	Percentage of Graduates (%)	51.15	60.45	62.5	65.71
小 学	**Primary Schools**				
毕业生数 (万人)	Number of Graduates (10 000 persons)	130.2	135.7	140.31	129.48
初级中等学校招生数 (万人)	New Student Enrollment of Junior Secondary Schools (10 000 persons)	126.34	132.85	138.54	129.26
升学率 (%)	Percentage of Graduates(%)	97.04	97.89	98.74	99.83
学龄儿童(万人)	**School-age Children (10 000 persons)**	**645.08**	**566.87**	**496.42**	**437.72**
已入学学龄儿童（万人）	School-age Children Enrolled in Schools (10 000 persons)	634.9	554.99	480.32	431.43
入学率 (%)	Enrollment Rate (%)	98.4	97.9	96.76	98.56

注：1. 高级中等学校招生数包括中专招收初中毕业生数、普通高中和职业高中的招生数、技工学校的招生数；

2. 初级中等学校招生数包括普通初中和职业初中招生数。初中毕业生包括普通初中和职业初中毕业生。

a. The number of new student enrollment in senior school includes that of students in specialized secondary schools, regular secondary schools and vocational schools and the technical schools.

b. The number of new student enrollment in junior school includes that of students in regular junior schools, and junior vocational schools.

14-16 幼儿园基本情况

Basic Statistics on Kindergartens

项目	Item	2000	2001	2002	2003
幼儿园个数（所）	Number of Kindergartens (unit)	5473	1333	1506	2331
班数（个）	Number of Classes (unit)	29896	25903	23747	25732
在园幼儿数（万人）	Student Enrollment (10 001 persons)	62.87	60.06	56.91	65.71
教职工数（万人）	Number of Staff and Teachers (10 001 persons)	3.98	1.61	1.85	2.42
#教师	#Teachers	3.39	0.98	0.96	1.27

14-17 教育经费总支出情况

Statistics on the Expenses of Educational Funds

单位：万元 (10 000 yuan)

年份	合计 Total	国家财政性教育经费 Government Appropriation for Education	#预算内教育经费 Budgetary	社会团体和公民个人办学经费 Funds of Social Organizations and Citizens for Running Schools	社会捐资和集资办学经费 Donations and Fund-Raising for Running Schools	学费和杂费 Tuition and Miscellaneous Fee	其他教育经费 Other Educational Funds
1996	870239.3	565019.8	374125.3	10502.8	70612.5	143251.6	80852.6
1997	989732.7	636639.5	428334.2	8013.5	91738.1	162014.4	91327.2
1998	1203245.1	710268.5	504295.0	10144.0	72342.6	253321.0	157169.0
1999	1375585.6	797469.8	573878.4	18527.2	71829.1	321773.5	165986.0
2000	1531180.5	862111.2	629976.6	27231.8	42117.6	403493.9	196226.0
2001	1777653.0	1009760.9	766718.4	35535.9	41326.2	471246.5	219783.5
2002	2063358.4	1160671.2	1034137.9	60413.3	33939.1	525885.7	282449.1
2003	2325331.0	1237512.0	1097560.0	114981.0	26073.8	621676.6	325087.6

14-18 各类专业技术人员

Various Specialized Technical Personnel

单位：人 (person)

项 目	Item	2002 合计 Total	2002 国有 State-owned	2002 集体 Collective-owned	2003 合计 Total	2003 国有 State-owned	2003 集体 Collective-owned
总 计	**Total**	**1262050**	**1229989**	**32061**	**1212866**	**1182432**	**30434**
#高级职称	Senior	63401	63069	332	65086	64725	361
中级职称	Secondary	449751	442444	7307	438120	430829	7291
#女性	Female	501117	490381	10736	487533	478059	9474
#自然科学	Natural Sciences	998718	985273	13445	981362	967763	13599
#社会及人文科学	Social Sciences and Humanities	263332	244716	18616	231504	214669	16835

注：此表未包括国家机关与人民团体中的专业技术人员；集体单位含供销社系统。2002年起含中央在湘单位.

Technicians from government offices and mass organizations were excluded. Supply and marketing cooperatives were included in the collective-owned units.Technicians from center units in Hunan province were included since 2002.

14-19 地方国有单位各行业自然科学技术人员(2003年)

Natural Scientific and Technical Personnel in Local State-Owned Units by Sector (2003)

单位：人 (person)

行 业	Sector	自然科学技术人员 Personnel of Natural Scientific and Technical	工程技术人员 Engineering Personnel	农业技术人员 Agricultural Personnel	科学研究人员 Scientific Research Personnel	卫生技术人员 Health Care Personnel	教学人员 Teaching Personnel
合 计	**Total**	**896105**	**123132**	**27828**	**4272**	**157173**	**583700**
农林牧渔业	Agriculture, Forestry, Farming of Animals and Fishing	40352	13161	25772	178	463	778
采矿业	Mining	5073	2882	1		1022	1168
制造业	Manufacturing	41174	31860	447	26	4156	4685
电力、煤气及水的生产和供应业	Production and Distribution of Electricity,Gas and Water	3039	2909	6	2	74	48
建筑业	Construction	13956	12964	1		643	348
交通运输仓储和邮政业	Traffic,Transport,Storage and Post	9476	8564	39	4	433	436
信息传输、计算机服务和软件业	Information Transfer,Computer Services and Software	623	475	2	62	3	81
批发和零售业	Wholesale and Retail Trade	2459	1367	187	7	855	43
住宿和餐饮业	Accommodation and Restaurants	98	87	3		7	1
金融业	Finance	212	182	18		10	2
房地产业	Real Estate	509	499		1	5	4
租赁和商务服务业	Tenancy and Business Services	993	835	85	3	36	34
科学研究、技术服务和地质勘查业	Scientific Research,Technical Service and Geologic Perambulation	16290	11904	309	2309	528	1240
水利、环境和公共设施管理业	Management of Water Conservancy, Environment and Public Establishment	21303	19194	324	123	390	1272
居民服务和其他服务业	Resident Services and Other Services	5983	4804	191	3	291	694
教育	Education	576933	2998	266	1402	1831	570436
卫生、社保和社会福利	Sanitation,Social Security&Social Welfare	149323	2468	70	75	145169	1541
文化、体育和娱乐业	Culture,Sports and Entertainment	5059	3697	33	69	393	867
其他行业	Others	3250	2282	74	8	864	22

14-20 地方集体单位各行业自然科学技术人员(2003年)

Natural Scientific and Technical Personnel in Local Collective-Owned Units by Sector (2003)

单位：人 (person)

行业	Sector	自然科学技术人员 Natural Scientific and Technical Personnel	工程技术人员 Engineering Personnel	农业技术人员 Agricultural Personnel	科学研究人员 Scientific Research Personnel	卫生技术人员 Health Care Personnel	教学人员 Teaching Personnel
合 计	**Total**	**13599**	**6138**	**808**	**29**	**5635**	**989**
农林牧渔水利	Farming,Forestry,Animal Husbandry and Fishery,Water Conservancy	605	151	394	1	25	34
工业、建筑房地产业	Industry, Construction,Real Estate	2884	2539	24	2	203	116
商业、饮食业	Wholesale and Retail Trade, Catering	1608	1104	305	24	114	61
文化教育卫生科研	Culture, Education,Health Care, Scientific Research	6453	473	41	2	5173	764
其他行业	Others	2049	1871	44		120	14
合计中：女性	**Female in Total**	**4138**	**976**	**120**	**6**	**2684**	**352**

14-21 自然科学研究获奖成果

Number of Achievements in Natural Scientific Research

单位：项 (item)

项 目	Item	2000	2001	2002	2003
省科技进步奖	Provincial Scientific Technological Progress Prize	360	150	150	147
国家科学技术进步奖	National Scientific Technological Progress Prize	13	14	13	18
国家批准授予的发明奖	National Invention Prize		1	1	1
国家自然科学奖	National Natural Sciences Prize	1			

14-22 科技成果情况(2003年)

Statistics on Achievements of Science and Technology (2003)

单位:项 (item)

项 目	Item	合 计 Total	科研院所 Research Institutions	大专院校 Universities and Colleges	工矿企业 Industrial and Mining Enterprises	其 他 Others
项目基本情况	**Basic Statistics on Items**					
登记项目数	Number of Registered Items	836	88	293	345	110
#鉴定项目数	# Number of Appraised Items	654	60	231	284	79
奖励项目数	Number of Prized Items	264	36	95	79	54
项目计划管理情况	**Statistics of Items Planned Management**					
国家计划项目	National Plan Items	103	7	55	34	7
省部计划项目	Provincial Plan Items	410	58	151	138	63
计划外项目	Non-plan Items	323	23	87	173	40
成果水平	**Level of Achievements**					
国际首创或领先	Originate and Keep Ahead at International	24	3	9	12	
国际先进	International Advanced Level	121	6	38	68	9
国内首创或领先	Originate and Keep Ahead at National	309	36	83	145	45
国内先进	Domestically Advanced Level	220	35	77	56	52
其他	Others	53	3		50	

14-23 三种专利申请与批准项数

Three Types of Patent Applications Examined and Certified

单位：项 (item)

项 目	Item	申请数 Applications Examined		批准数 Applications Granted	
		2002	2003	2002	2003
总 计	**Total**	**4860**	**6054**	**2347**	**3175**
按种类分	**By Types:**				
发 明	Creation and Inventions	1012	1492	158	346
实用新型	Utility Models	2789	3124	1600	1888
外观设计	Designs	1059	1438	589	941
按申请人类别分	**By Proposer:**				
个 人	Personal	3700	4626	1769	2284
大专院校	Universities and Colleges	137	213	36	72
科研单位	Research Institutions	17	33	20	27
工矿企业	Industrial and Mining Enterprises	986	1167	510	780
机关团体	Agencies and Organizations	20	15	12	12

14-24 各类技术合同签订及执行情况(2003年)

Statistics on Contracts Signed and Performed (2003)

项 目	Item	合同数 (项) Number of Contracts (item)	合同金额 (万元) Contracted Value (10 000 yuan)	#技术交易额 Value of Technical Trade
总 计	**Total**	**21315**	**369306**	**211218**
技术开发合同	Contracts of Technical Development	3325	148306	83556
技术转让合同	Contracts of Technical Alienation	2926	70680	44062
技术服务合同	Contracts of Technical Services	10611	131844	73122
技术咨询合同	Contracts of Technical Consultative	4453	18476	10478

14-25 各级科技计划项目进入技术市场情况(2003年)

Statitics on Different Levels of Scientific Plan Items Put into Technical Markets (2003)

开发类别	Item	合计 Total	国家部门计划 Country Level	省级计划 Province Level	市州县计划 Prefectures and County level
项目个数合计(项)	**Total (item)**	**7519**	**348**	**2427**	**4744**
#科研机构	Research Institutions	599	104	266	229
大中专院校	Universities and Colleges	582	41	219	322
企业	Industrial and Mining Enterprises	3177	80	928	2169
技术贸易机构	Institutions of Technical Trade	1326	45	652	629
个体经营	Personal and Partnership	671	43	175	453
其他	Others	1164	35	187	942
金额合计(万元)	**Total (10 000 yuan)**	**181977**	**29632**	**75729**	**76615**
#科研机构	Research Institutions	19418	5732	7067	6619
大中专院校	Universities and Colleges	7200	866	2163	4171
企业	Industrial and Mining Enterprises	30907	1820	4228	24860
技术贸易机构	Institutions of Technical Trade	87142	20615	61112	5415
个体经营	Personal and Partnership	11041	361	607	10073
其他	Others	26269	239	553	25478

14-26 高新技术产品情况(2003年)

Basic Statistics on High-tech Products (2003)

项目	Item	企业单位数（个）Number of Enterprises (unit)	高新技术产品总产值（万元）Gross Output Value of High-tech Products (10 000 yuan)	高新技术产品增加值（万元）Added Value of High-tech Products (10 000 yuan)
合计	Total	1019	9565468	3036395
# 高新技术企业	# High ang New Technology Enterprises	495	6519535	1999072
按市州分：	By Region:			
长沙市	Changsha City	308	3912195	1182524
株洲市	Zhuzhou City	135	1457031	455750
湘潭市	Xiangtan City	88	908248	316490
衡阳市	Hengyang City	122	575875	213128
邵阳市	Shaoyang City	36	88570	30650
岳阳市	Yueyang City	55	846767	271707
常德市	Changde City	54	335751	117670
张家界市	Zhangjiajie City	8	15524	8621
益阳市	Yiyang City	27	183227	48692
郴州市	Chenzhou City	103	286340	92120
永州市	Yongzhou City	20	576553	159274
怀化市	Huaihua City	23	175404	66282
娄底市	Loudi City	29	125301	42164
湘西自治州	West Hunan A.P	11	78683	31323
长沙高新技术开发区	Changsha High-tech Development District	231	3521928	1052849
株洲高新技术开发区	Zhuzhou High-tech Development District	68	1080949	346365
湘潭高新技术开发区	Xiangtan High-tech Development District	35	288107	105185
衡阳高新技术开发区	Hengyang High-tech Development District	26	280246	105400
岳阳高新技术开发区	Yueyang High-tech Development District	28	439316	166541
益阳高新技术开发区	Yiyang High-tech Development District	7	97046	24242
郴州高新技术开发区	Chenzhou High-tech Development District	8	13559	5309
按登记注册类型分：	By Registration Status			
内资企业	Domestic-Funded Enterprises	904	8210902.9	2616448.1
国有	State-owned Enterprises	179	1935305.1	664111.3
集体	Collective-owned Enterprises	78	119876.8	33387.7
股份合作	Cooperative Enterprises	49	145581.4	49628.5
国有联营	State Joint Ownership Enterprises	2	1460.3	435.5
集体联营	Collective Joint Ownership Enterprises	1	229.5	46.5
国有与集体联营	Joint State-collective Enterprises	1	494.8	173.2
其他联营	Other Joint Ownership Enterprises	1	160	52
国有独资公司	State-funded Corporations	16	1022793	280822.1
其他有限责任公司	Other Limited Liability Corporations	209	1649566.4	505931.8
股份有限公司	Share-holding Corporations Ltd.	126	2455355.3	778669.6
私营独资	Private-funded Enterprises	60	83511.7	33279.5
私营合伙	Private Partnership Enterprises	20	17480.9	5979.6
私营有限责任公司	Private Limited Liability Corporations	129	574001.6	175102.9
私营股份有限公司	Private Share-holding Corporations Ltd.	24	126257.8	48937.1
其他内资	Other Enterprises	9	78828.3	39890.8
港澳台商投资企业	Enterprises With Investment from H.K,Macao and Taiwan	61	522041	156906
外商投资企业	Enterprises With Foreign Investment	54	832524.5	263040.7
按企业规模分：	By Size:			
大型企业	Large	69	3916982.8	1190437.6
中型企业	Medium	165	2565276.3	838205.9
按高新技术领域分：	By High-tech Fields:			
电子与信息	Electron and Information	145	1214349.4	348495.4
生物医药技术	Medicine and Biotechnology	208	1511833.4	571279
新材料	New Materials	325	2858249.2	859500.5
光机电一体化	Optical and Mechatronics	174	2608841.4	742772.9
新能源、高效节能	New Energy Resources,Energy Saving	41	245808.5	84328.6
环境保护	Environmental Protection	15	29545.3	13292.1
航空航天	Avigation and Spaceflight	2	3557.8	1167.1
地球、空间及海洋工程	Earth,Airspace and Ocean	1	658.6	243.7
其他企业	Other Enterprises	108	1092624.8	415315.5

14-26 续表 continued

项目	Item	高新技术产品销售收入（万元）Sales Revenue of High-tech Products (10 000 yuan)	#出口收入（万美元）Exports Revenue (USD 10 000)	高新技术产品利税总额（万元）Peofits and Tax of High-tech Products (10 000 yuan)	#利润总额 Total of Profit and Tax
合计	**Total**	**9843197**	**100829**	**1290959**	**629570**
#高新技术企业	# High ang New Technology Enterprises	6753795	60701	873930	425204
按市州分:	**By Region:**				
长沙市	Changsha City	4414042	28507	567281	241409
株洲市	Zhuzhou City	1418877	22267	155791	81457
湘潭市	Xiangtan City	872989	16411	133384	68429
衡阳市	Hengyang City	540072	6636	50358	27524
邵阳市	Shaoyang City	86482	780	6777	2804
岳阳市	Yueyang City	820606	2124	93213	46102
常德市	Changde City	322280	3406	52625	28218
张家界市	Zhangjiajie City	4267	372	8307	6293
益阳市	Yiyang City	179814	2851	29294	18904
郴州市	Chenzhou City	284329	10267	35476	19935
永州市	Yongzhou City	508296	797	124337	69554
怀化市	Huaihua City	164193	379	9460	5956
娄底市	Loudi City	128956	1269	19601	10043
湘西自治州	West Hunan A.P	97993	4763	5058	2942
长沙高新技术开发区	Changsha High-tech Development District	4039257	25474	507544	208439
株洲高新技术开发区	Zhuzhou High-tech Development District	1053806	16669	102419	59494
湘潭高新技术开发区	Xiangtan High-tech Development District	265705	2828	19607	3044
衡阳高新技术开发区	Hengyang High-tech Development District	266681	4643	23577	14357
岳阳高新技术开发区	Yueyang High-tech Development District	437876	359	37308	18344
益阳高新技术开发区	Yiyang High-tech Development District	100351	1413	25816	18392
郴州高新技术开发区	Chenzhou High-tech Development District	13062	208	767	430
按登记注册类型分:	**By Registration Status**				
内资企业	Domestic-Funded Enterprises	8418154.2	76872.1	1079275.6	531760
国有	State-owned Enterprises	1874153	33840.8	263698.5	129001.5
集体	Collective-owned Enterprises	118132.8	2803.6	12425.9	5341.5
股份合作	Cooperative Enterprises	136891.9	1737	17861.7	8660.5
国有联营	State Joint Ownership Enterprises	1266.1	84.7	261.5	184.2
集体联营	Collective Joint Ownership Enterprises	206.8		11.6	11.6
国有与集体联营	Joint State-collective Enterprises	470		30	20
其他联营	Other Joint Ownership Enterprises	159		26.2	10.5
国有独资公司	State-funded Corporations	952687	5866.6	170408.2	94419
其他有限责任公司	Other Limited Liability Corporations	1673426.9	4889.8	202256.9	72134.8
股份有限公司	Share-holding Corporations Ltd.	2693390.9	15351.6	273823.2	135995.6
私营独资	Private-funded Enterprises	77610.7	995.3	13794.8	9165.4
私营合伙	Private Partnership Enterprises	17128.5	132.1	2973.4	2120.7
私营有限责任公司	Private Limited Liability Corporations	626249.3	7088.8	96221.4	55213.5
私营股份有限公司	Private Share-holding Corporations Ltd.	123674.1	1651.4	16872.1	11732.9
其他内资	Other Enterprises	122707.2	2430.4	8610.2	7748.3
港澳台商投资	Enterprises With Investment from H.K,Macao and Taiwan	569591.1	3882.1	84019.4	35561.4
外商投资	Enterprises With Foreign Investment	855451.3	20074.6	127664.3	62248.9
按企业规模分:	**By Size:**				
大型企业	Large	3764536.4	43872.1	530642.6	248058.6
中型企业	Medium	2577642.6	23918.2	306170.3	161235
按高新技术领域分:	**By High-tech Fields:**				
电子与信息	Electron and Information	1529915.5	15450.4	216283	72015.2
生物医药技术	Medicine and Biotechnology	1663058.3	9622.1	205583	111208.8
新材料	New Materials	2803483.1	46897.5	322341.9	155617
光机电一体化	Optical and Mechatronics	2359016.7	17059.7	326065.2	181118.7
新能源、高效节能	New Energy Resources,Energy Saving	241638.8	1831.3	28930.4	15142.1
环境保护	Environmental Protection	30263.9	825	2057.1	657.6
航空航天	Avigation and Spaceflight	3438.2		262.3	172.1
地球、空间及海洋工程	Earth,Airspace and Ocean	658.6		112	27.8
其他企业	Other Enterprises	1211723.5	9142.8	189324.4	93611

14-27 大中型工业企业科技活动情况（2003年）

Basic Statistics on Scientific and Technological Actives in Large and Medium-Sized Industrial Enterprises (2003)

指 标	Item	合 计 Total	#国有 State-owned	#大型 Large	#中型 Medium
大中型工业企业个数 （个）	Large and Medium-Sized Industrial Enterprises (unit)	522	219	56	466
#有科技活动的企业个数	# Number of Units Having S&T Activities	255	109	51	204
企业科技活动人员 （人）	Number of S&T Personnel of Enterprises (person)	42118	21243	21111	21007
#全时人员	Personnel	23069	10340	12977	10092
#具有高、中级职称	Senior and Medium	18995	10263	10581	8414
#研究与实验发展人员	R&D Employee	15573	7579	7487	8086
企业办科技机构数 （个）	Number of Institutions for S&T in Enterprises (unit)	203	75	57	146
企业办科研机构科技活动人员 （人）	Number of Persons of Institutions for S&T in Enterprises (person)	14210	6078	7229	6981
#具有高、中级职称	Senior and Medium	6844	2801	3501	3343
#博士毕业	Doctor	129	30	50	79
#硕士毕业	Master	678	160	249	429
#本科毕业	University	6731	2353	3527	3204
#研究与实验发展人员	R&D Personnel	6425	2967	3268	3157
当年科技活动经费筹集总额 （万元）	Funds of S&T Activities this Year (10 000 yuan)	352102	141932	222072	130029
#企业自筹	#Self-raised	285392	118713	177462	107930
金融机构贷款	Bank Loans	39698	10127	24436	15262
来自政府部门资金	Government Allocation	16951	8212	13830	3121
来自事业单位的资金	From Enterprises Allocation	3205	3044	37	3168
来自国外的资金	From Foreign Investment				
其他资金	Other Investment	6856	1837	6307	549
当年科技活动经费支出总额 （万元）	Expenditure for S&T Activities this Year (10 000 yuan)	295566	133894	178915	116651
#内部支出	#Intramural Expenditure	257630	121503	158094	99536
#研究与发展经费	#R&D	115931	69660	67618	48313
基础研究	Fundamental Research	3042	2177	2348	694
应用研究	Applied Research	12206	7196	7745	4460
实验发展	Experimental Development	100684	60287	57524	43159
#新产品开发经费	#New Products Development	92874	41734	58452	34422
#劳务费	#Labor Expenditures	83029	41796	49373	33656
#原材料费	#Raw and Processed Materials Expenditures	75321	34491	43956	31365
新产品产值 （万元）	Gross Output Value of New Products (10 000 yuan)	1978076	819274	1160196	817880
新产品销售收入 （万元）	Sales Revenue of New Products (10 000 yuan)	1944218	816641	1185558	758660
#出口	#Exported	262114	151745	207631	54484
新产品销售利润 （万元）	Sales Profits of New Products (10 000 yuan)	195966	80411	89253	106713
科技活动项目个数 （项）	Number of Projects for S&T (item)	2681	1519	1037	1644
#新产品开发	#New Products Development	1143	543	394	749
#研究与实验发展	#Research and Experimental Development	1688	896	605	1083
科技活动项目参加人员（人）	Personnel of Projects for S&T Activities (person)	22960	11119	10891	12069
科技活动项目经费支出总额 （万元）	Expenditures of Projects fo S&T Activities (10 000 yuan)	187848	83728	112529	75318
专利申请数 （件）	Patent Applications (item)	1285	789	406	879
拥有发明专利数 （件）	Applications of Inventions (item)	360	83	149	211

14-28 大中型工业企业科技活动人员与经费情况（2003年）

Basic Statistics on S&T Personnel and Funds of S&T Activities in Large and Medium-Sized Industrial Enterprises (2003)

类别	Item	企业科技活动人员（人） S&T Personnel in Enterprises (person)	#高中级职称人员 Senior and Medium	当年科技活动经费筹集总额（万元） Funds of S&T Activities this Year (10 000 yuan)	当年科技活动经费支出总额（万元） Expenditure for S&T Activities this Year (10 000 yuan)	#新产品开发 New Products Development
总计	**Total**	**42118**	**18995**	**352102**	**295566**	**92874**
按市州分组：	**By Region**					
长沙市	Changsha City	9319	4366	93199	88036	40015
株洲市	Zhuzhou City	7124	4500	93345	51200	24939
湘潭市	Xiangtan City	7619	2969	42114	39324	7442
衡阳市	Hengyang City	5613	1906	33800	26987	6761
邵阳市	Shaoyang City	691	436	10089	6221	3622
岳阳市	Yueyang City	3737	1746	19259	19286	1287
常德市	Changde City	2904	947	18513	21885	3122
张家界市	Zhangjiajie City	172	65		262	
益阳市	Yiyang City	1532	470	2204	2270	1035
郴州市	Chenzhou City	593	187	4225	4130	1391
永州市	Yongzhou City	1057	443	18221	19012	1002
怀化市	Huaihua City	477	217	1865	2027	857
娄底市	Loudi City	1027	707	14029	13866	1221
湘西自治州	West Hunan A.P	253	36	1239	1061	181
按企业规模分组	**By Size**					
大型企业	Large	21111	10581	222072	178915	58452
中型企业	Medium	21007	8414	130029	116651	34422
按登记注册类型分组	**By Registration Status**					
内资企业	Domestic-Funded Enterprises	40265	18705	344608	288182	91595
国有	State-owned Enterprises	21243	10263	141932	133894	41734
集体	Collective-owned Enterprises	397	130	3875	4649	1948
股份合作	Cooperative Enterprises	144	74	186	184	27
国有联营	State Joint Ownership Enterprises					
集体联营	Collective Joint Ownership Enterprises					
国有与集体联营	Joint State-collective Enterprises					
其他联营	Other Joint Ownership Enterprises					
国有独资公司	Statc-funded Corporations	4284	1865	20300	20393	7715
其他有限责任公司	Other Limited Liability Corporations	4406	1694	19966	23554	4645
股份有限公司	Share-holding Corporations Ltd.	8568	4220	148151	96502	32948
私营独资	Private-funded Enterprises	35	3	152	152	52
私营合伙	Private Partnership Enterprises					
私营有限责任公司	Private Limited Liability Corporations	911	260	8659	7487	2270
私营股份有限公司	Private Share-holding Corporations Ltd.	277	196	1386	1366	255
其他内资	Other Enterprises					
港澳台商投资	Enterprises With Investment from Hong Kong, Macao and Taiwan	641	107	5432	3513	1053
外商投资	Enterprises With Foreign Investment	1212	183	2062	3871	227

类　别	Item	企业科技活动人员（人） S&T Personnel in Enterprises (person)	#高中级职称人员 Senior and Medium	当年科技活动经费筹集总额（万元） Funds of S&T Activities this Year (10 000 yuan)	当年科技活动经费支出总额（万元） Expenditure for S&T Activities this Year (10 000 yuan)	#新产品开发 New Products Development
按工业行业大类分组	**By Industrial Branch**					
煤炭开采和洗选业	Mining and Washing of Coal	300	118	962	1279	23
黑色金属矿采选业	Mining of Ferrous Metal Ores					
有色金属矿采选业	Mining of Non-ferrous Metal Ores	228	77	997	967	48
非金属矿采选业	Mining and Processing of Nonmetal Ores	13	11	29	29	
其他采矿业	Mining of Other Ores N.E.C					
农副食品加工业	Processing of Food from Agricultural Products	537	214	5550	5509	1599
食品制造业	Manufacture of Foods	381	167	4678	2618	267
饮料制造业	Manufacture of Beverage	705	127	865	2002	167
烟草制品业	Manufacture of Tobacco	1376	476	15598	15592	2033
纺织业	Manufacture of Textile	997	288	3597	3529	641
纺织服装、鞋、帽制造业	Textile Wearing Apparel,Footware and Caps					
皮革毛皮羽毛(绒)及其制品	Leather,Fur,Feather and Its Products					
木材加工及木、竹、藤、棕、草制品业	Processing of Timbers,Manufacture of Wood, Bamboo, Rattan,Palm and Straw Products	20	16	2	2	
家具制造业	Manufacture of Furniture					
造纸及纸制品业	Manufacture of Paper and Paper Products	716	391	5224	4624	68
印刷业和记录媒介的复制	Printing,Reproduction of Recording Media	134	44	300	352	60
文教体育用品制造业	Manufacture of Articles for Culture, Education and Sport Activity					
石油加工炼焦及核燃料加工	Processing of Petroleum,Coking, Processing of Nucleus Fuel	767	307	5524	5937	247
化学原料及化学制品制造业	Manufacture of Chemical Raw Material and Chemical Products	3632	1914	25108	26811	6742
医药制造业	Manufacture of Medicines	1057	352	8283	7952	1415
化学纤维制造业	Manufacture of Chemical Fiber	334	160	6616	7727	1424
橡胶制品业	Manufacture of Rubber					
塑料制品业	Manufacture of Plastic	300	112	1927	1913	924
非金属矿物制品业	Non-metallic Mineral Products	1290	451	5796	4913	1031
黑色金属冶炼及压延加工业	Processing of Ferrous Metals	5036	2065	31902	29561	5884
有色金属冶炼及压延加工业	Processing of Non-ferrous Metals	2769	1613	64763	17395	9341
金属制品业	Manufacture of Metal Products	145	60	746	650	567
通用设备制造业	Manufacture of General Purpose Machinery	1615	831	3107	3615	1032
专用设备制造业	Manufacture of Special Purpose Machinery	5182	2341	62011	57187	27690
交通运输设备制造业	Manufacture of Transport Equipment	6623	3452	63345	56695	20141
电气机械及器材制造业	Electrical Machinery and Equipment	2450	1101	18238	15424	4204
通信设备、计算机及其他电子设备制造业	Manufacture of Communication Equipment, Computer and Other Electronic Equipment	1783	683	7018	7784	3726
仪器仪表及文化、办公用机械制造业	Measuring Instrument and Machinery for Cultural Activity and Office Work	612	173	4394	4394	2560
工艺品及其他制造业	Artwork,Other Manufacture N.E.C	126	72	267	267	153
废弃资源废旧材料回收加工	Recycling and Disposal of Waste					
电力、热力的生产和供应业	Production and Supply of Electric&Heat Power	2797	1199	4967	10549	887
燃气生产和供应业	Production and Distribution of Gas					
水的生产和供应业	Production and Distribution of Water	193	180	288	288	

14-29 大中型工业企业办科技机构情况（2003年）

Basic Statistics on Institutions for Scientific and Technological in Large and Medium-Sized Industrial Enterprises (2003)

类　别	Item	企业办科技机构（个）Number of Institutions for S&T in Enterprises (unit)	企业办科技机构人员（人）Number of Personnel in Institutions for S&T in Enterprises (person)	#高中级职称人员 Senior and Medium	#博士 Doctor	#硕士 Master
总计	**Total**	**203**	**14210**	**6844**	**129**	**678**
按市州分组:	**By Region**					
长沙市	Changsha City	71	4126	2590	63	382
株洲市	Zhuzhou City	38	2226	1313	37	127
湘潭市	Xiangtan City	12	1271	515		9
衡阳市	Hengyang City	8	946	445	7	35
邵阳市	Shaoyang City	4	144	92		1
岳阳市	Yueyang City	11	993	479	5	64
常德市	Changde City	16	2507	490	10	14
张家界市	Zhangjiajie City					
益阳市	Yiyang City	10	421	164	3	16
郴州市	Chenzhou City	5	147	59		4
永州市	Yongzhou City	10	762	337	3	14
怀化市	Huaihua City	5	163	41		2
娄底市	Loudi City	10	413	299		8
湘西自治州	West Hunan A.P	3	91	20	1	2
按企业规模分组	**By Size**					
大型企业	Large	57	7229	3501	50	249
中型企业	Medium	146	6981	3343	79	429
按登记注册类型分组	**By Registration Status**					
内资企业	Domestic-Funded Enterprises	191	13770	6751	126	653
国有	State-owned Enterprises	75	6078	2801	30	160
集体	Collective-owned Enterprises	7	308	89	10	26
股份合作	Cooperative Enterprises	1	4	2		
国有联营	State Joint Ownership Enterprises					
集体联营	Collective Joint Ownership Enterprises					
国有与集体联营	Joint State-collective Enterprises					
其他联营	Other Joint Ownership Enterprises					
国有独资公司	State-funded Corporations	13	556	326		9
其他有限责任公司	Other Limited Liability Corporations	27	2068	758	3	34
股份有限公司	Share-holding Corporations Ltd.	46	4412	2540	77	368
私营独资	Private-funded Enterprises	1	5	1		
私营合伙	Private Partnership Enterprises					
私营有限责任公司	Private Limited Liability Corporations	19	273	179	4	46
私营股份有限公司	Private Share-holding Corporations Ltd.	2	66	55	2	10
其他内资	Other Enterprises					
港澳台商投资	Enterprises With Investment from Hong Kong, Macao and Taiwan	8	329	47	2	21
外商投资	Enterprises With Foreign Investment	4	111	46	1	4

类别	Item	企业办科技机构（个）Number of Institutions for S&T in Enterprises (unit)	企业办科技机构人员（人）Number of Personnel in Institutions for S&T in Enterprises (person)	#高中级职称人员 Senior and Medium	#博士 Doctor	#硕士 Master
按工业行业大类分组	**By Industrial Branch**					
煤炭开采和洗选业	Mining and Washing of Coal	2	27	20	3	3
黑色金属矿采选业	Mining of Ferrous Metal Ores					
有色金属矿采选业	Mining of Non-ferrous Metal Ores	2	16	11		
非金属矿采选业	Mining and Processing of Nonmetal Ores					
其他采矿业	Mining of Other Ores N.E.C					
农副食品加工业	Processing of Food from Agricultural Products	12	311	103	29	56
食品制造业	Manufacture of Foods	4	97	46	1	2
饮料制造业	Manufacture of Beverage	4	88	25		2
烟草制品业	Manufacture of Tobacco	3	1376	288	9	29
纺织业	Manufacture of Textile	4	54	37		
纺织服装、鞋、帽制造业	Textile Wearing Apparel,Footware and Caps					
皮革毛皮羽毛(绒)及其制品	Leather,Fur,Feather and Its Products					
木材加工及木、竹、藤、棕、草制品业	Processing of Timbers,Manufacture of Wood, Bamboo, Rattan,Palm and Straw Products					
家具制造业	Manufacture of Furniture					
造纸及纸制品业	Manufacture of Paper and Paper Products	1	65	40	2	
印刷业和记录媒介的复制	Printing,Reproduction of Recording Media	2	56	8		2
文教体育用品制造业	Manufacture of Articles for Culture, Education and Sport Activity					
石油加工炼焦及核燃料加工	Processing of Petroleum,Coking, Processing of Nucleus Fuel	3	369	201		12
化学原料及化学制品制造业	Manufacture of Chemical Raw Material and Chemical Products	23	843	486	11	64
医药制造业	Manufacture of Medicines	11	426	123	3	20
化学纤维制造业	Manufacture of Chemical Fiber	3	96	60		2
橡胶制品业	Manufacture of Rubber					
塑料制品业	Manufacture of Plastic	4	80	34	3	11
非金属矿物制品业	Non-metallic Mineral Products	7	368	206		24
黑色金属冶炼及压延加工业	Processing of Ferrous Metals	7	1022	396	1	12
有色金属冶炼及压延加工业	Processing of Non-ferrous Metals	11	577	257	8	22
金属制品业	Manufacture of Metal Products					
通用设备制造业	Manufacture of General Purpose Machinery	6	325	266		20
专用设备制造业	Manufacture of Special Purpose Machinery	19	2818	1617	27	98
交通运输设备制造业	Manufacture of Transport Equipment	28	2472	1286	12	92
电气机械及器材制造业	Electrical Machinery and Equipment	26	1187	580	6	84
通信设备、计算机及其他电子设备制造业	Manufacture of Communication Equipment, Computer and Other Electronic Equipment	8	916	521	9	81
仪器仪表及文化、办公用机械制造业	Measuring Instrument and Machinery for Cultural Activity and Office Work	2	194	60	1	22
工艺品及其他制造业	Artwork,Other Manufacture N.E.C	1	106	72	0	2
废弃资源废旧材料回收加工	Recycling and Disposal of Waste					
电力、热力的生产和供应业	Production and Supply of Electric&Heat Power	9	302	85	4	17
燃气生产和供应业	Production and Distribution of Gas					
水的生产和供应业	Production and Distribution of Water	1	19	16		1

14-30 大中型工业企业科技活动新产品情况（2003年）

Basic Statistics on New Products in Large and Medium-Sized Industrial Enterprises (2003)

类别	Item	新产品产值（万元）Gross Output Value of New Products (10 000 yuan)	新产品销售收入（万元）Sales Revenue of New Products (10 000 yuan)	新产品销售利润（万元）Sales Profits of New Products (10 000 yuan)	专利申请数（件）Total Applications (item)	拥有发明专利数（件）Total Applications of Inventions (item)
总计	**Total**	**1978076**	**1944218**	**195966**	**1285**	**360**
按市州分组：	**By Region**					
长沙市	Changsha City	644975	646766	71828	380	98
株洲市	Zhuzhou City	353198	357122	29533	735	54
湘潭市	Xiangtan City	307397	309830	23172	28	52
衡阳市	Hengyang City	291114	261914	17186	35	11
邵阳市	Shaoyang City	25518	24224	2865	1	2
岳阳市	Yueyang City	96576	86686	12695	50	54
常德市	Changde City	93909	90591	12636	17	14
张家界市	Zhangjiajie City					
益阳市	Yiyang City	37245	36919	3071	1	8
郴州市	Chenzhou City	25985	30328	5375	2	2
永州市	Yongzhou City	17367	13668	1725	2	10
怀化市	Huaihua City	5098	3453	1085	4	21
娄底市	Loudi City	66026	72519	12098	21	24
湘西自治州	West Hunan A.P	13668	10200	2696	9	10
按企业规模分组	**By Size**					
大型企业	Large	1160196	1185558	89253	406	149
中型企业	Medium	817880	758660	106713	879	211
按登记注册类型分组	**By Registration Status**					
内资企业	Domestic-Funded Enterprises	1841004	1819259	172915	1271	350
国有	State-owned Enterprises	819274	816641	80411	789	83
集体	Collective-owned Enterprises	23859	24351	1173	4	9
股份合作	Cooperative Enterprises	11591	11525	1773		
国有联营	State Joint Ownership Enterprises					
集体联营	Collective Joint Ownership Enterprises					
国有与集体联营	Joint State-collective Enterprises					
其他联营	Other Joint Ownership Enterprises					
国有独资公司	State-funded Corporations	240128	235010	15171	25	26
其他有限责任公司	Other Limited Liability Corporations	121773	114266	11922	83	15
股份有限公司	Share-holding Corporations Ltd.	505435	500117	37641	325	163
私营独资	Private-funded Enterprises					
私营合伙	Private Partnership Enterprises					
私营有限责任公司	Private Limited Liability Corporations	118042	116549	24665	43	52
私营股份有限公司	Private Share-holding Corporations Ltd.	900	800	160	2	2
其他内资	Other Enterprises					
港澳台商投资	Enterprises With Investment from Hong Kong, Macao and Taiwan	97509	91955	19003	14	10
外商投资	Enterprises With Foreign Investment	39564	33005	4047		

类别	Item	新产品产值（万元） Gross Output Value of New Products (10 000 yuan)	新产品销售收入（万元） Sales Revenue of New Products (10 000 yuan)	新产品销售利润（万元） Sales Profits of New Products (10 000 yuan)	专利申请数（件） Total Applications (item)	拥有发明专利数（件） Total Applications of Inventions (item)
按工业行业大类分组	**By Industrial Branch**					
煤炭开采和洗选业	Mining and Washing of Coal	807	722	276	2	12
黑色金属矿采选业	Mining of Ferrous Metal Ores					
有色金属矿采选业	Mining of Non-ferrous Metal Ores				3	3
非金属矿采选业	Mining and Processing of Nonmetal Ores					
其他采矿业	Mining of Other Ores N.E.C					
农副食品加工业	Processing of Food from Agricultural Products	17483	17053	1584	17	15
食品制造业	Manufacture of Foods	18478	14981	3445	4	4
饮料制造业	Manufacture of Beverage	43493	43201	11848	12	13
烟草制品业	Manufacture of Tobacco	56178	57786	9380	18	4
纺织业	Manufacture of Textile	34726	33755	1736	10	
纺织服装、鞋、帽制造业	Textile Wearing Apparel,Footware and Caps					
皮革毛皮羽毛(绒)及其制品	Leather,Fur,Feather and Its Products					
木材加工及木、竹、藤、棕、草制品业	Processing of Timbers,Manufacture of Wood, Bamboo, Rattan,Palm and Straw Products	8925	8925	1123		
家具制造业	Manufacture of Furniture					
造纸及纸制品业	Manufacture of Paper and Paper Products	465	1000	26	10	2
印刷业和记录媒介的复制	Printing,Reproduction of Recording Media	925	870	18		
文教体育用品制造业	Manufacture of Articles for Culture, Education and Sport Activity					
石油加工炼焦及核燃料加工	Processing of Petroleum,Coking, Processing of Nucleus Fuel	40212	40212	6860	4	18
化学原料及化学制品制造业	Manufacture of Chemical Raw Material and Chemical Products	79565	75984	6789	71	59
医药制造业	Manufacture of Medicines	43239	30216	4901	9	33
化学纤维制造业	Manufacture of Chemical Fiber	3050	2998	137		
橡胶制品业	Manufacture of Rubber					
塑料制品业	Manufacture of Plastic	18515	20924	2878	2	3
非金属矿物制品业	Non-metallic Mineral Products	38214	33475	6050	19	3
黑色金属冶炼及压延加工业	Processing of Ferrous Metals	390136	402295	35752	21	13
有色金属冶炼及压延加工业	Processing of Non-ferrous Metals	311294	326892	27280	136	41
金属制品业	Manufacture of Metal Products	900	800	160	2	2
通用设备制造业	Manufacture of General Purpose Machinery	60409	48863	10657	6	8
专用设备制造业	Manufacture of Special Purpose Machinery	245057	247003	4937	220	49
交通运输设备制造业	Manufacture of Transport Equipment	296354	301378	15066	68	15
电气机械及器材制造业	Electrical Machinery and Equipment	217110	199761	33113	65	46
通信设备、计算机及其他电子设备制造业	Manufacture of Communication Equipment, Computer and Other Electronic Equipment	3689	3528	663	4	8
仪器仪表及文化、办公用机械制造业	Measuring Instrument and Machinery for Cultural Activity and Office Work	48341	31096	11278	3	
工艺品及其他制造业	Artwork,Other Manufacture N.E.C	513	503	10		8
废弃资源废旧材料回收加工	Recycling and Disposal of Waste					
电力、热力的生产和供应业	Production and Supply of Electric&Heat Power				1	1
燃气生产和供应业	Production and Distribution of Gas					
水的生产和供应业	Production and Distribution of Water				578	

14-31 大中型工业企业科技活动项目情况（2003）

Basic Statistics on Projects for Scientific and Technological Activies in Large and Medium-Sized Industrial Enterprises (2003)

类别	Item	科技活动项目数（项）Projects for S&T Activities (item)	#新产品开发 New Products R&D	参与项目人员（人）Personnel of Projects (person)	#高中级职称人员 Senior and Medium	项目经费支出（万元）Expenditure of Projects (10 000 yuan)
总计	**Total**	**2681**	**1143**	**22960**	**11864**	**187848**
按市州分组：	**By Region**					
长沙市	Changsha City	638	294	6258	2640	61147
株洲市	Zhuzhou City	617	247	4332	2682	36742
湘潭市	Xiangtan City	329	63	2770	1660	22262
衡阳市	Hengyang City	104	43	2094	1067	10876
邵阳市	Shaoyang City	124	86	549	352	5284
岳阳市	Yueyang City	178	64	2479	1311	11338
常德市	Changde City	143	49	1175	637	7049
张家界市	Zhangjiajie City					
益阳市	Yiyang City	228	201	593	232	1673
郴州市	Chenzhou City	47	9	593	187	3945
永州市	Yongzhou City	47	32	815	361	16589
怀化市	Huaihua City	35	16	259	92	1218
娄底市	Loudi City	178	33	854	611	9188
湘西自治州	West Hunan A.P	13	6	189	32	538
按企业规模分组	**By Size**					
大型企业	Large	1037	394	10891	6426	112529
中型企业	Medium	1644	749	12069	5438	75318
按登记注册类型分组	**By Registration Status**					
内资企业	Domestic-Funded Enterprises	2617	1099	21712	11655	182321
国有	State-owned Enterprises	1519	543	11119	6140	83728
集体	Collective-owned Enterprises	13	8	305	83	2887
股份合作	Cooperative Enterprises	9	8	136	67	75
国有联营	State Joint Ownership Enterprises					
集体联营	Collective Joint Ownership Enterprises					
国有与集体联营	Joint State-collective Enterprises					
其他联营	Other Joint Ownership Enterprises					
国有独资公司	State-funded Corporations	356	231	2620	1472	12847
其他有限责任公司	Other Limited Liability Corporations	165	79	1655	925	7877
股份有限公司	Share-holding Corporations Ltd.	506	207	4970	2643	67231
私营独资	Private-funded Enterprises	2	1	11	3	152
私营合伙	Private Partnership Enterprises					
私营有限责任公司	Private Limited Liability Corporations	38	20	660	203	6221
私营股份有限公司	Private Share-holding Corporations Ltd.	9	2	236	119	1302
其他内资	Other Enterprises					
港澳台商投资	Enterprises With Investment from Hong Kong, Macao and Taiwan	54	39	511	93	3319
外商投资	Enterprises With Foreign Investment	10	5	737	116	2208

14-31 续表 continued

类　别	Item	科技活动项目数（项）Projects for S&T Activities (item)	#新产品开发 New Products R&D	参与项目人员（人）Personnel of Projects (person)	#高中级职称人员 Senior and Medium	项目经费支出（万元）Expenditure of Projects (10 000 yuan)
按工业行业大类分组	**By Industrial Branch**					
煤炭开采和洗选业	Mining and Washing of Coal	13	2	161	71	411
黑色金属矿采选业	Mining of Ferrous Metal Ores					
有色金属矿采选业	Mining of Non-ferrous Metal Ores	33	3	226	77	760
非金属矿采选业	Mining and Processing of Nonmetal Ores					
其他采矿业	Mining of Other Ores N.E.C					
农副食品加工业	Processing of Food from Agricultural Products	32	26	371	148	3090
食品制造业	Manufacture of Foods	18	13	271	78	2397
饮料制造业	Manufacture of Beverage	32	25	356	81	463
烟草制品业	Manufacture of Tobacco	63	13	326	146	4329
纺织业	Manufacture of Textile	205	193	771	241	2664
纺织服装、鞋、帽制造业	Textile Wearing Apparel,Footware and Caps					
皮革毛皮羽毛(绒)及其制品	Leather,Fur,Feather and Its Products					
木材加工及木、竹、藤、棕、草制品业	Processing of Timbers,Manufacture of Wood, Bamboo, Rattan,Palm and Straw Products					
家具制造业	Manufacture of Furniture					
造纸及纸制品业	Manufacture of Paper and Paper Products	40	13	557	391	4003
印刷业和记录媒介的复制	Printing,Reproduction of Recording Media	6	4	60	22	202
文教体育用品制造业	Manufacture of Articles for Culture, Education and Sport Activity					
石油加工炼焦及核燃料加工	Processing of Petroleum,Coking, Processing of Nucleus Fuel	64	14	565	291	2357
化学原料及化学制品制造业	Manufacture of Chemical Raw Material and Chemical Products	282	57	2479	1201	17235
医药制造业	Manufacture of Medicines	59	30	427	164	3509
化学纤维制造业	Manufacture of Chemical Fiber	6	5	184	107	1424
橡胶制品业	Manufacture of Rubber					
塑料制品业	Manufacture of Plastic	15	8	192	84	1041
非金属矿物制品业	Non-metallic Mineral Products	67	32	595	351	3358
黑色金属冶炼及压延加工业	Processing of Ferrous Metals	170	17	1456	1239	16559
有色金属冶炼及压延加工业	Processing of Non-ferrous Metals	235	110	1738	807	14203
金属制品业	Manufacture of Metal Products	3	3	116	54	584
通用设备制造业	Manufacture of General Purpose Machinery	54	44	648	379	2348
专用设备制造业	Manufacture of Special Purpose Machinery	234	135	2320	1378	39004
交通运输设备制造业	Manufacture of Transport Equipment	547	200	3936	2103	43209
电气机械及器材制造业	Electrical Machinery and Equipment	231	105	1649	703	11906
通信设备、计算机及其他电子设备制造业	Manufacture of Communication Equipment, Computer and Other Electronic Equipment	87	56	1450	565	5700
仪器仪表及文化、办公用机械制造业	Measuring Instrument and Machinery for Cultural Activity and Office Work	19	8	440	158	3760
工艺品及其他制造业	Artwork,Other Manufacture N.E.C	8	6	106	72	187
废弃资源废旧材料回收加工	Recycling and Disposal of Waste					
电力、热力的生产和供应业	Production and Supply of Electric&Heat Power	147	21	1515	911	3082
燃气生产和供应业	Production and Distribution of Gas					
水的生产和供应业	Production and Distribution of Water	11		45	42	63

十五、文化、体育、卫生

CULTURE, SPORTS AND PUBLIC HEALTH

资料整理人员： 陈洲艳

十五、文化、体育、卫生

CULTURE, SPORTS AND PUBLIC HEALTH

15-1 文化产业机构和人员(2003年)

Cultural Institutions and Personnel (2003)

类 别	Item	合 计 Total		文化部门 Culture Department		其他部门 Other Department	
		机构(个) Institutions (unit)	人员(人) Personnel (person)	机构(个) Institutions (unit)	人员(人) Personnel (person)	机构(个) Institutions (unit)	人员(人) Personnel (person)
总 计	**Total**	**13941**	**83258**	**7550**	**36438**	**6019**	**24095**
出版发行业	Publication and Distribution	372	22725				
艺术业	Art	230	6930	230	6930	6019	24095
图书馆业	Libraries	115	1938	115	1938		
群众文化业	Mass Culture	2648	5984	2624	5944	24	40
艺术教育业	Culture and Education	5	575	5	575		
娱乐业	Recreational Services	7303	32368	2989	12683	4314	19685
文艺科研业	Art Research Institutions	1	29	1	29		
文物业	Culture Relics	202	2447	199	2228	3	219
其他文化产业	Other Culture	3053	9788	1375	5637	1678	4151
非文化产业	Non-Cultural Institutions	12	474	12	474		

15-2 艺术业机构和人员

Art Institutions and Personnel

类 别	Item	2002		2003	
		机构(个) Institutions (unit)	人员(人) Personnel (person)	机构(个) Institutions (unit)	人员(人) Personnel (person)
总 计	**Total**	**234**	**6669**	**10584**	**49069**
艺术表演团体	**Art Performance Troupes**	**87**	**4365**	**86**	**4328**
话剧团	Drama	1	102	1	75
歌剧、舞剧、歌舞剧团	Opera,Ballet and Dance Troupes	7	600	5	513
歌舞团、轻音乐团	Song and Dance Troupe, Light Music Troupes	5	199	8	390
文工团、文宣队	Culture and Performance Troupes	5	202	5	186
戏曲剧团	Local Opera Troupes	67	3036	65	2945
曲艺、杂技、木偶、皮影团	Recitation and Ballad Troupes,Acrobatics and Circus Troupes,Puppet Show Troupes and Shadow Play Troupes	2	226	2	219
艺术表演场所(剧场、影剧院)	**Art Centers (Theaters and Music Halls)**	**97**	**1935**	**94**	**2244**
艺术创作机构	**Art Creation Institutions**	**20**	**99**	**19**	**97**
艺术展览机构	**Art Exhibition Institutions**	**3**	**14**	**5**	**24**
其他	**Others**	**27**	**265**	**10380**	**42376**

15-3 出版发行、文物、图书馆、群众文化业机构人员(2003年)

Number of Institutions and Personnel in Publishing and Distribution, Cultural Relics, Library and Mass Culture (2003)

类别	Item	合计 Total 机构(个) Institutions (unit)	合计 Total 人员(人) Personnel (person)	文化部门 Culture Department 机构(个) Institutions (unit)	文化部门 Culture Department 人员(人) Personnel (person)	其他部门 Other Department 机构(个) Institutions (unit)	其他部门 Other Department 人员(人) Personnel (person)
出版发行事业	**Publishing and Distribution**	**372**	**22725**				
图书	Books Published	14	1370				
报纸	Newspaper Published	88	6746				
杂志	Magazines Published	229	1779				
音像出版	Image to Publish	5	225				
音像电复制	Image to copy	2	168				
出版物印刷	Publication to Print	31	6590				
发行	Distribution	1	5565				
印刷物质供销	Print Materiat Supply and Marketing	2	282				
文物事业	**Cultural Relics**	**200**	**2386**	**197**	**2167**	**3**	**219**
#文物保护管理机构	#Protection and Management Agencies	125	995	125	995		
博物馆	Museums	73	1314	70	1095	3	219
#综合性的	#Comprehensive Museum	31	719	31	719		
纪念性的	Memorial Museum	42	595	39	376		
文物商店	Cultural Relics Agencies	2	77	2	77		
图书馆事业	**Libraries**	**115**	**1938**	**115**	**1938**		
群众文化事业	**Mass Culture**	**2648**	**5984**	**2624**	**5944**	**24**	**40**
群众艺术馆	Mass Art Centers	15	466	15	466		
文化馆	Cultural Centers	125	1814	125	1814		
文化站	Cultural Stations	2508	3704	2484	3664	24	40

注：文物保护管理机构的人员包含文物行政主管机关中文物事业编制的人员。

Protection and management agencies include administrative departments and other agencies.

15-4 图书、杂志、报纸出版情况

Statistics on Books, Magazines and Newspapers Published

年份 Year	图书 Books Published 种数(种) Number of Publications (kind)	图书 总印数(万册) Printed Copies (10 000 copies)	图书 总印张(亿印张) Printed Sheets (100 million sheets)	杂志 Magazines Published 种数(种) Number of Publications (kind)	杂志 总印数(万册) Printed Copies (10 000 copies)	杂志 总印张(亿印张) Printed Sheets (100 million sheets)	报纸 Newspaper Published 种数(种) Number of Publications (kind)	报纸 总印数(万份) Printed Copies (10 000 copies)	报纸 总印张(亿印张) Printed Sheets (100 million sheets)
1995	2357	33677	14.90	208	7768	1.75	63	62425	6.90
1998	3513	36582	15.41	202	8920	1.93	55	75879	9.28
1999	3367	30765	13.99	214	12437	2.35	62	84995	11.83
2000	3156	24844	12.37	244	10504	2.11	95	83467	12.75
2001	3346	23808	12.70	251	10051	2.27	109	92273	18.65
2002	3504	32600	18.10	263	11207	2.66	109	95198	21.59
2003	3702	29556	16.80	269	12577	3.20	106	113514	31.50

注：图书种数不包括租型图书。The total collection books excludes the books for rental.

15-5 广播、电视事业情况

Statistics on Broadcasting and Television Stations

项 目	Item	2000	2001	2002	2003
广播电视系统全部职工(万人)	**Number of Staff and Workers in System of Broadcasting and Television (10000 persons)**	**2.32**	**2.39**	**2.24**	**2.27**
广播	**Broadcasting**				
广播电台数(座)	Number of Broadcasting Stations (set)	11	11	11	11
广播电台节目套数(套)	Number of Broadcasting Program (set)	53	53	53	53
平均每日播出时间(小时)	Broadcasting Hours per Day (hour)	483	486	495	531
中、短波发射台、转播台数(座)	Medium Wave and Short Wave Broadcast Transmission Station and Relaying Station (set)	25	25	25	25
中、短波发射机(部)	Medium Wave and Short Wave Broadcast Transmitters (set)	36	36	36	36
中、短波发射机功率(千瓦)	Power of Medium and Short Wave Broadcast Transmitters (kw)	579	579	579	579.5
覆盖率(%)	Listener-Coverage Rate (%)	81.46	81.62	81.73	81.79
电视	**Television**				
电视中心台数(座)	Number of Television Stations (set)	16	15	15	15
电视节目套数(套)	Number of Television Program (set)	33	101	101	103
平均每周播出时间(小时)	Broadcasting Hours per Week (hour)	2338	8224	8196	9178
电视发射台(座)	Television Transmission Stations (set)	542	534	461	443
#1千瓦以上(座)	#One KW and Over (set)	48	50	48	48
电视发射机(部)	Television Transmitters (set)	720	709	628	607
电视发射机功率(千瓦)	Power of Television Transmitters (kw)	291	291	291	300
覆盖率(%)	Viewer-Coverage Rate (%)	91.38	91.7	91.79	91.91

注：广播电台数、电视中心台数从1998年起不包括县级台数。

Note: Number of Broadcasting Stations and Number of Television Stations Exclude County Level Stations Since 1998.

15-6 各类卫生机构、床位和人员 (2003年)

类 别	Item	机 构 (个) Number of Institutions (unit)	床位数（张） Number of Beds (unit)		
			编制床位数 Number of Organization Beds	实有床位数 Number of Reality Beds	标准床位数 Number of Standard Beds
总 计	**Total**	**4016**	**152645**	**144933**	**85249**
医院	Hospitals	721	100633	96541	64341
市	City	443	65594	63121	42590
县	County	278	35079	33420	21751
综合医院	General Hospitals	515	74628	71855	48595
中医院	Hospitals of Chinese Medicine	111	16244	15003	9762
中西医结合医院	Hospitals Which Integrate Traditional Chinese Therapeutics with Western Therapeutics	6	552	502	330
专科医院	Specialized Hospital	89	9209	9181	5694
口腔医院	Hospitals for Oral Cavity Diseases	6	90	73	70
眼科医院	Ophthalmology Hospitals	4	80	80	40
耳鼻喉科医院	Otorhinolaryngology Hospitals	1	60	60	60
肿瘤医院	Tumor Hospitals	5	1109	1090	90
妇产科医院	Hospitals for Maternity and Child Care	3	52	52	30
儿童医院	Children's Hospitals	1	300	385	385
精神病院	Mental Hospitals	22	3852	4156	2603
传染病院	Hospitals for Infectious Diseases	4	703	592	582
皮肤病病院	Hospitals for Occupational Diseases	2	14	14	14
结核病院	Tuberculosis Hospitals	4	694	514	478
骨科医院	Orthopaedics Hospitals	9	440	485	304
康复医院	Rehabilitation Hospitals	9	647	542	440
整形外科医院	Plastic Hospitals	1	20	20	20
其他专科医院	Other Specialized Hospitals	18	1148	1118	538
疗养院	Sanatoriums	7	1950	1635	1150
社区卫生服务中心	Health Service Center for Community	13	195	205	71
卫生院	Health Center	2627	40258	37363	14665
门诊部	Clinics	41	649	605	392
急救中心	First-aid Station	1	2	2	
采供血机构	Institutions for Collection and Supply of Blood	18			
妇幼保健院	Maternity and Child Care Centers	132	4534	4196	2572
专科疾病防治院	Specialized Disease Prevention and Treatment Institute	100	3113	3084	1667
疾病预防控制中心	Disease Prevention & Control Center	167	224	222	71
卫生监督所	Medical Supervision Institute	27			
卫生监督检验所	Medical Supervision & Check Institute	6			
医学科学研究机构	Research Institutes of Medical Science	5	100	100	100
医学在职培训机构	Training Institutes of Medical Science	5	103	107	73
健康教育所	Health Education Institute	2			
其他卫生事业机构	Other Health Care Institutions	144	884	873	147

Health Care Institutions, Beds and Personnel by Type (2003)

卫生工作人员 (人) Health Personnel (person)	#卫生技术人员 Medical Technical Personnel	执业医师 Doctors	执业助理医师 Assistant Doctors	注册护士 Senior Nurse & Nurse	药剂人员 Pharmacist	检验人员 Laboratory Technician	其他 Others
232100	189529	55837	23840	54310	21976	9929	23637
132158	104466	32825	6397	41209	11239	5179	7617
82457	64152	21124	2966	26463	6229	3034	4336
49701	40314	11701	3431	14746	5010	2145	3281
98151	77571	24599	4300	31993	7399	3872	5408
23762	19269	5904	1558	6344	3154	922	1387
729	581	185	73	190	76	26	31
9516	7045	2137	466	2682	610	359	791
436	337	166	16	80	13	40	22
99	70	21	9	15	6	3	16
133	114	29	8	36	13	5	23
1448	1067	299	21	448	71	40	188
98	78	27	5	24	8	4	10
617	449	167		224	33	25	
3069	2166	582	87	1013	156	83	245
680	498	127	17	220	55	37	42
50	39	16	5	5	6	3	4
518	370	117	31	123	40	23	36
574	485	154	82	112	82	21	34
481	352	93	45	119	42	18	35
29	20	9		4	1	1	5
1284	1000	330	140	259	84	56	131
1022	597	164	38	286	58	26	25
405	342	138	54	74	52	20	4
70555	62990	14410	14546	9202	9344	2509	12979
756	635	273	26	203	66	39	28
3	3	1	1	1			
538	353	50	23	122	2	112	44
8556	6983	2651	805	1860	495	460	712
3887	3119	1018	375	670	242	267	547
10112	7761	3522	1198	462	222	1187	1170
729	372	146	91	18	4	28	85
73	54	29	9	1	3	7	5
447	202	85	3		64	9	41
603	158	56	36	33	13	5	15
7	5	2	1				2
2249	1489	467	237	169	172	81	363

15-7 医疗机构运营情况（2003年）

Basic Statistics of Operation on Health Care Institutions (2003)

类 别	Item	诊疗人次（人次） Number of Patients Treated (person-time)	#门诊、急诊人次 Out-Patients and Emergency Patients	入院人数（人） Number of Inpatients (person)
总 计	**Total**	**77918813**	**71246852**	**2644893**
医院	Hospitals	34531646	32476871	1796398
综合医院	General Hospitals	26551043	24907448	1452863
中医院	Hospitals of Chinese Medicine	5795485	5624248	252509
中西医结合医院	Hospitals Which Integrate Traditional Chinese Therapeutics with Western Therapeutics	177999	152570	13923
专科医院	Specialized Hospital	2007119	1792605	77103
口腔医院	Hospitals for Oral Cavity Diseases	349023	303393	500
眼科医院	Ophthalmology Hospitals	78992	72992	642
耳鼻喉科医院	Otorhinolaryngology Hospitals	41757	41757	494
肿瘤医院	Tumor Hospitals	122786	93905	13285
妇产科医院	Hospitals for Maternity and Child Care	15402	14700	730
儿童医院	Children's Hospitals	237095	237095	11018
精神病院	Mental Hospitals	301337	296595	19857
传染病院	Hospitals for Infectious Diseases	91095	81095	4815
皮肤病病院	Hospitals for Occupational Diseases	30600	30600	40
结核病院	Tuberculosis Hospitals	51920	34185	3281
骨科医院	Orthopaedics Hospitals	119671	99948	7179
康复医院	Rehabilitation Hospitals	205833	184038	3492
整形外科医院	Plastic Hospitals	3552	2125	427
其他专科医院	Other Specialized Hospitals	358056	300177	11343
疗养院	Sanatoriums	65836	57507	4513
社区卫生服务中心	Health Service Center for Community	296403	231772	7758
卫生院	Health Center	38962190	34712694	668201
门诊部	Clinics	342157	335098	1781
妇幼保健院	Maternity and Child Care Centers	3049232	2871520	135528
专科疾病防治院	Specialized Disease Prevention and Treatment Institute	671349	561390	30714

15-7 续表 (continued)

类 别	Item	治愈率 (%) Mend Rate (%)	好转率 (%) Improvement Rate (%)	死亡率 (%) Death Rate (%)	病床周转次数 (次) Turn Over of Beds (time)	病床工作日 (day) Days Per Bed in Use (day)	病床使用率 (%) Utilization Rate of Beds (%)
总 计	**Total**	**63.47**	**32.54**	**0.50**	**20.80**	**191.02**	**52.33**
医院	Hospitals	54.80	40.29	0.69	20.03	217.03	59.46
综合医院	General Hospitals	55.32	39.55	0.72	21.95	219.50	60.14
中医院	Hospitals of Chinese Medicine	51.72	44.67	0.61	18.23	201.38	55.17
中西医结合医院	Hospitals Which Integrate Traditional Chinese Therapeutics with Western Therapeutics	62.01	35.37	0.53	16.13	133.12	36.47
专科医院	Specialized Hospital	54.41	40.64	0.39	8.64	227.19	62.24
口腔医院	Hospitals for Oral Cavity Diseases	70.99	26.75	0.40	10.34	122.70	33.62
眼科医院	Ophthalmology Hospitals	73.48	22.46	0.00	14.50	108.32	29.68
耳鼻喉科医院	Otorhinolaryngology Hospitals	84.97	13.43	0.00	25.30	113.56	31.11
肿瘤医院	Tumor Hospitals	46.36	41.63	0.41	12.48	358.36	98.18
妇产科医院	Hospitals for Maternity and Child Care	78.51	14.46	0.00	23.81	140.03	38.36
儿童医院	Children's Hospitals	41.01	51.25	0.47	28.62	304.46	83.41
精神病院	Mental Hospitals	53.58	44.03	0.36	4.39	210.77	57.74
传染病院	Hospitals for Infectious Diseases	21.62	72.79	1.14	8.22	174.25	47.74
皮肤病病院	Hospitals for Occupational Diseases	66.67	33.33	0.00	2.14	25.43	6.97
结核病院	Tuberculosis Hospitals	6.77	87.32	0.40	11.03	261.73	71.71
骨科医院	Orthopaedics Hospitals	90.18	7.95	0.10	18.20	222.63	60.99
康复医院	Rehabilitation Hospitals	70.78	28.66	0.17	9.27	188.68	51.69
整形外科医院	Plastic Hospitals	100.00	0.00	0.00	21.35	164.25	45.00
其他专科医院	Other Specialized Hospitals	71.02	26.76	0.32	11.56	199.05	54.53
疗养院	Sanatoriums	43.87	53.35	1.18	6.87	255.99	70.13
社区卫生服务中心	Health Service Center for Community	84.97	12.91	0.06	46.95	243.97	66.84
卫生院	Health Center	81.32	16.38	0.11	22.06	114.64	31.41
门诊部	Clinics	80.05	16.44	0.65	16.08	191.77	52.54
妇幼保健院	Maternity and Child Care Centers	85.31	13.55	0.08	38.87	226.08	61.94
专科疾病防治院	Specialized Disease Prevention and Treatment Institute	77.06	21.16	0.17	11.18	132.57	36.32

15-8 县区其他卫生机构(2003年)

Other Health Care Institutions (2003)

项目	Item	县区诊所 Clinics	县区卫生所医务室 Health Center and Health-room	县区社区卫生服务站 Health Service Stations for Community
机构总数	**Number of Institutions**	**7554**	**3131**	**252**
总人员数（人）	Number of Personnel (person)	14987	7145	465
执业医师	#Doctors	4575	2819	146
#中医	#Chinese Medicine	803	309	25
执业助理医师	# Assistant Doctors	2044	1095	151
#中医	#Chinese Medicine	389	62	12
注册护士	#Senior Nurse and Nurse	2429	1405	91
药剂人员	Pharmacist	1158	490	26
检验人员	Laboratory Technician	420	78	11
其他	Others	4361	1258	40
诊疗人次数（人次）	Number of Visits (person-times)	15244097	5120090	335476
总收入（万元）	Annual Income (10 000 yuan)	48947	16469	623
总支出（万元）	Annual Expenditure (10 000 yuan)	43507	15673	490

15-9 县区村卫生室基本情况(2003年)

Basic of Villages Clinic (2003)

项目	Item	总计 Total	#村办 Setup by Village	#乡卫生院设点 Branch of Township Health Center	#私人 Private
机构数（个）	Number of Institutions	34054	17466	2056	11074
执业（助理）医师（人）	Number of Doctors and Assistant Doctors (person)	4257	1968	718	1203
乡村医生和卫生员（人）	Number of Village Doctors & Assistants (person)	34982	17687	1466	12571
#乡村医生数	#Number of Village Doctors	31227	15837	1366	11188
#大专及以上学历	#Above Three Years College	1385	587	134	563
#中专学历及中专水平	#Specialized Secondary School	13861	6713	488	5349
#在职培训合格者	#Up to Standard of Training	14009	8053	395	4152
乡村接生员数(人)	Number of Village Midwives (person)	133469	88191	1942	39135
年总收入（万元）	Annual Income (10 000 yuan)	51698	28038	1666	16141
年总支出（万元）	Annual Expenditure (10 000 yuan)	57625	25569	11386	14947
诊疗人次数（万人次）	Number of Visits (10 000 person-times)	4410.86	2279.46	191.85	1181.10
儿童疫苗接种人次数（万人次）	Number of Children Vaccinate (10 000 person-time)	1739.14	922.50	8.44	766.65

15-10 主要疾病死亡构成（2003年）

Death Composition of Major Disease(2003)

类　别	Item	合计 Total	男 Male	女 Female
总计	**Total**	72005	41255	30750
传染病和寄生虫病	Infectious Disease and Verminosis	1504	960	544
#传染病	#Infectious Disease	1478	940	538
呼吸道结核	Pulmonary Tuberculosis	1042	694	348
肿瘤	Tumor Disease	13128	7901	5227
#恶性肿瘤	#Malignant Tumor	12751	7797	4954
血液、造血器官及免疫的其他疾病	Blood and Apparatus of Blood-making Disease	69	26	43
内分泌、营养和代谢的其他疾病	Internal System,Nutrition,Metabolite and Immunity Disease	891	419	472
精神障碍	Psychosis	178	75	103
神经系统疾病	Nervous System Disease	459	245	214
循环系统	Circulative Disease	26320	14735	11585
#心脏病	Heart Trouble	12434	6514	5920
脑血管病	Cerebrovasular Disease	9452	5657	3795
呼吸系统	Respiratory Disease	12181	6825	5356
消化系统	Digestive Disease	2306	1476	830
肌肉骨骼和结缔组织疾病	Muscle、Skeleton and Tissue Disease	161	65	96
泌尿生殖系统	Urinary Disease	1219	702	517
妊娠、分娩和产褥期并发症	Complications of Pregnancy, Childbirth & the Puerperium	97	3	94
新生儿病	Newborn Baby Disease	595	304	291
损伤和中毒	Trauma and Poisoning	7928	5199	2729
诊断不明	Uncertain Diagnosis	212	127	85
其他	Others	4446	2021	2425

15-11 体育事业情况

Statistics on Sports

项 目	Item	2000	2001	2002	2003
体委系统职工人数(人)	**Staff and Workers in Sports Commissions (person)**	**5303**	**5587**	**4556**	**4795**
体育场(个)	**Stadiums (unit)**	**37**	**311**	**319**	**-**
体育馆(个)	**Gymnasiums (unit)**	**55**	**36**	**38**	**-**
游泳池、馆(个)	**Swimming Pools and Natatorums (unit)**	**111**	**43**	**44**	**-**
举办县级以上运动会(次)	**Number of Sports Meets Above County Level (time)**	**1705**	**1658**	**1714**	**4642**
国家体育锻炼标准达标人数(万人)	**Number of Persons Who Have Come up to the State Physical Training Standards (10000 persons)**	**1155.04**	**811.82**	**1387**	**963.8**
等级运动员发展人数(人)	**Number of Athletes in Grades (person)**	**5175**	**5571**	**863**	**1242**
#国际级运动健将	#International Master of Sports	2	2	-	-
国家级运动健将	National Master of Sports	31	11	29	20
一 级	First Grade Sportsmen	13	43	72	109
二 级	Second Grade Sportsmen	890	1047	755	1113
三 级	Third Grade Sportsmen	2191	2711	-	-
少年级	Juvenile Grade Sportsmen	2048	1757	-	-
等级裁判员发展人数(人)	**Number of Referees in Grades (person)**	**4173**	**3723**	**1201**	**1849**
#国家级裁判员	#National Referees	21	18	-	8
打破纪录情况(人/次/项)	**Basic Situation of Records Chalked Up (person/time/event)**				
世界纪录	#World Records	3 / 1 / 5	2 / 7 / 3	2 / 10 / 4	1/2/2
亚洲纪录	Asia Records		2 / 2 / 2	2 / 7 / 4	-
全国纪录	National Records	1 / 1 / 1	4 / 6 / 7	2 / 2 / 2	-
获奖情况	**Basic Situation of Medallion Won**				
参加全国比赛获奖	National Competitions				
金 牌(枚)	# Gold-plate (piece)	32	54.5	27	49
银 牌(枚)	Silver-plate (piece)	36	48	16	29
铜 牌(枚)	Copper-plate (piece)	36	44	23	33
参加国际比赛获奖	International Competitions				
金 牌(枚)	# Gold-plate (piece)	12	7	18	8
银 牌(枚)	Silver-plate (piece)	7	7	7	7
铜 牌(枚)	Copper-plate (piece)	6	6	6	3

注：1. 体育场、体育馆、游泳池只包括体委系统，2003年因全国普查，暂无数据。

2. 参加全国比赛指参加全国性的成人竞技比赛。参加国际比赛指参加世界锦标赛、世界杯赛、奥运会、亚洲锦标赛和亚运会。

3. 奖牌数包括我省运动员参加国家队集体项目所得的奖牌。

4. 从2002年起，等级运动员不含三级和少年级运动员。

a. Data of stadiums, gymnasiums and natatoriums only refer to those of sports commissions.The data is missing because national census in 2003.

b. National games refer to nation-wide adult athletics. International games include the world championship, the world cup, the Olympics, the Asia championship and the Asian Games.

c. The number of medals includes that of medals won by athletes of our province in national collective events.

d. The number of athletes in grades excludes third grade sportsmen and juvenile grade sportsmen since 2002.

十六、党群、政法和社会福利

PARTY AND MASS，POLITICS AND LAW，SOCIAL WELFARE

资料整理人员： 陈洲艳

16-1 历届省人民代表大会的代表人数

Number of Deputies to All the Previous Provincial People's Congress

单位：人 (person)

指标	Item	代表总数 Total Number of All Deputies	#女性代表 Female Deputies	占代表总数% As Percentage to Total (%)	#少数民族代表 Deputies From National Minorities	占代表总数% As Percentage to Total (%)	#中青年代表 Midlife and Youth Deputies	占代表总数% As Percentage to Total (%)
第一届 (1954)	First Congress (1954)	552	36	6.5	9	1.6	399	72.3
第二届 (1958)	Second Congress (1958)	552	36	6.5	9	1.6	399	72.3
第三届 (1964)	Third Congress (1964)	662	148	22.4	57	8.6	409	61.8
省革命委员会 (1968)	The Provincial Revolutionary Committee (1968)	160						
第五届 (1977)	Fifth Congress (1977)	1252	274	21.9	72	5.8	966	77.2
第六届 (1983)	Sixth Congress (1983)	988	225	22.8	84	8.5	570	57.7
第七届 (1988)	Seventh Congress (1988)	874	210	24.0	78	8.9	529	60.5
第八届 (1993)	Eighth Congress (1993)	870	191	22.0	87	10.0	587	62.0
第九届 (1997)	Ninth Congress (1997)	763	175	22.9	85	11.1	488	64.0
第十届 (2003)	Tenth Congress (2003)	762	149	19.6	82	10.8	72	9.5

注：1968年省革命委员会召开了全体委员会议，代表人数为委员人数。

The plenary meeting was held by the provincial revolutionary committee in 1968, and the number of delegates was that of committee members.

16-2 历届省政治协商会议的委员人数

Number of Deputies to All the Previous Chinese People's Political consultative Conferences

单位：人 (person)

指标	Item	委员总数 Total Number of All Deputies	#中国共产党代表 Deputies from the Communist Party of China	占代表总数% As Percentage to Total (%)	#少数民族代表 Deputies From National Minorities	占代表总数% As Percentage to Total (%)
第一届 (1955)	First Congress (1955)	175	39	22.3	6	3.4
第二届 (1959)	Second Congress (1959)	396	131	33.1	15	3.8
第三届 (1964)	Third Congress (1964)	398	134	33.7	20	5.0
第四届 (1977)	Fourth Congress (1977)	500	222	44.4	26	5.2
第五届 (1983)	Fifth Congress (1983)	732	270	36.9	38	5.2
第六届 (1988)	Sixth Congress (1988)	703	280	39.8	58	8.3
第七届 (1993)	Seventh Congress (1993)	724	288	39.8	61	8.4
第八届 (1997)	Eighth Congress (1997)	716	280	39.1	70	9.8
第九届 (2003)	Ninth Congress (2003)	716	281	39.3	72	10.6

16-3 工会工作情况

Labor Union Work

项　目	Item	2000	2001	2002	2003
工会基层组织个数（万个）	Number of Grassroots Unions (10 000 unit)	4.1	8.5	5.47	4.96
女职工委员会（万个）	Number of Women Workers Working Committees (10 000 units)	1.68			2.01
已建工会组织的基层单位在岗职工人数（万人）	Number of Staff and Workers in Grassroots Unions (10 000 persons)	487	589.21	651.94	658.93
#在岗女职工	#Female	186			245.49
工会专职干部数（万人）	Full-time Cadres (10 000 persons)	2.14		1.78	2.32
已建立职代会制度的单位个数（万个）	Number of Units Established With Workers Delegating Congress System (10 000 units)	1.34	1.56	1.59	1.01
召开职代会的单位个数（万个）	Number of Units Convoked Staff Congress (10 000 units)	1.21	1.56		1.06
开展合理化建议活动的单位个数（个）	Number of Units Developing Rationalization Proposals (unit)	9611	7000	5640	3036
本年度提出合理化建议（万件）	Advanced Rationalization Proposals This Year (10 000 piece)	66.6	100	21.85	17.57
开展民主评议领导干部的公有制单位个数（个）	Number of Units Developing Democratic Remark Public Owenrship on Leaders (unit)	9233	9417	12384	9307
建立工会劳动法律监督组织（个）	Number of Units Established With Labor Law Supervisional Organization (unit)	6295	8700	3434	1832
建立经费审查组织的单位个数（个）	Number of Units Established with Outlay Went Through (unit)	17904			19333

16-4 其他社会福利事业单位机构和人员

Institution and Personnel in Social Welfare and Special Care

项 目	Item	机构数（个） Number of Institutions (unit)		职工人数（人） Staff and Workers (person)	
		2002	2003	2002	2003
福利企业单位总计	**Social Welfare Institutions and Enterprises**	**796**	**793**	**28812**	**29132**
福利工厂	Welfare Factories	740	754	27310	27535
假肢厂	Artificial Limb Factories	1	1	87	88
商业服务业	Commercial Services	55	38	1415	1509
收容遣送安置单位总计	**Collecting and Repatriation Units**	**61**	**65**	**1393**	**1674**
收容遣送站	Collecting and Repatriation Stations	55	59	811	815
流浪儿童救助保护中心	The Centers of Salvation and Safeguard Children on the Tramp				
安置农场	Settle Down Farm	6	6	582	859
殡仪事业单位	**Funeral and Interment Institutions**	**72**	**75**	**1312**	**1411**

16-5 收养性社会福利、优抚事业单位基本情况(2003年)

Basic Statistics on Adoption Social Welfare and Special Care Units (2003)

项 目	Item	机构(个) Institution (unit)	职工(人) Staff and Workers (person)	床位(张) Beds (unit)	年末在院人数(人) Number of Persons Housed (person)
总计	**Total**	**1568**	**7222**	**41080**	**9936468**
国有收养性单位	Run by Government	262	4072	16129	4685390
集体收养性单位	Run by Collective Units	1303	3018	24736	5195613
民办收养性单位	Run by the Local People	3	132	215	55465
在总计中:	**Among Total:**				
荣誉军人康复医院	Rehabilitation Hospitals for Glory Soldiers	1	125	120	40850
复员军人疗养院	Convalescent Homes for Demobilized Soldiers	1	22	40	2640
复退军人精神病院	Mental Hospitals for Veteran and Demobilized Soldiers	7	489	945	93451
光荣院	Homes for Disabled Veterans	143	835	4685	1893387
社会福利院	Social Welfare Homes	75	1164	6327	1504011
儿童福利院	Baby Welfare Homes	15	329	1445	554541
社会福利医院	Psychopathic Welfare Homes	6	1005	1589	417854
城镇老年福利机构	Urban Elderly Welfare Units	196	641	6066	1226341
农村老年福利机构	Rural Elderly Welfare Units	1120	2487	19637	4188833
其他福利机构	Other Adopting Units	4	125	226	14560

16-6 社会救济和福利主要费用

Value of Major Social Relief and Welfare Funds

单位：万元 (10 000 yuan)

项 目	Item	2000	2001	2002	2003
总 计	**Total**	**120397**	**158784**	**235586**	**306937**
民政事业费支出	**Civil Administration Department Funds**	**80343**	**104818**	**158443**	**210815**
抚恤事业费	Commiserate	23214	26041	31739	38554
社会救济福利事业费	Subsidies of Welfare	27834	39123	73208	84354
离休、退休费	Pensions for Retired and Resigned Persons	11163	13443	14112	15963
安置事业费				12988	16809
社会残疾人福利事业费	Social Welfare Relief Funds for Handicapped	579	428		
自然灾害救济费	Relief Funds for Natural Disasters	8010	13821	22179	24171
其他民政事业费	Others	9543	11963	13979	15670
集体供给	**Collective Funds**	**40054**	**53966**	**77143**	**96122**
优抚对象优待总金额	Funds for Family Members of Martyrs and Disabled Veterans	10534	11952	11522	12333
农村困难户集体补助金额	Funds for Poor Households in Rural	1243			
农村五保户集体供养金额	Funds for Households with Livelihood Guaranteed in Five Aspects in Rural	13837	14468	12366	
城镇保障资金	Funds for Urban Social Security	13535	26634	52728	83309
农村保障资金	Funds for Rural Social Security	905	912	527	480

16-7 婚姻登记情况

Basic Statistics on Marriage Registration

项 目	Item	2000	2001	2002	2003
准予登记结婚 (万对)	**Registered Marriages (10 000 couples)**	**38.31**	**36.57**	**36.57**	**38.38**
初 婚 (万人)	First Marriages (10 000 persons)	71.77	66.71	66.68	69.58
再 婚 (万人)	Remarriages (10 000 persons)	4.85	5.50	5.51	6.31
离婚人数 (万对)	**Number of Divorces (10 000 couples)**	**6.45**	**7.34**	**5.40**	**6.00**
离婚率 (‰)	Divorce Rate (‰)	1.97	2.23	1.64	1.80

16-8 律师、公证、调解工作基本情况

Basic Statistics on Lawyers,Notarization and Mediation

类 别	Item	2000	2001	2002	2003
律师工作	**Lawyers**				
律师事务所 (个)	Number of Law Offices (unit)	352	380	394	412
律师 (人)	Number of lawyers (persons)	4888	4859	5206	5090
专职律师	Full-time Lawyers	2471	3204	3933	3994
兼职律师	Part-time Lawyers	1439	919	545	257
特邀律师	Specially Invited Lawyers	295	-		
担任法律顾问工作 (家)	Number of Units with Permanent Legal Advisors (unit)	7899	7210	8097	8142
刑事案件代理及辩护 (件)	Agent & Defender of Criminal Cases (case)	13664	13219	14479	14235
民事案件诉讼代理 (件)	Agent of Civil Cases (case)	25820	23941	26420	27219
经济案件诉讼代理 (件)	Agent of Economic Cases (case)	13455	11690	12540	11463
非诉讼法律事务 (件)	Agent of Non-Litigious Legal Affairs (case)	25883	24088	27207	34590
行政案件诉讼代理 (件)	Agent of Administrative Action (case)	2156	1951	2271	1817
解答法律询问 (人次)	Agent of Legal Advisory Services (person-time)	236553	172749	202613	219459
代写法律事务文书 (件)	Agent of Legal Documents Written on Behalf of Clients	35934	34854	37935	38745
公证工作	**Notarization**				
公证处 (个)	Number of Notary Offices (unit)	138	138	130	129
公证人员 (人)	Notarization Personnel (person)	604	619	604	591
受理公证文书 (件)	Number of Accept Notarized Documents (case)	319416	196827	172272	180134
出证公证文书 (件)	Number of Show Notarized Documents (case)	317705	195870	171478	178804
#国内经济合同公证 (件)	Number of Domestic Notarized Business Contracts (case)	81815	69417	61542	60690
人民调解工作	**Number of People's Mediation**				
专职司法助理员 (人)	Number of Full-time Judicial Assistants (person)	4114	3574	3703	3919
人民调解委员会 (个)	Number of People's Mediation Committees (person)	57231	59448	58810	61162
调解人员 (人)	Number of Mediators (person)	723389	275778	301121	313003
调解民间纠纷 (件)	Number of Civil Disputes Mediated (case)	340612	332876	301469	336309

16-9 交通事故发生情况

Statistics on Traffic Accidents

指标	Item	合计 Total	按事故发生程度分 By Serious Degree of Traffic Accidents 特大 Extraordinarily Serious	重大 Serious	一般 Ordinary
发生次数（起）	Number of Traffic Accidents (case)				
	1995	10361	151	3082	7128
	1996	10994	148	3113	7733
	1997	10401	155	2981	7265
	1998	10128	122	2951	7055
	1999	15337	138	3278	11921
	2000	23938	149	3094	20695
	2001	32504	9	232	32263
	2002	28056	154	3173	24729
	2003	23224	93	-	-
死亡人数（人）	Number of Deaths (person)				
	1995	3428	440	2983	5
	1996	3368	346	3022	
	1997	3308	422	2882	4
	1998	3290	325	2921	44
	1999	3698	411	3239	48
	2000	3401	375	3026	
	2001	3316	24	229	3063
	2002	3658	437	3221	
	2003	3664	387	-	-
受伤人数（人）	Number of Injuries (person)				
	1995	9176	697	2200	6279
	1996	10448	518	2614	7316
	1997	9978	742	2336	6900
	1998	9963	472	2144	7347
	1999	14714	617	2548	11549
	2000	22028	521	2272	19235
	2001	29434	81	81	29272
	2002	27468	788	2200	24480
	2003	23159	375	-	-
损失折款（万元）	Losses Coverted into Cash (10 000 yuan)				
	1995	6202.99	1122.50	1660.69	3419.80
	1996	6967.38	1048.38	1961.14	3957.86
	1997	6586.39	1183.34	1795.00	3608.05
	1998	6458.15	899.64	1713.18	3845.33
	1999	8314.70	981.60	1847.96	5485.14
	2000	9662.20	939.54	1937.15	6785.60
	2001	8799.48	51.36	145.22	860.29
	2002	9100.39	1020.35	1834.00	6246.04
	2003	10646.79	-	-	-
平均每起损失（元）	Average Loss per Traffic Accident (yuan)				
	1995	5986.86	74337.75	5388.36	4797.70
	1996	6337.44	70836.49	6299.84	5118.14
	1997	6332.46	76343.52	6021.47	4966.35
	1998	6376.53	73740.98	5805.42	5450.50
	1999	5421.33	71130.43	5673.46	4601.24
	2000	4036.38	63056.63	6261.00	3278.86
	2001	2707.22	5706.67	6259.48	2666.49
	2002	3243.65	66256.49	5780.00	2525.80
	2003	4584.39	-	-	-

16-10 火灾发生情况

Statistics on Fires

指标	Item	合计 Total	按事故发生程度分 By Serious Degree of Fires 特大 Extraordinarily Serious	重大 Serious	一般 Ordinary
发生次数（起）	Number of Fires Accidents (case)				
	1995	1128	18	133	977
	1996	1087	19	127	941
	1997	2467	6	29	3432
	1998	2908	5	32	2871
	1999	2871	6	28	2837
	2000	3440	5	19	3416
	2001	3979	1	19	3959
	2002	5040	3	18	5019
	2003	6221	2	16	6203
死亡人数（人）	Number of Deaths (person)				
	1995	73	9	21	43
	1996	106	16	36	54
	1997	130	41	33	56
	1998	89	4	28	57
	1999	86	4	22	60
	2000	102	19	16	67
	2001	95		21	74
	2002	70		19	51
	2003	122		34	88
受伤人数（人）	Number of Injuries (person)				
	1995	266	41	70	155
	1996	195	21	84	90
	1997	328	96	45	187
	1998	188	11	7	170
	1999	145	1	2	142
	2000	165	20	11	134
	2001	121		10	111
	2002	120	3	7	110
	2003	127	3	7	117
损失折款（万元）	Losses Coverted into Cash (10 000 yuan)				
	1995	6824.18	3157.17	2490.81	1176.20
	1996	5271.00	1894.18	2179.35	1197.47
	1997	7666.43	2802.15	1186.95	3677.33
	1998	5975.11	858.40	1481.69	3635.02
	1999	6275.00	1620.00	1220.00	3435.00
	2000	4799.00	878.00	683.00	3238.86
	2001	4397.35	347.00	1020.00	3030.35
	2002	5357.08	1382.94	766.17	3207.97
	2003	4834.52	924.89	517.46	3392.17
平均每起损失（万元）	Average Loss per Fire (10 000 yuan)				
	1995	6.05	175.40	18.73	1.20
	1996	4.85	99.69	17.16	1.27
	1997	3.11	467.03	40.93	1.51
	1998	2.05	171.68	46.30	0.79
	1999	2.19	270.00	43.56	1.21
	2000	1.40	175.63	35.93	0.95
	2001	1.10	347.00	53.68	0.77
	2002	1.06	460.98	42.57	0.64
	2003	0.78	462.45	32.34	0.55

十七、企业调查

ENTERPRISES SURVEY

资料整理人员： 刘于惠　夏普照

17-1 重点企业集团基本情况及主要经济指标(2003年)

Basic Conditions and Main Economic Indicators of Key Enterprises Group (2003)

分类	Item	单位数（个）Number of Enterprises (unit)	从业人员（人）Number of Employed Persons (person)	在岗职工 Number of Fully Employed Staff and Workers	其他人员 Others
总计	**Total**	**77**	**355674**	**340836**	**14838**
按集团审批部门分	**By Examining Department**				
国务院	The State Council	2	17906	17733	173
国务院主管部门	Governing Department of the State Council	5	12115	12058	57
省级人民政府	Provincial Government	25	175260	171748	3512
省级政府主管部门	Governing Department of the Provincial Government	19	44740	43508	1232
其他	Others	26	105653	95789	9864
按母公司控股情况分	**By Situation of Share Holding**				
国有绝对控股	Controlling Share Holding Absolutely by the State	49	252673	246637	6036
国有相对控股	Controlling Share Holding Comparatively by the State	8	21697	19040	2657
集体绝对控股	Controlling Share Holding Absolutely by the Collective				
集体相对控股	Controlling Share Holding Comparatively by the Collective				
其他	Others	20	81304	75159	6145
按企业规模分	**By Size of Enterprises**				
大型	Large	34	238989	231013	7976
中型	Medium	36	105130	99171	5959
小型	Small	3	4247	3883	364
其他	Others	4	7308	6769	539
按主营行业分	**By Sector**				
农、林、牧、渔业	Farming, Forestry, Animal Husbandry and Fishery				
采掘业	Mining and Quarrying	2	26318	26318	
制造业	Manufacturing	48	234498	222791	11707
电气水的生产和供应业	Production and Supply of Electric Power, Gas and Water	1	1854	1854	
建筑业	Construction	4	28894	27814	1080
运输邮电业	Transportation, Post and Telecommunication	2	6100	5099	1001
批发零售业	Wholesale and Retail Trade	13	33554	32789	765
住宿和餐饮业	Hotel and Catering Services	1	8061	8061	
金融保险业	Banking ang Insurance				
房地产业	Real Estate	1	286	286	
其他	Others	5	16109	15824	285
按母公司注册类型分	**By Type of Registration**				
国有企业	State-owned Enterprises	11	36875	35712	1163
国有独资企业	State Funded Corporations	25	143025	140764	2261
其他有限责任公司	Others Limited Liability Corporations	17	75790	72850	2940
股份有限公司	Share Holding Co. Ltd.	22	97455	89209	8246
其他	Others	2	2529	2301	228

continued

分类	Item	从业人员劳动报酬（万元）Labor Reward of Employed Persons (10 000 yuan)	在岗职工 Number of Fully Employed Staff and Workers	其他人员 Others	固定资产投资完成额（万元）Actually Completed Investment in Fixed Assets (10 000 yuan)
总计	**Total**	**569204**	**553593**	**15611**	**1037126**
按集团审批部门分	**By Examining Department**				
国务院	The State Council	25915	25684	231	45674
国务院主管部门	Governing Department of the State Council	32176	31969	207	74661
省级人民政府	Provincial Government	282126	279934	2192	769261
省级政府主管部门	Governing Department of the Provincial Government	56876	55718	1158	28343
其他	Others	172111	160288	11823	119187
按母公司控股情况分	**By Situation of Share Holding**				
国有绝对控股	Controlling Share Holding Absolutely by the State	416324	409945	6379	900400
国有相对控股	Controlling Share Holding Comparatively by the State	22882	21721	1161	10386
集体绝对控股	Controlling Share Holding Absolutely by the Collective				
集体相对控股	Controlling Share Holding Comparatively by the Collective				
其他	Others	129998	121927	8071	126340
按企业规模分	**By Size of Enterprises**				
大型	Large	392642	382930	9712	918313
中型	Medium	160903	155608	5295	98379
小型	Small	4141	3988	153	
其他	Others	11518	11067	451	20434
按主营行业分	**By Sector**				
农、林、牧、渔业	Farming, Forestry, Animal Husbandry and Fishery				
采掘业	Mining and Quarrying	28806	28806		7565
制造业	Manufacturing	390940	377976	12964	973517
电气水的生产和供应业	Production and Supply of Electric Power, Gas and Water	3992	3992		1085
建筑业	Construction	40204	39612	592	
运输邮电业	Transportation, Post and Telecommunication	6783	5743	1040	2396
批发零售业	Wholesale and Retail Trade	46160	45721	439	30570
住宿和餐饮业	Hotel and Catering Services	10516	10516		
金融保险业	Banking ang Insurance				
房地产业	Real Estate	421	421		
其他	Others	41382	40806	576	21993
按母公司注册类型分	**By Type of Registration**				
国有企业	State-owned Enterprises	55174	53351	1823	73480
国有独资企业	State Funded Corporations	226599	224447	2152	153675
其他有限责任公司	Others Limited Liability Corporations	131891	129483	2408	551689
股份有限公司	Share Holding Co. Ltd.	150449	141590	8859	256286
其他	Others	5091	4722	369	1996

单位：万元 17-1 续表 2 continued (10 000 yuan)

年末资产总计 Total Assets at the Year-end	固定资产原价合计 Original Value of Fixed Assets	累计折旧 Accumulated Deprecia-tion	#本年折旧 Deprecia-tion Charge of the Year	累计对外投资 Accumulated Value of Investing Abroad	#本年对外投资 Value of Investing Abroad of the Year	存货 Inventory	流动资产年均余额 Annual Average Balance of Circulation Funds	年末负债合计 Total Liabilities at the Year-end	流动负债 Liquid Liabilities
14020756	**7713251**	**2808950**	**388206**	**945744**	**73166**	**1916609**	**5692251**	**8676396**	**6497434**
756113	299438	105477	21193	148616		130783	390703	497832	432998
1007344	602349	262925	32339	20985	10956	171281	467461	633288	560910
7143267	3892448	1375745	197524	564924	21230	845714	2821314	4277652	3039004
1734696	825729	263864	34880	56659	7742	176413	598352	871154	742031
3379336	2093287	800939	102270	154560	33238	592418	1414421	2396470	1722491
10820087	6697625	2522716	319377	803047	37458	1214231	4058629	6840252	4995574
938857	387225	108952	15192	37878	7700	169657	520284	514955	455210
2261812	628401	177282	53637	104819	28008	532721	1113338	1321189	1046650
10067998	5652411	2025513	296990	628337	53005	1429584	3935698	6364119	4687510
3576359	1948563	756467	85376	273111	2750	440374	1575965	2137553	1654995
90479	20488	7212	135			5263	40762	59550	48571
285920	91789	19758	5705	44296	17411	41388	139826	115174	106358
215243	180653	68357	5624	4903	1615	11434	97689	107048	70217
10942100	6274765	2350531	325242	603910	42216	1556206	4423374	6801252	4889924
68483	50089	17207	2040			922	18507	43210	25856
154463	49170	24864	4589			68761	86820	50904	50903
84259	64605	23259	2169	3487	3487	1511		90835	68953
1435235	590567	185340	21483	196600	652	155309	677180	1058475	936559
331897	182749	46875	7142	6240		30644	14569	195009	165270
26545	5404	598	405	6269		4167	10599	13755	12554
762531	315249	91919	19512	124335	25196	87655	363513	315908	277198
1645722	1153416	478290	52222	191565	17054	187985	565650	1136963	813346
4992271	3282276	1275860	142386	258459	4297	652239	2285646	3255263	2669193
3412333	1987734	663605	120696	330165	14556	314755	987226	2094951	1390052
3885699	1219725	371324	69561	164793	37259	752231	1821069	2152108	1589036
84731	70100	19871	3341	762		9399	32660	37111	35807

单位：万元　　17-1 续表 3　continued　　(10 000 yuan)

分类	Item	所有者权益 Creditors' Equity	股本 Share Capital	营业收入 Business Revenue	主营收入 Major Business Revenue
总计	**Total**	**5344360**	**2580251**	**9985182**	**9839554**
按集团审批部门分	**By Examining Department**				
国务院	The State Council	258281	107001	463297	456592
国务院主管部门	Governing Department of the State Council	374056	183036	1488659	1418921
省级人民政府	Provincial Government	2865615	1097617	4256106	4221588
省级政府主管部门	Governing Department of the Provincial Government	863542	366842	1037968	1024405
其他	Others	982866	825755	2739152	2718048
按母公司控股情况分	**By Situation of Share Holding**				
国有绝对控股	Controlling Share Holding Absolutely by the State	3979835	2094163	7487489	7363575
国有相对控股	Controlling Share Holding Comparatively by the State	423902	158065	419855	413042
集体绝对控股	Controlling Share Holding Absolutely by the Collective				
集体相对控股	Controlling Share Holding Comparatively by the Collective				
其他	Others	940623	328023	2077838	2062937
按企业规模分	**By Size of Enterprises**				
大型	Large	3703879	1546393	7276097	7161687
中型	Medium	1438806	956074	2574156	2554012
小型	Small	30929	15915	32511	32418
其他	Others	170746	61869	102418	91437
按主营行业分	**By Sector**				
农、林、牧、渔业	Farming, Forestry, Animal Husbandry and Fishery				
采掘业	Mining and Quarrying	108195	68317	94771	75997
制造业	Manufacturing	4140848	1948340	7672830	7566629
电气水的生产和供应业	Production and Supply of Electric Power, Gas and Water	25273	14027	50847	50847
建筑业	Construction	103559	94737	147594	147489
运输邮电业	Transportation, Post and Telecommunication	-6576	8655	42151	36706
批发零售业	Wholesale and Retail Trade	376760	233806	1215521	1209135
住宿和餐饮业	Hotel and Catering Services	136888	50000	135765	134514
金融保险业	Banking ang Insurance				
房地产业	Real Estate	12790	8605	6475	6307
其他	Others	446623	153764	619228	611930
按母公司注册类型分	**By Type of Registration**				
国有企业	State-owned Enterprises	508759	454908	778147	764245
国有独资企业	State Funded Corporations	1737008	1018009	4524740	4419791
其他有限责任公司	Others Limited Liability Corporations	1317382	468932	1990245	1983317
股份有限公司	Share Holding Co. Ltd.	1733591	620198	2653251	2633813
其他	Others	47620	18204	38799	38388

单位：万元　　　　　　　　　　17-1 续表 4　　continued　　　　　　　　　　(10 000 yuan)

#出口额 Value of Exports	其他业务收入 Revenue of Others Business	主营业务成本 Accumulated Value of Investing Abroad	主营业务税金及附加 Pre-tax and Related Payment of Major Business	存货跌价损失及营业管理财务费用 Loss of Inventory Value-decrease and Expenditrue for Financial Management	#利息支出 Expenditrue for Interest	利润总额 Total Profits	应交所得税 Income Taxes Payable	应交增值税 Added Value Tax Payable	研究开发费用 Expenditrue for Research and Develop-ment
678368	**145628**	**8103014**	**131595**	**1379608**	**179198**	**274656**	**120689**	**367551**	**80176**
49908	6705	366458	1598	97026	10351	-5140	1398	9999	10165
6958	69738	1216413	55441	95212	14046	68135	26606	46436	12423
304186	34518	3432171	30603	643409	86467	165598	54755	208594	38452
128880	13563	782795	9088	193347	19666	52056	14352	27232	5403
188436	21104	2305177	34865	350614	48668	-5993	23578	75290	13733
491554	123914	6148817	110944	992141	127878	120186	93178	304692	70824
14268	6813	308692	10294	103038	15888	12762	3986	17749	2092
172546	14901	1645505	10357	284429	35432	141708	23525	45110	7260
493835	114410	5839339	114494	1022831	144067	290665	94609	310109	61474
171227	20144	2161397	15372	328225	31640	-18943	25578	55087	15749
6993	93	27707	285	6234	1277	376	23	927	
6313	10981	74571	1444	22318	2214	2558	479	1428	2953
	106201	6232807	110119	34022	570	1656	52	7167	461
520170		38964	281	1009879	150531	237393	92107	319413	70430
	105	127175	5251	5263	911	6024	2140	3125	
	5445	33600	1071	8219	141	6866	1768	59	
	6386	1052422	5534	35114	549	-28733	1279	38	
151885	1251	85482	4490	155819	19197	-3201	8100	21931	6834
				35636	4178	10063	3557	1646	
	168	4586	345	1533	602	31			
6313	7298	474300	3870	94123	2519	44557	11686	14172	2451
177055	13902	631996	7384	201340	15218	-112399	8315	11313	20084
184735	104949	3754325	89417	519125	63138	100992	48739	170763	29893
109879	6928	1611250	14297	234280	47295	124672	30757	113211	16660
206354	19438	2077104	19393	416398	52915	160648	31746	70305	13531
345	411	28339	1104	8465	632	743	1132	1959	8

17-2 建立现代企业制度的重点企业基本情况(2003年)

分类	Item	单位数（个）Number of Enterprises (unit)	注册资本合计（万元）Total Registered Capital (10 000 yuan)
总计	**Total**	**171**	**3612203**
按企业改制主管部门分	**By Department Responsible for Enterprises Restructure**		
国家重点企业	Key Enterprises in Contact with State	10	664904
重组集团的原512户企业	The Previous 512 Enterprises Rebuilding Groups	5	426610
中央企工委管理的企业	Enterprises Control by Enterprises Committee of the State	1	16112
省级重点企业	Key Enterprises in Contact with Province	60	1805399
原国家百户试点企业	Enterprises in Experiment of the State	2	51400
原省级试点企业	Enterprises in Experiment of the Province	57	922179
企业集团母公司	Parent Company of Enterprises Group		
按母公司控股情况分	**By Situation of Share Holding**		
国有绝对控股	Controlling Share Holding Absolutely by the State	114	3036443
国有相对控股	Controlling Share Holding Comparatively by the State	14	268340
集体绝对控股	Controlling Share Holding Absolutely by the Collective	5	15527
集体相对控股	Controlling Share Holding Comparatively by the Collective	1	3994
其他	Others	37	287899
按企业规模分	**By Size of Enterprises**		
特大型	Extra Large		
大型	Large	53	2103956
中型	Medium	100	1372304
小型	Small	14	70345
其他	Others	4	65598
按主营行业分	**By Sector**		
农、林、牧、渔业	Farming, Forestry, Animal Husbandry and Fishery		
采掘业	Mining and Quarrying	5	516645
制造业	Manufacturing	126	2650738
电气水的生产和供应业	Production and Supply of Electric Power, Gas and Water	9	122711
建筑业	Construction	6	35818
运输邮电业	Transportation, Post and Telecommunication	2	10322
批发零售贸易餐饮业	Wholesale and Retail Trade and Catering Services	18	132843
金融保险业	Banking ang Insurance		
房地产业	Real Estate	1	20480
其他	Others		
按母公司注册类型分	**By Type of Registration**		
国有企业	State-owned Enterprises	51	892362
国有独资企业	State Funded Corporations	34	1503393
其他有限责任公司	Others Limited Liability Corporations	37	491935
股份有限公司	Share Holding Co. Ltd.	40	681826
其他	Others	4	23547

Basic Conditions of Key Enterprises Building Modern Eenterprises System (2003)

固定资产投资完成额（万元） Actually Completed Investment in Fixed Assets (10 000 yuan)	从业人员（人） Number of Employed Persons (person)	在岗职工 Number of Fully Employed Staff and Workers	其他人员 Others	从业人员劳动报酬（万元） Labor Reward of Employed Persons (10 000 yuan)	在岗职工 Number of Fully Employed Staff and Workers	其他人员 Others
1490509	**412273**	**394310**	**17963**	**635839**	**619450**	**16389**
894397	91179	90987	192	182682	182478	204
73731	36527	35980	547	58214	57460	754
1024	654	637	17	2357	2323	34
1186725	219523	207459	12064	375272	364348	10924
4353	5531	5520	11	6409	6399	10
318485	137000	132607	4393	211725	209460	2265
1386124	351680	336752	14928	558603	543915	14688
38693	27250	24722	2528	36812	35564	1248
310	2775	2754	21	2307	2293	14
110	894	894		1492	1492	
65272	29674	29188	486	36625	36186	439
1064310	272449	264101	8348	434161	425587	8574
416026	127309	118013	9296	184467	177059	7408
7107	9094	8792	302	10463	10110	373
3066	3421	3404	17	6728	6694	34
14166	42877	35567	7310	48188	40525	7663
1367380	310645	301819	8826	501328	484581	6747
92396	10249	10048	201	23113	22683	430
2119	15412	14335	1077	17910	16757	1153
4540	6027	6027		4344	4344	
8384	17484	16952	532	27072	26710	362
	506	506		607	607	
326677	108360	105347	3013	166544	163859	2685
340876	160414	149254	11160	242910	231646	11264
734630	86187	85452	735	148336	147585	751
73766	51029	48013	3016	70112	68468	1644
8965	3379	3358	21	3503	3489	14

17-3 建立现代企业制度的重点企业主要经济指标(2003年)

单位：万元

分类	Item	年末资产总计 Total Assets at the Year-end	固定资产原价合计 Original Value of Fixed Assets	累计折旧 Accumulated Depreciation
总计	**Total**	**17795030**	**10347050**	**4154746**
按企业改制主管部门分	**By Department Responsible for Enterprises Restructure**			
520户国家重点企业	Key Enterprises in Contact with State	5801529	3151923	1271518
重组集团的原512户企业	The Previous 512 Enterprises Rebuilding Groups	1367373	1108357	522237
中央企工委管理的企业	Enterprises Control by Enterprises Committee of the State	75663	13030	4852
省级重点企业	Key Enterprises in Contact with Province	10476758	5583727	2169855
原国家百户试点企业	Enterprises in Experiment of the State	483110	162806	37936
原省级试点企业	Enterprises in Experiment of the Province	6688636	3066281	1284860
企业集团母公司	Parent Company of Enterprises Group			
按母公司控股情况分	**By Situation of Share Holding**			
国有绝对控股	Controlling Share Holding Absolutely by the State	14868716	8965560	3564547
国有相对控股	Controlling Share Holding Comparatively by the State	1489238	532059	151957
集体绝对控股	Controlling Share Holding Absolutely by the Collective	152633	28925	10979
集体相对控股	Controlling Share Holding Comparatively by the Collective	12761	12621	9188
其他	Others	1271682	807885	418075
按企业规模分	**By Size of Enterprises**			
特大型	Extra Large			
大型	Large	11143764	6096999	2389171
中型	Medium	6060431	4053359	1708886
小型	Small	283599	86985	30413
其他	Others	307236	109707	26276
按主营行业分	**By Sector**			
农、林、牧、渔业	Farming, Forestry, Animal Husbandry and Fishery			
采掘业	Mining and Quarrying	317432	261937	106234
制造业	Manufacturing	14288080	8613548	3379488
电气水的生产和供应业	Production and Supply of Electric Power, Gas and Water	847928	868140	451591
建筑业	Construction	323837	75611	30307
运输邮电业	Transportation, Post and Telecommunication	47582	43546	21717
批发零售贸易餐饮业	Wholesale and Retail Trade and Catering Services	1428423	427179	109444
金融保险业	Banking ang Insurance			
房地产业	Real Estate	96371	43400	4100
其他	Others			
按母公司注册类型分	**By Type of Registration**			
国有企业	State-owned Enterprises	5500972	2884866	1164079
国有独资企业	State Funded Corporations	5116695	3381610	1385120
其他有限责任公司	Others Limited Liability Corporations	3846438	2202499	785457
股份有限公司	Share Holding Co. Ltd.	3070267	1790574	788767
其他	Others	187979	50716	15452

Main Economic Indicators on Key Enterprises

Building Modern Eenterprises System (2003)

(10 000 yuan)

#本年折旧 Depreciation Charge of the Year	累计对外投资 Accumulated Value of Investing Abroad	#本年对外投资 Value of Investing Abroad of the Year	存货 Inventory	流动资产年均余额 Annual Average Balance of Circulation Funds	年末负债合计 Total Liabilities at the Year-end	流动负债 Liquid Liabilities	所有者权益 Creditors' Equity	股本 Share Capital
529823	**1364071**	**235880**	**2550819**	**7129733**	**10953038**	**7748802**	**6841992**	**3114768**
182901	391559	3169	1052351	2351216	3104275	2158490	2697254	758699
55527	392355	93301	200061	562720	958408	584170	408965	433391
444	48770	100	3553	16090	17331	14827	58332	16112
331141	676184	102084	1725607	4216565	5898065	4452287	4578693	1544779
5489	98010	12539	44160	223549	379301	332363	103809	60880
165516	575295	71234	1332018	3156194	3601423	2853643	3087213	1018644
470198	1169713	170240	2155081	5772922	9460342	6626678	5408374	2567671
22495	144084	46450	228367	744616	718492	621695	770746	268073
1195	2802		19589	88040	123139	54613	29494	20266
520	717		2603	8520	6287	5428	6474	3994
35415	46755	19190	145179	515635	644778	440388	626904	254764
351002	870641	117708	1841708	4853458	6656498	5121915	4487266	1584259
171715	384276	106741	656111	2043503	3965095	2349346	2095336	1410884
2755	9897	8	32956	137807	177200	140294	106399	72402
4351	99257	11423	20044	94965	154245	137247	152991	47223
11713	5270	1644	22180	135884	145473	88678	171959	86701
452506	1040831	161571	2296992	5998168	8409428	6226607	5878652	2567100
40485	1079	968	3545	176423	654229	112013	193699	107224
1726			51089	168719	258415	224045	65422	52665
1493			130	20958	36589	18623	10993	6261
14127	161137	51649	131366	569311	1175781	864701	252642	139751
150	9140	5700	11230	18106	27849	13929	68522	20480
132364	432673	6402	1033722	2385266	3389304	2203389	2111668	823342
164470	465789	149590	603198	1994109	3406627	2533094	1710068	1088367
148126	272270	14645	432174	1245597	2374433	1672400	1472005	502421
81669	189051	64149	442044	1370420	1584847	1222342	1485420	659562
1599	2802	1094	18992	95038	125234	70275	41499	28310

单位：万元

17-3 续表

分类	Item	营业收入 Business Revenue	主营收入 Major Business Revenue	#出口额 Value of Exports
总　计	**Total**	**12177281**	**11999016**	**629990**
按企业改制主管部门分	**By Department Responsible for Enterprises Restructure**			
国家重点企业	Key Enterprises in Contact with State	3954231	3941553	181338
重组集团的原512户企业	The Previous 512 Enterprises Rebuilding Groups	780025	779858	209593
中央企工委管理的企业	Enterprises Control by Enterprises Committee of the State	20307	16355	
省级重点企业	Key Enterprises in Contact with Province	7495250	7366750	378215
原国家百户试点企业	Enterprises in Experiment of the State	413896	411624	5896
原省级试点企业	Enterprises in Experiment of the Province	4778643	4739776	229886
企业集团母公司	Parent Company of Enterprises Group			
按母公司控股情况分	**By Situation of Share Holding**			
国有绝对控股	Controlling Share Holding Absolutely by the State	10594783	10444403	574437
国有相对控股	Controlling Share Holding Comparatively by the State	789168	781566	37290
集体绝对控股	Controlling Share Holding Absolutely by the Collective	67490	67022	1823
集体相对控股	Controlling Share Holding Comparatively by the Collective	11920	11859	171
其他	Others	713920	694166	16269
按企业规模分	**By Size of Enterprises**			
特大型	Extra Large			
大型	Large	8106903	8029913	534022
中型	Medium	3806253	3720111	93698
小型	Small	146680	144966	2270
其他	Others	117445	104026	
按主营行业分	**By Sector**			
农、林、牧、渔业	Farming, Forestry, Animal Husbandry and Fishery			
采掘业	Mining and Quarrying	180570	156526	37
制造业	Manufacturing	10069007	9941886	581071
电气水的生产和供应业	Production and Supply of Electric Power, Gas and Water	321906	321176	
建筑业	Construction	250904	239559	
运输邮电业	Transportation, Post and Telecommunication	13560	9574	46
批发零售贸易餐饮业	Wholesale and Retail Trade and Catering Services	1159611	1153879	48416
金融保险业	Banking ang Insurance			
房地产业	Real Estate	24066	24066	
其他	Others			
按母公司注册类型分	**By Type of Registration**			
国有企业	State-owned Enterprises	4021026	3991938	135411
国有独资企业	State Funded Corporations	3436907	3389465	310932
其他有限责任公司	Others Limited Liability Corporations	2236495	2221712	128586
股份有限公司	Share Holding Co. Ltd.	2286079	2201251	47371
其他	Others	91599	91151	1823

continued (10 000 yuan)

其他业务收入 Revenue of Others Business	主营业务成本 Accumulated Value of Investing Abroad	主营业务税金及附加 Pre-tax and Related Payment of Major Business	存货跌价损失及营业管理财务费用 Loss of Inventory Value-decrease and Expenditrue for Financial Management	#利息支出 Expenditrue for Interest	利润总额 Total Profits	应交所得税 Income Taxes Payable	应交增值税 Added Value tax Payable	研究开发费用 Expenditrue for Research and Development
178265	**9122280**	**833870**	**1557857**	**205312**	**499660**	**173732**	**607854**	**113972**
12678	2414746	705783	481376	57080	328666	93765	277204	47352
167	710968	2164	107250	18718	-88460	4278	32358	13909
3952	13069	59	3060	327	1296		105	708
128500	5154081	785491	939785	126642	517117	147452	423422	71390
2272	378382	1041	31867	6817	3281	1634	4063	132
38867	2945239	735776	717037	73188	363981	129879	326701	47849
150380	7932976	815393	1268272	169472	406437	156134	546729	95512
7602	625714	10657	147156	21107	33728	10065	21178	10068
468	58434	363	11097	1279	854	129	817	32
61	7129	106	3833	187	1028	20	885	157
19754	498027	7351	127499	13267	57613	7384	38245	8203
76990	5733832	769787	1081132	133410	480876	146270	453891	93506
86142	3185387	62665	432906	62218	10467	25137	150246	17877
1714	123499	421	21190	5023	3089	1600	2552	1184
13419	79562	997	22629	4661	5228	725	1165	1405
24044	114704	1811	43568	1321	2567	260	10233	560
127121	7401738	812808	1279759	177296	440812	160106	535703	111895
730	263672	1218	36358	1975	26327	702	26124	141
11345	217807	7710	16888	914	1055	654	720	
3986	6707	227	2565	434	185	61	10	
5732	1001619	4699	134734	16101	4704	8392	31825	578
	16505	842	2947	1360	593		1500	
29088	2589370	728112	466123	41511	203541	81780	281596	29465
47442	2782822	29954	476610	65811	73455	55485	156379	29311
14783	1763863	14100	306161	51953	147906	19075	89856	36028
84828	1819494	61022	284167	43134	69745	16484	76046	17916
448	78655	481	13166	1610	1907	316	1977	38

17-4 企业景气指数

Business Climate Indices

单位：点 (point)

指标	Item	2002 一季度 1st. Quarter	2002 二季度 2nd. Quarter	2002 三季度 3rd. Quarter	2002 四季度 4th. Quarter
全省总计	**Total**	**104.06**	**106.50**	**108.98**	**111.60**
按行业门类分	**By Sector**				
工业	Industry	102.30	110.28	114.93	121.37
建筑业	Construction	100.80	114.15	115.63	112.87
交通邮电仓储业	Transportation, Storage, Postal and Telecommunication Service	104.03	88.49	86.90	95.26
商贸餐饮业	Wholesale and Retail Trade & Catering Trade	102.43	97.35	98.07	102.05
房地产业	Real Estate	123.26	127.64	116.20	125.61
社会服务业	Social Services	106.77	105.95	109.59	102.24
按注册类型分	**By Registration**				
国有企业	State-owned	102.27	101.14	101.05	106.64
集体企业	Colletive-owned	80.32	87.85	83.98	89.59
有限责任公司	Limited-liability Companies	111.38	105.37	113.28	117.35
股份有限公司	Share Holding Ltd. Companies	110.67	129.96	138.57	140.65
港澳台外商投资	Funded by Overseas Entrepreneurs	124.41	125.77	127.04	126.72
按企业规模分	**By Size of Enterprises**				
大型企业	Large	138.68	128.68	141.80	153.07
中型企业	Medium	108.53	105.75	104.32	109.19
小型企业	Small	92.79	93.11	93.22	93.55
上市公司	**Share Listed Companies**	**120.09**	**136.96**	**148.90**	**158.79**

指标	Item	2003 一季度 1st. Quarter	2003 二季度 2nd. Quarter	2003 三季度 3rd. Quarter	2003 四季度 4th. Quarter
全省总计	**Total**	**115.64**	**96.43**	**116.04**	**116.77**
按行业门类分	**By Sector**				
工业	Industry	115.88	111.80	117.04	121.58
建筑业	Construction	113.94	118.34	123.66	134.24
交通邮电仓储业	Transportation, Storage, Postal and Telecommunication Service	103.90	54.82	91.43	88.62
商贸餐饮业	Wholesale and Retail Trade & Catering Trade	114.71	101.67	114.89	109.33
房地产业	Real Estate	119.41	117.60	104.07	114.07
社会服务业	Social Services	112.50	63.24	124.19	114.71
按注册类型分	**By Registration**				
国有企业	State-owned	109.15	96.75	113.77	110.54
集体企业	Colletive-owned	99.74	88.28	91.06	94.19
有限责任公司	Limited-liability Companies	119.57	107.19	119.34	127.94
股份有限公司	Share Holding Ltd. Companies	139.77	120.58	131.96	143.16
港澳台外商投资	Funded by Overseas Entrepreneurs	121.50	112.99	128.63	123.95
按企业规模分	**By Size of Enterprises**				
大型企业	Large	141.23	127.47	141.28	152.34
中型企业	Medium	109.15	99.63	112.84	115.01
小型企业	Small	106.26	92.24	106.49	103.51
上市公司	**Share Listed Companies**	**155.10**	**112.97**	**133.46**	**159.42**

17-5 企业家信心指数

Enterprepreneur Expectation Indices

单位：点 (point)

指标	Item	2002 一季度 1st. Quarter	二季度 2nd. Quarter	三季度 3rd. Quarter	四季度 4th. Quarter
全省总计	**Total**	**109.44**	**102.93**	**109.83**	**109.29**
按行业门类分	**By Sector**				
工业	Industry	104.14	99.97	109.87	114.59
建筑业	Construction	110.26	106.77	107.07	110.66
交通邮电仓储业	Transportation, Storage, Postal and Telecommunication Service	98.32	89.23	86.93	88.3
商贸餐饮业	Wholesale and Retail Trade & Catering Trade	101.31	95.66	103.16	99.61
房地产业	Real Estate	141.86	139.8	137.92	129.68
社会服务业	Social Services	124.25	111.82	120.52	109.99
按注册类型分	**By Registration**				
国有企业	State-owned	103.08	96.28	101.29	100.36
集体企业	Colletive-owned	87.94	83.85	94.52	90.69
有限责任公司	Limited-liability Companies	118.83	108.61	118.21	118.9
股份有限公司	Share Holding Ltd. Companies	108.15	115.5	127.96	139.29
港澳台外商投资	Funded by Overseas Entrepreneurs	145.74	138.5	142.82	138.86
按企业规模分	**By Size of Enterprises**				
大型企业	Large	107.92	106.82	119.84	132.91
中型企业	Medium	109.77	103.41	108.81	107.93
小型企业	Small	101.51	95.97	102.54	96.27
上市公司	**Share Listed Companies**	**110.08**	**103.99**	**124.73**	**144.93**

指标	Item	2003 一季度 1st. Quarter	二季度 2nd. Quarter	三季度 3rd. Quarter	四季度 4th. Quarter
全省总计	**Total**	**122.67**	**105.38**	**119.23**	**121.57**
按行业门类分	**By Sector**				
工业	Industry	125.93	120.54	123.47	128.53
建筑业	Construction	122.61	115.76	120.61	120.36
交通邮电仓储业	Transportation, Storage, Postal and Telecommunication Service	97.27	60.54	90.26	96.53
商贸餐饮业	Wholesale and Retail Trade & Catering Trade	107.63	96.36	111.13	107.68
房地产业	Real Estate	132.98	138.14	141.00	133.00
社会服务业	Social Services	128.13	83.82	116.13	122.06
按注册类型分	**By Registration**				
国有企业	State-owned	113.87	100.88	112.33	112.37
集体企业	Colletive-owned	102.18	88.28	100.11	100.84
有限责任公司	Limited-liability Companies	129.87	124.73	138.05	130.20
股份有限公司	Share Holding Ltd. Companies	142.30	126.54	135.02	150.90
港澳台外商投资	Funded by Overseas Entrepreneurs	132.98	126.77	144.53	134.90
按企业规模分	**By Size of Enterprises**				
大型企业	Large	146.30	134.09	143.76	154.97
中型企业	Medium	114.10	103.48	116.06	114.98
小型企业	Small	114.64	101.72	112.65	110.94
上市公司	**Share Listed Companies**	**155.56**	**125.41**	**136.09**	**167.73**

17-6 工业景气指数

Business Survey of Industry

单位：点 (point)

指标	Item	2002 一季度 1st. Quarter	2002 二季度 2nd. Quarter	2002 三季度 3rd. Quarter	2002 四季度 4th. Quarter
综合生产经营状况	**Comprehensive Conditions of Production and Management**	**102.46**	**110.28**	**114.93**	**121.37**
生产成本	Production Cost	85.08	97.38	99.83	101.10
生产总量	Total Production Quantity	98.66	137.15	118.72	123.97
产品订货	Production Order	85.78	84.4	86.68	90.19
产品销售量	Sales Volume of Products	95.27	129.03	117.59	123.16
产品销售价格	Selling Price of Products	81.84	82.39	84.78	95.96
产成品库存	Inventory of Products	93.73	94.63	95.75	97.08
税后利润	After-tax Profits	89.27	110.71	102.57	112
流动资金	Circulating Funds	54.49	53.27	58.81	63.81
货款拖欠	Payment Delinquent	100.16	99.46	97.85	111.28
设备利用	Utilization of Equipment				
用工	Employment	90.21	86.98	94.81	93.6
固定资产投资	Investment in Fixed Assets	102.31	105.86	114.09	120.72
科技开发	Scientific and Technical Development	109.57	115.02	120.67	122.5
原材料能源进价	Bid of Raw Materials and Energy				
原材料能源供应	Supply of Raw Materials and Energy	115.16	122.17	123.58	119.03

指标	Item	2003 一季度 1st. Quarter	2003 二季度 2nd. Quarter	2003 三季度 3rd. Quarter	2003 四季度 4th. Quarter
综合生产经营状况	**Comprehensive Conditions of Production and Management**	**115.46**	**111.87**	**117.04**	**121.57**
生产成本	Production Cost	79.24	93.54	88.06	62.90
生产总量	Total Production Quantity	119.39	131.63	123.22	132.01
产品订货	Production Order	119.81	113.90	119.14	124.36
产品销售量	Sales Volume of Products	115.85	124.58	126.51	134.27
产品销售价格	Selling Price of Products	101.68	94.81	102.85	117.55
产成品库存	Inventory of Products	120.63	107.84	118.27	110.63
税后利润	After-tax Profits	105.39	112.57	114.13	121.07
流动资金	Circulating Funds	74.17	75.52	75.17	76.22
货款拖欠	Payment Delinquent	106.94	102.45	110.86	113.48
设备利用	Utilization of Equipment				
用工	Employment	88.81	98.68	101.78	101.24
固定资产投资	Investment in Fixed Assets	116.49	124.08	127.05	124.95
科技开发	Scientific and Technical Development	121.81	122.20	121.71	118.87
原材料能源进价	Bid of Raw Materials and Energy	59.14	68.67	70.44	46.75
原材料能源供应	Supply of Raw Materials and Energy	110.77	115.92	109.18	85.41

17-7 建筑业景气指数

Business Survey of Construction

单位：点 (point)

指标	Item	2002 一季度 1st. Quarter	2002 二季度 2nd. Quarter	2002 三季度 3rd. Quarter	2002 四季度 4th. Quarter
综合生产经营状况	**Comprehensive Conditions of Production and Management**	**100.81**	**114.15**	**115.63**	**112.87**
工程合同签定	Signment of Project Contracts	88.84	111.49	121.59	118.27
建筑产品实物工程量	Volume of Projects in Physical Unit	78.37	129.83	146.67	144.28
施工产值	Output Value of Construction	85.90	133.49	142.57	146.10
竣工产值	Output Value of Completed Construction	83.64	104.28	108.20	145.45
工程结算收入	Income from Project Settlement	73.77	118.95	131.61	133.04
建筑材料进价	Bid of Construction Materials	101.54	94.37	96.39	82.45
工程结算成本	Cost of Project Settlement	92.65	89.57	87.20	75.16
税后利润	After-tax Profits	99.62	100.78	103.59	109.52
流动资金	Circulating Funds	39.72	38.57	46.66	48.18
货款拖欠	Payment Delinquent	79.21	65.03	75.19	84.18
用工	Employment	84.83	103.55	114.84	126.46
固定资产投资	Investment in Fixed Assets	93.27	102.57	104.83	109.93

指标	Item	2003 一季度 1st. Quarter	2003 二季度 2nd. Quarter	2003 三季度 3rd. Quarter	2003 四季度 4th. Quarter
综合生产经营状况	**Comprehensive Conditions of Production and Management**	**113.94**	**118.34**	**123.66**	**134.24**
工程合同签定	Signment of Project Contracts	110.77	123.53	126.50	138.09
建筑产品实物工程量	Volume of Projects in Physical Unit	103.80	142.70	145.15	164.73
施工产值	Output Value of Construction	101.37	154.98	147.91	163.28
竣工产值	Output Value of Completed Construction	87.02	114.15	122.13	148.04
工程结算收入	Income from Project Settlement	86.14	140.14	132.40	164.51
建筑材料进价	Bid of Construction Materials	82.07	75.21	49.41	13.99
工程结算成本	Cost of Project Settlement	95.62	72.83	55.15	22.25
税后利润	After-tax Profits	115.33	119.74	112.05	115.84
流动资金	Circulating Funds	48.90	48.15	51.16	43.32
货款拖欠	Payment Delinquent	95.86	78.69	69.62	64.87
用工	Employment	97.84	132.35	134.19	133.83
固定资产投资	Investment in Fixed Assets	93.96	108.73	110.79	109.50

17-8 交通邮电仓储业景气指数

Business Survey of Transportation, Storage, Postal and Telecommunication Services

单位：点 (point)

指标	Item	2002 一季度 1st. Quarter	2002 二季度 2nd. Quarter	2002 三季度 3rd. Quarter	2002 四季度 4th. Quarter
综合生产经营状况	**Comprehensive Conditions of Production and Management**	**102.77**	**88.49**	**86.90**	**95.26**
业务量	Business Volume	133.35	108.56	117.41	108.46
业务收入	Business Revenue	126.32	113.39	113.21	114.14
业务收费价格	Business Charges	96.46	74.66	81.75	86.08
营业成本	Business Cost	72.68	74.14	59.39	51.45
税后利润	After-tax Profits	123.60	80.53	69.85	68.42
流动资金	Circulating Funds	53.38	47.08	41.66	47.88
货款拖欠	Payment Delinquent	109.51	104.25	100.76	102.52
用工	Employment	80.06	71.42	79.99	77.85
固定资产投资	Investment in Fixed Assets	96.26	100.82	104.62	112.40

指标	Item	2003 一季度 1st. Quarter	2003 二季度 2nd. Quarter	2003 三季度 3rd. Quarter	2003 四季度 4th. Quarter
综合生产经营状况	**Comprehensive Conditions of Production and Management**	**105.38**	**55.55**	**91.43**	**87.26**
业务量	Business Volume	121.17	54.15	106.39	113.50
业务收入	Business Revenue	125.90	47.16	113.79	107.87
业务收费价格	Business Charges	111.19	89.97	100.24	103.05
营业成本	Business Cost	73.97	72.26	71.50	50.27
税后利润	After-tax Profits	122.63	61.79	86.36	66.00
流动资金	Circulating Funds	55.90	35.93	40.01	35.39
货款拖欠	Payment Delinquent	120.60	88.80	86.89	107.59
用工	Employment	94.69	79.86	91.63	89.10
固定资产投资	Investment in Fixed Assets	105.80	99.79	104.41	87.08

17-9 批发、零售贸易与餐饮业景气指数

Business Survey of Wholesales, Retail Trade and Catering Services

单位：点 (point)

指标	Item	2002 一季度 1st. Quarter	2002 二季度 2nd. Quarter	2002 三季度 3rd. Quarter	2002 四季度 4th. Quarter
综合生产经营状况	**Comprehensive Conditions of Production and Management**	**102.67**	**97.35**	**98.07**	**102.05**
商品购进额	Commodity Purchases	98.26	99.01	101.63	107.49
商品购进价格	Bid of Commodities	109.43	97.78	92.37	90.12
商品销售额	Sales of Commodities	94.35	95.61	102.4	110.61
# 出口销售额	#Export				
商品销售价格	Selling Price of Commodities	81.71	85.44	87.24	100.06
商品库存	Inventory of Commodities	108.23	109.34	110.99	111.98
经营费用（营业费用）	Business Cost	95.85	91.18	82.17	81.78
税后利润	After-tax Profits	93.29	85.37	95.7	103.97
流动资金	Circulating Funds	68.03	73.6	65.81	67.16
货款拖欠	Payment Delinquent	115.1	113.45	109.49	114.56
用工	Employment	87.39	82.71	88.61	90.75
固定资产投资	Investment in Fixed Assets	95.7	101.14	101.1	102.31

指标	Item	2003 一季度 1st. Quarter	2003 二季度 2nd. Quarter	2003 三季度 3rd. Quarter	2003 四季度 4th. Quarter
综合生产经营状况	**Comprehensive Conditions of Production and Management**	**114.55**	**101.19**	**114.89**	**109.62**
商品购进额	Commodity Purchases	100.55	86.50	112.78	118.36
商品购进价格	Bid of Commodities	77.07	95.95	88.09	73.17
商品销售额	Sales of Commodities	107.51	82.26	116.34	119.25
# 出口销售额	#Export	94.98	90.29	91.39	104.73
商品销售价格	Selling Price of Commodities	109.96	83.64	103.68	126.06
商品库存	Inventory of Commodities	113.24	102.20	114.93	109.48
经营费用（营业费用）	Business Cost	97.98	94.06	78.46	68.74
税后利润	After-tax Profits	110.94	86.33	111.75	109.63
流动资金	Circulating Funds	74.49	73.23	74.84	66.58
货款拖欠	Payment Delinquent	118.48	112.07	115.18	119.62
用工	Employment	84.70	72.51	86.91	90.69
固定资产投资	Investment in Fixed Assets	101.97	101.91	104.05	108.16

17-10 房地产业景气指数

Business Survey of Real Estate Trade

单位：点 (point)

指标	Item	2002 一季度 1st. Quarter	2002 二季度 2nd. Quarter	2002 三季度 3rd. Quarter	2002 四季度 4th. Quarter
综合生产经营状况	**Comprehensive Conditions of Production and Management**	**123.26**	**127.64**	**116.20**	**125.61**
土地开发面积	Area of Land Development	103.61	116.39	107.03	106.17
完成投资	Completed Investment	108.41	120.66	125.02	127.71
房屋施工面积	Floor Space under Construction	117.86	123.82	102.18	98.78
房屋竣工面积	Floor Space Completed	89.16	94.32	97.90	107.79
商品房预售面积	Presold Space of Commercial Buildings	102.41	116.20	112.82	109.41
商品房销售面积	Sold Space of Commercial Buildings	98.79	110.20	106.79	105.61
商品房销售价格	Selling Price of Commercial Buildings	100.00	104.65	95.29	99.73
空置商品房面积	Vacant Space of Commercial Buildings	150.60	146.99	143.90	147.62
税后利润	After-tax Profits	101.18	110.20	112.67	110.16
流动资金	Circulating Funds	70.93	82.56	71.76	82.08
货款拖欠	Payment Delinquent	108.24	113.68	107.06	122.89
用工	Employment	113.95	119.50	110.04	111.76
固定资产投资	Investment in Fixed Assets	116.28	121.82	116.20	124.71

指标	Item	2003 一季度 1st. Quarter	2003 二季度 2nd. Quarter	2003 三季度 3rd. Quarter	2003 四季度 4th. Quarter
综合生产经营状况	**Comprehensive Conditions of Production and Management**	**120.26**	**118.44**	**104.07**	**113.94**
土地开发面积	Area of Land Development	107.53	102.18	107.60	100.07
完成投资	Completed Investment	109.08	124.95	125.20	112.95
房屋施工面积	Floor Space under Construction	111.30	103.69	102.50	102.47
房屋竣工面积	Floor Space Completed	98.68	97.95	89.87	100.08
商品房预售面积	Presold Space of Commercial Buildings	102.97	100.97	99.92	98.07
商品房销售面积	Sold Space of Commercial Buildings	101.87	106.24	104.93	98.00
商品房销售价格	Selling Price of Commercial Buildings	100.81	96.80	102.00	113.00
空置商品房面积	Vacant Space of Commercial Buildings	141.94	147.26	142.86	140.48
税后利润	After-tax Profits	112.95	105.72	112.07	103.04
流动资金	Circulating Funds	72.23	74.95	73.88	79.21
货款拖欠	Payment Delinquent	121.28	111.90	116.00	124.75
用工	Employment	103.73	96.86	102.67	97.10
固定资产投资	Investment in Fixed Assets	113.68	114.36	112.07	105.02

17-11 社会服务业景气指数

Business Survey of Social Services

单位：点 (point)

指标	Item	2002 一季度 1st. Quarter	2002 二季度 2nd. Quarter	2002 三季度 3rd. Quarter	2002 四季度 4th. Quarter
综合生产经营状况	**Comprehensive Conditions of Production and Management**	**105.86**	**105.95**	**109.59**	**102.24**
业务量	Business Volume	91.35	97.65	88.03	104.57
客房出租（限于旅馆业）	Rent of Guest Rooms(hotels)	87.27	91.23	91.98	98.67
旅游客源（限于旅游业）	Tourists(tourism)	87.66	125	99.6	88.58
业务收费（服务）价格	Business(services) Charges	90.38	89.42	84.96	84.31
营业收入	Business Revenue	94.42	95.15	88.75	101.64
营业成本	Business Cost	82.54	85.08	82.21	82.44
税后利润	After-tax Profits	95.64	95.42	83.9	92.02
流动资金	Circulating Funds	73.26	75.81	64	75.58
货款拖欠	Payment Delinquent	98.81	97.15	88.22	100
用工	Employment	90.51	98.66	96.04	92.37
固定资产投资	Investment in Fixed Assets	114.88	108.88	113.47	100.93

指标	Item	2003 一季度 1st. Quarter	2003 二季度 2nd. Quarter	2003 三季度 3rd. Quarter	2003 四季度 4th. Quarter
综合生产经营状况	**Comprehensive Conditions of Production and Management**	**112.5**	**63.24**	**124.19**	**114.71**
业务量	Business Volume	106.25	59.7	120.97	117.91
客房出租（限于旅馆业）	Rent of Guest Rooms(hotels)	139.68	121.54	144.26	138.46
旅游客源（限于旅游业）	Tourists(tourism)	87.88	30.56	133.33	111.9
业务收费（服务）价格	Business(services) Charges	95.24	74.24	96.77	88.06
营业收入	Business Revenue	78.13	52.94	117.74	111.94
营业成本	Business Cost	76.56	80.88	72.58	82.35
税后利润	After-tax Profits	76.19	52.24	111.48	100
流动资金	Circulating Funds	80.95	53.73	77.05	79.1
货款拖欠	Payment Delinquent	100	106.9	107.27	94.92
用工	Employment	96.88	75	122.58	107.35
固定资产投资	Investment in Fixed Assets	117.46	105.88	126.67	128.36

十八、各市、州、县主要经济和社会统计指标

MAIN ECONOMIC AND SOCIAL STATISTICS INDICATORS OF CITIES, PREFECTURE AND COUNTIES

资料整理人员： 石　梅　欧阳普　肖首雄　梁尔郁
龙立珍　杨　未　彭　蕾　唐双全
李生春　陈洲艳　熊　丽

18-1 各市、州、县年末人口(2003年)

Population at the Year-end (2003)

市县名称	Cities and Counties	总户数（万户） Households (10 000 households)	总人口（万人） Total Population (10 000 persons)	男 Male	女 Female	城镇人口 Urban	乡村人口 Rural	城市化水平(%) City Level (%)
长沙市	**Changsha City**	**177.10**	**601.76**	**309.39**	**292.37**	**295.83**	**305.93**	**49.16**
芙蓉区	Furong District	10.49	34.58	17.61	16.97	34.58		100.00
天心区	Tianxin District	11.21	40.10	20.68	19.42	40.10		100.00
岳麓区	Yuelu District	9.50	37.62	19.66	17.96	37.62		100.00
开福区	Kaifu District	13.43	39.54	19.72	19.82	39.54		100.00
雨花区	Yuhua District	12.64	44.42	22.79	21.63	44.42		100.00
长沙县	Changsha County	22.41	73.47	37.49	35.98	20.00	53.47	27.22
望城县	Wangcheng County	21.53	70.50	36.10	34.40	17.73	52.77	25.15
宁乡县	Ningxiang County	38.79	128.94	66.66	62.28	27.37	101.57	21.23
浏阳市	Liuyang City	37.10	132.59	68.68	63.91	34.47	98.12	26.00
株洲市	**Zhuzhou City**	**104.80**	**373.60**	**192.00**	**181.60**	**152.40**	**221.20**	**40.79**
荷塘区	Hetang District	6.55	23.50	12.20	11.30	23.50		100.00
芦淞区	Lousong District	7.20	19.30	9.80	9.50	19.30		100.00
石峰区	Shifeng District	7.50	25.80	13.40	12.40	25.80		100.00
天元区	Tianyuan District	3.60	11.60	5.80	5.80	8.60	3.00	74.14
株洲县	Zhuzhou County	12.38	43.80	22.70	21.10	20.70	23.10	47.26
攸县	You County	20.57	75.15	38.50	36.70	14.10	61.10	18.76
茶陵县	Chaling County	15.41	57.03	29.20	27.80	8.80	48.20	15.43
炎陵县	Yanling County	5.20	17.70	9.10	8.60	4.70	13.00	26.55
醴陵市	Liling City	26.38	99.68	51.30	48.40	26.90	72.80	26.99
湘潭市	**Xiangtan City**	**84.97**	**282.03**	**145.61**	**136.42**	**111.9**	**170.13**	**39.68**
雨湖区	Yuhu District	10.91	36.78	18.95	17.83	36.78		100.00
岳塘区	Yuetang District	10.58	33.41	17.38	16.03	33.41		100.00
湘潭县	Xiangtan County	32.39	112.44	58.17	54.27	22.15	90.29	19.70
湘乡市	Xiangxiang City	28.04	89.25	45.95	43.3	17.98	71.27	20.15
韶山市	Shaoshan City	3.05	10.15	5.16	4.99	1.58	8.57	15.57
衡阳市	**Hengyang City**	**201.31**	**713.90**	**375.95**	**337.95**	**206.43**	**507.47**	**28.92**
珠辉区	Zhuhui District	8.26	26.83	13.72	13.11	24.65	2.18	91.87
雁峰区	Yanfeng District	6.13	19.48	9.90	9.58	19.48		100.00
石鼓区	Shigu District	6.52	19.70	10.09	9.61	19.70		100.00
蒸湘区	Zhengxiang District	6.01	20.07	10.40	9.67	18.45	1.62	91.93
南岳区	Nanyue District	1.86	5.39	2.74	2.65	4.96	0.43	92.02
衡阳县	Hengyang County	32.62	112.27	59.41	52.86	18.04	94.23	16.07
衡南县	Hengnan County	27.4	100.63	53.12	47.51	14.43	86.20	14.34
衡山县	Hengshan County	11.3	40.70	21.10	19.60	5.87	34.83	14.42
衡东县	Hengdong County	18.71	66.63	34.55	32.08	9.76	56.87	14.65
祁东县	Qidong County	27.98	92.35	48.74	43.61	17.65	74.70	19.11
耒阳市	Leiyang City	32.65	124.49	66.30	58.19	29.31	95.18	23.54
常宁市	Changning City	21.87	85.36	45.88	39.48	24.13	61.23	28.27
邵阳市	**Shaoyang City**	**203.71**	**732.35**	**384.16**	**348.19**	**179.12**	**553.23**	**24.46**
双清区	Shuangqing District	8.21	25.46	13.15	12.31	25.46		100.00
大祥区	Daxiang District	8.40	29.58	14.93	14.65	29.58		100.00
北塔区	Beita District	2.53	8.33	4.15	4.17	5.54	2.78	66.56

18-1 续表 1

市县名称	Cities and Counties	总户数（万户） Households (10 000 households)	总人口（万人） Total Population (10 000 persons)	男 Male	女 Female	城镇人口 Urban	乡村人口 Rural	城市化水平 (%) City Level (%)
邵东县	Shaodong County	32.80	117.62	61.90	55.72	37.18	80.44	31.61
新邵县	Xinshao County	21.12	73.10	38.89	34.22	10.61	62.49	14.51
邵阳县	Shaoyang County	25.15	96.36	51.51	44.85	13.28	83.08	13.78
隆回县	Longhui County	30.44	110.54	58.35	52.19	11.99	98.55	10.84
洞口县	Dongkou County	22.20	79.15	41.52	37.64	15.33	63.82	19.37
绥宁县	Shuining County	9.32	34.68	18.11	16.57	4.47	30.21	12.90
新宁县	Xinning County	15.98	58.24	30.14	28.10	7.01	51.23	12.03
城步县	Chengbu County	6.79	25.72	13.17	12.55	4.43	21.29	17.23
武冈市	Wugang City	20.78	73.58	38.34	35.23	14.24	59.33	19.36
岳阳市	**Yueyang City**	**165.48**	**527.83**	**275.50**	**252.33**	**193.34**	**334.49**	**36.63**
岳阳楼区	Yueyanglou District	23.77	55.13	28.86	26.27	51.01	4.12	92.53
云溪区	Yunxi District	5.65	16.15	8.37	7.78	9.99	6.16	61.86
君山区	Junshan District	8.08	22.85	12.48	10.37	9.27	13.58	40.57
岳阳县	Yueyang County	22.13	75.06	39.29	35.77	22.02	53.04	29.34
华容县	Huarong County	20.79	71.48	36.62	34.86	21.44	50.04	29.99
湘阴县	Xiangying County	21.04	69.15	36.15	33.00	18.15	51.00	26.25
平江县	Pingjiang County	27.61	99.73	52.03	47.70	23.45	76.28	23.51
汨罗市	Miluo City	21.55	70.48	36.66	33.82	22.91	47.57	32.51
临湘市	Linxiang City	14.86	47.80	25.04	22.76	15.10	32.70	31.59
常德市	**Changde City**	**192.20**	**600.20**	**308.50**	**291.70**	**181.90**	**418.30**	**30.31**
武陵区	Wuling District	16.70	46.30	23.30	23.00	43.10	3.20	93.09
鼎城区	Dingcheng District	26.90	90.50	46.10	44.40	16.30	74.20	18.01
安乡县	Anxiang County	17.40	57.90	29.20	28.70	17.90	40.00	30.92
汉寿县	Hanshou County	23.80	81.10	42.40	38.70	18.60	62.50	22.93
澧　县	Li County	28.80	87.80	44.90	42.90	22.80	65.00	25.97
临澧县	Linli County	14.20	43.60	22.20	21.40	10.40	33.20	23.85
桃源县	Taoyuan County	31.50	97.30	50.60	46.70	23.20	74.10	23.84
石门县	Shimen County	23.20	69.20	36.00	33.20	14.40	54.80	20.81
津市市	Jinshi City	9.70	26.50	13.80	12.70	15.20	11.30	57.36
张家界市	**Zhangjiajie City**	**50.34**	**157.43**	**81.49**	**75.94**	**44.48**	**112.95**	**28.25**
永定区	Yongding District	14.60	42.03	21.66	20.37	16.85	25.18	40.09
武陵源区	Wulingyuan District	1.68	4.54	2.35	2.19	2.30	2.24	50.66
慈利县	Cili County	21.25	67.69	35.02	32.67	17.41	50.28	25.72
桑植县	Sangzhi County	12.81	43.17	22.46	20.71	7.92	35.25	18.35
益阳市	**Yiyang City**	**132.65**	**456.51**	**235.21**	**221.30**	**134.61**	**321.90**	**29.49**
资阳区	Ziyang District	11.96	41.11	21.20	19.91	19.69	21.42	47.90
赫山区	Heshan District	24.63	86.89	44.57	42.32	43.23	43.66	49.75
南县	Nan County	23.07	77.31	39.67	37.64	18.85	58.46	24.38
桃江县	Taojiang County	23.45	82.45	42.40	40.05	13.42	69.03	16.28
安化县	Anhua County	26.22	95.84	49.83	46.01	13.38	82.46	13.96
沅江市	Yuanjiang City	23.32	72.91	37.54	35.37	26.04	46.87	35.72
郴州市	**Chenzhou City**	**135.18**	**455.27**	**238.10**	**217.17**	**145.72**	**309.55**	**32.01**
北湖区	Beihu District	10.41	29.87	15.44	14.43	20.71	9.16	69.35
苏仙区	Suxian District	10.88	33.86	17.39	16.47	16.65	17.21	49.20
桂阳县	Guiyang County	21.73	78.71	41.23	37.48	23.99	54.72	30.48
宜章县	Yizhang County	15.28	55.57	28.93	26.64	13.85	41.72	24.92
永兴县	Yongxing County	17.54	63.33	32.90	30.43	15.36	47.97	24.26

18-1 续表 2

市县名称	Cities and Counties	总户数（万户）Households (10 000 households)	总人口（万人）Total Population (10 000 persons)	男 Male	女 Female	城镇人口 Urban	乡村人口 Rural	城市化水平(%) City Level (%)
嘉禾县	Jiahe County	10.29	34.48	18.12	16.36	8.24	26.24	23.89
临武县	Linwu County	9.09	31.1	16.37	14.73	7.52	23.58	24.18
汝城县	Rucheng County	10.84	35.8	18.76	17.04	8.30	27.50	23.19
桂东县	Guidong County	4.86	16.95	8.75	8.20	3.99	12.96	23.51
安仁县	Anren County	12.39	39.49	21.54	17.95	8.80	30.69	22.28
资兴市	Zixing City	11.87	36.11	18.67	17.44	18.31	17.80	50.71
永州市	**Yongzhou City**	**153.52**	**570.56**	**299.73**	**270.83**	**141.71**	**428.85**	**24.84**
芝山区	Zhishan District	15.90	57.97	30.48	27.49	19.13	38.84	33.00
冷水滩区	Lengshuitan District	14.82	50.43	25.92	24.51	23.45	26.98	46.50
祁阳县	Qiyang County	26.05	99.12	51.99	47.13	27.01	72.11	27.25
东安县	Dongan County	16.34	58.89	30.18	28.71	11.50	47.39	19.53
双牌县	Shuangpai County	4.96	17.10	9.10	8.00	3.25	13.85	19.01
道县	Dao County	17.50	66.69	35.54	31.15	15.27	51.42	22.90
江永县	Jiangyong County	6.64	24.97	12.83	12.14	5.19	19.78	20.78
宁远县	Ningyuan County	19.41	78.04	41.48	36.56	14.20	63.84	18.20
蓝山县	Lanshan County	9.41	34.82	18.50	16.32	8.28	26.54	23.78
新田县	Xintian County	10.60	36.70	19.50	17.20	7.50	29.20	20.44
江华县	Jianghua County	11.89	45.83	24.21	21.62	6.93	38.90	15.12
怀化市	**Huaihua City**	**136.62**	**492.92**	**255.25**	**237.67**	**122.25**	**370.67**	**24.80**
鹤城区	Hecheng District	11.23	32.44	16.68	15.76	28.29	4.15	87.21
中方县	Zhongfang County	7.12	26.25	13.75	12.50	3.28	22.97	12.50
沅陵县	Yuanling County	17.48	64.84	32.84	32.00	10.70	54.14	16.50
辰溪县	Chenxi County	12.92	51.81	26.80	25.01	11.29	40.52	21.79
溆浦县	Xupu County	23.07	85.59	44.69	40.90	15.23	70.36	17.79
会同县	Huitong County	10.14	34.71	17.99	16.72	5.48	29.23	15.79
麻阳县	Mayang County	9.20	36.45	19.04	17.41	5.29	31.16	14.51
新晃县	Xinhuang County	6.95	25.61	13.63	11.98	4.48	21.13	17.49
芷江县	Zhijiang County	10.58	35.75	18.70	17.05	5.65	30.10	15.80
靖州县	Jingzhou County	6.65	26.01	13.42	12.59	9.44	16.57	36.29
通道县	Tongdao County	5.49	22.23	11.50	10.73	4.16	18.07	18.71
洪江市	Hongjiang City	13.29	43.73	22.39	21.34	13.16	30.57	30.09
洪江区	Hongjiang District	2.50	7.49	3.82	3.67	5.79	1.70	77.30
娄底市	**Loudi City**	**120.36**	**403.89**	**210.55**	**193.34**	**113.49**	**290.40**	**28.10**
娄星区	Louxing District	15.95	41.23	21.30	19.93	32.20	9.03	78.10
双峰县	Shuangfeng County	27.28	89.38	47.24	42.14	12.66	76.72	14.16
新化县	Xinhua County	33.14	128.83	67.06	61.77	18.35	110.48	14.24
冷水江市	Lengshuijiang District	12.73	35.15	18.14	17.01	20.12	15.03	57.24
涟源市	Liangyuan City	31.26	109.30	56.81	52.49	30.16	79.14	27.59
湘西自治州	**West Hunan A.P**	**71.35**	**265.55**	**137.36**	**128.19**	**68.66**	**196.89**	**25.86**
吉首市	Jishou City	8.79	28.53	14.54	13.99	15.81	12.72	55.42
泸溪县	Louxi County	7.62	28.69	14.82	13.87	6.98	21.71	24.33
凤凰县	Fenghuang County	9.46	37.31	19.36	17.95	6.42	30.89	17.21
花垣县	Huayuan County	6.79	27.08	14.03	13.05	5.47	21.61	20.20
保靖县	Baojing County	7.42	27.41	14.38	13.03	5.91	21.50	21.56
古丈县	Guzhang County	4.16	13.74	7.11	6.63	3.93	9.81	28.60
永顺县	Yongshun County	12.89	49.01	25.38	23.63	11.64	37.37	23.75
龙山县	Longshan County	14.22	53.78	27.74	26.04	12.50	41.28	23.24

18-2 各市、州、县计划生育指标(2003年)

Indicators of Family Plan (2003)

市县名称	City and County	出生率(‰) Birth Rate (‰)	死亡率(‰) Death Rate (‰)	自然增长率(‰) Natural Growth Rate (‰)	计划内生育率(%) Birth Within Plan Rate (%)	多孩率(%) More Childrens Rate (%)	已婚育龄妇女人数(万人) Married Women at Child-Bearing Age (10 000 persons)	节育率(%) Contra-ceptive Rate (%)	措施落实率(%) Contra-ception Using Rate (%)	节育手术(万例) Birth Control Opera-tion (10 000 cases)
长沙市	**Changsha City**	**10.24**	**7.11**	**3.13**	**97.84**	**0.29**	**128.66**	**89.73**	**96.23**	**8.66**
芙蓉区	Furong District	7.88	6.32	1.56	99.41	0.08	6.96	91.16	97.37	0.20
天心区	Tianxin District	7.06	6.34	0.71	99.06	0.04	6.03	83.87	97.83	0.23
岳麓区	Yuelu District	8.92	6.12	2.81	99.37	0.14	6.19	83.17	88.84	0.33
开福区	Kaifu District	7.98	7.09	0.89	98.94	0.15	8.36	82.95	88.61	0.32
雨花区	Yuhua District	9.61	6.66	2.95	97.80	0.18	8.53	91.67	97.92	0.34
长沙县	Changsha County	10.34	7.41	2.93	98.03	0.10	16.83	91.00	97.20	1.26
望城县	Wangcheng County	9.79	6.57	3.21	97.02	0.70	16.12	90.15	96.30	1.05
浏阳市	Liuyang City	11.34	7.60	3.74	96.20	0.35	29.69	90.97	97.17	2.77
宁乡县	Ningxiang County	11.98	7.52	4.47	98.70	0.30	29.95	91.11	97.32	2.17
株洲市	**Zhuzhou City**	**10.45**	**6.74**	**3.71**	**97.37**	**0.31**	**85.79**	**90.45**	**96.61**	**5.89**
荷塘区	Hetang District	10.19	6.75	3.45	98.73	0.09	4.24	90.43	96.59	0.22
芦淞区	Lousong District	9.37	6.32	3.05	98.47	0.08	4.31	84.92	90.71	0.14
石峰区	Shifeng District	9.42	6.81	2.61	98.79	0.08	5.30	87.65	93.63	0.30
天元区	Tianyuan District	11.10	6.64	4.46	98.58	0.28	3.00	90.96	97.16	0.16
醴陵市	Liling City	9.36	6.86	2.50	96.42	0.67	22.58	90.84	97.03	1.34
株洲县	Zhuzhou County	8.84	6.69	2.15	97.83	0.20	10.85	91.15	97.36	0.78
攸 县	You County	11.81	6.64	5.16	97.54	0.16	18.55	91.11	97.32	1.68
茶陵县	Chaling County	12.62	6.67	5.94	96.64	0.36	12.89	90.85	97.05	0.94
炎陵县	Yanling County	10.94	7.42	3.52	97.37	0.20	4.06	91.25	97.47	0.32
湘潭市	**Xiangtan City**	**10.69**	**6.96**	**3.73**	**95.66**	**0.87**	**61.19**	**90.96**	**97.16**	**4.61**
雨湖区	Yuhu District	9.00	6.88	2.12	99.13	0.06	7.42	90.45	96.62	0.42
岳塘区	Yuetang District	9.86	6.76	3.11	98.47	0.21	7.99	90.39	96.56	0.57
韶山市	Shaoshan City	9.53	6.99	2.54	99.28	0.31	2.26	91.07	97.28	0.14
湘乡市	Xiangxiang City	12.25	7.27	4.98	94.36	1.19	19.09	90.91	97.11	1.39
湘潭县	Xiangtan County	10.33	6.80	3.53	94.84	1.02	24.42	91.32	97.54	2.10
衡阳市	**Hengyang City**	**12.94**	**7.08**	**5.86**	**89.95**	**0.89**	**157.12**	**89.77**	**95.89**	**14.61**
珠辉区	Zhuhui District	10.38	6.89	3.49	98.25	0.14	6.11	88.47	94.51	0.31
雁峰区	Yanfeng District	11.91	6.66	5.25	98.11	0.18	4.32	89.04	95.11	0.26
石鼓区	Shigu District	11.48	6.96	4.52	98.99	0.18	4.89	87.84	93.83	0.27
蒸湘区	Zhengxiang District	12.90	6.80	6.09	98.65	0.17	4.34	90.48	96.65	0.23
南岳区	Nanyue District	12.01	6.79	5.22	98.59	0.31	1.16	89.62	95.73	0.11
耒阳市	Leiyang City	13.02	6.96	6.06	88.59	1.02	26.18	89.30	95.39	2.93
衡阳县	Hengyang County	12.92	7.52	5.40	89.60	1.43	25.84	89.22	95.30	2.41
衡南县	Hengnan County	12.59	7.22	5.37	90.96	0.90	23.22	90.97	97.17	1.75
衡山县	Hengshan County	11.65	7.06	4.59	84.57	0.55	8.66	89.95	96.08	0.94
衡东县	Hengdong County	13.27	7.59	5.68	85.05	1.25	14.60	90.18	96.33	1.53
常宁市	Changning City	14.18	6.71	7.47	91.40	0.82	18.06	89.17	95.25	1.64
祁东县	Qidong County	13.79	6.77	7.02	88.11	0.62	19.75	90.77	96.96	2.23
邵阳市	**Shaoyang City**	**12.86**	**6.70**	**6.15**	**89.42**	**0.90**	**155.08**	**90.75**	**96.94**	**14.28**
双清区	Shuangqing District	13.11	7.42	5.69	97.05	0.16	6.86	90.81	97.00	0.48
大祥区	Daxiang District	12.38	6.68	5.70	95.86	0.06	6.60	90.74	96.93	0.53
北塔区	Beita District	12.56	7.72	4.84	91.92	0.39	1.78	90.81	97.00	0.12
邵东县	Shaodong County	13.22	6.48	6.74	87.34	0.93	26.43	90.87	97.07	2.91
新邵县	Xinshao County	12.08	6.84	5.24	88.08	0.90	14.60	90.85	97.05	1.65

市县名称	City and County	出生率(‰) Birth Rate (‰)	死亡率(‰) Death Rate (‰)	自然增长率(‰) Natural Growth Rate (‰)	计划内生育率(%) Birth Within Plan Rate (%)	多孩率(%) More Childrens Rate (%)	已婚育龄妇女人数(万人) Married Women at Child-Bearing Age (10 000 persons)	节育率(%) Contra-ceptive Rate (%)	措施落实率(%) Contra-ception Using Rate (%)	节育手术(万例) Birth Control Opera-tion (10 000 cases)
邵阳县	Shaoyang County	13.03	6.45	6.57	89.91	1.00	19.25	90.83	97.03	1.38
隆回县	Longhui County	13.04	6.72	6.33	93.82	0.68	22.83	90.84	97.03	1.88
洞口县	Dongkou County	12.71	6.68	6.02	84.86	0.79	16.56	90.10	96.24	1.62
武冈市	Wugang City	14.40	7.03	7.38	84.56	1.09	16.55	90.88	97.08	1.93
绥宁县	Shuining County	11.39	6.60	4.79	97.11	0.40	7.13	90.26	96.42	0.60
新宁县	Xinning County	11.60	6.56	5.04	84.41	2.02	11.54	90.98	97.18	0.88
城步县	Chengbu County	13.23	6.70	6.53	95.62	1.33	4.96	90.90	97.10	0.32
岳阳市	**Yueyang City**	**11.24**	**6.91**	**4.33**	**93.94**	**0.96**	**113.80**	**90.82**	**97.01**	**9.18**
岳阳楼区	Yueyanglou District	11.91	6.60	5.32	97.75	0.14	8.87	90.57	96.75	0.51
云溪区	Yunxi District	11.97	6.74	5.24	98.19	0.62	3.50	90.97	97.17	0.30
君山区	Junshan District	10.54	6.96	3.58	92.48	1.10	4.80	91.10	97.31	0.35
汨罗市	Miluo City	10.73	7.25	3.48	97.56	0.32	14.47	90.30	96.45	1.06
岳阳县	Yueyang County	11.34	6.84	4.50	92.66	1.17	18.11	90.52	96.69	1.42
临湘市	Linxiang City	12.59	6.87	5.73	93.75	0.97	10.23	91.00	97.20	0.72
华容县	Huarong County	9.61	6.83	2.78	97.47	0.51	16.16	91.39	97.62	1.33
湘阴县	Xiangying County	12.01	7.24	4.78	92.56	1.70	15.15	90.92	97.12	1.52
平江县	Pingjiang County	11.21	6.84	4.37	88.76	1.41	21.10	90.87	97.06	1.84
屈原区	Quyuan District	9.94	6.15	3.79	97.26	1.06	1.42	90.91	97.10	0.12
常德市	**Changde City**	**8.93**	**6.82**	**2.11**	**95.96**	**0.13**	**136.28**	**90.86**	**97.06**	**12.97**
武陵区	Wuling District	9.19	6.86	2.33	97.92	0.14	9.80	90.78	96.97	0.53
鼎城区	Dingcheng District	8.00	6.80	1.20	96.41	0.12	20.05	90.86	97.05	1.08
津市市	Jinshi City	9.20	6.79	2.41	97.95	0.04	5.66	90.84	97.03	0.35
安乡县	Anxiang County	7.83	6.67	1.16	96.42	0.18	11.98	91.12	97.33	1.05
汉寿县	Hanshou County	9.02	6.85	2.17	87.46	0.39	16.57	89.98	96.12	1.26
澧 县	Li County	9.13	7.21	1.91	97.63	0.10	22.07	91.32	97.55	5.37
临澧县	Linli County	9.26	6.98	2.29	97.95	0.02	9.53	90.96	97.16	0.57
桃源县	Taoyuan County	9.38	6.74	2.64	96.71	0.04	21.98	90.95	97.15	1.46
石门县	Shimen County	9.80	6.44	3.36	97.47	0.10	17.00	90.81	97.00	1.18
西洞庭区	Xidongting District	5.73	6.87	-1.14	98.98	0.00	0.83	91.43	97.67	0.04
西湖区	Xihu District	6.60	6.03	0.57	97.86	0.00	0.80	90.82	97.01	0.06
张家界市	**Zhangjiajie City**	**11.86**	**7.12**	**4.75**	**95.41**	**0.90**	**32.38**	**90.79**	**96.98**	**2.29**
永定区	Yongding District	12.44	6.79	5.65	96.34	0.92	8.31	90.89	97.09	0.57
武陵源区	Wulingyuan District	15.36	6.76	8.61	96.04	0.57	0.98	92.11	98.39	0.10
慈利县	Cili County	9.80	7.21	2.59	95.57	0.24	14.72	91.17	97.39	0.91
桑植县	Sangzhi County	14.17	7.31	6.85	94.36	1.63	8.38	89.85	95.98	0.71
益阳市	**Yiyang City**	**9.61**	**6.69**	**2.93**	**96.20**	**0.83**	**94.19**	**91.02**	**97.22**	**6.26**
资阳区	Ziyang District	10.87	6.76	4.12	96.83	0.86	9.06	91.03	97.24	0.56
赫山区	Heshan District	9.78	6.82	2.96	96.60	0.80	17.40	90.88	97.08	1.01
沅江市	Yuanjiang City	8.04	6.69	1.36	97.27	0.73	14.85	90.95	97.15	0.93
南县	Nan County	8.32	6.73	1.59	97.19	0.73	13.86	91.33	97.56	1.20
桃江县	Taojiang County	11.18	6.86	4.33	95.05	0.86	17.88	91.01	97.21	1.18
安化县	Anhua County	9.94	6.39	3.55	95.26	0.92	19.10	90.92	97.12	1.22
大通湖区	Datonghu District	6.50	6.40	0.10	98.76	0.77	2.04	91.50	97.74	0.15
郴州市	**Chenzhou City**	**12.04**	**6.69**	**5.35**	**93.10**	**0.95**	**93.54**	**90.89**	**97.08**	**6.91**
北湖区	Beihu District	12.07	6.29	5.78	97.64	0.49	6.35	89.79	95.91	0.47
苏仙区	Suxian District	13.18	6.36	6.82	97.19	0.74	7.10	90.86	97.05	0.43
资兴市	Zixing City	11.75	6.64	5.11	98.31	0.54	7.98	90.82	97.01	0.57
桂阳县	Guiyang County	11.94	6.74	5.20	91.99	1.11	15.25	91.20	97.42	1.31

18-2 续表 2 continued

市县名称	City and County	出生率(‰) Birth Rate (‰)	死亡率(‰) Death Rate (‰)	自然增长率(‰) Natural Growth Rate (‰)	计划内生育率(%) Birth Within Plan Rate (%)	多孩率(%) More Childrens Rate (%)	已婚育龄妇女人数(万人) Married Women at Child-Bearing Age (10 000 persons)	节育率(%) Contra-ceptive Rate (%)	措施落实率(%) Contra-ception Using Rate (%)	节育手术(万例) Birth Control Opera-tion (10 000 cases)
永兴县	Yongxing County	10.86	6.30	4.56	95.89	0.56	12.87	90.89	97.09	0.82
宜章县	Yizhang County	10.75	6.76	4.00	88.08	0.75	10.95	90.85	97.04	0.78
嘉禾县	Jiahe County	12.02	6.80	5.22	91.55	1.13	7.08	90.81	97.00	0.51
临武县	Linwu County	12.80	6.66	6.14	84.04	1.91	6.15	90.98	97.19	0.48
汝城县	Rucheng County	14.48	7.32	7.15	95.69	1.05	7.68	90.94	97.14	0.65
桂东县	Guidong County	13.86	7.79	6.07	91.03	1.68	3.42	91.59	97.83	0.31
安仁县	Anren County	11.53	6.61	4.92	92.95	0.85	8.72	90.92	97.12	0.58
永州市	**Yongzhou City**	**10.37**	**6.74**	**3.63**	**92.75**	**0.94**	**112.96**	**90.54**	**96.71**	**8.10**
芝山区	Zhishan District	10.75	6.75	4.01	95.61	0.64	11.55	90.85	97.04	0.60
冷水滩区	Lengshuitan District	10.37	6.48	3.89	94.85	0.44	10.07	90.81	97.00	0.65
东安县	Dongan County	9.91	6.75	3.16	95.03	0.65	11.89	89.59	95.70	0.70
道县	Dao County	9.61	6.72	2.89	90.25	1.73	13.12	90.84	97.03	0.91
宁远县	Ningyuan County	9.44	6.75	2.69	91.32	1.37	14.51	91.20	97.41	1.26
江永县	Jiangyong County	10.38	6.63	3.75	93.96	0.54	4.84	90.95	97.15	0.36
江华县	Jianghua County	11.95	6.80	5.15	90.28	1.45	8.98	89.88	96.01	0.67
蓝山县	Lanshan County	10.99	6.74	4.25	88.34	1.71	6.95	90.30	96.46	0.51
新田县	Xintian County	10.27	6.84	3.42	91.23	0.70	7.33	89.94	96.07	0.57
双牌县	Shuangpai County	9.38	6.76	2.62	95.85	0.38	3.39	89.00	95.07	0.28
祁阳县	Qiyang County	10.88	6.80	4.08	93.97	0.47	20.31	90.87	97.07	1.59
怀化市	**Huaihua City**	**11.93**	**6.73**	**5.20**	**95.76**	**1.36**	**102.50**	**90.56**	**96.73**	**8.04**
鹤城区	Hecheng District	15.35	6.41	8.94	96.09	0.77	6.60	91.38	97.61	0.47
洪江市	Hongjiang City	10.51	6.77	3.74	96.24	0.82	9.72	90.93	97.13	0.67
洪江区	Hongjiang District	8.12	6.59	1.53	97.17	0.47	2.33	88.34	94.36	0.11
中方县	Zhongfang County	12.82	7.18	5.64	93.86	2.25	5.69	91.61	97.86	0.57
沅陵县	Yuanling County	11.63	7.01	4.62	96.72	0.61	12.54	91.55	97.79	1.01
辰溪县	Chenxi County	10.75	6.62	4.12	93.63	1.53	10.01	91.06	97.26	0.74
溆浦县	Xupu County	11.15	6.63	4.52	96.51	0.84	17.82	91.08	97.29	1.21
麻阳县	Mayang County	12.65	6.48	6.17	98.12	0.75	7.04	89.28	95.36	0.58
新晃县	Xinhuang County	11.66	7.06	4.60	95.00	1.76	5.40	90.90	97.10	0.50
芷江县	Zhijiang County	13.58	6.81	6.77	94.87	2.09	8.33	90.92	97.12	0.88
会同县	Huitong County	11.24	6.68	4.56	94.95	2.58	7.68	90.18	96.33	0.62
靖州县	Jingzhou County	12.35	6.59	5.76	96.47	1.36	5.08	87.45	93.41	0.30
通道县	Tongdao County	13.68	6.64	7.04	94.50	3.37	4.26	87.26	93.20	0.38
娄底市	**Loudi City**	**12.91**	**6.89**	**6.02**	**88.78**	**1.70**	**83.95**	**90.98**	**97.18**	**7.87**
娄星区	Louxing District	10.86	6.96	3.90	97.19	0.18	8.81	90.81	97.00	0.65
冷水江市	Lengshuijiang District	11.75	6.75	5.01	96.05	0.36	8.24	90.86	97.05	0.62
涟源市	Liangyuan City	15.05	7.32	7.73	82.97	2.81	22.48	91.00	97.20	2.66
双峰县	Shuangfeng County	13.09	6.65	6.44	96.33	0.89	19.31	91.27	97.49	1.57
新化县	Xinhua County	11.99	6.70	5.29	84.74	1.95	25.11	90.85	97.04	2.36
湘西自治州	**West Hunan A.P**	**12.84**	**6.65**	**6.19**	**87.23**	**3.13**	**49.57**	**89.90**	**96.03**	**4.60**
吉首市	Jishou City	10.20	6.48	3.71	92.92	1.85	5.08	90.83	97.03	0.46
泸溪县	Louxi County	10.73	6.64	4.10	86.54	2.69	5.20	90.81	97.00	0.44
凤凰县	Fenghuang County	12.50	6.67	5.83	89.89	2.65	6.65	90.82	97.01	0.60
花垣县	Huayuan County	13.48	6.72	6.77	82.06	3.06	4.99	90.99	97.19	0.52
保靖县	Baojing County	13.51	6.46	7.05	83.76	2.59	5.50	89.78	95.90	0.55
古丈县	Guzhang County	11.26	7.18	4.08	89.38	2.38	2.42	89.10	95.17	0.24
永顺县	Yongshun County	15.22	6.61	8.61	88.54	2.44	9.36	89.14	95.21	0.92
龙山县	Longshan County	13.10	6.71	6.39	86.21	5.39	10.35	88.82	94.88	0.88

18-3 各市、州、县从业人员年末人数(2003年)

Employment at the Year-end (2003)

单位：万人 (10 000 persons)

市县名称	City and County	从业人员人数 Number of Employed Persons	在岗职工 Staff and Workers on the Job	#国有经济 State-owned Units	#城镇集体经济 Urban Collective Owned Units	城镇个体从业人员 Empoly-Persons in Urban Self Employed Individuals	城镇私营企业从业人员 polyed Persons in Urban Private Enterprises	农村从业人员 Rural Employed Persons	其他从业人员 Other Employed Persons	离开本单位仍保留劳动关系的职工 Staff and Workers Left Self-Unit and Remind
长沙市	**Changsha City**	**356.35**	**59.84**	**39.67**	**4.16**	**22.26**	**24.22**	**230.50**	**3.28**	**16.25**
芙蓉区	Hurong District	27.97	12.60	8.08	0.86	5.96	5.05	0.90	0.50	2.96
天心区	Tianxin District	17.45	7.14	4.74	0.54	2.84	3.87	0.72	0.21	2.67
岳麓区	Yuilu District	16.03	6.80	4.49	0.18	1.20	2.24	3.94	0.23	1.62
开福区	Kaifu District	22.31	7.30	4.06	0.92	3.21	5.22	2.73	0.30	3.55
雨花区	Yufua District	26.64	11.16	7.71	0.58	3.29	5.97	1.58	1.66	2.98
长沙县	Changsha County	46.23	4.22	2.16	0.11	1.17	0.45	40.01	0.11	0.27
望城县	Wangcheng County	39.19	3.04	2.09	0.48	0.40	0.14	34.79	0.09	0.73
宁乡县	Ningxiang County	81.80	3.99	3.28	0.21	1.39	0.31	74.89	0.15	1.07
浏阳市	Liuyang City	78.73	3.59	3.06	0.28	2.80	0.97	70.94	0.03	0.40
株洲市	**Zhuzhou City**	**208.10**	**26.32**	**19.16**	**3.26**	**11.31**	**5.84**	**152.83**	**2.26**	**9.54**
荷塘区	Hetang District	10.40	4.14	2.77	0.44	0.84	0.73	3.06	0.41	1.22
芦淞区	Lusong District	12.50	4.78	3.40	0.64	1.72	1.16	1.48	0.82	2.54
石峰区	Shifeng District	13.48	6.46	4.42	0.74	0.60	0.88	2.98	0.29	2.27
天元区	Tianyuan District	6.04	1.86	1.48	0.25	0.34	0.43	3.01	0.12	0.28
株洲县	Zhuzhou County	24.55	1.21	0.94	0.17	0.96	0.31	21.77	0.19	0.11
攸县	You County	44.05	2.12	1.87	0.20	2.43	0.52	38.20	0.11	0.67
茶陵县	Chaling County	30.27	1.72	1.50	0.14	0.70	0.12	27.08	0.08	0.57
炎陵县	Yanling County	10.62	0.90	0.76	0.11	0.62	0.42	8.44	0.05	0.19
醴陵市	Liling City	56.19	3.13	2.02	0.57	3.10	1.27	46.81	0.19	1.69
湘潭市	**Xiangtan City**	**171.89**	**22.96**	**17.68**	**2.80**	**10.42**	**5.56**	**123.39**	**0.52**	**9.04**
雨湖区	Yuhu District	5.36	0.60	0.27	0.24	1.83	0.15	2.76		0.02
岳塘区	Yuetang District	5.59	0.42	0.27	0.13	0.66	0.05	4.37	0.01	0.08
湘潭县	Xiangtan County	67.54	3.51	3.03	0.41	0.82	0.60	61.97	0.01	0.63
湘乡市	Xiangxiang City	57.13	4.04	2.59	0.58	1.56	1.54	49.26	0.09	0.64
韶山市	Shaoshan City	6.82	0.56	0.50	0.04	0.76	0.35	5.03	0.01	0.11
衡阳市	**Hengyang City**	**379.81**	**39.78**	**29.10**	**4.80**	**14.51**	**7.73**	**298.16**	**3.03**	**16.60**
珠晖区	Zhuhui District	6.70	0.54	0.28	0.20	1.45	0.10	4.57	0.01	0.03
雁峰区	Yanfeng District	2.90	0.47	0.25	0.11	0.51	0.07	1.78	0.01	0.06
石鼓区	Shigu District	3.27	0.29	0.23	0.04	0.63	0.03	2.17	0.07	0.08
蒸湘区	Zhengxiang District	4.11	0.59	0.28	0.29	0.45	0.06	2.75	0.22	0.04
南岳区	Nanyue District	2.87	0.51	0.43	0.06	0.34	0.02	1.82	0.16	0.02
衡阳县	Hengyang County	63.05	4.58	3.44	1.07	1.22	1.10	55.11	0.10	0.94
衡南县	Hengnan County	50.94	4.19	3.28	0.59	1.38	0.13	44.17	0.16	0.91
衡山县	Hengshan County	24.95	1.61	1.32	0.15	1.00	0.37	21.59	0.07	0.31
衡东县	Hengdong County	35.70	2.27	1.75	0.32	1.00	0.40	31.05	0.16	0.82
祁东县	Qidong County	46.62	3.00	2.62	0.38	1.00	0.27	41.09	0.24	1.02
耒阳市	Leiyang City	65.47	5.28	3.53	0.30	3.28	1.48	53.65	0.26	1.52
常宁市	Changning City	46.34	3.92	3.44	0.40	1.93	0.20	38.41	0.11	1.77
邵阳市	**Shaoyang City**	**411.13**	**29.14**	**25.14**	**2.06**	**13.04**	**2.53**	**351.69**	**1.42**	**13.32**
双清区	Shuangqing District	16.37	4.97	4.29	0.14	1.44	0.94	4.27	0.11	4.63
大祥区	Da xiang District	13.92	3.99	3.20	0.30	0.52	0.22	7.44	0.22	1.52
北塔区	Beita District	4.24	0.63	0.48	0.05	0.02	0.01	3.15		0.44

单位：万人　　18-3 续表 1　continued　　(10 000 persons)

市县名称	City and County	从业人员人数 Number of Empolyed Persons	在岗职工 Staff and Workers on the Job	#国有经济 State-owned Units	#城镇集体经济 Urban Collective Owned Units	城镇个体从业人员 Empoly-Persons in Urban Self Empolyed Individuals	城镇私营企业从业人员 polyed Persons in Urban Private Enterprises	农村从业人员 Rural Empolyed Persons	其他从业人员 Other Empolyed Persons	离开本单位仍保留劳动关系的职工 Staff and Workers Left Self-Unit and Remind
邵东县	Shaodong County	56.44	3.52	2.91	0.61	2.37	0.52	48.88	0.11	1.04
新邵县	Xinshao County	38.54	1.92	1.65	0.17	0.41	0.25	35.02	0.11	0.84
邵阳县	Shaoyang County	54.73	2.24	2.05	0.09	0.74	0.07	51.05	0.03	0.61
隆回县	Longhui County	61.72	2.48	2.26	0.07	2.37	0.08	56.11	0.20	0.47
洞口县	Dongkou County	49.93	2.48	2.29	0.17	1.71	0.11	44.21	0.17	1.25
绥宁县	Shuining County	20.55	1.20	0.99	0.07	0.52	0.10	18.25	0.16	0.32
新宁县	Xinning County	35.61	1.93	1.65	0.10	0.79	0.04	31.76	0.08	1.01
城步县	Chengbu County	14.02	1.47	1.31	0.05	0.20	0.05	11.87	0.04	0.40
武冈市	Wugang City	45.04	2.32	2.06	0.23	1.95	0.13	39.67	0.18	0.79
岳阳市	**Yueyang City**	**257.75**	**30.69**	**25.27**	**2.59**	**11.33**	**3.01**	**202.13**	**2.58**	**8.01**
岳阳楼区	Yueyanglou District	11.20	0.84	0.65	0.18	4.26	0.13	5.92		0.05
云溪区	Yunxi District	5.63	0.58	0.39	0.17	0.78	0.08	4.03	0.08	0.08
君山区	Junshan District	7.07	1.30	1.17	0.08			5.65		0.12
岳阳县	Yueyang County	34.69	2.25	1.94	0.12	1.26	0.17	30.20	0.14	0.67
华容县	Huarong County	34.42	2.20	1.90	0.21	0.97	0.14	30.41	0.10	0.60
湘阴县	Xiangyin County	37.18	2.46	1.94	0.31	0.20	0.19	33.16	0.14	1.03
平江县	Pingjiang County	50.11	2.70	2.25	0.25	0.71	0.15	45.62	0.12	0.81
汨罗市	Miluo City	37.60	5.13	4.74	0.38	1.01	0.53	29.12	1.13	0.68
临湘市	Linxiang City	22.44	1.98	1.73	0.18	1.37	0.26	18.02	0.16	0.65
常德市	**Changde City**	**306.91**	**23.12**	**18.07**	**1.48**	**15.86**	**5.43**	**257.46**	**0.84**	**4.20**
武陵区	Wuling District	12.01	0.91	0.60	0.10	1.65	0.25	9.08	0.02	0.10
鼎城区	Dingchen District	45.54	2.79	2.22	0.24	4.58	0.39	37.19	0.03	0.56
安乡县	Anxiang County	27.84	2.25	1.44	0.16	0.83	0.45	23.75	0.02	0.54
汉寿县	Hanshou County	44.52	1.98	1.56	0.20	1.67	0.60	39.80	0.08	0.39
澧县	Li County	43.29	2.62	2.05	0.30	1.95	0.53	37.50	0.02	0.67
临澧县	Linli County	24.84	1.36	1.10	0.14	0.85	0.51	21.77	0.14	0.21
桃源县	Taoyuan County	51.75	2.19	2.09	0.08	1.42	0.70	46.92	0.05	0.47
石门县	Shimen County	39.25	2.39	1.83	0.16	1.95	0.52	34.05	0.09	0.25
津市市	Jinshi City	10.42	1.71	1.33	0.05	0.74	0.28	7.40	0.01	0.28
张家界市	**Zhangjiajie City**	**84.79**	**7.46**	**5.84**	**0.65**	**2.01**	**1.30**	**72.62**	**0.08**	**1.32**
永定区	Yongding District	20.73	3.01	2.53	0.06	0.85	0.30	16.29	0.01	0.27
武陵源区	Wulingyuan District	2.86	0.47	0.39	0.01	0.01	0.12	2.22	0.02	0.02
慈利县	Cili County	37.57	2.25	1.70	0.48	0.65	0.58	33.55	0.01	0.53
桑植县	Sangzhi County	23.63	1.73	1.22	0.10	0.50	0.30	20.56	0.04	0.50
益阳市	**Yiyang City**	**248.39**	**26.04**	**21.57**	**2.11**	**5.72**	**2.25**	**201.80**	**0.77**	**11.81**
资阳区	Ziyang District	20.86	1.24	1.01	0.17	0.56	0.09	17.86	0.07	1.04
赫山区	Heshan District	49.65	6.63	4.80	0.65	2.12	1.28	35.61	0.36	3.65
南县	Nan County	44.06	8.15	7.03	0.55	0.73	0.34	32.82	0.12	1.90
桃江县	Taojiang County	46.22	2.77	2.29	0.27	0.89	0.19	40.52	0.12	1.73
安化县	Anhua County	46.03	2.31	2.15	0.16	0.47	0.11	41.86	0.08	1.20
沅江市	Yuanjiang City	41.57	4.94	4.29	0.31	0.95	0.24	33.13	0.02	2.29
郴州市	**Chenzhou City**	**263.27**	**23.49**	**20.08**	**1.42**	**15.55**	**3.50**	**212.53**	**1.99**	**6.21**
北湖区	Beihu District	19.99	5.21	4.21	0.24	2.55	1.38	8.02	0.77	2.06
苏仙区	Suxian District	16.90	2.76	2.31	0.15	1.19	0.48	11.39	0.30	0.78
桂阳县	Guiyang County	46.83	2.43	2.28	0.12	2.45	0.21	41.48	0.03	0.23
宜章县	Yizhang County	35.37	2.11	1.87	0.13	1.81	0.27	30.60	0.11	0.47
永兴县	Yongxing County	30.93	2.14	1.80	0.31	1.42	0.25	26.59	0.03	0.50

市县名称	City and County	从业人员人数 Number of Empolyed Persons	在岗职工 Staff and Workers on the Job	#国有经济 State-owned Units	#城镇集体经济 Urban Collective Owned Units	城镇个体从业人员 Empoly-Persons in Urban Self Empolyed Individuals	城镇私营企业从业人员 polyed Persons in Urban Private Enterprises	农村从业人员 Rural Empolyed Persons	其他从业人员 Other Empolyed Persons	离开本单位仍保留劳动关系的职工 Staff and Workers Left Self-Unit and Remind
嘉禾县	Jiahe County	17.27	1.24	1.18	0.05	0.69	0.13	15.06	0.01	0.14
临武县	Linwu County	18.92	1.27	1.20	0.07	1.30	0.15	15.93		0.27
汝城县	Rucheng County	20.57	1.07	1.00	0.05	1.26	0.03	17.80	0.02	0.39
桂东县	Guidong County	10.24	0.74	0.61	0.08	0.43	0.07	8.81	0.05	0.14
安仁县	Anren County	25.33	1.39	1.26	0.12	0.65	0.30	22.44	0.01	0.54
资兴市	Zixing City	20.92	3.13	2.36	0.1	1.8	0.23	14.41	0.66	0.69
永州市	**Yongzhou City**	**303.39**	**22.95**	**19.71**	**1.52**	**5.38**	**1.60**	**265.72**	**0.94**	**6.80**
芝山区	Zhishan District	30.83	3.49	3.07	0.26	0.57	0.35	25.05	0.15	1.22
冷水滩区	Lengshuitan District	26.04	3.88	2.79	0.23	1.54	0.37	18.04	0.07	2.14
祁阳县	Qiyang County	50.53	4.02	3.36	0.20	0.91	0.25	44.12	0.17	1.06
东安县	Dongan County	27.44	1.79	1.61	0.16	1.22	0.07	23.84	0.03	0.49
双牌县	Shuangpai County	8.20	0.83	0.75	0.08	0.21	0.10	6.76	0.01	0.29
道县	Dao County	34.92	1.96	1.83	0.10	0.08	0.06	32.08	0.11	0.63
江永县	Jiangyong County	13.06	1.04	0.96	0.07	0.02	0.02	11.79	0.03	0.16
宁远县	Ningyuan Couny	45.40	1.83	1.66	0.13	0.23	0.07	43.07	0.06	0.14
蓝山县	Lanshan County	19.67	1.12	0.95	0.14	0.24	0.07	17.94	0.13	0.17
新田县	Xintian County	21.52	1.22	1.12	0.06	0.30	0.20	19.58	0.07	0.15
江华县	Jianghua County	25.78	1.77	1.61	0.09	0.06	0.04	23.45	0.11	0.35
怀化市	**Huaihua City**	**265.11**	**22.52**	**17.38**	**2.00**	**7.32**	**1.97**	**225.75**	**1.13**	**6.42**
鹤城区	Hecheng District	15.83	4.42	3.30	0.30	2.61	0.84	6.38	0.33	1.25
中方县	Zhongfang County	14.32	0.89	0.79	0.03	0.30	0.05	12.92	0.03	0.13
沅陵县	Yuanling County	34.45	2.51	1.85	0.18	1.09	0.07	29.72	0.07	0.99
辰溪县	Chenxi County	25.46	2.33	1.88	0.25	0.40	0.09	21.80	0.19	0.65
溆浦县	Xupu County	45.92	2.95	2.27	0.26	0.60	0.12	41.28	0.04	0.93
会同县	Huitong County	21.31	1.25	0.90	0.07	0.26	0.13	19.36	0.09	0.22
麻阳县	Mayang County	18.82	1.26	1.10	0.14	0.42	0.08	16.72	0.05	0.29
新晃县	Xinhuang County	14.79	0.89	0.78	0.09	0.13	0.12	13.42	0.03	0.20
芷江县	Zhijiang County	20.48	1.49	1.06	0.22	0.41	0.05	18.32	0.06	0.15
靖州县	Jingzhou County	14.25	1.19	0.93	0.15	0.21	0.05	12.58	0.06	0.16
通道县	Tongdao County	12.68	0.87	0.75	0.09	0.15	0.02	11.51	0.07	0.06
洪江市	Hongjiang City	26.80	2.47	1.77	0.22	0.74	0.35	21.74	0.11	1.39
娄底市	**Loudi City**	**216.22**	**22.36**	**18.92**	**2.06**	**6.12**	**2.86**	**175.35**	**2.37**	**7.16**
娄星区	Louxing District	19.86	6.57	3.13	0.61	1.84	1.36	5.74	1.73	2.62
冷水江市	Lengshuijiang City	50.52	5.54	5.54	0.50	0.88	0.47	9.78	0.24	1.33
涟源市	Lianyuan City	71.69	3.98	3.98	0.49	1.50	0.40	48.52	0.24	1.27
双峰县	Shuangfrng County	18.24	2.64	2.64	0.09	0.90	0.20	46.03	0.11	0.64
新化县	Xinhua County	55.91	3.63	3.63	0.37	1.00	0. 43	65.28	0.05	1.30
湘西自治州	**West Hunan A.P**	**157.83**	**12.12**	**10.61**	**0.77**	**13.58**	**2.52**	**125.97**	**0.67**	**2.97**
吉首市	Jishou City	16.85	3.10	2.51	0.17	2.30	0.74	9.77	0.32	0.63
泸溪县	Luxi County	16.97	1.16	1.07	0.08	0.84	0.32	14.16	0.01	0.49
凤凰县	Fenghuang County	21.46	1.27	1.12	0.10	1.36	0.12	18.48	0.04	0.19
花垣县	Huayuan County	17.23	1.43	1.16	0.06	1.63	0.41	13.61	0.03	0.12
保靖县	Baojing County	16.89	1.00	0.91	0.09	1.30	0.45	13.79	0.03	0.32
古丈县	Guzhang County	8.65	0.64	0.56	0.07	0.58	0.12	7.11	0.01	0.19
永顺县	Yongsun County	28.47	1.76	1.62	0.11	2.29	0.14	23.86	0.10	0.32
龙山县	Longshan County	31.30	1.77	1.65	0.09	3.29	0.23	25.19	0.12	0.70
未列入地区的单位	**Not Classified by Region**	**12.77**	**10.66**	**10.66**					**0.91**	**1.20**

18-4 各市、州、县国有经济各行业在岗职工年末人数(2003年)

单位：人

市县	Cities and Counties	农林牧渔业 Agriculture, Forestry, Farming of Animals and Fishing	采掘业 Mining	制造业 Manufacturing	电力燃气及水的生产和供应 Production and Spply of Elrctricity Gas and Water	建筑业 Construction	交通运输仓储和邮政业 Traffic, Transport, Storage and Post	信息传输计算机服务软件业 Information Transfer, Computer Services and Software	批发和零售业 Wholesale and Retail Trade
长沙市	**Changsha City**	**2112**	**5904**	**37038**	**8246**	**34006**	**25888**	**3822**	**19074**
芙蓉区	Hurong District			2094	93	1940	7900	1249	8555
天心区	Tianxin District	25		6489	4152	13727	356	34	2099
岳麓区	Yuilu District	129		5177	76	370	984		314
开福区	Kaifu District	215	10	3321	1083	918	3894	519	3890
雨花区	Yufua District	61	32	11397	240	16503	5815	1144	1273
长沙县	Changsha County	164		2562	737		3334	68	223
望城县	Wangcheng County	340		4626	186	143	671	334	1431
宁乡县	Ningxiang County	386	4918	848	912	372	1792	218	550
浏阳市	Liuyang City	792	944	524	767	33	1142	256	739
株洲市	**Zhuzhou City**	**3696**	**2462**	**52529**	**6886**	**6880**	**8643**	**1114**	**3758**
荷塘区	Hetang District								
芦淞区	Lusong District								
石峰区	Shifeng District					22			
天元区	Tianyuan District			29		35	1439		10
株洲县	Zhuzhou County	301	22	525	304	8	371	68	260
攸县	You County	628	945	2004	719		392	106	499
茶陵县	Chaling County	2110	316	562	420		696	139	259
炎陵县	Yanling County	477	4	24	870		305	81	216
醴陵市	Liling City	114		2266	1118		1537	62	898
湘潭市	**Xiangtan City**	**772**	**5056**	**63422**	**2884**	**17704**	**3943**	**696**	**4241**
雨湖区	Yuhu District								
岳塘区	Yuetang District								
湘潭县	Xiangtan County	233	4687	716	91	6905	328	92	382
湘乡市	Xiangxiang City	210		3840	830		1016	55	1146
韶山市	Shaoshan City	8		46	48	1000	75	21	192
衡阳市	**Hengyang City**	**4893**	**9656**	**52737**	**8910**	**15069**	**9412**	**1916**	**14197**
珠晖区	Zhuhui District	282						3	
雁峰区	Yanfeng District	325							
石鼓区	Shigu District								
蒸湘区	Zhengxiang District			183					11
南岳区	Nanyue District	270			100		231	21	71
衡阳县	Hengyang County	1043	633	5096	270		720	360	2816
衡南县	Hengnan County	1499	583	1338	10	7242	524		1793
衡山县	Hengshan County	106	497	1364	273		317	139	509
衡东县	Hengdong County	509		1772	1529	19	566	47	1119
祁东县	Qidong County	88	10	4229	441	24	819	274	1296
耒阳市	Leiyang City	217	4069	1727	2164	280	846	176	1711
常宁市	Changning City	354	2671	9984	836	931	492	205	1009
邵阳市	**Shaoyang City**	**13225**	**11597**	**23188**	**12404**	**17615**	**15086**	**2072**	**11158**
双清区	Shuangqing District	183	928	8162	1585	14871	7516	389	1705
大祥区	Da xiang District	370		6511	563	800	2345	133	1191
北塔区	Beita District	168		3120			9		28

Employed Staff and Workers in State – Owned Units by Sector at the Year-end (2003)

(person)

住宿和餐饮业 Accommodation and Restaurants	金融业 Finance	房地产业 Real Estate Trade	租赁和商务服务业 Tenancy and Business Services	科学研究技术服务地质勘查 Scientific Research, Technical Services, Geologic Perambulation	水利环境和公共设施管理业 Management of Water Conservancy, Environment and Public Establishment	居民服务和其他服务业 Resident Services and Other Services	教育 Education	卫生、社会保障和社会福利 Sanitation Social Security and Social Welfare	文化体育和娱乐业 Culture, Sports and Entertainment	公共管理和社会组织 Public Management and Social Organization
8917	**14659**	**4660**	**8052**	**24270**	**5599**	**1439**	**80868**	**27652**	**17089**	**67422**
3629	9674	813	5407	4784	341	717	6059	5292	3908	18329
787	1439	653	560	1956	739	108	6919	1432	1537	4378
889	323	271	53	3161	1173	48	22229	3234	390	6110
1549	679	1122	75	1643	244	430	2863	5212	5743	7158
1572	598	634	1057	10450	455	54	6731	4891	4356	9855
48	243	10	66	997	414		7751	815	181	4006
46	437		41	108	331		6574	1504	186	3917
144	533	713	423	509	1117	82	10521	2557	228	6020
253	733	444	370	662	785		11221	2715	560	7649
1542	**4371**	**1734**	**2232**	**4362**	**4437**	**73**	**30516**	**8881**	**3082**	**31317**
				15	407	10		111	753	839
							722	310		1029
					147		771			939
430	201	133	68	537	432		866	289	208	4371
45	100	84		9	167		3867	568	88	2633
117	342	44	274	320	559		6107	929	117	4559
122	266	77	80	22	178		4666	1017	185	3897
137	92	61	341	30	179		1160	582	878	2128
95	439	138	89	174	727	11	6204	1647	299	4350
1151	**3906**	**971**	**1147**	**3635**	**2467**	**277**	**29648**	**8799**	**1047**	**25011**
		88			99		1145	59		1290
			75		51		1106	170		1257
31	266		12	101	127		8953	1317	109	5980
169	559	151	90	114	813	23	7776	2468	145	6478
412	131	9	44	24	158	18	910	364	168	1330
2445	**6007**	**3149**	**1368**	**4742**	**6631**	**319**	**68453**	**22558**	**3242**	**55318**
		26			300		1027	186		1105
			3	19	278		605	264	8	1019
			22	22	261		797	286	13	932
		88	10		145		1150	268	4	971
565	**108**	61	24	117	356	62	575	484	225	1071
290	558	97	139	60	796	60	9629	1582	412	6800
123	205	30	107	520	757		9637	2540	164	5771
80	459	85	63	460	138		4113	1215	108	4262
85	313	73	70	29	344	16	5684	1362	225	4741
55	393	296	119	525	190	29	8904	2635	130	6593
329	514	142	134	596	2012	30	10564	2547	278	6915
219	343	182	228	150	238	25	6974	2719	170	6702
1082	**5561**	**1148**	**1485**	**1954**	**2682**	**1040**	**58481**	**15460**	**3440**	**52728**
41	219	497	154	328	8	60	2495	1451	168	2139
316	2367	179	583	825	493		3857	2269	578	8635
		1	97	16	11		713	36		577

市县	Cities and Counties	农林牧渔业 Agri-culture, Forestry, Farming of Animals and Fishing	采掘业 Mining	制造业 Manu-facturing	电力燃气及水的生产和供应 Produc-tion and Spply of Elrctricity Gas and Water	建筑业 Construc-tion	交通运输仓储和邮政业 Traffic, Transport, Storage and Post	信息传输计算机服务软件业 Informa-tion Transfer, Computer Services and Software	批发和零售业 Whole-sale and Retail Trade
邵东县	Shaodong County	317	5334	795	900	1548	743	216	902
新邵县	Xinshao County	266	1319	938	398		710	130	672
邵阳县	Shaoyang County	644	1094	525	973		715	79	854
隆回县	Longhui County	556	222	1505	874		501	245	1023
洞口县	Dongkou County	5355	774	36	1245		372	183	1759
绥宁县	Shuining County	742			792		447	405	136
新宁县	Xinning County	1304	347	213	1839		897	62	1087
城步县	Chengbu County	2021	26	1026	1142	396	491	104	722
武冈市	Wugang City	1299	1553	357	2093		340	126	1079
岳阳市	**Yueyang City**	**37170**	**98**	**50531**	**5170**	**4399**	**12972**	**1463**	**9748**
岳阳楼区	Yueyanglou District	65		41			32		583
云溪区	Yunxi District			83	12	82	246		263
君山区	Junshan District	3476		341	210	146	220		312
岳阳县	Yueyang County	1073		1681	705	23	682	117	1112
华容县	Huarong County	2160		76	634	50	516	46	752
湘阴县	Xiangyin County	1106		365	399		952	112	2015
平江县	Pingjiang County	712	98	925	543	12	1528	214	653
汨罗市	Miluo City	25742		3043	371	302	940	126	1181
临湘市	Linxiang City	961		2965	335	195	672	148	915
常德市	**Changde City**	**5131**	**4343**	**12866**	**6255**	**690**	**7188**	**1767**	**6042**
武陵区	Wuling District	54							89
鼎城区	Dingchen District	1252		28	242		497	8	1083
安乡县	Anxiang County	290		342	167		318		455
汉寿县	Hanshou County	331		623	224	461	361	3	888
澧县	Li County	1397	1467	93	172	43	145	122	220
临澧县	Linli County	117		51	225		213		806
桃源县	Taoyuan County	374		28	618		855		939
石门县	Shimen County	795	2876		1138		315		346
津市市	Jinshi City			4428	213		254		312
张家界市	**Zhangjiajie City**	**2601**	**1306**	**2129**	**3856**	**434**	**3689**	**1812**	**1766**
永定区	Yongding District	738		1488	947	420	2216	1173	792
武陵源区	Wulingyuan District			12	65		51	13	38
慈利县	Cili County	1021	381	629	1780	14	759	142	912
桑植县	Sangzhi County	842	925		1064		663	484	24
益阳市	**Yiyang City**	**68839**	**356**	**15065**	**4136**	**1377**	**6988**	**2498**	**6506**
资阳区	Ziyang District	210		87		115	25		307
赫山区	Heshan District	49891		6717	1699	1183	4650	1480	1672
南县	Nan County	816	20	663	271		533	191	793
桃江县	Taojiang County	589	194	3100	654		535	84	880
安化县	Anhua County	1018	142	1006	1176		517	322	931
沅江市	Yuanjiang City	16315		3492	336	79	728	421	1923
郴州市	**Chenzhou City**	**5312**	**28838**	**14318**	**8157**	**5374**	**4402**	**4432**	**6309**
北湖区	Beihu District	6	4680	7588	1616	3465	636	2485	724
苏仙区	Suxian District	303	2130	3152	1179	1277	469	1065	334
桂阳县	Guiyang County	555	4213		792		543		1019
宜章县	Yizhang County	764	2905	433	132		420	34	852
永兴县	Yongxing County	183	1196	581	841	457	438	444	917

continued (person)

住宿和餐饮业 Accommodation and Restaurants	金融业 Finance	房地产业 Real Estate Trade	租赁和商务服务业 Tenancy and Business Services	科学研究技术服务地质勘查 Scientific Research, Technical Services, Geologic Perambulation	水利环境和公共设施管理业 Management of Water Conservancy, Environment and Public Establishment	居民服务和其他服务业 Resident Services and Other Services	教育 Education	卫生、社会保障和社会福利 Sanitation Social Security and Social Welfare	文化体育和娱乐业 Culture, Sports and Entertainment	公共管理和社会组织 Public Management and Social Organization
8	584	98	86	127	243	12	9089	1217	89	6748
91	298	6	71	6	287		6042	1376	76	3843
18	238	66	60	106			7104	678	429	6952
51	420	97	99	92	372		8419	1815	202	6117
125	355	10	39	133	47		6398	1812	233	4065
59	238			90			2466	863	1227	2401
114	258	8	15	82	353	968	3635	1377	176	3731
134	219	50	100	56	131		2923	795	99	2663
125	365	136	181	93	737		5340	1771	163	4857
1873	**5121**	**1017**	**902**	**2048**	**6802**	**116**	**49383**	**13600**	**1864**	**48456**
		87	77	24	126		2791	435	61	2192
							1137	39		2029
	125	54			603		1944	407		3837
18	224	15	97	359	298	32	6290	1746	38	4908
278	330		236	129	1036	18	6664	1571	71	4486
162	256	142	42	414	792	6	6489	1770	293	4060
135	327	158	154	159		19	8638	2621	154	5407
44	285	19	27	148	252	11	6088	1094	402	7330
55	263	58	66	153	704		4705	983	139	4040
1467	**4496**	**1324**	**4258**	**2334**	**7043**	**667**	**53126**	**17127**	**2099**	**42467**
	342	82	19	19	69		2039	865	12	2364
	437	146	648	289	1489	14	7525	2754	250	5609
	337		304	213	704	36	5276	1695	91	4162
35	367	109	112	239	174	10	5850	1262	394	4177
	398	294	268	111	1511	409	7194	1868	235	4511
134	363	99	8	81	271		4500	800	143	3187
	377	70	1780	39	456		8086	2401	146	4721
100	335	13	65	438	214		5486	2112	60	4048
128	384	72	45	82	259	5	2427	765	68	3859
1049	**2139**	**309**	**765**	**1067**	**1164**	**23**	**9755**	**4101**	**4739**	**15660**
281	1449	154	640	721	505		4810	1754	535	5751
435	102				312		132	73		2847
333	325	147	61	91	347	23	4797	1071	336	3642
	263	8	64	255			16	1203	3868	3420
977	**3819**	**1274**	**1777**	**1681**	**5006**	**115**	**47189**	**12423**	**1571**	**34091**
25	99	282	58	6	762		4125	1185	102	2744
407	2027	170	860	952	1201	66	11332	3326	930	11418
269	319	249	368	161	1295	14	6868	1335	205	3979
89	376	209	138	155	258	25	7932	2061	127	5469
78	304	151	191	135	261	2	7072	2288	129	5750
109	694	213	162	272	1229	8	9860	2228	78	4731
1762	**3817**	**762**	**1716**	**4276**	**2943**	**118**	**43434**	**14618**	**6038**	**44136**
626	1171	81	461	2346	67	29	3037	3011	3209	6856
130	574	81	358	956	50	13	3583	1515	1395	4465
238	304	138	111	282	455	40	7354	2027	126	4620
165	333	136	45	55	290		5191	1580	167	5227
142	210	77	191	259	300		5315	1270	197	5026

单位：人 18-4 续表 2

市县	Cities and Counties	农林牧渔业 Agriculture, Forestry, Farming of Animals and Fishing	采掘业 Mining	制造业 Manufacturing	电力燃气及水的生产和供应 Production and Spply of Elrctricity Gas and Water	建筑业 Construction	交通运输仓储和邮政业 Traffic, Transport, Storage and Post	信息传输计算机服务软件业 Information Transfer, Computer Services and Software	批发和零售业 Wholesale and Retail Trade
嘉禾县	Jiahe County	566	1851		433	20	271	136	293
临武县	Linwu County	510	2048	313	578		286	61	1058
汝城县	Rucheng County	564		156	565	3	318	26	210
桂东县	Guidong County	258			323		249	53	275
安仁县	Anren County	631		863	454	22	399	30	506
资兴市	Zixing City	972	9815	1232	1244	130	373	98	121
永州市	**Yongzhou City**	**8635**	**2120**	**17179**	**9383**	**2481**	**6400**	**2498**	**7177**
芝山区	Zhishan District	1054	5	3513	1530	1877	1047	39	813
冷水滩区	Lengshuitan District	451	409	3177	1042	109	1433	909	1039
祁阳县	Qiyang County	1378	1245	2883	2419	332	977	938	698
东安县	Dongan County	543		1136	845		690	68	860
双牌县	Shuangpai County	21		1007	503	7	313	79	196
道县	Dao County	560	75	3396	243	8	201	98	632
江永县	Jiangyong County	1123		965	370		354	57	491
宁远县	Ningyuan Couny	67		235	765		342	72	722
蓝山县	Lanshan County	200		137	736	143	149	81	451
新田县	Xintian County	256		480	302		455	45	529
江华县	Jianghua County	2982	386	250	628	5	439	112	746
怀化市	**Huaihua City**	**6619**	**3917**	**6463**	**7946**	**3900**	**8126**	**1699**	**5485**
鹤城区	Hecheng District	464	116	1226	1143	2567	2863	682	1107
中方县	Zhongfang County	293	83	306	36		262	120	60
沅陵县	Yuanling County	934	221	52	1559	8	1354	46	770
辰溪县	Chenxi County	576	2090	2371	156	1161	424	89	538
溆浦县	Xupu County	1150	261	1022	1391	48	365	423	771
会同县	Huitong County	566	129	7	59	5	484	59	234
麻阳县	Mayang County	501	723	189	691		294	28	432
新晃县	Xinhuang County	112		245	615		326	25	247
芷江县	Zhijiang County	261		15	637		340	34	315
靖州县	Jingzhou County	1018		143	94	53	402	42	422
通道县	Tongdao County	412		298	367	7	375	45	133
洪江市	Hongjiang City	332	294	589	1198	51	637	106	456
娄底市	**Loudi City**	**2425**	**15962**	**43085**	**4232**	**7178**	**5754**	**1282**	**6918**
娄星区	Louxing District	584	1022	18372	1061	5374	3388	594	1307
冷水江市	Lengshuijiang City	107	9831	14697	1954	1024	1077	95	2278
涟源市	Lianyuan City	1059	1537	4610	651	535	519	239	913
双峰县	Shuangfrng County	149	2524	119	269		225	134	1312
新化县	Xinhua County	526	1048	5287	297	245	545	220	1108
湘西自治州	**West Hunan A.P**	**2302**	**682**	**6121**	**7962**	**546**	**4339**	**1339**	**4479**
吉首市	Jishou City	181	5	768	1039	275	2326	460	1150
泸溪县	Luxi County	668		1739	1096		391	182	188
凤凰县	Fenghuang County	58	40	196	826	112	253	76	876
花垣县	Huayuan County	308	56	1224	1567		237	189	559
保靖县	Baojing County	219	171	315	538		220	79	492
古丈县	Guzhang County	336		430	324		152	53	189
永顺县	Yongsun County	327	38	762	1198	109	240	222	305
龙山县	Longshan County	205	372	687	1374	50	520	78	720
未列入地区	**Not Classified by Region**		**297**	**686**		**4948**	**76453**	**115**	**1127**

continued (person)

住宿和餐饮业 Accommodation and Restaurants	金融业 Finance	房地产业 Real Estate Trade	租赁和商务服务业 Tenancy and Business Services	科学研究技术服务地质勘查 Scientific Research, Technical Services, Geologic Perambulation	水利环境和公共设施管理业 Management of Water Conservancy, Environment and Public Establishment	居民服务和其他服务业 Resident Services and Other Services	教育 Education	卫生、社会保障和社会福利 Sanitation Social Security and Social Welfare	文化体育和娱乐业 Culture, Sports and Entertainment	公共管理和社会组织 Public Management and Social Organization
62	174	38	237	15	370	18	3095	898	223	3090
63	212	43	110	56	202	18	2857	745	198	2593
90	186	23	123	20	153		3455	529	38	3519
31	78		50	75	47		1659	529	133	2348
31	195	32	3	117	467		4176	1419	255	3038
184	380	113	27	95	542		3712	1095	97	3354
1742	**4078**	**666**	**1804**	**2681**	**3278**	**124**	**48010**	**14570**	**10394**	**53670**
85	947	50	70	596	717	33	6450	2866	1166	7261
607	1052	72	408	603	855	67	5712	1656	1199	7970
266	413	109	488	1054	280		6043	2597	2867	8513
123	286	21	191	40	363		4656	1406	723	3809
54	87	28	31	30	56		1837	368	329	2804
42	269	129	138	32	263		4913	1478	862	4644
23	137	34	69	110	69		2622	577	513	2522
50	278	100	285	83	186	24	4729	752	982	6073
26	150	14	24	56	123		2812	680	701	3577
22	258	58	7	28	283		4269	905	487	2707
444	201	51	93	49	83		3967	1285	565	3790
2365	**4991**	**1086**	**1439**	**1970**	**3770**	**128**	**48570**	**13713**	**2238**	**49326**
691	2300	256	627	912	1581	49	5684	2622	667	7452
39	77	21	18	52			2724	441	17	3351
228	342	125	94	123	262		6258	1057	174	4875
189	226	45	35	74	117		4811	778	184	4948
319	439	409	82	197	578		7079	2236	95	5873
216	277	23	81	31	235	17	3217	622	213	2563
60	187		89	70	286		3004	827	472	3147
138	179		32	50	100	5	2196	758	70	2672
236	185	79	77	88	138		3607	639	50	3899
	276		74	55	93		2904	718	69	2844
117	182	31	64	62	15	17	2187	688	56	2435
132	321	97	166	256	365	40	4899	2327	171	5267
1163	**3409**	**1361**	**3016**	**2420**	**4972**	**153**	**39165**	**11713**	**1166**	**33871**
563	1697	625	1723	1307	1242	131	11514	3704	721	12927
178	534	382	376	370	1116	4				
81	327	124	327	608	768		9570	3223	91	7850
194	400	79	202	38	197		7764	1775	116	6245
147	451	151	388	97	1649	18	10317	3011	238	6849
597	**2745**	**290**	**1007**	**1509**	**2401**	**52**	**28704**	**9520**	**1253**	**30287**
223	1338	52	449	1020	989		5309	2371	569	6571
9	215	45	68	81	162		2898	832	119	2031
61	171	46	96	115	236	39	3391	1006	80	3522
81	184	27	41	83	166		2717	748	82	3295
7	167	14	80	38	67	13	2817	948	83	2870
3	52	8	117	25	56		1591	467	39	1783
113	201	37	96	80	412		5109	1463	70	5461
100	417	61	60	67	313		4872	1685	211	4754
985	**50**	**209**	**886**	**154**			**4006**	**3163**	**15**	**13436**

18-5 各市、州、县城镇集体经济各行业在岗职工年末人数(2003年)

单位：人

市县	Cities and Counties	农林牧渔业 Agriculture, Forestry, Farming of Animals and Fishing	采掘业 Mining	制造业 Manufacturing	电力燃气及水的生产和供应 Production and Spply of Elrctricity Gas and Water	建筑业 Construction	交通运输仓储和邮政业 Traffic, Transport, Storage and Post	信息传输计算机服务软件业 Information Transfer, Computer Services and Software	批发和零售业 Wholesale and Retail Trade
长沙市	**Changsha City**	**34**	**377**	**16640**		**10930**	**1146**	**40**	**3703**
芙蓉区	Hurong District	20		2255		3894	119		585
天心区	Tianxin District			3692		269	53		836
岳麓区	Yuilu District		144	1066		262			119
开福区	Kaifu District			2556		5191	228		425
雨花区	Yufua District		233	3930		302	16	40	679
长沙县	Changsha County			333		102			347
望城县	Wangcheng County	8		2688		6	716		591
宁乡县	Ningxiang County	6		52		304	14		37
浏阳市	Liuyang City			68		600			84
株洲市	**Zhuzhou City**	**783**	**35**	**12687**	**20**	**2527**	**2368**	**15**	**2065**
荷塘区	Hetang District					344			21
芦淞区	Lusong District			164		81			139
石峰区	Shifeng District			137		19			
天元区	Tianyuan District					29			7
株洲县	Zhuzhou County	226			6	448	242		4
攸县	You County	234		2		375			77
茶陵县	Chaling County	276				120	249		89
炎陵县	Yanling County	15		19		102	525		41
醴陵市	Liling City	17	1	2595	14		350		825
湘潭市	**Xiangtan City**	**30**	**100**	**9511**	**70**	**8420**	**2828**	**1**	**3211**
雨湖区	Yuhu District		100	645		1022			43
岳塘区	Yuetang District			519		274	307		115
湘潭县	Xiangtan County			14		2122	331		65
湘乡市	Xiangxiang City	5		1074	70	1807	1553		656
韶山市	Shaoshan City			23		58			92
衡阳市	**Hengyang City**	**1260**	**133**	**14372**		**14020**	**1609**		**6753**
珠晖区	Zhuhui District			223		1584			
雁峰区	Yanfeng District			298		644			78
石鼓区	Shigu District			188		70	5		
蒸湘区	Zhengxiang District			334		1910			
南岳区	Nanyue District			10		162			39
衡阳县	Hengyang County	430		3135		1875	125		2292
衡南县	Hengnan County	450		768		2438	260		1141
衡山县	Hengshan County			1081			143		69
衡东县	Hengdong County		123	826		1380	287		55
祁东县	Qidong County	29		91		1856	126		848
耒阳市	Leiyang City			777		242	484		866
常宁市	Changning City	351		2248		110	179		485
邵阳市	**Shaoyang City**	**78**	**430**	**2866**	**82**	**7527**	**1296**	**93**	**1825**
双清区	Shuangqing District		61	211	24	325	273		391
大祥区	Da xiang District			709		1678	6		109
北塔区	Beita District	9		328		18			17

Employed Staff and Workers in Urban Collective-Owned Units by Sector at the Year-end (2003)

(person)

住宿和餐饮业 Accommodation and Restaurants	金融业 Finance	房地产业 Real Estate Trade	租赁和商务服务业 Tenancy and Business Services	科学研究技术服务地质勘查 Scientific Research, Technical Services, Geologic Perambulation	水利环境和公共设施管理业 Management of Water Conservancy, Environment and Public Establishment	居民服务和其他服务业 Resident Services and Other Services	教育 Education	卫生、社会保障和社会福利 Sanitation Social Security and Social Welfare	文化体育和娱乐业 Culture, Sports and Entertainment	公共管理和社会组织 Public Management and Social Organization
1312	**2006**	**447**	**881**	**22**	**10**	**161**	**651**	**3140**	**89**	**4**
859		31	509	22		36	6	260	84	
35		211	108			50	6	160		
17		26				65	31	89		
401		84	16		10	10	84	162	5	4
	316	39	115					122		
	23	56					143	52		
	370		20				358			
	638		25				23	1039		
	659		88					1256		
357	**2102**	**594**	**705**		**76**	**629**	**29**	**3180**	**27**	**223**
			9					228		159
3							12	69		9
36								151		
								37		
	280							473		17
	305	19						987		
	286	12	16		76			279		
46	170		24					136		
240	611	7	18			184	17	820	27	
277	**1505**	**36**	**191**		**119**	**72**		**1424**	**218**	**18**
41	265		24					233		
	22	12	17		20	12		37		
	578							1013		18
	555		28		68	26				
	85		9		31			119		
564	**3291**	**123**	**390**		**1005**	**309**	**55**	**3666**	**30**	**418**
						6		212		
						10		112		
					4		4	113	8	
	103	17	18					531		
4	49							47	22	300
	704									
	769	15						2032		
	214					18				
	246		21					454		
	486		29		205					85
37	374							165		33
	346		27		296					
121	**3069**	**31**	**732**		**488**	**69**	**7**	**1761**	**14**	**150**
	117		11					29	6	
51	349	14	37			42	7			15
	53							49		10

单位：人 18-5 续表 1

市县	Cities and Counties	农林牧渔业 Agriculture, Forestry, Farming of Animals and Fishing	采掘业 Mining	制造业 Manufacturing	电力燃气及水的生产和供应 Production and Spply of Elrctricity Gas and Water	建筑业 Construction	交通运输仓储和邮政业 Traffic, Transport, Storage and Post	信息传输计算机服务软件业 Information Transfer, Computer Services and Software	批发和零售业 Wholesale and Retail Trade
邵东县	Shaodong County	36	3	148	19	3410	740		230
新邵县	Xinshao County		60	237	39	523	6		301
邵阳县	Shaoyang County			80		266			86
隆回县	Longhui County			38					
洞口县	Dongkou County		306	128		5			116
绥宁县	Shuining County	33		228		108		93	
新宁县	Xinning County			60		280			157
城步县	Chengbu County			126		40			189
武冈市	Wugang City			573		874	271		229
岳阳市	**Yueyang City**	**692**	**250**	**7377**	**148**	**4107**	**1721**		**5405**
岳阳楼区	Yueyanglou District	5	91	585		519	6		
云溪区	Yunxi District			262	33	729	61		34
君山区	Junshan District		62	620					54
岳阳县	Yueyang County			9		104			543
华容县	Huarong County		20	7		107	200		1200
湘阴县	Xiangyin County	275		344		1060	457		197
平江县	Pingjiang County			260	57	835			895
汨罗市	Miluo City	121	7	158	58	25	929		613
临湘市	Linxiang City	17	70	246		502			366
常德市	**Changde City**	**604**		**1781**	**807**	**1959**	**621**		**1520**
武陵区	Wuling District			432		61	48		
鼎城区	Dingchen District	306		886		97	102		35
安乡县	Anxiang County			209		697			400
汉寿县	Hanshou County			79					62
澧县	Li County	298		8		688	398		
临澧县	Linli County				144				66
桃源县	Taoyuan County			33	45	4	29		35
石门县	Shimen County			35	366	396	27		691
津市市	Jinshi City								130
张家界市	**Zhangjiajie City**	**706**	**41**	**772**	**62**	**1446**	**421**		**364**
永定区	Yongding District			279					126
武陵源区	Wulingyuan District								
慈利县	Cili County	586	41	493	62	1446	421		226
桑植县	Sangzhi County	120							12
益阳市	**Yiyang City**	**374**		**5120**	**202**	**4005**	**2469**	**177**	**2042**
资阳区	Ziyang District			815					162
赫山区	Heshan District	14		2720	105	2200	435	167	265
南县	Nan County	325		1161		730	165	10	1221
桃江县	Taojiang County	2		32		854	350		120
安化县	Anhua County			75	97	30	294		81
沅江市	Yuanjiang City	33		317		191	1225		193
郴州市	**Chenzhou City**	**625**	**1400**	**2087**	**110**	**2020**	**886**	**88**	**2159**
北湖区	Beihu District		133	409		569	355	62	275
苏仙区	Suxian District		56	184		366	15	26	193
桂阳县	Guiyang County		594	185					21
宜章县	Yizhang County	149	337	84	109	197			151
永兴县	Yongxing County	327		625		10	472		354

continued (person)

住宿和餐饮业 Accommodation and Restaurants	金融业 Finance	房地产业 Real Estate Trade	租赁和商务服务业 Tenancy and Business Services	科学研究技术服务地质勘查 Scientific Research, Technical Services, Geologic Perambulation	水利环境和公共设施管理业 Management of Water Conservancy, Environment and Public Establishment	居民服务和其他服务业 Resident Services and Other Services	教育 Education	卫生、社会保障和社会福利 Sanitation Social Security and Social Welfare	文化体育和娱乐业 Culture, Sports and Entertainment	公共管理和社会组织 Public Management and Social Organization
2	374		75		353	10		666		
	257	1	7					230		
	274				118					108
	398							219	8	
	341		586					240		
57	174							52		
	258	16			17			235		17
	177		16							
11	297					17		41		
10	**2095**	**29**	**349**	**1152**	**114**	**13**	**134**	**1844**	**70**	**476**
4		29	45	76	69	13	27	272	18	84
				52	45			286		76
	70							21		
	432		37						31	
6	343		39				101			120
	346		32					440		
	357		89					17		
	246		55	1001				575		
	301		31					233		96
12	**3281**	**15**	**562**		**779**	**20**	**74**	**2598**	**123**	**70**
	442	12								
	478		324						38	
	274		42							
	401				323		73	893	10	29
	350	3	56		232			944	49	
	317		12		135	20		610	26	29
12	512		102				1			
	348		26		89					
	159							151		12
319	**898**	**11**	**117**	**44**	**201**		**111**	**1036**		
71	332	4	117	44						
66	32				16					
182	282	7			185		111	1036		0
	252									
14	**3126**	**98**	**167**		**648**		**19**	**2595**	**93**	
8	247		12					461	37	
	670	98	51						32	
6	424		46		460		18	631	24	
	543		34		188			608		
	657		23				1	371		
	585		1					524		
57	**2509**	**3**	**847**	**163**	**18**	**122**	**17**	**1007**		**58**
25	334	3	57	114			17			23
	289		39	49				25		10
	371		16					10		
	213									25
	235		621		18	122		321		

市县	Cities and Counties	农林牧渔业 Agriculture, Forestry, Farming of Animals and Fishing	采掘业 Mining	制造业 Manufacturing	电力燃气及水的生产和供应 Production and Spply of Elrctricity Gas and Water	建筑业 Construction	交通运输仓储和邮政业 Traffic, Transport, Storage and Post	信息传输计算机服务软件业 Information Transfer, Computer Services and Software	批发和零售业 Wholesale and Retail Trade
嘉禾县	Jiahe County	86					29		3
临武县	Linwu County		199	16		67			256
汝城县	Rucheng County			77					
桂东县	Guidong County	63		150		383			53
安仁县	Anren County		81	130	1	428	15		299
资兴市	Zixing City			227					554
永州市	**Yongzhou City**	**839**	**4**	**2868**		**6258**	**388**	**290**	**1265**
芝山区	Zhishan District			883		1044			293
冷水滩区	Lengshuitan District	46	4	257		1034	82		356
祁阳县	Qiyang County			811		311		278	126
东安县	Dongan County	270		327		635			174
双牌县	Shuangpai County	156		79		287			
道县	Dao County			195		617	16		44
江永县	Jiangyong County	56		18		478			
宁远县	Ningyuan Couny	290				420	248		23
蓝山县	Lanshan County			233		703	34	12	
新田县	Xintian County	21		5		367			21
江华县	Jianghua County			60		362	8		228
怀化市	**Huaihua City**	**144**		**2671**	**856**	**4749**	**2425**	**30**	**2624**
鹤城区	Hecheng District			347		1113	273		311
中方县	Zhongfang County								92
沅陵县	Yuanling County			181	446	10	67		139
辰溪县	Chenxi County			294	143	509	254		226
溆浦县	Xupu County			550	165	582	472	30	318
会同县	Huitong County	75				67			45
麻阳县	Mayang County			205		420	242		162
新晃县	Xinhuang County			40		248	197		60
芷江县	Zhijiang County			451	102	668	131		284
靖州县	Jingzhou County			418		129	356		156
通道县	Tongdao County	57				354	221		150
洪江市	Hongjiang City			185		649	212		681
娄底市	**Loudi City**	**46**	**1219**	**7418**	**14**	**1012**	**4563**		**3884**
娄星区	Louxing District		1027	2964		387	875		309
冷水江市	Lengshuijiang City		112	1763		398	1706		532
涟源市	Lianyuan City	46		692	14	36	922		2838
双峰县	Shuangfrng County						359		
新化县	Xinhua County		80	1999		191	701		205
湘西自治州	**West Hunan A.P**	**228**		**560**	**30**	**2765**	**645**		**1801**
吉首市	Jishou City			114		639	272		313
泸溪县	Luxi County			155		450	50		34
凤凰县	Fenghuang County					521			249
花垣县	Huayuan County			31	30	104			213
保靖县	Baojing County			8		377	25		288
古丈县	Guzhang County			32		90	213		312
永顺县	Yongsun County			3		554			300
龙山县	Longshan County	228		217		30	85		92

continued (person)

住宿和餐饮业 Accommodation and Restaurants	金融业 Finance	房地产业 Real Estate Trade	租赁和商务服务业 Tenancy and Business Services	科学研究技术服务地质勘查 Scientific Research, Technical Services, Geologic Perambulation	水利环境和公共设施管理业 Management of Water Conservancy, Environment and Public Establishment	居民服务和其他服务业 Resident Services and Other Services	教育 Education	卫生、社会保障和社会福利 Sanitation Social Security and Social Welfare	文化体育和娱乐业 Culture, Sports and Entertainment	公共管理和社会组织 Public Management and Social Organization
	152		26					221		
	154		27							
	159		17					218		
	134		14							
32	208		31					12		
	260									
95	**2422**	**94**	**141**	**5**			**35**	**340**	**40**	**97**
	348	8							40	
	427		51							
	448	86								20
	229									
	116							152		23
95										24
	117		18							
	241									30
	151		54				35	188		
	135									
	210		18	5						
110	**3184**	**89**	**143**	**45**	**122**	**15**	**10**	**2513**	**54**	**219**
48	469	13	27					381		25
	184		18							
19	371		14					587		
	264				122			593	26	21
	382					14			28	28
	214							231		20
	189		29				10	112		
	184							150		16
	193		42					338		18
38	222		3					121		73
	145			45						18
5	367	76	10			1				
111	**1760**	**41**	**140**	**43**		**36**		**230**	**27**	**32**
70	758		75	14					27	32
17	305	38	20	29		36		7		
24	340									
	357							223		
		3	45							
22	**1365**		**89**		**5**		**21**	**125**		**21**
3	251		39		5		21	13		
	134									
	181		34							
	118							112		
	137		16							
	84									
19	235									
	225									21

18-6 各市、州、县在岗职工工资总额和年平均工资(2003年)

Total Wage Bill and Average Annual Wage of Employed Staff and Workers (2003)

市县名称	City and County	在岗职工工资总额(万元) Total Wages of Staff and Workers on the Job (10 000 yuan)	#国有经济 State-owned Units	#城镇集体经济 Urban Collective Owned Units	在岗职工年平均工资(元) Average Annual Wages of Staff and Workers on the Job (yuan)	#国有经济 State-owned Units	#城镇集体经济 Urban Collective Owned Units	在岗职工年平均工资为上年% Average Annual Wages as Percentage of Preceding Year (%)
长沙市	**Changsha City**	**1019924**	**742005**	**41234**	**16987**	**18639**	**9830**	**118.4**
芙蓉区	Hurong District	219823	160477	8645	17569	19864	10212	118.9
天心区	Tianxin District	107312	76809	5859	15089	16317	10421	113.6
岳麓区	Yuilu District	134171	106509	1615	19581	23511	8827	114.1
开福区	Kaifu District	128965	83342	8216	17302	20133	8819	117.3
雨花区	Yufua District	204858	155158	6370	18127	19956	10855	123.3
长沙县	Changsha County	69975	30470	1111	16720	14128	10455	133.3
望城县	Wangcheng County	38059	27722	3251	12575	13398	6705	118.3
宁乡县	Ningxiang County	57434	48804	2834	14356	14840	13156	122.0
浏阳市	Liuyang City	59327	52714	3333	16481	17208	11998	107.9
株洲市	**Zhuzhou City**	**359855**	**265030**	**26815**	**13453**	**14583**	**9084**	**110.8**
荷塘区	Hetang District	3735	3048	687	12940	14372	8971	116.5
芦淞区	Lusong District	3708	3081	387	13238	15064	8117	108.3
石峰区	Shifeng District	7235	2787	262	12704	14849	7644	97.4
天元区	Tianyuan District	20997	14898	53	14291	16673	7614	107.0
株洲县	Zhuzhou County	13388	10972	1659	10484	11626	8157	113.9
攸县	You County	25263	22773	1909	11434	11850	9073	115.8
茶陵县	Chaling County	19556	17677	1315	11606	10956	8600	117.4
炎陵县	Yanling County	9983	8639	1030	11064	11500	9741	110.6
醴陵市	Liling City	33705	24955	4633	10544	12440	7774	111.4
湘潭市	**Xiangtan City**	**272925**	**223508**	**23330**	**11935**	**12639**	**8661**	**107.0**
雨湖区	Yuhu District	6312	3670	1910	10910	13684	8738	103.6
岳塘区	Yuetang District	4489	3506	843	10972	13175	6781	113.7
湘潭县	Xiangtan County	37514	33213	3904	10866	11159	9343	109.9
湘乡市	Xiangxiang City	44787	31063	4850	10960	11736	8581	102.8
韶山市	Shaoshan City	5768	5312	321	10347	10644	7684	106.2
衡阳市	**Hengyang City**	**433854**	**335094**	**36637**	**10935**	**11535**	**7691**	**111.2**
珠晖区	Zhuhui District	4496	2955	1050	8385	10482	5183	108.0
雁峰区	Yanfeng District	4201	2830	652	9022	11241	5711	104.0
石鼓区	Shigu District	3280	2813	308	11207	11651	8667	104.3
蒸湘区	Zhengxiang District	5141	3261	1695	8661	11280	6347	100.9
南岳区	Nanyue District	7432	6522	706	14707	14239	10333	129.3
衡阳县	Hengyang County	42164	34321	7432	9379	10067	6861	100.2
衡南县	Hengnan County	39252	31626	5102	9561	9757	8885	120.5
衡山县	Hengshan County	15689	13817	974	9807	10378	6389	108.9
衡东县	Hengdong County	21831	18215	2046	9537	10041	6177	107.1
祁东县	Qidong County	33174	29554	3517	11032	10801	8925	108.7
耒阳市	Leiyang City	56317	37822	2675	10750	10650	7528	108.0
常宁市	Changning City	40898	36885	3569	10274	10536	8479	112.8
邵阳市	**Shaoyang City**	**286265**	**249235**	**18455**	**9929**	**10005**	**8913**	**107.9**
双清区	Shuangqing District	40337	27837	1438	7942	6922	9937	109.6
大祥区	Da xiang District	45342	40611	2765	12032	12568	9170	111.5
北塔区	Beita District	3872	3081	520	7316	6610	10805	71.8

市县名称	City and County	在岗职工工资总额 (万元) Total Wages of Staff and Workers on the Job (10 000 yuan)	#国有经济 State-owned Units	#城镇集体经济 Urban Collective Owned Units	在岗职工年平均工资 (元) Average Annual Wages of Staff and Workers on the Job (yuan)	#国有经济 State-owned Units	#城镇集体经济 Urban Collective Owned Units	在岗职工年平均工资为上年% Average Annual Wages as Percentage of Preceding Year (%)
邵东县	Shaodong County	39488	34157	5178	11325	11897	8596	108.9
新邵县	Xinshao County	16460	14962	1087	8349	8770	6343	106.9
邵阳县	Shaoyang County	21993	20575	1015	9944	10032	10863	110.1
隆回县	Longhui County	27003	25513	622	10933	11299	9377	110.5
洞口县	Dongkou County	22934	21570	1309	9249	9402	7617	103.5
绥宁县	Shuining County	13624	11827	713	11390	12022	9446	115.2
新宁县	Xinning County	15412	13595	1086	8364	8241	10422	122.1
城步县	Chengbu County	14132	12236	491	9596	9287	8967	111.9
武冈市	Wugang City	25668	23270	2233	11041	11285	9432	117.5
岳阳市	**Yueyang City**	**341424**	**280519**	**20683**	**11034**	**10990**	**7952**	**107.1**
岳阳楼区	Yueyanglou District	8951	7828	1124	10733	12048	6096	104.7
云溪区	Yunxi District	5564	3792	1654	9597	9747	9855	97.3
君山区	Junshan District	11187	10210	591	8518	8673	7123	104.2
岳阳县	Yueyang County	25526	22701	1066	11354	11657	8358	108.8
华容县	Huarong County	21560	19487	1630	9778	10205	7605	108.0
湘阴县	Xiangyin County	23262	19373	2764	9489	10028	8748	114.1
平江县	Pingjiang County	27657	23956	1995	10272	10708	7958	117.4
汨罗市	Miluo City	36460	33680	2691	7123	7117	7092	84.3
临湘市	Linxiang City	21498	18963	1957	10779	10841	10937	106.1
常德市	**Changde City**	**293503**	**244377**	**15427**	**12526**	**13271**	**9804**	**111.2**
武陵区	Wuling District	11088	8148	1251	12310	13563	12843	106.2
鼎城区	Dingchen District	29533	25269	2104	10310	10845	9304	118.4
安乡县	Anxiang County	21578	15400	1698	9597	10331	9156	108.0
汉寿县	Hanshou County	21219	17718	1980	10655	11238	10527	105.3
澧县	Li County	27545	23482	2182	10335	11439	6523	106.8
临澧县	Linli County	18349	15475	1501	13296	13909	11092	123.3
桃源县	Taoyuan County	27837	26371	1231	12307	12327	11900	115.2
石门县	Shimen County	31149	24931	2397	12691	13243	11713	113.6
津市市	Jinshi City	21705	18709	606	12287	13433	12369	103.1
张家界市	**Zhangjiajie City**	**93365**	**78269**	**5256**	**12283**	**12987**	**8236**	**112.5**
永定区	Yongding District	45106	36120	1281	14985	14277	10231	141.3
武陵源区	Wulingyuan District	4326	3544	74	8744	8571	8540	100.5
慈利县	Cili County	27252	22988	3506	11411	12497	7331	108.0
桑植县	Sangzhi County	16680	15617	395	11536	12008	10255	114.7
益阳市	**Yiyang City**	**231620**	**196911**	**15295**	**8909**	**9054**	**7442**	**110.3**
资阳区	Ziyang District	12871	10951	1291	10435	10863	7429	110.7
赫山区	Heshan District	103484	84636	4731	8395	8400	7637	98.1
南县	Nan County	23542	19471	2960	9465	10426	5741	108.1
桃江县	Taojiang County	26769	22741	2238	9660	9930	8212	105.9
安化县	Anhua County	25859	23954	1906	10397	10399	10363	114.7
沅江市	Yuanjiang City	39095	35158	2169	8331	8362	7475	113.1
郴州市	**Chenzhou City**	**285896**	**248098**	**12718**	**12131**	**12308**	**9050**	**110.5**
北湖区	Beihu District	69702	57719	2162	13305	13596	9268	114.2
苏仙区	Suxian District	37081	31595	1494	13428	13639	10647	110.9
桂阳县	Guiyang County	30121	28212	1437	12286	12235	11953	110.0
宜章县	Yizhang County	21143	19403	943	10047	10409	6890	111.8
永兴县	Yongxing County	22867	20619	2022	10788	11445	6962	114.4

18-6 续表 2 continued

市县名称	City and County	在岗职工工资总额（万元）Total Wages of Staff and Workers on the Job (10 000 yuan)	#国有经济 State-owned Units	#城镇集体经济 Urban Collective Owned Units	在岗职工年平均工资（元）Average Annual Wages of Staff and Workers on the Job (yuan)	#国有经济 State-owned Units	#城镇集体经济 Urban Collective Owned Units	在岗职工年平均工资为上年% Average Annual Wages as Percentage of Preceding Year (%)
嘉禾县	Jiahe County	14743	14064	535	11676	11737	10359	114.0
临武县	Linwu County	15052	14554	498	12065	12377	6950	115.9
汝城县	Rucheng County	12877	12188	531	12110	12195	11419	119.7
桂东县	Guidong County	7602	6750	543	10246	10987	6856	113.7
安仁县	Anren County	15422	14199	1032	11023	11257	8315	114.6
资兴市	Zixing City	39286	28795	1521	12370	12125	13694	109.4
永州市	**Yongzhou City**	**236079**	**203445**	**11197**	**10290**	**10301**	**7533**	**114.0**
芝山区	Zhishan District	35323	32713	1278	10307	10957	4898	123.9
冷水滩区	Lengshuitan District	49366	33506	1888	12529	11577	8769	128.7
祁阳县	Qiyang County	40074	34344	1706	10089	10274	9493	121.9
东安县	Dongan County	20048	18367	1479	11159	11400	9043	112.3
双牌县	Shuangpai County	8454	8043	411	10248	10809	5085	120.2
道县	Dao County	16898	15823	649	8735	8727	6624	114.1
江永县	Jiangyong County	10339	9572	720	9541	9606	8809	104.0
宁远县	Ningyuan Couny	18142	17087	816	9941	10304	6520	113.8
蓝山县	Lanshan County	8904	7743	918	8035	8215	6686	113.6
新田县	Xintian County	12032	11162	493	9581	9721	8886	125.8
江华县	Jianghua County	16499	15085	839	9302	9372	9484	105.3
怀化市	**Huaihua City**	**239138**	**189050**	**17595**	**10584**	**10821**	**8852**	**112.0**
鹤城区	Hecheng District	57800	45894	2962	13352	14143	10095	138.6
中方县	Zhongfang County	9255	7914	293	10416	10049	9969	108.9
沅陵县	Yuanling County	28891	19785	2508	11494	10714	13723	116.7
辰溪县	Chenxi County	19633	16622	1652	7999	8172	6629	106.0
溆浦县	Xupu County	25943	19649	1980	8775	8644	7618	109.2
会同县	Huitong County	12691	9662	713	9793	10695	10923	109.5
麻阳县	Mayang County	11979	10962	862	9484	9970	6257	117.7
新晃县	Xinhuang County	10410	9207	881	11663	11819	9668	114.4
芷江县	Zhijiang County	16827	12604	2165	11267	11867	9781	108.7
靖州县	Jingzhou County	11842	9247	1424	9882	10008	9337	104.2
通道县	Tongdao County	9317	8303	834	10603	11028	8323	113.8
洪江市	Hongjiang City	24550	19201	1321	9909	10894	6462	114.9
娄底市	**Loudi City**	**244123**	**216396**	**15475**	**10999**	**11519**	**7480**	**110.0**
娄星区	Louxing District	95306	85413	5460	11256	12351	9013	115.2
冷水江市	Lengshuijiang City	55067	46163	4611	10019	10187	9070	109.0
涟源市	Lianyuan City	37116	33363	2345	9445	10192	4756	105.6
双峰县	Shuangfrng County	23776	20847	810	9148	9673	8855	107.8
新化县	Xinhua County	32858	30610	2249	9043	9377	6087	107.2
湘西自治州	**West Hunan A.P**	**132703**	**118105**	**7210**	**10875**	**11050**	**9108**	**110.8**
吉首市	Jishou City	33160	28247	1414	10848	11327	8715	107.5
泸溪县	Luxi County	12063	11344	703	10531	10684	8529	112.6
凤凰县	Fenghuang County	14302	12949	782	11144	11402	7935	110.1
花垣县	Huayuan County	16157	12591	707	11046	10699	10033	116.5
保靖县	Baojing County	11419	10562	832	10625	10876	8339	111.0
古丈县	Guzhang County	7287	6412	846	11185	11237	10780	107.2
永顺县	Yongsun County	19546	18108	1192	11179	11211	10690	113.9
龙山县	Longshan County	18770	17892	732	10546	10759	8322	109.9
未列入地区	**Not Classified by Region**	179268	179268		**16518**	**16518**		**105.1**

18-7 离开本单位仍保留劳动关系的职工生活费和年平均生活费(2003年)

Living Income and Annual Average Living Income of Staff and Workers Left-Self Units and Remind Labor Relations (2003)

市县名称	City and County	离开本单位仍保留劳动关系的职工生活费 Living Income of Staff and Workers Left-Self Units and Remind Labor Relations			年平均生活费 Annual Average Living Income		
		合计 (万元) Total (10 000 yuan)	#国有经济 State-owned Units	城镇集体经济 Urban Collective Owned Units	合计 (元) Total (yuan)	#国有经济 State-owned Units	城镇集体经济 Urban Collective Owned Units
长沙市	**Changsha City**	**61629**	**41640**	**7547**	**3799**	**4492**	**1842**
芙蓉区	Hurong District	12896	8418	1783	4253	4927	2327
天心区	Tianxin District	7584	5037	1440	2770	3576	1372
岳麓区	Yuilu District	7368	4034	237	4580	4615	1278
开福区	Kaifu District	11195	6929	1483	3327	4097	1711
雨花区	Yufua District	13607	9389	1601	4550	5022	2799
长沙县	Changsha County	910	785	95	3171	2963	5086
望城县	Wangcheng County	1893	1086	746	2559	4052	1764
宁乡县	Ningxiang County	3478	3322	106	3235	3936	619
浏阳市	Liuyang City	2698	2640	56	6986	7733	1254
株洲市	**Zhuzhou City**	**30265**	**20421**	**2364**	**3001**	**3252**	**1211**
荷塘区	Hetang District	328	284	44	7159	8187	3946
芦淞区	Lusong District	116	37	63	2246	7176	1725
石峰区	Shifeng District	279	3	107	3899	1333	3340
天元区	Tianyuan District	572	415	7	4065	7687	1458
株洲县	Zhuzhou County	348	325	23	2986	3585	900
攸县	You County	2302	2226	75	3301	3426	2124
茶陵县	Chaling County	1655	1604	51	1850	1913	900
炎陵县	Yanling County	552	503	49	3009	3283	1633
醴陵市	Liling City	2139	1526	225	1268	1959	376
湘潭市	**Xiangtan City**	**22789**	**18848**	**1877**	**2471**	**2947**	**873**
雨湖区	Yuhu District	38	31	3	2000	4394	739
岳塘区	Yuetang District	163	142	21	2027	2573	943
湘潭县	Xiangtan County	2053	1986	37	3258	4494	232
湘乡市	Xiangxiang City	2453	1196	346	3731	3343	2967
韶山市	Shaoshan City	316	307	8	2737	3212	636
衡阳市	**Hengyang City**	**24903**	**17558**	**1825**	**1523**	**1617**	**537**
珠晖区	Zhuhui District	106	100	4	3487	4784	923
雁峰区	Yanfeng District	156	121	35	2643	3083	773
石鼓区	Shigu District	86	16	50	699	2104	640
蒸湘区	Zhengxiang District	58	21	37	1446	1247	1593
南岳区	Nanyue District	109	107	2	5150	5090	1500
衡阳县	Hengyang County	719	512	207	814	960	591
衡南县	Hengnan County	1001	840	30	1108	1510	126
衡山县	Hengshan County	892	742	60	1315	2211	439
衡东县	Hengdong County	655	568	84	803	1201	252
祁东县	Qidong County	1328	1099	229	1289	1680	609
耒阳市	Leiyang City	3167	1403	98	2280	1991	670
常宁市	Changning City	2085	1929	142	1211	1627	288

市县名称	City and County	离开本单位仍保留劳动关系的职工生活费 Living Income of Staff and Workers Left-Self Units and Remind Labor Relations			年平均生活费 Annual Average Living Income		
		合计 (万元) Total (10 000 yuan)	#国有经济 State- owned Units	城镇集体经济 Urban Collective Owned Units	合计 (元) Total (yuan)	#国有经济 State- owned Units	城镇集体经济 Urban Collective Owned Units
邵阳市	**Shaoyang City**	**17899**	**14833**	**1398**	**1338**	**1657**	**444**
双清区	Shuangqing District	6339	5021	363	1362	1532	634
大祥区	Da xiang District	3011	2319	372	1990	1986	1521
北塔区	Beita District	536	443	90	1253	1944	450
邵东县	Shaodong County	1232	1119	113	1156	1663	287
新邵县	Xinshao County	535	488	33	634	1050	99
邵阳县	Shaoyang County	926	654	165	1511	2561	604
隆回县	Longhui County	933	909	5	1929	1913	2000
洞口县	Dongkou County	1372	1324	48	1102	1706	102
绥宁县	Shuining County	997	767	91	3117	3151	3820
新宁县	Xinning County	416	374	2	417	706	7
城步县	Chengbu County	326	210	46	814	649	681
武冈市	Wugang City	1277	1206	72	1614	2232	335
岳阳市	**Yueyang City**	**20070**	**16363**	**1377**	**2507**	**2793**	**1041**
岳阳楼区	Yueyanglou District	127	119	9	2683	5126	351
云溪区	Yunxi District	223	159	64	2646	2630	2686
君山区	Junshan District	482	461	9	3735	3943	1071
岳阳县	Yueyang County	1453	1361	83	2144	2439	719
华容县	Huarong County	1097	951	134	1848	2093	1055
湘阴县	Xiangyin County	715	594	94	700	1225	332
平江县	Pingjiang County	1014	878	89	1260	1707	439
汨罗市	Miluo City	1345	1183	155	1951	2361	839
临湘市	Linxiang City	842	779	55	1293	1518	415
常德市	**Changde City**	**18707**	**15845**	**768**	**4347**	**5292**	**953**
武陵区	Wuling District	645	570	18	6598	11463	958
鼎城区	Dingchen District	1457	1136	237	2338	3857	869
安乡县	Anxiang County	1078	1044	20	1838	3238	88
汉寿县	Hanshou County	1725	1532	193	4481	6763	1217
澧县	Li County	1102	1043	23	1643	1714	553
临澧县	Linli County	1318	1150	123	6329	6422	6955
桃源县	Taoyuan County	1184	1059	52	2498	2731	1205
石门县	Shimen County	1584	1170	45	5951	5605	9489
津市市	Jinshi City	2058	1982	35	7537	7719	5915
张家界市	**Zhangjiajie City**	**3711**	**3340**	**244**	**3024**	**3691**	**903**
永定区	Yongding District	1443	1185	190	2571	2923	1309
武陵源区	Wulingyuan District	61	58		4087	4455	
慈利县	Cili County	1483	1414	48	3284	4347	409
桑植县	Sangzhi County	724	683	6	3912	4453	11600
益阳市	**Yiyang City**	**14865**	**12949**	**1287**	**1264**	**1562**	**447**
资阳区	Ziyang District	338	274	64	322	454	143
赫山区	Heshan District	5964	5380	146	1460	1672	342
南县	Nan County	1162	885	259	821	946	562
桃江县	Taojiang County	2394	1985	338	1386	1646	748
安化县	Anhua County	1348	1018	330	1138	1416	707
沅江市	Yuanjiang City	3659	3407	150	1588	2117	238
郴州市	**Chenzhou City**	**16319**	**14057**	**879**	**2645**	**3207**	**786**
北湖区	Beihu District	5753	4916	369	2823	3571	1100
苏仙区	Suxian District	2465	2107	186	3122	3522	2017
桂阳县	Guiyang County	1067	937	24	4631	4497	3414

市县名称	City and County	离开本单位仍保留劳动关系的职工生活费 Living Income of Staff and Workers Left-Self Units and Remind Labor Relations			年平均生活费 Annual Average Living Income		
		合计 (万元) Total (10 000 yuan)	#国有经济 State- owned Units	城镇集体经济 Urban Collective Owned Units	合计 (元) Total (yuan)	#国有经济 State- owned Units	城镇集体经济 Urban Collective Owned Units
宜章县	Yizhang County	1064	828	134	2355	3360	798
永兴县	Yongxing County	517	482	11	1082	1483	77
嘉禾县	Jiahe County	434	390	6	3121	3586	909
临武县	Linwu County	747	715	32	2860	3583	518
汝城县	Rucheng County	1145	1090	42	2894	3119	1082
桂东县	Guidong County	198	164	17	1337	1939	502
安仁县	Anren County	589	557	25	1100	1691	124
资兴市	Zixing City	2340	1871	33	3432	3503	1159
永州市	**Yongzhou City**	**16212**	**13552**	**1034**	**2382**	**2639**	**976**
芝山区	Zhishan District	2285	2083	10	1895	2138	48
冷水滩区	Lengshuitan District	4770	3432	371	2221	2291	1635
祁阳县	Qiyang County	2792	2257	209	2702	2877	1431
东安县	Dongan County	1381	1190	181	2818	4237	881
双牌县	Shuangpai County	721	672	49	2407	3118	582
道县	Dao County	624	614	10	981	1171	102
江永县	Jiangyong County	515	511	4	3239	3230	5000
宁远县	Ningyuan Couny	476	457	20	3458	4128	723
蓝山县	Lanshan County	991	963	25	5758	5913	2744
新田县	Xintian County	682	584	7	4504	4632	9125
江华县	Jianghua County	975	789	148	2742	2822	2603
怀化市	**Huaihua City**	**11862**	**9569**	**606**	**1798**	**2250**	**360**
鹤城区	Hecheng District	3463	2896	180	2776	2964	1575
中方县	Zhongfang County	244	232		1714	1992	
沅陵县	Yuanling County	1510	1237	59	1520	2073	162
辰溪县	Chenxi County	1177	932	142	1627	2129	592
溆浦县	Xupu County	1484	834	49	1500	1200	210
会同县	Huitong County	606	391	5	2712	3308	97
麻阳县	Mayang County	873	847	7	3030	3682	143
新晃县	Xinhuang County	468	437	25	2286	3537	369
芷江县	Zhijiang County	416	379	17	2838	5370	275
靖州县	Jingzhou County	329	277	13	2007	3422	185
通道县	Tongdao County	244	169	74	4101	5235	3008
洪江市	Hongjiang City	1048	938	35	743	768	90
娄底市	**Loudi City**	**18354**	**15917**	**1407**	**2617**	**2886**	**1195**
娄星区	Louxing District	8079	7277	359	2780	3216	1460
冷水江市	Lengshuijiang City	4421	3451	227	3109	3266	1564
涟源市	Lianyuan City	2099	1576	444	1633	1760	1288
双峰县	Shuangfrng County	2150	2124	261	4212	4208	4500
新化县	Xinhua County	1605	1489	116	1231	1627	299
湘西自治州	**West Hunan A.P**	**6845**	**6068**	**445**	**2301**	**2620**	**879**
吉首市	Jishou City	2233	1767	256	3542	3618	2572
泸溪县	Luxi County	380	378		777	907	
凤凰县	Fenghuang County	378	347	28	1991	3418	410
花垣县	Huayuan County	375	368		3197	3562	
保靖县	Baojing County	744	725	17	2243	2348	735
古丈县	Guzhang County	281	278	0	1403	1522	12
永顺县	Yongsun County	1150	1064	69	3627	4217	1179
龙山县	Longshan County	1303	1141	74	1865	2469	452
未列入地区	**Not Classified by Region**	**9784**	**9784**		**9000**	**9000**	

18-8 各市、州、县生产总值(2003年)

Gross Domestic Products (2003)

市县	Cities and Counties	生产总值(万元) GDP (10 000 yuan)	第一产业 Primary Industry	第二产业 Secondary Industry	#工业 Industry	第三产业 Tertiary Industry	GDP为上年% Index (preceding year=100)	人均GDP(元) Per Capita GDP (yuan)
长沙市	**Changsha City**	**9294858**	**832886**	**3936734**	**2682806**	**4525238**	**114.0**	**14810**
长沙市区	Urban District	5523787	87064	2112716	1336513	3324007	114.5	24132
长沙县	Changsha County	1254233	193905	732061	610628	328267	115.9	16291
望城县	Wangcheng County	669362	132123	304719	190581	232520	112.2	9870
宁乡县	Ningxiang County	838684	218111	329446	220490	291127	112.0	6795
浏阳市	Liuyang City	1008792	201683	457792	324595	349317	112.3	7732
株洲市	**Zhuzhou City**	**3830868**	**496005**	**1877981**	**1577713**	**1456882**	**111.1**	**10707**
株洲市区	Urban District	1890642	44537	1044033	891109	802072	111.8	21509
株洲县	Zhuzhou County	300381	70351	115091	73170	114939	110.3	6994
攸县	You County	530547	137757	191529	146071	201261	110.3	7811
茶陵县	Chaling County	255481	87955	86764	69474	80762	109.3	5188
炎陵县	Yanling County	101326	25994	30440	23076	44892	110.3	6148
醴陵市	Liling City	752491	129411	410124	374813	212956	110.9	8066
湘潭市	**Xiangtan City**	**2676868**	**369788**	**1086831**	**859818**	**1220249**	**111.2**	**10056**
湘潭市区	Urban District	1498863	29079	719328	584492	750456	111.6	21209
湘潭县	Xiangtan County	565529	185839	133219	101961	246471	110.6	5527
湘乡市	Xiangxiang City	521574	141486	202430	149109	177658	110.8	6169
韶山市	Shaoshan City	90902	13384	31854	24256	45664	110.8	10509
衡阳市	**Hengyang City**	**4454628**	**1051355**	**1573436**	**1304750**	**1829837**	**110.1**	**6754**
衡阳市区	Urban District	1262746	47606	470085	303239	745055	111.5	15492
衡阳县	Hengyang County	565939	206929	186824	154232	172186	109.7	5459
衡南县	Hengnan County	576825	210423	202042	170116	164360	109.0	6145
衡山县	Hengshan County	230772	67279	74460	52194	89033	109.7	6105
衡东县	Hengdong County	361582	105848	101670	73368	154064	110.1	5862
祁东县	Qidong County	511780	140199	180907	147838	190674	109.4	6032
耒阳市	Leiyang City	584173	150641	179682	145175	253850	111.5	5068
常宁市	Changning City	476910	118377	200784	153703	157749	109.6	5894
邵阳市	**Shaoyang City**	**2850856**	**852893**	**824401**	**626174**	**1173562**	**109.3**	**4338**
双清区	Shuangqing District	91509	12993	35439	31717	43077	113.4	3423
大祥区	Daxiang District	82040	13880	34515	21276	33645	111.6	2692
北塔区	Beita District	31019	8266	14831	12276	7922	112.2	3728
邵东县	Shaodong County	774808	131314	273412	209037	370082	109.4	7410
新邵县	Xinshao County	247903	68523	84673	47973	94707	109.7	3824
邵阳县	Shaoyang County	219935	84125	41242	30650	94568	109.0	2633
隆回县	Longhui County	313433	99092	89858	41181	124483	107.1	3238
洞口县	Dongkou County	358578	142623	67619	49585	148336	109.6	5040
绥宁县	Shuining County	184519	72761	53355	46343	58403	109.4	5975
新宁县	Xinning County	167391	57337	30823	21552	79231	110.0	3259
城步县	Chengbu County	88613	26683	34642	29873	27288	112.2	3940
武冈市	Wugang City	260198	121553	36942	24416	101703	108.0	3934

注:总量指标按当年价格计算,指数按可比价格计算。

Aggregate data are calculated at current prices, while indices are calculated at comparable prices.

市县	Cities and Counties	生产总值 (万元) GDP (10 000 yuan)	第一产业 Primary Industry	第二产业 Secondary Industry	#工业 Industry	第三产业 Tertiary Industry	GDP 为上年% Index (preceding year=100)	人均GDP (元) Per Capita GDP (yuan)
岳阳市	**Yueyang City**	**4951877**	**1046632**	**2108831**	**1816632**	**1796414**	**111.0**	**9860**
岳阳楼区	Yueyanglou District	338411	23473	105327	78937	209611	112.1	11280
云溪区	Yunxi District	122214	28465	47233	38493	46516	111.6	11551
君山区	Junshan District	167146	72056	48339	39617	46751	110.8	7315
岳阳县	Yueyang County	458974	160824	142510	109840	155640	111.0	6524
华容县	Huarong County	501007	210811	150612	124679	139584	110.6	7288
湘阴县	Xiangyin County	504725	173406	200597	165895	130722	110.9	7590
平江县	Pingjiang County	399039	124572	132657	98796	141810	110.5	4642
汨罗市	Miluo City	468100	130360	214641	183588	123099	111.8	7624
临湘市	Linxiang City	311581	77335	126047	110278	108199	110.8	6803
常德市	**Changde City**	**4865833**	**1157149**	**1976756**	**1600695**	**1731928**	**111.3**	**9229**
武陵区	Wuling District	1775707	33144	1160039	994640	582524	116.3	28687
鼎城区	Dingchen District	563773	189240	145290	90259	229243	109.3	6906
安乡县	Anxiang County	330340	142921	78903	65905	108516	110.7	6687
汉寿县	Hanshou County	354536	121510	81551	61221	151475	111.5	5126
澧 县	Li County	557874	177666	142991	106026	237217	110.5	7001
临澧县	Linli County	309077	96501	112855	102874	99721	107.2	8322
桃源县	Taoyuan County	573320	217997	145998	89703	209325	107.1	7258
石门县	Shimen County	386150	118871	126944	97384	140335	111.8	6323
津市市	Jinshi City	180745	46594	73442	64262	60709	110.7	7063
张家界市	**Zhangjiajie City**	**819087**	**154551**	**205923**	**133223**	**458613**	**110.3**	**5708**
永定区	Yongding District	183476	49161	43370	32052	90945	111.0	4522
武陵源区	Wulingyuan District	74601	4962	7469	1797	62170	99.6	16078
慈利县	Cili County	231868	72401	64746	46554	94721	109.3	3875
桑植县	Sangzhi County	93683	29607	23180	18426	40896	109.9	2474
益阳市	**Yiyang City**	**2396731**	**577990**	**696894**	**523809**	**1121847**	**109.4**	**5840**
资阳区	Ziyang District	182889	43590	56158	43430	83141	109.6	4926
赫山区	Heshan District	317864	85068	92109	60904	140687	109.6	4384
南县	Nan County	282665	113532	83852	63458	85281	109.5	4685
桃江县	Taojiang County	263406	80924	90841	72196	91641	109.6	3550
安化县	Anhua County	260956	94620	72290	60456	94046	108.6	3030
沅江市	Yuanjiang City	403305	131303	125962	106251	146040	110.2	6149
郴州市	**Chenzhou City**	**3242609**	**642645**	**1257165**	**1047407**	**1342799**	**111.3**	**7597**
北湖区	Beihu District	545516	33504	274685	229208	237327	113.0	16431
苏仙区	Suxian District	335116	45344	143604	127259	146168	112.3	9477
桂阳县	Guiyang County	441863	127373	141395	118353	173095	111.3	6128
宜章县	Yizhang County	306130	64659	101856	83624	139615	112.0	5823
永兴县	Yongxing County	362060	77200	138138	117387	146722	113.0	6332
嘉禾县	Jiahe County	210119	53467	68210	58806	88442	111.9	7470
临武县	Linwu County	218750	46178	100812	88351	71760	111.5	7353
汝城县	Rucheng County	167485	44285	59073	47929	64127	112.1	5095
桂东县	Guidong County	55546	15702	16296	10972	23548	110.7	3502
安仁县	Anren County	199258	65802	48853	38198	84603	110.2	5704
资兴市	Zixing City	390300	69590	199370	159613	121340	114.5	11251

市县	Cities and Counties	生产总值 (万元) GDP (10 000 yuan)	第一产业 Primary Industry	第二产业 Secondary Industry	#工业 Industry	第三产业 Tertiary Industry	GDP 为上年% Index (preceding year=100)	人均GDP (元) Per Capita GDP (yuan)
永州市	**Yongzhou City**	**2803566**	**853117**	**756971**	**572388**	**1193478**	**110.6**	**5607**
芝山区	Zhishan District	349625	104617	106505	89598	138503	110.7	6034
冷水滩区	Lengshuitan District	443225	76885	213947	184038	152393	115.9	9224
祁阳县	Qiyang County	466223	143847	149956	102498	172420	111.0	4935
东安县	Dongan County	323702	107658	96304	63299	119740	110.8	6017
双牌县	Shuangpai County	82890	25123	31986	24077	25781	110.4	5717
道县	Dao County	300957	110897	71871	55163	118189	109.3	6200
江永县	Jiangyong County	129092	57990	21354	15732	49748	109.5	5189
宁远县	Ningyuan County	208115	80505	45667	28717	81943	109.0	2944
蓝山县	Lanshan County	134389	41704	40534	31064	52151	110.7	4072
新田县	Xintian County	111543	50683	22626	16452	38234	109.2	3577
江华县	Jianghua County	130784	57864	29144	24137	43776	109.6	3333
怀化市	**Huaihua City**	**2496138**	**567534**	**709601**	**549889**	**1219003**	**109.8**	**5621**
鹤城区	Hecheng District	170343	23099	61596	60078	85648	109.9	5765
中方县	Zhongfang County	113105	40577	23866	16400	48662	110.1	4985
沅陵县	Yuanling County	348620	61301	213128	197525	74191	112.2	6226
辰溪县	Chenxi County	141674	43148	40104	32339	58422	109.6	2972
溆浦县	Xupu County	253705	115602	63463	43536	74640	108.2	3529
会同县	Huitong County	140590	44956	37272	30080	58362	109.5	4843
麻阳县	Mayang County	98544	40113	21776	15454	36655	109.5	2927
新晃县	Xinhuang County	82417	22380	27266	25334	32771	109.3	3286
芷江县	Zhijiang County	149885	50208	42511	33240	57166	110.4	4247
靖州县	Jingzhou County	142333	44324	30762	27158	67247	109.5	5608
通道县	Tongdao County	57654	24655	11702	10170	21297	108.0	2854
洪江市	Hongjiang City	158561	58744	41860	25491	57957	109.5	3934
娄底市	**Loudi City**	**2112509**	**388584**	**890554**	**682618**	**833371**	**109.0**	**5634**
娄星区	Louxing District	544442	29485	284116	224316	230841	110.0	13597
双峰县	Lengshuijiang City	373229	142795	115772	76875	114662	106.3	4482
新化县	Lianyuan City	317497	110176	67065	48493	140256	107.6	2667
冷水江市	Shuangfrng County	387317	18515	223335	208878	145467	113.4	11405
涟源市	Xinhua County	335600	89105	123470	92679	123025	109.1	3402
湘西自治州	**West Hunan A.P**	**826378**	**223739**	**304768**	**216790**	**297871**	**108.1**	**3393**
吉首市	Jishou City	210694	25640	94769	64422	90285	107.5	7123
泸溪县	Luxi County	77610	23577	29984	22860	24049	111.5	2940
凤凰县	Fenghuang County	98637	23619	24588	16568	50430	107.8	2984
花垣县	Huayuan County	73357	20696	32037	29207	20624	112.6	2765
保靖县	Baojing County	78078	22249	34344	17936	21485	112.6	2945
古丈县	Guzhang County	33040	11593	8396	4886	13051	108.8	2767
永顺县	Yongsun County	110271	45878	28411	17382	35982	108.0	2436
龙山县	Longshan County	144691	50487	52239	43529	41965	103.3	3139

18-9 各市、州、县耕地面积及播种面积(2003年)

Cultivated Area and Sown Area (2003)

单位：千公顷 (1 000 hectares)

市县名称	City and County	耕地面积 Cultivated Area	水田 Paddy Fields	旱地 Dry Fields	农作物播种面积 Total Sown Area	#粮食作物 Grain Crops
长沙市	**Changsha City**	**283.57**	**253.92**	**29.65**	**570.11**	**340.16**
芙蓉区	Furong District	0.25	0.01	0.24	3.27	0.03
天心区	Tianxin District	1.06	0.81	0.25	2.18	0.56
岳麓区	Yuelu District	2.39	1.82	0.56	5.21	0.70
开福区	Kaifu District	4.50	4.19	0.30	10.03	3.92
雨花区	Yuhua District	2.36	1.78	0.59	4.54	0.19
长沙县	Changsha County	57.69	54.20	3.49	120.28	74.52
望城县	Wangcheng County	48.33	43.87	4.46	109.83	66.26
宁乡县	Ningxiang County	92.54	79.35	13.18	171.83	113.93
浏阳市	Liuyang City	74.45	67.88	6.57	142.94	80.05
株洲市	**Zhuzhou City**	**203.59**	**167.49**	**36.09**	**329.40**	**231.50**
荷塘区	Hetang District	4.24	3.45	0.79	6.96	4.71
芦淞区	Lousong District	1.23	0.93	0.30	1.50	0.59
石峰区	Shifeng District	4.42	3.49	0.93	7.66	3.32
天元区	Tianyuan District	4.16	3.44	0.73	7.06	4.82
株洲县	Zhuzhou County	31.90	27.77	4.13	53.47	40.31
攸县	You County	53.68	42.26	11.42	89.10	59.07
茶陵县	Chaling County	37.22	29.85	7.37	61.06	45.68
炎陵县	Yanling County	14.09	12.18	1.90	20.38	15.36
醴陵市	Liling City	52.65	44.12	8.52	82.21	57.64
湘潭市	**Xiangtan City**	**141.03**	**125.82**	**15.20**	**274.85**	**189.72**
雨湖区	Yuhu District	1.65	1.28	0.37	3.26	1.35
岳塘区	Yuetang District	4.37	3.42	0.95	7.19	3.57
湘潭县	Xiangtan County	76.04	71.36	4.67	138.95	106.54
湘乡市	Xiangxiang City	53.06	44.47	8.59	113.25	69.60
韶山市	Shaoshan City	5.91	5.28	0.63	12.20	8.66
衡阳市	**Hengyang City**	**371.08**	**303.61**	**67.47**	**795.03**	**461.75**
珠晖区	Zhuhui District	5.97	4.36	1.60	11.37	3.10
雁峰区	Yanfeng District	1.99	1.57	0.42	2.26	1.49
石鼓区	Shigu District	3.17	2.70	0.47	4.46	3.14
蒸湘区	Zhengxinag District	3.35	3.02	0.33	5.98	3.47
南岳区	Nanyue District	1.88	1.59	0.29	3.90	1.90
衡阳县	Hengyang County	65.76	58.07	7.69	165.17	87.35
衡南县	Hengnan County	59.62	54.35	5.26	149.35	88.71
衡山县	Hengshan County	23.55	19.58	3.98	40.58	27.00
衡东县	Hengdong County	43.19	34.87	8.32	96.03	56.53
祁东县	Qidong County	54.43	40.51	13.92	88.88	51.48
耒阳市	Leiyang City	61.15	43.59	17.56	130.58	75.75
常宁市	Changning City	47.01	39.39	7.62	96.47	61.83
邵阳市	**Shaoyang City**	**400.43**	**289.05**	**111.38**	**716.55**	**470.14**
双清区	Shuangqing District	4.68	3.21	1.47	6.65	4.11
大祥区	Daxiang District	8.07	5.16	2.91	13.05	8.61
北塔区	Beita District	2.69	1.79	0.90	4.86	2.68
邵东县	Shaodong County	56.70	35.91	20.78	91.91	58.83

单位：千公顷　　18 - 9 续表 1　continued　　(1 000 hectares)

市县名称	City and County	耕地面积 Cultivated Area	水田 Paddy Fields	旱地 Dry Fields	农作物播种面积 Total Sown Area	#粮食作物 Grain Crops
新邵县	Xinshao County	36.86	25.31	11.55	62.38	46.55
邵阳县	Shaoyang County	60.99	41.05	19.93	94.41	61.61
隆回县	Longhui County	61.34	44.65	16.69	112.28	67.73
洞口县	Dongkou County	49.71	38.30	11.41	105.26	66.52
绥宁县	Suining County	22.09	20.16	1.93	39.91	21.54
新宁县	Xinning County	38.17	26.96	11.21	72.05	50.86
城步县	Chengbu County	15.13	11.83	3.30	26.33	17.25
武冈市	Wugang City	44.00	34.71	9.29	87.46	63.85
岳阳市	**Yueyang City**	**322.78**	**231.06**	**91.72**	**713.12**	**381.65**
岳阳楼区	Yueyanglou District	3.44	1.15	2.28	5.79	2.54
云溪区	Yunxi District	8.67	4.73	3.94	13.81	6.11
君山区	Junshan District	25.90	13.15	12.75	49.62	16.82
岳阳县	Yueyang County	47.03	28.78	18.25	114.32	66.01
华容县	Huarong County	67.30	42.50	24.81	132.61	46.37
湘阴县	Xiangyin County	38.75	35.07	3.67	115.16	66.20
平江县	Pingjiang County	53.94	44.77	9.17	106.39	70.37
汨罗市	Miluo City	43.73	35.75	7.98	100.75	65.79
临湘市	Linxiang City	34.02	25.16	8.86	74.67	41.44
常德市	**Changde City**	**461.22**	**343.78**	**117.45**	**965.04**	**475.61**
武陵区	Wuling District	9.23	7.80	1.43	18.16	6.85
鼎城区	Dingcheng District	82.34	64.83	17.51	177.08	96.21
安乡县	Anxiang County	45.65	30.92	14.73	79.83	23.86
汉寿县	Hanshou County	57.84	45.72	12.13	125.13	66.19
澧县	Li County	71.00	49.85	21.15	145.88	64.05
临澧县	Linli County	40.69	30.91	9.78	73.16	37.10
桃源县	Taoyuan County	92.33	69.19	23.14	203.78	102.14
石门县	Shimen County	43.93	32.86	11.07	103.18	60.62
津市市	Jinshi City	18.21	11.71	6.50	38.84	18.59
张家界市	**Zhangjiajie City**	**106.00**	**68.15**	**37.85**	**212.14**	**123.87**
永定区	Yongding District	31.90	18.88	13.01	58.57	29.88
武陵源区	Wulingyuan District	3.46	2.05	1.41	5.09	2.81
慈利县	Chili County	47.80	30.78	17.02	95.15	55.89
桑植县	Sangzhi County	22.84	16.44	6.40	53.33	35.29
益阳市	**Yiyang City**	**275.76**	**208.62**	**67.15**	**552.12**	**285.69**
资阳区	Ziyang District	23.13	20.00	3.13	45.10	33.01
赫山区	Heshan District	45.77	39.75	6.03	87.40	60.15
南县	Nan County	58.54	39.55	18.99	129.97	48.05
桃江县	Taojiang County	43.81	38.24	5.58	68.44	45.41
安化县	Anhua County	42.05	29.84	12.21	99.45	56.46
沅江市	Yuanjiang City	62.46	41.25	21.21	121.76	42.61
郴州市	**Chenzhou City**	**274.83**	**198.83**	**75.99**	**529.87**	**323.74**
北湖区	Beihu District	7.53	6.09	1.44	22.87	9.33
苏仙区	Suxian District	15.39	12.93	2.46	31.17	22.15
桂阳县	Guiyang County	60.30	34.96	25.34	98.36	56.15
宜章县	Yizhang County	31.04	19.52	11.52	65.72	40.10
永兴县	Yongxing County	33.65	24.64	9.01	71.73	45.88

单位：千公顷 18 - 9 续表 2 continued (1 000 hectares)

市县名称	City and County	耕地面积 Cultivated Area	水田 Paddy Fields	旱地 Dry Fields	农作物播种面积 Total Sown Area	#粮食作物 Grain Crops
嘉禾县	Jiahe County	19.08	12.47	6.62	42.85	25.10
临武县	Linwu County	17.60	12.39	5.21	36.61	21.13
汝城县	Rucheng County	24.73	20.65	4.08	43.13	27.65
桂东县	Guidong County	10.83	9.67	1.15	13.72	10.02
安仁县	Anreng County	27.61	22.63	4.98	53.99	36.63
资兴市	Zixing City	20.77	17.97	2.80	49.72	29.60
永州市	**Yongzhou City**	**337.71**	**259.84**	**77.88**	**763.83**	**456.39**
芝山区	Zhishan District	37.46	32.56	4.90	95.61	56.04
冷水滩区	Lengshuitan District	32.63	24.73	7.90	62.02	44.32
祁阳县	Qiyang County	52.66	42.17	10.49	133.51	91.14
东安县	Dongan County	39.97	34.88	5.09	94.85	55.87
双牌县	Shuangpai County	8.11	7.15	0.97	19.19	11.76
道县	Dao County	44.21	30.89	13.32	99.99	55.22
江永县	Jiangyong County	21.41	15.70	5.71	42.18	20.59
宁远县	Ningyuan County	38.36	28.33	10.03	75.41	43.29
蓝山县	Lanshan County	18.80	13.31	5.49	36.35	21.00
新田县	Xintian County	18.47	11.84	6.63	46.33	22.98
江华县	Jianghua County	25.62	18.27	7.35	58.39	34.18
怀化市	**Huaihua City**	**299.41**	**259.18**	**40.24**	**599.97**	**328.28**
鹤城区	Hecheng District	11.10	9.87	1.23	20.35	9.50
中方县	Zhongfang County	19.55	17.23	2.32	39.76	19.87
沅陵县	Yuanling County	39.04	35.19	3.85	85.46	49.18
辰溪县	Chenxi County	26.24	22.65	3.59	55.33	28.96
溆浦县	Xupu County	45.59	35.09	10.50	105.48	64.93
会同县	Huitong County	22.12	19.90	2.22	42.94	21.37
麻阳县	Mayang County	19.07	17.38	1.70	43.35	24.00
新晃县	Xinhuang County	18.95	12.78	6.18	35.74	18.74
芷江县	Zhijiang County	29.97	27.33	2.64	54.08	30.61
靖州县	Jinzhou County	22.53	20.09	2.44	36.27	16.56
通道县	Tongdao County	17.87	15.84	2.03	29.23	14.17
洪江市	Hongjiang City	27.38	25.82	1.56	51.98	30.39
娄底市	**Loudi City**	**180.53**	**116.27**	**64.26**	**347.21**	**258.91**
娄星区	Louxing District	11.56	7.57	3.98	22.88	15.29
双峰县	Shuangfeng County	51.71	40.88	10.83	107.40	77.88
新化县	Xinhua County	55.67	31.67	24.00	106.56	80.56
冷水江市	Lenshuijiang City	7.69	4.69	3.00	12.19	7.89
涟源市	Lianyuan City	53.91	31.46	22.45	98.18	77.29
湘西自治州	**West Hunan A.P**	**175.79**	**111.01**	**64.78**	**362.00**	**202.38**
吉首市	Jishou City	11.14	7.25	3.89	24.82	9.37
泸溪县	Louxi County	16.54	13.03	3.51	32.63	14.61
凤凰县	Fenghuang County	32.26	20.44	11.81	57.67	26.27
花垣县	Huayuan County	23.56	11.80	11.76	28.59	18.64
保靖县	Baojin County	17.87	10.00	7.87	38.08	22.89
古丈县	Guzhang County	8.56	7.22	1.34	18.67	9.59
永顺县	Yongshun County	34.33	23.52	10.81	86.40	55.55
龙山县	Longshan County	31.55	17.76	13.78	75.14	45.46

18-10 各市、州、县机耕、灌溉面积及水库、塘坝和堤防(2003年)

Tractor-Ploughed Area and Irrigated Area,Reservoirs,Small Reservoirs and Dikes (2003)

市县名称	City and County	机耕面积(千公顷) Tractor Ploughed Area (1 000 hectares)	有效灌溉面积(千公顷) Irrigated Area (1 000 hectares)	水库(座) Number of Reservoirs (set)	容量(万立方米) Capacity (10 000 cu.m)	塘坝(座) Number of Small Reservoirs (set)	容量(万立方米) Capacity (10 000 cu.m)	堤防长度(公里) Total Length of Dikes (km)
长沙市	**Changsha City**	**315.91**	**218.83**	**760**	**118110**	**242210**	**104381**	**533**
芙蓉区	Furong District		0.30	1	80	200	60	15
天心区	Tianxin District	1.15	1.17	2	48	800	320	16
岳麓区	Yuelu District	2.50	2.05	12	522	1978	1400	37
开福区	Kaifu District	4.15	3.86	18	728	3920	3876	75
雨花区	Yuhua District	2.34	1.35	11	507	1850	4409	30
长沙县	Changsha County	71.58	45.12	173	18122	64646	23236	98
望城县	Wangcheng County	53.00	37.44	85	6494	37550	15612	201
宁乡县	Ningxiang County	94.19	67.40	277	32358	76094	39298	61
浏阳市	Liuyang City	87.00	60.14	181	59251	55172	16170	
株洲市	**Zhuzhou City**	**193.74**	**144.84**	**887**	**84319**	**97697**	**44846**	**176**
荷塘区	Hetang District	3.10	3.08	17	571	2389	1321	14
芦淞区	Lousong District		0.61	2	40	935	400	7
石峰区	Shifeng District	2.54	2.98	13	668	2641	1586	7
天元区	Tianyuan District	3.70	3.22	12	157	2022	1474	32
株洲县	Zhuzhou County	34.59	24.93	144	7936	17206	11700	112
攸 县	You County	58.01	40.06	299	38033	21987	16870	2
茶陵县	Chaling County	37.00	24.96	196	9010	22439	4829	
炎陵县	Yanling County	9.80	10.80	11	630	2100	220	
醴陵市	Liling City	45.00	34.20	193	27274	25978	6446	2
湘潭市	**Xiangtan City**	**187.87**	**115.58**	**383**	**94072**	**141670**	**69582**	**268**
雨湖区	Yuhu District	0.99	1.45	1	20	1760	1334	17
岳塘区	Yuetang District	5.55	2.97	6	362	2830	1950	30
湘潭县	Xiangtan County	112.00	63.39	146	19925	60041	46058	143
湘乡市	Xiangxiang City	62.10	43.35	181	71789	72600	18900	78
韶山市	Shaoshan City	7.23	4.42	49	1976	4439	1340	
衡阳市	**Hengyang City**	**421.74**	**254.38**	**1529**	**188958**	**422806**	**82505**	**461**
珠晖区	Zhuhui District	3.66	2.84	13	377	5620	3200	62
雁峰区	Yanfeng District	0.27	1.33	6	242	893	841	18
石鼓区	Shigu District	1.60	2.33	8	727	2500	470	21
蒸湘区	Zhengxinag District	3.01	1.96	11	300	2260	1410	24
南岳区	Nanyue District	1.71	0.88	8	568	1537	169	
衡阳县	Hengyang County	85.41	49.72	235	31000	109698	21000	31
衡南县	Hengnan County	116.78	52.09	348	24017	97000	15800	119
衡山县	Hengshan County	25.88	13.89	109	9915	22500	4500	72
衡东县	Hengdong County	50.60	29.68	189	20266	35468	10621	93
祁东县	Qidong County	45.76	30.67	147	22205	83130	14120	3
耒阳市	Leiyang City	44.06	39.01	275	60447	27900	7300	17
常宁市	Changning City	43.00	29.98	180	18894	40813	7115	1
邵阳市	**Shaoyang City**	**241.09**	**254.75**	**1234**	**141183**	**259648**	**61095**	**49**
双清区	Shuangqing District	2.24	2.81	15	652	5267	1066	
大祥区	Daxiang District	2.17	4.64	27	2143	8310	1143	
北塔区	Beita District	0.79	1.89	13	387	2560	494	6
邵东县	Shaodong County	37.89	38.76	126	19588	73900	12800	

注：有效灌溉面积、水库、塘坝、堤防长度数据由水利部门提供。

The date of irrigated area, reservoirs, small reservoirs and length of dikes are provided by the water conservancy department.

18-10 续表 1 continued

市县名称	City and County	机耕面积(千公顷) Tractor Ploughed Area (1 000 hectares)	有效灌溉面积(千公顷) Irrigated Area (1 000 hectares)	水库(座) Number of Reservoirs (set)	容量(万立方米) Capacity (10 000 cu.m)	塘坝(座) Number of Small Reservoirs (set)	容量(万立方米) Capacity (10 000 cu.m)	堤防长度(公里) Total Length of Dikes (km)
新邵县	Xinshao County	22.33	20.44	95	12785	30127	6959	7
邵阳县	Shaoyang County	18.85	32.80	270	19616	44000	12000	8
隆回县	Longhui County	30.24	36.95	245	32406	27518	5204	9
洞口县	Dongkou County	49.89	36.08	151	16801	17400	3936	6
绥宁县	Suining County	22.40	16.60	39	2808	5200	2980	3
新宁县	Xinning County	20.01	25.33	107	17660	18020	8265	
城步县	Chengbu County	9.03	9.59	26	2039	2246	2398	4
武冈市	Wugang City	25.25	28.86	120	14298	25100	3850	6
岳阳市	**Yueyang City**	**407.14**	**245.90**	**1457**	**161514**	**99467**	**30789**	**1114**
岳阳楼区	Yueyanglou District	0.62	1.40	22	913	1685	379	8
云溪区	Yunxi District	7.30	4.38	47	2147	2500	2100	77
君山区	Junshan District	43.56	23.03	24	584	178	20	207
岳阳县	Yueyang County	66.04	38.08	357	83850	8001	3482	88
华容县	Huarong County	68.82	48.07	60	5617	6394	1720	323
湘阴县	Xiangyin County	64.32	35.30	75	4142	7980	2809	247
平江县	Pingjiang County	31.13	33.40	290	20184	26733	5931	2
汨罗市	Miluo City	87.73	36.13	283	22113	28466	3380	111
临湘市	Linxiang City	37.62	26.11	299	21964	17530	10968	51
常德市	**Changde City**	**425.07**	**389.57**	**1201**	**243674**	**175471**	**65708**	**1476**
武陵区	Wuling District	10.00	6.51					150
鼎城区	Dingcheng District	106.00	73.94	189	30023	18631	7395	127
安乡县	Anxiang County	37.00	35.38					398
汉寿县	Hanshou County	72.00	46.40	211	11865	6919	600	195
澧县	Li County	72.50	59.30	117	50784	30052	11690	301
临澧县	Linli County	44.00	34.32	138	27493	29603	9446	49
桃源县	Taoyuan County	55.00	81.62	352	96094	58990	14630	167
石门县	Shimen County	18.57	39.95	163	25000	23750	19501	33
津市市	Jinshi City	10.00	12.15	31	2415	7526	2446	56
张家界市	**Zhangjiajie City**	**18.10**	**48.02**	**212**	**210241**	**17751**	**8894**	**81**
永定区	Yongding District	7.00	12.35	87	13785	2795	1509	26
武陵源区	Wulingyuan District		0.96	5	736	226	392	14
慈利县	Chili County	8.50	26.21	103	193617	13619	6393	32
桑植县	Sangzhi County	2.60	8.50	17	2103	1111	600	9
益阳市	**Yiyang City**	**379.60**	**219.19**	**548**	**412303**	**50072**	**18092**	**1000**
资阳区	Ziyang District	36.50	17.40	29	3998	2900	654	133
赫山区	Heshan District	73.00	34.37	138	10647	10989	6914	159
南县	Nan County	97.00	56.13					356
桃江县	Taojiang County	54.00	36.81	210	19264	13139	5045	42
安化县	Anhua County	8.80	21.13	168	369217	21635	5065	2
沅江市	Yuanjiang City	110.30	53.35	3	9177	1409	414	308
郴州市	**Chenzhou City**	**199.60**	**169.48**	**912**	**1023158**	**89416**	**24203**	**43**
北湖区	Beihu District	10.01	8.23	13	4211	2528	1033	6
苏仙区	Suxian District	13.95	13.85	47	6927	6368	2256	8
桂阳县	Guiyang County	31.80	26.89	187	16829	23465	3376	
宜章县	Yizhang County	18.11	17.98	130	7770	4906	3426	1
永兴县	Yongxing County	24.07	21.73	128	27073	13400	3758	9

市县名称	City and County	机耕面积(千公顷) Tractor Ploughed Area (1 000 hectares)	有效灌溉面积(千公顷) Irrigated Area (1 000 hectares)	水库(座) Number of Reservoirs (set)	容量(万立方米) Capacity (10 000 cu.m)	塘坝(座) Number of Small Reservoirs (set)	容量(万立方米) Capacity (10 000 cu.m)	堤防长度(公里) Total Length of Dikes (km)
嘉禾县	Jiahe County	13.80	11.13	74	9660	8906	1113	
临武县	Linwu County	14.30	10.22	67	8232	5570	1175	5
汝城县	Rucheng County	22.43	18.54	63	6441	1335	1069	
桂东县	Guidong County	6.50	6.33	30	1120	2982	542	6
安仁县	Anreng County	28.33	19.22	112	14230	14993	3809	4
资兴市	Zixing City	16.30	15.36	61	920665	4963	2646	4
永州市	**Yongzhou City**	**213.38**	**236.00**	**1283**	**178975**	**177902**	**83537**	**98**
芝山区	Zhishan District	23.00	29.50	146	13393	10000	13212	6
冷水滩区	Lengshuitan District	16.44	21.84	137	7073	19358	13202	4
祁阳县	Qiyang County	41.00	38.44	206	15186	78000	37320	21
东安县	Dongan County	40.50	30.50	262	11422	18133	3791	
双牌县	Shuangpai County	4.60	6.44	27	70080	1619	651	1
道县	Dao County	22.00	28.95	103	9123	17106	5820	36
江永县	Jiangyong County	9.90	13.74	115	10317	1968	1177	7
宁远县	Ningyuan County	25.03	25.32	87	10714	11896	3500	8
蓝山县	Lanshan County	10.57	12.30	33	2465	1237	561	7
新田县	Xintian County	5.60	11.75	72	13312	16520	1833	7
江华县	Jianghua County	14.74	17.22	95	15890	2065	2470	1
怀化市	**Huaihua City**	**89.41**	**184.11**	**1581**	**706264**	**68374**	**40783**	**28**
鹤城区	Hecheng District	2.16	6.14	45	6132	1474	776	3
中方县	Zhongfang County	3.06	10.84	138	7344	1576	1156	
沅陵县	Yuanling County	13.71	24.99	196	617213	4864	6449	
辰溪县	Chenxi County	13.71	18.00	239	11622	3100	2297	2
溆浦县	Xupu County	10.21	27.85	153	15458	21176	14640	6
会同县	Huitong County	5.02	14.82	129	5746	6302	1408	
麻阳县	Mayang County	1.60	13.03	258	13085	5947	1535	4
新晃县	Xinhuang County	3.18	7.85	66	3080	1198	422	4
芷江县	Zhijiang County	11.04	16.70	135	11600	5860	1566	5
靖州县	Jinzhou County	10.01	13.97	46	4300	7439	4590	2
通道县	Tongdao County	7.10	11.31	34	900	4378	3698	
洪江市	Hongjiang City	8.61	18.61	142	9784	5060	2246	2
娄底市	**Loudi City**	**125.41**	**112.36**	**696**	**62215**	**179471**	**33304**	**12**
娄星区	Louxing District	11.74	6.01	36	1216	15305	3164	
双峰县	Shuangfeng County	74.50	32.95	205	13060	71900	13880	5
新化县	Xinhua County	16.66	35.02	271	28815	28760	8204	5
冷水江市	Lenshuijiang City	2.51	5.34	30	2176	6059	1025	2
涟源市	Lianyuan City	20.00	33.04	154	16948	57447	7031	
湘西自治州	**West Hunan A.P**	**25.80**	**82.33**	**612**	**42466**	**4865**	**4929**	**10**
吉首市	Jishou City	0.99	4.90	23	3300	500	420	2
泸溪县	Louxi County	1.55	8.19	127	8047	1418	2097	7
凤凰县	Fenghuang County	2.68	13.39	92	7860	823	819	
花垣县	Huayuan County	4.06	10.15	55	3190	243	148	
保靖县	Baojin County	3.90	8.20	57	4900	528	390	
古丈县	Guzhang County	0.22	4.38	47	1800	338	220	1
永顺县	Yongshun County	7.20	15.30	146	8129	66	395	
龙山县	Longshan County	5.20	17.82	65	5240	949	440	

18-11 各市、州、县主要农业机械年末拥有量(2003年)

Year-End Possession of Major Agriculture Machinery (2003)

市县名称	City and County	农业机械总动力(千瓦) Power of Agricultural Machinery (kw)	大中型拖拉机 Large and Medium Tractors		小型及手扶拖拉机 Mini and Walking Tractors		排灌机械 Machinery for Agricultural Drainage and Irrigation		农用载重汽车(辆) Trucks for Agricultural Use (unit)
			台 (unit)	千瓦 (kw)	台 (unit)	千瓦 (kw)	台 (unit)	千瓦 (kw)	
长沙市	**Changsha City**	**2895027**	**2492**	**74501**	**18774**	**167373**	**145947**	**618871**	**9558**
芙蓉区	Furong District	65088	275	7312	52	457	3762	14489	207
天心区	Tianxin District	26168	70	2182	50	456	845	5915	150
岳麓区	Yuelu District	45059	10	220	98	862	1030	8651	346
开福区	Kaifu District	62880	27	550	246	2087	2593	23623	245
雨花区	Yuhua District	50212	9	242	135	1049	1102	5894	367
长沙县	Changsha County	701255	51	2813	2716	25598	48997	157577	2301
望城县	Wangcheng County	456625	125	7367	3518	31064	33427	176885	1156
宁乡县	Ningxiang County	769062	569	14225	4877	43472	34123	109420	2074
浏阳市	Liuyang City	718678	1356	39590	7082	62328	20068	116417	2712
株洲市	**Zhuzhou City**	**1349050**	**486**	**9445**	**11208**	**107160**	**40771**	**238063**	**4749**
荷塘区	Hetang District	26595	47	1478	110	1169	2379	8327	145
芦淞区	Lousong District	8426			154	1412	228	1591	34
石峰区	Shifeng District	27951	1	37	136	1363	1152	4748	195
天元区	Tianyuan District	33026			192	1747	2301	7299	110
株洲县	Zhuzhou County	183988	10	334	841	7422	11075	56500	813
攸 县	You County	385279	203	3367	1914	19081	9160	47729	1943
茶陵县	Chaling County	235390			3395	33093	5789	37580	701
炎陵县	Yanling County	77915	225	4229	651	5885	925	6303	86
醴陵市	Liling City	370480			3815	35988	7762	67986	722
湘潭市	**Xiangtan City**	**1166002**			**9239**	**82309**	**119461**	**297296**	**2404**
雨湖区	Yuhu District	18841			148	1306	1023	3277	76
岳塘区	Yuetang District	52985			932	8069	3790	11185	275
湘潭县	Xiangtan County	654092			5790	51992	58000	192505	1388
湘乡市	Xiangxiang City	391500			1645	14585	53911	78819	600
韶山市	Shaoshan City	48584			724	6357	2737	11510	65
衡阳市	**Hengyang City**	**1939858**	**3580**	**81381**	**9428**	**88373**	**97449**	**403937**	**6997**
珠晖区	Zhuhui District	47975	234	7624	180	1600	3925	17617	69
雁峰区	Yanfeng District	20737			52	459	783	4178	163
石鼓区	Shigu District	42907			145	1452	2953	15359	106
蒸湘区	Zhengxinag District	51419	275	8800	160	1413	942	2468	134
南岳区	Nanyue District	11180			75	661	2643	2106	26
衡阳县	Hengyang County	249397	801	17655	1574	15846	16693	43649	974
衡南县	Hengnan County	448066	710	12238	1351	12172	18058	87744	2447
衡山县	Hengshan County	196144			649	5731	6795	27936	754
衡东县	Hengdong County	235802	1	26	1204	11161	9116	42444	498
祁东县	Qidong County	221926	527	11144	321	3185	16237	58693	746
耒阳市	Leiyang City	224083	377	8444	2173	20838	8725	37875	736
常宁市	Changning City	190222	655	15450	1544	13855	10579	63868	344
邵阳市	**Shaoyang City**	**2027535**	**3103**	**73265**	**18109**	**171933**	**122410**	**428662**	**5992**
双清区	Shuangqing District	66890	108	3224	400	3528	3132	13516	178
大祥区	Daxiang District	33960			457	4791	3145	11992	77
北塔区	Beita District	37921			72	631	1550	11477	117
邵东县	Shaodong County	400904	469	9116	3130	27638	27608	74061	1432

18-11 续表 1 continued

市县名称	City and County	农业机械总动力（千瓦）Power of Agri-cultural Machinery (kw)	大中型拖拉机 Large and Medium Tractors		小型及手扶拖拉机 Mini and Walking Tractors		排灌机械 Machinery for Agricultural Drainage and Irrigation		农用载重汽车（辆）Trucks for Agri-cultural Use (unit)
			台 (unit)	千瓦 (kw)	台 (unit)	千瓦 (kw)	台 (unit)	千瓦 (kw)	
新邵县	Xinshao County	149528	358	11132	1766	18713	6653	31071	361
邵阳县	Shaoyang County	212185			181	1596	25608	95762	513
隆回县	Longhui County	158179	411	10790	1332	15659	17516	54787	232
洞口县	Dongkou County	300844	953	21212	3489	31466	12092	39595	1453
绥宁县	Suining County	180746	185	3145	1018	8753	2972	15888	470
新宁县	Xinning County	143626	105	2451	1138	11562	3450	14598	357
城步县	Chengbu County	96734	91	1620	2145	19818	2498	12259	343
武冈市	Wugang City	246018	423	10575	2981	27778	16186	53656	459
岳阳市	**Yueyang City**	**3328496**	**2195**	**85763**	**19565**	**178297**	**103217**	**792102**	**8612**
岳阳楼区	Yueyanglou District	47486	4	209	335	2958	528	4308	538
云溪区	Yunxi District	89842	18	990	329	2616	1518	16000	491
君山区	Junshan District	188490	736	33309	695	6627	2199	31716	540
岳阳县	Yueyang County	503723	80	3513	2235	19728	13173	91739	1430
华容县	Huarong County	502809	325	9866	3097	27530	28958	277335	369
湘阴县	Xiangyin County	539868	1	55	2198	19408	13082	70596	853
平江县	Pingjiang County	344422			3010	25585	9278	70439	1062
汨罗市	Miluo City	662580	669	27307	5225	50785	15568	110921	1501
临湘市	Linxiang City	449276	362	10514	2441	23060	18913	19048	1828
常德市	**Changde City**	**2537392**	**2480**	**67803**	**21922**	**196505**	**175756**	**1076873**	**6494**
武陵区	Wuling District	145165	8	485	854	7795	5484	28165	481
鼎城区	Dingcheng District	478552	219	4978	4558	40221	27670	149448	1923
安乡县	Anxiang County	294305	205	10804	2320	21429	16438	110836	162
汉寿县	Hanshou County	347735	30	750	2972	25220	28813	318043	411
澧县	Li County	400152	611	13752	1639	14751	40862	223555	1104
临澧县	Linli County	214299			3667	32949	15917	73456	594
桃源县	Taoyuan County	297798	625	18476	1862	17097	19927	84613	956
石门县	Shimen County	254421	670	15258	3322	30615	13685	42023	696
津市市	Jinshi City	104965	112	3300	728	6428	6960	46734	167
张家界市	**Zhangjiajie City**	**607575**	**1959**	**47818**	**6041**	**56458**	**12933**	**68639**	**2537**
永定区	Yongding District	199492	556	13908	2687	24233	2266	22378	877
武陵源区	Wulingyuan District	6789	2	37	285	2517	49	245	29
慈利县	Chili County	275796	1327	31962	1624	14930	8334	38795	1057
桑植县	Sangzhi County	125498	74	1911	1445	14778	2284	7221	574
益阳市	**Yiyang City**	**2578071**	**2718**	**85702**	**15160**	**159530**	**150877**	**803162**	**4477**
资阳区	Ziyang District	311467	228	5563	2295	18855	20790	108344	556
赫山区	Heshan District	486106	453	10146	2535	30420	38689	170323	1214
南县	Nan County	541640	260	15889	4225	39415	33293	238997	252
桃江县	Taojiang County	495021	505	9428	1602	20709	18228	71471	896
安化县	Anhua County	298754	933	35742	1022	11695	8864	30535	1093
沅江市	Yuanjiang City	445083	339	8934	3481	38436	31013	183492	466
郴州市	**Chenzhou City**	**2072921**	**3070**	**85035**	**11373**	**109720**	**51893**	**244248**	**9101**
北湖区	Beihu District	119800			1400	17478	775	5318	583
苏仙区	Suxian District	238444	397	8735	574	5218	4687	21257	1013
桂阳县	Guiyang County	264653	446	10088	2563	23578	10365	36550	875
宜章县	Yizhang County	413615	754	27249	171	1508	13137	75899	2119
永兴县	Yongxing County	172313	608	16696	1428	13089	4376	24115	640

市县名称	City and County	农业机械总动力(千瓦) Power of Agricultural Machinery (kw)	大中型拖拉机 Large and Medium Tractors 台 (unit)	大中型拖拉机 千瓦 (kw)	小型及手扶拖拉机 Mini and Walking Tractors 台 (unit)	小型及手扶拖拉机 千瓦 (kw)	排灌机械 Machinery for Agricultural Drainage and Irrigation 台 (unit)	排灌机械 千瓦 (kw)	农用载重汽车(辆) Trucks for Agricultural Use (unit)
嘉禾县	Jiahe County	201826	403	8493	1515	14126	6783	25429	1197
临武县	Linwu County	223110	1	40	240	2119	3342	15417	1358
汝城县	Rucheng County	146236	106	2275	1060	9478	2925	12564	409
桂东县	Guidong County	36642	105	2456	857	9307	474	2080	59
安仁县	Anreng County	106608	103	3300	680	6004	1424	9683	468
资兴市	Zixing City	149674	147	5703	885	7815	3605	15936	380
永州市	**Yongzhou City**	**2329051**	**6882**	**156097**	**11314**	**119820**	**191199**	**846328**	**5125**
芝山区	Zhishan District	271866	465	13918	587	6719	41777	155493	96
冷水滩区	Lengshuitan District	271448	837	22504	784	6925	25482	80116	418
祁阳县	Qiyang County	467361	508	15640	421	3704	62263	318712	1267
东安县	Dongan County	210560	513	7742	591	5365	16480	66352	259
双牌县	Shuangpai County	64044	207	4076	263	2186	743	5164	21
道县	Dao County	112393	1328	20029	982	6496	2488	23242	355
江永县	Jiangyong County	81570	175	3713	610	5386	6758	41258	204
宁远县	Ningyuan County	274924	1394	35356	297	2623	16008	65136	366
蓝山县	Lanshan County	222577			4423	57619	3553	19713	1438
新田县	Xintian County	205992	558	13553	2100	19962	6382	27376	600
江华县	Jianghua County	146316	897	19566	256	2835	9265	43766	101
怀化市	**Huaihua City**	**1523516**	**3686**	**101760**	**5594**	**56460**	**52533**	**277815**	**4133**
鹤城区	Hecheng District	146519	22	484	578	6988	2973	32307	440
中方县	Zhongfang County	108873	114	4060	515	7227	1809	9809	470
沅陵县	Yuanling County	187602	294	7862	360	3174	6847	28139	429
辰溪县	Chenxi County	134374	294	8096	504	4712	5450	22488	427
溆浦县	Xupu County	237500	503	12129	507	5662	12336	60749	346
会同县	Huitong County	99753	495	9105	828	7022	2918	12609	192
麻阳县	Mayang County	73501	292	7061	220	1943	2808	24909	199
新晃县	Xinhuang County	62197	1	26	484	4228	1562	8163	143
芷江县	Zhijiang County	124863	507	17679	622	5646	4985	34695	252
靖州县	Jinzhou County	92834	298	8940	440	4400	6000	15135	369
通道县	Tongdao County	94322	308	6039	339	2994	1345	8666	360
洪江市	Hongjiang City	161178	558	20279	197	2464	3500	20146	506
娄底市	**Loudi City**	**1500324**	**1477**	**51289**	**10289**	**106240**	**85326**	**317186**	**7089**
娄星区	Louxing District	180845	43	2386	1855	19145	11012	32653	901
双峰县	Shuangfeng County	439948	385	8271	1650	15294	42637	111849	2180
新化县	Xinhua County	365976	1045	40401	2091	28620	11648	72264	1228
冷水江市	Lenshuijiang City	102141	4	231	280	2823	2218	19719	596
涟源市	Lianyuan City	411414			4413	40358	17811	80701	2184
湘西自治州	**West Hunan A.P**	**789722**	**3103**	**84361**	**7587**	**72551**	**16854**	**98434**	**1686**
吉首市	Jishou City	80335	438	7884	734	6454	693	4182	283
泸溪县	Louxi County	80142	260	5720	330	2475	3924	26840	286
凤凰县	Fenghuang County	93776	4	221	1047	11555	3502	26956	94
花垣县	Huayuan County	88478	642	18886	1407	13603	1600	7397	96
保靖县	Baojin County	78532	447	14751	579	5179	1355	6114	213
古丈县	Guzhang County	44013	96	2304	340	2962	554	2675	184
永顺县	Yongshun County	120098	824	24720	1105	9835	2824	10341	175
龙山县	Longshan County	204348	392	9875	2045	20488	2402	13929	355

18-12 各市、州、县农村用电及化肥农药施用量(2003年)

E1ectricity Consumed and Fertilizer，Pesticide Applied in Rural Areas (2003)

市县名称	City and County	农村小水电(个数) Small Hydropower Station in Rural Areas (unit)	装机容量(千瓦) Capacity of Power Generating Sets (kw)	农村用电量(万千瓦小时) Electricity Consumed in Rural Area (10 000 kw.h)	化肥施用量（折纯量）(吨) Consumption of Chemical Fertilizer (ton)	每公顷播种面积施用量(公斤) Consumption of Per Hectare Sown Area (kg)	农药施用量(吨) Consumption of Chemical Pesticide (ton)
长沙市	**Changsha City**	**47**	**8577**	**103944**	**135988**	**239**	**8203**
芙蓉区	Furong District			2710	332	102	19
天心区	Tianxin District			1600	567	260	64
岳麓区	Yuelu District			5598	1337	257	80
开福区	Kaifu District			2168	2685	268	153
雨花区	Yuhua District			4018	1267	279	81
长沙县	Changsha County	2	750	39938	27319	227	1974
望城县	Wangcheng County	1	500	11885	17445	159	1245
宁乡县	Ningxiang County	28	3512	17697	45354	264	2153
浏阳市	Liuyang City	16	3815	18330	39682	278	2434
株洲市	**Zhuzhou City**	**176**	**40200**	**39937**	**92477**	**281**	**3597**
荷塘区	Hetang District			2086	1084	156	72
芦淞区	Lousong District			1850	384	256	40
石峰区	Shifeng District			3687	1094	143	43
天元区	Tianyuan District			548	1956	277	105
株洲县	Zhuzhou County	9	337	3035	16389	307	650
攸 县	You County	45	12140	8680	28133	316	690
茶陵县	Chaling County	8	3000	3338	16085	263	698
炎陵县	Yanling County	31	17295	8026	4552	223	96
醴陵市	Liling City	83	7428	8687	22800	277	1203
湘潭市	**Xiangtan City**	**22**	**1675**	**28919**	**87243**	**317**	**3849**
雨湖区	Yuhu District			1817	818	251	26
岳塘区	Yuetang District			2703	1789	249	60
湘潭县	Xiangtan County	22	1675	13672	47890	345	2323
湘乡市	Xiangxiang City			8015	34283	303	1343
韶山市	Shaoshan City			2712	2463	202	97
衡阳市	**Hengyang City**	**136**	**9574**	**34044.62**	**177413**	**223**	**13346**
珠晖区	Zhuhui District			965	2768	243	237
雁峰区	Yanfeng District			705	728	322	68
石鼓区	Shigu District	1	20	1086	1349	302	111
蒸湘区	Zhengxinag District			1380	1135	190	78
南岳区	Nanyue District	4	68	270	905	232	50
衡阳县	Hengyang County	8	895	6821	32543	197	1612
衡南县	Hengnan County	10	849	5084	32678	219	2275
衡山县	Hengshan County	17	2510	3625	10771	265	913
衡东县	Hengdong County	12	690	3108	21142	220	1278
祁东县	Qidong County	8	99	4365	23908	269	1163
耒阳市	Leiyang City	26	880	4375	25563	196	1242
常宁市	Changning City	50	3563	2260.62	23923	248	4319
邵阳市	**Shaoyang City**	**265**	**38563**	**44167.99**	**176070**	**246**	**7483**
双清区	Shuangqing District	1	375	517.36	1480	223	76
大祥区	Daxiang District			713.32	2601	199	114
北塔区	Beita District			512	1236	254	54
邵东县	Shaodong County	5	895	12241	36057	392	1020

市县名称	City and County	农村小水电（个数）Small Hydropower Station in Rural Areas (unit)	装机容量（千瓦）Capacity of Power Generating Sets (kw)	农村用电量（万千瓦小时）Electricity Consumed in Rural Area (10 000 kw.h)	化肥施用量（折纯量）（吨）Consumption of Chemical Fertilizer (ton)	每公顷播种面积施用量（公斤）Consumption of Per Hectare Sown Area (kg)	农药施用量（吨）Consumption of Chemical Pesticide (ton)
新邵县	Xinshao County	10	2396	3471	12998	208	494
邵阳县	Shaoyang County	4	278	4178.1	24246	257	687
隆回县	Longhui County	12	6650	8993.21	30130	268	1660
洞口县	Dongkou County	21	8150	4336	22723	216	1560
绥宁县	Suining County	58	7550	2430	8025	201	511
新宁县	Xinning County	64	2201	3113	15628	217	670
城步县	Chengbu County	66	7617	1066	4059	154	147
武冈市	Wugang City	24	2451	2597	16887	193	490
岳阳市	**Yueyang City**	**65**	**13512**	**38444**	**168734**	**237**	**9967**
岳阳楼区	Yueyanglou District			6180	1220	211	355
云溪区	Yunxi District			1483	5050	366	527
君山区	Junshan District			1890	14727	297	700
岳阳县	Yueyang County	9	1504	2275	23054	202	747
华容县	Huarong County			3913	39210	296	3600
湘阴县	Xiangyin County			4985	21787	189	624
平江县	Pingjiang County	44	8663	7168	27112	255	870
汨罗市	Miluo City	1	150	6984	21775	216	2186
临湘市	Linxiang City	11	3195	3566	14799	198	358
常德市	**Changde City**	**58**	**12264**	**64520.12**	**286435**	**297**	**7824**
武陵区	Wuling District			2962	5689	313	100
鼎城区	Dingcheng District	3	220	11052.2	46664	264	1721
安乡县	Anxiang County			7054	38450	482	886
汉寿县	Hanshou County			9007.22	42477	339	1355
澧县	Li County	7	1041	7198	48850	335	1658
临澧县	Linli County	1	260	11482	21105	288	295
桃源县	Taoyuan County	32	8802	9682.24	37739	185	710
石门县	Shimen County	15	1941	4658.46	34414	334	781
津市市	Jinshi City			1424	11047	284	318
张家界市	**Zhangjiajie City**	**74**	**16717**	**6472.07**	**45875**	**216**	**1776**
永定区	Yongding District	20	3216	1278	11603	198	588
武陵源区	Wulingyuan District			313	903	177	24
慈利县	Chili County	42	7871	3620	21803	229	842
桑植县	Sangzhi County	12	5630	1261.07	11566	217	322
益阳市	**Yiyang City**	**274**	**20602**	**37692.2**	**143714**	**260**	**8623**
资阳区	Ziyang District			2665	12000	266	1406
赫山区	Heshan District	4	350	9557.2	20818	238	2253
南县	Nan County			9722	45109	347	2028
桃江县	Taojiang County	48	3559	7592	14861	217	448
安化县	Anhua County	222	16693	2234	14208	143	497
沅江市	Yuanjiang City			5922	36718	302	1991
郴州市	**Chenzhou City**	**944**	**165119**	**34442.18**	**143967**	**272**	**5860**
北湖区	Beihu District	89	28576	1984.44	5487	240	248
苏仙区	Suxian District	64	20390	3976	9301	298	319
桂阳县	Guiyang County	381	21610	6755.49	27809	283	905
宜章县	Yizhang County	76	33065	3602.92	14122	215	536
永兴县	Yongxing County	127	5695	2825.11	20046	279	696

市县名称	City and County	农村小水电(个数) Small Hydropower Station in Rural Areas (unit)	装机容量(千瓦) Capacity of Power Generating Sets (kw)	农村用电量(万千瓦小时) Electricity Consumed in Rural Area (10000 kw.h)	化肥施用量（折纯量）(吨) Consumption of Chemical Fertilizer (ton)	每公顷播种面积施用量(公斤) Consumption of Per Hectare Sown Area (kg)	农药施用量(吨) Consumption of Chemical Pesticide (ton)
嘉禾县	Jiahe County	6	3245	2244.06	13290	310	401
临武县	Linwu County	45	10934	2051.82	9806	268	303
汝城县	Rucheng County	50	26055	1456	13919	323	728
桂东县	Guidong County	48	4335	1105	3549	259	135
安仁县	Anreng County	17	4031	2095.34	12857	238	624
资兴市	Zixing City	41	7183	6346	13781	277	965
永州市	**Yongzhou City**	**1418**	**74614**	**35309.5**	**184871**	**242**	**8081**
芝山区	Zhishan District	113	4697	2826	16764	175	703
冷水滩区	Lengshuitan District	5	1290	4390	13873	224	635
祁阳县	Qiyang County	74	7034	7663.5	31865	239	1851
东安县	Dongan County	64	7440	4216	16692	176	881
双牌县	Shuangpai County	164	6296	1887	5140	268	188
道县	Dao County	155	1471	1332	29474	295	842
江永县	Jiangyong County	138	477	576	14328	340	657
宁远县	Ningyuan County	272	853	2620	19093	253	831
蓝山县	Lanshan County	234	3446	1899	9970	274	506
新田县	Xintian County	140	280	1400	15029	324	370
江华县	Jianghua County	59	41330	6500	12643	217	617
怀化市	**Huaihua City**	**248**	**51989**	**31844.21**	**102507**	**171**	**10541**
鹤城区	Hecheng District	7	2375	1635	2528	124	326
中方县	Zhongfang County	26	5515	2186.3	7250	182	610
沅陵县	Yuanling County	10	4690	6530	8097	95	615
辰溪县	Chenxi County	8	1452	1998	8988	162	650
溆浦县	Xupu County	79	3483	2916.8	27300	259	5547
会同县	Huitong County	23	6121	2387	5380	125	389
麻阳县	Mayang County	10	3035	1640	5467	126	377
新晃县	Xinhuang County	5	2200	2138.28	3433	96	210
芷江县	Zhijiang County	14	2808	3478	9432	174	481
靖州县	Jinzhou County	13	3950	1107.83	6379	176	283
通道县	Tongdao County	14	2435	1200	3951	135	110
洪江市	Hongjiang City	39	13925	4627	14302	275	943
娄底市	**Loudi City**	**85**	**19896**	**27863**	**84127**	**242**	**3494**
娄星区	Louxing District	8	3940	2788	3648	159	201
双峰县	Shuangfeng County			7993	35244	328	1348
新化县	Xinhua County	52	8318	4285	18452	173	615
冷水江市	Lenshuijiang City	3	581	4956	2729	224	282
涟源市	Lianyuan City	22	7057	7841	24054	245	1048
湘西自治州	**West Hunan A.P**	**100**	**23275**	**10775.6**	**53917**	**149**	**2716**
吉首市	Jishou City	9	1490	1552	6022	243	955
泸溪县	Louxi County	10	2495	910.52	4615	141	298
凤凰县	Fenghuang County	13	3696	842.57	7015	122	318
花垣县	Huayuan County	19	5080	1075	6305	221	169
保靖县	Baojin County	9	1659	2553	5942	156	304
古丈县	Guzhang County	12	1725	291.05	2023	108	70
永顺县	Yongshun County	13	2640	996.12	10888	126	383
龙山县	Longshan County	15	4490	2555.34	11107	148	219

18-13 各市、州、县农林牧渔业总产值(2003年)

Gross Output Value of Farming,Forestry,Animal Husbandry and fishery (2003)

单位：万元 (10 000 yuan)

市县名称	Cities and Counties	农林牧渔业总产值 Gross Output Value of Farming, Forestry, Animal Husbandry and Fishery	指数(上年=100) Indices (preceding year=100)	农业产值 Output Value of Farming	林业产值 Output Value of Forestry	牧业产值 Output Value of Animal Husbandry	渔业产值 Output Value of Fishery	服务业产值 Output Value of Services
长沙市	**Changsha City**	**1371608**	**105.4**	**694002**	**70917**	**527412**	**61035**	**18242**
芙蓉区	Furong District	20522	103.5	12478	63	5839	2089	53
天心区	Tianxin District	13121	105.2	6129	1397	3932	1632	31
岳麓区	Yuelu District	30927	105.0	17797	128	11904	1013	85
开福区	Kaifu District	38343	105.5	18118	457	16423	3319	26
雨花区	Yuhua District	31808	105.1	19680	67	10358	1688	16
长沙县	Changsha County	317297	105.1	169918	12457	122571	8964	3387
望城县	Wangcheng County	216055	105.6	104553	4946	88944	14491	3121
宁乡县	Ningxiang County	371548	105.0	180581	16780	152554	15950	5685
浏阳市	Liuyang City	331986	106.0	164749	34623	114887	11888	5838
株洲市	**Zhuzhou City**	**779227**	**103.6**	**371436**	**55146**	**292860**	**34964**	**24822**
荷塘区	Hetang District	16485	103.0	8446	637	6065	1012	325
芦淞区	Lousong District	10324	102.4	3941	516	4580	934	354
石峰区	Shifeng District	24975	103.6	13283	412	9869	1028	384
天元区	Tianyuan District	20612	102.9	10666	469	8399	632	446
株洲县	Zhuzhou County	111484	103.8	56543	5406	39367	6420	3748
攸 县	You County	219500	103.9	103130	16224	79245	7957	12945
茶陵县	Chaling County	135096	103.9	60473	10081	55310	6682	2550
炎陵县	Yanling County	42367	103.3	15478	11440	12217	437	2796
醴陵市	Liling City	198385	103.3	99478	9962	77808	9863	1274
湘潭市	**Xiangtan City**	**625042**	**104.4**	**246304**	**15781**	**309070**	**36800**	**17088**
雨湖区	Yuhu District	26814	105.0	6688	104	16692	1195	2135
岳塘区	Yuetang District	30631	105.2	10722	151	15178	1398	3183
湘潭县	Xiangtan County	318733	104.4	133470	6969	152996	18936	6362
湘乡市	Xiangxiang City	225410	104.4	85907	8143	112556	13841	4964
韶山市	Shaoshan City	23455	104.3	9517	414	11649	1431	444
衡阳市	**Hengyang City**	**1692246**	**103.2**	**752904**	**61486**	**718002**	**125986**	**33868**
珠晖区	Zhuhui District	25067	103.4	14265	265	7827	2174	536
雁峰区	Yanfeng District	9323	103.3	4629	16	3513	977	188
石鼓区	Shigu District	12452	103.2	6880	20	3820	1593	140
蒸湘区	Zhengxiang District	14331	102.8	8690	320	3560	1460	301
南岳区	Nanyue District	12047	104.9	6541	942	4051	327	185
衡阳县	Hengyang County	342501	103.3	136334	11895	159514	28628	6130
衡南县	Hengnan County	327702	103.1	150223	9775	137673	24739	5292
衡山县	Hengshan County	105491	103.2	44889	4588	48166	5629	2219
衡东县	Hengdong County	171263	103.1	74383	8123	77517	7546	3693
祁东县	Qidong County	234528	103.1	118236	3179	82457	26106	4550
耒阳市	Leiyang City	249362	103.4	107827	10983	109775	14437	6340
常宁市	Changning City	188218	103.1	80045	11380	80129	12370	4294
邵阳市	**Shaoyang City**	**1338968**	**103.1**	**636508**	**75304**	**553954**	**42691**	**30511**
双清区	Shuangqing District	23846	105.8	6214	60	12456	1205	3910
大祥区	Daxiang District	26452	105.1	11350	267	10103	982	3750
北塔区	Beita District	13804	105.4	5782	112	5997	823	1091
邵东县	Shaodong County	203722	102.2	120241	1761	65060	14130	2530

单位：万元 18-13 续表 1 (10 000 yuan)

市县名称	Cities and Counties	农林牧渔业总产值 Gross Output Value of Farming, Forestry, Animal Husbandry and Fishery	指数(上年=100) Indices (preceding year=100)	农业产值 Output Value of Farming	林业产值 Output Value of Forestry	牧业产值 Output Value of Animal Husbandry	渔业产值 Output Value of Fishery	服务业产值 Output Value of Services
新邵县	Xinshao County	111070	102.5	55317	3759	48050	3072	872
邵阳县	Shaoyang County	131130	103.8	69451	6100	48683	4563	2333
隆回县	Longhui County	163945	101.2	83032	6057	66183	4022	4651
洞口县	Dongkou County	240742	104.6	100286	7508	121442	6174	5332
绥宁县	Suining County	111079	103.9	45331	32852	29900	1079	1917
新宁县	Xinning County	89599	103.4	51933	4436	29749	2285	1196
城步县	Chengbu County	42284	105.0	18225	6534	16433	365	726
武冈市	Wugang City	181296	102.0	69346	5857	99897	3992	2203
岳阳市	**Yueyang City**	**1662765**	**105.1**	**814915**	**50236**	**570634**	**213455**	**13525**
岳阳楼区	Yueyanglou District	39845	104.9	11551	953	16592	10245	505
云溪区	Yunxi District	44238	105.0	16167	1632	15998	10059	383
君山区	Junshan District	114092	105.1	64525	1850	28523	18625	569
岳阳县	Yueyang County	259526	105.3	128214	6570	96391	26248	2103
华容县	Huarong County	346939	105.5	196421	3883	92290	52260	2085
湘阴县	Xiangyin County	256533	104.2	112527	7685	80391	53824	2106
平江县	Pingjiang County	194519	104.5	100740	16020	71769	3836	2155
汨罗市	Miluo City	272469	105.5	108990	3364	135855	22375	1885
临湘市	Linxiang City	134603	105.1	75781	8279	32825	15984	1734
常德市	**Changde City**	**1832771**	**105.5**	**813114**	**36317**	**702557**	**228436**	**52347**
武陵区	Wuling District	51941	103.5	24077	138	17023	8759	1944
鼎城区	Dingcheng District	301083	107.0	135643	5624	101460	50130	8226
安乡县	Anxiang County	211359	106.5	96521	1692	54489	51821	6836
汉寿县	Hanshou County	215256	106.0	105500	2950	55307	44358	7141
澧县	Li County	281638	103.3	131944	2650	111849	24234	10961
临澧县	Linli County	155613	100.1	56910	5196	77648	11514	4345
桃源县	Taoyuan County	349137	104.8	148465	12587	161310	21466	5309
石门县	Shimen County	189178	113.3	82728	4836	93079	4523	4012
津市市	Jinshi City	77566	103.8	31326	644	30392	11631	3573
张家界市	**Zhangjiajie City**	**259897**	**103.0**	**131986**	**26893**	**84745**	**4872**	**11401**
永定区	Yongding District	84901	102.9	41296	7473	26641	2041	7450
武陵源区	Wulingyuan District	8367	103.3	3562	1709	2545	14	536
慈利县	Chili County	117751	102.6	60610	11110	41176	2413	2442
桑植县	Sangzhi County	48879	104.4	26518	6601	14383	404	973
益阳市	**Yiyang City**	**910202**	**104.1**	**467574**	**48825**	**274241**	**107802**	**11760**
资阳区	Ziyang District	67691	104.0	37425	1124	19584	9068	490
赫山区	Heshan District	142359	103.8	66477	5898	57358	11156	1470
南县	Nan County	217215	103.7	131498	1764	46669	34204	3080
桃江县	Taojiang County	130044	104.1	60716	19538	44400	2660	2730
安化县	Anhua County	147839	104.0	64354	17205	56806	7906	1569
沅江市	Yuanjiang City	205055	104.3	107104	3297	49425	42808	2421
郴州市	**Chenzhou City**	**1025866**	**103.5**	**490858**	**72677**	**393373**	**49915**	**19042**
北湖区	Beihu District	54860	103.2	27274	3778	20947	1884	976
苏仙区	Suxian District	75276	104.0	30726	5700	32578	4943	1329
桂阳县	Guiyang County	195421	103.4	118436	13395	52887	7135	3569
宜章县	Yizhang County	100625	103.0	47243	4203	43812	3506	1860
永兴县	Yongxing County	127875	103.9	52220	6978	57435	8758	2484

单位：万元　　18-13 续表 2　　(10 000 yuan)

市县名称	Cities and Counties	农林牧渔业总产值 Gross Output Value of Farming, Forestry, Animal Husbandry and Fishery	指数 (上年=100) Indices (preceding year=100)	农业产值 Output Value of Farming	林业产值 Output Value of Forestry	牧业产值 Output Value of Animal Husbandry	渔业产值 Output Value of Fishery	服务业产值 Output Value of Services
嘉禾县	Jiahe County	89547	103.2	41118	2669	42449	1653	1659
临武县	Linwu County	73447	103.0	38495	3590	28005	2057	1300
汝城县	Rucheng County	68947	103.2	34007	7663	25282	646	1350
桂东县	Guidong County	23839	103.0	12229	2440	8328	370	472
安仁县	Anreng County	105810	103.6	51035	6684	41173	4929	1988
资兴市	Zixing City	110219	104.1	38075	15577	40477	14034	2055
永州市	**Yongzhou City**	**1385042**	**103.9**	**711254**	**84280**	**500365**	**72843**	**16299**
芝山区	Zhishan District	169297	104.1	98546	4545	58276	6131	1800
冷水滩区	Lengshuitan District	124980	104.3	59399	4106	51551	9279	645
祁阳县	Qiyang County	228668	104.4	112253	12937	80137	22760	580
东安县	Dongan County	170064	103.9	96478	10999	53317	8478	792
双牌县	Shuangpai County	40740	103.5	17905	7694	11320	1522	2300
道县	Dao County	176540	103.5	84262	8484	72537	10007	1250
江永县	Jiangyong County	91593	105.1	59440	4282	23860	2353	1658
宁远县	Ningyuan County	134376	103.2	65665	4651	55087	7222	1750
蓝山县	Lanshan County	70947	103.7	30363	6207	31320	1157	1900
新田县	Xintian County	83290	103.6	45059	2541	32702	2700	288
江华县	Jianghua County	94547	103.5	41885	17833	30259	1234	3336
怀化市	**Huaihua City**	**884782**	**103.2**	**435637**	**101650**	**306425**	**23961**	**17110**
鹤城区	Hecheng District	35719	105.2	16457	4984	11859	2313	107
中方县	Zhongfang County	64800	103.9	33086	5949	21193	1849	2724
沅陵县	Yuanling County	90473	101.4	42958	15897	26678	3610	1331
辰溪县	Chenxi County	67904	103.6	36545	5725	23995	1069	571
溆浦县	Xupu County	169885	103.8	92969	10390	62950	3116	460
会同县	Huitong County	69716	103.5	30449	10633	24802	1647	2184
麻阳县	Mayang County	61130	102.9	32718	6998	19281	1392	740
新晃县	Xinhuang County	43977	102.3	15973	3818	21815	856	1516
芷江县	Zhijiang County	80368	104.1	36530	8869	30284	2128	2559
靖州县	Jinzhou County	65506	103.1	31690	7568	21304	2624	2320
通道县	Tongdao County	39239	103.1	18141	8681	10842	1017	558
洪江市	Hongjiang City	96068	102.5	48123	12142	31422	2341	2040
娄底市	**Loudi City**	**608018**	**99.3**	**260913**	**13673**	**298293**	**29944**	**5196**
娄星区	Louxing District	46919	99.0	19457	757	22371	2763	1570
双峰县	Shuangfeng County	223742	99.3	101129	4780	103570	13195	1068
新化县	Xinhua County	169938	96.9	56556	4890	100019	7188	1285
冷水江市	Lenshuijiang City	28817	99.7	10094	897	15738	1683	405
涟源市	Lianyuan City	138602	102.4	73677	2349	56594	5115	868
湘西自治州	**West Hunan A.P**	**360969**	**103.1**	**210501**	**45269**	**89895**	**11314**	**3990**
吉首市	Jishou City	41926	103.2	26803	3990	9177	1275	681
泸溪县	Louxi County	37446	100.3	20624	4830	10110	1121	761
凤凰县	Fenghuang County	36485	102.4	24692	3419	7028	1211	135
花垣县	Huayuan County	33525	103.4	16748	3212	11410	1760	396
保靖县	Baojin County	38632	102.4	21856	4361	11149	955	312
古丈县	Guzhang County	17800	102.5	7749	4197	4486	844	525
永顺县	Yongshun County	72395	104.5	44520	8603	18160	997	115
龙山县	Longshan County	82758	103.8	47508	12658	18376	3152	1065

18-14 各市州、县主要农产品产量(2003年)

Output of Major Farm Crops (2003)

单位：吨 (ton)

市县名称	City and County	粮食合计 Total Grain	稻谷 Rice	小麦 Wheat	玉米 Corn	大豆 Beans	薯类 Tubers
长沙市	**Changsha City**	**2163732**	**1939536**	**3091**	**62120**	**17403**	**121342**
芙蓉区	Furong District	90				30	40
天心区	Tianxin District	2982	2040		404	433	48
岳麓区	Yuelu District	4825	3775		47	10	946
开福区	Kaifu District	26093	24243		70	649	845
雨花区	Yuhua District	1506	838			83	511
长沙县	Changsha County	506272	469237	225	21210	3162	11222
望城县	Wangcheng County	411261	354532	285	8131	1202	44166
宁乡县	Ningxiang County	716690	658174	1827	7596	6951	36821
浏阳市	Liuyang City	494013	426697	754	24662	4883	26743
株洲市	**Zhuzhou City**	**1645029**	**1566930**	**59**	**20381**	**12424**	**38395**
荷塘区	Hetang District	35035	33870		40	40	1007
芦淞区	Lousong District	3748	3640			35	73
石峰区	Shifeng District	21347	18525		326	764	1137
天元区	Tianyuan District	35899	35183			35	558
株洲县	Zhuzhou County	285348	277955	59	585	1245	4357
攸 县	You County	433289	420950		963	1975	8484
茶陵县	Chaling County	318774	300878		2025	5040	9629
炎陵县	Yanling County	85953	79871		262	1305	4001
醴陵市	Liling City	425636	396058		16180	1985	9149
湘潭市	**Xiangtan City**	**1326881**	**1268858**	**1109**	**35429**	**3777**	**13311**
雨湖区	Yuhu District	9661	9661				
岳塘区	Yuetang District	25576	24907		141		446
湘潭县	Xiangtan County	747398	706467	450	30111	1384	6948
湘乡市	Xiangxiang City	483785	469158	557	4462	2279	5177
韶山市	Shaoshan City	60461	58665	102	715	114	740
衡阳市	**Hengyang City**	**2738985**	**2481327**	**9754**	**42557**	**34331**	**125378**
珠晖区	Zhuhui District	17763	16772		220	151	550
雁峰区	Yanfeng District	8737	8443			1	110
石鼓区	Shigu District	17720	17286	53		15	196
蒸湘区	Zhengxinag District	17999	17045		414	110	367
南岳区	Nanyue District	11211	10050		94	34	896
衡阳县	Hengyang County	553999	509303	487	2288	6441	26070
衡南县	Hengnan County	549170	494694	840	16611	7758	15992
衡山县	Hengshan County	155668	150286		491	849	2555
衡东县	Hengdong County	345174	301737		3042	3894	32168
祁东县	Qidong County	317022	283842	740	8127	4433	15789
耒阳市	Leiyang City	392155	351149	3300	9656	4895	16155
常宁市	Changning City	352367	320720	4334	1614	5750	14530
邵阳市	**Shaoyang City**	**2634482**	**2110823**	**36131**	**250113**	**50813**	**162839**
双清区	Shuangqing District	21591	19083	78	308	564	1316
大祥区	Daxiang District	42157	34327	344	3081	1380	2646
北塔区	Beita District	16815	13042	263	305	615	2410
邵东县	Shaodong County	324939	258152	1400	31383	8598	19566

市县名称	City and County	粮食合计 Total Grain	稻谷 Rice	小麦 Wheat	玉米 Corn	大豆 Beans	薯类 Tubers
新邵县	Xinshao County	254415	190760	9281	9286	5246	36068
邵阳县	Shaoyang County	308490	257890	3725	19419	9643	14568
隆回县	Longhui County	346374	280545	6584	22947	6210	27915
洞口县	Dongkou County	430809	368246	6455	24759	7770	20369
绥宁县	Suining County	129350	114229	225	1864	2393	9641
新宁县	Xinning County	283303	215828	2575	52193	2201	10022
城步县	Chengbu County	76419	55395	728	15890	870	2939
武冈市	Wugang City	399820	303326	4473	68678	5323	15379
岳阳市	**Yueyang City**	**2271721**	**2003785**	**3529**	**116153**	**31011**	**96368**
岳阳楼区	Yueyanglou District	12211	8518		790	7	2062
云溪区	Yunxi District	31382	26612	35	819	1032	2408
君山区	Junshan District	98440	92890		2688	1192	612
岳阳县	Yueyang County	392013	327969	485	23325	8362	27054
华容县	Huarong County	273660	258000		6700	4000	3380
湘阴县	Xiangyin County	418480	378400	650	17800	1820	14400
平江县	Pingjiang County	425058	385069	1907	8066	7100	19140
汨罗市	Miluo City	414761	344491	244	54435	1987	12020
临湘市	Linxiang City	205716	181836	208	1530	5511	15292
常德市	**Changde City**	**2451332**	**2162038**	**6844**	**118998**	**34092**	**107285**
武陵区	Wuling District	33071	32049			174	673
鼎城区	Dingcheng District	488041	473791	375	602	4766	6415
安乡县	Anxiang County	149876	142960	180	1534	1631	1778
汉寿县	Hanshou County	371727	360505		1455	2146	6051
澧县	Li County	337523	290047	2928	22554	3300	13606
临澧县	Linli County	184696	164695	577	4929	4422	7270
桃源县	Taoyuan County	500550	448928	75	14683	9297	22748
石门县	Shimen County	288461	158477	2451	72076	5702	46867
津市市	Jinshi City	97387	90586	258	1165	2654	1877
张家界市	**Zhangjiajie City**	**548588**	**313212**	**9534**	**99326**	**15096**	**105269**
永定区	Yongding District	148498	97965	777	15908	3008	29580
武陵源区	Wulingyuan District	11574	7228	66	1850	435	1756
慈利县	Chili County	260617	149800	6275	56510	5450	38656
桑植县	Sangzhi County	127899	58219	2416	25058	6203	35277
益阳市	**Yiyang City**	**1566885**	**1394713**	**2287**	**40414**	**13968**	**97765**
资阳区	Ziyang District	162596	152336		348	103	9519
赫山区	Heshan District	346958	337285	70	665	961	7089
南县	Nan County	302097	282004	698	3462	2633	7556
桃江县	Taojiang County	235874	201432	180	6075	976	25990
安化县	Anhua County	256003	179639	1339	24243	8280	35769
沅江市	Yuanjiang City	263357	242017		5621	1015	11842
郴州市	**Chenzhou City**	**1811727**	**1445231**	**3974**	**164078**	**38173**	**147881**
北湖区	Beihu District	50672	40388		2832	1471	5647
苏仙区	Suxian District	127786	110285		7419	1895	7645
桂阳县	Guiyang County	298894	233349	833	13848	13775	36188
宜章县	Yizhang County	226391	158057		42933	3124	21607
永兴县	Yongxing County	250299	211418	2027	17482	2135	13835

单位：吨　　18-14 续表 2　continued　　(ton)

市县名称	City and County	粮食合计 Total Grain	稻谷 Rice	小麦 Wheat	玉米 Corn	大豆 Beans	薯类 Tubers
嘉禾县	Jiahe County	142492	89666	750	27087	4272	19042
临武县	Linwu County	117416	78446	239	18710	2508	15959
汝城县	Rucheng County	141797	125142	105	8161	1462	6552
桂东县	Guidong County	55135	51732	20	780	582	1718
安仁县	Anreng County	247921	231691		578	4135	10925
资兴市	Zixing City	152924	115057		24248	2814	8763
永州市	**Yongzhou City**	**2434515**	**2050231**	**15284**	**80974**	**74963**	**177367**
芝山区	Zhishan District	316619	291669	964	2410	6450	9169
冷水滩区	Lengshuitan District	247313	217937		10135	5661	11903
祁阳县	Qiyang County	527178	440632	11751	12918	18563	27517
东安县	Dongan County	312860	274173	601	12535	8818	15310
双牌县	Shuangpai County	55560	45584		2538	1322	5532
道县	Dao County	246864	189888	756	6423	13689	32074
江永县	Jiangyong County	105936	85189	65	4983	2504	12873
宁远县	Ningyuan County	222596	180577	1051	3213	5062	30368
蓝山县	Lanshan County	119562	103927		1402	1380	12344
新田县	Xintian County	121661	90606	74	13557	6782	8588
江华县	Jianghua County	158366	130049	22	10860	4732	11689
怀化市	**Huaihua City**	**1619385**	**1379248**	**15579**	**70451**	**23207**	**117681**
鹤城区	Hecheng District	57650	54151	42	598	610	1806
中方县	Zhongfang County	114099	100563	360	3700	1969	5876
沅陵县	Yuanling County	209124	170894		7852	7527	21827
辰溪县	Chenxi County	145054	126268	675	5150	2900	9770
溆浦县	Xupu County	325199	258242	9055	22540	6472	24990
会同县	Huitong County	102745	87799	1197	5040	1061	6149
麻阳县	Mayang County	109734	99800	1260	1580	320	5980
新晃县	Xinhuang County	75119	44636	2102	14200	223	12777
芷江县	Zhijiang County	149994	131347	770	4964	850	11316
靖州县	Jinzhou County	94813	88680	38	759	291	4002
通道县	Tongdao County	73980	67850		1490	450	4000
洪江市	Hongjiang City	161874	149018	80	2578	534	9188
娄底市	**Loudi City**	**1292350**	**1014400**	**39898**	**87434**	**26611**	**94912**
娄星区	Louxing District	79385	66287	1805	840	2530	4552
双峰县	Shuangfeng County	466869	400691	3384	21208	10642	22261
新化县	Xinhua County	350006	256153	10585	41566	3668	31771
冷水江市	Lenshuijiang City	41002	32656	2109	420	225	5162
涟源市	Lianyuan City	355088	258613	22015	23400	9546	31166
湘西自治州	**West Hunan A.P**	**780858**	**489761**	**17847**	**97092**	**21132**	**145127**
吉首市	Jishou City	46223	34760	72	2673	2079	5608
泸溪县	Louxi County	69264	61368	369	1380	1620	3409
凤凰县	Fenghuang County	88196	67457	858	8151	2484	9045
花垣县	Huayuan County	81025	55198	2125	13774	1442	8401
保靖县	Baojin County	85901	49446	1917	17580	2132	13461
古丈县	Guzhang County	32406	26255	5	3418	781	1777
永顺县	Yongshun County	206606	111342	6475	25432	5691	52143
龙山县	Longshan County	171237	83935	6026	24684	4903	51283

单位：吨　　　　18-14 续表 3 continued　　　　(ton)

市县名称	City and County	棉花 Cotton	油料 Oil-bearing	#油菜籽 Rapeseeds	黄红麻 Jute and Ambary Hemp	苎麻 Ramie	烤烟 Fluecured Tobacco	茶叶 Tea	柑桔 Citrus
长沙市	**Changsha City**	**906**	**21738**	**9921**	**1**	**508**	**14102**	**9374**	**54197**
芙蓉区	Furong District								50
天心区	Tianxin District		77	32					70
岳麓区	Yuelu District		15	15				40	620
开福区	Kaifu District		73	49				7	1340
雨花区	Yuhua District								327
长沙县	Changsha County	39	2251	1250		8	43	5157	16577
望城县	Wangcheng County		3186	2283				502	7582
宁乡县	Ningxiang County	501	8854	1659	1	17	2654	2907	15085
浏阳市	Liuyang City	366	7282	4633		483	11405	761	12546
株洲市	**Zhuzhou City**	**1144**	**27677**	**16112**		**1071**	**1125**	**1245**	**32732**
荷塘区	Hetang District		115	115				28	501
芦淞区	Lousong District		12					22	178
石峰区	Shifeng District		1650	394				16	621
天元区	Tianyuan District		443	181				38	332
株洲县	Zhuzhou County	240	2301	328				227	3826
攸 县	You County	480	8737	5185		83		260	3750
茶陵县	Chaling County	315	10634	7644		968	1125	234	15237
炎陵县	Yanling County	37	1774	1233				120	2689
醴陵市	Liling City	72	2011	1032		20		300	5598
湘潭市	**Xiangtan City**	**484**	**8298**	**1798**		**27**		**1169**	**6009**
雨湖区	Yuhu District							2	95
岳塘区	Yuetang District		224	62				41	409
湘潭县	Xiangtan County	172	4907	1008		9		510	2710
湘乡市	Xiangxiang City	285	2645	386		18		556	2615
韶山市	Shaoshan City	27	522	342				60	180
衡阳市	**Hengyang City**	**14371**	**166197**	**125962**	**93**	**246**	**15956**	**1769**	**66071**
珠晖区	Zhuhui District		990	626					2019
雁峰区	Yanfeng District		160	156					3024
石鼓区	Shigu District	8	204	154					901
蒸湘区	Zhengxinag District	20	254	228					265
南岳区	Nanyue District		80	34				40	600
衡阳县	Hengyang County	8432	56137	48371	10	43	513	39	10267
衡南县	Hengnan County	3735	36089	26331			5782	376	13949
衡山县	Hengshan County	55	3292	1428		20		236	3706
衡东县	Hengdong County	341	16349	11752		5	17	360	4385
祁东县	Qidong County	123	9584	3828			2515	55	10771
耒阳市	Leiyang City	1285	26454	22638	71	50	3960	173	9682
常宁市	Changning City	372	16604	10416	12	128	3169	490	6502
邵阳市	**Shaoyang City**	**520**	**100869**	**67168**	**25**	**316**	**6320**	**3006**	**222948**
双清区	Shuangqing District		468	256				3	5555
大祥区	Daxiang District	70	1532	716				9	11407
北塔区	Beita District		522	292				16	1371
邵东县	Shaodong County	38	10419	6034		86		257	18599

单位：吨　　　　18-14　续表 4 continued　　　　(ton)

市县名称	City and County	棉花 Cotton	油料 Oil-bearing	#油菜籽 Rapeseeds	黄红麻 Jute and Ambary Hemp	苎麻 Ramie	烤烟 Flucured Tobacco	茶叶 Tea	柑桔 Citrus
新邵县	Xinshao County	110	4084	1940		30	898	94	9487
邵阳县	Shaoyang County	86	17751	9317	17	49	1848	22	9377
隆回县	Longhui County	48	12708	8816			1953	162	8416
洞口县	Dongkou County	72	23970	17957		99	66	1640	74840
绥宁县	Suining County	7	4851	3845		16		72	31819
新宁县	Xinning County	36	9737	6535	8	10	1111	14	37795
城步县	Chengbu County		5000	4260				137	1780
武冈市	Wugang City	53	9827	7200		26	444	580	12502
岳阳市	**Yueyang City**	**46252**	**107585**	**82935**	**3260**	**15414**		**12964**	**63169**
岳阳楼区	Yueyanglou District		821	306		1		103	2000
云溪区	Yunxi District	100	2641	1932		20		190	1345
君山区	Junshan District	9028	9789	9210		264		7	9100
岳阳县	Yueyang County	1310	22771	11250		40		1742	5901
华容县	Huarong County	32400	30290	29940	2510	12000		837	22957
湘阴县	Xiangyin County	800	10845	7235	750	940		1490	5950
平江县	Pingjiang County	823	11286	7736		30		2170	6559
汨罗市	Miluo City	651	8435	6719				2385	8272
临湘市	Linxiang City	1140	10707	8607		2119		4040	1085
常德市	**Changde City**	**88131**	**337258**	**310478**	**237**	**26117**	**5430**	**7775**	**311120**
武陵区	Wuling District	763	3298	2617				70	13546
鼎城区	Dingcheng District	14500	42594	38237	12	327		221	32477
安乡县	Anxiang County	26409	40763	40581		953		10	16702
汉寿县	Hanshou County	6979	24166	21975	210	6691	23	1250	19391
澧县	Li County	19583	71394	68911	15	49		96	14515
临澧县	Linli County	6455	34601	32040		75	1025	98	7218
桃源县	Taoyuan County	7527	70178	61503		17700	1688	3328	64846
石门县	Shimen County	1624	34344	30632		320	2694	2623	134833
津市市	Jinshi City	4291	15920	13982		2		79	7592
张家界市	**Zhangjiajie City**	**1455**	**65649**	**51556**		**6707**	**9818**	**1429**	**102164**
永定区	Yongding District	122	20399	15575		2520	2011	152	19011
武陵源区	Wulingyuan District		1624	1205		13	240	7	1307
慈利县	Chili County	1320	30850	26758		4050	3150	1152	75150
桑植县	Sangzhi County	13	12776	8018		124	4417	118	6696
益阳市	**Yiyang City**	**30948**	**97914**	**84149**	**40**	**73237**	**3410**	**11347**	**112366**
资阳区	Ziyang District	178	1700	1420		606		460	7151
赫山区	Heshan District	55	2175	1205		566		1676	6819
南县	Nan County	21355	35066	34438	40	25049			27663
桃江县	Taojiang County	106	2867	1594		20	8	3600	5033
安化县	Anhua County	331	27240	16800		346	3402	5250	12340
沅江市	Yuanjiang City	8923	28866	28692		46650		361	53360
郴州市	**Chenzhou City**	**460**	**48930**	**18326**	**1**	**111**	**69614**	**1888**	**81848**
北湖区	Beihu District		1519				2839	111	2682
苏仙区	Suxian District	63	1860	52			1160	44	3468
桂阳县	Guiyang County	7	7693				44538	283	7358
宜章县	Yizhang County	6	4199	835			3739	49	6646
永兴县	Yongxing County	79	3652	2287		81	7402	188	19765

单位：吨　　　　18-14 续表 5 continued　　　　(ton)

市县名称	City and County	棉花 Cotton	油料 Oil-bearing	#油菜籽 Rapeseeds	黄红麻 Jute and Ambary Hemp	苎麻 Ramie	烤烟 Fluecured Tobacco	茶叶 Tea	柑桔 Citrus
嘉禾县	Jiahe County	3	5025	314		1	6009	76	10376
临武县	Linwu County		2603	11			1896	28	1742
汝城县	Rucheng County	180	2854	1800	1		50	92	717
桂东县	Guidong County	16	354	33			90	150	895
安仁县	Anreng County	41	14085	11255		3	1747	461	3894
资兴市	Zixing City	65	5086	1739		26	144	406	24305
永州市	**Yongzhou City**	**2558**	**63895**	**13143**	**77**	**39**	**30854**	**1391**	**206336**
芝山区	Zhishan District	659	6013	272	6		594	466	17946
冷水滩区	Lengshuitan District	735	3716	850			374		18945
祁阳县	Qiyang County	503	18133	7443	53		992	319	41382
东安县	Dongan County	285	7038	229		7	149	5	14177
双牌县	Shuangpai County	9	572					36	3752
道县	Dao County	34	7874	112			1419	17	35713
江永县	Jiangyong County		5471	1877			3007	66	29456
宁远县	Ningyuan County	288	4144	213	18	17	6781	124	29000
蓝山县	Lanshan County		1660				5065	71	8093
新田县	Xintian County		3074	137		15	8453	75	3037
江华县	Jianghua County	45	6200	2010			4020	212	4835
怀化市	**Huaihua City**	**1866**	**96767**	**78662**	**52**	**41**	**2734**	**1294**	**224664**
鹤城区	Hecheng District	4	3422	2601	2		4		3432
中方县	Zhongfang County	282	6894	5200			46	30	9760
沅陵县	Yuanling County	27	15324	11848			32	496	3517
辰溪县	Chenxi County	350	8710	5850			220	16	15704
溆浦县	Xupu County	1020	16750	15223			358	662	34238
会同县	Huitong County	24	7394	7116	43	8	200	38	27281
麻阳县	Mayang County	52	11242	6120		18		2	29570
新晃县	Xinhuang County	3	4083	3605	7	15	738	1	3351
芷江县	Zhijiang County	37	8190	7165			784	6	29097
靖州县	Jinzhou County	37	6141	5730			79	2	11912
通道县	Tongdao County	20	2850	2780				1	2073
洪江市	Hongjiang City	10	5767	5424			273	40	54729
娄底市	**Loudi City**	**692**	**27330**	**11828**		**127**	**964**	**5326**	**24410**
娄星区	Louxing District	10	1543	389		15		1150	3900
双峰县	Shuangfeng County	541	11282	5512		58	35	2108	4169
新化县	Xinhua County	28	8888	4795			747	900	3582
冷水江市	Lenshuijiang City		363	43			2	38	6331
涟源市	Lianyuan City	113	5254	1089		54	180	1130	6428
湘西自治州	**West Hunan A.P**	**302**	**86921**	**66745**		**366**	**16295**	**596**	**166353**
吉首市	Jishou City	60	7328	5568		99	754		28742
泸溪县	Louxi County	52	8772	7589			50	4	30578
凤凰县	Fenghuang County	31	11401	9141		166	2711	40	26226
花垣县	Huayuan County	12	6702	4842			849	5	3615
保靖县	Baojin County	50	9831	6013			785	72	27223
古丈县	Guzhang County	47	3316	3097			71	305	7623
永顺县	Yongshun County	38	25875	19151		101	2649	107	25251
龙山县	Longshan County	12	13696	11344			8426	63	17095

18-15 各市、州、县主要林产品产量(2003年)

Output of Major Forest Products (2003)

市县名称	City and County	油茶籽(吨) Tea-oil Seeds (ton)	油桐籽(吨) Tung-oil Seeds (ton)	松脂(吨) Pine Resin (ton)	板栗(吨) Chestnuts (ton)	棕片(吨) Palm Leaf (ton)	竹笋干(吨) Bamboo Shoots (ton)	木材采伐量(万方) Woods Cuts (10 000 cu.m)	竹材采伐量(万根) Bamboo Cuts (10 000 roots)
长沙市	**Changsha City**	**48134**	**975**	**720**	**1645**	**380**	**1003**	**18.99**	**96.42**
芙蓉区	Furong District								
天心区	Tianxin District								
岳麓区	Yuelu District	1			6		2		
开福区	Kaifu District	12	20	10	4	1		0.30	3.40
雨花区	Yuhua District			10	2				
长沙县	Changsha County	2230	143	130	21	37	1	2.64	6.72
望城县	Wangcheng County	156	12	50	50	20			
宁乡县	Ningxiang County	4020		260	120	2		1.90	29.00
浏阳市	Liuyang City	41715	800	260	1442	320	1000	14.15	57.30
株洲市	**Zhuzhou City**	**51884**	**1166**	**2158**	**1971**	**552**	**3101**	**24.23**	**780.00**
荷塘区	Hetang District	1490				50	13	0.02	1.82
芦淞区	Lousong District	1500						0.05	1.10
石峰区	Shifeng District	1460		18	2	30	8	0.11	
天元区	Tianyuan District	686			2			0.02	1.08
株洲县	Zhuzhou County	6850	28	220	340	18	48	1.60	126.00
攸 县	You County	17380	330	40	495	200	760	4.94	142.00
茶陵县	Chaling County	12358	763	1500	782	187	812	5.44	166.00
炎陵县	Yanling County	1080	20	300	150	45	1395	12.05	342.00
醴陵市	Liling City	9080	25	80	200	22	65	1.80	62.00
湘潭市	**Xiangtan City**	**14831**	**116**	**478**	**134**	**107**	**351**	**4.95**	**155.06**
雨湖区	Yuhu District	10			2			0.03	
岳塘区	Yuetang District	116		6				0.18	0.31
湘潭县	Xiangtan County	5600	105	370	130	90	70	2.75	129.75
湘乡市	Xiangxiang City	9000	10	80		17	280	1.94	24.00
韶山市	Shaoshan City	105	1	22	2		1	0.05	1.00
衡阳市	**Hengyang City**	**63516**	**2897**	**620**	**7279**	**192**	**1707**	**10.68**	**520.00**
珠晖区	Zhuhui District	30	2		4	5	8	0.01	50.00
雁峰区	Yanfeng District							0.02	
石鼓区	Shigu District							0.01	
蒸湘区	Zhengxinag District							0.03	
南岳区	Nanyue District							0.45	33.00
衡阳县	Hengyang County	2100	10	20	2000		150	2.00	150.00
衡南县	Hengnan County	320	1804	280	180	61	110	2.19	30.00
衡山县	Hengshan County	4765	360	210	294			1.08	80.00
衡东县	Hengdong County	11000	610		2500	35	18	2.20	50.00
祁东县	Qidong County	5001	51		101	11	101	0.99	55.00
耒阳市	Leiyang City	15800	40	110	1450		320		
常宁市	Changning City	24500	20		750	80	1000	1.70	72.00
邵阳市	**Shaoyang City**	**3781**	**1032**	**620**	**923**	**224**	**1396**	**66.17**	**899.67**
双清区	Shuangqing District							0.04	
大祥区	Daxiang District							0.44	
北塔区	Beita District								
邵东县	Shaodong County	130	40	60	40			2.40	2.50

市县名称	City and County	油茶籽(吨) Tea-oil Seeds (ton)	油桐籽(吨) Tung-oil Seeds (ton)	松脂(吨) Pine Resin (ton)	板栗(吨) Chestnuts (ton)	棕片(吨) Palm Leaf (ton)	竹笋干(吨) Bamboo Shoots (ton)	木材采伐量(万方) Woods Cuts (10 000 cu.m)	竹材采伐量(万根) Bamboo Cuts (10 000 roots)
新邵县	Xinshao County	235	250	50	120	20	45	3.58	73.00
邵阳县	Shaoyang County	3030	310	136	405	16	12	2.86	22.00
隆回县	Longhui County	108	245	2	5	25	480	9.50	95.80
洞口县	Dongkou County	20	30	80	30	5	1	9.57	135.45
绥宁县	Suining County	39	6	52	21	16	602	21.22	268.80
新宁县	Xinning County	5	20	150	100	30	50	5.57	110.00
城步县	Chengbu County	130	95	90	150	50	170	8.69	188.12
武冈市	Wugang City	84	36		52	62	36	2.30	4.00
岳阳市	**Yueyang City**	**6426**	**629**	**301**	**1154**	**300**	**245**	**20.38**	**635.26**
岳阳楼区	Yueyanglou District				5			0.43	0.13
云溪区	Yunxi District	6	1		45		1	0.45	10.00
君山区	Junshan District							0.36	0.50
岳阳县	Yueyang County							2.60	60.00
华容县	Huarong County		48	26	126	17	32	2.00	80.00
湘阴县	Xiangyin County	30	40	70				1.28	3.30
平江县	Pingjiang County	6100	500		768	130	180	8.74	177.26
汨罗市	Miluo City	240	20	200	80	3	12	2.40	19.30
临湘市	Linxiang City	50	20	5	130	150	20	2.12	284.77
常德市	**Changde City**	**24145**	**2024**	**338**	**1474**	**338**	**112**	**17.00**	**447.00**
武陵区	Wuling District	500						0.20	
鼎城区	Dingcheng District	6500	5	240	40	3	3	3.54	172.00
安乡县	Anxiang County							0.80	
汉寿县	Hanshou County	2000	40					1.10	39.00
澧县	Li County	896	69					1.70	
临澧县	Linli County	5673	34	8	529	6	61	0.50	
桃源县	Taoyuan County	7636	1355	80	314	189	48	8.60	236.00
石门县	Shimen County	940	421	10	533	140		0.06	
津市市	Jinshi City		100		58			0.50	
张家界市	**Zhangjiajie City**	**1024**	**1041**	**650**	**1569**	**733**	**52**	**16.49**	**494.00**
永定区	Yongding District	270	127		530	210	12	8.01	100.00
武陵源区	Wulingyuan District				3			0.11	
慈利县	Chili County	382	500	300	506	427	40	4.21	44.00
桑植县	Sangzhi County	372	414	350	530	96		4.16	350.00
益阳市	**Yiyang City**	**7339**	**559**	**443**	**615**	**1155**	**383**	**27.20**	**1220.00**
资阳区	Ziyang District	200	2		20	2	2		
赫山区	Heshan District	2020	25		10			3.32	68.70
南县	Nan County							1.50	
桃江县	Taojiang County	2100	150	200	200	300	30	3.88	750.00
安化县	Anhua County	3004	382	243	385	841	351	14.30	401.30
沅江市	Yuanjiang City	15				12		4.20	
郴州市	**Chenzhou City**	**40972**	**853**	**3316**	**2279**	**809**	**2515**	**57.32**	**614.22**
北湖区	Beihu District	3145	10	260	307		366	2.45	51.12
苏仙区	Suxian District	3220	31	225	75	11	127	3.46	146.00
桂阳县	Guiyang County	8120	107	880	96	180	194	4.59	39.00
宜章县	Yizhang County	1254	12	633	70	105	65	3.80	65.62
永兴县	Yongxing County	5762	21	267	221	16	329	4.34	31.00

市县名称	City and County	油茶籽(吨) Tea-oil Seeds (ton)	油桐籽(吨) Tung-oil Seeds (ton)	松脂(吨) Pine Resin (ton)	板栗(吨) Chestnuts (ton)	棕片(吨) Palm Leaf (ton)	竹笋干(吨) Bamboo Shoots (ton)	木材采伐量(万方) Woods Cuts (10 000 cu.m)	竹材采伐量(万根) Bamboo Cuts (10 000 roots)
嘉禾县	Jiahe County	2732	69	179	211	1	21	2.40	7.80
临武县	Linwu County	2300	175	100	195	90	140	3.00	26.50
汝城县	Rucheng County	4000	25	100	380	190	330	9.98	37.00
桂东县	Guidong County	350	29	10	24	40	174	3.42	40.00
安仁县	Anreng County	6189	78	602	260	51	69	4.08	22.18
资兴市	Zixing City	3900	296	60	440	125	700	15.80	148.00
永州市	**Yongzhou City**	**41207**	**1209**	**4702**	**2526**	**963**	**1609**	**62.45**	**486.11**
芝山区	Zhishan District	2450	50	80	156	75	116	1.88	80.31
冷水滩区	Lengshuitan District	5580	20	601	19		10	1.29	7.29
祁阳县	Qiyang County	9950	350	865	1020	95	610	2.88	16.66
东安县	Dongan County	3250	13	8	33	152	30	2.74	88.22
双牌县	Shuangpai County	128	31	41	59	34	87	15.35	110.00
道县	Dao County	8066	169	80	156	75	116	3.58	20.31
江永县	Jiangyong County	519	17	10		330		7.62	4.55
宁远县	Ningyuan County	6000	42	10	40	80	20	5.29	46.08
蓝山县	Lanshan County	1380	28	87	31	47	60	5.75	62.83
新田县	Xintian County	1800	8	60	910	15	20	1.85	33.83
江华县	Jianghua County	7700	600	2860	102	60	540	14.22	16.03
怀化市	**Huaihua City**	**25214**	**15098**	**2878**	**4542**	**1562**	**1026**	**74.03**	**484.40**
鹤城区	Hecheng District	2175	1036	790	801	305	60	1.88	0.20
中方县	Zhongfang County	5120	2700		510	840	90	3.67	8.00
沅陵县	Yuanling County	718	395	25	1113	101	123	10.30	14.00
辰溪县	Chenxi County	1870	182	10	110	36	30	3.30	21.00
溆浦县	Xupu County	2000	1000	50	47	43	41	5.40	40.00
会同县	Huitong County	6362	4904	426	337	56	317	7.50	74.00
麻阳县	Mayang County	300	340		500			1.01	10.00
新晃县	Xinhuang County	90	1700	30	112	120	6	3.50	13.50
芷江县	Zhijiang County	1283	962	25	518	36	14	5.32	36.00
靖州县	Jinzhou County	842	125	511	98	1	60	14.30	63.50
通道县	Tongdao County	2400	560	870	70	1	45	11.80	65.20
洪江市	Hongjiang City	2054	1194	141	326	23	240	6.05	139.00
娄底市	**Loudi City**	**4688**	**469**	**161**	**471**	**179**	**826**	**7.60**	**220.00**
娄星区	Louxing District							0.15	0.50
双峰县	Shuangfeng County	4251	182	64	98	78	146	1.10	70.00
新化县	Xinhua County	268	170	50	250	25	450	5.20	87.00
冷水江市	Lenshuijiang City	48	19		16	21	16	0.15	2.50
涟源市	Lianyuan City	121	98	47	107	55	214	1.00	60.00
湘西自治州	**West Hunan A.P**	**6555**	**9645**	**14**	**2787**	**128**	**84**	**4.61**	**12.20**
吉首市	Jishou City	122	114		114	10	3	0.18	
泸溪县	Louxi County	664	628		368	15	8	0.58	
凤凰县	Fenghuang County	150	250		250	4	1	0.37	3.00
花垣县	Huayuan County	120	40		60	10	27	0.03	6.00
保靖县	Baojin County	180	210		800	30	15	0.28	3.20
古丈县	Guzhang County	350	150		95	4	2	2.07	
永顺县	Yongshun County	3859	2801	8	510	20	23	0.62	
龙山县	Longshan County	1110	5452	6	590	35	5	0.48	

18-16 各市、州、县牲畜头数、畜产品及水产品产量(2003年)

Number of Livestocks,Output of Livestock Products and Aquatic Products (2003)

市县名称	City and County	大牲畜年末存栏数(头) Large Animals (head)	#牛 Cattle and Buffaloes	生猪存栏(万头) Hogs (10 000 heads)	肉猪出栏(万头) Slaughtered Fattened Hogs (10 000 heads)	猪肉产量(吨) Output of Pork (ton)	牛肉产量(吨) Output of Beef (ton)	羊肉产量(吨) Output of Mutton (ton)	水产品(吨) Aquatic Products (ton)	#鱼 Fish
长沙市	**Changsha City**	**352338**	**351520**	**391.77**	**683.13**	**466179**	**14195**	**10304**	**94235**	**91553**
芙蓉区	Furong District	85	85	2.5	9	5715			1018	895
天心区	Tianxin District	305	300	5	6	4000	12	3	2400	2400
岳麓区	Yuelu District	223	223	5.95	19	12350	38	6	1917	1917
开福区	Kaifu District	2370	2370	17.1	26.49	16550	246	23	5500	5490
雨花区	Yuhua District	305	305	7.82	16.5	10725	318	36	1830	1830
长沙县	Changsha County	132696	132696	99.8	179.8	125125	5550	360	14250	14050
望城县	Wangcheng County	17352	17352	72.8	116	76346	767	99	20049	18374
宁乡县	Ningxiang County	122593	122580	107.4	170.14	118630	5105	1965	28321	28267
浏阳市	Liuyang City	76409	75609	73.4	140.2	96738	2159	7812	18950	18330
株洲市	**Zhuzhou City**	**188014**	**187291**	**229.28**	**370.55**	**241411**	**6353**	**5025**	**56345**	**54888**
荷塘区	Hetang District	980	980	7.48	8.3	5300	40	210	1682	1680
芦淞区	Lousong District	700	700	3.04	5.61	3647	70	155	1470	1438
石峰区	Shifeng District	2100	2100	7.1	13.32	8658	60	362	1652	1631
天元区	Tianyuan District	655	655	5.5	8.5	5607	70	110	1040	1030
株洲县	Zhuzhou County	8731	8664	26.4	50.86	33059	150	660	10170	9591
攸 县	You County	54248	54100	58.5	104.78	68107	1825	409	12782	12563
茶陵县	Chaling County	69032	68624	46.2	72	46800	2780	280	11000	10763
炎陵县	Yanling County	23568	23568	10.61	16.3	10595	196	46	749	713
醴陵市	Liling City	28000	27900	64.45	90.88	59638	1162	2793	15800	15479
湘潭市	**Xiangtan City**	**104169**	**104124**	**213.85**	**456.17**	**307565**	**714**	**772**	**63380**	**60375**
雨湖区	Yuhu District	308	308	10.7	30.58	20927		19.	2050	2035
岳塘区	Yuetang District	744	699	9.6	24.29	16229	10	228	2080	1844
湘潭县	Xiangtan County	9712	9712	96.5	216.34	145353	336	295	32500	31270
湘乡市	Xiangxiang City	91102	91102	83.1	167.36	112856	260	168	24400	22885
韶山市	Shaoshan City	2303	2303	13.95	17.6	12200	108	62	2350	2341
衡阳市	**Hengyang City**	**249762**	**246903**	**416.1**	**805.81**	**547712**	**7703**	**7119**	**209486**	**199120**
珠晖区	Zhuhui District	1253	1253	4.95	10.71	6952		2	3090	2930
雁峰区	Yanfeng District	543	543	3.09	4.5	2970			1616	1612
石鼓区	Shigu District	841	841	3.2	4.94	3408			2326	2203
蒸湘区	Zhengxinag District	200	200	1.64	4.64	3016	20	6	2115	2000
南岳区	Nanyue District	5340	5340	2.76	4.7	3055	309	40	510	498
衡阳县	Hengyang County	54600	54600	87.2	167	116112	928	918	46890	44093
衡南县	Hengnan County	53489	53489	58.7	140	100660	1240	155	42086	39530
衡山县	Hengshan County	8600	8600	21.36	51.9	34254	160	115	9620	9288
衡东县	Hengdong County	34814	32108	59.7	96	63685	700	391	14500	11382
祁东县	Qidong County	15890	15780	47.4	104.7	69102	770	4500	43213	43032
耒阳市	Leiyang City	40200	40200	60	121	82280	3006	540	24000	23550
常宁市	Changning City	33992	33949	66.1	95.72	62218	570	452	19520	19002
邵阳市	**Shaoyang City**	**868907**	**853980**	**463.82**	**726.59**	**497649**	**31078**	**5772**	**71249**	**68968**
双清区	Shuangqing District	4377	4377	5.8	14.52	11676	808	122	1929	1924
大祥区	Daxiang District	7625	7441	7.38	13.73	9566	528	111	1510	1463
北塔区	Beita District	4428	4428	2.45	5.32	3507	135	49	1305	1266
邵东县	Shaodong County	34810	34810	62	117	80500	1550	233	24240	22700

市县名称	City and County	大牲畜年末存栏数(头) Large Animals (head)	#牛 Cattle and Buffaloes	生猪存栏(万头) Hogs (10 000 heads)	肉猪出栏(万头) Slaughtered Fattened Hogs (10 000 heads)	猪肉产量(吨) Output of Pork (ton)	牛肉产量(吨) Output of Beef (ton)	羊肉产量(吨) Output of Mutton (ton)	水产品(吨) Aquatic Products (ton)	#鱼 Fish
新邵县	Xinshao County	85575	85467	48.83	62.50	41610	1826	440	4843	4717
邵阳县	Shaoyang County	94687	89424	41.65	61.30	42297	3200	494	7520	7482
隆回县	Longhui County	124118	122927	51.13	67.92	46182	4890	824	6566	6518
洞口县	Dongkou County	85266	85066	88.86	157.40	112243	4365	1005	10119	10000
绥宁县	Suining County	98498	97962	29.8	34.00	22356	5052	780	1710	1668
新宁县	Xinning County	150798	146340	39.15	26.86	18444	4612	404	4098	4076
城步县	Chengbu County	104804	103947	15.47	16.84	10272	1962	617	609	609
武冈市	Wugang City	73921	71791	71.3	149.20	98996	2150	693	6800	6545
岳阳市	**Yueyang City**	**212021**	**210492**	**345.39**	**722.54**	**481296**	**8671**	**4179**	**303963**	**287364**
岳阳楼区	Yueyanglou District	1160	1160	6.47	22.60	16785	70	21	14519	14179
云溪区	Yunxi District	4773	4773	5	18.00	13500	56	100	13500	12509
君山区	Junshan District	10700	10700	23	35.60	23140	243	62	26700	26050
岳阳县	Yueyang County	22862	22862	66.39	125.00	85000	2400	250	37100	35753
华容县	Huarong County	23880	23000	34.4	74.62	48503	900	360	77000	70984
湘阴县	Xiangyin County	17460	17460	59.2	102.00	66300	1368	168	80000	78497
平江县	Pingjiang County	48451	48174	47	100.50	64320	1700	2880	5680	5605
汨罗市	Miluo City	64828	64828	93.27	201.20	134496	1830	160	28967	24783
临湘市	Linxiang City	17907	17535	10.66	43.02	29252	104	178	20497	19004
常德市	**Changde City**	**373119**	**371937**	**289.34**	**503.44**	**342829**	**19164**	**38825**	**272768**	**261437**
武陵区	Wuling District	3505	3501	8.45	15.82	10762	300	343	11324	10974
鼎城区	Dingcheng District	36920	36867	44.46	71.68	48742	2028	2471	52378	51110
安乡县	Anxiang County	13301	13076	18.82	35.11	23875	1212	831	55208	53745
汉寿县	Hanshou County	23510	23410	32.63	52.16	35872	972	508	46883	42448
澧县	Li County	31529	31479	41.58	77.91	52982	1872	3696	37910	37687
临澧县	Linli County	34361	34344	27.96	45.02	30612	2412	3061	14392	12921
桃源县	Taoyuan County	125824	125416	60.34	108.06	73481	6060	12547	33104	31434
石门县	Shimen County	89189	88874	41.69	69.09	46985	3408	14477	7591	7574
津市市	Jinshi City	14980	14970	13.41	28.59	19518	900	891	13978	13544
张家界市	**Zhangjiajie City**	**166349**	**163248**	**76.29**	**106.81**	**80419**	**7249**	**4191**	**7694**	**7626**
永定区	Yongding District	40295	40024	23.41	31.58	23685	3612	1294	2855	2855
武陵源区	Wulingyuan District	3164	3121	2	2.80	2184	183	255	23	23
慈利县	Chili County	68660	67630	33.2	50.33	37748	2760	2228	4202	4160
桑植县	Sangzhi County	54230	52473	17.68	22.10	16802	694	414	614	588
益阳市	**Yiyang City**	**288555**	**286053**	**204.11**	**321.04**	**223504**	**11404**	**6026**	**186077**	**179080**
资阳区	Ziyang District	6315	6315	18	29.54	19791	85	25	15099	14728
赫山区	Heshan District	9679	9317	31.44	62.37	46792	766	240	17103	16637
南县	Nan County	14640	13300	33.6	57.78	40432	1012	350	60419	59123
桃江县	Taojiang County	45900	45800	40.57	54.33	36495	847	534	4900	4789
安化县	Anhua County	195000	194300	42	55.00	36580	8064	4785	12500	12214
沅江市	Yuanjiang City	17021	17021	38.5	62.02	43414	630	92	76056	71589
郴州市	**Chenzhou City**	**407612**	**406505**	**306.51**	**512.99**	**360800**	**12833**	**5462**	**80380**	**78356**
北湖区	Beihu District	26719	26447	11.9	24.03	16821	1210	611	3140	3057
苏仙区	Suxian District	67465	67465	18.94	39.85	25619	1340	1613	8268	8200
桂阳县	Guiyang County	48100	48000	46.26	71.25	49745	1043	460	11820	11707
宜章县	Yizhang County	47099	46587	38.55	57.78	41334	1253	281	5684	5583
永兴县	Yongxing County	64824	64800	47	68.92	48270	2410	416	14540	14248

市县名称	City and County	大牲畜年末存栏数(头) Large Animals (head)	#牛 Cattle and Buffaloes	生猪存栏(万头) Hogs (10 000 heads)	肉猪出栏(万头) Slaughtered Fattened Hogs (10 000 heads)	猪肉产量(吨) Output of Pork (ton)	牛肉产量(吨) Output of Beef (ton)	羊肉产量(吨) Output of Mutton (ton)	水产品(吨) Aquatic Products (ton)	#鱼 Fish
嘉禾县	Jiahe County	17889	17867	35	58.76	41619	1436	181	2611	2494
临武县	Linwu County	18931	18774	23.24	33.36	24293	926	1017	3231	2679
汝城县	Rucheng County	28900	28900	27.5	35.60	25020	700	85	1015	950
桂东县	Guidong County	22500	22500	8.5	11.24	7868	330	165	600	598
安仁县	Anreng County	31700	31700	24.47	59.20	43111	545	75	8285	7864
资兴市	Zixing City	33485	33465	25.15	53.00	37100	1640	558	21186	20976
永州市	**Yongzhou City**	**708345**	**702231**	**378.7**	**588.69**	**425412**	**22881**	**5573**	**116617**	**111656**
芝山区	Zhishan District	66473	66333	36.66	60.50	43560	853	193	9880	9012
冷水滩区	Lengshuitan District	33957	33882	36.5	59.50	42840	638	169	15025	14679
祁阳县	Qiyang County	16408	16408	47.88	98.74	72200	1228	560	35788	34568
东安县	Dongan County	77924	75019	32.4	53.94	38837	1870	411	13580	12874
双牌县	Shuangpai County	24069	24000	9.8	11.90	8211	666	1256	2389	2261
道县	Dao County	155452	153211	59.01	79.45	58963	7435	1006	16450	15654
江永县	Jiangyong County	140752	140200	17.63	33.06	23803	5486	321	3608	3193
宁远县	Ningyuan County	49803	49750	48.65	71.15	50274	1219	92	11700	11472
蓝山县	Lanshan County	36749	36717	31	44.20	31824	658	225	1870	1785
新田县	Xintian County	16747	16700	26.57	38.85	27972	792	312	4300	4214
江华县	Jianghua County	90011	90011	32.6	37.40	26928	2036	1028	2027	1944
怀化市	**Huaihua City**	**695599**	**692314**	**248.46**	**338.10**	**261183**	**19789**	**10408**	**35255**	**33794**
鹤城区	Hecheng District	13951	13909	12.04	15.00	9903	540	479	3596	3497
中方县	Zhongfang County	32000	32000	18.5	29.60	22792	755	425	3020	2875
沅陵县	Yuanling County	110639	110639	24.7	29.00	23200	1101	1205	5258	4946
辰溪县	Chenxi County	42130	42130	21.8	28.90	18785	792	400	1735	1695
溆浦县	Xupu County	65605	65400	40.02	65.90	54098	1328	1376	5173	5162
会同县	Huitong County	72920	72682	17.56	23.50	18330	2272	3440	2306	2200
麻阳县	Mayang County	46130	46100	15.4	18.00	13253	720	860	2235	2207
新晃县	Xinhuang County	101800	101000	25.24	28.45	20199	6659	853	1020	990
芷江县	Zhijiang County	48408	48177	22.43	36.40	29692	721	407	3037	3036
靖州县	Jinzhou County	58934	57710	18.7	18.90	15451	3239	459	2726	2278
通道县	Tongdao County	57800	57600	13	10.70	8025	811	174	1440	1355
洪江市	Hongjiang City	45282	44967	19.07	33.75	27455	851	330	3709	3553
娄底市	**Loudi City**	**313942**	**311872**	**249.89**	**406.94**	**253635**	**9194**	**2206**	**50483**	**48798**
娄星区	Louxing District	20200	20100	16.4	22.74	14099	980	300	4500	4062
双峰县	Shuangfeng County	38492	38492	84.83	157.20	99036	570	104	21500	20975
新化县	Xinhua County	171294	169536	76.56	128.89	77710	5985	752	12384	12135
冷水江市	Lenshuijiang City	17884	17874	13	20.01	12806	639	348	2749	2692
涟源市	Lianyuan City	66072	65870	59.1	78.10	49984	1020	702	9350	8934
湘西自治州	**West Hunan A.P**	**475174**	**474784**	**110.59**	**117.39**	**79216**	**6725**	**6268**	**18015**	**17697**
吉首市	Jishou City	33745	33745	6.01	9.93	6752	338	762	1725	1657
泸溪县	Louxi County	49378	49378	7.97	11.34	7798	396	595	1551	1433
凤凰县	Fenghuang County	62636	62632	12.78	10.20	7344	551	284	2380	2366
花垣县	Huayuan County	56322	56322	18.12	14.39	9354	1020	1184	2894	2882
保靖县	Baojin County	63406	63406	14.1	16.79	11082	789	1378	1554	1540
古丈县	Guzhang County	36921	36909	5.64	6.13	3985	332	273	1157	1153
永顺县	Yongshun County	118174	117813	24.93	23.16	15054	2531	869	1545	1501
龙山县	Longshan County	54592	54579	21.04	25.45	17847	768	923	5209	5165

18-17 各市、州、县规模以上工业总产值(2003年)

Gross Output Vale of Industrial Enterprises Above Designated Size (2003)

单位：万元　　　　(10 000 yuan)

市县名称	City and County	工业总产值 Gross Industrial Output Value	轻工业 Light Industry	重工业 Heavy Industry	#国有经济 State-owned Economic	#集体经济 Collective Owned Economic	指数(上年为100) Indices (precending year=100)
长沙市	**Changsha City**	**5643301**	**2249507**	**3393793**	**1282779**	**170314**	**132.86**
芙蓉区	Furong District	218487	65077	153409	9178	10329	125.48
天心区	Tianxin District	330621	101391	229230	167258	18009	111.42
岳麓区	Yuelu District	684855	106300	578555	60096	4398	137.83
开福区	Kaifu District	364099	280635	83464	38339	4831	112.91
雨花区	Yuhua District	1304086	946993	357093	934981	18864	97.14
长沙县	Changsha County	1746334	304541	1441793	10773	23585	150.77
望城县	Wangcheng County	260510	141550	118960	47760	17043	139.74
宁乡县	Ningxiang County	354896	170673	184223	6209	34975	138.29
浏阳市	Liuyang City	379413	132347	247067	8185	38280	165.41
株洲市	**Zhuzhou City**	**2620980**	**464565**	**2156415**	**608594**	**134956**	**108.99**
荷塘区	Hetang District	373913	29950	343964	135559	10714	114.37
芦淞区	Lusong District	312340	175408	136933	135523	4727	101.57
石峰区	Shifeng District	1294309	27189	1267119	296847	30280	105.71
天元区	Tianyuan District	111228	18888	92340	31		119.68
株洲县	Zhuzhou County	29841	9522	20319	5416	2325	106.30
攸　县	You County	121908	29017	92890	8108	11919	119.28
茶陵县	Chaling County	33436	6075	27361	9639	10600	134.45
炎陵县	Yanling County	9348	2597	6751	3593		137.58
醴陵市	Liling City	334657	165918	168738	13879	64392	118.68
湘潭市	**Xiangtan City**	**2025509**	**476959**	**1548549**	**959100**	**93413**	**116.10**
雨湖区	Yuhu District	264391	74232	190159	61905	20117	132.12
岳塘区	Yuetang District	1306739	225847	1080892	861186	25609	110.91
湘潭县	Xiangtan County	130487	40371	90116	23961	27909	138.75
湘乡市	Xiangxiang City	296811	117650	179161	11759	17660	118.41
韶山市	Shaoshan City	27081	18859	8222	290	2119	103.66
衡阳市	**Hengyang City**	**2112036**	**519322**	**1592715**	**689166**	**346158**	**127.22**
珠晖区	Zhuhui District	223288	19632	203656	128519	5977	138.73
雁峰区	Yanfeng District	293031	97999	195033	71740	10057	123.34
石鼓区	Shigu District	64795	17234	47561	28165	6853	117.71
蒸湘区	Zhengxiang District	284804	8373	276431	235331	4879	120.44
南岳区	Nanyue District	1061	717	344	171	344	98.46
衡阳县	Hengyang County	186150	93118	93032	18930	133737	121.68
衡南县	Hengnan County	156324	27861	128463	14965	82006	126.96
衡山县	Hengshan County	51005	25324	25681	15873	3151	123.38
衡东县	Hengdong County	119614	34932	84682	15169	7340	145.00
祁东县	Qidong County	218415	176990	41425	14733	2288	128.80
耒阳市	Leiyang City	269857	15144	254713	127434	24393	166.47
常宁市	Changning City	243693	2001	241693	18138	65134	110.89
邵阳市	**Shaoyang City**	**845098**	**410520**	**434578**	**249510**	**68731**	**119.74**
双清区	Shuangqing District	188850	93083	95767	71254	12979	115.92
大祥区	Daxiang District	80779	30631	50147	26577	12943	107.58
北塔区	Beita District	40194	32548	7646	4686	5673	149.64

市县名称	City and County	工业总产值 Gross Industrial Output Value	轻工业 Light Industry	重工业 Heavy Industry	#国有经济 State-owned Economic	#集体经济 Collective Owned Economic	指数(上年为100) Indices (precending year=100)
邵东县	Shaodong County	146271	55874	90397	63219	15354	123.81
新邵县	Xinshao County	52771	22279	30492	17740	4040	130.91
邵阳县	Shaoyang County	38191	20655	17537	5645	710	141.97
隆回县	Longhui County	45005	28011	16994	20869	4255	77.12
洞口县	Dongkou County	47491	24938	22553	11906	3528	133.82
绥宁县	Suining County	78077	25436	52641	4527	4386	120.79
新宁县	Xinning County	25742	9463	16279	9354	4386	128.92
城步县	Chengbu County	72325	61944	10381	7065	4386	136.95
武冈市	Wugang City	29403	5658	23745	6668	4865	132.61
岳阳市	**Yueyang City**	**4359114**	**1381984**	**2977130**	**497915**	**319258**	**115.99**
岳阳楼区	Yueyanglou District	2967017	621365	2345653	377281	62235	112.30
云溪区	Yunxi District	50331	11749	38583	360	3179	146.79
君山区	Junshan District	59306	48359	10947	10617	3694	159.29
岳阳县	Yueyang County	117465	90124	27340	18367	44254	133.67
华容县	Huarong County	195738	89848	105890	5722	97011	101.03
湘阴县	Xiangyin County	263722	192489	71233	5920	24465	113.67
平江县	Pingjiang City	78673	26081	52593	10817	530	114.52
汨罗市	Miluo City	475971	256559	219412	19820	33149	138.22
临湘市	Linxiang County	150891	45411	105481	49012	50741	112.05
常德市	**Changde City**	**2204544**	**1483704**	**720840**	**1025267**	**130642**	**117.46**
武陵区	Wuling District	1135455	966860	168595	769627	1931	116.03
鼎城区	Dingcheng District	144151	55129	89022	839	19826	120.27
安乡县	Anxiang County	104976	86296	18680	7294	36668	116.63
汉寿县	Hanshou County	112273	89640	22633	5708	1922	138.20
澧　县	Li County	141457	96834	44623	24155	11164	119.17
临澧县	Linli County	131565	90896	40669	32689	37380	118.99
桃源县	Taoyuan County	152030	56593	95438	11270	18562	122.77
石门县	Shimen County	146996	7541	139455	88466	3191	122.37
津市市	Jinshi City	135643	33916	101727	85218	7491	101.18
张家界市	**Zhangjiajie City**	**157787**	**54684**	**103103**	**45211**	**4461**	**144.29**
永定区	Yongdi District	62657	22286	40371	10109	3578	152.97
武陵源区	Wulingyuan District	1276	256	1020	1229		108.34
慈利县	Cili County	71520	19802	51718	26992	883	138.13
桑植县	Sangzhi County	22335	12341	9994	6881		143.15
益阳市	**Yiyang City**	**831141**	**386841**	**444301**	**242269**	**112309**	**125.05**
资阳区	Ziyang District	38540	20297	18243	6301	3756	104.01
赫山区	Heshan District	411039	161865	249174	116897	28296	140.08
南　县	Nan County	93429	81083	12346	14650	30038	96.36
桃江县	Taojiang County	85154	7042	78112	22964	10060	127.27
安化县	Anhua County	64476	8737	55739	26111	18448	105.82
沅江市	Yuanjiang City	138504	107817	30687	55346	21712	126.58
郴州市	**Chenzhou City**	**1675898**	**304283**	**1371615**	**444794**	**275761**	**142.63**
北湖区	Beihu District	413118	184512	228606	180314	50331	111.10
苏仙区	Suxian District	206313	17773	188541	66054	42379	140.92
桂阳县	Guiyang County	135046	5416	129630	24389	19635	168.57
宜章县	Yizhang County	132356	19990	112367	14033	49852	140.37

单位：万元 18-17 续表 2 continued (10 000 yuan)

市县名称	City and County	工业总产值 Gross Industrial Output Value	轻工业 Light Industry	重工业 Heavy Industry	#国有经济 State-owned Economic	#集体经济 Collective Owned Economic	指数（上年为100） Indices (precending year=100)
永兴县	Yongxing County	159664	3448	156216	2155	6590	176.68
嘉禾县	Jiahe County	75922	5770	70152	6750	11846	156.63
临武县	Linwu County	110390	6829	103561	14768	33344	145.72
汝城县	Rucheng County	89142	661	88481	4247		156.37
桂东县	Guidong County	11960		11960	1544	7461	181.42
安仁县	Anren County	65108	32053	33055	1752	33945	162.14
资兴市	Zixing City	276878	27833	249046	128789	20379	176.79
永州市	**Yongzhou City**	**987690**	**228903**	**758787**	**231945**	**37634**	**125.27**
芝山区	Zhishan District	138030	85279	52751	95011	2844	108.36
冷水滩区	Lengshuitan District	524988	76831	448157	31970	7421	140.09
祁阳县	Qiyang County	111688	30718	80970	32376	10819	119.20
东安县	DonganCounty	41128	285	40842	8871	6805	131.22
双牌县	Shuangpai County	41120	640	40480	14394	2586	110.06
道　县	Dao County	32688	15054	17634	20018	4835	106.37
江永县	Jiangyong County	19752	336	19416	2991	2227	122.29
宁远县	Ningyuan County	23200	10792	12408	11066		128.46
蓝山县	Lanshan County	19695	2908	16787	5310		121.33
新田县	Xintian County	12777	3527	9250	6219	97	53.47
江华县	Jianghua County	22625	2531	20094	3720		72.43
怀化市	**Huaihua City**	**870582**	**247929**	**622653**	**357717**	**48102**	**123.60**
鹤城区	Hecheng District	177063	89079	87984	37510	24864	113.85
中方县	Zhongfang County	30384	4931	25453	2200	1032	131.80
沅陵县	Yuanling County	231896	2871	229025	159424	2440	118.35
辰溪县	Chenxi County	57363	3101	54261	22176	2835	121.43
溆浦县	Xupu County	85558	53275	32283	71620	4591	116.37
会同县	Huitong County	32676	7158	25519			125.14
麻阳县	Mayang County	20868	5089	15779	6577	2241	130.10
新晃县	Xinhuang County	43137	17826	25311	23474	2835	125.84
芷江县	Zhijiang County	43232	12895	30338	5546	1165	192.65
靖州县	Jingzhou County	33501	1565	31935	11235	3170	109.16
通道县	Tongdao County	21475	4426	17049	1610	2119	169.96
洪江市	Hongjiang City	93430	45714	47716	16347	811	137.21
娄底市	**Loudi City**	**1390558**	**55685**	**1334873**	**823984**	**97224**	**117.78**
娄星区	Louxing District	693992	9636	684357	575615	48403	109.47
双峰县	Shuangfeng County	61415	4377	57038	464	11488	119.33
新化县	Xinhua County	57254	8364	48890	18681	10965	127.25
冷水江市	Lengshuijiang County	446331	7966	438365	170619	9016	133.12
涟源市	Lianyuan County	131566	25342	106224	58606	17352	120.36
湘西自治州	**West Hunan A.P**	**390298**	**82283**	**308015**	**163056**	**7406**	**109.81**
吉首市	Jishou County	104692	48829	55863	17302	4685	84.75
泸溪县	Luxi County	65677	452	65225	52635	1437	143.45
凤凰县	Fenghuang County	15402	2221	13180	5779		78.19
花垣县	Huayuan County	101842	1743	100099	43506		129.69
保靖县	Baojing County	47871	1846	46025	5520	262	141.94
古丈县	Guzhang County	7226	834	6393	4154		152.19
永顺县	Yongshun County	15033	7499	7534	8855	389	142.08
龙山县	Longshan County	32556	18860	13696	25305	632	84.39

18-18 各市、州、县国有经济固定资产投资新增固定资产及房屋竣工面积(2003年)

Investment in Fixed Assets,Newly Increased Fixed Assets and Completed Building Floor Space of State-Owned Units (2003)

市县名称	Cities and Counties	固定资产投资(万元) Total Investment in Fixed Assets (10 000 yuan)	基本建设 Investment in Capital Construction	更新改造 Investment in Innovation	其他投资 Others Investment	房地产开发 Real Estate Development	新增固定资产(万元) Newly Increased Fixed Assets (10 000 yuan)	房屋建筑竣工面积(平方米) Floor Space of Buildings Completed (sq.m)	#住宅 Residential Buildings
长沙市	**Changsha City**	**2011322**	**1545178**	**177888**	**61492**	**226764**	**1211778**	**2729080**	**943054**
芙蓉区	Furong District	212818	153833	4927	12423	41635	127002	399450	275333
天心区	Tianxin District	163111	100400	20880	12522	29309	66897	145801	34567
岳麓区	Yuelu District	242557	180617	960	2200	58780	272652	602994	42778
开福区	Kaifu District	343586	288714	5720	1077	48075	276816	265339	96621
雨花区	Yuhua District	448665	341879	89164		17622	271319	238324	37007
长沙县	Changsha County	103893	85712	13331	650	4200	20931	74213	46575
望城县	Wangcheng County	98886	60869	11334	23433	3250	40166	174400	54100
宁乡县	Ningxiang County	180758	153482	8377	2912	15987	102414	568570	176692
浏阳市	Liuyang City	217048	179672	23195	6275	7906	33581	259989	179381
株洲市	**Zhuzhou City**	**428490**	**177393**	**209820**	**19876**	**21401**	**322639**	**707702**	**269835**
荷塘区	Hetang District	53351	19143	33408		800	48352	73666	30256
芦淞区	Lousong District	68328	21145	27827	13112	6244	41696	98746	67127
石峰区	Shifeng District	162488	30563	131225		700	107812	75317	31400
天元区	Tianyuan District	57427	48281	2136	500	6510	27470	131222	43659
株洲县	Zhuzhou County	9934	9050	329	555		7586	14917	12316
攸 县	You County	30560	15579	5750	3530	5701	34631	105456	59665
茶陵县	Chaling County	23284	21336	1045	443	460	30008	123702	9880
炎陵县	Yanling County	5055	2843		1226	986	4881	26071	12350
醴陵市	Liling County	18063	9453	8100	510		20203	58605	3182
湘潭市	**Xiangtan City**	**369556**	**159729**	**189268**	**1300**	**19259**	**183701**	**609537**	**362590**
雨湖区	Yuhu District	120594	68509	37403		14682	81745	270320	152755
岳塘区	Yuetang District	190169	51585	135188		3396	61042	161866	119660
湘潭县	Xiangtan County	18710	14471	3274		965	18506	108090	56025
湘乡市	Xiangxiang City	29119	16200	11403	1300	216	11833	46500	23700
韶山市	Shaoshan City	10964	8964	2000			10575	22761	10450
衡阳市	**Hengyang City**	**415353**	**292919**	**101089**	**9649**	**11696**	**391624**	**833566**	**503008**
珠晖区	Zhuhui District	34419	20062	13792	562	3	13898	68268	46411
雁峰区	Yanfeng District	47026	16396	29494		1136	33970	115162	72385
石鼓区	Shigu District	61368	47733	8002	1060	4573	91907	81025	
蒸湘区	Zhengxiang District	22212	21207			1005	29073	257503	207439
南岳区	Nanyue District	2220	1970			250	2625		
衡阳县	Hengyang County	40325	29634	10691			57079	80870	60400
衡南县	Hengnan County	17657	13427	3580		650	24051	81717	33128
衡山县	Hengshan County	16461	4191	3842	7520	908	20002	25101	21978
衡东县	Hengdong County	13915	10737	1497		1681	6477	42822	17686
祁东县	Qidong County	20267	12151	6569	507	1040	14031	31515	18608
耒阳市	Leiyang City	113954	102030	11824		100	79488	14128	5200
常宁市	Changning City	25529	13381	11798		350	19023	35455	19773

市县名称	Cities and Counties	固定资产投资（万元） Total Investment in Fixed Assets (10 000 yuan)	基本建设 Investment in Capital Construction	更新改造 Investment in Innovation	其他投资 Others Investment	房地产开发 Real Estate Development	新增固定资产（万元） Newly Increased Fixed Assets (10 000 yuan)	房屋建筑竣工面积（平方米） Floor Space of Buildings Completed (sq.m)	#住宅 Residential Buildings
邵阳市	**Shaoyang City**	**217485**	**192802**	**18903**	**1713**	**4067**	**131627**	**619441**	**240084**
双清区	Shuangqing District	16641	8248	6021		2372	12653	68071	15859
大祥区	Daxiang District	26217	23213	2074		930	11788	77343	41100
北塔区	Beita District	10343	10343				5393	35458	23458
邵东县	Shaodong County	16610	16068	542			9543	63789	37005
新邵县	Xinshao County	23195	20503	2692			13125	78253	25780
邵阳县	Shaoyang County	23232	20232	3000			10587	47550	8200
隆回县	Longhui County	18196	16729	1467			8715	68980	26210
洞口县	Dongkou County	18459	17799		660		9267	51302	16700
绥宁县	Suining County	16214	16214				8988	26290	18578
新宁县	Xinning County	23517	23517				15238	45790	
城步县	Chengbu County	13700	9532	3107	1053	8	19963	38931	9510
武冈市	Wugang City	11161	10404			757	6367	17684	17684
岳阳市	**Yueyang City**	**558559**	**343656**	**191020**	**2516**	**21367**	**373430**	**836818**	**516425**
岳阳楼区	Yueyanglou District	257281	113584	139431	1066	3200	158402	110008	65350
云溪区	Yunxi District	13935	12005	1930			1670		
君山区	Junshan District	27898	25848	2050			33500	102433	80294
岳阳县	Yueyang County	35133	31810	1200	1000	1123	12148	55380	41820
华容县	Huarong County	22409	20969	200		1240	18755	149981	121850
湘阴县	Xiangyin County	46724	37974	6100		2650	18134	83462	37895
平江县	Pingjiang County	24275	19062	5213			40048	104016	54850
汨罗市	Miluo City	90695	61232	27963		1500	20373	67214	28650
临湘市	Linxiang City	30132	21172	6933	450	1577	63450	91459	26471
常德市	**Changde City**	**406081**	**302908**	**74495**	**14634**	**14044**	**394931**	**781910**	**259092**
武陵区	Wuling District	222306	131616	70045	9673	10972	243794	287259	74029
鼎城区	Dingcheng District	11361	10861	500			7479	68764	8100
安乡县	Anxiang County	17073	16369			704	17641	58949	20422
汉寿县	Hanshou County	15986	13836	770		1380	14790	111938	42353
澧县	Li County	38239	38239				57834	63571	20579
临澧县	Linli County	13845	13437			408	2837	29800	10846
桃源县	Taoyuan County	12995	12995				29605	61413	26448
石门县	Shimen County	57324	51783		4961	580	14147	81755	41800
津市市	Jinshi City	16952	13772	3180			6804	18461	14515
张家界市	**Zhangjiajie City**	**92847**	**51986**	**20063**	**17321**	**3477**	**58443**	**117310**	**54278**
永定区	Yongding District	31190	17254	11558		2378	9865	31630	7830
武陵源区	Wulingyuan District	21287	14551	2494	4242		19444		
慈利县	Chili County	11236	7811	880	1887	658	9544	52795	24704
桑植县	Sangzhi County	29134	12370	5131	11192	441	19590	32885	21744
益阳市	**Yiyang City**	**223943**	**182141**	**35169**	**4726**	**1907**	**141613**	**305173**	**96018**
资阳区	Ziyang District	20118	18278	1750		90	9763	27100	13600
赫山区	Heshan District	81632	64856	15759		1017	38814	133336	29942
南县	Nan County	34730	32030	1900		800	16504	18705	
桃江县	Taojiang County	14589	13713	520	356		7045		
安化县	Anhua County	26405	21105	930	4370		29788	95232	49476
沅江市	Yuanjiang City	46469	32159	14310			39699	30800	3000
郴州市	**Chenzhou City**	**341042**	**258610**	**51771**	**13902**	**16759**	**216070**	**1063318**	**465332**
北湖区	Beihu District	59781	41169	12697	5020	895	36026	161726	91708
苏仙区	Suxian District	59534	47236	5134		7164	36073	170761	71738
桂阳县	Guiyang County	38063	30906	2696	321	4140	22022	149450	113261

市县名称	Cities and Counties	固定资产投资(万元) Total Investment in Fixed Assets (10 000 yuan)	基本建设 Investment in Capital Construction	更新改造 Investment in Innovation	其他投资 Others Investment	房地产开发 Real Estate Development	新增固定资产(万元) Newly Increased Fixed Assets (10 000 yuan)	房屋建筑竣工面积(平方米) Floor Space of Buildings Completed (sq.m)	#住宅 Residential Buildings
宜章县	Yizhang County	16027	13967	560	1500		10967	95505	55355
永兴县	Yongxing County	34428	32568	1500		360	22707	62408	39480
嘉禾县	Jiahe County	23642	16282	7360			14082	47894	28494
临武县	Linwu County	20448	14577	3420	2451		10033	45340	26380
汝城县	Rucheng County	7817	6518	1299			2336	12879	3222
桂东县	Guidong County	11247	11247				9345	25953	12509
安仁县	Anreng County	24473	19830	4143	500		31169	225380	4315
资兴市	Zixing City	45582	24310	12962	4110	4200	21310	66022	18870
永州市	**Yongzhou City**	**315109**	**224938**	**48357**	**36384**	**5430**	**129347**	**611165**	**203274**
芝山区	Zhishan District	58012	47893	6868	871	2380	28436	189696	72959
冷水滩区	Lengshuitan District	112214	74963	21057	15014	1180	27204	124546	24980
祁阳县	Qiyang County	51605	44207	6694	324	380	21376	55344	14770
东安县	Dongan County	19246	8406	3381	6880	579	13097	18633	15033
双牌县	Shuangpai County	10724	8861	1863			4634	23500	500
道县	Dao County	16827	9856	1180	4940	851	7280	44475	17953
江永县	Jiangyong County	4465	3744	341	380		3207	11480	6280
宁远县	Ningyuan County	10172	6972	3200			5902	28154	10654
蓝山县	Lanshan County	7651	5358	2103	190		4311	24936	12500
新田县	Xintian County	10599	3372		7167	60	706	13650	10250
江华县	Jianghua County	13594	11306	1670	618		13194	76751	17395
怀化市	**Huaihua City**	**212495**	**119798**	**80367**		**12330**	**83768**	**181123**	**89439**
鹤城区	Hecheng District	48638	35000	11398		2240	8004	19872	13638
中方县	Zhongfang County	5401	5046	355			337	7376	6882
沅陵县	Yuanling County	40054	2632	31880		5542	3593	25881	8680
辰溪县	Chenxi County	11736	5248	6488			14053	22210	5150
溆浦县	Xupu County	19734	10054	9680			10844		
会同县	Huitong County	10518	9673	845			1469	5317	2860
麻阳县	Mayang County	6811	4750	2061			2752	31897	3400
新晃县	Xinhuang County	5855	4475	1260		120	5792	13377	7899
芷江县	Zhijiang County	25234	18935	5231		1068	12866	6600	3000
靖州县	Jinzhou County	6561	4967	1594			7346	3000	3000
通道县	Tongdao County	3715	1565	1590		560	2627	20300	15600
洪江市	Hongjiang City	28238	17453	7985		2800	14085	25293	19330
娄底市	**Loudi City**	**519164**	**113741**	**398843**	**1294**	**5286**	**356311**	**508981**	**265773**
娄星区	Louxing District	407010	54283	349301		3426	274281	234904	120670
双峰县	Shuangfeng County	18982	17419	500	808	255	8875	30385	19400
新化县	Xinhua County	17426	14626	1850		950	15449	117873	53433
冷水江市	Lengshuijian City	55322	9270	46052			39721	70800	47626
涟源市	Lianyuan City	20424	18143	1140	486	655	17985	55019	24644
湘西自治州	**West Hunan A.P**	**296082**	**241826**	**42352**		**11904**	**155366**	**517455**	**241998**
吉首市	Jishou City	94330	66894	20972		6464	33806	168096	86070
泸溪县	Louxi County	16709	16314	395			8131	27020	2162
凤凰县	Fenghuang County	17561	16580	858		123	12448	31739	9130
花垣县	Huayuan County	13006	11783	1223			3067	16410	11396
保靖县	Baojin County	81926	65909	15000		1017	22790	43180	28760
古丈县	Guzhang County	12835	10503	2332			2350	34053	16246
永顺县	Yongshun County	33192	32705			487	56777	82454	42828
龙山县	Longshan County	26523	21138	1572		3813	15997	114503	45406
不分地区	**Not Classified by Region**	**605810**	**597756**	**8054**			**501303**		

18-19 各市、州、县社会消费品零售总额(2003年)

Total Value of Retail Sales of Consumer Goods (2003)

单位：万元 (10 000 yuan)

市县名称	City and County	消费品零售总额 Total Retail Sales of Consumer Goods	批发零售贸易业 Wholesales and Retail Sales Trade	#限额以上 #Above Designated Size	餐饮业 Catering Trade	其他 Others
长沙市	**Changsha City**	**4519993**	**3821602**	**1219898**	**649747**	**48644**
芙蓉区	Furong District	414882	352365	35747	62517	
天心区	Tianxin District	262100	204155	3574	57945	
岳麓区	Yuelu District	164152	120015	12709	44137	
开福区	Kaifu District	306482	249674	52928	49356	7451
雨花区	Yuhua District	261035	191281	5476	69009	745
长沙县	Changsha County	227523	205446	72083	19550	2528
望城县	Wangcheng County	160936	140625	12938	14038	6273
宁乡县	Ningxiang County	270085	246927	23335	20247	2911
浏阳市	Liuyang City	309106	271614	22505	35952	1540
株洲市	**Zhuzhou City**	**1400470**	**1207097**	**143373**	**159735**	**33638**
荷塘区	Hetang District	71631	54181	7380	17450	
芦淞区	Lusong District	287442	259262		28180	
石峰区	Shifeng District	85541	70895		14646	
天元区	Tianyuan District	53612	32005		20365	1242
株洲县	Zhuzhou County	94049	85587	3202	5668	2794
攸　县	You County	168303	156489	11017	11814	
茶陵县	Chaling County	81201	76436	8027	4765	
炎陵县	Yanling County	30619	25441	2780	3012	2166
醴陵市	Liling City	297805	271144	24701	22605	4056
湘潭市	**Xiangtan City**	**902986**	**713859**	**91133**	**149004**	**40123**
雨湖区	Yuhu District	209656	169549		31050	9057
岳塘区	Yuetang District	110799	86853		19072	4874
湘潭县	Xiangtan County	164698	137782	2621	18905	8011
湘乡市	Xiangxiang City	173275	139948	9307	24551	8776
韶山市	Shaoshan City	29093	24281	78	3620	1192
衡阳市	**Hengyang City**	**1560339**	**1315190**	**174931**	**235050**	**10099**
珠晖区	Zhuhui District	178970	155511	3531	23137	322
雁峰区	Yanfeng District	169237	140070	24595	27084	2083
石鼓区	Shigu District	154953	136955	51823	17706	292
蒸湘区	Zhengxiang District	49236	38997	18521	10052	187
南岳区	Nanyue District	30976	25304		5367	305
衡阳县	Hengyang County	176460	149612	12446	25446	1402
衡南县	Hengnan County	148131	135957	8916	11884	290
衡山县	Hengshan County	53727	45419	5926	8163	145
衡东县	Hengdong County	109221	90565	4450	17657	999
祁东县	Qidong County	145672	119736	9436	22584	3352
耒阳市	Leiyang City	204969	158132	27220	46365	472
常宁市	Changning City	138784	118928	8060	19606	250
邵阳市	**Shaoyang City**	**1002612**	**907990**	**65410**	**92264**	**2358**
双清区	Shuangqing District	87395	64438		22957	
大祥区	Daxiang District	60124	51660		8464	
北塔区	Beita District	7682	6608		1074	

单位：万元　　18-19 续表 1 continued　　(10 000 yuan)

市县名称	City and County	消费品零售总额 Total Retail Sales of Consumer Goods	批发零售贸易业 Wholesales and Retail Sales Trade	#限额以上 #Above Designated Size	餐饮业 Catering Trade	其他 Others
邵东县	Shaodong County	255927	242295	13205	13632	
新邵县	Xinshao County	72977	62937	2986	9837	203
邵阳县	Shaoyang County	85224	77944	4082	7280	
隆回县	Longhui County	75519	67853	9497	7666	
洞口县	Dongkou County	80974	75287	6625	4722	965
绥宁县	Suining County	50643	47358	4590	2802	483
新宁县	Xinning County	37015	32401	6516	4268	346
城步县	Chengbu County	32266	30175	3132	1730	361
武冈市	Wugang City	94361	88357	8540	6004	
岳阳市	**Yueyang City**	**1723297**	**1545232**	**150449**	**127949**	**50116**
岳阳楼区	Yueyanglou District	126973	111088		12297	3588
云溪区	Yunxi District	32472	28701		2686	1085
君山区	Junshan District	26840	18872		2798	5170
岳阳县	Yueyang County	149968	133056	4385	10628	6284
华容县	Huarong County	158839	140704	12214	14386	3749
湘阴县	Xiangyin County	109762	99214	6159	6905	3643
平江县	Pingjiang City	95092	80323	10206	11907	2862
汨罗市	Miluo City	113768	100010	8795	9880	3878
临湘市	Linxiang County	110255	103822	4800	5808	625
屈原区		12790	8139		1006	3645
常德市	**Changde City**	**1562997**	**1341195**	**125065**	**180206**	**41596**
武陵区	Wuling District	276279	227914	96951	39925	8440
鼎城区	Dingcheng District	264677	255932	644	8580	165
安乡县	Anxiang County	105569	88275	5748	14744	2550
汉寿县	Hanshou County	121220	106100	5653	12081	3039
澧　县	Li County	177709	160479	12415	11760	5470
临澧县	Linli County	104282	87950	9898	12194	4138
桃源县	Taoyuan County	253249	194771	14020	49433	9045
石门县	Shimen County	161439	130260	8201	23154	8025
津市市	Jinshi City	98573	89514	7535	8335	724
张家界市	**Zhangjiajie City**	**283475**	**244457**	**24319**	**37969**	**1049**
永定区	Yongdi District	115565	100415	1086	15150	
武陵源区	Wulingyuan District	18338	11811		6527	
慈利县	Cili County	85638	75320	9141	9339	979
桑植县	Sangzhi County	50258	44301	2747	5938	20
益阳市	**Yiyang City**	**905673**	**812093**	**73035**	**86422**	**7158**
资阳区	Ziyang District	146043	133197	14015	11974	872
赫山区	Heshan District	177702	157159	2157	18806	1737
南　县	Nan County	122376	109502	7039	11849	1025
桃江县	Taojiang County	125400	111975	9899	12364	1061
安化县	Anhua County	147785	132812	4181	13833	1140
沅江市	Yuanjiang City	127072	112314	9224	13731	1027
郴州市	**Chenzhou City**	**1402243**	**1167108**	**121531**	**180106**	**55029**
北湖区	Beihu District	166887	120421	8672	43283	3183
苏仙区	Suxian District	85989	71866	4522	11894	2229
桂阳县	Guiyang County	146261	120118	7484	22330	3813
宜章县	Yizhang County	131711	111449	8955	18212	2050

单位：万元 18-19 续表 2 continued (10 000 yuan)

市县名称	City and County	消费品零售总额 Total Retail Sales of Consumer Goods	批发零售贸易业 Wholesales and Retail Sales Trade	#限额以上 #Above Designated Size	餐饮业 Catering Trade	其他 Others
永兴县	Yongxing County	150208	132922	4591	13364	3922
嘉禾县	Jiahe County	64694	43333	4241	13589	7772
临武县	Linwu County	60767	48915	8759	11216	636
汝城县	Rucheng County	41388	38247	1028	3141	
桂东县	Guidong County	15242	10977		640	3625
安仁县	Anren County	51214	28622	4244	5500	17092
资兴市	Zixing City	169540	157248	8341	9775	2517
永州市	**Yongzhou City**	**876561**	**786336**	**53708**	**86762**	**3463**
芝山区	Zhishan District	134560	111453	249	22509	598
冷水滩区	Lengshuitan District	179959	161041	14439	18510	409
祁阳县	Qiyang County	121269	113091	18043	8042	136
东安县	DonganCounty	91184	81288	2248	9285	611
双牌县	Shuangpai County	20371	17967		2195	209
道　县	Dao County	94649	84456	1536	9832	361
江永县	Jiangyong County	36691	34128		2288	275
宁远县	Ningyuan County	93438	86220	7790	6915	303
蓝山县	Lanshan County	37828	35359	4927	2139	330
新田县	Xintian County	27884	26002	2394	1710	172
江华县	Jianghua County	38727	35331	2082	3337	59
怀化市	**Huaihua City**	**852701**	**699711**	**28701**	**130598**	**22393**
鹤城区	Hecheng District	88300	62509	5842	16357	9435
中方县	Zhongfang County	30785	25983		3684	1118
沅陵县	Yuanling County	82024	64652	4802	14331	3041
辰溪县	Chenxi County	65015	56414	6445	8237	364
溆浦县	Xupu County	118600	97938	2810	19199	1464
会同县	Huitong County	39325	36524	20	2698	103
麻阳县	Mayang County	40614	37116	247	3211	287
新晃县	Xinhuang County	28181	21854		3770	2557
芷江县	Zhijiang County	51898	43768	30	6267	1863
靖州县	Jingzhou County	45473	39058	1942	6290	125
通道县	Tongdao County	31220	26050		3970	1200
洪江市	Hongjiang City	70600	58835	2127	11489	276
洪江区	Hongjiang District	38559	30832	190	7696	31
娄底市	**Loudi City**	**754176**	**679523**	**80058**	**68536**	**6117**
娄星区	Louxing District	178368	162886	39360	14504	978
双峰县	Shuangfeng County	120825	115377	7860	5160	288
新化县	Xinhua County	145257	135703	9365	8425	1129
冷水江市	Lengshuijiang County	137505	113048	4682	24175	282
涟源市	Lianyuan County	172222	152510	18792	16272	3440
湘西自治州	**West Hunan A.P**	**415499**	**342779**	**21461**	**61255**	**11465**
吉首市	Jishou County	141176	111515	10247	27883	1778
泸溪县	Luxi County	29888	26684	1765	3069	135
凤凰县	Fenghuang County	56952	45501	1991	9121	2330
花垣县	Huayuan County	27751	25338	686	2230	183
保靖县	Baojing County	24156	21317	629	2155	685
古丈县	Guzhang County	15160	13017	1031	1977	166
永顺县	Yongshun County	61606	49696	3450	7479	4432
龙山县	Longshan County	58810	49712	1663	7342	1756

18-20 各市、州、县财政收入与支出(2003年)

Government Revenue and Expenditures (2003)

单位：万元 (10 000 yuan)

市县名称	City and County	财政收入 Total Revenue	财政支出 Total Expenditures
长沙市	**Changsha City**	**598930**	**784168**
本级	City Level	324001	344134
芙蓉区	Furong District	29564	39627
天心区	Tianxin District	24273	37224
岳麓区	Yuelu District	23526	32608
开福区	Kaifu District	26966	41147
雨花区	Yuhua District	36168	44182
长沙县	Changsha County	42565	71186
望城县	Wangcheng County	30436	48641
宁乡县	Ningxiang County	25235	52949
浏阳市	Liuyang City	36196	72470
株洲市	**Zhuzhou City**	**168180**	**307238**
本级	City Level	72228	131670
荷塘区	Hetang District	5642	10166
芦淞区	Lousong District	6446	9290
石峰区	Shifeng District	6867	10268
天元区	Tianyuan District	16089	20487
株洲县	Zhuzhou County	8735	19074
攸县	You County	15598	28951
茶陵县	Chaling County	10203	23666
炎陵县	Yanling County	5288	13894
醴陵市	Liling City	21084	39772
湘潭市	**Xiangtan City**	**100735**	**194085**
本级	City Level	48255	93000
雨湖区	Yuhu District	8264	12710
岳塘区	Yuetang District	6833	9855
湘潭县	Xiangtan County	16431	35067
湘乡市	Xiangxiang City	17481	35562
韶山市	Shaoshan City	3471	7891
衡阳市	**Hengyang City**	**149375**	**335968**
本级	City Level	43631	108525
珠晖区	Zhuhui District	2865	7453
雁峰区	Yanfeng District	3038	7044
石鼓区	Shigu District	2870	6907
蒸湘区	Zhengxiang District	2351	6559
南岳区	Nanyue District	2830	6154
衡阳县	Hengyang County	14734	32130
衡南县	Hengnan County	16912	33781
衡山县	Hengshan County	7393	16146
衡东县	Hengdong County	10093	20672
祁东县	Qidong County	11659	28355
耒阳市	Leiyang City	18401	35835
常宁市	Changning City	12598	26407
邵阳市	**Shaoyang City**	**119559**	**314078**
本级	City Level	12912	63277
双清区	Shuangqing District	6815	9498
大祥区	Daxiang District	6082	9672
北塔区	Beita District	1492	3461
邵东县	Shaodong County	16883	32840
新邵县	Xinshao County	7886	23984
邵阳县	Shaoyang County	12894	30619
隆回县	Longhui County	12393	33366
洞口县	Dongkou County	9647	24179
绥宁县	Suining County	8191	18702
新宁县	Xinning County	8500	23132
城步县	Chengbu County	5313	16267
武冈市	Wugang City	10551	25081
岳阳市	**Yueyang City**	**205835**	**364247**
本级	City Level	81838	126933
岳阳楼区	Yueyanglou District	15824	21337
云溪区	Yunxi District	6536	9888
君山区	Junshan District	3405	9729
岳阳县	Yueyang County	11362	29605
华容县	Huarong County	15561	31612
湘阴县	Xiangyin County	11597	27144
平江县	Pingjiang County	16721	38897
汨罗市	Miluo City	25455	41076
临湘市	Linxiang City	17536	28026
常德市	**Changde City**	**192935**	**359221**
本级	City Level	62519	106504
武陵区	Wuling District	11630	18602
鼎城区	Dingcheng District	18456	36467
安乡县	Anxiang County	11659	23890
汉寿县	Hanshou County	12879	28390
澧县	Li County	18406	36828
临澧县	Linli County	13127	22846

单位：万元　　18-20 续表 continued　　(10 000 yuan)

市县名称	City and County	财政收入 Total Revenue	财政支出 Total Expenditures	市县名称	City and County	财政收入 Total Revenue	财政支出 Total Expenditures
桃源县	Taoyuan County	19693	35702	道县	Dao County	9359	23235
石门县	Shimen County	15308	32567	江永县	Jiangyong County	5970	12137
津市市	Jinshi City	9258	17425	宁远县	Ningyuan County	8760	25060
张家界市	**Zhangjiajie City**	**37883**	**107357**	蓝山县	Lanshan County	7046	15217
本级	City Level	9888	21875	新田县	Xintian County	4236	14779
永定区	Yongding District	7683	23072	江华县	Jianghua County	5995	20390
武陵源区	Wulingyuan District	7022	10761	**怀化市**	**Huaihua City**	**92038**	**252342**
慈利县	Cili County	8735	26841	本级	City Level	20386	41773
桑植县	Sangzhi County	4555	24808	鹤城区	Hecheng District	4553	11860
益阳市	**Yiyang City**	**74642**	**211938**	中方县	Zhongfang County	2712	11960
本级	City Level	19288	53583	沅陵县	Yuanling County	11588	28637
资阳区	Ziyang District	5212	18401	辰溪县	Chenxi County	7050	21016
赫山区	Heshan District	12324	27436	溆浦县	Xupu County	10456	27151
南县	Nan County	8215	22688	会同县	Huitong County	5694	14280
桃江县	Taojiang County	9321	27412	麻阳县	Mayang County	4326	16575
安化县	Anhua County	9315	32630	新晃县	Xinhuang County	3571	14123
沅江市	Yuanjiang City	10967	29788	芷江县	Zhijiang County	5025	15317
郴州市	**Chenzhou City**	**214922**	**350706**	靖州县	Jinzhou County	4888	12894
本级	City Level	46232	75775	通道县	Tongdao County	3290	11560
北湖区	Beihu District	15607	26943	洪江市	Hongjiang City	8499	25196
苏仙区	Suxian District	16848	26053	**娄底市**	**Loudi City**	**91331**	**198600**
桂阳县	Guiyang County	26138	37485	本级	City Level	25376	47404
宜章县	Yizhang County	20039	29359	娄星区	Louxing District	8104	20400
永兴县	Yongxing County	19531	31156	双峰县	Shuangfeng County	13279	32664
嘉禾县	Jiahe County	13663	20718	新化县	Xinhua County	13912	39004
临武县	Linwu County	15194	23612	冷水江市	Lenshuijiang City	15141	25233
汝城县	Rucheng County	9296	18383	涟源市	Lianyuan City	15519	33895
桂东县	Guidong County	4000	11345	**湘西自治州**	**West Hunan A.P**	**41381**	**206743**
安仁县	Anreng County	9996	18209	本级	City Level	6679	42236
资兴市	Zixing City	18378	31668	吉首市	Jishou City	8851	22698
永州市	**Yongzhou**	**108074**	**273227**	泸溪县	Louxi County	2686	15783
本级	City Level	26281	53243	凤凰县	Fenghuang County	3273	25154
芝山区	Zhishan District	6090	22179	花垣县	Huayuan County	4927	19039
冷水滩区	Lengshuitan District	8291	20945	保靖县	Baojin County	3449	17518
祁阳县	Qiyang County	13572	33602	古丈县	Guzhang County	1278	12619
东安县	Dongan County	7615	21159	永顺县	Yongshun County	4241	24995
双牌县	Shuangpai County	4859	11281	龙山县	Longshan County	5997	26701

18-21 各市、州、县各级学校(2003年)

Schools by Level (2003)

单位：所 (unit)

市县名称	City and County	普通高等学校 Regular Institutions of Higher Education	中等学校 Secondary Schools	中等职业教育 Vocational Secondary Education	普通中学 Regular Secondary Schools	普通小学 Primary Schools
长沙市	**Changsha City**	**37**	**463**	**105**	**358**	**1580**
芙蓉区	Furong District		20	8	12	36
天心区	Tianxin District		20	4	16	43
岳麓区	Yuelu District		29	12	17	47
开福区	Kaifu District		26	10	16	64
雨花区	Yuhua District		38	15	23	44
长沙县	Changsha County		59	10	49	305
望城县	Wangcheng County		48	2	46	209
宁乡县	Ningxiang County		108	10	98	426
浏阳市	Liuyang City		115	34	81	406
株洲市	**Zhuzhou City**	**6**	**272**	**36**	**236**	**1029**
荷塘区	Hetang District		23	12	11	40
芦淞区	Lusong District		17	4	13	22
石峰区	Shifeng District		24	5	19	23
天元区	Tianyuan District		10	1	9	31
株洲县	Zhuzhou County		33	1	32	160
攸　县	You County		42	3	39	255
茶陵县	Chaling County		31	1	30	193
炎陵县	Yanling County		21	1	20	47
醴陵市	Liling City		71	8	63	258
湘潭市	**Xiangtan City**	**5**	**290**	**58**	**232**	**734**
雨湖区	Yuhu District		38	17	21	36
岳塘区	Yuetang District		37	16	21	54
湘潭县	Xiangtan County		101	10	91	365
湘乡市	Xiangxiang City		102	13	89	247
韶山市	Shaoshan City		12	2	10	32
衡阳市	**Hengyang City**	**4**	**539**	**60**	**479**	**2510**
珠晖区	Zhuhui District		25	6	19	51
雁峰区	Yanfeng District		36	17	19	36
石鼓区	Shigu District		13	3	10	36
蒸湘区	Zhengxiang District		19	11	8	36
南岳区	Nanyue District		3		3	30
衡阳县	Hengyang County		78	3	75	364
衡南县	Hengnan County		67	6	61	361
衡山县	Hengshan County		35	3	32	135
衡东县	Hengdong County		50	3	47	314
祁东县	Qidong County		72	3	69	380
耒阳市	Leiyang City		77	5	72	458
常宁市	Changning City		70	6	64	309
邵阳市	**Shaoyang City**	**2**	**596**	**34**	**562**	**2424**
双清区	Shuangqing District		25	5	20	37
大祥区	Daxiang District		30	8	22	49
北塔区	Beita District		7	1	6	15

单位：所 18-21 续表 1 continued (unit)

市县名称	City and County	普通高等学校 Regular Institutions of Higher Education	中等学校 Secondary Schools	中等职业教育 Vocational Secondary Education	普通中学 Regular Secondary Schools	普通小学 Primary Schools
邵东县	Shaodong County		83	2	81	290
新邵县	Xinshao County		64	2	62	194
邵阳县	Shaoyang County		63	1	62	355
隆回县	Longhui County		100	3	97	388
洞口县	Dongkou County		61	3	58	296
绥宁县	Suining County		40	1	39	216
新宁县	Xinning County		43	2	41	152
城步县	Chengbu County		20	2	18	201
武冈市	Wugang City		60	4	56	231
岳阳市	**Yueyang City**	**3**	**433**	**39**	**394**	**1764**
岳阳楼区	Yueyanglou District		54	16	38	68
云溪区	Yunxi District		12	0	12	45
君山区	Junshan District		14		14	48
岳阳县	Yueyang County		56	2	54	289
华容县	Huarong County		60	3	57	158
湘阴县	Xiangyin County		59	2	57	286
平江县	Pingjiang City		77	6	71	440
汨罗市	Miluo City		67	10	57	219
临湘市	Linxiang County		36	2	34	211
常德市	**Changde City**	**3**	**383**	**59**	**324**	**1588**
武陵区	Wuling District		46	19	27	67
鼎城区	Dingcheng District		65	8	57	273
安乡县	Anxiang County		28	3	25	137
汉寿县	Hanshou County		43	3	40	310
澧　县	Li County		51	8	43	206
临澧县	Linli County		27	4	23	124
桃源县	Taoyuan County		56	5	51	197
石门县	Shimen County		52	6	46	225
津市市	Jinshi City		15	3	12	49
张家界市	**Zhangjiajie City**	**1**	**127**	**11**	**116**	**724**
永定区	Yongdi District		44	6	38	180
武陵源区	Wulingyuan District		4	0	4	20
慈利县	Cili County		45	3	42	286
桑植县	Sangzhi County		34	2	32	238
益阳市	**Yiyang City**	**1**	**352**	**40**	**312**	**1277**
资阳区	Ziyang District		31	5	26	115
赫山区	Heshan District		68	16	52	245
南　县	Nan County		52	3	49	198
桃江县	Taojiang County		65	4	61	223
安化县	Anhua County		67	7	60	273
沅江市	Yuanjiang City		69	5	64	223
郴州市	**Chenzhou City**	**2**	**417**	**42**	**375**	**2261**
北湖区	Beihu District		46	15	31	117
苏仙区	Suxian District		41	7	34	100
桂阳县	Guiyang County		51	3	48	466
宜章县	Yizhang County		55	2	53	271

市县名称	City and County	普通高等学校 Regular Institutions of Higher Education	中等学校 Secondary Schools	中等职业教育 Vocational Secondary Education	普通中学 Regular Secondary Schools	普通小学 Primary Schools
永兴县	Yongxing County		38	3	35	240
嘉禾县	Jiahe County		29	2	27	191
临武县	Linwu County		32	2	30	123
汝城县	Rucheng County		30	2	28	253
桂东县	Guidong County		15	1	14	104
安仁县	Anren County		37	2	35	184
资兴市	Zixing City		43	3	40	212
永州市	**Yongzhou City**	**2**	**442**	**43**	**399**	**2528**
芝山区	Zhishan District		56	9	47	301
冷水滩区	Lengshuitan District		48	6	42	166
祁阳县	Qiyang County		60	4	56	143
东安县	DonganCounty		50	3	47	214
双牌县	Shuangpai County		20	2	18	94
道　县	Dao County		50	4	46	359
江永县	Jiangyong County		19	2	17	90
宁远县	Ningyuan County		55	7	48	438
蓝山县	Lanshan County		28	2	26	276
新田县	Xintian County		26	2	24	200
江华县	Jianghua County		30	2	28	247
怀化市	**Huaihua City**	**3**	**454**	**59**	**395**	**2910**
鹤城区	Hecheng District		67	28	39	77
中方县	Zhongfang County		24	1	23	75
沅陵县	Yuanling County		71	9	62	594
辰溪县	Chenxi County		41	2	39	299
溆浦县	Xupu County		65	2	63	440
会同县	Huitong County		30	3	27	234
麻阳县	Mayang County		28	2	26	234
新晃县	Xinhuang County		23	1	22	224
芷江县	Zhijiang County		33	2	31	228
靖州县	Jingzhou County		21	1	20	134
通道县	Tongdao County		13	2	11	168
洪江市	Hongjiang City		38	6	32	203
娄底市	**Loudi City**	**3**	**360**	**42**	**318**	**1343**
娄星区	Louxing District		37	13	24	73
双峰县	Shuangfeng County		83	6	77	275
新化县	Xinhua County		111	6	105	521
冷水江市	Lengshuijiang County		48	8	40	79
涟源市	Lianyuan County		81	9	72	395
湘西自治州	**West Hunan A.P**	**1**	**221**	**32**	**189**	**2001**
吉首市	Jishou County		41	17	24	172
泸溪县	Luxi County		21	2	19	191
凤凰县	Fenghuang County		33	3	30	319
花垣县	Huayuan County		23	2	21	175
保靖县	Baojing County		20	2	18	201
古丈县	Guzhang County		13	1	12	160
永顺县	Yongshun County		39	2	37	430
龙山县	Longshan County		31	3	28	353

18-22 各市、州、县各级学校教职工(2003年)

School Staff and workers by Level (2003)

单位：人 (person)

市县名称	City and County	普通高等学校 Regular Institutions of Higher Education	中等学校 Secondary Schools	中等职业教育 Vocational Secondary Education	普通中学 Regular Secondary Schools	普通小学 Primary Schools
长沙市	**Changsha City**	**35386**	**34470**	**6041**	**28429**	**19762**
芙蓉区	Furong District		2057	692	1365	1430
天心区	Tianxin District		1422	297	1125	1287
岳麓区	Yuelu District		2188	491	1697	1673
开福区	Kaifu District		2675	791	1884	1646
雨花区	Yuhua District		4014	1268	2746	1607
长沙县	Changsha County		4420	814	3606	2508
望城县	Wangcheng County		3781	341	3440	2409
宁乡县	Ningxiang County		7052	825	6227	4138
浏阳市	Liuyang City		6861	522	6339	3064
株洲市	**Zhuzhou City**	**5174**	**21088**	**3023**	**18065**	**11977**
荷塘区	Hetang District		2204	1078	1126	827
芦淞区	Lusong District		1583	586	997	821
石峰区	Shifeng District		1508	432	1076	925
天元区	Tianyuan District		829	37	792	482
株洲县	Zhuzhou County		2406	141	2265	1450
攸　县	You County		3898	377	3521	2135
茶陵县	Chaling County		2604	34	2570	2202
炎陵县	Yanling County		1075	52	1023	677
醴陵市	Liling City		4981	286	4695	2458
湘潭市	**Xiangtan City**	**6811**	**16279**	**2769**	**13510**	**10317**
雨湖区	Yuhu District		2942	1042	1900	1279
岳塘区	Yuetang District		2053	710	1343	1400
湘潭县	Xiangtan County		5891	507	5384	3801
湘乡市	Xiangxiang City		4893	433	4460	3467
韶山市	Shaoshan City		500	77	423	370
衡阳市	**Hengyang City**	**4316**	**36587**	**5657**	**30930**	**31074**
珠晖区	Zhuhui District		1905	554	1351	1191
雁峰区	Yanfeng District		3353	2208	1145	967
石鼓区	Shigu District		864	50	814	750
蒸湘区	Zhengxiang District		1661	931	730	855
南岳区	Nanyue District		228		228	278
衡阳县	Hengyang County		4721	306	4415	4784
衡南县	Hengnan County		4647	554	4093	4624
衡山县	Hengshan County		2142	183	1959	1872
衡东县	Hengdong County		2921	86	2835	2411
祁东县	Qidong County		4965	298	4667	3812
耒阳市	Leiyang City		5495	487	5008	5909
常宁市	Changning City		4050	365	3685	3621
邵阳市	**Shaoyang City**	**1340**	**33256**	**2509**	**30747**	**27569**
双清区	Shuangqing District		1446	308	1138	1289
大祥区	Daxiang District		2549	919	1630	1252
北塔区	Beita District		366	32	334	366

单位：人 18-22 续表 1 continued (person)

市县名称	City and County	普通高等学校 Regular Institutions of Higher Education	中等学校 Secondary Schools	中等职业教育 Vocational Secondary Education	普通中学 Regular Secondary Schools	普通小学 Primary Schools
邵东县	Shaodong County		5475	152	5323	4181
新邵县	Xinshao County		3155	156	2999	2650
邵阳县	Shaoyang County		3039	34	3005	3578
隆回县	Longhui County		4794	222	4572	3917
洞口县	Dongkou County		3179	130	3049	2820
绥宁县	Suining County		1957	105	1852	1749
新宁县	Xinning County		2667	67	2600	1719
城步县	Chengbu County		1472	70	1402	1327
武冈市	Wugang City		3157	314	2843	2721
岳阳市	**Yueyang City**	**2616**	**27897**	**2302**	**25595**	**21710**
岳阳楼区	Yueyanglou District		4383	987	3396	2836
云溪区	Yunxi District		966		966	784
君山区	Junshan District		884		884	756
岳阳县	Yueyang County		3442	185	3257	2867
华容县	Huarong County		3913	146	3767	2755
湘阴县	Xiangyin County		3333	180	3153	2962
平江县	Pingjiang City		4582	226	4356	3808
汨罗市	Miluo City		4093	578	3515	2673
临湘市	Linxiang County		2470	169	2301	2269
常德市	**Changde City**	**1968**	**29241**	**3895**	**25346**	**22551**
武陵区	Wuling District		4567	1884	2683	1924
鼎城区	Dingcheng District		4433	410	4023	3865
安乡县	Anxiang County		2782	138	2644	2044
汉寿县	Hanshou County		3522	122	3400	3301
澧　县	Li County		3921	445	3476	3365
临澧县	Linli County		2059	179	1880	1716
桃源县	Taoyuan County		3679	334	3345	2734
石门县	Shimen County		2972	235	2737	2702
津市市	Jinshi City		1306	148	1158	900
张家界市	**Zhangjiajie City**	**460**	**6580**	**577**	**6003**	**6298**
永定区	Yongdi District		2001	185	1816	2345
武陵源区	Wulingyuan District		183	9	174	207
慈利县	Cili County		2591	244	2347	1976
桑植县	Sangzhi County		1805	139	1666	1770
益阳市	**Yiyang City**	**918**	**26124**	**2975**	**23149**	**18121**
资阳区	Ziyang District		2358	253	2105	1861
赫山区	Heshan District		6717	1452	5265	3640
南　县	Nan County		4159	229	3930	3445
桃江县	Taojiang County		4458	328	4130	3450
安化县	Anhua County		4009	340	3669	2865
沅江市	Yuanjiang City		4423	373	4050	2860
郴州市	**Chenzhou City**	**1450**	**24309**	**2201**	**37770**	**21447**
北湖区	Beihu District		2912	827	2085	1643
苏仙区	Suxian District		2648	477	2171	1800
桂阳县	Guiyang County		3118	65	3053	3449
宜章县	Yizhang County		2931	115	2816	2567

单位：人　　18-22 续表 2 continued　　(person)

市县名称	City and County	普通高等学校 Regular Institutions of Higher Education	中等学校 Secondary Schools	中等职业教育 Vocational Secondary Education	普通中学 Regular Secondary Schools	普通小学 Primary Schools
永兴县	Yongxing County		3165	135	3030	2388
嘉禾县	Jiahe County		1515	59	1456	1689
临武县	Linwu County		1416	33	1383	1581
汝城县	Rucheng County		1851	91	1760	1523
桂东县	Guidong County		833	28	805	701
安仁县	Anren County		2009	89	1920	2195
资兴市	Zixing City		2451	282	2169	1911
永州市	**Yongzhou City**	**1525**	**28916**	**2204**	**26712**	**28267**
芝山区	Zhishan District		3255	309	2946	2756
冷水滩区	Lengshuitan District		3053	238	2815	2700
祁阳县	Qiyang County		6190	354	5836	5670
东安县	DonganCounty		2924	121	2803	2306
双牌县	Shuangpai County		837	64	773	971
道　县	Dao County		3033	480	2553	3357
江永县	Jiangyong County		1201	127	1074	1333
宁远县	Ningyuan County		3201	266	2935	3528
蓝山县	Lanshan County		1348	58	1290	1598
新田县	Xintian County		1804	71	1733	1791
江华县	Jianghua County		2070	116	1954	2257
怀化市	**Huaihua City**	**1352**	**23373**	**3211**	**20162**	**24812**
鹤城区	Hecheng District		4067	1803	2264	2026
中方县	Zhongfang County		1331	105	1226	1378
沅陵县	Yuanling County		2477	226	2251	3744
辰溪县	Chenxi County		1978	86	1892	3008
溆浦县	Xupu County		3204	158	3046	3818
会同县	Huitong County		1496	90	1406	1603
麻阳县	Mayang County		1345	70	1275	1723
新晃县	Xinhuang County		1046	76	970	1089
芷江县	Zhijiang County		1499	163	1336	1668
靖州县	Jingzhou County		1390	94	1296	1212
通道县	Tongdao County		1134	45	1089	976
洪江市	Hongjiang City		2406	295	2111	2567
娄底市	**Loudi City**	**1195**	**23274**	**3171**	**20103**	**16806**
娄星区	Louxing District		4053	1447	2606	2179
双峰县	Shuangfeng County		5119	322	4797	3605
新化县	Xinhua County		5748	303	5445	4600
冷水江市	Lengshuijiang County		3027	766	2261	2039
涟源市	Lianyuan County		5327	333	4994	4383
湘西自治州	**West Hunan A.P**	**1573**	**11226**	**1319**	**9907**	**15100**
吉首市	Jishou County		2201	821	1380	1489
泸溪县	Luxi County		1190	55	1135	1647
凤凰县	Fenghuang County		1394	105	1289	2128
花垣县	Huayuan County		963	46	917	1613
保靖县	Baojing County		1142	55	1087	1600
古丈县	Guzhang County		575	16	559	878
永顺县	Yongshun County		1852	61	1791	2884
龙山县	Longshan County		1909	160	1749	2861

18-23 各市、州、县各级学校专任教师(2003年)

Full-time Teachers and workers by Level (2003)

单位：人 (person)

市县名称	City and County	普通高等学校 Regular Institutions of Higher Education	中等学校 Secondary Schools	中等职业教育 Vocational Secondary Education	普通中学 Regular Secondary Schools	普通小学 Primary Schools
长沙市	**Changsha City**	**16055**	**28102**	**3710**	**24392**	**18265**
芙蓉区	Furong District		1499	431	1068	1230
天心区	Tianxin District		1101	180	921	1172
岳麓区	Yuelu District		1607	238	1369	1216
开福区	Kaifu District		2048	516	1532	1499
雨花区	Yuhua District		2833	708	2125	1488
长沙县	Changsha County		3617	412	3205	2433
望城县	Wangcheng County		3311	283	3028	2307
宁乡县	Ningxiang County		6014	527	5487	3899
浏阳市	Liuyang City		6072	415	5657	3021
株洲市	**Zhuzhou City**	**2643**	**16839**	**1751**	**15088**	**11421**
荷塘区	Hetang District		1465	550	915	729
芦淞区	Lusong District		1072	336	736	757
石峰区	Shifeng District		1068	245	823	837
天元区	Tianyuan District		667	21	646	425
株洲县	Zhuzhou County		2052	109	1943	1424
攸　县	You County		3112	220	2892	2094
茶陵县	Chaling County		2058	23	2035	2142
炎陵县	Yanling County		874	39	835	593
醴陵市	Liling City		4471	208	4263	2420
湘潭市	**Xiangtan City**	**3721**	**13864**	**1791**	**12073**	**9872**
雨湖区	Yuhu District		2154	632	1522	1162
岳塘区	Yuetang District		1558	424	1134	1270
湘潭县	Xiangtan County		5285	366	4919	3694
湘乡市	Xiangxiang City		4415	299	4116	3380
韶山市	Shaoshan City		452	70	382	366
衡阳市	**Hengyang City**	**2658**	**28786**	**3319**	**25467**	**29445**
珠晖区	Zhuhui District		1413	337	1076	1115
雁峰区	Yanfeng District		2049	1187	862	782
石鼓区	Shigu District		677	31	646	638
蒸湘区	Zhengxiang District		1138	553	585	813
南岳区	Nanyue District		188		188	260
衡阳县	Hengyang County		4017	205	3812	4587
衡南县	Hengnan County		3618	325	3293	4490
衡山县	Hengshan County		1822	121	1701	1774
衡东县	Hengdong County		2362	59	2303	2238
祁东县	Qidong County		3917	216	3701	3592
耒阳市	Leiyang City		4569	285	4284	5791
常宁市	Changning City		3202	186	3016	3365
邵阳市	**Shaoyang City**	**733**	**28340**	**1523**	**26817**	**26123**
双清区	Shuangqing District		1041	149	892	1096
大祥区	Daxiang District		1759	495	1264	1107
北塔区	Beita District		280	22	258	341

单位：人 18-23 续表 1 continued (person)

市县名称	City and County	普通高等学校 Regular Institutions of Higher Education	中等学校 Secondary Schools	中等职业教育 Vocational Secondary Education	普通中学 Regular Secondary Schools	普通小学 Primary Schools
邵东县	Shaodong County		4647	99	4548	3808
新邵县	Xinshao County		2816	107	2709	2592
邵阳县	Shaoyang County		2774	21	2753	3528
隆回县	Longhui County		4286	164	4122	3770
洞口县	Dongkou County		2886	98	2788	2719
绥宁县	Suining County		1625	86	1539	1646
新宁县	Xinning County		2238	37	2201	1585
城步县	Chengbu County		1309	60	1249	1273
武冈市	Wugang City		2679	185	2494	2658
岳阳市	**Yueyang City**	**1459**	**24457**	**1560**	**22897**	**21169**
岳阳楼区	Yueyanglou District		3381	597	2784	2696
云溪区	Yunxi District		839	0	839	735
君山区	Junshan District		781		781	704
岳阳县	Yueyang County		3079	171	2908	2799
华容县	Huarong County		3600	105	3495	2740
湘阴县	Xiangyin County		3083	134	2949	2938
平江县	Pingjiang City		4188	189	3999	3770
汨罗市	Miluo City		3500	364	3136	2565
临湘市	Linxiang County		2111	105	2006	2222
常德市	**Changde City**	**1244**	**24302**	**2518**	**21784**	**21853**
武陵区	Wuling District		3117	1080	2037	1825
鼎城区	Dingcheng District		3786	246	3540	3712
安乡县	Anxiang County		2449	89	2360	2024
汉寿县	Hanshou County		3230	93	3137	3282
澧　县	Li County		3344	356	2988	3285
临澧县	Linli County		1638	130	1508	1651
桃源县	Taoyuan County		3112	231	2881	2622
石门县	Shimen County		2477	176	2301	2581
津市市	Jinshi City		1149	117	1032	871
张家界市	**Zhangjiajie City**	**161**	**5528**	**415**	**5113**	**5846**
永定区	Yongdi District		1630	108	1522	2220
武陵源区	Wulingyuan District		156	9	147	191
慈利县	Cili County		2233	192	2041	1818
桑植县	Sangzhi County		1509	106	1403	1617
益阳市	**Yiyang City**	**530**	**22496**	**2033**	**20463**	**17435**
资阳区	Ziyang District		2012	157	1855	1783
赫山区	Heshan District		5330	881	4449	3491
南　县	Nan County		3562	174	3388	3288
桃江县	Taojiang County		3854	236	3618	3348
安化县	Anhua County		3544	259	3285	2721
沅江市	Yuanjiang City		4194	326	3868	2804
郴州市	**Chenzhou City**	**721**	**20431**	**1313**	**19118**	**20000**
北湖区	Beihu District		2161	513	1648	1520
苏仙区	Suxian District		2039	264	1775	1701
桂阳县	Guiyang County		2677	54	2623	3208
宜章县	Yizhang County		2392	29	2363	2380

单位：人　　18-23 续表 2 continued　　(person)

市县名称	City and County	普通高等学校 Regular Institutions of Higher Education	中等学校 Secondary Schools	中等职业教育 Vocational Secondary Education	普通中学 Regular Secondary Schools	普通小学 Primary Schools
永兴县	Yongxing County		2746	102	2644	2310
嘉禾县	Jiahe County		1362	25	1337	1597
临武县	Linwu County		1196	28	1168	1423
汝城县	Rucheng County		1652	63	1589	1460
桂东县	Guidong County		696	20	676	675
安仁县	Anren County		1618	47	1571	2055
资兴市	Zixing City		1892	168	1724	1671
永州市	**Yongzhou City**	**909**	**23581**	**1535**	**22046**	**25450**
芝山区	Zhishan District		2672	203	2469	2510
冷水滩区	Lengshuitan District		2371	169	2202	2392
祁阳县	Qiyang County		5123	250	4873	4991
东安县	DonganCounty		2611	91	2520	2131
双牌县	Shuangpai County		728	55	673	927
道　县	Dao County		2321	342	1979	3082
江永县	Jiangyong County		989	73	916	1262
宁远县	Ningyuan County		2485	159	2326	3088
蓝山县	Lanshan County		1105	38	1067	1458
新田县	Xintian County		1520	52	1468	1589
江华县	Jianghua County		1656	103	1553	2020
怀化市	**Huaihua City**	**848**	**19774**	**2109**	**17665**	**23538**
鹤城区	Hecheng District		3014	1157	1857	1855
中方县	Zhongfang County		1213	78	1135	1292
沅陵县	Yuanling County		2098	149	1949	3483
辰溪县	Chenxi County		1751	58	1693	2886
溆浦县	Xupu County		2927	119	2808	3703
会同县	Huitong County		1265	66	1199	1529
麻阳县	Mayang County		1175	49	1126	1651
新晃县	Xinhuang County		908	60	848	1008
芷江县	Zhijiang County		1277	91	1186	1609
靖州县	Jingzhou County		1209	79	1130	1169
通道县	Tongdao County		938	17	921	905
洪江市	Hongjiang City		1999	186	1813	2448
娄底市	**Loudi City**	**673**	**19799**	**1931**	**17868**	**16246**
娄星区	Louxing District		2919	823	2096	2002
双峰县	Shuangfeng County		4681	238	4443	3555
新化县	Xinhua County		5071	192	4879	4532
冷水江市	Lengshuijiang County		2387	434	1953	1902
涟源市	Lianyuan County		4741	244	4497	4255
湘西自治州	**West Hunan A.P**	**874**	**9300**	**810**	**8490**	**14041**
吉首市	Jishou County		1644	465	1179	1394
泸溪县	Luxi County		1022	33	989	1575
凤凰县	Fenghuang County		1175	64	1111	1963
花垣县	Huayuan County		798	32	766	1491
保靖县	Baojing County		960	36	924	1439
古丈县	Guzhang County		448	12	436	775
永顺县	Yongshun County		1566	48	1518	2637
龙山县	Longshan County		1687	120	1567	2767

18-24 各市、州、县各级学校在校学生(2003年)

Students Enrollment by Level (2003)

单位：人 (person)

市县名称	City and County	普通高等学校 Regular Institutions of Higher Education	中等学校 Secondary Schools	中等职业教育 Vocational Secondary Education	普通中学 Regular Secondary Schools	高中 Senior Secondary Schools	初中 Junior Secondary Schools	普通小学 Primary Schools
长沙市	**Changsha City**	**268613**	**540301**	**107475**	**432826**	**112950**	**319876**	**313587**
芙蓉区	Furong District		31653	13984	17669	6271	11398	21713
天心区	Tianxin District		32985	17265	15720	5385	10335	18096
岳麓区	Yuelu District		31582	10247	21335	7346	13989	21525
开福区	Kaifu District		32172	7320	24852	8163	16689	20526
雨花区	Yuhua District		51780	17608	34172	12635	21537	25269
长沙县	Changsha County		63269	7537	55732	12675	43057	39361
望城县	Wangcheng County		64220	8416	55804	10933	44871	33601
宁乡县	Ningxiang County		119248	14433	104815	26288	78527	70016
浏阳市	Liuyang City		113392	10665	102727	23254	79473	63480
株洲市	**Zhuzhou City**	**45006**	**337897**	**39096**	**298801**	**67265**	**231536**	**223938**
荷塘区	Hetang District		30340	12370	17970	6667	11303	15516
芦淞区	Lusong District		21101	7580	13521	4906	8615	15514
石峰区	Shifeng District		22516	9227	13289	4430	8859	14959
天元区	Tianyuan District		12843	271	12572	2777	9795	8293
株洲县	Zhuzhou County		36527	1478	35049	4996	30053	22596
攸　县	You County		60558	4018	56540	12556	43984	44264
茶陵县	Chaling County		48759	278	48481	10368	38113	31816
炎陵县	Yanling County		14579	451	14128	2969	11159	9682
醴陵市	Liling City		90674	3423	87251	17596	69655	61298
湘潭市	**Xiangtan City**	**63175**	**268320**	**40400**	**227920**	**58816**	**169104**	**176239**
雨湖区	Yuhu District		41221	16682	24539	10180	14359	20557
岳塘区	Yuetang District		26628	8219	18409	6161	12248	20537
湘潭县	Xiangtan County		103249	7279	95970	19505	76465	70274
湘乡市	Xiangxiang City		89793	7210	82583	21597	60986	57693
韶山市	Shaoshan City		7429	1010	6419	1373	5046	7178
衡阳市	**Hengyang City**	**43435**	**553887**	**58525**	**495362**	**96606**	**398756**	**523480**
珠晖区	Zhuhui District		28551	9472	19079	5285	13794	21023
雁峰区	Yanfeng District		34309	18237	16072	5825	10247	14629
石鼓区	Shigu District		15669	2818	12851	3251	9600	14890
蒸湘区	Zhengxiang District		24513	12390	12123	2767	9356	16648
南岳区	Nanyue District		3175		3175	925	2250	3898
衡阳县	Hengyang County		79513	3451	76062	15292	60770	81449
衡南县	Hengnan County		69419	6272	63147	11454	51693	69833
衡山县	Hengshan County		31980	1040	30940	5577	25363	30810
衡东县	Hengdong County		51603	721	50882	8900	41982	48101
祁东县	Qidong County		74403	2194	72209	14997	57212	64118
耒阳市	Leiyang City		81924	1930	79994	11967	68027	96580
常宁市	Changning City		61885	3057	58828	10366	48462	61501
邵阳市	**Shaoyang City**	**10626**	**595612**	**29338**	**566274**	**126416**	**439858**	**532481**
双清区	Shuangqing District		20091	1639	18452	3890	14562	18905
大祥区	Daxiang District		42935	16536	26399	9962	16437	20796
北塔区	Beita District		4971	186	4785	368	4417	4622

单位：人　　　　18-24 续表 1 continued　　　　(person)

市县名称	City and County	普通高等学校 Regular Institutions of Higher Education	中等学校 Secondary Schools	中等职业教育 Vocational Secondary Education	普通中学 Regular Secondary Schools	高中 Senior Secondary Schools	初中 Junior Secondary Schools	普通小学 Primary Schools
邵东县	Shaodong County		100379	2525	97854	26435	71419	87395
新邵县	Xinshao County		53588	1217	52371	11042	41329	53967
邵阳县	Shaoyang County		59894		59894	7920	51974	77157
隆回县	Longhui County		93731	2561	91170	20566	70604	77597
洞口县	Dongkou County		60189	485	59704	14500	45204	59115
绥宁县	Suining County		30113	428	29685	6308	23377	27993
新宁县	Xinning County		49864	591	49273	8825	40448	33099
城步县	Chengbu County		20716	222	20494	3623	16871	17233
武冈市	Wugang City		59141	2948	56193	12977	43216	54602
岳阳市	**Yueyang City**	**16356**	**448969**	**37633**	**411336**	**84020**	**327316**	**390014**
岳阳楼区	Yueyanglou District		69034	21518	47516	15407	32109	50389
云溪区	Yunxi District		16106	1386	14720	5031	9689	13209
君山区	Junshan District		14302		14302	2727	11575	15677
岳阳县	Yueyang County		60303	2629	57674	11259	46415	52180
华容县	Huarong County		58825	2100	56725	11469	45256	45737
湘阴县	Xiangyin County		57520	1841	55679	9032	46647	51905
平江县	Pingjiang City		75335	2066	73269	11659	61610	69879
汨罗市	Miluo City		61325	6093	55232	9554	45678	53885
临湘市	Linxiang County		37530	1311	36219	7882	28337	37153
常德市	**Changde City**	**14596**	**446789**	**53776**	**393013**	**99227**	**293786**	**377299**
武陵区	Wuling District		63756	28166	35590	10846	24744	35667
鼎城区	Dingcheng District		72677	4289	68388	16580	51808	62506
安乡县	Anxiang County		40945	723	40222	11402	28820	30381
汉寿县	Hanshou County		56829	2013	54816	10755	44061	57730
澧　县	Li County		59709	6946	52763	12686	40077	55222
临澧县	Linli County		28834	2143	26691	8582	18109	26162
桃源县	Taoyuan County		61215	4455	56760	13634	43126	52521
石门县	Shimen County		44254	3635	40619	10551	30068	41444
津市市	Jinshi City		18570	1406	17164	4191	12973	15666
张家界市	**Zhangjiajie City**	**2790**	**111547**	**11038**	**100509**	**20012**	**80497**	**111186**
永定区	Yongdi District		32942	4967	27975	5253	22722	32820
武陵源区	Wulingyuan District		3488	151	3337	824	2513	3781
慈利县	Cili County		44405	4377	40028	8885	31143	45453
桑植县	Sangzhi County		30712	1543	29169	5050	24119	29132
益阳市	**Yiyang City**	**10078**	**406244**	**37917**	**368327**	**81623**	**286704**	**273995**
资阳区	Ziyang District		32716	2658	30058	6247	23811	25390
赫山区	Heshan District		100236	20030	80206	25159	55047	54594
南　县	Nan County		56331	1900	54431	11906	42525	46136
桃江县	Taojiang County		72714	2515	70199	16631	53568	47828
安化县	Anhua County		76590	4978	71612	9285	62327	55107
沅江市	Yuanjiang City		67657	5836	61821	12395	49426	44940
郴州市	**Chenzhou City**	**12449**	**379682**	**17984**	**361698**	**64605**	**297093**	**332904**
北湖区	Beihu District		40493	8856	31637	9404	22233	25953
苏仙区	Suxian District		31675	5109	26566	7520	19046	20505
桂阳县	Guiyang County		55837	573	55264	7955	47309	59339
宜章县	Yizhang County		50800	381	50419	7622	42797	45649

单位：人　　　　　18-24 续表 2 continued　　　　　(person)

市县名称	City and County	普通高等学校 Regular Institutions of Higher Education	中等学校 Secondary Schools	中等职业教育 Vocational Secondary Education	普通中学 Regular Secondary Schools	高中 Senior Secondary Schools	初中 Junior Secondary Schools	普通小学 Primary Schools
永兴县	Yongxing County		50537	331	50206	7290	42916	40866
嘉禾县	Jiahe County		25207	22	25185	3427	21758	31504
临武县	Linwu County		23855	131	23724	3480	20244	21485
汝城县	Rucheng County		28447	248	28199	4662	23537	26880
桂东县	Guidong County		14862	223	14639	1806	12833	11627
安仁县	Anren County		33304	671	32633	6359	26274	26238
资兴市	Zixing City		24665	1439	23226	5080	18146	22858
永州市	**Yongzhou City**	**13436**	**431334**	**35895**	**395439**	**92971**	**302468**	**467757**
芝山区	Zhishan District		55280	14020	41260	14185	27075	37749
冷水滩区	Lengshuitan District		38740	1616	37124	13865	23259	39671
祁阳县	Qiyang County		69514	5969	63545	19451	44094	74928
东安县	DonganCounty		49403	869	48534	11769	36765	33971
双牌县	Shuangpai County		13569	818	12751	2530	10221	11586
道　县	Dao County		47709	5342	42367	6931	35436	59232
江永县	Jiangyong County		15136	229	14907	2703	12204	20902
宁远县	Ningyuan County		52760	2870	49890	8716	41174	68689
蓝山县	Lanshan County		24832	957	23875	3800	20075	32382
新田县	Xintian County		29925	446	29479	4590	24889	35622
江华县	Jianghua County		34466	2759	31707	4431	27276	53025
怀化市	**Huaihua City**	**11802**	**371655**	**49077**	**322578**	**55523**	**267055**	**340792**
鹤城区	Hecheng District		67137	34113	33024	7518	25506	33655
中方县	Zhongfang County		19716	1341	18375	2821	15554	14343
沅陵县	Yuanling County		40127	2626	37501	6439	31062	41354
辰溪县	Chenxi County		34555	599	33956	6192	27764	34862
溆浦县	Xupu County		56146	1770	54376	8727	45649	50819
会同县	Huitong County		22853	748	22105	3514	18591	22901
麻阳县	Mayang County		23731	826	22905	3987	18918	29477
新晃县	Xinhuang County		15806	547	15259	2263	12996	16068
芷江县	Zhijiang County		22128	1956	20172	2883	17289	28914
靖州县	Jingzhou County		21149	805	20344	3154	17190	17103
通道县	Tongdao County		15859	120	15739	1773	13966	16442
洪江市	Hongjiang City		32448	3626	28822	6252	22570	34854
娄底市	**Loudi City**	**8377**	**381687**	**38347**	**343340**	**79018**	**264322**	**325159**
娄星区	Louxing District		60988	23367	37621	13694	23927	34497
双峰县	Shuangfeng County		83324	3791	79533	19051	60482	59829
新化县	Xinhua County		106734	2204	104530	18401	86129	104455
冷水江市	Lengshuijiang County		38339	5511	32828	9942	22886	24937
涟源市	Lianyuan County		92302	3474	88828	17930	70898	101441
湘西自治州	**West Hunan A.P**	**16481**	**183615**	**13272**	**170343**	**26688**	**143655**	**298061**
吉首市	Jishou County		30927	10555	20372	5138	15234	29106
泸溪县	Luxi County		19904	88	19816	3675	16141	35501
凤凰县	Fenghuang County		21411	331	21080	2771	18309	44809
花垣县	Huayuan County		15418	302	15116	1801	13315	31501
保靖县	Baojing County		18089	384	17705	2541	15164	27727
古丈县	Guzhang County		8503	104	8399	1045	7354	13033
永顺县	Yongshun County		31700	535	31165	5508	25657	51383
龙山县	Longshan County		37663	973	36690	4209	32481	65001

18-25 各市、州、县卫生机构、人员与床位(2003年)

Health Care Institutions, Personnel and Beds (2003)

市县名称	City and County	机构(个) Health Care Institution (unit)	#医院卫生院 Hospitals	卫生工作人员(人) Personnel in Health Care Institution (person)	#卫生技术人员 Medical Technical Personnel	#执业医师 Doctors	#执业助理医师 Assistant Doctors	实有床位(张) Beds (unit)	#医院卫生院 Hospitals
长沙市	**Changsha City**	**368**	**281**	**33211**	**24966**	**8336**	**1648**	**22785**	**20404**
芙蓉区	Furong District	35	21	5995	4269	1669	95	3842	3227
天心区	Tianxin District	30	14	2132	1649	604	66	1644	1357
岳麓区	Yuelu District	39	23	4263	3140	1130	49	2792	2703
开福区	Kaifu District	34	27	5098	3595	1368	89	3032	2758
雨花区	Yuhua District	43	35	5258	3772	1262	135	4612	4177
长沙县	Changsha County	39	37	1473	1279	370	236	1199	1169
望城县	Wangcheng County	43	39	1394	1136	308	141	1159	887
宁乡县	Ningxiang County	45	41	3557	2758	766	356	2106	1805
浏阳市	Liuyang City	60	44	4041	3368	859	481	2399	2321
株洲市	**Zhuzhou City**	**204**	**180**	**14503**	**12058**	**3747**	**1058**	**9920**	**9617**
荷塘区	Hetang District	14	10	1604	1253	409	95	1431	1401
芦淞区	Lusong District	15	12	2891	2282	767	52	2102	2000
石峰区	Shifeng District	17	14	2364	1919	628	77	1857	1855
天元区	Tianyuan District	6	3	201	165	63	18	60	60
株洲县	Zhuzhou County	27	25	960	834	221	112	568	554
攸县	You County	35	33	2021	1774	530	243	1071	1056
茶陵县	Chaling County	27	25	1288	1123	308	84	688	648
炎陵县	Yanling County	20	17	728	620	137	160	514	464
醴陵市	Liling City	43	41	2446	2088	684	217	1629	1579
湘潭市	**Xiangtan City**	**134**	**116**	**11919**	**9571**	**3069**	**990**	**7890**	**7519**
雨湖区	Yuhu District	32	27	3574	2598	891	118	2487	2425
岳塘区	Yuetang District	22	18	2710	2151	764	166	1933	1793
湘潭县	Xiangtan County	35	32	2429	2110	560	321	1370	1290
湘乡市	Xiangxiang City	36	33	2685	2291	714	349	1863	1786
韶山市	Shaoshan City	9	6	521	421	140	36	237	225
衡阳市	**Hengyang City**	**397**	**333**	**28059**	**22097**	**6534**	**2976**	**14119**	**13074**
珠晖区	Zhuhui District	22	19	2971	2354	817	67	1936	1934
雁峰区	Yanfeng District	25	18	2128	1664	655	72	1327	1132
石鼓区	Shigu District	16	13	2708	2188	822	25	1867	1867
蒸湘区	Zhengxiang District	14	9	1237	807	255	90	680	600
南岳区	Nanyue District	10	7	609	436	137	30	625	485
衡阳县	Hengyang County	34	31	3299	2229	662	571	738	718
衡南县	Hengnan County	32	29	2706	2168	628	577	972	954
衡山县	Hengshan County	31	29	1152	1021	257	198	633	613
衡东县	Hengdong County	33	31	1807	1435	418	283	797	748
祁东县	Qidong County	40	15	2560	2019	686	251	1444	1026
耒阳市	Leiyang City	66	63	3414	2833	656	363	1766	1696
常宁市	Changning City	74	69	3468	2943	541	449	1334	1301
邵阳市	**Shaoyang City**	**331**	**288**	**18088**	**15090**	**4136**	**1721**	**10928**	**10362**
双清区	Shuangqing District	10	7	1387	1060	341	49	928	910
大祥区	Daxiang District	20	15	2134	1635	562	67	1353	1353
北塔区	Beita District	6	5	48	47	9	15	50	50

注:本表资料未含医务室、卫生保健所、诊所。 The clinics, health care centres were excluded.

市县名称	City and County	机构(个) Health Care Institution (unit)	#医院卫生院 Hospitals	卫生工作人员(人) Personnel in Health Care Institution (person)	#卫生技术人员 Medical Technical Personnel	#执业医师 Doctors	#执业助理医师 Assistant Doctors	实有床位(张) Beds (unit)	#医院卫生院 Hospitals
邵东县	Shaodong County	42	40	2309	1986	631	278	1416	1416
新邵县	Xinshao County	20	17	1619	1355	337	161	1594	1172
邵阳县	Shaoyang County	50	47	1765	1551	371	191	832	804
隆回县	Longhui County	32	30	2194	1883	529	240	1080	1050
洞口县	Dongkou County	44	41	1822	1504	426	248	888	868
绥宁县	Suining County	29	26	786	685	231	100	512	512
新宁县	Xinning County	34	23	1531	1231	228	89	883	853
城步县	Chengbu County	15	12	753	621	159	65	501	498
武冈市	Wugang City	29	25	1740	1532	312	218	891	876
岳阳市	**Yueyang City**	**289**	**225**	**15818**	**13127**	**3985**	**1506**	**10231**	**8593**
岳阳楼区	Yueyanglou District	45	31	3643	2961	1126	204	2950	2646
云溪区	Yunxi District	14	10	954	779	256	103	718	648
君山区	Junshan District	10	5	521	421	136	43	427	360
岳阳县	Yueyang County	33	25	1541	1346	362	235	893	683
华容县	Huarong County	34	24	1403	1144	364	111	1028	748
湘阴县	Xiangyin County	51	43	1900	1608	473	247	1205	978
平江县	Pingjiang City	32	29	2539	2175	517	233	965	835
汨罗市	Miluo City	38	32	1882	1545	449	162	1095	876
临湘市	Linxiang County	32	26	1435	1148	302	168	950	819
常德市	**Changde City**	**323**	**270**	**18669**	**15551**	**4581**	**2224**	**11724**	**10361**
武陵区	Wuling District	32	22	3502	2681	964	147	2538	2285
鼎城区	Dingcheng District	45	39	2645	2386	547	432	1399	1174
安乡县	Anxiang County	31	23	1584	1352	401	176	1147	960
汉寿县	Hanshou County	41	35	1692	1423	448	217	1127	897
澧　县	Li County	40	34	2483	1947	468	429	1434	1196
临澧县	Linli County	24	20	1374	1149	273	172	732	692
桃源县	Taoyuan County	50	45	2473	2074	650	328	1508	1468
石门县	Shimen County	44	41	2064	1833	633	223	1237	1187
津市市	Jinshi City	16	11	852	706	197	100	602	502
张家界市	**Zhangjiajie City**	**133**	**109**	**5032**	**4159**	**1084**	**817**	**3317**	**3013**
永定区	Yongdi District	40	30	1796	1456	436	302	1336	1201
武陵源区	Wulingyuan District	7	5	113	90	20	26	84	84
慈利县	Cili County	40	34	1968	1644	416	281	1251	1112
桑植县	Sangzhi County	46	40	1155	969	212	208	646	616
益阳市	**Yiyang City**	**217**	**172**	**14951**	**12633**	**4408**	**1460**	**8489**	**7467**
资阳区	Ziyang District	19	17	1613	1303	425	139	872	807
赫山区	Heshan District	42	29	3205	2606	1014	297	1969	1769
南　县	Nan County	38	28	2480	2128	653	212	1328	1116
桃江县	Taojiang County	33	31	2551	2235	735	337	1254	1234
安化县	Anhua County	30	28	2459	2125	676	246	1573	1463
沅江市	Yuanjiang City	55	39	2643	2236	905	229	1493	1078
郴州市	**Chenzhou City**	**340**	**302**	**16227**	**13444**	**3586**	**2057**	**10454**	**10153**
北湖区	Beihu District	39	31	3126	2507	778	191	2343	2311
苏仙区	Suxian District	28	24	1902	1486	413	214	1409	1361
桂阳县	Guiyang County	45	43	1815	1508	377	288	1094	1044
宜章县	Yizhang County	34	32	1620	1358	327	171	1207	1187

18-25 续表 2 continued

市县名称	City and County	机构(个) Health Care Institution (unit)	#医院卫生院 Hospitals	卫生工作人员(人) Personnel in Health Care Institution (person)	#卫生技术人员 Medical Technical Personnel	#执业医师 Doctors	#执业助理医师 Assistant Doctors	实有床位(张) Beds (unit)	#医院卫生院 Hospitals
永兴县	Yongxing County	31	28	1712	1426	343	251	859	848
嘉禾县	Jiahe County	22	20	1021	869	167	133	512	485
临武县	Linwu County	21	19	738	617	164	76	494	484
汝城县	Rucheng County	27	23	858	726	199	154	582	540
桂东县	Guidong County	22	20	456	372	118	61	311	296
安仁县	Anren County	27	23	1216	1090	303	130	655	624
资兴市	Zixing City	44	39	1763	1485	397	388	988	973
永州市	**Yongzhou City**	**337**	**285**	**15902**	**13498**	**3283**	**2501**	**9118**	**8480**
芝山区	Zhishan District	28	24	2826	2302	672	392	1660	1605
冷水滩区	Lengshuitan District	29	22	2083	1727	583	112	1559	1267
祁阳县	Qiyang County	54	31	2840	2372	382	587	1093	1033
东安县	DonganCounty	22	20	1434	1193	239	419	591	574
双牌县	Shuangpai County	20	18	550	482	126	103	308	308
道　县	Dao County	29	25	1317	1158	276	225	852	772
江永县	Jiangyong County	18	16	577	531	95	50	430	394
宁远县	Ningyuan County	51	49	1476	1305	280	250	733	713
蓝山县	Lanshan County	31	29	842	726	154	122	448	418
新田县	Xintian County	25	23	848	744	232	89	578	558
江华县	Jianghua County	30	28	1109	958	244	152	866	838
怀化市	**Huaihua City**	**455**	**401**	**16271**	**13665**	**3622**	**1934**	**11513**	**11083**
鹤城区	Hecheng District	35	28	3351	2685	956	253	2144	2066
中方县	Zhongfang County	25	23	454	414	67	102	266	266
沅陵县	Yuanling County	73	62	1767	1469	372	213	1269	1206
辰溪县	Chenxi County	43	40	1627	1433	355	216	1230	1210
溆浦县	Xupu County	62	58	1805	1568	344	219	1395	1367
会同县	Huitong County	29	26	748	659	191	84	668	630
麻阳县	Mayang County	33	27	861	757	198	103	596	516
新晃县	Xinhuang County	27	24	788	646	201	110	614	594
芷江县	Zhijiang County	34	31	1008	854	217	93	601	579
靖州县	Jingzhou County	20	17	743	634	146	125	459	444
通道县	Tongdao County	24	21	621	531	128	67	422	408
洪江市	Hongjiang City	50	44	2498	2015	447	349	1849	1797
娄底市	**Loudi City**	**168**	**143**	**14724**	**12438**	**3397**	**1995**	**8466**	**7978**
娄星区	Louxing District	33	26	3408	2515	688	306	2216	2019
双峰县	Shuangfeng County	26	22	2222	2026	495	496	1172	1088
新化县	Xinhua County	41	36	3411	2885	816	467	1514	1493
冷水江市	Lengshuijiang County	32	27	2019	1729	525	206	1357	1302
涟源市	Lianyuan County	36	32	3664	3283	873	520	2207	2076
湘西自治州	**West Hunan A.P**	**320**	**243**	**8726**	**7232**	**2069**	**953**	**5979**	**5800**
吉首市	Jishou County	35	21	2110	1606	632	120	1483	1433
泸溪县	Luxi County	23	20	789	689	167	152	412	412
凤凰县	Fenghuang County	39	34	910	793	226	154	547	530
花垣县	Huayuan County	30	21	801	642	211	92	585	560
保靖县	Baojing County	56	27	900	782	181	104	571	554
古丈县	Guzhang County	20	16	394	340	76	35	290	285
永顺县	Yongshun County	52	50	1337	1119	296	148	1146	1116
龙山县	Longshan County	65	54	1485	1261	280	148	945	910

18-26 各市、州、县农民平均每人纯收入(2003年)

Per Capita Annual Net Income of Rural Residents by Region (2003)

市县名称	City and County	调查户数(户) Number of Households Surveyed (household)	调查户常住人口(人) Number of Residents Surveyed (person)	平均每人纯收入 (元) Per Capita Annual Net Income (yuan)	工资性收入 Laborers' Remuneration	家庭经营收入 Income from Family Business	转移性收入 Transfer Income	财产性收入 Property Income	人均生活消费支出 (元) Per Capita Living Expenditure (yuan)	#食品 #Foods
长沙市	**Changsha City**	**770**	**2999**	**3745.74**	**1446.49**	**2027.90**	**143.09**	**128.26**	**3172.11**	**1382.79**
芙蓉区	Furong District	30	117	5733.67	1633.58	2296.87	262.65	1540.57	4384.07	1567.99
天心区	Tianxin District	30	108	5639.49	1907.89	2855.93	431.50	444.17	3985.88	1754.73
岳麓区	Yuelu District	40	140	5386.36	2628.51	1800.42	348.90	608.52	5234.49	1499.10
开福区	Kaifu District	40	138	5295.23	1386.89	3438.19	107.85	362.30	4420.96	1823.39
雨花区	Yuhua District	30	123	5463.59	1847.07	2774.89	11.75	829.88	3788.70	1390.73
长沙县	Changsha County	130	514	4110.32	1345.84	2502.24	148.30	113.94	3225.70	1545.55
望城县	Wangcheng County	150	577	3700.11	1486.40	2039.45	145.75	28.51	2971.33	1443.81
宁乡县	Ningxiang County	170	656	3351.69	1127.24	1908.61	159.32	156.51	3030.08	1175.35
浏阳市	Liuyang City	150	626	3791.77	1791.35	1818.03	110.71	71.68	3243.97	1481.36
株洲市	**Zhuzhou City**	**660**	**2624**	**3029.62**	**1381.60**	**1471.73**	**100.65**	**75.64**	**2332.01**	**1081.10**
荷塘区	Hetang District	40	111	3910.38	1590.56	1590.94	229.18	499.69	3170.41	1565.14
芦淞区	Lusong District	30	107	3895.23	1682.39	1768.45	256.12	188.27	2749.24	1219.91
石峰区	Shifeng District	30	112	3908.71	1766.31	1930.05	68.29	144.06	2662.85	1084.35
天元区	Tianyuan District	30	167	3660.57	826.22	2179.89	133.50	520.97	2676.04	1123.45
株洲县	Zhuzhou County	100	383	3101.47	1103.46	1943.93	44.32	9.75	2659.34	1283.62
攸县	You County	110	435	3379.16	1797.78	1427.74	77.81	75.83	2435.93	1084.35
茶陵县	Chaling County	100	400	1866.24	672.46	1119.31	58.70	15.78	1531.69	671.00
炎陵县	Yanling County	100	413	1807.94	659.75	1006.27	120.00	21.93	1569.93	907.81
醴陵市	Liling City	120	496	3441.85	1721.28	1484.44	152.80	83.34	2595.71	1219.93
湘潭市	**Xiangtan City**	**330**	**1299**	**3218.47**	**1166.81**	**1913.82**	**88.19**	**49.65**	**2407.67**	**1156.87**
雨湖区	Yuhu District	30	109	4722.61	1629.35	2596.74	230.39	266.14	3484.74	1284.27
岳塘区	Yuetang District	40	143	4442.58	1522.01	2401.52	227.35	291.70	3069.42	1365.75
湘潭县	Xiangtan County	100	468	3165.38	1175.34	1896.33	60.23	33.48	2172.19	1076.85
湘乡市	Xiangxiang City	130	493	3012.80	1125.87	1772.74	84.29	29.90	2550.01	1222.58
韶山市	Shaoshan City	30	86	3661.12	814.02	2545.24	242.78	59.07	2679.02	1241.00
衡阳市	**Hengyang City**	**860**	**3300**	**3030.96**	**1278.05**	**1648.54**	**75.26**	**29.12**	**2264.34**	**1197.96**
珠晖区	Zhuhu District	30	123	3204.26	1781.07	1184.06	204.88	34.25	2440.49	1219.70
雁峰区	Yanfeng District	30	119	3175.84	1456.21	1612.65	91.75	15.24	2476.77	1191.14
石鼓区	Shigu District	30	123	3156.52	1027.50	1601.93	450.15	76.93	2347.01	1164.11
蒸湘区	Zhenxiang District	30	122	3019.81	1536.21	1311.35	109.92	62.33	2403.15	1195.11
南岳区	Nanyue District	50	178	3263.03	980.41	2008.68	221.64	52.28	2275.75	1004.31
衡阳县	Hengyang County	100	336	2995.42	960.58	1849.13	119.05	66.67	2165.13	1045.85
衡南县	Hengnan County	100	378	2992.68	1242.03	1628.44	64.08	58.14	2475.50	1356.56
衡山县	Hengshan County	80	329	3184.46	1147.34	1856.31	172.28	8.54	2490.76	1081.97
衡东县	Hengdong County	100	404	3045.85	965.57	2073.80	5.43	1.04	2243.87	1235.90
祁东县	Qidong County	100	397	2986.72	1418.25	1456.39	83.19	28.89	2247.46	1211.58
耒阳市	Leiyang City	100	367	3045.88	1447.51	1577.98	15.42	4.97	2313.55	1326.54
常宁市	Changning City	110	424	3016.99	1643.52	1303.48	66.06	3.92	1947.03	1053.65
邵阳市	**Shaoyang City**	**1180**	**4384**	**2019.71**	**836.85**	**1036.98**	**135.63**	**10.25**	**1962.78**	**1059.82**
双清区	Shuangqing District	60	208	3155.54	1407.96	1671.77	58.13	17.68	2717.91	1219.71
大祥区	Daxiang District	60	238	3039.04	698.94	2086.00	204.41	49.69	2653.22	1657.19
北塔区	Beita District	40	152	2838.44	842.62	1717.84	221.80	56.18	2489.26	1535.86

市县名称	City and County	调查户数(户) Number of Households Surveyed (household)	调查户常住人口(人) Number of Residents Surveyed (person)	平均每人纯收入(元) Per Capita Annual Net Income (yuan)	工资性收入 Laborers' Remuneration	家庭经营收入 Income from Family Business	转移性收入 Transfer Income	财产性收入 Property Income	人均生活消费支出(元) Per Capita Living Expenditure (yuan)	#食品 #Foods
邵东县	Shaodong County	100	378	3197.52	1454.51	1483.06	254.36	5.58	3000.15	1665.76
新邵县	Xinshao County	120	506	1560.10	835.33	642.94	74.66	7.17	1449.62	826.09
邵阳县	Shaoyang County	120	456	1188.32	554.29	597.96	33.43	2.64	1340.78	792.92
隆回县	Longhui County	120	462	1210.37	541.92	576.60	80.64	11.21	1287.43	640.26
洞口县	Dongkou County	90	322	2391.92	976.99	1237.65	164.99	12.28	2260.51	1139.86
武冈市	Wugang City	170	374	2149.59	678.51	1319.23	142.80	9.06	1839.66	1004.02
绥宁县	Suining County	80	340	2578.98	913.20	1414.62	221.85	29.32	2485.91	1477.53
新宁县	Xinning County	120	507	1160.29	427.77	689.50	40.31	2.71	1426.91	761.04
城步县	Chengbu County	100	441	1221.09	313.02	875.72	29.95	2.40	1241.41	765.03
岳阳市	**Yueyang City**	**780**	**3069**	**2945.95**	**958.40**	**1840.78**	**88.09**	**58.67**	**2586.79**	**1216.44**
岳阳楼区	Yueyanglou District	30	114	4440.86	2137.31	1446.29	361.59	495.67	4255.03	1369.22
云溪区	YungXi District	50	209	3833.99	1142.41	2458.97	133.73	98.88	3213.39	1333.49
君山区	JungShang District	80	301	3136.34	592.21	2505.47	34.43	4.24	3003.75	1370.60
岳阳县	Yueyang County	100	379	3055.71	645.02	2246.30	135.51	28.88	2914.29	1323.38
华容县	Huarong County	100	378	3037.87	818.49	2181.18	20.32	17.89	3029.63	1457.54
湘阴县	Xiangyin County	100	414	3008.68	1417.03	1510.28	61.88	19.48	2495.34	1222.55
平江县	Pingjiang County	120	504	1345.56	659.08	630.26	47.37	8.85	1484.52	859.78
汨罗市	Miluo City	100	376	3361.84	864.90	2202.37	204.66	89.90	2564.47	1156.18
临湘市	Linxiang City	100	394	3051.50	981.12	1863.52	88.53	118.33	2540.67	1190.87
常德市	**Changde City**	**870**	**3009**	**2550.22**	**900.95**	**1527.72**	**90.68**	**30.87**	**2211.01**	**1101.54**
武陵区	Wuling District	70	279	3779.28	917.56	2417.31	95.34	349.08	2870.58	1094.61
鼎城区	Dingcheng District	100	328	2566.66	996.86	1500.56	55.69	13.55	2182.51	1109.53
安乡县	Anxiang County	100	339	2601.52	653.13	1904.08	29.55	14.76	2160.61	1175.50
汉寿县	Hanshou County	100	383	2386.81	978.48	1257.79	147.15	3.39	2369.34	1158.90
澧县	Li County	110	383	2579.12	938.74	1581.60	55.12	3.65	2350.53	1155.98
临澧县	Linli County	100	317	2711.38	800.74	1780.98	102.22	27.45	2256.54	970.50
桃源县	Taoyuan County	100	367	2646.95	1098.62	1447.30	91.42	9.61	2088.84	1044.42
石门县	Shimen County	110	353	2035.22	674.45	1131.88	143.51	85.37	1971.75	1121.59
津市市	Jinshi City	80	260	2459.74	457.67	1855.25	144.26	2.56	1815.54	886.76
张家界市	**Zhangjiajie City**	**330**	**1275**	**1863.86**	**713.11**	**1048.34**	**87.57**	**14.84**	**1691.35**	**900.99**
永定区	Yongding District	100	412	1714.66	576.65	1040.81	89.38	7.81	1843.70	926.50
武陵源区	Wulingyuan District	30	105	1949.70	393.09	961.29	549.92	45.40	1742.53	643.21
慈利县	Cili County	100	343	1701.38	564.06	1086.38	48.79	2.15	1658.35	882.30
桑植县	Sangzhi County	100	415	1223.29	490.63	660.39	69.58	2.69	1195.35	673.85
益阳市	**Yiyang City**	**630**	**2511**	**2362.45**	**975.18**	**1252.16**	**117.49**	**17.62**	**2233.96**	**1103.87**
资阳区	Ziyang District	100	419	2546.40	839.71	1301.36	355.11	50.21	2402.60	1027.43
赫山区	Heshan District	100	363	2628.16	971.03	1517.15	80.77	59.21	2595.60	1236.10
南县	Nan County	110	432	2397.61	823.51	1565.38	33.13	-24.40	2185.33	1200.18
桃江县	Taojiang County	100	378	2520.26	1305.42	1072.48	129.60	12.76	2593.44	1191.59
安化县	Anhua County	120	549	1392.22	867.17	490.77	33.96	0.32	1281.20	695.61
沅江市	Yuanjiang City	100	370	2653.03	591.89	1806.87	226.64	27.63	2484.51	1280.76
郴州市	**Chenzhou City**	**970**	**4188**	**2812.13**	**989.38**	**1686.94**	**79.23**	**56.59**	**2283.60**	**1085.40**
北湖区	Beihu District	80	315	3671.35	1466.17	1749.28	133.63	322.27	3210.19	1206.84
苏仙区	Suxian District	60	219	3675.21	1202.95	2310.92	138.98	22.37	2489.35	1244.39
桂阳县	Guiyang County	90	340	3161.33	869.52	2176.19	97.97	17.64	2473.50	1244.83
宜章县	Yizhang County	120	524	2347.75	729.77	1422.13	101.64	94.21	1907.32	910.37
永兴县	Yongxing County	100	419	3313.70	1413.21	1792.77	51.11	56.61	2799.85	1069.60

市县名称	City and County	调查户数(户) Number of Households Surveyed (household)	调查户常住人口(人) Number of Residents Surveyed (person)	平均每人纯收入					人均生活消费支出	
				(元) Per Capita Annual Net Income (yuan)	工资性收入 Laborers' Remuneration	家庭经营收入 Income from Family Business	转移性收入 Transfer Income	财产性收入 Property Income	(元) Per Capita Living Expenditure (yuan)	#食品 #Foods
嘉禾县	Jiahe County	80	324	3166.35	1354.28	1750.76	33.64	27.68	2733.27	1291.57
临武县	Linwu County	120	465	3200.20	993.88	1906.63	118.62	181.07	2521.97	1211.11
汝城县	Rucheng County	90	368	1528.24	519.25	960.03	39.69	9.27	1281.95	714.23
桂东县	Guidong County	80	347	1486.56	440.22	1003.46	37.10	5.78	1316.28	846.05
安仁县	Anreng County	100	411	1948.87	934.82	968.16	33.36	12.52	1937.18	1021.35
资兴市	Zixing City	120	456	3639.88	1267.25	2227.04	115.04	30.56	2535.16	1135.57
永州市	**Yongzhou City**	**1050**	**4397**	**2122.09**	**691.79**	**1346.67**	**62.56**	**21.07**	**1820.43**	**991.24**
芝山区	Zhishan District	100	403	2501.21	706.29	1735.57	15.10	44.24	2165.81	1230.98
冷水滩区	Lengshuitan District	110	398	2529.97	956.20	1469.91	37.79	66.07	1902.88	903.84
祁阳县	Qiyang County	100	416	2497.49	867.20	1436.21	158.02	36.07	2073.95	1050.01
东安县	Dongan County	100	377	2481.05	607.23	1830.12	35.86	7.84	1875.60	1067.64
双牌县	Shuangpai County	80	335	1665.65	634.96	1008.98	13.73	7.97	1390.11	808.82
道县	Dao County	100	427	2462.55	808.59	1593.79	35.82	24.35	2226.17	1201.01
江永县	Jiangyong County	100	410	2370.90	743.21	1624.28	0.46	2.95	2033.23	1148.30
宁远县	Ningyuan County	120	488	1375.02	531.41	744.95	89.06	9.59	1421.33	812.06
蓝山县	Lanshan County	70	301	2302.18	789.18	1407.65	96.76	8.58	2082.42	1165.99
新田县	Xintian County	90	383	1451.31	322.66	1094.74	32.64	1.27	1445.86	794.16
江华县	Jianghua County	100	459	1341.77	565.25	754.67	18.28	3.57	1046.56	601.82
怀化市	**Huaihua City**	**940**	**3996**	**2032.10**	**568.62**	**1368.55**	**84.88**	**10.05**	**1745.16**	**1033.10**
鹤城区	Hecheng District	30	121	2750.42	530.35	1914.28	276.87	28.93	2210.30	1084.11
中方县	Zhongfang County	60	227	2001.67	270.70	1408.91	284.89	37.17	1791.12	1061.61
沅陵县	Yuanling County	100	419	1347.87	405.36	864.60	72.58	5.33	1240.22	770.98
辰溪县	Chenxi County	90	352	1762.00	465.95	1175.91	120.14	0.00	1589.77	1002.40
溆浦县	Xupu County	100	365	2610.78	695.91	1867.54	36.52	10.80	2017.24	1220.03
会同县	Huitong County	110	413	2300.00	1192.23	1059.77	41.66	6.35	1999.88	1299.53
麻阳县	Mayang County	90	399	1428.24	422.69	1005.47	0.00	0.08	1341.60	820.26
新晃县	Xinhuang County	100	384	1301.87	181.04	996.23	123.39	1.20	1433.96	913.47
芷江县	Zhijiang County	100	370	1776.01	604.90	1118.80	40.10	12.22	1667.38	1018.06
靖州县	Jinzhou County	70	221	2471.04	775.10	1616.80	42.79	36.36	2179.09	1208.01
通道县	Tongdao County	100	455	1289.19	398.88	639.16	244.88	6.27	1028.17	596.08
洪江市	Hongjiang City	80	270	2674.97	597.79	2052.22	20.82	4.13	2226.29	1071.38
娄底市	**Loudi City**	**480**	**1871**	**1878.31**	**967.66**	**817.59**	**79.41**	**13.64**	**1763.75**	**895.49**
娄星区	Louxing District	50	139	2928.64	1091.48	1556.75	144.24	136.17	2284.12	1210.52
双峰县	Shuangfeng County	100	374	2450.48	1171.48	1145.02	132.43	1.55	2322.53	1070.35
新化县	Xinhua County	130	581	1320.20	675.13	579.60	62.57	2.90	1260.95	700.18
冷水江市	Lenshuijiang City	80	301	2547.70	1086.06	1235.10	188.13	38.41	2113.50	887.98
涟源市	Lianyuan City	120	476	1737.12	1113.34	590.23	21.55	12.01	1749.47	940.68
湘西自治州	**West Hunan A.P**	**720**	**3218**	**1400.71**	**377.09**	**909.42**	**103.59**	**10.61**	**1283.39**	**753.67**
吉首市	Jishou City	70	325	1975.24	605.17	1203.54	110.88	55.65	1603.35	745.83
泸溪县	Louxi County	90	400	1245.76	399.87	566.02	277.32	4.55	992.23	658.67
凤凰县	Fenghuang County	100	472	1354.22	294.08	959.03	99.99	1.12	1361.69	752.90
花垣县	Huayuan County	90	450	1262.24	374.95	802.49	70.28	14.52	1039.32	641.69
保靖县	Baojin County	100	444	1266.87	369.89	856.33	37.07	3.58	1279.31	766.31
古丈县	Guzhang County	70	274	1234.06	265.23	791.92	176.95	-0.04	1168.12	721.83
永顺县	Yongshun County	100	404	1337.52	211.61	1068.57	57.20	0.15	1158.45	725.36
龙山县	Longshan County	100	449	1464.70	483.54	879.63	90.06	11.48	1482.89	890.43

十九、各省、市、自治区
主要经济社会统计指标

MAIN ECONOMIC AND SOCIAL STATISTICS INDICATORS BY PROVINCES, MUNICIPALITIES AND AUTONOMOUS REGIONS

资料整理人员： 李生春

19-1 各省(市、区)地区生产总值(2003年)

Gross Domestic Product (2003)

地区	Region	地区生产总值(亿元) Gross Domestic Product (100 million yuan)	第一产业 Primary Industry	第二产业 Secondry Industry	工业 Industry	建筑业 Construction
全国	**Total National**	**116898.4**	**17092.1**	**61131.3**	**52963.4**	**8167.9**
北京	Beijing	3611.9	95.3	1298.5	1017.3	281.2
天津	Tianjin	2386.9	89.7	1212.3	1103.4	109.0
河北	Hebei	7095.4	1064.3	3675.4	3251.5	423.9
山西	Shanxi	2445.6	213.3	1400.1	1190.1	210.0
内蒙古	Inner Mongolia	2092.9	421.9	947.9	707.2	240.7
辽宁	Liaoning	6002.5	622.5	2852.6	2510.4	342.2
吉林	Jilin	2521.8	488.8	1140.8	926.0	214.8
黑龙江	Heilongjiang	4433.1	513.1	2532.5	2248.6	283.9
上海	Shanghai	6250.8	93.0	3130.7	2865.9	264.9
江苏	Jiangsu	12451.8	1106.8	6782.3	5954.7	827.6
浙江	Zhejiang	9200.0	722.0	4830.0	4310.0	520.0
安徽	Anhui	3973.2	749.1	1780.6	1445.6	335.0
福建	Fujian	5241.7	705.5	2495.6	2149.9	345.7
江西	Jiangxi	2830.0	560.0	1227.0	842.0	385.0
山东	Shandong	12430.0	1505.0	6650.0	5855.2	794.8
河南	Henan	7025.9	1237.0	3550.5	3034.1	516.3
湖北	Hubei	5395.9	792.6	2580.6	2254.5	326.1
湖南	Hunan	4638.7	886.5	1794.2	1452.9	341.4
广东	Guangdong	13449.9	1051.6	7048.1	6358.1	690.0
广西	Guangxi	2733.2	628.2	1005.9	811.5	194.4
海南	Hainan	677.5	257.1	150.9	102.3	48.6
重庆	Chongqi	2250.1	343.1	976.0	768.4	207.6
四川	Sichuan	5456.3	1128.6	2266.1	1771.4	494.7
贵州	Guizhu	1344.3	294.5	571.9	450.5	121.4
云南	Yunnan	2458.8	499.0	1067.8	866.4	201.4
西藏	Tibet	184.59				
陕西	Shanxi	2398.6	320.0	1133.6	834.8	298.8
甘肃	Gansu	1301.1	240.0	607.6	449.8	157.8
青海	Qinghai	390.2	47.0	184.3	120.8	63.5
宁夏	Ningxia	384.9	55.5	191.7	143.3	48.4
新疆	Xinjiang	1849.8	388.0	795.5	571.0	224.5

注: 1.本表绝对数按当年价格计算,增长速度按可比价格计算。

2.以下各表均为国家统计局为确保时效,反馈较早的初步统计数,正式数据以即将出版的《中国统计年鉴(2004)》为准。

a. Absolute figures in this table are calculated at current prices, and the growth rate is calculated at comparable prices.

b. Data were initial from the National Bureau of Statistics. Please refer to the China Statistical Yearbook(2004) for official data.

地 区	Region	第三产业 Tertiary Industry (100 million yuan)	#交通运输仓储邮电通信业 Transportation, Storage,Postal and Telecom-munications	#批发和零售贸易餐饮业 Wholesale and Retail, Catering Trade	地区生产总值比上年增长(%) Increase Rate of GDP in 2001 over 2000 (%)	人均地区生产总值(元/人) Per Capita GDP (yuan/person)
全 国	**Total National**	**38675.0**	**6715.6**	**9027.7**	**9.1**	**9073**
北 京	Beijing	2218.2	253.4	271.3	10.5	31613
天 津	Tianjin	1084.9	256.0	211.9	14.5	25874
河 北	Hebei	2355.7	615.2	602.9	11.6	10508
山 西	Shanxi	832.2	191.8	181.2	13.2	7402
内蒙古	Inner Mongolia	723.1	225.0	181.7	16.3	8734
辽 宁	Liaoning	2527.5	495.2	835.5	11.5	14258
吉 林	Jilin	892.2	151.9	315.5	10.2	9334
黑龙江	Heilongjiang	1387.6	289.6	424.5	10.3	11623
上 海	Shanghai	3027.1	418.4	649.1	11.8	46718
江 苏	Jiangsu	4562.7	827.2	1207.3	13.5	16796
浙 江	Zhejiang	3648.0	687.8	1135.3	14.0	19730
安 徽	Anhui	1443.5	253.8	397.9	9.1	6889
福 建	Fujian	2040.6	531.0	492.6	11.5	15006
江 西	Jiangxi	1043.0	261.2	232.2	13.0	6677
山 东	Shandong	4275.0	716.1	1194.1	13.7	13654
河 南	Henan	2238.5	546.2	575.1	10.5	7530
湖 北	Hubei	2022.8	334.6	558.5	9.3	9001
湖 南	Hunan	1958.1	359.8	465.8	9.6	7554
广 东	Guangdong	5350.3	1250.7	1249.7	13.6	16990
广 西	Guangxi	1099.1	243.0	349.1	10.2	5964
海 南	Hainan	269.5	58.3	83.7	10.5	8655
重 庆	Chongqi	931.1	136.6	199.2	11.4	8075
四 川	Sichuan	2061.7	387.3	575.6	11.8	6418
贵 州	Guizhu	477.9	93.1	101.5	10.1	3601
云 南	Yunnan	892.1	162.9	234.6	8.6	5647
西 藏	Tibet					6874
陕 西	Shanxi	945.0	226.0	152.1	10.9	6480
甘 肃	Gansu	453.4	70.9	142.7	10.1	4984
青 海	Qinghai	158.9	32.0	27.9	12.1	7276
宁 夏	Ningxia	137.7	27.0	27.6	12.2	6685
新 疆	Xinjiang	666.3	133.7	150.1	10.8	9686

19-2 各省(市、区)地区生产总值构成(2003年)

Constrcture of Gross Domestic Product(2003)

(地区生产总值=100) (GDP=100)

地 区	Region	地区生产总值 Gross Domestic Product	第一产业 Primary Industry	第二产业 Secondary Industry	工业 Industry	建筑业 Construction	第三产业 Tertiary Industry	#交通运输仓储邮电通信业 Transportation, Storage, Postal and Telecommunications	#批发和零售贸易餐饮业 Wholesale, and Retial, Catering Trade
全 国	**Total National**	**100.0**	**18.3**	**49.7**	**43.1**	**6.6**	**32.0**	**5.4**	**8.3**
北 京	Beijing	100.0	2.6	36.0	28.2	7.8	61.4	7.0	7.5
天 津	Tianjin	100.0	3.8	50.8	46.2	4.6	45.5	10.7	8.9
河 北	Hebei	100.0	15.0	51.8	45.8	6.0	33.2	8.7	8.5
山 西	Shanxi	100.0	8.7	57.3	48.7	8.6	34.0	7.8	7.4
内蒙古	Inner Mongolia	100.0	20.2	45.3	33.8	11.5	34.6	10.8	8.7
辽 宁	Liaoning	100.0	10.4	47.5	41.8	5.7	42.1	8.3	13.9
吉 林	Jilin	100.0	19.4	45.2	36.7	8.5	35.4	6.0	12.5
黑龙江	Heilongjiang	100.0	11.6	57.1	50.7	6.4	31.3	6.5	9.6
上 海	Shanghai	100.0	1.5	50.1	45.9	4.2	48.4	6.7	10.4
江 苏	Jiangsu	100.0	8.9	54.5	47.8	6.7	36.6	6.6	9.7
浙 江	Zhejiang	100.0	7.9	52.5	46.9	5.7	39.7	7.5	12.3
安 徽	Anhui	100.0	18.9	44.8	36.4	8.4	36.3	6.4	10.0
福 建	Fujian	100.0	13.5	47.6	41.0	6.6	38.9	10.1	9.4
江 西	Jiangxi	100.0	19.8	43.4	29.8	13.6	36.9	9.2	8.2
山 东	Shandong	100.0	12.1	53.5	47.1	6.4	34.4	5.8	9.6
河 南	Henan	100.0	17.6	50.5	43.2	7.4	31.9	7.8	8.2
湖 北	Hubei	100.0	14.7	47.8	41.8	6.0	37.5	6.2	10.4
湖 南	Hunan	100.0	19.1	38.7	31.3	7.4	42.2	7.8	10.0
广 东	Guangdong	100.0	7.8	52.4	47.3	5.1	39.8	9.3	9.3
广 西	Guangxi	100.0	23.0	36.8	29.7	7.1	40.2	8.9	12.8
海 南	Hainan	100.0	38.0	22.3	15.1	7.2	39.8	8.6	12.4
重 庆	Chongqi	100.0	15.3	43.4	34.2	9.2	41.4	6.1	8.9
四 川	Sichuan	100.0	20.7	41.5	32.5	9.1	37.8	7.1	10.6
贵 州	Guizhu	100.0	21.9	42.5	33.5	9.0	35.6	6.9	7.6
云 南	Yunnan	100.0	20.3	43.4	35.2	8.2	36.3	6.6	9.5
西 藏	Tibet								
陕 西	Shanxi	100.0	13.3	47.3	34.8	12.5	39.4	9.4	6.3
甘 肃	Gansu	100.0	18.5	46.7	34.6	12.1	34.9	5.5	11.0
青 海	Qinghai	100.0	12.0	47.2	31.0	16.3	40.7	8.2	7.2
宁 夏	Ningxia	100.0	14.4	49.8	37.2	12.6	35.8	7.0	7.2
新 疆	Xinjiang	100.0	21.0	43.0	30.9	12.1	36.0	7.2	8.1

注:本表按当年价格计算。

Data in value terms in this table are calculated at current prices.

19-3 各省(市、区)总人口和从业人员(2003年)

Total Poputation and Employed Persons (2003)

地 区	Region	总人口 (万人) Total Population (10 000 persons)	出生率 Birth Rate ‰	死亡率 Death Rate ‰	自然增长率 Natural Growth Rate ‰	从业人员 (万人) Number of Employed Persons (10 000 persons)
全 国	**National Total**	**129227**	**12.41**	**6.4**	**6.01**	**74432**
北 京	Beijing	1456	5.1	5.2	-0.10	737.0
天 津	Tianjin	1011	7.14	6.04	1.10	419.7
河 北	Hebei	6769	11.43	6.27	5.16	3389.5
山 西	Shanxi	3314	12.26	6.04	6.22	1469.5
内蒙古	Inner Mongolia	2380	9.24	6.17	3.07	1005.2
辽 宁	Liaoning	4210	6.9	5.83	1.07	1861.3
吉 林	Jilin	2704	7.25	5.64	1.61	1044.6
黑龙江	Heilongjiang	3815	7.48	5.45	2.03	1622.4
上 海	Shanghai	1711	4.85	6.2	-1.35	771.5
江 苏	Jiangsu	7406	9.04	7.03	2.01	3610.3
浙 江	Zhejiang	4680	9.66	6.38	3.28	2961.9
安 徽	Anhui	6410	11.15	5.2	5.95	3416.0
福 建	Fujian	3488	11.43	5.58	5.85	1756.7
江 西	Jiangxi	4254	14.07	5.98	8.09	1972.3
山 东	Shandong	9125	11.42	6.64	4.78	4850.6
河 南	Henan	9667	12.1	6.46	5.64	5535.7
湖 北	Hubei	6002	8.26	5.94	2.32	2537.3
湖 南	Hunan	6663	11.82	6.87	4.95	3694.8
广 东	Guangdong	7954	13.66	5.31	8.35	4119.5
广 西	Guangxi	4857	13.86	6.57	7.29	2601.4
海 南	Hainan	811	14.68	5.52	9.16	353.8
重 庆	Chongqi	3130	9.89	7.2	2.69	1659.5
四 川	Sichuan	8700	9.18	6.06	3.12	4449.6
贵 州	Guizhu	3870	15.91	6.87	9.04	2118.4
云 南	Yunnan	4376	17	7.2	9.80	2349.6
西 藏	Tibet	270	17.4	6.3	11.10	130.7
陕 西	Shanxi	3689.5	10.67	6.38	4.29	1911.3
甘 肃	Gansu	2603.34	12.58	6.46	6.12	1304.0
青 海	Qinghai	533.8	16.94	6.09	10.85	254.3
宁 夏	Ningxia	580.3	15.68	4.73	10.95	290.6
新 疆	Xinjiang	1933.95	16.01	5.23	10.78	721.3

19-4 各省(市、区)职工人数(2003年底)

Namber of Staff and Workers (2003)

单位：万人 (10 000 persons)

地区	Region	年末人数 Number of Staff and Workers at the Year-end	国有经济单位 State-owned Units	集体经济单位 Collective Owned Units	股份合作单位 Share Holding Units	联营单位 Joint-owned Units	有限责任公司 Limited Liability Corpra-tions	股份有限公司 Share Holding Corpra-tions Ltd.	港澳台商投资单位 Funded by Enter-preneurs from HongKong Macro and Taiwan	外商投资单位 Foreign Funded Economic Units
全　国	**National Total**	**10492.0**	**6621.3**	**950.5**	**164.1**	**41.2**	**1201.5**	**546.8**	**394.1**	**425.6**
北　京	Beijing	436.3	197.6	26.1	13.7	3.5	88.3	26.7	15.0	27.7
天　津	Tianjin	174.9	85.8	11.8	1.1	0.9	22.0	8.0	10.6	31.7
河　北	Hebei	486.8	367.3	41.1	6.3	0.4	35.9	17.8	6.4	9.7
山　西	Shanxi	347.9	248.8	37.4	3.1	0.2	43.8	10.7	2.0	1.3
内蒙古	Inner Mongolia	240.3	166.1	15.5	2.0	0.3	39.8	11.8	1.6	2.5
辽　宁	Liaoning	483.5	310.2	48.5	6.1	0.5	55.3	22.6	8.5	28.6
吉　林	Jilin	286.8	204.4	27.6	2.4	0.2	22.4	19.9	2.3	6.2
黑龙江	Heilongjiang	487.8	321.3	55.2	17.0	1.8	35.3	36.0	3.4	3.4
上　海	Shanghai	279.2	140.7	15.5	3.4	1.9	25.9	26.0	21.7	43.4
江　苏	Jiangsu	579.1	305.0	52.6	11.8	2.5	72.0	43.6	31.0	45.2
浙　江	Zhejiang	373.2	170.4	30.5	16.4	1.7	85.4	26.5	20.9	20.8
安　徽	Anhui	337.8	212.2	40.7	4.2	0.6	48.2	21.4	2.5	4.9
福　建	Fujian	334.1	147.1	23.1	4.0	3.7	22.4	10.8	75.9	44.4
江　西	Jiangxi	256.7	196.1	20.0	3.7	0.2	17.4	8.4	4.0	2.4
山　东	Shandong	762.3	487.5	74.1	11.8	1.6	79.0	37.2	14.4	53.6
河　南	Henan	682.5	388.0	113.7	7.5	1.9	117.8	37.0	8.0	5.5
湖　北	Hubei	486.1	330.2	38.3	4.2	1.7	43.2	26.8	5.9	5.1
湖　南	Hunan	379.4	297.5	31.3	3.4	0.5	23.0	16.9	3.1	3.3
广　东	Guangdong	763.5	365.6	77.0	13.1	6.1	66.1	30.2	140.3	64.0
广　西	Guangxi	255.7	189.9	20.1	1.9	1.0	23.4	10.0	4.1	4.0
海　南	Hainan	71.6	57.3	3.9	0.4	1.0	3.5	2.2	1.8	1.6
重　庆	Chongqi	205.6	121.9	18.9	4.1	5.7	37.6	10.7	2.5	3.2
四　川	Sichuan	486.7	315.9	48.7	7.0	1.0	66.7	33.6	3.1	5.7
贵　州	Guizhu	188.7	141.7	13.7	1.5	0.4	20.3	8.9	0.8	1.1
云　南	Yunnan	244.0	181.8	14.6	3.5	0.3	24.1	11.7	1.8	1.3
西　藏	Tibet	14.5	13.7	0.4	…	…	0.2	0.1		
陕　西	Shanxi	319.4	246.4	23.3	3.6	0.6	26.9	13.8	1.1	1.9
甘　肃	Gansu	189.0	155.1	14.7	4.5	0.8	6.7	3.1	0.5	1.5
青　海	Qinghai	41.1	33.3	2.4	0.8	0.1	2.7	1.6	0.1	
宁　夏	Ningxia	59.4	38.7	2.2	1.1	0.1	12.6	3.1	0.1	0.9
新　疆	Xinjiang	237.9	184.0	7.6	0.6	0.3	33.3	9.7	0.6	0.7

19-5 各省(市、区)职工平均工资(2003年)

Averge Wage of Staff and Workers by Region (2003)

单位：元 (yuan)

地区	Region	全部职工年平均工资 Annual Average Wages of All Staff and Workers	国有经济单位 State-owned Units	集体经济单位 Collective Owned Units	股份合作单位 Share Holding Units	联营单位 Joint-owned Units	有限责任公司 Limited Liability Corpra-tions	股份有限公司 Share Holding Corpra-tions Ltd.	港澳台商投资单位 Funded by Enter-preneurs from HongKong Macro and Taiwan	外商投资单位 Foreign Funded Economic Units
全 国	**National Total**	**14040**	**14577**	**8678**	**10575**	**13531**	**13392**	**15857**	**14691**	**19366**
北 京	Beijing	25312	28464	13580	13282	15642	22191	24417	28517	44653
天 津	Tianjin	18648	19352	11285	17556	16860	19226	24272	16385	19278
河 北	Hebei	11189	11783	6919	8461	12310	10945	10757	12414	10978
山 西	Shanxi	10729	11213	6629	6121	8161	11977	10848	9033	10898
内蒙古	Inner Mongolia	11279	11929	7620	6495	10356	10410	12078	6691	8530
辽 宁	Liaoning	13008	13603	7629	8685	8810	12839	16165	13846	15060
吉 林	Jilin	11081	11124	8018	7470	8151	11214	13648	10342	17323
黑龙江	Heilongjiang	11038	11034	5425	12360	10488	9918	20531	11634	11846
上 海	Shanghai	27304	28406	16973	18091	21930	25327	27084	22061	32674
江 苏	Jiangsu	15712	17502	9836	9887	11949	13813	15129	14748	17921
浙 江	Zhejiang	21367	27293	16058	12533	16829	15771	20976	16016	15788
安 徽	Anhui	10581	11220	6407	7145	9130	10694	13136	8912	12107
福 建	Fujian	14310	16460	11386	12005	13779	13267	15910	11845	13277
江 西	Jiangxi	10521	10918	6905	8405	11361	10347	13327	8058	10448
山 东	Shandong	12567	13975	8442	8131	11048	10753	10663	10881	11246
河 南	Henan	10749	11397	7894	9228	8689	10930	12093	12175	13240
湖 北	Hubei	10692	11806	7137	7066	8074	8837	9182	9209	14282
湖 南	Hunan	12221	12604	8546	10631	10013	11562	13316	12217	13614
广 东	Guangdong	19986	22944	10836	13512	21072	22429	24810	15259	20748
广 西	Guangxi	11953	12331	7962	7243	14110	12154	12452	8711	16828
海 南	Hainan	10397	10305	7029	14618	11465	11446	15427	8835	13401
重 庆	Chongqi	12425	13586	8552	9791	9710	10254	14831	12779	14529
四 川	Sichuan	12441	13923	8723	9018	10359	9319	11001	12354	13518
贵 州	Guizhu	11037	11390	7504	8562	7285	10792	12236	9821	10365
云 南	Yunnan	12870	13471	8519	8761	15062	11899	13722	13243	14409
西 藏	Tibet	26931	27611	9348	21264	16554	24306	13603		
陕 西	Shanxi	11461	11833	6858	7048	10688	11083	13539	14730	18074
甘 肃	Gansu	12307	12929	7573	12765	8696	8273	13342	11477	16037
青 海	Qinghai	15356	16692	8306	10086	19558	9802	10731	14244	
宁 夏	Ningxia	12981	13721	8924	8839	10405	12434	11579	12299	13240
新 疆	Xinjiang	13255	13199	9966	9371	10839	12434	21496	11946	13439

19-6 各省(市、区)固定资产投资

Investment in Fixed Assets

地区	Region	固定资产投资 (亿元) Investment in Fixed Assets (100 million yuan)		基本建设投资 Capital Construction		更新改造 Investment in Innotation	
		2002	2003	2002	2003	2002	2003
全 国	**National Total**	**43201.6**	**55117.9**	**17251.26**	**22728.95**	**6584.16**	**8443.94**
北 京	Beijing	1681.6	1986.2	414.59	555.73	169.63	216.09
天 津	Tianjin	703.7	923.6	361.85	501.37	166.02	210.89
河 北	Hebei	1161.6	1619.3	597.11	843	374.21	509.45
山 西	Shanxi	676.0	931.7	375.39	498.02	193.12	253.04
内蒙古	Inner Mongolia	618.2	1052.4	409.11	750.37	107.55	173.59
辽 宁	Liaoning	1315.9	1664.9	529	677.71	365.41	459.6
吉 林	Jilin	693.4	849.4	371.6	435.66	160.59	206.59
黑龙江	Heilongjiang	906.6	1014.6	496.79	573.05	213.19	225.6
上 海	Shanghai	1970.2	2213.2	779.28	874.14	415.7	381.6
江 苏	Jiangsu	2320.0	3664.8	1141.31	1864.51	448.44	668.86
浙 江	Zhejiang	2296.6	3057.1	1180.56	1642.5	360.18	356.9
安 徽	Anhui	792.0	1093.9	406.77	513.57	222.27	319.63
福 建	Fujian	964.5	1182.0	397.9	471.84	194.49	226.8
江 西	Jiangxi	611.6	975.4	347.53	566.14	133.41	194.03
山 东	Shandong	2288.7	3564.8	1070.72	1789.01	637.59	916.35
河 南	Henan	1116.1	1554.0	694.43	948.15	233.79	364.86
湖 北	Hubei	1259.5	1460.8	735.73	804.95	308.45	368.42
湖 南	Hunan	906.8	1160.2	535.26	599.75	227.96	301.76
广 东	Guangdong	3022.9	3835.2	1275.46	1798.73	467.91	618.91
广 西	Guangxi	542.2	717.5	352.65	441.35	105.51	142.64
海 南	Hainan	188.4	237.8	152.02	182.88	11.53	12.35
重 庆	Chongqi	735.9	970.2	375.11	526.91	108.02	109.44
四 川	Sichuan	1408.1	1788.6	793.45	949.54	257.49	370.74
贵 州	Guizhu	527.6	653.6	308.69	381.33	118.22	141.72
云 南	Yunnan	612.8	775.6	390.38	485.18	112.77	146.15
西 藏	Tibet	109.4	134.8	98.63	121.3	7.62	9.31
陕 西	Shanxi	750.6	1007.7	456.75	616.03	143.44	164.13
甘 肃	Gansu	448.9	536.2	263.06	307.31	137.92	161.8
青 海	Qinghai	205.2	225.0	157.63	159.09	25.13	37.46
宁 夏	Ningxia	173.1	245.9	119.8	156.06	21.42	37.21
新 疆	Xinjiang	700.3	833.2	483.89	604.09	110.2	113.8

注:各地区数据不包括城乡集体和个人投资。

The regional data on the collective and individual investment were not included.

19-7 各省(市、区)房地产开发企业完成投资额及住宅竣工、销售面积

Investment Completed in Real Estate Development and Floor Space Completed of Residential Buildings and Floor Space of Selling Houses

地区	Region	完成投资额(亿元) Investment Completed (100 million yuan)		住宅竣工面积(万平方米) Floor Space Completed (10 000 sq.m)		住宅销售面积(万平方米) Floor Space of Selling Houses (10 000 sq.m)	
		2002	2003	2002	2003	2002	2003
全　国	**National Total**	**7790.92**	**10106.12**	**34975.75**	**39509.75**	**26808.29**	**32247.24**
北　京	Beijing	989.41	1202.48	2384.44	2593.65	1708.34	1895.77
天　津	Tianjin	175.84	211.39	746.44	911.27	564.00	786.50
河　北	Hebei	175.04	251.98	839.04	1062.56	658.85	845.03
山　西	Shanxi	67.43	94.88	447.00	441.00	299.05	328.68
内蒙古	Inner Mongolia	72.53	90.93	583.38	618.13	422.13	555.73
辽　宁	Liaoning	388.31	486.17	1984.29	2107.61	1277.46	1476.18
吉　林	Jilin	116.77	139.27	755.85	542.71	518.28	385.44
黑龙江	Heilongjiang	145.79	163.12	803.59	874.47	692.47	803.22
上　海	Shanghai	748.89	901.24	1984.68	2491.84	1971.47	2376.40
江　苏	Jiangsu	544.13	809.17	2696.69	3068.11	2321.85	2751.42
浙　江	Zhejiang	728.80	972.39	2660.60	3052.83	2219.30	2613.96
安　徽	Anhui	146.49	240.65	1062.48	1326.21	794.82	1093.27
福　建	Fujian	248.99	362.07	1323.49	1368.08	1047.05	1257.31
江　西	Jiangxi	103.64	173.78	688.21	871.21	562.09	755.07
山　东	Shandong	391.16	579.57	2189.65	2458.81	1695.84	2000.44
河　南	Henan	138.36	185.56	892.32	991.32	639.94	851.10
湖　北	Hubei	178.64	239.04	1072.45	1332.51	805.69	1073.48
湖　南	Hunan	150.92	230.03	807.80	1146.70	602.29	846.87
广　东	Guangdong	1115.25	1209.92	3908.76	4048.07	2530.81	2789.94
广　西	Guangxi	75.28	120.26	352.49	543.03	339.63	490.67
海　南	Hainan	20.11	35.95	54.46	104.82	76.74	108.31
重　庆	Chongqi	245.91	327.89	1390.73	1678.44	1016.58	1318.23
四　川	Sichuan	344.38	449.33	2312.34	2644.38	1865.94	2303.71
贵　州	Guizhu	83.01	104.06	514.10	496.39	424.85	434.16
云　南	Yunnan	96.26	112.15	561.53	529.50	400.22	457.53
西　藏	Tibet	2.77	1.72	16.16	0.29	16.16	0.00
陕　西	Shanxi	123.57	188.56	642.07	713.78	477.54	581.45
甘　肃	Gansu	37.71	50.80	220.26	260.67	165.83	218.63
青　海	Qinghai	16.92	22.31	133.60	156.99	68.04	100.34
宁　夏	Ningxia	30.86	50.91	219.65	407.28	118.36	232.38
新　疆	Xinjiang	87.71	98.54	727.21	667.09	506.66	516.02

19-8 各省(市、区)财政收入决算情况(2003年)

Final Statement of Government Revenue (2003)

单位：万元 (10 000 yuan)

地区	Region	收入合计 Total Revenue	增值税 Value-Added Tax	营业税 Operation Tax	企业所得税 Income Income Tax of Enterprises	企业所得税退税 Return for Income Tax of Enterprises	个人所得税 Individual Income Tax	资源税 Resources Tax	城市建设维护税 Tax on Town Maintenance and Construction	房产税 Tax on Real Estates
地方合计	**Total**	**98499846**	**18109889**	**27675639**	**10435040**	**-1403**	**5672469**	**832962**	**5467075**	**3238610**
北 京	Beijing	5925388	752553	2636946	937007		572106	2848	288542	307915
天 津	Tianjin	2045295	451925	643231	238022	-6	125347	3755	107987	71989
河 北	Hebei	3358263	687193	653546	286917	-1	181460	58092	187733	90009
山 西	Shanxi	1860547	513574	366306	142312	-2	85860	80305	129631	52527
内蒙古	Inner Mongolia	1387157	225940	363318	71615	-5	54288	20144	69675	58620
辽 宁	Liaoning	4470490	854907	1190908	359313	-38	235562	61245	257669	207190
吉 林	Jilin	1540033	306877	350192	118021	-72	78070	14776	93277	63792
黑龙江	Heilongjiang	2488643	586400	461394	107808	-2	109793	144485	210205	90352
上 海	Shanghai	8862277	1701998	3323140	1461501		718127	0	356155	224086
江 苏	Jiangsu	7981065	1814325	2072215	926878		401547	17731	463216	231595
浙 江	Zhejiang	7065607	1550060	2200657	1065165		457895	6338	421743	172580
安 徽	Anhui	2207487	369517	459731	190470	-29	82408	26472	133121	59682
福 建	Fujian	3047095	543961	847298	368133	-63	212552	14501	139206	131463
江 西	Jiangxi	1681670	230683	431628	97435	-7	72763	12664	82215	35392
山 东	Shandong	7137877	1260824	1447077	664382		260262	104760	444019	244706
河 南	Henan	3380535	579478	753089	291370	-49	156041	35884	205386	91636
湖 北	Hubei	2597636	456411	574219	213471		114805	18995	173749	82399
湖 南	Hunan	2686469	361183	602304	134574		121622	9089	163264	65418
广 东	Guangdong	13155151	2336835	4158122	1700183		947674	15274	477462	455607
广 西	Guangxi	2036578	286917	479121	130545		103496	11294	95192	59819
海 南	Hainan	513205	63637	160617	26044		27801	5494	27447	26268
重 庆	Chongqi	1615618	246601	466392	87694		78711	20172	86520	42134
四 川	Sichuan	3365917	480965	896047	247547		143575	29744	206002	94439
贵 州	Guizhu	1245552	194261	314589	84133	-828	54412	9731	86919	36655
云 南	Yunnan	2289992	391100	451702	214963	-3	83851	14585	235834	69915
西 藏	Tibet	81499	9364	40160	7160	-1	2851	1999	3168	0
陕 西	Shanxi	1773300	316393	510441	127942		68506	26337	122833	65942
甘 肃	Gansu	876561	181229	240704	53110	-31	36776	12332	70084	34316
青 海	Qinghai	240411	52503	73079	12177	-1	7831	6252	15483	8401
宁 夏	Ningxia	300310	50424	108953	16846		13021	1301	18485	12012
新 疆	Xinjiang	1282218	251851	398513	52302	-265	63456	46363	94853	51751

单位：万元　　19-8 续表 continued　　(10 000 yuan)

地区	Region	印花税 Stamp Tax	农业税 Agri-cultural Tax	农业特产税 Tax on Special Agri-cultural Products	契税 Contract Tax	国有企业计划亏损补贴 Planning Subsidies to Loss-suffering State-owned Enterprises	行政性收费收入 Income From Adimini-strative Fees	罚没收入 Penalty and Confisca-tory Income	专项收入 Expert Project Income	其它收入 Other Income
地方合计	**Total**	**911130**	**3365576**	**896002**	**3580454**	**-1940433**	**7141325**	**4312379**	**3417288**	**1384914**
北京	Beijing	73524	5609	906	203975	-510546	181240	102177	215243	26973
天津	Tianjin	20708	3595	138	82543	-30000	147274	59786	60031	26025
河北	Hebei	23300	249978	8306	59877	-15560	294368	259740	166549	57726
山西	Shanxi	17682	39350	941	15613	-17987	134890	122860	109097	23558
内蒙古	Inner Mongolia	12052	70152	10450	28108	-6149	123014	61011	51762	31584
辽宁	Liaoning	47453	72322	30935	156920	-33307	378573	204765	180998	29679
吉林	Jilin	14564	101705	20622	48553	-62948	150066	96015	60639	14353
黑龙江	Heilongjiang	12362	162802	16652	55374	-21795	151960	105347	140902	49412
上海	Shanghai	131908	1186	0	634831	-361866	227976	141381	197772	20230
江苏	Jiangsu	79339	265992		402796	-73058	508231	349877	234098	27391
浙江	Zhejiang	64799	54442	14	478227	-472124	203224	312889	259011	19762
安徽	Anhui	16674	266789	166	71027	-22920	229728	103739	76418	28628
福建	Fujian	34770	11785	37141	115484	-2944	214450	165018	82689	43619
江西	Jiangxi	9698	156977	3181	68503	-2192	182076	133723	49309	57840
山东	Shandong	46613	424030	120176	153276	-48894	757389	251479	285982	95003
河南	Henan	16398	377052	27121	59071	-17060	300409	191958	141795	40204
湖北	Hubei	24721	231984	26792	57511	-42408	243369	192457	76810	60530
湖南	Hunan	18550	181682	80452	55541	-39804	348640	228507	99509	131153
广东	Guangdong	141344	79777	13801	485211	-28582	876579	448339	335068	208172
广西	Guangxi	8728	67753	111904	45355	-15372	220037	141645	65425	66539
海南	Hainan	4439	4816	35025	13949	0	47247	25144	13822	3580
重庆	Chongqi	12939	62348	13848	41920	-23319	259343	79978	48764	20653
四川	Sichuan	23067	211223	18501	116586	-27401	422951	179529	111470	45463
贵州	Guizhu	5653	51639	49668	17562	-5369	117114	67559	52411	59887
云南	Yunnan	16015	47912	200736	40530	-23597	123962	111629	88781	127155
西藏	Tibet	482			0	-9186	6318	2928	2580	12572
陕西	Shanxi	12825	66480	42066	25364	-13006	102627	74630	67904	19411
甘肃	Gansu	6754	52691	11093	10432	-12904	57504	31427	49334	21419
青海	Qinghai	1538	5043	2703	2814	-40	12467	5798	14557	6473
宁夏	Ningxia	2482	7438	42	8046	-11	20394	12942	11846	5062
新疆	Xinjiang	9749	31024	12622	25455	-84	97905	48102	66712	4858

19-9 各省(市、区)财政支出决算情况(2003年)

Final Statement of Government Expenditure (2003)

单位：万元 (10 000 yuan)

地区	Region	支出合计 Total Expenditure	基本建设支出 Expenditure for Capital Construction	挖潜改造支出 Expenditure for Innovation Enterprises	地质勘探费 Expenditure for Geological Prospecting	科技三项费用 Expenditure for Science and Technology Promotion	流动资金 Expenditure for Circulating Funds	农业支出 Expenditure for Agriculture
地方合计	**Total**	**172298382**	**19065766**	**6342642**	**813626**	**1903799**	**13984**	**5739956**
北　京	Beijing	7348043	719875	458741	9140	63736		178125
天　津	Tianjin	3120771	524274	293732	11241	78023		55028
河　北	Hebei	6467439	415300	99938	20805	54058		190704
山　西	Shanxi	4156866	368678	68039	17523	29874	2399	154706
内蒙古	Inner Mongolia	4472566	781312	147553	36051	30112		159636
辽　宁	Liaoning	7843764	680144	156750	40867	162423		281979
吉　林	Jilin	4092265	318364	104058	32987	30797		116888
黑龙江	Heilongjiang	5649080	387665	127258	22600	57873		206589
上　海	Shanghai	10884386	2447362	1545172	1614	15383		138058
江　苏	Jiangsu	10476812	759687	511946	22230	135056		415909
浙　江	Zhejiang	8967740	633046	489049	27185	195284		402093
安　徽	Anhui	5074398	474481	148824	35359	27109		169118
福　建	Fujian	4522167	373496	143434	13097	58128	315	172626
江　西	Jiangxi	3820981	338935	68589	56914	17248		154592
山　东	Shandong	10106395	636760	462915	21837	140670	2684	425229
河　南	Henan	7165978	502569	166891	25856	57218		210074
湖　北	Hubei	5404356	307235	123936	21727	61746	4323	175539
湖　南	Hunan	5737453	513964	101835	53731	49090		226221
广　东	Guangdong	16956324	2408689	220378	30684	364417	3095	416297
广　西	Guangxi	4436763	399988	126696	28202	28805	682	168211
海　南	Hainan	1053984	134463	1917	3171	5881		38686
重　庆	Chongqi	3415775	640685	72583	6609	27969		91157
四　川	Sichuan	7322993	750182	232608	41255	61228	486	268650
贵　州	Guizhu	3323547	316396	54909	31141	23103		145073
云　南	Yunnan	5873475	706605	176952	27642	45658		256144
西　藏	Tibet	1459054	594347	2233	14544	3603		40011
陕　西	Shanxi	4182008	462523	93786	46292	28706		141922
甘　肃	Gansu	3000092	329959	63901	42937	12759		99523
青　海	Qinghai	1220438	295285	10488	13216	7490		41566
宁　夏	Ningxia	1057793	203563	39719	11236	7500		51442
新　疆	Xinjiang	3684676	639934	27812	45933	22852		148160

单位：万元 19-9 续表1 continued (10 000 yuan)

地区	Region	林业支出 Expenditure for Forestry	水利和气象支出 Expenditure for Water Conservancy and Meteorology	工业交通等部门的事业费 Operating Expenses of Departments of Industry and Transportation	流通部门事业费 Operating Expenses for Department of Commerce	文体广播事业费 Operating Expenses of Departments of Culture, Sport and Broadcasting	教育事业费 Expenditure for Operating Expenses of Education	科学事业费 Operating Expenses of Department of Science
地方合计	**Total**	**1956720**	**2295192**	**1714403**	**292797**	**4346468**	**26973098**	**1097450**
北京	Beijing	46295	37401	41309	2429	164145	988222	107629
天津	Tianjin	7194	18141	16272	220	71864	475804	19403
河北	Hebei	56367	58528	106779	10785	170256	1190712	26922
山西	Shanxi	63263	43964	45436	7153	114282	674140	15867
内蒙古	Inner Mongolia	148624	47227	38046	5970	105711	543525	16572
辽宁	Liaoning	70974	84706	88672	16125	144850	983397	37469
吉林	Jilin	67086	33628	57391	13379	105212	536908	20429
黑龙江	Heilongjiang	184849	53342	83421	23912	141932	810979	35049
上海	Shanghai	49758	49585	39850	1533	169554	1313724	113439
江苏	Jiangsu	29157	214275	99016	10326	256666	1790766	55235
浙江	Zhejiang	49748	146709	165706	11293	276526	1642075	71680
安徽	Anhui	34848	122420	34324	5677	118748	845575	18204
福建	Fujian	38734	59998	70219	11363	137150	929672	42526
江西	Jiangxi	41412	38953	50577	9799	92796	644665	18547
山东	Shandong	68101	124786	89036	14466	307350	1791484	58375
河南	Henan	53144	97693	59539	8146	238910	1311582	30337
湖北	Hubei	43405	64675	45475	16048	139234	890687	21776
湖南	Hunan	65871	70006	58892	18599	155101	900570	22267
广东	Guangdong	114954	428841	117926	39310	381087	2652474	152589
广西	Guangxi	62568	69446	30280	4066	135794	790977	35027
海南	Hainan	16011	15454	5291	1211	23079	147959	3887
重庆	Chongqi	57025	21642	10871	3229	74597	429462	8666
四川	Sichuan	134181	82962	62928	15786	177801	1089036	38508
贵州	Guizhu	57591	44006	41009	8215	115871	601258	19641
云南	Yunnan	144157	87938	64342	16980	138045	933394	42064
西藏	Tibet	12770	9806	30864	484	35893	130664	2545
陕西	Shanxi	83160	65651	80227	11951	121122	663304	17968
甘肃	Gansu	64137	42650	23515	1769	88741	475673	16739
青海	Qinghai	21169	12148	13799	299	25618	126319	3756
宁夏	Ningxia	18157	16798	11915	1361	31619	137830	5771
新疆	Xinjiang	52010	31813	31476	913	86914	530261	18563

地区	Region	卫生经费 Expenditure for Public Health	其他部门的事业费 Opreating Expenses for Other Departments	抚恤和社会福利救济费 Expenditure for Pensions and Relief Funds for Social Welfare	行政事业单位离退休经费 Expenditure for Retired Persons in Adminis-trative Department	社会保障补助支出 Expenditure on Subsidies to Social Security Programs	行政管理费 Expenditure on Government Adminis-tration	外交外事支出 Expenditure for Foreign Affairs
地方合计	**Total**	**7559910**	**8866106**	**4936859**	**8056373**	**11177708**	**16577460**	**98712**
北京	Beijing	496358	315935	228318	339052	128102	390900	1335
天津	Tianjin	153135	81941	59350	11029	275049	175505	4404
河北	Hebei	348275	481874	190083	355094	560816	670410	6789
山西	Shanxi	203272	198278	132787	262100	468907	454411	1089
内蒙古	Inner Mongolia	170878	258935	109468	302696	244960	456517	1037
辽宁	Liaoning	251624	416685	307939	384032	1276451	622468	15725
吉林	Jilin	161382	229029	160270	287777	495632	312315	3588
黑龙江	Heilongjiang	230611	383160	188269	169275	620253	489551	2726
上海	Shanghai	364420	391940	155024	61114	331291	447886	8130
江苏	Jiangsu	555684	536722	265957	363917	339492	1071724	5383
浙江	Zhejiang	453797	664839	180694	73186	220311	952162	6958
安徽	Anhui	170815	178608	208102	322677	491158	512911	3372
福建	Fujian	207346	250767	96399	273825	84737	366705	1933
江西	Jiangxi	150613	220192	134785	141237	414471	359542	623
山东	Shandong	396107	523771	281244	444158	345457	1123337	3971
河南	Henan	301893	398718	241193	506498	536876	831015	669
湖北	Hubei	242474	331140	251717	239215	485471	570864	972
湖南	Hunan	168303	332605	218603	339042	478624	591494	1651
广东	Guangdong	735442	908202	304539	837492	370069	1754697	6057
广西	Guangxi	210155	325073	112174	193680	220519	463286	6858
海南	Hainan	46470	69272	31048	51076	87269	105078	1402
重庆	Chongqi	108218	73557	128237	240926	339682	368357	670
四川	Sichuan	314235	242844	254623	465885	535911	945994	2960
贵州	Guizhu	172994	131443	88755	27572	197285	433298	1351
云南	Yunnan	327510	274211	172517	452154	423636	554504	2870
西藏	Tibet	52805	13980	21094	17490	36360	200566	430
陕西	Shanxi	167206	254390	155448	202954	413506	469146	1367
甘肃	Gansu	117896	122194	80087	178267	370844	313188	2065
青海	Qinghai	52972	37836	35463	131365	107051	111201	707
宁夏	Ningxia	44812	37186	26717	53414	88764	77326	969
新疆	Xinjiang	182208	180779	115955	328174	188754	381102	651

单位：万元　　19-9 续表3 continued　　(10 000 yuan)

地区	Region	城市维护费 Expenditure for City Maintenance	政策性补贴支出 Expenditure for Price Subsidies	支援不发达地区支出 Expenditure for Supporting Undeveloped Areas	海域开发建设和场地使用费支出 Expenditure for Developing Land and Sea Area	专项支出 Expenditure for Special Items	其他支出 Others Expenditure
地方合计	**Total**	**7618224**	**3797871**	**1560106**	**23868**	**3096786**	**13511412**
北京	Beijing	361534	44901		400	238454	1419447
天津	Tianjin	276061	31147	39	1738	55272	212713
河北	Hebei	212357	216263	51674	1870	147568	332601
山西	Shanxi	117745	92200	55251	12	85525	208985
内蒙古	Inner Mongolia	185405	198437	66952	43	45247	117681
辽宁	Liaoning	480929	259170	32410	2215	154099	341987
吉林	Jilin	118799	415377	30787	677	49094	103831
黑龙江	Heilongjiang	250618	446546	34312	13	141288	155298
上海	Shanghai	447399	10092			199818	1934667
江苏	Jiangsu	926665	142070	8358	1044	209398	860642
浙江	Zhejiang	596096	51750	33121	673	225035	591637
安徽	Anhui	141734	216787	48315	252	69203	359372
福建	Fujian	128799	68662	29845	1002	77685	505107
江西	Jiangxi	129612	111274	50103	60	45097	245697
山东	Shandong	685165	194468	13790	4279	259129	1003154
河南	Henan	220220	277590	70896	304	124616	401127
湖北	Hubei	178897	154425	46019	373	80879	516791
湖南	Hunan	234149	140698	62699	98	89750	427442
广东	Guangdong	634956	124757	91898	2341	305155	1778223
广西	Guangxi	187385	53162	83635	917	56899	257200
海南	Hainan	35434	13867	21282	665	11574	109311
重庆	Chongqi	198820	53581	39372		47287	120735
四川	Sichuan	241893	154624	103376	260	95074	441285
贵州	Guizhu	85189	29988	106567	72	48255	295288
云南	Yunnan	181702	42685	142495	118	58906	186179
西藏	Tibet	5020	18151	29242		4620	114941
陕西	Shanxi	152771	53043	68647	46	51779	116021
甘肃	Gansu	66241	53501	99331	50	40769	150871
青海	Qinghai	12089	11371	43244		8521	39153
宁夏	Ningxia	27957	19375	34583	65	10940	44223
新疆	Xinjiang	96583	97909	61863	4281	59850	119803

19-10 各省(市、区)居民消费价格分类指数(2003年)

General Consumer Price Indices by Category (2003)

(上年=100) (preceding year=100)

地区	Region	居民消费价格指数 General Consumer Price Indices	食品 Foods	烟酒及用品 Beverages Tobacco and Liquor	衣着 Clothing	家庭设备用品服务 Household Facilities Articles and Services	医疗保健 Medcine and Medical Services	交通和通信 Transportation and Communications	娱乐教育文化 Recreation Education and Cultural Services	居住 Residence
全国	**National Total**	**101.2**	**103.4**	**99.8**	**97.8**	**97.4**	**100.9**	**97.8**	**101.3**	**102.1**
北京	Beijing	100.2	103.2	100.2	97.1	97.7	100.1	97.8	98.3	101.6
天津	Tianjin	101.0	103.3	98.8	88.1	96.5	94.0	97.0	110.7	101.7
河北	Hebei	102.2	104.5	100.1	97.8	97.0	106.0	98.1	100.7	104.5
山西	Shanxi	101.8	104.7	100.7	97.5	98.8	99.0	98.2	100.4	106.7
内蒙古	Inner Mongolia	102.2	102.8	99.4	98.7	98.1	98.9	97.3	112.0	99.7
辽宁	Liaoning	101.7	105.3	98.6	97.8	96.4	103.5	97.7	99.6	101.7
吉林	Jilin	101.2	104.0	100.4	99.6	97.9	101.8	97.9	99.2	100.4
黑龙江	Heilongjiang	100.9	103.3	98.8	98.4	97.0	99.4	98.5	101.9	101.2
上海	Shanghai	100.1	101.3	99.8	97.5	98.4	100.0	96.3	100.3	101.1
江苏	Jiangsu	101.0	103.3	99.5	99.0	96.6	100.3	97.4	102.5	101.0
浙江	Zhejiang	101.9	102.8	101.2	96.7	96.9	100.1	95.1	111.2	101.2
安徽	Anhui	101.7	106.0	99.9	97.3	97.7	99.9	97.9	100.9	100.7
福建	Fujian	100.8	102.0	100.4	96.5	97.3	98.7	97.3	104.3	102.8
江西	Jiangxi	100.8	102.9	99.8	97.2	97.5	97.8	99.3	100.1	102.1
山东	Shandong	101.1	104.9	99.6	96.9	98.0	100.3	98.8	100.1	101.0
河南	Henan	101.6	104.7	100.3	98.0	97.7	102.5	99.2	99.4	102.3
湖北	Hubei	102.2	104.3	99.8	101.0	97.3	99.6	98.5	102.7	103.5
湖南	Hunan	102.4	105.8	99.8	98.8	97.2	105.9	98.0	100.4	103.1
广东	Guangdong	100.6	102.3	101.4	97.7	98.0	100.4	97.9	98.0	103.1
广西	Guangxi	101.1	102.9	100.0	98.5	97.4	102.8	96.4	100.6	102.3
海南	Hainan	100.1	102.9	100.1	95.9	98.1	100.1	91.8	98.7	101.7
重庆	Chongqi	100.6	104.3	98.2	94.2	95.5	99.3	98.7	99.6	102.2
四川	Sichuan	101.7	102.7	100.2	98.5	98.3	102.9	99.8	100.7	102.9
贵州	Guizhu	101.2	103.2	99.6	97.6	97.2	104.3	100.2	100.7	101.0
云南	Yunnan	101.2	101.7	99.9	97.2	98.4	99.3	98.6	106.4	101.9
西藏	Tibet	100.9	100.5	103.0	101.5	101.4	101.0	100.1	99.7	98.8
陕西	Shanxi	101.7	105.2	99.6	99.0	97.1	106.6	95.6	98.9	101.0
甘肃	Gansu	101.1	103.0	99.8	98.4	98.5	101.9	98.7	100.5	101.5
青海	Qinghai	102.0	104.1	99.0	101.9	100.1	104.8	98.7	100.9	99.9
宁夏	Ningxia	101.7	104.5	101.1	99.4	95.7	100.2	98.1	105.6	100.0
新疆	Xinjiang	100.4	102.5	99.8	99.2	98.9	94.8	99.1	99.1	104.2

19-11 各省(市、区)城镇居民家庭人均收支情况(2003年)

Per Capita Annual Income and Expenditure of Urban Households (2003)

地区	Region	全部收入 (元) Total Income (yuan)	#可支配收入 Disposable Income	实际支出 (元) Real Expenditure (yuan)	消费性支出 Living Expenditure	非消费性支出 Non-living Expenditure	恩格尔系数 (%) Engler Quotiety (%)
全国	**National Total**	**9061.2**	**8472.2**	**8731.6**	**6510.9**	**2220.6**	**37.12**
北京	Beijing	14959.3	13882.6	13762.9	11123.8	2639.0	31.67
天津	Tianjin	10971.6	10312.9	11088.0	7867.5	3220.5	37.67
河北	Hebei	7608.4	7239.1	7284.2	5439.8	1844.4	35.16
山西	Shanxi	7446.9	7005.0	7435.1	5105.4	2329.7	33.54
内蒙古	Inner Mongolia	7351.6	7012.9	6984.4	5419.1	1565.3	31.47
辽宁	Liaoning	7832.7	7240.6	8220.2	6077.9	2142.3	39.40
吉林	Jilin	7311.2	7005.2	7171.0	5492.1	1678.9	35.65
黑龙江	Heilongjiang	6968.0	6678.9	6327.0	5015.2	1311.8	35.57
上海	Shanghai	16380.2	14867.5	17110.0	11040.3	6069.6	37.16
江苏	Jiangsu	9912.1	9262.5	9107.7	6708.6	2399.1	38.26
浙江	Zhejiang	14295.4	13179.5	13692.1	9712.9	3979.2	36.64
安徽	Anhui	7155.9	6778.0	7100.9	5064.3	2036.5	44.21
福建	Fujian	10816.3	9999.5	9879.3	7356.3	2523.0	42.21
江西	Jiangxi	7153.7	6901.4	6387.5	4914.6	1473.0	40.29
山东	Shandong	9057.6	8399.9	8290.0	6069.4	2220.6	33.80
河南	Henan	7245.0	6926.1	6465.6	4941.6	1524.0	33.64
湖北	Hubei	7745.8	7322.0	7551.1	5963.3	1587.9	38.23
湖南	Hunan	8145.1	7674.2	8441.6	6082.6	2359.0	35.83
广东	Guangdong	13451.1	12380.4	12825.5	9636.3	3189.2	37.19
广西	Guangxi	8293.9	7785.0	7582.3	5763.5	1818.8	40.01
海南	Hainan	7605.7	7259.3	7055.0	5502.4	1552.6	44.76
重庆	Chongqi	8671.9	8093.7	8584.8	7118.1	1466.7	37.96
四川	Sichuan	7488.5	7041.9	7506.6	5759.2	1747.4	38.91
贵州	Guizhu	6746.4	6569.2	6081.2	4949.0	1132.3	39.77
云南	Yunnan	8202.6	7643.6	7650.6	6023.6	1627.0	41.61
西藏	Tibet	9696.8	8765.5	10498.7	8045.3	2453.4	44.04
陕西	Shanxi	7314.4	6806.4	7552.2	5666.5	1885.7	34.59
甘肃	Gansu	7132.8	6657.2	7027.8	5298.9	1728.9	36.01
青海	Qinghai	7155.1	6745.3	7090.3	5400.2	1690.1	36.79
宁夏	Ningxia	6991.3	6530.5	7911.8	5330.3	2581.5	36.01
新疆	Xinjiang	7866.9	7173.5	7141.6	5540.6	1601.0	35.87

19-12 各省(市、区)农民家庭收支情况(2003年)

Per Capita Annual Income and Expendture of Rural Households (2003)

地 区	Region	总收入 (元) Total Income (yuan)	#纯收入 Net Income	总支出 (元) Total Expenditure (yuan)	#生活消费 Living Expenditure	现金收入 (元) Cash Income (yuan)	现金支出 (元) Cash Expenditure (yuan)	恩格尔系数 (%) Engler Quotiety (%)
全 国	**National Total**	**3582.42**	**2622.24**	**3024.99**	**1943.30**	**2929.47**	**2537.42**	**45.6**
北 京	Beijing	6477.54	5601.55	5242.32	4147.30	6316.16	5173.49	32.1
天 津	Tianjin	5900.25	4566.01	3836.88	2319.52	5532.10	3702.06	38.2
河 北	Hebei	3785.51	2853.38	2617.95	1600.10	3202.47	2326.68	39.9
山 西	Shanxi	2879.28	2299.17	2091.84	1434.40	2255.05	1812.75	43.3
内蒙古	Inner Mongolia	3862.02	2267.65	3583.91	1770.56	2934.13	2879.15	41.3
辽 宁	Liaoning	4458.53	2934.44	3618.71	1884.08	3771.51	3115.27	43.2
吉 林	Jilin	3862.08	2530.41	3379.37	1815.57	3118.86	2951.97	44.0
黑龙江	Heilongjiang	4268.18	2508.94	3863.93	1661.70	3700.08	3482.42	40.7
上 海	Shanghai	7227.15	6653.92	6930.96	5669.57	6936.31	6642.29	35.3
江 苏	Jiangsu	5202.45	4239.26	3858.64	2704.37	4652.67	3393.33	41.4
浙 江	Zhejiang	6666.79	5389.04	5906.53	4285.13	6316.00	5617.04	38.2
安 徽	Anhui	2842.58	2127.48	2378.84	1596.27	2255.26	1928.65	46.0
福 建	Fujian	4640.13	3733.89	3737.89	2715.50	4158.43	3449.69	45.0
江 西	Jiangxi	3180.95	2457.53	2731.14	1907.57	2542.57	2152.45	51.7
山 东	Shandong	4482.15	3150.49	3521.42	2133.20	3887.25	3087.77	41.8
河 南	Henan	3036.19	2235.68	2320.17	1444.45	2228.33	1885.26	45.9
湖 北	Hubei	3378.80	2566.76	2755.26	1801.63	2560.51	2127.96	51.7
湖 南	Hunan	3515.52	2532.87	3184.26	2139.15	2866.96	2607.77	51.9
广 东	Guangdong	4946.68	4054.58	3888.37	2927.35	4376.87	3418.54	47.9
广 西	Guangxi	2916.20	2094.51	2631.28	1751.23	2323.17	2122.86	51.3
海 南	Hainan	3428.68	2588.06	2502.13	1644.79	2880.31	2000.23	57.6
重 庆	Chongqi	2922.12	2214.55	2333.87	1583.31	2019.62	1672.00	52.5
四 川	Sichuan	3255.78	2229.86	2828.43	1747.02	2327.84	1985.92	53.9
贵 州	Guizhu	2147.25	1564.66	1840.51	1185.17	1463.64	1213.30	56.9
云 南	Yunnan	2554.36	1697.12	2320.36	1405.70	1709.81	1616.54	53.0
西 藏	Tibet	1973.18	1691.00	1434.29	1030.13	1287.57	938.95	65.0
陕 西	Shanxi	2281.01	1675.66	2189.11	1455.39	1849.67	1923.02	39.3
甘 肃	Gansu	2336.79	1673.05	2053.15	1336.85	1644.19	1611.71	43.9
青 海	Qinghai	2410.04	1794.13	2286.65	1563.15	1740.29	1679.44	49.6
宁 夏	Ningxia	3268.02	2043.30	3029.84	1637.13	2624.54	2457.34	41.5
新 疆	Xinjiang	3564.10	2106.19	3082.75	1465.31	2930.35	2599.41	45.5

注:现金收支为已经扣除储蓄借贷后的现金收支。

Data on the cash income and expenditure are calculated with removing the factor of debit and credit.

19-13 各省(市、区)农林牧渔业总产值和指数(2003年)

Gross Output Value and the Related Indices of Farming, Forestry, Animal Husbandry and Fishery (2003)

地 区	Region	农林牧渔业总产值（亿元） Gross Output Value (100 million yuan)	农业 Framing	林业 Forestry	牧业 Animal Husbandry	渔业 Fishery	指数 (上年=100) Related Indices (precending year=100)
全 国	**National Total**	**29691.8**	**14870.1**	**1239.9**	**9538.8**	**3137.6**	**103.9**
北 京	Beijing	246.8	88.8	13.5	125.5	10.2	104.1
天 津	Tianjin	213.9	88.2	1.6	77.2	26.4	106.9
河 北	Hebei	1956.9	958.3	41.3	820.6	57.7	106.3
山 西	Shanxi	403.6	249.5	20.4	111.9	2.0	104.7
内蒙古	Inner Mongolia	666.4	336.0	47.9	267.1	4.9	106.2
辽 宁	Liaoning	1215.0	497.3	38.4	422.0	224.0	107.1
吉 林	Jilin	792.1	438.3	33.8	298.4	13.6	106.3
黑龙江	Heilongjiang	903.3	502.9	59.1	294.2	23.1	103.0
上 海	Shanghai	247.3	98.2	13.1	81.1	49.2	101.1
江 苏	Jiangsu	1952.2	981.2	31.5	458.9	371.6	101.0
浙 江	Zhejiang	1184.0	529.4	65.7	233.0	337.1	104.2
安 徽	Anhui	1305.4	617.9	73.4	443.5	129.7	94.0
福 建	Fujian	1151.2	466.8	79.3	237.3	351.9	103.7
江 西	Jiangxi	841.6	383.7	70.5	254.0	118.5	102.7
山 东	Shandong	2902.5	1599.3	53.7	831.3	370.0	105.5
河 南	Henan	2193.1	1137.7	69.1	835.9	23.3	98.0
湖 北	Hubei	1342.1	733.4	34.8	383.7	170.4	105.3
湖 南	Hunan	1453.0	671.7	81.7	575.1	97.0	103.7
广 东	Guangdong	1908.7	851.7	55.7	482.8	432.7	103.8
广 西	Guangxi	1030.9	500.8	53.8	342.8	115.5	104.3
海 南	Hainan	380.0	152.7	53.3	64.8	103.1	109.0
重 庆	Chongqi	488.6	270.1	14.6	177.6	18.3	106.7
四 川	Sichuan	1784.5	804.7	59.3	832.3	53.3	106.2
贵 州	Guizhu	466.7	275.5	25.9	139.5	6.1	105.4
云 南	Yunnan	799.3	433.9	73.2	242.5	16.6	106.6
西 藏	Tibet	58.6	25.3	5.3	27.1	0.0	105.0
陕 西	Shanxi	535.0	334.4	26.8	145.6	4.5	106.4
甘 肃	Gansu	400.8	275.8	19.8	93.9	1.0	105.9
青 海	Qinghai	76.9	29.7	2.6	40.7	0.1	103.0
宁 夏	Ningxia	103.4	54.1	7.5	36.4	2.6	106.0
新 疆	Xinjiang	688.3	482.8	13.7	162.0	3.2	106.3

注:本表绝对数按当年价格计算,指数按可比价格计算。

Absolute data were calculated at current prices while the indices were calculated at comparable prices.

19-14 各省(市、区)主要农产品产量(2003年)

Output of Major Farm Production (2003)

单位：万吨 (10 000 tons)

地区	Region	粮食 Grain	#谷物 Cereal	油料 Oil-bearing Crops	棉花 Cotton	糖料 Sugar Crops	水果 Fruitage
全国	**National Total**	**43069.5**	**37428.7**	**2811.0**	**486.0**	**9641.6**	**14517.4**
北京	Beijing	58.0	52.0	3.3	0.3		114.2
天津	Tianjin	119.3	112.0	3.1	9.5		84.3
河北	Hebei	2387.8	2205.9	163.1	52.2	22.0	1270.7
山西	Shanxi	958.9	807.1	36.4	9.2	11.4	328.8
内蒙古	Inner Mongolia	1360.7	1092.3	102.3	0.5	99.4	123.3
辽宁	Liaoning	1498.3	1360.1	61.4	0.3	3.4	396.9
吉林	Jilin	2259.6	2015.6	57.1	0.1	7.0	253.2
黑龙江	Heilongjiang	2512.3	1792.0	44.7		71.4	356.7
上海	Shanghai	98.8	96.0	6.4	0.1	13.1	114.5
江苏	Jiangsu	2471.9	2302.2	199.5	29.1	34.4	601.9
浙江	Zhejiang	793.4	700.6	43.8	2.1	123.9	568.4
安徽	Anhui	2214.8	1946.2	231.4	24.1	26.1	609.1
福建	Fujian	713.2	540.5	26.0		118.1	522.0
江西	Jiangxi	1450.3	1371.1	76.0	7.6	118.2	273.2
山东	Shandong	3435.5	3075.4	361.8	87.7	0.0	2526.0
河南	Henan	3569.5	3355.3	309.9	37.7	21.2	1318.5
湖北	Hubei	1921.0	1692.2	272.7	32.5	76.0	611.6
湖南	Hunan	2442.7	2225.6	125.7	16.3	142.3	512.4
广东	Guangdong	1430.4	1231.4	81.9		1134.1	836.9
广西	Guangxi	1465.1	1366.0	55.7	0.1	4861.8	641.2
海南	Hainan	204.6	150.4	9.6		402.1	193.5
重庆	Chongqi	1087.1	799.3	38.3		11.3	128.6
四川	Sichuan	3054.1	2483.0	217.1	2.5	170.8	464.9
贵州	Guizhu	1104.3	864.2	72.3	0.1	75.7	78.8
云南	Yunnan	1471.0	1212.9	29.7	…	1695.2	126.2
西藏	Tibet	96.6	93.0	4.9			1.1
陕西	Shanxi	968.4	863.3	41.3	5.3	0.8	730.9
甘肃	Gansu	789.3	600.3	46.0	8.7	19.9	247.7
青海	Qinghai	86.8	49.7	26.2			2.4
宁夏	Ningxia	270.2	239.0	13.2		0.0	71.2
新疆	Xinjiang	775.5	734.1	50.1	160.0	381.6	408.3

单位：万吨　　19-14 续表 Continued　　(10 000 tons)

地 区	Region	肉类总产量 Total Output of Meat	猪肉 Pork	牛肉 Beef	羊肉 Mutton	奶类 Milk	水产品 Aquatic Products
全 国	**National Total**	**6932.94**	**4518.6**	**630.5**	**357.2**	**1848.6**	**4704.5**
北 京	Beijing	70.26	32.7	5.2	4.7	63.7	7.1
天 津	Tianjin	53.42	32.2	5.4	3.1	43.2	29.8
河 北	Hebei	502.41	290.3	78.6	29.0	207.6	86.3
山 西	Shanxi	66.51	46.8	6.7	7.2	55.6	3.1
内蒙古	Inner Mongolia	162.72	71.3	24.0	45.3	312.2	7.3
辽 宁	Liaoning	280.15	147.9	33.9	5.1	46.4	382.0
吉 林	Jilin	218.50	84.5	40.3	3.8	23.3	10.9
黑龙江	Heilongjiang	151.46	85.6	29.9	6.7	303.9	41.9
上 海	Shanghai	50.84	24.6	0.1	0.9	27.1	35.5
江 苏	Jiangsu	354.78	221.2	5.6	17.6	50.0	342.9
浙 江	Zhejiang	153.93	117.2	1.4	3.6	24.7	482.8
安 徽	Anhui	329.64	209.7	34.9	15.1	9.0	165.3
福 建	Fujian	146.23	116.4	2.5	1.6	19.5	572.8
江 西	Jiangxi	195.22	142.7	7.0	1.4	10.9	146.1
山 东	Shandong	662.11	332.6	79.7	32.9	148.4	706.2
河 南	Henan	603.55	386.0	93.0	42.0	52.6	39.0
湖 北	Hubei	301.14	238.6	14.9	4.9	11.1	286.8
湖 南	Hunan	503.79	419.3	16.1	9.4	5.3	156.6
广 东	Guangdong	359.60	234.5	5.8	0.6	10.8	648.5
广 西	Guangxi	227.13	179.8	12.9	2.8	3.8	264.6
海 南	Hainan	47.00	28.4	2.7	1.3	0.1	123.1
重 庆	Chongqi	160.55	132.1	5.3	2.7	9.1	22.5
四 川	Sichuan	581.77	461.6	25.6	17.4	45.8	76.4
贵 州	Guizhu	152.53	126.9	10.1	4.5	3.4	8.0
云 南	Yunnan	253.69	208.8	17.6	8.2	23.4	20.4
西 藏	Tibet	19.01	0.9	10.8	7.4	25.1	
陕 西	Shanxi	92.07	62.0	10.5	7.9	107.1	6.7
甘 肃	Gansu	75.88	48.7	10.7	10.6	22.6	1.4
青 海	Qinghai	23.67	7.4	7.1	8.5	23.5	0.1
宁 夏	Ningxia	23.38	10.7	3.7	5.5	38.7	5.0
新 疆	Xinjiang	110.00	17.4	28.8	45.5	120.8	6.7

19-15 各省(市、区)规模工业增加值和指数

Added Value of Industry and It's Indices

地 区	Region	工业增加值 (亿元) Added Value of Industry (100 million yuan)					2003年比上年增长 % Increase Rate in 2003 Over 2002
		1999	2000	2001	2002	2003	
全 国	**National Total**	**21564.7**	**25394.8**	**28329.4**	**32994.8**	**41045.0**	**17.0**
北 京	Beijing	584.5	722.7	751.2	840.4	970.8	12.3
天 津	Tianjin	490.1	630.1	728.1	843.4	1027.8	20.1
河 北	Hebei	976.6	1132.7	1244.1	1413.5	1810.3	20.1
山 西	Shanxi	400.7	428.7	499.8	633.0	882.2	24.2
内蒙古	Inner Mongolia	235.7	279.5	307.6	375.8	509.7	31.5
辽 宁	Liaoning	935.8	1194.0	1255.7	1377.7	1764.3	18.5
吉 林	Jilin	412.2	496.2	589.1	669.3	806.7	17.9
黑龙江	Heilongjiang	933.8	1213.1	1207.9	1262.0	1380.2	13.6
上 海	Shanghai	1541.7	1687.2	1988.4	2131.9	2767.1	22.0
江 苏	Jiangsu	2234.6	2604.4	2943.5	3546.7	4620.6	22.7
浙 江	Zhejiang	1267.8	1560.1	1874.4	2403.9	3194.0	23.7
安 徽	Anhui	494.5	507.4	577.2	690.6	834.7	19.8
福 建	Fujian	665.0	797.1	875.4	1177.6	1461.4	23.9
江 西	Jiangxi	249.0	269.7	308.2	362.7	440.3	21.0
山 东	Shandong	2098.8	2549.4	2900.7	3500.5	4695.2	22.7
河 南	Henan	993.6	1116.4	1249.8	1387.9	1754.1	19.9
湖 北	Hubei	946.4	1011.8	1072.8	1170.5	1356.2	12.5
湖 南	Hunan	461.8	528.1	605.5	706.6	886.5	20.7
广 东	Guangdong	2788.2	3423.9	3738.3	4361.1	5606.3	21.9
广 西	Guangxi	281.8	323.9	342.7	370.4	436.9	17.6
海 南	Hainan	54.6	63.3	65.3	82.3	86.4	24.9
重 庆	Chongqi	239.5	283.7	308.2	360.1	477.9	21.1
四 川	Sichuan	634.3	662.4	790.4	977.5	1156.0	21.0
贵 州	Guizhu	196.0	217.0	236.6	271.1	331.9	13.5
云 南	Yunnan	491.1	531.5	582.1	659.1	719.7	9.1
西 藏	Tibet	8.4	9.3	9.5	10.5	11.0	9.5
陕 西	Shanxi	346.0	411.2	459.7	533.7	664.7	16.8
甘 肃	Gansu	225.6	244.7	296.5	340.6	389.8	13.0
青 海	Qinghai	58.3	65.3	71.8	80.2	95.5	15.9
宁 夏	Ningxia	61.6	73.7	82.9	80.6	105.1	17.5
新 疆	Xinjiang	256.7	356.6	365.2	373.7	463.2	10.8

注:1.本表绝对数按当年价格计算;指数按可比价格计算。

2.本表综合范围是全部国有和年产品销售收入500万元以上的非国有企业。(下三表同)

a. Absolute data were calculated at current prices while the indices were calculated at comparable prices.

b. The coverage of this table was to cover all state-owned enterprises and the non-state-owned enterprises with an annual sales income of over 5 million yuan. (The same as in the following three tables.)

19-16 各省(市、区)工业主要经济指标(2003年)

Main Indicators of Industrial Economy (2003)

单位：亿元 (100 million yuan)

地区	Region	产品销售收入 Sales Revenue	#产品销售成本 Cost of Sales	#产品销售费用 Fees of Sales	#产品销售税金及附加 Sales Tax and Extra Charges	税金总额 Total Tax	利润总额 Total Profits
全　国	**National Total**	**140610.31**	**116259.26**	**4874.12**	**2036.09**	**7295.22**	**8152.35**
北　京	Beijing	3732.81	3093.29	173.46	35.69	179.56	219.55
天　津	Tianjin	4115.15	3467.66	165.13	39.74	159.18	231.88
河　北	Hebei	5861.80	4879.83	146.57	63.18	309.65	387.84
山　西	Shanxi	2320.55	1764.00	143.98	29.24	181.04	135.49
内蒙古	Inner Mongolia	1351.71	1099.55	58.52	17.94	88.73	64.97
辽　宁	Liaoning	6213.27	5199.62	159.99	79.41	314.88	235.40
吉　林	Jilin	2598.56	2089.16	75.45	68.13	175.03	157.17
黑龙江	Heilongjiang	2866.12	1887.03	78.72	67.36	281.45	592.55
上　海	Shanghai	10982.62	9020.04	396.30	139.30	524.05	805.65
江　苏	Jiangsu	17969.35	15606.13	537.75	137.16	687.75	789.12
浙　江	Zhejiang	12520.98	10611.99	380.69	136.77	557.82	785.82
安　徽	Anhui	2638.55	2146.24	96.59	66.59	188.19	135.57
福　建	Fujian	4712.77	3958.23	162.99	59.34	191.09	281.36
江　西	Jiangxi	1489.22	1221.87	54.47	33.60	104.47	52.11
山　东	Shandong	14919.49	12581.93	436.88	153.43	690.01	915.08
河　南	Henan	5223.94	4372.06	169.22	82.86	292.14	251.53
湖　北	Hubei	4072.52	3268.85	175.52	81.56	250.84	178.40
湖　南	Hunan	2580.32	2050.60	98.68	105.01	231.68	100.08
广　东	Guangdong	20760.22	17444.41	794.02	152.76	653.38	1033.68
广　西	Guangxi	1388.74	1116.91	57.58	24.82	105.36	63.68
海　南	Hainan	286.05	223.34	17.52	6.92	19.62	15.92
重　庆	Chongqi	1595.07	1283.11	75.84	31.34	105.17	85.97
四　川	Sichuan	3345.64	2655.74	168.04	66.24	223.08	162.80
贵　州	Guizhu	923.17	652.28	49.89	41.44	99.30	31.96
云　南	Yunnan	1500.22	1005.24	55.90	207.24	325.31	102.33
西　藏	Tibet						
陕　西	Shanxi	1814.85	1351.32	66.16	43.05	136.45	147.69
甘　肃	Gansu	1130.27	929.32	29.18	32.46	91.18	30.36
青　海	Qinghai	264.48	210.02	7.49	3.27	19.30	12.72
宁　夏	Ningxia	362.89	304.04	12.16	4.25	21.40	7.68
新　疆	Xinjiang	1068.97	765.44	29.42	25.96	88.12	137.99

单位：亿元　　19-16 续表 continued　　(100 million yuan)

地 区	Region	亏损企业亏损额 Loss Value of Loss-making Enterprises	应收帐款净额 Net Value Receivables	产成品 Finished Goods	资产总计 Total Capital	负债总计 Total Liabilities	职工平均人数(万人) Average Staff and Workers (10 000 persons)
全　国	**National Total**	**1072.25**	**18623.90**	**8172.36**	**167074.16**	**98656.19**	**5707.80**
北　京	Beijing	40.32	559.45	247.36	5158.26	2764.49	100.58
天　津	Tianjin	45.75	585.39	184.07	4471.36	2597.48	117.12
河　北	Hebei	41.37	552.52	368.52	6867.55	4232.22	269.45
山　西	Shanxi	17.79	286.55	196.42	4315.24	2779.95	180.02
内蒙古	Inner Mongolia	11.14	157.07	92.83	2437.52	1443.32	72.18
辽　宁	Liaoning	68.19	845.84	408.83	9169.86	5394.84	243.14
吉　林	Jilin	35.28	340.28	154.36	3713.42	2380.87	103.39
黑龙江	Heilongjiang	33.82	393.62	195.10	4381.96	2517.46	140.73
上　海	Shanghai	95.89	1691.73	433.60	11601.52	5765.47	219.63
江　苏	Jiangsu	84.18	2425.46	846.04	16558.65	10282.64	572.64
浙　江	Zhejiang	35.79	1706.33	746.10	11731.62	6703.53	475.16
安　徽	Anhui	16.62	330.26	172.96	3851.13	2336.79	149.12
福　建	Fujian	23.45	638.90	245.80	4870.14	2600.53	209.01
江　西	Jiangxi	10.20	173.90	96.77	2223.46	1468.20	96.05
山　东	Shandong	48.06	1191.31	746.91	14536.24	8609.78	595.38
河　南	Henan	35.44	574.68	290.90	6541.50	4140.34	318.04
湖　北	Hubei	32.27	555.91	228.92	7095.31	4234.54	202.54
湖　南	Hunan	29.64	348.32	165.25	3709.49	2377.38	152.39
广　东	Guangdong	157.48	3105.65	1304.22	18905.05	10561.49	722.03
广　西	Guangxi	22.07	175.78	113.60	2215.91	1456.77	82.50
海　南	Hainan	4.58	38.85	24.34	413.45	225.83	9.71
重　庆	Chongqi	14.08	334.36	102.00	2377.73	1446.06	84.33
四　川	Sichuan	26.29	544.40	246.69	5821.01	3520.34	199.85
贵　州	Guizhu	15.44	188.40	72.51	1818.74	1210.46	64.97
云　南	Yunnan	34.56	166.59	82.24	2946.44	1691.67	64.49
西　藏	Tibet						
陕　西	Shanxi	30.66	314.90	160.41	3522.54	2253.62	110.75
甘　肃	Gansu	28.36	169.97	99.53	2195.32	1420.63	77.83
青　海	Qinghai	6.20	54.30	16.86	857.29	575.44	13.55
宁　夏	Ningxia	4.74	63.83	39.18	710.72	486.80	22.42
新　疆	Xinjiang	22.58	109.34	90.04	2055.74	1177.26	38.81

19-17 各省(市、区)工业经济效益指标(2003年)

Indicators on Industrial Economic Benefit (2003)

地区	Region	综合指数 (%) Index of Synthesis (%)	总资产贡献率 (%) Ratio of Ratio of Total Assets to Industrial Output Value(%)	资本保值增值率 (%) Ratio of Assets Keeping Value and Increment (%)	资产负债率 (%) Assets Liability Ratio (%)	流动资产周转次数 (次/年) Number of Times of Annual of Turnover Circulating Funds (times/year)	成本费用利润率 (%) Ratio of Pprofits to Industrial Cost (%)	全员劳动生产率 (元/人) Overall Labor Productivity (yuan/person-year)	产品销售率 (%) Proportion of Products Sold (%)
全 国	**National Total**	**144.67**	**11.13**	**113.48**	**59.05**	**1.96**	**6.24**	**66943**	**98.06**
北 京	Beijing	153.91	8.96	113.41	53.59	1.61	6.13	95268	98.23
天 津	Tianjin	154.67	9.94	105.07	58.09	2.11	6.01	87780	98.88
河 北	Hebei	144.60	12.34	114.14	61.63	2.15	7.16	54760	98.70
山 西	Shanxi	115.46	9.37	114.15	64.42	1.51	6.31	33233	97.69
内蒙古	Inner Mongolia	125.56	8.56	116.09	59.21	1.73	5.11	53483	98.74
辽 宁	Liaoning	118.93	7.31	104.64	58.83	1.67	4.01	56880	97.99
吉 林	Jilin	143.00	10.21	108.06	64.12	1.69	6.61	72419	97.60
黑龙江	Heilongjiang	234.24	21.53	101.84	57.45	1.69	27.02	60211	97.89
上 海	Shanghai	195.80	12.85	113.40	49.70	1.99	7.93	134862	99.02
江 苏	Jiangsu	143.91	10.84	114.26	62.10	2.26	4.61	72792	97.87
浙 江	Zhejiang	159.25	14.48	125.00	57.14	2.19	6.72	71562	97.69
安 徽	Anhui	127.87	10.23	116.56	60.68	1.66	5.55	50680	98.66
福 建	Fujian	155.10	11.86	118.71	53.40	2.22	6.43	75488	97.60
江 西	Jiangxi	108.16	9.19	109.13	66.03	1.67	3.72	36932	98.13
山 东	Shandong	151.27	13.40	120.62	59.23	2.54	6.58	57748	97.90
河 南	Henan	120.68	10.52	113.67	63.29	1.93	5.10	38352	98.52
湖 北	Hubei	125.63	8.22	116.62	59.68	1.61	4.72	58896	98.35
湖 南	Hunan	121.55	11.07	112.56	64.09	1.79	4.21	46204	100.07
广 东	Guangdong	152.06	10.43	111.21	55.87	2.16	5.34	84214	97.44
广 西	Guangxi	121.92	9.45	112.61	65.74	1.70	4.86	50539	97.43
海 南	Hainan	151.72	10.00	106.53	54.62	1.62	6.05	90737	96.16
重 庆	Chongqi	131.44	10.14	115.83	60.82	1.55	5.71	58111	97.83
四 川	Sichuan	126.39	8.43	112.10	60.48	1.44	5.18	60536	98.74
贵 州	Guizhu	107.53	8.80	112.53	66.56	1.26	3.98	41991	96.80
云 南	Yunnan	159.94	16.56	107.06	57.41	1.34	8.42	73112	99.10
西 藏	Tibet								
陕 西	Shanxi	134.91	10.10	117.84	63.98	1.32	9.14	47526	97.72
甘 肃	Gansu	94.42	7.15	104.34	64.71	1.39	2.86	30996	97.90
青 海	Qinghai	102.51	5.34	115.94	67.12	1.02	5.21	40072	97.20
宁 夏	Ningxia	90.72	6.40	103.14	68.49	1.39	2.20	33660	96.83
新 疆	Xinjiang	172.36	12.49	111.86	57.27	1.73	15.71	53500	98.57

19-18 各省(市、区)主要工业产品产量(2003年)

Output of Major Industrial Production (2003)

地区	Region	原煤(万吨) Coal (10 000 tons)	原油(万吨) Oil (10 000 tons)	发电量(亿千瓦小时) Electicity Hydropower (100 million kw.h)	钢(万吨) Steels (10 000 tons)	生铁(万吨) Pig Iron (10 000 tons)	成品钢材(万吨) Steel Products (10 000 tons)	水泥(万吨) Cement (10 000 tons)
全国总计	**National Total**	**166700.0**	**16960.5**	**19107.6**	**22233.6**	**20231.2**	**24119.4**	**86226.6**
北京	Beijing	822.6		192.2	816.4	788.2	785.3	996.0
天津	Tianjin		1316.3	320.1	566.0	342.7	1083.5	451.0
河北	Hebei	6600.2	511.0	1088.3	4065.1	4070.7	3729.4	6811.4
山西	Shanxi	29508.7		965.0	1002.7	2017.8	823.5	1949.0
内蒙古	Inner Mongolia	11959.4	5.5	647.7	576.8	602.6	558.3	940.5
辽宁	Liaoning	5870.7	1332.2	837.1	2227.8	2060.6	2359.4	2439.7
吉林	Jilin	2037.6	476.4	311.1	381.6	318.7	369.1	1119.1
黑龙江	Heilongjiang	6669.2	4840.1	493.8	165.7	136.7	141.4	1169.4
上海	Shanghai		38.0	687.6	1728.8	1300.2	1779.8	744.7
江苏	Jiangsu	2760.4	166.4	1366.3	1742.2	784.2	2961.5	7825.1
浙江	Zhejiang	69.4		1101.7	334.2	173.3	527.0	7168.0
安徽	Anhui	6726.4		557.2	692.7	693.6	720.1	3073.0
福建	Fujian	778.2		610.7	257.9	214.8	462.0	2400.2
江西	Jiangxi	951.7		320.9	599.5	496.4	664.1	2524.2
山东	Shandong	14667.3	2665.5	1397.0	1415.4	1329.3	1437.7	9935.0
河南	Henan	11871.0	549.8	1025.1	873.9	658.9	744.7	4722.6
湖北	Hubei	366.4	77.5	780.5	1254.3	1034.6	1126.3	3445.8
湖南	Hunan	2366.7		537.8	592.2	540.8	562.0	3135.0
广东	Guangdong	202.3	1275.7	1882.7	599.8	348.8	846.3	7530.0
广西	Guangxi	417.1	3.3	362.9	206.2	250.4	242.2	2665.2
海南	Hainan	2.0	7.6	58.6	0.2	6.4	10.8	397.8
重庆	Chongqi	1484.2		204.1	225.2	203.5	242.3	2037.7
四川	Sichuan	3133.9	13.9	849.3	738.9	695.1	827.3	4059.9
贵州	Guizhu	7802.5		641.0	206.2	182.8	193.1	1591.0
云南	Yunnan	1399.4		474.8	294.8	423.3	286.5	2052.8
西藏	Tibet	2.2						124.9
陕西	Shanxi	7392.8	1267.4	419.2	180.2	162.7	133.0	1828.0
甘肃	Gansu	2603.3	73.4	404.9	223.9	237.2	245.6	1160.8
青海	Qinghai	310.6	220.0	130.5	47.7		40.3	307.0
宁夏	Ningxia	2047.9		206.1	13.3	13.2	12.7	494.1
新疆	Xinjiang	1845.7	2120.4	233.5	204.1	143.9	204.2	1127.7

19-18 续表 continued

地区	Region	布（亿米）Cloth (100 million meter)	家用电冰箱（万台）Household Refrigerators (10 000 units)	农用化肥（万吨）Chemical Fertilizers (10 000 tons)	汽车（万辆）Motor Vehicls (10 000 units)	程控交换机（万线）Telephone Exchanges (10 000 lines)	移动电话机（万部）Mobile Telephone (10 000 subscribers)	微型电子计算机（万部）Micro Computers (10 000 units)
全国总计	**National Total**	**374.6**	**2242.6**	**4200.9**	**444.4**	**7379.9**	**18231.4**	**3216.7**
北京	Beijing	1.0	22.7	2.4	34.9	1934.7	3330.5	470.6
天津	Tianjin	2.5	29.6	16.8	17.3	21.9	3139.7	0.4
河北	Hebei	19.7		230.1	11.2	20.4		
山西	Shanxi	3.4		201.1	0.1			
内蒙古	Inner Mongolia	0.5		50.3	0.3		222.6	5.1
辽宁	Liaoning	4.0	109.7	107.5	13.0	21.4	123.1	178.3
吉林	Jilin	1.0	5.4	9.6	64.1	3.3		
黑龙江	Heilongjiang	1.3	4.9	52.6	20.0	0.1		4.0
上海	Shanghai	2.9	34.5	4.9	58.7	1884.0	2178.2	739.5
江苏	Jiangsu	67.1	243.8	216.7	21.3	139.8	333.5	605.6
浙江	Zhejiang	71.3	130.0	55.8	8.2	94.4	1893.3	7.4
安徽	Anhui	6.8	274.9	204.9	20.6			15.8
福建	Fujian	14.1		60.7	8.7	0.01	626.7	241.7
江西	Jiangxi	3.2	30.0	51.9	18.5	2.9		10.6
山东	Shandong	72.3	499.0	530.1	7.5	221.3	582.1	48.6
河南	Henan	17.9	145.9	330.2	2.8	6.8		0.5
湖北	Hubei	20.1		298.0	36.9	0.1	305.4	2.0
湖南	Hunan	3.6	44.7	180.5	4.4	1.0		
广东	Guangdong	28.1	564.9	84.6	18.9	2935.7	5355.2	881.1
广西	Guangxi	0.5		68.9	18.1			
海南	Hainan	0.1		33.5	5.5			
重庆	Chongqi	13.5		96.6	40.5	0.02	100.1	1.0
四川	Sichuan	6.5	33.4	432.0	4.8	0.04		2.5
贵州	Guizhu	0.5	50.4	188.8	0.1	1.7	33.6	
云南	Yunnan	0.3		260.6	4.1			
西藏	Tibet							
陕西	Shanxi	10.5	17.3	106.3	4.3	90.6	7.4	2.2
甘肃	Gansu	0.5	1.5	74.2				
青海	Qinghai			90.0				
宁夏	Ningxia			76.3				
新疆	Xinjiang	1.5		85.3				

19-19 各省(市、区)建筑业总产值和房屋建筑面积

Total Output Value of Construction and Floor Space of Building Constrution

地区	Region	总产值(亿元) Total Output Value of Construction (100 million yuan)		施工面积(万平方米) Floor Space of Buildings under Construction (10 000 sq.m)		竣工面积(万平方米) Floor Space of Buildings Completed (10 000 sq.m)	
		2002	2003	2002	2003	2002	2003
全国	**National Total**	**18527.2**	**21865.5**	**215608.7**	**263467.4**	**110217.1**	**118259.3**
北京	Beijing	1055.1	1269.9	10240.9	11971.8	3827.0	4405.7
天津	Tianjin	406.2	498.7	2817.8	3348.2	1332.1	1601.0
河北	Hebei	711.2	730.4	8297.9	8744.9	4741.2	4178.4
山西	Shanxi	446.9	492.9	2912.4	3360.3	1432.9	1191.3
内蒙古	Inner Mongolia	220.0	245.7	2178.3	2434.2	1497.1	1257.4
辽宁	Liaoning	839.3	1016.5	7234.9	8195.1	4037.0	3514.6
吉林	Jilin	292.6	373.3	2475.6	3818.6	1597.5	1731.9
黑龙江	Heilongjiang	407.9	426.9	3325.9	3516.5	2120.5	1961.6
上海	Shanghai	822.3	1055.9	6240.1	8547.1	2426.8	2802.4
江苏	Jiangsu	2199.5	2560.2	27753.4	35040.0	15478.6	17116.1
浙江	Zhejiang	2283.0	2973.7	28512.8	40250.0	12781.8	17627.9
安徽	Anhui	528.2	641.8	6344.3	11567.5	3847.6	4087.2
福建	Fujian	402.7	495.4	5541.0	6586.7	2518.5	2521.7
江西	Jiangxi	245.1	344.3	3530.8	6139.7	1915.7	2679.6
山东	Shandong	1151.2	1402.2	15184.1	17920.7	8064.9	9137.4
河南	Henan	536.7	613.6	7118.4	7913.6	3630.8	3138.6
湖北	Hubei	636.5	703.8	7227.5	7034.0	4151.2	4053.6
湖南	Hunan	595.6	674.4	7155.9	8970.0	3661.1	3905.6
广东	Guangdong	1341.8	1479.8	18882.4	22434.2	7947.9	9378.5
广西	Guangxi	221.2	290.8	2997.8	4094.1	1325.6	1663.8
海南	Hainan	41.5	24.0	544.9	413.5	208.8	53.6
重庆	Chongqi	500.7	563.3	8707.4	9007.1	4711.1	4033.6
四川	Sichuan	1072.5	1323.7	14903.8	15325.3	8491.6	8978.8
贵州	Guizhu	181.1	207.3	2309.4	2514.8	1054.3	816.2
云南	Yunnan	358.2	348.8	3406.1	3525.3	2226.2	1795.7
西藏	Tibet	21.7	12.0	124.7	67.5	95.0	18.1
陕西	Shanxi	346.6	422.5	3325.0	3873.8	1453.9	1440.0
甘肃	Gansu	192.4	200.3	2456.7	2544.1	1495.7	1179.7
青海	Qinghai	73.4	73.4	451.3	511.9	244.1	238.8
宁夏	Ningxia	83.9	104.4	834.7	1068.1	430.9	535.0
新疆	Xinjiang	312.3	295.6	2572.6	2728.6	1469.6	1215.4

19-20 各省(市、区)建筑业主要效益指标(2003年)

Main Value Indicators of Construction (2003)

地区	Region	企业个数(个) Number of Construction Enterprises (unit)	计算劳动生产率的平均人数(万人) Average Persons Calculated Overall Labor Productivity (10 000 persons)	按建筑业总产值计算的劳动生产率(元/人) Overall Labor Productivity in Terms of Total Output Value (yuan/person)	人均竣工产值(元/人) Per Capita Output Value of Completed (yuan/person)	人均施工面积(平方米) Per Capita Floor Space of Buildings under Construction (sq.m)	人均竣工面积(平方米) Per Capita Floor Space of Buildings Completed (sq.m)
全　国	**National Total**	**50568**	**2626.65**	**83245**	**57061**	**100.3**	**45.0**
北　京	Beijing	2126	97.44	130315	95410	122.9	45.2
天　津	Tianjin	887	32.70	152497	99959	102.4	49.0
河　北	Hebei	1673	103.92	70284	47429	84.1	40.2
山　西	Shanxi	1113	55.11	89443	39365	61.0	21.6
内蒙古	Inner Mongolia	721	47.08	52196	41229	51.7	26.7
辽　宁	Liaoning	2499	130.30	78012	51083	62.9	27.0
吉　林	Jilin	790	39.76	93901	69826	96.0	43.6
黑龙江	Heilongjiang	1476	63.85	66864	54087	55.1	30.7
上　海	Shanghai	1679	68.62	153864	93975	124.5	40.8
江　苏	Jiangsu	4737	297.46	86070	57866	117.8	57.5
浙　江	Zhejiang	3509	225.19	132052	87248	178.7	78.3
安　徽	Anhui	1730	96.94	66211	40566	119.3	42.2
福　建	Fujian	1433	46.03	107613	99521	143.1	54.8
江　西	Jiangxi	1042	52.98	64997	42084	115.9	50.6
山　东	Shandong	4372	220.12	63703	43837	81.4	41.5
河　南	Henan	2076	94.74	64764	41706	83.5	33.1
湖　北	Hubei	1816	88.87	79192	59394	79.1	45.6
湖　南	Hunan	1495	99.95	67474	44944	89.7	39.1
广　东	Guangdong	3890	163.56	90477	75583	137.2	57.3
广　西	Guangxi	990	40.54	71741	51912	101.0	41.0
海　南	Hainan	118	3.12	76764	34271	132.3	17.1
重　庆	Chongqi	1708	94.03	59903	38445	95.8	42.9
四　川	Sichuan	3521	207.50	63790	45639	73.9	43.3
贵　州	Guizhu	552	27.34	75848	41566	92.0	29.9
云　南	Yunnan	1286	51.50	67730	46917	68.5	34.9
西　藏	Tibet	97	2.05	58435.00	28957.00	32.9	8.8
陕　西	Shanxi	854	71.21	59329	28522	54.4	20.2
甘　肃	Gansu	861	45.92	43620	31056	55.4	25.7
青　海	Qinghai	371	11.90	61694	38793	43.0	20.1
宁　夏	Ningxia	429	15.93	65513	49188	67.0	33.6
新　疆	Xinjiang	717	30.98	95410	64314	88.1	39.2

19-21 各省(市、区)客运量和旅客周转量(2003年)

Passenger Traffic and Turnover Volume of Passenger Traffic (2003)

地 区	Regions	客运量 (万人) Volume of Passenger Traffic (10 000 persons)	铁路 Railways	公路 Highways	水运 Waterways	旅客周转量 (亿人公里) Turnover Volume of Passenger Traffic (100 million person-km)	铁路 Railways	公路 Highways	水运 Waterways
全 国	**National Total**	**1587497**	**97261**	**1464335**	**17142**	**13811**	**4789**	**7696**	**63**
北 京	Beijing	29300	4360	24940		132	62	69	
天 津	Tianjin	3403	1291	2109	3	92	70	22	…
河 北	Hebei	65209	4442	60767		780	384	397	
山 西	Shanxi	37225	2861	34328	36	247	85	162	…
内蒙古	Inner Mongolia	23599	2768	20831		205	83	122	
辽 宁	Liaoning	50349	8731	41076	542	481	310	164	7
吉 林	Jilin	24505	4306	20112	87	207	122	84	…
黑龙江	Heilongjiang	47842	8319	39347	176	355	151	203	…
上 海	Shanghai	6481	3391	2052	1038	101	38	58	5
江 苏	Jiangsu	123297	5104	118046	147	958	183	774	…
浙 江	Zhejiang	141148	5197	133968	1983	718	181	532	6
安 徽	Anhui	62727	2987	59544	196	621	224	397	…
福 建	Fujian	47766	1576	45483	707	334	75	258	1
江 西	Jiangxi	36909	3325	33196	388	482	300	181	1
山 东	Shandong	77212	3343	72754	1115	623	220	398	5
河 南	Henan	81228	4864	76301	63	812	462	350	…
湖 北	Hubei	61961	3017	58371	573	545	232	309	4
湖 南	Hunan	96207	5061	90353	793	818	431	385	2
广 东	Guangdong	131199	7237	122265	1697	1263	267	988	8
广 西	Guangxi	42932	1623	40524	785	463	94	367	2
海 南	Hainan	24787	13	24037	737	78	…	76	2
重 庆	Chongqi	58159	1069	55673	1417	236	35	188	13
四 川	Sichuan	141148	4233	133782	3133	548	145	400	2
贵 州	Guizhu	55074	1796	52695	583	249	112	135	1
云 南	Yunnan	34785	1364	33039	382	230	36	193	1
西 藏	Tibet	125		125		6		6	
陕 西	Shanxi	30977	2497	28159	321	383	208	174	1
甘 肃	Gansu	14961	989	13732	240	244	156	87	…
青 海	Qinghai	4265	395	3870		38	16	22	
宁 夏	Ningxia	5856	251	5605		51	18	34	
新 疆	Xinjiang	18103	852	17251		250	88	161	
不分地区	Not Classified by Region	8759				1263			

注:不分地区合计中,包括公路和水运部门的直属企业、民航、管道完成数。

The total includes the quantities transported by highways, waterways, civil aviation and pipelines.

19-22 各省(市、区)货运量和货物周转量(2003年)

Freight Traffic and Turnover Volume of Freight Traffic (2003)

地区	Regions	货运量 (万吨) Volume of Freight Traffic (10 000 tons)	铁路 Railways	公路 Highways	水运 Waterways	货物周转量 (亿吨公里) Turnover Volume of Freight Traffic (100 million ton-km)	铁路 Railways	公路 Highways	水运 Waterways
全 国	**National Total**	**1561422**	**221178**	**1159957**	**158070**	**53859**	**17247**	**7099**	**28716**
北 京	Beijing	30729	2368	28361		462	383	79	
天 津	Tianjin	32014	5664	20072	6278	6521	320	68	6133
河 北	Hebei	77089	14347	61570	1172	3223	2019	592	612
山 西	Shanxi	106720	39020	67671	29	1259	923	336	…
内蒙古	Inner Mongolia	50820	12288	38532		1160	918	242	
辽 宁	Liaoning	83515	13885	65981	3649	2385	1028	226	1131
吉 林	Jilin	31436	6153	25211	72	531	440	91	…
黑龙江	Heilongjiang	54350	14267	39031	1052	991	809	163	19
上 海	Shanghai	58507	1208	30678	26621	8492	38	69	8385
江 苏	Jiangsu	92845	5204	64321	23320	1773	412	365	995
浙 江	Zhejiang	103833	3328	70907	29598	2047	253	314	1481
安 徽	Anhui	54643	8744	39918	5981	1329	810	318	200
福 建	Fujian	34415	4207	23884	6324	1223	194	194	835
江 西	Jiangxi	27709	4784	21047	1878	769	556	162	50
山 东	Shandong	117051	14009	97977	5065	3909	1039	528	2342
河 南	Henan	69688	12925	56100	663	1892	1463	405	23
湖 北	Hubei	41261	4718	30348	6195	1213	612	224	377
湖 南	Hunan	60306	5570	51136	3600	1351	773	455	122
广 东	Guangdong	100565	6391	73087	21087	3158	286	553	2318
广 西	Guangxi	31525	4587	24164	2774	863	527	217	119
海 南	Hainan	8008	368	5689	1951	251	2	46	203
重 庆	Chongqi	32563	1943	28406	2214	368	103	107	158
四 川	Sichuan	57527	7278	47467	2782	768	534	220	15
贵 州	Guizhu	18224	4971	12886	367	547	466	77	4
云 南	Yunnan	58170	4146	53864	160	612	253	358	2
西 藏	Tibet	266		266		27		27	
陕 西	Shanxi	34961	6686	28165	110	849	668	181	…
甘 肃	Gansu	24539	3783	20713	43	739	615	124	…
青 海	Qinghai	5653	858	4795		124	81	43	…
宁 夏	Ningxia	7344	2296	5048		244	181	63	
新 疆	Xinjiang	27078	4416	22662		637	383	254	
不分地区	Not Classified by Region	28070	768		5085	4142	155		3190

注:不分地区合计中,包括公路和水运部门的直属企业、民航、管道完成数。

The total includes the quantities transported by highways, waterways, civil aviation and pipelines.

19-23 各省(市、区)社会消费品零售总额(2003年)

Total Retail Sales of Consumer Goods (2003)

地 区	Region	社会消费品零售总额 (亿元) Total Retail Sales of Consumer Goods (100 million yuan)	按地域分类 By Location 市 City	县 County	县以下 Under County Level	按行业分类 By Sector 批发零售贸易业 Wholesale and Retail Trades	餐饮业 Catering Trade	其他行业 Others	比上年增长(%) Increase Rate in 2003 over 2002 (%)
全 国	**National Total**	**45842.00**	**29777.30**	**5247.80**	**10816.90**	**37692.50**	**6065.70**	**2083.80**	**9.1**
北 京	Beijing	1916.72	1535.80	88.75	292.16	1611.22	121.44	184.05	14.5
天 津	Tianjin	922.27	859.19	35.26	27.82	727.10	109.91	85.25	10.9
河 北	Hebei	2177.87	1064.38	421.12	692.38	1894.76	233.49	49.63	10.6
山 西	Shanxi	729.30	471.34	135.19	122.77	614.24	81.71	33.35	13.7
内蒙古	Inner Mongolia	726.76	449.46	166.53	110.77	592.24	99.20	35.32	21.3
辽 宁	Liaoning	2330.80	1963.66	111.96	255.18	1935.63	338.88	56.30	12.3
吉 林	Jilin	1110.28	857.68	76.82	175.78	951.04	153.83	5.41	10.1
黑龙江	Heilongjiang	1376.45	1019.42	186.63	170.40	1191.93	152.29	32.24	10.1
上 海	Shanghai	2220.64	1905.90	17.62	297.11	1990.24	214.83	15.57	9.1
江 苏	Jiangsu	3566.48	2516.34	217.82	832.32	3072.62	434.44	59.42	13.7
浙 江	Zhejiang	3157.09	1999.88	329.46	827.74	2696.42	358.88	101.78	10.9
安 徽	Anhui	1331.25	666.60	285.64	379.00	1143.68	159.37	28.20	9.8
福 建	Fujian	1740.45	1057.54	218.33	464.58	1423.06	211.22	106.16	13.1
江 西	Jiangxi	923.21	455.31	206.61	261.29	812.02	85.25	25.94	11.7
山 东	Shandong	3936.52	2525.62	396.35	1014.55	3251.68	497.22	187.62	22.2
河 南	Henan	2426.41	1234.76	494.21	697.44	2009.72	343.11	73.58	10.8
湖 北	Hubei	2358.69	1603.34	222.86	532.49	1884.70	298.30	175.69	10.8
湖 南	Hunan	1816.31	997.12	332.48	486.70	1558.40	224.57	33.33	10.8
广 东	Guangdong	5606.02	3718.27	269.42	1618.33	4681.08	877.29	47.65	11.8
广 西	Guangxi	857.71	458.52	169.69	229.50	716.79	115.28	25.64	12.2
海 南	Hainan	191.64	128.10	16.64	46.89	150.53	30.99	10.11	10.9
重 庆	Chongqi	835.53	482.31	112.71	240.51	719.13	107.32	9.07	9.5
四 川	Sichuan	2091.05	1004.16	357.27	729.62	1621.48	349.41	120.16	13.0
贵 州	Guizhu	458.76	271.95	85.80	101.01	374.29	75.46	9.02	10.2
云 南	Yunnan	782.46	425.26	180.49	176.71	635.42	124.63	22.41	10.0
西 藏	Tibet	58.30	26.08	25.01	7.21	46.58	8.17	3.55	9.2
陕 西	Shanxi	853.23	565.55	149.14	138.53	646.28	184.34	22.60	17.2
甘 肃	Gansu	474.60	307.95	76.25	90.40	388.27	66.88	19.46	9.5
青 海	Qinghai	102.66	66.14	24.70	11.82	83.37	16.44	2.85	11.5
宁 夏	Ningxia	120.75	81.54	20.75	18.46	98.78	19.65	2.33	15.1
新 疆	Xinjiang	421.17	311.34	49.20	60.63	341.91	60.64	18.62	11.1

注: 1. 社会消费品零售总额及其增长速度均按当年价格计算。

2. 全国总计数字有调整,不等于各省合计(下两表同)。

a、Total retail sales of consumer goods and increase rate are calculated at current prices.

b、The national total was adjusted, The sum of provincial figures do not add up to the national total. Similarly in following two tables.

19-24 各省(市、区)海关进出口总额

Total Value of Import and Export (Customs Statistics)

单位：亿美元 (USD 100 million)

地 区	Region	2002			2003		
		进出口总额 Imports and Exports	出口额 Exports	进口额 Imports	进出口总额 Imports and Exports	出口额 Exports	进口额 Imports
全 国	**National Total**	**6207.7**	**3255.7**	**2952**	**8509.9**	**4382.3**	**4127.6**
北 京	Beijing	525.1	126.1	398.9	684.6	168.5	516.1
天 津	Tianjin	227.5	115.7	111.8	293.6	143.7	149.9
河 北	Hebei	66.7	45.9	20.7	89.8	59.3	30.5
山 西	Shanxi	23.1	16.6	6.54	30.8	22.7	8.2
内蒙古	Inner Mongolia	24.4	8.1	16.3	28.3	11.6	16.7
辽 宁	Liaoning	217.4	123.7	93.7	265.6	146.3	119.3
吉 林	Jilin	37.1	17.7	19.4	61.7	21.6	40.1
黑龙江	Heilongjiang	43.5	19.9	23.6	53.3	28.7	24.5
上 海	Shanghai	726.4	320.5	405.9	1123.5	484.6	639.0
江 苏	Jiangsu	703	384.7	318.3	1136.2	591.2	545.0
浙 江	Zhejiang	419.6	294.2	125.5	614.2	416.0	198.2
安 徽	Anhui	41.8	24.5	17.3	59.4	30.6	28.8
福 建	Fujian	284	173.7	110.3	353.3	211.4	141.9
江 西	Jiangxi	16.9	10.5	6.4	25.3	15.0	10.2
山 东	Shandong	339.4	211.1	128.3	446.4	265.6	180.8
河 南	Henan	32	21.2	10.8	47.1	29.8	17.3
湖 北	Hubei	39.5	21	18.5	51.1	26.6	24.5
湖 南	Hunan	28.8	18	10.8	37.3	21.5	15.9
广 东	Guangdong	2211.1	1184.7	1026.4	2836.5	1529.4	1307.0
广 西	Guangxi	24.3	15.1	9.2	31.9	19.7	12.2
海 南	Hainan	18.7	8.2	10.5	22.8	8.7	14.1
重 庆	Chongqi	17.9	10.9	7	25.9	15.9	10.1
四 川	Sichuan	44.7	27.1	17.6	56.4	32.1	24.3
贵 州	Guizhu	6.9	4.4	2.5	9.8	5.9	4.0
云 南	Yunnan	22.3	14.3	8	26.7	16.8	9.9
西 藏	Tibet	1.3	0.8	0.5	1.6	1.2	0.4
陕 西	Shanxi	22.3	13.8	8.5	27.8	17.4	10.5
甘 肃	Gansu	8.8	5.5	3.3	13.3	8.8	4.5
青 海	Qinghai	2	1.5	0.5	3.4	2.7	0.7
宁 夏	Ningxia	4.4	3.3	1.1	6.5	5.1	1.4
新 疆	Xinjiang	26.9	13.1	13.8	47.7	25.4	22.3

19-25 各省(市、区)外商直接投资额

Actually Used Foreign Direct Investment

单位：万美元 (USD 10 000)

		1997	1998	1999	2000	2001	2002	2003
全　国	**National Total**	**4525704**	**4546275**	**4031871**	**4071481**	**4687759**	**5274286**	**5350467**
北　京	Beijing	159286	216800	197525	168368	176818	172464	219126
天　津	Tianjin	251135	211361	176399	116601	213348	158195	153473
河　北	Hebei	110064	142868	104202	67923	66989	78271	96405
山　西	Shanxi	26592	24451	39129	22472	23393	21164	21361
内蒙古	Inner Mongolia	7325	9082	6456	10568	10703	17701	8854
辽　宁	Liaoning	220470	219045	106173	204446	251612	341168	282410
吉　林	Jilin	40227	40917	30120	33701	33766	24468	19059
黑龙江	Heilongjiang	73485	52639	31828	30086	34114	35511	32180
上　海	Shanghai	422536	360150	283665	316014	429159	427229	546849
江　苏	Jiangsu	543511	663179	607756	642550	691482	1018960	1056365
浙　江	Zhejiang	150345	131802	123262	161266	221162	307610	498055
安　徽	Anhui	43443	27673	26131	31847	33672	38375	36720
福　建	Fujian	419666	421211	402403	343191	391804	383837	259903
江　西	Jiangxi	47768	46496	32080	22724	39575	108197	161202
山　东	Shandong	249294	220274	225878	297119	352093	473404	601617
河　南	Henan	69204	61654	52135	56403	45729	40463	53903
湖　北	Hubei	79019	97294	91488	94368	118860	142665	156886
湖　南	Hunan	91702	81816	65374	68182	81011	103089	148907
广　东	Guangdong	1171083	1201994	1165750	1128091	1193203	1133400	782294
广　西	Guangxi	87986	88613	63512	52466	38416	41726	41856
海　南	Hainan	70554	71715	48449	43080	46691	51196	42125
重　庆	Chongqi	38675	43107	23893	24436	25649	19576	26083
四　川	Sichuan	24846	37248	34101	43694	58188	55583	41231
贵　州	Guizhu	4977	4535	4090	2501	2829	3821	4521
云　南	Yunnan	16566	14568	15385	12812	6457	11169	8384
西　藏	Tibet							
陕　西	Shanxi	62816	30010	24197	28842	35174	36005	33190
甘　肃	Gansu	4144	3864	4104	6235	7439	6121	2342
青　海	Qinghai	247		459		3649	4726	2522
宁　夏	Ningxia	671	1856	5134	1741	1680	2200	1743
新　疆	Xinjiang	2472	2167	2404	1911	2035	1899	1534

19-26 各省(市、区)外商投资企业进出口商品总值

Total Value of Import and Export Goods of Foreign – Funded Enterprises

单位：万美元　　　　　　　　　　　　　　　　　　　　　　　　　　　(USD 10 000)

地区	Region	2002			2003		
		进出口总额 Imports and Exports	出口额 Exports	进口额 Imports	进出口总额 Imports and Exports	出口额 Exports	进口额 Imports
全　国	**National Total**	**33023948**	**16998509**	**16025439**	**47225181**	**24033755**	**23191426**
北　京	Beijing	877384	401640	475745	1180654	512473	668181
天　津	Tianjin	1831326	909006	922320	2328980	1141831	1187149
河　北	Hebei	225227	143722	81504	305669	184636	121032
山　西	Shanxi	24149	16089	8060	41227	26390	14836
内蒙古	Inner Mongolia	25031	12489	12543	20930	14906	6024
辽　宁	Liaoning	1346998	720003	626996	1656935	874599	782336
吉　林	Jilin	172414	40392	132022	270414	41056	229358
黑龙江	Heilongjiang	64718	28162	36556	63223	29288	33935
上　海	Shanghai	4501428	1915697	2585731	7195227	3079445	4115782
江　苏	Jiangsu	4988156	2424878	2563278	8598191	4111856	4486335
浙　江	Zhejiang	1458388	920127	538261	2193179	1305000	888179
安　徽	Anhui	112891	46184	66708	153315	57917	95398
福　建	Fujian	1879764	1046590	833174	2367421	1346529	1020892
江　西	Jiangxi	40650	18067	22583	67215	27706	39509
山　东	Shandong	1941081	1098793	842288	2435767	1376753	1059014
河　南	Henan	67033	37201	29832	106329	53652	52676
湖　北	Hubei	146268	66922	79346	201845	84242	117604
湖　南	Hunan	66298	24304	41994	76867	33406	43461
广　东	Guangdong	12860694	6962505	5898189	17467761	9537313	7930449
广　西	Guangxi	78204	30688	47515	103708	37732	65976
海　南	Hainan	95336	35466	59871	82681	27756	54925
重　庆	Chongqi	37812	9732	28080	61754	13695	48058
四　川	Sichuan	66785	32046	34738	95710	45192	50518
贵　州	Guizhu	12810	5423	7387	27763	11056	16708
云　南	Yunnan	25382	13067	12315	26776	14403	12374
西　藏	Tibet	290	243	48	379	175	204
陕　西	Shanxi	40409	11453	28956	52999	15522	37478
甘　肃	Gansu	13510	10000	3510	14162	10750	3412
青　海	Qinghai	1138	312	826	1411	1295	116
宁　夏	Ningxia	9339	6153	3186	11913	7799	4114
新　疆	Xinjiang	9847	6209	3638	14779	9382	5397

19-27 各省（市、区）国际旅游业接待情况

Basic Indicators of International Tourisn

地区	Region	2002			2003		
		旅游人数（万人次）Number of Tourists (10 000 person-times)	#外国人 Foreigners	旅游创汇总额（亿美元）Foreign Exchange Earnings from Tourisn (USD 100 million)	旅游人数（万人次）Number of Tourists (10 000 person-times)	#外国人 Foreigners	旅游创汇总额（亿美元）Foreign Exchange Earnings from Tourisn (USD 100 million)
北　京	Beijing	310.4	266.5	31.1	185.1	152.7	19.0
天　津	Tianjin	50.6	45.3	3.4	48.9	45.6	3.3
河　北	Hebei	47.4	42.7	1.7	28.0	25.8	0.8
山　西	Shanxi	24.8	16.2	0.7	11.6	7.9	0.4
内蒙古	Inner Mongolia	43.9	43.5	1.5	41.4	41.0	1.4
辽　宁	Liaoning	92.9	79.4	5.5	77.9	66.8	4.5
吉　林	Jilin	29.4	25.9	0.9	21.2	18.5	0.7
黑龙江	Heilongjiang	71.7	66.9	2.9	58.7	54.6	2.4
上　海	Shanghai	272.5	215.9	22.7	244.7	199.0	20.5
江　苏	Jiangsu	222.6	138.9	10.5	223.2	143.5	11.3
浙　江	Zhejiang	204.1	121.1	9.3	180.8	106.9	8.7
安　徽	Anhui	45.9	23.9	1.2	28.1	16.4	0.8
福　建	Fujian	184.8	52.8	11.0	149.7	45.9	9.1
江　西	Jiangxi	24.1	6.6	0.7	16.6	4.5	0.5
山　东	Shandong	97.7	74.1	4.7	77.7	61.6	3.7
河　南	Henan	41.0	25.5	1.5	18.9	11.3	0.6
湖　北	Hubei	102.4	75.6	2.8	40.5	32.3	1.4
湖　南	Hunan	56.6	22.4	3.1	15.4	10.5	0.5
广　东	Guangdong	1525.9	298.1	50.9	1197.0	245.8	42.7
广　西	Guangxi	136.3	65.9	3.2	65.0	32.9	1.6
海　南	Hainan	38.9	16.5	0.9	29.3	14.4	0.8
重　庆	Chongqi	46.2	31.1	2.2	23.5	18.2	1.1
四　川	Sichuan	66.7	41.2	2.0	45.2	24.4	1.5
贵　州	Guizhu	22.8	8.5	0.8	7.7	2.4	0.3
云　南	Yunnan	130.4	78.1	4.2	100.0	65.7	3.4
西　藏	Tibet	14.2	12.9	0.5	5.1	4.6	0.2
陕　西	Shanxi	85.0	71.8	3.5	46.6	30.8	2.0
甘　肃	Gansu	23.7	16.3	0.5	10.2	6.8	0.2
青　海	Qinghai	4.4	1.9	0.1	1.8	0.8	…
宁　夏	Ningxia	0.6	0.4	0.0	0.3	0.2	…
新　疆	Xinjiang	27.5	23.4	1.0	17.1	15.0	0.5

中国统计出版社最新资料书简目

中国统计年鉴-2004
中国统计摘要-2004
2004中国发展报告
中国城市统计年鉴-2003
中国农村统计年鉴-2004
中国劳动统计年鉴-2004
中国人口统计年鉴-2004
中国工业经济统计年鉴-2004
中国市场统计年鉴-2004
2003中国城市发展报告
中国建筑业统计年鉴-2003
中国价格及城镇居民家庭收支调查统计年鉴-2004
国际统计年鉴-2004
中国对外经济贸易统计年鉴-2003
中国基本单位统计年鉴-2003
中国民政统计年鉴-2004
中国高技术产业统计年鉴-2004
中国房地产行业名录

北京统计年览-2004
天津统计年鉴-2004
河北经济年鉴-2004
山西统计年鉴-2004
内蒙古统计年鉴-2004
辽宁统计年鉴-2004
吉林统计年鉴-2004
黑龙江统计年鉴-2004
上海统计年鉴-2004
江苏统计年鉴-2004
浙江统计年鉴-2004
安徽统计年鉴-2004
福建统计年鉴-2004
江西统计年鉴-2004
山东统计年鉴-2004
河南统计年鉴-2004
湖北统计年鉴-2004
湖南统计年鉴-2004
广东统计年鉴-2004
广西统计年鉴-2004
海南统计年鉴-2004
重庆统计年鉴-2004
四川统计年鉴-2004
贵州统计年鉴-2004
云南统计年鉴-2004
西藏统计年鉴-2004
陕西统计年鉴-2004
甘肃年鉴-2004

青海统计年鉴-2004
宁夏统计年鉴-2004
新疆统计年鉴-2004
新疆生产建设兵团统计年鉴-2004
石家庄统计年鉴-2004
唐山统计年鉴-2004
邯郸统计年鉴-2004
呼和浩特经济统计年鉴-2004
鄂尔多斯市统计年鉴-2004
包头统计年鉴-2004
赤峰统计年鉴-2004
沈阳年鉴-2004
大连统计年鉴-2004
鞍山统计年鉴-2004
长春统计年鉴-2004
吉林市社会经济统计年鉴-2004
四平统计年鉴-2004
延吉统计年鉴-2004
哈尔滨统计年鉴-2004
齐齐哈尔经济统计年鉴-2004
牡丹江统计年鉴-2004
大庆统计年鉴-2004
黑龙江垦区统计年鉴-2004
上海浦东新区统计年鉴-2004
南京统计年鉴-2004
苏州统计年鉴-2004
无锡统计年鉴-2004
常州统计年鉴-2004
徐州统计年鉴-2004
南通统计年鉴-2004
盐城统计年鉴-2004
镇江统计年鉴-2004
杭州统计年鉴-2004
宁波统计年鉴-2004
绍兴统计年鉴-2004
台州统计年鉴-2004
舟山统计年鉴-2004
温州统计年鉴-2004
金华统计年鉴-2004
嘉兴统计年鉴-2004
丽水统计年鉴-2004
福州年鉴-2004
厦门经济特区年鉴-2004
福州经济技术开发区年鉴-2004
南昌经济社会统计年鉴-2004
九江经济统计年鉴-2004
济南统计年鉴-2004

青岛统计年鉴-2004
潍坊统计年鉴-2004
郑州统计年鉴-2004
洛阳统计年鉴-2004
三门峡统计年鉴-2004
平顶山统计年鉴-2004
南阳经济统计年鉴-2004
武汉统计年鉴-2004
宜昌统计年鉴-2004
十堰统计年鉴-2004
荆州统计年鉴-2004
广州统计年鉴-2004
东莞统计年鉴-2004
惠州统计年鉴-2004
深圳统计年鉴-2004
南宁统计年鉴-2004
桂林经济社会统计年鉴-2004
柳州经济统计年鉴-2004
来宾统计年鉴-2004
河池地区经济社会统计年鉴-2004
海口统计年鉴-2004
成都统计年鉴-2004
贵阳统计年鉴-2004
昆明统计年鉴-2004
西安统计年鉴-2004
兰州年鉴-2004
西宁统计年鉴-2004
银川统计年鉴-2004
乌鲁木齐统计年鉴-2004
巴音郭楞统计年鉴-2004
吐鲁番统计年鉴-2004

CHINA
凡在中国境内从
请您依法按照有关规